Materials on Canadian INCOME TAX

15th Edition

Editors

Tim Edgar, Arthur Cockfield and Martha O'Brien

Contributors

Neil Brooks, Catherine A. Brown, Art Cockfield, Donna Eansor,
Tim Edgar, M. Michelle Gallant, Colin Jackson, Tamara Larre,
Geoffrey Loomer, Carl MacArthur, Darcy MacPherson,
Martha E.C. O'Brien, Anthony F. Sheppard,
Chris Sprysak, Saul Templeton, Ellen Zweibel

CARSWELL®

ISBN 978-0-7798-6695-3 (15th ed.)

A cataloguing record for this publication is available from Library and Archives Canada.

Composition: Computer Composition of Canada

Printed in the United States by Thomson Reuters.

THOMSON REUTERS

CARSWELL, A DIVISION OF THOMSON REUTERS CANADA LIMITED

One Corporate Plaza
2075 Kennedy Road
Toronto, Ontario
M1T 3V4

Customer Relations
Toronto 1-416-609-3800
Elsewhere in Canada/U.S. 1-800-387-5164
Fax 1-416-298-5082
www.carswell.com
E-mail www.carswell.com/email

Preface

Consistent with earlier editions, this 15th edition is intended to be used primarily as a teaching tool for an introductory income tax course at Canadian law schools. As a result, we have focused on provisions of the *Income Tax Act* that we consider pertinent to a basic income tax course. Extracts from selected cases, as well as the notes, questions, and problems, are all intended to raise issues associated with the relevant statutory provisions. Legislative developments since the last edition are reflected to the extent that they affect such issues.

We are pleased to welcome to this edition three new contributors: Colin Jackson, Saul Templeton and Darcy MacPherson. Martha O'Brien is expanding her role in this edition to include co-editorship. Perhaps most importantly, we want to thank Faye Woodman, Ruth Kuras, Lorna Turnbull and John Burghardt, who are saying goodbye as contributors. We are also grateful for the efforts of Daniel Sandler, who has stepped down as one of the co-editors after several editions. As always, this edition builds on the past contributions of our colleagues to the earlier editions.

The contributors to the chapters of the 15th edition are as follows:

Chapter	*Title*	*Contributors*
1	The Logic, Policy and Politics of Tax Law	Neil Brooks
2	Source Concept of Income	Martha O'Brien Tamara Larre
3	Who Is Subject to Canadian Income Tax?	Geoffrey Loomer Colin Jackson
4	Income from Employment	Donna Eansor Saul Templeton
5	Income from Business or Property	Michelle Gallant Darcy MacPherson
6	Computation of Profit and Timing Principles for the Recognition of Revenue and Expense	Arthur Cockfield Tim Edgar
7	Capital Gains	Tony Sheppard
8	Refining the Basis of Liability	Ellen Zweibel
9	Taxation of Intermediaries and the Relevance of Income Tax to Other Areas of Law	Catherine Brown Chris Sprysak
10	Dispute Resolution, Statutory Interpretation and Tax Avoidance	Colin Campbell Carl MacArthur

We would also like to thank Heather Cant Woodward at Carswell for her production assistance and support for this project.

The 15th edition reflects the law as of March 31, 2015.

Tim Edgar
Arthur Cockfield
Martha O'Brien

Table of Contents

1

The Logic, Policy and Politics of Tax Law

I. THE JOY OF LEARNING TAX LAW

A. Accounting for the Attraction of Tax Law

Proving only, some would say, that there is no accounting for taste, a surprisingly large group of students find the study of tax law the most interesting, challenging and fascinating course in law school. Nevertheless, many students approach their first tax law course with trepidation. They anticipate that it will be both tedious and daunting. This chapter will reflect on what makes tax law attractive to some students, with the aim of enticing other students to approach it with a more open mind, or at least persuade them of its potential value. Moreover, thinking hard about why you are taking a tax course should serve to reduce your alienation and enable you to plan your approach to the course to maximize its educational value.

Some law students find tax law interesting for obvious practical reasons — both personal and professional. Every individual resident in Canada who owes tax must file a tax return annually. Filing your annual tax return and paying tax is one of the most important obligations of citizenship. Consequently, tax law is of personal interest to almost everyone since knowing a little tax law will make the annual ritual of filing a tax return more understandable, will perhaps make it more profitable, and might even make it a joyful experience.

For an aspiring lawyer, an even more compelling practical reason to study income tax law is that tax law is pervasive. No matter what area of legal practice you engage in, tax matters are likely to be relevant. Any advice that a lawyer gives a client about such apparently uncomplicated transactions as the sale, lease or encumbrance of property; the dissolution of marriage; the drafting of wills and the administration of estates; the negotiation of employment and other contracts; or the settlement of claims for personal injuries and other losses will be inadequate unless the tax consequences are considered. More complex commercial and business transactions, from the incorporation of a private business to the capitalization or reorganization of a public company, are permeated, if not dominated, by tax considerations. Obviously, all lawyers do not need a specialized knowledge of tax law, even the tax law relevant to their particular area of practice. They must, however, be sufficiently aware of the potential tax consequences of the transactions to which they commit their clients in order to advise them when to consult a tax specialist. Many practising lawyers go through their careers blissfully ignorant of most of the esoteric rules of private law and cause their clients little grief on that account; however, if lawyers are not sensitive to the possible income tax implications of the transactions upon which they advise their clients they might irrevocably send them on a course of action that results in adverse tax consequences. These will not be happy clients.

As a consequence of its pervasiveness, one of the aspects of tax law that makes it particularly interesting is that it provides a superb vantage point from which to study many related legal subjects, if not the whole fabric of the law. Studying the income taxation consequences of transactions such as sale and leasebacks, weak currency loans, commodity straddles, financial derivatives and corporate mergers is a good way to learn about those transactions themselves. Every new fashion in the capitalization of corporations, corporate reorganizations and most other areas of transactional law must pass before tax lawyers.

Aside from its obvious practical value, the study of income tax law is intellectually fascinating. At its most elemental level, it involves taking one simple idea — the idea that everyone should pay tax on his or her income — and then applying that idea to the full panoramic variety of economic and property relations and transactions that characterize our modern, complex society. To determine each individual's income, the infinite variety of human activity must be classified under this single rubric. Do individuals earn taxable income in the following situations: When they receive an interest-free loan from their parents? When they are awarded a scholarship? When they benefit from the use of the heavily subsidized recreational facilities at university? When they accept a free trip from their law firm in recognition of the hard work they have done as an associate? When they earn frequent flier miles on the value of that trip? When someone discharges a debt they owe? When they exchange their legal services for the roofing services of their neighbour (does the neighbour also receive taxable income from this transaction)? When they sell their university poster collection? When they live in a residence they own? When they look after their own children? When they receive an inheritance?

Even the contributors to this volume are bedeviled with these kinds of questions in their personal lives. For example, the publishers of this volume usually send the contributors an extra free copy. Should the contributors include the value of this gift in their taxable income? If so, should they include the subjective value of the book to them in their income, or should they include its fair market value (as a new or second-hand book?)? Does your answer change if they give it away to a deserving student? If they include its value in their employment income as a benefit they have received by virtue of their employment, can they deduct its value from their business income if they use it to assist them in earning that income? If they give it away should the person who receives it have to include its value in his or her income? These are straightforward examples drawn from the countless situations in which a person might have to recognize gross income for tax purposes. Now think about the difficulties of determining what expenses individuals should be entitled to deduct from gross income in order to arrive at their net taxable income, or the complex problems of determining at what point in time income should be recognized even in the most straightforward financial transaction, and you will begin to appreciate what an intensely intellectual endeavour studying tax law can be. Incidentally, the answer to the question of which of the above situations should result in gross income is arguably all of them, although the income generated in many of those transactions is in fact not subject to tax under the Act, as you are about to learn.

Tax law is also intellectually exciting because it constitutes the rules of a fast game played by dedicated people for high stakes. Bright tax lawyers, accountants and economists in the Department of Finance attempt to implement government policy by drafting provisions of the income tax law. As soon as these provisions are announced, a small army of dedicated and imaginative tax lawyers and accountants — being paid an indecent amount of money — begin to apply their minds to how they might advise their clients to find ways around the laws. The courts are called in to resolve disputes. Department of Finance officials respond with proposed amendments to the legislation, in an often vain attempt to preserve the integrity of the government's initial policy judgments. Wealthy individuals, their representatives, and the business community frantically lobby for relief. The financial press takes sides. Politicians fulminate. Tax teachers pontificate. As tax law students you have front-row seats to this high stakes game. Take time to reflect on it as a disinterested observer before you join in the fray upon graduation.

Tax law is also interesting because almost every social and economic policy has a tax angle. The Act is laden with social and economic legislative judgments that have nothing to do with administering an equitable, efficient and simple technical tax system. Consequently, there are few better vantage points from which to observe the unfolding drama of public policy. The government publishes an account every year of the provisions in the Act that are deliberately used as instruments to further specific social and economic policies. In the most recent annual account of tax expenditures, the Department of Finance estimated that the personal income tax legislation alone contains over 125 such provisions in policy areas such as culture and recreation, education, family, health, income maintenance and retirement, general business and investment, and small business. To give some sense of the importance of these tax expenditures for Canadian economic and social policy, if their individual cost estimates are added together, they amount to over $50 billion of foregone tax revenue. Recently, the public policy debate has included the need for tax breaks for sports stadiums and NHL hockey teams, the need for additional green taxes to protect the environment, the need for tax changes to support traditional family values, the need for more tax breaks for talented workers in the hi-tech industry and other tax concessions to increase the innovative capacity and productivity of the Canadian economy, and the need for more tax breaks for students pursuing higher education.

At a macro level, over the past few years many Canadians have been caught up in a debate over whether the level of taxes in Canada is causing a "brain drain" to the United States and generally whether tax levels are reducing work incentives, savings behaviour and investment activity and thus resulting in Canadians falling further behind the standard of living of Americans. As illustrative of the importance of tax in public policy, and of its potential interest, scan the major newspapers on almost any day of the week and mark the references to tax law. During budget season (from the end of February to about the end of April), when the federal and provincial governments are tabling their budgets, announcements of major tax law changes dominate the news. Indeed, the public debate over the federal budget and related tax changes every year is about the closest Canadians get to a national conversation about our collective goals and values.

Tax laws are such important instruments of economic and social policy that they are the subject of examination by scholars from almost every discipline. Thus the study of tax law is greatly enriched by the fact that tax lawyers share an interest in this subject with accountants, philosophers, economists, political scientists, sociologists, psychologists and historians. No matter what your undergraduate training, you ought to be able to find aspects of tax law to which it is highly relevant.

Finally, tax law holds the attention of many students because it is shot through with politics. Often it is at the centre of politics. Historically, it has been the immediate cause of countless revolutions, including of course the American War of Independence. The refusal to pay taxes is a traditional and still sometimes used form of protest against government policy. In the late 1980s, the introduction of the Goods and Services Tax (GST) in Canada gave rise to one of the most divisive political battles in recent history. In the last few years, in what has become referred to as the era of post-deficit politics, the need for tax cuts has become one of the defining issues of Canadian politics. No other public policy issue has been so consistently at the centre of ideological conflict over the proper role, size, and functions of the modern welfare state.

Modern political parties define themselves by their stance on tax issues. This should not be surprising since tax laws are the most visible policy instrument that modern governments use to position themselves along the two fundamental axes upon which political ideologies have traditionally been arrayed: an axis in which political ideologies are ordered from those concerned primarily with individualism to those concerned primarily with collectivism; and, an axis upon which they are arrayed from those concerned with the need for hierarchy or elitism to those concerned primarily with achieving a high degree of social and economic equality. To implement collective decision-making, and thus move from concerns over individualism to concerns about community, taxes are an important policy instrument. Similarly, taxes are normally seen as an important policy instrument in achieving a more egalitarian society. Taxes thus raise fundamental questions not only about public policy but also about morality, including the central question of what is a morally acceptable distribution of the income and wealth that members of a society collectively produce. As such, tax laws are a particularly reliable barometer of shifts in prevailing ideologies. The tax system has been called "a mirror of democracy".[1] Joseph Schumpeter, a widely admired economic historian, observed that "nothing shows so clearly the character of a society and of a civilization as does the fiscal policy that its political sector adopts."[2]

Altogether, aside from the rational use of tax laws as an instrument of government policy, taxes are at the centre of political debate because they are so clearly about money. Although money is not everything — we are told — it appears that most people think it is not without its advantages. At the end of the day, the debate over taxes is a debate over who will pay. Although it is a rather obvious point that taxes "reflect a continuing struggle among contending interests for the privilege of paying the least",[3] a few of the many frequently repeated quotes provide the flavour of this debate. T. S. Adams, a prominent American economist who worked in the U.S. Treasury when the American income tax was being implemented observed that "modern taxation or tax-making in its most characteristic aspect is a group contest in which powerful interests vigorously endeavour to rid themselves of present and proposed tax burdens. It is, first of all, a hard game in which he who trusts wholly in economics, reason, and justice, will in the end retire beaten and disillusioned. Class politics is the essence of taxation."[4] Louis Eisenstein, a leading American tax lawyer in the 1940s and 1950s, and a tax commentator of uncommon brilliance and originality, in a book that every tax student should read, *The Ideologies of Taxation*, was equally blunt. He stated, "taxes ... are a changing product of earnest efforts to have others pay them. In a society where the few control the many, the efforts are rather simple. Levies are imposed in response to the preferences of the governing groups. Since their well-being is equated with the welfare of the community, they are inclined to burden themselves as lightly as possible. Those who have little say are expected to pay."[5]

In attempting to account for the attraction of tax law, perhaps the last word should be left to Eisenstein who, after a lifetime of practising, studying, and writing about tax law observed, "Any intelligent thinking on taxes eventually reaches the ultimate purpose of life on this planet as each of us conceives it."[6]

---

1 C. Webber & A. Wildavsky, *A History of Taxation and Expenditure in the Western World* (New York: Simon and Schuster, 1986) at 326.

2 J. Schumpeter, *History of Economic Analysis* (New York: Oxford University Press, 1954) at 769.

3 L. Eisenstein, *The Ideologies of Taxation* (New York: Ronald Press, 1961) at 3-4.

4 T. S. Adams, "Ideals and Idealism in Taxation" (1928) 18 *American Economic Review* 12.

5 *Supra* note 3 at 11.

6 L. Eisenstein, "A Discussion of 'The Ideologies of Taxation'" (1962) 18 Tax L. Rev. 1 at 22.

B. Objectives of the Basic Course in Tax Law

Some law students express anxiety about taking a tax law course because in numerous respects tax law seems different from other law subjects. It is detailed and complex and contains mathematical formulas and accounting concepts; it appears to be dominated by economic analysis and principles; the policy issues appear unique; it is entirely statutory; and, the politics are largely driven by the concerns of business interests. Hopefully, what this introductory chapter will show is that these characteristics of tax law should not be off-putting, no matter what your background, and that tax law is not different from other legal subjects; indeed, in a tax law course you can learn everything you need to know about the law.

The purpose of this chapter on the logic, policy and politics of tax law is to provide students with a brief overview of the concepts and vocabulary of tax law, the tools of tax analysis, tax policy principles, and some of the basic frameworks that are essential in understanding and evaluating tax law and policy issues. It may seem somewhat odd to present these frameworks here since — and this is the point that was made above — they are the same frameworks that underlie most areas of law. Nevertheless, as they apply to tax law they are sufficiently unique that it seems justifiable to set them out in this context. Moreover, the application of these explanatory frameworks is really all there is that is very difficult to learn in law school and they can be thoroughly mastered only by applying them again and again across the diverse subject areas of the law.

Some law students still seem to resist the idea that it is worthwhile learning what they consider "theory". They came to law school to learn the practice of law, not to apply theoretical frameworks. It has always been a mystery to many of us who teach law why this feeling still seems to linger among some law students. Where do students get the idea that practical matters can be divorced from so-called theory? Presumably not from ordinary experience. Without a theory you cannot explain why a Koala is not a bear, a whale is not a fish, or a tomato is not a vegetable. Moreover, you have no basis for arguing that professional wrestling is not a sport, that men should not be allowed to compete in synchronized swimming events, or about anything else that matters. Why would anyone suppose that the study of law is any different than these gripping issues? Even if you think that law, or tax law, generally makes no sense, or is simply a set of discrete rules to be memorized, you implicitly hold some view about what does make sense or why tax law is only a set of discrete rules divorced from any context and, therefore, the premises underlying that intuition should be exposed and subject to examination. As someone once said, "there is nothing more practical than a good theory." As aspiring practising lawyers, you ought to take this dictum seriously. On the other hand, in the interests of disclosing contrary authorities, as all ethical lawyers would, Yogi Berra is reputed to have said, "In theory there is no difference between theory and practice. In practice there is."

It is a commonplace view that law, as practised by lawyers, is a process of decision-making, not the regurgitation of a discrete set of rules. It does not take three years to train lawyers how to find the black-letter rules that might be relevant to a legal problem. First-year law students are able to find those rules with relative ease. Learning to think like a lawyer involves learning to solve public policy problems, normally at the level of the implementation of the law in judicial and other adjudicative forums, and not infrequently before administrative and legislative bodies. Like participants in all decision-making processes, in order to practise law well lawyers must be prepared to bring to bear on their work the full variety of approaches, knowledge and disciplines relevant to it. Moreover, they must understand the basic principles, the conceptual frameworks, and the factors that animate the law and the different perspectives from which it can be viewed. That is to say, they must understand the law, and be able to place legal problems in their widest possible context.

As with all law courses, at the heart of the basic tax law course are issues for which there is no one answer and which require the full range of the skills of a lawyer to determine the preferred outcome. Tax law involves the kind of intellectual work needed for figuring out the best of a number of alternative answers. It is complex and requires sophisticated and careful reasoning and the exercise of thoughtful judgment. That is why competency in law requires so much training and, incidentally, one of the reasons that good lawyers are so well remunerated: not many people are prepared to devote the time required for the formal education and practical experience necessary nor do they not have the aptitude (or inclination) required to develop the skills of perceiving similarities between situations and factors, drawing normative distinctions, and theorizing about and mustering evidence relating to the relationship between legally relevant variables. Parenthetically, the high salaries of some lawyers are also likely accounted for by their innate abilities, personal connections, the government regulation of legal practice, and several market failures in the delivery of legal services. One such failure is the fact that the value of legal services is almost impossible for clients to judge (legal services are a classic illustration of what economists refer to as post-experience goods in which consumers are generally unable to judge the causality between consumption and some of its effects, and therefore, markets are unlikely to deliver them efficiently). Another is the fact that the practice of law is increasingly taking the form of a winner-take-all tournament in which marginal differences in skill levels are making huge differences in remuneration. All of these considerations suggest strong normative justifications for the regulation of legal salaries, including progressive income taxation. More on this later.

The following brief reviews of the various logics, policies and politics — or as they might be collectively referred, the explanatory frameworks — that underlie tax law are somewhat conventional. They very briefly summarize a vast literature, much of which some of you will have covered in great depth in your undergraduate courses. You may not find these frameworks particularly useful; however, you should then attempt to develop your own frameworks, whether drawn from disciplines as diverse as feminist theory or classical economics, so that you can coherently, from your own perspective, grasp the law in action and understand and evaluate its consequences.

You need to develop theories about all aspects of the tax system, for a number of reasons. First, to help you understand tax law. Without an intellectual framework, you will be simply learning what must appear as a bunch of incoherent rules. Perhaps more so than in any other area of law, the details of tax law can only be truly understood if you understand the deeper structures that underlie the income tax. Even though much of tax law is accounted for by the pleadings of special interest groups, the log-rolling of politicians, or even the incompetence of the drafters, you will not be able to identify these rules and make sense out of them without an explanatory framework.

Second, although these explanatory frameworks for thinking about legal issues should help you understand the law, they are obviously indispensable in critiquing the law. Aside from your obligations as citizens, as lawyers you bear an increased responsibility for the quality of our laws and their administration. As lawyers we are constantly called upon to react to and evaluate the flow of proposals concerning legal change and the government's role in the economy more generally. Having a systematic framework for organizing your thoughts about various government programs and laws not only ensures that you will be applying your values consistently, but will also assist you in avoiding the kind of armchair empiricism and ad hoc judgments that lawyers are sometimes accused of engaging in. Moreover, understanding the policies and principles that underlie the law will help you avoid falling into the trap of false necessity, that is, the irresistible temptation to assign a degree of inevitability to existing arrangements and convert "what is" into "what ought to be".

A third reason for theorizing about tax law in the basic tax course is that two of the overriding purposes of university education are to further the ability of students to think effectively and to assist them in clarifying their beliefs and values, with the consequence of making the world a better place. The development of these attributes of citizenship is, of course, the reason that there are numerous tax credits for university students and large (but unfortunately diminishing) government subsidies. Hopefully, thinking about the important public policy issues raised in tax law will contribute in a small way to furthering these important missions of the university.

Finally, mapping, or understanding complex conceptual interrelationships, is an important learning strategy. There has been a considerable amount of research into student approaches to learning that reveals that whether you are an abstract or concrete learner or a sequential or network learner, there are important differences between deep and surface approaches to learning. Those students whose learning is most effective appear to have the following characteristics: they focus on what is "signified", that is, the author or the instructor's argument or the concepts applicable to understanding the issues under discussion; they relate previous knowledge to new knowledge; they relate knowledge from different courses; they relate theoretical ideas to everyday experience; they relate and distinguish evidence and arguments; and, they organize and structure content into a coherent whole. These explanatory frameworks are intended to assist you to do all of these things as you proceed through the tax course.

The following sections of this introductory chapter briefly describe some of the explanatory frameworks that underlie tax law. By and large, learning the frameworks is presented as an objective of the basic course in tax law, but naturally each instructor will have his or her own objectives for the course (as will students). Nevertheless, normally the objectives of individual instructors (and students) will be embraced within some number of the objectives as stated here, although the emphasis will obviously vary widely. These objectives include learning the following: some of the details of the taxation of individuals, the vocabulary and classification of taxes, the methodology of tax law and policy analysis, some of the important analytical tools for tax analysis, the normative justifications for tax laws, the criteria for evaluating technical tax laws, the criteria for evaluating tax expenditures, the conceptual framework that underlies the income tax laws relating to the taxation of individuals, the fundamentals of tax planning, the principles of statutory interpretation, the political and other determinants of tax laws, and the various perspectives from which tax law can be viewed. Only the most basic outlines of these frameworks are presented here. Students who wish to advance their knowledge of these frameworks beyond the elementary level presented here should consult one of the standard texts in the relevant area. However, your knowledge and skill in applying these frameworks can only be enriched and deepened by using them to assist your thinking about the issues that are raised throughout the course.

Introductory tax materials commonly contain brief overviews of topics such as the history of Canadian income tax law, the sources of tax law (in tax law the various branches of government – the legislative, executive, administrative and the judicial – all play a central role), the structure of the income tax statute, and a review of the numerous texts, looseleaf services and other secondary sources and explanations of tax law. This chapter does not contain a review of these topics in part because of limitations of space and in part because there are so many good and accessible discussions of them.[7]

---

[7] One of the most thorough is Ted Cook, *Canadian Tax Research: A Practical Guide*, 5th ed. (Toronto: Carswell, 2010). Students with a real interest in tax law should study this book. Another useful source for this kind of background information is Bob Neale and Murray Pearson, *Ernst & Young's Guide to Tax Research and Writing*, 7th ed. (Toronto: Canadian Institute of Chartered Accountants, 2014). As well, most single volume tax textbooks have a chapter that provides an overview of these topics, see, in particular, Peter Hogg, Joanne Magee and Jinyan Li, *Principles of Canadian Income Tax Law*, 8th ed. (Toronto: Carswell, 2013). Finally, a good sense of the structure of the legislation can be gained by examining and using Arthur Cockfield, Martha O'Brien and Catherine Brown, *Student Edition of The Income Tax Act 2015* (Toronto: Carswell, 2015). This booklet also contains an entertaining tax novella that provides an insightful introduction to basic tax concepts.

II. THE RELATIVE UNIMPORTANCE OF THE DETAILS OF TAX LAW

One obvious, if not particularly important, purpose of the basic course is to learn some of the details of tax law. At the end of the course, you might not have a working knowledge of income tax law, but you will be aware of the kinds of transactions involving individuals that are likely to have tax consequences, what principles would apply in giving shape to the details that govern the transaction, and where in the conceptual structure of the tax law answers to particular tax problems are likely to be found.

There is no question that tax law is comprised of a formidable quantity of detailed rules. The Act itself is now consolidated in an over 1,400 page document. Thousands and thousands of additional pages are needed to embrace the regulations, rulings and other pertinent government documents. It is detailed because the environment of tax law — the economy — is complex and sophisticated and tax laws must be drafted to apply to the minutia of the transactions that the economy generates.

However, you should not be overly concerned with learning the details of tax law, and in most basic tax courses little effort is made to survey much of the detail. Although a fair amount of technical detail is covered in most courses — in fact students are often shocked by how much has been covered come exam day — covering detail is not an end in itself. The detailed tax law should serve primarily to introduce you to the vocabulary of income tax law and to illustrate and give content to the deeper, conceptual structure of the law. Having said that, however, you should not shy away from the detail. As a lawyer you will often be called upon to learn, categorize, and make sense out of massive details of the law in many areas and, therefore, you should begin to learn to cope with the details of the law. A tax law course is a wonderful vehicle to assist you in learning this skill. Moreover, concentrating on the details in some areas is absolutely essential if you are to learn the skill of reading statutes carefully and for all of their nuances. One of the most important objectives of a basic tax law course is to assist students in learning how to read a complex statute. This often requires concentrating on the precise language used in the Act and an attempt to understand the logic of obscure and arcane refinements to the provisos to the exceptions.

In case you are still feeling tempted to begin memorizing by rote vast chunks of tax law, a few more words of caution. First, in any area where you are familiar with the underlying business, economic or legal context, to be frank, the details of tax law are not all that hard. They are about equivalent to the instructional details one has to understand in assembling IKEA furniture. As someone once quipped — although it was not a very nice thing to quip — the details of tax law are so simple to learn that even accountants are expected to learn them. Second, rest assured that no matter how many details of tax law you learn in the basic course, given the voluminous details of the law, you will have probably covered only 1 or 2 per cent of tax law. Could anything possibly turn on whether you have in your head 1.5 per cent as opposed to 1.7 per cent of the tax laws? Third, no area of law is more susceptible to change than income taxation. So even if you remember a few rules, you will be only slightly ahead of the game. They will inevitably change. A major tax amending bill is enacted almost every year. But while the details change, the fundamental structure of the Act, and the fundamental normative principles underlying it, have not changed almost since its inception. Fourth, if all you learn in a tax course are some of the details of tax law you will forget them almost the minute you walk out of the exam. You will have largely wasted your time, and missed an excellent educational opportunity. Fifth, a somewhat more cynical reason for not attempting to memorize the details of tax law is that you can look them up, particularly when someone is paying you to do so.

One aspect of tax law that contributes to the sense that it is extremely detailed is that tax law is more number-oriented than most law school courses and draws upon concepts in accounting and finance. However, this also should not be a matter of undue concern. In fact, you should see this as an opportunity. Law students should develop skills in basic numeracy. Some forms of quantitative analysis increasingly are becoming more important skills of lawyers. Moreover, many statutes, including the Act, use arithmetic functions and you should be familiar with how arithmetic functions (especially ratios, which can be tricky) are expressed in statutory language. Tax law, like most business oriented courses, does draw upon corporate, accounting and finance concepts and is laced with the vocabulary of those subject areas. However, there is a surprisingly small number of concepts that are used. If you are unfamiliar with them now is the time to learn them. Their use is becoming increasingly common in all areas of law. Moreover, the computations in tax law, and other areas of law, are only used to illustrate concepts. Normally the concepts are not so difficult that they cannot be expressed and understood verbally — and you should be able to understand them that way. However, for some people, at least, an arithmetic function makes the concept more readily understandable. Invariably the arithmetic functions involve simple addition, subtraction, multiplication or division. The math is not difficult. Of course, in some areas such as calculating tax liabilities or alternative tax planning opportunities, the math is not so simple. However, none of these calculations are required in order to understand tax law or even to practice tax law, as opposed to tax accounting. Even if you practice in this area, you will not necessarily need to do the complex math since you will invariably have computer programs (and accountants!) to assist you.

III. TAX TAXONOMY: THE DEFINITION, CLASSIFICATION AND TERMINOLOGY OF TAXES

A. What is a Tax?

Although there is not much question that the income tax is a tax, in order to locate a discussion of the income tax analytically there is some value in thinking about what distinguishes a tax from other methods by which the government might raise revenue and from other government policy instruments more generally. A dictionary definition of a tax would be something like, "a compulsory transfer of money from private individuals or organizations to the government not paid in exchange for some specific good or benefit". The distinguishing characteristics of taxes are that they are compulsory and unrequited.

It is normally easy to distinguish between a tax paid to the government and an amount paid that would not be classified as a tax. The latter would include fines and penalties imposed by governments to deter or punish unacceptable behaviour; royalty payments to compensate the government for the right to extract oil and gas or to exploit other natural resources from government-owned land or resources; and prices charged by the government for some goods and services that it sells to individuals. However, in some cases one of these types of payments to the government might contain a tax. For example, if the amount paid to the government in return for a particular good or service is not performing the economic function of a price, namely to bring the supply and demand of a good or service into balance, then it should be regarded as a tax.

Is the amount paid for a government-sponsored lottery ticket a price or a tax? One might argue that it is a price because it is voluntary and the purchaser receives a chance to win a prize in exchange. However, an amount can sensibly be treated as a tax even though it can be avoided by not purchasing the good or engaging in the activity to which it attaches. All taxes can be avoided in that sense. Liquor taxes can be avoided by not buying liquor, gas taxes can be avoided by not buying gas, the GST can be avoided by buying only exempt or zero-rated goods and services, and the income tax can be avoided by not working. If one wants to buy a lottery ticket, the full price must be paid, even the portion that far exceeds the government's cost of the ticket. It is the case that by buying a lottery ticket the purchaser is obtaining a chance to win a prize, however, the government sets the price of lottery tickets far above the expected value of the prizes. About 40 per cent of the price is not returned to winners. Consequently, the payment to the government for a lottery ticket is probably sensibly treated as in part a price and in part a tax. The government's 40 per cent monopoly profit is equivalent to a tax. One way to think about this is that the government might have sold the ticket for a price that equaled the cost of running the lottery, including the expected value of the prizes, and then imposed an explicit

40 per cent tax (actually, a 66.6 per cent tax on the price of the lottery ticket); the economic result would have been identical.

What is the significance of classifying an amount as a tax, as in the example of 40 per cent of the cost of lottery tickets? Like many questions in tax law and policy, the question of whether an amount paid to the government should be regarded as a tax or some other type of payment is purely a conceptual question. That is, it is not a question the answer to which can be empirically verified. Nor is it a question about values. In asking whether a payment represents a tax we are not being asked to assign some value to lotteries whether good or bad, wise or unwise, right or wrong, politically desirable or not. It is a pure question of concept. In order to clarify our thinking about the government's 40 per cent monopoly profits made from the sale of lottery tickets, is it more helpful to think about it as a price, perhaps like tuition fees paid to the government for a university education, or is it more helpful to think about it as a tax, like the income tax? If it is analogous to other taxes, then the normative justifications required in imposing taxes, and the criteria applied in evaluating those taxes, should be applied to this portion of the price of a lottery ticket. Selective sales taxes, also referred to as excise taxes, are normally justified on the grounds that the consumption of the items taxed impose social costs and, therefore, the tax is an attempt to ensure that the price of the good reflects its full cost; both the private costs of producing it and the social costs imposed by its consumption. What cost do purchasers of lottery tickets impose on society? One of the criteria used in evaluating taxes is whether the cost of the tax is fairly distributed across income classes. The empirical evidence suggests that low-income individuals spend a much larger percentage of their income on lottery tickets than high-income individuals. Assuming that the winners announced in the newspapers — who always seem to be folks down on their luck — are a random sample of the people who buy lottery tickets, this seems like an obvious point. But then the normative question becomes more urgent: what possible justification is there for this viciously regressive tax?

Another kind of situation in which the decision to label a payment to the government as a tax is contentious is where there is only a loose connection between the amount an individual pays for government goods and services and the value of the goods and services provided. For example, there is an ongoing debate in Canadian public policy as to whether the premiums paid for employment insurance and coverage under the Canada pension plan should be regarded as a price or a tax. Basically, everyone pays a fixed percentage of his or her income in these premiums, around 10 per cent in the case of the Canada pension plan (on the assumption that the amount paid by the employer is, in the long run, paid by the employee in the form of lower wages), until his or her income reaches slightly under $54,000 (the annual maximum pensionable earnings). Then the premiums remain a fixed amount. Consequently, someone earning $100,000 pays a significantly lower percentage of his or her income in these premiums than someone earning $50,000. If these premiums are regarded as a price, this might be unobjectionable since the employment insurance coverage purchased by the high-income individual is about equal to the coverage received by the middle-income individual. Similarly, both will receive about the same amount from the Canada Pension Plan. However, if the premiums bear little relationship to the benefits that different individuals receive, then they can fairly be regarded as taxes and the fairness of their incidence, that is who pays them, becomes a matter of concern.

Public finance texts frequently divide government charges into public prices, service fees, specific benefit taxes, taxes in lieu of charges, general benefit taxes, earmarked taxes (divided further into pure earmarking, notional earmarking, and effective earmarking), and taxes. However, for the purposes of simply locating taxes analytically within the broader range of government policy instruments that require payments to governments enough has been said. But more generally on this issue about what is a tax, it is important to bear in mind that while in some contexts it is analytically useful to distinguish between a tax and other government policy instruments such as prices, regulation, government subsidies and confiscation, in many respects taxes are no different than these other policy instruments. In particular, a sharp distinction is often drawn between the government's use of taxes and the government's use of property and contract laws to achieve particular policy objectives. Unlike property and contract laws, taxes, it is sometimes alleged, are burdensome impositions, reduce freedom, usurp private choices, and are an interference with private property. At one level, whether taxes reduce freedom, for example, is a normative question. Many people would argue that taxes, in fact, greatly enhance the amount of freedom available in a society by redistributing income. By any measure, $1,000 in the hands of someone whose income is otherwise $20,000 increases the options confronting that person by much more than taking $1,000 from a person earning $300,000 could conceivably reduce freedom. Moreover, taxes increase people's freedom by allowing them to pursue their collective aspirations. There are important differences between governing policy instruments such as taxes, subsidies, regulation, credit controls, the rules of contract and property law, government ownership, and government suasion. However, the differences are much more subtle than they are often made out to be in discussions over tax law and policy.

B. Classification of Taxes

All taxes have five components, and they are usually classified by reference to an attribute of one or the other of these components. First, each tax must have a base upon which it is levied. Second, each tax must have a tax-filing unit that is responsible for paying the tax. Third, taxes must have a rate that is to be applied to the base in arriving at the tax owing. Fourth, unless they are imposed on individual transactions, taxes must have a period over which the base is measured and the taxes collected. Fifth, each tax must have a set of administrative arrangements for its collection. Although taxes can be classified by reference to the characteristics of each of these components, only the tax classification schemes relating to the tax base and tax rates will be reviewed here since they are by far the most important.

1. The Tax Base

The most common way for classifying taxes is by reference to their base, that is, the amount, transaction or property upon which the tax is levied. The concept of the "tax base" is an important part of the specialized terminology of tax. There are three obvious bases upon which a broad-based tax might be levied: the amount that an individual earns (income); the amount that an individual spends (consumption); or, the amount represented by an individual's property (wealth). The base of most taxes is expressed in monetary terms: the dollar value of income earned, goods and services consumed, or property held. The tax is calculated simply by applying the rate of tax, almost always expressed as a percentage, to this base.

An income tax is, of course, a tax in which the base is income. A good deal of the basic course in income tax law is taken up with learning how this base is defined in the Act. In the Act income is defined, by and large, by reference to the sources side of the household budget as the net amount an individual earns from sources such as employment, property and business. However, income can also be defined on the uses side of the household budget: the value of the individual's personal consumption plus the increase in his or her net wealth. The equivalence between defining income on the sources and uses side of the household budget is easy to see. If an individual earns income from some sources he or she can either use it to purchase consumption goods and services or save it and thus increase his or her net wealth.

In addition to taxing income comprehensively, a government might impose a tax on only some aspect of income, such as wages and salaries. These taxes are commonly referred to as payroll taxes and are primarily used to finance social insurance schemes. In Canada, federal payroll taxes consist of premiums for employment insurance and Canada/Quebec pension plan contributions. Provincial payroll taxes include workers compensation premiums and, in some provinces, taxes on payrolls to help finance health care.

Consumption is potentially another comprehensive tax base. Recall that the definition of income, on the uses side of the household budget, is consumption plus increase in net wealth. Hence a consumption tax is essentially equivalent to an income tax that exempts the value of the taxpayer's savings from tax. If consumption is the desired tax base, there are numerous ways the tax can be imposed and collected. The federal GST is a value-added tax in which the tax rate is applied to the value added to goods and services at each stage of their production. By contrast, the provincial retail sales taxes are single-stage taxes that are collected by retailers when goods and services are sold to consumers. Over the years, there has been an extended debate over which form of sales tax is to be preferred; however, the multi-stage sales tax appears to have emerged triumphant and is now used around the world. Generally, it appears easier to extend to all goods and services, easier to remove from production goods, and more difficult to evade than a single-stage sales tax.

In addition to a tax on sales transactions, a broad-based consumption tax could take the form of a personal expenditure tax. For example, if individuals calculated all of their income and then deducted their savings at the end of the year presumably the balance would be the value of the goods and services they consumed in the year. Some economists argue that a personal consumption tax would be more equitable, efficient and administratively simpler than an income tax, but no country has yet implemented one.

Consumption taxes that are only imposed on selected goods and services are commonly referred to as excise taxes. In Canada, excise taxes are imposed both by the federal government and the provinces on products such as gasoline, cigarettes, alcoholic beverages, lotteries, automobile air conditioners, and a few luxury goods. The normative justification for most of these excise taxes is that the consumption of these goods creates social costs so that the tax is necessary in order to ensure that the price of the good reflects these social costs.

In addition to income and consumption, an individual's wealth is a third possible comprehensive tax base. Wealth taxes can take many forms. Some European countries impose an annual tax on the net wealth of individuals. More commonly, countries impose a tax on the value of a person's wealth when he or she transfers it to some other person either by way of gift or upon death. Wealth transfer taxes are referred to, depending upon their form, as estate or inheritance taxes, or more prosaically as death taxes. The justifications for wealth taxes include the need to achieve a more equitable distribution of wealth, to increase the progressivity of the tax system, to act as a backdrop to the income tax system, and generally to increase the efficiency of the tax system. Not surprisingly, all of these arguments are contentious. Nevertheless, Canada remains only one of a few industrialized countries in the world that does not have a general tax on wealth. Canada does, however, have substantial partial wealth taxes. All provinces or local governments in Canada impose a tax on real property.

This brief review of possible tax bases does not exhaust the list of taxes. Taxes can be levied on any base and in most countries there are a number of miscellaneous taxes that are levied on bases such as business activities, corporate capital, gross receipts, and the use of natural resources.

The following statistics provide a sense of the importance of these various tax bases and sources of revenue to the Canadian federal government. In 2014-2015, the revenue of the federal government was estimated in the February 11, 2014 Federal Budget papers to be $276 billion. This will be comprised of the following estimated amounts: personal income tax - $138 billion (50 per cent); corporate income tax -

$37 billion (13 per cent); non-resident income tax - $5 billion (2 per cent); goods and services tax - $31 billion (11 per cent); custom import duties – $4 billion (1 per cent); excise taxes - $11 billion (4 per cent); employment insurance premiums - $23 billion (8 per cent); and, other revenues - $26 billion (9 per cent). From the point of view of students enrolled in a basic course in income tax, the most salient statistic is that income tax accounts for over one-half of federal government revenue.

In the public finance literature there is heated debate over what is the proper mix of taxes in a country. Generally, left-wing commentators argue for more reliance on income and wealth taxes because they are progressive; right-wing analysts call for more reliance on consumption taxes because they do not tax income from capital. The latter argue that taxing income from capital creates economic distortions that impair the rate of growth in the economy and that this problem has become more serious in the new globalized economy in which capital is almost completely mobile. The owners of capital — multinationals and high net wealth individuals — are free to move their capital across the world seeking those jurisdictions in which it can earn the highest after-tax rate of return.

2. The Rates of Tax

In addition to their base, the other major way that taxes are classified is by reference to their rates. Here, only the concepts that apply to the rates of an income tax will be considered. In considering both the progressivity and the economic effects of income taxes, it is important to distinguish between several concepts of tax rates, most notably, statutory, marginal, average and effective rates.

The statutory rate structure is straightforward and is set out in section 117 of the Act. Although this is not evident from the rate scale established in section 117, the Act provides for a personal tax credit that offsets the tax liability on a taxpayer's first $11,327 of income (in year 2015). (In a rather convoluted way, the tax credit is expressed as 15 per cent of $11,327 in section 118. Since the rate of tax on this income is 15 per cent, the credit completely offsets the tax liability on this amount of income and in this way acts as a zero rate bracket. Incidentally, all these numbers are indexed for inflation every year, thus they are not nice round numbers.) Once the amount sheltered by the personal tax credit is exceeded the statutory rates apply. The tax-schedule in section 117 contains four tax brackets: 15 per cent on taxable income up to $44,701; 22 per cent on additional taxable income up to $ 89,401; 26 per cent on additional taxable income up to $138,586; and 29 per cent on additional taxable income above $138,586 (the dollar amounts of these brackets are for year 2015). Parenthetically, these rates are, of course, only the rates of tax in the federal Act. All of the provinces also impose an income tax, which is imposed on the taxpayer's federal taxable income. The federal government collects the provincial income taxes (in all provinces except Quebec) and remits them to the provinces. Thus taxpayers only have to file one tax return. The provincial rates vary considerable, but simply by way of example, the Manitoba rates for 2015 are 10.8 per cent on taxable income up to $31,000; 12.75 per cent on additional taxable income up to $67,000; and, 17.4 per cent on taxable income over $67,000. Thus in Manitoba the top combined marginal tax rate will be 46.4 per cent on income in excess of $138,586 (29% + 17.4%).

In tax terminology, the rate of tax that applies to an additional dollar a taxpayer earns within each income bracket is called the marginal rate of tax, while the rate that is applicable to the taxpayer's income as a whole — that is the fraction of total income that is paid in taxes — is called the average rate. The percentage figures in the statutory rate schedules are marginal rates; average rates are not set out in the statute. An individual with $150,000 of taxable income, for example, is subject to a federal rate of 15 per cent on taxable income from $11,327 to $44,701; a rate of 22 per cent on taxable income from $44,701 to $89,401; 26 per cent on taxable income from $89,401 to $138,586; and a rate of 29 per cent on taxable income from $138,586 to $150,000. The taxpayer would pay a total federal tax of $30,938. Thus although the individual's federal marginal rate of tax is 29 per cent — that is the rate paid on next dollar earned — the average rate of tax is only 20.6 per cent ($30,938/ $150,000). Notice that when taxpayers earn an additional dollar, even though it might cause them to be moved into a higher marginal tax bracket, it cannot affect the amount of tax they pay on their other income. Thus the popular expression, "I cannot afford to earn more money because it will throw me into a higher bracket," if it is taken to imply that taxpayers might actually sustain an after-tax loss if they earn more money because they will be paying more tax on their income earned up to that point, rests upon a misunderstanding of marginal tax rates.

The expression "effective tax rate" is similar to the expression average tax rate except that it is usually computed by reference to some broader measure of the taxpayer's income than taxable income. In the example above, the taxpayer with taxable income of $150,000 had an average rate of tax of 20.6 per cent. But suppose that the taxpayer had also earned $25,000 of income that was exempted from tax and had also claimed a $25,000 deduction because he or she made a tax-preferred investment. The taxpayer's real income thus exceeded his or her taxable income by $50,000. The individual's effective tax rate would be only 15.4 per cent ($30,938/ $200,000). The concept of effective tax rate can be used to illustrate the effect of exemptions, deductions and tax credits on tax liabilities.

Most commonly, taxes are classified, in relation to their rates, as either being progressive, proportional or regressive. A progressive tax is one that takes an increasing proportion of income as income rises, a proportional tax takes a constant proportion of income, and a regressive tax takes a declining proportion of income. Note that progressive taxation does not simply mean that the rich pay more than the poor. This is true even in the case of the regressive tax. A progressive tax is one where the proportion of income paid in taxes rises with income.

Whether a tax is progressive, proportional or regressive cannot be determined by examining only who legally pays the tax, their taxable income and the rate scale of the tax. These terms are usually used to refer to the reduction in an individual's actual income because of a tax (that is after taking into account the economic incidence of a tax) and are based upon a broad measure of the individual's income. Consequently, whether a particular tax is progressive, proportional or regressive depends upon such things as who really pays the tax, how broadly their income is defined, over what period of time their income is measured, and who is assumed to benefit from exemptions, deductions and credits in the tax base.

Over the years several studies have examined the incidence of the taxes imposed in Canada and whether they are progressive, proportional or regressive. Generally, the studies find that all taxes in Canada are regressive except the income tax. This should occasion no surprise. Consumption taxes tend to be regressive, even though the rate of tax is constant, for example 5 per cent for the GST, because high-income individuals do not consume all of their income. They save a good portion of it. One study[8] found that in 1988 individuals earning under $10,000 spend about 14.6 per cent of their income on commodity taxes, while individuals earning between $100,000 and $150,000 spent only 7 per cent of their income on commodity taxes. On the assumption that renters paid the property taxes levied on apartment buildings, even the property tax was found to be regressive. Individuals earning under $10,000 paid 7 per cent of their income in property taxes, while individuals with incomes between $100,000 and $150,000 paid only 2.8 per cent of their income in property taxes. Even the individual income tax turned regressive over high-income ranges. Thus while individuals earning between $20,000 and $30,000 paid 7.6 per cent of their broad income in income taxes and individuals earning between $100,000 and $150,000 paid 15.5 per cent, those earning over $300,000 paid only 14.5 per cent. The reason for this is that very high-income individuals disproportionately earn sources of income that receive favourable tax treatment, such as capital gains. The authors of this study found that overall the Canadian tax system was about proportional. Everyone, regardless of his or her income, paid between 30 per cent and 35 per cent of his or her income broadly defined in taxes. The progressivity of the income tax was completely offset by the regressivity of the other taxes in the Canadian tax system.

C. Income Tax Terminology

It is difficult to understand any part of the income tax law, or any specific provision in the Act, without knowing something about the whole structure and where the particular piece being studied fits into the overall puzzle. Although this

---

[8] F. Vermaeten, W.I. Gillespie and A. Vermaeten, "Tax Incidence in Canada" (1994) 42 Can. Tax J. 348.

problem of the interrelatedness of the law applies in all areas of the law it might be slightly more serious in tax law because the income tax law is embedded in a statutory scheme that few can grasp by the exercise of pure intuition. Therefore, you should take time to study the logic of the scheme of the Act and be sure to locate any specific provision that you are examining within the larger structure of the Act. A very condensed version of that structure will be presented here for the purpose of defining some of the key terms used in the Act.

In calculating their tax liability, taxpayers first determine their net income for tax purposes. The rules for calculating net income are contained in Division B of Part I of the Act. Although there is no formal definition of gross or net income, section 3 provides a formula for calculating net income for tax purposes. Most of the major ideas you need for understanding the Division B calculation of net income are embedded in section 3. Very basically, it contemplates the following steps. First, the taxpayer "determines the total of all amounts each of which is the taxpayer's income for the year...[other than capital gains] from a source inside or outside Canada, including, without restricting the generality of the foregoing, the taxpayer's income for the year from each office, employment, business and property". Second, taxpayers add their net taxable capital gains to this total. Third, they subtract the deductions permitted in subdivision e. Fourth, they subtract any losses from employment, business, and property.

Even though this formula for the determination of income appears to be relatively comprehensive, a number of items that clearly increase a taxpayer's ability to pay are exempt from tax either because the courts have held that they do not fit within the concept of income as used in section 3 or because the Act specifically exempts them from tax. Strike pay is an example of the former. The Supreme Court of Canada (the "Supreme Court") has held that strike pay is exempt from tax since it is not "income from a source". Other exempt items that might be thought to be income but which have been held or accepted not to be included in section 3 include gambling gains, gifts and inheritances, windfalls, and personal injury awards. The Act explicitly exempts from income one-half of any capital gains realized by a taxpayer. Section 81 exempts from tax a number of other very particular types of income including certain allowances paid to elected officials, and various types of compensation such as that paid by the Federal Republic of Germany to victims of Nazi persecution.

This is not the place to review all the exemptions from tax, but simply to make the definitional point that an item exempted from tax simply does not enter the computation of income. It is important to note that the benefit to an individual taxpayer of having an amount exempted from income for tax purposes depends upon his or her marginal tax rate, which in turn will depend upon the amount of the taxpayer's taxable income. Suppose that a taxpayer sells a publicly-traded share and earns $1,000 of capital gains, that is, he or she sells the share for $1,000 more than what was paid for it. What is the value to the taxpayer of the fact that one-half of this gain is exempt from tax? It depends upon the taxpayer's marginal tax rate. If the taxpayer's income is so low that the taxpayer owes no tax then obviously the exclusion is of no value to him or her whatsoever. The taxpayer would not have paid any tax on it even if it were fully included in income for tax purposes. If the taxpayer's income is $25,000, and the combined marginal tax rate is, let's say, 25 per cent, then the value of being able to exclude $500 from income is 25 per cent of $500 or $125. For a taxpayer whose income is say $150,000, and who is in the 50 per cent combined marginal tax bracket, the value of being able to exclude $500 from income is 50 per cent of $500 or $250. That is, if the tax rates are progressive, exempting amounts from income has much greater value to high-income taxpayers than low-income taxpayers.

In arriving at income for tax purposes, section 3 contemplates that taxpayers earning business or property income will be able to deduct all the business expenses which represent the cost of earning business or property income, such as wages paid to employees, depreciation on business assets, and fees paid to investment advisors. All expenses of earning income should be deductible to arrive at the taxpayer's ability to pay. But in addition to business expenses, in subdivision e of Division B, taxpayers are able to deduct numerous expenses that are clearly personal expenses or investments, that is, expenses that were not incurred in order to earn income but that are in the nature of personal consumption expenses or personal savings. These personal deductions include deductions for such things as contributions to Registered Retirement Savings Plans, expenses for spousal support, moving expenses, and child care expenses. Like business expenses, these personal expenses are allowed as deductions, that is, as offsets against the taxpayer's income before applying the tax rates. As a matter of tax arithmetic, the value of a deduction for personal expenses is the same as an exclusion from income tax is taxable. Thus, if a taxpayer who has no tax liability incurs eligible child care expenses of $2,000, he or she receives no benefit from the tax deduction that is allowed for these expenses. If he or she is in the 25 per cent marginal tax bracket and incurs the same expense, the value of the deduction to him or her is $500. That is, by being able to deduct $2,000 of personal expenses he or she saves $500 in taxes. If he or she is a high-income taxpayer and in the 50 per cent tax bracket, the value of being able to deduct $2,000 of child care expenses is $1,000. This result is sometimes referred to as the upside-down effect of personal tax deductions.

Once taxpayers have arrived at what is sometimes referred to as net income for tax purposes, or Division B income, they then turn to Division C of Part I in order to calculate their "taxable income". Division C allows for the deduction of a few additional amounts. They include the following: a deduction of one-half of the employment income realized on the exercise of certain employee stock options; a deduction for business and other allowable losses that have been carried forward from prior years or back from subsequent years; payments such as worker's compensation and social assistance that are required to be included in the taxpayer's net income under Division B; the equivalent of an interest free $25,000 employee home relocation loan; and certain deductions for individuals residing in prescribed northern and isolated areas.

For many taxpayers, their net income for tax purposes will be the same as their taxable income. They will not be entitled to claim any of the deductions in Division C. However, if taxpayers qualify for any of the deductions in Division C then obviously their taxable income will be less than their net income. Why does the Act distinguish between net income and taxable income? That is to say, why aren't the deductions in Division C found in Division B? The reason is that the drafters wanted a concept of income in the Act that corresponded more closely to the taxpayer's economic income than taxable income since some of the tax expenditures in the Act are conditioned on the taxpayer's income. For example, in one-earner families, the income earning spouse can claim a tax credit of $11,327 × 15 per cent (in 2015) if he or she supports a spouse or common-law partner working at home. However, the base amount of this tax credit must be reduced by the spouse or common-law partner's net income for tax purposes. The drafters wanted a concept of income for the purposes of determining how much the base for the spousal tax credit should be reduced that corresponded as closely as possible to that person's economic income. Similarly, the basic GST tax credit for eligible individuals of $268 (in 2015) is reduced by 5 per cent of the amount that the individual's adjusted income exceeds $34,872. Eligibility for these credits, and several others in the Act, are dependent upon the spouse or taxpayer's net income as determined under the Act, not taxable income. The need to have a concept of income that corresponds somewhat closely to the taxpayer's economic income leads to the odd result that taxpayers receiving worker's compensation payments, for example, will include the payment in their income under Division B but then subtract it under Division C. Thus, although these amounts are not taxable, they must be included in the taxpayer's income so that, for example, individuals receiving them cannot also claim the full GST credit if their income, including these payments, exceeds $34,872. In addition to conditioning some of the provisions in the Act, people using tax statistics in tax and economic policy analysis find the concept of net income more useful for many purposes than taxable income since it corresponds more closely to economic income. It is arguable that some of the deductions for personal expenses, including the deduction for contributions to RRSPs, that are now found in Division B of the Act, should be moved to Division C since they do not reduce a taxpayer's economic income.

Once taxpayers determine their taxable income, they then turn to Division E of Part I to calculate their basic federal tax payable. In calculating this amount, taxpayers first apply the rate schedule in section 117. Once they have determined their total federal income tax on taxable income by applying the rate schedule to their taxable income they can deduct from this amount a number of tax credits. Tax credits are amounts that are offset directly against the taxpayer's tax liability. Thus, unlike tax deductions, their value does not depend upon the taxpayer's marginal tax rate. They have the same value for all taxpayers, at least all taxpayers who owe tax in excess of their eligible credits.

The federal tax credits that can be deducted from federal income tax on taxable income in arriving at basic federal tax payable include the basic, married, equivalent-to-married, and dependent tax credits; the caregiver tax credit; age credit; employment insurance credit; Canadian (Quebec) pension plan credit; disability credit; tuition fee credit; education credit; interest on student loan credit; transfer of tuition fee and education credits; transfer of spouse's credits; medical expense credit; charitable donations credit; and dividend tax credit.

All the tax credits listed above are non-refundable. This means that if the taxpayer's tax credits exceed the tax that is otherwise owed, the government does not make a payment to the taxpayer. The value of the credit is simply lost to the taxpayer. Tax credits can be made refundable. If they are made refundable that means that if a tax credit exceeds the taxpayer's tax that is otherwise payable, the government makes a payment to the taxpayer of the excess, creating in effect a negative tax. The Act contains four refundable credits: the GST credit, the Canada child tax benefit, the medical expense credit for taxpayers eligible for the mental or physical impairment credit, and the working income tax benefit.

In addition to being refundable, tax credits might also be income-tested so that they vanish as income increases. This targets them on low- and middle-income taxpayers. All three of the refundable tax credits in the Act, as well as the age credit, are income-tested. For example, as mentioned above, the GST tax credit of $268 (in 2015) is reduced by 5 per cent of the amount that a taxpayer's family income exceeds $34,872.

A final concept that should be briefly defined here is the tax expenditure concept. It has already been referred to a number of times in this chapter. The income tax law is composed of two analytically distinct provisions, technical tax provisions and tax expenditures. The technical tax provisions establish and define the basic structural elements of the tax system: the base, the tax filing unit, the accounting period, the rates and the administrative apparatus. These rules are necessary so that the tax system can achieve its principal objectives of raising revenue and redistributing income and they are evaluated using the traditional tax policy criteria of equity, neutrality and simplicity. These criteria are considered in more detail in Part VII, below. However, the Act contains over 125 provisions that have nothing to do with achieving the principal objectives of the tax system or defining one of its essential elements. Instead, their purpose is to provide implicit subsidies to taxpayers to encourage them to engage in particular types of activities or to provide particular taxpayers with a transfer payment. These provisions are now widely referred to as tax expenditures, and should be evaluated using budgetary criteria, the same criteria applied to spending programs.

IV. METHODOLOGY OF TAX LAW AND POLICY ANALYSIS

A. Forms of Reasoning About Tax (or Anything Else)

The term "methodology" is normally used to refer to philosophy of science issues in the social sciences: the study of how, in practice, economists, sociologists, historians, and political scientists go about their work; how they conduct investigations and assess evidence; and, how they decide what is true and false, or whether they can. In the past, lawyers sometimes assumed that they did not have to be bothered with issues of methodology. They assumed that finding and applying tax law, for example, or thinking like a lawyer more generally, involved quite a different reasoning process than that involved in other social sciences and was mainly deductive and largely learned by doing. Almost no one believes this any longer. It is now widely accepted that legal reasoning, even statutory interpretation, is essentially policy-making and is not all that different than policy-making in any other context. Like all policy-making, determining the tax law to apply in some contentious area involves postulating a range of plausible, alternative options; a consideration of the consequences of each in terms (in the case of tax law issues) of tax fairness, the neutrality of the tax system, administrative practicality and other relevant evaluative criteria; and a choice of the preferred option. Like all important decisions in which the consequences are serious — as invariably they are in deciding what the tax law is — all relevant principles, theories and tools of analysis should be brought to bear on the decision-making process. Of course, this methodology is no different than that followed when we make important decisions in our personal lives, although few of us do it systematically. But the more important the decision, even in our everyday lives, the more likely we will think about it carefully and follow this kind of reasoning process. So why not in tax law analysis?

To assist students to engage seriously in an analytical approach to tax law, this section reviews the three different forms of reasoning commonly used in all policy analysis. Whether undertaken in law offices, government departments, Parliament, or the courts, all reasoning involves the explication of issues that can be usefully classified as analytical, normative or empirical. Analytical issues involve reasoning about concepts; normative issues involve reasoning about values; and, empirical issues involve reasoning about facts. Naturally, like all attempts to classify phenomena, this classification can easily be deconstructed, no great trick to that. The world does not come in nice identifiable chunks. Along with other reasons, the distinction cannot be absolute because, on the one hand, normative theories make empirical assumptions about the kind of social order that will result if certain principles are acted upon; while, on the other hand, explanatory theories always rest upon judgments about which phenomena are significant enough to warrant our attempts to explain them. Nevertheless, this classification of issues is frequently useful in clarifying thinking and advancing debates. As an example, the question of whether some type of activity amounts to tax evasion would in most cases be usefully classified as a conceptual question; the question of the appropriate treatment of tax evaders as a normative question; and the question of what causes tax evasion as an empirical question.

Practitioners from almost every social science discipline have tackled issues relating to tax law. The interdisciplinary literature in tax is broad and deep. Thus, the other reason for reviewing the distinction between these forms of policy reasons here is that like all well-educated lawyers, tax lawyers need to be aware of, and appreciate the range and validity of, the different forms of research across a broad range of disciplines and methodologies that bear on their work. No one expects tax lawyers to become social scientists, but they necessarily must be critical consumers of the work of social scientists. Many students will have an extensive background in various social sciences; this brief review of how some of that work bears on tax law is meant only to be suggestive. However, it will assist in alerting students as they proceed throughout the study of tax law to the types of arguments that must be made in particular contexts and the acceptable forms of reasoning in resolving those issues.

B. Analytical Reasoning

Analytical reasoning does not involve an inquiry into values or facts, but instead it is an inquiry into the methods by which we search for such values or facts, the basis on which we assert them, and the concepts we use in formulating them. In effect, it is thinking about what is thinking. It aims to clarify. The pursuit of analytical knowledge is, of course, the domain of philosophy. However, practitioners in all disciplines must engage in conceptual analysis. Indeed, because of their professional training and practice, lawyers are characteristically good at conceptual analysis. At some level, determining and applying the law often simply involves classifying situations with similar facts together, or being able to distinguish between particular fact patterns depending upon the context in which they arise.

Although analytical reasoning involves several methodologies, one that everyone is familiar with, at least superficially, is the methodology of logic. Logic is the study of the validity or invalidity of what follows from what. Developing a facility with the logical assessment of arguments traditionally involves becoming familiar with the recurrent patterns of reasoning and their common pathologies. Even though no one believes any longer that legal reasoning can be reduced to formal logic, it clearly has logical qualities. Therefore, as in every area of law, in engaging in tax law and policy analysis students should be alert to the common fallacies and errors in personal inquiry such as over-generalizing, begging the question, the proneness to see things in terms of extremes, the fallacy of composition (the assumption that what is true for a part will be true for the whole, or the reverse), the fact that correlation does not imply causation, and the fallacy of the transplanted category.

As you begin the study of each new area of tax law, or begin to construct an argument about an important issue in tax analysis, you should attempt to ensure that you understand the definition of the terms, are able to articulate and apply the basic principles, and that you understand the underlying logical structures of the area. A good deal of tax law involves simply conceptual reasoning. Indeed, many of the most important advances in tax analysis, such as the development of the Haig-Simons definition of income and the tax expenditure concept, have been due largely to increased conceptual clarity.

The most distinctive form of legal logic is that of analogy: of comparing and contrasting similar and dissimilar examples. Analogical reasoning is frequently used in tax law for the same reason it is used in other areas of law, to ensure consistency, equal treatment and continuity. For example, the tax law provides that individuals resident in Canada are subject to tax on their worldwide income. The concept of "residency" is used in this context to implement the principle that if an individual has sufficiently strong social and economic ties with Canada, and is benefiting from Canadian government services and organized social and economic life in Canada, as a normative matter he or she can be justifiably taxed on his or her worldwide income. In most cases it will be obvious whether this principle applies to particular individuals, for example, if they have been physically present in Canada and have lived here most of their lives. However, in some cases, where an individual perhaps does not live in Canada year-round and has only tenuous social and economic connections, whether the general principle underlying the concept of residency applies will be less obvious. The case will have to be decided simply by arguing by analogy to similar previously decided cases. Is the case more like those previous cases in which the individual was held to be resident or more like those in which the individual was held not to be resident? But once again, even though it is traditionally regarded as a distinctive form of legal reasoning, in fact, analytical reasoning is frequently used in everyday life and in many policy-making contexts. It is by no means unique to the law.

C. Normative Reasoning

This type of reasoning involves making moral, ethical or value judgments. It deals with what ought to be. There is a great dispute about the nature of normative knowledge and, in particular, about whether moral judgments are any different than just feelings and thus can have no status as knowledge. However, for purposes of briefly explaining the types of normative arguments usually made in tax law and policy analysis, that debate can be set aside.

Most social science disciplines have both an empirical and a normative branch and in most disciplines practitioners can be divided into those who concern themselves primarily with normative issues and those who concern themselves primarily with empirical issues. This distinction is perhaps drawn most sharply in economics. Positive economics, which is the primary concern of most economists, deals with the explanations and predictions of decisions made by consumers and producers. In the policy context, these economists make assertions that take the form, if policy X is followed outcome Y will result. Many economists confine themselves to positive analysis. They seem to think they have a comparative advantage over other social scientists and nonspecialists in the description of the economy if they confine themselves to positive analysis but no such advantage in the production of normative or value judgments. So they confine themselves to questions such as what effect an increase in taxes might have on labour supply and savings behaviour and do not deal with the question of whether taxes are too low or high in terms of the goals and values of society.

Even though most economists purport to engage in positive economics, there is an important branch of economics that deals exclusively with normative issues relating to government action. This normative branch of economics is referred to as welfare economics. It should not be confused with government welfare programs. Basically, it provides a normative framework for assessing all of the government's activities and, therefore, is the normative framework that is most frequently invoked in tax policy analysis. It provides a framework for thinking about questions such as should the tax system provide tax concessions for research and development, tuition fees, child care expenses, principal residences, charitable contributions and almost every other tax rule that might influence individual behaviour. It is hard to make any normative sense out of much of the tax system without having a basic understanding of welfare economics and therefore it is briefly examined in the next section.

The study of politics can also be divided into a branch that is descriptive, often referred to as political science, and a branch that is normative and concerned with the characteristics of political values, often referred to as political theory. Empirical studies in political science have become increasingly separate fields of inquiry: the study of government, of public administration, of international relations, and of political behaviour and public policy analysis. Although political scientists have examined numerous empirical issues relating to taxation, much of their work has concentrated on attempting to provide political and other explanations for the details and design of the tax system.

Normative political theory is directly concerned with the justification of political institutions and policies. It aims to lay down principles of authority, liberty, justice, equality and so forth and then to specify what kind of social order would most adequately fulfil these principles. There is of course a broad range of opinions about taxation held by political theorists. Libertarians who are skeptical of the ability of democratic governments to pursue public ends argue that most social ordering should be left to the market economy. The more extreme proponents of this political theory argue that tax is not only an illegitimate exercise of government power but that it is equivalent to forced labour. Many liberal political philosophers, however, see an important role for taxation in ordering the good society. Prominent here have been various versions of contractarian political theory. Contractarian theorists hold that there is a set of basic political principles which all rational people would agree to given appropriate conditions. The most influential example has been John Rawl's theory of justice, which understands justice as the principles that rational individuals would choose to be governed by in an "original position" in which they were ignorant of their personal characteristics, their ideals of a good life, and their social position. He argues that in this "original position" alongside the familiar liberal principles of equal liberty and equality of opportunity, people would choose the difference principle, which permits social and economic inequalities only to the extent that they benefit the least advantaged members of society. Most would agree that if the state's normative role is to see that its least fortunate members have the best life it is possible to provide to them, then there is a large role for the tax system.

Moving to the left on the political philosophy spectrum, some left liberals claim that the state is responsible for guaranteeing the preconditions for effective choice and even that freedom must be distributed equally to everyone. Again, tax laws would presumably play a large role in ordering such a society. Of course on the far left, political philosophers view most major economic and social problems as being deeply rooted in the structure of basic capitalist institutions and therefore they see little role for the tax system as an instrument of social transformation. Karl Marx was scornful of attempts to achieve equality by taxation: "Tax reform is the hobby-horse of every radical bourgeois, the specific element in all bourgeois economic reforms. From the earliest medieval philistines to the modern English free-thinkers, the main struggle has revolved around taxation. The further it slips from his grasp in practice, the more keenly does the bourgeois pursue the chimerical ideal of equal distribution of taxation. ... The reduction of taxes, their more equitable distribution, etc., ... is banal bourgeois reform."

There is a range of liberal-democratic values employed in policy arguments: equality, fairness, efficiency, freedom, autonomy, community, participation, authority, tolerance and order. Clearly they frequently clash with one another and must be reconciled. Although there is no form of argument that is widely accepted among policy analysts for resolving the clash of values, at the very least normative arguments should be subject to the common standards of rationality. Thus, at the most basic level, any normative claim should be accompanied by reasons; the argument should be clear, that is, steps in reasoning should not be left out, words used should be unambiguous, and the arguments should be systematically presented and complete; the arguments should be consistent and free of contradiction, that is, the claim should follow logically from the reasons, and the claims should be consistent with each other; the argument should be complete, that is, it should address all of the important values involved with the policy; and, to the extent the argument rests upon empirical claims, they should be true.

But assuming the argument satisfies these criteria, it then must be judged simply upon a direct appeal to our intuition of what is just. In testing our intuition about value judgments there are a number of common techniques. We can apply the principle to a number of particular cases and examine the implications of each of those against our intuition. We can abstract the principle to a higher level of generality and examine its consistency with other more fundamental principles that are perhaps more widely held. We can use heuristics like the Rawlsian original position to see whether we think that the principle would have reasonably been chosen by people who were unable to consider their own self-interest. Once these strategies are exhausted, we must simply accept that individuals with different perspectives hold different values and ensure that we have in place a fair procedure for taking action whether in relation to the tax system or any other area of public policy.

D. Empirical Reasoning

Many of the most contentious issues in tax law involve empirical questions. What effect do tax laws have on the decision of individuals to work, save and invest? What effect do they have on who performs household labour and the formation of families? What effect do they have on compensation packages, the financial structure of firms, and the legal forms in which businesses are conducted? Are taxes a drag on the economy? These are only a sampling of the countless empirical questions that will confront you in a basic tax course; therefore, it is important to understand the logic and methods of empirical research, or the way that trained social scientists go about answering these questions.

What all empirical or scientific research is about is finding and explaining causal relationships: "if A occurs, does B occur, and why?" All empirical or scientific knowledge is knowledge of relationships. The basic idea is straightforward. Only a difference or change can explain another difference or change: only variables can explain variables. So the language of variables is the language of science. In biology, scientists explain the causal relationships between biological phenomena; in astronomy, they explain the relationships between celestial phenomena. In the social sciences, scientists attempt to explain a variation in human behaviour by discovering some related variation. Of course, the idea of causality is complex and debating causality is what makes science so endlessly fascinating.

In investigating causal relationships, the variable that the investigator wishes to explain is referred to as the dependent variable (this variable depends on the action of another variable), and the hypothesized explanation is referred to as the independent variable (this variable is defined by the experimenter and hence is independent or outside the experimental situation). The most salient characteristic that distinguishes the different disciplines in the social sciences is simply the independent variables they usually invoke in order to explain whatever it is that needs explanation (the dependent variable). Within disciplines, what distinguishes different perspectives is, again, most often the nature of the independent variables they study.

In studying the relationship between two variables, a social scientist will inevitably begin with a theory about why and how the variables might be related. Naturally, that theory will usually be derived from the conventional wisdom about human behaviour that informs the social scientist's particular discipline. Thus, the choice about what independent variables to study in large part rests upon different theories of human behaviour that each social science discipline by and large assumes. In addition to studying different independent variables in attempting to explain changes in behaviour, the different disciplines have also developed different scientific procedures for testing causal relationships, based upon their relative expertise.

The characteristics and tools of empirical research, as they are applied to tax policy issues, could be illustrated by reference to any one of the dozens and dozens of empirical questions that bedevil tax analysts. In recent years one of the most contentious issues in tax policy has been the effect of income tax rates on labour supply, savings, investment, and tax evasion. Therefore, one of these issues, the effect of tax rates on evasion behaviour, will be used to illustrate the different approaches that the social sciences use to answer this empirical question. Posing the question more broadly, the phenomenon that interests social scientists in this context is why some people comply with tax laws and others do not. What explains this variation in behaviour, or, in the language of variables, what independent variable or variables explain the dependent variable of whether or not individuals evade the payment of taxes?

Economists approaching the question of why people choose not to comply with the tax laws generally begin by constructing a theory based upon the assumption about human behaviour that underlies all of economics, namely, that individuals generally act rationally in evaluating the costs and benefits of any chosen activity. Consequently, in modelling the choice confronting individuals who are deciding whether to engage in tax evasion, their basic model assumes that people would commit evasion when the expected utility of their criminal act exceeds its expected disutility. Therefore, the independent variables they examine include all phenomena that affect this rational calculus, most notably the tax rate, since that determines the benefits of evading paying tax on a given amount of income; the penalty structure, since that is part of the expected cost of evading; and, the probability of being caught and sanctioned, since that is also relevant in determining the expected disutility of evading.

Naturally, economists have developed various theoretical models of taxpayer evasion behaviour that are considerably more complex than a simple model that assumes that taxpayers optimize their conduct in reacting passively to whatever tax rules are in force. For example, since in reality there is a high degree of interaction between taxpayers and revenue departments, a number of economists have attempted to model the tax evasion decision in terms of game theory. Also, some economists have used partial and general equilibrium models to take account of factors such as the degree of substitutability in the consumption of goods and services produced in the evasion and non-evasion sectors that are ignored in standard theories of choice under risk models.

Once a social scientist has constructed a theoretical model to explain what variables might be related to a taxpayer's choice to engage in tax evasion, he or she must test this model empirically to determine if it has any explanatory force in the real world. Because economists are familiar with aggregate economic variables, and because they have developed highly sophisticated techniques for statistically controlling variables, most economists use actual data and statistical methods to attempt to scientifically estimate the casual relationship between variables. Thus, for example, as a first cut, if they wanted to know whether high tax rates cause individuals to evade tax, they might compare the amount of tax evaded at different income levels. Since in a progressive income tax system marginal income tax rates increase as income increases, if high-income taxpayers are more likely to evade taxes than low-income taxpayers one might infer that high rates cause evasion. Of course, the problem with this simple kind of correlational study is that it does not control for confounding variables. Even if it were found that high-income taxpayers cheated more than low-income taxpayers there might be explanations for this that are equally plausible as the higher marginal tax rates these individuals faced; for example, maybe high-income taxpayers have more opportunity to cheat because of the types of income they earn, or maybe high-income people are generally more dishonest than low-income people, indeed, maybe that is how many people get rich, by cheating.

To ensure that a correlation between income and tax evasion is not just an effect of some variable associated with income other than tax rates, in comparing evasion between high-income and low-income taxpayers the economist would have to attempt to control for all other plausible explanations. They might do this by finding two jurisdictions with different tax rates, and undertake what is called a cross-sectional study. In comparing the tax evasion behaviour of individuals in the same income class in the two jurisdictions they would attempt to statistically control for all other plausible independent variables (type of income, marital status and so on). If, having controlled for all other variables, it is found that high-income individuals in the high-tax jurisdiction engage in more tax evasion behaviour than high-income individuals in the low-tax jurisdiction, the difference might be reasonably attributable to the effect of high tax rates. Another common method used by economists to control for extraneous variables is a longitudinal study. The tax evasion of high-income individuals is examined before and after a reduction in their tax rates, for example. There have been countless studies of this type, empirically testing for the various variables that economists predict would influence a taxpayer's decision to evade.

Psychologists would begin to approach the question of why people evade taxes in the same way that economists do, that is, by postulating a theory of human behaviour that would explain this particular type of behaviour. However, psychologists tend to view the model of human behaviour used by economists as too simplistic. Although, like economists, psychologists tend to explain human behaviour in terms of variables that relate to individuals, they model human behaviour in much more complex terms than economists. Unlike economists, for example, they would not think of modelling taxpayers, in this context, as perfectly amoral, risk-averse utility-maximizers. Instead, they might be interested, as key independent variables in the tax evasion decision, in factors such as the individual's views about the moral acceptability of tax evasion. That is, unlike economists, psychologists tend to assume that individuals are moral beings with ideas and values of their own and that legal commands and their own impulses filter through and are affected by this moral screen. Furthermore, they would note that variables such as tax rates, the probability of detection, and the size of fines are mediated through individual attitudes and perceptions.

In addition, psychologists would likely be troubled by the fact that economic theories of compliance are premised on the assumption that noncompliance is the result of considered and conscious decisions by taxpayers. The assumption overlooks the considerable force of habit in accounting for behaviour. In many situations compliance or noncompliance may be simply the result of habit, doing what is easiest, or indifference. So in studying compliance psychologists would want to explore the factors that might affect the movement of taxpayers from inertia to active decision-making and back to inertia again. How do tax issues become salient? What causes people to begin thinking about changing their behaviour? How do people form habits? They would also likely note that the assumption that taxpayers make a rational calculus of the costs and benefits of evasion overlooks the fact that decision-making is inevitably a process. Likely, most people do not approach taxpaying in terms of simply making a decision at one point in time of whether to comply or not. Rather, they undertake or fail to undertake a series of actions whose cumulative result is compliance or noncompliance, for example, keeping track of all income, maintaining records, padding a particular expense, making a guess at what the law is. These are discrete actions and decisions that people may confront and make without reference to an overarching decision to comply or not to comply. Finally, psychologists would want to consider the subjective framing of tax decisions. As an example, there is now an extensive body of empirical research suggesting that decision-makers typically frame their choices in terms of gains or losses from some initial or neutral reference point rather than in terms of net assets after an action.

Since they are primarily interested in variables related to the individual, psychologists frequently use simulations and laboratory experiments to test the explanatory power of their chosen independent variables. By way of illustration, simulations undertaken by psychologists in testing their hypothesis about tax evasion have often involved small-scale experiments, in which subjects might be paid a monthly salary. Subjects might then be given tax tables and asked to assess their tax liability and pay tax under a hypothetical tax system in which evasion will be penalized and audits will be conducted at varying frequencies. Subjects are informed that it is a game and that the winner will be the persons with the largest amount of net earnings after-tax at the end of the simulation. To determine their effects on tax compliance, independent variables, such as the fairness of the game, tax rates and penalties, would be varied in separate conditions. These simulations are highly artificial. They often make it difficult to generalize the results to actual tax evasion behaviour. However, they can make an important contribution to the accumulation of knowledge about tax evasion.

Sociologists tend to see the cause of variation in human behaviour in the structure of the social system. Thus they explain people's actions by examining the forces that impinge on the positions that individuals occupy within the system. Among other things, this means that they extend the basic economic model of crime control by making the point that law is not the only source of punishments and rewards. Taxpayers live and work in society. They have families, friends, and co-workers who are sources of rewards and punishments. These social forces shape behaviour just as effectively as the rewards and punishments administered by the state. Given their basic assumptions about human behaviour, sociologists are also likely to look at independent variables such as attitudes toward government, views relating to the enforcement of tax laws, views about the fairness of the tax system, contact with the tax department, and demographic characteristics.

In testing their hypotheses, sociologists frequently use so-called soft methods of research, such as participant-observer research, but they also attempt to test for structural explanations of behaviour using randomized controlled field experiments and social surveys. One of the most famous randomized controlled field experiments undertaken in the area of tax evasion was conducted in the early 1960s by Schwartz and Orleans.[9] The study has since become somewhat of a classic in social experimentation. A homogeneous sample of taxpayers was selected and randomly assigned to either one of two experimental groups or a control group. Members of the experimental groups were interviewed about one month before filing their returns on 1961 income. During the interview they were subjected to comments by the interviewers. To one experimental group the interviewers stressed the severity of government sanctions against tax evasion. To the other, they stressed the obligations of citizens to the government and the importance of personal integrity. After the subjects' tax returns were filed, the IRS supplied the investigators with data relating to the adjusted gross income, tax deductions, and tax payment data, for the groups interviewed as a whole for both 1961 and 1962. Based on comparisons of the change in reported adjusted gross income and tax payment figures for the two experimental subgroups

[9] R.D. Schwartz and S. Orleans, "On Legal Sanctions" (1967) 34 U. Chicago L. Rev. 274.

and the control group, which received no communication, Schwartz and Orleans concluded that both threats of sanctions and appeals to conscience encouraged compliance, but moral appeals were more effective than threats.

Sociologists have also conducted a large number of surveys relating to tax evasion. Basically, based on the surveyed population's answers to a number of questions, researchers have attempted to divide the sampled population into evaders and non-evaders and then have attempted to determine the salient differences between the two populations. Assuming that the dependent variable can be accurately operationalized, any number of possible independent variables can be examined: perceived likelihood of apprehension, perceived severity of legal sanctions, perceived disapproval from others, perception of evasion by others, moral acceptability of tax evasion, views on enforcement of tax laws, views on the fairness of tax system, and demographic characteristics.

The point of this brief review of the empirical research related to tax evasion is not to determine what has been learned about the causes of tax evasion, but simply to examine the various approaches that social scientists take to such questions. Empirical questions will arise throughout the basic tax course. Students cannot be expected, of course, to set about collecting and evaluating the empirical research that relates to these questions. However, you should carefully identify such questions; conceptualize them as an issue involving the relationship between variables; attempt to operationalize the dependent variable and hypothesize relevant independent variables; search for a theory of human behaviour that might explain why a given independent variable might be expected to cause the dependent variable; and examine your own experience and your knowledge of widely accepted social or economic facts for evidence that might constitute empirical grounds confirming your hypothesis.

E. Methodological Pluralism

Tax policy analysis seldom involves pure analytical, normative or empirical questions. The resolution of those questions is the domain of philosophers and social scientists. Instead, tax policy analysis is concerned with identifying and defining problems in the tax system, specifying ends to be achieved, evaluating alternatives and selecting options. At one level it involves simply the application of clear thinking. In trying to reach decisions as rationally as possible we should formulate the issues as analytically as possible and we should make our values and empirical assumptions explicit. But even though it is essentially an instrumental exercise, since it involves the resolution of important questions with serious consequences, it should draw upon all the relevant principles, theories and tools of analysis helpful in reaching an informed decision.

As mentioned above, no one believes that even the most routine court decisions are uniquely determined by pre-existing legal rules and that courts either do or should reach their decisions by logical deduction from a conjunction of a statement of the relevant legal rule or statutory provision and a statement of the facts of the case. When judges decide cases they are making policy decisions and, therefore, judges and the lawyers who argue before them should engage in the full range of techniques of policy analysis.

In tax classes the discussions can become heated since the policy issues often deal with such fundamental questions about the nature of our collective lives together and our moral responsibilities toward one another. Even those who believe most strongly in the rationality of normative reasoning and the verifiability of empirical reasoning usually concede that there is no one true answer to every question. Therefore, like all policy analysts, it is important that tax analysts remain skeptical and cautious about all claims, that they attempt to achieve clarity and civility, and that they respect the importance of perspective in addressing any issue.

V. ANALYTICAL TOOLS FOR TAX ANALYSIS

An understanding of a few accounting, financial and economic concepts will greatly clarify a number of tax policy and tax planning issues. The ones discussed here are most important in terms of influencing the design of the tax laws and are the primary tools of positive tax analysis.

A. Inflation: Nominal Versus Real Values

Inflation is the persistent rise in the general price level. Assume that in 2015 you earned $40,000 and in 2016 you earned $44,000. The money or nominal value of your wages increased by 10 per cent from 2015 to 2016. Your experience will suggest, however, that the purchasing power or real value, of your income did not increase by 10 per cent because the price of goods and services that you have to purchase also increased. Indeed, if prices increased by 10 per cent, it would require $44,000 in 2016 to purchase what $40,000 purchased in 2015. In this case, although the nominal value of your income rose, the real value remained unchanged. "Nominal" refers to the value of a concept measured in terms of current dollars; "real" refers to the value of a concept measured in terms of the number of units of goods and services that can be purchased.

In any given year the nominal and real value of money will be the same. However, the nominal value of money earned (or any other dollar figure) in a prior year must be adjusted for the rate of inflation to arrive at its real value in the current year. The rate of inflation is the percentage change in the price level from period to period. A widely used measure of the average price of goods and services is the consumer price index (CPI). It measures the average cost of the goods and services bought by a typical consumer. The percentage change in the consumer price index is the key measure of the inflation rate. In the early 1980s, the inflation rate was over 10 per cent a year. In recent years, it has been between 1 per cent and 3 per cent and, therefore, not of as great concern. Nevertheless, any amount of inflation affects the real value of money over time.

Inflation gives rise to at least three problems for the tax system. First, it means that if the dollar figures used in the Act to express the value of deductions and credits and to establish the income level at which tax rates increase (the tax brackets) are not adjusted for inflation they will lose their real value over time. This means that inflation will generate increasingly larger amounts of government revenue without any change in the dollar amount of tax deductions and credits or any change in the tax brackets or rates. In 1974 tax brackets and deductions and credits were fully indexed for inflation. In 1986, however, in order to raise increasingly more revenue every year and in order to reduce the deficit without explicitly increasing tax rates, the federal government adopted a system of partial indexation. Indexing adjustments were to be made only for annual increases in the CPI in excess of 3 per cent. Over the years this resulted in billions of dollars of additional tax revenues for Canadian governments. Finally, after much pressure from numerous constituencies and from the popular press, the federal government restored full indexing in its February 2000 Budget.

A second way in which inflation may affect the tax system, if it is not taken into account by those who write the tax laws, is that it will result in the taxation of the nominal value of income from capital instead of its real value. Since the Canadian income tax system takes no account of the declining real value of capital due to inflation, it imposes a hidden and in some cases quite substantial additional tax on some taxpayers' income from capital. Although the failure to index the cost of capital affects all forms of capital, an illustration using capital property will serve to make the point. Suppose in 2000 you used some of your savings to buy stock in a company for $10. In 2016 you sell the stock for $30. You would have to recognize $20 of capital gains for tax purposes. But suppose the overall price level doubled from 2000 to 2016. In this case, the $10 you invested in 2000 is equivalent (in terms of purchasing power) to $20 in 2016. When you sell your stock for $30 you have a real gain (an increase in purchasing power) of only $10. Yet the tax system treats your gain as being $20, namely the full amount of your nominal gain. Capital gains have always been given preferential tax treatment. Under the present Act you only have to include one-half of your capital gains in your income for tax purposes. In part, this preferential treatment is designed to be a crude proxy for indexing. However, for this purpose it is clearly too generous in many cases and not sufficiently generous in others. Furthermore, the taxation of all forms of income from capital is distorted by not properly accounting for the real value of capital. Thus a fully indexed tax system would allow for the indexation of interest income, inventories and depreciable property.

Finally, whenever a dollar amount is carried forward or backward under the Act, it is the nominal dollar value and not the real value that is used. For example, taxpayers who realize a $10,000 loss in one year, if they have no other income to offset this amount, can carry the amount forward and deduct it from income the next year. The Act contains a complicated set of rules for the carryforward and carryback of losses. But clearly in principle it is the real value of the loss that should be carried forward, that is the loss adjusted for inflation, and not its nominal value. By not allowing taxpayers to carryforward the real value of their losses the tax system is, in effect, only allowing them to carry forward part of their loss.

B. Tax Deferral and the Time Value of Money

Questions relating to the time value of money, and the correct period for reporting income or claiming deductions, present some of the most critical and vexing issues in the design of an income tax. They are the key to understanding the taxation of financial instruments, installment sales, prepaid income and expenses, compensation arrangements, and important aspects of international and corporate tax. Tax legislators have only recently recognized the importance of time-value analysis. This recognition has resulted in numerous tax amendments and it will undoubtedly continue to inform a broad range of tax issues. Tax planners continue to structure transactions to exploit gaps in the tax system's treatment of transactions taking place in different years. The importance of time-value analysis is that it neutralizes the time dimension so that transactions occurring at different times can be compared. Students sometimes misleadingly think that the important issues in tax are whether an item is included in or deducted from income and that questions of timing could not be all that important. In fact, in tax, timing is almost everything. A few of the foundational concepts that are important in understanding basic income tax laws are reviewed here.

1. Future value

The fundamental idea underlying the time value of money is that the value of capital increases over time because it can be used to earn additional income. Therefore, $100 received this year is worth less than $100 received last year and more than $100 to be received next year. This is not a very difficult concept. If someone offered you $100 today or $100 next year which would you take? Naturally, you would take the $100 today since you could invest it and earn say a 10 per cent rate of return and have $110 next year (instead of the $100 that was otherwise offered). If you invested it in an Internet stock, and got lucky, you might be able to double it to $200 in one year. The point is that because of the time value of money $100 today is worth more than $100 next year. This assumes, of course, that you earn a rate of return greater than the rate of inflation. To keep the math simple, these examples assume that there is no inflation.

How much more is $100 worth if it is received this year instead of next year? The future value of an amount is the amount that it will grow over the period. Normally in calculating the future value of an amount, the amount that it will grow is assumed to be the rate of interest on relatively risk-free investments. If we assume that the interest rate is 10 per cent, which is greater than it is in fact these days, but assuming this keeps the calculations simple, then the value of $100 one year from now is $110. In the example above, unless the person offered you more than $110 one year from now, you would be wise to take the $100 now.

Often we want to know the future value of $100 for a period of greater than one year. What is the future value of $100 20 years from now? If an investor only earned simple interest on the $100, that is, if he or she were paid the interest the $100 earned each year than, assuming the rate of interest were 10 per cent, at the end of 20 years the investor would have the $100 principal plus $200 of interest ($10 of interest each year for 20 years). So the value of $100 in 20 years would seem to be $300. But in doing these kinds of future value calculations it is normally assumed that the interest earned at the end of every year is not paid to the investor, but instead is reinvested. That is, it is assumed that the interest earned each year is, in effect, loaned to the borrower which itself will earn interest, and so on. The earning of interest on interest is called "compounding". When interest is compounding there is a simple formula for deriving future amounts (the compound interest formula) which need not be set out here. However, as anyone who has heard a sales pitch by a banker knows, the effect of compounding is "magic". For example, in the simple example above, over 20 years simple interest yields an amount of $300 while compound interest (at the same rate of interest and over the same period) yields $673. Quite a difference. The difference becomes even greater over longer periods of time. Thus at the end of 30 years simple interest in the example would yield $400 while compound interest would yield $1,745; at the end of 40 years, simple interest would yield $500 while compound interest would yield $4,526.

What accounts for the dramatic difference between simple interest and compound interest? The reason is that accumulating interest, which is available to earn further interest, grows exponentially. Calculators or tables are frequently used in calculating the future value of amounts. However, the "rule of 72" is a straightforward method of arriving at an approximate amount. This rules states that money will approximately double at a given rate of interest over the number of years obtained by dividing 72 by the interest rate. For instance, money doubles approximately every 6 years at a 12 per cent rate of compounding interest and approximately every 8 years at 9 per cent.

2. Present Value

Future value analysis neutralizes the time factor by taking a current year amount and converting it to a future year amount. Thus $100 this year is the same as $110 next year, assuming a 10 per cent rate of interest. The alternative means of neutralizing the time factor is the exact reverse of the future value method, namely, the present-value method, which converts future values into present values for purposes of comparison. We know that $110 one year from now is worth $100 this year, assuming the interest rate is 10 per cent, what is $100 one year from now worth today? Again, there is a relatively straightforward formula for discounting a future payment to its present value and it is easy to determine with a calculator or a present-value table. However, the concept is all that is important here. The answer you could guess at; it is approximately $91. Present value computations are important and have many applications in both tax policy analysis and in tax planning.

3. Asset valuation

The processing of calculating the present value of a future amount is, of course, the key tool in the valuation of assets. Conceptually, the value of an asset is simply the sum of the present values of all future returns that will be generated by the investment, regardless of whether such future returns take the form of interest, dividends, or capital gains.

4. Value of Tax Deferral

Often people assert that the ability to contribute, say, $10,000 to an RRSP (or make any other tax shelter investment) is not such a great tax break since it only defers tax and does not result in an exemption of tax. Taxpayers who contribute to an RRSP pay no tax on the income they contribute to the plan (they can deduct it from their income for tax purposes) and they pay no tax on the investment income earned in the plan. However, both the principal contributed and the investment income earned are taxed when they are withdrawn from the plan. However, compounding interest on the tax that is deferred explains the benefits of deferral and it can be huge. In the above example, if taxpayers in the 50 per cent tax bracket pay tax on the $10,000 and then invest the after-tax amount of $5,000 and earn 10 per cent interest upon which they pay tax, after 20 years they will have only $13,260. If they invest in an RRSP and are able to defer paying tax on the $10,000 and the earned interest until they withdraw it after 20 years they will have $33,363 after-tax. If the period of saving is extended to 30 or 40 years the benefits of deferral become even greater because of the effect of compounding.

There are many ways to describe the tax benefits of deferral. One way is to say that the tax deferred (which in the above example would be $5,000 in the initial year, assuming the taxpayer was in the 50 per cent marginal tax bracket) and the tax that would otherwise be payable each year on the earned interest is essentially an interest-free loan from the government to the taxpayer without collateral and without a definite time for repayment of the loan. The higher the taxpayer's tax bracket, the larger the interest-free loan.

Another way of expressing the advantages of deferral in the above example is that it is equivalent to the government completely exempting the taxpayer's earned income from capital income from tax. That is, deferral is equivalent to exemption of the yield on the amount deferred. To see this conceptual point, think of the above example this way. If the taxpayer had been taxed on the $10,000 of earned income she would have only had $5,000 left to invest after-tax. In effect, because she was able to deduct this amount from her taxes in that year, she put $5,000 of her own money in the RRSP and the government gave her an interest-free loan of $5,000 to put in as well. When the principal and earned interest is withdrawn the government will recover, in effect, its interest-free loan and, again assuming the tax rate is 50 per cent it will recover one-half the earned interest. The other one-half of the interest, which conceptually one might say was earned on the taxpayer's $5,000, will never be subject to tax. Among other assumptions, this equivalence between deferral and exempting the return on after-tax income only holds if the tax rate is the same in all relevant years. In fact, in most cases the taxpayer's marginal tax rate will be higher in the year that she contributes to the RRSP than when she withdraws it. Therefore, tax advantages of RRSPs, and other forms of tax deferral, are likely to be greater than exempting the yield on after-tax income from tax.

As you read through the materials in this casebook the importance of the time value of money will become clearer to you not only in tax planning but also in tax policy analysis. Many of the provisions in the present Act do not fully account for the relationships between present and future value and consequently provide unintended tax breaks for taxpayers.

C. Capitalization Effect of Taxes

To the extent that the tax system favours one type of investment over another, the demand for, and supply of, particular investments will be affected. Money and other resources will be shifted from the unfavoured type of investment to the tax-favoured type of investment and in response the relative prices of the investments will change. For example, if a tax is imposed or increased on income from a particular type of asset, the value of that asset will likely fall as investors sell it off. Conversely, if a tax is removed or reduced on income from an asset, the value of the asset will likely rise as investors increase their demand for the investment. The fall or rise in the price of assets due to the imposition or removal of a tax is referred to as the capitalization effect of a tax. The effect is simply an application of the obvious proposition that the world does not stand still when taxes (or anything else) change.

A simple, and simplified, example can be used to illustrate tax capitalization. Assume a bond that has a value of $100 pays $10 interest annually, which is taxed at a rate of 50 per cent, for an after-tax return of $5. Now suppose that the government decides, for whatever reason, to remove the tax from the income of this type of bond. What should happen to the price of the bond? It would likely rise to $200. Since investors will now be able to earn $10 after-tax from this type of bond, presumably they would be willing to pay twice as much for it as they would for bonds from which they could only earn $5 after-tax.

Although analysts disagree about the extent of tax capitalization, and whether the price of assets in most markets ever rise to completely discount the tax benefits, as assumed in the above example, there is no question that tax capitalization is a wide-spread phenomenon in the economy and an absolutely essential concept to take into account in tax policy analysis, tax reform, tax planning and in interpreting the Act. A few implications of the concept can be drawn from the example above. First, when the tax on the bond is removed, notice that all existing holders of this type of bond receive a windfall. The value of their bond increases from $100 to $200. The more general point is: that whenever taxes are changed there will be windfall gains and losses to some taxpayers. The random and undeserved effect of these gains or losses is the concern that gave rise to the old adage "an old tax is a good tax."

Second, once the tax change is made, and at some time in the future, most holders of the tax-favoured bonds will be investors who bought them for $200. It will appear as if they are receiving a tax concession since the income on their bonds is not being taxed. But in fact they are no better off than investors holding the taxable bonds. Both sets of investors are earning a rate of return of 5 per cent after-tax. Consequently, although economic inefficiencies have been created by increasing the demand for the particular bonds by exempting their income from tax (assuming that the exemption was not correcting a market failure), once the change has been made there are arguably no tax inequities — both investors in the unfavoured and the tax-favoured bonds are in the same after-tax position. Incidentally, as another illustration of the adage "an old tax is a good tax" notice how arguably unfair it would be to remove the tax concession. All those investors who purchased the tax favoured bond for $200 would suffer an immediate $100 windfall loss. Would that be unfair?

Third, if you were a tax planner would you advise your clients to buy the tax-favoured bond simply because it was tax favoured? Presumably not. It bears an implicit tax in the form of a reduced rate of return. In deciding on the best investment for a client both explicit and implicit taxes have to be considered. Does the tax effect of capitalization mean that in fact because of the forces of demand and supply it is pointless to invest in tax-favoured investments?

Fourth, it is sometimes difficult to determine who benefits from the capitalization effect of taxes. For example, years ago when the government introduced a tax-sheltering scheme for investors in multiple-unit residential buildings in order to increase the stock of rental units and hopefully reduce rents, some analysts suggested that the only large winners from the scheme were those speculators who owned urban land upon which such units could be built. Such land was in short supply and when the scheme was announced, since these speculators could see that the tax concession was going to reduce the cost to developers of building such units, they simply raised the price of their land and captured a good chunk of the expected tax savings.

D. The Incentive Effect of Taxes: The Income and Substitution Effects

Taxes affect human behaviour in two ways, first, by reducing people's income and, second, by increasing the relative prices of the activities, transactions and goods and services upon which they fall. Although hardly any human behaviour escapes the effect of taxes, the most important effects, from the point of view of the economy, are the effects of taxes on people's work and savings behaviour and the effects of taxes on the investment decisions of businesses. Social scientists in most disciplines have examined the effects of taxes (or related phenomena) on human behaviour, however, the issues raised by this concern have been studied most extensively by economists. Standard consumer demand theory in economics notes that when the price of a good changes, it has two effects on consumer's behaviour: an income effect and a substitution effect. The importance of these effects can be illustrated by attempting to answer a straightforward question: Will people work more or fewer hours a week if the income tax they have to pay for each hour worked is increased?

A simple example might help in thinking about this question. Assume that A earns $60,000 a year (she earns $40 an hour and works 1,500 hours a year) as an employee in a firm. The income tax rate is a flat 25 per cent, with no exemptions. Consequently, she pays $12,500 a year in tax and is left with $47,500 of disposable income. How is she likely to vary the number of hours she works if the tax rate is increased to 30 per cent with the result that her taxes are increased by $2,500 and her disposable income reduced to $45,000? In attempting to answer this question, economists would assume that A is a rational individual seeking to maximize her utility (seeking to make herself as well off as possible), given her disposable income. In deciding whether to increase or decrease the number of hours she works, she would feel the influence of two competing pressures, a substitution and an income effect.

She might decide to work fewer hours because of the tax increase. She might reduce her hours of work so that her disposable income is, say, only $42,500 instead of $45,000. Why might she work fewer hours after the tax increase? Since the tax increase means that she is only earning $28 after-tax for every hour she works, instead of the $30 that she earned before the tax increase, she might decide that it is not worthwhile to work so hard. She might decide that at this lower after-tax wage she would rather be wind-surfing or listening to Holly Cole albums a few more hours a week instead of working. The way that economists talk about this effect is to say that the effect of a tax increase is to reduce the cost of leisure and, therefore, people will consume more of it, that is, they will substitute leisure for work. Before the tax increase the opportunity cost of her leisure was $30; after the tax increase it was only $28. When the price of a good goes down economists predict that consumers will consume more of it by substituting it for other goods. Hence the term, the substitution effect. The force of this effect is what presumably lies behind people's intuition when they predict that tax increases will cause workers to work less. However, this theorizing ignores the income effect of taxes.

The tax increase reduced A's disposable income by $2,500; therefore, in theory, she might decide to work additional hours in order to restore the level of her disposable income. This effect is called the income effect for the obvious reason that it results from the fall in the taxpayer's real income. "A" may enjoy foreign travel and with the fall in her income would not be able to afford her annual trip abroad; therefore, she may rationally decide to work more hours after the tax increase.

The relative size of the income and substitution effect is likely to differ for different types of people. Given these two effects, what types of persons, or persons in what situations, do you think would work more if taxes are increased, and who would work less? In theory, the income effect is likely to prevail if taxpayers have fixed income commitments such as family obligations, mortgages or if they have low incomes and therefore an increase in tax represents a substantial cut in income. In theory, the substitution effect is likely to prevail if taxpayers have a weak commitment to the labour force because they have a good deal of discretionary income. The important point is that if we assume that individuals act rationally in deciding how many hours to work, then a fall in the after-tax wage rate because of a tax increase does not lead to an unambiguous prediction about the quantity of work effort supplied. Economic theory is silent on which of these two opposing effects will dominate. Therefore, the case for one prediction or the other can only be made with empirical evidence. Nevertheless, although they may sound abstract, the income and substitution effects are useful tools in thinking about a number of tax law and policy issues.

The income effect is largely determined by the average tax rate (since it depends upon the effect of the tax on the taxpayer's total disposable income), while the substitution effect is largely determined by the marginal tax rate (since it depends upon the effect of the tax on the taxpayer's next increment of income). This observation has led some economists concerned about the effect of the tax system on economic growth to support a tax system with high average tax rates and low marginal tax rates. In practice, the easiest way to achieve a tax system where average rates are high and marginal rates are low is to make the tax base as comprehensive as possible.

E. Tax Incidence: Who Pays?

The notion of tax incidence is indispensable in tax analysis. While it is one of the most important topics in tax analysis, it is also one of the most intractable. Basically, the question that tax incidence seeks to answer is: when a tax is imposed (or changed) whose real income is reduced by the tax? A few things can be said reasonably confidently about tax incidence: (1) It is always some individual's income that is reduced. Corporations or other legal constructs cannot themselves bear the incidence of taxes. (2) It is not necessarily the person who actually writes the tax cheque to the government or who is legally obliged to pay it, since some part of taxes are almost inevitably shifted backward and forward from the payer. (3) The more difficult it is for the person who is taxed to substitute other goods or activities for the taxed goods or activity the more likely it is that he or she will bear the tax. (4) The incidence of tax is likely to vary between the short-term and the long-term. The last three points require a slight elaboration.

The proposition that the formal incidence of a tax, that is who is legally obliged to pay it, is largely irrelevant to its effective incidence is so well established that it has a name: the invariance of incidence proposition. The reason that the formal incidence of a tax tells you very little about who in fact pays it is that the incidence of a tax is ultimately determined not by legal formalities but by the forces of supply and demand operating through the economy. Take a straightforward example. If a new tax were introduced on the sale of televisions and required to be paid by television retailers, it is unlikely the retailers would bear the tax, or much of it. On the one hand, if consumer demand for televisions was fairly inelastic, that is if consumers simply had to have televisions and were unable to substitute other products for them, then very likely retailers would simply add the cost of the tax on to the price of television. Tax analysts would say that the tax has been shifted forward. Forward shifting takes place if the tax falls on the user, rather than the supplier of the commodity or service in question. On the other hand, if consumers could easily substitute other products for televisions (by buying computers, for example) then their demand for televisions would decline if its price were increased and it is likely that the cost of the tax would be shifted backward to those engaged in producing televisions through lower wages and salaries, lower prices for raw materials, or a lower return on borrowed money. Or, the tax might not be shifted at all and reduce the net income of the owner of the business. The point is that since the incidence of tax is determined by the forces of demand and supply its legal incidence is irrelevant. There is no reason for believing that the person whose real income is reduced if a tax is imposed on televisions would vary depending upon whether the tax was imposed on manufacturers, retailers, or directly on consumers.

Another well accepted proposition about tax incidence is that the harder it is for people to substitute other things for the taxed activity, the greater the proportion of the incidence they are likely to bear. In the above example, if there are no substitutes for televisions, and every consumer demands a television, it seems reasonably certain that consumers of televisions will bear the incidence of the tax no matter who it is legally imposed upon.

Finally, in determining the incidence of taxes it is sometimes necessary to distinguish between the short-term and the long-term. In the short-term the individual who is legally obliged to pay the tax might not be able to shift it forward or backward. However, in the long run, as the economy adjusts to the tax, it is likely shared between several parties.

Simply to illustrate the application of these propositions, one can ask who likely bears the incidence of the payroll tax. In Canada, the employee's contribution rate to employment insurance is 1.73 per cent, and the employer's rate is 2.42 per cent. Whose real income is likely reduced by this tax? In the short-run employers might pay their portion of the tax if it is increased, but in the long run as salaries are renegotiated it is likely shifted. In negotiations over salaries, employers presumably only care about their gross labour costs; employees presumably only care about their after-tax take home pay. Neither of these considerations would suggest that in the long run it should matter who bears the formal incidence of the tax. Is it likely that workers can avoid the tax by substituting some other activity for working? Not likely. Empirical studies on labour supply in Canada suggest that for most of the workforce the elasticity of labour supply is close to zero. This would suggest that in the long run the payroll tax in Canada is probably borne by workers.

What is the likely incidence of the tax on corporate profits? In a perfectly competitive economy, if the tax is not shifted it must be paid out of profits and thus it reduces the real income of shareholders. If this is its incidence the tax is extremely progressive since shareholders tend to be high-income individuals. However, some analysts contend that corporations in many industries are able to treat the tax as simply a cost of doing business and, therefore, they are able to add it to the price of the goods and services that they sell. In this case it would be borne by consumers. In effect, it acts as a disguised sales tax. Others suggest that firms are unlikely to be able to add the tax to prices since their products have to compete against the products of foreign corporations which do not bear the tax and, therefore, it likely falls on the most immobile factor of production, namely workers. Unfortunately, empirical studies have been unable to lend much certainty to the theoretical ambiguity about who pays the corporate tax.

Incidence analysis can be applied not just to overall tax changes, but also to changes in specific tax laws. For example, what would be the incidence of increasing the tax on business meal and entertainment expenses by making them completely nondeductible? (At present, business people can deduct 50 per cent of the cost of business meals and entertainment.)

Although useful things can be said about the incidence of a tax change based upon an application of the theoretical propositions mentioned above, in fact, the effective incidence of any tax change is almost impossible to determine. There are at least two reasons for this. First, in deciding what the incidence of a particular tax change is, it is necessary to make a judgment about what would happen if the change were not made. That is, there is always an implicit counterfactual hypothesis underlying the judgment about the incidence of a tax change. In the theoretical literature on tax incidence economists have developed several different concepts of incidence to attempt to account for different ways that the revenue might be raised if, for example, the tax under examination were not enacted. Second, the examples above might be generously described as an illustration of partial equilibrium analysis. We concentrated on the market of the tax product and ignored other markets. But in a market economy the introduction or change in a tax starts a series of adjustments that ripple through the entire economy. Ultimately, the price of totally unrelated products might be affected. Economists use general equilibrium theory to attempt to identify and incorporate economy-wide repercussions and implications of taxation. However, although general equilibrium models can sometimes be usefully applied to policy problems, including questions of tax incidence, limitations in data and problems of tractability usually lead economists to evaluate policies in one market at a time.

Several studies have been done on the overall incidence of taxes in Canada. Using various assumptions about the incidence of the taxes levied in Canada, most studies have concluded that the overall tax burden in Canada is about proportional. That is, that regardless of your income (broadly defined) you will pay about 35 per cent of it in tax.

F. The Deadweight Loss of Taxation

The cost of taxes to taxpayers includes the amount they have to pay to government. This amount concerns some economists since they think that individuals can make better choices about how to spend their income and increase their well-being than governments. Nevertheless, assuming that the government is spending the tax revenues raised wisely, most would agree we are likely better off paying at least some taxes and receiving government services since, altogether aside from issues relating to the fair distribution of income, there are many services that the market cannot provide efficiently. At the very least, the public services that individuals receive as a result of the taxes they pay are presumably worth something to them. But in addition to the cost to taxpayers of actually paying a tax, there is an additional cost of taxes that no one benefits from; this cost is variously described as the deadweight loss of taxation or the excess burden of taxation (the burden in excess of the amounts actually paid). It arises because when a tax is imposed on a particular good or activity it causes some people to avoid the tax by substituting a less valued good or activity for the taxed good or activity. As a result of this substitution of valued for less valued goods, the individual's welfare will be diminished because of the tax, even though he or she do not pay it.

Consider a simple example. Suppose that a pizza slice costs $4. "A" would pay $7 for a slice of pizza because he values it so highly. When he buys the pizza he has $3 of what economists call consumer surplus, which is the difference between the maximum amount a person is willing to pay for a good and its current market price. "B", on the other hand, would only pay $5 for a slice of pizza. She still buys the pizza for $4, but she has only $1 of consumer surplus. Notice that when A and B buy a slice of pizza $4 of individual welfare is created in the form of consumer surplus. That is, after the exchange of their money for pizza, A and B are in total $4 better off. The pizza salesperson is likely better off as well, but in this simple example we will ignore the producer's surplus. Of course, increasing individual welfare, or the social surplus, is what voluntary exchanges are all about.

Now look what happens if the government imposes a $2 tax on a pizza slice. "A" will continue to buy pizza slices, but will now pay $6, leaving him with only $1 of consumer surplus. "B", on the other hand, will not buy the pizza for $6 and will forgo the $1 of consumer surplus such a purchase brought when she only had to pay $4. What is the effect of the tax? The consumer surplus, or the well-being of the two parties, has been reduced by $3, from $4 to $1. Of this $3 in reduced welfare, $2 has been paid to the government and we assume that the parties will benefit from it in some way. But that still leaves a $1 loss of consumer surplus that is unaccounted for. Thus in addition to the $2 of revenue that it raises, the tax causes a $1 deadweight loss. It is called a deadweight loss since no one benefits from it. Notice that the deadweight loss arises only because B changed her behaviour because of the tax and thus lost the consumer surplus that buying a pizza at the pre-tax price of $4 provided her. If individuals do not change their behaviour because of a tax there is no deadweight loss. Economists are prepared to assume that they derived an equal benefit from the tax they paid. Since as a normative matter economists are primarily interested in increasing the social surplus through voluntary exchanges, the deadweight loss of taxes is of great concern to them.

The concept of deadweight loss is usually explained in microeconomic textbooks much more thoroughly, with the aid of diagrams and algebraic formulae. However, the basic idea behind the concept is straightforward: taxes — like any form of legal regulation — can reduce individual welfare by preventing individuals from achieving some of the gains to be realized through voluntary exchanges. Taxes should be designed, most economists argue, to minimize deadweight loss.

G. General Theory of the Second Best

In one of the most frequently quoted passages in economic policy literature, R.G. Lipsey and K. Lancaster assert, "The general theorem for the second best optimum states that if there is introduced into a general equilibrium system a constraint which prevents the attainment of one of the Paretian conditions [see VI.C, below], the other Paretian conditions, although still attainable, are, in general, no longer desirable."[10] At the most general level, what this theorem appears to suggest is that once the economy has deviated from the ideal of perfect competition, piecemeal tax (or any other) reforms to improve the allocation of resources might make things worse off, not better off. This might suggest that all reform efforts to achieve efficiency are hopeless. To prevent complete paralysis of action, in tax policy analysis the policy prescription suggested by the theorem has been applied loosely to simply act as a caution that the tax system, or any individual part of it, does not operate in a vacuum. When making a change to one tax law, the whole system must be considered as well as other government policies. For example, the theory posits that removing a preference from that tax system that appears to induce behaviour that might not otherwise occur cannot be assumed to improve the efficiency of the economy because there might exist some other government policy, or tax provision, that the tax preference is counterbalancing. Although efficiency would be promoted if both measures were repealed, if the other government intervention cannot be changed the tax provision might be acting as a "second best" alternative in promoting economic neutrality. All tax changes have to be evaluated in the context of other tax provisions as well as non-tax government policies. Put another way, a tax provision that distorts behaviour might actually be desirable when other distortions exist in the economy. As you proceed throughout the course, see if you can identify measures that can be justified by the use of second best analysis.

When a measure is referred to as a second best it is a way of drawing attention to the fact that there is a first-best policy but it cannot be achieved because of resource, technological or institutional constraints. Obviously all economic policy is likely second best in this sense; however generally, the context does not call for the point to be made or the term used. It is well known, for example, that the first-best tax system, that is one that would not affect people's behaviour, is a "lump-sum" tax; a tax that is a fixed amount for each individual regardless of his or her income, consumption or any other attribute that might relate to his or her behaviour. This is the first-best solution. On moral grounds, no one argues that government should be financed with a lump-sum tax. But in this sense our present mix of taxes is clearly second-best. However, when the term first-best is applied to the income tax, for example, it is normally taken to mean an income tax with a comprehensive

---

[10] R.G. Lipsey and K.J. Lancaster, "The General Theory of the Second Best" (1956) 24 Review of Economic Studies 11.

tax base. In some cases, policy decisions have so many constraints that they are referred to as "third best" or "seventh best".

VI. NORMATIVE JUSTIFICATIONS FOR TAX LAWS

A. Why We Need Tax Laws

The short two-fold answer to the question of why we need tax laws is to raise revenue to finance government spending and to redistribute income. These are not bad answers. However, in thinking about tax laws in Canada, or any other market economy for that matter, it makes sense to start at the beginning. At the most basic level, we have taxes because we have governments. Collecting taxes is simply one of the ways that the government has to achieve its broad social and economic objectives. Consequently, the question of why we have taxes can be reduced to the question of why we have governments. Although examining normative theories of government might appear far removed from the study of tax law, because tax laws are so deeply embedded in the structure of government, and are such a pervasive instrument of government policy, at least a superficial understanding of the normative theory of government is required to make sense out of tax laws. A discussion of the normative justifications for government, or stated more broadly, a discussion of the principles that should guide the selection of forms of social organization to coordinate social life, could quickly become mired in competing versions of libertarian, liberal and collectivist theory. What follows is a brief account of the conventional way of thinking about normative justifications for government for the purpose of tax policy analysis.

Although there are much richer normative theories of government than that provided by economists, because welfare and public finance economists have developed the most highly articulated and arguably the most explanatory theory of government, that discipline's conceptual framework is the one emphasized here. This normative model of government is the one most frequently used in discussions of tax law and policy and the one that has driven the structural economic reforms, including tax reforms, in western industrial countries over the past 20 years.

Public finance economists divide the functions of government in a market economy into three categories: the allocation, distribution and stabilization functions. In addition to these functions, this section will briefly discuss the government's role in constituting the marketplace and encouraging economic growth.

B. The Role of the Tax System in Constituting the Marketplace

In identifying the functions of government, economists often begin by assuming that a marketplace exists in which individuals exchange goods and services. They then identify "market failures" that require government intervention. This might seem like a harmless convention; however, conceptually it is wrong and failing to adequately recognize how markets are constituted can lead to a misconception of the nature of tax laws and mistaken public policies.

There is no such thing as a free, neutral and self-regulating marketplace in which exchanges between individuals take place. As any first-year law student knows only too well, what economists refer to as the marketplace is in fact a domain of economic activity that is regulated by countless detailed and complex rules of property, contract, tort and even criminal law. In the eighteenth and nineteenth centuries many of these rules were developed by judges deciding the concrete cases that formed the common law. As such, they represented the value judgments and policy decisions of those judges. Since the writings of the legal realists, it has not been disputed that in formulating these common law rules judges considered issues of loss distribution and social welfare. At present, most of these areas of law are shot through with legislative enactments and regulations and are thus even more obviously subject to the same political forces as rules in any other area of law. The rules that govern the marketplace are every bit as socially and politically constructed as the tax system and other government policy instruments. There is nothing inevitable or natural about these rules. Moreover, they have distributional consequences in the same way that taxes do and they are as coercive.

Once the government's role in constituting the marketplace is recognized a number of consequences follow; in particular, such recognition renders incoherent a good deal of rhetoric comparing private market rules to regulatory rules such as taxes. However, perhaps most importantly, there is no neutral position in thinking about public policy issues. That is, in discussions over the relative merits of the market or taxes and public provision there is no default position. Both are forms of government intervention and both require justification.

One purpose of taxation is to assist in constituting the marketplace. The revenues raised through taxation are required to fund the elaborate public infrastructure — such as law reform bodies, the judicial system, the police and the prison system — that is needed to develop and enforce the private law rules regulating markets. There could be no property without taxation.

C. The Role of the Tax System in Achieving an Efficient Allocation of Resources

The efficient allocation of resources, and thus the maximization of social welfare, is the normative government objective that preoccupies economists. The term efficiency in ordinary usage refers to the absence of waste or an effective (efficient) strategy for achieving a particular objective. The technical economic usage of the term includes this notion of carrying on a given activity at least cost; however, the term is used in a much wider sense in normative economics. In welfare economics the economy is said to be efficient not only if goods and services are produced with the least amount of waste but also if they are distributed among members of society in such a way that no redistribution could take place among them that benefits some without harming others. This state of affairs is referred to as Pareto efficient, or Pareto optimal, after the Italian economist and sociologist Vilfredo Pareto (1848-1923) who developed the concept.

In thinking about the role of government, and therefore the objectives of the tax system, economists begin by demonstrating that private markets are generally capable of achieving an efficient allocation of resources without government intervention and, thus, without taxation. They claim that so long as economic markets are competitive (and a limited number of other assumptions are made), the actions of individuals pursuing their self-interest can alone solve the three major coordinating tasks that must be accomplished in any society: exchange efficiency, goods will be allocated to those individuals who value them most; production efficiency, the given output of goods will be produced with the fewest possible inputs; and product mix efficiency, those goods produced will correspond with those desired by consumers. Basically, the claim is that competitive markets will ensure that all potential gains from trade will be exhausted so that no additional exchange of goods could make anybody better off without making someone worse off. In this idealized world not only are taxes unnecessary but they will almost invariably have the undesirable effect of reducing the efficiency of the economy. For example if taxes increase the price of labour, then less labour will be devoted to producing goods that others value, and the economy will be less efficient. If taxes increase the price of some consumer goods relative to others, then people will buy less of the taxed goods and more of other goods even though at prices set in the market they would have preferred the former. By distorting people's behaviour taxes destroy social welfare.

A simple story can be told to show the intuition that lies behind the claim that competitive markets alone can result in an efficient allocation of resources. In a competitive marketplace, individual consumers will presumably purchase those goods that will maximize their own satisfaction, given their budget. In selecting between goods and services in pursuit of their own well-being, consumers have no need for governments. How could a government bureaucrat possibly know more about what individuals should consume in order to satisfy their wants than those individuals themselves? Business people, the people in society who produce the goods and services individuals consume, will try to make as much profits as they can, but they cannot exploit consumers. If they produce shoddy goods, produce inefficiently, or try to profiteer, consumers will turn to the goods produced by other business people. Workers will try to get the best pay and conditions of employment they can, but they cannot get more than the value of their labour or it would profit their employer to sack them. They cannot be required to accept less than the value of what they produce for then it would pay another capitalist to employ them at a slightly higher wage rate. Investors will always invest their financial capital in businesses they think will yield them the highest rate of return; therefore, by attempting to maximize their own wealth, they will be ensuring that capital is always allocated to its highest use, to the benefit of society. Exchanges will always be fair in competitive markets because each party to a transaction must benefit, whether buying or selling goods or services, or else he or she would refuse to deal.

Although one might gain a sense from this description of the operation of markets about how the self-interested actions of individuals exchanging with one another might lead to an efficient allocation of resources, economists make two very strong claims about the virtues of markets that to most people are counterintuitive. First, they allege that no matter how large and complicated the economy, if all markets are competitive, an equilibrium point will be reached at which all markets will be cleared: individual prices will be established for all goods and services so that the demand for all these goods and services will be met. Second, at this equilibrium point social welfare will be as great as it can be: the total benefits that consumers derive from consuming the goods and services produced, minus the cost of producing them, will be maximized. That is, the allocation of resources will be Pareto efficient. The proofs for these points are boring and complicated, but are given in simplified form in any basic microeconomic textbook. Nevertheless, it is important to be clear about this virtue of markets since it is the reason that most economists so passionately support markets and often express so much concern about the effect of taxes. Taxes almost invariably distort prices set by the market forces of supply and demand and thus impair the efficient operation of the economy, resulting in reduced consumer or producer surplus and thus reduced welfare.

I do not mean to belabour the concept of efficiency, however, the concept of social surplus, or gains from trade, or social welfare (hence "welfare" economics), is so important in understanding the virtues of markets and the concern that economists have with taxes (or any other government policy instruments that interfere with markets) that a simple illustration might firm up the point. Assume that I stop to buy a cup of coffee at my favourite coffee shop. It is early in the morning, and I would be willing to pay $1.20 for a cup of coffee. It costs the owners of the coffee shop only 80 cents to serve a cup of coffee to go. They sell it for $1. When I agree to pay $1 for the coffee, it is clear that this exchange has made both me and the coffee shop owner better off. I am 20 cents better off. The coffee was worth 20 cents more to me than I had to pay. This is referred to as my consumer surplus. The coffee shop is also 20 cents better off. The amount they received for the coffee exceeded their cost by 20 cents. This is referred to as their producer surplus. It is easy to see that after this simple exchange — my $1 for a cup of coffee — there has been a social gain, or welfare gain, of 40 cents due to the existence of this market. And, of course, the remarkable thing about gains from trade is that while both the consumer and producer have both gained, no one has lost. The process of trade creates welfare gains that simply did not exist before the trade took place. It is important to realize it is the exchange that created the wealth not the production of the coffee. That is, if the coffee was produced but no one valued it, no wealth would be created. Or, if I stepped outside the coffee shop with my coffee and someone else who at that moment valued a coffee at $1.40 offered me that amount for my coffee (because the shop had closed), upon this exchange the wealth of society would increase by another 20 cents. A good that was only valued at $1.20 (by me) was now in the hands of someone who assigned a value of $1.40 to it.

Since it is exchanges that create welfare in society, economists argue that to increase social welfare we ought to generate as many markets as we can to allow people to trade freely. To repeat the claim made by welfare economists, in a competitive equilibrium, the sum of all the gains to all the market participants is as large as possible, without making anyone worse off. Thus one can see why neo-classical economists attach such a strong normative value to regimes of private exchange and private ordering.

The concept of efficiency, as understood by welfare economists, might appear to be uncontentious as a normative standard. Basically, it says that if two (or any number of) people are made better off in their own estimation by exchanging goods and services, and no one is harmed, then society is better off if we allow people to exchange. The principle does, however, rest upon a number of ethical judgments all of which could be challenged, for example, that the most important goal of public policy is the maximization of social welfare as opposed to the achievement of other values such as fairness, justice, or economic security; it assumes that when responding to marketplace forces, individuals are always the best judge of their own welfare; it assumes that an individual's welfare does not depend upon the welfare of others; and, it assumes that a dollar to each individual should be given the same weight in measuring social welfare whether the person is poor or rich. Nevertheless, setting aside the possible ethical objections to the principle of efficiency, markets will only achieve an efficient allocation of resources if certain conditions are met. When one of these conditions is not met in a particular market there is a normative justification for some form of government action.

Economists refer to the types of situations in which individual behaviour will not lead to an efficient allocation of resources as market failures. Market failures have been studied, refined, and disputed endlessly in the literature. Right-wing economists have difficulty seeing them; left-wing economists find market failures everywhere they look. The following is a brief list of some of the major market failures. They can be discussed with almost unimaginable degrees of complexity; however, the point of this brief list is simply to illustrate the types of normative arguments that are made to justify tax laws on the grounds of promoting efficiency. Governments attempt to correct many of these market failures by subsidizing or directly providing goods and services that will not be supplied or will be undersupplied in markets. Obviously, governments must raise taxes in order to do this. Also, the great majority of tax expenditures are justified on the grounds that they are necessary in order to correct a market failure. Hence you need to know something about market failures not only to understand why tax laws are required generally, but also in order to make any sense out of most of the over 100 tax expenditures in the Act.

1. Public goods

The market will only allocate resources efficiently if goods consumed by one person cannot be consumed by someone else (the good has the characteristic of rivalry in consumption); if those who do not pay for a good can be excluded from its consumption (the good has the characteristic of excludability in ownership and use); and, if individuals can decide whether or not to purchase the good. There is a long list of goods that do not meet these criteria to some degree. They are referred to as public goods. The classic example is national defence. There is no way that one person, by himself or herself, could purchase national defence. But even assuming that individuals could, if they were able to protect themselves and their home from a missile attack at least all of their immediate neighbours would be protected without having to purchase the good and there is no way that the consumer could exclude them from the benefits of the good. Other familiar examples of public goods include law and order, public parks, and public infrastructure like street lighting and highways. The only way that people can provide themselves with these goods, all of which presumably promote their well-being, is by paying taxes and providing them publicly for everyone. Notice that it would not do to simply ask for donations for the purchase of these goods. Some individuals would not contribute and "free-ride" on other individuals' contributions. One purpose of taxes is to prevent "free-riders".

2. Externalities

The market will only allocate resources efficiently if all the costs and benefits of the production and consumption of a good are borne and enjoyed exclusively by the producers and consumers of that good. But both the production and consumption of all sorts of goods generate negative and positive externalities (or as they are variously called spillover effects, social costs and benefits, or neighbourhood effects). The standard example of a negative production externality is pollution. Smoke from a local factory will impose medical, cleaning and other costs on households that do not use the factory's output. Governments may regulate, impose taxes (emission taxes), issue tradeable emission permits, or use some other policy instrument in an attempt to deal with these negative production externalities. They may even subsidize the businesses causing pollution in order to encourage them to internalize these externalities. Thus, the Act contains fast write-off provisions for investments in pollution control equipment.

Education is an example of a good that generates positive consumption externalities. Why does the government provide free public education and generous tax credits, as well as subsidies, for individuals who attend institutions of higher education? One reason is that we assume that society generally benefits if its citizens are well educated. Therefore, since there are social benefits to education, in addition to private benefits, in order to ensure that individuals consume the efficient amount of education it must be subsidized. Again, taxes are obviously required to pay for the social benefits of education as well as many other goods that generate social benefits. Notice that this argument for taxes is made simply on the grounds that they are required to ensure that resources in the economy are allocated efficiently. That is, it accepts as its premise the normative standard of welfare economics. Naturally, a case can also be made for the public provision of education and other goods on the grounds of social justice.

3. Asymmetric Information

Markets can only achieve an efficient result — that is a result in which both parties are made better off — if both parties have access to all relevant information. Yet in many markets one party knows more about the product or service to be traded than the other and, therefore, there is a market failure. The most obvious way to attempt to correct this market failure is for the government to mandate consumer and investor disclosure requirements or product standards. However, in addition to the availability of information, for markets to operate efficiently, individuals have to be prepared to inform themselves about their exchanges. Yet fully informing oneself and making choices is not costless; in fact it is often burdensome. For this reason, it is reasonable that for some complex but essential products or services individuals would favour taxes and government designed and provided services over prices and market-provided services. For example, with respect to retirement pensions, government pensions can provide much greater security than private pensions and thus alleviate the anxieties of choosing among often insecure private alternatives. Moreover, the time and costs involved in requiring each individual to make an informed judgment about issues relating to private pension design and investment policies is enormous. It is a curious kind of person who enjoys the literature of pension and life insurance companies. Many people would, presumably, rather be reading Robertson Davies.

4. Cognitive Limitations

Markets will only achieve an efficient result not only if individuals have all the relevant information to make an informed choice but also if people are able to make rational judgments on the basis of the information they receive. Yet, psychologists have documented dozens and dozens of types of situations in which people consistently make errors of judgment. One of countless examples that might be given to illustrate this market failure is the notorious difficulty that people have in making rational intertemporal choices, particularly if the costs of those choices have to be borne immediately and the benefits will not be realized until sometime in the distant future. So, for example, one of the most compelling normative arguments supporting the tax deduction for contributions to RRSPs is that if the government did not bias people's choices about whether to spend all of their money now or save some for retirement, many people would make the wrong choice, even in terms of their own best interest, and not save for retirement. The RRSP deduction is designed, in part, to correct this market failure.

5. Incomplete Markets

In order for markets to allocate resources efficiently there must be markets for everything for which consumers are prepared to pay a price that covers their production costs. However, in some instances, even where this is the case, no market will emerge. This is particularly the case in markets for insurance because of problems of moral hazard and adverse selection. For example, even though consumers might demand employment insurance it is unlikely that a private market for employment insurance would develop since insurance companies would be concerned that the presence of insurance would cause more individuals to become unemployed (the moral hazard problem) and that only individuals who were likely to lose their jobs would purchase the insurance policy (adverse selection). Therefore, if individuals think that employment insurance would increase their well-being, the only way it can be provided is if they pay taxes to cover its cost and administer it through government agencies. Other obvious cases of incomplete markets include capital markets for loans to students, loans to small businesses, and loans to companies engaged in international trade. In all of these areas the government has stepped in, in some cases with tax measures.

This list of market failures could go on at length; the need for taxation even on grounds of economic efficiency is much more pervasive than most people seem to realize. However, the main point to be made here is simply that one important purpose of taxes is to allow for the correction of market failures and thus further the efficient allocation of resources and the maximization of social welfare. As you proceed through the study of tax law attempt to discern the normative justification for tax expenditures by identifying the market failures they were designed to correct. Of course not all tax expenditures are designed to correct market failures; some can be justified as instruments to achieve other government objectives.

Before turning to other normative justifications of tax, by way of clarifying the role of taxes in correcting market failures a few further points might be made. Once a market failure has been identified the government does not, of course, necessarily have to invoke taxes in order to correct it. The government has a broad range of policy instruments at its disposal including the reformulation of rules of property and contract law, regulation, the criminal law, minimum standards, enhanced private remedies, direct subsidies, public ownership and moral suasion. For example, assume that the government decides that the marketplace left to itself will not result in the optimal amount of indigenous cultural activity and there are positive externalities to such activities including the provision of public creative ideas and aesthetic standards; the development of national feeling, pride and identity; and, the social improvement of the participants in such cultural activities. Having made this normative judgment the government must then make an instrumental judgment about which is the best policy instrument to achieve this end. It could directly provide such activities through public ownership, such as the Canadian Broadcasting Corporation and the National Film Board; it could provide direct grants to non-profit organizations involved in such activities; it could impose Canadian-content regulation on the media; or, it could provide tax expenditures in the form of tax credits or fast write-offs for businesses engaged in Canadian cultural activities. The point is that once the government decides that as a normative matter a particular activity should be encouraged (or discouraged) in an attempt to correct for a market failure, an equally difficult task involves selecting the appropriate instrument to achieve that end. Tax laws are only one such instrument. In recent years, reflecting the rise of neo-liberalism, there has been much discussion about the general inadequacy or inappropriateness of the use of rule-bound forms of policy instruments and the advantages of flexible market-based instruments. Hence, the generally accepted preferred government intervention to reduce pollution externalities has shifted from so-called command and control regulations, to taxes, to tradeable emission permits.

Simply because a market failure is identified does not necessarily justify taxation or some other form of government intervention. Market failures are a necessary condition for government action but not a sufficient condition. Governments also fail. Even though the market might fail to produce an efficient result does not mean that governments can do any better. Again, reflecting the shift in prevailing ideologies, economists who used to spend most of their time examining market failures are these days preoccupied with studying government failures. There is now a branch of economics, public choice theory, devoted exclusively to this study. These economists point out the tendency of politicians to make decisions that provide short-run obvious benefits at the expense of long-run hidden costs; the numerous incentives for politicians to support special interest groups; the fact that majority voting does not always lead to what is in the public interest because of the problem of the oppressive majority (in some situations, the majority will benefit but not by as much as the minority will lose); the voting paradox (in which majority voting leads to no clear winner); and the fact that politicians frequently engage in log rolling (in which one politician votes for a policy supported by another because that politician will return the favour); and other strategic forms of behaviour. Also, they point to all the problems of bureaucracies, including the difficulty of controlling and evaluating a department's performance and the tendency for government agencies and their budgets to expand. As is well known, based in part on these trends in public sector economics, governments have increasingly reduced the role of monetary policy, privatized government services, deregulated private industries, reduced social security programs, reduced taxes, constrained their own ability to collect taxes, and moved to impose legislative limits on what democratically elected governments can do in the field of economic policy.

Finally, in concluding this discussion of market failures, it should be noted that maximizing welfare is not the only virtue that some economists and political philosophers claim for markets. Some defend markets largely on epistemological grounds. They argue that the limitations of human knowledge make rational planning impossible and that markets allow for the influence of tacit knowledge that is embedded in practices and institutions. Others defend markets largely on the ethical grounds that they promote individual freedom, choice and autonomy. Others defend them on the political grounds that they diffuse power and act as a shield against coercion by others and by a tyrannous state. Others defend them on the practical grounds that they provide incentives for action and for dynamic growth. The role of government and taxes become less clear-cut if one of these other justifications for markets is accepted.

D. The Role of the Tax System in Achieving a Morally Acceptable Distribution of Income

While many people are prepared to defend private markets on the grounds that they maximize social welfare or individual freedom of choice, only a few defend the market's ability to achieve a just distribution of income. Therefore, most people are prepared to assign some role to the government in achieving a socially acceptable distribution of income and wealth, that is, in redistributing resources from the rich to the poor. (There have been few serious claims that the market, absent government intervention, generates too much income equality.)

The government's distributive function might embrace one or both of two different conceptions stated here in the form of questions. First, to what extent should government raise the living standards of low-income individuals? Second, to what extent should the government attempt to increase the equality of the distribution of income throughout society by reducing the income and wealth of the rich? Even though there are different views about the justification for assisting the poor, the fact that the government should do so is seldom in dispute. The question of to what extent the state should attempt to equalize incomes has been much more contentious.

There are several contending theories of distributive justice. At one end of the spectrum are theories based upon notions of entitlement in a market economy. Some theorists apply a principle of entitlement without qualification; individuals are entitled to keep whatever they earn in the market. Only a small number of political philosophers hold this view; however, it appears to be surprisingly widely held among the general population, particularly among business people and others who have done well in the marketplace. Other theorists who espouse entitlement-based arguments normally qualify them in some way: individuals are only entitled to keep what they earn in markets that are competitive, or only in markets in which everyone was given an equal starting position. At the other end of the spectrum are theorists who apply some form of egalitarian criteria in making judgments about the just distribution of income. At the extreme, strict egalitarians call for perfect equality in the distribution of economic resources. Others argue for a distribution of income in which the welfare of the lowest group is maximized.

Most theories of distributive justice clearly contemplate that, if implemented, some people will be made better off and others worse off than they would be in an economy that sought solely to maximize social welfare, as that term is understood by economists. Some economists, reluctant to rest the case for redistribution on strong value judgments, have posited two bases for redistribution that might actually make it Pareto efficient; that is, they have posited circumstances under which after redistribution all individuals might be at least as well off as under the status quo. First, redistribution might be Pareto efficient if individuals have interdependent preferences. If individuals derive utility from making gifts to the less fortunate, then both the rich donor and the poor donee are better off after the transfer. While this would only argue for voluntary redistribution, if it is the overall distribution of income that affects the utility of the rich, and not just the income of specific individual poor people, then distribution has the characteristics of a public good. Unless the government intervenes and redistributes through taxation there will be a sub-optimal amount of transfers because of the free-rider problem.

A second set of circumstances under which self-interested individuals might consent to income redistribution is if they are risk-averse and uncertain about their economic futures. In these circumstances, progressive income tax and means-tested transfers can be justified as a form of social insurance it is a way for individuals to spread the risks of income variation. Collective provision of this form of insurance can be justified because of problems of moral hazard in analogous private insurance plans and imperfections in capital markets.

This is not the place to review critically, or even summarize, the many hundreds of years of debate over the most appropriate theory of distributive justice. However, simply because the view that it is departures from the market distribution of income — through taxation for example — that require justification appears so widespread, it seems worthwhile to note a few of the many problems with the intuitions underlying the justness of the market distribution of income. There would appear to be two such intuitions.

One intuition suggesting that the market distribution of income is just rests upon the assumption that people's earnings are a measure of the value of their contribution to social welfare and therefore their personal dessert. However, to be at all persuasive there are a number of obvious problems such a theory would have to overcome. To list just a few: the value of individual contributions to social welfare is impossible to determine since all contributions are of an intrinsically social nature and all income is co-operatively generated, therefore, the rules of property and contract cannot sensibly distinguish between individual contributions in the production of goods and services; the demand side of the labour market does not reward skills that are socially valuable but skills that individuals with money demand; in the same way, the supply side of the market does not reward skills that are valuable or admirable but skills that are scarce; large earnings are often the result of morally irrelevant factors because the contributor has no control over them, such as the accident of being born into a family of wealth, the chance of being raised in a wealthy country, the good fortune of remaining able-bodied and working for a firm that remains profitable and in Canada, the good luck of investing in the right stock, or the fortuity of being born with an inherited talent that is in scarce supply; and finally, even if an individual's contributions were morally relevant in determining the amount to which he or she should have a moral claim, in real markets, factors such as social conventions, discrimination, monopoly power, and government regulation are much more likely than productivity to determine the size distribution of income.

A second intuition that appears to underlie the notion that the market distribution of earnings is presumptively just rests upon the judgment that the process by which earnings are distributed appears to be fair. However, this process-claim arbitrarily assumes that the initial distribution of income and wealth is just; that people only have property and not broader social rights; that the marketplace in which people trade is free (that is, that people's choices are always fully informed and non-coerced) and neutral (that is, that the rules that define the marketplace do not favour some over others); and, that individuals only have entitlements to goods and services allocated through markets but not to those allocated by other social forms of organization. None of these assumptions is easy to support.

If any role is assigned to the government to redistribute earnings, on whatever ethical basis, most commentators are of the view that the taxation system is an important policy instrument to achieve that objective. Even libertarians have traditionally preferred that redistribution be achieved through the tax system as opposed to other forms of government intervention because the tax system preserves the basic processes of free exchange. A reasonable level of taxes poses little threat to either producer or consumer sovereignty. Even with a tax on income, individuals are still free to make whatever career or investment choices they wish, and free to choose whatever goods and services they wish to consume. The only liberty seriously infringed by an income tax is the liberty to retain all the income one is able to gain by entering into profitable market transactions. But, since prices continue to be determined largely by supply and demand, and since the effect of the tax on income would be known before individuals made the choices they thought would maximize their well-being, it is hard to imagine that this loss of liberty is serious at all. Indeed, unless one assumes that economic freedom needs absolutely no instrumental justification, it would appear to be hardly affected at all.

Of course, the tax system itself, even if it were extremely progressive, is unlikely to be able to seriously affect the distribution of income, or turn back the rising tide of inequality now being experienced in most industrialized countries, including Canada. Concerted action on almost every front would be necessary to achieve the distribution of income that most political philosophers would regard as just including the enrichment of early childhood education, providing increased economic security and bargaining power for workers, and glutting high-skill labour markets with university graduates. Those on the far left, if there are any remaining, would argue that no redistributional policy can be effective without changing fundamentally the economic system of production.

E. The Role of the Tax System in Stabilizing the Economy

From the great depression in the 1930s until the 1980s, the prevailing economic wisdom was that full employment and stable prices did not necessarily come about automatically in a market economy, even if the government corrected the misallocation of resources and inequalities in the distribution of income. In the absence of public policy guidance, market economies tended to be subject to substantial fluctuations, and could suffer from sustained periods of unemployment, inflation or both.

The overall level of employment and prices depends upon the level of aggregate demand for consumer and investment goods relative to potential output in the economy at prevailing prices. The level of aggregate demand depends, in turn, upon the spending decisions of individuals, consumers and investors. In the nineteenth century, classical economists argued that market economies would tend to move toward full employment. However, the performance of western economies after World War I and, in particular, the prolonged depression of the 1930s, threw the assumption of inherent stability of free market economies into question. John Maynard Keynes, in his classic text, *The General Theory of Employment, Interest and Money*,[11] argued that aggregate demand, which is the chief determinant of the level of economic activity, might stabilize the economy at points other than full employment. He suggested, therefore, that government intervention in the economy was important in order to manage aggregate demand, and to ensure the economy was operating near its potential output.

Keynes argued that government fiscal instruments — spending and tax policies — were the most effective tools for demand management. In order to increase aggregate demand in periods of economic downturns, for example, the government should increase its spending on public works, provide more money for social assistance, offer loans and other forms of relief to small businesses hurt by a decline in demand for their goods and services, and cut taxes for people who tend to consume most of their incomes, namely those in low-income brackets. Keynes suggested that monetary instruments to control the money supply, such as bank reserve requirements, discount rates, open market policies, and selective credit controls, might also be used to achieve the government's stabilization policy, but these instruments were not as important, or as effective, as fiscal instruments.

"Keynesianism", the term that came to be applied to government policies aimed at reducing the severity and duration of downturns in the business cycle, became widely accepted among industrialized countries. By the late 1960s, many economists were predicting that the prudent use of fiscal policy to manage aggregate demand would ensure that business cycles were a thing of the past.

To make a long story short, with the advent of stagflation (a sharp rise in both the rate of inflation and unemployment coupled with declining output) in the 1970s, there was a sharp retreat from Keynesianism at every level. The economic doctrine of monetarism, which questions the effectiveness of any stabilization role for government, not only began dominating economic studies but also was adopted by many industrialized countries as part of their general drift towards neo-liberal policies. In Canada, the triumph of monetarism was almost complete; the federal government appeared to have abandoned any meaningful stabilization function. In the early 1990s, during one of Canada's most severe recessions, the government not only refused to implement any special counter-cyclical measures, but instead reduced spending and increased taxes on middle-income Canadians. It attributed this stance to the persistent high deficits and high public debt.

Nevertheless, in late 2008 when the financial and economic crises threatened to plunge the world into a global depression, Keynesianism and stabilization policy made a stunning comeback. Most of the major countries affected by the crisis, including Canada, embarked on an unprecedented level of multilateral economic cooperation and an ambitious program of stimulus spending in order to attempt to restore consumer and business confidence. However, although there were tax cuts

---

[11] (London: MacMillan, 1936).

in some countries, most of the policy developments involved government spending programs. Particularly in view of the large deficits run up by most governments, it seems reasonably clear that in the immediate future the structure of the tax system will not be influenced by a concern over its potential use as an instrument of economic stabilization.

F. The Role of the Tax System in Increasing the Rate of Economic Growth

In recent years, the most contentious debate over the role of the tax system has been its role in assisting or hindering economic growth. From the mid-1970s until only fairly recently, there was a dramatic slowdown in economic growth and in particular productivity. Although there is some dispute about the cause of this slowdown, many economists and business persons blame it squarely on structural impediments in the economy caused by excessive government intervention, and most importantly, excessive taxation. They argue that reducing taxes will usher in a new era of unconstrained prosperity.

The precise behavioural mechanisms through which lower taxes are supposed to unleash unbridled economic growth are sometimes difficult to discern from the arguments of those who support the reduction of taxes, however, they appear to include the following. If high-income individuals face lower marginal tax rates they will work more hours per week, more weeks per year, and more years per lifetime since the amount they can earn after-tax from working will have increased; they will save more because the government will take less of the interest, dividends and capital gains they can earn on their savings; and, rich and talented Canadians will be more likely to remain in Canada and contribute to the economy instead of emigrating to more tax-hospitable countries. If taxes are lowered generally, and in particular are lowered on the profits earned from buying and selling corporate shares or cashing in employee stock options then more individuals will be encouraged to become entrepreneurs or otherwise make risky investments since they will be allowed to keep more of the resulting profits. Reduced taxes on high-income individuals will also signal to international businesses that Canada is friendly to business and, therefore, encourage them to locate their plant and head office here. Reduced corporate taxes will allow Canadian firms to retain more of their profits to invest back in their business and attract more international investment.

These arguments were popularized by the so-called "supply-siders" during the Reagan administration in the United States. As briefly described above, according to traditional Keynesian doctrine, employment and economic growth are determined by aggregate demand. Unemployment and low rates of economic growth are caused by insufficient spending. During the late 1970s, when many western economies were suffering from stagflation, supply-side economists stepped in and argued that the preoccupation of Keynesians with demand had blinded them to the need for analyzing the effect of changing tax rates on productivity, investment and incentives to work. They argued that instead of concentrating on demand, governments should concentrate on increasing the supply of goods and services. Although supply-side economics addresses all aspects of aggregate supply, it focuses in particular on the appropriate role of government in encouraging growth through its taxation policies.

No one doubts the existence of the kind of incentive effects supply-side economics teaches. However, the question is how important they are within a range of reasonable tax rates. Although it seems to be almost an article of faith among the converted that high taxes have significant adverse effects on economic growth, many others take the view that this proposition is not obvious in theory, nor is it supported by the weight of empirical evidence.

The debate over the role of taxes in encouraging economic growth cannot be resolved here. At some time you may want to turn your mind to it, but the important point for the purpose of understanding the foundations of income tax law is that the concern over the effect of taxes on economic growth is reflected throughout the Act. Unlike stabilization policy, which no longer appears to be a matter of concern in structuring the tax system, the role of the tax system in promoting economic growth is a central preoccupation of the tax drafters. However, precisely how this concern becomes reflected in tax laws will naturally depend on which model the government bases its policies of what makes the economy productive . The model for increasing productivity that underlies supply-side economics and the resulting tax design were suggested above. But there is another model for increasing productivity and international competitiveness in which the public sector and taxes play a substantial role. This model rests on the premise that an economy will be productive if there is a highly trained, well paid, secure, and co-operative labour force that is willing and able to adapt to changing technologies and innovations, a well-developed public infrastructure including high quality health, education and transportation systems; a professional public sector that is capable of taking the lead in the process of gathering information, targeting potential high-growth areas of the economy, and allocating public resources; and, a society in which equality is actively promoted.

VII. CRITERIA FOR EVALUATING TECHNICAL TAX MEASURES

A. Role of Evaluative Criteria

A good income tax system is one that functions as an effective instrument for achieving its assigned government goals. In broad terms, this means that it should be designed so that it can be used to assist in raising the revenue required to finance government spending, in stabilizing the economy, in achieving a socially acceptable distribution of income, and in pursuing the appropriate rate of economic growth. However, as well as being designed to ensure that it is an effective instrument in achieving the goals the government wishes to pursue through its use, the tax system must be designed so that it satisfies the criteria that are used in evaluating all policy instruments. These criteria arise from the value judgments and assumptions underlying a country's basic social and economic institutions. In tax law they are traditionally classified under the headings of equity, neutrality and simplicity. In recent years, because of the increasing internationalization of domestic economies, a further criteria has been added: international harmonization or competitiveness. Indeed, those on the right argue that in this age of globalization the most important consideration in designing a tax system is ensuring that a country's system does not differ greatly from those of other countries, particularly major trading partners, and particularly as it affects income from capital and high-income, mobile taxpayers.

A few general comments will provide some context for examining each of these criteria. First, it is conceptually important to distinguish these evaluative criteria from the purposes of the tax system itself. Tax systems are not enacted to ensure that equally situated individuals are treated the same, or to leave the choices of individuals unaffected, or to make life simpler for people. The fairest, most neutral, and simplest tax system would be no tax system at all. The purpose of the tax system is to assist the government in achieving its broad objectives. However, once it is conceded that a tax system is required for these purposes, then it clearly should be designed in a way that satisfies the familiar criteria of equity, neutrality, and simplicity.

Second, although these criteria appear to be relied upon more explicitly in understanding and evaluating tax law, they are no different than the criteria used for good policy analysis in every area of law. In legal analysis generally, most of the policy arguments that are made can be categorized as fairness arguments, arguments about the incentive effects of the law, and arguments about whether the law can be administered. Every policy question in law — which means every legal question — requires you to consider the fairness of competing outcomes. In tax law these considerations are discussed under the heading, sensibly enough, of equity. Every legal policy question requires you to consider what effect the proposed rule will have on people's behaviour and thus on the economy and society generally. In tax law these considerations are usually somewhat misleadingly discussed under the heading of neutrality. Finally, policy questions in every area of law can only be sensibly answered after a thorough consideration of the administrative practicality of alternative solutions. How will the legal rules actually be administered? Will they be convenient to comply with? Will they lead to too much uncertainty? Will they be enforceable? Often the answer to these questions will require the familiar rehearsal of the pros and cons of implementing a bright-line test as opposed to a more flexible standard. All these considerations are referred to compendiously in tax policy analysis as considerations relating to simplicity.

Third, in tax law there is an ongoing debate about whether, based upon these criteria, the base of our most comprehensive tax should be income or consumption. Many economists argue that a personal consumption tax would be more equitable, more economically neutral and simpler than the present personal income tax. This debate is not pursued here. However, as you proceed with your study of tax law you might consider how different a personal consumption tax base would be from the income tax base that you are studying and whether it in fact would be more equitable, neutral and simple.

Fourth, an obvious point, no element of the tax system can be designed in a way that simply follows deductively from some general overriding principles. Inevitably difficult trade-offs between these three criteria have to be made. For example, one reason for the complexity of the tax system is the frequent attempts to fine-tune the rules to ensure that an equitable result is reached in most cases. Some commentators argue that more inequities should be tolerated in order to have a simpler tax system.

Fifth, the importance of learning to apply these criteria can be underlined by noting that they have never changed. The details of the law change constantly; yet the norms underlying the Act and the basic structure of the Act have remained essentially unchanged because they reflect a balancing of these criteria. By understanding the application of these criteria you can spot rules that conflict with them and, therefore, are possible candidates for revision.

Finally, these criteria only apply to the elements of the technical tax system. That is, you apply them in attempting to understand the design of the technical tax base, the definition of the tax units and the attribution of income to them, the rules relating to the period of income measurement, the tax rates, and the rules of administration. These tax criteria do not apply to an evaluation of tax expenditures. It is a common mistake among students taking the basic tax course (and even judges) to apply these criteria to all provisions in the Act. Tax expenditures are implicit government spending programs and, therefore, they should be evaluated using budgetary criteria, not tax criteria.

B. Equity

One of the most fundamental axioms of social justice is that people in the same circumstances should be treated the same. In tax policy analysis this evaluative criteria is referred to as horizontal equity: people who are "similarly situated" should pay the same amount of tax. Vertical equity refers to the ethical requirement that unequals be treated appropriately differently. Arguably, equity is the most important criterion with which to evaluate a tax system. If the government was not concerned about horizontal equity, it could raise revenue simply by confiscating resources or by printing money. What distinguishes a tax from other methods of reducing private consumption is that a tax is premised on some notion of equity or fairness. The difficult question is: in determining whether two people are similarly circumstanced or have the same ability to pay, and, therefore, should bear the same tax burden, which of their personal circumstances should be considered?

Although the criteria of horizontal and vertical equity are routinely used in tax analysis, they in fact have no normative content. They are simply used as devices for alerting analysts to potential normative issues. With respect to horizontal equity, since individuals are always alike in some respects and different in others, the difficult question is what personal circumstances are to be counted in determining whether two persons are equal for tax purposes. A normative theory is required in order to determine the relevancy of various personal characteristics. Similarly, with respect to vertical equity, a normative theory is required to judge what degree of differentiation between dissimilar persons is appropriate. For example, if one believes the fairest manner of raising revenue to finance public goods is to require individuals to make an equal sacrifice, and that income is an appropriate and manageable proxy for sacrifice, then horizontal equity simply requires that those with the same income pay the same amount of tax. Vertical equity requires that the rate structure be set so that those with different incomes pay an amount that requires them to make the same sacrifice. That is to say, basically, these criteria simply require that once a normative theory of a fair tax system has been chosen, it ought to be applied across taxpayers as consistently as possible. Or to put this another way, if we say that not allowing individuals to deduct their child care expenses, or any other expenses, violates horizontal equity, all we are really saying is that, given our normative definition of income, individuals should not have to pay tax on income spent for child care. While the concept of horizontal equity might be used to indicate there is a problem here, obviously the real issue is whether or not our normative definition of income should include amounts spent on child care. Horizontal equity is simply a way of referring to the consistency with which the normative theory underlying the tax base is implemented.

How should income be defined in an equitable income tax system? There have been numerous suggestions. The most commonly accepted theory of tax fairness equates a fair tax system with one based upon a taxpayer's ability to pay. The rationale of the ability-to-pay approach is that the payment of taxes involves the individual in a loss of utility, a sacrifice. A fair system of taxation based on the ability-to-pay approach is defined as one in which the sacrifices of utility by all taxpayers are equal. In the public finance literature at the turn of the century there was considerable discussion of precisely what ultimately should amount to a sacrifice of utility, both in the sense of treating taxpayers with the same ability to pay the same (horizontal equity) and ensuring that those with greater ability to pay were required to make the same subjective sacrifice as those with less ability to pay (vertical equity).

Some commentators assumed that a taxpayer's ability to pay should be measured by reference to the flow of psychic satisfactions to an individual. However, since a tax base must be measurable, even in theory, this definition makes no sense. There is no known scale or metric that allows the satisfaction experienced by one person to be compared with that experienced by another. Other commentators assumed, and some economists still do, that taxpayers' ability to pay should be measured ideally by reference to their "full income"; that is, basically, the amount they could earn if they realized their full earning potential. Full income is obviously an unobtainable ideal. Most people never reveal their earnings potential and if it were taxed they would of course have even less incentive to do so. Thus there is no administrative way of taxing it. Moreover, most commentators concede that, in Rawlsian terms, a tax on full income would violate the liberty principle. It would require highly endowed individuals to adopt a life plan that would provide them with the funds to pay the tax on their full income, notwithstanding a preference they might have for a different life plan. Nevertheless, many commentators still view the concept of income that should be implemented in the income tax as being a proxy for a taxpayer's ability to pay as understood by the sacrifice and earning potential theory.

In 1938, Henry Simons launched a blistering attack on these theories of tax fairness in his classic text, *Personal Income Taxation.*[12] He scornfully dismissed them as "pseudo-scientific" and noted that the concepts upon which theories of ability to pay were based — "sacrifice" and "faculty" — were incapable of measurement. In their place, he argued that income should be defined as in essence the power to consume: "Personal income connotes, broadly, the exercise of control over the use of society's scarce resources".[13] Simons is often accused of not being clear about the normative principle underlying his proposed definition of income. However, his definition is derived not from any principle of tax fairness, but followed from his strongly held view that the only justification for a progressive income tax was the redistribution of income. Simons is frequently quoted as favouring redistribution on "the ethical or aesthetic judgment that the prevailing distribution of wealth and income reveals a degree (and/ or kind) of inequality which is distinctly evil or unlovely."[14] But Simons' strong commitment to progressive taxation reflected more than a mere aesthetic judgment; he believed that progressive taxes were a vital step in the creation of a more stable and non-monopolistic capitalism. He felt that not only was an excessive inequality of economic power "unlovely", but more signifi-

---

[12] Henry C. Simons, *Personal Income Taxation: The Definition of Income as a Problem of Fiscal Policy* (Chicago: University of Chicago Press, 1938).

[13] *Ibid.* at 49.

[14] *Ibid.* at 18-19.

cantly, it seriously threatened the legitimacy of the capitalist economy. Reflecting, in part, the pragmatic public philosophy accepted by most social scientists during the 1930s, most economists almost immediately adopted Simons' line, or a variant of it, as the justification for progressive taxation.

Although most contemporary commentators accept Simons' concept of income there is still wide disagreement over precisely what it means. In recent years, largely in the context of attempting to justify the treatment of personal expenses in a fair tax system, such as the treatment of medical expenses and charitable contributions, a number of different normative theories justifying the income tax have been proposed, each leading to a slightly different concept of income. However, the primary debate has been between those who think that income should be defined by reference to the economic resources that taxpayers benefit from (often referred to as the standard-of-living concept of income) and those who think that income should be defined by the economic resources that individuals control (often referred to as the ability-to-pay concept of income).

Whether income is defined by reference to the benefit theory or the control theory has implications throughout the tax system. However, the importance of the debate might be illustrated by reference to the question of whether the individual or the family should be the basic taxpaying unit. Under the Canadian tax system, the individual is the basic unit of taxation. However, some commentators and political constituencies argue that the family should be the basic unit of taxation. They use the following example to give force to their argument. Under the present tax system a family in which one spouse earns $100,000 and the other works in the home pays much more tax than a family in which both spouses work outside the home and earn $50,000 each. Under our progressive tax system an individual earning $100,000 in Ontario in 2014 will pay about $26,500 in income tax, while an individual earning $50,000 will only pay about $8,700. Hence, the one-earner family will pay about $9,000 more tax in this example than the two-earner family. Those who support family-unit taxation argue that in a fair tax system two families with the same income should pay the same amount of tax regardless of how that income is earned by the individual spouses. What do you think?

As a conceptual matter, the debate is not really over whether the family or the individual is the correct unit of account. Few people claim that the household is the natural unit to which utility — or anything else that matters for tax purposes — accrues. Instead, the individual is the proper focus of fairness in any social institution; therefore, the proper question is, in determining an individual's tax liability, should that individual's marital status, or other personal relationships, be relevant? Those who argue for family-unit taxation argue that income should be defined by reference to the economic resources that an individual benefits from and, therefore, if an individual has a sharing relationship with another the economic resources provided by that person, and from which the individual benefits, should be included in his or her income. On the assumption that married couples share all their economic resources, this reasoning leads to the conclusion that the earned and other taxable income of both spouses should be totalled and then divided equally between them in determining their individual tax liabilities. Those who argue for individual taxation presumably take a different view of the definition of income. Individuals should be taxed on the income they control whether they share it with another or not. Thus taxpayers' conjugal, or any other sharing relationships, should be ignored in assessing their tax liability.

Which leads to a fairer tax base, the benefit theory or the control theory of income? This is clearly a normative question. The benefit theory obviously has some intuitive appeal. It would seem just that two individuals with the same material standard of living contribute the same amount to support government programs. Similarly the control theory has intuitive appeal. It would seem just that two individuals who confronted the same options pay the same amount of tax. Some individuals might decide to spend their income on expensive vacations, others might decide to share it with a spouse. Arguably these are personal decisions that should not affect the individual's tax liabilities. More could be said about these two potential definitions of income in order to clarify our intuitions about their relative fairness; however, the point here is simply to illustrate one important implication of these two concepts of income. There is not much question that the control theory of income underlies the design of the Canadian income tax system, even though it is not applied entirely consistently.

The relative fairness of the benefit or control theory of income does not, of course, exhaust the debate over which is the most appropriate tax base. For example, if one believes that the market distribution of income is unjust, and that the tax system should be used to achieve a more socially acceptable distribution of income, then there is a strong case for adopting the control theory since that means the tax would be levied directly on the earned income of individuals, regardless of its perceived fairness compared to the benefit theory. Also, even if the benefit theory of income is adopted, that does not necessarily lead to family-unit taxation. Family-unit taxation would only be the correct result in terms of fairness if it could be shown that spouses generally pool all of their income and that the value of the labour performed by the spouse who works in the home in the one-earner family should be ignored for tax purposes. Finally, even if the benefit theory of income were considered to be fairer than the control theory, before family-unit taxation were adopted an analyst would also have to consider the neutrality and simplicity of individual versus family-unit taxation.

In the basic tax course horizontal and vertical equity are frequently applied to tax measures, particularly to personal expenses such as child care expenses, medical expenses, charitable contributions, the expenses of raising children, and casualty losses. This rather extended discussion of family-unit taxation was simply to make the point that invariably what is at stake in these discussions is some normative theory of income and its reach.

C. Neutrality

The second traditional criterion by which taxes are evaluated is frequently referred to as neutrality: taxes should avoid distorting the workings of the market mechanism or personal decisions. The assumption underlying this criterion is that in free markets individuals will make decisions about how hard to work, how much to save, what goods to purchase, what relationships to enter into, and so forth, by comparing the benefits they derive from these actions with their costs. Since individuals are the best judges of the benefits and costs to themselves with respect to particular choices, their welfare will be maximized if their decisions are made freely on the basis of market prices and personal preferences. Taxes that distort individual choices will give rise to an excess burden or deadweight loss. The neutrality criterion requires that tax rules be drafted to minimize the excess burden of taxation.

Taxes can obviously affect a wide range of personal and business decisions; the difficult questions are in what contexts do taxes matter and how much do they matter. Most public finance scholars now distinguish between a hierarchy of responses to tax changes. Standing at the top of the hierarchy is the timing of transactions. Timing decisions appear to be very responsive to tax changes. In the second tier of the hierarchy are financial and accounting changes, essentially compensation and portfolio changes. They are also somewhat responsive to tax changes. On the bottom of the hierarchy are real decisions by individuals and firms, for example, decisions about how much to work, how much to save, and where to live. These are least responsive to tax changes.

As you proceed through the basic course, always explore the effects that the various rules might have on the behaviour of individuals. In most areas it is almost impossible to draft a completely neutral rule. Moreover, some would argue that the economic concept of excess burden rests upon shaky empirical and hidden normative judgments underlying the presumptive appropriateness of the free market allocation of resources. Therefore, instead of asking whether the rules are neutral, it is perhaps more useful to ask whether the likely incentive effects are appropriate (based upon an explicit normative judgment).

D. Simplicity

Simplicity is a term used by tax analysts to refer compendiously to a variety of desirable administrative attributes of a tax system. It is increasingly recognized as an important criterion in assessing tax rules. Some argue that people are beginning to despair at the complexity of tax laws and thus the legitimacy of taxation is being threatened. Also, the more complex the tax system the larger the tax planning and compliance industry. Some argue that people in this industry are imposing an increasingly large deadweight loss on the economy.

Many major design features of the income tax law, such as the failure to tax the imputed rental value of homes, the taxation of capital gains only when they are realized and the pre-set depreciation schedules, are explained, in part, by administrative considerations. Once again, as you proceed through the basic course you should identify the ways in which almost all the detailed rules have been shaped by administrative considerations. The following is a brief list of those considerations.

Comprehensibility. The tax system should be understandable to the people to whom it applies. This does not mean that lay persons should be able to read and understand it, but it means that the principles that underlie the rules should have an intuitive appeal and that they should be consistently implemented. The logic of the Act should be obvious.

Certainty. The application of the tax system to particular transactions should be determinable, predictable, and reasonably certain. The rules are most likely to be applied consistently if their underlying purposes are evident. In some areas, to provide certainty, bright-line tests or factual presumptions should be used.

Compliance Convenience. Taxpayers should not have to devote undue time or incur undue costs in complying with the tax system. However, a body of empirical literature is developing on the magnitude of the various compliance costs that the tax system imposes on individuals and businesses. By almost any measure, it appears that the cost to taxpayers of complying with the income tax is high.

Administrative Convenience. The administrative cost of collecting and enforcing the law should be reasonable. In many cases, administrative costs (costs borne by the government) and compliance costs (costs borne by individual taxpayers) are close substitutes. In most cases the costs are more equitably distributed if they are borne by the government.

Difficult to Avoid and Evade. The tax system should offer minimal opportunity for noncompliance. A tax system that is difficult to enforce creates arguably the most serious form of unfairness: the tax burden is shifted from dishonest to honest taxpayers.

VIII. CRITERIA FOR EVALUATING TAX EXPENDITURES

A. Definition of Tax Expenditures

As alluded to a number of times in this introductory chapter, the Act is not only a tax collecting statute; it is also a significant government spending statute. This insight that the Act is comprised of two analytically distinct types of provisions is without question one of the most important for those who wish to understand, apply and interpret the Act. Technical tax provisions are those provisions that establish the basic structural elements of the tax system: the tax base, the filing unit, the accounting period rules, the rates, and the rules of administration. These rules are required in order to make the statute effective for raising revenue and redistributing income and are drafted and evaluated using the traditional tax policy criteria of equity, neutrality and simplicity. But there are over 100 provisions that deal with individual taxation in the Act that cannot be explained by reference to these criteria. These provisions have nothing to do with defining the basic elements of the tax system. Instead their purpose is to provide implicit subsidies for those who behave in ways that the government wishes to encourage or who are deemed to be entitled to some form of relief because of their personal circumstances. These provisions are now widely referred to as tax expenditures. They take the form of special tax exemptions or deductions, tax credits, lower rates of tax or provisions that allow taxes to be deferred.

The Department of Finance publishes annually a document entitled, *Government of Canada: Tax Expenditures,* in which it lists, describes and estimates the cost of these tax expenditures to the federal government. To provide a sense of the pervasiveness of these provisions, the following is a sample of provisions under only three of the subject area headings and their projected cost for 2014 (all dollars figures are millions). Under the heading "Education" the Department lists: tuition fee credit ($310), education credit ($210); education and tuition fee credits transferred ($575); carry-forward of tuition and education credits ($740); student loan interest credit ($46); exemption of scholarships and bursary income ($45); and, registered education savings plan ($155). Under the heading "Family" the Department lists: spousal credit ($1,570); eligible dependent credit ($810); infirm dependent credit ($7); and caregiver credit ($65). Under the heading "Health" they list: non-taxation of business-paid health and dental benefits ($2,065); disability credit ($750); medical expense credit ($1,425); and, children's fitness tax credit ($130).

The concept of tax expenditures was developed largely by Stanley Surrey, a professor of law at Harvard Law School and Assistant Secretary of Tax Policy in the U.S. Treasury Department during the 1960s. Over the years there has been an extensive debate in the tax policy literature about the definition of tax expenditures and whether it was coherent at all to try to distinguish between technical tax provisions and tax expenditures because many provisions, such as the medical expense and charitable contributions credits, could be rationalized as either technical tax provisions or tax expenditures. That debate need not be rehearsed here, since it was largely unproductive and the concept has been widely accepted since the 1980s, except to make this point. The arguments that many economists and business people, in particular, made to show that the concept was in some way incoherent, reflected a misunderstanding about the nature of conceptual reasoning. The term "tax expenditure" refers only to a concept. It does not purport to rest upon an empirical or normative judgment. It simply suggests a way of categorizing provisions in the tax system in order to clarify our thinking about them. Just because many provisions that are sometimes labelled tax expenditures might also arguably be justified in terms of traditional tax criteria does not mean the concept is not useful. Any concept, tax expenditures are no exception, can be deconstructed. There is simply no phenomena in the world that can be divided up into incontestable categories. The most we can ask of our concepts, or the way that we categorize phenomena, is that they promote clarity of thought. That would seem to be a standard the concept of tax expenditure can easily meet.

Generally, two methods are used in classifying tax provisions as tax expenditures. One method involves constructing a benchmark tax system using the traditional tax policy criteria. All deviations in the Act from this benchmark are labelled tax expenditures. A second method involves labelling as tax expenditures all those tax provisions that are justified by reference to a government spending objective and that are arguably being used as alternatives to direct government spending programs.

The fact that tax expenditures are functionally equivalent to a direct government spending program can be easily illustrated. Assume that the government wished to subsidize 50 per cent of the cost of child care expenses of two-earner families. It has two straightforward ways of doing so. It can invite qualifying individuals to submit their child care receipts every year and write it a cheque for 50 per cent of the expenses, or the government can allow the qualifying individuals to deduct their expenses from their income for tax purposes. If the individuals are in the 50 per cent tax bracket a deduction of say $7,000 for child care expenses will save them $3,500 tax. In terms of the after-tax income of the individuals and of the revenues and expenditures of the government, the tax expenditure is equivalent to the direct spending program. In effect, with the tax deduction, instead of writing individuals a cheque directly, the government has simply allowed them to offset their government subsidy against their tax liability.

B. Evaluating Tax Expenditures

In terms of studying and understanding the Act, the significance of identifying tax expenditures is that while technical provisions are evaluated using tax criteria — equity, neutrality and simplicity — tax expenditures are evaluated using budgetary criteria, the same criteria that are used in evaluating spending programs (since that is what they are). If a provision might be justified using either tax or budgetary criteria, instead of entering into an often fruitless analysis of whether it is a technical or tax expenditure provision, it should be analyzed using both sets of criteria.

Three budgetary questions might be asked about every tax expenditure. First, what government objective is being served by the tax expenditure? Normally, the answer to this question will involve the identification of some market failure that the subsidy program is attempting to correct. However, it may involve the identification of some objective other than the furtherance of social welfare such as social justice or gender equity.

Second, assuming that the tax expenditure is serving some valid government objective, then it should be assessed using the same budgetary criteria used in assessing government spending programs: Are the benefits distributed fairly? Is the program target efficient, that is, are the benefits well targeted at the intended beneficiaries and not unreasonably over- or under-inclusive of those beneficiaries? Does the program avoid causing any unintended distorting effects? Are the administrative and compliance costs of the program reasonable? Does the government have control over the spending program and is it politically accountable for it? Is the program appropriately implemented?

Third, can the objective served by the tax expenditure be better served by some other governing policy instrument? In most cases, the obvious alternative instrument would be a direct spending program; however, in some cases the objectives served by tax expenditures could also be served by government regulation or public provision. Those who favour the use of the tax system to deliver subsidies argue that the advantages of tax expenditures include the fact that they tend to be simpler in design than direct subsidies, they involve less bureaucratic discretion than direct subsidies, they encourage private decision-making, they use an established framework of administration, and they involve less stigma than direct government handouts. Those who oppose the use of the tax system to deliver subsidies argue that almost all these claimed virtues of tax expenditures are not advantages of placing spending programs in the tax system, but instead are alleged advantages of automatic cheque-writing programs as opposed to discretionary grant programs. That is, they are alleged advantages of the design of the program not whether they are delivered as direct spending programs or an offset against tax liabilities.

Those who oppose the use of the tax system to deliver subsidies argue that the disadvantages of tax expenditures include the fact that they are open-ended programs over which the government has little control; if they are delivered as tax deductions (as opposed to credits) they have a perverse upside-down effect (the greater the taxpayer's marginal tax rate the greater the implicit subsidy); even if they are delivered as tax credits they are not available to non-taxpaying individuals unless the credits are refundable; when placed in the tax system these spending programs are almost inevitably subject to more abuse than direct spending programs; they increase the complexity of the tax system and tax administration; they increase the perceived unfairness of the tax system; since they are not reported in government budgetary documents the government is less accountable for them; and, they are less transparent than direct subsidies.

Some tax analysts argue that almost all tax expenditures should be removed from the income tax system, and that removing these subsidies is the only true pathway to tax reform. Those that are not serving any valid government objective should be simply repealed; those that are serving a valid government objective should be redesigned as direct subsidy programs. Those that remain in the Act should be placed in a separate part of the Act where they would not obscure the logic of the technical tax system and would not complicate its interpretation and administration. As you proceed through the basic course, ask yourself which tax expenditures you think should be repealed, which should be replaced with a direct subsidy program, and which should be redesigned.

IX. PRINCIPLES OF STATUTORY INTERPRETATION

Many law school courses still emphasize the study of common law cases; however, most lawyers in practice spend much more time working with legislative materials and the courts' treatment of these materials. Furthermore, in the modern welfare state, legislation and regulations are obviously far more significant instruments of public policy than common law judgments. A course in income tax law provides an excellent opportunity to continue to develop your skills in working with legislative materials. Like skills in policy analysis, and most other skills that are learned in the basic tax course, these skills are readily transferable to other areas of law.

Income tax law is entirely statutory in origin: unlike some other areas of legislative law it is not a codification of previously developed judicial principles. The common law did not impose an obligation on individuals to share in the financing of public goods or to redistribute some of their wealth to others. Most of the details of tax law are expressed in statutory language. Amendments to tax legislation are proposed and implemented annually. All of the institutions of government involve themselves in the scrutiny of tax law. It is administered by the largest bureaucracy in government, by far. That bureaucracy, the Canada Revenue Agency, publishes a bewildering variety of administrative documents ranging from interpretation bulletins to pamphlets and leaflets. For all these reasons, tax law is a perfect area in which to learn about statutes and the legislative and administrative processes.

At one level, learning about legislative materials involves simply learning to read and understand complex statutes. There is only one way to do this: read statutes. To assist in developing this skill, you should, of course, not only read statutes, but also read them critically and purposefully. When studying a provision in the Act always observe where it is located in the structure of the Act. There is a basic logic, even symmetry, to the structure of the Act, as there is to all statutes, and a familiarity with this structure greatly assists in understanding individual sections. When reading provisions in the Act you should note the various levels of paragraphing within each provision, their relationship to one another, and the functions they serve; the use of defined terms; the formatting of each section, particularly the word patterns for describing mathematical formulas; and, the common grammatical patterns used in statutes. A familiarity with these features of statutes will make reading them much easier.

At another level, learning about statutes involves learning about the problems of drafting. Which sections of the Act reflect bad drafting techniques and which present exemplary and imaginative solutions to drafting problems? In drafting, what are the trade-offs involved in using specific language as opposed to general legislative formulations? When should bright-line tests be used and what form should they take? What types of issues should the drafter delegate for resolution to the courts or to an administrative agency of government? Are there categories of problems that do not yield to statutory resolution and is it possible to generalize about them? Much of what lawyers do involves attempting to order affairs by verbal formulation. Studying tax law, and the techniques used by some of the country's best (certainly busiest) drafters, can be an effective way of learning this important skill of every well-educated lawyer.

Most importantly, and also most perplexing, learning about statutes means learning how to interpret them and apply them to an infinite variety of factual contexts. This involves learning to read statutes with a sensitivity to the variety of potential usages that every word has and with a sensitivity to the multiple contexts that can be drawn upon to assist in determining the appropriate usage of a word in a statute. It involves learning how to identify and work with the purposes that underlie statutory formulation and how to use tax and budgetary criteria to determine the reach of these purposes. A skillful advocate can draw upon an immensely rich source of materials in arguing that a particular usage should be attributed to a statutory formulation; to creatively mine these materials you should be thoroughly familiar with the various theories of statutory interpretation and the argumentative strategies that each would allow. Again, tax law provides an unrivalled opportunity to learn these skills. One reason for this is that in dealing with tax law cases, judges often seem much more self-conscious about the problems of statutory interpretation than they do in other areas of the law where interpretive issues arise. Judges of the Supreme Court of Canada feel the need to expound a theory of statutory interpretation in almost every tax case they decide. Every new Supreme Court of Canada tax case brings forth a predictable deluge of comments from tax lawyers. Consequently, the tax literature is rich with articles and opinions on the problems of statutory interpretation.

For every tax case that you study you should try to discern which approach the court took, why it took that approach, and whether there was a more appropriate approach. That is, in proceeding through the course you should not only develop an understanding of the approaches taken to statutory interpretation by Canadian courts and the range of arguments that they find legitimate and persuasive but also develop your own theory of what approach the courts should be taking. Some of the principles of statutory interpretation applied by the courts are considered in more detail in Part II of Chapter 10.

X. MAKING SENSE OF INCOME TAX LAWS

The central message of this introductory chapter is that a thorough understanding of the principles of technical tax policy and of tax expenditure analysis is needed, not only to critique tax law rules, but also to understand and interpret them. When drafters are drafting a tax provision they begin by considering the goals of the provision. They then try to formulate an approach that will achieve these goals in a way that is equitable, neutral and simple. That is, drafters begin with an overall understanding of both the problem they are dealing with and the evaluative criteria that need to be balanced. Only then do they attempt to write language that will implement these policies. In attempting to understand tax law it makes sense to try to place yourself in the position of the drafters and retrace their steps. Also, in interpreting the provisions, to make sense out of them and to be fair to the drafters, you should take the same approach that the drafters did, namely, determine the tax principles at stake and then look at the language. Since the drafters inevitably had this larger tax policy context in mind when they wrote the provisions, it is an essential part of the context in interpreting the provisions. Consequently, understanding tax policy analysis is as important to the person who wishes to understand and interpret tax law as it is to the policy-makers themselves.

In developing skills of policy analysis it is necessary to assume that the tax policy outcomes you are studying are the result of rational policy choices. But many provisions in the Act cannot be justified in these terms and there is little value in trying to rationalize the irrational. As in every other area of law, the social, economic and political determinants of tax law are diverse. Political scientists who study the public policy process have developed a number of theories or explanations to account for legislative outputs. Some stress the importance of prevailing ideas and ideologies; others argue that environmental factors, such as Canada's proximity to the United States, largely determine policy outputs; others argue that policy outputs are largely determined by the distribution of economic power in Canadian society (some are of the view that economic power is widely dispersed, others take that view that it is highly concentrated); others argue that policy outputs are determined, or at least are severely constrained, by the structure of the economy and by the reliance on private investment; public choice theorists argue that policy outputs can largely be explained by examining the self-interest of the proximate decision-makers, civil servants seeking to increase their own power and prestige, politicians hoping to get re-elected and interest group leaders attempting to appease their members. As you examine each aspect of tax law you will greatly enrich your understanding if you speculate on the influence of these different factors on the law's development.

Each of us has a world-view, or a set of assumptions about how the world works, that we resort to in attempting to organize and understand the confusing welter of information we receive about the political and social world. This is what the person meant who said "when you are a hammer everything looks like a nail."

Since tax law is so intimately connected with many of the most pressing issues of the day, our ideological view of the world tends to have a decisive effect on our understanding of it. However, like everything else in life, tax law can be reasonably and usefully viewed from a number of different perspectives. There is no ascertainable "truth" in tax law but only partial truths that are dependent upon one's perspective. Thus theoretical and methodological pluralism is the only way to understand the tax (or any other) world. By any account, a well-educated lawyer must be able to view issues from different points of view. Also, by attempting to view tax law from different perspectives, students will be better able to explore their own values and the values of others.

2

Source Concept of Income

I. LEGISLATIVE AND JUDICIAL DEVELOPMENT OF THE SOURCE CONCEPT OF INCOME

A. Legislative Framework

There is no definition of "income" in the *Income Tax Act*. Instead, Canada's income tax system has, from its earliest enactment in the *Income War Tax Act*, been based on the source concept of income. This means that the system's structure requires the various items of revenue received by a taxpayer to be analyzed and allocated to a source which is either expressly enumerated in the Act or recognized by the case law.

Paragraph 3(a) of the Act contains the legislative expression of the source concept of income:

> 3. The income of a taxpayer for a taxation year for the purposes of this Part is the taxpayer's income for the year determined by the following rules:
>
> (a) determine the total of all amounts each of which is the taxpayer's income for the year (other than a taxable capital gain from the disposition of a property) *from a source* inside or outside Canada, including, without restricting the generality of the foregoing, the taxpayer's income for the year from each office, employment, business and property, (...).
>
> (Emphasis added)

The "taxpayer's income for the year" as described in section 3 is the net income from each source, plus net taxable capital gains. The detailed rules requiring inclusions or permitting deductions for the enumerated sources are found in subdivision a (office or employment) and subdivision b (business or property). Under section 4, income from each source is calculated separately, and then the income (or loss) from each source is aggregated to compute a taxpayer's total income. A loss from one source may thus offset income from another source.

Subdivision d, "Other Sources of Income", in particular section 56, includes in income certain specific types of receipts such as pension benefits, employment insurance benefits, amounts received out of a registered retirement savings plan, retiring allowances, and scholarships and bursaries, which otherwise might not be considered attributable to a source. Subdivision g (section 81) excludes certain amounts from income.

B. Role of the Courts in Defining Sources of Income

Since the Act does not define income, the courts have played a critical role in determining what amounts are to be considered income from a source. In an early American case, *Eisner v. Macomber*, 252 U.S. 189 (1919), at pp. 206-7, the distinction between capital, or the source of income, and income itself was famously expressed by Mr. Justice Pitney as follows:

> The fundamental relation of "capital" to "income" has been much discussed by economists the former being likened to the tree or the land, the latter to the fruit or the crop; the former depicted as a reservoir supplied from springs, the latter as the outlet stream, to be measured by its flow during a period of time.

Income is thus differentiated from the source of the income. A capital asset which produces income is considered to be a source of income; the recurring income which flows from exploitation of the asset is income from a source. This approach results in the fundamental distinction, still operative in Canadian income tax law, between income and capital gains.

A capital gain or loss is realized on the sale (or other disposition) of a capital asset. That is, it results from the disposition of the source itself. Capital gains became partially taxable with the major tax reform of 1972. Paragraph 3(b) includes a taxpayer's net taxable capital gains in determining a taxpayer's income for the year. Capital gains and losses are covered in detail in Chapter 7.

The application of the source concept of income means that an amount received by a taxpayer that has no recognized source is not subject to tax. A loss that is not from a recognized source is correspondingly not deductible.

The following case describes the historical origins of the source concept of income and various types of receipts that are not considered to be income from a source.

BELLINGHAM v. THE QUEEN
[1996] 1 C.T.C. 187, 96 D.T.C. 6075 (F.C.A.)

[Lands belonging to several persons, including the taxpayer, were expropriated by the Town of Grand Centre (the "Town"). The compensation was ultimately determined by the Land Compensation Board at almost six times the Town's offer, so that the Board had no difficulty finding fault on the Town's part. Despite the Board's

award, litigation ensued, with the landowners eventually accepting an offer substantially less than the Board's award. The taxpayer's share of the settlement was agreed by the parties to have three components: $377,015 as compensation for the value of the land, $181,319 as ordinary interest, and $114,272 as "additional interest" under the Alberta Expropriation Act subsections 66(4) and (5). The land having been acquired by the taxpayer as a business venture, the compensation of $377,015 was included in the taxpayer's income from a business. The ordinary interest was taxable pursuant to paragraph 12(1)(c) of the Act. The additional interest was held by the Federal Court-Trial Division to be income from a business under subsection 9(1) of the Act. The taxpayer appealed the rulings on the character of the compensatory payment and the additional interest.]

Robertson J.A. (Stone and Décary, JJ.A. concurring):

This is an appeal from a decision of the Trial Division involving the taxation of monies received by the appellant (the "taxpayer") following an expropriation of her lands. Two issues arise for our consideration. One focuses on whether a specific award of "additional interest", made under subsection 66(4) of the *Expropriation Act*, R.S.A. 1980, c. E-16, constitutes "income". The other issue involves the perennial question of whether "proceeds of disposition" were received on account of income or capital.

In regard to the income/ capital issue, I am in agreement with the learned Trial Judge who concluded that the proceeds of disposition were received on account of income. With great respect, however, I cannot subscribe to his conclusion that an award of additional interest is income within the meaning of the relevant provisions of the *Income Tax Act*, S.C. 1970-71-72, c. 63 as amended (the "Act"). Such an award is imposed for purposes of censuring and discouraging unacceptable conduct on the part of an expropriating authority. It has no compensatory element and, in my view, it is tantamount to a punitive damage award and, therefore, falls outside the charging provisions of the Act. Specifically, additional interest is not "income from a business" under subsection 9(1), nor is it "income from a source" as contemplated by paragraph 3(a) of the Act. Succinctly stated, it is my opinion that punitive damage awards fall within the tax-exempt category of "windfall gains". My reasoning begins with a recitation of relevant facts.

...

The notion of what receipts constitute income for purposes of taxation is central to the workings of the Act. Standing alone, the term income is susceptible to widely diverging interpretations. Narrowly construed, income may be defined to include only those amounts received by taxpayers on a recurring basis. Broadly construed, income may be defined so as to capture all accretions to wealth. Canadian taxpayers are more likely to embrace the former definition. The latter approach reflects the economist's concern for achieving horizontal and vertical equity in a taxation system. Such a concern translates into a broad understanding of what receipt items should be included in income. This perspective is reflected in the Report of the Carter Commission. Working from the Haig-Simons definition of income, that Commission recommended a modified, but comprehensive tax base. Had its recommendations become law we would have witnessed, for example, the taxation of gifts and inheritances. Instead, the concept of income under the Act remains undefined, except to the extent that income must be from a source.

There can be no doubt that the source doctrine serves to narrow the reach of the charging provisions of the Act so as to permit certain receipts to escape taxation, including gifts and inheritances. The more difficult question relates to the precise scope of the doctrine and the legal criteria to be applied when assessing whether a particular receipt is taxable. The statutory source of the doctrine itself is, of course, section 3 of the Act which provides the basic framework for determining a taxpayer's income for a taxation year for purposes of Part I of the Act. It is paragraph 3(a) which introduces the concept of income from a source: [text of section 3 omitted].

The historical origins of the source doctrine are well known and worth highlighting when contrasted with the manner in which it has been recast in the above paragraph [paragraph 3(a)]. The adoption of the source concept of income can be traced to England's taxing statutes of the 19th century, which required taxpayers to file separate returns for each source of income. The legislated objective was to ensure that no one official knew a person's total income. More importantly, the source doctrine distinguished between the receipt of income from a source and the disposition of the source itself. In an agrarian society, land is considered to be the source of income. Profits are derived from the annual harvest and represent income. A disposition of the land itself, that is to say the capital, is considered to be of a different character and, hence, the distinction between income and capital is critical. The distinction is as important today as it was in centuries past.

The English taxation system retains the source concept of income, now referred to as the schedule system. Unless a receipt comes within one of six named schedules it is simply not taxable. Thus gifts, inheritances and windfalls, not being from a specified source, are treated as non-taxable receipts. The distinction drawn between income and capital is preserved and, thus, capital gains are exempt from income taxation.

The Canadian approach is similar to its English counterpart, but only to the extent that the definition of income is circumscribed by the source doctrine. The critical distinction between the two approaches lies in the fact that paragraph 3(a) refers initially to income from any source and then goes on to identify the traditional sources: income from each office, employment, business and property. Paragraph 3(a) makes it clear that the named sources are not exhaustive and, thus, income can arise from other unidentified sources. In summary, Parliament has chosen to define income by reference to a restrictive doctrine while recasting it in such a manner as to achieve broader ends. Commentators, however, are agreed that paragraph 3(a) continues to receive a narrow construction: see ... V. Krishna, *The Fundamentals of Canadian Income Tax,* 4th ed., (Toronto: Carswell 1993) at 129-130, and J.A. Rendall, "Defining the Tax Base", in B.G. Hansen, V. Krishna and J.A. Rendall, eds., *Canadian Taxation* (Toronto: Richard De Boo, 1981) at 59.

The rule of strict construction might explain the reluctance of the courts to recognize new sources of income. Unfortunately, not even the application of the contextual and teleological approaches to statutory construction sheds light on the scope of the source doctrine. Turning to two related provisions of the Act we find that Parliament has chosen to include and exclude items from income without regard to whether their tax treatment offends the source doctrine. Section 12 of the Act prescribes a multitude of inclusions to income from a business or property. The list of exclusionary items found in section 81 is even longer. Arguably, several of the items would be treated differently under the source doctrine were it not for these two sections of the Act. I recognize that it is necessary for Parliament to include and exclude items from income as a means of pursuing various social and economic objectives. The result, however, is that it is futile to pursue the contextual or teleological approach to the interpretation of paragraph 3(a). The parameters of the source doctrine cannot be distilled from provisions intended to contradict the very precepts underlying the doctrine itself.

Against this background, we are left to pursue the judicial understanding of what items fall outside the grasp of paragraph 3(a). I begin with the recognized exclusionary categories: gambling gains, gifts and inheritances, and the residual category of windfall gains. I shall deal briefly with the first two categories as they provide the underlying framework for the third.

Gambling gains are non-taxable provided the taxpayer is not in the business of gambling: see *Graham v. Green (Inspector of Taxes)*, [1925] 2 K.B. 37; *M.N.R. v. Walker*, [1951] C.T.C. 334, 52 DTC 1001 (Ex. Ct.), *M.N.R. v. Morden*, [1961] C.T.C. 484, 61 DTC 1266 (Ex. Ct.). The classical reason for excluding such receipts from income is that a "bet" is based on an "irrational agreement". A more compelling argument is that a gambling gain does not flow from a productive source. That is, a source that is capable of producing income: see F.G. La Brie, *The Principles of Canadian Income Taxation,* (Toronto: CCH Canadian Ltd., 1965) at 25.

There is no need to cite authorities for the proposition that gifts and inheritances are immune from taxation. It is well accepted that these items represent non-recurring amounts and the transfer of old wealth. Underlying the source doctrine is the understanding that income involves the creation of new wealth. Gifts do not flow from a productive source of income. Where a gift emanates from what otherwise is regarded as a productive source, e.g., the taxpayer's employment, then the issue is one of concealed wages and employee benefits (see section 6 of the Act). To qualify as a gift, there must be a voluntary and gratuitous transfer of property. There must be an absence of valuable consideration. Hence, a payment that takes the form of a *quid pro quo* will not be characterized as a gift.

The precise scope of the residual category — windfall gains — has proven problematic. At best, it can be said that a payment which is unexpected or unplanned and not of a recurring nature, is more likely than not to be characterized as a windfall gain. But like all generalizations, this observation must be scrutinized meticulously. I turn now to the jurisprudence which reasonably bears on the issue at hand.

As a starting point, it might be felt that the decision of the Tax Appeal Board in *Cartwright and Sons Ltd. v. M.N.R.*, 61 D.T.C. 499 (T.A.B.) offers the definitive answer. In that case it was held that a punitive damage award was not taxable on the basis that the sum paid to the taxpayer "had no income feature" (at 501). The legal reasoning of the Board goes no further. A more extensive analysis of paragraph 3(a) was pursued in *The Queen v. Cranswick*, *supra* [[1982] C.T.C. 69, 82 D.T.C. 6073 (F.C.A.), leave to appeal refused (1982), 42 N.R. 355 (S.C.C.)]. In that case this Court had to determine whether an unsolicited payment to a minority shareholder of a Canadian company constituted income. The majority shareholder was the American parent of the Canadian company. The payment was made to thwart possible litigation arising from the sale of part of the Canadian company's assets below book value. The Court concluded that the payment in question was not taxable because it "was of an unusual and unexpected kind that one could not set out to earn as income from shares" (at 820). The Court also referred to several indicia which could be applied when assessing whether a receipt constitutes income from a source. The Court was careful, however, to stipulate that while each of the following may be relevant, none is conclusive in determining whether a payment represents a windfall gain (at 818-19):

(a) [The taxpayer] had no enforceable claim to the payment;

(b) There was no organized effort on the part of [the taxpayer] to receive payment;

(c) The payment was not sought after or solicited by [the taxpayer] in any manner;

(d) The payment was not expected by [the taxpayer], either specifically or customarily;

(e) The payment had no foreseeable element of recurrence;

(f) The payor was not a customary source of income to [the taxpayer];

(g) The payment was not in consideration for or in recognition of property, services or anything else provided or to be provided by [the taxpayer]; it was not earned by [the taxpayer], either as a result of any activity or pursuit of gain carried on by [the taxpayer] or otherwise.

There is one aspect of *Cranswick* which does not appear to have been pursued on appeal. It is open to question whether the taxpayer in that case received the payment in return for relinquishing the right to seek compensation for losses suffered as a result of the disadvantageous sale. It would appear that that issue had to be abandoned since the agreed statement of facts stipulated that the payment in question was not made by reason of an enforceable claim by the minority shareholders against the Canadian company. That concession on the part of the Minister cannot be ignored for as the law presently stands monies paid in exchange for the discharge of even a questionable legal right may constitute income in the hands of the taxpayer. This is one of the teachings of *Mohawk Oil Co. v. Canada (C.A.), supra* [[1992] 1 C.T.C. 195 (app. for leave to SCC dismissed)].

Finally there are two decisions of the Supreme Court which must be acknowledged. The first is *Curran v. MNR* (1959), [1959] S.C.R. 850. In that case the taxpayer received $250,000 from a third party as an inducement to leave his present employment. The agreement between the taxpayer and the third party stipulated that the payment was "in consideration of the loss of pension rights, chances for advancement, and opportunities for re-employment ..." (at 853). A majority of the Supreme Court recognized that the source of the payment was the taxpayer's employment with the third party. The payment of $250,000 received by the taxpayer was held to be income within the meaning of what is now paragraph 3(a) of the Act.

The other decision of the Supreme Court which must be acknowledged is *Canada v. Fries* [1990] 2 S.C.R. 1322. In that case the Supreme Court held that strike pay does not constitute income from a source under paragraph 3(a). The taxpayer had gone on strike and received weekly strike pay, from his union, equal to his normal net take-home pay. The union's strike fund was accumulated from the tax deductible dues paid by its members. At the time the union members voted to go on strike they were aware of a union recommendation that they be reimbursed for their loss of salary and benefits in return for their strike support. In reversing the judgment of the Federal Court of Appeal, the Supreme Court restored the decision of the Tax Review Board. The analysis offered by the Supreme Court is limited to the conclusion that "the benefit of the doubt must go to the taxpayer" (at 1323) see [1989] 3 F.C. 362 (C.A.); aff'g [1985] 2 F.C. 378 (T.D.); rev'g [1983] C.T.C. 2124, 83 DTC 117 (T.R.B.).

I do not find it necessary to rely on the residual presumption to support the conclusion that a punitive damage award constitutes a windfall gain. Nor am I prepared to base my decision on the fact that an award of additional interest is, arguably, non-recurring, unexpected or an unusual form of income. As a general proposition, I accept that monies received by a taxpayer from an expropriating authority constitute income from a productive source. As well, I accept that the taxpayer has an enforceable right to additional interest once the Board concludes that there was fault on the part of the expropriating authority. Furthermore, it matters not whether the taxpayer actively sought payment of additional interest. The critical factor is that the punitive damage award does not flow from either the performance or breach of a market transaction. Of course, no distinction should be drawn between voluntary and involuntary market exchanges.

In the case at hand, the source of the additional interest award is not the expropriating authority. That body is merely the payor. The true source of the award is the *Expropriation Act* which dictates as a matter of public policy that expropriating authorities are obligated to pay a penal sum in circumstances where their behaviour falls below a prescribed standard. An award of additional interest under subsection 66(4) of the *Expropriation Act* is unrelated to the issue of fair compensation for expropriated lands. That concern is dealt with fully under section 42 and subsection 66(2). In certain respects an award of additional interest possesses the attributes of a gift. The taxpayer is the beneficiary, not of the expropriating authority's largesse, but of the legislature's desire to ensure that minimum standards of commercial behaviour are observed. The taxpayer's gain is the expropriating authority's loss. The payment in question does not flow from either an express or implied agreement between the parties. There is no element of bargain or exchange. There is no consideration. There is no *quid pro quo*, on the part of the taxpayer. The payment is simply a windfall, and, therefore, not income within paragraph 3(a) of the Act.

In reaching the above conclusion, I have not lost sight of the fact that the payment of additional interest is as much a part of the statutory scheme as is the payment of compensation for expropriated lands. But for the expropriation, the possibility of obtaining additional interest would not have materialized and, therefore, it is arguable that we should not isolate specific awards which are woven into the compensatory fabric of legislation. As much as that line of reasoning may be attractive to some, I do not find it persuasive.

In my view, you cannot treat a non-compensatory receipt in the same manner as a compensatory one simply because both arise from the same transaction. As the law presently stands we must look to the nature and purpose of a particular payment or award when assessing how it will be dealt with for tax purposes. This is certainly true with respect to the tax treatment of awards or settlements stemming from contractual or tortious claims. Such receipts are not treated automatically as a unitary sum. In regard to personal injury claims, the tax treatment accorded to general and special damages by the Minister is not the same as that attributable to restitution for the loss of income from employment: see Interpretation Bulletin IT-365R2 and IT-183. In cases involving breach of contract, allocations may be made according to the type of loss for which compensation has been paid: see *Mohawk Oil Co. v. Canada* [92 DTC 6135; [1992] 1 CTC 95 (F.C.A.)], *supra.* The same approach is applicable to a receipt item which is characterized as a punitive damage award.

Appeal allowed in part.

As noted in *Bellingham*, Canadian courts have not interpreted the expansive language of paragraph 3(a) to add unenumerated sources of income to the four sources that are specifically enumerated. However, amounts that are received by a taxpayer in the place of income from a source may be included in income as if such amounts were income from that source. This is the "surrogatum principle", which is applied to amounts received as civil damages, or amounts paid in settlement of a claim for breach of contract or tort, to determine if the amount received is a "surrogate" for income from a source. The principle was stated by Diplock L.J. in *London and Thames Haven Oil Wharves Ltd. v. Attwooll*, [1967] 2 A11 E.R. 124 (C.A.) at p. 134-135:

> ... The question whether a sum of money received by a trader ought to be taken into account in computing the profits or gain arising in any year from his trade is one which ought to be susceptible of solution by applying rational criteria; and so, I think, it is. I see nothing in experience as embalmed in the authorities to convince me that this question of law, even though it is fiscal law, cannot be solved by logic, and that, with some temerity, is what I propose to try to do.
>
> I start by formulating what I believe to be the relevant rule. Where, pursuant to a legal right, a trader receives from another person compensation for the trader's failure to receive a sum of money which, if it had been received, would have been credited to the amount of profits (if any) arising in any year from the trade carried on by him at the time when the compensation is so received, the compensation is to be treated for income tax purposes in the same way as that sum of money would have been treated if it had been received instead of the compensation. The rule is applicable whatever the source of the legal right of the trader to recover the compensation. It may arise from a primary obligation under a contract, such as a contract of insurance; from a secondary obligation arising out of non-performance of a contract, such as a right to damages, either liquidated, as under the demurrage clause in a charterparty, or unliquidated; from an obligation to pay damages for tort, as in the present case: from a statutory obligation; or in any other way in which legal obligations arise.

In the following case, the surrogatum principle was not applied to a sum received as compensation for anticipatory breach of an employment contract, although the general validity of the principle was not questioned.

SCHWARTZ v. THE QUEEN
[1996] 1 C.T.C. 303, 96 D.T.C. 6103 (S.C.C.)

[*The taxpayer had agreed to take a senior position with a new employer, Dynacare, Inc., and a written employment contract was executed. However, before the taxpayer's employment commenced, Dynacare, Inc. advised him that his services would not be required. Following negotiations, the taxpayer accepted a lump sum of $360,000 in settlement of his claim for breach of contract, plus $40,000 on account of legal costs. The Minister included the settlement amount in the taxpayer's income as a retiring allowance under subparagraph 56(1)(a)(ii). At trial, the Minister argued that the amount was either a retiring allowance, an employment benefit, or income from a source under section 3 of the Act, the source being the employment contract, and the Tax Court Judge rejected all three arguments. On appeal, the Federal Court of Appeal overturned certain findings of fact made by the Tax Court Judge and found that the sum of $342,000 had been allocated by the parties to the settlement as $75,000 for loss of salary, and $267,000 for lost stock options. On appeal to the Supreme Court of Canada, the Minister did not argue that the settlement payment was a substitute for employment income or benefits, despite the success of this argument at the Federal Court of Appeal. The Minister instead argued that most of the settlement was taxable as income from an unenumerated source under paragraph 3(a). The Supreme Court of Canada restored the Tax Court Judge's finding of fact that there had been no allocation of the settlement; rather the amount paid to the taxpayer by Dynacare was primarily to compensate the taxpayer for embarrassment, anxiety and inconvenience (which is, presumably, non-taxable).*]

La Forest J. (L'Heureux-Dubé, Gonthier and McLachlin JJ. concurring):

Before this Court, the Crown argued that the damages received by the appellant were taxable in two ways. Its main contention was that the money received by Mr. Schwartz relating to lost salary and stock options was taxable as income from an unenumerated source under the general provision of section 3(a) of the Act — such unenumerated source being the employment contract terminated by Dynacare. The Crown also put forward an alternative argument, namely that the whole of the damages ($360,000) received by Mr. Schwartz were taxable under s. 56(1)(a)(ii) of the Act as a retiring allowance.

For the reasons that follow, I am of the opinion that the appeal should be allowed. To deal with the substance of the Minister's main argument, it is necessary to address the correctness of the Federal Court of Appeal's decision to overturn Rip, JTCC's finding of fact with respect to the allocation made by Dynacare and Mr. Schwartz of the compensation agreed upon. I conclude that the Federal Court of Appeal was wrong in doing so, a conclusion that is sufficient, technically to dispose of the Crown's main argument in favour of the appellant. However, the substance of the Minister's main argument raises important questions that merit attention by this Court and it having been fully argued by the parties, I think it appropriate to deal with it on its merits. Regarding this issue, I have come to the conclusion that section 3(a) of the Act does contemplate taxability of income arising from sources other than those specifically provided for in section 3(a) and in subdivision d of Division B of Part I of the Act. However, in the case at bar, an analysis of the way Parliament handled the taxability of payments such as the one received by Mr. Schwartz demonstrates that it is to the rules relating to retiring allowances that one should turn in assessing taxability.

...

As I noted at the outset, the Minister argued that the amount of compensation relating to lost salary and stock options ($342,000) constitutes income from a source taxable under the general provision of s. 3(a) of the Act, such source being the contract of employment. I pause here to mention that what the Crown argued before us differs somewhat from the approach adopted by the Federal Court of Appeal. Mahoney, J.A. found that $342,000 of the $360,000 was income from employment since it had been received by Mr. Schwartz to compensate for loss of moneys that, if duly received, would have constituted income from employment taxable under s. 5(1). Before us, the Crown did not argue that this amount constitutes income from employment. It first submitted that the application of the *surrogatum* principle, developed in the *London & Thames* case, *supra*, leads to the conclusion that $342,000 of the $360,000 received by Mr. Schwartz must be characterized as income from a source, since it compensates Mr. Schwartz for loss of moneys that, if received, would have constituted income from a source. The Minister then identifies that source as being the employment contract, a source other than the five enumerated in s. 3(a) and the "other sources" provided for in subdivision d of Division B of Part I of the Act. The difference lies in the Minister's argument relating to the specific *source* of the damages received by the appellant.

...

[La Forest J. then addressed the issue of when it is permissible for an appellate court to overturn a finding of fact made by the trial judge, and the circumstances where a second appellate court should interfere with the ruling of the first appellate court.]

As mentioned earlier, the conclusion that the Federal Court of Appeal was wrong in interfering with the trial judge's finding of fact respecting apportionment disposes of the Minister's main argument. This is so because in order to find that some of the amount received by Mr. Schwartz was taxable under s. 3(a) as income from the employment contract, one must be able to identify what portion of the $360,000 was paid to Mr. Schwartz in compensation for amounts that he would have been entitled to receive under the contract of employment.

Since the Federal Court of Appeal erred in its decision relating to the trial judge's assessment of the evidence, the factual situation is that there is evidence that the amounts received by Mr. Schwartz were, in part, received to compensate for the loss of amounts to which he would have been entitled under the employment contract entered into with Dynacare and, in part, to compensate for embarrassment, anxiety and inconvenience suffered by the appellant, and that there is no evidence tending to establish what portion of the $360,000 was allocated to which head. Thus, absent a proper determination of that factual situation, the damages received by Mr. Schwartz cannot, in whole or in part, be found to be taxable under s. 3(a) of the Act as income from the employment contract.

As I mentioned at the beginning of my analysis, however, I propose to deal with the substance of the Minister's main contention since it raises important issues that merit attention and have been fully argued by the parties. I, therefore, turn to these submissions.

...

The Crown relies on the principle developed by Diplock, L.J. in *London & Thames, supra,* and argues that the portion of damages received by Mr. Schwartz related to lost salary and stock options constitutes income from a source. In *London & Thames,* Diplock, L.J. had this to say, at p. 134:

> Where, pursuant to a legal right, a trader receives from another person compensation for the trader's failure to receive a sum of money which, if it had been received, would have been credited to the amount of profits (if any) arising in any year from the trade carried on by him at the time when the compensation is so received, the compensation is to be treated for income tax purposes in the same way as that sum of money would have been treated if it had been received instead of the compensation.

The Minister, quite correctly, noted that this principle was adopted and applied by the Federal Court of Appeal in *Manley, supra,* [85 DTC 5150; [1985] 1 CTC 186 (FCA)]. ...

In the present case, the Federal Court of Appeal applied this principle and found that, since part of the damages received by the appellant replaced lost salary and stock options which, if they had been paid to Mr. Schwartz, would have constituted income from employment taxable under s. 5(1), such damages had to be treated in the same manner for tax purposes, i.e., as income from office or employment taxable under s. 5(1) of the Act.

The solution arrived at by the Federal Court of Appeal is in contradiction with the findings in the *Atkins* case, supra, [[1976] C.T.C. 497, 76 D.T.C. 6258 (F.C.A.)] where the same court held that such damages [in lieu of damages for wrongful dismissal] could not be characterized as income from office or employment under s. 5(1). ...

However, the correctness of *Atkins* is not at issue before us since the Minister, as I have explained, is not arguing that the amounts are taxable as income from employment, but submits, rather, that they are income from an unenumerated source taxable under the general provision of s. 3(a) of the Act.

...

Parliament has stated very clearly in that section that the five sources identified in s. 3(a) do not constitute an exhaustive enumeration. This is evident from the emphasized words in the paragraph, which I here reproduce:

> 3. ...
>
> (a) determine the aggregate of amounts each of which is the taxpayer's income for the year (other than a taxable capital gain from the disposition of a property from a source inside or outside Canada, *including, without restricting the generality of the foregoing,* his income for the year from each office, employment, business and property;
>
> [Emphasis added.]

Mr. Schwartz argues that the sources of income other than those contemplated in s. 3(a) are the "other sources" referred to in subdivision d of Division B of Part I of the Act and relies on this statement by E.C. Harris, *Canadian Income Taxation* (4th ed. 1986), at p. 99:

> While the Act recognizes that there may be other sources of income than [those specifically provided for in s. 3(a)], the case law under the former Act suggests that the only other sources of income and loss that are likely to be recognized are those that are specifically recognized in the Act.

However, this conclusion disregards the fact that Parliament, in the introductory part of s.56(1) of the Act, made clear that the enumeration that followed was not to be interpreted as restricting the generality of s. 3. (...)

Mr. Schwartz also submitted that, for policy reasons, an interpretation to the contrary would defeat the purpose and fundamental structure of the Act. However, as noted by Krishna, similarly valid policy concerns can be invoked to support an interpretation to the contrary. In his textbook *The Fundamentals of Canadian Income Tax, supra,* at pp. 129-30, he writes:

> The better view is that the named sources (office, employment, business, and property) are not exhaustive and income can arise from any other unnamed source. Hence, income from any source inside or outside Canada should be taxable under paragraph 3(a) of the Act. *This is justifiable both on the basis of the language of the statute and on policy grounds. To the extent that the*

> *income tax is based on the ability to pay, all accretions to wealth of an income nature are a measure of that ability and should be taxable regardless of source.*
>
> [Emphasis added.]

In any event, policy concerns such as those raised by the appellant should not and cannot be relied on in disregard of Parliament's clearly expressed intention: *interpretatio cessat in claris.* In s. 3(a), when Parliament used the words "without restricting the generality of the foregoing", great care was taken to emphasize that the first step in calculating a taxpayer's "income for the year" was to determine the total of all amounts constituting income inside or outside Canada and that the enumeration that followed merely identified examples of such sources. The phrasing adopted by Parliament, in s. 3(a) and in the introductory part of s. 56(1) is probably the strongest that could have been used to express the idea that income from *all* sources, enumerated or not, expressly provided for in subdivision d or not, was taxable under the Act.

This interpretation is also consistent with the approach adopted by this Court in the few other cases where this question was at issue. In *Curran v. Minister of National Revenue* 59 DTC 1247; [1959] SCR 850, the taxpayer had received a $250,000 payment by a third party in return for which he was to resign from his employment and start working for another company. The payment did not constitute income from employment, since it had not been paid by the taxpayer's employer, but was assessed as constituting "income from a source" under the general provision of s. 3 of the Act. This assessment was upheld by the Exchequer Court of Canada (57 DTC 1270). The relevant provisions found in s. 3 of the Act were, at that time, similar to those found in s. 3(a) in today's version of the Act: ...

This decision [of the Exchequer Court in *Curran*] was later confirmed by this Court. More recently, in *Canada v. Fries* [89 DTC 5240], [1989] 3 F.C. 363, the Federal Court of Appeal expressly recognized that income from unenumerated sources was taxable under the general provision of s. 3(a) of the Act. In that case, the taxpayer was contesting the Minister's assessment, including in his yearly income strike pay he had received from his union. The court dismissed the taxpayer's claim and found that the amounts were taxable as constituting income from a source within the purview of s 3(a) of the Act. Our Court, however, while implicitly holding that income from unenumerated sources was in fact taxable under the general provision of s. 3(a) of the Act, reversed this decision on the basis that the payments were not in the nature of "income ... from a source" within the meaning of s. 3(a); see *Canada v. Fries,* [1990] 2 S.C.R. 1322.

In the case at bar, I do not think the Minister's argument should be accepted. In order to determine if a specific amount is taxable under the general provision of s. 3(a) of the Act, various considerations should be taken into account. Without providing a list of such considerations or attempting to suggest an approach to taxation under the general provision of s. 3(a) in an exhaustive way, I note that one must obviously go back to the concept of income and consider the whole scheme of the Act in order to properly analyze the issue in a given case. In the present case, accepting the argument made by the Crown would amount to giving precedence to a general provision over the detailed provisions enacted by Parliament to deal with payments such as that received by Mr. Schwartz pursuant to the settlement.

As indicated earlier, Parliament adopted a specific solution to a specific problem that resulted from a number of rulings by the courts respecting the taxability of payments similar to the one received by the appellant. Under these rulings, damages paid with respect to wrongful dismissal were not taxable as income from office or employment under s. 5(1); nor were they taxable as constituting retiring allowances. The Crown had at that point many options. The Minister could have argued that such damages were taxable as income from a source under the general provision in s. 3(a) of the Act. It could also have sought an amendment to the Act making such payments expressly taxable as income from office or employment. But neither of these courses was taken. Instead, the Act was amended twice so that such amounts could be taxable under s. 56 as income from "another" source. First, it was provided that termination payments were taxable. Then, the Act was amended to make such a payment taxable as constituting a retiring allowance. It is thus pursuant to these provisions that taxability should be assessed. To do otherwise would defeat Parliament's intention by approving an analytical approach inconsistent with basic principles of interpretation.

This Court has always refused to interpret the Act in such a manner. For example, in *The Queen v. Savage* [83 DTC 5409], [1983] 2 S.C.R. 428, the taxpayer received $300 from her employer as a prize for achievement. Section 56(1)(n) of the Act provided that such gifts, when worth over $500, constituted taxable income. The prize was not, therefore, caught by this provision. The Minister, however, argued that the amount also fell within the purview of s. 6(1)(a) of the Act as a general benefit, and as such was taxable as income from an office or employment. Dickson, J., as he then was, rejected this argument. At page 446, he stated:

> If a prize under $500 would still be taxable under ss. 5 and 6, it would have to follow on the Crown's argument that a prize under $500 would equally be taxable under s. 3. That cannot be right. That would mean that a prize over $500 would be taxable under s. 56(1)(n) and a prize up to $500 would be taxable under s. 3. The $500 exclusion in s. 56(1)(n) would never have any effect. It seems clear that the first $500 of income received during the year falling within the terms of s. 56(1)(n) is exempt from tax. Any amount in excess of $500 falls under s. 56(1)(n) and is taxable accordingly. If that is not the effect, what purpose is served by the subsection?

The situation here is analogous. To find that the damages received by Mr. Schwartz are taxable under the general provision of s. 3(a) of the Act would disregard the fact that Parliament has chosen to deal with the taxability of such payments in the provisions of the Act relating to retiring allowances. It is thus to those provisions that I will turn in assessing taxability.

...

The essence of the Minister's argument is that "employment" as understood in s. 248(1) of the Act commences the moment the contract of employment is entered into by the parties, regardless of whether or not the employee has the obligation to provide services from that point. Therefore Mr. Schwartz, by losing the benefit of the contract of employment entered into with Dynacare, lost "employment", and the damages received fall within the purview of s. 56(1)(a)(ii) of the Act [the section defining "retiring allowance"]. I do not think the Minister's position is correct in law, in light of the definitions given by Parliament to the word "employment" and of the ordinary meaning of the words chosen by Parliament to define this term. The Minister's position is also inconsistent with the way Parliament has used the term "employment" in at least one other provision of the Act, while also being untenable when one considers the context in which the 1983 amendment was made.

The key element in the words chosen by Parliament to deal with this situation is the definition of "employment" which is the "position of an individual *in the service* of some other person". The statutory requirement that one must be "in the service" of another person to be characterized as an "employee" excludes, in my opinion, any notion of prospective employment when the phrase is given its ordinary meaning. An employee is "in the service" of his or her employer from the moment he or she becomes under obligation to provide services under the terms of the contract. At the basis of every situation of employment is a contract of employment; however, employment does not necessarily begin from the moment the contract is entered into. Before having an obligation to provide services, one cannot be considered to be "in the service" of his or her employer or, more accurately, his or her future employer. Consequently, there cannot be any *loss* of a position that has yet to be held, under the definition of "retiring allowance" found in s. 248(1). I cannot see how, in the present case, Mr. Schwartz could be "in the service" of Dynacare from the moment the contract of employment was entered into in the spring of 1988 and how he could have "lost" employment when the contract was unilaterally cancelled by Dynacare. (...) Mr. Schwartz was not in any way — and had never been — obliged to provide any services to Dynacare at that moment; he was not "in the service" of Dynacare.

...

The $360,000 received by Mr. Schwartz cannot, therefore, be considered a retiring allowance. ... For all these reasons, I would allow the appeal and restore the decision of the Tax Court of Canada with costs throughout.

[In a minority judgment, Major, J. (Sopinka and Iacobucci, JJ. concurring) agreed with the conclusion reached by La Forest, J. that a settlement for loss of intended employment is not subject to tax under subparagraph 56(1)(a)(ii) and that there was no factual foundation on which to argue that the settlement could be taxed as income from the employment contract. However, Major, J. took the position that it was not necessary to discuss the issue of whether the settlement could be taxed as income from an unenumerated source. He disagreed with the obiter dicta of La Forest, J. that indicated that income from unenumerated sources are as a general matter taxable under subsection 3(a). After citing the passage from Krishna at p. 130, supra, that "all accretions to wealth of an income nature are a measure of [the] ability [to pay] and should be taxable regardless of source", Major, J. stated:]

However, a literal adoption of this position would arguably constitute a dramatic departure from established tax jurisprudence. It has long been recognized that not all "accretions to wealth" are included as income. Inheritances and gifts are "accretions to wealth" but are nevertheless not taxed because they are not income from employment, property or business. Profits from hobbies are accretions to wealth, but they, too, are not taxed for the same reason.

...

If this Court intends to conclude that s. 3(a) should be applied literally, and permit taxation on income from any source whatsoever, it should only do so in circumstances which warrant such a decision because such a result is of fundamental importance. Moreover, as I have mentioned, so deciding can be viewed as a marked departure from previous tax jurisprudence. In 1966, the Carter Commission recommended the extension of taxation to all sources of income and all accretions to purchasing power, but its recommendations were not implemented by Parliament and it is hardly the role of the judiciary to do so.

Appeal allowed.

In *Tsiaprailis v. The Queen*, [2005] 2 C.T.C. 1, 2005 D.T.C. 5119, 2005 D.T.C. 5126 (S.C.C.), the taxpayer disputed the inclusion in her income of a portion of a lump sum paid to her to settle a law suit in which she claimed entitlement to continued benefits, in the form of monthly payments, under a group disability insurance policy provided by her former employer. The agreed statement of facts provided as follows:

> In October 1996, the Appellant entered into a settlement agreement with [the insurer] and received a lump sum payment of $105,000 in lieu of continued benefits pursuant to the terms of settlement. The sum of $105,000 essentially meant [the insurer] was paying:
>
> (i) the Appellant's entitlement to past benefits, plus interest;

(ii) 75% of the present value of the Appellant's entitlement to future benefits under the policy;

(iii) 6,455 for costs, GST and disbursements.

The majority decision of the Supreme Court (written by Madame Justice Charron, Bastarache, Binnie and Deschamps concurring) dismissed the appeal, ruling that the allocation of the settlement amount was clear from the letters exchanged between the parties, and was confirmed in the agreed statement of facts. The majority decision clearly affirmed the surrogatum principle and set out the following two tests for applying the principle:

(1) What was the payment intended to replace? And, provided the answer to this question is sufficiently clear:

(2) Would the replaced amount have been taxable in the recipient's hands?

The narrow issue was whether the portion of the settlement allocable to the past benefits was a replacement for an amount payable to the taxpayer on a periodic basis pursuant to a disability insurance plan under subparagraph 6(1)(f)(ii) of the Act. The majority found that the evidence was "clear and cogent" that a portion of the lump sum was intended to replace past monthly disability payments, and such payments would have been taxable. In the majority's view, to draw a distinction between an amount paid to settle a claim for past benefits under the insurance contract and a payment made pursuant to the insurance contract "is to render the surrogatum principle meaningless".

The taxpayer's position, (accepted by the dissenting opinion of Madame Justice Abella, concurred in by Major and LeBel JJ.), was that the amount was not paid "pursuant to a disability insurance plan", as required by subparagraph 6(1)(f)(ii), but was paid by the defendant insurer pursuant to a settlement agreement. This meant that the surrogatum principle was not applicable.

Even if the surrogatum principle could be applied, the dissent considered the general nature of the payment was to release the insurance company from liability and to extinguish the taxpayer's claim for benefits. Since the insurer expressly denied liability in the release, the payment was not made "pursuant to" the policy, in the sense of "in accordance with" or "in compliance with" the policy. Further, the amounts to which the taxpayer felt she was entitled under the policy were not directly replaced by the settlement amounts; they were "used more as a way to gauge the reasonableness of any compromise".

The majority disagreed with this approach, approving the reasoning of the Federal Court of Appeal that "Ms. Tsiaprailis cannot assert the insurer's liability under the policy in her action, recover an amount from the insurer in that action, and then argue that the payment does not flow from the obligations of the insurer under the policy" (paragraph 14).

Notes and Questions

1. Do you think that *Curran* would be decided the same way today, given the reasoning in *Schwartz* and the fact that Mr. Curran received the payment several months before his new employment commenced?
2. Review subsection 6(3) of the Act. Could the amount received by Mr. Schwartz be included in income applying this provision?
3. In *Manley v. The Queen*, [1985] 1 C.T.C. 186, 85 D.T.C. 5150 (F.C.A.), leave to appeal refused (1986), 67 N.R. 400 (note) (S.C.C.), the surrogatum principle was applied to treat an award of damages for breach of warranty of authority as income of the taxpayer. The taxpayer had contracted to receive a finder's fee in connection with the sale of a business with a person who had no authority to make the contract to pay the finder's fee. For further discussion of the surrogatum principle, see M. O'Brien, "Surrogatum, Source and Tsiaprailis: Is There a Principled Basis for the Taxation of Replacement Payments?" (2006) 54 Can. Tax J. 862.
4. Was the Court more willing in *Tsiaprailis* to allocate the settlement between taxable and non-taxable amounts than in *Schwartz*? Was this due to a difference in the evidentiary formulation, or a difference in the legal reasoning? See *Canada v. Siftar*, [2003] 3 C.T.C. 386, 2003 D.T.C. 5243 (F.C.A.).
5. Is there anything in the Act which indicates that gifts or bequests are not included in income? What statutory authority does Robertson J.A. rely on for the conclusion that gifts are non-taxable windfalls? As a general policy matter, should the value of all gifts or bequests received by a taxpayer during the year be included in income for the year?
6. In Interpretation Bulletin IT-365R2: Damages, Settlements and Similar Receipts (May 8, 1987), noted by Robertson J.A. in *Bellingham*, the CRA states (at paragraph 2):

    > All amounts received by a taxpayer or a taxpayer's dependant, as the case may be, that qualify as special or general damages for personal injury or death will be excluded from income regardless of the fact that the amount of such damages may have been determined with reference to the loss of earnings of the taxpayer in respect of whom the damages were awarded. However, an amount which can reasonably be considered to be income from employment rather than an award of damages will not be excluded from income.

    What policy objectives does the CRA's published position in IT-365R2 serve? How does it compare to the law regarding taxation of damages as expressed in the cases? Should personal injury damages, particularly those calculated by reference to lost earnings, be taxable? See T. Larre, "Taxing Personal Injury Damages" (2010) 58 Can. Tax J. 577.

7. Both the *Bellingham* and *Schwartz* decisions refer to *Fries,* in which the Supreme Court held that strike pay was not income from a source. Is this good tax policy? See B. Alarie & M. Sudak, "The Taxation of Strike Pay" (2006) 54 Can. Tax J. 426.
8. The courts have been confronted with the issue of whether a source of income existed in the context of fraudulent schemes. In *Johnson v. Canada,* [2013] 1 C.T.C. 10, 2013 D.T.C. 5004 (F.C.A.), leave to appeal refused [2012] S.C.C.A. No. 492, 2013 CarswellNat 633, the Federal Court of Appeal overturned the lower court's decision and held that the profits earned by an innocent investor from a Ponzi scheme were, in fact, income from a source. In doing so, the Court examined the factors set out in *Cranswick,* and held that they did not indicate that the payments were a non-taxable windfall. The Court's decision turned on the finding that the income was tied to an investment contract, and it reasoned that it did not matter that the money invested was used in a Ponzi scheme. It was on these grounds that the Court distinguished the case from *Hammill v. Canada,* [2005] 4 C.T.C. 29, 2005 D.T.C. 5397 (F.C.A.), leave to appeal refused 2006 CarswellNat 58 (S.C.C.), where the taxpayer was denied losses where the taxpayer had entrusted a fraudster with gems and paid him substantial fees in order to facilitate the sale of the gems. In that case, it was held that there was no source of income, and it was suggested that a fraudulent scheme could not give rise to a business. The Court in *Johnson* was careful to point out that the situation at hand was different because the contractual rights were respected. Do you agree that the two cases can be distinguished on these grounds?

II. LOSSES

A. Current Year Losses

The logical extension of the source concept of income is a schedular income tax under which income from the defined sources is calculated separately, separate tax rates are applied to each source, and losses from one source can only be offset against income from that same source. Section 4 reflects this schedular character in its requirement that taxpayers calculate income separately by source, both as to type and place. For example, if a taxpayer carries on two or more businesses or carries on business in different locations, section 4 requires separate determinations of the income from each business at each location.

Although the application of section 3 is premised on the source concept of income and, in particular, the separate computation of income from each source, the provision implements a "global income tax" under which income from the various sources is aggregated, and the total is subjected to a single tax rate structure. This process of aggregation also takes losses into account. Under paragraph 3(d), losses from a business, property or employment incurred in a taxation year reduce the taxpayer's income from all these sources. Allowable capital losses, however, are "quarantined" by paragraph 3(b) and can only offset taxable capital gains in a manner consistent with a schedular income tax. Current year losses from business, property, or employment can offset taxable capital gains.

As the Carter Commission recognized in its report (Vol. 4 at 252-55), there are some valid arguments for a full recognition of losses through the payment of a subsidy to the taxpayer calculated by multiplying the loss amount by a specified tax rate. A full recognition of losses would be more equitable because the tax system would recognize the losses of all taxpayers, not just those with sources of positive income. The payment of subsidies in loss years could also help to stabilize the economy. However, the Commission also recognized that full loss recognition would not be politically attractive.

The quarantining rule for allowable capital losses is justified generally as a response to taxpayers' ability to control the realization of capital gains and losses. In the absence of such a limitation, taxpayers might manipulate the timing of the realization of their capital gains and losses so that they are able to deduct the losses earlier than the inclusion of the gains, and thus substantially impair tax revenues. An exception from the quarantining rule is made for a special category of allowable capital losses referred to as "allowable business investment losses" ("ABILs"). This exception was apparently enacted to encourage investment in Canadian-controlled private corporations: see paragraphs 3(d) and 39(1)(c). An ABIL is deductible against all sources of income. The quarantining rule for allowable capital losses, its rationale, and the exception for ABILs are discussed in more detail in Chapter 7.

Section 31 limits the deduction of certain farming losses to $17,500 in any one year, with the amounts not deductible – the "restricted farm losses" – being available for carryover against other farming income. The targeted taxpayers are those persons whose chief source of income is neither farming nor a combination of farming and some other subordinate source of income. The concern here is that farming could be a "hobby" of the taxpayer, rather than a true business endeavor. Indeed, there are examples in the case law that would seem to support this concern, such as horseracing operations carried out by taxpayers with other significant sources of income that could offset any losses. However, there is a policy question about whether there is anything particularly unique about farming as opposed to other activities that makes it more likely to be carried out as a personal endeavor. The alternative would be to scrutinize farming using the same tests as are applied to all businesses, which are intended to separate commercial and personal activities, such that only the former are considered to be a "source" of income (or losses). This issue is discussed in Chapter 5.

B. Loss Carryovers

Tax payable is calculated by applying the relevant tax rates to taxable income and then reducing this amount by any available tax credits. See Chapter 8. Subsection 2(2) defines a taxpayer's taxable income as his or her income for the year under section 3, plus the additions and minus the deductions permitted by Division C of Part I of the Act (sections 110–13). Division C amounts are an eclectic set of inclusions and deductions with unrelated rationales. The loss carryover provisions described below are some of the more significant taxable income deductions. Other deductions are noted in subsequent chapters where they are relevant to the particular topic.

To the extent that current year losses cannot be used in the year that they arise (section 3 does not permit a negative balance that would entitle a taxpayer to a refund of tax), the losses may be carried over to another year (either forward or backward) and deducted in the calculation of taxable income for that other year. The carryover period and deductibility rules differ depending on the nature of the loss.

1. Non-Capital Losses

Paragraph 111(1)(a) permits the deduction of non-capital losses, defined in subsection 111(8), over a 23-year period (the three taxation years before the loss was incurred and the 20 subsequent taxation years). Allowing taxpayers to offset losses against income of the three preceding years should produce tax refunds close to the time when the loss was incurred, a time when the money is particularly needed. As a general rule, there is no restriction on the source of income of the taxpayer from which the loss is deductible. This creates a potential tax advantage for taxpayers who purchase corporations with undeducted losses realized in previous years. After buying such a corporation, a taxpayer could transfer a business to it and future profits from the business could be reduced by the losses carried forward.

However, subsections 111(5) to (5.4) and 249(4) have been enacted to limit this perceived abuse of the non-capital loss carryforward provisions and limit the availability of unused losses on a change in control of a corporation.

2. Farm Losses and Restricted Farm Losses

Farm losses, as defined in subsection 111(8), and restricted farm losses, as defined in section 31, may be carried back three years and forward 20 years in accordance with paragraphs 111(1)(d) and (c). Subject to the change of control rules for the non-capital losses of a corporation, farm losses may be deducted against income from any source. However, restricted farm losses are only deductible from farming income.

3. Net Capital Losses

Net capital losses, as defined in subsection 111(8), may be carried back three years and carried forward indefinitely (paragraph 111(1)(b)), but are deductible only from taxable capital gains (subsection 111(1.1)). In the taxation year ending immediately before an individual's death and the preceding tax year, net capital losses are deductible as if they were non-capital losses (subsection 111(2)). Where control of a corporation is acquired, the net capital losses of the corporation are not deductible (subsection 111(4)). Capital losses accrued at the time of the change of control are similarly restricted, although the corporation may elect to realize accrued gains against which the non-deductible capital losses may be offset.

Questions and Problems

1. Why does paragraph 111(1)(a) refer to non-capital losses for the 20 taxation years immediately preceding and the three years immediately following the particular year in which a loss carryover is claimed? How does this wording result in a 20-year carryforward and a 3-year carryback for a non-capital loss? See also the similar wording for the taxable income deduction in paragraphs 111(1)(b) and (c) and the recognition of listed personal property losses in subsection 41(2).
2. In 2009, X had income from employment of $20,000. He had income of $30,000 from a restaurant that he owns and a loss of $12,000 from a consulting business. He had income from property of $15,000 and realized taxable capital gains of $5,000 in addition to a taxable net gain of $2,000 from the disposition of listed personal property in the year. His allowable capital losses for the year were $8,000. He also incurred moving expenses of $1,000. Apply section 3 to determine X's net income for 2009.
3. Given the following amounts, calculate Y's income and taxable income for 2009 and 2010. Assume that Y has exhausted her entitlement to the capital gains exemption.
   (a) employment income for each of 2009 and 2010 of $50,000;
   (b) a loss of $57,000 incurred in 2010 from the carrying on of a consulting business;
   (c) a loss of $9,000 incurred in 2009 from the carrying on of the same consulting business;
   (d) a taxable capital gain of $6,000 and an allowable capital loss of $30,000 from the disposition of shares in 2010.

III. NEXUS BETWEEN A TAXPAYER AND A SOURCE OF INCOME

The income calculation rules in the Act attempt to resolve three basic questions:
(1) What amounts of revenue must be recognized as income?
(2) What amounts of expenses are recognized as deductible?
(3) When must the relevant amounts be recognized?

More often than not, resolution of this first issue proceeds on the apparent assumption that the person liable to tax on the revenue has been identified. In these instances, the focus tends to be on the deductibility and timing consequences following from the appropriate classification of the particular revenue stream as income from employment, business, property, or a capital gain or loss arising on the disposition of property. In some instances, however, the identification of the appropriate taxpayer is problematic, and the courts have been required to articulate criteria that effectively define the required nexus between a taxpayer and a source of income.

The calculation rules for the four conventional sources of income — employment, business, property and capital gains — arguably suggest the broad contours of the nexus sufficient to attract liability to tax. Employment income belongs to the employee as a *quid pro quo* for the employee's labour. The owner of a business or property is the person entitled to the profits from these sources. Capital gain or loss of a taxpayer is defined as the gain or loss from the disposition of property, which suggests that the owner of the property, who controls its disposition, must recognize the gain or loss.

As discussed in Part IV of this chapter, taxpayers sometimes attempt to shift income or a source of income to another person in an effort to reduce tax payable. Indeed, to the extent that the nexus for a particular source of income depends on private law relationships, it can be a relatively easy matter to manipulate that nexus in a tax-effective manner. Perhaps not surprisingly, therefore, Canadian courts and the Department of Finance have sometimes responded to these tax avoidance techniques by redefining the nexus between a taxpayer and a source of income. In a select few cases outside of an explicit tax-avoidance context, Canadian courts have also been required to articulate some of the basic criteria that define the taxpayer subject to tax on a source of income.

Consider, for example, the following case in which the tax authorities sought to tax an individual in respect of amounts that his former spouse had appropriated and to which she was not entitled as a matter of private law.

PETER D. FIELD v. THE QUEEN

[2001] 2 C.T.C. 2462, 2001 D.T.C. 236, 2001 CarswellNat 497 (T.C.C.)

[The taxpayer's estranged wife forged RRSP withdrawal forms to withdraw funds from his RRSP, which were paid into their still-open joint account. She then withdrew the funds. In the course of the settlement of the division of their matrimonial property, the wife admitted having taken the funds, but the taxpayer did not pursue recovery of the money on the advice of his lawyer. The taxpayer was assessed under subsection 146(8), which includes in a taxpayer's income "all amounts received by the taxpayer in the year as benefits out of or under registered retirement savings plans" .... The taxpayer appealed, arguing that he had never received any of the funds fraudulently withdrawn by his estranged wife, and could therefore not be subject to tax in respect of these amounts.]

Rowe D.J.T.C.C.: ...

[14] I agree that one must be cautious when making a finding of fact that involves dishonesty or fraud — even in the civil context — especially when the party alleged to have committed the act did not participate in the proceedings before the court. However, it is sufficient for the purposes of the within appeal — from a standpoint of determining the facts — for me to conclude that the actions taken by the appellant's estranged wife to redeem the particular CI Mutual Funds RRSP were unauthorized and that the signature on the requisite form — Exhibit A-1 — is not that of the appellant. In my opinion, this is obvious when compared to his actual signature as it appears on the Notice of Appeal — Exhibit A-5. One does not have to be a handwriting expert to spot the clumsy attempt at duplicating the somewhat peculiar signature of the appellant which appears to be composed of his initials in a form not unlike that of a logo or symbol. There is no evidence whatsoever that the appellant was careless in permitting such an action to have been taken by his wife following their separation and the fact she had been his investment broker in accordance with her license and special qualifications is no more significant than if he had been the victim of a fraud perpetrated by an officer at a financial institution that had been handling his RRSP portfolio. The court Order forming part of Exhibit A-5 — at paragraph 13 — referred to certain mutual funds as being the property of the appellant free and clear from any claim from his wife. In paragraph 14, there is reference to a Schedule A — not filed as an exhibit — which contained a list of certain mutual funds declared to be owned by the wife free and clear from the appellant. The testimony of the appellant was that he had read the handwritten copy of Schedule A and the particular CI Mutual Funds RRSP was not the subject of any mention in the agreement or subsequent Order. He also stated that in accepting the advice of his solicitor — in the context of the overall resolution of their marital affairs — he elected not to pursue his soon-to-be ex-wife in civil court, even though she had admitted cashing in the RRSP and he had obtained

proof in the form of a paper trail in order to demonstrate she had done so without his authorization.

[15] Counsel for the respondent pointed out that when placing monies into the RRSP, the appellant had obtained the benefit of deducting the amounts from his taxable income. That may be so, but when a taxpayer is the victim of a defalcation by someone licensed to deal with his or her investments, it cannot be the law that the victim — in the meantime — must pay the applicable amount of income tax on the unauthorized withdrawal and then be compelled to pursue the offender through the courts, a bonding company, a bankruptcy trustee, an employer — if relevant — or to wait for relief to be granted by either the federal or provincial government — several years later — following a lengthy investigation and/or public inquiry. It is more sensible — in my view — for the Minister to include the amount of the fraudulently acquired funds into the income of the offending party, especially where the requisite evidence is handed over in sufficient detail to support any such assessment. Further, the Minister could assess the tax-payer — if and when recovery is actually made on the wrongly appropriated funds — on the basis the amount initially realized through the involuntary withdrawal from the plan had not lost its tax-exempt characterization and could still be regarded as money remaining within an RRSP and, as a result, the taxpayer would have to include the recovered amount into income. It might not stand up to a challenge by the taxpayer but it would have a better chance of survival than the proposition currently advanced on behalf of the Minister as the basis for assessment in the within appeal.

[16] I cannot see how the appellant — in the plain and ordinary sense — "received" any amounts as "benefits out of or under" an RRSP within the language used in subsection 146(8) of the Act. He did not receive any money from the RRSP withdrawal and he did not receive any benefit thereof. The joint account previously operated by the appellant and his wife was used as a conduit to funnel the misappropriated funds into a new account in her sole name and this procedure did not provide any benefit to him.

[17] It is true the appellant previously obtained some tax relief when depositing monies into the said RRSP. Whether the marginal rate avoided by a taxpayer in participating in an RRSP will prove — ultimately — to have been greater than the amount attributable to a withdrawal is arguable when one considers — by way of example — that the combined federal and provincial tax rates deferred in 1984 were substantially less than the applicable rate on a withdrawal of the original funds — together with earned interest — during the 1999 taxation year. I cannot see the fact situation suffered by the appellant to be sufficiently common so as to require a special sitting of Parliament to debate an amendment to the legislation in order to require tax to be paid on any withdrawal from a taxpayer's RRSP, without regard to the manner by which it occurred. Similarly, I doubt there will be a rash of conspiracies springing up whereby people will

now plot to structure a purported unauthorized withdrawal of an RRSP — when it was actually done with the consent of the plan holder — so that the culpable parties could then grow fat on the marginal difference in tax rates, or even enjoy a complete windfall if the person responsible for the actual withdrawal — as in the within appeal — could avoid having the amount included into income. One can imagine the challenge facing the advertising agency retained by a firm doing business as an RRSP-qualified investment vendor attempting to sell a product — during the period just before the tax filing deadline — which would require disclosure to potential investors that they risked paying income tax on any future unauthorized and/or fraudulent withdrawals by the particular retirement fund/ plan agent, employee, or manager. However, the Minister's assessment was obviously premised on the legislation permitting such an interpretation. I cannot agree and have not been provided with any jurisprudence supporting such a radical departure from the ordinary rules which apply to the process of determining the meaning of statutory language. The facts in the within appeal are not based on any alleged negligent handling of an account or on some misunderstanding arising from a miscommunication to a broker concerning a withdrawal of funds inside a registered retirement savings plan. The within appeal involves an unauthorized act by a person previously in a position of trust as a licensed investment dealer, from which improper conduct she derived a benefit — and in so doing — harmed the appellant.

[18] The appeal is allowed with costs and the assessment is referred back to the Minister for reconsideration and reassessment on the basis the sum of $10,815 — previously included into income as a benefit out of the CI Mutual Funds RRSP — be deleted.

BUCKMAN v. M.N.R.

[1991] 2 C.T.C. 2608, 91 D.T.C. 1249 (T.C.C.)

[The taxpayer was a lawyer who embezzled funds from his clients. The Minister of National Revenue assessed the taxpayer for the 1983, 1984 and 1985 taxation years, including in his income unreported misappropriations.]

Sobier T.C.J.: — ...

The Appellant's position is that the embezzled funds (the "Funds") were not income in his hands. He contends that "income must be designated as derived from a particular source which may be:

i) office;

ii) employment;

iii) business;

iv) property; or

v) other source [Appellant's Factum, page 2]."

He also contends that once the particular source of a receipt is determined, that receipt is taxed in accordance with the rules applicable to that particular source [Appellant's Factum, page 2.].

Since the Funds were misappropriated in the course of [the Appellant's] law practice, the source, if any, must be business [Appellant's Factum, page 3.]. Accordingly, his income for a taxation year from a business is his profit therefrom for the year [Appellant's Factum, page 3.].

To determine "profit", says the Appellant, generally accepted accounting principles ("GAAP") will govern unless there are specific provisions in the *Income Tax Act* (the "Act") which require a departure from GAAP [Appellant's Factum, page 4.].

Under GAAP, the Funds would not be included in profit from a business and therefore could not be "income" from a business, since the Appellant did not have use of the Funds absolutely without restriction since they, at all times, belonged to their rightful owners. In addition, by making payments to the rightful owners which he claims were interest payments, he became a borrower of the Funds [Appellant's Factum, page 4.].

The Appellant claims that because he recognized his obligation to repay the Funds, he is to be treated as a borrower rather than a thief [Appellant's Factum, page 5.]. Finally, he contends that the misappropriation of the Funds in the course of carrying on a business is a situation different from other "illegal businesses" such as gambling, prostitution, bootlegging etc. where receipts of business are paid voluntarily [Appellant's Factum, page 5.].

The Respondent has adopted two alternative positions. The first is that the receipt of the Funds is income from a source and therefore taxable under section 3 of the Act. The second, that receipt of the Funds was income from a business and taxable even though the Funds were received from illegal operations.

...

Viscount Haldane speaking for the Judicial Committee of the Privy Council in *Minister of Finance v. Smith*, 1 D.T.C. 92 dealt with the issue of the taxability of unlawful businesses at page 93 where he said:

> Nor does it seem to their Lordships a natural construction of the Act to read it as permitting persons who come within its terms to defeat taxation by setting up their own wrong. There is nothing in the Act which points to any intention to curtail the statutory definition of income, and it does not appear appropriate under the circumstances to impart any assumed moral or ethical standard as controlling in a case such as this the literal interpretation of the language employed. There being power in the Dominion Parliament to levy the

> tax if they thought fit, their Lordships are therefore of opinion that it has levied income tax without reference to the question of Provincial wrongdoing.

Counsel for the Appellant referred to the dissenting opinion of Mr. Justice Black of the United States Supreme Court in *James v. United States*, 61-1 U.S.T.C. 9449. In James, the majority of the U.S. Supreme Court overruled *Commissioner v. Wilcox*, 46-1 U.S.T.C. 9188 (U.S.S.C.) by holding that embezzled funds are includable in income and taxable. However, counsel still urged the Court to ignore the majority decision and apply Mr. Justice Black's dissenting opinion. However, there was no doubt in *James* that the previous position in *Wilcox* was overruled and the law concerning the treatment of embezzled funds was from thenceforth changed.

Counsel also referred to *Gilbert v. Commissioner of Internal Revenue*, 582 F. 2d 478 (1977, 2d Cir.). That case is distinguished by the single fact the Appellant in *Gilbert* fully intended to repay the funds; whereas, it is clear Mr. Buckman was embezzling the Funds with no intention to repay. He did all in his power to keep his clients in the dark concerning his activities. Mr. Gilbert did not attempt to hide the fact. "He immediately informed several of the corporation's officers and directors and he made a complete accounting to all of them within two weeks [*Gilbert, supra* at page 481.]." The lack of intention on the Appellant's part to repay the funds may be deduced from the delivery of false documents as well as the payment of so-called interest to the clients. These actions were in furtherance of the deception.

The Queen v. Poynton, 72 D.T.C. 6329 (Ont. C.A.) is the leading authority dealing with fraudulently obtained funds as income. There, the Respondent fraudulently acquired about $21,000 of funds from the company in which he was a director and secretary-treasurer. The Court of Appeal held that the money was taxable in his hands as a benefit to an officer or employee under subsection 5(1) of the Act.

In his Reasons for Judgment in *Poynton*, Evans J.A. quotes with approval the Reasons of Lord Haldane in *Smith, supra*. The argument in *Poynton* that the moneys did not have the quality of income since the Appellant did not enjoy the right to the monies absolutely, with no restriction, contractual or otherwise, as to its disposition use or enjoyment was put to rest. (...)

Later at page 6335, Mr. Justice Evans went on to say:

> I am of the opinion that there is no difference between money and money's worth in calculating income. They are both benefits and fall within the language of s. 3 and 5 of the Act, being benefits received or enjoyed by the respondent in respect of, in the course of, or by virtue of his office or employment. I do not believe the language to be restricted to benefits that are related to the office or employment in the sense that they represent a form of remuneration

> for services rendered. If it is a material acquisition which confers an economic benefit on the taxpayer and does not constitute an exemption, e.g. loan or gift then it is within the all-embracing definition of s. 3.

Counsel for the Respondent argues that *Poynton* is distinguishable from this appeal because the Funds were not obtained by the Appellant as a result of his employment but were derived from a business source.

To say, as the Appellant does, that the application of *Poynton* must be limited to theft, embezzlement, etc. between employer and employee is incorrect.

It is clear from *Curlett, supra*, that the application is not limited to an employer/employee relationship. The Court in *Curlett* found that the money was income from a business (see *Curlett* page 431.) (...)

The Appellant received the money, appropriated it unto himself and used and enjoyed it for his own benefit. It was never treated by him as a loan. There was no intention to repay the Funds. Mr. Buckman was engaged in an ongoing, long term scheme to steal from his clients. In reality, he intended to hold the Funds for his own account and did so in fact.

The number of misappropriations and the methods employed by the Appellant had all the earmarks of a business. He took risks in stealing the Funds and being found out. His reward however, was his hope of escaping detection and keeping the Funds for his own use. There is no difference whether the thief acted as a solicitor, agent or employee. The fact that the Funds are to be treated as income flows from the realities of the situation. Paraphrasing Evans J.A. in *Poynton:* What is being sought to be taxed didn't accrue to Mr. Buckman *qua* solicitor or *qua* mortgage broker but *qua* thief.

Mr. Buckman was engaged in a business separate and apart from his law practice and mortgage brokerage activities and what he received from this business was income. Based upon *Curlett* and *Poynton,* the Funds received were income from a business and therefore taxable. This was the reality of the situation regardless of GAAP.

Because of this finding, I need not canvass the other argument that the Funds emanated from another source.

For the above reasons the appeal is dismissed.

Notes and Questions

1. Why were the restrictions on the taxpayer's entitlement to the business revenue ignored in *Buckman*? What does this suggest about the content of the concept of "entitlement" as the nexus between a taxpayer and income from a business? What are the consequences to the taxpayer in *Buckman* of a repayment of all or a portion of the embezzled funds?

2. The concept of "constructive receipt" refers to those instances in which an amount of revenue is available to the taxpayer who earned it, but is not reduced to his or her possession. In these circumstances, the taxpayer may be considered to have constructively received the revenue at the time that it becomes available. Could Mr. Field have been considered to have received the amount his former wife withdrew from his RRSP, given that he did not demand that she repay or account for it as part of their matrimonial property settlement?

IV. INCOME SPLITTING

Income splitting involves the transfer of income from one person to another who is taxed on the income at a lower marginal tax rate than that applicable to the transferor. The transfer is usually to a person with whom the transferor forms an economic unit, such as family members, corporations controlled by family members, family trusts, and the like. In that way, the taxpayer may relinquish legal ownership of the income but its use is retained within the economic unit for the benefit of the transferor who has earned the income. If the plan is successful, the tax payable on the income is lower because the income is taxed at a lower marginal rate, and the amount of after-tax income for the economic group is increased.

The motivation for income splitting is made obvious in the following example. Consider a person earning $100,000. Assuming the tax rates and brackets below, which are similar to federal rates in 2015, this person will pay $18,500 in federal income tax.

Rate	Tax Bracket	Taxable Amount	Tax Payable
0%	$0-$10,000	$10,000	$0
15%	$10,000-$40,000	$30,000	$4,500
22%	$40,000-$80,000	$40,000	$8,800
26%	$80,000-138,000	$20,000	$5,200
29%	Over $138,000	$0	$0
Total		$100,000	$18,500

If the person was able to shift half of her income over to a family member with no other income (a child or a spouse, for example), each would pay tax of $6,700, resulting in $13,400 in total tax payable by the two of them — a savings of $5,100. Note that no income is taxed in the two higher brackets, so that the marginal rate for these taxpayers is 22 per cent, while the marginal rate for the single taxpayer above was 26 per cent.

Rate	Tax Bracket	Taxable Amount to Each	Tax Payable by Each
0%	$0-$10,000	$10,000	$0
15%	$10,000-$40,000	$30,000	$4,500
22%	$40,000-$80,000	$10,000	$2,200
26%	$80,000-$138,000	Nil	Nil
29%	Over $138,000	Nil	Nil
Total		$50,000	$6,700

There are four basic techniques that attempt to split income by shifting the nexus between a taxpayer and a particular source of income. The first technique involves the direction of payment by a third party to a person other than the taxpayer who earned the income or is otherwise entitled to it. The second technique involves the assignment of a right to income from one taxpayer to another. The third technique involves the transfer of property that generates the income or gain. The fourth technique involves the use of low-interest or non-interest bearing loans.

The Act contains several provisions designed to counteract income splitting. These provisions generally attribute income from its legal owner to someone else for tax purposes. See, for example, sections 74.1, 74.2, 74.3, 74.4, 74.5 and 75.1. See also subsection 75(2) and subsections 56(2) to (4.3).

The Act also specifically endorses certain types of income splitting. A pensioner is permitted to split up to half of his or her pension income with a spouse or common-law partner by filing a joint election under section 60.03. The pensioner is permitted a subdivision e deduction from income under paragraph 60(c), and the spouse or common-law partner must include the split income as a subdivision d amount pursuant to paragraph 56(1)(a.2). The spouse or common-law partner is subject to tax on the pension income split with the pensioner, despite not having received it or having control over it.

Income splitting is also permitted through a spousal registered retirement savings plan (RRSP). An individual can contribute to the RRSP of his or her spouse or a common-law partner and take a deduction for that contribution (see Chapter 8).Withdrawals from the spousal RRSP will be included in the income of the spouse or common-law partner. In 2014, the federal government announced plans to permit income splitting of up to $50,000 between spouses, to a maximum benefit of $2,000 per couple, in the form of a credit against federal tax payable (see Chapter 8).

Notes and Questions

1. Subsection 56(2) requires an income inclusion for a taxpayer who directs payment to be made to another person. For example, in *Hasiuk v. Canada*, [2008] 3 C.T.C.

2262, 2008 D.T.C. 2157 (T.C.C.), aff'd [2009] 2 C.T.C. 7, 2008 D.T.C. 6703 (F.C.A.), the provision applied where a taxpayer diverted money owing to his company to his sons' company.

In *Neuman v. The Queen*, [1998] 3 C.T.C. 177, 98 D.T.C. 6297 (S.C.C.), the Court described the four requirements in subsection 56(2):

(1) the payment must be to a person other than the reassessed taxpayer;

(2) the allocation must be at the direction or with the concurrence of the reassessed taxpayer;

(3) the payment must be for the benefit of the reassessed taxpayer or for the benefit of another person whom the reassessed taxpayer wished to benefit; and

(4) the payment would have been included in the reassessed taxpayer's income if it had been received by him or her.

In *Neuman,* the taxpayer incorporated a company which paid relatively large dividends to his spouse, who was the shareholder of a particular class of shares. Justice Iacobucci decided that as the taxpayer was not entitled to the dividend income, the fourth requirement was not met.

2. Where a taxpayer transfers a right to receive money to a non-arm's length person, subsection 56(4) may require the taxpayer to include the amount in her or his income. In *Boutilier v. The Queen,* [2007] 3 C.T.C. 2007, 2007 D.T.C. 479 (T.C.C.), the provision applied to a financial planner who was owed fees as a result of his clients continuing to hold mutual fund units he had sold to them. The taxpayer arranged to have these "trailer fees" paid to his corporation, which paid tax on the fees and paid the remainder out to a family trust. The Court held that the "beneficial entitlement test" was met because it was the taxpayer, and not his corporation, who was beneficially entitled to the trailer fees.

3. The concept of "indirect receipt" requires a taxpayer to recognize as income those amounts that are not received directly but are, instead, applied for his or her benefit. The doctrine is said to apply only to the extent that the relevant amount would have been included in the taxpayer's income if received directly. Subsection 56(2) is a statutory version of this doctrine. Marceau J.A. in *Winter v. Canada,* [1989] 2 C.T.C. 55, 89 D.T.C. 5304 (F.C.T.D.), aff'd [1991] 1 C.T.C. 113, 90 D.T.C. 6681 (F.C.A.), (cited in *Neuman* and *Boutilier*) mistakenly refers to this provision as an embodiment of the doctrine of "constructive receipt".

4. Does the wording in subsection 56(2) require that a taxpayer be otherwise entitled to an amount that is paid to another person? Compare the wording in subsection 56(2) with that in subsection 56(4). On what statutory basis does the Supreme Court of Canada in *Neuman* derive this apparent requirement? Why was the requirement met in *Boutilier*, but not in *Neuman*?

5. In *M.N.R. v. Alan Bronfman*, [1965] C.T.C. 378, 65 D.T.C. 5235 (Exch. Ct.), the taxpayer, his three brothers and his brother-in-law were shareholders and directors in a private company, Brintcan, but they did not own enough shares to control the company. During 1950 to 1955, the company made gifts totalling $97,000 to relatives of the directors who were not shareholders of Brintcan. One-fifth of the value of the gifts was added to the appellant's income, the Minister relying on subsection 16(1) (now subsection 56(2)). In considering the application of this provision, Dumoulin J. stated: (at 383; 5238):

   > One fourth and paramount requirement remains to be satisfied: does the inclusion of the payments so made "in computing the taxpayer's income to the extent that it would be if the payment ... had been made to him", entail correlatively the personal ownership of the moneys thus paid out?
   >
   > I would think not, because, firstly, the section's clear enough purpose is the taxation of indirect payments under circumstances such as the instant ones. ...

   How does this interpretation differ from that of the Supreme Court in *Neuman?* What is the significance of the role of the taxpayer as a corporate director? What significance should that role have?

6. What "transfers of property" are contemplated by subsection 56(2)? Is there overlap in the application of subsections 56(2) and (4) to property transfers? Does it matter?

7. Section 120.4 imposes tax at the highest marginal personal rate on certain income of individuals under 18 years of age. This "kiddie tax" applies generally to: (1) taxable dividends and shareholder benefits on shares of a corporation that are not listed for trade on a recognized exchange; and (2) income from a partnership or trust that is derived by the provision of goods or services by the partnership or trust to a business carried on by either a person related to the particular minor or a corporation in which such a person is a shareholder. An exception is provided for income from property received by a minor on certain inheritances. The kiddie tax was presumably introduced as a response to both the Supreme Court's decision in *Neuman* and the income-splitting structures like that in *Ferrel* (cited in *Boutilier*) where a trust was used to split income between a professional and his minor children. What possible reasons would support the limitation of the application of the approach in section 120.4 to minors? Why does the provision not apply to the same categories of income derived by spouses? What assumptions underlie the imposition of the kiddie tax and its limited exception for certain inheritances? For further discussion, see M. Donnelly, J. McGee and A. Young, "Income Splitting and the New Kiddie Tax: Major Changes for Minor Children" (2000), 48 Can. Tax J. 979.

8. What is the policy justification for income splitting? For some of the policy issues surrounding income splitting, see Frances Woolley, "Policy Forum: Liability

Without Control: The Curious Case of Pension Income Splitting" (2001) 55 Can. Tax J. 603 and the papers in the policy forum on income splitting in (2013) 61:3 Can. Tax J. 677-721.

3

Who is Subject to Canadian Income Tax?

I. WHAT JURISDICTIONAL BASES ARE AVAILABLE?

A. General

In beginning to discuss the operation of a tax system, we must first ask one critical question: who does the state claim authority to tax? To some extent the theoretical component of this question has been addressed in Chapter 1. To get at the question more directly, this chapter uses cases, domestic legislation, international tax treaties and administrative statements to explore Canada's answer. It discusses the bases on which Canada taxes both residents and non-residents. It then proceeds to discuss exemptions from tax, including exemptions for Aboriginal peoples.

B. Alternative Jurisdictional Bases for Income Taxation

The common jurisdictional bases for imposing income taxation are citizenship or nationality, residence, and the source of income.

1. Citizenship or Nationality

Citizenship or nationality is used as a basis for taxation in a few countries, the most notable of which is the United States (which also uses residence). The rationale for this basis may be expressed in terms of the obligation of every citizen or national to help support the state through taxation, whether or not the citizen is living within the state's borders. This view rests on the "costs and benefits" view of taxation in the sense that each citizen ought to pay the cost of the government's services in accordance with the particular benefits conferred on the individual. However, given today's mobility, taxation based on citizenship or nationality attributes an exaggerated importance to the jurisdiction in which an individual (or corporation) was born or obtained nationality. But more importantly, taxation based on citizenship or nationality may unduly emphasize the political connection between a person and a country and minimize the importance of the economic connection. Taxation based on citizenship or nationality does, in most cases, have the virtue of being easy to apply (because citizenship rules are relatively clear) but may be difficult to enforce (for example, where a non-resident citizen has no assets in the country for the government to seize).

2. Residence

As will be seen in the next section of this chapter, residence is the primary basis for income taxation in Canada. Without trying to define the term at this point, residence can be described as being a closer relationship with a country than citizenship but not as close as domicile. Domicile of choice involves two main elements: a fact of presence within the jurisdiction and present intention on the part of the individual to maintain a permanent home in the jurisdiction. Residence consists of present ties to (but not necessarily physical presence in) a jurisdiction. It is not, at least directly, a matter of a person's intention. It is noteworthy, however, that the courts have on occasion blurred the distinction between residence and domicile.

Although residence is the main connecting factor for Canadian income tax, there does not seem to be a fully articulated explanation of why Canada adopted it. One might suggest that its use in Canada was just another Canadian "colonial" copy of the U.K. experience. Although the term does not give rise to precise formulation or interpretation, residence emphasizes an economic association with a country. That association prompted the Royal Commission on Taxation (the "Carter Commission") to recommend the continuation of residence as the principal basis for determining liability to income tax.

Two other reasons for the adoption of residence (with source of income) as the basis of taxation are the ability to pay principle and enforceability. The ability to pay principle is the basis of a progressive personal income tax system, as discussed in Chapter 1. Even a system based on taxation of consumption rather than income usually rests partially on the computation of net income. Residence also implies attachments to a jurisdiction that tend to make the enforceability of the tax regime easier.

3. Source of Income

Most countries impose income tax on non-residents who derive income from a source in the country. Tax is imposed because income is derived from the country of source through working, investing, or carrying on business therein. For example, Canada imposes an income tax on persons who are employed in Canada, carry on business in Canada, or receive income from sources in Canada (including income arising from the disposition of specified types of property), even though they are not resident here.

On the other hand, Canada also imposes income tax on the income earned by residents who work in foreign countries, or carry on business or receive income from investments in foreign countries. In other words, Canadian residents are taxed on their worldwide income.

II. RESIDENTS: WHAT IS RESIDENCE?

Under subsection 2(1) of the Act, the worldwide income of taxpayers who are resident in Canada at any time in a taxation year is subject to tax. In contrast, non-resident taxpayers are liable to tax only on income from Canadian sources under subsection 2(3) and Part XIII of the Act. The impact of subsection 2(1) on individuals is reduced by the operation of the part-time residence rules in section 114.

A. Individuals

1. Case Law Principles

Except for the provisions in subsection 250(1) and the general language in subsection 250(3), the Act does not define the residence of an individual. The case law has held that residence is a question of fact, and that "residence" and "ordinarily resident" have no special or technical meaning. Indeed, Thorson P. in *Thomson v. M.N.R.*, [1945] C.T.C. 63 at 73 (Exch. Ct.) said: "The cases ... really carry one no further than the dictionary, and, in the main, are but useful illustrations of the circumstances under which a person may be considered as residing or ordinarily resident in a place or country."

THOMSON v. M.N.R.
[1946] C.T.C. 51, 2 D.T.C. 812 (S.C.C.)

Rand J.:

The appeal raises a question of interpretation of the charging section of the *Income War Tax Act*. The appellant has been assessed on income received for the year 1940 and his liability depends on whether he is within the following provisions of Section 9:

> 9. There shall be assessed, levied and paid upon the income during the preceding year of every person
>
> (a) residing or ordinarily resident in Canada during such year; or
>
> (b) who sojourns in Canada for a period or periods amounting to one hundred and eighty-three days during such year.

He claims that during 1940 he was neither residing nor ordinarily resident in Canada, nor did he sojourn here for the number of days specified.

The material facts may be shortly stated. Born in Saint John, New Brunswick, in 1872, the appellant lived in that city and later at the Village of Rothesay, a short distance from it, until 1923 and in that time had become a man of means. As a result of a dispute over assessment by the village, he took up arms against what has become a sea of taxing troubles, sold his home, declared Bermuda to be his domicile, and proceeded to that island; and at the end of a week, armed with a British passport obtained there, returned to the mainland to set up residence in the United States. This continued until 1930 with his chief abode at Pinehurst, North Carolina. There in that year he built an expensive dwelling which ever since has been kept in readiness for occupancy. In 1932, marking his return to Canada, he rented a house at St. Andrew's, New Brunswick, where he spent a summer season of 134 days. This was repeated during the next two years, with 134 days in 1933 and 81 days in 1934. In the latter year he built a house at East Riverside near Rothesay costing, with furniture, close to $90,000. The reason given for this was his wife's desire to be near her relatives and friends in New Brunswick, but he protests against harbouring any like sentiment. Since then and up to 1942, between May and October he has spent there an average of 150 days each year. After the season at East Riverside, his life has centered around Pinehurst, with a stay of a month or two at Belleair, Florida. During that time, the New Brunswick house is closed except the quarters of a housekeeper and wife which are open the year around; but it could at any time become a winter or all year home if desired. With him in these mass movements are his wife and only child, motor cars and servants, and at all three places he indulges himself as an addict of golf, to which he devotes most of his time and a substantial part of his money. His passport was renewed in 1933 for a further period of ten years at a British Consulate in the United States, and on it his domicile was again stated to be in Bermuda. Apart from the brief visit in 1923, leasing a house for one or two years which he never occupied, a stay of six days in 1926 and eight in 1938, that island was stranger to him for the twenty years after leaving Rothesay. From 1930 to 1941 he was taxed on income in the United States as a non-resident; but in 1942 he was classed as a resident and taxed accordingly.

The President of the Exchequer Court properly, I think, characterizing his motions in relation to Bermuda as "pure farce", found him to be ordinarily resident in Canada for the year in question and maintained the action; and from that judgment this appeal is brought. ...

As interpreted, the English Act used the word "residing" or the expression "ordinarily resident" in the sense of the general acceptation, without special or technical meaning; and the Tax Commissioners find first the actual circumstances of a case and then as fact whether they are within that acceptation.

An appeal is allowed on a point of law, and where the person charged is appealing, the question invariably is whether there was any evidence to justify the finding. This strictly limited jurisdiction prevents us from assuming that a court sitting in appeal generally would have come to the same view of liability; and there are frequent intimations by individual judges that their own finding might have been different. But notwithstanding this limited function, these [U.K.] decisions reveal many aspects of residence under modern conditions and the extreme scope of interpretation to which the courts have felt themselves driven by the generality of the terms used and from the wide administrative jurisdiction conferred upon the Commissioners. ...

The gradation of degrees of time, object, intention, continuity and other relevant circumstances shows, I think, that in common parlance "residing" is not a term of invariable elements, all of which must be satisfied in each instance. It is quite impossible to give it a precise and inclusive definition. It is highly flexible, and its many shades of meaning vary not only in the contexts of different matters, but also in different aspects of the same matter. In one case it is satisfied by certain elements, in another by others, some common, some new.

The expression "ordinarily resident" carries a restricted signification, and although the first impression seems to be that of preponderance in time, the decisions on the English Act reject that view. It is held to mean residence in the course of the customary mode of life of the person concerned, and it is contrasted with special or occasional or casual residence. The general mode of life is, therefore, relevant to a question of its application.

For the purposes of income tax legislation, it must be assumed that every person has at all times a residence. It is not necessary to this that he should have a home or a particular place of abode or even a shelter. He may sleep in the open. It is important only to ascertain the spatial bounds within which he spends his life or to which his ordered or customary living is related. Ordinary residence can best be appreciated by considering its antithesis, occasional or casual or deviatory residence. The latter would seem clearly to be not only temporary in time and exceptional in circumstances, but also accompanied by a sense of transitoriness and of return.

But in the different situations of so-called "permanent residence", "temporary residence", "ordinary residence", "principal residence" and the like, the adjectives do not affect the fact that there is in all cases residence; and that quality is chiefly a matter of the degree to which a person in mind and fact settles into or maintains or centralizes his ordinary mode of living with its accessories in social relations, interests and conveniences at or in the place in question. It may be limited in time from the outset, or it may be indefinite, or so far as it is thought of, unlimited. On the lower level, the expressions involving residence should be distinguished, as I think they are in ordinary speech, from the field of "stay" or "visit".

In that view, it is scarcely open to doubt that if the word "residing" or the expression "ordinarily resident" had been used as in the English statute, it would have been impossible not to hold the appellant in the year in question both residing and ordinarily resident at East Riverside for the full 160 days of living there. His life is a good example of what Viscount Sumner in the *Lysaght* case had in mind when he spoke of the "fluid and restless character of social habits" to which modern life has introduced us. His ordinary residence throughout the year 1940 was indisputably within a strip of North America bordering on the Atlantic and running from Florida to New Brunswick. In that area, enabling him to keep pace with a benign climate, he had at least two and possibly three dwelling places, each of which coupled with his presence for the time being constituted, so far as he had any, his home. When he moved to East Riverside, he moved not only himself but that home; ambulatory over a considerable part of the continent, it became residence where so set up. From each radiated his living and interests and from them in turn he might make occasional departures or visits or temporary stays amounting even to limited residence. ...

The Canadian Act taxes the person "residing" on the whole of his income, and provides only for a deduction of the amount of tax which the taxpayer may have been compelled to pay in a foreign country on the income arising from sources there. In the English Act, on the contrary, there is an elaborate classification of income with varying taxabilities and to hold a person liable for income from foreign possessions beyond what was received in the United Kingdom it is necessary under Schedule D to find not only that he resides in the United Kingdom but, where he is a British subject, that he is both ordinarily resident and domiciled there. These taxes are, in theory, justified by the protection to life and property which the laws of the country imposing them may give. They are conceived to be intended to apply fairly and equally to all persons and an apparent gross violation of that assumption is relevant to the enquiry into what Parliament by its general language has intended. That a person should be liable for tax upon the whole of his income even with the deduction mentioned merely because he has spent, say, two months in Canada as a temporary change of scene, whether or not part of his routine of life, is too unreasonable an intention to attribute to the language of Parliament unless it is beyond doubt. I would, therefore, treat the word "sojourns" as applying to presence in Canada where the nature of the stay is either outside the range of residence or is what is commonly understood as temporary residence or residence for a temporary purpose.

But that qualified stay is not the character of the appellant's. Apart from any question of domicile which would appear to be still in New Brunswick, his living in Canada is substantially as deep rooted and settled as in the United States. In terms of time, Pinehurst may take precedence but at best it is a case of *primus inter pares*. He is at East Riverside at his "home"; and the mere limitation of time does not qualify that fact; *Attorney-General v. Coote*, 4 Price 183. That brings him within the most exacting of any reasonable interpretation of "resides" or "ordinarily resident".

For these reasons I would dismiss the appeal with costs.

Taschereau, J. (dissenting): ... For some years [Thomson] lived in rented houses in Pinehurst, North Carolina, building a house there in 1930, and for the years 1930 to 1942, he paid the United States income taxes, as a resident of the United States. ...

The fundamental error of the court below has been, I believe, to consider Thomson as a resident of Canada, making occasional visits to the United States, when he should have been classified as a resident of the United States, making occasional visits to Canada. The retaining of his Canadian citizenship has no bearing upon the matter. Nationality is not an ingredient for the purpose of the Act. ...

[Kerwin, Kellock, and Estey JJ., gave separate judgments dismissing the appeal.]

Notes and Questions

1. Part XXVI of the Regulations provides rules for the determination of income earned in a province by an individual. The rules provide that a province may tax any individual who resided in that province on the last day of the year. In consequence, it is immaterial that the individual may have resided for most of the taxation year in another province(s). All income whether arising in Canada or abroad is taxed by the individual's province of residence on the last day of the year. An exception is income from an (unincorporated) business which has a permanent establishment outside of the province. In that case, special rules apply for the allocation and taxation of its profits among the provinces and the federal government.

   Because the provinces have substantially different tax rates, the determination of an individual's province of residence is significant.

2. An individual may be considered a resident of Canada for Canadian income tax purposes and a resident of another country under its fiscal legislation. Accordingly, an individual may be liable to taxation in both countries on the same income unless relief is provided under a tax treaty. For a discussion of the application of tax treaties, see Part IV of this chapter. For recent examples of the application of the tax treaty rules where a taxpayer was resident of both Canada and the United States see *Allchin v. The Queen* [2005] 2 C.T.C. 2701, 2005 D.T.C. 603 (T.C.C.), and *Trieste v. The Queen*, 2012 TCC 91, 2012 D.T.C. 1125 (T.C.C.), affirmed 2012 FCA 320, 2013 D.T.C. 5020 (F.C.A.).

3. Should an individual's citizenship influence residence status? What do you think of Mr. Justice Tashereau's dissent in *Thomson* where he refers to Mr. Thomson's Canadian citizenship?

DENIS M. LEE v. M.N.R.
[1990] 1 C.T.C. 2082, 90 D.T.C. 1014 (T.C.C.)

Teskey T.C.J.: The appellant appeals his 1981, 1982 and 1983 reassessments.

...

The single issue is whether the appellant, in any or all of the years, was resident in Canada within the meaning of subsection 2(1) of the *Income Tax Act* (notwithstanding that Immigration Canada treated him as a visitor).

...

The appellant is an electronic engineer. He was born in Erith, England on July 7, 1946. During the relevant times, the appellant held a valid passport for the United Kingdom of Great Britain and Northern Ireland. ...

Each time the appellant entered Canada, the passport was stamped by Immigration Canada, with the majority of entries setting out a date upon which he must leave Canada. The authorized period of stay varied from 5 days to 45 days. On some of the stamps the word "visitor" was written in by an immigration official. Throughout the three-year period, the appellant was employed full time by a non-resident corporation and all work was performed outside Canada.

All income was deposited directly into a Canadian bank. In 1981, the appellant married Cathy Lewis, a Canadian citizen residing in Canada, who had no income of her own and was wholly dependent on the appellant. She has always resided continuously in Canada.

In June of 1981, a house near Apsley, Ontario was purchased by Cathy Lewis with money supplied by the appellant. The appellant's wife in September of 1982 borrowed money by way of a mortgage. The appellant guaranteed the mortgage which has an affidavit attached dated September 13, 1982 where he swore that he was not then a non-resident of Canada.

During the three-year period, the appellant regularly returned to Canada when not working. The appellant pleads in his notice of appeal that he was charged in Provincial Court for failure to file an income tax return for 1981 and was acquitted. However, no evidence of any kind was adduced to support this allegation.

Prior to the appellant's marriage, his parents maintained a bedroom for him in Kent, England.

During the three-year period, the appellant:

(1) never filed or paid income tax anywhere;

(2) was not allowed to work in Canada;

(3) was given a fixed date to leave Canada on each entry (i.e., not allowed to stay in Canada);

(4) claims he could not join O.H.I.P, pay U.I. or maintain an R.R.S.P. or join a pension plan;

(5) if he purchased property in Ontario, he would have had to pay a 20 percent non-resident land transfer tax;

(6) was out of the country more than 183 days a year;

(7) had no desire to work in Canada;

(8) had a residence in Britain in the home of his mother and father;

(9) held a mortgage in Britain on his first wife's house;

(10) claims he could not live a normal life in Canada as he had to leave every 27 days;

(11) had a bank account with the Royal Bank of Canada both in Canada and in the Caribbean.

The appellant was also asked the following questions and gave the following answers:

Q. Every time you finished your stint on the rig you would come back home to Canada to visit your wife?

A. I came back for the periods that Immigration would allow me to come.

Q. As often as you could.

A. Yes.

...

Q. You certainly wouldn't call your place in Canada an occasional residence or a casual residence. You would call it a home, would you not?

A. No, I wouldn't call it a home.

Q. What did you call it, a casual residence?

A. As I said before, I keep restating it, to me a home is somewhere where you're allowed to work, where you can enjoy a normal life, and I was not allowed to lead a normal life. Immigration Canada insisted that I left the country every 27 days.

Q. Was Canada a place where you occasionally resided?

A. We keep coming back to the word "reside". In my definition I didn't reside here. I was not allowed to do any of the things that I would regard as normal for a resident of an area.

Q. When people asked you on the rig where you lived what did you say?

A. Obviously I said Canada.

In 1984, the appellant purchased a car in Canada. In 1985 the appellant:

1. obtained a Canadian driver's licence;
2. obtained a Canadian visa;
3. became a landed immigrant in Canada.

[After referring to the relevant provisions of the Act and Thomson case, supra, the judge continued.]

The question of residency is one of fact and depends on the specific facts of each case. The following is a list of some of the indicia relevant in determining whether an individual is resident in Canada for Canadian income tax purposes. It should be noted that no one or any group of two or three items will in themselves establish that the individual is resident in Canada. However, a number of factors considered together could establish that the individual is a resident of Canada for Canadian income tax purposes:

— past and present habits of life;
— regularity and length of visits in the jurisdiction asserting residence;
— ties within the jurisdiction;
— ties elsewhere;
— permanence or otherwise of purposes of stay;
— ownership of a dwelling in Canada or rental of a dwelling on a long-term basis (for example, a lease for one or more years);
— residence of spouse, children and other dependent family members in a dwelling maintained by the individual in Canada;
— memberships with Canadian churches or synagogues, recreational and social clubs, unions and professional organizations;
— registration and maintenance of automobiles, boats and airplanes in Canada;
— holding credit cards issued by Canadian financial institutions and other commercial entities including stores, car rental agencies, etc;
— local newspaper subscriptions sent to a Canadian address;
— rental of Canadian safe deposit box or post office box;
— subscriptions for life or general insurance including health insurance through a Canadian insurance company;
— mailing address in Canada;
— telephone listing in Canada;

— stationery including business cards showing a Canadian address;
— magazine and other periodical subscriptions sent to a Canadian address;
— Canadian bank accounts other than a non-resident bank account;
— active securities accounts with Canadian brokers;
— Canadian driver's licence;
— membership in a Canadian pension plan;
— holding directorship of Canadian corporations;
— membership in Canadian partnerships;
— frequent visits to Canada for social or business purposes;
— burial plot in Canada;
— will prepared in Canada;
— legal documentation indicating Canadian residence;
— filing a Canadian income tax return as a Canadian resident;
— ownership of a Canadian vacation property;
— active involvement in business activities in Canada;
— employment in Canada;
— maintenance or storage in Canada of personal belongings including clothing, furniture, family pets, etc;
— obtaining landed immigrant status or appropriate work permits in Canada;
— severing substantially all ties with former country of residence.

The appellant claims that he did not want to be a resident of Canada during the years in question. Intention, or free choice, is an essential element in domicile, but is entirely absent in residence.

After considering all of the relevant factors brought out at trial and applying the law as set out, I am satisfied that the appellant at the beginning of 1981 was not a resident of Canada. The appellant was obviously a resident of Canada on September 13, 1982 not only because he swore he was not a non-resident but he also on that day guaranteed the mortgage on the residence that became on marriage the matrimonial residence. The question for determination is at what time between January 1, 1981 and September 13, 1982 did the appellant become a resident of Canada. Although marriage can be a neutral factor, in this case it is the additional factor that tips the scales from one of non-residency to one of residency.

The appeal for the 1981 taxation year is allowed with costs. The reassessment is sent back to the Minister for reconsideration and reassessment on the basis that the appellant was not a resident of Canada on January 1, 1981 and stayed a non-resident up to the date of his marriage in 1981, whereupon he became a resident of Canada and has remained a resident of Canada from then on. It therefore follows that the appeals with respect to the 1982 and 1983 taxation years are dismissed.

Notes and Questions

1. In *Fisher v. The Queen* (1994), [1995] 1 C.T.C. 2011, 95 D.T.C. 840 at paragraph 40 [C.T.C.] Bowman T.C.J. said of the taxpayer:

> He had a right to come home whenever he chose. That can be said of no other country. One is reminded of the passage in Robert Frost's poem, "The Death of the Hired Man": "Home is the place where, when you have to go there, They have to take you in."

2. Where did Mr. Lee reside when he was not a resident of Canada? See also section 255 of the Act, which addresses the geographical scope of "Canada".
3. In *Lee*, the Tax Court tied Mr. Lee's residence for tax purposes to the date of his marriage. The significance of a taxpayer's legal marriage, common-law relationship, separation and independent life style has been discussed in several cases dealing with residence. See for example, *Ferguson v. M.N.R.*, [1989] 2 C.T.C 2387, 89 D.T.C. 634 (T.C.C.); *Erikson v. The Queen*, [1975] C.T.C. 624, 75 D.T.C. 5429 (F.C.T.D.); *The Queen v. Sherwood*, [1978] C.T.C. 713, 78 D.T.C. 6470 (F.C.T.D.); *Mazerolle v. The Queen*, [1994] 2 C.T.C. 2162, 94 D.T.C. 1381 (T.C.C.); *Guo v. The Queen*, [2003] 2 C.T.C. 2745 (T.C.C.), affirmed (2004), [2005] 1 C.T.C. 126, 2004 D.T.C. 6728 (F.C.A.).
4. In some cases, a taxpayer has managed to establish non-residence even where his spouse of an intact marriage continued to reside in Canada. See *Schujahn v. M.N.R.*, [1962] C.T.C. 364, 62 D.T.C. 1225 (Can. Ex. Ct.), *infra*, in the section on part-time residence. See also *Shih v. The Queen*, [2000] 2 C.T.C. 2921, 2000 D.T.C. 2072 (T.C.C.). In that case, the Tax Court held that Mr. Shih was not resident of Canada even though his wife and three sons lived in Regina in a family home owned jointly by Mr. and Mrs. Shih. Mr. Shih had immigrated with his family in 1991 under the immigrant entrepreneurial program. The program required him to establish a business in Canada. Mr. Shih complied with this responsibility but after less than two years this condition was removed by immigration authorities and the business was closed. From the time of acquiring permanent resident status in Canada in 1991, Mr. Shih maintained his employment as a pharmaceutical salesman in Taiwan. During the period August 11, 1991 to 1994, Mr. Shih visited his family 12 times and spent generally less than 20 per cent of his time in Canada. His wife visited Taiwan once or twice a year for short visits. Mr. Shih explained that he and his wife brought their sons to Canada so that they would receive a Western education. It was the only reason for the family coming to Canada. Mr. Shih's aged parents remained in Taiwan

and he was responsible, as the eldest son, for their care and support. Mr. Shih maintained membership in Taiwan in a tennis club and was a member of a church there. Initially he rented an apartment in Taiwan but subsequently he bought a house. Mogan T.C.J. held that Mr. Shih was a non-resident of Canada. At paragraph 10 (C.T.C.) he stated:

> On the evidence, the Appellant was a stranger to Regina (and Canada) throughout the years under appeal even though he probably was a much loved husband and father to his wife and children when he came to visit them. He not only resided in Taiwan but he also maintained a personal home there. He was not a resident of Canada ...

2. Deemed Residence (subsections 250(1), (2))

An individual who is not resident in Canada under the case law principles may be considered resident by virtue of the deeming provisions in subsections 250(1) and (2).

Paragraph 250(1)(a) deems an individual to be resident in Canada for the entire taxation year if he or she "sojourned" in the country for a period or periods aggregating 183 days or more in the calendar year. What do you think sojourning means? For example, must an individual do more than commute to work in Canada in order to be a sojourner? If so, why? There have been few cases interpreting the word.

R & L FOOD DISTRIBUTORS LIMITED v. M.N.R.
[1977] C.T.C. 2579, 77 D.T.C. 411 (T.R.B.)

Prociuk A.W.: ...

The appellant corporation of Tecumseh, Ontario appeals from the respondent's reassessment of its income for the 1973 taxation year wherein the small business deduction pursuant to subsection 125(1) of the *Income Tax Act*, S.C. 1970-71-72, c. 63, as amended, was disallowed on the ground that the appellant was not a Canadian-controlled private corporation in that the controlling shareholders were not resident in Canada.

The appellant is a wholesale food distributor and sells to all major chains in Ontario. It was incorporated before 1970, pursuant to the laws of the Province of Ontario. There are three common shares issued and outstanding and there are three shareholders, two of whom are employed by the appellant and claim that each of them sojourns more than 183 days a year in Canada in the course of their employment and are deemed residents thereof pursuant to subsection 250(1) of the *Income Tax Act*, which reads, in part, as follows:

> 250. (1) For the purposes of this Act, a person shall, subject to subsection (2), be deemed to have been resident in Canada throughout a taxation year if

(a) he sojourned in Canada in the year for a period of, or periods the aggregate of which is, 183 days or more.

Paragraphs (b) to (f) are inapplicable.

The said two shareholders, Ben Labe and Joseph Rosenthal, testified in support of the appellant's appeal. It was conceded at the commencement of the hearing that the third shareholder, Helen Labe, was not a resident.

Ben Labe (hereinafter referred to as "Labe") stated that the address of his home was 28190 Tavistock, Southfield, Michigan, U.S.A. He was employed as a general manager of the appellant. The appellant owns the land and buildings where it conducts its business and the said assets are worth about $225,000. Mr. Labe's home was and is in Michigan from where he commuted daily to Windsor, Ontario to work. In 1973 he stayed overnight in Canada about 6 or 7 times when he had to travel to Toronto to call on accounts. If he took an early plane to Toronto from Windsor, he would stay overnight in the business premises and slept on a couch. He would also spend some of his holiday time in Toronto with family friends. He is also involved in another business in Windsor, Ontario, of which he is part owner. His estimate is that he spent about 300 work days in 1973 in Canada. He filed an income tax return in Canada as well as in the United States. When asked why he had not moved to Canada, he replied that it was a family decision and as long as he and his wife have children living with them, they would not consider moving. It takes him 25 to 30 minutes to travel from home to the place of business in Canada. He does not own or maintain a residence in Canada. He is a member of the Synagogue in Michigan and makes his contributions there. He is a member of the Detroit Chapter of B'nai Brith. He has no business interests in the United States at all.

Mr. Joseph Rosenthal (hereinafter referred to as "Rosenthal") owned a home at 15390 Jay Street, Oak Park, Michigan, U.S.A. and resided there in 1973. He also commuted daily to work for the appellant where he was and is a general sales manager. He worked five days a week and got home every evening. He also does not own or maintain a residence in Canada but all his investments are in Canada. He belongs to a social club in Windsor and is a member of a Masonic Order in the United States. He filed his personal income return in Canada and in the United States. He is also a member of the Zadeche Synagogue in Michigan to which he makes contributions.

This is a brief résumé of the evidence of each of the witnesses. The issue here is whether on the evidence before the Board these shareholders are deemed residents of Canada. If they are, then the appellant is entitled to the small business deduction by reason of the fact Labe and Rosenthal control the company.

It has been established beyond any doubt that both shareholders have spent more than 183 work days in 1973 in Canada in the employ of the appellant.

Each has a home in Michigan and the family ties are there. With the exception of a few days in the case of Labe, each returned to his home every evening after work. Neither had a residence in Canada. Does this mode of activity or life style amount to sojourning in Canada in the year for a period or periods, the aggregate of which is 183 days or more, within the meaning of subsection 250(1) of the said Act?

In *The Shorter Oxford English Dictionary* the meaning of "sojourn" is given as "to make a temporary stay in a place; to remain or reside for a time". In perusing numerous cases decided by the Canadian and British courts, it is obvious that coming from one country to work for the day at a place of business in another country and thereafter returning to one's permanent residence in the evening is not tantamount to making a temporary stay in the sense of establishing even a temporary residence in the country where the business enterprise is situate. Assuming that Labe and Rosenthal had established a temporary residence in Windsor, Ontario, each of them would still have the burden of establishing that the residence in each case was not casual and uncertain but that it was in the ordinary regular course and that the usual relationship of such residence was beyond doubt. See *Thomson v. M.N.R.,* [1946] C.T.C. 51; 2 D.T.C. 812.

The evidence here is that home and social ties for each witness were clearly in Michigan and not in Windsor. I am of the opinion that neither Labe nor Rosenthal qualify as a deemed resident of Canada. The appellant, accordingly, was not a Canadian-controlled private corporation in 1973 and the appeal herein is dismissed.

Question

Do you agree with Mr. Procuik's remarks at the end of *R & L Food Distributors* that, even had the taxpayers established that they had a temporary residence in Canada, they would "still have the burden of establishing that the residence in each case was not casual and uncertain but that it was the ordinary regular course. ..."?

Income Tax Folio S5-F1-F1
Determining an Individual's Residence Status

Summary

The purpose of this Chapter is to explain the position of the CRA concerning the determination of an individual's residence status for income tax purposes and the factors to be taken into account in making that determination.

Under the Canadian income tax system, an individual's liability for income tax is based on his or her status as a **resident** or a **non-resident** of Canada. An individual who is **resident** in Canada during a tax year is subject to Canadian income tax on his or her worldwide income from all sources. Generally, a **non-resident** individual is only subject to Canadian income tax on income from sources inside Canada.

An individual who is resident in Canada can be characterized as **ordinarily resident** or **deemed resident**. An individual who is **ordinarily resident** in Canada will be subject to Canadian tax on his or her worldwide income during the part of the year in which he or she is resident in Canada; during the other part of the year, the individual will be taxed as a non-resident. An individual who is **deemed resident** in Canada in a particular year will be subject to Canadian income tax on his or her worldwide income throughout that year. In certain situations, an individual who would otherwise be ordinarily resident or deemed resident in Canada may be deemed not to be resident in Canada pursuant to subsection 250(5) and the tie-breaker rules of an income tax treaty.

The factors to be considered in the determination of an individual's residence status are discussed throughout this Chapter. Many of the comments in this Chapter apply to determinations of residence status for provincial, as well as federal, tax purposes. Taxpayers seeking a less technical overview of these matters may prefer to first review Residency – Individuals on the CRA website.

DISCUSSION AND INTERPRETATION

General Overview

1.1 Under the Canadian income tax system, an individual's liability for income tax is based on his or her status as a **resident** or a **non-resident** of Canada. An individual who is **resident** in Canada during a tax year is subject to Canadian income tax on his or her worldwide income from all sources. Generally, a **non-resident** individual is only subject to Canadian income tax on income from sources inside Canada. An individual may be resident in Canada for only part of a year, in which case the individual will only be subject to Canadian tax on his or her worldwide income during the part of the year in which he or she is resident; during the other part of the year, the individual will be taxed as a non-resident.

...

Factual residence – leaving Canada

Residential ties in Canada

1.10 The most important factor to be considered in determining whether an individual leaving Canada remains resident in Canada for tax purposes is whether the individual maintains residential ties with Canada while abroad. While the residence status of an individual can only be determined on a case-by-case basis after taking into consideration all of the relevant facts, generally, unless an individual severs all significant residential ties with Canada upon leaving Canada, the individual will continue to be a factual resident of Canada and subject to Canadian tax on his or her worldwide income.

Significant residential ties

1.11 The residential ties of an individual that will almost always be significant residential ties for the purpose of determining residence status are the individual's:

- dwelling place (or places);
- spouse or common-law partner; and
- dependants.

1.12 Where an individual who leaves Canada keeps a dwelling place in Canada (whether owned or leased), available for his or her occupation, that dwelling place will be considered to be a significant residential tie with Canada during the individual's stay abroad. However, if an individual leases a dwelling place located in Canada to a third party on arm's-length terms and conditions, the CRA will take into account all of the circumstances of the situation (including the relationship between the individual and the third party, the real estate market at the time of the individual's departure from Canada, and the purpose of the stay abroad), and may consider the dwelling place not to be a significant residential tie with Canada except when taken together with other residential ties (see ¶1.26 for an example of this situation and see ¶1.15 for a discussion of the significance of secondary residential ties).

1.13 If an individual who is married or cohabiting with a common-law partner leaves Canada, but his or her spouse or common-law partner remains in Canada, then that spouse or common-law partner will usually be a significant residential tie with Canada during the individual's absence from Canada. Similarly, if an individual with dependants leaves Canada, but his or her dependants remain behind, then those dependants will usually be considered to be a significant residential tie with Canada while the individual is abroad. Where an individual was living separate and apart from his or her spouse or common-law partner prior to leaving Canada, by reason of a breakdown of their marriage or common-law partnership, that spouse or common-law partner will not be considered to be a significant tie with Canada.

Secondary residential ties

1.14 Generally, secondary residential ties must be looked at collectively in order to evaluate the significance of any one such tie. For this reason, it would be unusual for a single secondary residential tie with Canada to be sufficient on its own to lead to a determination that an individual is factually resident in

Canada while abroad. Secondary residential ties that will be taken into account in determining the residence status of an individual while outside Canada are:

- personal property in Canada (such as furniture, clothing, automobiles, and recreational vehicles);
- social ties with Canada (such as memberships in Canadian recreational or religious organizations);
- economic ties with Canada (such as employment with a Canadian employer and active involvement in a Canadian business, and Canadian bank accounts, retirement savings plans, credit cards, and securities accounts);
- landed immigrant status or appropriate work permits in Canada;
- hospitalization and medical insurance coverage from a province or territory of Canada;
- a driver's license from a province or territory of Canada;
- a vehicle registered in a province or territory of Canada;
- a seasonal dwelling place in Canada or a leased dwelling place referred to in ¶1.12;
- a Canadian passport; and
- memberships in Canadian unions or professional organizations.

Other residential ties

1.15 Other residential ties that the courts have considered in determining the residence status of an individual while outside Canada, and which may be taken into account by the CRA, include the retention of a Canadian mailing address, post office box, or safety deposit box, personal stationery (including business cards) showing a Canadian address, telephone listings in Canada, and local (Canadian) newspaper and magazine subscriptions. These residential ties are generally of limited importance except when taken together with other residential ties, or with other factors such as those described in ¶1.16.

Application of term ordinarily resident

1.16 Where an individual has not severed all of his or her residential ties with Canada, but is physically absent from Canada for a considerable period of time (that is, for a period of time extending over several months or years), the courts have generally focused on the term **ordinarily resident** in determining the individual's residence status while abroad. The strong trend in decisions of the courts on this issue is to regard temporary absence from Canada, even on an extended basis, as insufficient to avoid Canadian residence for tax purposes. Accordingly, where an individual maintains residential ties with Canada while abroad, the following factors will be taken into account in evaluating the significance of those ties:

- evidence of intention to permanently sever residential ties with Canada;
- regularity and length of visits to Canada; and
- residential ties outside Canada.

For greater certainty, the CRA does not consider that intention to return to Canada, in and of itself and in the absence of any residential ties, is a factor whose presence is sufficient to lead to a determination that an individual is resident in Canada while abroad.

Evidence of intention to permanently sever residential ties

1.17 Whether an individual intended to permanently sever residential ties with Canada at the time of his or her departure from Canada is a question of fact to be determined with regard to all of the circumstances of each case. Although length of stay abroad is one factor to be considered in making this determination (that is, as evidence of the individual's intentions upon leaving Canada), the courts have indicated that there is no particular length of stay abroad that necessarily results in an individual becoming a non-resident. Generally, if there is evidence that an individual's return to Canada was foreseen at the time of his or her departure, the CRA will attach more significance to the individual's remaining residential ties with Canada (see ¶1.11 – 1.15), in determining whether the individual continued to be a factual resident of Canada subsequent to his or her departure. For example, where, at the time of an individual's departure from Canada, there exists a contract for employment in Canada if and when the individual returns to Canada, the CRA will consider this to be evidence that the individual's return to Canada was foreseen at the time of departure. However, the CRA would have to review each individual's situation on a case-by-case basis to determine whether the individual's remaining residential ties with Canada, including the contract of employment, are sufficient to conclude that the individual continues to be resident in Canada.

Steps taken to comply with the Act

1.18 Another factor that the CRA will consider in determining whether an individual intended to permanently sever all residential ties with Canada at the time of his or her departure from Canada, is whether the individual took into account and complied with the provisions of the Act dealing with the taxation of:

- individuals ceasing to be resident in Canada; and
- individuals who are not resident in Canada.

For example, upon ceasing to be resident in Canada, an individual is required to either pay, or post acceptable security for, the Canadian tax payable with respect to capital gains arising from the deemed disposition of all of the individual's property (with the exception of certain types of property that are listed in paragraph 128.1(4)(b)). Where applicable, the CRA will look at whether this requirement has been met as an indication of the individual's intention to permanently sever his or her residential ties with Canada at the time the individual left Canada.

1.19 Similarly, the CRA will take into account whether the individual informed any Canadian residents making payments to the individual that the individual intended to become a non-resident upon leaving Canada, with the result that certain payments (including interest, dividend, rent and pension payments) made to the individual after that time might be subject to withholding tax under Part XIII.

...

Sojourners as deemed residents

1.32 An individual who has not established sufficient residential ties with Canada to be considered factually resident in Canada, but who sojourns (that is, is temporarily present) in Canada for a total of 183 days or more in any calendar year, is deemed to be resident in Canada for the entire year, under paragraph 250(1)(a). As a result, an individual who sojourns in Canada for a total of 183 days (or more) is taxed differently under the Act than an individual who is factually resident in Canada throughout the same period of time and has subsequently become a non-resident. In particular, an individual who is factually resident in Canada for part of a year is only taxed on his or her worldwide income for that part of the year, in accordance with the rules under section 114. An individual who is deemed to be resident in Canada pursuant to paragraph 250(1)(a) is liable for tax on his or her worldwide income throughout the year.

1.33 The CRA considers any part of a day to be a **day** for the purpose of determining the number of days that an individual has sojourned in Canada in a calendar year. However, it is a question of fact whether an individual who is not resident in Canada is **sojourning** in Canada. An individual is not automatically considered to be sojourning in Canada for every day (or part day) that the individual is present in Canada; the nature of each particular stay must be determined separately. To sojourn means to make a temporary stay in the sense of establishing a temporary residence, although the stay may be of very short duration. For example, if an individual is commuting to Canada for his or her employment and returning each night to his or her normal place of residence outside of Canada, the individual is not sojourning in Canada. On the other hand, if the same individual were to vacation in Canada, then he or she would be sojourning in Canada and each day (or part day) of that particular time period (the length of the vacation) would be counted in determining the application of paragraph 250(1)(a). In distinguishing a **commuter** from a **sojourner**, relevance should be placed on the country in which an individual spends his or her time away from work. In other words, an individual who comes to Canada for work purposes may nevertheless be considered sojourning in Canada if that individual does not leave the country to spend his or her time away from work.

...

Notes and Questions

1. Paragraphs 250(1)(b) to (f) deal with Canadians and their families who are abroad in some official capacity. See paragraphs 1.34 to 1.35 of Income Tax Folio S5-F1-C1 and Interpretation Bulletin IT-106R3: Crown Corporation Employees Abroad (November 19, 2002).
2. Inconsistent treatment resulting from the application of paragraph 250(1)(c) is illustrated by the case of *Laramée v. M.N.R.*, [1976] C.T.C. 2152, 76 D.T.C. 1116 (T.R.B.), where the taxpayer, a teacher, was a member of the Public Service Commission who was sent to teach at an Armed Forces base in Germany. The Tax Review Board held that she was a federal employee and, therefore, within paragraph 250(1)(c), whereas other teachers abroad were not, because they were school board employees and not federal employees.
3. Paragraph 250(1)(d) deems those who perform services for a "prescribed international development assistance program of the Government of Canada" to be resident in Canada throughout the taxation year. The taxpayer need not be directly employed by the program to fall within the scope of paragraph 250(1)(d) as was shown in *Marois v. M.N.R.*, [1979] C.T.C. 2174, 79 D.T.C. 18 (T.R.B.).
4. Paragraph 250(1)(e) was repealed in 1998. It provided that a "spouse ... living with that person [the deemed resident]" would also be a deemed resident. What is the policy underlying this change? Note that a child of a deemed resident who is dependent for support generally assumes, subject to income limitations, the Canadian tax status of his or her parent.

3. Part-Time Residence (section 114)

Section 114 provides special rules for calculating the taxable income of an individual who is resident in Canada during only part of a taxation year.

The provision is an exception to the rule in subsection 2(1) that a person resident in Canada at any time in a taxation year is taxed on world income for the whole year. In order for an individual to establish part-time residence in Canada, the facts must disclose either that the individual commenced to reside or ceased to reside in Canada.

SCHUJAHN v. M.N.R.
[1962] C.T.C. 364, 62 D.T.C. 1225 (Exch. Ct.)

[In 1954, the appellant, an American citizen and an employee of a U.S. corporation with world-wide affiliations, was transferred from Minneapolis, U.S.A., the head office of the corporation, to Toronto to take charge of the operations of a Canadian subsidiary. The appellant and his family moved to Toronto where he purchased a house and lived from 1954 to August 2, 1957 on which date he was recalled and returned to the parent company in Minneapolis on what he was told by company officials was a permanent basis. His wife and one son remained in Toronto in their home in order to facilitate the sale of the house which took place in February 1958. The appellant maintained small bank accounts and a car for his wife in Toronto. Upon his return to Minneapolis, the appellant rejoined his club as a resident member, having resigned from his club in Toronto, and after his wife and son's arrival in Minneapolis in February, 1958, bought a house in Minneapolis. Between August 2, 1957 and the end of 1957, the appellant was in Toronto on three occasions, once on his way on a business trip to England, once on his return trip, and the third time during the Christmas holidays. The question for determination was whether the appellant ceased to be a resident in Canada for tax purposes on August 2, 1957 (and therefore entitled to the benefits of section 29 [now 114] of the Income Tax Act) or remained a resident in Canada for the whole of the year 1957.]

Noël J.: ...

The appellant admits that for the taxation year 1957, which is in appeal, up until August 2, 1957, he was a resident in Canada for income tax purposes within the meaning of Section 139(4) of the *Income Tax Act*. However, he submits that when he left Toronto on August 2, 1957, to take another appointment in the United States, he then ceased as of that date to be a resident of Canada and that, consequently, he is entitled to the benefits of Section 29 [now 114] of the *Income Tax Act* and should not report as income the revenue he has earned in the United States from August 2, 1957 to December 31, 1957.

... It is quite a well settled principle in dealing with the question of residence that it is a question of fact and consequently that the facts in each case must be examined closely to see whether they are covered by the very diverse and varying elements of the terms and words "ordinarily resident" or "resident". It is not as in the law of domicile, the place of a person's origin or the place to which he intends to return. The change of domicile depends upon the will of the individual. A change of residence depends on facts external to his will or desires. The length of stay or the time present within the jurisdiction, although an element, is not always conclusive. Personal presence at some time during the year, either by the husband or by the wife and family, may be essential to establish residence within it. A residence elsewhere may be of no importance as a man may have several residences from a taxation point of view and the mode of life, the length of stay and reason for being in the jurisdiction might counteract his residence outside the jurisdiction. Even permanency of abode is not essential since a person may be a resident though travelling continuously and in such a case the status may be acquired by a consideration of the connection by reason of birth, marriage or previous long association with one place. Even enforced coerced residence might create residential status. ...

[His Lordship then quoted from the judgment of Rand J., in Thomson and referred to the difference in procedure between U.K. and Canadian tax cases.]

...The evidence here discloses that the taxpayer's house in Toronto was occupied by the appellant's wife and child until February 1958 when it was sold; at all times from August 2, 1957, until the end of the 1957 taxation year he had a home where he could return at any moment as of right; he in fact returned on three occasions: before going to Europe on a business trip, then on his way back and a few days around Christmas. A car belonging to him but used by his wife, remained in Toronto until the latter's departure; he maintained two bank accounts, one for his mortgage payments on the house in Toronto and the other for his wife's household expenses. On the other hand, in July 1957, he put up his house in Toronto for sale, resigned his membership in a Toronto club, transferred all his personal belongings, clothes and hobbies to Minneapolis, reapplied and obtained resident membership in his club in Minneapolis, brought his own car back and allowed his wife to stay in Toronto as caretaker for the home and in order to ensure its sale.

The majority of the cases reviewed dealt with taxpayers whose original abode was either in the United Kingdom or Canada and who took up residence in other countries. As pointed out by Taschereau, J., in the *Thomson* case [[1946] C.T.C. 51 at p. 58]:

> Moreover in the majority of these cases, the taxpayer was held liable not because his visits to England were of such a nature that they were considered sufficient to qualify him as a "resident", but for the reason that he had never ceased to be a resident of England, and that his occasional absence had never deprived him of the status of British resident.

In the present instance we are dealing with the case of a man whose original residence was in the United States; he was sent to Canada to take charge of a new operation for his company and once the Canadian company was properly set up and running smoothly, he was called back to the parent company to take over new responsibilities and there and then, but for the sale of his house in Toronto, severed himself entirely from Canada.

From the evidence, I am satisfied that the only reason why the appellant's wife and son remained in Toronto until February 1958 was for the sole purpose of ensuring the sale of the house and that the retaining of two bank accounts, one for the mortgage payments and the other for his wife's household expenses, as well as the use of one of his cars by his wife, was a logical consequence of the necessary means taken by him to sell his house in Toronto.

The three visits made by the appellant during the period under review were, as far as the Christmas visit is concerned, of such a singular occurrence and as far as the stop-overs, of such a transitory and incidental nature, that I fail to see how this could be construed as implying residence in Canada. I would see here the simple gesture of a husband who has changed residence but visits with his family when going through the city where they had to temporarily live ...

Had the retention of the house in Toronto and the fact that the appellant's wife and child remained there been indicative of something other than that of wishing to sell the house without sustaining too great a loss, I would be inclined to hold as a matter of fact that the appellant had two residences for taxation purposes, one in Toronto and another in Minneapolis, U.S.A. However, such is not the case, indeed from the evidence it appears that as of August 2, 1957 the house in Toronto became, as far as the appellant is concerned, merely a house to sell and his wife and son remained there for that sole purpose, departing as soon as it was sold.

I therefore feel that the appellant, in this case, has established to my satisfaction that he had on August 2, 1957 divorced himself completely from his residence in Canada and that the fact of his wife and son remaining in Canada until the sale of his house was explained in a satisfactory manner. For the reasons which I have set forth above, I am of the opinion that the appellant must succeed and I therefore find that the appellant did not reside in Canada from August 2, 1957 to December 31 of that year and that, therefore, he is entitled to the deductions provided by Section 29 of the *Income Tax Act*. Therefore, there will be judgment allowing the appeal and declaring that the appellant is entitled for the year 1957, but from August 2, 1957 only, to the deductions provided by Section 29 of the *Income Tax Act*. The appellant is also entitled to the costs of the appeal.

Note

The Act contains a number of significant provisions that apply when a taxpayer ceases to be resident in Canada or commences to be resident in Canada. These rules are found in section 128.1 of the Act.

Paragraph 128.1(4)(b) provides that a taxpayer who ceases to be resident in Canada is deemed, immediately before becoming non-resident, to have disposed of each property owned by the taxpayer at that time for proceeds equal to fair market value and to have reacquired the property after becoming non-resident for the same amount. Hence accrued increases in value of properties held by the taxpayer before departure will be realized and taxed (departure tax). Certain properties are excepted from the deemed disposition. They are generally those that will be subject to tax in

Canada even though they are held by non-residents. The main exceptions are real or immovable property situated in Canada, and property of a business carried on in Canada by a taxpayer. In addition, property owned by an individual on previously becoming a resident of Canada or inherited after becoming resident is excluded if the individual was resident in Canada during the ten year period preceding the cessation of residence for 60 months or less.

The departure tax, as it has been labeled, prevents residents who leave Canada from avoiding the payment of income tax in respect of their properties unless the properties fall within the excepted categories (and the taxpayer is an individual). If the properties fall within the recognized exceptions, the individual's liability for tax is deferred until the actual disposition of the property or a subsequent deemed disposition.

When a taxpayer becomes resident in Canada, the taxpayer is deemed by paragraph 128.1(1)(b) to have acquired at that time each property owned by the taxpayer at a cost equal to its fair market value. This deemed acquisition cost establishes a base from which gains or losses on a subsequent disposition of the property in Canada are calculated. There are specific exemptions for certain types of property.

See Chapter 7 for further discussion.

4. Ordinarily Resident (subsection 250(3))

Subsection 250(3) states that a reference to a person resident in Canada includes a person who was at the relevant time ordinarily resident in Canada. The courts have failed to clarify the relationship between the meaning of "resident" in subsection 2(1) and "ordinarily resident" in subsection 250(3). B. Hansen in "Individual Residence," 1977 *Conference Report* (Toronto: Canadian Tax Foundation, 1978), 682 has said (at 693):

> ... "ordinarily resident" should be narrower than "resident". Any situation where an adverb qualifies an adjective must lead to this result. This is clearly the attitude of Rand J. in *Thomson v. M.N.R.,* where he stated that "ordinarily resident" has a "restricted significance". In fact, if "resident" was given its fullest connotation it should encompass any sort of residence be it "casual", "transitory", "permanent", or "ordinary". In other words, technically the two phrases mean the same thing. However, from a practical point of view, in my view "ordinarily resident" has a wider scope than "resident". Where a court considers whether a taxpayer is "resident" in Canada, there is a natural tendency to focus on the taxation year in question. I believe it is this factor which has occasionally led courts to suggest that physical presence is essential to a finding of residence in any one taxation year. On the other hand, "ordinarily resident" permits the court to review a taxpayer's activities over a period of years. [footnote omitted]

Since Hansen's article was published, the number of cases in which taxpayers have been found to be "ordinarily resident" in Canada has increased. See, for example, *The Queen v. Sherwood, supra*; *Rajotte v. M.N.R.*, [1979] C.T.C. 2555, 79 D.T.C. 436 (T.R.B.); *Saunders v. M.N.R.*, [1980] C.T.C. 2436, 80 D.T.C. 1392 (T.R.B.); and *Roy v. M.N.R.*, [1983] C.T.C. 2644, 83 D.T.C. 576 (T.R.B.).

The use of the term "ordinarily resident" to widen the scope of "resident" gained importance with the decision in the following case.

THE QUEEN v. K. F. REEDER
[1975] C.T.C. 256, 75 D.T.C. 5160 (F.C.T.D.)

Mahoney J.: ...

The issues in this appeal are whether or not the defendant was "not resident in Canada" as that phrase is used in section 114 of the *Income Tax Act* between March 29 and December 1, 1972, and, if it is found that he was resident in Canada during that period, whether the Income Tax Convention between Canada and France relieves him of the liability to pay income tax to Canada in respect of that period. The facts are not in dispute.

The defendant was born in Canada in 1947 and resided here continuously until and since the period in issue. He graduated in civil engineering in 1970, at the age of 23, and was employed from June through December 1970 in Sherbrooke, Quebec and from January 1, 1971 until March 1, 1972 in Alexandria, Ontario. He married in October 1970 and was, prior to the period in issue, living with his wife in an apartment in Alexandria.

On February 16, 1972 he was offered employment by Michelin Tire Manufacturing Company of Canada Limited (herein called "Michelin Canada"). The relevant portions of the offer follow:

> We would like you to begin employment with the Company on March 13, 1972, at our plant at Granton, Pictou County, Nova Scotia. For two days we would like to introduce you to the Canadian Company, and answer your questions on your training and future. We will then ask you to spend your initial training period with the Company in France.
>
> ...
>
> We undertake, of course, to pay your fare, and if your training is to be more than six months, we will pay that of your family should you wish them to accompany you, together with an allowance to cover your basic living expenses. However, we would ask you to go alone to France for the first month, to facilitate your installation there.
>
> It is anticipated that following training, you shall be employed in Nova Scotia, and the Company agrees to pay your removal costs from your present location to Nova Scotia.

> We wish to inform you that we have a full Canadian style benefits plan which is compulsory for all our employees. Details of this and your participation in it, as well as vacation particulars, plus other benefits, will be given at a later date.
>
> ...
>
> With your acceptance, we will require the address and account number of your bank to which you wish us to send your salary.

The defendant accepted the offer, resigned his Alexandria position effective March 1, gave up his apartment March 16, presented himself in Granton March 27 and left for France on March 29.

After leaving Alexandria, the defendant and his wife visited and stayed with friends and relatives in Canada until their respective departures. Their furniture and household effects were stored with a commercial storage company in Ottawa, Ontario. After an unsuccessful effort to sell his car, the defendant stored it in a rented garage in Saint John, New Brunswick. From March 27 to 29, the defendant stayed at a motel in New Glasgow, Nova Scotia. His wife followed him to France on April 27.

The defendant had been covered by his previous employer under the Ontario Health Insurance Plan. He did not cancel that coverage when he terminated but simply allowed it to lapse. The defendant was not covered under the counterpart Nova Scotia plan until his return to Canada.

The correct corporate name of the "Company in France" referred to in the offer of Employment is not in evidence. I will, for convenience, refer to it as Michelin France.

Immediately upon arrival in France, the defendant commenced work for Michelin France at Clermont. He bought a motorcycle and stayed in a hotel. On April 14, in anticipation of his wife's arrival, he bought a car and on April 23 he rented a fully furnished apartment complete with dishes and linen. He operated his vehicles on the authority of his Ontario driver's licence. He took out his insurance in France.

The defendant maintained a bank account at New Glasgow, Nova Scotia, in which, throughout his absence from Canada, Michelin Canada deposited his pay cheques. The expense allowance paid him by Michelin France covered ordinary living expenses. Unusual outlays, like the down-payment on the car, were drawn from the New Glasgow bank account by cheques cashed for him by Michelin France. Their child was born on July 21. All medical expenses in connection with the confinement and any others incurred in France were paid by Michelin France. The evidence does not disclose whether Michelin France was reimbursed by Michelin Canada.

The Michelin France establishment at Clermont closed for vacation all of August. The defendant was offered two weeks paid vacation with the option of an unpaid vacation for the balance of the month or to work elsewhere in Europe. He chose the latter and was employed in Germany from August 14 to September 14. He sold the motorcycle before going to Germany. His wife and child accompanied him and they lived in a furnished apartment. On returning to France, the defendant was assigned to a plant at Tours. He then gave up the apartment in Clermont and took another in Tours.

He worked in France and Germany as an ordinary production worker on the various machines and processes which he was expected to supervise when he returned to Canada although he was paid at the supervisor's rate. The length of his stay was determined both by the necessity of mastering the operations he was to oversee and by the fact that the Michelin Canada plant was not complete and those operations had not yet begun in Canada. It would appear, however, that it was intended that the stay be at least six months since that was the term necessary to obligate Michelin Canada to pay his wife's passage to France which, in fact, it did.

The arithmetic of the calculation of tax is not in issue and it is not, therefore, necessary to recite section 114 in full. Suffice it to say, the section provides for a calculation that results in a reduced tax liability, from that imposed on a taxpayer resident in Canada throughout the entire taxation year.

The Act does not define the word "resident". It does however expand its meaning somewhat. *[Mahoney J. cited subsection 250(3).]*

The bulk of judicial prose generated on the subject of fiscal residence has related to the peripatetic lifestyle of the leisurely wealthy — the jet setters of yesteryear. In *Levene v. Commissioners of Inland Revenue,* [1928] A.C. 217, per Viscount Sumner at 227, the taxpayer

> ... continued to go to and fro during the years in question, leaving at the beginning of winter and coming back in summer. His home thus remained as before. He changed his sky but not his home. On this I see no error in law in saying of each year, that his purpose in leaving the United Kingdom was occasional residence abroad only. The occasion was the approach of an English winter and when with the promise of summer here that occasion passed away, back came Mr. Levene to attend to the calls of interest, of friendship and of piety.

In *P.W. Thomson v. M.N.R.*, [1946] S.C.R. 209, per Rand, J. at 225; [1946] C.T.C. 51 at 64-5; 2 D.T.C. 812, the taxpayer's

> ... ordinary residence throughout the year 1940 was indisputably within a strip of North America bordering on the Atlantic and running from Florida to New Brunswick. In that area, enabling him to keep pace with a benign climate, he

> had at least two and possibly three dwelling places, each of which coupled with his presence for the time being constituted, so far as he had any, his home. When he moved to East Riverside, he moved not only himself but that home; ambulatory over a considerable part of the continent, it became residence where so set up. From each radiated his living and interests and from them in turn he might make occasional departures or visits or temporary stays amounting even to limited residence.

It would be artless to think that these lifestyles were not tailored, to some extent at least, with pertinent income tax laws very much in mind.

While the defendant here is far removed from the jet set, including any possible imputation of a preconceived effort to avoid taxation, the factors which have been found in those cases to be material in determining the pure question of fact of fiscal residence are as valid in his case as in theirs. While the list does not purport to be exhaustive, material factors include:

(a) past and present habits of life;
(b) regularity and length of visits in the jurisdiction asserting residence;
(c) ties within that jurisdiction;
(d) ties elsewhere;
(e) permanence or otherwise of purposes of stay abroad

The matter of ties within the jurisdiction asserting residence and elsewhere runs the gamut of an individual's connections and commitments: property and investment, employment, family, business, cultural and social are examples, again not purporting to be exhaustive. Not all factors will necessarily be material to every case. They must be considered in the light of the basic premises that everyone must have a fiscal residence somewhere and that it is quite possible for an individual to be simultaneously resident in more than one place for tax purposes.

The general effect of the authorities was succinctly stated by Estey, J. in the *Thomson* case:

> A reference to the dictionary and judicial comments upon the meaning of these terms indicates that one is "ordinarily resident" in the place where in the settled routine of his life he regularly, normally or customarily lives.

The defendant was at a stage in life when he was highly mobile. He was able, willing, even eager, to travel. In that, he was not atypical of his contemporaries and the relevant factors must be considered in that context. It is not contested that he was, before March 29, 1972, and has, since December 1, 1972, been resident in Canada. Throughout, his ties of whatever description have all been with Canada, save only those ties, undertaken during the term of his absence, which were necessary to permit him and his family to enjoy an acceptable and expected lifestyle while in France. That absence was temporary even though, strictly speaking, indeterminate in length. The ties in France were temporarily undertaken and abandoned on his return to Canada.

I am satisfied that had the defendant been asked, while in France, where he regularly, normally or customarily lived, Canada must have been the answer. I find that the defendant was resident in Canada throughout all of 1972. Since he paid no income tax in France, section 126 of the Act is not in play; however, it remains to be determined whether he is exempted from paying income tax to Canada by virtue of the *Canada-France Income Tax Convention Act*, 1951, S.C. 1951, c. 40. ...

[Mahoney J. found that Mr. Reeder was not exempt by virtue of the treaty provisions.]

Notes and Questions

1. Compare the position taken by Mahoney J. in *Reeder* with that of the CRA in Income Tax Folio S5-F1-C1, *supra*. Are there any important differences?
2. *Robert Leslie Midyette v. The Queen*, [1985] 2 C.T.C. 362, 85 D.T.C. 5565 (F.C.T.D.) centred on the question whether a person ordinarily resident in Canada within subsection 250(3) was deemed to be resident in Canada. If so, this would have allowed Mr. Midyette to deduct moving expenses associated with a move outside Canada under the provisions of section 62 as modified by former section 63.1. McNair J. held that the taxpayer did not come within the provision. He said (at 369-70; 5570):

> Dickson, J. gave this excellent and succinct explanation of the purpose of a deeming clause in *R. v. Sutherland,* [1980] 2 S.C.R. 451 at 456:
>
> > The purpose of any "deeming" clause is to impose a meaning, to cause something to be taken to be different from that which it might have been in the absence of the clause.
>
> Driedger, *Construction of Statutes* (2nd ed.) concludes his discourse of the meaning of "deemed" with this cautionary note at 27-28:
>
> > The purpose to be served by a deeming clause must always be borne in mind, for it obviously could not serve any purpose other than that stated in the statute that contains it.
>
> Viewed in this light, it is my opinion that subsection 250(3) of the Act is not a deeming clause and that the plain meaning of the words used therein bespeaks an intention to extend any narrow or limited signification of residence in the sense of actual

physical presence at any given time to the circumstantial concept of the person who has centralized his ordinary mode of living at some place in Canada or has maintained a sufficient nexus or connection therewith as to be logically regarded as being ordinarily resident in Canada, even though physically absent therefrom. In my view the subsection is not capable of being strained beyond the plain and proper meaning of the words to read as though a person ordinarily resident in Canada shall be deemed to be "a person resident in Canada" so as to come within the deeming scope of section 250, which is the construction for which the plaintiff contends. The linchpin of subsection 250(3) has failed to hold. And now the final point.

The modernized principle for the interpretation of fiscal legislation is well stated by Estey, J. in *Stubart Investments Limited v. The Queen,* [1984] 1 S.C.R. 536 at 578; [1984] C.T.C. 294 at 316; 84 D.T.C. 6305 at 6323:

> While not directing his observations exclusively to taxing statutes, the learned author of *Construction of Statutes* (2nd ed., 1983), E. A. Driedger, put the modern rule succinctly (at p. 87):
>
> > Today there is only one principle or approach, namely, the words of an Act are to be read in their entire context and in their grammatical and ordinary sense harmoniously with the scheme of the Act, the object of the Act, and the intention of Parliament.

In my opinion, the plain meaning of the words of section 63.1 read in conjunction with those of section 250 in their entire context and in keeping with the object and spirit of the Act indissolubly links the deemed "taxpayer" to the person "deemed to have been resident in Canada" within the rubric of subsections 250(1), (2) and (4) and more particularly to those sorts of persons described in paragraphs (a), (b), (c) and (d) of subsection 250(1) thereof.

3. The deductibility of moving expenses incurred by a taxpayer in circumstances similar to that in *Midyette* is now specifically ensured by paragraph (c) of the definition of "eligible relocation" in section 248 (this rule was contained within section 64.1 until 1998). See the discussion, in Chapter 8, of the special deductions under subdivision e of Division B of Part I of the Act.
4. What are the income tax consequences for an individual who is resident at the same time in Canada and another country under the relevant domestic law? What if Canada has a tax treaty with the other country asserting residence jurisdiction to tax? See, for example, Article IV of the *Canada-U.S. Tax Convention* and the material in Part IV of this chapter.
5. What is the effect and purpose of subsection 250(5)? Although the original version of this provision applied only to corporations (see Part II. B below), the rule was amended in 1998 such that it now applies to all persons. For analysis see *Allchin v. The Queen, supra*, and paragraphs 1.37-1.38 of Income Tax Folio S5-F1-C1, *supra.*

Problem

Y is a commercial pilot employed by Air Canada. She is based in Toronto and flies both domestic and international routes. Y is divorced, with two adult children, who live in Calgary and Winnipeg. Her ex-spouse and her mother live in Toronto.

Y is a high-income individual subject to a high effective tax rate. Not surprisingly perhaps, she has been approached by a financial adviser with the following plan intended to eliminate her Canadian tax liability:

(1) sell her home in Toronto and purchase a condominium in Buffalo, New York;

(2) transfer title to a cottage in Northern Ontario to her mother;

(3) obtain Costa Rican citizenship and a passport, along with a vacation home in that country;

(4) transfer all Canadian bank accounts to the United States;

(5) resign membership in all Canadian social clubs; and

(6) give up season tickets to the Toronto Symphony and the Toronto Maple Leafs hockey club.

Y would live in Buffalo and would spend 3 months of the year in Costa Rica. Aside from being extremely pleasant, the Costa Rican residency is required to maintain her citizenship and passport. Y would fly only international routes for Air Canada out of Toronto. She would stay with her mother, her ex-spouse, or friends when she must stay in Toronto either before or after flights. Summer months would be spent at the Northern Ontario cottage.

Y has an interest in a pension plan with Air Canada. The plan is administered by a Canadian financial institution. She also has an interest in a mutual fund administered by a Canadian subsidiary corporation of the same financial institution and an interest in several life insurance policies issued by a Canadian insurer. Y maintains her Ontario Health Insurance Plan membership card and receives all medical care in Toronto.

Y has asked for your opinion regarding the effectiveness of this tax plan. In addition to considering the issue of Canadian residency, you should consider Y's possible Canadian tax liability as a non-resident. In this respect, see the material in Part III of this chapter.

B. Corporations

1. General

Under the Act, a corporation is considered to be a "person" and a "taxpayer". This approach is consistent with the general legal principle that a corporation is an entity separate from its shareholders. As a separate taxpayer, a corporation may be a resident or non-resident of Canada for income tax purposes.

The residence of a corporation is determined by applying statutory rules, case law principles, and tax treaty provisions. The statutory rules and case law principles are discussed in this part. The application of tax treaties is discussed in Part IV of this chapter.

2. Deemed Residence (subsection 250(4))

Paragraph 250(4)(a) deems a corporation incorporated in Canada to be resident in Canada throughout a taxation year. The rule does not apply to corporations incorporated in Canada before April 27, 1965. These corporations are deemed to be resident in Canada under paragraph 250(4)(c) only if, at any time in the taxation year or at any time in a preceding taxation year ending after April 26, 1965, they were resident in Canada (presumably under the case law principles) or carried on business in Canada. See Part III. B, on the meaning of "carrying on business".

3. Case Law Principles

The concept of corporate residence developed in the case law remains relevant for corporations incorporated in Canada before April 27, 1965 and for corporations incorporated or continued outside Canada. For example, a corporation incorporated in Bermuda might be resident in Canada according to Canadian case law principles.

Both U.K. and Canadian courts have held that a corporation is resident where its "central management and control" is located, a concept drawn from the following case.

DE BEERS CONSOLIDATED MINES LIMITED v. HOWE
[1906] A.C. 455 (H.L.)

[The appellant company carried on a diamond-mining business in South Africa. The company was registered there. Regular meetings were held at the head office in South Africa, where some of the directors resided. However, the majority of the directors resided in England, and the meetings in London were those at which much of the company's business was conducted.]

Lord Loreburn L.C. ...

The question in this appeal is whether the De Beers Consolidated Mines Limited ought to be assessed to income tax on the footing that it is a company resident in the United Kingdom. ...

Under the 2nd section of the Income Tax Act 1853, schedule D, any person residing in the United Kingdom must pay on his annual profits or gains arising or accruing to him "from any kind of property whatever, whether situate in the United Kingdom or elsewhere", and also "from any profession, trade, employment, or vocation, whether the same shall be respectively carried on in the United Kingdom or elsewhere." Now, it is easy to ascertain where an individual resides, but when the inquiry relates to a company, which in a natural sense does not reside anywhere, some artificial test must be applied.

Mr Cohen propounded a test which had the merits of simplicity and certitude. He maintained that a company resides where it is registered and nowhere else. If that be so, the appellant company must succeed, for it is registered in South Africa.

I cannot adopt Mr Cohen's contention. In applying the conception of residence to a company, we ought, I think, to proceed as nearly as we can upon the analogy of an individual. A company cannot eat or sleep, but it can keep house and do business. We ought, therefore, to see where it really keeps house and does business. An individual may be of foreign nationality, and yet reside in the United Kingdom. So may a company. Otherwise it might have its chief seat of management and its centre of trading in England under the protection of English law, and yet escape the appropriate taxation by the simple expedient of being registered abroad and distributing its dividends abroad. The decision of Kelly C.B. and Huddleston B. in *Calcutta Jute Mills v. Nicholson* and *Cesena Sulphur Company v. Nicholson* [(1876), 1 Ex. D. 428], now 30 years ago, involved the principle that a company resides, for purposes of income tax, where its real business is carried on. Those decisions have been acted upon ever since. I regard that as the true rule; and the real business is carried on where the central management and control actually abides.

It remains to be considered whether the present case falls within that rule. This is a pure question of fact, to be determined, not according to the construction of this or that regulation or by-law, but upon a scrutiny of the course of business and trading.

The case stated by the commissioners gives an elaborate explanation of the way in which this company carried on its business. The head office is formally at Kimberley, and the general meetings have always been held there. Also the profits have been made out of diamonds raised in South Africa, and sold under annual contracts to a syndicate for delivery in South Africa upon terms of division of profits realized on resale between the company and the syndicate. And the annual contracts contain provisions for regulating the market in order to realize the best profits on resale. Further, some of the directors and life governors live in South Africa, and there are directors meetings at Kimberley, as well as in London. But it is clearly established that the majority of directors and life governors live in England; that the directors' meetings in London are the meetings where the real control is always exercised in practically all the important business of the company, except the mining operations. London has always controlled the negotiation of the contracts with the diamond syndicates, has determined policy in the disposal of diamonds and other assets, the working and development of mines, the application of profits, and the appointment of directors. London has also always controlled matters that require to be determined by the majority of all the directors, which include all questions of expenditure except wages, materials, and such like at the mines, and a limited sum which may be spent by the directors at Kimberley.

The commissioners, after sifting the evidence, arrived at the two following conclusions, *viz*: (1) that the trade or business of the appellant company constituted one trade or business and was carried on, and exercised by, the appellant company within the United Kingdom, at their London office; (2) that the head and seat and directing power of the affairs of the appellant company were at the office in London, from whence the chief operations of the company, both in the United Kingdom and elsewhere, were in fact controlled, managed, and directed.

These conclusions of fact cannot be impugned, and it follows that this company was resident within the United Kingdom for purposes of income tax, and must be assessed on that footing. I think, therefore, that this appeal fails. ...

[Lord James of Hereford gave a separate concurring judgment; Lord Macnaghten and Lord Robertson concurred.]

Lord Loreburn's formulation of the test of corporate residence has been adopted in various Canadian decisions, most notably *Birmount Holdings Ltd. v. The Queen*, [1978] C.T.C. 358, 78 D.T.C. 6254, 1978 CarswellNat 198 (Fed. C.A.).

Central management and control usually refers to the exercise of power and control by the board of directors of a corporation. In rare cases the board of directors may have abdicated the exercise of its powers. "[T]he businesses ... [may be] conducted in a manner irregular, unauthorized, and perhaps unlawful" as stated by Viscount Simons in *Unit Construction Co. Ltd. v. Bullock* (1959), [1959] 3 All E.R. 831, [1960] A.C. 351 (H.L.) at 362. Nonetheless, he continues at 363, "it is the actual place of management, not that place in which it ought to be managed, which fixes the residence of a company."

Viscount Simons justifies the rule at 363 as follows:

> If it were not so, the result to the Revenue would be serious enough. In how many cases would a limited company register in a foreign country, prescribe by its articles that its business should be carried on by its directors meeting in that country, and then claim that its residence was in that country though every act of importance was directed from the United Kingdom?

Consider, however, the problems of proof faced by revenue authorities who allege the board of directors of a corporation does not exercise central management and control of a corporation. Note in *Unit Construction* that the taxpayer itself argued that the central management and control of the particular corporations were not in their boards of directors in order to obtain a better tax result for the corporate group. See also some early Canadian cases: *Sifneos v. M.N.R.*, [1968] Tax A.B.C. 652, 68 D.T.C. 522; and *Bedford Overseas Freighters Limited v. M.N.R.* (1968), 68 D.T.C. 529; aff'd [1970] C.T.C. 69, 70 D.T.C. 6072 (Exch. Ct.).

The degree of central management and control that must be located in a jurisdiction before residence can be established remains a difficult question. It is sometimes suggested that the decision in *Unit Construction* indicates that a subsidiary corporation in a multinational corporate group, the directors of which implement strategies and policies of the parent corporation, is managed and controlled by the parent corporation (and thus resident in the same jurisdiction). However, more recent cases have demonstrated that corporate residence depends on the exercise of board powers at the level of each corporation in a corporate group, even if that exercise is somewhat ceremonial. In other words, a shareholder exercising influence over a corporation's board of directors is not the same as usurping their decision-making. See, for example, *Wood v. Holden*, [2006] EWCA Civ 26, [2006] 1 W.L.R. 1393 (Eng. C.A.).

If the central management and control of a corporation is located in two or more jurisdictions, the corporation can potentially have more than one residence. See, for example, *Swedish Central Ry. Co. Ltd. v. Thompson,* [1925] A.C. 495. The likelihood of such a finding depends on whether a court requires merely that some part of the mind and management of the corporation be located in a jurisdiction, or requires instead that there be final and supreme authority located in a jurisdiction. Application of the first approach would greatly increase the likelihood of a corporation being considered resident in a particular jurisdiction since it would only be necessary to locate some part of the superior authority there. Canadian courts have not indicated clearly which is the preferred approach.

C. Trusts and Estates

Sections 104 to 108 of the Act deal with the taxation of trusts and estates, which are taxed separately in a manner similar to, but not identical with, the tax treatment of individuals.

In *Fundy Settlement v. Canada*, 2012 SCC 14, [2012] 3 C.T.C. 265, 2012 D.T.C. 5063, the Supreme Court of Canada clarified that the factual residence of a trust, like that of a corporation, is "where 'its real business is carried on', which is where the central management and control of the trust actually takes place" (paragraph 15, quoting *De Beers*). While we might expect that the central management and control of a trust would be in the jurisdiction where the trustee resides, *Fundy Settlement* showed that this will not always be the case. The Tax Court judge found that the Canadian resident beneficiaries exercised central management and control in Canada and that the trustee, a corporation resident in Barbados, had a limited role and little responsibility. Accordingly, the trust was held to be resident in Canada.

Even where a trust is factually not a resident of Canada under the central management and control test, it may be deemed to be resident in Canada by section 94 of the Act for certain purposes, including computing the income of the trust and determining its liability for income tax under Part I of the Act.

III. NON-RESIDENTS: CANADIAN-SOURCE INCOME

A. Introduction

Non-residents are subject to Canadian tax if they earn income in Canada or receive income from Canada.

Part I of the Act deals with non-residents who earn income in Canada from employment, the carrying on of a business, or the disposition of taxable Canadian property (subsection 2(3)). These non-residents file an income tax return in the same way as all residents of Canada and are taxed on this income at the relevant marginal rates.

Part XIII of the Act deals with a non-resident's income from property that is situated in Canada. Section 212 provides that, where certain payments are made by a resident of Canada to a non-resident, such as interest, rents and royalties, a withholding tax must be paid on the gross amount by the payer on behalf of the recipient non-resident. Non-residents do not file a tax return with respect to this income, although they may do so in some circumstances (sections 216-217).

B. Non-Residents Employed or Carrying on Business in Canada or Disposing of Taxable Canadian Property

Subsection 2(3) provides that, where a non-resident was employed in Canada, carried on a business in Canada, or disposed of a taxable Canadian property at any time in a taxation year or a previous year, the non-resident shall pay an income tax on taxable income earned in Canada determined in accordance with Division D (sections 115 and 116) of Part I of the Act. Why are the words "or a previous year" included?

The first point to note is the number of defined terms appearing in subsection 2(3). Examine the definitions of "employed", "employee", "employer", and "employment" in subsection 248(1), "Canada" in section 255, "taxation year" in section 249, "carrying on business" in section 253, and "taxable Canadian property" in subsection 248(1).

1. Employed in Canada

Employment in Canada requires that the non-resident be employed and carry out at least some part of the employment in Canada. The residence of the employer is irrelevant. The part of the income allocated to Canada is included in the non-resident's income earned in Canada for the particular taxation year. If the non-resident employee resides in a country with which Canada has a bilateral tax treaty, the treaty will typically restrict Canada's right to tax unless the employee is present in Canada for a period or periods exceeding 183 days, the remuneration is paid by a person resident in Canada, or the remuneration is borne by a "permanent establishment" in Canada.

2. Carrying on Business

A number of cases have considered the meaning of the term "business" (defined in subsection 248(1)) and the phrase "carrying on business". Under subsection 2(3), it must be determined that a non-resident was carrying on a business and that the business was carried on in Canada.

The meaning of "carrying on business in Canada" is illustrated in *Grainger* and *McKinlay Transport*, both reproduced below. In considering whether a non-resident exercised a trade within the United Kingdom, the U.K. courts have given substantial weight to whether the contract that formed the basis of the transaction was made in the U. K. under common law contract principles. It should be noted, however, that the meaning of "carrying on business in Canada" is extended by section 253 of the Act, in particular to include situations where a non-resident "solicits orders or offers anything for sale in Canada through an agent or servant".

A non-resident found to be carrying on business in Canada, either under case law principles or the extended definition in section 253, ultimately may be exempt from Canadian income tax because of a tax treaty between Canada and the jurisdiction in which the non-resident resides. Canada's tax treaties, like most bilateral tax treaties, generally require that to be taxable the non-resident must be carrying on business through a "permanent establishment" situated in Canada.

GRAINGER & SON v. GOUGH (SURVEYOR OF TAXES)
[1896] A.C. 325 (H.L.)

Lord Herschell:

My Lords, the appellants are wine merchants carrying on business in the City of London. They act as agents in this country for certain purposes, which will require careful consideration, for M. Louis Roederer, a wine merchant, whose chief place of business is at Reims, in the Republic of France. Two questions arise for determination: first, whether M. Roederer exercises any trade, employment, or vocation within the United Kingdom; and next, whether if so, he is liable to be assessed to the income tax in the name of the appellants as being his agents within the meaning of s. 41 of 5 & 6 Vict. c. 35.

The first step to be taken is to ascertain with accuracy what are the facts in the present case. ... The nature of the appellants' agency is plain enough. They canvass for orders for Roederer's wine, and receive a commission on all orders from Great Britain, if executed. The functions of the sub-agents whom they appoint are the same. When orders are received they "are transmitted by the appellants to Louis Roederer at Reims, and he exercises his discretion as to executing the said orders". This is the statement in the original case. In the amendment it is stated that "orders are sought by them as agents on behalf of Louis Roederer as their principal, that such orders are given by customers to Messrs. Grainger & Son, and received by them; but the appellants allege that the said Louis Roederer in his arrangements with them as his agents has reserved a right to reject any particular order". The commissioners add that, in their opinion, this right is, in fact, intended to protect Roederer in cases where there is doubt as to the pecuniary position of the customer giving the order, and that no special notice is given to the customer of the right so reserved.

The commissioners appended to the amended case certain documents produced by the appellants as specimens indicative of the manner and style of business transacted by them on behalf of M. Louis Roederer. One of them is an order addressed to the appellants. It commences — "Please ship per G. & J. Porter," and then specifies certain quantities and descriptions of Roederer's wine. The appellants in reply to this write: — "In compliance with your obliging order of yesterday we shall have much pleasure in requesting M.L. Roederer to ship for your account, through Messrs. G. & J. Porter of Calais," the wine specified.

Taking the findings together, I think it clear that no contracts to sell wine were ever made by the appellants on behalf of Roederer. All that they did was to transmit to him the orders received, and until he had agreed to comply or complied with them there was no contract. He was under no obligation to the persons giving the orders to the appellants to execute any one of them. I think the statement in the original case was, having regard to the documents, a perfectly correct one, and that it is not accurate to speak of Roederer's having reserved to himself a right to reject any particular order. An order given to a merchant for the supply of goods does not of itself create any obligation. Until something is done by the person receiving the order which amounts to an acceptance there is no contract. It is clear that the appellants in receiving an order did not accept or purport to accept it on Roederer's behalf so as to constitute a contract, and that they had no authority so to do.

...

Taken in connection with the facts stated, I think the finding that the appellants "are agents in Great Britain for the sale" of Roederer's wine means no more than this, that they are engaged by him to canvass for custom, to seek to obtain from persons in this country orders for his wine. The wine is sold to the customers as it lies in Reims cellar or "pris en Cave". The customer pays the cost of packing and carriage from the cellars and takes all risk. The delivery to the purchaser, therefore, takes place in France. The wine is invoiced to the purchaser in Roederer's name as vendor, the invoice being sent to the appellants, and by them transmitted to the purchaser. The amounts due in respect of the wines sold are sometimes collected by the appellants on behalf of Roederer, and sometimes remitted direct to him. When the payments are made to the appellants in cash or in cheques on London banks, cashed by them, the moneys so received are credited to Roederer against the amount of the commission due to them and charges incurred by them on his behalf. ...

All that the appellants have done in this country on behalf of M. Roederer has been to canvass for orders, to transmit to him those orders, when obtained, and in some cases to receive payment on his behalf. Beyond this he has done nothing in this country, either personally or by agents. Does he, then, exercise his trade within the United Kingdom? It has been sometimes said that it is a question of fact whether a person so exercises his trade. In a sense this is true; but, in order to determine the question in any particular case, it is essential to form an idea of the elements which constitute the exercise of a trade within the meaning of the Act of Parliament. In the first place, I think there is a broad distinction between trading *with* a country and carrying on a trade *within* a country. Many merchants and manufacturers export their goods to all parts of the world, yet I do not suppose any one would dream of saying that they exercise or carry on their trade in every country in which their goods find customers. When it is said, then, that in the present case England is the basis of the business, that the wine was to be consumed here, and that the business done would remain undone but for the existence of the customers in England, I cannot accept this as proof that M. Roederer carries on his trade in this country. It would equally prove that every merchant carries on business in every country to which his goods are exported. Moreover, the proposition would be just as true if English customers gave their orders personally at Reims. Something more must be necessary in order to constitute the exercise of a trade *within* this country. How does a wine merchant exercise his trade? I take it, by making or buying wine and selling it again, with a view to profit. If all that a merchant does in any particular country is to solicit orders, I do not think he can reasonably be said to exercise or carry on his trade in that country. What is done there is only ancillary to the exercise of trade in the country where he buys or makes, stores, and sells his goods. Indeed, I do not think it was contended that the solicitation of custom in this country by a foreign merchant would in all cases amount to an exercise by him of his trade "within" this country. The learned counsel shrank from maintaining that if, for example, he sought custom only by sending circulars to persons residing here, or advertised in British newspapers, he could on that account be said within the meaning of the statute to be exercising his trade in this country. They relied on the circumstances that he had appointed agents in this country who regularly solicited and received orders and transmitted them to M. Roederer. If in each case the other circumstances are the same, the contract of sale being made abroad, and the delivery taking place there, I find myself quite unable to see how the mode in which orders are solicited and obtained, whether by an agent or by circulars or advertisements, can make the difference, and cause the trade in the one case to be exercised, and in the other not to be exercised within this country. If the mere employment by a foreign merchant of an agent to solicit and to transmit orders does not amount to an exercise of his trade in this country, I do not think that it becomes an exercise of his trade here if, in addition, the agent in some cases receives the price of the goods sold for transmission to his principal. Still less does it appear to me material that in the London Post Office Directory there was inserted by the authority and with the knowledge of Grainger & Son (but not, I may observe, so far as is stated, by the authority or with the knowledge of Roederer): "Roederer, Louis, Reims, champagne merchant (Grainger & Son, agents), 21 Mincing Lane."

For these reasons I have come to the conclusion that the taxing section does not apply in the present case. This view renders it unnecessary to decide the question whether the appellants are agents within the meaning of s. 41 of 5 & 6 Vict.

It was said that if M. Roederer was not liable to income tax in this case it would give foreigners an unfair advantage over British traders. This does not appear to me to be the case. I do not think such considerations can legitimately influence our decision; but if they are to be introduced, I think it would be much more prejudicial to British traders if we were to lay down that, though the sale and delivery of their goods take place in this country only, they carry on business in every other country from which they obtain orders for their goods through solicitation by an agent, or, indeed, in any other way; for I do not think it can logically or reasonably make any difference in principle what the method of soliciting custom may be.

I think the appeal should be allowed with costs both here and in the Courts below.

[Lord Watson and Lord Davey gave separate judgments allowing the appeal; Lord Macnaghten concurred in their judgments; and Lord Morris delivered a dissenting judgment.]

Following *Grainger*, the U.K. courts have considered factors other than the place where the contract was made in deciding whether a non-resident exercised a trade or carried on business in the jurisdiction. See, for example, *F. L. Smidth and Company v. Greenwood,* [1921] 3 K.B. 583 (C.A.); aff'd [1922] 1 A.C. 417 (H.L.) where the taxpayer, a Danish firm resident in Copenhagen, manufactured and dealt in cement-making and other similar machinery for export all over the world. The taxpayer had an office in London in the charge of a qualified engineer who was a full-time servant. He received inquiries for machinery, sent to Denmark particulars of the work which the machinery was required to do, including samples of materials to be dealt with, and, when the machinery was supplied, he was available to give the English purchaser the benefit of his experience in assembling it. The contracts between the respondents and their customers were made in Copenhagen and the goods were shipped f.o.b. Copenhagen. The Commissioners held that the respondents exercised a trade within the United Kingdom and were assessable to income tax. This decision was reversed on appeal by Rowlatt J.

Atkin L.J. in the Court of Appeal dismissed the further appeal and in so doing made the following observations (at 593):

> There are indications in the ... cases that it is sufficient to consider only where it is that the sale contracts are made which result in a profit. It is obviously a very important element in the inquiry, and if it is the only element the assessments are clearly bad. The contracts in this case were made abroad. But I am not prepared to hold that this test is decisive. I can imagine cases where the contract of resale is made abroad, and yet the manufacture of the goods, some negotiation of the terms, and complete execution of the contract take place here under such circumstances that the trade was in truth exercised here. I think that the question is, Where do the operations take place from which the profits in substance arise?

The location where "the operations take place from which the profits in substance arise" may lead a court to consider such factors as the place of solicitation, manufacture, delivery, payment and provision of support services, if any. Additionally, a court may look to determine whether the non-resident maintained a bank account, inventory, branch office, agent and telephone listing in Canada.

See also *Cutlers Guild Limited v. The Queen,* [1981] C.T.C. 115, 81 D.T.C. 5093 (F.C.T.D.) where Dubé J. remarked (at 117; 5095):

Whether or not a taxpayer is carrying on a business in another country is a question of fact to be determined in each case. Courts have ruled that the place where sales, or contracts of sale, are effected is of substantial importance. However, the place of sale may not be the determining factor if there are other circumstances present that outweigh its importance. *Firestone Tyre & Rubber Co. Ltd. v. Lewellin* (1957), 37 T.C. 111.

Another test emanating from the jurisprudence is "Where do the operations take place from which the profits arise?" Soliciting orders in one country may only be ancillary to the exercise of a trade in another country *F.L. Smidth & Co. v. Greenwood* (1922), 8 T.C. 193. Certain authorities establish that activities and operations other than contracts for sale constitute the carrying on of a business, specially where these respective activities and operations produce or earn income. While income may be realized through sales, it may not arise entirely from that one activity or operation STJ in *Wm. Wrigley Jr. Company Limited v. Provincial Treasurer of Manitoba,* [1947] C.T.C. 304; confirmed by the Privy Council, [1949] CTC 377. Purchasing of merchandise in one country (ie Japan) with the view of trading in it elsewhere (Canada) does not, of course, constitute an exercise of the trade in the former country *Grainger & Son v. William Lane Gough,* [1896] A.C. 325.

More recent Canadian cases have tended to look at a multiplicity of criteria in attempting to determine if a non-resident is carrying on a business in Canada. In the following cases, note the attempts of the Courts to apply both the common law principles with respect to carrying on business as well as the extended definition in section 253.

G.L.S. LEASCO INC., McKINLAY TRANSPORT LTD. v. M.N.R.
[1986] 2 C.T.C. 2034, 86 D.T.C. 1484 (T.C.C.)

Brulé, T.C.J.:—...

The only issue involved in these appeals is the determination of whether G.L.S. was carrying on business in Canada during the years in question.

...

G.L.S. Leasco is a corporation incorporated under the laws of the State of Michigan and is a wholly-owned subsidiary of Centra Inc., a corporation incorporated under the laws of the State of Delaware, one of the United States of America.

McKinlay is a corporation incorporated under the laws of the Province of Ontario. McKinlay is a wholly-owned subsidiary of Central Cartage Co., a corporation incorporated under the laws of the State of Michigan, one of the United States of America. Central Cartage Co. is a wholly-owned subsidiary of Centra Inc.

G.L.S. carries on the business of leasing transportation equipment, transportation terminal properties and other capital assets associated with the transportation business in the United States. During each of its 1977 to 1980 taxation years it leased transportation equipment in Canada, primarily to McKinlay.

G.L.S. submitted that it carried on business in Canada throughout each of its 1977 to 1980 taxation years and realized the following income or losses:

TAXATION YEAR	INCOME OR (LOSSES)
1977	($53,069.80)
1978	($690,545.71)
1979	$80,081.74
1980	$558,149.86

G.L.S. computed that its taxable income for each of its 1979 and 1980 taxation years was nil. This computation resulted from the appellant deducting its non-capital losses realized by its 1977 and 1978 taxation years from the income the appellant earned in its 1979 and 1980 taxation years.

By reassessments, notices of which were posted on October 29, 1983, the respondent determined that G.L.S. did not maintain a permanent establishment in Canada during each of its 1977 to 1980 taxation years and therefore the respondent stated that the original losses claimed by the appellant were "disallowed".

...

McKinlay carries on the business as a common carrier in Canada. During the 1976 taxation years G.L.S. entered into an agreement with McKinlay whereby G.L.S. agreed that the appellant would be a preferred and primary customer of its Canadian business and that the appellant would have a right of first refusal for the rental of all transportation equipment owned by G.L.S. and used by it in Canada.

During each of McKinlay's 1976 to 1980 taxation years, McKinlay leased transportation equipment owned by G.L.S. and used it in its Canadian business. As a result of these rentals, McKinlay made rental payments (net of the seven percent Ontario retail sales tax) to G.L.S.

By assessments, notices of which were each posted on the 27th day of August, 1982, the respondent assessed McKinlay in respect of each of its 1976 to 1980 taxation years and stated that it had failed to deduct or withhold 15 percent of the rental payments made to G.L.S. and had failed to remit the said 15 percent amount to the Receiver General as required by Part XIII of the *Income Tax Act.*

...

Counsel for the appellants pointed out that if G.L.S. is found to have carried on business in Canada then the appeal of McKinlay should be allowed. In support of his argument for G.L.S. it was said that no one factor can determine whether or not a company is carrying on business in Canada. All the facts must be reviewed. It was admitted that G.L.S. did not have much infra-structure in Canada, and such was not necessary because of its captive customers from its group of related companies.

G.L.S. has no outward commercial trappings in Canada but such were not necessary because of its *modus operandi.* G.L.S. maintained that what it did was purchase equipment in Canada, lease this out and receive rent. This, G.L.S. maintained was its business. While it did not have a permanent office in Canada, nor employees, it did have the use of an office at McKinlay Transport, and it used this office physically for signing documentation and as a mailing address. There was a bank account in Canada and two employees of McKinlay helped G.L.S. as required.All purchase orders were made in Canada under the name "G.L.S. Leasco-Canada", paid for in Canadian dollars and delivery of the equipment taken in Canada for use in Canada. Because of the streamlined nature of the group of Centra Inc. companies, the accounting was done in the United States, cheques were issued from there, requisitioned by a Mr. Mason, a vice-president of the parent company, who supervised the Canadian operation, and who did much of the supervision while in Canada on frequent trips.

The decision by G.L.S. to carry on business in Canada arose when McKinlay had trouble financing for new equipment needed in its Canadian operation. G.L.S. then made a survey and proposed to carry on in Canada as they did in the United States. This involved a separate Canadian operation albeit controlled by United States employees and adapted to a part of the United States computer accounting system which included some 24 separate companies. A memo showing this analysis for a proposed Canadian operation was introduced as evidence to the Court. This memo outlined some 34 steps required to set up a proper Canadian operation and included a cash flow sheet for the transaction with a projected seven-year analysis.

...

There is no argument that the question of whether or not a company is "carrying on business" is a matter of fact. This is supported by the authorities. Mr. Justice Urie in the recent Federal Court of Appeal decision of *The Queen v. Gurd's Products Company Limited*, [1985] 2 C.T.C. 85; 85 D.T.C. 5314 reiterated at 92 (D.T.C. 5319) what was said as far back as 1881 in the case of *Erichsen v. Last* [(1881), 4 T.C. 422, 8 Q.B.D. 414] by the Master of the Rolls as follows:

> Now the facts as I understand them are clear enough, and the question is whether what the Company do amounts to carrying on trade within the meaning of the Act. I do not think there is any principle of law which lays down what carrying on of trade is. There are a multitude of incidents which together make the carrying on a trade, but I know of no one distinguishing incident which makes a practice a carrying on of trade, and another practice not a carrying

on of trade. If I may use the expression, it is a compound fact made up of a variety of incidents.

The facts, of course, must be considered in accordance with the provisions of the *Income Tax Act.* "Business" is defined in subsection 248(1) as including a profession, calling, trade, manufacture, or undertaking of any kind whatever, and an adventure in the nature of trade. The meaning of "carrying on business" in Canada has been more particularly defined by section 253 of the Act which provides:

> 253. Where, in a taxation year, a non-resident person
>
> ...
>
> (b) solicited orders or offered anything for sale in Canada through an agent or servant whether the contract or transaction was to be completed inside or outside Canada or partly in and partly outside Canada,
>
> he shall be deemed, for the purposes of this Act, to have been carrying on business in Canada in the year.

Further, when a non-resident company is involved, the provisions of the *Income Tax Act* in paragraph 2(3)(b) and in subparagraph 115(1)(a)(ii) make the company liable for tax if the company is carrying on business in Canada.

Counsel for the Minister agreed that the substance of the operation must be examined, and in so doing he said that it would be seen that not all the necessary indicia were present to conclude that G.L.S. was carrying on business in Canada. From the cases listed above by the respondent, two points were put forth as being the basis of certain decisions.

Where an agent was the representative in the foreign jurisdiction, and that was the only principal factor, as in the *Standard Ideal* and *Loeck* cases (*supra*) the courts held that the respective appellants were not carrying on business in the other jurisdiction.

The place where the contract was made was held to be paramount in the *Erichsen, Grainger, Geigy, Smidth, Firestone* and *Capitol Life cases (supra).*

In *United Geophysical Co. of Canada v. M.N.R.*, [1961] Ex. C.R. 283, [[1961] C.T.C. 134], there is a closer comparison to be made to the present case. This Exchequer Court decision dealing with the rental of equipment to a Canadian subsidiary was carrying on business in Canada and not the United States parent. There were five points raised by the Court:

(1) The governing contract was made in the United States.

(2) The amount of the rental was to be determined in the United States.

(3) Rental was to start when the equipment was supplied to the appellant in the United States.

(4) Payment was received in the United States.

(5) Rental was as a result of the use by the appellant in Canada of the equipment and not because the U.S. company was obliged to service or repair it in Canada.

For these reasons the Court held that the parent United States company was not carrying on business in Canada and that the Canadian subsidiary was liable for withholding tax on the payments made to the parent. This, it was argued by the respondent, is the situation in the present case and should be taxed accordingly.

There are many distinguishing factors in the *United Geophysical* case and the G.L.S. case. First of all G.L.S. executed by its officer the contracts in Canada as was stated in evidence and supported by exhibits. Where the amount of the rental was determined it was not disclosed in evidence. Mr. Mason the vice-president of the appellant McKinlay's parent company, Central Cartage Co., was also responsible for G.L.S. He was involved in all aspects of the purchasing and leasing of equipment both in the United States and Canada. He frequently used the office provided to G.L.S. by McKinlay in Windsor and whether or not the amounts of rental were determined in Windsor or Detroit was not disclosed, but in any event I do not consider this significant.

All purchases of equipment were made in Canada and delivered to McKinlay. All purchase orders were labelled "G.L.S. Leasco-Canada". Payments were made by McKinlay in Canadian dollars to a Canadian bank account of G.L.S. but forwarded to Detroit where all the accounting took place. There is a similarity in that the equipment was used in Canada and rental payments resulted.

...

The decision of *The Queen v. Gurd's Products (supra)* dealt with a similar problem and the Federal Court of Appeal held that a business was being carried on in Canada because the company:

(1) intended to carry on business in Canada;

(2) established a bank account in Canada;

(3) purchased product in Canada and earned a profit therefrom;

(4) had an official agent in Canada; and

(5) its associates involved were not dealing at arm's length.

While the Minister's counsel suggested that the *Gurd's* case does not set out the guiding principles of what carrying on business in Canada should be, I believe there is enough similarity to reach a similar conclusion.

G.L.S. intended to do business in Canada as was set out in evidence and supported by a memorandum provided to the Court. There was a Canadian bank account and the equipment was all purchased in Canada. While there was no official agent in Canada, two employees of McKinlay were always available to help G.L.S. in Canada. In addition Mr. Mason spent a great deal of time in Canada supervising the operation. In the *Gurd's* case, the company did not have an office, no phone number, no employees and all decisions and negotiations were performed in the United States. Still the Federal Court of Appeal said the company was carrying on business in Canada.

G.L.S. in the United States did not have any employees, offices, signs, nor telephones yet carried on business there, as was admitted by the Minister. In Canada the office made available by McKinlay was used physically by Mr. Mason, all documentation used this address, mail was received there, such address was accepted by the Government, and a sales tax exemption permit was given to G.L.S. treating the company as doing business in Canada.

While perhaps not all the form was present, the substance of doing business in Canada was evident in this case with the result that the appeals of both appellants are allowed with costs, to be taxed on a party and party basis.

Appeals allowed.

SUDDEN VALLEY INC. v. M.N.R.

[1976] 2 F.C. 462, 68 D.L.R. (3d) 376, [1976] C.T.C. 297, 76 D.T.C. 6178 (F.C.T.D.), aff'd. (1976), [1977] 1 F.C. 617, 72 D.L.R. (3d) 158, [1976] C.T.C. 775, 76 D.T.C. 6448 (Fed. C.A.)

[Sudden Valley Inc. appealed from a decision of the Tax Review Board which held it was not carrying on business in Canada. The company was a U.S. developer selling recreational land in Washington State near Seattle when a downturn in a large local industry and the extremely high unemployment depressed the land market so much as to make it practically non-existent. The Company therefore turned to the nearby Vancouver market. It leased office space in Vancouver and hired telephone operators to contact local people and to set up dinners and social occasions in which the land in Washington State was pitched. During this time invitations were issued to Canadians to visit Sudden Valley and some did.

The corporation had no licence to sell real estate in Canada and indeed the evidence showed not one sale was made in Canada. There was also no evidence of any legally binding offer to purchase ever having been obtained at any time in Canada. Offers were made and deposits were accepted in the United States. No *agent or representative in Canada had any authority to accept an offer or bind the company. The advertising campaign in Canada, which cost $1,000,000, resulted in over 70 per cent of the lots being purchased by Canadian residents from the Vancouver area.*

It is noteworthy that the advertising did not state that there was land for sale but merely invited Canadians to visit the beauties of Sudden Valley, which was proximate to and easily accessible from Vancouver. The potential buyer was given a gate pass which allowed access to the Sudden Valley Development.]

Addy J. (F.C.T.D.):

The Company, which had not made any profit during the years in question, claims that it is taxable and should be taxed as a company actually doing business in Canada and, therefore, be subject to tax pursuant to ... section 2(3)(b) of the current Act. It alleges that the interest payable on the outstanding balances is reasonably attributable to the business of selling land and is taxable under ... Part I and not Part XIII of the current Act.

...

Section 253(b) of the current Act does change the common law to some extent and the matter therefore turns on whether the facts of the present case fall within the provisions of that section.

...

In considering whether the plaintiff was "soliciting orders" in Canada, I do not agree that the words can be extended to include "a mere invitation to treat." Soliciting orders means that orders must be sought and attempts made to obtain them within the jurisdiction and the word "offer," in my view, must be given its ordinary meaning in contract law, that is, a binding offer which, if accepted, would create a contract between the offeror and the offeree. This becomes all the more evident when one considers that the question at common law depended specifically on the existence of a binding contract and that the section was intended to amend the former common law to the effect that the contract need not be made within the jurisdiction. ... From a glance at the evidence in this case, which I have summarized above, it is abundantly clear that no offer was obtained and no attempt was made to obtain any in Canada and it is equally clear that nothing was offered for sale in Canada either through an agent or otherwise. One must therefore conclude that the real estate business of the plaintiff was not being carried on in Canada even within the extended meaning given to that term by section 253(b).

The only activity carried on in Canada by the plaintiff was that of attempting to induce Canadians to visit Sudden Valley in the hope that some might eventually become interested in buying property there. There was no Canadian income from this business undertaking and the payment of interest on the agreements resulting from its United States real estate business is without a doubt much too remote from the Canadian activities.

Appeal dismissed.

[The taxpayer's appeal to the Federal Court of Appeal was dismissed. The Court referred to Justice Addy's reasons.]

Notes and Questions

1. In *Maya Forestales S.A. v. The Queen* (2006), [2007] 2 C.T.C. 68, 2008 D.T.C. 6100 (F.C.A.), a Costa Rican company offering portions of its Costa Rican plantation for sale in Canada through two Canadian agents was considered to be soliciting orders within the meaning of paragraph 253(b), and thus carrying on business in Canada, even though the contracts were concluded in Costa Rica. Dussault J. in the Tax Court observed that "Parliament's intent in enacting [paragraph 253(b)] was to subject non-resident persons to Canadian tax provided they carry out a minimum amount of commercial activity within Canada's borders" and that the words "solicits orders or offers anything for sale" are very broad; the subject matter "can be tangible or intangible, moveable or immoveable, personal or real" ([2005] 2 C.T.C. 2655, 2005 D.T.C. 514 (T.C.C.) at paragraph 34).
2. The development of electronic commerce has presented a considerable challenge to the maintenance of the source jurisdiction to tax business income. Does a U.S.-based retailer carry on business in Canada where orders are placed by Canadian consumers over the Internet? Assume the retailer stores all products in the United States in a warehouse, with delivery made in Canada. What if the retailer's product is simply downloaded by the consumer?
3. Even where a non-resident carries on business in Canada, Canada's tax treaties restrict further the source jurisdiction to tax by requiring that the non-resident maintain a "permanent establishment" in Canada. See, for example, Articles V and VII of the *Canada-U.S. Tax Convention*. How does the concept of a permanent establishment affect Canada's source jurisdiction to tax income from electronic commerce? What if the supplier is based in a low-tax country with which Canada has not concluded a tax treaty? See the material in Part IV of this chapter.
4. These jurisdictional issues are discussed briefly in *Electronic Commerce and Canada's Tax Administration — A Report to the Minister of National Revenue from the Minister's Advisory Committee on Electronic Commerce* (April 1998), at paragraphs 4.2.2.2 and 4.2.2.4. For more recent international analysis, see Organisation for Economic Co-operation and Development (OECD), *Report on the Attribution of Profits to Permanent Establishments* (July 2008) and OECD, *2010 Report on the Attribution of Profits to Permanent Establishments* (July 2010).

TARA EXPLORATION AND DEVELOPMENT CO. LTD. v. M.N.R.
[1970] C.T.C. 557, 70 D.T.C. 6370 (Exch. Ct.)

[The facts as to the residence of the company were as follows: although the company was incorporated in Ontario before April 7, 1965, it had no employees at its head office in Toronto, and no person resident in Canada had the authority to contract or conduct business on its behalf. All management and executive decisions were made in Ireland. The company maintained a bank account in Toronto, but all important decisions in respect of it were made in Ireland by the company's president who was resident and domiciled in Ireland.]

Jackett P.:

This is an appeal from assessments under Part I of the *Income Tax Act* for the 1965 and 1966 taxation years, in which the question is whether the respondent erred in assessing the appellant, a company incorporated under the laws of Ontario, on the basis that it had a taxable income for those years by reason of profits that it made on a purchase of shares in Gortdrum Mines Limited and the resale of those shares partly in the 1965 taxation year and partly in the 1966 taxation year.

[There were 180,000 shares which were held for approximately two years.]

There is no dispute as to whether the appellant made the profits in question or as to the amounts thereof.

The first problem to be solved is whether, looking only at Part I of the *Income Tax Act*, the profits in question are subject to tax. To resolve this problem, the following questions must be answered:

(a) Were the profits in question profits from a "business" within the meaning of that word as used in the *Income Tax Act*, as the respondent contends, or were they profits from realization of an investment of a capital nature, as the appellant contends? And

(b) Is the appellant subject to Part I of the *Income Tax Act* in respect of the two years in question, either

  (i) because the appellant was resident in Canada in those years so as to have been taxable under Part I by virtue of Section 2(1) of the *Income Tax Act*, as the respondent contends, and the appellant disputes, or

  (ii) because the appellant "carried on business in Canada" in those years so as to be taxable under Part I by virtue of Section 2(2) [2(3)] of the *Income Tax Act*, as the respondent contends and the appellant disputes?

If the answers to these questions are such that the assessments could be supported under Part I of the *Income Tax Act,* if that Act were the only law involved, the further problem will have to be solved as to whether the profits in question are "not subject to Canadian tax" by virtue of paragraph 1 of Article III of the agreement between Canada and Ireland that is set out in the Schedule to the *Canada-Ireland Income Tax Agreement Act*, 1955 (S.C. 1955, c. 10) read with the provisions of that statute.

...

[President Jackett assumed that what was involved was a "business" transaction because, in the light of the decided cases on the point, it was an adventure in the nature of trade, and decided that the appellant was not resident in Canada.]

The final question, in so far as the *Income Tax Act* is concerned, is whether the appellant "carried on business" in Canada in the taxation years in question so as to be taxable by virtue of Section 2(2) of that Act. To appreciate the problem that is raised, Section 2(2) should be read with Section 3 and Section 31(1) [now subsection 115(1)] in the light of Section 139(1)(e) [now subsection 248(1)]. Those provisions read as follows:

...

> 3. The income of a taxpayer for a taxation year for the purposes of this Part is his income for the year from all sources inside or outside Canada and, without restricting the generality of the foregoing, includes income for the year from all
>
> (a) businesses,
>
> (b) property, and
>
> (c) offices and employments.
>
> 31. (1) For the purposes of this Act, a non-resident person's taxable income earned in Canada for a taxation year is
>
> (a) his income for the year from all duties performed by him in Canada and all businesses carried on by him in Canada,
>
> minus
>
> (b) the aggregate of such of the deductions from income permitted for determining taxable income as may reasonably be considered wholly applicable and of such part of any other of the said deductions as may reasonably be considered applicable.
>
> 139. (1) In this Act,
>
> (e) "business" includes a profession, calling, trade, manufacture or undertaking of any kind whatever and includes an adventure or concern in the nature of trade but does not include an office or employment.

For the purpose of this discussion, I assume that the purchase and sale of Gortdrum shares was an "adventure ... in the nature of trade" so as to be a "business" within the meaning established by Section 139(1)(e). It follows that profits therefrom must be included, for the purposes of Part I of the *Income Tax Act*, in computing the appellant's "income", for each of the years in which such profits were made.

For the purpose of the question that arises concerning Section 2(2), I make two further findings of fact, namely:

> 1. The adventure in the nature of trade from which the profits in question arose took place in Canada. The shares were bought in Canada by a broker acting for the appellant and were sold in Canada by a broker acting for the appellant. This, in my opinion, establishes that the "adventure" was in Canada even though the appellant was a corporation resident outside Canada. (In my opinion, the fact that the officer of the appellant who communicated the appellant's instructions to the broker came to Canada to do so is irrelevant.)
>
> 2. The adventure in the nature of trade by which the appellant made the profits in question did not in itself constitute "carrying on business in Canada" within the ordinary meaning of the words "carrying on business" and was not part of a larger activity that falls within those words. It was an isolated transaction and it was not a part of the "business" for which the appellant had raised its capital or that it was actually carrying on. [Footnote deleted.]

On these facts, the question arises as to whether Section 139(1)(e) operates, not only to enlarge the definition of income in Section 3 to include profits from certain adventures, but also to enlarge the concept of "carrying on business" in the charging section to make non-residents subject to Canadian income tax when they have not actually been carrying on business in Canada but have had only an adventure in the nature of trade consisting of an isolated purchase and sale transaction that was carried out in Canada through brokers.

As far as I can recall, the statutory definition of "business" that operates to make it include an "adventure or concern in the nature of trade" has heretofore been used freely to expand the profits in respect of which a person resident in Canada is taxable but has never heretofore been used to apply Part I of the *Income Tax Act* to non-resident persons who do not, in fact, carry on business in Canada.

...

It follows that if, by virtue of Section 139(1)(e) of the *Income Tax Act*, a non-resident person who has made a profit from an adventure in the nature of trade in Canada is to be deemed to have "carried on business in Canada" for the purpose of the charging provision in Section 2(2) of that Act, that statutory definition will have gone beyond making explicit the scope of the "income" in respect of which residents were taxable under the old law and will have brought within the charging provisions of the new law a group of non-resident persons who were not previously subject to Canadian income tax law.

Nevertheless, if, properly understood, the statute has the effect of casting its net over a group of non-resident persons who would not have been subject to the *Income War Tax Act*, effect must be given to it.

Having revealed the possibly irrelevant background against which I see the matter, I turn to the problem of statutory interpretation involved, which is whether Section 2(2) can be read as requiring an income tax to be paid, not only upon the taxable income of a non-resident person who actually "carried on business in Canada" in a taxation year, but also on the taxable income of a non-resident person who "carried on" an "adventure ... in the nature of trade" in Canada in a taxation year. In other words, does Section 139(1)(e) permit the substitution of the words "adventure ... in the nature of trade" for the word "business" in Section 2(2) as well as in Section 3?

In considering this question, it is worthy of note that the *Income Tax Act* does contain a provision that provides that, where a non-resident person does certain things in Canada, he shall be deemed "to have been carrying on business in Canada". See Section 139(7) [now section 253] of the *Income Tax Act* which reads as follows:

> 139. (7) Where, in a taxation year, a non-resident person
>
> (a) produced, grew, mined, created, manufactured, fabricated, improved, packed, preserved or constructed, in whole or in part, anything in Canada whether or not he exported that thing without selling it prior to exportation, or
>
> (b) solicited orders or offered anything for sale in Canada through an agent or servant whether the contract or transaction was to be completed inside or outside Canada or partly in and partly outside Canada,
>
> he shall be deemed, for the purposes of this Act, to have been carrying on business in Canada in the year.

It has never been suggested to my knowledge that an isolated purchase and sale falls within this subsection.

With great doubt as to the correctness of my conclusion, I am of opinion that Section 139(1)(e) does not operate to make a non-resident person subject to Canadian income tax in respect of a profit from an adventure that otherwise does not amount to, and is not part of, a "business". With considerable hesitation, I have concluded that the better view is that the words "carried on" are not words that can aptly be used with the word "adventure". To carry on something involves continuity of time or operations such as is involved in the ordinary sense of a "business". An adventure is an isolated happening. One *has* an adventure as opposed to *carrying on* a business.

My conclusion is, therefore, that the appeal succeeds on the ground that the appellant does not fall within the charging section of the *Income Tax Act*.

...

Appeal allowed.

The Supreme Court of Canada (per Abbott, J.) dismissed the Minister's appeal, agreeing with the assumption that the profits were made from an adventure in the nature of trade but preferring to dispose of the appeal by applying the *Canada-Ireland Income Tax Agreement*. In this respect, the Court held that, since the profits were not attributable to a permanent establishment in Canada under Article I of the treaty, the taxpayer was not liable for tax. See [1972] C.T.C. 328, 72 D.T.C. 6288.

Subsequent cases have confirmed the view of the Exchequer Court in *Tara* that, although a taxpayer might engage in an adventure in the nature of trade and thus a "business" as defined in the Act, that is not the same thing as "carrying on business".

Paragraph 253(c) now provides that a non-resident is deemed to be carrying on business in Canada in respect of business income derived from the disposition of certain Canadian resource property, timber resource property, and real or immovable property situated in Canada. For dispositions of these types of property, section 253 supersedes the decision of the Exchequer Court in *Tara*. Any gain realized by a non-resident from an adventure or concern in the nature of trade involving such property will be liable to Canadian tax, subject to available treaty relief.

3. Disposition of Taxable Canadian Property

Paragraph 2(3)(c) provides the third category of income of a non-resident subject to tax: taxable capital gains from dispositions of "taxable Canadian property". This term is defined at length in subsection 248(1). Among other things, it includes real or immovable property situated in Canada, shares of unlisted or closely-held corporations and interests in certain trusts and partnerships where more than half of the value of the share or interest is derived from real or immovable property situated in Canada, and certain property used in a business carried on in Canada. Reference should be made to sections 115 and 116 and to the taxation of capital gains generally.

In general, anyone undertaking a real estate transaction should be aware of these provisions, since both the purchaser and vendor of real estate are affected. It is also important to consider the possible effect of the provisions of any tax treaties between Canada and other countries.

C. Non-Resident Withholding Tax

Non-residents are subject to tax on certain investment income derived from Canadian sources. Part XIII (sections 212 to 218.1) imposes a flat rate (generally 25 per cent) on the gross amounts specified therein. As mentioned earlier, Part XIII deals basically with property income whereas subsection 2(3) covers the business income, employment income and taxable capital gains of a non-resident.

Part XIII tax has three main aspects. First, a non-resident must be paid or credited, or deemed to be paid or credited, an amount by a person resident in Canada.

Second, the amount must be paid or credited as, on account of or in lieu of payment of, or in satisfaction of, specified types of amounts including management fees, some interest payments, dividends, rents, royalties, pension benefits, annuity payments, and estate or trust income. Third, specified percentages of the amounts are payable by the resident person as a withholding tax on behalf of the non-resident. However, a recipient of certain Part XIII payments (such as rent) may file a separate tax return in respect of them as though a resident of Canada. For a general discussion of the Canada Revenue Agency's interpretation of the provisions of Part XIII, see Information Circular 77-16R4: Non-Resident Income Tax (May 11, 1992). This circular also contains references to Interpretation Bulletins that deal with specific types of Part XIII payments.

Where a non-resident carries on business in Canada through a resident corporation, there are generally two levels of Canadian tax: once on the income as earned by the corporation, and again on any dividends paid by the corporation to the non-resident. Can a non-resident avoid the withholding tax on dividends by carrying on business through a Canadian branch? See section 219 of the Act which imposes a special additional tax (normally referred to as the "branch tax") on the after-tax profits of a branch at a 25 per cent rate. No tax is imposed under section 219 if the after-tax profits are reinvested in Canada.

The Part XIII withholding tax rate of 25 per cent is often reduced (or eliminated) by Canada's tax treaties, particularly for dividends, interest and royalties. The reduction varies depending on the treaty and the type of investment income. It is noteworthy that the *Canada-U.S. Tax Convention* was amended by the Fifth Protocol in 2007 (effective December 2008) to eliminate withholding tax on interest payments between residents of Canada and the United States.

IV. TAX TREATIES

A. Canadian Tax Treaty Network and the Foreign Tax Credit

To date, Canada has entered into some 92 bilateral tax treaties. The preamble to most of these treaties states that:

> The Government of Canada and the Government of [whatever country], desiring to conclude a convention for the avoidance of double taxation and the prevention of fiscal evasion with respect to taxes on income and on capital have agreed as follows: ...

There are, however, several other reasons for Canada's expanding network of tax treaties. They include promoting international trade and investment and, less commonly today, assisting developing nations to establish tax incentives for foreign investors.

1. Avoiding Double Taxation

The most commonly cited reason for Canada's tax treaty network is the one mentioned first in the preamble, namely, to avoid double taxation. Canada and many other countries also provide relief from double taxation by way of unilateral tax credits and exemptions. As we have seen in the first part of this chapter, residents of Canada are taxed on their worldwide income, while non-residents are taxed on income derived from sources in Canada. If we assume, albeit somewhat unrealistically, that all other countries in the world have exactly the same basis of liability for taxation as Canada, the potential for double taxation is obvious. For example, a resident of Canada who carries on business in Country A and receives investment income from Country B will be doubly taxed. All income, including the business income from Country A and the investment income from Country B, will be taxed in Canada. The business income will also be taxed in Country A, and the investment income will be taxed in Country B. Nevertheless, because the resident of Canada may be able to deduct the amount of foreign taxes from the amount of Canadian taxes (the foreign tax credit), there may be no double taxation, even if Canada has not concluded a tax treaty with either Country A or Country B.

The foreign tax credit provisions allow a taxpayer to claim a credit against "tax otherwise payable under Part I" of the Act in respect of income taxes paid to a foreign government. Subsection 126(1) provides that a taxpayer may claim a credit for income taxes paid to a foreign government in respect of "non-business income" not exceeding the lesser of the amount of foreign non-business income taxes paid for the taxation year and, roughly, the amount of Canadian tax payable on the income. The formula is as follows:

$$\text{tax otherwise payable under Part I} \times \frac{\text{foreign non-business income}}{\text{Division B income from all sources minus certain amounts}}$$

A similar formula is applied, with some significant modifications, to the calculation of foreign "business income". Constitutionally, the provinces cannot tax foreign business income received by individuals. Therefore, a calculation needs to be made regarding the section 120(1) federal surtax on individuals with business income not taxed in a province.

In the preceding example, if the tax levied on the business income by Country A is equal to the tax otherwise payable under Part I on the business income, and, if the tax levied on the investment income by Country B is equal to the tax otherwise payable under Part I on the investment income, the Canadian resident will pay no tax to the Canadian government. However, if the rate of foreign tax on the foreign income is lower than the rate of Canadian tax on the income, the Canadian tax will not be offset completely. If the rate of foreign tax on the foreign income is higher than the Canadian rate of tax, no foreign tax credit can be claimed for the excess. If the foreign income is business income, the unused foreign tax credit may be carried back three years and forward ten years. There is no carryover provision for foreign tax credits in respect of non-business income. Furthermore, the non-business income foreign tax credit of an individual is limited to 15 per cent of gross foreign income if the income is income from property other than real property. Foreign taxes in excess of 15 per cent are deductible in computing income under subsection 20(11).

In reality, the tax system of the other country is never a mirror image of the Canadian system. This may provide scope for tax planning, but it also may subject persons to overtaxation. One difficult problem occurs when the source rules of the other country treat certain income as derived from a particular source within that country and the source rules of Canada provide otherwise. This problem is dealt with to a limited extent in Canada's tax treaties. Most treaties provide rules that operate to determine the sources of dividends, interest, and royalties. In addition, the double taxation relief article of Canadian tax treaties generally provides that, if a country is permitted to tax profits, income or gains of a resident of the other country, then those profits, income or gains, as the case may be, are deemed to be from sources in the country.

In any discussion of how Canada's tax treaties eliminate double taxation, reference should be made to the competent authority provisions. Where a taxpayer feels aggrieved by the application of a treaty, the taxpayer may apply for redress to the competent authority (in the case of Canada, the Minister of National Revenue or an authorized representative) of the taxpayer's country of residence. The competent authority is then required, if the objection is justified and if there is no satisfactory unilateral solution, to attempt to resolve the case by mutual agreement with the competent authority of the other country. The right of appeal by a resident of a country to the competent authority is in addition to any rights under the domestic laws of either party to the treaty. The competent authority route provides an alternative to potentially lengthy and expensive litigation in both countries. In cases not provided for by the treaty, the competent authorities may also consult and reach agreements on rules, guidelines or procedures for the elimination of double taxation.

2. Preventing Tax Avoidance and Evasion

The prevention of fiscal evasion is another important reason for the conclusion of tax treaties. In this regard, a tax treaty will normally provide that the competent authorities of Canada and the other country shall exchange such information as is necessary for carrying out the provisions of the treaty or of the domestic laws of each country. Thus, for example, information may be exchanged between Canada and another country in connection with taxpayers not dealing at arm's length (e.g., a U.S. parent and its wholly-owned Canadian subsidiary), with a view to the proper allocation of revenues and expenditures according to the economic realities rather than according to the relative tax burdens of each jurisdiction. The treaties require that any information received by a party to a treaty pursuant to the treaty is to be treated in the same manner as information obtained under the taxation laws of that country. Even where Canada does not have a comprehensive tax treaty with another state, it may negotiate a Tax Information Exchange Agreement. To date, Canada has entered into such agreements with 22 countries.

3. Promoting International Trade

One of the most important, but often unexpressed, reasons for Canada to enter into a tax treaty with another country is to help promote the stability necessary for international trade with, and investment in, the other country. Hence, if the other country experiences budgetary or balance of payments problems, it will not be able to substantially change its tax system to the detriment of Canadian businesses or investors. Of course, tax treaties can be modified or terminated. In either case, however, taxpayers will normally get some advance notice. In addition, because a tax treaty enshrines the basis of liability, as well as some maximum rates of tax, the ability to tax cross-border transactions is effectively allocated between the treasuries of the two countries. The allocation of taxing powers is particularly important if Canada and the other country have differently developed economies. Canada was a net capital importer until the late 1990s and, until recently, has favoured higher levels of withholding taxes. Furthermore, in its dealings with less developed countries Canada has been inclined to permit them to levy high withholding taxes, sometimes unilaterally, and to provide foreign incentives for Canadian investors.

Tax treaties also promote international trade and investment by eliminating the right of a country to tax individuals or corporations whose activities are not closely connected to the country. Thus, treaties provide that residents of one country are not subject to tax on business profits derived from the other country unless they have a "permanent establishment" in the other country. In most treaties the term "permanent establishment" is defined as a fixed place of business through which the business of the non-resident is wholly or partly carried on, such as an office or a factory, and also extends to a dependent agent who has and habitually exercises authority to conclude contracts in the name of the non-resident. See, for example, Articles V and VII of the *Canada-U.S. Tax Convention*. If an American accountant flies into Halifax for a few weeks to consult on financial aspects of off-shore oil and gas exploration, the treaty will preclude Canadian tax unless according to Articles V and VII of the Convention the accountant has a "permanent establishment" in Halifax. In 2008, the tax treaty was amended to deem the provision of cross-border services to emanate from a permanent establishment in certain circumstances (see Article V, paragraph 9).

Finally, further reference should be made to Canada's previous efforts in its tax treaties with less developed nations to accommodate tax incentives granted by them to Canadians, known as tax sparing. A tax treaty between Canada and a developing country may provide that, for the purposes of the computation of the Canadian foreign tax credit, "tax paid" to the other country shall be deemed to include an amount equal to the amount that would have been paid as tax to the other country but for certain exemptions and deductions granted by that other country. The effectiveness of tax sparing has been questioned by the Organisation for Economic Co-operation and Development (OECD) and others. Canada and some other countries are phasing out such measures.

B. History and Development of Canada's Tax Treaties

The first Canadian income tax was introduced in 1917, but it was not until 1928 that a bilateral agreement was concluded for the elimination of double taxation. It consisted of an exchange of notes between Canada and the United States which provided for the relief from double taxation of shipping profits. In 1936, the two countries concluded a more formal agreement which dealt with rates of withholding tax on interest and dividends. That agreement was terminated in 1941 and replaced by the *Canada-U.S. Tax Convention*. This convention is generally considered to be Canada's first tax treaty.

During the period before the conclusion of the *Canada-U.S. Tax Convention*, a number of model tax conventions were developed — the first in 1928 — under the auspices of the League of Nations. It was not, however, until 1963 that the Fiscal Committee of the Organisation for European Economic Co-operation, later to become the Organisation for Economic Co-operation and Development (OECD), produced the first of the modern model treaties (the 1963 Draft Convention).

The 1963 Draft Convention consisted of 30 articles. A commentary was published on each article and member countries were permitted to express exception to or reservations concerning particular articles. The 1977 Model Convention (a new model treaty which essentially evolved from the 1963 Draft Convention and was adopted by the Council of the OECD in 1977) has generally been used as the basis for the conclusion or revision of tax treaties, even those involving countries that are not members of the OECD. Canada has been a member of the OECD since 1964, and has used the 1963 Draft Convention or the 1977 Model Convention as a basis for its tax treaties. In 1992, the OECD Model Convention was issued in looseleaf format. This change reflects a policy of periodic revisions to the Convention and its commentary. The OECD Model Convention has been substantially updated several times since then, most recently in 2014.

The United Nations also has a model tax convention. The 1980 *UN Model Tax Convention* was revised and updated in 2001 and again in 2011. Although the UN Model Convention is identical to the OECD Model Convention in most respects, it contains several provisions that reflect the interests of developing countries. The

OECD Model Convention reflects the interests of the member countries of the OECD, which includes the world's wealthiest countries.

Canada has not adopted the OECD Model Convention or its revisions without reservation. It has deviated from the Model Convention in two particular respects: (a) withholding taxes; and (b) non-discrimination.

1. Withholding Taxes

One of the assumptions underlying the OECD Model Convention is that all bilateral tax treaties will be concluded between two equally developed nations. Thus, the OECD Model Convention tends to reflect a capital and technology export bias. The interests of the country of residence are sometimes favoured over the interests of the country of source. Less developed, capital- and technology-importing nations may be penalized because the amount of withholding tax the source country may levy on investment income and royalties is limited.

As a former net capital- and technology-importer, Canada traditionally deviated in its treaties from the OECD Model Convention by insisting on withholding taxes on certain royalties and higher withholding tax rates on dividends and interest. More recently, however, in an attempt to attract foreign investment, and perhaps reflecting a different economic philosophy, the Canadian position has changed. The federal government is now prepared to reduce the withholding tax on direct dividends to 5 per cent. This change has been reflected in protocols to conventions with various countries, most notably the United States. The federal government is also prepared to eliminate its withholding tax on arm's length interest payments, as well as arm's length payments in respect of rights to use patented information, for information concerning scientific experience, and for the use of computer software.

Article XI of the *Canada-U.S. Tax Convention* now exempts most interest payments from withholding taxes. Article XI of the *Canada-U.K. Tax Convention* is a more limited provision. In any case, paragraph 212(1)(b) of the Act exempts from Part XIII tax, *inter alia*, all interest paid to arm's length persons, whatever country they are resident in, except for "participating debt interest" (defined in subsection 212(3)). This change was announced in conjunction with the Fifth Protocol amending the *Canada-U.S. Tax Convention*. Further, interest paid by the federal and provincial governments, municipalities, and certain Crown corporations to non-residents is exempt from withholding tax. These exemptions were introduced in attempts to reduce the cost of public-sector debt and the corporate cost of capital. Such exemptions would not be as necessary if the Part XIII withholding tax were fully creditable in the lenders' countries. Part XIII tax is assessed on gross interest, whereas most countries' foreign tax credits (and, it should be added, Canadian foreign tax credits) are calculated on the assumption that the foreign tax paid is based on net interest. Net interest is the amount by which the interest earned on a loan made by a financial intermediary exceeds the interest paid on money it has borrowed to make the loan.

2. Non-Discrimination

Canada has reserved its position on the non-discrimination article in the OECD Model Convention (Article 24). Essentially, the non-discrimination article in the OECD Model Convention prohibits discrimination on the grounds of nationality and, in certain circumstances, residence. The Act contains some provisions that, more or less, promote economic and cultural nationalism. It is noteworthy, however, that "Canadian-controlled private corporations" as defined in subsection 125(7) of the Act, which receive important high profile tax concessions, are not really *Canadian* controlled but Canadian *resident*-controlled corporations. Nationality does not matter.

The non-discrimination provisions of the *Canada-U.S. Tax Convention* are illustrative. Generally, Article XXV provides that citizens of a contracting state who are residents of the other contracting state shall not be subject to any more onerous taxation than resident citizens of the other contracting state in the same circumstances. Citizens of a contracting state who are non-residents of the other state, however, are entitled only to most favoured-nation treatment in the other state. Thus, an American citizen who is resident outside Canada and derives income from Canada is not entitled to the same treatment as Americans or Canadians resident in Canada; instead, such a person is entitled to the treatment accorded citizens of third countries who are not resident in Canada. Article XXV also provides most favoured-nation protection to foreign corporations. Hence, Canada can legitimately levy the branch tax (Part XIV of the Act). Paragraph 5 guarantees that residents of a contracting state carrying on business in the other state through a permanent establishment are entitled to the same treatment as residents of that state engaged in the same activities. Article XXV also forbids limitations on the deductibility of interest, royalties and other disbursements paid by a resident of a contracting state to residents of the other contracting state. An exception is made, however, for the Canadian thin capitalization rules.

C. Implementation of Canada's Tax Treaties

It is generally accepted that the executive of the Government of Canada has the power to enter into international treaties. However, the implementation of provisions of international treaties depends on the enactment of implementing legislation by the Canadian Parliament and provincial legislatures. Since all of Canada's treaties extend special tax concessions to residents of the other state and modify the tax liability of Canadian taxpayers, every tax treaty must be implemented by statute before it can be effective in conferring rights on taxpayers. The implementing statute for a tax treaty will typically annex a copy of the treaty as a schedule and provide:

> In the event of any inconsistency between the provisions of this Act or the Convention and the operation of any other law, the provisions of the Act and the Convention prevail to the extent of the inconsistency.

Canada's tax treaties do not apply to taxes imposed by the provinces. Therefore, there is the possibility that a province will impose taxes that conflict with the scheme of taxation of residents and non-residents worked out in any or all of Canada's tax treaties. For those provinces that levy their own individual or corporation income tax (Alberta levies its own corporation income tax and Quebec levies its own individual and corporation income tax), specific provisions are necessary to give recognition to international tax treaties. The Alberta and Quebec statutes contain provisions that incorporate all of the effects of a tax treaty.

Only Quebec has concluded a tax agreement with another country. Pursuant to Article 29, paragraph 10 of the *Canada-France Tax Convention*, which allows interested provinces to sign separate taxation agreements with the French government (to the extent that such agreements are not inconsistent with the federal treaty), Quebec and France entered into an agreement that became effective in 1988.

D. Interpretation of Canada's Tax Treaties

Even a brief examination of any of Canada's tax treaties will show that their simple and general drafting style is very different from the complex and quasi-mathematical style of the Act. In *H.P. Bulmer Ltd. v. Bollinger S.A.*, [1974] 2 All E.R. 1226 at 1237, Lord Denning discussed the differences between the interpretation of domestic legislation and the European Economic Community Treaty and its Regulations:

> The draftsmen of our statutes have striven to express themselves with the utmost exactness. They have tried to foresee all possible circumstances that may arise and to provide for them. They have sacrificed style and simplicity. They have forgone brevity. They have become long and involved. In consequence, the judges have followed suit. They interpret a statute as applying only to the circumstances covered by the very words. ...
>
> How different is this treaty. It lays down general principles. It expresses its aims and purposes. All in sentences of moderate length and commendable style. But it lacks precision. ...
>
> Seeing these differences, what are the English courts to do when they are faced with a problem of interpretation? They must follow the European pattern. No longer must they examine the words in meticulous detail. No longer must they argue about the precise grammatical sense. They must look to the purpose or intent. ...

Even when Canadian courts were taking a strict approach to the interpretation of the Act, they consistently accepted the view that treaties should be given a broad, liberal interpretation. Thus, as early as in *Saunders v. M.N.R.* (1954), 11 Tax A.B.C. 399 at 402, Mr. Fordham, then Chair of the Tax Appeal Board, wrote:

> The accepted principle appears to be that a taxing Act must be construed against either the Crown or the person sought to be charged, with perfect strictness-so far as the intention of Parliament is discoverable. Where a tax convention is involved, however, the situation is different and a liberal interpretation is usual, in the interests of the comity of nations. Tax conventions are negotiated primarily to remedy a subject's tax position by the avoidance of double taxation rather than to make it more burdensome. This fact is indicated in the preamble to the Convention.

In *The Queen v. Crown Forest Industries,* [1995] 2 C.T.C. 64, 95 D.T.C. 5389, the Supreme Court again considered the appropriate approach to the interpretation of tax treaties. The decision constitutes a firm commitment to the traditional liberal, Anglo-Canadian approach to treaty interpretation. To quote Mr. Justice Iacobucci, writing for the Court (at 71; 5393):

> In interpreting a treaty the paramount goal is to find the meaning of the words in question. This process involves looking to the language used and the intentions of the parties. Both upon the plain language reading of Art. IV and through an interpretation of the goals and purposes of the *Canada-United States Income Tax Convention* (1980), I reach the same destination: to allow the appeal.

Further, and very significantly, the Supreme Court in *Crown Forest* signalled a permissive attitude regarding the use of extrinsic evidence in the interpretation of tax treaties. Even in the absence of ambiguity, the Court was prepared to consider extrinsic evidence (at 77; 5396):

> Clearly, the purpose of the Convention has significant relevance to how its provisions are to be interpreted. I agree with the intervenor Government of the United States' submission that, in ascertaining these goals and intentions, a court may refer to extrinsic materials which form part of the legal context (these include accepted model conventions and official commentaries thereon) without the need first to find an ambiguity before turning to such materials.

The reference to "extrinsic materials which form part of the legal context" is puzzling. It avoids reference to articles 31 and 32 of the *Vienna Convention on the Law of Treaties* which deal with the use of extrinsic materials in the interpretation of treaties. Rather, the words reflect the arguments of the American intervenor, which unlike Canada, has not ratified the *Vienna Convention*. As a result, the decision may provide for the greater use of extrinsic materials in the interpretation of treaties, but it leaves the rules governing their admission unclear. The broad and vague term "form part of the legal context" may not incorporate the same rules as articles 31 and 32 of the *Vienna Convention*. Article 31 of the Convention provides that a treaty shall be interpreted in its context. Context is defined, generally, to mean agreements made or accepted by the parties to the treaties. Article 31 also provides that certain subsequent agreements and practices must be taken into account. Article 32 allows reference to supplementary means of interpretation, which include preparatory work of the treaty and the circumstances of its conclusion, to confirm the meaning resulting from the application of article 31 or to determine the meaning if the result under article 31 is ambiguous, obscure, manifestly absurd or unreasonable. The Supreme Court referred to the OECD Model Convention and the commentary on the Model Convention as being (at 80; 5398):

> ... of high persuasive value in terms of defining the parameters of the *Canada-United States Tax Convention* (1980) and also has world-wide recognition as a basic document of reference in the negotiation, application and interpretation of multi-lateral or bilateral tax conventions.

The Supreme Court also noted that the OECD Model Convention is not the only international convention worthy of consideration and referred specifically to the UN Model Convention. It also mentioned the relevance of other international conventions. It can be expected that less weight will be given to other international conventions to which Canada is not a signatory.

It is not surprising that in *Crown Forest* the Supreme Court referred to the Technical Explanation of the *United States-Canada Tax Convention*. The United States Treasury Department has adopted the practice of publishing technical explanations of the tax conventions it enters into. Normally, of course, such material would not have much cogency because it reflects only the viewpoint of one party to the treaty. However, in the case of the *Canada-United States Tax Convention*, opportunities were given to officials of the Departments of Finance and Revenue Canada who participated in the negotiations to review and comment on the technical explanations. Canada has publicly indicated its agreement with the interpretations. Hence, these technical interpretations probably form part of the context of the *Canada-United States Tax Convention* by virtue of article 31(2) of the *Vienna Convention*.

Finally, the Supreme Court in *Crown Forest* referred to two other types of extrinsic materials: foreign jurisprudence and U.S. Senate hearings. Undoubtedly, Canadian courts will exercise caution in relying on these materials.

Decisions subsequent to *Crown Forest* have confirmed that, in interpreting Canada's tax treaties, due consideration should be given to various extrinsic materials. These materials would include commentaries on the OECD Model Convention issued subsequent to the date that Canada and its treaty partner concluded the treaty in question. See, for example, *Prévost Car Inc. v. The Queen*, [2009] 3 C.T.C. 160, 2009 D.T.C. 5053, 2009 CarswellNat 480 (F.C.A.).

Any discussion of the interpretation of Canada's tax treaties must take into account the *Income Tax Conventions Interpretation Act,* R.S.C. 1985, c. I-4 and the Supreme Court of Canada decision in *The Queen v. Melford Developments,* [1982] C.T.C. 330, 82 D.T.C. 6281 (S.C.C.). The Supreme Court considered in *Melford* whether the meaning of undefined terms in a treaty is static or ambulatory. A German bank had guaranteed a loan made by one Canadian resident taxpayer to another. The bank received fees for the guarantee. The Canadian borrower argued that no withholding tax under Part XIII of the *Income Tax Act* should be exigible. The *Canada-Germany Tax Convention* provided that withholding tax could be levied on "interest". In 1956, at the time the treaty was ratified, the definition of interest in the *Income Tax Act* did not include loan guarantee fees. Subsequently, however, in 1974 the Act was amended to deem guarantee fees to be interest.

According to Mr. Justice Estey (at 331; 6281), the appeal involved the "principles applicable to the interpretation of domestic tax law and international tax conventions where their provisions are said to be competing". In holding for the payer he concluded (at 337; 6286) "the introduction of provisions relating to interest by the amendments of 1974 to the *Income Tax Act* of Canada evidences no intention by Parliament to amend the [treaty]." Thus while the Supreme Court was not prepared to declare that tax conventions can never override domestic tax legislation, the Court required evidence of an express statement of Parliamentary intention to do so.

To succeed in *Melford*, it was necessary for the Crown to argue that treaties should be interpreted in an ambulatory manner. In other words, a term should take its meaning from the domestic law as amended from time to time, rather than the meaning it had at the time the treaty was ratified. This ambulatory approach to the interpretation of international treaties troubled Mr. Justice Estey who said (at 336; 6286):

> What the position of the appellant amounts to is an assertion that Canada can simply amend the Agreement by the device of redefining the term interest.

In response to the decision in *Melford*, section 3 of the *Income Tax Conventions Interpretation Act* provides:

> 3. Meaning of undefined terms. — Notwithstanding the provisions of a convention or the Act giving the convention the force of law in Canada, it is hereby declared that the law of Canada is that, to the extent that a term in the convention is
>
> (a) not defined in the convention,
>
> (b) not fully defined in the convention, or
>
> (c) to be defined by reference to the laws of Canada,

that term has, except to the extent that the context otherwise requires, the meaning it has for the purposes of the *Income Tax Act*, as amended from time to time, and not the meaning it had for the purposes of the *Income Tax Act* on the date the convention was entered into or given the force of law in Canada if, after that date, its meaning for the purposes of the *Income Tax Act* has changed.

V. EXEMPTIONS FROM TAX

Section 149 of the *Income Tax Act* exempts from tax certain specified persons. This group includes municipalities, federal and provincial Crown corporations, registered charities, non-profit organizations, and labour organizations. Paragraph 149(1)(f) exempts registered charities from income tax, and section 149.1 contains a fairly comprehensive set of rules that govern the registration and activities of charities. Non-profit organizations, which are distinct from charities, are exempt from tax pursuant to paragraph 149(1)(l) if, in the opinion of the Minister, they are organized and operated exclusively for social welfare, civic improvement, pleasure or recreation or for any other purpose except profit, and no part of their income was payable to, or available for the benefit of, any member, proprietor, or shareholder.

Section 143 provides that a communal organization, other than a registered charity, which carries on a business and whose members as a matter of religious conviction do not own any property in their own right, is required either to pay tax as an *inter vivos* trust or elect to pay the aggregate of taxes of the individual families in the organization as if the income had been apportioned and taxed in their hands.

Paragraph 81(l)(a) provides that an amount declared to be exempt from income tax by any other enactment of Parliament shall not be included in the income of a taxpayer. The *Indian Act*, R.S.C. 1985, c. I-5 provides an exemption for some types of income received by status Indians. This exemption is discussed further in Part VI below. Section 81 also lists several other types of receipts that are not required to be included in income (and are therefore exempt from income tax). These amounts include the following: personal injury awards where the recipient has not reached 21 years of age before the end of the year; income from the office of the Governor General; expense allowances (up to prescribed limits) provided to members of provincial legislative assemblies and municipal officers; certain Armed Service pensions; and travel expenses paid by employers to some part-time employees.

It is noteworthy that members of the Armed Forces, when deployed in certain high-risk international operational missions, must include their wages in income but then are allowed to deduct their wages (not exceeding the maximum amount earned by a non-commissioned member) under paragraph 110(1)(f) of the *Income Tax Act*. See the discussion of Division C deductions in Chapter 8.

VI. ABORIGINAL TAXATION

The topic of aboriginal taxation has two sides. On one side, some Aboriginal persons are exempt from taxation on certain types of income. Much of the litigation has centered on the exemptions from tax provided in the *Indian Act*; however, the courts have also considered whether certain treaties concluded between First Nations and the Crown or specific aboriginal rights may ground exemptions from taxation.

On the other side, aboriginal governments impose taxes on their members and on others. The right of aboriginal governments to impose municipal-type taxes on real property on a reserve has been a long-time provision of the *Indian Act*. That legislation and agreements between First Nations and the federal government concerning taxation matters including the imposition of income taxes by First Nations are inextricably linked with the progress of Aboriginal peoples to self-government. There are now at least 12 income tax collection and sharing agreements which are discussed below. It remains to be decided whether there is, in addition, an aboriginal right to tax (which also might imply an exemption) that is constitutionally protected. The acquisition of powers of self-government by First Nations both through political and judicial means could found ancillary rights, including the right to taxation, on a number of bases: the Crown/Aboriginal fiduciary relationship, the need to uphold the honour of the Crown, or the common law principle that certain rights exist if they are necessarily incidental to other recognized rights.

A. Exemption from Liability to Tax

1. Exemption on the Basis of Aboriginal Right(s)

The position of some First Nations is that their members do not have to pay taxes to the federal or provincial governments. They contend that the governments of Canada have no more right to levy taxes on their members than they do on the citizens of other sovereign nations — although we have seen that the federal and provincial governments have a limited ability to tax non-residents and arguably would have some power to tax First Nation individuals with economic ties beyond First Nations' lands. So far, however, no general exemption of aboriginal persons from taxation has been recognized by the courts or through the CRA's administrative practice. The case of *Mitchell v. M.N.R.* (2001), [2002] 3 C.T.C. 359, [2001] 1 S.C.R. 911 (S.C.C.) does, however, provide an indication of the issues and complexities arising from First Nations' claims of exemption from taxation as ancillary to a particular aboriginal right. In *Mitchell*, the Supreme Court of Canada considered the assertion of a right by Chief Mitchell of Akwesasne, Ontario, a descendent member of the Mohawk Nation, to "enter Canada from the United States with personal and community goods, without paying customs or duties, and the right to trade these goods with other First Nations" (*Mitchell* at paragraph 16). The Supreme Court held that the evidence adduced was insufficient to establish an aboriginal right even under the liberal rules of evidence permitted in ancestral aboriginal rights cases. In the course of her judgment, Chief Justice McLachlin, (Gonthier, Iacobucci, Arbour and LeBel JJ concurring), recharacterized the right claimed as "the right to bring goods across the St. Lawrence River for the purposes of trade" (*Mitchell* at paragraph 25). The right could not be to cross the border since the border did not exist in pre-contact times. The tax exemption that was claimed was only ancillary to the exercise of the alleged aboriginal right.

The majority of the Supreme Court held that there was no evidence of an ancestral Mohawk practice of transporting goods across the St. Lawrence River for the purposes of trade. Accordingly, it was unnecessary to determine, first, whether the right had been extinguished before the coming into force in 1982 of the protective provisions of section 35 of the *Charter of Rights and Freedoms*, and second, assuming that the right had not been extinguished, whether the imposition of customs duties could be justified as an infringement of the aboriginal trading right.

Section 35 of the *Charter* provides that "[t]he existing aboriginal and treaty rights of the aboriginal peoples of Canada are hereby recognized and affirmed." It is noteworthy that in *Mitchell* both the Federal Court-Trial Division ([1998] 1 C.T.C. 63) and the Federal Court of Appeal ((1998), 233 N.R. 129) found an aboriginal right that they held had not been extinguished by the imposition of customs duties on aboriginal persons traveling across the border. Neither the long-standing existence of customs legislation nor its "sporadic" and "inconsistent" imposition on Mohawks crossing the border exhibited a "clear and plain intention" by the Crown to extinguish the aboriginal right.

Properly viewed, the requirement to pay customs duties, if the right to cross the St. Lawrence to trade is found to be an aboriginal right, can be considered an infringement of the aboriginal right. In constitutional terms the justification stage is where the Crown seeks to justify infringements, such as taxation, on aboriginal rights. The Federal Court-Trial Division held that the government did not lead any evidence on infringement and hence the infringement could not be justified. The Federal Court of Appeal did not consider the matter.

2. Exemption by Treaty

None of the treaties concluded (before recent land claims settlements) between First Nations and the Crown contain specific reference to taxation. Although the terms of Treaty #8, which governs vast tracts of British Columbia, Alberta, Saskatchewan and the Northwest Territories, do not refer to taxation, specific oral assurances regarding taxation were made to the First Nations at the time of its negotiation. The report of the Treaty Commissioners, Laird, Ross and McKenna, to Ottawa states:

> There was expressed at every point the fear that the making of the Treaty would be followed by the curtailment of the hunting and fishing privileges, and many were impressed with the notion that the Treaty would lead to taxation and enforced military service.
>
> We assured them that the Treaty would not lead to any forced interference with their mode of life, *that it did not open the way to the imposition of any tax*, and that there was no fear of enforced military service [emphasis added].

The significance of this oral statement was canvassed by the Federal Court of Appeal in *Benoit v. The Queen*, 2003 D.T.C. 5366 (F.C.A.), leave to appeal refused (2004), 330 N.R. 200 (note) (S.C.C.), where it was held that, even if the oral assurance were to be incorporated as one of the terms of Treaty #8, it did not mean that the beneficiaries of Treaty #8 were to be forever exempt from taxation. The Commissioners, the Court concluded, did not overstep their mandate, which was to negotiate terms not better than previously concluded treaties. These other treaties did not provide a general exemption from taxation. The evidence supported a finding that the Commissioners' assurances to the First Nations meant that Treaty #8 would not, by itself, result in the imposition of taxes on the beneficiaries. There was no evidence supporting the conclusion that the First Nation signatories to the treaty understood the words to mean otherwise.

Even where a treaty does not provide a specific exemption from tax, First Nations have claimed that its terms should be interpreted to imply an exemption from taxes that are linked to benefits the Crown has promised to provide under the treaty. See, in this respect, *R. v. Johnston* (1966), 56 D.L.R. (2d) 749, where the Saskatchewan Court of Appeal held that an Indian beneficiary of Treaty #6 was liable to pay provincial hospitalization tax even though the treaty guaranteed Johnston "a medicine chest ... kept at the house of each Indian agent for the use or benefit of the Indians at the direction of such agent ...." Note that section 88 of the *Indian Act* provides that provincial laws of general application will apply to Indians "subject to the terms of any treaty".

3. Exemption Under the Indian Act

Although treaties and aboriginal rights may found claims for exemption from taxation for some Aboriginal peoples, much of the litigation of exemptions for Aboriginal peoples has focused on the provisions of the *Indian Act*, which provide a limited exemption for status Indians on certain real property and "personal property ... situated on a reserve". The relevant sections are reproduced below:

> s. 2(1) In this Act,

...

"Indian" means a person who pursuant to this Act is registered as an Indian or is entitled to be registered as an Indian;

...

87(1) Notwithstanding any other Act of Parliament or any Act of the legislature of a province..., the following property is exempt from taxation:

(a) the interest of an Indian or a band in reserve lands or surrendered lands; and

(b) the personal property of an Indian or a band situated on a reserve.

The Supreme Court recently considered the purpose and application of section 87 of the *Indian Act* in two cases, *Bastien Estate v. Canada*, 2011 SCC 38, [2011] 5 C.T.C. 111, 2011 CarswellNat 2717, 2011 D.T.C. 5118, and *Dubé v. Canada*, 2011 SCC 39, [2011] 5 C.T.C. 149, 2011 CarswellNat 2720, 2011 D.T.C. 5120.

BASTIEN ESTATE v. CANADA
2011 SCC 38, [2011] 5 C.T.C. 111, 2011 CarswellNat 2717, 2011 D.T.C. 5118

Cromwell J. (McLachlin C.J. and Binnie, Fish, Charron JJ. concurring):

...

II. Facts, Proceedings and Issue

1. *Facts*

...

The late Rolland Bastien was a status Indian and belonged to the Huron-Wendat Nation. He was born and died on the Wendake Reserve near Quebec City. His wife and children who succeed him are also Huron and live on the reserve. From 1970 until 1997 when he sold the business to his children, Mr. Bastien operated a moccasin manufacturing business on the Wendake Reserve: Les Industries Bastien enr. He invested some of the income from the operation and sale of his business in term deposits with two caisses populaires situated on Indian reserves, the Caisse populaire Desjardins du Village Huron (the "Caisse") situated on the Wendake Reserve and the Caisse populaire Desjardins de Pointe-Bleue situated on the Mashteuiatsh Reserve. Only the income from the investments with the Caisse on the Wendake Reserve is in issue on this appeal. The Caisse has since its founding in 1965 had its head office, its only place of business and its sole fixed asset on the reserve (partial agreed statement of facts, A.R., vol. II, at p. 200).

In 2001, Mr. Bastien held certificates of deposit at the Caisse and these investments paid interest that was deposited in a transaction savings account at the Caisse. Mr. Bastien considered this income to be property exempt from taxation. However, in 2003, the Minister of National Revenue made an assessment in which he added the investment income to Mr. Bastien's income for the 2001 taxation year. The Minister confirmed the assessment and Mr. Bastien's estate appealed unsuccessfully to the Tax Court and the Federal Court of Appeal.

...

3. *Issue*

There is only one question before the Court: Was Mr. Bastien's interest income earned on the term deposits with the Caisse populaire Desjardins du Village Huron exempt from income taxation because it was personal property situated on a reserve?

III. Analysis

...

2. *Determining the Location of Income*

Where, because of its nature or the type of exemption in question, the location of property is not objectively easy to determine, courts must apply the connecting factors approach set out in *Williams v. Canada*, [1992] 1 S.C.R. 877, in order to attribute a location to the property. While this search for location may seem at times to be more the stuff of metaphysics than of law, the attribution of location is what the *Indian Act* provisions require. The difficulty of doing so means that it is not generally possible to apply a simple, standard test to determine the location of intangible property. Gonthier J. recognized this in *Williams*, at p. 891, where he was considering whether unemployment insurance benefits were exempt from taxation under s. 87:

> Because the transaction by which a taxpayer receives unemployment insurance benefits is not a physical object, the method by which one might fix its *situs* is not immediately apparent. In one sense, the difficulty is that the transaction has no *situs*. However, in another sense, the problem is that it has too many. There is the *situs* of the debtor, the *situs* of the creditor, the *situs* where the payment is made, the *situs* of the employment which created the qualification for the receipt of income, the *situs* where the payment will be used, and no doubt others. The task is then to identify which of these locations is the relevant one, or which combination of these factors controls the location of the transaction.

As the location of such property will always be notional, there is a risk that attributing a location to it will be arbitrary. An alternative would be to apply consistently a single strict rule, but that solution is not without its limitations. Gonthier J. expressed caution against a single criteria test. Indeed, where one or two factors have a controlling force, there could be manipulation or abuse, and there is cause to worry that such an analysis would miss the purpose of the *Indian Act* exemption: *Williams*, at p. 892.

To address this challenge, Gonthier J. in *Williams* set out a two-step test. At the first step, the court identifies potentially relevant factors connecting the intangible personal property to a location. "A connecting factor is only relevant", wrote Gonthier J. "in so much as it identifies the location of the property in question for the purposes of the *Indian Act*" (p. 892). Thus, even in this somewhat metaphysical sphere, the focus is clearly on ascribing a physical location to the property in question. Connecting factors mentioned in *Williams* include things such as the residence of the payor and the payee, the place of payment and where the employment giving rise to qualification for the benefit was performed: *Williams*, at p. 893. As Gonthier J. noted, potentially relevant connecting factors have different relevance depending on the categories of property and the types of taxation in issue. So, for example, "connecting factors may have different relevance with regard to unemployment insurance benefits than in respect of employment income, or pension benefits" (p. 892). To take this into account, as well as to ensure that the analysis serves to identify the location of the property for the purposes of the *Indian Act*, at the second step, the court analyses these factors purposively in order to assess what weight should be given to them. This analysis considers the purpose of the exemption under the *Indian Act*; the type of property in question; and the nature of the taxation of that property (p. 892).

Williams thus establishes a clearly structured analysis, but one that turns on careful consideration of the particular circumstances of each case assessed against the purpose of the exemption. As Gonthier J. noted at p. 893, the *Williams* approach "preserves the flexibility of the case by case approach, but within a framework which requires the court to assess the weight which is to be placed on the various connecting factors". The *Williams* approach applies here because we are dealing with the location of a transaction – the payment of interest pursuant to a contract – for the purposes of taxation.

(i) <u>The Purpose of the Exemption</u>

In *Mitchell v. Peguis Indian Band*, [1990] 2 S.C.R. 85, La Forest J. discussed the purpose of both the tax exemption and the immunity from seizure in the *Indian Act*. With respect to the exemption from taxation, he observed that it serves to "guard against the possibility that one branch of government, through the imposition of taxes, could erode the full measure of the benefits given by that branch of government entrusted with the supervision of Indian affairs" (p. 130). He summed up his discussion of the purpose of the provisions by noting that since the *Royal Proclamation* of 1763, R.S.C. 1985, App. II, No. 1, "the Crown has always acknowledged that it is honour-bound to shield Indians from any efforts by non-natives to dispossess Indians of the property which they hold *qua* Indians". He added an important qualification: the purpose of the exemptions is to preserve property reserved for their use, "not to remedy the economically disadvantaged position of Indians by ensuring that [they could] acquire, hold and deal with property in the commercial mainstream on different terms than their fellow citizens": p. 131. As La Forest J. put it:

> These provisions are not intended to confer privileges on Indians in respect of any property they may acquire and possess, wherever situated. Rather, their purpose is simply to insulate the property interests of Indians in their reserve lands from the intrusions and interference of the larger society so as to ensure that Indians are not dispossessed of their entitlements. [Emphasis added; p. 133.]

However, La Forest J. was careful to emphasize that even with respect to purely commercial arrangements, the protections from taxation and seizure always apply to property situated on a reserve. As he put it, at p. 139:

> ... if an Indian band concluded a purely commercial business agreement with a private concern, the protections of ss. 87 and 89 would have no application in respect of the assets acquired pursuant to that agreement, except, of course, if the property was situated on a reserve. It must be remembered that the protections of ss. 87 and 89 will always apply to property situated on a reserve. [Emphasis added.]

The Court returned to the purpose of the exemptions in *Williams*. Gonthier J. confirmed that the purpose of the exemptions "was to preserve the entitlements of Indians to their reserve lands and to ensure that the use of their property on their reserve lands was not eroded by the ability of governments to tax, or creditors to seize" (p. 885). Echoing the limitation described by La Forest J. in *Mitchell*, Gonthier J. added that "the purpose of the sections was not to confer a general economic benefit upon the Indians" (at p. 885) and that "[w]hether the Indian wishes to remain within the protected reserve system or integrate more fully into the larger commercial world is a choice left to the Indian" (p. 887). In light of this, Gonthier J. held that the purpose of the requirement in s. 87 that the property be "situated on a reserve" is to "determine whether the Indian holds the property in question as part of the entitlement of an Indian *qua* Indian on the reserve" (p. 887). In both *Union of New Brunswick Indians* and *God's Lake*, the Court confirmed that the purpose of the exemptions was as set out in *Mitchell* and *Williams*.

...

The reference to rights of an "Indian *qua* Indian" in *Mitchell*, which was repeated in *Williams*, and the linking of the tax exemption to the traditional way of life have been criticized: C. MacIntosh, "From Judging Culture to Taxing 'Indians':

Tracing the Legal Discourse of the 'Indian Mode of Life'" (2009), 47 *Osgoode Hall L.J.* 399, at p. 425. However, I do not read either judgment as departing from a focus on the location of the property in question when applying the tax exemption. The exemption provisions must be read in light of their purpose, but not, as Professor MacIntosh puts it, be "let loose from the moorings of their express language" (p. 425). A purposive interpretation goes too far if it substitutes for the inquiry into the location of the property mandated by the statute an assessment of what does or does not constitute an "Indian" way of life on a reserve. I do not read *Mitchell* or *Williams* as mandating that approach.

...

(v) Applying the *Williams* Analysis to Mr. Bastien's Interest Income

In my view, the connecting factors identified in *Williams* are potentially relevant here. When they are considered and weighed in light of the purpose of the exemption, the type of property and the nature of the taxation of that property, all point to the reserve as the location of the interest income in this case.

I turn first to the location of the debtor, a factor traditionally relied on to determine the location of the obligation to pay. Here the debtor is the Caisse whose head office and only place of business as well as its only fixed asset is located on the Wendake Reserve. The income – interest agreed to be paid by the Caisse to Mr. Bastien – arises from a contractual obligation between the taxpayer and the Caisse which was entered into on the reserve. By virtue of the contract, the income was to be paid (and was paid) by the Caisse by depositing it into the taxpayer's account on the reserve: see art. 1566 of the *Civil Code of Québec*. Thus, the location of the debtor and the place where payment must be made are clearly on the reserve....

Having regard to the purpose of the exemption, the type of property and the nature of the taxation of that property, the connecting factors of the location of the debtor, the place where the legal obligation to pay must be performed and the location of the term deposits giving rise to the income should in my view be given significant weight in the circumstances of this case. As noted, the property flows from a contractual obligation which, both under the contract and the terms of the *Civil Code* (art. 1566), is to be performed on the reserve. The deposits themselves and the account into which the interest on them is paid are on the reserve. The debtor's only place of business is on the reserve. Thus, the type of property supports the view that the connecting factors of the place of contracting, the place of performance and the residence of the debtor should weigh heavily in attributing a location to the interest income. The nature of the taxation – the income is income from property – reinforces this view. And so does the purpose of the exemption, which is to preserve Indian property on a reserve.

The analysis must also take account of other potentially relevant connecting factors. Here, those factors reinforce rather than detract from the conclusion that the interest income is property situated on the reserve.

Consider the residence of the payee, Mr. Bastien. That of course was on the reserve. As for the source of the capital which was invested to produce the interest income, it too was earned on the reserve. There is some parallel with *Williams* in this regard. In *Williams*, the employment income which gave rise to the entitlement to unemployment insurance benefits had been earned on the reserve. Gonthier J. noted that the connection between the benefits and the qualifying employment was strong because the benefits are based on premiums arising from the previous employment: p. 896. In this case, while the interest income was derived from the loan to the Caisse, it was Mr. Bastien's business income, generated on the reserve and not assessed by the Minister, which produced the capital which in turn was invested to produce that income. These other potentially relevant connecting factors do not point to any other location than the reserve and tend to strengthen rather than undermine the connection between the investment income and the reserve.

The Tax Court and the Federal Court of Appeal attached great weight to the fact that the Caisse's income-generating activities were in general commercial markets off the reserve. While that factor may have weight with respect to other types of investments, it has been given significantly too much weight with respect to the term deposits in issue here. I agree with the following comments by Maclagan, at pp. 1516-17:

> In the case of a fixed-income security, there is legally no further income-generating activity of anyone that needs to take place beyond that which takes place when a taxpayer purchases the securities. ... The mere step of acquiring a fixed-income investment generates the right to receive a certain fixed amount of income. The income-generating activity that matters is the generation of the original capital and the acquisition of the securities. Of course, the issuer has to pay the income to the investor, but this might be paid out of capital, other borrowings, or unrelated earnings ... . [Emphasis added.]
>
> ...
>
> As I mentioned earlier, La Forest J. in *Mitchell* also noted that the purpose of the legislation is not to permit Indians to "acquire, hold, and deal with property in the commercial mainstream on different terms than their fellow citizens": p. 131. However, he was clear that, even if an Indian acquired an asset through a purely commercial business agreement with a private concern, the exemption would nonetheless apply if the asset were situated on a reserve. As he emphasized, "[i]t must be remembered that the protections of ss. 87 and 89 will always apply to property situated on a reserve": p. 139.

...

> When one focuses, as required by *Williams*, on the connecting factors relevant to the location of Mr. Bastien's interest income arising from his contractual relationship with the Caisse, it is apparent that the other commercial activities of the Caisse should have been given no weight in this case. Mr. Bastien's investment was in the nature of a debt owed to him by the Caisse and did not make him a participant in those wider commercial markets in which the Caisse itself was active.

Of course, in determining the location of income for the purposes of the tax exemption, the court should look to the substance as well as to the form of the transaction giving rise to the income. The question is whether the income is sufficiently strongly connected to the reserve that it may be said to be situated there. Connections that are artificial or abusive should not be given weight in the analysis. For example, if in substance the investment income arises from an Indian's off-reserve investment activities, that will be a significant factor suggesting that less weight should be given to the legal form of the investment vehicle. There is nothing of that nature present in this case. Cases of improper manipulation by Indian taxpayers to avoid income tax may be addressed as they are in the case of non-Indian taxpayers.

Applying the exemption of interest income in this case is broadly consistent with the purpose of preserving Indian property situated on the reserve. It provides an investment option protected from taxation for Mr. Bastien's property while preserving it against possible seizure.

4. Conclusion

All potentially relevant factors in this case connect the investment income to the reserve. In the circumstances of this case, the fact that the Caisse produced its revenue in the "commercial mainstream" off the reserve is legally irrelevant to the nature of the income it was obliged to pay to Mr. Bastien. This is true as to both form and substance. Mr. Bastien's investment income should therefore benefit from the s. 87 *Indian Act* exemption.

...

[Appeal allowed. Deschamps J., writing for herself and Rothstein J., concurred in the result but disagreed with Cromwell J.'s analysis.]

Notes and Questions

1. The concurring judges in *Bastien Estate* expressed concern that the application of the test articulated by Cromwell J. was vulnerable to manipulation. Deschamps J. wrote (at para 102):

> In principle, I cannot agree that significant weight should be given to connecting factors that can easily be manipulated. In my view, that is the effect of the importance attached to the contractual aspects of the investment contract rather than to the property's concrete and discernible connections with the reserve. Cromwell J. accepts the argument that the Tax Court of Canada failed to give sufficient weight to the contractual nature of the deposit at the Caisse populaire in determining the location of the property in issue (paras. 11 and 13). In my opinion, the Tax Court of Canada was right not to dwell on that aspect of the property.

Do you agree?

2. The taxpayer in *Dubé* also received the benefit of the exemption in section 87 of the *Indian Act*. In dissent, Deschamps J. (for herself and Rothstein J.) wrote the following:

> Where a taxpayer has a right to be paid interest that is provided for in an investment contract, the particular nature of this type of property makes it necessary, in order to take account of the purpose of the exemption, to consider the activity that resulted in the accumulation of the capital deposited with the financial institution. If that capital results from an on-reserve activity that generates exempt property, this factor could justify giving the interest provided for in the contract the same tax treatment as the product of the activity. This approach would make it possible to maintain a form of symmetry between the tax treatment of the property that results in the accumulation of the capital and the tax treatment of the interest.

3. For Deschamps and Rothstein JJ., the most important difference between *Bastien Estate* and *Dubé* was the source of the capital that was deposited in the Caisse populaire to earn the interest in question. Because the Tax Court judge was "unable to establish a connection between the deposited capital and the [on reserve] transportation company operated by Mr. Dubé", the dissenting judges were concerned that "[t]o grant the exemption ... would be tantamount to turning the reserve into a tax haven for Indians engaged in unspecified for-profit activities off the reserve."
4. Consider the application of the general anti-avoidance rule ("GAAR") in section 245 of the Act. Does the provision apply where an intermediary is used in an attempt to situate income on-reserve? The exemption in section 87 of the *Indian Act* is recognized in paragraph 81(1)(a) of the Act but the paragraph is unnecessary since the income would be exempt even without its application.
5. Corporations cannot claim the exemption under section 87. In *R. v. Kinookimaw Beach Association,* [1979] 4 C.N.L.R. 101, the Saskatchewan Court of Appeal held that a corporation incorporated by seven Indian bands to develop reserve lands as a resort area was liable to pay provincial tax on the purchase of certain property. The corporation was being taxed, not its shareholders and therefore it was not entitled to the tax exemption of its shareholders.

6. Status Indians resident on a reserve may be required to pay federal and provincial commodity taxes. In *Union of New Brunswick Indians v. New Brunswick (Minister of Finance)*, [1998] 1 S.C.R. 1161 the respondent Union contended that status Indians should not be forced to pay provincial sales tax on items purchased outside the reserve which were to be used primarily (consumed) on the reserve. The Court held that "Sales taxes attach at the moment of sale. At this point, the property has but one location-the place of sale." Therefore tax was exigible. In considering whether the use of property by Indians would be facilitated by such an exemption, Justice McLachlin commented at (1184–86):

> A ... difficulty with this argument [for exemption] is that it rests on the assumption that providing a tax exemption to Indians for property purchased off-reserve will benefit Indians uniformly. The argument is that Parliament must have intended the tax to apply to off-reserve purchases because this is required to protect and enhance the position of Indians. Yet it is far from clear that Indians across Canada would benefit from such an interpretation.
>
> Confining s. 87 to property situated on a reserve and excluding off-reserve sales taxes will have varying effects. It is said that in New Brunswick the effects are negative. There are very few retail establishments on New Brunswick reserves where 65-75 percent of status Indians live. Delivery of goods to reserves may partially offset the problem; the trial judge, Savoie J., found that delivery of goods and services to Indians resident on reserves in New Brunswick was available from many of the retail establishments close to reserves. However, delivery may involve additional charges equivalent to a sales tax and, in any event, will not be available in many situations. The reality is that, at present, New Brunswick Indians are unable to live on their reserves without paying a certain amount of provincial sales tax.
>
> At the same time, adopting the "paramount location" test would have adverse consequences for Indians who live off the reserve. They would presumably have to pay tax on purchases made on and off the reserve because the "paramount location" of the goods would be off-reserve.
>
> In addition, the "point of sale" test is beneficial to on-reserve Indians in many part of Canada. First it provides an incentive for Indians to establish their own retail outlets on reserves and gives a competitive edge to reserve businesses, thereby increasing economic activity and employment. Although the exemption may not yet have been a catalyst in New Brunswick, where until recently off-reserve sales were exempt from tax, it has fostered aboriginal economic development elsewhere.
>
> ...
>
> Second, the "point of sale" approach to the tax exemption permits reserves to impose their own taxes on reserve sales, thus creating a tax base for aboriginal governments: .... For example, in the *Budget Implementation Act*, 1997, S.C. 1997, c. 26, Parliament granted the Cowichan tribes the authority to impose a direct tax on the on-reserve purchase of tobacco by status Indians. This legislation enabled the Cowichan Tribes to fill the tax void created by s. 87 and raise revenue for the community. If s. 87 is interpreted

to provide an exemption for all off-reserve purchases of tobacco destined for use on the reserve, the purpose of this amendment would be frustrated.

B. Taxes Imposed by First Nations

First Nations have always had limited powers of municipal-type taxation under section 83(1)(a) of the *Indian Act*. This provision permits Indian Bands, with the approval of the Minister of Indian Affairs and Northern Development, to pass by-laws for the purpose of imposing local taxation on land, or interests in land on the reserve, including rights to occupy, possess or use land on the reserve. First Nations have also sought power to levy their own taxes concomitant with their acquisition of powers of self-government. Thus, there is the example of the *First Nation Self-Government Agreement*, brought into effect by the *Yukon First Nations Self-Government Act,* S.C. 1994, c. 35, and by the *First Nations (Yukon) Self Government Act*, S.Y., 1993, c. 5, which permits Yukon First Nations to enter into tax collection and sharing agreements with the federal government and the Yukon government. Some important parts of the standard memorandum of agreement between the federal government and various First Nations are reproduced at the end of this chapter.

The introduction of a new level of taxation by First Nations governments presents substantial challenges. In a draft document called *A Working Paper on Indian Government Taxation* issued in March 1993, the Indian Taxation Policy Group of the Department of Finance outlined some "guiding principles". These principles, which have not been formally adopted and have been criticized on a number of grounds, nonetheless provide a basis for discussion. They include (articulated on pages 12-13 of the working paper):

- *The property of Indians which is situated on reserves would continue to be exempt from non-Indian government taxation.*

The corollary is that First Nations governments may want to fill the lacunae.

- *Decisions on the exercise of taxation powers should be the prerogative of the governments of First Nations.*

Taxation is only one method of raising revenue for self-government. In many First Nations, the concept of taxation as an instrument of government is not familiar, although First Nations have traditionally shared revenues.

- *Expanded Indian government tax powers should operate concurrently with federal and provincial tax powers.*

The standard agreement below sets out a co-ordinated system of sharing revenues between the federal government and First Nations. Provincial taxation must be the subject of separate agreements between First Nations and provincial governments.

• *The overall integrity of the Canadian Tax system should be maintained.*

This principle includes both the prevention of tax avoidance and unintended over- taxation. The other is that First Nations governments exercise their tax powers without significantly adding to the total federal and provincial tax burden already shouldered by taxpayers.

• *The recognition of Indian government taxation powers should not be seen as an alternative to continued federal funding for Indian people.*

It was the opinion of the Working Group that Indian government taxation in most cases should be seen as an avenue for the development of independent revenues not as a mechanism for replacing existing funding arrangements. First Nations taxation powers should be considered in future funding arrangements only when a First Nation has in place an institutional infrastructure and level of service that is reasonably equivalent to surrounding communities.

MEMORANDUM OF AGREEMENT DATED AS OF XXX BETWEEN THE GOVERNMENT OF CANADA AND THE FIRST NATION

WHEREAS the First Nation desires to exercise its power of direct taxation pursuant to the *First Nation Self-Government Agreement*, brought into effect by the *Yukon First Nations Self-Government Act*, S.C. 1994, c.35, and by the *First Nations (Yukon) Self-Government Act*, S.Y., 1993, c.5;

AND WHEREAS the First Nation *Income Tax Act* imposes taxes on the income of individuals and provides that the First Nation may enter into a tax collection agreement;

AND WHEREAS the First Nation wishes to enter into an agreement with Canada, pursuant to which Canada will collect taxes payable under the First Nation *Income Tax Act* on behalf of the First Nation and will make payments to the First Nation in respect of the taxes so collected, in accordance with such terms and conditions as the tax collection agreement prescribes;

...

NOW, THEREFORE, in consideration of the terms, exchange of promises, covenants and conditions in this agreement, the parties to this agreement agree as follows:

COVENANTS BY CANADA

2. (1) Canada, as agent of the First Nation, shall collect for and on behalf of the First Nation income tax for each taxation year to which this Agreement applies, and shall remit amounts in respect thereof to the First Nation in accordance with this Agreement.

3. (1) Canada agrees, in respect of each of the first ten taxation years of this Agreement, to vacate 75% of the federal tax payable by an individual residing within Settlement Land pursuant to the Yukon Land Claims settlements on the last day of the taxation year.

(2) Canada agrees, in respect of each subsequent taxation year, to vacate 95% of the federal tax payable by an individual residing within Settlement Land on the last day of the taxation year.

...

COVENANTS BY THE FIRST NATION

4. The First Nation agrees, in respect of each taxation year to which this Agreement applies, to impose an income tax under the First Nation *Income Tax Act* in the following manner:

(a) in the case of an individual who resides within Settlement Land on the last day of the taxation year and who has no income earned in the year outside the Yukon, income tax shall be expressed, for the first ten years of this Agreement, as 75% of the federal tax payable by that individual for the year and, for subsequent years as 95% of the federal tax payable;

(b) in the case of an individual who resides within Settlement Land on the last day of the taxation year and who has income earned in the year outside the Yukon, income tax shall be the amount that bears the same relation to 75% of the federal tax payable for the first ten years of this Agreement, or 95% for subsequent years, that the income earned in the year on Settlement Land bears to his income for the year.

5. The income tax imposed under the First Nations *Income Tax Act* shall be imposed at the same rate for all residents within Settlement Land, whether Citizen [of First Nation] or non-citizen.

Notes and Questions

1. Compare the anti-discrimination provision in the above standard agreement with similar provisions in Canada's tax treaties, described in Part IV of this chapter.
2. How does the taxation of non-Yukon source income of residents of settlement land compare to that of Canadian residents who receive income from outside Canada? What is the reason for the differences?

4

Income from Employment

I. WHO IS AN EMPLOYEE?

For income tax purposes, an individual who is retained to provide services to another person is either an "employee" or an "independent contractor". The expression "independent contractor" is synonymous with "business person", "self-employed" and "freelancer"; it connotes an individual engaged in "business" activities as distinct from an employee who works in a "master-servant" relationship and earns "employment income".

"Office" is defined in subsection 248(1) of the *Income Tax Act* (the "Act"). An office-holder may include an elected official, director, executor or executrix, judge, tribunal member, chairperson or union officer. Subsection 248(1) also includes definitions of "employed", "employee", "employment", and "employer". Unfortunately, these definitions are not particularly helpful in determining whether an individual is an employee or an independent contractor.

A. Tax Implications of Distinguishing Between Income from Employment and Income from Business

The distinction between an employee and an independent contractor is important because different rules apply depending on whether the income earned is employment income or business income. The major differences include the following:

(1) *Payment and Withholding of Tax* — An employer must withhold and remit a prescribed amount from each payment made to an employee (section 153). There is no withholding obligation on payments to an independent contractor, although the recipient may be required to make quarterly or monthly instalments of tax (section 156). An employer who fails to withhold as required is liable to both civil and criminal penalties.

(2) *Basis of Measurement* — Income from an office or employment is generally calculated on a "cash basis", whereas income from business is calculated on an "accrual basis". Income from an office or employment is recognized when it is "received" and permitted employment expenses are deductible when "paid". In contrast, business income is recognized when "earned" and business expenses when "incurred". The distinction is largely a question of timing, and is discussed in greater detail in Chapter 6.

(3) *Reporting Period: Taxation Year* — Section 249 stipulates that the taxation year of an individual is the calendar year. Income from an office or employment is calculated on a calendar-year basis while business income is calculated and reported on the basis of a fiscal period. "Fiscal period" is defined in subsection 249.1(1). For individuals, a fiscal period cannot generally extend beyond the end of the calendar year in which it begins. Prior to 1995, it was possible for an individual who derived business income to significantly defer the recognition of income for tax purposes by setting the fiscal period of the business so that it ended early in the calendar year (e.g., February 1 – January 31). Although an individual may elect to retain an off-calendar year end (subsection 249.1(4)) for business income purposes, an income adjustment is made to approximate the income earned in a calendar year (subsections 34.1(1) and 34.1(3)).

(4) *Scope of Deductions* — An employee may deduct the limited set of expenses authorized in section 8. A self-employed businessperson has considerably wider scope to deduct income-earning expenses under sections 9 and 20.

B. Characterizing Working Relationships: Employee or Independent Contractor

Because the Act does not adequately differentiate an employee from an independent contractor, the issue has been left primarily to the courts. Ultimately, the characterization of an individual as an employee or independent contractor is a question of fact.

Historically, under the common law, the courts distinguished between an employee, engaged in a contract *of service,* and an independent contractor, performing a contract *for service*, by assessing the nature and degree of control over the work to be done. If a worker has no control over the work and how it is to be done, he or she is considered an employee under the common law control test as set out by Baron Bramwell in *R. v. Walker* (1858), 27 L.J.M.C. 207 at 208 (C.C.R.):

> It seems to me that the difference between the relations of master and servant and of principal and agent is this: A principal has the right to direct what the agent has to do; but a master has not only that right, but also the right to say how it is done.

In assessing the nature and degree of control, the courts historically have considered four aspects:

(1) the power of selection of the servant;

(2) the payment of wages;

(3) control over the method of work; and

(4) the master's right of suspension or dismissal.

The traditional control test relies on the degree and nature of control over the person purported to be an employee. In *Di Francesco v. M.N.R.* (1964), 34 Tax A.B.C. 380, 64 D.T.C. 106 (T.A.B.), which involved the characterization of the activities of a real estate agent, the Tax Appeal Board stated:

> A servant acts under the direct control and supervision of his master, and is bound to conform to all reasonable orders given him in the course of his work; an independent contractor, on the other hand, is entirely independent of any control or interference, and merely undertakes to produce a specified result, employing his own means to produce that result.

However, societal changes have contributed to the dissolution of a master's ability to direct and control workers. Many workers are professionals or highly trained individuals who possess knowledge and skills which transcend those of the masters. Traditional master/servant relationships have been replaced by modern relationships that are governed more and more by contracts. Technology has provided individuals with the ability to work away from a set work place, in home offices or otherwise away from a work site. Unionization and collective agreements govern many workers and their conditions of work.

All of these developments have limited the appropriateness and usefulness of the control test as the means to determine whether a worker is an employee engaged in a contract *of service*, or an independent contractor working under a contract *for service*. Initially in response to these changes, courts developed additional tests to determine the nature of each working relationship. The following case suggests a move away from single criterion tests, including the "control test", toward an examination of the whole scheme of operations to determine the total relationship of the parties.

WIEBE DOOR SERVICES LTD. v. M.N.R.
[1986] 2 C.T.C. 200, 87 D.T.C. 5025 (F.C.A.)

MacGuigan J.:

This section 28 application is brought to set aside a decision by the Tax Court, which upheld an assessment against the applicant for the payment of Unemployment Insurance Premiums and Canada Pension Plan Contributions for the years 1979, 1980 and 1981. Counsel for the applicant admitted before this Court that the assessment for the 1979 year was correct, in that the only two persons then in question were admittedly employees in that year, but contended that the 12 persons in relation to whom the applicant was assessed in 1980 and 1981 were all independent contractors rather than employees.

The applicant is in the business of installing doors and repairing overhead doors in the Calgary area, with about 75 per cent of its business being on the repair side. It carries on its business through the services of a considerable number of door installers and repairers, with each of whom it has a specific understanding that they would be running their own businesses and would therefore be responsible for their own taxes and any contributions for workers' compensation, unemployment insurance and Canada Pension Plan. Such an agreement is not of itself determinative of the relationship between the parties, and a court must carefully examine the facts in order to come to its own conclusion. ...

The traditional common-law criterion of the employment relationship has been the control test, as set down by Baron Bramwell in *R. v. Walker* (1858), 27 L.J.M.C. 207, 208:

> It seems to me that the difference between the relations of master and servant and of principal and agent is this: A principal has the right to direct what the agent has to do; but a master has not only that right, but also the right to say how it is to be done.

That this test is still fundamental is indicated by the adoption by the Supreme Court of Canada in *Hôpital Notre-Dame de l'Espérance and Theoret v. Laurent et al.*, [1978] 1 S.C.R. 605 at 613, of the following statement: "The essential criterion of employer-employee relations is the right to give orders and instructions to the employee regarding the manner in which to carry out his work".

Nevertheless, as Professor P.S. Atiyah, *Vicarious Liability in the Law of Torts*, London, Butterworths, 1967, p. 41, has put it, "the control test as formulated by Bramwell, B., ... wears an air of deceptive simplicity, which ... tends to wear thin on further examination". A principal inadequacy is its apparent dependence on the exact terms in which the task in question is contracted for: where the contract contains detailed specifications and conditions, which would be the normal expectation in a contract with an independent contractor, the control may even be greater than where it is to be exercised by direction on the job, as would be the normal expectation in a contract with a servant, but a literal application of the test might find the actual control to be less. In addition, the test has broken down completely in relation to highly skilled and professional workers, who possess skills far beyond the ability of their employers to direct.

Perhaps the earliest important attempt to deal with these problems was the development of the entrepreneur test by William O. (later Justice) Douglas, "Vicarious Liability and the Administration of Risk" (1928-29), 38 *Yale L.J.* 584, which posited four differentiating earmarks of the entrepreneur: control, ownership, losses, and profits. It was essentially this test which was applied by Lord Wright in *Montreal v. Montreal Locomotive Works Ltd. et al.*, [1947] 1 D.L.R. 161 at 169-70; [1946] 3 W.W.R. 748 at 756-58:

In earlier cases a single test, such as the presence or absence of control, was often relied on to determine whether the case was one of master and servant, mostly in order to decide issues of tortious liability on the part of the master or superior. In the more complex conditions of modern industry, more complicated tests have often to be applied. It has been suggested that a fourfold test would in some cases be more appropriate, a complex involving (1) control; (2) ownership of the tools; (3) chance of profit; (4) risk of loss. Control in itself is not always conclusive. Thus the master of a chartered vessel is generally the employee of the shipowner though the charterer can direct the employment of the vessel. Again the law often limits the employer's right to interfere with the employee's conduct, as also do trade union regulations. *In many cases the question can only be settled by examining the whole of the various elements which constitute the relationship between the parties. In this way it is in some cases possible to decide the issue by raising as the crucial question whose business is it, or in other words by asking whether the party is carrying on the business, in the sense of carrying it on for himself or on his own behalf and not merely for a superior.* In the present case the business or undertaking is the manufacture of the warlike vehicles. The respondent might have been making them with a view to selling them to the Government for its own profit. The Government as purchaser might in that case advance funds or subsidize the work: The Crown might, as it would presumably, take powers of supervision, inspection and regulation, having specified the tests which each vehicle is to satisfy. The Government might even provide the material or the factory to the actual manufacturer. These and kindred powers might be very wide, without the result being that the manufacturer was not doing the work for his own profit and at his own risk. But in reviewing in the present case the contracts which are the determining matters, their Lordships with great respect to the Judges below who have taken a different view, find themselves in agreement with the judgment of the Supreme Court. *The combined force of the whole scheme of operations* seems to them to admit of no other conclusion. The factory, the land on which it was built, the plant and machinery were all the property of the Government which had them appropriated or constructed for the very purpose of making the military vehicles. The materials were the property of the Government and so were the vehicles themselves at all stages up to completion. The respondent supplied no funds and took no financial risk and no liability, with the significant exception of bad faith or wanton neglect: every other risk was taken by the Government. It is true that the widest powers of management and administration were entrusted to the respondent but all was completely subject to the Government's control. A 'fee' was payable in respect of each completed vehicle, but when the whole plan is considered, that was solely as a reward for personal services in managing the whole undertaking. It was something very different from the risk of profit or loss which an independent contractor has to assume; every item of expense was borne by the Crown, just as the Government took every possible risk of loss or damage except in the very unlikely event, as already noted, of bad faith or wilful neglect on the part of the respondent. The undertaking throughout was the undertaking of the

> Government and not the undertaking of the respondent which was simply an agent or mandatory or manager on behalf of the Crown. The accuracy of the positive announcement in each of the contracts that the respondent was acting throughout under the contracts for and on behalf of the Government and as its agent cannot be controverted. [Emphasis added.]

Taken thus in context, Lord Wright's fourfold test is a general, indeed an overarching test, which involves "examining the whole of the various elements which constitutes the relationship between the parties". In his own use of the test to determine the character of the relationship in the *Montreal Locomotive Works* case itself, Lord Wright combines and integrates the four tests in order to seek out the meaning of the whole transaction.

A similar general test, usually called the "organization test" (though termed the "integration test" by the Tax Court here), was set forth by Denning, L.J. (as he then was) in *Stevenson, Jordan and Harrison, Ltd. v. MacDonald and Evans*, [1952] 1 T.L.R. 101, 111:

> One feature which seems to run through all the instances is that, under a contract of service, a man is employed as part of the business, and his work is done as an integral part of the business; whereas under a contract for services, his work, although done for the business, is not integrated into it but is only accessory to it.
>
> ...

The organization test was approved by the Supreme Court of Canada in *Cooperators Insurance Association v. Kearney*, [1965] S.C.R. 106 at 112, 48 D.L.R. (2d) 1 at 22-33, where Spence, J. for the Court quoted with approval the following passage from Fleming, *The Law of Torts* (2nd ed. 1961) 328-29:

> Under the pressure of novel situations, the courts have become increasingly aware of the strain on the traditional formulation [i.e., the control test], and most recent cases display a discernible tendency to replace it by something like an "organization" test. Was the alleged servant part of his employer's organization? Was his work subject to co-ordinational control as to "where" and "when" rather than to "how"?

The organization test has recently been described by MacKinnon, A.C.J.O. for the Ontario Court of Appeal as an enlargement of, and presumably an advance upon, Lord Wright's test: *Mayer v. J. Conrad Lavigne Ltd.* (1979), 27 O.R. (2d) 129 at 132, 105 D.L.R. (3d) 734 at 737. However, it has had less vogue in other common-law jurisdictions. In fact A. N. Khan, "Who Is a Servant?" (1979), 53 Austr. L.J. 832, 834, makes bold to say of the English and Australian cases:

> However, the "integration" or "organisation" test if applied in isolation can lead to as impractical and absurd results as the control test. The courts, therefore, came to the conclusion that a "multiple" test should be applied, in that all the factors should be taken into account. Thus in *Morren v. Swinton & Pendlebury Borough Council* [[1965] 1 W.L.R. 576] Lord Parker C.J. stated that the control test was perhaps an over-simplification. His Lordship added that: "clearly superintendence and control cannot be the decisive test when one is dealing with a professional man, or a man of some particular skill and experience". Thus the courts started modifying and transforming the test into [a] "common sense" test [Somervell L.J. in Cassidy v. Minister of Health, [1975] 2 K.B. 343] or "multiple" test [Mocatta J. in *Whittaker v. Minister of Pensions & National Insurance*, [1967] 1 Q.B. 156].

Professor Atiyah, supra, at 38-9 ends up with Lord Wright's test from the *Montreal Locomotive Works* case, as he finds it more general than Lord Denning's which he sees as decisive in only some cases.

I am inclined to the same view, for the same reason. I interpret Lord Wright's test not as the fourfold one it is often described as being but rather as a four-in-one test, with emphasis always retained on what Lord Wright, supra, calls "the combined force of the whole scheme of operations", even while the usefulness of the four subordinate criteria is acknowledged.

Lord Denning's test may be more difficult to apply, as witness the way in which it has been misused as a magic formula by the Tax Court here and in several other cases ... in all of which the effect has been to dictate the answer through the very form of the question, by showing that without the work of the "employees" the "employer" would be out of business ("Without the installers, the Appellant would be out of business"). As thus applied, this can never be a fair test, because in a factual relationship of mutual dependency it must always result in an affirmative answer. If the businesses of both parties are so structured as to operate through each other, they could not survive independently without being restructured. But that is a consequence of their surface arrangement and not necessarily expressive of their intrinsic relationship.

What must always remain of the essence is the search for the total relationship of the parties. Atiyah's counsel in this respect, supra, at 38, is, I believe, of great value:

> [I]t is exceedingly doubtful whether the search for a formula in the nature of a single test for identifying a contract of service any longer serves a useful purpose. ... The most that can profitably be done is to examine all the possible factors which have been referred to in these cases as bearing on the nature of the relationship between the parties concerned. Clearly not all of these factors will be relevant in all cases, or have the same weight in all cases. Equally clearly no magic formula can be propounded for determining which factors should, in any given case, be treated as the determining ones. The

> plain fact is that in a large number of cases the court can only perform a balancing operation, weighing up the factors which point in one direction and balancing them against those ... pointing in the opposite direction. In the nature of things it is not to be expected that this operation can be performed with scientific accuracy. This line of approach appears to be in keeping with what Lord Wright said in the little-known Privy Council decision in *Montreal Locomotive Works* ...

Of course, the organization test of Lord Denning and others produces entirely acceptable results when properly applied, that is, when the question of organization or integration is approached from the persona of the "employee" and not from that of the "employer", because it is always too easy from the superior perspective of the larger enterprise to assume that every contributing cause is so arranged purely for the convenience of the larger entity. We must keep in mind that it was with respect to the business of the employee that Lord Wright addressed the question "Whose business is it?"

Perhaps the best synthesis found in the authorities is that of Cooke, J. in *Market Investigations, Ltd. v. Minister of Social Security*, [1968] 3 All E.R. 732 at 738-39:

> The observations of Lord Wright, of Denning L.J., and of the judges of the Supreme Court in the U.S.A. suggest that the fundamental test to be applied is this: 'Is the person who has engaged himself to perform these services performing them as a person in business on his own account?' If the answer to that question is 'yes,' then the contract is a contract for services. If the answer is 'no' then the contract is a contract of service. No exhaustive list has been compiled and perhaps no exhaustive list can be compiled of considerations which are relevant in determining that question, nor can strict rules be laid down as to the relative weight which the various considerations should carry in particular cases. The most that can be said is that control will no doubt always have to be considered, although it can no longer be regarded as the sole determining factor; and that factors, which may be of importance, are such matters as whether the man performing the services provides his own equipment, whether he hires his own helpers, what degree of financial risk be taken, what degree of responsibility for investment and management he has, and whether and how far he has an opportunity of profiting from sound management in the performance of his task. The application of the general test may be easier in a case where the person who engages himself to perform the services does so in the course of an already established business of his own; but this factor is not decisive, and a person who engages himself to perform services for another may well be an independent contractor even though he has not entered into the contract in the course of an existing business carried on by him.

There is no escape for the trial judge, when confronted with such a problem, from carefully weighing all of the relevant factors, as outlined by Cooke, J.

It is patently obvious that the applicant's content on that Lord Denning's test should be applied only in the case of highly skilled workers is in no way supportable. It is, however, equally apparent that the Tax Court has erred in law in its use of that test. ...

What was the effect of the error of law in this case? If we excise the Tax Court's erroneous application of the organization or integration test from its decision, we are left with an inconclusive result, though on two tests out of three it found for the applicant. This Court cannot on a section 28 application engage in an examination of the evidence as such, unless a particular result is so inevitable on the facts that any other conclusion would be perverse. I would therefore allow the application, set aside the decision of the Tax Court judge in respect of the 1980 and 1981 tax years, and refer the matter back to the Tax Court judge for a determination consistent with these reasons.

Application allowed.

Notes and Questions

1. How does MacGuigan J. suggest that courts determine whether a working relationship is a contract of service or a contract for service?
2. According to MacGuigan J., what role does the entrepreneur/economic reality test, the integration test, the organization test and the control test play in the characterization of an employer-employee relationship? MacGuigan J. says that the best synthesis of the authorities is by Cooke, J. in *Market Investigations, Ltd. v. Minister of Social Security*, [1968] 3 All E.R. 732. Does this synthesis include all of the above tests?
3. The "specific results" test is also relied upon by the courts in characterizing an employment relationship. This test was set out by Jackett C.J. of the Exchequer Court in *Alexander v. M.N.R.*, [1969] C.T.C. 715, 70 D.T.C. 6006 at 724 [6011]. Dr. Alexander was a radiologist under contract to a hospital. The contract required Dr. Alexander to discharge administrative responsibilities and provide professional services, which included the securing of the services of more than one radiologist to provide twenty-four hour emergency work and a minimum of 9,000 examinations per year. Jackett C.J. found that Dr. Alexander was self-employed because his contract with the hospital provided for the "accomplishment of a specified job or task" rather than providing for the disposal of his personal services to the master hospital.
4. The "specific results" test was also applied in *Hauser v. M.N.R.*, [1978] C.T.C. 2728, 78 D.T.C. 1532 (T.R.B.). The Chairman concluded that Dr. Hauser was an employee of the hospital partly because, unlike Dr. Alexander, Dr. Hauser had

to personally perform the work set out in his contract to the hospital and his professional services were at the disposal of the hospital.

5. In *671122 Ontario Ltd. v. Sagaz Industries Canada Inc.*, [2001] 4 C.T.C. 139, [2001] 2 S.C.R. 983 (S.C.C.), reconsideration refused 2001 CarswellOnt 4155 (S.C.C.) (a vicarious liability case), the test in *Wiebe Door* was affirmed by the Supreme Court of Canada. The Court stated (at paragraph 46) that "... there is no one conclusive test which can be universally applied to determine whether a person is an employee or an independent contractor ... what must always occur is a search for the total relationship of the parties". The Supreme Court went on to describe the application of the test as follows (at paragraph 47):

> The central question is whether the person who has been engaged to perform the services is performing them as a person in business on his own account. In making this determination, the level of control the employer has over the worker's activities will always be a factor. However, other factors to consider include whether the worker provides his or her own equipment, whether the worker hires his or her own helpers, the degree of financial risk taken by the worker, the degree of responsibility for investment and management held by the worker, and the worker's opportunity for profit in the performance of his or her tasks.

The list of relevant factors for consideration is not exhaustive, and different weight is given to different factors depending on the circumstances of each case.

6. In *Wiebe Door*, MacGuigan J. acknowledges that Wiebe Door Services had a "specific understanding" with the door installers and repairers "that they would be running their own businesses and would therefore be responsible for their own taxes and any contributions for workers' compensation, unemployment insurance and Canada Pension Plan". At the same time, he stated that "Such an agreement is not of itself determinative of the relationship between the parties ..." As MacGuigan J. points out, courts are not bound by the intention of the parties to a contract and can characterize the source of income on the basis of the "substance" of the relationship (*Boardman v. The Queen*, [1979] C.T.C. 159, 79 D.T.C. 5110 (F.C.T.D.)). If the substance of a relationship is to prevail, how does this impact on the parties' freedom to contract?

7. More recent decisions of the Federal Court of Appeal have focused on the parties' intention although the cases are not consistent about the role of the intention of the parties in the determination of the issue. In *Wolf v. The Queen*, [2002] 3 C.T.C. 3, 2002 D.T.C. 6853 (Fed. C.A.), the Federal Court of Appeal reversed the Tax Court of Canada finding that the appellant was an independent contractor and not an employee. Two of the three justices, Justices Décary and Noël considered the intention of the parties in determining whether the appellant was an independent contractor or an employee. According to Décary at paragraph 117:

> ... I say, with great respect, that the courts in their propensity to create artificial legal categories have sometimes overlooked the very factor which is the essence of a contractual relationship, i.e. the intention of the parties ...

Justice Décary then said at para. 119:

> ... When a contract is genuinely entered into as a contract for services and is performed as such, the common intention of the parties is clear and that should be the end of the search.

Whereas Décary J.A. sees common intention as determinative, Noël J.A. at para. 122 treats intention as a balancing factor if the traditional *Wiebe Door* test does not yield a conclusive result:

> ... In my view, this is a case where the characterization which the parities have placed on their relationship ought to be given great weight. I acknowledge that the manner in which parties choose to describe their relationship is not usually determinative particularly where the applicable legal tests point in the other direction. But in a close case such as the present one, where the relevant factors point in both directions with equal force, the parties' contractual intent, and in particular their mutual understanding of the relationship cannot be disregarded.

In *Royal Winnipeg Ballet v. M.N.R.*, [2008] 1 C.T.C. 220, 2006 D.T.C. 6323 (F.C.A.), a majority of the Federal Court of Appeal determined that the intentions of the parties should always be taken into account in determining the total relationship of the parties. The Federal Court of Appeal reversed the Tax Court of Canada and held that the ballet dancers were independent contractors (Sharlow and Desjardins JJ.A. majority, Evans J.A. dissenting). Sharlow J.A. stated at paragraphs 60-61:

> ... One principle is that in interpreting a contract, what is sought is the common intention of the parties *rather than the adherence to the literal meaning of the words* .... The inescapable conclusion is that the evidence of the parties' understanding of their contract must always be examined and given appropriate weight. ... [t]his does not mean that the parties' declaration as to the legal character of their contract is determinative. Nor does it mean that the parties' statements as to what they intended to do must result in a finding that their intention has been realized ... [if] it is established that the terms of the contract, considered in the appropriate factual context, do not reflect the legal relationship that the parties profess to have intended, then their stated intention will be disregarded.

Justice Sharlow then said at paragraph 64:

> ... In these circumstances, it seems to me wrong in principle to set aside, as worthy of no weight, the uncontradicted evidence of the parties as to their common understanding of their legal relationship, even if that evidence cannot be conclusive. The judge should have considered the *Wiebe Door Services Ltd.* factors in light of this uncontradicted evidence and asked himself whether, on balance, the facts were consistent with the conclusion that the dancers were self-employed, as the parties understood to be the case, or were more consistent with the conclusion that the dancers were employees.

Finally, in *Lang v. M.N.R.* (2007), 2007 D.T.C. 1754 (T.C.C. [Employment Insurance]) D.G.H. Bowman C.J. did a comprehensive review of both the *Wolf* and *Royal Winnipeg Ballet* cases in determining that the appellants were independent contractors. He concluded at paragraph 34:

> Intent is a test that cannot be ignored but its weight is as yet undetermined. It varies from case to case from being predominant to being a tie-breaker. It has not been considered by the Supreme Court of Canada ... Trial judges who ignore intent stand a very good chance of being overruled in the Federal Court of Appeal.

See also *Gilpin Furniture & Funeral Service Ltd. v. The Queen*, 2009 TCC 192 (T.C.C. [Employment Insurance].

8. How much importance should be placed upon who is responsible for taxes and other contributions? See, for example, *Moose Jaw Kinsmen Flying Fins Inc. v. M.N.R.*, [1988] 2 C.T.C. 2377, 88 D.T.C. 6099 (F.C.A.). In *Moose Jaw*, the taxpayer engaged the services of a head swimming coach and assistant coaches on a part time basis. They were engaged under written contracts and paid at hourly rates. The head coach co-ordinated the assistants and supervised them on behalf of the taxpayer. The taxpayer owned some office equipment, and miscellaneous speed swimming equipment. The coaches provided their own whistles and stop watches. The taxpayer did not make unemployment contributions on behalf of the coaches. The Minister determined that the coaches were employees of the taxpayer and issued Notices of Assessment for the 1984 and 1985 taxation years for arrears of Unemployment Insurance contributions on behalf of the coaches. These assessments were confirmed by the Tax Court and the Federal Court of Appeal. In examining the nature of the relationship, the Federal Court of Appeal suggested (at paragraph 12) that "[i]n this case, perhaps the most cogent evidence was the employment contract. ... Properly construed, it seems to me that it points to a contract of service, i.e. an employer/employee relationship ..." See also *Baxter v. The Queen*, [1996] 3 C.T.C. 2311, 96 D.T.C. 3292 (T.C.C.). Baxter was an elevator technician who received a T-4 information return from Schindler Elevator Corporation showing contributions for Canada Pension Plan, registered pension plan, Unemployment Insurance and income tax deductions. In considering the importance of this fact to the characterization of the working relation-

ship, Bowman T.C.J. stated that: "None of these factors is in itself necessarily determinative, but cumulatively they are indicative of the status of an employee and not an independent contractor".

9. For a more recent enunciation of the *Wiebe Door* principles applied in distinguishing a contract of service from a contract for services, see *TBT Personnel Services Inc. v. The Queen,* 2011 FCA 256, 343 D.L.R. (4th) 100 (F.C.A.), leave to appeal refused 2012 CarswellNat 983 (S.C.C.) and *1392644 Ontario Inc. v. Canada*, 2013 FCA 85, 358 D.L.R. (4th) 363 (F.C.A.).

Consider the following decision in which the taxpayer had a contract with the university and received T-4 returns which accounted for his income as employment income. Do the courts consider the employer's T-4 reporting to be an important factor in determining if the relationship is one of employment or independent contracting? Should they?

CAVANAUGH v. THE QUEEN
[1997] 3 C.T.C. 2155, 97 D.T.C. 3292 (T.C.C.)

[The appellant Cavanagh was a tutorial leader and marker for a university course. He did not have an ongoing contract with the university. He had control over the scheduling and number of tutorials as well as marking. With the exception of a course outline and a solution manual, Cavanagh provided his own supplies to complete the work and was responsible for all off-campus expenses. He was not supervised by the university and received only limited supervision from the professor of the course which he was tutoring. The university issued Cavanagh a T-4 setting out the income as income from employment. Cavanagh reported the income as employment income but later claimed that he was in error. The Minister determined that Cavanagh was an employee of the university and denied him a deduction for automobile expenses for the 1991 taxation year. Cavanagh appealed the assessment on the basis that he was an independent contractor and therefore entitled to the deduction as expenses from business or professional income.]

Margeson T.C.J. (Orally):

... The Court is satisfied on the basis of all the evidence that this was an independent contractor situation. ...

The Court refers to the case of *Wiebe Door, supra*, which case directs that we consider the four-in-one test. In looking at the matter of control, the Court is satisfied that there was not a significant amount of control by York or the professors. There was none by York, there was a little bit by the professors, but under the circumstances of this case, the Court is satisfied that it was minimal and is not the type of control that one would expect to find in a normal employer/employee relationship.

With respect to the ownership of tools, the Court is satisfied that a proper consideration of the facts here militates against a finding of an employer/employee relationship. It has already indicated in its summary of the evidence that many of the tools of the trade were supplied by the Appellant himself. He supplied pens, the grade sheets, the floppy disks, he supplied to a large extent the marking materials and his own briefcase. He paid parking fees at York when he went there, he paid for outside material, he was given only the course outline and the solution manual by York.

The Appellant also indicated, significantly I think, that off-campus expenses were his own. He was free to set up tutorials at other places and he would have to pay for the expenses if he did. He said that he had autonomy. The Court is satisfied that he had a certain amount of autonomy with respect to presentation. Certainly with respect to the marking there did not seem to be any restriction or control over this marking and he did the marking whenever he wanted to. All he had to do was pick up the papers, he marked them and returned them to the professor. That is not control as envisioned by *Wiebe Door, supra*, as far as this Court is concerned.

With respect to supervision, if it is any different from control, the Court is satisfied that the only supervision he received was a minimal amount of supervision by the professor, not by York but by the professor who was running the course. According to the evidence it was probably only with respect to seeing if he was following the course content. With respect to marking, if a question arose with respect to the grade the professor might look at it but, other than that, there was very little control over him.

He could postpone a tutorial if he wanted to, he could set up another time, he could have extra tutorials if he wanted to. These were all factors which one would not expect to find with a university professor at least if he were an employee.

There was no real evidence as to what is expected generally of a university professor who is generally an employee but when the Court considers generally what a normal employee is reasonably expected to do, it finds that a normal employee would not be entitled to the amount of freedom that the Appellant had here.

The Court is satisfied that the Appellant followed a syllabus to a certain extent but that was a minimum amount of control. The Court is impressed to a certain extent by the fact that the Appellant was not a lecturer. That differentiates this case from some of the others. He was a course leader or a tutorial leader and he did some marking.

When the relationship was over, when the Appellant finished the marking, when the course and the tutorials were over, that was the end of any relationship that he had with York. He had to go back and re-solicit another contract or renegotiate a new relationship. He had no tenure whatsoever with York.

He stated that he might be rehired again, he might not ever be rehired again. He was asked the question if York was under any obligation to rehire him and he said no. He was also asked what would happen in the event that he got into difficulty and his answer basically on that was he did not expect really that York would look after him although he hoped that they might. He did not believe that it had any responsibility there. The course coordinator, or the professor in charge of the course decided who was retained for these contracts, it was not York itself.

With respect to his income tax return the Court is satisfied that he explained adequately what happened to that tax return. His actions were a bit surprising because he was an accountant but nonetheless even accountants make mistakes. The Court is satisfied that he explained sufficiently why the return was completed as it was. ...

It is significant and this was not in any of the other cases that were referred to, that the Appellant had the right to hire somebody else to do his work, to mark his papers, to do the tutorial if he wanted to and indeed he did this. It is satisfied also that this case is different from the other cases cited because the Appellant himself had the right to decide where the tutorials would be held. He could change the scheduling of the tutorials. He could have more tutorials if he found that the question put in one tutorial had to be carried over to another time or if he found that the students were not understanding particular questions in the tutorial. For that matter, he may have scheduled additional tutorials on his own initiative.

The Court is also satisfied that this case is different from the ones referred to because of the profit and loss argument. The Court is satisfied that there was a possibility of profit for him. There was an opportunity for profit, there was a possibility of loss. How much money he made depended to a certain extent upon how accurate he was in concluding how many students there were going to be and what the drop-out rate would be. In the end result, if he made a mistake, he could have earned less income. His time per hour would have been much less than it would have been if he had calculated it properly. To that extent there was a chance of profit. There was also a risk of loss.

With respect to the ownership of tools, the Appellant had many of the tools of the trade, so to speak. They were his own and not those of York. ...

With respect to integration, the integration test is a very difficult one, but the Court is satisfied here that to a certain extent the work of the Appellant was integrated into that of York in the sense that universities are there to teach courses and the Appellant was there to provide a tutorial for certain classes. He was there also to mark papers and that is part of the work of a university so to that extent it was integrated into the work of York, at least part of York. But it was not an integral part in the sense that the work of York could not be carried on in the event that this Appellant was not hired. York would have hired somebody else and indeed the Appellant was free himself to hire somebody else. That is a significant factor. ...

The manner of payment was of some importance. The Appellant was not paid on a regular basis as one would expect an employee to be paid. He might be without pay for three months or more and then was paid regularly, periodically a portion of what he was entitled to. However, it was impossible to calculate what he would ultimately earn due to the mortality rate of the class. ...

It is true that there was a T-4 which was given by York setting out the income as income from employment, but York is not entitled to decide whether it was an employer/employee relationship or that of an independent contractor. That is for the Court to decide. Just because York referred to this as employment income in a T-4 does not mean that it was correct.

...

The appeal is allowed and the matter is referred back to the Minister for reconsideration and reassessment based upon the Court's finding that the Appellant was entitled to deduct the amount of expenses in the year, of $4,770.12 as properly deductible expenses from income from a business or from professional income.

C. Attempts to Avoid Characterization as an Office or Employment

The obvious advantage of an independent contractor being able to deduct business expenses instead of being limited to the specific deductions in section 8 as an employee has led to certain arrangements designed to avoid the status of an employee. The following are three of the more common arrangements.

1. Interposing a Contract for Services

The employment relationship is characterized by an underlying contract of service whereas independent contractors are engaged on the basis of a contract for services. In certain instances, employees have been successful in shifting income to a business source by redefining the relationship through the introduction of a new and different form of contract (*D.B. MacDonald v. M.N.R.*, [1974] C.T.C. 2204, 74 D.T.C. 1161 (T.R.B.)). However, the courts are not bound by the terminology used in the contract and can characterize the source of income on the basis of the "substance" of the relationship (*Boardman v. The Queen*, [1979] C.T.C. 159, 79 D.T.C. 5110 (F.C.T.D.)).

2. Interposing a Corporation or Trust

Some taxpayers have attempted to alter their employment relationship by interposing a trust (of which the taxpayer and family members are the beneficiaries) or a corporation owned by the former employee, thereby shifting income to the trust or corporation where greater tax planning opportunities often exist. See Part III of Chapter 2 for a discussion of the tax-effectiveness of some of these arrangements.

3. Capitalization of the Employment Benefit

The expression "capitalization of the employment benefit" refers to various methods intended to convert what would otherwise be income from an office or employment into income from a capital source, which is either exempt or only partially taxed as a capital gain. Opportunities for capitalizing employment benefits arise during, at the beginning, and at the end of an employment relationship. Consider the following case and the role of subsection 6(3).

CURRAN v. M.N.R.
(1959), [1959] C.T.C. 416, 59 D.T.C. 1247 (S.C.C.)

[Curran, a 42-year-old geologist who was highly regarded in his field, was the manager of production for Imperial Oil. He was receiving $25,000 per year in salary and on his retirement at age 65 would have been entitled to a substantial pension. In 1951, Curran was induced by Brown, a substantial shareholder of Federated Petroleums Ltd. and Home Oil Ltd., to become the general manager of Federated Petroleums.

On August 15, 1951, two agreements were entered into. In the first, Brown, the grantor, agreed as follows:]

Now therefore this indenture witnesseth

1. The grantor hereby agrees to pay the grantee the sum of $250,000 in consideration of the loss of pension rights, chances for advancement, and opportunities for re-employment in the oil industry, consequent upon the resignation of the grantee from his present position with Imperial Oil Limited, the said sum to be paid forthwith upon the grantee informing his present employers that he is leaving their employ and whether or not employment has been offered to him by Federation Petroleums Limited or accepted by him, prior to that time.
2. In consideration of the agreement of the grantor to pay the said sum, the grantee hereby agrees to resign his position with Imperial Oil Limited, such resignation to take effect not later than the 15th day of September, A.D. 1951.

[Brown paid the $250,000 to the appellant, but Calta Assets Ltd. actually furnished the funds out of its own assets and from money borrowed from a bank. The second agreement was between Curran and Federated Petroleums. The appellant was also given the option, within a limited time, to purchase 25,000 shares of Home Oil Co. at a given price.]

Taschereau J. (dissenting): ...

The learned trial Judge [[1957] Ex. C.R. 377] has reached the conclusion that the sum of $250,000 paid to the appellant in 1951, constituted income within the meaning of the Act and was properly assessed as such.

I cannot escape the conclusion that a substantial part of this amount paid to the appellant by Robert A. Brown Jr., was a capital receipt in the circumstances of this case, and not taxable as such.

The appellant had been with Imperial Oil Ltd. since 1933, with one short interval, and in August, 1951 was manager of the Producing Department. He enjoyed a very high reputation as a geologist, and was a man of extensive knowledge. He earned a salary of $25,000 a year, and on two occasions had been invited to become a director of the company. If the appellant had remained in the employment of Imperial Oil Ltd. or an affiliated company, he would have been entitled, when reaching the retirement age of 65, to an annual pension of approximately $12,500, and as an employee of the company, many other privileges were available to him, such as group insurance, sick benefits, and a stock-purchase privilege. There were also great possibilities of salary increases.

It would indeed have been a very poor bargain for the appellant to enter into, without insisting upon a fair compensation, as he did in his written agreement with Brown, for foregoing such substantial actual and eventual benefits. I do not think however that the total of this amount of $250,000, which is in my view divisible, was paid to the appellant as consideration of the loss of those benefits. I believe that a proportion was for personal services to the new employer. As this division has not been made by the trial Judge, I would allow the appeal with costs, and refer the case back to the Exchequer Court so that it may apportion the part of this sum of $250,000 which is income, and therefore taxable, and the other part which is of a capital nature.

Martland, J.:

The facts of this case are contained in the judgment of the Chief Justice, including the contents of the agreement dated August 15, 1951, made between the appellant and Mr. R.A. Brown Jr. I agree with counsel for the respondent that this agreement must be considered in conjunction with the agreement of the same date, between the appellant and Federated Petroleums Ltd. (hereinafter referred to as "Federated"), which was executed immediately following the execution of the first-mentioned agreement. The agreement with Mr. Brown specifically recites that Brown, the holder of a substantial interest in Federated, is very desirous of persuading the appellant to resign from his position with Imperial Oil Ltd. in order to be free to accept an offer of employment from Federated. The employment contract with Federated enabled it to require the appellant to serve as manager of any other company or companies in which Federated had a financial interest.

These circumstances make it clear that the $250,000 payment was made by Brown to the appellant and received by the appellant to induce him to serve as manager of Federated or of Home and preferably, if possible, the latter. This being so, it seems to me that it constituted a payment for services to be rendered by the appellant.

For the appellant it is contended that the payment represented a capital receipt and not income. The argument is based upon the proposition that the agreement made by him with Brown was to provide compensation for loss or relinquishment of a source of income, which source was of itself a capital asset of the appellant.

In support of this submission several English decisions and an Australian case were cited. All of these were, however, cases in which an employer purchased from its employee a surrender by the latter of rights which he had previously held as against the employer. ...

[Martland J. reviewed the English and Australian jurisprudence and continued:]

In the present case it is clear that Mr. Brown was not seeking to acquire any rights which the appellant had under his existing employment contract with Imperial Oil Ltd. The agreement made by Brown with the appellant and Brown's evidence make it clear that he was seeking to acquire the skilled services of the appellant as a manager. In order that those services might be available it was necessary that the appellant should resign from his position with Imperial Oil Ltd. and such resignation resulted in the foregoing by him of various advantages which his employment with Imperial Oil Ltd. carried and which are referred to in the agreement. However, the essence of the matter was the acquisition of services and the consideration was paid so that those services would be made available.

I, therefore, think that the payment made to the appellant by Brown, under the agreement of August 15, 1951, was income to the appellant within the meaning of Section 3 of the *Income Tax Act,* 1948 (Can.), c. 52 [now paragraph 3(a)]. ...

Counsel for the respondent conceded that Section 24A [now subsection 6(3)] was not applicable to the circumstances of this case. Counsel for the appellant, however, urged that Section 24A was enacted in order to broaden the scope of Section 5 [now paragraph 5(1)(a)] so as to tax certain kinds of income not otherwise taxable under Section 5. He pointed out that Section 24A might have applied to the payment in question here if it had been made to the appellant by Federated or by Home. Since it did not apply, because the payment was not made by the appellant's employer, he contended that the payment could not be regarded as income within Section 3, because to so hold would make Section 24A meaningless in its application.

It seems to me, however, that Section 24A was essentially a provision dealing with onus of proof and deemed certain payments as therein defined to be payments within Section 5, unless the recipient could establish affirmatively that a payment did not reasonably fall within the provisions of paragraphs (i), (ii) or (iii) of Section 24A [now paragraphs 6(3)(c), (d) and (e)]. I do not think that it follows that payments which would fall within Section 24A, except for the fact that they were made by someone other than the employer, of necessity cannot be income within the provisions of Section 3.

In my opinion the appeal should be dismissed with costs.

[Judson J. concurred with Kerwin C.J.C.]

[Locke J. concurred with Kerwin C.J.C. and Martland J.]

Notes and Questions

1. Opportunities for capitalizing employment benefits arise at the end of an employment relationship when an employer makes an extraordinary payment to a departing employee. Employees in receipt of such extraordinary payments have attempted to characterize these amounts as something other than income. The Minister, however, has an array of statutory tools to prevent tax avoidance in this area. These include:
   (1) subparagraph 56(1)(a)(ii), which includes "retiring allowances" in income; and
   (2) subsection 6(3), which can include in employment income amounts received both before and after the period of actual employment.
2. In *Richstone v. The Queen*, [1974] C.T.C. 155, 74 D.T.C. 6129 (F.C.A.), subsection 6(3) was applied to bring into employment income an amount paid, upon the termination of employment, for a covenant not to compete made by the employee.
3. Subsection 6(3) was also applied in *Choquette v. The Queen*, [1974] C.T.C. 742, 74 D.T.C. 6563 (F.C.T.D.) to a payment made to an employee on the surrendering of his rights under an employment contract in return for a "capital indemnity". The employee continued to work for the company in a different capacity. If he had left his employer entirely, would subsection 6(3) still bring the "capital indemnity" into the employee's income?
4. In *Schwartz v. The Queen*, [1996] 1 C.T.C. 303, 96 D.T.C. 6103 (S.C.C.), the taxpayer received $360,000 in damages on the unilateral termination of his employment contract before he had commenced his employment duties. The Tax

Court of Canada found that the amount was neither a "retiring allowance", nor income from a source under section 3 of the Act. That decision was reversed by the Federal Court of Appeal, but upheld by the Supreme Court of Canada. The case is considered further in Part I of Chapter 2.

5. It is interesting to contrast the result in *Curran* with U.K. jurisprudence. Consider *Pritchard v. Arundale*, [1971] 3 All E.R. 1011 (Ch. Div.). In this case Mr. A had been in private practice in a firm of chartered accountants for 26 years. He was an auditor of a company set up by a Mr. L., who persuaded him to leave his job and become a managing director of Mr. L's company. As well as his salary, Mr. A, in consideration for his undertaking to serve the company, received an option to purchase shares from Mr. L. The Inland Revenue contended that the shares represented emoluments of the taxpayer's office and hence were taxable. However, Mr. A argued that the shares were merely compensation and an inducement for leaving his practice. The taxpayer succeeded. Would the result be the same under subsection 6(3) of the Act?
6. Contrast the decision in *Au v. The Queen*, [2005] 3 C.T.C. 2155, 2005 D.T.C. 794 (T.C.C.), appeal dismissed [2006] 2 C.T.C. 235, 2006 D.T.C. 6074 (F.C.A.). Are these cases distinguishable?

II. AMOUNTS INCLUDED IN COMPUTING INCOME FROM AN OFFICE OR EMPLOYMENT

A. Salary, Wages and Other Remuneration

Section 5 includes in a taxpayer's income any amounts received as salary, wages, gratuities and "other remuneration". "Salary and wages" have been given their ordinary meaning and include compensation for services rendered by employees in the course of their duties. "Gratuities" are voluntary payments made in consideration of services rendered in the course of a taxpayer's office or employment. "Other remuneration" includes honoraria, commissions, bonuses, gifts, rewards, gratuities and prizes provided as compensation for services.

B. Benefits

1. Introduction

Although the term "other remuneration" in section 5 is sufficiently broad to include most benefits received other than by way of salary or wages, paragraph 6(1)(a) was enacted to ensure that the value of all benefits (cash and non-cash) are included in the computation of a taxpayer's income. The paragraph requires the inclusion of the value of "board", "lodging" and "other benefits of any kind whatever".

The taxation of benefits is influenced by many considerations. Obviously, one of the more important policy concerns is the potential for erosion of the income tax base of the government. There could be a substantial revenue loss if employees received part of their remuneration in the form of indirect benefits rather than in the form of direct cash payments and the benefits were excluded from income. Equally important, however, is the policy concern for equity. Is it fair for a taxpayer who receives remuneration in the form of indirect benefits to exclude such benefits from income when other taxpayers in receipt of an equivalent amount in cash are fully taxed?

In addition to revenue and equity considerations, the tax authorities must bear in mind two other concerns. First, they must be satisfied that the cost of administering the tax system (in this context, the cost of collecting the tax on benefits) does not outweigh the incremental revenue derived from the taxation of benefits. For example, although it is easy to accept that an employer that supplies subsidized meals to its employees confers a benefit on the employees who consume the meals, it is neither easy nor cheap to administer a system that can keep an accurate record of the value of benefits conferred. How does one record, for example, which employees consume the meals and how does one calculate the amount of the subsidy in each meal?

Second, there are important political considerations in taxing benefits. Transportation passes for bus, rail and air travel issued to employees of transportation companies usually confer a benefit on employees who use them. These companies have powerful labour unions. Passes are also issued to Members of Parliament who are allowed to travel first class on a space confirmed basis. Thus, Revenue Minister William Rompkey may have had broader concerns on his mind when he indicated in the House of Commons on January 22, 1982 that he had "... no intention of taxing the value of free passes on the railways available for railway employees".

Historically, only money or something convertible into money was included in income for tax purposes, as explained in the following background study prepared for the Carter Commission.

STUDIES OF THE ROYAL COMMISSION ON TAXATION — NO. 16 — SPECIFIC TYPES OF PERSONAL INCOME

D. Sherbaniuk
(1967), pp. 33-35 [Footnotes deleted]

Chapter 3

THE TAXATION OF BENEFITS AND ALLOWANCES FROM AN OFFICE OR EMPLOYMENT

THE TAX TREATMENT OF BENEFITS

A fundamental principle of the common law concept of income is that only money or something capable of being turned into money can constitute income for tax purposes; a mere benefit or advantage, which may be of value to the person who enjoys it, is not includible in his income. The leading authority for this proposition is the decision of the House of Lords in *Tennant v. Smith*. In that case the appellant, a bank agent, was bound, as part of his duty, to occupy the bank house in order to care for the premises and to be on hand for the transaction of any special bank business after hours. He was not allowed to sublet the house or use it for other than bank business. In deciding whether the appellant was entitled to certain relief from taxation which was granted to persons whose total income was below a stipulated amount, the House of Lords held that the value of his residence had been improperly included as part of his income from an office or employment. As has been pointed out elsewhere, the ground for the court's decision may have been that, since a free residence was not "beneficially received" by the appellant, its value did not constitute income to him. That is to say, just as a sum of money paid by a master to his servant to be expended by the servant on the master's behalf and for which the servant is accountable, is not income to the servant, so, too, the value of living accommodation occupied free of charge by a servant in the course of his duties *and for the benefit of his master is not income to the servant*, even though he derives some advantage by not having to rent other quarters. However that may be, certain statements made by members of the court have since been interpreted as establishing the principle *that only money or what is convertible into money can constitute income.* Some of their Lordships based their decision on the narrow ground that the language of Schedules D and E, under which alone the appellant fell to be taxed, extended only to money payments or payments convertible into money, and was not apt to tax other benefits. Lord Macnaghten was not content to rest his judgment on any strict interpretation of the language of the schedules:

> The real answer is, that the thing which the Crown now seeks to charge is not income. ... [The duty under Schedules D and E] is a tax on income in the proper sense of the word. It is a tax on what "comes in"-on actual receipts. ... No doubt if the appellant had to find lodgings for himself he might have to pay for them. His income goes further because he is relieved from that expense. But a person is chargeable for income tax under Schedule D, as well as under Schedule E, not on what saves his pocket, but on what goes into his pocket. And the benefit which the appellant derives from having a rent-free house provided for him by the bank, brings in nothing which can be reckoned up as a receipt or properly described as income.

Furthermore, a conclusion contrary to that reached by their Lordships would have involved the proposition that the taxability of free accommodation depended upon the suitability of the premises to the taxpayer. This proposition was quite unacceptable to Lord Halsbury:

> ... in every case where such a question arose it would be necessary to examine the particular circumstances of each man's family. If he had a large family that could not be accommodated in the house, and he must hire a house elsewhere, one result would follow. If he was a bachelor, and the house was appropriate to his wants, then another result would follow.
>
> I cannot think that the legislature ever contemplated such an examination or discrimination of persons subject to taxation as such a system of assessment would imply.

Both Lord Watson and Lord Macnaghten remarked that, although the Act contained express directions for estimating and calculating the value of property for certain purposes, it contained no direction for estimating or bringing into account any benefit or advantage or enjoyment derived from free residence.

The rule in *Tennant v. Smith* that only money or what is convertible into money can constitute income has probably been part of Canadian income tax law from its inception in 1917. The rule appears to have been regarded as applicable under the *Income War Tax Act*, although there is no Canadian judicial authority to that effect. In a recent case arising under the *Income Tax Act, McCullagh Estate v. M.N.R.*, Thurlow J. quoted with approval from the judgment of Lord Macnaghten in *Tennant v. Smith* that a person is taxable not on what saves his pocket, but on what goes into his pocket.

In *Waffle v. M.N.R.*, [1968] C.T.C. 572, 69 D.T.C. 5007 (Ex. Ct.), Cattanach J. dealt with the problem of applying *Tennant v. Smith,* [1892] A.C. 150, in the context of Canadian tax law. Noting that this House of Lords decision was decided under the United Kingdom taxation legislation, which did not contain a provision similar to paragraph 6(1)(a), he stated:

> I think that the language employed in Section 5 [now 6] to the effect that the "value of board, lodging and other benefits of any kind whatsoever" is to be included in taxable income, overcomes the principle laid down in *Tennant v. Smith*. Obviously board which has been consumed and lodging which has been engaged cannot be converted into money by the taxpayer either subsequently or prior thereto and, in my view, identical considerations apply to "other benefits of any kind whatsoever".

The only specified benefits in paragraph 6(1)(a) are "board" and "lodging". The question of whether an employee received lodging was considered in the following case.

SORIN v. M.N.R.
(1964), 34 Tax A.B.C. 263, 64 D.T.C. 62 (T.A.B.)

Weldon J.O.:

During Philip Sorin's 1958 taxation year, which is now under appeal, the City Hotel in St. Catharines, Ontario, was operated by a partnership composed of Mr. Sorin and Albert Taube. ... When the partnership was formed in 1952 the appellant agreed to manage the two beverage rooms and to look after the renting of the hotel rooms, and Albert Taube agreed to look after the book-keeping, the payment of accounts and the banking for the partnership. ... By Notice of Re-assessment, mailed to the appellant on April 4, 1960, the Minister charged [Sorin] with a benefit, allegedly received by him, in the form of a room in the City Hotel, which was valued at $4 per week [1/2 the normal rate] for 52 weeks or $208.

... Philip Sorin testified that he was unmarried, and made his home with a brother living in St. Catharines. He said that, on the average, he was unable to get away from the hotel until from about 3:30 a.m to 4:30 a.m. four or five nights a week, because of certain duties which he had to perform after the beverage rooms were closed, and also, there were always the problems to be dealt with created by obstreperous visitors of the hotel guests. So, rather than disturb his brother's home at 4:00 a.m. or thereabouts he followed the practice of staying at the hotel on late nights in room 23, situated in the back part of the main floor. Mr. Sorin also followed the custom of having an afternoon nap in the room because of his strenuous night duties. The room is also used for storing 15 to 20 cartons of hotel records, tools, a spare television set, which is very essential to a beverage room and other articles. In listening to the appellant's evidence in respect of this room, I could not help but come to the conclusion, that he would have much preferred to have spent more time in his room in his brother's home if his hotel duties had permitted him to do so. Mr. Sorin's demeanour in the witness box was convincing, and he appeared to come through his cross-examination by counsel for the respondent unscathed.

To succeed in his contention, the respondent was bound to establish that room 23, under all of the circumstances, was "lodging" to the appellant for the purposes of Section 5(1)(a) of the Act. It should be mentioned that the City Hotel does not serve meals. Mr. Sorin's uncontradicted evidence was that he made his home with his brother. Therefore, it seems unrealistic to me to argue that Parliament intended to levy a tax on the appellant herein for the privilege of using a room for cat naps and short rest periods each business day, under the pretext that he was being provided "lodging", where the taxpayer in question was obliged to perform his duties under very exhausting conditions. I have, therefore, come to the conclusion that room 23 in the City Hotel did not in the taxation year under appeal represent "lodging" to the appellant within Section 5(1)(a) of the Act.

Notes and Questions

1. Why did the Minister include only $208 in Sorin's income? Why wasn't $416 the proper amount to be included?
2. Is there any substance to the Tax Appeal Board's conclusion that Sorin did not receive "lodging"? If he did not have other lodging would the result in the case have been different?
3. Are there any other arguments which support the result in the case?

Other than "board" or "lodging" and subject to the exceptions contained in paragraphs 6(1)(a)(i) to (v), an amount is taxable under paragraph 6(1)(a) if it is:

- a "benefit of any kind whatever"; and
- "received or enjoyed in the year in respect of, in the course of, or by virtue of an office or employment".

If both of these requirements are satisfied, the "value" of the benefit is included in the taxpayer's income under paragraph 6(1)(a).

The second requirement is considered first.

2. "In Respect of, in the Course of, or by Virtue of an Office or Employment"

The fact that a taxpayer "received or enjoyed" a "benefit" does not automatically mean that the "benefit" is taxable. Paragraph 6(1)(a) requires that the benefit is "received or enjoyed in respect of, in the course of, or by virtue of an office or employment". Initially, following U.K. law, Canadian courts interpreted this part of paragraph 6(1)(a) to require a causal connection between the services rendered by the employee or officer and the receipt or enjoyment of the benefit. In order to be a taxable benefit, the benefit had to be of the character of remuneration for services. In the following case the Supreme Court of Canada adopted a much broader interpretation of the necessary relationship between a benefit and a taxpayer's employment or office.

THE QUEEN v. SAVAGE
[1983] C.T.C. 393, 83 D.T.C. 5409 (S.C.C.)

Dickson J:

... The question is whether the sum of $300 received by Elizabeth Joan Savage from her employer, Excelsior Life Insurance Company ("Excelsior"), for successful completion of the Life Office Management Association series of examinations, is subject to income tax.

...

Mrs. Savage was employed by Excelsior as a research assistant. During 1976, she took three Life Office Management Association courses: Life Insurance Law, Economics and Investment, and Life Insurance Actuary Mathematics. The courses are designed to provide a broad understanding of modern life insurance and life insurance company operations, including management practices and personnel needs. The courses were voluntarily taken by Mrs. Savage to improve her knowledge in the life insurance field. She received from Excelsior $300 ($100 per course) as a result of passing the examinations. Such payment per course was available to all employees of Excelsior in accordance with company policy, designed to encourage self-upgrading of staff members. The courses, in both study time required and complexity of material, were comparable to university courses. Approximately 61 per cent of those taking the examinations in 1976 in the United States and Canada passed. One hundred or so Excelsior employees wrote the examinations in the spring and fall of 1976; the percentage passing slightly exceeded the overall United States and Canadian average results.

Excelsior reported the amount of $300 on a T4A Supplementary under "Other Income", indicating it was a "prize for passing LOMA examinations", and claimed it as an expense of doing business.

Receipt of a prize comes under paragraph 56(1)(n) of the *Income Tax Act*, SC 1970-71-72, c 63. ...

Mrs. Savage did not include the payment to her of $300 in the computation of her income for the 1976 taxation year. The Minister, by notice of reassessment, assessed the amount in the computation of her income on the basis that it constituted income of the taxpayer from an office or employment.

By notice of objection Mrs. Savage took issue with the assessment on the basis that the amount was a prize for achievement, and as it was less than $500 it did not have to be included in income.

The Minister confirmed the assessment by notification "on the ground that the prize in the amount of $300 paid to you by your employer, the Excelsior Life Insurance Company, had been properly included in the computation of your income for the year in accordance with the provisions of sections 3 and 5 of the Act". ...

A Benefit in Respect of Employment

As I noted, all members of the Federal Court of Appeal concluded the payments aggregating $300 were not within subsection 5(1) or paragraph 6(1)(a) because they were not payments "for services as an employee". LeDain, J. said:

> The sum of $100 paid to the appellant for successful completion of a course was not a payment for services rendered as an employee. It was not related in any way to her services as an employee. The courses were taken voluntarily, on her own time. There was no obligation as an employee to take them. The interest of the employer was that the courses would make her a more valuable employee. The payment was in the nature of a gift to encourage employees to take the courses and successfully complete them. The employment was certainly a condition of being able to receive the payment, but the payment was not received by reason of the employment but by reason of the successful completion of the course.

LeDain, J. relied on *Estate of Phaneuf v. The Queen*, [1978] 2 F.C. 564 (T.D.) and *Ball (H M Inspector of Taxes) v. Johnson* (1971), 47 Tax Cas. 155 (Ch. D.).

The *Ball* case was much like the one at bar. The Midland Bank expected its staff, among whom was Mr. Johnson, to study and sit for examinations of the Institute of Banks, to qualify themselves better as bankers. The bank paid cash awards to those who passed, including Johnson. It was held the reason for the payments was Johnson's personal success in passing the examinations and they were not remuneration for his services with the bank. The case is of little relevance, however, because of the language of Rule 1 of Schedule E of the *Income Tax Act* 1952 (Eng). The tax, if any, arose under section 156 of that Act, as amended by section 10 of the *Finance Act* 1956 (Eng). The relevant parts of section 156 were as follows:

> The Schedule referred to in this Act as Schedule E is as follows — 1. Tax under this Schedule shall be charged in respect of any office or employment or emoluments therefrom ...

The result reached by the Court was unexceptional having regard to the language being construed and in particular "emoluments therefrom". The significance of these words, not found in our Act, was touched on by Lord Reid in *Laidler v. Perry (Inspector of Taxes)*, [1965] 2 All E.R. 121 (H.L.) at 124:

> Section 156 however, applies only to "emoluments *therefrom*", i.e., from the office or employment of the recipient, and it is well settled that not every sum or other profit received by an employee from his employer in the course of his employment is to be regarded as arising from the employment. So the question in this case is whether these profits or emoluments of £10 did or did not arise from the taxpayer's employment.
>
> There is a wealth of authority on this matter and various glosses on or paraphrases of the words in the Act of 1952 appear in judicial opinions, including speeches in the House. No doubt they were helpful in the circumstances of the cases in which they were used, but in the end we must always return to the words in the statute and answer the question — did this profit arise from the employment? The answer will be no if it arose from something else.

And in *Hochstrasser* (*Inspector of Taxes) v. Mayes*, [1960] A.C. 376 (H.C.) Viscount Simonds adopted, at p. 388, the language of Upjohn, J., before whom the matter first came:

> Indeed, in my judgment, the authorities show that to be a profit arising from the employment the payment must be made in reference to the services the employee renders by virtue of his office, and it must be something in the nature of a reward for services past, present or future.
>
> In this passage the single word 'past' may be open to question, but apart from that it appears to me to be entirely accurate.

The *Hochstrasser* case and *Ball v. Johnson* are of little assistance. The provisions of section 156 of the *Income Tax Act* 1952 of England are not unlike subsection 5(1) of the Canadian *Income Tax Act* but our Act goes further in paragraph 6(1)(a). In addition to the salary, wages and other remuneration referred to in subsection 5(1), paragraph 6(1)(a) includes in income the value of benefits "of any kind whatever ... received or enjoyed ... in respect of, in the course of, or by virtue of an office or employment".

In *Phaneuf, supra*, the issue was whether Mr. Phaneuf was liable for income tax in respect of a benefit received by him on the purchase of shares. He acquired the shares in Charles Ogilvy Limited, his employer, pursuant to a bequest of the Company's principal shareholder. The bequest gave the right to the Company's employees to acquire a number of shares at par value. The Company's Board of Directors revised the list of employees entitled to purchase shares and approved a formula for distribution based on service to some extent. Mr. Phaneuf bought shares of a par value of $2 although they had a market value at the time of $17.25. In the Federal Court, Mr. Justice Thurlow, then ACJ of the Trial Division, held that the benefit was conferred on Mr. Phaneuf as a person and not as an employee and as a personal gift rather than as remuneration, and hence not a taxable benefit. Thurlow, ACJ followed *Ransom v. M.N.R.*, [1968] 1 Ex. C.R. 293. In *Ransom* Noël, J. referred to the difference between Rule 1 of Schedule E of the English statute and the provisions of our *Income Tax Act* and then observed, at 307:

> I now come to section 5(1)(a) and (b) [now paragraphs 6(1)(a) and (b)] of the Act which, as already mentioned, is couched in language which appears to be wider than the English taxation rule on which the taxpayers in *Hochstrasser v. Mayes* and *Jennings v. Kinder (supra)* were held not to be taxable. The Canadian taxation section indeed uses such embracing words that at first glance it appears extremely difficult to see how anything can slip through this wide and closely interlaced legislative net.
>
> In order, however, to properly evaluate its intent it is, I believe, necessary to bear in mind firstly, that section 5 of the Act is concerned solely with the taxation of income identified by its relationship to a certain entity, namely, an office or employment and in order to be taxable as income from an office or employment, money received by an employee must not merely constitute income as distinct from capital, but it must arise from his office or employment. Similar comments were made in Hochstrasser v. Mayes with reference to the English legislation by Viscount Simmonds at p 705 and by Lord Radcliffe, at p 707. Secondly, the question whether a payment arises from an office or employment depends on its causative relationship to an office or employment, in other words, whether the services in the employment are the effective cause of the payment. I should add here that the question of what was the effective cause of the payment is to be found in the legal source of the payment, and here this source was the agreement which resulted from the open offer of the employer to compensate its employee for his loss and the acceptance by him of such offer. The cause of the payments is not the services rendered, although such services are the occasion of the payment, but the fact that because of the manner in which the services must be rendered or will be rendered, he will incur or have to incur a loss which other employees paying taxes do not have to suffer.

Thurlow, ACJ adopted that passage and the following words of Viscount Cave LC in *Seymour v. Reed*, [1927] A.C. 554 (H.L.) at 559:

> The question, therefore, is whether sum of £939, 16s fell within the description, contained in r 1 of Sch E of "salaries, fees, wages, perquisites or profits whatsoever therefrom" (ie, from an office or employment of profit) "for the year of assessment", so as to be liable to income tax under that Schedule. These words and the corresponding expressions contained in the earlier statutes (which were not materially different) have been the subject of judicial interpretation in cases which have been cited to your Lordships; and must now (I think) be taken as settled that they include all payments made to the holder of an office or employment as such, that is to say, by way of remuneration for his services, even though such payments may be voluntary, but that they do not include a mere gift or present (such as a testimonial) which is made to him

> on personal grounds and not by way of payment for h s services. The question to be answered is, as Rowlatt J put it: "Is it in the end a personal gift or is it remuneration?" If the latter, it is subject to the tax; if the former, it is not.

Mr. Justice Thurlow then said, at 572:

> While the language of the statutes differ, the test expressed by Viscount Cave LC *(supra)* appears to me to express, as well as it can be expressed, the essence of what falls within the taxing provision of the *Income Tax Act*. Is the payment made "by way of remuneration for his services" or is it "made to him on personal grounds and not by way of payment for his services"? It may be made to an employee but is it made to him as employee or simply as a person. Another way of stating it is to say is it received in his capacity as employee, but that appears to me to be the same test. To be received in the capacity of employee it must, as I see it, partake of the character of remuneration for services. That is the effect that, as it seems to me, the words "in respect of, in the course of or by virtue of an office or employment" in paragraph 6(1)(a) have.

I agree that the appropriate test in *Phaneuf* was whether the benefit had been conferred on Mr. Phaneuf as an employee or simply as a person. It would seem that Mr. Phaneuf received, as a person, the right to acquire the shares and therefore the case was correctly decided. With great respect, however, I do not agree with the latter part of the passage last quoted and in particular the statement that, to be received in the capacity of employee, the payment must partake of the character of remuneration for services. Such was the conclusion in the English cases but based on much narrower language. Our Act contains the stipulation, not found in the English statutes referred to, "benefits of any kind whatever ... in respect of, in the course of, or by virtue of an office or employment". The meaning of "benefit of whatever kind" is clearly quite broad; in the present case the cash payment of $300 easily falls within the category of "benefit". Further, our Act speaks of a benefit "in respect of" an office or employment. In *Nowegijick v. The Queen*, [1983] C.T.C. 20, 83 D.T.C. 5041 [[1983] 1 S.C.R. 29 (S.C.C.)], this Court said, at 25 [5045], that:

> The words "in respect of" are, in my opinion, words of the widest possible scope. They import such meanings as "in relation to", "with reference to" or "in connection with". The phrase "in respect of" [is] probably the widest of any expression intended to convey some connection between two related subject matters.

See also *Paterson v. Chadwick*, [1974] 2 All E.R. 772 (Q.B.D.) at 775.

I agree with what was said by Evans, JA in *R v. Poynton*, [1972] 3 O.R. 727 at 738, speaking of benefits received or enjoyed in respect of, in the course of, or by virtue of an office or employment:

> I do not believe the language to be restricted to benefits that are related to the office or employment in the sense that they represent a form of remuneration for services rendered. If it is a material acquisition which confers an economic benefit on the taxpayer and does not constitute an exemption, eg. loan or gift, then it is within the all-embracing definition of s. 3.

It is difficult to conclude that the payments by Excelsior to Mrs. Savage were not in relation to or in connection with her employment. As Mr. Justice Grant said, the employee took the course to improve his or her knowledge and efficiency in the company business and for better opportunity of promotion.

As Crown counsel submits, the sum of $300 received by Mrs. Savage from her employer was a benefit and was received or enjoyed by her in respect of, in the course of or by virtue of her employment within the meaning of paragraph 6(1)(a) of the *Income Tax Act*; it was paid by her employer in accordance with the company policy upon the successful completion of courses "designed to provide a broad understanding of modern life insurance and life insurance company operations" and "to encourage self-upgrading of staff members"; the interest of the employer "was that the courses would make her a more valuable employee"; Mrs. Savage took the courses to "improve [her] knowledge and efficiency in the company business and for better opportunity for promotion". Distinguishing this case from *Phaneuf*, there was no element of gift, personal bounty or of considerations extraneous to Mrs. Savage's employment.

I would hold that the payments received by Mrs. Savage were in respect of employment. That, of itself, makes them income from a source under section 3 of the Act.

[Appeal dismissed]

As noted in Chapter 2, certain monetary receipts are not income. For example, gambling gains, windfalls such as lottery prizes, and gifts are not income. However, what if an employer "gives" something to his employee? If the thing given is required by the employment contract, it is clearly a "benefit" given in "in respect of, in the course of, or by virtue of" the job.

But what about a gratuitous benefit, given by way of the employer's munificence, and not by virtue of a legal obligation? Clearly gifts are a benefit. The issue is whether they are "received or enjoyed in respect of, in the course of, or by virtue of an office or employment". Is "intention" a factor in determining the "source" of income? Consider the following case.

LAIDLER v. PERRY
[1965] 2 W.L.R. 1171, [1965] 2 All E.R. 121 (H.L.)

Lord Reid:

My Lords, the Appellant appeals against additional assessments to Income Tax of £10 for each of the years 1955-56 to 1960-61. Each assessment of £10 is in respect of a voucher given to the Appellant by his employer at Christmas. He is research manager of Associated Lead Manufacturers, Ltd., a company formed by amalgamation of a number of old family businesses. It had been the custom of these businesses to make Christmas gifts in kind, such as turkeys, to members of their staffs and to provide entertainment for their manual workers and after amalgamation this custom was continued. When it became impossible during the last war to make gifts in kind, National Savings Certificates were given instead. After the war it was decided to give a voucher for £10 to each member of the staff, including ex-members drawing pensions, to be spent in shops of their choice. In 1960 about 2,300 vouchers for £10 were so given. Each year the gift is enclosed with a letter from the chairman sending Christmas greetings and expressing the thanks of the board for past services and their confidence that good relations with the staff would continue. Letters received in reply show that this was much appreciated.

The Appellant and other members of the staff are taxable under Schedule E of the Income Tax Act, 1952, as amended by the Finance Act, 1966, of which the leading provision in Section 156 is:

> Tax under this Schedule shall be charged in respect of any office or employment on emoluments therefrom; ...

and in the Second Schedule to the Finance Act, 1956, it is provided that

> the expression 'emoluments' shall include all salaries, fees, wages, perquisites and profits whatsoever.

It is not disputed that this definition is wide enough to include these vouchers, and it is not now disputed that, by reason of the very wide range of choice in spending them, each is worth its face value of £10. But Section 156 applies only to "emoluments *therefrom*", i.e., from the office or employment of the recipient, and it is well settled that not every sum or other profit received by an employee from his employer in the course of his employment is to be regarded as arising from the employment. So the question in this case is whether these profits or emoluments of £10 did or did not arise from the Appellant's employment.

There is a wealth of authority on this matter, and various glosses on or paraphrases of the words in the Act appear in judicial opinions including speeches in this House. No doubt they were helpful in the circumstances of the cases in which they were used, but in the end we must always return to the words in the Statute and answer the question — did this profit arise from the employment? The answer will be no if it arose from something else. ...

The Commissioners have found as a fact the reason why these vouchers were given:

> The directors of the group followed this policy because the distribution of personal presents at Christmas time was one of several measures which help to maintain a feeling of happiness among the staff and to foster a spirit of personal relationship between the management and staff; the directors believing that a contented staff was a good thing in itself and likely to be of advantage to the group.

The Appellant argues that this shows that these gifts were not rewards for services; it would have been derisory if not insulting to give £10 to a man in his high position as a reward for his services. I would accept that, but I think that, although the word "reward" has been used in many of the cases, it is not apt to include all the cases which can fall within the statutory words. To give only one instance, it is clear that a sum given to an employee in the hope or expectation that the gift will produce good service by him in future is taxable. But one can hardly be said to reward a man for something which he has not yet done and may never do.

The Appellant's argument is that these gifts were made not as rewards but to promote loyalty and good relations. That may be so. But each voucher must have been given to promote the loyalty of and good relations with the recipient. The case is quite different where, out of benevolence, a gift is made to an employee who is in difficulties. That may be justified as a payment which it is proper for a public company to make because indirectly it will benefit the company by showing that they are good employers. But the gift is not made merely because the donee is an employee. His employment is not the *causa causans*. Here it is. Vouchers are given to all members of the staff alike.

The real question appears to me to be whether these vouchers can be said to be mere personal gifts, inspired not by hope of some future quid pro quo from the donee but simply by personal goodwill appropriately signified at Christmas time. That is a question of fact, and in their decision the Commissioners say:

> ... we hold that the vouchers were made available in return for services rather than as gifts not constituting a reward for services.

The expression "in return for services" and "reward for services" may not be very aptly chosen, but this finding does appear to me to negative mere personal gift, and it appears to me to be unassailable.

Whatever might be said if the gifts to the Appellant were considered in isolation, we must I think consider them in their context. Leaving pensioners aside, vouchers for £10 were given to over 2,000 members of the staff of whom some part-time employees received as little as £4 10s. per week. So the company spent over £20,000 making these gifts at Christmas, 1960. And it is not suggested that the vouchers given to the Appellant can be put in a different category from those given to those part-time employees. I agree with Lord Denning, M.R., who, having said that if each voucher had been for £100 the case would be clear, continued:

> But now suppose that, instead of £100, it was a box of chocolates or a bottle of whisky or £2, it might be merely a gesture of goodwill at Christmas without regard to services at all. So it is a question of degree. It seems to me that in this case, when you find that £10 a year was paid to each of the staff year after year, each of them must have come to expect the £10 as a regular thing which went with their service.

I can find nothing in the facts found by the Commissioners to contradict their decision. Perhaps the most important is that set out in the passage I quoted earlier giving the reason why the directors decided to make these gifts; and that points to their object being to obtain beneficial results for the company in future. It is true that not only did the salaries paid compare favourably with those paid for comparable work elsewhere, but good work by particular employees (including the Appellant) was rewarded by bonuses independent of these vouchers: and that has in some cases been held to be an element telling in favour of the taxpayer. And it is possible that the gifts in kind in the old days could have been treated differently. But on balance I think that the Commissioners were well entitled to come to the decision which they made.

I do not think it necessary to deal with the other authorities cited or referred to in argument. In some it is said that one ought to look at the matter primarily from the point of view of the recipient, and that may well be right where the donor is not the employer. But if one is looking for the *causa causans* of gifts made by the employer it must surely be right to see why he made the gifts. Other cases were about gifts made once and for all on special occasions, and there other arguments may be valid. But this is a case of gifts regularly made by the employer and I have only thought it necessary to direct my observations to that kind of case.

...

For the reasons which I have given I would dismiss this appeal, and costs must follow the event.

Notes and Questions

1. The CRA's administrative practice concerning fringe benefits is found in Interpretation Bulletin IT-470R: Employees' Fringe Benefits (April 8, 1999). Examine IT-470R carefully. What is its legal status?
2. On what basis could an employee demonstrate that the connection between a benefit and an employment were insufficient to trigger the application of paragraph 6(1)(a)? In *Savage*, the Court approved of the test in *Phaneuf*. Is the test helpful in demonstrating an insufficient connection between the benefit and the employment?
3. If an employee is in receipt of a gift from an employer, the Canada Revenue Agency (the "CRA") takes the position that the gift is excluded from the employee's income if it satisfies certain criteria. Its current policy, announced on January 1, 2010 (included in T4130 Employer's Guide-Taxable Benefits and Allowances), and effective as of the 2010 taxation year is as follows:

> A gift has to be for a special occasion such as a religious holiday, a birthday, a wedding, or the birth of a child. An award has to be for an employment-related accomplishment such as outstanding service or employees' suggestions. It is recognition of an employee's overall contribution to the workplace, not recognition of job performance. You may give an employee an unlimited number of non-cash gifts and awards with a combined total value of $500 or less annually. If the FMV of the gifts and awards you give your employee is greater than $500, the amount over $500 must be included in the employee's income. For example, if you give gifts and awards with a total value of $650, there is a taxable benefit of $150 ($650 – $500).

   What is the rationale for this policy?

4. In *Dunlap v. The Queen*, [1998] 4 C.T.C. 2644, 98 D.T.C. 2053 (T.C.C.), the taxpayer's employer held an annual Christmas party for all its employees (and one guest each), providing dinner, an open bar and accommodation at a hotel. The Minister assessed the employees with a taxable benefit under paragraph 6(1)(a) equal to the per person cost of the event. The Court dismissed the taxpayer's appeal. In considering some of the concessions granted in IT-470R, the Court stated (at paragraph 14):

> The purported concessions found in [IT-470R] referred to by Counsel for the Appellant are not supported by the *Act* and they cannot be permitted to determine the result of an appeal. Such a decision would be in direct conflict with the

> economic policy objectives of Parliament as expressed by this legislative provision. I must also note that I would be loathe to equate an administrative approach taken by the Minister of National Revenue (which conflicts with the clear provisions of statutory provision) to "public policy".

5. When an employee receives a benefit from a third party such as a supplier, advertiser or other firm providing services to the company of which the taxpayer is an officer or employee, the issue is whether or not the benefit is from office or employment. In *Waffle v. M.N.R.*, *supra*, the taxpayer was an officer of T Ltd., a franchised Ford dealership. As part of a sales incentive program offered by Ford Motor Company, the president of T Ltd. became eligible to take a Caribbean cruise at Ford's expense. When the president became unable to take the trip, Waffle and his wife were substituted. It was purely a pleasure cruise. The Minister added the value of the cruise to Waffle's income as a benefit from his office or employment. The Exchequer Court held that the benefit had been received by Waffle as a benefit of his employment.
6. When a car dealership has reached its sales quota its officers do not automatically become eligible for a trip. Rather, they have their names entered into a lottery from which certain winners will be drawn. Mr. X, an officer of a dealership, is chosen by such a lottery and he spends two weeks on a Caribbean cruise. What result? See *Poirier v. M.N.R.*, [1968] Tax A.B.C. 319, 68 D.T.C. 234 (T.A.B.).

   Would it make any difference if everyone in the lottery was a winner of some prize, and the draw merely determined what the prize would be?

3. "Benefit of Any Kind Whatever"

Despite the Supreme Court's suggestion in *Savage* that "the meaning of 'benefit of whatever kind' is clearly quite broad", the courts have had difficulty determining whether various apparent economic advantages enjoyed by employees are taxable "benefits". Consider the following cases.

LOWE v. THE QUEEN
[1996] 2 C.T.C. 33, 96 D.T.C. 6226 (F.C.A.)

Stone J.A. (Strayer and Décary concurring):

This appeal from a judgment of the Tax Court of Canada arises out of an assessment of the appellant's income for the taxation year 1990, which included a portion of the cost of an expense-paid trip taken by the appellant and his wife to New Orleans on the basis that the appellant received in that year a taxable "benefit" under paragraph 6(1)(a) of *the Income Tax Act* ...

At all material times, the appellant was an account executive in the London, Ontario office of the Wellington Insurance Company and as such had responsibility for maintaining and developing relationships with independent insurance brokers and encouraging them to sell general insurance including home, auto and business policies. As Wellington had no sales force of its own, it relied on independent brokers who also sold the insurance of its competitors. According to the evidence at trial, all general insurers sell the same basic coverage. The appellant's job, therefore, was to promote his employer's insurance to the independent brokers and to create smooth relationships with them.

... The appellant testified at trial as did two officers of Wellington — Messrs. Evans and McConachie. The latter two witnesses had also attended in New Orleans. No witnesses were called by the respondent. The evidence of the witnesses is summarized by the Tax Court Judge at pages 4-7 of his reasons:

> ... Lowe attended the program in New Orleans as an employee of Wellington at the direction of his supervisor. The trip was not a holiday to Lowe and was not considered by Wellington to be a 'perk' to Lowe. He was to be present for four days to make sure the brokers for whom he was responsible had a good time. Wellington asked the account executives to go to New Orleans. They could not refuse; it was part of their job. Lowe testified it was his view he could not turn down the trip. His job in New Orleans, according to Evans and McConachie, was to maintain and promote the relationship with the brokers. At the same time, according to Evans and Lowe, Lowe's wife was to accompany him. The spouses of the brokers would be present and Wellington expected the spouses of its account executives to be present. Wellington paid for any babysitting expenses incurred by an account executive by virtue of his spouse attending at New Orleans. Evans said that unless there were compelling reasons, the spouse was expected to attend. Lowe considered his wife's presence in New Orleans as 'part of my job'. Her reason to be there, he said, was to be with brokers and build a rapport. 'Anything she could do to improve relationships, she should do.' Because he was 'not given the choice for his wife not to attend', he felt he did not have the option of her not attending.
>
> The initial brochure to the brokers offered:
>
> ... a fabulous trip-for-two to New Orleans! Spend four sun-filled days and fun-filled nights at the breathtaking Royal Orleans Hotel in the French Quarter. Take a starlight Mississippi Riverboat cruise, ... And dine as you have never dined before! ...
>
> Lowe testified that throughout the four days of the program, he and his wife had less than one hour to themselves (a bus trip through New Orleans); otherwise, he said, they were constantly occupied with the brokers and their wives. He admitted he enjoyed the trip, as he enjoyed his job. However, he said he was not free to do as he wished when in New Orleans. He was in New Orleans to serve his employer.

The Tax Court Judge concluded from the evidence that the Minister had erred in allowing only 38% as the business portion of the expenses incurred by the appellant. He was of the view that only 20% of this cost represented a taxable benefit. At the same time he left unchanged the Minister's assessment of the benefit enjoyed by the appellant's spouse

[being 75% of the cost of her trip].

The Minister's assumption that the primary purpose of the trip was personal pleasure was rejected by the Tax Court Judge who found, at pages 9-10:

> The evidence suggests the primary purpose of the trip to New Orleans as far as Lowe is concerned was not personal pleasure. To the brokers and their spouses, it may have been so. As far as Lowe was concerned, he was present in New Orleans for the purposes of his employer's business and this function was the main purpose of his trip. ... Lowe's day was not the eight hours assumed by the Minister. The evidence states he was occupied from 7:30 in the morning to approximately 11:00 p.m. He did derive some enjoyment and pleasure from the trip, he admitted.
>
> Evans revealed that not all Wellington account executives went to New Orleans. The account executives who went to New Orleans were those [who] had the most brokers travelling to New Orleans as well as the importance of the business relationship with the brokers. If an account executive convinced brokers to sell more Wellington policies, his chances of going to New Orleans increased.
>
> An account executive did not go to New Orleans if he had no brokers going there. To this extent, I believe, the trip to New Orleans was some type of reward to the account executive.

... In his work *The Fundamentals of Canadian Income Tax*, 4th ed. (Toronto: Carswell, 1993), Professor V. Krishna discusses the purpose of paragraph 6(1)(a) as follows, at page 161:

> The purpose of para. 6(1)(a) is simple: it is intended to equalize the tax payable by employees who receive their compensation in cash with the amount payable by those who receive compensation in cash and in kind. In the absence of this rule, the tax system would provide an incentive for employees to barter for non-cash benefits. The result would be a capricious and irrational tax system where tax burdens would be determined more by fortuitous circumstances of bargaining power than by principles of fairness.

He goes on immediately thereafter to suggest what should constitute a benefit for tax purposes:

> What, then, constitutes a benefit for tax purposes? There is no single test or determinative criterion which answers the question. Generally, the starting point is to determine whether the item under review provides the employee with *an*

> *economic advantage that is measurable in monetary terms.* If there is an advantage, one asks: does the primary advantage enure for the benefit of the employee or the employer?
>
> [emphasis added]

... It seems clear that the appellant was sent by his employer to New Orleans to be present with the successful brokers and their wives who were expected to enjoy what was described in the programme as 'four sun-filled days and fun-filled nights'. The business purpose behind the trip lay in the fact that the employer had a direct stake in maintaining and improving its relationships with brokers who had experienced significant success in selling its insurance contracts. The employer's evident objective was to foster or even strengthen business relationships by entertaining the brokers and their wives in New Orleans and thereby rewarding the brokers for that success. To this end, the appellant was much assisted by his wife who, with him, attended a two hour meeting with the account executives and their wives as well as a two and one-half hour meeting with the brokers and their wives. The Tax Court Judge found that the account executives were instructed 'to make sure that the brokers sign up for the tours and other activities and to accompany them with their own spouses'. Evans met with the account executives each day to 'make sure the brokers were happy'. According to the appellant's evidence, which was not challenged, he and his wife were constantly occupied with the brokers and their wives and had little time left over for personal pleasure.

I agree with counsel for the respondent that whether travelling expenses in a case such as this are to be viewed as a personal benefit turns heavily on the facts. In *Hale v. Minister of National Revenue*, 68 DTC 5326 (Ex. Ct.), the Court refused to treat an amount paid by a life insurance company for the expenses of the employee's wife in attending with him at a sales conference in Phoenix, Arizona as a taxable benefit under the predecessor of paragraphs 6(1)(a). It was clear that the taxpayer's wife, although having no formal connection to her husband's employer, was seen with her husband, as it was put by Cattanach J. at page 5327, 'as the selling unit' in the employer's business. Again, in *Arsens v. Minister of National Revenue*, 69 DTC 81, the Tax Appeal Board held that the cost of a trip to Disneyland in California which was undertaken primarily as a publicity promotion for the benefit of the employer's company should not be taxed as personal benefits in the hands of the several employees who attended on the trip. In the words of J.O. Weldon, Q.C., the presiding member of the Board, at page 87:

> However, looking at the substance of this particular matter, it has not been possible for me to see any sound basis for levying income tax against 30 employees of Paul's Restaurants Ltd., who went on the Disneyland trip, with the actual cost of the trip because it was, obviously, undertaken primarily for

the benefit of their employer, the interests of the said employees being completely incidental thereto.

In *Philp v. Minister of National Revenue*, [1970] C.T.C. 330, 70 D.T.C. 6237 (Can. Ex. Ct.), the Court was called upon to determine to what extent, if any, a taxable benefit had been conferred by a grocery chain on employees and independent retail store managers in awarding them an expense-paid trip to Nassau in the Bahamas as a result of a competition in selling the chain's products. The appeal was allowed in part on the basis that 'something of value in an economic sense' apart from the business purpose of the trip had been conferred on the recipients and should be taxed accordingly. At page 6244, Thurlow, J., as he then was, called attention, inter alia, to evidence which he regarded as supporting 'something of value' to the taxpayer:

> ... apart from what was arranged for and carried out in the usual leisure or after hours of the day *a considerable portion of the usual business or working hours of each day was made available for leisure with an organized programme of recreational activities arranged for those who wished to participate in them.* These activities as well as a transportation, hotel rooms, meals and receptions were all included in the project and were paid for by Oshawa. To my mind *it is clear therefore that to persons interested in such an outing as a holiday, as indeed many people are, the right to take such a trip represents something of value in the material sense.* [emphasis added]

This 'something of value' test was applied both by the Trial Division and by this Court in *Hart v. The Queen*, [1981] C.T.C. 91, 81 D.T.C. 5070 (F.C.T.D), affirmed [1982] C.T.C. 275, 82 D.T.C. 6237 (F.C.A.). That case involved a twenty-three day trip by the appellant and his wife, a farming couple, to Australia and New Zealand in 1977. Some of their activities involved visits to agricultural institutions and meeting with government agricultural officials, farmers or ranchers. The Trial Judge, Mahoney, J., as he then was, found, however, at page 5071, that:

> A good deal of this activity related to matters of no immediate interest to Hartholm [the employer], notably sheep.

He went on to conclude, at pages 5071-5072, that:

> ... the tour was of personal value to the Harts entirely apart from its business value. There may well be an incidental personal value inherent in many purely business trips but the personal benefit to the Harts in this case was not a mere incident of a business trip. A holiday oriented towards one's business or professional interests remains a holiday; it is not, per se, a business trip.

Viewing the cost of the trip as for a combination of business and pleasure, Mahoney, J. treated one-half of the husband's expenses as a personal benefit and upheld the Minister's assessment with respect to the expenses of the spouse... In dismissing the appeal from that decision, this Court saw no ground for interfering with what it regarded as "purely questions of fact and opinion", when "the view taken by the Trial Judge is not unreasonable or based on some erroneous principle" and the finding being "well supported by the evidence". Thurlow CJ described the tour to Australia and New Zealand, at page 276 (DTC 6239), in the following terms:

> The tour program, while predominantly concerned with activities that would be of interest to persons engaged in agricultural operations and which, for that reason, might be of little interest to persons of other callings was...nevertheless a holiday. *It was a tour of such activities and entertainment quite unrelated to agricultural pursuits. It is impossible, in my view, to conclude that such a tour was purely or even essentially a business trip* or that it had no value as a holiday and represented no economic benefit as a holiday trip received or enjoyed by the appellant. [emphasis added]

Although the *Philp* test is expressed in different words, it is not dissimilar from that of *Poynton* as approved in *Savage*, *supra*, – 'a material acquisition which confers an economic benefit on the taxpayer'. It seems to me in light of existing jurisprudence that no part of the appellant's trip expenses should be regarded as a personal benefit unless that part represents a material acquisition for or something of value to him in an economic sense and that if the part which represents a material acquisition or something of value was a mere incident of what was primarily a business trip it should not be regarded as a taxable benefit within subparagraph 6(1)(a) of the Act. The Tax Court Judge found that the primary purpose of the appellant's trip to New Orleans was not for personal pleasure but for the purposes of the employer's business and allowed 80% of the appellant's costs as the business portion of the trip. His refusal to allow the whole as business expenses was based on the view that the trip to New Orleans was to an extent to 'reward' him and because he derived some pleasure from the trip. When the time spent in New Orleans by the appellant on the employer's business is considered, it can be readily seen that the appellant had precious little time left over for personal pleasure. Nor is it clear that there was any element of 'reward' for the appellant. It may well be, depending on the circumstances, that a true 'reward' situation could support a conclusion that a trip was somehow earned by an employee so as to make the cost thereof, in whole or in part, taxable in the hands of the employee. The essential question in the present case, it seems to me, is whether on the facts the principal purpose of the trip was business or pleasure. Here it was found to be the former. Any pleasure derived by the appellant must, in my view, be seen as merely incidental to business purposes having regard to the fact that the overwhelming portion of the appellant's time in New Orleans was devoted to business activities.

I am similarly of the view, with respect, that the Tax Court Judge erred in treating the expenses of the appellant's spouse as a personal benefit under paragraph 6(1)(a). In concluding that the presence of the spouse in New Orleans was not necessary, the trial judge appears to have drawn heavily on his view that as a matter of law the spouse was under no obligation to be present and the employer could not require her presence in New Orleans. As he put it, at pages 10-11:

> In these days, as in 1989 and 1990, spouses, wives in particular, are under no obligation to follow the dictates of their spouses' employers, if this was ever the case. Times have changed. There was no evidence Lowe's wife was subject to the interview and 'education' process described in *Hale v. MNR*, 68 DTC 5326, at 5327. I am not satisfied that Lowe's wife's attendance in New Orleans was tantamount to being obligatory, as described by Cattanach, J. in *Hale* at page 5328.

In my view, while the existence of a legal obligation as in *Hale* is not present in the case at bar, the Tax Court ought nevertheless to have considered on the evidence, which was not contradicted, whether the spouse's presence with her husband in New Orleans at the request of the employer was primarily to serve the employer's business. The evidence seems clear that during the period of her stay in New Orleans the appellant's spouse attended the same meetings as did her spouse with the same objectives in mind and that she, like him, devoted the vast percentage of her time attending to the brokers and their wives. That evidence was not rejected or even commented upon unfavourable [*sic*] by the Tax Court Judge. No doubt she, like her husband, 'enjoyed the trip', but enjoying a trip which is devoted primarily to the husband's role as an employee on behalf of his employer over the course of very lengthy work days should not, in my view, be seen in the circumstances of this case as giving rise to a personal benefit either to the spouse or to the employee. Any personal enjoyment of the trip by the spouse should, like that of the appellant, be viewed as merely incidental to what was primarily a business trip by both spouses for the purpose of advancing the employer's business interests.

... I would allow the appeal with costs, set aside the Judgment of the Tax Court of Canada of February 27, 1995 except for the awarding of costs and would refer the matter back to the Minister for reconsideration and reassessment on a basis consistent with these reasons.

THE QUEEN v. HUFFMAN
[1990] 2 C.T.C. 132, 90 D.T.C. 6405 (F.C.A.)

Heald J.A.: ...

At all relevant times, the respondent was a plainclothes police officer in the employ of the Niagara Regional Police Force and was assigned to the Identification Unit in the Criminal Investigation Branch. His duties involved general criminal investigatory work at crime scenes and inspecting for physical evidence. The respondent worked in the field about ninety per cent of the time. His duties included examining for fingerprints, footprints, blood stains, etc. As a consequence, his clothing often became soiled, torn or contaminated with odours which made frequent cleaning necessary. The respondent's evidence which was accepted by the Trial Judge was to the effect that the jacket and overcoat purchased by him and required to be worn by him while on duty, were necessarily a size larger than he customarily wore when he was off duty. This was necessary in order to accommodate the on-duty equipment which he was required to carry (e.g., billy-club, walkie-talkie, revolver, etc.). According to the Trial Judge, these clothes were chosen "... with employment requirements in mind and were worn only at work". ...

The evidence also established that the equipment carried by the respondent as a plainclothes officer caused extra wear on his clothing: for example, the inner lining of his jacket was often torn by the holster, the trouser pockets became frayed and torn from constant removal and return of the billy-club to the pocket and the centre seam of the jacket often became torn from the strain and constant movement caused by the equipment being carried underneath the jacket. It is apparent from the evidence that the active nature of the respondent's duties as a plainclothes officer substantially curtailed the life of the clothing which he was required to wear.

Article 17.01 of the Collective Agreement between the respondent's employer and the Niagara Police Association, of which the respondent was a member provided:

> 17.01 Each member covered by this agreement who is required to provide and wear ordinary clothing as part of his regular duties, shall be re-imbursed by the Board for expenses in the purchase of such clothing, upon presentation of the necessary receipts. Such reimbursement shall be in an amount not to exceed five hundred ($500.00) per annum.

Article 26 of the Collective Agreement provides that each uniformed member of the Niagara Region Police Force is to be provided with normal working gear for both winter and summer. The evidence shows, however, that plainclothes officers are not provided with the full complement of clothing issued to uniformed officers. They were only issued one dress uniform for ceremonial occasions.

The object of Article 17.01 was to address the fact that plainclothes officers had not been previously reimbursed for the cost of plainclothes they were required to wear on duty. A transfer to plainclothes duty was only a lateral transfer and did not result in any pay increments. Consequently, since uniformed officers were provided with their working clothes (i.e., uniforms) at no cost to them, plainclothes officers, prior to the addition of Article 17.01, suffered an economic loss while on plainclothes duty. Article 17.01 reimbursed them for that economic loss.

...

The appellant submits that the learned Trial Judge erred in law in finding that the sum of $500.00 paid to the respondent pursuant to Article 17.01, *supra*, was not a benefit conferred upon him pursuant to paragraph 6(1)(a) of the *Income Tax Act*. ...

Counsel for the appellant relied on the decision of the Supreme Court of Canada in the case of The *Queen v. Savage*, [1983] C.T.C. 393, 83 D.T.C. 5409. In *Savage*, the Court approved of a passage from an earlier decision of the Court in the case of *Nowegijick v. The Queen*, [1983] S.C.R. 29 at p. 39 to the effect that the phrase "in respect of" contained words of "the widest of any expression intended to convey some connection between two related subject matters". Accordingly, counsel submitted that the $500.00 paid to the respondent by his employer was paid to him in respect of his employment. I have no difficulty with that particular submission. However such a conclusion does not address the critical issue as to whether or not, on these facts, the respondent is taxable pursuant to paragraph 6(1)(a) in respect of the $500.00 payment. In my view, the Trial Judge applied the proper test in deciding this issue. He commented that the Supreme Court of Canada in *Savage*, *supra*, specifically adopted the view of Mr. Justice Evans in the case of *R. v. Poynton*, [1972-73] O.R. 727 (Ont. C.A.) where he stated at p. 738:

> I do not believe the language to be restricted to benefits that are related to the office or employment in the sense that they represent a form of remuneration for services rendered. If it is a material acquisition which confers an economic benefit on the taxpayer and does not constitute an exemption, e.g., loan or gift, then it is within the all-embracing definition of section 3 [now paragraph 6(1)(a)].

Based on this passage, the learned Trial Judge set out the test which he applied to the facts at bar:

> It is therefore necessary to consider whether the facts here show that there was a material acquisition conferring an economic benefit on the taxpayer.

He then proceeded to review the evidence and to make the findings of fact referred to *supra*. In applying the *Savage* test, as enunciated *supra*, to the factual situation at bar, he stated:

> Based on the jurisprudence defining benefit in s. 6(1)(a) of the *Income Tax Act*, I am unable to conclude in these circumstances that the plaintiff received a benefit. The plaintiff was required, in order to carry out his duties as a plain-clothes officer and receive a salary as such, to incur certain expenses regarding his clothing, and reimbursement of these expenses should not be considered as conferring a benefit under paragraph 6(1)(a) of the Act. ...The taxpayer was simply being restored to the economic situation he was in before his employer ordered him to incur the expenses.

I agree with the Trial Judge. The findings of fact which he made are amply supported by the evidence. I also think that he correctly applied the relevant jurisprudence to the facts in this case.

[The Court went on to consider an alternative submission of the appellant that, in effect, the $79.57 difference between the $500 payment to the taxpayer and his actual expenses of $420.43 was a taxable allowance under paragraph 6(1)(b). This part of the decision appears below in this chapter.]

Notes and Questions

1. According to Stone J.A. in *Lowe*, what is the test for the existence of a benefit under paragraph 6(1)(a)?
2. Would Huffman have been able to deduct the cost of the jacket and overcoat under section 8 had he incurred the expense himself? Is this a relevant consideration? Contrast the decision in *Huffman* with *Bure v. The Queen*, [2000] 1 C.T.C. 2407, 2000 D.T.C. 1507 (T.C.C.). Bure was a hockey player for the Vancouver Canucks. When his contract was renegotiated in 1996, the Canucks agreed (in a separate agreement) to pay Bure's agent US$250,000 for each of the 5 years under the contract (representing 5 per cent of the amount paid to Bure). The Canucks reported the Canadian dollar equivalent as a taxable benefit on Bure's T4s. Bure did not report these amounts as income. In concluding that the amount paid to Bure's agent was a taxable benefit, the Court stated that "Had the Canucks not paid [the agent], the Appellant would have had to pay his agent with after-tax dollars. The parties agree that such payment would not be tax deductible by the Appellant".

CYRIL JOHN RANSOM v. M.N.R.
[1967] C.T.C. 346, 67 D.T.C. 5235 (Exch. Ct.)

Noël J.:

This is an appeal from an assessment dated November 8, 1965, whereby the appellant was assessed for additional tax in the amount of $773.04 by reason of adding to his declared taxable income for the year 1963 the amount of $2,809, a portion of the loss incurred by him on the sale of his home in Sarnia, which amount had been reimbursed by DuPont of Canada Limited, his employer. ...

[The appellant was transferred from Sarnia to Montreal on June 20, 1961, and as soon as he was notified of his transfer, the house in Sarnia was put up for sale. He advertised in the newspaper and shortly thereafter it was placed in the hands of a real estate agent until it was sold. He had considerable difficulty in selling his house in Sarnia because at that time Imperial Oil had decided to move a fairly large number of its senior personnel from Sarnia to Toronto, with the result that there were about 60 homes in the same price bracket as his for sale at the same time.]

The appellant herein states that as his employer, DuPont of Canada Limited, required as a condition of his employment, that he move from Sarnia, Ontario, to Montreal, P.Q., reimbursement to the extent above mentioned constituted reimbursement of expenses caused to him by reason of his employment.

The appellant further urged (although this allegation was not established at the trial) that the said reimbursement by the employer was a matter of convenience for the employer who preferred to make the above-mentioned reimbursement rather than purchase the employee's house (as it could have done under the company's housing scheme) at the appraised selling price and then incur expenses of subsequently disposing of it.

The appellant, therefore, takes the position that as the expenses incurred by him were caused wholly and exclusively by reason of the terms and conditions of his employment in respect of which his employer, by reason of its General Company Procedure, undertook to reimburse him, this reimbursement constituted one of the expenses incurred by him in the course of his employment, and one provided for as a term and condition of his employment.

It does not, he says, in any manner whatsoever, constitute a benefit for services as an employee under the provisions of Section [6(1)] of the *Income Tax Act* or any other section of the said Act. ...

There are no decisions in this country on the taxability of an indemnity paid to an employee against the loss sustained on the sale of his house when he is transferred from one locality to another and the present appeal is a test case of special interest to a number of employees who, like the appellant, do not wish to be taxed on amounts which they consider to be reimbursement for expenses incurred in the course of their employment. ...

I can deal with Section [6(3)] of the Act briefly by saying that the appellant has, in my view, rebutted by the production of adequate evidence the presumption this section creates that the payment he received from his employer is remuneration for services rendered. It indeed appears clearly that the indemnity paid to the appellant in respect of the capital loss sustained upon the sale of his house when transferred, cannot reasonably be regarded as falling within any of the following categories: (i) "as consideration or partial consideration for accepting the office or entering into the contract of employment" as the evidence discloses that it had nothing to do with his engagement as an employee; (ii) "as remuneration or partial remuneration for services as officer or under the contract of employment" as the evidence discloses that the appellant was receiving under his service contract the full salary appropriate to his appointment. Furthermore, the source of the payment was not the services rendered by the appellant but resulted from the fact that he availed himself of the procedure whereby he could claim compensation for the capital loss sustained as a result of his transfer from Sarnia to Montreal. ... (iii) nor can it be said that the payment received by the appellant was "in consideration or partial consideration for covenant with reference to what the officer or employee is, or is not, to do before or after the termination of the employment".

I now come to Section [6(1)(a) and (b)] of the Act which, as already mentioned, is couched in language which appears to be wider than the English taxation rule on which the taxpayers in *Hochstrasser v. Mayes*, [1959] 1 Ch. 22 and *Jennings v. Kinder*, [1958] 3 W.L.R. 215 were held not to be taxable. The Canadian taxation section indeed uses such all-embracing words that at first glance it appears extremely difficult to see how anything can slip through this wide and closely interlaced legislative net.

[Noël J. first considered the nexus between the payment and the taxpayer's employment, suggesting that in order to be included under paragraph 6(1)(a), the "cause of the payment" must be the services rendered. On this point, the case has been overruled by the Supreme Court of Canada decision in Savage. Noël, J. continued:]

There can, I believe, be no difference in principle between the reimbursement of an expense or of a loss nor, in my view, can anything turn on the fact that the loss or expense which is the subject matter of the present reimbursement covers the value of a capital asset.

Although I have no doubt, as a matter of substance, that the payment received by the appellant should not be included in his income, I have had some difficulty in expressing the reasons why such a result should be obtained. The English House of Lords' decision has been of some use in dealing with

Section [6(3)] of the Act, it has not, however, been too helpful in applying Section [6(1)] to the instant case, as the wording of the English rule is quite different from our Section [6(1)] even though some of the facts are similar.

The correctness of the conclusion arrived at under Section [6(1)] can, however, I believe, be sustained by a mere examination of the notion of *remuneration, reimbursement* for money disbursed in the course of or by reason of the employment and *allowance*. These seem to me to be three distinctively different concepts.

In a particular case, it may be difficult to decide as a question of fact into which category a particular payment falls. There is, however, no difficulty when an employee is required to disburse money in the course of his employment, i.e., to make payments on behalf of the employer. A clear example is where a cashier pays wages. There would equally be no difficulty with reimbursement of such an expense paid out of an employee's own pocket and then reimbursed, i.e., if a lawyer's clerk or stenographer paid search fees out of his or her own pocket and, upon returning to the office, took the money out of petty cash. Such transactions are too obvious for debate.

Another class of payment by an employer to an employee is also so well established as to be beyond debate. Where an employment contract contemplates an employee being away from his home base from time to time, the employee must eat and sleep while away from home. The expenses involved in providing himself with food and shelter while away from home are personal expenses, but they are personal expenses that arise because the employee is required to perform the duties of his employment away from his home base temporarily. Such a payment is money disbursed "by reason of" but not "in the course of" his employment. Nobody questions that reimbursement of such an expense is something quite different from remuneration for the services performed by the employee. Such personal expenses are incurred *by reason of* the employment. Until the employee has been reimbursed for such expenses, he is out of pocket *by reason of* the employment. His remuneration can only be what he receives over and above such reimbursement.

In a case such as here, where the employee is subject to being moved from one place to another, any amount by which he is out of pocket by reason of such a move is in exactly the same category as ordinary travelling expenses. His financial position is adversely affected *by reason* of that particular facet of his employment relationship. When his employer reimburses him for any such loss, it cannot be regarded as remuneration, for if that were all that he received under his employment arrangement, he would not have received any amount for his services. Economically, all that he would have received would be the amount that he was out of pocket *by reason* of the employment.

An *allowance* is quite a different thing from reimbursement. It is, as already mentioned, an *arbitrary* amount usually paid in lieu of *reimbursement*. It is paid to the employee to use as he wishes without being required to account for its expenditure. For that reason it is possible to use it as a concealed increase in remuneration and that is why, I assume, "allowances" are taxed as though they were remuneration.

It appears to me quite clear that reimbursement of an employee by an employer for expenses or losses incurred by reason of the employment (which as stated by Lord Macnaghten in *Tennant v. Smith*, [1892] A.C. 162, puts nothing in the pocket but merely saves the pocket) is neither remuneration as such or a *benefit* "of any kind whatsoever" so it does not fall within the introductory words of Section [6(1)] or within paragraph (a). It is equally obvious that it is not an allowance within paragraph (b) for the reasons that I have already given.

...

... Such a loss, in my view, is in the same category as those other "removal expenses" (such as the expenses incurred by the employee in moving himself, his family and his household effects) which are considered by the respondent as conferring no benefit on the employee and which, as a matter of fact, are not added by the respondent to the appellant's income. ...

THE QUEEN v. PHILLIPS
[1994] 1 C.T.C. 383, 94 D.T.C. 6177 (F.C.A.)

Robertson J.: (Stone J.A concurring): ...

[The taxpayer was moved by his employer Canadian National Railway ("CNR") from Moncton, New Brunswick to Winnipeg, Manitoba. The taxpayer sold his house in Moncton and purchased a replacement house in Winnipeg. Pursuant to a relocation agreement between the employer and the union, the taxpayer received a $10,000 payment to compensate him, as an eligible employee, for increased housing costs in Winnipeg, although no restrictions were placed on the use of the $10,000 payment.]

The scheme of the Act as it relates to taxable income is deceptively straightforward. Subsection 5(1) directs the taxpayer to include in employment income conventional remuneration, such as "salary" and "wages", received in a taxation year. Section 6 seeks to capture in employment income various ancillary or "fringe" benefits, whether or not they are strictly monetary. ...

Paragraph 6(1)(a) brings into employment income "the value of ... other benefits of any kind whatever received or enjoyed ... in respect of, in the course of, or by virtue of an office or employment". The early jurisprudence held that this provision only applied to benefits received as remuneration in exchange for employment services. ...

In *Savage*, the Supreme Court accepted that a taxable benefit must be conferred on the taxpayer in his or her capacity as an employee. It rejected, however, the understanding that to be received in this capacity, the payment must be in exchange for services performed by the employee. ...

An economic advantage received by an employee from his or her employer will be deemed a benefit within the meaning of paragraph 6(1)(a) unless the employee can demonstrate that the payment was not a benefit in respect of employment, but made in his or her capacity as a person. Framed in this manner, the test is able to embrace conveniently the categories of gifts, loans and other contractual arrangements.

The question of whether a payment is a gift, loan or the result of considerations extraneous to the employment relationship is often approached with reference to the employer's intention or the purpose of the payment. The terms of CNR's agreement with the respondent clearly defeat the characterization of the $10,000 as a gift or a loan. In my view, it is also apparent that if an employee receives a payment on the condition that he or she continues to work for the employer, as is the case before us, then that payment can hardly be said to have stemmed from considerations extraneous to the employment relationship.

Collateral contracts, like all contracts, are only a means of providing objective evidence of subjective intent. By itself, a collateral contract cannot therefore be conclusive of whether a payment is received in the capacity of person or employee. To focus on the existence of a collateral contract to the exclusion of its context — the employment relationship — is to allow the form of the document to prevail over its substance.

The fact that the parties in the case at Bar chose to effect a post-contractual modification supported by consideration does not in any way diminish the employment relationship in question. On the contrary, the employees' continuing employment was facilitated. Considering that one of the terms of CNR's agreement with the respondent is that he remain in CNR's employ, I fail to see how it can be said that the respondent received the payment other than as an employee. This is not to suggest that the "collateral contract theory" will necessarily be inapplicable in all cases; ...

Putting aside the form-substance issue, the respondent sought to persuade us that CNR's motivation in making the payment was somehow relevant to the issue at hand — that it, in effect, manifested a consideration extraneous to the employment relationship. This approach would be understandable if the facts before us involved a $10,000 payment to an employee whose uninsured house was destroyed by fire. All but the extreme skeptic would likely concede that the employer was motivated primarily by altruism. It is difficult to appreciate how motivation could be the deciding factor on the facts before us.

It is indisputable that CNR's agreement with the respondent was motivated primarily by a desire to protect and promote both parties' economic interests by providing a mutually acceptable solution to a labour dispute. Any secondary motivations for entering the agreement are irrelevant. The unvarnished reality is that labour negotiations and relocation compensation schemes are, today, integral aspects of the employer-employee relationship. This is especially true in an economy where the downsizing of work forces has become commonplace. The closure of the Moncton Shops, while tragic for its employees, is by no means an extraordinary occurrence.

Applying the law as outlined in *Savage*, I am driven to the inescapable conclusion that the respondent received the $10,000 payment in his capacity as employee. That determination, however, does not dispose of the appeal. The appellant had to consider whether the $10,000 payment was a non-taxable reimbursement of an expense incurred as a consequence of employment and whether it conferred an economic advantage on the respondent. ...

... The rule in *Ransom* is straightforward. Reimbursement by an employer for the loss suffered by an employee in selling a house following a job transfer is not taxable to the extent that the payment reflects the employee's actual loss;

...

The potential dangers of applying an abstract rule of law to variegated factual circumstances is highlighted by the wholesale application of *Ransom* to employee relocation cases. A review of the relevant jurisprudence reveals that relocation compensation packages are intended to address the financial repercussions of employee relocation on two levels: the losses suffered on the sale of the employee's house and the expenses incurred in purchasing a replacement property. Payments made to compensate for increased housing costs on the purchase of a replacement property are the subject of this appeal. I turn now to the matter of identifying specifically the types of losses which fall within each category, as reflected in the jurisprudence.

...

As a general proposition, relocation payments which reimburse the employee for actual losses incurred on a sale are immune from taxation. This is the thrust of the legal rule articulated in *Ransom*....

Two kinds of losses can arise upon the sale of an employee's house: a capital loss and a loss associated with the discharge of a mortgage with an interest rate lower than prevailing market rates. It is necessary to distinguish these losses from the expenses occasioned by a new mortgage with both a higher interest rate and a principal amount which reflects the higher housing prices at the new work location.

For example, if an employee had a $50,000 outstanding mortgage at 10 per cent and relocated to purchase a house requiring a $70,000 mortgage at

15 per cent, only the 5 per cent differential on the $50,000 can truly be considered a loss. Assuming that the $20,000 difference in principal is attributable solely to higher housing costs at the new work location (a task which itself is fraught with uncertainty), interest rate compensation with respect to that amount must be classified as reimbursement for an expense incurred in the purchase of a replacement house.

The tax treatment of compensation directed only to the loss of a favourable mortgage rate on the sale of a house is, in my view, governed by *Splane*, [[1990] 2 C.T.C. 199, 90 D.T.C. 6442 (F.C.T.D.), aff'd. [1991] 2 C.T.C. 224, 91 D.T.C. 5549 (F.C.A.) which held that such payment is not taxable]. ...

Compensation may be awarded for two kinds of expenses incurred in acquiring a new house. The first is a larger capital outlay on the employee's part as a result of on-average higher housing prices at the new work location. The other relates to higher financing costs with respect to that portion of the mortgage principal attributable to higher housing costs as explained above. It is recognized that paragraph 62(3)(f) of the Act deals explicitly with the tax treatment of certain acquisition expenses — legal fees and transfer taxes — but the Act goes no further. ...

The case under appeal is distinguishable from *Ransom* in one salient respect: CNR's compensation scheme made no provision for losses incurred on the sale of the respondent's house. Yet it is one matter to distinguish Ransom on the facts and quite another to determine whether that distinction is, in law, valid. The appellant argues that if no valid distinction exists in law then *Ransom* must be regarded as having been wrongly decided.

On what legal basis can one conclude that relocation compensation directed toward losses suffered on the sale of a house is not subject to tax while that directed toward expenses incurred in purchasing its replacement, is? The answer to that question lies in the legal rationale underlying *Ransom.* Once that rationale is isolated, it is apparent that it has no application to relocation compensation directed at defraying higher housing costs at a new work location. ...

It cannot be denied that the wisdom of *Ransom* has been questioned not only by the appellant but by at least one commentator; see B.G. Hansen, "The Taxation of Employees" in B.G. Hansen, V. Krishna & J.A. Rendall, eds, *Canadian Taxation* (Toronto: De Boo, 1981) 117 at 133-135. ... Not surprisingly, the appellant argues that the $10,000 payment is nothing but a *de facto* subsidy for a personal living expense.

The foundation of the appellant's argument doubtless rests upon the following excerpt from Noël J.'s reasons in *Ransom*, where he draws an analogy between travelling expenses and a capital loss on the sale of a house ...

Noël J.'s analogy seems to conflate all travelling expenses incurred in respect of employment and suggests that compensation for all out-of-pocket expenses be tax-free. Yet there are at least two disparate types of "travelling expenses". There are, for example, those incurred travelling to and from work and those incurred when an employer sends an employee on a business trip.

It could be argued on behalf of the Minister that a capital loss incurred when selling a house is to be treated as a personal or living expense. Like the transportation costs of travelling to and from work, these expenses are matters of personal choice unrelated to employment. It could be maintained with some force that losses associated with a general decline in housing market prices or attributable to the employee's folly in paying "too much" for "too little" should not be accorded special tax treatment. This position is weakened, of course, when the capital loss is a consequence of the forced and hasty disposition of a house.

The taxpayer could counter that a capital loss suffered on the sale of a house is akin to travelling expenses of an employee dispatched on a business trip by his or her employer. Such an employee has little choice but to incur an expense. For this reason, reimbursement is not viewed as a benefit but as righting a potential injustice. It accords with the equitable principle of *restitutio in integrum*. Similarly, a general decline in housing markets, of itself, results only in a paper loss to the employee. It is not until the employee is required by the employer to relocate that a capital loss is thrust upon him or her. Thus, any reimbursement received from the employer in respect of a capital loss should be a tax-free benefit.

The merits of these competing arguments can only be properly assessed by reference to the object and purpose of section 6, as understood through the "words in context" canon of statutory interpretation ...

It is well recognized that any decision to include or exclude benefits from employment income impacts significantly on government's ability to raise revenue. ... Quite obviously, section 6 of the Act seeks to limit tax avoidance relating to monetary and non-monetary compensation not reflected in wages or salaries.

Another primary and, for the purposes of this appeal, overriding objective of section 6 is to ensure that "employees who receive their compensation in cash are on the same footing as those who receive compensation in some combination of cash and kind. ... Two employees performing the same work for the same employer should receive the same tax treatment in respect of their employment. This is simply one manifestation of our conception of tax equity and, in my view, is the true rationale underlying *Ransom*. ...

This explanation accords with Parliament's intent that employees receive equal tax treatment in respect of their employment incomes. Every employee incurs some expense travelling to and from work. This is a necessary cost of being available for employment. Not every employee however, is required by his or her employer to travel or relocate to perform his or her office. It is simply not equitable for one of two employees to bear that capital loss; see also *The Queen v. Huffman*, [1990] 2 C.T.C. 132, 90 D.T.C. 6405.

Once policy considerations are brought into play, it is admittedly proper to ask whether it is the prerogative of Parliament alone to decide whether or not a particular kind of "reimbursement" should or should not be taxed. I would respond by noting that nothing in the Supreme Court's reasons in *Savage* indicates that *Ransom* was overruled per se. *Ransom* was cited and quoted, but only set aside in respect of its conclusion that taxable benefits must have been received in exchange for services performed by the employee.

In the 27 years since *Ransom* was decided, the Act has undergone extensive revisions which touch on the issues under consideration. None, however, contradicts or represents a threat to the rule in *Ransom*. Some even complement it; see, for example, paragraph 62(3)(d) of the Act, which addresses the loss suffered by a tenant/employee in canceling a lease. Moreover, *Ransom* has been applied by this Court on several occasions. In my opinion, *Ransom* has become so enmeshed in our conception of taxable benefits that it is, in my view, for the Supreme Court or Parliament to set aside its logic.

...

Just as the appellant sought to convince us that *Ransom* should be deemed to have been wrongly decided, so would the respondent have us extend *Ransom* to embrace CNR's $10,000 payment to him. While I support the rule in *Ransom*, it has no application in a case concerning an expenditure as opposed to a capital loss. This interpretation is compelled both by the Supreme Court's decision in *Savage*, the concept of tax equity underlying section 6 and the structure of the Act as a whole.

It is apparent on the facts before us that the respondent's net worth *qua* employee increased. Even if the $10,000 payment is taxable, he gains considerable disposable income. The compensatory payment effectively represents a temporary wage increase not available to all employees. Second, he gains an advantage over fellow employees resident in the community with higher housing costs. I find it difficult to accept that the respondent has a valid claim to a $10,000 tax-free benefit which can be used in the purchase of a house, while other Winnipeg employees are forced to expend after-tax dollars in order to gain entry into the housing market.

The extension of the *Ransom* principle as a stop-gap cost-of-living equalizer may well also negate the effect of other provisions of the Act. Parliament has explicitly recognized and addressed potential injustices relating to dramatic cost-of-living variations from one part of the country to another: see *Report of the Task Force on Tax Benefits for Northern and Isolated Areas* (Ottawa: Supply and Services Canada, 1989). Section 110.7 of the Act, for example, entitles taxpayers in prescribed areas of Canada to make special deductions with respect to housing and travel expenses in computing taxable income. Similarly, section 80.4 brings into income the benefit accrued when an employer loans an employee funds at lower than the prevailing interest rate, subject to a deduction created in paragraph 110(1)(j). ...

Perhaps the most persuasive rationale for limiting the application of *Ransom* lies in the myriad expenses which its extension could exempt from taxation. The respondent effectively argues that any payment received from an employer to compensate an employee for higher housing costs in a new work location only serves to make the employee whole. As we have seen, this rationale is flawed. Moreover, nothing bars the extension of this same faulty reasoning to other purchases, such as new cars or appliances, in provinces with higher costs of living.

I also observe that the problem of compensation directed at tax equalization is apparently of concern to tax lawyers familiar with the U.S. multi-national practice of "grossing up" salaries of executives transferred to Canada ... What of the employee who moves to a province with higher marginal rates of taxation? Why should he or she not be able to claim a tax-free benefit as well, assuming the employer is willing to provide such compensation? In my opinion, it is evident that the decision below creates a window of opportunity for those intent on structuring tax-free compensation packages for employees required to relocate to urban centres where costs of living are appreciably higher.

When the above concerns are contemplated in light of the clear wording of paragraph 6(1)(a) of the Act, the reasoning in *Savage* and Parliamentary intent, it seems plain that the $10,000 payment is a taxable benefit unless the respondent can satisfy this Court that it did not confer an economic advantage upon him. This marks the respondent's final effort to gain a $10,000 tax-free benefit and his real complaint.

The respondent relies on the finding of the Tax Court judge that his house in Winnipeg is inferior to the one in Moncton and argues that he is still out-of-pocket from being required to pay $28,000 "more" for "less". Leaving aside the fact that such a finding is clearly irrelevant on an appeal from a *de novo* decision, I note that the Trial judge made no similar finding, most likely for compelling reasons.

Comparative analyses of floor space and house amenities comprise personal value judgments. To contrast a storey-and-a-half house in Moncton with a Winnipeg bungalow by reference to "ball park figures" regarding on-average housing costs is valuable to the consumer but unacceptable as a legal benchmark for determining so-called actual loss. There is an obvious reason why an employer would only partially compensate employees for higher housing costs.

House selection is as dependent on personal taste and lifestyle as it is on cost. After all, location is the touchstone for determining value in real estate.

The foregoing criticisms are not intended to detract from the respondent's conviction that he received "less" for "more". What is important for him and the other CNR employees who await the outcome of this decision to recognize is that "economic benefit" cannot be assessed on the basis of subjective criteria and that the taxation of benefits cannot be made to depend on the perceptions of individual taxpayers. ...

Once the subjective value argument is dismissed, it is quite evident that the $10,000 payment enabled the respondent to acquire a more valuable asset. CNR did more than save his pocket-it put money into it. Of course, the respondent will doubtless suffer short-term hardships which inevitably accompany job relocation. However, grasping for a tax-free benefit is neither an appropriate nor meaningful way of acknowledging the true costs of employment relocation....

Notes and Questions

1. Do you agree that the payment by Ransom's employer put nothing in his pocket but merely saved his pocket? Ransom would have avoided the loss if he had not been required to move from Sarnia to Montreal in the course of his employment. However, Ransom's net worth increased in relation to that of other Sarnia homeowners. In this respect, is the decision consistent with the tax policy principle of horizontal equity? What other policy considerations may have influenced the court's decision as well as the apparent acceptance of it by the CRA in IT-470R, *supra*?

2. *Krull v. Canada (A.G.)*, [1996] 1 C.T.C. 131, (*sub nom.* Canada (A.G.) v. Hoefele) 95 D.T.C. 5602 (F.C.A.), leave to appeal refused (1996), (*sub nom.* Minister of National Revenue v. Hoefele) 204 N.R. 398 (note) (S.C.C.) dealt with a moving package offered by Petro Canada to certain employees relocated from Calgary to Toronto. The employer reimbursed the employees for higher mortgage interest costs incurred at the new work location, both because of increased interest rates and because of increased mortgages reflecting the higher costs of similar homes in the new location. The Federal Court of Appeal applied *Ransom* and concluded that the payments were not taxable benefits because there was no increase in the taxpayers' equity in the new homes. The Court distinguished the *Phillips* case on the basis that in *Phillips* the taxpayer's net worth was increased. The Court did not, however, provide any reasoning in support of this assertion. Is there any difference between the reimbursement of mortgage interest and principal costs? Is it fair to treat Mr. Phillips differently from Mr. Krull?

3. Compare *Ransom* and *Krull* with *Gernhart v. The Queen*, [1996] 3 C.T.C. 2369, 96 D.T.C. 1672 (T.C.C.), affirmed (1997), 98 D.T.C. 6026, [1998] 2 C.T.C. 102 (F.C.A.), leave to appeal refused (1998), 227 N.R. 397 (note) (S.C.C.). Gernhart,

an employee of General Motors in the United States, accepted a posting at GM Canada in Windsor. GM had a tax equalization policy applicable to international postings of its employees. Under this policy, the amount of income tax during the taxpayer's assignment in Canada would approximate what she would have paid had she remained in her home country (i.e., the company would pay her the difference). Although the tax equalization payment was reported in the taxpayer's T4, she argued that the amount was not income based on the principle in *Ransom* and *Krull*. According to Bonner T.C.C.J. (at paragraphs 12-13):

> As I see it, the position of the appellant is hardly comparable to that of the taxpayers in *Ransom*, *Splane* and *Hoefele* [one of the Tax Court decisions consolidated in the *Krull* appeal]. Each of the three was called upon by his employer to move in the course of employment. The reimbursement of a cost associated with such a move can, at least arguably, be regarded in the context of such employment as a "zero-sum transaction". Here, however, the payment was made pursuant to an element of the appellant's overall, ongoing compensation package and was designed to induce her to serve, as she did, outside the United States. It therefore constituted part of the appellant's remuneration for services within the meaning of subsection 5(1) of the Act even though it was intended to compensate the appellant for the tax disadvantage inherent in rendering those services outside the United States. Remuneration is commonly adjusted to reflect advantages and disadvantages inherent in rendering services under an employment contract but does not for that reason cease to be remuneration for such services. In my view this case is clearly governed by the decision of the Supreme Court of Canada in *Curran v. M.N.R.* ...
>
> The payment may also be viewed as a benefit taxable under paragraph 6(1)(a) of the Act. It is necessary to guard against the sort of creeping erosion of clear statutory language which may arise from a repeated process of comparison of particular cases to earlier "similar-fact" cases decided under that language. The "zero-sum transaction" analysis in the cases relied on by the appellant rests on a comparison of the position of the taxpayer before and after moving. At first blush it appears to assist the appellant. In this case, however, such an analysis is not helpful because it ignores the true nature of the payments as remuneration for services under a contract of employment. It leads to a result which is contrary to the plain meaning not only of section 5 but also of section 6. The tax equalization payment is an obvious benefit when the appellant's position is compared with that of any other resident of Canada in receipt of the same income but not in receipt of tax equalization. Inherent in the tax treatment sought by the appellant is a privilege offensive to the principle that individuals in similar financial circumstances should pay similar amounts of tax.

In a brief oral judgment, the Federal Court of Appeal dismissed Gernhart's appeal: [1998] 2 C.T.C. 102, 98 D.T.C. 6026 (F.C.A.). Even if the taxpayer initially paid and was reimbursed by the employer for the amount of the tax differential, the Court would have distinguished *Ransom* and cases following it on the basis that (at paragraph 2) "those cases dealt with losses or payments made by the employee in order to perform the services and not as here, an expense made by him as a consequence of the receipt of remuneration". Does the Tax Court or the Federal Court of Appeal in *Gernhart* adequately distinguish *Ransom* and *Krull*?

4. In 1998, subsections 6(19) to (23) were added to the Act to deal explicitly with relocation packages similar to those in *Ransom* and *Krull*. What is the effect of these provisions? Why, under these provisions, is the reimbursement of a housing loss treated more favourably than the reimbursement of increased housing costs at the new work location?
5. X, a lawyer, is employed by A Corporation. X was required to travel to Vancouver from the company's head office in Toronto to negotiate various business deals for the company. X spent a total of 8 days in Vancouver and all his expenses were paid by the company. How should X reflect these facts on his tax return?
6. Paragraph 6(1)(a) excludes certain non-cash benefits from an employee's income. Why are those benefits excluded?
7. T is a drill operator for Canarc Oil Company which is exploring the oil reserves of the Canadian Arctic. Canarc transfers T from Alberta to a remote drilling site near the northwestern shore of Baffin Island. T lives with 25 other employees of the company in living quarters provided by the company. Each employee has a two-room apartment in a large building. There are central kitchen and washroom facilities. The company provides T with his meals and lodging without charge. It also supplies him with special down insulated clothing to withstand the Arctic cold. T spends a year and a half on Baffin Island. He receives three round trips to Calgary during that time at the company's expense. He consults you as to whether the free meals, lodging, clothing and transportation will result in taxable income to him. Consider subsection 6(6).
8. What is the basis of the deduction for clergy in paragraph 8(1)(c)? Would an exclusion such as that in subsection 6(6) have been more appropriate? What is the difference between an exclusion and a deduction for income tax purposes?
9. What if an employee receives an interest-free loan from his employer? See section 80.4 and subsection 6(9).

4. Valuation

Paragraph 6(1)(a) requires that the "value" of a taxable benefit be included in the taxpayer's income. The critical issue is the definition of "value". In the United Kingdom, the leading case is *Wilkins v. Rogerson*, [1961] 1 All E.R. 358 (C.A.), where an employer arranged with a tailor to supply each of his employees with a suit of clothes as a Christmas present. The cost to the employer of the taxpayer's suit was £14 15s. On appeal the employee conceded that he had received a taxable benefit but maintained that its value in terms of money's worth was the price for which he could have sold the suit in the open market if he had sold it immediately after he had received it. It was agreed this price was £5 due to the fact that it should be classified as a second hand suit the moment it was delivered. On appeal the court held that the £5 value was the measure of the benefit rather than the cost to the employer in providing the suit. The court said in part:

> The only controversy was whether he was to pay tax on the cost of that perquisite to his employer or on the value of it to him, and it appears to me that this perquisite is a taxable subject-matter because it is money's worth. It is money's worth because it can be turned into money and, when turned into money, the taxable subject matter is the value received. I cannot myself see how it is connected directly with the cost to the employers. ... The taxpayer has to pay on what he gets. Here he has got a good suit. He can realize it only for £5. The advantage to him is therefore £5. The detriment to his employers has been considerably more, but that seems to me to be irrelevant. ...

Following the *Tennant v. Smith* principle, the *Wilkins* decision found that the suit was a taxable benefit because it was convertible into money. Assessing the value of the benefit on the basis of the amount of money into which the suit could be converted is consistent with the principle in *Tennant v. Smith.*

Under Canadian law, the value of a benefit under paragraph 6(1)(a) is generally the fair market value of the benefit. The generally accepted definition of fair market value is the amount a person not obligated to buy would pay to a person not obligated to sell: *Steen v. The Queen*, [1988] 1 C.T.C. 256, 88 D.T.C. 6171 (F.C.A.). Determining the fair market value of a benefit should be straightforward in most cases. Nevertheless, difficulties do arise, as the following two cases illustrate.

GIFFEN et al. v. THE QUEEN
[1995] 2 C.T.C. 2767, 96 D.T.C. 1011 (T.C.C.)

[The appellants, Giffen and Mommersteeg, were employees of Hiram Walker ("HW") and were required to travel frequently in the course of their employment. The air fares were paid by HW. Both appellants were members of frequent flyer plans and earned frequent flyer points ("air miles") which could be redeemed for free airline tickets ("reward tickets"). Giffen's air miles were earned on employer-paid first class and business class tickets. Mommersteeg's air miles were earned on employer-paid economy class tickets. The appellants redeemed the air miles for reward tickets, which were used by their family members. The Tax Court of Canada found that the free travel rewards were benefits under paragraph 6(1)(a) and that they were "received" when the appellants' family members travelled free. The Court then turned to the issue of the "value" of the benefits.]

BONNER T.C.J.

... In the case of Mr. Giffen all reward tickets used were for passage in either business class or first class. Counsel for the respondent argued that the value of a free ticket to Mr. Giffen was the amount that Mr. Giffen would have been required to pay for a revenue ticket in first or business class. Counsel noted that such tickets are not discounted. In the case of Mr. Mommersteeg the value, according to counsel for the respondent, was the discounted economy class fare if available on that flight or, if not, the full economy fare for the flight taken.

Counsel for the respondent submitted further that the reward tickets had a measurable value to HW equal to the cost to HW of tickets which it might have gotten free had the appellants not used points for personal purposes. That argument is devoid of merit. It ignores the fact that in order to reap the benefits HW would first have had to extract from its employees a contractual obligation to join frequent flyer plans, to keep records of points earned qua employee and points earned personally and to redeem points in accordance with HW's direction. The administrative cost to HW of all of this would have been considerable...

Counsel for the appellant submitted that the value of the benefit is equal to the incremental cost to the airline of filling the reward seat. He referred to the discussion of the House of Lords in *Pepper (Inspector of Taxes) v. Hart*, [1992] [B.]T.C. 591. ... It is of no assistance because it turned on the statutory provision which has no equivalent in the Act. The argument that cost to the employer is the proper test must be rejected as well. The decisions of the Exchequer Court in *Philp v. M.N.R.*, ... and *Waffle v. M.N.R.*, ... are not authority for the proposition that cost to the employer is a universally applicable measure of the value of a benefit from employment. Here the benefits were not acquired by ordinary purchase in the open market.

In my view the proper measure of the value of a benefit in the form of a reward ticket is the price which the employee would have been obliged to pay for a revenue ticket entitling him to travel on the same flight in the same class of service and subject to the same restrictions as are applicable to reward tickets. The sale price of a revenue ticket for travel in the same class on the same flight is only the starting point in the calculation. Care must be taken to adjust for the differences in value between revenue tickets and reward tickets attributable to restrictions on the latter. The testimony of William Young, a truthful and knowledgeable witness, makes it clear that:

a) within economy class a wide variety of prices is charged and price varies inversely with the number of restrictions attached to the ticket;

b) the restrictions imposed on reward tickets, though not the same as those imposed on discounted economy tickets are, nevertheless, onerous; and,

c) reward tickets are intended to fill and generally do fill seats which cannot be sold.

On that evidence I conclude that an economy class reward ticket is unlikely to be worth more than the most heavily discounted economy ticket sold for the flight in question. Business class and first class revenue tickets are not discounted but, just as in the case of economy tickets, reward tickets for travel in those two classes cannot, because of restrictions, be regarded as equal in value to unrestricted revenue tickets. It seems likely that restrictions to which first class and business class reward tickets are subject reduce the value of them to the same extent that restrictions on economy class reward tickets reduce their value. Thus the value of a reward ticket in either business or first class is equal to that proportion of an unrestricted business or first class fare which the price of the most heavily discounted economy class fare on that flight is of the price of a full fare economy class ticket.

It follows that the value attributed by the Minister to the reward tickets issued at Mr. Giffen's request is excessive. In the case of Mr. Mommersteeg it is clear that the two round trip reward tickets issued cannot be worth more than the $268 price of the discounted economy class round trip revenue used by Mr. Mommersteeg. They may be worth less if less expensive economy class tickets were available for that flight.

The appeals will therefore be allowed and the assessments referred back to the Minister for reassessment on the basis that the value of the benefits in issue is to be determined by the formula set out in these reasons. Success was divided. In the circumstances each side will bear its own costs.

YOUNGMAN v. THE QUEEN
[1990] 2 C.T.C. 10, 90 D.T.C. 6322 (F.C.A.)

[The appellant, his wife and his three children owned all of the shares of Andrich Developments Limited. In 1966, the company acquired 16 acres of land near Guelph, Ontario, for the purpose of subdividing and developing it. When the municipal authorities rejected the subdivision project, the appellant decided to have the company build a home for his family. The home was completed in 1978 at a total cost of $395,549. Of this amount, approximately $80,000 was borrowed from Canada Trust. The appellant also made interest-free loans to the company to assist in financing construction. The appellant and his family moved into the house and commencing February 1, 1979, the appellant paid the company a monthly rent of $1,100 (including $300 for utilities). The Minister reassessed the appellant and his wife as having received a shareholder benefit under paragraph 15(1)(c). The appellant appealed.]

Pratte J.A. (Heald and Stone JJ.A. concurring): ...

After having unsuccessfully challenged that reassessment before the Tax Review Board [unreported], the appellant appealed to the Trial Division and alleged that the fair market value of the rental of the house he had occupied in 1979 did not exceed the rent that he had paid and that, as a consequence, he had received no benefit from his company during the year [86 D.T.C. 6584].

In her statement of defence, the respondent stated that in reassessing the appellant, the Minister of National Revenue had made the following assumptions:

(a) the Plaintiff, his wife Beatrice, and their three children at all relevant times owned all of the issued voting shares of Andrich Developments Limited ("the corporation"), the Appellant and his wife holding 1400 shares each, and the children 400 shares each;

(b) in 1978, the corporation, at the direction of and for the benefit of the Plaintiff and his wife, constructed a luxury single-family residence ("the residence") on a 16-acre lot owned by the corporation, at a cost of $395,549.34;

(c) the Plaintiff, his wife and his three children, occupied the house in or about January of 1979, and in February of 1979 and throughout the rest of the year, the Plaintiff paid rent to the corporation of $800.00 per month, and paid other expenses related to the operation of the house, including utilities, of $300.00 per month, a total of $12,100.00 in the 1979 taxation year;

(d) the residence was charged with a first mortgage of $79,413.55;

(e) the corporation's equity in the residence was $316,135.79;

(f) during the 1979 taxation year, the corporation paid mortgage interest of $7,566.00, municipal taxes of $420.00 and insurance premiums of $813.00, a total of $8,799.00, in respect of the said residence;

(g) a reasonable estimate of the value of the benefit conferred upon the plaintiff by the corporation in the 1979 taxation year was $6,526.00;

(h) in 1977, an investor could expect a 9% return on capital from an effectively risk-free investment;

(i) the corporation did not build the residence for the purpose of producing or gaining income from a business or property.

Moreover, in a schedule to the statement of defence, the respondent indicated that the amount of the benefit allegedly conferred on the appellant had been calculated in the following manner:

Corporation's equity in the residence	$316,135.79
Return on investment of $316,135.79 at 9%	$28,452.00
Mortgage interest, municipal taxes and insurance paid by the corporation	8,799.00
Gross Benefit to Plaintiff and wife received from corporation	37,251.00
Less: Amount of benefit attributable to Plaintiff's wife	18,625.00
Amount of benefit attributable to Plaintiff	$18,625.00
Less: Rent and expenses paid by Plaintiff	12,100.00
Net amount of benefit to the Plaintiff	$6,526.00

At trial, the appellant and his wife testified as to the circumstances in which the house had been built. The appellant said that the decision to have his company build that house had been made not only for the purpose of providing him and his family with a bigger and better home but also in the hope that the building of such a nice home in that area would serve to eliminate opposition to the proposed subdivision development. The appellant also introduced expert evidence as to the rental value of the house. According to one expert, the free market rental value of the house was approximately $800 per month plus utilities; the other expert fixed it at approximately $950. Both agreed that there was no comparable house on the market in the area. One said that, in that area, the free market rental value of houses bore no relation to their real value.

The appellant's basic argument at trial was that the assessment was wrong because, instead of being based on the value of the benefit that the appellant had received from his company — which value was established by the uncontradicted evidence of the two experts — it was based on the costs that the company had incurred to provide him with that benefit. The trial judge rejected that argument. He first found that the appellant's company had not built the house for a business purpose since, in his view, it had been, from the outset, built for the personal use of the appellant. He also found that, in the circumstances, the fair market rental value was totally inappropriate for measuring the value of the benefit conferred on the appellant because that fair market rental value bore no relation to the actual costs of that benefit. ...

I will deal first with the question of onus of proof. The rule is well known. When the Minister has, in his pleadings, disclosed the assumptions of facts on which the assessment was made, and when, as is the case here, it is not contested that the assessment was in fact based on those assumptions, the taxpayer has the onus of disproving the Minister's assumptions. Here, the Minister's basic assumption was that "a reasonable estimate of the value of the benefit conferred upon the plaintiff by the corporation in the 1979 taxation year was $6,526.00. The argument of the appellant on this point, as I understand it, is that this assumption has been rebutted since the evidence shows that it was made for the reason that the Minister considered arbitrarily, according to the appellant, that the company that had built the house was entitled to a 9% return on its investment. It follows, says the appellant, that the only evidence as to the value of the benefit conferred on the appellant is that of his experts. I do not see merit in that argument. In order to rebut the Minister's assumption, the appellant had to prove that the value of the benefit in question was less than $6,526. The assumption of the Minister could be correct even if it was made for a wrong reason. It follows, therefore, that the question to be resolved in this case is whether the appellant adduced evidence showing that, in 1979, the appellant did not receive a benefit or advantage of $6,526 from Andrich Developments Limited.

As to the attack made by the appellant on the Trial Judge's finding that Andrich Developments Limited had not built the house for a business purpose, I shall simply say that I cannot say that the Judge was plainly wrong in reaching that conclusion. Moreover, as will now become apparent, this finding was not without importance.

The appellant's main proposition is that, under paragraph 15(1)(c), what is to be added to the income of the shareholder is the value of the benefit that he received rather than the cost of that benefit to the corporation. That proposition is certainly well founded. However, it does not support the appellant's conclusion. In determining the value of benefit, one may take its cost into consideration. Free market value is not, in all circumstances, the sole indication of real value. ...

In order to assess the value of a benefit, for the purposes of paragraph 15(1)(c), it is first necessary to determine what that benefit is or, in other words, what the company did for its shareholder; second, it is necessary to find what price the shareholder would have had to pay, in similar circumstances, to get the same benefit from a company of which he was not a shareholder. In the present case, the benefit or advantage conferred on the appellant was not merely the right to use or occupy a house for as long as he wished; it was the right to use or occupy for as long as he wished a house that the company, at his request, had built specially for him in accordance with his specifications. How much would the appellant have had to pay for the same advantage if he had not been a shareholder of the company? Certainly more than what the two experts referred to as the free market rental value since, in my view, the company would have then charged a rent sufficient to produce a decent return on its investment. It is impossible to determine with accuracy the amount of that rent. However, subject to one important reservation, I cannot say that it would have been less than what the Minister assumed it to be. That reservation is that if the appellant had been dealing with a company of which he was not a shareholder, consideration would certainly have been given, in determining the rent payable, to the fact that he had himself lent more than $100,000 without interest to the company in order to help to finance the construction of the house. As long as that loan remained outstanding, the rent otherwise payable would, in my view, have been reduced by an amount equal to the interest that should normally have been paid on the balance of the loan.

I would, therefore, allow the appeal and refer the reassessment back to the Minister for reconsideration and reassessment in accordance with these reasons. I would grant the appellant his costs in this Court and in the Trial Division.

Notes and Questions

1. Consider the new suit of clothes provided to the employee in *Wilkins v. Rogerson.* Under paragraph 6(1)(a), would the clothes be valued as new or used? What if the clothing has a company logo? See *Wisla v. The Queen*, [2000] 1 C.T.C. 2823, 2000 D.T.C. 3563 (T.C.C.).
2. Placing a value on a taxable benefit is difficult in cases where the item provided to the employee has a work-related purpose and also provides a personal benefit. The apportionment of dual character benefits is well illustrated in cases where an employee travels on an employer-paid trip that has a business purpose and a personal enjoyment component.
3. In *Ferguson v. M.N.R.*, [1972] C.T.C. 2105, 72 D.T.C. 1097, only 10 per cent of the value of the trip (value in this case being equal to the employer's cost) was a benefit. In this case, Mr. Ferguson was a director and chief financial officer of the employer company, which requested him to attend a convention in Greece where he could meet present and prospective customers, even though he had no selling responsibilities in the company. No prize or award was involved. The taxpayer testified that although he traveled to foreign lands frequently for pleasure, the trip to Greece was for business and he had "slight interest" in it. He argued that if it had been a pleasure trip he would have taken his wife. However, he did take a number of planned tours in Athens. The Court found a "nominal" portion of the trip to be a taxable benefit.
4. In *Philp et al. v. M.N.R.*, [1970] C.T.C. 330, 70 D.T.C. 6237 (Exch. Ct.), the "benefit" in issue was an expense paid six-day trip to the Caribbean given by a supermarket chain to certain employees after they had met or exceeded a sales quota. The only scheduled events were three two-hour business sessions referred to as "College of Profit", and the president's dinner. The Court decided that a benefit had been conferred on each taxpayer consisting of one-half of the employer's cost for each taxpayer's trip.
5. Contrast the decisions in *Ferguson* and *Philp* with *Lowe*, supra.

6. Do you agree with the manner in which the Court valued the benefit in *Giffen*? The CRA's current administrative position (set out in *Income Tax Technical News 40*, June 11, 2009) with regard to loyalty points (such as frequent flyer points) collected by employees on credit card purchases that are reimbursed by employers is that no employee benefit has to be included in income provided that: the points are not converted to cash; the plan is not indicative of another form of remuneration; and the plan or arrangement is not for tax avoidance purposes. The CRA indicated that the change in administrative practice is due to the difficulty of valuing the benefits as well as tracking and identifying the benefits attributable to points accumulated by way of employment versus personal use of the credit cards.
7. What happens when a benefit is provided to an employee but is not used? In *Richmond v. The Queen*, [1998] 3 C.T.C. 2552, 98 D.T.C. 1804 (T.C.C.), the taxpayer was given a parking space at no charge by his employer. The CRA assessed the taxpayer with a taxable benefit of $1,800, equating the value to an unreserved parking space in the near neighbourhood Richmond only used the spot about 20 per cent of the year, and therefore argued that he should only have been assessed on $360. Bell T.C.J. dismissed the taxpayer's appeal, concluding (at paragraph 7): "Whether the Appellant used the property is of little consequence. It was available to him and was accordingly a benefit to him. He adduced no evidence to establish that the value of the assigned exclusive parking spot was less than that assessed by the Minister". Do you agree? Contrast *Richmond* with *Rachfalowski v. The Queen* (2008), [2009] 1 C.T.C. 2073, 2008 D.T.C. 3626 (T.C.C.).
8. In *Rachfalowski*, the taxpayer was an executive who received a golf club membership paid for by his employer. The taxpayer testified that he hated golf, could not and did not golf. His request for cash instead of the membership was declined and when he tried to refuse the membership outright, he was persuaded not to do so. He used the golf club occasionally to entertain clients and a couple of times he took his wife for dinner. In allowing the taxpayer's appeal from an assessment that included the full cost of the club membership in his income, Bowman C.J. commented (at paragraph 18): "I have a fair idea what our friend on the Clapham omnibus would probably say. I think the more reasonable view is that the value to a particular taxpayer of such a benefit under paragraph 6(1)(*a*) should be determined on an individual basis of actual use as opposed to availability". Bowman C.J. determined that, in this case, the golf club membership primarily benefited the employer and, even if he was wrong in that determination, the value of the benefit was minimal at best. Do you agree with Bowman C.J. that the value of the benefit should be determined on an individual basis based on the use made by the employee of the benefit?
9. A presumption in favour of using the fair market value method of valuing employee benefits has been established by the Federal Court of Appeal in *Spence v.*

Canada, 2011 FCA 200, [2011] 5 C.T.C. 188, 2011 D.T.C. 5111 (F.C.A.), relying on the analysis in Kim Brooks, "Delimiting the Concept of Income: The Taxation of In-Kind Benefits" (2004) 49 McGill L.J. 255. *Spence* allows that there might be facts demonstrating that the fair market value method is inappropriate, but since there was no evidence suggesting this was the case the fair market value method was applied. What facts and evidence might suggest that the fair market value method is inappropriate?

C. Allowances

Subject to certain specific exceptions, paragraph 6(1)(b) requires allowances received by a taxpayer to be included in income from an office or employment. Recall the decision in *Ransom, supra*. The case is important not only for its interpretation of the word "benefit" in paragraph 6(1)(a) but also for its discussion of the distinction between the concepts of an allowance and a reimbursement for income tax purposes.

STUDIES OF THE ROYAL COMMISSION ON TAXATION — No. 16 — SPECIFIC TYPES OF PERSONAL INCOME

D. Sherbaniuk
(1967) pp. 87-90 [Footnotes deleted]

Chapter 3

THE TAXATION OF BENEFITS AND ALLOWANCES FROM AN OFFICE OR EMPLOYMENT ALLOWANCES

Section 3(1)(e) of the *Income War Tax Act* provided for the inclusion in income of

> (e) personal and living expenses when such form part of the profit, gain or remuneration of the taxpayer or the payment of such constitutes part of the gain, benefit or advantage accruing to the taxpayer under any estate, trust, contract, arrangement or power of appointment, irrespective of when created.

This provision was invoked by the Minister of National Revenue in the leading case of *Samson v. M.N.R.* to tax an employee in respect of a per diem living allowance. He was assessed in respect of the $20 per day living allowance, less a deduction of $2 per day, but was not charged in respect of the transportation expenses. It was not disputed that the taxpayer actually disbursed more than the amount of the allowance while absent from his place of residence and in connection with his duties. He kept no vouchers in respect of these expenditures, and did not produce itemized accounts of travelling expenses. Thorson, P. held that the allowance was not taxable. It involved no element of remuneration or net gain or profit or gratuity to the appellant, he said, and did not result in any gain or profit to him, but was paid and received only as reimbursement to the appellant of living expenses over and above ordinary personal and living expenses to which he would be put by reason of his necessary absences from his residence in connection with his duties. His Lordship acknowledged that, in some circumstances, an allowance would be taxable:

> It may well be that an arrangement made between individuals under which a fixed amount is paid for certain expense purposes may result in net gain or profit to the recipient of the fixed amount through his actually spending less than the fixed amount on such expenses and the recipient may be properly assessable for income tax in respect of such net gain or profit in that it becomes remuneration to him.

But such was not the case here where the Order in Council made it clear that the essential character of the payment was reimbursement. *He went on to point out that the assessability for income tax purposes of any particular amount did not depend upon what it was called, but rather upon what it really was:* ... This decision may be explained on the basis of the doctrine of beneficial receipt, according to which an amount received by a taxpayer will have the quality of income only if his right to it is absolute and under no restriction, contractual or otherwise, as to its disposition, use or enjoyment.

As one writer has pointed out,

> ... where cash is supplied to an employee who is under a duty to apply it according to his employer's needs and objects it is not income of the employee.
>
> There is no difference in principle where an employee is required to spend his own money in this manner and is reimbursed at a later date.

The potential for abuse suggested by the *Samson* case was dealt with legislatively in a series of provisions culminating in paragraph 6(1)(b). Subject to the exceptions contained in subparagraphs 6(1)(b)(i)–(xi), an allowance is taxable under paragraph 6(1)(b) if it is "an allowance for personal or living expenses or as an allowance for any other purpose".

The Queen v. MacDonald, [1994] 2 C.T.C. 48, 94 D.T.C. 6262 (F.C.A.), is the leading case on what constitutes an allowance under paragraph 6(1)(b). The taxpayer was an RCMP officer who was transferred from Regina to Toronto. He received a housing subsidy of $700.00 per month following his transfer. The subsidy was authorized by the Treasury Board and paid by the Department of Supply and Services. The taxpayer did not include the subsidy in his income. The Minister reassessed and included the subsidy in MacDonald's income for the taxation year in issue. The Federal Court of Appeal (Linden, J.A., Mahoney, MacGuigan, JJ.A. concurring) held that the subsidy was an allowance under paragraph 6(1)(b). The court set out the definition of an allowance for the purposes of paragraph 6(1)(b):

> First, an allowance is an arbitrary amount in that it is a predetermined sum set without specific reference to any actual expenseor cost. ... [T]he amount of the allowance may be set through a process of projected or average expenses or costs. Second, paragraph 6(1)(b) encompasses allowances for personal or living expenses, or for any other purpose, so that an allowance will usually be for a specific purpose. Third, an allowance is in the discretion of the recipient in that the recipient need not account for the expenditure of the funds towards an actual expense or cost.

The following cases illustrate the treatment of allowances for income tax purposes and deal with the distinction between a reimbursement of expenses and an allowance.

CAMPBELL v. M.N.R.
(1955), 13 Tax A.B.C. 273, 55 D.T.C. 434 (T.A.B.)

W.S. Fisher:

... The appellant has appealed against her income tax assessment for the year 1948 made under the provisions of the *Income War Tax Act* and her assessments for the years 1949, 1950 and 1951 made under the provisions of The 1948 *Income Tax Act*.

When assessing her for the year 1948, the respondent added to the income disclosed in her return the sum of $600 received by her from her employer representing an allowance paid at the rate of $50 per month in connection with the use of the appellant's car on her employer's business. Amounts of $900 in each of the years 1949 and 1950 and $1,200 in the year 1951 were added by the respondent to her income for those years, respectively, and for the same reason, namely, that the said amounts represented payments of $75 per month in 1949 and 1950 and $100 per month in 1951, paid to her by her employer in respect of the use of her car on the employer's business.

The taxpayer objected to the inclusion of these amounts as part of her income for the said years on the ground that they were not allowances, as such, to the appellant, but were monies advanced to her for the furnishing of services apart from any office or employment held by her, and she alleged that they were rentals for the use of her car from which there should be deducted the relevant expenses of running the car plus depreciation in connection with the various motor vehicles owned by the appellant during the period under review. ...

On the [above] branch of the appeal, Mrs. Campbell's evidence was that during the years under appeal she was the Superintendent of Nurses at the East Windsor Hospital, a hospital owned and operated by the East Windsor Health Association. In the year 1951 this hospital had approximately 250 patients. It was a hospital for chronic invalids, and from time to time a large number of these patients had had to be taken to a general hospital for treatment. In the year 1948, the appellant had supervision over 80 or 90 nurses and also over the maintenance staff, and, in addition, assisted in the kitchen with the preparation of diets, etc. Her evidence was that the transportation of patients from the East Windsor Hospital to a general hospital for treatment was not part of her duties but that, prior to the year 1948, there had been no definite arrangements at the hospital for the transportation of such patients to and from their places of treatment. The hospital maintained no transportation service of its own, and the appellant's evidence was that she used to transport these patients in her own car and at her own expense.

In the year 1947 she asked the hospital to purchase a hospital car for the transportation of the patients back and forth between treatment centres and the East Windsor Hospital, the said hospital car to be used for other duties such as obtaining maintenance supplies and taking deposits to the bank, etc. While these items were not part of her duties any more than the transporting of patients, she had been performing them for the hospital up until that time. Although the hospital did not purchase a car of its own, it offered her $50 per month if she would continue to use her own car to transport the patients and their wheelchairs back and forth and would permit the use of her car for obtaining maintenance supplies and doing the hospital's banking, among certain other matters which might arise.

The appellant's evidence was that this fifty dollars a month for the use of her car was on a rental basis, according to her understanding, but apparently the arrangement was a verbal one, only, and the evidence of the business administrator of the hospital — who was not present when the arrangement was made as he did not become an employee of the hospital until a later date — was that the various amounts paid to the appellant in connection with her car were charged in the books of the hospital under the heading of "Miscellaneous Expense" and had not been shown as rentals paid for the use of the car.

The appellant's evidence was that she paid for the gas and oil used in the car and also for any repairs which became necessary in connection with her own car, and that her car was used not only by herself for the purposes indicated above, but was also available for the use of other employees of the hospital such as maintenance men, the chef, and in fact anyone who might be designated to transfer the hospital's patients to other hospitals for treatment therein. She pointed out that many of the chronic invalids spent most of their time in wheelchairs and therefore wheelchairs for the use of patients while they were receiving treatment in other hospitals had to be transported in her car also, and the resultant wear and tear on the vehicle in all these circumstances was considerable. She gave an estimate of the mileage covered by the car (or cars) owned by her during the years in question in this appeal but she was able to furnish estimates only of the amounts expended by her for gas, oil and repairs during the years in question. She had understood that the monthly amounts received by her for the use of her car were not subject to income tax and, as she paid cash for her gas and oil, it was impossible at this date to verify the actual amounts expended on these items.

[At this point the opinion recites the applicable legislation, substantially incorporated in sections 6 and 8 of the present Act.]

In view of these provisions of the law and in the light of the appellant's evidence that the transportation of the patients back and forth between hospitals in her own motorcar was not part of her ordinary duties but, apparently, was voluntarily performed by her, and that the use of her car for hospital purposes was not a part of her contract nor did it arise out of her duties as Superintendent of Nurses at the hospital, I am of the opinion that her appeal in respect of the amounts added to her income in respect of the monthly amounts received by her in the years 1948 to 1951, both inclusive, for the use of her automobile have been properly assessed as income in her hands as an allowance paid to her by her employer on a periodic basis and without allowing any deductions in respect of the expenses incurred in running and maintaining the said automobile.

It was submitted further on behalf of the appellant that the use of her motorcar in the above circumstances might be considered to be engaging in the business of transporting goods and passengers, but I am unable to concur in this submission.

THE QUEEN v. HUFFMAN
[1990] 2 C.T.C. 132, 90 D.T.C. 6405 (F.C.A.)

[See the facts, supra, 261.]

... I am unable to agree that the sum of $79.57, being the difference between the $500.00 payment to the respondent and the receipts submitted by him ($420.43) can be held to be an allowance and thus taxable pursuant to paragraph 6(1)(b). The Trial Judge found, on the evidence, that the reimbursement was increased from $400.00 to $500.00 pursuant to the 1979 Collective Agreement. An administrative decision was taken that officers would not be required to submit receipts above $400.00 even though they would receive reimbursement of $500.00. The rationale for this decision was said to be the avoidance of extra paperwork. In any event, the Trial Judge said that he accepted the respondent's evidence that he spent more than $500.00. He added:

> I therefore find, as a fact, that the plaintiff spent more than $500.00 in the year in question and was reimbursed for that expenditure the maximum allowable under the contract of employment, $500.00.

This reimbursement cannot be said to be an allowance as that term is used in paragraph 6(1)(b). In interpreting the use of the word "allowance" in another section of the *Income Tax Act*, this Court said in the case of *The Queen v. Pascoe*, [1975] C.T.C. 656 at 658; 75 D.T.C. 5427 at 5428:

> An allowance is, in our view, a limited predetermined sum of money paid to enable the recipient to provide for certain kinds of expense, its amount is determined in advance and, once paid, it is at the complete discretion of the recipient who is not required to account for it. A payment in satisfaction of an obligation to indemnify or reimburse someone or to defray his or her actual expenses is not an allowance; it is not a sum allowed to the recipient to be applied in his or her discretion to certain kinds of expense.

Applying that test to these facts, it is obvious that the $500.00 here in issue or any part of it cannot be said to be an allowance. Article 17.01 provides for reimbursement only upon presentation of receipts. As noted by the Trial Judge *supra*, a special exception was made in 1979 but only in respect of the $100.00 increase that year and in the interests of avoiding undue extra paperwork. This circumstance cannot operate so as to change the nature of the payment. It is still a reimbursement, not an allowance and the Trial Judge did not err in so finding.

For these reasons, it is my conclusion that the within appeal should be dismissed with costs.

Notes and Questions

1. In *The Queen v. MacDonald*, *supra*, the Minister also argued that the housing subsidy was a taxable benefit under paragraph 6(1)(a). The Court resolved the case under paragraph 6(1)(b) and did not deal with subparagraph 6(1)(a). Is the housing subsidy received by MacDonald a taxable benefit under paragraph 6(1)(a)?
2. Could Mrs. Campbell have mitigated her tax liability by adopting a different procedure? For example, if you were entertaining customers for your employer which procedure would you adopt:
   (a) Paying for the entertainment and receiving a reimbursement?

(b) Taking a petty cash advance from the employer and accounting for its use?

(c) Receiving a fixed stipend each month to cover estimated expenses?

(d) Using a credit card that is billed directly to the employer?

3. Could Mrs. Campbell deduct her actual expenses from the added income assessed to her by the Minister?
4. What is the critical distinction between an allowance and a reimbursement of expenses?
5. Note the treatment of the expense allowances for MLAs and municipal officers (subsections 81(2) and (3)).
6. X tried out for a football club. He travelled to the training camp and took board and lodging in the city at his own expense. X failed to make the team but received $275 from the club. When the Minister added this amount to his income, X objected, saying that it was a repayment of his costs of transportation and living expenses. What result? See *Lukas v. M.N.R.* (1960), 25 Tax A.B.C. 283, 60 D.T.C. 630 (T.A.B.).
7. What is the rationale for each of the exclusions in subparagraphs 6(1)(b)(i)–(ix)?

Problem

Joe Deakes is an employee of the Acme Sales Co. From October to May, Joe works at the company's head office in Toronto. From May to September, he travels across Canada demonstrating his company's clothing products. His usual practise is to stage a fashion show at a large department store. These fashion shows are sometimes the joint effort of several clothing manufacturers. Joe is also responsible for the entertainment of prospective buyers. However, he has no authority to conclude contracts on behalf of the company. The clothing is transported from store to store and city to city by means of a station wagon which the company provides.

Joe receives reimbursement of his expenses in operating the station wagon to the extent of 40 cents per kilometre totalling $10,000. He also receives $13,000 as an allowance for living expenses while he is travelling in the company's interests. However, his total living expenses while travelling for the company were $15,000.

How should the above facts be treated for tax purposes?

III. DEDUCTIONS IN COMPUTING INCOME FROM OFFICE OR EMPLOYMENT

A. General

Section 8 authorizes a number of deductions in respect of employment income. Subsection 8(2) limits the deductions that may be claimed by an officer or employee to those expenses set out in section 8. Therefore, if an expenditure is not listed in section 8, an employee is not entitled to deduct it from gross income. This is the case even though a good argument can be made in favour of permitting a taxpayer to deduct all expenses incurred in earning employment income. The cost of commuting to and from work, the purchase price of clothes and the cost of meals consumed in the course of employment are examples of expenditures which may be considered legitimate expenses incurred in earning income. An employee can argue that, had the expense not been incurred, the employment income could not have been earned. However, this "but for" reasoning could lead to the deduction of many personal expenses. For example, if the employee had not purchased clothes, he or she would not have been able to retain employment; if the employee had not eaten, he or she would not have been alive to earn income.

Consider why the Act limits the deduction of employment expenses as compared to expenses deductible by an independent contractor. Can the limitation be justified on the basis of equity and neutrality? If yes, would restricting deductions available to independent contractors in a similar way provide a sound solution? In addition to equity and neutrality, what policy considerations should be addressed prior to equalizing the deduction?

Would a better solution be to broaden the scope of employee deductions? Is it relevant that the tax base would be narrowed or eroded if the scope of employee deductions were broadened?

Apart from the general limitation in subsection 8(2), a number of limitations are imposed on the permitted deductions under section 8. For example, subsection 8(4) permits the deduction of meals only if the officer or employee has been away from the employer's work site for a period of not less than 12 hours. Other limitations apply to the deduction of dues (subsection 8(5)) and workspace in the home (subsection 8(13)).

Section 67 applies to all deductions from any source including income from an office or employment. The provision states that the amount of an expense which is otherwise deductible must also be reasonable. Only that portion of the expense which is found to be reasonable will be deductible. It is a question of fact whether or not an expense is reasonable in the circumstances. In this respect, review section 67.1, which arbitrarily restricts the deduction of expenses incurred for food, beverages and entertainment to 50 per cent of the cost of those items. Sections 67 and 67.1 are discussed in more detail in Part IV, Chapter 5.

Particular attention should be paid to the difference between exclusions and deductions. Look closely at the subparagraphs of paragraph 6(1)(b) and the paragraphs of subsection 8(1). Consider cases in which an exclusion may be more advantageous than a deduction for an employee and cases in which a deduction may be more advantageous. Consider which may be more favourable for the employer. For example, the treatment of certain travelling expenses can be dealt with by way of an exclusion (subparagraph 6(1)(b)(vii)) or by a deduction (paragraph 8(1)(h)). Note the cross-references between sections 6 and 8.

B. Specific Deductions

1. Travelling Expenses (paragraphs 8(1)(e), (f), (g), (h), (h.1), (j); subsection 8(4))

There are several possible arrangements between an employer and employee concerning the payment of travel expenses. In the case of automobile expenses, for example, the employer may provide the automobile and take care of all expenses, or the employee may provide the automobile. In the latter event, if the employee is to have the same amount of after-tax income, the employer will have to provide further sums of money to the employee. The employer may reimburse the employee for the expenses incurred or may provide an allowance.

If the employee must pay for travel expenses out of income, are the expenses deductible? What if the employer paid all or a portion of them?

MARTYN v. M.N.R.
(1962), 29 Tax A.B.C. 305, 62 D.T.C. 341 (T.A.B.)

[The taxpayer, a pilot with Trans-Canada Air Lines, attempted to deduct the cost of commuting between his home and the airport, a round trip distance of 27 miles. The evidence disclosed that public transportation was at best very inconvenient and often unavailable.]

J.O. Weldon, Q.C. (with whom C.L. Snyder, Q.C. concurred):

... A complicated formula is used to calculate the pilot's pay, which takes into account such things as the speed of the aircraft, its weight, the flying time which is especially important, and a small base pay. There is a minimum guaranteed pay equivalent to 60 hours per month actual flying time, and a pilot is permitted to work a total of 85 hours per month. Actual flying time is calculated from the time the engines commence to run to the time they are stopped. A pilot must arrive at the airport one hour before flight departure. During that hour he checks the weather reports and forecasts, makes out a flight plan, checks the aircraft, makes sure all the systems are working satisfactorily, checks the airport facilities, the en route facilities and the navigation facilities. ... The appellant is on call five days a week, twenty-four hours a day. During his duty period he must not leave his home without leaving a telephone number where he can be reached. The appellant ordinarily goes to the airport and in due course returns to his home by his own motor car. During normal working hours he said he could take an air line conveyance from its terminal in Toronto costing $3 for the round trip. In the early hours of the morning there is no other way than by air line cab which would cost about $8 for the round trip. The appellant has claimed $2.70 car expense covering a round trip between his home and the airport made up as follows: 27 miles at $0.10 per mile = $2.70.

In his Notice of Objection the appellant contended that to carry out his duties as a pilot it was necessary for him to travel to and from the airport by motor car. He stated that "public transportation is not provided on a 24-hour basis and at times when all flights are departing and arriving", and further states: "Should I use public transportation I would not be able to get sufficient rest between flights to carry out my duties in a safe and healthy manner". The Notification By The Minister dated November 22, 1961, confirmed the assessment disallowing the automobile expenses amounting to $392.30 and stated that these expenses were not incurred by the taxpayer for travelling in the course of his employment within the meaning of subsection (9) of Section 11 of the Act [now paragraph 8(1)(h.1)].

To succeed the appellant must bring himself within all the requirements set forth in paragraphs (a), (b) and (c) of the above-mentioned section. ...

The appellant would, prima facie, appear to satisfy paragraphs (a), (b) and (c) of subsection (9) above. On a closer scrutiny of paragraph (a) it will be obvious that the "car expenses" in question were not incurred by the taxpayer while he was carrying on the duties of his employment away from his employer's place of business, but rather in proceeding from his home to his employer's place of business and in returning in due course to his home. That brings up the question as to when the appellant's employment actually commenced. His counsel argued at the hearing of this appeal that it commenced when he got into his motor car to drive to the airport. However there was no evidence given by any official of Trans-Canada Air Lines or by any other person to show this to be a fact. ...

There is no evidence in this appeal to warrant a finding that the appellant's employment commenced when he stepped into his motor car to go to his employer's place of business.

Paragraphs (b) and (c) of subsection (9) above do not appear to present any obstacles to the appellant. He made it clear that when he has to stay overnight at his destination Trans-Canada Air Lines pays for his hotel room and taxis.

As the Chairman of the Board indicated several times during the hearing of the appeal, the appellant assumed a heavy burden when he undertook to prove that his automobile expenses as a "reserve pilot" were expended by him for travelling in the course of his employment. On quick reflection it can readily be seen that every employee to reach his place of work expends amounts for transportation. The amounts expended may vary greatly from the cost of a motor car complete with chauffeur to the cost of shoe leather. Every employee must accommodate his place of residence to his work. He is free to decide whether he will walk to his work, drive his motor car or use public transportation, and the cost of the mode of travel used is ordinarily considered part of the personal or living expenses of the taxpayer. Therefore, the appellant must give very convincing reasons why he should be treated differently from the great mass of employees. The term "travelling expenses" is usually used in connection with transportation while on duty, by private motor car, bus, train and aircraft, and includes hotel expenses, meals, taxis and gratuities, while the employee is away from his employer's place of business. The appellant's "travelling expenses" do not fit into the above statement and it must be concluded that he cannot deduct his automobile expenses under subsection (9) of Section 11. If the appellant has a point to make with regard to his automobile expenses relative to his employment it would seem that it could best be considered by his employer. ...

Counsel for the appellant placed reliance on the case of *Coron v. M.N.R.* (1957), 18 Tax A.B.C. 97; 57 DTC 518. The appellant in that case, who lived in Montreal, was a professional river pilot subject to the by-laws of the Pilotage District of Montreal. While subject to certain rules and regulations applicable to his trade he was a self-employed person, and was permitted to deduct the part of his expenses which were considered reasonable for the purpose of earning his income while living away from home. The aeroplane pilot in the present appeal was not self-employed as was the river pilot but was an employee of Trans-Canada Air Lines. As a result a different ruling under the *Income Tax Act* must apply. ...

The law applicable to the present appeal is set out in the case of *Luks v. M.N.R.* No. 2, [1959] Ex. C.R. 45; [1958] C.T.C. 345; 58 DTC 1194, wherein Mr. Justice Thurlow said:

> In the present case, travelling between the appellant's home and the several places where he was employed was not part of the duties of his employment. ... The journeys were not made for the employer's benefit, nor were they made on the employer's behalf or at his direction, nor had the employer any control over the appellant when he was making them. The utmost that can be said of them is that they were made in consequence of the appellant's employment. That is not sufficient for the present purpose.

It therefore follows in this present appeal that the claim made by Mr. Martyn for the deduction of $392.30 for automobile expenses incurred in taking him from his home to his place of employment and return cannot be allowed as a deductible item for income tax purposes.

Notes and Questions

1. Commuting expenses are traditionally disallowed on the ground that a taxpayer's choice of place of residence is a consumption decision. Compare the following cases:
   (a) H and W are married and both work. They decide to live close to his place of business; as a result W has a round trip each day of 20 miles.
   (b) S, a single woman, works in the city but prefers to live in the country; as a result she commutes daily 10 miles each way.
2. Consider *Evans v. The Queen*, [1999] 1 C.T.C. 2609, 99 D.T.C. 168 (T.C.C.). Evans was employed as a school psychologist. She was required to travel from her home to a number of schools each day. She received a travel allowance (28 cents per kilometre) from her employer for travel between the schools but no allowance for travel to the first school and home from last school. She claimed these expenses as a deduction under paragraph 8(1)(h.1). According to Potter T.C.J., the provision of a travel allowance did not preclude the deduction of travel expenses provided that the expenses related to travel not covered by the allowance. As to the deductibility of travel from and to her home, Potter, T.C.J. concluded (at paragraphs 36-37):

   > If the Appellant had simply to get herself between her residence and the various schools where she started and finished her days, it would seem to me that her travel expenses would properly be limited to the cost of such travel less the amount that she would have expended to travel on a daily basis to and from the administrative centre. In the normal course of events, her cost of travel between her residence and the administrative centre would be considered personal in nature.
   >
   > ...
   >
   > However, it seems to me that there is a further wrinkle in this particular case as it relates to the requirement to transport the voluminous amount of paper and materials around to her various work places requiring the exclusive use of the trunk of her car on a permanent basis throughout the school year. In my opinion, she had no alternative as part of her duties but to transport these back and forth between her residence and the first and last schools she visited on a daily basis. I have no hesitation in finding that it was an implied term of the contract not only that she had to have a car available to transport herself around, but also that she had to have all these materials on hand in order to carry out her duties. There was no other practical way in which she could do this but to take them back and forth to her residence. ...

3. Consider again the decision in *Ransom, supra.* If it is persuasive to say that commuting expenses represent personal living expenses because a taxpayer's choice of residence is a consumption decision, is it not equally persuasive to say that Ransom's loss on the sale of his house was a personal expense inasmuch as

he made a consumption decision to buy a house in Sarnia rather than lodging his family in rented accommodations?

4. Compare paragraphs (e), (f), (g), (h), and (h.1) of subsection 8(1), noting the many differences of detail, but remarking also on the possibility that a particular taxpayer might have a case for relief under two or more of the paragraphs. In *The Queen v. Little*, [1974] C.T.C. 678, 74 D.T.C. 6534 (F.C.T.D.) the taxpayer was a CPR engineer who lived in Moose Jaw where the CPR divisional office was located. The Moose Jaw foreman was responsible for work assignments in Moose Jaw, Swift Current, Outlook, Estevan and North Portal. In the tax year, the taxpayer was assigned to yard work in Swift Current. A claim for relief under paragraph 8(1)(g) was denied on the ground that Swift Current was the location of his "employer's establishment to which he reported for work". Consider whether the taxpayer might have had a better chance of success under paragraph 8(1)(e). If Little did satisfy paragraph 8(1)(e), would that paragraph permit deduction of all his travel expenses?
5. If Little had been required to drive engines from Swift Current to other places, and while away from Swift Current had made disbursements for meals and lodging, he would have been entitled to relief under paragraph 8(1)(g). If he had expenses for meals, but no lodging expenses, while away from Swift Current would he qualify? Although subparagraph 8(1)(g)(ii) speaks of a taxpayer who makes disbursements for meals and lodging, Cattanach J. decided in favour of a taxpayer who had expenses for meals but not for lodging. See *The Queen v. Deimert*, [1976] C.T.C. 301, 76 D.T.C. 6187 (F.C.T.D.).
6. Note the variety of restrictions expressed in paragraphs 8(1)(e) to (h), and the number of interpretive difficulties to which they give rise. For example, observe that a claim under paragraph 8(1)(f) is subject to ten limitations. The *Little* case illustrates the necessity of satisfying all the conditions of a paragraph in order to obtain the deduction. Even if Moose Jaw had been "the employer's establishment to which he reported for work", could it be said that Little travelled "away from" Moose Jaw "on vehicles used by the employer to transport the goods or passengers"?
7. *Little* helps to explain the rococo appearance of paragraphs 8(1)(e) to (h) and similar relieving provisions in the Act (for example, section 110 and former section 109) by showing the *ad hoc* manner in which they are introduced and amended. A good statement of one of the reasons for some of the strange gaps in the relieving provisions may be found in *Gervais v. M.N.R.*, [1981] C.T.C. 2496, 81 D.T.C. 414 (T.R.B.). The taxpayer, a relieving telegrapher for the CNR, failed in his claim for automobile expenses incurred in travelling more than 8,000 miles to provide relief in six towns and cities other than his home town. M. Tremblay observed "... there is no provision for deducting [travel expenses other than meals and lodging] in paragraph 8(1)(e). The legislator doubtless assumed that railway

company employees may or must travel only by rail or that provision is made elsewhere in the Act for the deduction of their travelling expenses".

8. Under paragraphs 8(1)(f), (h) and (h.1), the taxpayer must be "ordinarily required" to carry on the duties of his employment away from his employer's place of business; in paragraph 8(1)(g) the phrase is "required ... regularly". What do these phrases mean? Do they mean the same thing? In *Ondrey v. M.N.R.* (1961), 26 Tax A.B.C. 89, 61 D.T.C. 135 (T.A.B.) a taxpayer who spent two-thirds of each day travelling was found to satisfy the "ordinarily required" condition. Would the result be the same if a taxpayer spent 4 months of each year travelling and the remainder of the time at head office?

9. Ondrey would not be entitled to deduct the cost of his meals: see subsection 8(4). Why does subsection 8(4) limit the deduction for meal expenses under paragraphs (f) and (h) and not under paragraphs (e) and (g)?

10. Several cases deal with the requirement that the taxpayer be "ordinarily required to carry on the duties of his employment away from his employer's place of business". See, for example, *Klue v. M.N.R.*, [1976] C.T.C. 2401, 76 D.T.C. 1303 (T.R.B.); *Patterson v. M.N.R.*, [1982] C.T.C. 371, 82 D.T.C. 6326 (F.C.T.D.); *Bubnick v. M.N.R.*, [1981] C.T.C. 2015, 81 D.T.C. 25 (T.R.B.), and *Imray v. The Queen*, [1998] 4 C.T.C. 221, 98 D.T.C. 6580 (F.C.T.D.).

11. John T. Klue was a Detective Sergeant with the Metropolitan Toronto Police Force. Under *The Police Act* of Ontario, he was obliged to appear in court whenever he was needed and irrespective of whether he was at the time on or off duty. He claimed parking costs and automobile expenses relating to 84 occasions in 1974 on which, being off duty, he had to appear in courts located about 25 miles from his home. The Tax Review Board Chairman, Mr. Cardin, found that Klue was ordinarily required to appear in court as part of his duties, that this was away from his employer's place of business, and that the 84 trips were not equivalent to commuting to the police station to which Klue was assigned and which was also about 25 miles from his home. None of the claimed expenses related to appearances while Klue was "on duty". Klue's claim was allowed under paragraph 8(1)(h).

12. In *Patterson*, the Federal Court–Trial Division accepted that it was part of the duties of a school principal to use his car to transport students to various events and competitions, to hospital, and on camping trips, and that such travel was "ordinarily required". In *Bubnick*, the Tax Review Board, per J.B. Goetz Q.C., conceived a quite different job description for a school principal whose auto expenses arose from numerous errands which Mr. Goetz described as sounding like "a pick-up and delivery service". In dismissing the claim, he expressed disbelief that the school board would expect the principal to spend his time on such errands.

13. The Imrays were teachers who both attended an annual two-day teacher's convention pursuant to terms of their employment. They claimed expenses incurred for attending the convention as deductions under section 8(1)(h)(i). In dealing with the meaning of "ordinarily required", the Court concluded (at paragraphs 23-24):

> The requirement of the Imrays' attendance at Teachers' Conventions is a function of legal, administrative and ethical expectations which apply to all teachers in Alberta. Within this context, the fact that Teachers' Conventions occur only once per year is a minor factor. As is the case for Mr. Imray, who has attended every year since being a teacher, save one, when because of a flood in his school he was unable to attend, the evidence establishes that most teachers in Alberta accept this responsibility.
>
> On this basis, I have no hesitation in finding that Teachers' Convention attendance is 'normal', 'a matter of regular occurrence', 'commonly' and 'usually' occurs, and is a requirement which takes teachers 'from time to time away from the places which they usually work'.

14. In *Neufeld v. M.N.R.*, [1981] C.T.C. 2010, 81 D.T.C. 18 (T.R.B.) "ordinarily required" was held to be an issue of contractual obligation. The taxpayer, a clothing store manager, spent about 25 per cent of his working hours away from the store, making deliveries to customers, exchanging stock with another store, making promotional appearances and soliciting new business, and attending company sales meetings. The Tax Review Board, per D.E. Taylor, held that "ordinarily" is not proven by a percentage argument. He also held that the requirement in subparagraph 8(1)(f)(ii) that the employee be "ordinarily ... away from his employer's place of business" must be a clear requirement of the employment contract, just like the employee's obligation to pay his own expenses.
15. Compare this statement in *Neufeld* with the decision in *Verrier v. Canada*, [1990] 1 C.T.C. 313, 90 D.T.C. 6202 (F.C.A.); leave to appeal to S.C.C. refused (1990), 120 N.R. 80 where it was held that the taxpayer, an automobile salesperson on commission, could deduct certain expenses under paragraph 8(1)(f) even though there was no written employment contract. The Court found the conditions in subparagraphs 8(1)(f)(i) and (ii) to be satisfied on the basis that the employment of the taxpayer would be terminated if he did not sell a certain number of automobiles, and he could satisfy the quota only by operating, in part, away from his employer's place of business. For a similar "practical" approach to the deduction of employment expenses, see *McKee v. The Queen*, [1990] 1 C.T.C. 317, 90 D.T.C. 6205 (F.C.A.); *The Queen v. Moore*, [1990] 1 C.T.C. 311, 90 D.T.C. 6200 (F.C.A.); and *The Queen v. Betz*, [1990] 1 C.T.C. 321, 90 D.T.C. 6201 (F.C.A.).

16. The range of deductions available to commission salespersons under paragraph 8(1)(f) is wider than that for "travel expenses" or "meal and lodging" expenses permitted by paragraphs (e), (g) and (h). Why?

2. Legal Expenses (paragraph 8(1)(b))

An employee is entitled to deduct amounts paid on account of legal expenses incurred to establish a right to salary or wages, as well as to collect any such amount that is owed. "Salary or wages" is defined for this purpose in subsection 248(1), and includes any amount under sections 5, 6 and 7. What is the difference between establishing a right to salary or wages and collecting these amounts? See *Lyonde v. M.N.R.*, [1988] 2 C.T.C. 2032, 88 D.T.C. 1397 (T.C.C.). This distinction is crucial for taxation years before 1990, because in those years paragraph 8(1)(b) covered only amounts paid for legal expenses incurred to collect salary or wages.

Must the employee succeed in establishing the right to the salary or wages in order for the expense to be deductible? The CRA's view is set out in Interpretation Bulletin IT-99R5: Legal and Accounting Fees (December 11, 1998), paragraph 23:

> A deduction under paragraph 8(1)(b) is allowed only in respect of an amount "owed" by an employer or a former employer. If the taxpayer is not successful in court or otherwise fails to establish that some amount is owed, no deduction for expenses is allowed. However, failure to collect an amount established as owed to the taxpayer does not preclude a deduction under this paragraph.

Is this view correct? See *Loo v. The Queen*, [2004] 3 C.T.C. 247, 2004 D.T.C. 6540 (F.C.A.).

Would legal expenses incurred to prevent a breach of contract and preserve the particular source of employment income be deductible under paragraph 8(1)(b)? Courts have distinguished between legal expenses incurred to protect one's livelihood and legal expenses incurred in an effort to collect salary or wages owing. For example, in *Blagdon v. The Queen*, [2003] 4 C.T.C. 107, 2003 D.T.C. 5491 (F.C.A.), the Court concluded that expenses incurred by a shipmaster to defend his competence and right to command a ship were non-deductible because they were incurred to protect his means of livelihood, not to collect salary or wages owing to him. According to the Court (at paragraph 4), "We can understand that a broad entitlement to a deduction for legal expenses for persons in the situation of Captain Blagdon might be justified on policy grounds but that is a matter for Parliament not the courts".

Paragraph 6(1)(j) requires an award or reimbursement received by a taxpayer in respect of an amount deductible under subsection 8(1) to be included in income unless otherwise included or taken into account in reducing the amount claimed as a deduction. This provision ensures that legal expenses are deducted under paragraph

8(1)(b) only to the extent that they represent a cost of earning income, net of any awards or reimbursements in respect of the expenses.

3. Professional and Union Dues (subparagraphs 8(1)(i)(i), (iv), (v); subsection 8(5))

Paragraph 8(1)(i) provides a deduction for annual professional and union dues. Because the dues must be annual in nature, the payment of an additional fee on entry into a profession is not a deductible employment expense.

Why is it necessary that the professional status be recognized by statute? The same type of restrictive condition is imposed on trade union dues. Also, the deduction is available to those who are required to pay union dues as a condition of employment, even though they are not members of the union (subparagraph 8(1)(i)(v)).

Dues used to provide benefits to members, such as malpractice insurance, are deductible provided that the insurance is required to maintain a professional status (subsection 8(5)).

Despite the restrictive language of subparagraph 8(1)(i)(i), taxpayers often claim annual dues paid to organizations that do not involve a professional status of any sort, much less a status recognized by statute. Such claims are often "successful", not as a result of favourable decisions, judicial or administrative, but simply because the deductions were not audited. Consider the following "test case".

THE QUEEN v. SWINGLE
[1977] C.T.C. 448, 77 D.T.C. 5301 (F.C.T.D.)

Collier J.:

This is an appeal by the plaintiff, through the Minister of National Revenue, from a decision of the Tax Review Board.

The defendant is a chemist. He holds a doctorate degree in applied science. He also has a post-doctorate degree. Since February 1, 1971 he has been employed in the Public Service of Canada. Until December 1973 he was with the Royal Canadian Mounted Police crime detection laboratory. He worked as a forensic chemist evaluating physical evidence for prosecutions contemplated or carried out.

He then went to the Department of Transport. Again his employment was in the field of chemistry and analysis. He was designated as an analyst pursuant to subsection 731(1) of the *Canada Shipping Act.* That was in the area of pollution and pollution prevention. Under the relevant legislation a certificate of an analyst is admissible in evidence in any prosecution and, in the absence of any evidence to the contrary, is proof of the statements contained in the certificate.

The defendant is presently Manager of Laboratory Services (Pacific Region), Department of Fisheries and Environment, Environmental Protection Services. He has 17 persons working under him. He is responsible for the quality of the work coming out of the laboratory.

He is, as well, a designated analyst pursuant to the *Northern Inland Waters Act,* the *Arctic Waters Pollution Prevention Act* and the *Clean Air Act.* He retains his designation as an analyst pursuant to the *Canada Shipping Act.* In his present employment he has prepared reports in regard to matters such as oil spills. He has, of course, issued certificates of analysis. They have similar evidentiary characteristics as those authorized by the *Canada Shipping Act.* Since his employment with the Public Service he has given and still gives expert evidence in courts. His educational and professional credentials have been accepted.

He practically and realistically, has to keep up with most modern technical developments in chemistry. This is necessary in order to remain up to date in his present position as manager. It is equally necessary in order to make himself available for promotion, or for employment elsewhere, including the private sector.

In competitions in the Public Service, membership in so-called professional societies is considered a desirable qualification. This is perhaps even more so in the private sector.

All of the above facts were testified to by the defendant. His evidence was uncontradicted.

The appeal earlier referred to arises this way. The defendant, to keep abreast of rapidly changing developments in chemistry, has taken membership in a reasonable selection of chemical and allied societies. These organizations publish learned journals. They provide valuable technical information and knowledge. The defendant has, himself, published papers in some of the journals.

He is a member of the Forensic Society. That is a well-known organization in the United Kingdom. Its members are chemists and other professionals. He also belongs to and receives literature from the Chemical Society of Britain. The Royal Institute of Chemistry is amalgamated, in part, with that society. The *United Kingdom Food and Drug Act* (1952) requires a chemist giving evidence under that Act to have membership in the Royal Institute. The defendant is a member as well of the American Chemical Society. Lastly, he has membership in the Canadian Institute of Chemistry.

All these organizations require payment of annual dues. In his 1974 tax return the defendant claimed as deductions the sum of $193.15. That amount was made up as follows:

(a) The Professional Institute of the Public Service of Canada	$ 72.00
(b) The Forensic Society	$ 15.00
(c) The American Chemical Society	$ 51.00
(d) The Chemical Society of Britain	$ 20.70
(e) The Canadian Institute of Chemistry	$ 34.45
Total	$193.15

The Minister of National Revenue allowed the deduction of $72 paid to the Professional Institute of the Public Service of Canada. The balance of $121.15 was disallowed. The assessment increased the defendant's tax liability by $38.

[Collier J. indicated his assumption that the $72 allowed by the Minister was authorized by subparagraph 8(1)(i)(iv).] ...

It is common ground that the payments made by the defendant to the four organizations are "annual professional membership dues". The plaintiff concedes the defendant is a "professional", in the sense he is qualified and skilled in the general field of chemistry. The nub of the dispute is whether the payment of the amounts was "necessary to maintain a professional status recognized by statute". The Tax Review Board found the payments were allowable deductions. The Minister now appeals that judgment to this Court.

Some legislative and legal history is, in considering paragraph 8(1)(i), appropriate.

The *Income War Tax Act*, R.S.C. 1927, c. 97 and amendments, had no counterpart to 8(1)(i). But several decisions dealt with the deductibility, under that legislation, of annual dues paid by employees in respect of the carrying on of their employment.

Bond v. M.N.R., [1946] C.T.C. 281, 2 D.T.C. 907, is the leading authority. The taxpayer was a salaried employee of the City of Winnipeg. He was by profession a lawyer. He performed legal duties for his employer. He was a member of the governing body for lawyers in Manitoba. He paid annual dues to that organization. He could not legally practise as a lawyer without maintaining membership in the Law Society and paying those annual dues. He sought to deduct them, as an expense, from income. Thorson, P. held the dues to be a permissible deduction. ...

A similar conclusion was reached in *Rutherford v. M.N.R.*, [1946] C.T.C. 293, 2 D.T.C. 914. The taxpayer there was a lawyer employed by a provincial government as legislative counsel. Thorson, P. found there was no distinction in principle between his status and that of the taxpayer in the *Bond* case.

Cooper v. M.N.R., [1949] C.T.C. 146, 4 D.T.C. 573, followed the reasoning of the *Bond* decision. Cooper was a salaried motion picture projectionist. He sought to deduct annual dues paid to his trade union. He had to be a union member in order to be employed as a projectionist. The Court held the dues were permissible deductions.

As I see it, the effect of the three decisions referred to was this. Where a taxpayer's income was derived from an office or employment he could deduct dues he was required to pay in order to exercise the very right to carry on his profession or calling, and thus earn salary or remuneration.

[Collier, J. traced, in detail, the history of the Income Tax Act provisions antecedent to the present paragraph 8(1)(i).]

I turn now to the case before me. Counsel for the plaintiff contends that, even if the defendant has a professional status recognized by statute, the payment of the dues in question was not necessary to maintain that status. The defendant, it is said, retains his professional status as a chemist or analyst whether he pays annual dues to these societies or not; his legal right to carry on his profession is not dependent on belonging to any of them. *M.N.R. v. Montgomery*, [1970] C.T.C. 115; 70 D.T.C. 6080, was relied on. The taxpayer, in addition to being a self-employed practising lawyer, was an officer in the RCNR. He sought, unsuccessfully, to deduct wardroom dues. The essence of the reasons of Kerr, J. is at pages 120-21 [6084]:

> ... I am satisfied that as an officer in the RCNR the respondent is a person with a "profession", that the status of an officer in the RCNR is a professional status recognized by statute, ie the National Defence Act, that the wardroom mess of HMCS Tecumseh is composed of RCNR officers, and that it was necessary for the respondent to pay wardroom dues.
>
> But it does not follow that those wardroom dues fall within Section 11(10)(a). It is my opinion that the necessity that Parliament was contemplating in that subsection is directly related to the essential purpose to be served by the payment of the professional membership dues. Inherent in the subsection is a direct relationship between membership in a professional society and professional status. The status recognized by statute is a professional status that is dependent upon membership in the professional society. No membership, no status. Such dues are no doubt used for the needs of the society, but the primary purpose of their payment is retention of membership, with its rights and privileges. It is clear to me that wardroom dues are paid for a very different purpose, namely, to defray operational costs of the mess, which is a room or suite where the members meet, eat, converse, entertain, etc. A wardroom mess can be established by a very few officers, even three or four. I understood LCDR Gwillim to say that he had served in 50 messes. The purpose of the payment of wardroom dues is not, in my opinion, to maintain a professional status. The status of a navy officer does not call for membership in a mess, unlike the practice of medicine, for example, which calls for membership in a medical society established by statute.

> Officers receive their commissions from the Crown. No dues are paid to obtain or maintain their commissions and officer status. My attention was not drawn to any specific recognition of a wardroom mess in a statute and I scarcely think that the status of membership in a wardroom mess is a professional status recognized by statute.
>
> The consequence of failure on the part of an officer to pay his wardroom dues conceivably might be loss of his status as an officer, and in that negative and limited sense it may be said that payment is necessary to maintain his status, but, in my opinion, that possibility is remote from what Parliament was contemplating and endeavouring to provide in the *Income Tax Act* when enacting Section 11(10)(a). If it were intended to include dues payable for operation of messes in the armed forces, it would have been easy to have said so expressly.
>
> In my opinion, therefore, the wardroom dues in question are not deductible under Section 11(10)(a).

The plaintiff argues the *Montgomery* case holds that the only deductible dues are those which have the effect of maintaining one's professional status and, at the same time, are the source of the right to carry on the practice of the particular profession. I do not think the *Montgomery* case goes that far.

I can visualize situations where a profession is recognized by statute, but where no annual dues are required to be paid in order to carry on that profession; yet at the same time it may be "necessary" to belong to organizations in order to remain qualified, in the practical and business sense; to be able effectively to perform, and earn income, in a particular profession.

For example, I think it indisputable that accountancy is a profession; that an accountant is a "professional". A particular person may be a highly qualified and skilled accountant. That profession is, in British Columbia for example, recognized by statute: see the *Chartered Accountants Act*, R.S.B.C. 1960, c. 51, and the *Certified General Accountants Act*, R.S.B.C. 1960, c. 47. But one is not bound to be a member of the Institute of Chartered Accountants or of the Association of Certified General Accountants in order to practise the general profession of an accountant. An outsider is merely prevented from using the designation chartered accountant or certified general accountant. I can foresee, however, that a highly qualified and skilled accountant (in the general sense) may well find it necessary to pay annual dues to an appropriate professional organization in order to maintain his high qualifications and skills, and so be able to continue selling his services to others, including an employer.

Subparagraph 8(1)(i)(i) must not be read in isolation. In subparagraph (iv), for example, there is no requirement that the union dues there specified must be paid by the taxpayer in order to obtain or keep employment in a particular calling (the situation in the *Cooper* case). On the other hand, the dues specified in subparagraph (v) are those that must be paid in order for the taxpayer to retain employment, even though he is not a member of the particular union (the so-called "union shop" situation). ...

To my mind, the defendant has not proved one essential matter, quite necessary before the so-called main issue can be met. The defendant is a chemist or an analyst, or perhaps both. If he is viewed as a chemist, it has not, as I see it, been shown, on the materials before me, that the professional status of a chemist is one "recognized by statute". I am convinced the defendant has indeed a "professional" status in his particular field-just as much as a doctor or lawyer. But no statutes recognizing that professional status were put before me, nor cited.

If the defendant is viewed merely as an analyst, I have difficulty in holding, on the evidence before me, that an analyst has a "professional status recognized by statute". I assume there are many kinds of analysts. The legislation earlier referred to (the *Canada Shipping Act*, the *Northern Inland Waters Act*, the *Arctic Waters Pollution Prevention Act* and the *Clean Air Act*) do not define an "analyst". Nor do they describe that occupation in any manner from which a "professional status" can be inferred. The statutes merely provide that "any person", or sometimes a "qualified person" may be designated as an analyst. Subsection 731(1) of the *Canada Shipping Act* (to use it as an example) reads:

> 731. (1) The Minister may designate any person as a pollution prevention officer or an analyst for the purposes of this Part.

But when one turns to subparagraph 8(1)(i)(i) of the *Income Tax Act* the use of the term "professional" seems to infer special skills, abilities, or qualifications. The statutes relied on by the defendant are silent as to those matters. The defendant has not brought his claim for the deductions clearly within the terms of this subparagraph conferring the right.

Notes and Questions

1. For the CRA's views on the deduction of membership dues by employees see Interpretation Bulletin IT-158R2: Employees' Professional Membership Dues (July 14, 1989).
2. The *Swingle* case illustrates again the different tax treatment of the employee and the business taxpayer. There is little doubt that a practising lawyer can deduct annual membership dues in the Canadian Bar Association as part of normal business expenses. Following *Swingle*, it seems clear that the same dues are not deductible by a lawyer who is an employee (as contrasted with a partner) of a law firm, or who is employed as a corporate counsel or as a law teacher. Is this difference justified?
3. Undoubtedly, part of the impetus to take *Swingle* as a "test case" was the observation that thousands of taxpayers were making claims under paragraph 8(1)(i)

— as under numerous other provisions — which were in no way justified. Thousands of unwarranted claims, each rather negligible in amount, add up to significant revenue leakage; frequently, they lead either to legislative action or to a judgment which, in either case, may introduce a restrictive rule of law which prohibits some arguably meritorious claims along with forestalling those which were vexatious. In the tax world, "throwing the baby out with the bathwater" is a very apposite saying; the history of tax law is replete with such examples.

4. In *Lemieux v. M.N.R.*, [1982] C.T.C. 2018, 82 D.T.C. 1039 (T.R.B.) the taxpayer claimed the following amounts:

Association des médecins de langue francaise du Canada	$ 5.00
Canadian Medical Protection Association	200.00
Association des médecins du Québec	30.00
	$235.00

All three amounts were disallowed. The $5 and $30 claims were denied on the basis of evidence that the taxpayer paid them not to preserve his status as a resident physician, but because they provided him with medical information. The $200 was, admittedly, the "cost of professional liability insurance which is essential to the practice of my profession", but did not qualify as professional membership dues.

5. A practising physician or lawyer (i.e., a non-employee) will have no difficulty in deducting, as a normal business expense, the cost of professional liability insurance and the cost of professional journals which "provide medical (or legal) information". Similarly, it is unlikely that the payment or reimbursement of such expenses by an employer would constitute a taxable benefit under paragraph 6(1)(a). Thus, understandably, the inclination on the part of doctors, lawyers and other professionals who cannot escape the "employment" characterization and who do not have generous employers is to claim equivalent deductions under such statutory reliefs as are available in section 8, no matter how ill-suited the relief may be to the particular claim.

6. At times, the employment contract may oblige an employee to provide an office, supplies or an assistant. Subparagraphs 8(1)(i)(ii) and (iii) permit the deduction of such expenses when they are paid. In *Watts v. M.N.R.* (1961), 27 Tax A.B.C. 432, 61 D.T.C. 592 (T.A.B.) the taxpayer, a secretary, attempted to deduct the expenses of a housekeeper on the ground that she was an assistant within the meaning of subparagraph 8(1)(i)(ii). The Tax Appeal Board disallowed the expense since the housekeeper did not assist the taxpayer in performing her employment duties. Could a teacher deduct the cost of books by virtue of this section? Could a carpenter deduct the cost of tools?

7. Subsection 8(13) limits the deduction for home office expenses in much the same way as subsection 18(12) applicable to self-employed individuals (see Part IV of

Chapter 5). What kinds of home office expenses of an employee are deductible under paragraph 8(1)(f) or 8(1)(i)? For a statement of the CRA's position on this issue, see Interpretation Bulletin IT-352R2: Employee's Expenses, Including Work Space in Home Expenses (August 26, 1994).

8. Amounts are frequently deducted from an employee's income, either in compliance with a statute or by reason of the employment contract. Paragraphs 8(1)(m) and (m.2) permit the deduction of some of these amounts from the taxpayer's income. The amounts which are deducted will generally create taxable income when the taxpayer receives them. Unemployment insurance premiums and Canada Pension Plan contributions give rise to a tax credit under section 118.7. Such contributions were formerly deductible in calculating the employment income of a taxpayer (see former paragraphs 8(1)(k) and (l)). The significance of the conversion of an income deduction to a tax credit is discussed generally in Chapter 7.

5

Income from Business or Property

I. THE STATUTORY SETTING

Section 9 provides that "a taxpayer's income for a taxation year from a business or property is the taxpayer's profit from that business or property for the year." Sections 10 to 37 set out more detailed rules for the computation of profit.

The concept of "profit" is undefined in the Act. The courts have generally interpreted profit to be a net amount — that is, a calculation which determines the difference between total receipts and the costs and expenses necessary to produce such receipts. The determination of profit is a question of law to be determined according to the test of "well-accepted principles of business (or accounting) practice" or "generally-accepted accounting principles" ("GAAP") except where these principles are inconsistent with the specific provisions of the Act or principles of law. For further discussion of the concept of profit and timing principles for profit computation, see Chapter 6.

The difference between total receipts and the expenses necessary to produce those receipts can, of course, result in a loss. Recall that the treatment of losses is found in Chapter 2. Generally, losses from one source of income, such as a business, can be offset against income from a different source, such as employment income. This rule applies only to non-capital losses. Capital losses are "ring-fenced" in that they may only be set off against capital gains.

While the use of the term "profit" in section 9 invites the calculation of receipts minus expenses, section 12 of the Act specifically requires that certain items be included in computing income from business or property. These items include:

- amounts received for goods and services to be rendered in the future (paragraph 12(1)(a)),
- amounts receivable for property sold or services rendered in the course of business (paragraph 12(1)(b)),
- interest (paragraph 12(1)(c)),
- amounts deducted in a preceding year as a reserve for doubtful debts (paragraph 12(1)(d));
- amounts received based on production or use of property (paragraph 12(1)(g)),
- dividends (paragraph 12(1)(j) or (k)),
- income from partnerships (paragraph 12(1)(l)),

- income from trusts (paragraph 12(1)(m));
- benefits from profit sharing plan and employee trust to employer (paragraph 12(1)(n));
- inducement or assistance payments (paragraph 12(1)(x)); and
- cash bonus on Canada Savings Bonds (section 12.1).

For the most part, income from a business and income from property are subject to the same treatment (see sections 9, 18 and 20). In some cases, however, the Act treats them differently and it is necessary to characterize a receipt either as property income or as business income. The distinction is important, for example, in the following circumstances:

(1) Active business income of a Canadian-controlled private corporation is taxed at a special low tax rate because of a tax credit under section 125 known as the "small business deduction". The low rate is unavailable for property income of a "specified investment business".

(2) A dividend refund available to private corporations under section 129 is computed in a way that excludes income from an active business.

(3) The attribution rules in sections 74.1 and 74.2 apply to income from property, but not to income from a business.

(4) Certain rules with respect to rental and leasing properties apply if this type of income is income from property, not income from a business. These rules are designed to prevent taxpayers from creating or increasing losses from rental property through the deduction of capital cost allowance (regulations 1100(11) and (15)).

(5) The deduction under paragraph 20(1)(b) for cumulative eligible capital is available only in respect of a business, not property.

(6) The tax liability of non-resident taxpayers is tied to the source of income. For example, income from a business carried on in Canada is taxable under Part I of the Act on a net basis, whereas income from property is generally subject to a 25 per cent withholding tax under Part XIII on a gross basis. See Chapter 3.

(7) Sections 91-95 of the Act are targeted mainly at property income earned by foreign corporations controlled by Canadian residents, certain foreign trusts and foreign-based investment funds.

(8) Where a Canadian resident pays foreign income taxes on income earned

from a foreign country, the method of relief for international double taxation (i.e., foreign tax credit under section 126 or deductions under subsections 20(11) or (12)) is different for foreign-source business income and foreign-source non-business income. See Chapter 3.

II. INCOME FROM A BUSINESS

Subsection 9(1) provides little assistance in deciding what is income from a business. The profit element distinguishes taxpayer activities that are in relation to business or property from those taxpayer activities that are purely personal in nature. This distinction is important because, under the source concept of income, taxpayers' receipts that are not from a source are not included in income and are not subject to tax. See Chapter 2. Similarly, if the taxpayers' activities yield losses, only losses incurred in the course of business activities are deductible; taxpayers may not claim deductions in respect of activities that are personal in nature. Finally, as noted above, business income must be distinguished from other sources of income, where the Act provides different rules for the computation of income from each source. What follows is a discussion of the meaning of the term "business" and the distinction between business income and income from other sources.

A. What Constitutes a "Business"?

Subsection 248(1) defines a "business" to include "a profession, calling, trade, manufacture or undertaking of any kind whatever and ... an adventure or concern in the nature of trade but does not include an office or employment". This definition is not exhaustive and is supplemented by a vast body of case law. Many cases use the late nineteenth century statement from *Smith v. Anderson* (1880), 15 Ch. D. 247 (C.A.) as a starting point for considering what constitutes a business. The court in that case stated that "anything which occupies the time, attention and labour of a man [sic] for the purpose of profit" is a business.

In general, the case law has established that a business is an organized activity that is carried on for the purpose of profit. Many of the earliest cases dealt with the question of whether a taxpayer's gambling activities constituted a business. These cases illustrate the difficult problem of deciding: a) under what circumstances a taxpayer is considered to have organized his or her gambling effort in the same way as a bookmaker organizes the business; and b) whether or not such activity could be considered to be undertaken for the purpose or pursuit of profit?

1. Organized Activity

GRAHAM v. GREEN (INSPECTOR OF TAXES)
[1925] 2 K.B. 37, 9 T.C. 309

Rowlatt J.:

In this case the appellant was in the habit of betting on horses at starting prices. He did it on a large and sustained scale, and he did it with such shrewdness that he made an income out of it, and it is found that substantially it was his means of living. Under those circumstances he has been assessed to income tax in respect of those emoluments, and hence this appeal. ...

[T]he question [arises] whether the winnings on the appellant's bets as bets are "profits or gains" ... [or] whether, assuming the winnings from the bets themselves are not profits or gains, the aggregate of his winnings, as the result of his sustained and continued action, are the profits or gains of a "vocation" or possibly, as it might have been put, of a trade or adventure. ...

... [O]ne is faced with the difficult question of what is profit or gain. My attention, of course, was drawn to my decision in *Ryall v. Hoare*. ... In the course of my judgment I said that a mere receipt by finding an object of value, or a mere gift, was not a profit or gain, and I do not feel much doubt about that. I further said that the winning of a bet did not result in a profit or gain. Until I am corrected, I think I was right in that. Whether it is a gift or whether it is a finding, there is nothing on which there is a profit. There is no increment, there is no service, there is merely the picking up of something either by the will of the person who had it before or because there is no person to oppose the picking up. When one comes to the question of a bet, it seems to me that the position is substantially the same. What is a bet? A bet is merely an irrational agreement that one person should pay another person something on the happening of an event. A agrees to pay B something if C's horse runs quicker than D's or if a coin comes one side up rather than the other side up. There is no relevance at all between the event and the acquisition of property. The event does not really produce it at all. It rests, as I say, on a mere irrational agreement. ...

Now we come to betting, pure and simple. It has been settled that a bookmaker carries on a taxable vocation. What is the bookmaker's system? He knows that there are a great many people who are willing to back horses, and that they will back horses with anybody who holds himself out to give reasonable odds as a bookmaker. By calculating the odds in the case of various horses over a long period of time and quoting them so that on the whole the aggregate odds, if I may use the expression, are in his favour, he makes a profit. That seems to me to be organizing an effort in the same way that a person organizes an effort if he sets out to buy himself things with a view to securing a profit by the difference in their capital value in individual cases.

Now we come to the other side, the man who bets with the bookmaker, and that is this case. These are mere bets. Each time he puts on his money at whatever may be the starting price. I do not think he could be said to organize his effort in the same way as a bookmaker organizes his, for I do not think the subject matter from his point of view is susceptible to it. In effect all he is doing is just what a man does who is a skillful player at cards, who plays every day. He plays today, and he plays tomorrow, and he plays the next day, and he is skillful on each of the three days, more skillful on the whole than the people with whom he plays, and he wins. But it does not seem that one can find, in that case, any conception arising in which his individual operations can be said to be merged in the way that particular operations are merged in the conception of a trade. I think all you can say of that man, in the fair use of the English language, is that he is addicted to betting. It is extremely difficult to express, but it seems to me that people would say he is addicted to betting, and could not say that his vocation is betting. The subject is involved in great difficulty of language, which I think represents great difficulty of thought. There is no tax on a habit. I do not think "habitual" or even "systematic" fully describes what is essential in the phrase "trade, adventure, employment, or vocation". All I can say is that in my judgment the income which this gentleman succeeded in making is not profits or gains, and that the appeal must be allowed, with costs.

Notes and Questions

1. In later cases the courts maintained their focus on the organization of the taxpayer's activity in determining whether or not there was a business. In *Walker v. M.N.R.*, [1951] C.T.C. 334, 52 D.T.C. 1001 (Ex. Ct.) the court stated (at 339; 1003):

> ... [E]ach case must depend on its own particular facts, the important feature being whether or not there was an intention on the bettor's part to make profit, and not as a form of amusement or hobby. Although in view of my finding above it is not necessary to decide this latter point, nevertheless when it is considered that the taxpayer did have an interest in several race horses; had the benefit of inside information from jockeys and other interested persons on the probable outcome of races, which he admits he had due to the fact that he was running some horses which he owned or had an interest in; and the further fact that for ten years or more he systematically attended all the races in sometimes four different cities and bet on most of the events, one is almost driven to the conclusion that this set of facts constitutes a business or calling within the meaning of the tax Acts, and the monies made thereby would therefore be taxable. There does not seem to be any doubt that money made on casual bets made for pure amusement, or a hobby, is not assessable. Where to draw the line is the difficulty, but should I be compelled to make a decision on this aspect of the case, I think I would have to find on the facts and circumstances of the case that such winnings are assessable to tax ...

2. In *M.N.R. v. Morden*, [1961] C.T.C. 484, 61 D.T.C. 1266 (Ex. Ct.) the court also considered the efforts devoted by the taxpayer to his gambling activities (at 486-89; 1267-69):

> His gambling activities up to the year 1948 were so extensively organized and occupied so much of his time and attention that, had they continued throughout the years in question, any net gain therefrom might possibly have been income from a business within the definition of "business" contained in Section 127(1)(e). It is submitted, however, that from 1949 to 1955, a period which includes all the taxation years in question, his gambling activities were only occasional and amounted to nothing more than indulging in a hobby or recreation, and that therefore his net income therefrom was not taxable ...
>
> In the present case, I find no evidence that the respondent during the years in question in relation to his betting activities conducted an enterprise of a commercial character or had so organized these activities as to make them a business, calling or vocation. ... True, he was an inveterate gambler ... Gambling was in his blood and it provided him with the excitement which he craved. It was his hobby ... but for the years in question it was not his vocation, calling or business. ...

3. How might contemporary gambling activities be considered? In 2004, a thirty-year old Winnipeg man made an estimated $50,000 playing online poker and international live tournaments for which he qualified by his success in online games. Will Clarke has been playing poker since he was five years old and has been playing online for the past seven years. He gave up his job as a personal trainer and devotes 30 hours a week to playing, balancing four online games at once. His success at the online games qualifies him for two or three international, all-expenses paid trips to live tournaments. Would the money Will Clarke receives from his online poker games qualify as business income?
4. The issue of business income from gambling has been revisited in a number of cases: *Luprypa v. The Queen*, [1997] 3 C.T.C. 2363, 97 D.T.C. 1416, 1997 CarswellNat 765 (T.C.C.), *Epel v. The Queen*, 2003 D.T.C. 1361 (T.C.C.), and *Leblanc v. The Queen*, [2007] 2 C.T.C. 2248, 2007 D.T.C. 307 (T.C.C.). In *Luprypa*, the taxpayer claimed that a difference between reported and assessed income was primarily attributable to gambling on pool, and was consequently not taxable income. However, the Court found that pool was the taxpayer's business – the taxpayer worked to minimize his risk (by practicing every afternoon, playing Monday to Friday every week, playing inebriated opponents after 11:00 p.m., drinking only when not playing pool, etc.) and playing pool was his primary source of income. In *Epel*, regular poker winnings by the taxpayer were found to not be business income, as they were attributed to a run of luck by the taxpayer without a significant element of risk management. In *Leblanc*, a pair of brothers regularly made massive bets on sports parlay games in both Ontario and Quebec. However, expert evidence on the statistical nature of the bets and the

fact that the system effectively maximized risk led the Court to conclude that the betting did not constitute a business. If the brothers were actually attempting to minimize risk with their system, would this ruling undermine the rule that a court should not question the business judgment of a taxpayer who is clearly pursuing profit? In *Cohen v. The Queen*, 2011 TCC 262, [2011] 5 C.T.C. 2199, 2011 D.T.C. 1195 (T.C.C.), a lawyer who left his law practice to gamble full-time, spending upwards of eight hours a day in gambling activities, was not found to be engaged in a business. In *Radonjic v. The Queen*, 2013 FC 916, [2013] 3 C.T.C. 37, 2013 D.T.C. 5063 (F.C.), the fact of winning at gambling was not, on its own, evidence of a reasonable expectation of profit.

2. The Pursuit of Profit

In the gambling cases reviewed in the previous section, the courts generally held that it was not reasonable to expect to make a profit gambling on horse races. As a result, these activities could not be characterized as having been undertaken by the taxpayers for the purpose of profit and, therefore, there was held to be no business. In *Moldowan v. M.N.R.*, [1977] C.T.C. 310, 77 D.T.C. 5213 (S.C.C.), the Court (per Dickson J.) stated (at 313; 5215): "Although originally disputed, it is now accepted that in order to have a 'source of income' the taxpayer must have a profit or a reasonable expectation of profit. Source of income, thus, is an equivalent term to business ..." Over time this statement evolved into a judicial requirement that a taxpayer's expectation of profit from his or her activities be reasonable. This requirement came to be known as the "REOP test". In addition to his broad statement, Dickson J. also considered how to determine "reasonableness" in the expectation of profit (at 313; 5215):

> In my view, whether a taxpayer has a reasonable expectation of profit is an objective determination to be made from all of the facts. The following criteria should be considered: The profit and loss experience in past years, the taxpayer's training, the taxpayer's intended course of action, the capability of the venture as capitalized to show a profit after charging capital cost allowance. The list is not intended to be exhaustive. The factors will differ with the nature and extent of the undertaking. ... One would not expect a farmer who purchased a productive going operation to suffer the same start-up losses as the man who begins a tree farm on raw land.

Since *Moldowan,* the REOP test was often used by the Minister to deny the recognition of losses on the basis that they were not derived from a business. For example, in *Landry v. The Queen*, [1995] 2 C.T.C. 3, 94 D.T.C. 6624 (F.C.A.), the taxpayer, who was 71 years of age, began practicing law after 23 years away from the profession. He did so without adjusting his methods to compensate for the realities of modern legal practice. In reviewing the losses suffered by the taxpayer, the majority of the Federal Court of Appeal took the position that the taxpayer, although practicing full time, was conducting his practice so inefficiently that there was no reasonable expectation of profit and, therefore, there was no business. The Court reached this conclusion based on an assessment of the taxpayer's business judgment, not because of any finding that he was practicing as a hobby or otherwise for enjoyment. Under the REOP test there were many cases involving a broad spectrum of taxpayers, including professionals, restaurateurs, artists and real estate syndicates, in which losses from various activities and undertakings have been denied because the courts found that there was no reasonable expectation of profit.

In 2002, the Supreme Court of Canada sought to clarify the test that should be applied in determining whether the taxpayer has a business or property source of income. The taxpayer, an experienced real estate investor, acquired four condominium units from which he earned rental income. All units were highly leveraged with the taxpayer paying only $1,000 cash for each unit. The taxpayer was provided with projections of rental income and expenses in respect of each of the properties. The projections contemplated negative cash flow and income tax deductions for a ten year period. Thus for the taxation years in question the taxpayer claimed losses, mainly as a result of significant interest expenses on money borrowed to acquire the units. These losses were disallowed by the Minister of National Revenue on the basis that the taxpayer had no reasonable expectation of profit and therefore no source of income for the purposes of section 9 of the Act, and that the interest expenses were not deductible pursuant to subparagraph 20(1)(*c*)(i). Both the Tax Court of Canada and the Federal Court of Appeal upheld the Minister's position, and the taxpayer appealed to the Supreme Court of Canada.

STEWART v. THE QUEEN
[2002] 3 C.T.C. 439, 2002 D.T.C. 6969 (S.C.C.)

The judgment of the Court was delivered by

Iacobucci and Bastarache JJ.—

...

This appeal requires the Court to consider the appropriate use of what has come to be known as the "reasonable expectation of profit" test. ...

Since [the decision in *Moldowan*], decisions have varied in the application of this test. Although some cases have held that the reasonable expectation of profit test should only be used at the threshold stage of distinguishing between commercial and personal activities, others have used the test as a tool to assess the profitability of various *bona fide* commercial ventures in order to determine whether the taxpayer has a source of income, and is therefore entitled to deduct losses relating to that source.

The present appeal is just such a case. The appellant, Brian Stewart, purchased four condominium units from which he earned rental income. For the tax years in question, the appellant incurred losses, mainly as a result of significant interest expenses. These losses were disallowed by the Minister on the basis that the taxpayer had no reasonable expectation of profit, and therefore no source of income ...

Since this Court's decision in *Moldowan*, the "reasonable expectation of profit" or "REOP" test has been applied by the Minister and the courts in a variety of situations in order to determine whether a taxpayer has a source of income, whether business or property. However, ... equating the phrase "reasonable expectation of profit" with a "source" of income for the purposes of the Act is a case law expansion of the use of that phrase in the definition of "personal or living expenses" in the Act. As such, it is appropriate to examine the REOP test closely in order to determine whether it should be accepted as a stand-alone source test, or whether there is a better approach to assessing the existence of a source. Indeed, the wide range of approaches that courts have taken to the REOP test alone calls for clarification ...

... It has been pointed out that, as a matter of logic, the fact that an activity carried on with a reasonable expectation of profit is a *sufficient* requirement for a source of income (the proposition from *Dorfman*) does not entail that a reasonable expectation of profit is a *necessary* requirement for a source of income (the proposition from *Moldowan*): see B. S. Nichols, "Chants and Ritual Incantations: Rethinking the Reasonable Expectation of Profit Test", 1996 Conference Report, *Report of Proceedings of the Forty-Eighth Tax Conference*, vol. 1, 28:1, at pp. 28:4-28:5; S. Silver, "Great Expectations: Are they Reasonable?", *Corporate Management Tax Conference 1995*, 6:1, at pp. 6:6-6:7. In other words, it is argued that by taking the comments from *Dorfman* out of their particular context and applying them generally, *Moldowan* mistakenly equated "source of income" with "reasonable expectation of profit".

Indeed, equating the term "business" with the phrase, "reasonable expectation of profit" does not accord with the traditional common law definition of business, which is that "anything which occupies the time and attention and labour of a man for the purpose of profit is business" (*Smith v. Anderson* (1880), 15 Ch. D. 247 (C.A.), at p. 258; *Terminal Dock and Warehouse Co. v. M.N.R.*, [1968] 2 Ex. C.R. 78, aff'd 68 D.T.C. 5316 (S.C.C.)). In addition, early cases dealing with the proper definition of a business rejected looking exclusively at one factor. For example, in *Erichsen v. Last* (1881), 4 T.C. 422, at p. 423, the English Court of Appeal stated:

I do not think there is any principle of law which lays down what carrying on of trade is. There are a multitude of incidents which together make the carrying on [of] a trade, but I know of no one distinguishing incident which makes a practice a carrying on of trade, and another practice not a carrying on of trade. If I may use the expression, it is a compound fact made up of a variety of incidents.

Thus, to equate "source of income" with "reasonable expectation of profit", at least in the instance of a business source, is not in line with these earlier characterizations of "business".

The view has also been taken that Dickson J. did not intend to set out a broadly applicable source test in *Moldowan*, but instead that he was simply distinguishing between mere hobbies and *bona fide* businesses: see J. R. Owen, "The Reasonable Expectation of Profit Test: Is There a Better Approach?" (1996), 44 *Can. Tax J.* 979, at p. 1002. This view stems from the fact that in the same paragraph where Dickson J. equates a business with a reasonable expectation of profit, he states "[i]f the taxpayer in operating his farm is merely indulging in a hobby, with no reasonable expectation of profit, he is disentitled to claim any deduction at all in respect of expenses incurred": *Moldowan*, *supra*, at p. 485. As well, various cases have held that the *Moldowan* test is only applicable where there is some personal element to the taxpayer's endeavour: *Hickman Motors Ltd. v. The Queen*, [1997] 2 S.C.R. 336, [1998] 1 C.T.C. 213, 97 D.T.C. 5363 at paras. 69 and 72; *Allen, supra; Nichol, supra; Bélec, supra*.

In light of the definition of "business" developed in earlier cases, as well as the dubious scope of Dickson J.'s *obiter* reference to "reasonable expectation of profit" in *Moldowan*, which may also have been a mistaken application of that phrase as used in *Dorfman*, the REOP test should not be blindly accepted as the correct approach to the "source of income" determination. This conclusion is strengthened by the fact that subsequent cases have run the gamut with respect to the application of the REOP concept.

It has also been argued that the limited use of the phrase, "reasonable expectation of profit" in the Act, does not support its use as a stand-alone source test. As mentioned above, the phrase first appeared in the Act in the definition of "personal or living expenses". The current version of that definition, in s. 248(1) (R.S.C. 1985, c. 1 (5th Supp.)), reads:

> "personal or living expenses" includes
>
> (*a*) the expenses of properties maintained by any person for the use or benefit of the taxpayer or any person connected with the taxpayer by blood relationship, marriage or common-law partnership or adoption, and not maintained in connection with a business carried on for profit or with a reasonable expectation of profit;

The phrase "personal or living expenses" relates to s. 18(1) (*h*) of the Act which now reads:

> 18. (1) In computing the income of a taxpayer from a business or property no deduction shall be made in respect of
>
> ...

> *h*) personal or living expenses of the taxpayer, other than travel expenses incurred by the taxpayer while away from home in the course of carrying on the taxpayer's business;

Silver, *supra*, at p. 6:4, contrasts this limited statutory use of the phrase "reasonable expectation of profit" with its broader judicial application:

> In any event, while the definition of "personal or living expenses" in subsection 248(1) is inclusive rather than exhaustive, it is clear that the provision and paragraph 18(1)(h) have limited application. The legislation establishes a "reasonable expectation of profit" test only in connection with expenses incurred in the maintenance of properties and only in connection with expenses from which the taxpayer may derive some use or benefit.
>
> It can be seen, therefore, from an examination of the Act that the statutory provisions that employ a "reasonable expectation of profit" test are specific in nature and would not appear to support a broad application of this test by Revenue Canada and the courts ...

To summarize, in recent years the *Moldowan* REOP test has become a broad-based tool used by both the Minister and courts in any manner of situation where the view is taken that the taxpayer does not have a reasonable expectation of profiting from the activity in question. From this it is inferred that the taxpayer has no source of income, and thus no basis from which to deduct losses and expenses relating to the activity. The REOP test has been applied independently of provisions of the Act to second-guess *bona fide* commercial decisions of the taxpayer and therefore runs afoul of the principle that courts should avoid judicial rule-making in tax law: see *Ludco, supra*; *Royal Bank v. Sparrow Electric Corp.*, [1997] 1 S.C.R. 411, (sub nom. *The Queen v. Royal Bank*) 97 D.T.C. 5089 (S.C.C.); *Canderel, supra*; *Shell Canada Ltd. v. Canada*, [1999] 3 S.C.R. 622, [1999] 4 C.T.C. 313, 99 D.T.C. 5669 (S.C.C.). As well, the REOP test is problematic owing to its vagueness and uncertainty of application; this results in unfair and arbitrary treatment of taxpayers. As a result, "reasonable expectation of profit" should not be accepted as the test to determine whether a taxpayer's activities constitute a source of income.

In our view, the determination of whether a taxpayer has a source of income, must be grounded in the words and scheme of the Act.

The Act divides a taxpayer's income into various sources. Under the basic rules for computing income in s. 3, the Act states:

> 3. The income of a taxpayer for a taxation year for the purposes of this Part is his income for the year determined by the following rules:
>
> (*a*) determine the aggregate of amounts each of which is the taxpayer's income for the year ... *from a source* inside or outside Canada, including,

without restricting the generality of the foregoing, *his income for the year from each office, employment, business and property*; [Emphasis added.]

With respect to business and property sources, the basic computation rule is found in s. 9:

9. (1) Subject to this Part, a taxpayer's income for a taxation year from a business or property is his profit therefrom for the year.

(2) Subject to section 31, a taxpayer's loss for a taxation year from a business or property is the amount of his loss, if any, for the taxation year from that source computed by applying the provisions of this Act respecting computation of income from that source *mutatis mutandis*.

It is clear that in order to apply s. 9; the taxpayer must first determine whether he or she has a source of either business or property income. As has been pointed out, a commercial activity which falls short of being a business may nevertheless be a source of property income. As well, it is clear that some taxpayer endeavours are neither businesses, nor sources of property income, but are mere personal activities. As such, the following two-stage approach with respect to the source question can be employed:

(i) Is the activity of the taxpayer undertaken in pursuit of profit, or is it a personal endeavour?

(ii) If it is not a personal endeavour, is the source of the income a business or property?

The first stage of the test assesses the general question of whether or not a source of income exists; the second stage categorizes the source as either business or property.

Equating "source of income" with an activity undertaken "in pursuit of profit" accords with the traditional common law definition of "business", i.e., "anything which occupies the time and attention and labour of a man for the purpose of profit": *Smith*, *supra*, at p. 258; *Terminal Dock*, *supra*. As well, business income is generally distinguished from property income on the basis that a business requires an additional level of taxpayer activity: see Krishna, *supra*, at p. 240. As such, it is logical to conclude that an activity undertaken in pursuit of profit, regardless of the level of taxpayer activity, will be either a business or property source of income.

The purpose of this first stage of the test is simply to distinguish between commercial and personal activities, and, as discussed above, it has been pointed out that this may well have been the original intention of Dickson J.'s reference to "reasonable expectation of profit" in *Moldowan*. Viewed in this light, the criteria listed by Dickson J. are an attempt to provide an objective list of factors for determining whether the activity in question is of a commercial or personal nature. These factors are what Bowman J.T.C.C. has referred to as "*indicia* of commerciality" or "badges of trade": *Nichol*, *supra*, at p. 1218. Thus, where the nature of a taxpayer's venture contains elements which suggest that it could be considered a hobby or other personal pursuit, but the venture is undertaken in a sufficiently commercial manner, the venture will be considered a source of income for the purposes of the Act.

We emphasize that this "pursuit of profit" source test will only require analysis in situations where there is some personal or hobby element to the activity in question. With respect, in our view, courts have erred in the past in applying the REOP test to activities such as law practices and restaurants where there exists no such personal element: see, for example, *Landry*, *supra*; *Sirois*, *supra*; *Engler v. The Queen*, 94 D.T.C. 6280 (sub nom. *Engler v. Canada*) [1994] 2 C.T.C. 64 (F.C.T.D.). Where the nature of an activity is clearly commercial, there is no need to analyze the taxpayer's business decisions. Such endeavours necessarily involve the pursuit of profit. As such, a source of income by definition exists, and there is no need to take the inquiry any further.

It should also be noted that the source of income assessment is not a purely subjective inquiry. Although in order for an activity to be classified as commercial in nature, the taxpayer must have the subjective intention to profit, in addition, as stated in *Moldowan*, this determination should be made by looking at a variety of objective factors. Thus, in expanded form, the first stage of the above test can be restated as follows: "Does the taxpayer intend to carry on an activity for profit and is there evidence to support that intention?" This requires the taxpayer to establish that his or her predominant intention is to make a profit from the activity and that the activity has been carried out in accordance with objective standards of businesslike behaviour.

The objective factors listed by Dickson J. in *Moldowan*, at p. 486, were: (1) the profit and loss experience in past years; (2) the taxpayer's training; (3) the taxpayer's intended course of action; and (4) the capability of the venture to show a profit. As we conclude below, it is not necessary for the purposes of this appeal to expand on this list of factors. As such, we decline to do so; however, we would reiterate Dickson J.'s caution that this list is not intended to be exhaustive, and that the factors will differ with the nature and extent of the undertaking. We would also emphasize that although the reasonable expectation of profit is a factor to be considered at this stage, it is not the only factor, nor is it conclusive. The overall assessment to be made is whether or not the taxpayer is carrying on the activity in a commercial manner. However, this assessment should not be used to second-guess the business judgment of the taxpayer. It is the commercial nature of the taxpayer's activity which must be evaluated, not his or her business acumen ...

In addition to the fact that the deductibility, or otherwise, of an expense is a separate question from the existence of the underlying source of income, it is also true that the profitability of the activity to which the expense relates does not affect the deductibility of the expense. In particular, there have been a number of cases where a taxpayer's large interest expenses have resulted in net losses, which in turn have caused the Minister to conclude that there is no reasonable expectation of profit, and therefore no source of income from which the interest expenses can be deducted. However, as stated above, reasonable expectation of profit is but one factor to consider in determining whether an activity has a sufficient degree of commerciality to be considered a source of income. Once that determination has been made, then the deductibility inquiry is undertaken according to whether the expense in question falls within the words of the relevant deduction provision(s) of the Act. Although it is true that the phrase "personal or living expenses" in s. 18(1)(*h*) is defined with reference to the phrase "reasonable expectation of profit", as we pointed out above, this definition has a narrow scope. In addition, it has been pointed out that the definition refers to a business carried on "for profit or with a reasonable expectation of profit". However, since, to get to s. 18, it must already have been determined under s. 9 that a business or property source exists, and since a business is defined as an activity undertaken "in pursuit of profit", it is hard to imagine a situation where the phrase "business carried on for profit or with a reasonable expectation of profit" would add any further restrictions to the activity in question: see Owen, *supra*, at p. 1009 ...

Clearly the existence of financing does not indicate that the underlying activity should not be characterized as a source of income. On the contrary, the fact that an activity has been financed externally is an indication that the taxpayer is operating his or her activity in a businesslike manner. As such, the existence of financing is an element which *adds* to the commerciality of a venture, and thus operates *in favour* of characterizing the activity as a source of income.

In summary, the issue of whether or not a taxpayer has a source of income is to be determined by looking at the commerciality of the activity in question. Where the activity contains no personal element and is clearly commercial, no further inquiry is necessary. Where the activity could be classified as a personal pursuit, then it must be determined whether or not the activity is being carried on in a sufficiently commercial manner to constitute a source of income. However, to deny the deduction of losses on the simple ground that the losses signify that no business (or property) source exists is contrary to the words and scheme of the Act. Whether or not a business exists is a separate question from the deductibility of expenses ...

... In this case, the appellant was engaged in property rental activities. He owned four rental condominium units from which he earned rental income. The fact that there was no personal element to these properties was never questioned. The units were all rented to arm's length parties and there was no evidence that the appellant intended to make use of any of the properties for his personal benefit. In our view, a property rental activity which lacks any element of personal use or benefit to the taxpayer is clearly a commercial activity. For what purpose would the taxpayer have spent his time and money in this activity if not for profit? As a result, the appellant satisfies the test for source of income. Although this is sufficient to dispose of the appeal, in our view a few additional remarks are warranted.

Even if the appellant had made use of one or more of the properties for his personal benefit, the Minister would not be entitled to conclude that no business existed without further analysis. A taxpayer in such circumstances would have the opportunity to establish that his or her predominant intention was to make a profit from the activity and that the activity was carried out in accordance with objective standards of businesslike behaviour. Whether a reasonable expectation of profit existed may be a factor that is taken into consideration in that analysis.

The Minister and the courts below made much of the fact that the appellant anticipated a capital gain from the eventual sale of the properties. It was argued that it was this anticipated gain, and not rental profits, which motivated the taxpayer. As well, the Minister argued that an anticipated capital gain should not be included in assessing whether the taxpayer had a reasonable expectation of profit ...

In response to this argument, it must be remembered that s. 20(1)(c)(i) is not a tax avoidance mechanism, and it has been established that, in light of the specific anti-avoidance provisions in the Act, courts should not be quick to embellish provisions of the Act in response to tax avoidance concerns: *Ludco, supra*, at para. 39; *Neuman v. M.N.R.*, [1998] 1 S.C.R. 770, [1998] 3 C.T.C. 177, (sub nom. *Neuman v. The Queen*) 98 D.T.C. 6297 (S.C.C.), at para. 63. In addition, in *Walls v. The Queen*, [2002] 3 C.T.C. 421, 2002 D.T.C. 6960, (sub nom. *Walls v. Canada*) [2002] 2 S.C.R. 684 (S.C.C.), the companion to this case, we point out at para. 22 that a tax motivation does not affect the validity of transactions for tax purposes. As such, the appellant's hope of realizing an eventual capital gain, and expectation of deducting interest expenses do not detract from the commercial nature of his rental operation or its characterization as a source of income. Moreover, in *Ludco, supra*, at para. 59, this Court specifically stated that s. 20(1)(*c*)(i) does not require the taxpayer to earn a net profit in order for interest to be deductible:

> The plain meaning of s. 20(1)(*c*)(i) does not support an interpretation of "income" as the equivalent of "profit" or "net income". Nowhere in the language of the provision is a quantitative test suggested. *Nor is there any support in the text of the Act for an interpretation of "income" that involves a judicial assessment of sufficiency of income.* Such an approach would be too subjective

> and certainty is to be preferred in the area of tax law. *Therefore, absent a sham or window dressing or similar vitiating circumstances, courts should not be concerned with the sufficiency of the income expected or received.* [Emphasis added.] ...

With respect to whether or not an anticipated capital gain should be included in assessing whether the taxpayer has a reasonable expectation of profit, we reiterate that the expected profitability of a venture is but one factor to consider in assessing whether the taxpayer's activity evidences a sufficient level of commerciality to be considered either a business or a property source of income. Having said this, in our view, the motivation of capital gains accords with the ordinary business person's understanding of "pursuit of profit", and may be taken into account in determining whether the taxpayer's activity is commercial in nature. Of course the mere acquisition of property in anticipation of an eventual gain does not provide a source of income for the purposes of s. 9; however, an anticipated gain may be a factor in assessing the commerciality of the taxpayer's overall course of conduct.

...

For these reasons, we conclude that the appellant's rental activities constituted a source of income. As a result, we would allow the appeal with costs throughout, set aside the judgment of the Federal Court of Appeal and refer the assessments for the taxation years in issue back to the Minister for reassessment on the basis that the taxpayer had a source of income from which he was entitled to deduct losses from the rental properties in question.

Notes and Questions

1. *The Queen v. Walls*, [2002] 3 C.T.C. 421, 2002 D.T.C. 6960 (S.C.C.) was the companion case to *Stewart*. In *Walls*, the taxpayers were limited partners in a partnership. A mini-warehouse was purchased on behalf of the partnership for $2,200,000 paid for with $1 in cash and the balance financed with debt on which interest was payable at 24 per cent per annum. The partnership generated losses on the mini-warehouse of which the respondents deducted their proportionate share for income tax purposes. On reassessment, the Minister of National Revenue reduced the losses by reducing the purchase price of the mini-warehouse to reflect a fair market value of $1,180,000 and also reduced the allowable interest expense by disallowing interest on debt in excess of the fair market value and by lowering the interest rate to 16 percent. On the basis that the partnership did not carry on business with a reasonable expectation of profit and, therefore, that the losses from the storage park operation were not losses from a business, the Minister determined that the losses could not be deducted by the taxpayers. The Federal Court-Trial Division upheld this assessment, but the Federal Court of Appeal set aside the judgment, holding that the trial judge erred in applying the reasonable

expectation of profit doctrine. The Supreme Court of Canada agreed, stating (at 429; 6964):

> Applying these principles to this case, we find that it is clear that the storage park operation constituted a source of income for the purposes of s. 9 of the Act. It is self-evident that such an activity is commercial in nature, and there was no evidence of any element of personal use or benefit in the operation. Although we state in Stewart, that reasonable expectation of profit may be used as one factor in making the overall determination as to whether or not the taxpayer's activities are personal or commercial, where, as here, the activities have no personal aspect, reasonable expectation of profit does not arise for consideration.

2. *Stewart* decided that the factors listed in *Moldowan* may still be considered in cases where the reasonable expectation of profit is a factor in determining whether the taxpayer's activities were commercial in nature. In *Sipley v. The Queen*, [1995] 2 C.T.C. 2073 (T.C.C.), the Tax Court of Canada held that the amount of time the taxpayer devotes to the activity in question is a further factor to be considered.
3. In response to the decisions in *Stewart* and *Walls*, the Department of Finance introduced draft legislation (see Canada, Department of Finance, *News Release 2003-055*, October 31, 2003) that would amend the Act to effectively reintroduce the requirement that a taxpayer have a reasonable expectation of profit in order to claim a loss. See Chapter 2. Proposed subsection 3.1(1) requires that the taxpayer reasonably expect to "realize a cumulative profit" over the course of the business, and proposed subsection 3.1(2) provides that profit is "determined without reference to capital gains or losses" for the purposes of subsection (1). This provision applies only to situations in which the taxpayer has a loss, and thus there would be no statutory reasonable expectation of profit requirement in determining whether income is from a source.
4. Consider the situation of a taxpayer who invested in shares in offshore companies that over the course of eight years yielded $600,000 in dividends. Over the same period, the taxpayer paid out approximately $6 million in interest expenses associated with the money borrowed to finance the purchase of the shares. How would this taxpayer's activities be characterized under the law as it has developed to this point? See *Ludco Enterprises Ltd. v. The Queen*, [2002] 1 C.T.C. 95, 2001 D.T.C. 5505.
5. As mentioned above, Stewart clearly restricted the application of the REOP test from *Moldowan*. In *Canada v. Craig*, [2012] 2 S.C.R. 489, [2012] 5 C.T.C. 205, 2012 D.T.C. 5115, a case considering the limitation on farming losses imposed by subsection 31(1), *Moldowan* was overruled. However, the ruling in *Moldowan* on farming losses was resurrected legislatively in 2013 by an amendment to subsection 31(1).

3. Adventure or Concern in the Nature of Trade

An adventure or concern in the nature of trade is specifically included in the statutory definition of "business". Therefore, subsection 9(1) applies even if the taxpayer did not conduct a "business" in what might be the usual sense of the word. It is enough if the taxpayer engaged in "an adventure or concern" that was similar to, or had the characteristics of, a business or trade. In other words, where a taxpayer enters into an isolated transaction, if the transaction is speculative and intended to yield a profit, although the taxpayer is not a trader, the profit is taxable as business income. There is a vast body of case law interpreting what constitutes an "adventure or concern in the nature of trade", as this is the borderline area between income from a "business" and a capital gain. The relevant cases are discussed in Chapter 7.

B. Income from a Business Distinguished from Other Sources of Income

The character of income is important for purposes of the Act because income from different sources is taxed differently. However, the Act does not contain any detailed rules on income characterization. Whether an item of income is income from a business or income from another source must be determined on the basis of case law.

1. Income from Office or Employment Compared

The distinction between income from a business (that is, income from service as an independent contractor or as a self-employed person) and income from an office or employment is crucial because the scope of deductions and the payer's withholding obligations are vastly different. This distinction is discussed in detail in Chapter 4.

2. Capital Gains Compared

A profit from the sale of property may be characterized as either a capital gain or income from a business. When a taxpayer is in the business of buying and selling property, the profit is clearly income from a business. When a taxpayer buys property for investment purposes and eventually sells the property for a gain, the gain is generally a capital gain. Cases in between are difficult to characterize. The characterization is important because capital gains and losses are treated differently from business income or losses. Capital gains are treated more favourably than business income. Only one-half of capital gains is included in income. Therefore, where a speculative transaction is profitable, taxpayers generally prefer to characterize the transaction as a capital transaction. On the other hand, where a speculative transaction produces a loss, taxpayers want to characterize the transaction as an adventure or concern in the nature of trade so that the loss is fully deductible in computing income, whereas only one-half of a capital loss would be deductible and only against capital gains. For further discussion of this issue, see Chapters 2 and 7.

3. Income from Property Compared

Because property is involved in earning both income from property and income from a business, distinguishing these two sources of income is often difficult. For example, a number of assets falling within the definition of property, such as building and machinery, will also be used in the course of a taxpayer's business. Is income from those assets to be categorized as income from property or a business?

Based on case law, the distinction generally depends on the extent of activity of the owner (or the owner's agents) in earning the income. In *Lois Hollinger v. M.N.R.*, [1972] C.T.C. 592, 73 D.T.C. 5003 (F.C.T.D.), the Court considered this issue and said (at 599-600; 5008):

> Counsel for the appellant further says that the question of whether income is from a business or property is one that must be resolved on the facts of each particular case and no simple criterion is determinative. The criteria which may, he says, be drawn from the authorities and which may serve as indicia are:
>
> (1) whether the income was the result of efforts made or time and labour devoted by the taxpayer;
>
> (2) whether there was a trading character to the income;
>
> (3) can the income be fairly described as income from a business within the meaning of that term as used in the Act; and, finally
>
> (4) the nature and extent of services rendered or activities performed.
>
> I believe that most of those criteria are what may be termed subjective ones, i.e., which deal or apply to the person receiving the income rather than to the objective question of the source of the income which, in my view, is always the overriding consideration which must determine the matter. The source here is clearly a business source. If income from property has any meaning at all, it can only mean the production of revenue from the use of such property which produces income without the active and extensive business-like intervention of its owner or someone on his behalf. I have in mind, for instance, property such as bonds or debentures or shares or real property which do not require the exertion of much activity or energy in order to produce the revenue.

Therefore, if income is derived principally from the ownership of property, the income is generally considered to be income from property. On the other hand, if the earning of the income involves a significant amount of activity, the income is often income from a business. Interest is clearly business income to a financial institution whose business is to make loans to borrowers. Interest earned by individuals from a savings account or private loan is generally income from property. Similarly, dividends generally constitute income from property, although they may constitute business income to an investment dealer in some circumstances. Rental income is more difficult to characterize because the owner of the property typically provides some services to tenants. The level of the services will generally determine whether rentals are from a property source or from a business source. In *Walsh and Micay v. M.N.R.*, [1965] C.T.C. 478, 65 D.T.C. 5293 (Exch. Ct.), the taxpayers were lawyers who had an interest in some rental properties. The court said (at 484; 5296-97):

> It is a question of fact at what point mere ownership of real property and the letting thereof has passed into commercial enterprise and administration. ...
>
> In my opinion the question remaining to be determined is whether the extent and nature of the services provided to tenants as above outlined can affect *[sic]* the rentals received with a trading character as distinct from mere income receipts from property.
>
> On the evidence I think that the rentals received by the appellants should be regarded as having accrued to them as owners of the properties rather than as traders and that the rentals accrued from use by the tenants of the property in that the rentals represent payments for their occupation thereof rather than from a combination of such use and the other services from which the tenants benefited. I regard the additional services which were provided to tenants as being relatively insignificant and insufficient to convert the appellants from landowners into the conductors of a business. The services such as the provision of heat, electric stoves and refrigerators, janitorial services to the common hallways, snow removal, carpeting in some rooms of the suites and drapes for windows are those which tenants have come to expect and are those which landlords normally provide in living accommodation of this kind. These are refinements offered to the tenants in connection with the occupation of suites and, in most instances, are also property for the use of which, along with the suites themselves, rent is paid. The heating of the building and snow removal are ancillary to the property itself and are exercised in the landlord's capacity as owner of the property rather than as a service to tenants although the tenants incidentally enjoy the benefits thereof. While the nature of services provided has a bearing on the question, the services above described are not such as would characterize the rental received therefor as income from a business rather than income from property, as services such as the provisions of breakfast, maid, linen, laundry and such like services might do.

Rental and other types of income earned by a corporation pursuant to the objects of its incorporation are generally presumed to be income from a business. See, for example, *Etoile Immobiliere S.A. v. M.N.R.*, [1992] 2 C.T.C. 2367, 92 D.T.C. 1984 (T.C.C.) and *Burri v. The Queen*, [1985] 2 C.T.C. 42, 85 D.T.C. 5287 (F.C.T.D.).

Question

1. "Server farms" – or data centres – have become an integral part of the growth of cloud computing (internet accessible data and programs) and the Internet. They are used in a wide variety of applications, such as cluster computing (building supercomputers out of a network of small, low-cost computers), web hosting, and other tasks that require computing resources beyond that of a single server. Assume that a taxpayer has purchased a warehouse. However, instead of providing physical storage for a fee, the taxpayer wants to convert the warehouse to house several small server farms, each of which could be rented to outside businesses. The taxpayer wants to allow renters as close to full control of their rented systems as possible, and intends to limit her involvement with the servers to installing the operating system, conveying passwords to new users, and disconnecting servers when a renter falls behind in payment. Does this scheme result in income from business or income from property? Is this similar to renting apartments or commercial premises? Are there any steps the taxpayer should take to maximize the likelihood of this being business income? See "Computing: Down on the Server Farm" *The Economist* 380:8581 (22 May 2008) 93.

III. INCOME FROM PROPERTY

A. Concept of Property and Liability to Tax

Section 12 expressly brings into income certain items that are typically derived from a property source. The meaning of "property", income from property, and specific inclusions of income from property are discussed below.

Subsection 248(1) defines "property" widely to mean property of any kind whatever, whether real, personal, corporeal or incorporeal. The definition specifically includes the following:

(1) a right of any kind, a share or a chose in action;
(2) unless a contrary intention is evident, money;
(3) a timber resource property; and
(4) the work in progress of a business that is a profession.

For a tracing of the historical roots of the amendment of the definition and a good summary of the current definition, see *Manrell v. Canada*, [2003] 3 F.C. 727, [2003] 3 C.T.C. 50, 2003 D.T.C. 5225 (Fed. C.A.), per Sharlow J. for the Court.

The extension of the definition to include money was added in 1971. Whether this extension was necessary is another matter. There is a dictum of Cattanach, J. in

M.N.R. v. Minden, [1963] C.T.C. 364, 63 D.T.C. 1231, which suggests that money is "property" for the purposes of the attribution rules.

The broad definition of property means that something of value is generally considered to be property for purposes of the Act. Typical types of property are personal property, real property and intangible property. Despite the broad definition, dispute may arise as to whether or not something of value is property. For example, in *Fasken Estate v. M.N.R.*, [1948] C.T.C. 265, 49 D.T.C. 491, Thorson, P. held that "property" included a contingent right to receive income from a trust. On the other hand, in *No. 481 v. M.N.R.* (1957), 18 Tax A.B.C. 294, 58 D.T.C. 41, Mr. Boisvert held that the benefit obtained by the covenantee under a covenant not to compete was not "property" since "it has no character of ownership, which is the condition *sine qua non* of the meaning of the word 'property'." Can *No. 481* be considered overruled by *Manrell*? Similarly, the knowledge and skills of the taxpayer are not considered "property": see *Rapistan Canada Ltd. v. Minister of National Revenue*, [1974] 1 F.C. 739, [1974] C.T.C. 495, 74 D.T.C. 6426 (Fed. C.A.), affirmed [1976] C.T.C. 296, 76 D.T.C. 6177, 9 N.R. 42 (S.C.C.), per Jackett C.J. for the Court. Finally, the right to do what is available to all (such as to carry on a business) is not a property right for the purposes of the Act. See *Manrell, supra*.

Income from property is generally income derived from the ownership of property. For example, a taxpayer who owns real property earns rental income from leasing the property. In certain circumstances where a property is transferred by a taxpayer to a related person, or where income from property is diverted to a corporation or trust, income from the property transferred may be attributed to the transferor in accordance with one of the anti-avoidance rules in the Act. For further discussion of income splitting, see Chapter 2.

Property income earned by a non-resident from a source in Canada is subject to Canadian taxation in accordance with Part XIII of the Act. Part XIII levies a special withholding tax of 25 per cent on most income items related to property sources — such as interest, dividends, rent and royalties. The 25 per cent rate is generally reduced by a tax treaty concluded by Canada with other countries. See Chapter 3.

B. Income from Property Distinguished from Other Sources of Income

Typical types of income from property include interest, rent, royalties, and dividends. For purposes of the Act, income from property should be distinguished from business income and capital gains. Moreover, income from property should be distinguished from the economic value of the use of property by the owner of the property (imputed income).

1. Business Income Compared

See Part I, above.

2. Capital Gains Compared

Income from property and capital gains are two separate sources of income for purposes of section 3 of the ITA. The former is included in income under paragraph 3(a) and the latter under paragraph 3(b). A major difference in tax treatment of these two types of income is that income from property is fully included in income, while only a portion of capital gains is included in income, the remaining portion being exempt.

Subsection 9(3) expressly provides that income from a property does not include any capital gain from the disposition of that property. The "fruit and tree" analogy is useful in demonstrating the distinction between income from property and capital gains. A taxpayer may hold a "tree" (property) to realize the fruit (interest, dividends, rent or royalties), in which case the fruit is either business income or property income. If the tree is sold for a gain, it is a capital gain.

The issue of distinguishing between income from property and capital gains often arises in cases where a capital property is sold and the sale price is paid in installments or the amount paid is dependent on the use or production of the property. Because of the preferential treatment of capital gains, taxpayers generally prefer to characterize the transaction as a sale of capital property, giving rise to capital gains. Subsection 16(1) and paragraph 12(1)(g) are designed as anti-avoidance measures. As discussed further below, subsection 16(1) treats certain deferred payments as including a disguised loan, giving rise to interest income. Paragraph 12(1)(g) treats payments that are based on the use or production of the property sold as rent or royalties.

3. Imputed Income Compared

Income from property is the value derived by the owner of a property from allowing another person to use the property. The economic value derived by the owner from the use of his or her own property is generally considered to be imputed income and not taxable under the Act. The following definition of imputed income is advanced by Professor A.F. Sheppard in his article, "The Taxation of Imputed Income and the Rule in *Sharkey v. Wernher*" (1973), *Can. Bar Rev.* 617-41, at 617-18:

> The two salient qualities of imputed income are: (1) it is non-cash income or, income in kind, and (2) it arises outside the market place. Some examples will help to

clarify the definition of imputed income. A taxpayer who occupies his own home instead of deriving rental income from letting to a tenant enjoys imputed income to the extent of the rent foregone. The owner-occupant enjoys a benefit, which increases his economic power, and the value of which is imputed income to him. However, a landlord who receives rent in kind from his tenant does not thereby gain imputed income because the transaction is an exchange in the market, albeit without cash. Although such barter transactions give rise to income in kind, they do not involve imputed income. Further, when a farmer consumes his own produce instead of selling it and buying groceries with the proceeds, the value of this benefit is imputed income. Similarly, when a taxpayer cuts his own lawn instead of hiring a gardener, he thereby enjoys a benefit which can be measured by the going wages of gardeners. Thus, broadly, imputed income "includes any gain, benefit or satisfaction from a non-market transaction or event".

...

How does imputed rent arise from owner-occupied homes? Suppose that two taxpayers have equal money incomes, family sizes, and consumption patterns, and that each taxpayer was furnished with $40,000.00. One bought a home for $30,000.00 and invested the other $10,000.00 using the $500.00 income (after income tax) to defray property taxes, maintenance and so on. The other invested the $40,000.00, became a tenant and used the $2,000.00 income (after income tax) to pay rent. While both taxpayers are in the same financial position, the owner-occupier's taxable income is increased by only $500.00 and the renter's taxable income includes the $2,000.00. Thus, the renter bears a greater tax burden than does the owner-occupier, because the rental value of owner occupied homes is excluded from taxable income. Moreover, the renter will be liable to capital gains on his investments and succession duties may be exigible on his death.

Many critics have elaborated on the drawbacks of excluding imputed rent. As the example indicates, by imposing a heavier tax burden on the renter, such an exclusion violates horizontal equity. Further, it contravenes the principle of neutrality by influencing those taxpayers who can do so, to purchase a home. As a subsidy to homeowners, it is inefficient, for its benefit increases directly with the size of the taxpayer's home and with his marginal rate of tax. The subsidy provides the greatest benefit where it is needed the least. Thus, even if one accepts that tax incentives should encourage home ownership, the exclusion of imputed rent is "an upside-down subsidy". And, it is argued, the exclusion substantially reduces revenue yield and cuts down the progressive effect of the personal income tax.

C. Interest Income

Under paragraph 12(1)(c) of the Act, any amount received or receivable "as, on account of or in lieu of payment of, or in satisfaction of, interest ..." is included in the taxpayer's income. Two significant issues arise under paragraph 12(1)(c): (1) when can an amount be considered "interest" subject to the provision and, (2) if interest, when must the amount be included in income?

1. Characterization as Interest

(a) Legal Meaning of Interest

The Act does not contain a definition of "interest"; the meaning of the term has been considered in a number of non-tax cases. See, for example, *Re Reference as to the Validity of Section 6 of the Farm Security Act, 1944 of the Province of Saskatchewan*, [1947] S.C.R. 394 and *A.G. Ont. v. Barfried Enterprises Ltd.*, [1963] S.C.R. 570. As determined in these cases, interest is compensation for the use of money belonging to another person; it must be referable to a principal amount and must either accrue daily or be allocable on a day-to-day basis. These criteria have generally been accepted for income tax purposes. See, for example, *Miller v. The Queen*, [1985] 2 C.T.C. 139, 85 D.T.C. 5354 (F.C.T.D.), *Sherway Centre Ltd. v. Canada*, [1998] 2 C.T.C. 343, 98 D.T.C. 6121 (Fed. C.A.) and Interpretation Bulletin IT-396R: Interest Income (May 29, 1984), paragraphs 11–14, setting out the Canada Revenue Agency's (the "CRA") administrative position as to whether certain types of payments may be considered interest.

The amount of interest is determined by the interest rate and the principal amount of a debt obligation. Interest rates in the financial markets are determined by the supply of and demand for money, which are in turn affected by a number of factors, including the anticipated rate of inflation, the general economic outlook, the creditworthiness of the borrower, the value of any security provided by the borrower, and the term of the loan. Debt obligations typically include loans, bonds, promissory notes, bank accounts, mortgages, guaranteed investment certificates, debentures, and other forms of evidence of indebtedness.

(b) Discounts

The term "discount" generally refers to the excess of the principal or face amount of a debt obligation over its issue price. A discount may arise on the issue of a debt obligation, in which case it is referred to as "original issue discount" ("OID"), or it may arise on a subsequent purchase of a debt obligation because of an increase in interest rates or a decrease in the credit worthiness of the issuer.

The characterization of a discount as interest is a question of fact. In general, OID is regarded as the equivalent of interest where the debt is either non-interest-bearing or carries an interest rate substantially lower than the market rate at the time of issue. For example, government treasury bills do not provide a stipulated interest rate but, instead, are issued at a discount from their stated face value. The discount rate (i.e., the difference between the face amount and the issue price of the bills) is directly related to current interest rate. In three different cases, (*O'Neil v. M.N.R.* (1991), 91 D.T.C. 692 (T.C.C.), *Gestion Guy Ménard Inc. v. M.N.R.*, [1993] 2 C.T.C. 2793, 93 D.T.C. 1058 (T.C.C.); and *Satinder v. The Queen* (1995), 95 D.T.C. 5340

(F.C.A.)) discounts arising on the issue of the bills were characterized as interest income of the debt-holders. When an appropriate commercial rate of interest is charged and, in addition, there is a discount, the courts generally have characterized the discount as a capital receipt. See *Lomax v. Peter Dixon & Son Ltd.*, [1943] 2 All E.R. 255 (C.A.), *Willingale v. International Commercial Bank Ltd.*, [1978] A.C. 834 (H.L.).

The Act contains rules dealing with the inclusion in income of certain deep discount debt obligations (subsections 16(2) and (3)) and zero coupon bonds (Regulation 7000(1)(a)). If a debt obligation is issued at a "deep" discount by a government body or other tax-exempt issuer, the discount is treated as income for the recipient under subsections 16(2) and (3). The formulas for determining when the discount is "deep" are complicated. Subsection 16(3) provides that the discount will be treated as income if the yield (including the discount) is more than four-thirds of the stated interest rate.

When a debt obligation is purchased at a discount from another taxpayer, the discount is either taxed as income or capital gain. If the taxpayer is engaged in the business of purchasing debt obligations, the amount of any discount is included in income on realization. If the taxpayer purchases the debt obligation as an investment, the discount is generally treated as a capital gain. (See *Wood v. M.N.R.*, [1969] C.T.C. 57, 69 D.T.C. 5073.)

(c) Bonuses

A bonus or penalty is an amount in excess of the stated interest and principal payable on maturity of a debt obligation, early repayment, or an event of default. Case law has generally held that bonus payments are not interest. See, for example, *Campbellton Enterprises Limitee v. M.N.R.* (1978), 90 D.T.C. 1890, [1990] 2 C.T.C. 2413 (T.C.C.); *Neonex International Ltd. v. The Queen* (1990), 78 D.T.C. 6339, [1978] C.T.C. 485 (F.C.A.); *Riviera Hotel Co. Ltd. v. M.N.R.* (1972), 72 D.T.C. 6142, [1972] C.T.C. 157 (F.C.T.D.). However, if a bonus varies with the term of a loan where no rate of interest is stipulated, the bonus may be regarded as interest. See *Puder v. M.N.R.*, 62 D.T.C. 555, (1962), 30 Tax A.B.C. 219. This characterization recognizes that the bonus is economically similar to OID, which is the economic equivalent of interest, as discussed above.

The case law characterization of bonus or penalty is overridden by statutory provisions in certain circumstances. For example, subsection 18(9.1) deals specifically with the tax treatment of a payment made as a bonus or penalty on the early redemption of a debt obligation as well as a payment made to reduce the rate of interest. For the purposes of paragraph 12(1)(c), the provision deems such payments to be receivable and received as interest. Similarly, section 12.1 deems cash bonus on Canada Savings Bonds to be interest and one-half of the cash bonus must be included in income when it is received.

(d) Participating Payments, Income Bonds, and Indexed Amounts

A participating debt obligation is commonly considered to include any debt obligation with a return that is calculated, in part, as a percentage of the return realized by the debtor from a particular business or property. Under the general legal definition of interest, a participating payment may not qualify as interest because it is not calculated as a percentage of the principal sum and is not thereby sufficiently linked with that sum. However, in certain circumstances, a participating payment is treated as interest for purposes of the Act. For example, regulation 7000(1)(d) requires debt holders to recognize on an annual accrual basis any amount of interest that is dependent on a contingency existing after a particular year. By implication, participating payments can be interest. A similar implication is found in paragraph 212(1)(b), which excludes contingent interest from a number of the enumerated exceptions to non-resident withholding tax on interest. This exclusion applies to any amount of interest that is contingent or dependent on the use of or production from property in Canada, or that is computed with reference to revenue, profit, cash flow, commodity price, or dividends.

Income bonds provide a return that is calculated as a fixed percentage of the principal sum but is payable only to the extent that the borrower has realized any profits in the relevant period. The return is generally treated as interest, even though it arguably does not accrue on a daily basis because it depends on the satisfaction of a contingency (the availability of profits) and is not payable solely with the passage of time. As an incentive for Canadian financial institutions to lend money to corporations in financial difficulty, the return on income bonds issued by such corporations is deemed to be a dividend (subsection 15(3)) so that it is received on a tax-free basis by the corporate lender (section 112).

All nominal interest payments include compensation for the loss in value of the loan principal attributable to inflation. Indexation for inflation attempts to measure the amount of this compensation accurately. However, amounts indexed for inflation may not be considered as interest because they are not referable to the principal sum of a loan and do not accrue on a daily basis as required under the general definition of interest. Subsection 16(6) overcomes that problem by specifically treating the amounts paid on indexed debt obligations (as defined in subsection 248(1)) as interest.

(e) Late Payment Charges

A supplier of goods or services who does not receive payment on the due date will often levy a late payment charge. Such a charge is generally calculated as a percentage of the amount outstanding in respect of the price of the goods or services for the period from the due date to the time of payment. The particular rate often reflects prevailing commercial interest rates. In effect, although no actual amount of money is advanced, the debt obligation arising from the supply of goods or services is economically equivalent to a loan from the supplier followed by receipt of payment of the price for goods or services. Late payment charges have been considered to be interest (see *Lebern Jewelry Co. Ltd. v. M.N.R.*, 76 D.T.C. 1313 (T.R.B.) and *Wenger's Ltd. v. M.N.R.*, [1992] 2 C.T.C. 2479 (T.C.C.)).

(f) Blended Payment or Capitalized Interest

Where a taxpayer receives a single payment under a contract or other arrangement which includes both the repayment of capital and interest (or other income), the payment is referred to as a blended payment. Subsection 16(1) requires that the interest (or other income) component of the blended payment be segregated and included in the taxpayer's income.

A blended payment may be found in the following situations:

- Original issue discount. Assume that the taxpayer loaned $1,000 to X in return for a promissory note with a face amount of $1,050 due six months after the date of the loan. The $1,050 is arguably a blended payment under subsection 16(1).
- Mortgage payments. Many residential mortgages require the borrower to make regular payments that are partly interest and partly the repayment of the principal sum. In fact, the amount of the principal sum is steadily reduced over the life of the loan.
- Deferred payments for the sale of capital property. A capital property is sold and the sale price is payable in installments over a period of time.

Whether or not a single payment is a blended payment is a question of fact. Consider the following case. What facts do the courts look at to determine whether a single payment constitutes a blended payment subject to subsection 16(1)?

GROULX v. M.N.R.
[1967] C.T.C. 422, 67 D.T.C. 5284 (S.C.C.)

Hall J. (for the Court):

... The only question in issue in this appeal is whether sums of $15,000 and $19,136.20 which the appellant received in 1958 and 1959 respectively pursuant to the terms of a contract of sale, can reasonably be regarded as having been received by the appellant by way of interest as provided in section 7(1) of the *Income Tax Act,* R.S.C. 1952, c. 148 [now subsection 16(1)].

The appellant was the owner of a farm in the Parish of St. Laurent for about twenty years. He resided, and at the time of the sale he was still residing in a house located on the farm, and he had operated this farm for many years until 1952.

Between 1950 and 1956 the appellant was approached by various persons with proposals that he sell his farm, but he refused every offer, being unwilling to accept the condition that he leave this farm which he had operated for so long a time. Eventually, around July 20, 1956, when land values were at their highest, the appellant was approached by a company Thorndale Investment Corporation, who made him an offer to purchase for the sum of $350,000. Once more he refused this offer, stating the price he required for his farm was $450,000.

Intense negotiations took place between the appellant and Thorndale Investment Corporation during the two days which followed. In fact, the appellant began by asking $450,000 while Thorndale Investment Corporation offered $350,000. After discussion the appellant dropped his price to $400,000, but the purchaser considered this too high. The appellant finally agreed to a further reduction of $5,000 which the purchasing company did not regard as sufficient. The appellant therefore decided to forgo interest in order to conclude the sale.

A notarial contract was signed on July 19, 1956, whereby Mr. Groulx sold a large part of his farm, with a total area of 1,256,859 square feet to Thorndale Investment Corporation for the price of $395,000, i.e. $0.17742 per square foot, of which $85,000 was paid immediately and the balance of $310,000 was to be paid before June 1, 1964, by annual instalments commencing in 1958. The balance bore no interest except in the event of delay in payment, in which case interest was to be 6%.

...

In the reasons for his judgment, the learned judge of the Exchequer Court stated:

> ... we are dealing here, more particularly, with two questions of fact. In the first place, was the Minister justified in assuming that, if the taxpayer had in this transaction followed recognized business practice, the balance of $310,000, payable by instalments, would have carried interest at the rate of 5% or 6% until final payment?
>
> There must be an affirmative reply to this question, since it has not been contested. Furthermore, I am of opinion that the evidence submitted by the appellant shows that it is almost invariable practice, in similar cases, for any balance of price secured by hypothec to carry interest at 5%.

By way of defence, the respondent [appellant in the present appeal] submits that, notwithstanding his admission that the above mentioned rates of interest apply as a general rule, this is a case involving special circumstances which therefore merits special consideration. In support of this submission the respondent states that he did not follow the practice of charging interest since his farm was non-productive.

The second question is whether, on the evidence, the property was sold at a price higher than its market value.

Counsel for the appellant had admitted that the method used by Mr. Lemire to establish that the property was sold at a price higher than its market value seemed somewhat weak from certain points of view, since it was based on his own experience and did not take into account the definition of "market value" established by the Supreme Court. However, he submitted that this did not mean that his valuation was erroneous. In any event, the directives of the Supreme Court do not prevent me from analyzing the evidence of Mr. Lemire, to the best of my ability, in order that I may extract therefrom a reliable estimate of the real value of this property. Further, I consider that it is our duty, under the circumstances, to act in this way.

...

It is not denied that the question in issue is that of determining the market or real value of this property.

...

In the first place, I am of the opinion that the appellant has at least established a *prima facie* case that the property was sold at a price higher than its market value and that the respondent has not discharged the onus, which fell upon him, to prove the contrary.

...

In my view, the respondent was not an ordinary farmer. As appears from his tax returns, which were lodged with this Court, his taxable income for the year 1958 exceeded $12,500 and for 1959 was about $15,000. He received part of these amounts by way of salary from a company of which he was president, but the greater part came from his investments. His evidence discloses that he was no stranger to real estate transactions. As to his statement that he had never thought of evading tax when forgoing interest, a child can calculate that interest of 5% on the balance of $310,000 exceeds $15,000 p.a.

A taxpayer who is as involved in business as the respondent must quickly appreciate the pecuniary advantage of not doubling his taxable income.

The *Interest Act*, R.S.C. 1952, c. 156, s. 2 provides:

2. Except as otherwise provided by this or by any other Act, of the Parliament of Canada, any person may stipulate for, allow and exact, on any contract or agreement whatsoever, any rate of interest or discount that is agreed upon.

> I believe that the respondent has disclosed that in sacrificing interest his intention was to ensure his receiving a price of $395,000 as capital ... and his evidence could scarcely be more indicative of a characteristic capitalization of interest.
>
> One might add that other circumstances — namely, the fact that the respondent himself proposed the non-payment of interest, the weakness of his reasons for making this proposal and the vague replies given by Mr. Feinstein when he was asked whether he would have paid the price of $395,000 regardless of interest — militate against the respondent. I must therefore conclude that there is sufficient evidence to justify the assessments in question.

The evidence fully justifies the conclusions at which the Honourable Mr. Justice Kearney arrived as to the facts. The appeal is dismissed and the judgment of the Exchequer Court is confirmed with costs against the appellant.

Notes and Questions

1. Would the *Groulx* case be decided the same way if the payments were spread over the same time period but there was no evidence of the question of interest being discussed? What if there was no clear provision for a discount in the case of a repayment? Do you believe that the fact that the sale price was approximately equal to the fair market value of the property should be determinative? In *Vanwest Logging Co. Ltd. v. M.N.R.*, [1971] C.T.C. 199, 71 D.T.C. 5120 and *Carter v. M.N.R.* (1964), 37 Tax A.B.C. 174, 65 D.T.C. 31, great emphasis was placed on the fact that the sale price was no greater than the fair market value. The matter was put even more emphatically in *Rodmon Construction Inc. v. The Queen*, [1975] C.T.C. 73, 75 D.T.C. 5038 (F.C.T.D.):

   > It is well established that in similar cases the prime factor to be considered is whether or not the fair market value has been paid: if the price paid is in excess of fair market value, the excess is deemed interest; if the price reflects the fair market value then there is no element of interest in the payment.

2. Would it be reasonable to assume that whenever a payment for the sale of property is deferred, there is a disguised interest element in the deferred payment? Could a deferred payment transaction be considered the equivalent of the seller receiving the full price up front and then providing a loan to the purchaser? Why would the seller allow the purchaser to use his or her money free of charge? If it is not reasonable to assume that a seller is willing to provide an interest-free loan to the purchaser, why is the fair market value of the property sold relevant?
3. If a taxpayer is injured in an auto accident, and the negligent driver pays the taxpayer $5,000 damages, the $5,000 is seen to be a capital receipt on the taxpayer's part and not income. If the negligent party agrees to pay the taxpayer $1,200 a year for the next five years, does that change the nature of the receipt?

In Interpretation Bulletin IT-365R2: Damages, Settlements and Similar Receipts (May 8, 1987), the CRA presents this interpretation of the law:

> Where an amount in respect of damages for personal injury or death has been awarded by a Court or resolved in an out-of-court settlement, no part of such amount will be income to the recipient even though the amount includes or is augmented by an amount which, pursuant to the terms of the Court order or the settlement agreement, is referred to as interest. However, where an amount that has been awarded for damages is held on deposit, the amount of interest earned will be included in the income of the injured taxpayer unless paragraph 81(1)(g.1) or (g.2) has application. Where an amount that has been awarded for damages is held in trust, any interest earned on the amount is income of the trust or of the beneficiary, depending on the circumstances.

2. Timing of Interest Inclusion

Paragraph 12(1)(c) requires interest to be included in income when it is received or receivable, "depending upon the method regularly followed by the taxpayer in computing his profit". The CRA has interpreted this phrase to permit a taxpayer to select either the received or receivable method of reporting interest income for each debt obligation held by the taxpayer, provided that the method chosen is followed consistently for the particular obligation and all similar obligations. The method that a taxpayer uses to report income other than interest is generally irrelevant.

Subsections 12(3) and (4) modify the rule in paragraph 12(1)(c) governing when interest must be included in income. To the extent that interest has not been included as received or receivable by the taxpayer, these provisions require inclusion on an accrual basis. Subsection 12(3) requires corporations, partnerships and certain trusts to include in income for a taxation year all interest accrued on a debt obligation during the year. Interest accrues on a daily basis. Subsection 12(4) requires an individual who holds a debt obligation to include in his or her income for a taxation year all interest accrued to the anniversary date of the debt obligation occurring in the year. The anniversary date of a debt obligation is one year after the day before the issue date, the same day every year thereafter, as well as the day the taxpayer disposes of the obligation (subsection 12(11)).

For certain "prescribed debt obligations", such as zero-coupon bonds and indexed debt obligations, the actual amount of interest accrued is determined in accordance with regulations 7000 and 7001. Section 12.2 contains comparable accrual rules for income from certain annuities and life insurance policies.

Problems

1. What is the difference between an amount of interest that is received and an amount that is receivable?

2. Assume X holds an investment certificate with a principal amount of $10,000 which pays simple interest at an annual rate of 10 per cent. The certificate was issued on July 1, for a term of five years. On the date of maturity, X is entitled to a return of the $10,000 principal plus $5,000 in interest. The certificate may be redeemed at any time, but in the event of an early redemption, the right to any interest is forfeited. If the certificate is held for the full five-year term, how must X report the interest income?

3. Sale of Obligations with Accrued Interest

The timing rules for interest income in paragraph 12(1)(c) and subsections 12(3) and (4) realize an appropriate result where a debt obligation is held by only one taxpayer. Problems arise, however, where an obligation with accrued interest is transferred and the interest becomes payable after the transfer. The issue is one of the proper allocation of income as between the transferor and the transferee. Subsection 20(14) provides that, in these circumstances, where the transferee of a debt instrument has become entitled to interest that has accrued on the instrument for a time prior to the transfer but is not payable until after the transfer, the accrued interest will be included as interest in the income of the transferor for the year of the transfer, to the extent that it is not otherwise included (for example, under subsection 12(4)). The same amount may be deducted from the transferee's income under subsection 20(14).

Is the deduction under subsection 20(14) available only if the transferor has included the accrued interest in income? See *Antosko v. The Queen*, [1994] 2 C.T.C. 25, 94 D.T.C. 6314 (S.C.C.) reproduced in Part II. B. of Chapter 10.

Problem

P buys from S a $1,000 bond. The bond has a 10 per cent coupon attached representing interest due for the period from January 1 to December 31. P buys the bond on June 30 for $1,050. When the $100 interest becomes payable to P on December 31, how much interest income must P report? Is S required to report any interest income?

D. Rent and Royalties

1. Meaning of "Rent" or "Royalty"

Paragraph 12(1)(g) provides that "any amount received by the taxpayer in the year that was dependent on the use of or production from property whether or not that amount was an instalment of the sale price of the property ..." must be included in the taxpayer's income. Although the word "rent" or "royalty" is not used in this provision, amounts that typically fall within paragraph 12(1)(g) are rents or royalties.

A "rent" is generally a fixed payment (usually periodic) for the use of property for a given period of time, after which the right to use the property expires (i.e., the right would revert back to the owner). See *The Queen v. Saint John Shipbuilding & Dry Dock Co.*, [1980] C.T.C. 352, 80 D.T.C. 6272 (F.C.A.). Rents are generally paid in respect of the use of tangible personal property or real property. The term "royalty" is defined to generally include mineral royalties and royalties for the use of intangible property (such as copyright, invention, trade-name, patent, trade-mark, design or model, plan, and secret formula or process). In *Vauban Productions v. The Queen*, [1975] C.T.C. 511, 75 D.T.C. 5371 (F.C.T.D.) (appeal dismissed, [1979] C.T.C. 262, 79 D.T.C. 5186 (F.C.A.)), Addy J. in the Federal Court–Trial Division stated:

> The term "royalties" normally refers to a share in the profits or a share or percentage of a profit based on use or on the number of units, copies or articles sold, rented or used. When referring to a right, the amount of the royalty is related in some way to the degree of use of that right. ... Royalties, which are akin to rental payments, ... are either based on the degree of use of the right or on the duration of use to be made of it ...

Rents and royalties represent payments for the use of property. The concept of "use" has been interpreted very broadly. A property is used by a person where the owner of the property allows the person to take possession or make use of the property. For example, land is used where the owner allows another person to excavate and remove gravel from the land. Intangible property is used where the assignee/ licensee is allowed to exploit the bundle of rights protected by law.

2. Payments Based on Production or Use

Royalties or rents need to be distinguished from sales profit. In the absence of statutory rules, the distinction is generally a question of fact. In general, if all the legal rights in a property are transferred, the transaction constitutes a sale, giving rise to sales profits; if less than all the rights are transferred, the transaction is a lease or license and the payments are rents or royalties. Difficulties of characterization arise where property that is sold is difficult to value and the consideration depends on productivity or use of the property.

Intangible property is often difficult to value. Payments for transfers of intangible property are often based on the use of the property or the production or sales of goods or services. Are these payments purchase payments or royalties for tax purposes? Moreover, difficulties of characterization arise because both a license and a sale of intangible property involve the grant of rights to the transferee. For example, with respect to copyright that expires after a prescribed term, a grant of an exclusive right to use the copyright for the remainder of its life can be identical in effect to a transfer in the form of a sale of the copyright. In an extreme case where there is a transfer of the exclusive right to exploit the copyright in all fields of use and media of publication for the remainder of the life of the copyright, the transaction is a sale rather than a license. A transfer of any lesser bundle of rights may be more difficult to classify.

A similar issue arises in the case of a sale by an owner of land of a profit à prendre, such as oil, found on the land. Neither the vendor nor the purchaser knows how much oil there is, so the purchaser may wish to base the price on the number of gallons of oil extracted, perhaps paying a guaranteed minimum. Are such payments capital (resulting in capital gain) or royalty income for the recipient? The leading case on the characterization of such payments for tax purposes was *Spooner v. M.N.R.* (1933), [1928-34] C.T.C. 184, 33 D.T.C. 258 (P.C.). The taxpayer in that case owned a ranch in Alberta. She sold twenty acres of it to Vulcan Oils Ltd. for $5,000 cash, 25,000 fully paid shares of Vulcan, plus a royalty of "10 per cent of all the petroleum, natural gas and oil purchased and saved from the said lands free of costs". The royalty right reserved was to receive oil, not money, although, in fact, the taxpayer accepted money in lieu of oil — some $95,000 in 1927, which the Minister sought to tax. It was held that the taxpayer had simply sold her property and realized capital gains.

As a result of the *Spooner* decision, the Act was revised in 1934 to include what is now paragraph 12(1)(g). Under that provision, any amount received by a taxpayer that is dependent on the use of, or production from, property, even if the amount is an installment payment of the sale price of property, is income in the hands of the recipient. The purpose of this provision is to prevent taxpayers from converting what would otherwise be fully taxable rent or royalty income into capital gains.

Paragraph 12(1)(g) generally applies to the sale of property where the sale price is dependent on the production or use of the property. Examples include (a) a sale of gravel, sand, shale and topsoil where the purchase price is payable in fixed installments (e.g. a fixed amount per cubic yard of gravel, etc. removed) (see, for example, *Pallett v. M.N.R.* (1959), 59 D.T.C. 230 (Ex. Ct.) and *Lackie v. The Queen*, [1979] C.T.C. 389 (F.C.A.); (b) a sale of a franchise to supply natural gas in return for an amount based on gross receipts from all sales of natural gas under the franchise (*Wain-Town Gas & Oil Company Ltd.*, [1952] C.T.C. 147, 52 D.T.C. 1138); and (c) proceeds of an assignment by an author to the publisher of the right to publish and sell his or her work where the amount of proceeds was based on the number of copies sold (see *Hould v. M.N.R.* (1965), 65 D.T.C. 624 (T.A B.).

For the purposes of non-resident withholding tax, paragraph 212(1)(d) deems certain types of payments to be rents or royalties. In particular, it includes payments for information or services of an industrial, commercial or scientific nature where the payments are determined, in whole or in part, by the use to be made of, or the benefits to be derived from, the information or services. It also includes payments for the use or right to use certain intellectual property in Canada, but it specifically excludes royalties or payments in respect of copyright in respect of the production or reproduction of any literary, dramatic, musical or artistic work, and certain other payments for the use of such things as railway rolling stock or aircraft.

3. Payments for Computer Software

Payments for computer software may be characterized as royalties or purchase prices. Because software transactions generally take the form of a "license" rather than a "sale", the characterization for tax purposes may be difficult. There are no statutory guidelines for this characterization. The CRA's administrative policy is to distinguish two types of software — shrink-wrap and custom software. Whether or not a software program is shrink-wrap software or custom software is a question of fact which can only be determined by reviewing the licensing agreement associated with the right to use the particular program. "Shrink-wrap software" basically refers to over-the-counter software that is licensed pursuant to a standard unsigned license agreement the terms of which the licensee may or may not have been aware at the time of purchase. Where software is purchased on the Internet, the so-called "click-wrap" or "web-wrap" software may also be treated as "shrink-wrap" software. On the other hand, if software is subject to a license agreement where it is clear that the customer was aware of its terms (usually verified by signing the license agreement) when acquiring the software, the software would be considered custom software.

Fees paid for acquiring a copy of custom software are treated as royalties. Fees paid for the right to use shrink-wrap software are treated as sale proceeds rather than license fees or royalties. In other words, where pre-packaged or standard software is "purchased" by a consumer, although the transaction is formally referred to as a "license", the transaction is classified for tax purposes as a purchase of a good. In such cases, the customer does not obtain the copyright to the software (i.e., the right to produce or reproduce the software).

Notes and Questions

1. The taxpayer holds a licence to reproduce and distribute copies of a software program from the non-resident company that owns the copyright for the program. For each reproduction of the software a new software licence agreement was executed and royalties were paid. Is the taxpayer required to withhold tax from its payments to the non-resident copyright holder? See ITA paragraph 212(1)(d) and *Syspro Software Ltd. v. The Queen*, [2003] 4 C.T.C. 3001, 2003 D.T.C. 931 (T.C.C.).
2. eBooks – electronic copies of books – are a growing portion of publication industry sales. Amazon's Kindle, an eBook reader, allows users to download eBooks wirelessly. Unlike physical books, eBooks "sold" are subject to greater

control by the vendor; in 2009, Amazon deleted copies of George Orwell's books (including "1984") that the publisher determined had been illegally sold. If Amazon (the American corporation, not its Canadian subsidiary) were to "sell" eBooks in Canada subject to that same degree of control, would the proceeds of those payments be subject to non-resident withholding tax? See "Amazon CEO apologizes for Kindle controversy" *Ottawa Citizen* (24 July 2009).

E. Dividends

1. Meaning of "Dividend"

A dividend paid on the shares of a corporation represents the return on equity investment in a corporation. The Act does not define "dividend". Subsection 248(1) simply provides that a dividend includes a stock dividend. The ordinary meaning of "dividend" has been established by the courts. In some old English cases, which have been generally accepted for Canadian tax purposes, the courts have determined that any *pro rata* distribution from a corporation to its shareholders is a dividend, unless the distribution is made on the liquidation of the corporation or on an authorized reduction of corporation capital. See, for example, *Hill v. Permanent Trustee of New South Wales*, [1930] A.C. 720 (P.C.) and *IRC v. Burrell*, [1924] 2 K.B. 52 (C.A.). Where a distribution is made on the liquidation of the corporation or on an authorized reduction of corporate capital, a distribution may give rise to a capital gain or loss on the particular shares, subject to the deemed dividend rules in the Act.

Section 84 deems a dividend to be paid where a corporation: (a) increases the paid-up capital in respect of the shares of any class of its capital stock; (b) distributes funds or property on the winding-up, discontinuance or reorganization of its business; (c) redeems, or purchases for cancellation, its shares; or (d) reduces the paid-up capital in respect of any class of shares of its capital stock otherwise than by way of a redemption, acquisition or cancellation of the shares.

Dividends may be paid in cash, in kind, or with new stock of the corporation (i.e., stock dividends). The amount of dividends received is included in income. Dividends paid by certain private corporations out of tax-free income (e.g. the tax-free portion of capital gains) are exempt from tax (subsection 83(2)). In addition to receiving dividends, a shareholder may receive economic benefits from a corporation, such as receiving interest-free loans from the corporation or using corporate property for personal purposes. The value of such shareholder benefits must be included in the shareholder's income under subsection 15(1).

2. Special Treatment of Dividends

Taxpayers are generally required to include in income any dividends received by them in the year (paragraphs 12(1)(j), 82(1)(a) and 12(1)(k)). However, the Act contains a number of special rules designed to provide relief from double taxation of income earned through a corporation. Double taxation occurs where the corporation earning the income pays corporate income tax and the shareholder receiving dividends paid out of the corporate earnings pays income tax on the dividends received.

The Act provides relief from double taxation by allowing individual shareholders a dividend tax credit in computing tax payable (paragraph 82(1)(b) and section 121) and allowing corporate shareholders to receive dividends on a tax-free basis (section 112).

IV. DEDUCTIONS IN RESPECT OF INCOME FROM BUSINESS OR PROPERTY

A. Structure of the Act

Subsection 9(1) defines a taxpayer's income from a business or property as the "profit from that business or property for the year". The term "profit" is not defined in the Act, The ordinary meaning of this term implies a net concept. Net profit is generally determined according to accounting or commercial principles unless these principles are overridden by other provisions of the Act or case law principles. Therefore, subsection 9(1) contains the primary rule for deductions.

Other provisions of the Act either disallow or allow various deductions from business or property income. Key provisions include:

- Section 18, which specifically limits a deduction for certain expenses, such as expenses that are not incurred for purposes of earning business or property income (paragraph 18(1)(a)), capital expenditures (paragraph 18(1)(b)), and personal or living expenses (paragraph 18(1)(h)).
- Section 20, which overrides section 18 and specifically allows a deduction of capital cost allowance (paragraph 20(1)(a)), interest (paragraph 20(1)(c)), and other amounts. In overriding the more general prohibitions on the deductibility of certain expenses, section 20 usually imposes limits on the availability and amount of any deduction. These limits are crucial because, to the extent that they are not met, section 18 applies to prohibit the deduction of the particular expenses.
- Section 67, which denies a deduction of expenses that are otherwise deductible to the extent that the amount of the expense is unreasonable.

- A deduction of certain expenses is prohibited on the ground of public policy according to provisions of the Act (such as sections 67.5 and 67.6) or case law principles.

The rest of this chapter discusses the general principles underlying the deductibility of business expenses and the non-deductibility of personal or living expenses, expenses contrary to public policy, and unreasonable expenses. Chapter 6 discusses the relevance of accounting and commercial principles in computing profit, inventory accounting, and the deduction of capital cost allowance and cumulative eligible capital.

B. General Approach to Deductions

In a series of decisions, Thorson P. of the Exchequer Court of Canada developed an approach to the determination of profit. In *Daley v. M.N.R.*, [1950] C.T.C. 254, 4 D.T.C. 877, he said (at 260; 880):

> ... The correct view, in my opinion, is that the deductibility of the disbursements and expenses that may properly be deducted "in computing the amount of the profits or gains to be assessed" is inherent in the concept of "annual net profit or gain" in the definition of taxable income contained in Section 3 [now subsection 9(1)]. The deductibility from the receipts of a taxation year of the appropriate disbursements or expenses stems, therefore, from Section 3 of the Act, if it stems from any section, and not at all, even inferentially, from paragraph (a) of Section 6 [now paragraph 18(1)(a)].
>
> ...
>
> That being so, it follows that in some cases the first enquiry whether a particular disbursement or expense is deductible should not be whether it is excluded from deduction by Section 6(a) or Section 6(b) but rather whether its deduction is permissible by the ordinary principles of commercial trading or accepted business and accounting practice. ...

Following *Daley*, an expenditure properly deducted under accounting principles will be deductible for tax purposes, *unless* prohibited by some provision of the Act. Conversely, an amount not deductible pursuant to accounting principles will not be deductible for tax purposes, unless the Act provides a specific deduction.

This approach has been recently confirmed by the Supreme Court of Canada in *Canderel v. Canada,* [1998] 2 C.T.C. 35, 98 D.T.C. 6100 (see Chapter 6). Speaking for the majority, Iacobucci J. confirmed the general proposition that the concept of profit in subsection 9(1) is a net concept. He also confirmed the accepted wisdom that, in determining the deductibility of an expense, recourse must first be had to subsection 9(1).

Thorson P.'s approach in *Daley* suggests that paragraph 18(1)(a) is unnecessary. However, the Minister relies on the provision in most cases rather than just relying on subsection 9(1) and generally accepted accounting principles. It is arguable that paragraph 18(1)(h) is unnecessary too. Paragraph 18(1)(h) is just a refinement of paragraph 18(1)(a); indeed, a taxpayer's personal or living expenses would not be deducted using accounting principles to determine the net income from a business or property. The structure envisioned by the various provisions of the Act is one in which the focus is progressively narrowed. Although a personal or living expense prohibited by paragraph 18(1)(h) would also be prohibited by paragraph 18(1)(a), and by subsection 9(1) according to *Daley,* the Minister often focuses attention on the specific characterization of a disputed expense as a personal expense expressly prohibited by paragraph 18(1)(h).

C. Income-earning Purpose Test

Paragraph 18(1)(a) provides that an expense is deductible to the extent that it is incurred for the purpose of earning income from a business or property. This provision is worded as a limitation on deductibility. However, as previously suggested, it does not limit the deductibility of expenses to any greater extent than the application of generally accepted accounting principles used to determine profit under subsection 9(1). Perhaps this was not always the case. The predecessor to paragraph 18(1)(a) was paragraph 6(a) of the *Income War Tax Act* which provided:

> 6. In computing the amount of the profits or gain to be assessed, a deduction shall not be allowed in respect of
>
> (a) disbursements or expenses not wholly, exclusively and necessarily laid out or expended for the purpose of earning the income.

The present paragraph 18(1)(a) appears less restrictive because the requirement that the expenditures be "wholly" and "exclusively" laid out to earn the income has been removed.

Through his clearly written judgments in *Daley, supra*, and the following two cases, Thorson P. established the general principles to be applied in the determination of the deductibility of expenses in arriving at net income from a business or property.

IMPERIAL OIL LIMITED v. M.N.R.
[1947] C.T.C. 353, 3 D.T.C. 1090 (Exch. Ct.)

Thorson P.:

The issue in this appeal under the Income War Tax Act, R.S.C. 1927, chap. 97, is whether in computing the amount of its profits or gains to be assessed for the year 1930 a deduction of $526,995.35 should be allowed, this being the amount which the appellant was obliged to pay in settlement of damage claims arising out of a collision at sea between its motorship "Reginalite" and the steamship "Craster Hall" owned by the United States Steel Products Company. ...

The appellant's business is described on its return as the manufacturing and marketing of petroleum products. In addition to producing and refining petroleum it is engaged in the transportation of petroleum and petroleum products. ...

Counsel for the appellant argued that the transporting of petroleum and petroleum products was part of the appellant's business, that the income from its marine operations was part of the income earned by it, that the ordinary risks and hazards of that business must be accepted as part thereof including the possibilities of loss inherent in it, that the risk of collision at sea was an ordinary hazard of a shipping company and that negligence on the part of its seamen resulting in damages to another ship was a contingency that was to be expected, and that, while the amount of damage done in the present case was large, the accident was not extraordinary or unusual. His contention was that, under the circumstances, the amount which the appellant had to pay was a proper expense wholly and exclusively incurred in the course of and for the purpose of the marine operations portion of its business and the earning of income therefrom, and representing a liability inherent in such business which it was obliged to meet, that it was not a capital item but an operating one, that it was properly deductible as a matter of accounting practice and that it was not excluded from deduction by Section 6(a). I think that counsel's position was well taken, both on the facts and as a matter of law.

...

The leading English authority is *Strong & Co. Limited v. Woodifield,* [1905] 2 K.B. 350; [1906] A.C. 448. ...

The reason for disallowing the deduction was "that the loss sustained by the appellants was not really incidental to their trade as innkeepers, and fell upon them in their character not of traders, but of householders". The decision turned on whether the loss was or was not really incidental to the business. If it had been it seems clear beyond doubt that the deduction would have been allowed. The case is, therefore, strong authority for the statement that if a trader has to pay damages for the negligence of his servants under such circumstances that the loss is really incidental to his trade then the amount so paid is deductible.

... The issue of fact [in the present case] is whether the payment made was in respect of a liability for a happening that was really incidental to the business. In my view, there is no doubt that it was. The undisputed evidence is that the transportation of petroleum and petroleum products by sea was part of the marine operations of the appellant and part of the business from which it earned its income, that the risk of collision between vessels is a normal and ordinary hazard of marine operations generally, and that, while the amount of the appellant's liability in the present case was unusually large, there was nothing abnormal or unusual about the nature of the collision itself. Negligence on the part of the appellant's servants in the operation of its vessels, with its consequential liability to pay damages for a collision resulting therefrom, was a normal and ordinary risk of the marine operations part of the appellant's business and really incidental to it.

That being so, the question is whether the law under section 6(a) [now paragraph 18(1)(a)] of the *Income War Tax Act* is so fundamentally different from that of the other jurisdictions referred to as to exclude deductibility of the amount claimed. I have come to the conclusion that it is not. ...

The argument of counsel for the respondent against allowing the deduction claimed by the appellant was strongly and clearly put. It can be summarized briefly. His first contention was that the test of the deductibility of an expenditure is whether it was wholly, exclusively and necessarily laid out for the purpose of earning the income, that each expenditure has to be isolated and the question asked, what income did it wholly, exclusively and necessarily earn? And he answered his own question with regard to the expenditures under review by saying that it did not earn income either in 1927 when the collision occurred or in 1930 when the amount of the appellant's liability was finally ascertained and paid, and that since it did not earn any income it was not deductible. Counsel also took the position that there was a radical and fundamental difference between the wording of Section 6(a) and that of the corresponding section in the English Act, and that there was a larger measure of deduction under the English Act than under the Canadian one. In this connection he went so far as to urge that the decision of the Supreme Court of Canada in the *Dominion Natural Gas Company* case (supra) in applying the test in the *Addie* case (supra) to Section 6(a) was wrong, that the statement of Duff, C.J. in that case to the effect that the words "for the purpose of earning the income" in Section 6(a) meant "in the process of earning the income" was inconsistent with the language of the section and had been overruled by the Judicial Committee in the *Montreal Coke Company* case (*supra*) and that the definition given by him must be disregarded in the light of Lord Macmillan's statement that, to be deductible, an expenditure "must be directly related to the earning of income". From this premise counsel then argued that the expenditure was not primarily for the purpose of earning income but primarily for the purpose of settling a legal liability, that the liability was for the negligence of the appellant's servants which could not be related to the earning of its income, that the expenditure was not laid out for the purpose of earning profit at all but solely to satisfy a legal liability and thus keep the sheriff away from the appellant's door and that since this was the true purpose of the expenditure it could not be regarded as being directly related to the earning of the income. Then, in addition, counsel took a position similar to that taken by Collins, M.R. in the Court of Appeal in *Strong & Co., Limited v. Woodifield* (supra) that the expenditure was not deductible because it was not laid out for the purpose of earning profits but was made out of profits after they were earned.

I am unable to accept any of the contentions thus put forward. In my judgment, counsel assigned a much narrower range of permissible deductibility under Section 6(a) than its language warrants. For example, while the section by implication prescribes that the expenditure should be made for the purpose of earning the income it is not a condition of its deductibility that it should actually earn any income. The view that an item of expenditure is not deductible unless it can be shown that it earned some income is quite erroneous. It is never necessary to show a causal connection between an expenditure and a receipt. An item of expenditure may properly be deductible even if it is not productive of any income at all and even if it results in a loss: *Commissioners of Inland Revenue v. The Falkirk Iron Co., Ltd.* (1933), 17 T.C. 625. ...

It is obvious that the words "for the purpose of earning income" in Section 6(a), as applied to disbursements or expenses, cannot be construed literally, for the laying out or expending of disbursement or expense cannot by itself ever accomplish the purpose of earning the income. As Watermeyer, A.J.P. pointed out in *Port Elizabeth Electric Tramway Company v. Commissioner for Inland Revenue* (supra), income is earned not by the making of expenditures but by various operations and transactions in which the taxpayer has been engaged or the services he has rendered, in the course of which expenditures may have been made. These are the disbursements or expenses referred to in Section 6(a), namely, those that are laid out or expended as part of the operations, transactions or services by which the taxpayer earned the income. They are properly, therefore, described as disbursements or expenses laid out or expended as part of the process of earning the income. This means that the deductibility of a particular item of expenditure is not to be determined by isolating it. It must be looked at in the light of its connection with the operation, transaction or service in respect of which it was made so that it may be decided whether it was made not only in the course of earning the income but as part of the process of doing so.

It is no answer to say that an item of expenditure is not deductible on the ground that it was not made primarily to earn the income but primarily to satisfy a legal liability. This was the kind of argument that was expressly rejected by the High Court of Australia in the *Herald & Weekly Times, Ltd.* case (supra), and it should be rejected here. In a sense, all disbursements are made primarily to satisfy legal liabilities. The fact that a legal liability was being satisfied has, by itself, no bearing on the matter. It is necessary to look behind the payment and enquire whether the liability which made it necessary — and it makes no difference whether such liability was contractual or delictual — was incurred as part of the operation by which the taxpayer earned his income. Where income is earned from certain operations, as it was by the appellant from its marine operations, all the expenses wholly, exclusively and necessarily incidental to such operations must be deducted as the total cost thereof in order that the amount of the profits or gains from such operations that are to be assessed may be computed. Such cost includes not only all the ordinary operations costs but also all moneys paid in discharge of the liabilities normally incurred in the operations. When the nature of the operations is such that the risk of negligence on the part of the taxpayer's servants in the course of their duties or employment is really incidental to such operations, as was the fact in the present case, with its consequential liability to pay damages and costs, then the amount of such damages and costs is properly included as one of the items of the total cost of such operations. It may, therefore, properly be described as a disbursement or expense that is wholly, exclusively and necessarily laid out as part of the process of earning the income from such operations. It cannot be said, under the circumstances, that the payment of such damages and costs is made out of profits. It is no such thing. Being an item of the total cost of the operations it must be deducted, along with the other items of cost, before the amount of the profits from the operations can be ascertained.

For the reasons given I have no hesitation in finding that the amount sought to be deducted by the appellant would properly be deductible according to the ordinary principles of commercial trading and well established principles of business and accounting practice as an item in the total cost of its marine operations, and that it falls outside the excluding provisions of Section 6(a). The amount was, therefore, improperly added to the assessment and it should be amended accordingly. The appeal must, therefore, be allowed with costs.

Judgment accordingly.

THE ROYAL TRUST CO. v. M.N.R.
[1957] C.T.C. 32, 57 D.T.C. 1055 (Exch. Ct.)

[The taxpayer company had developed a policy of requiring certain of its employees to join social clubs and other community organizations. The company paid all fees involved. In its 1952 tax year, the company claimed, under the head of "Sundries", the sum of $9,527.29 of which $1,200 represented admission fees and the remainder was for annual membership dues.

The evidence established that the club memberships resulted in business advantage to the company and that its competitors followed the same practice. An experienced chartered accountant gave the opinion that the amount paid in dues was a proper and necessary deduction in determining the company's income.]

Thorson P.: ...

It is clear that the range of deductibility of an outlay or expense under the *Income Tax Act* is greater than that of disbursements or expenses under the *Income War Tax Act*. But there are certain tests of deductibility that are as applicable in the case of the later enactment as they were in the case of the earlier one.

This Court had occasion in several cases under the *Income War Tax Act* to consider what should be the primary approach to the question whether a disbursement or expense was deductible for income tax purposes. I dealt with this question at length in *Imperial Oil Limited v. M.N.R.*, [1947] Ex. C.R. 527; [1947] C.T.C. 353; 3 D.T.C. 1090, and need not repeat what I said there beyond pointing out that it was held there that the deductibility of disbursements or expenses was to be determined according to the ordinary principles of commercial trading or well accepted principles of business and accounting practice unless their deduction was prohibited by reason of their coming within the express terms of the excluding provision of Section 6(a). I went on to say the section ought not to be read with a view to trying to bring a particular disbursement or expense within the scope of its excluding provisions, but that if it was not within the express terms of the exclusions its deduction ought to be allowed if such deduction would otherwise be in accordance with the ordinary principles of commercial trading or well accepted principles of business and accounting practice. It is manifest from the reasons for judgment in that case that the first approach to the question whether a particular disbursement or expense was deductible for income tax purposes was to ascertain whether its deduction was consistent with ordinary principles of commercial trading or well accepted principles of business and accounting practice and that if it was the next enquiry should be whether the deduction was within or without the exclusions of Section 6(a). My only present observation is that I should have omitted the reference to accounting practice which I made in that case.

In the case of *Daley v. M.N.R.*, [1950] Ex. C.R. 516, [1950] C.T.C. 251, 4 D.T.C. 877, I carried the analysis a step further and expressed the opinion that it was not correct to look at Section 6(a) as the authority, even inferentially, for permitting the deduction of a disbursement or expense. I put my view, at page 521, as follows:

> The correct view, in my opinion is that the deductibility of the disbursements or expenses that may properly be deducted "in computing the amount of the profits and gains to be assessed" is inherent in the concept of "annual net profit or gain" in the definition of taxable income contained in Section 3. The deductibility from the receipts of a taxation year of the appropriate disbursements or expenses stems, therefore, from Section 3 of the Act, if it stems from any section, and not at all, even inferentially, from paragraph (a) of Section 6.

This led to the statement that in some cases it was not necessary to consider Section 6(a) (now section 18(1)(a)) at all, for if the deduction of a disbursement or expense was not permissible by the ordinary principles of commercial trading or accepted business and accounting practice, such as, for example, that of the disbursement in question in that case, that was the end of the matter and it was not necessary to make any further enquiry, for if ordinary business practice could not sanction the deduction the expenditure could not possibly fall outside the exclusions of Section 6(a) but must automatically fall within its prohibition.

...

It follows from this line of reasoning, which is as applicable in the case of the *Income Tax Act* as it was in that of the *Income War Tax Act*, that instead of saying that the range of deductibility of an outlay or expense is greater under Section 12(1)(a) than that of a disbursement or expense under Section 6(a) of the *Income War Tax Act* it would be more accurate to say that the extent of the prohibition of the deduction of an outlay or expense is less under Section 12(1)(a) of the *Income Tax Act* than that of a disbursement or expense under the *Income War Tax Act*. Indeed, it was plainly intended that it should be so, with the result that the gap, if it may be so described, between the kind of an outlay or expense that is deductible according to ordinary principles of commercial trading and business practice and that which is deductible for income tax purposes is narrower now than it was under the former Act.

Consequently, if the correct approach to the question of whether a disbursement or expense was properly deductible in a case under the *Income War Tax Act* was the one which I have outlined, it follows, a fortiori, that it is the correct approach to the question of whether an outlay or expense is properly deductible in a case under the *Income Tax Act*. Thus, it may be stated categorically that in a case under the *Income Tax Act* the first matter to be determined in deciding whether an outlay or expense is outside the prohibition of Section 12(1)(a) of the Act is whether it was made or incurred by the taxpayer in accordance with the ordinary principles of commercial trading or well accepted principles of business practice. If it was not, that is the end of the matter. But if it was, then the outlay or expense is properly deductible unless it falls outside the expressed exception of Section 12(1)(a) and, therefore, within its prohibition.

There is, in my opinion, no doubt that it was consistent with good business practice for a trust company like the appellant to make the payments in question. They were made as a matter of business policy that had been carefully considered, was well regulated and had been in effect for many years prior to the year in question. It was considered that the use of social club facilities by the appellant's officers was particularly suited to the kind of personal business done by a trust company and was a means for promoting business beyond that which advertising could produce. The experience over the years showed that the policy had worked out well and that its benefits to the appellant were real. Business contacts were made at the club and business was discussed there. Membership in the clubs had produced profitable business for the appellant. Moreover, the appellant's competitors followed policies similar to the appellant's and the evidence is that it was considered good business practice for a trust company to have its business-getting officers become members of social clubs and pay their admission fees and annual membership dues. In addition to the business and commercial judgment of the appellant's officers that the payments made by them were properly deductible as business expenses there was the opinion of Mr. A. Gilmour as an accountant, for what it is worth, that from an accounting point of view the deduction of the amount of the payments made by the appellant was a proper and necessary one for the ascertainment of its true profits and gains. Thus I find as a fact that the payments made by the appellant were made in accordance with principles of good business practice for trust companies.

I now come to the enquiry whether the deduction of the amount in question is prohibited by Section 12(1)(a) of the Act or falls within its expressed exception.

The mere fact that an outlay or expense was made or incurred by a taxpayer in accordance with the principles of commercial trading and was consistent with good business practice does not automatically make it deductible for income tax purposes. If it were not so there would have been no need to couch the exception in Section 12(1)(a) in the terms that were used. A similar thought was expressed in respect of the corresponding provision of the United Kingdom Act by Kennedy, L.J., when he said in *Smith v. Lion Brewery Company Limited* (1910), 5 T.C. 568 at 581:

> It is clear that it is not every expenditure which is made by a trader for the promotion of his trade, and which, in fact, contributes to the earning of profits, which is a permissible deduction from the estimate of profits for Income Tax purposes.

...

There is a specific limitation in the exception expressed in Section 12(1)(a) on the kind of outlay or expense that may be deducted. It must have been made or incurred, in the case of a taxpayer engaged in a business, for the purpose of gaining or producing income from its business.

It is not necessary that the outlay or expense should have resulted in income. In *Consolidated Textiles Limited v. M.N.R.*, [1947] Ex. C.R. 77 at 81; [1947] C.T.C. 63; 3 D.T.C. 958, I expressed the opinion that it was not a condition of the deductibility of a disbursement or expense that it should result in any particular income or that any income should be traceable to it and that it was never necessary to show a causal connection between an expenditure and a receipt. And I referred to *Vallambrosa Rubber Co. v. C.I.R.* (1910), 47 S.C.L.R. 488 as authority for saying that an item of expenditure may be deductible in the year in which it is made although no profit results from it in such year and to *C.I.R. v. The Falkirk Iron Co. Ltd.* (1933), 17 T.C. 625, as authority for saying that it may be deductible even if it is not productive of any profit at all. I repeated this opinion in the *Imperial Oil Limited* case. The statements made in the cases referred to, which were cases governed by the *Income War Tax Act*, are equally applicable in a case under the *Income Tax Act*. The discussion of this point in the present case is, in a sense, academic, for even if it were necessary to show a causal connection between an expenditure and income it could be done in the present case. Both Mr. Pembroke and Mr. Harrington gave evidence of specific instances of profit actually resulting to the appellant from its expenditure.

The essential limitation in the exception expressed in Section 12(1)(a) is that the outlay or expense should have been made by the taxpayer "for the purpose" of gaining or producing income "from the business". It is the purpose of the outlay or expense that is emphasized but the purpose must be that of gaining or producing income "from the business" in which the taxpayer is engaged. If these conditions are met the fact that there may be no resulting income does not prevent the deductibility of the amount of the outlay or expense. Thus, in a case under the *Income Tax Act* if an outlay or expense is made or incurred by a taxpayer in accordance with the principles of commercial trading or accepted business practice and it is made or incurred for the purpose of gaining or producing income from his business its amount is deductible for income tax purposes.

That is plainly the situation in the present case. I have already found that the payments by the appellant were made in accordance with principles of good business practice for a trust company. It is equally clear, in my opinion, that they were made by the appellant for the purpose of gaining or producing income from its business. The appellant's purpose was to increase its business through personal contacts of its officers with persons whom it would not otherwise readily reach. The clubs were to be used as extensions of its office facilities for persons who would rather go there than to its office. Its whole policy was for the purpose of furthering its business and so gaining or producing income from it. In my view, the payments in question were properly deductible and the Minister was in error in adding their amount to the taxable income reported by the appellant.

There are some further observations to be made. It was contended by counsel for the respondent that the deduction of the amount of the appellant's payments was prohibited by Section 12(1)(a) on the ground that they were only remotely connected with its income earning process and not directly connected as the law required. In support of this contention he relied upon the statement of Lord Macmillan in *Montreal Coke and Manufacturing Company v. M.N.R.* and *Montreal Light, Heat and Power Consolidated v. M.N.R.*, [1944] A.C. 126 at 133; [1944] C.T.C. 94; 2 D.T.C. 654, where he said:

Expenditure, to be deductible, must be directly related to the earning of income.

[Thorson, P. emphasized that the amount at issue in Montreal Coke represented the cost of refinancing by redeeming $3 million in bonds and issuing new bonds at a lower rate of interest. Lord Macmillan's statement was directed at drawing a sharp distinction between expenditures connected with the taxpayer's financial structure and those connected with its business.]

... Thus, counsel was not justified in using the statement in support of his contention. Moreover, the connection between the appellant's gain or production of income from its business and the payments made by it was not remote in any sense of the term.

Counsel's specific contention regarding the amount of the payments made for admission fees presents more difficulty. Put briefly, the submission was that when the appellant paid the admission fee when one of its officers joined a club this was a payment made once and for all in respect of that officer and it was, therefore, a payment on account of capital within the meaning of Section 12(1)(b) of the Act, to which I have already referred, and its deduction was prohibited. In my opinion, there is no realistic reason for drawing a distinction between the payments of admission fees and those for annual membership dues. Both were made for the same purpose. The reality is that in the first year of an officer's membership in a club the payments are higher than in subsequent years. The admission fee is only the first in a series of payments. It does not create any asset for the appellant or confer any lasting or enduring benefit upon it. It would be lost if the annual membership dues were not paid. Mr. Pembroke and Mr. Harrington did not see any difference between the two kinds of payments. As Mr. Harrington put it the admission fees were paid, just as the annual membership dues were, to get the advantage of the club facilities for the advancement of the appellant's business and Mr. Pembroke considered that since they were not recoverable and no asset was acquired they were ordinary expenses of longer duration than the others. Moreover, although the admission fees were paid once and for all for the officers for whom they were paid they were recurring expenses so far as the appellant was concerned.

... The appeal herein must be allowed and the assessment referred back to the Minister for the necessary revision. The appellant is also entitled to costs.

Notes and Questions

1. The principle in *Royal Trust* continues to be of fundamental importance. However, the expenses at issue in that case would now be prohibited by paragraph 18(1)(l).
2. In *Royal Trust,* Thorson, P. says: "Indeed, it was plainly intended that it should be so, with the result that the gap, if it may be so described, between the kind of

an outlay or expense that is deductible according to ordinary principles of commercial trading and business practice and that which is deductible for income tax purposes is narrower now than it was under the former Act". Is there a "gap" between subsection 9(1) and paragraph 18(1)(a)? Can you think of an expense that would be deductible according to generally accepted accounting principles (GAAP) and subsection 9(1) but excluded because of paragraph 18(1)(a)?

3. For a more current statement of the relationship between "ordinary principles of commercial trading", GAAP and tax law principles, see *Canderel Ltd. v. The Queen*, [1998] 1 S.C.R. 147, [1998] 2 C.T.C. 35, 98 D.T.C. 6100 at paragraphs 31-35.

D. Personal or Living Expenses

Personal or living expenses are generally not deductible in computing income from a business or property. The deduction is prohibited by the general requirements in subsection 9(1) and paragraph 18(1)(a). In addition, paragraph 18(1)(h) specifically denies a deduction, with the exception for expenditures that are incurred by taxpayers while away from home in the course of carrying on business.

The list of expenses that are included in the definition of "personal or living expenses" in subsection 248(1) is not exhaustive and expenditures not listed there could be considered "personal or living expenses" for the purposes of paragraph 18(1)(h).

Despite the breadth and clarity of paragraph 18(1)(h), some expenses with personal elements are nonetheless deductible. From time to time, the case for recognizing as a deductible expense amounts that were previously disallowed as personal expenses is convincingly made and the Act is amended. In this respect, section 63 now authorizes a deduction for child care expenses and section 62 allows certain moving expenses. These expenses have not been characterized as "business expenses". Sections 62 and 63 are not in subdivision b of Division B of Part I of the Act. However, unlike some of the deductions authorized by subdivision e, sections 62 and 63 contain their own limitations which restrict the deduction of moving expenses and child care expenses by reference to income generated by the taxpayer's move or by the freedom from domestic duties. For a further discussion of subdivision e deductions, see Chapter 8.

The following sections consider various approaches to the characterization of an expense as a personal or living expense.

1. Variability of the Expense

THOMAS HARRY BENTON v. M.N.R.
(1952), 6 Tax A.B.C. 230, 52 D.T.C. 196

R.S.W. Fordham:

This appeal was dismissed at the conclusion of its hearing, at Calgary. It remains to state the reasons therefor.

Appellant is a farmer about sixty-two years of age and single, who operates a farm of some 480 acres. He manages to do so without any regularly-employed male help. He testified to being a semi-invalid, that he had had a slight stroke and undergone an abdominal operation for cancer. He said, too, that as a result, and due also to high blood pressure, he was subject to dizzy spells and must not be alone, but have someone near him in case further affliction overtook him. On this account and because of the milking, washing of milk utensils, general chores and work in and about the house that had to be done, he had a housekeeper, a Mrs. H.E. Reed, aged between sixty-five and sixty-seven, to whom he paid wages of $65 per month (which included board and lodging valued at $25), at $780.00 in 1949.

Appellant sought to deduct the last-mentioned sum as an expense of farm management or operation in reporting his taxable income for 1949. The Minister of National Revenue disallowed any such deduction in excess of $325.00, however, on the ground that wages paid to Mrs. Reed to the extent of $455 were personal or living expenses within the meaning of Section 12(1)(h) of the *Income Tax Act* [now 18(1)(h)] and, therefore, not deductible. As may be gathered, the Minister has considered the sum of $325 a sufficient proportion of the total amount paid, to allocate for farm work done that helped to earn the appellant's income during the year.

The evidence given satisfied me that Mrs. Reed was primarily a housekeeper engaged in the usual domestic duties performable on a farm and that her contribution to the income-earning work of the farm was necessarily of a secondary nature, however helpful it may have been to the appellant.

The appellant, who conducted his own case, stated it in a way that evoked some degree of sympathy. Nevertheless, nothing was advanced before me that appeared to warrant interference with the Minister's disposition of the matter, and the appeal must be dismissed accordingly.

Appeal dismissed.

LEDUC v. THE QUEEN

[2005] 1 C.T.C. 2858, 2005 D.T.C. 250 (T.C.C. [General Procedure])

Lamarre T.C.J.:

This is an appeal against an assessment made by the Minister of National Revenue ("Minister") under the Income Tax Act ("ITA") disallowing the deduction of legal expenses in the amount of $140,000 that were claimed by the appellant as a business expense in computing his income for his 2000 taxation year.

The facts which gave rise to the present appeal are partly summarized in the Admitted Statement of Facts jointly filed by the parties. Those facts read as follows:

The Appellant, a lawyer practicing in Cornwall, Ontario filed his 2000 income tax return and claimed $140,000 legal expenses as business expenses.

The Appellant paid $40,000 to the law firm of Edelson and Associates and $100,000 to the law firm of Skurka Pringle for defending him at a trial in the Superior Court of Ontario [2001 CarswellOnt 5013 (Ont. S.C.J.)] on an indictment charging six counts of sexual exploitation, one count of sexual interference and one count of offering sexual services for consideration. The indictment related to three complainants, one as young as 12 years old when the alleged sexual exploitation began. The charges arose following an O.P.P. [Ontario Provincial Police] criminal investigation of an alleged "pedophile ring" in the Cornwall area.

The Minister disallowed the deduction for legal expenses.

On July 24, 2003, the Ontario Court of Appeal reversed the Superior Court decision dated March 1, 2001 staying the indictment and ordered a new trial. A copy of the Court of Appeal decision is attached as Appendix "A" [*R. v. Leduc* (2003), 66 O.R. (3d) 1 (Ont. C.A.), leave to appeal refused (2004), (S.C.C.)]. An application for leave to appeal to the Supreme Court of Canada was dismissed without reasons on January 12, 2004. To the extent that they are relevant to this appeal, the parties admit the statement of facts found in the Court of Appeal decision.

In addition, the appellant testified. According to that testimony, he was called to the Ontario Bar in 1978 and is carrying on in the city of Cornwall a general law practice, which includes real estate, estates, and corporate and commercial work. He was charged in June and July 1998 with the above-mentioned criminal offences. In March 1999, the appellant received a letter from the Law Society of Upper Canada ("LSUC") (Exhibit A-1) that stated:

> The Law Society has been advised that you have been charged with the criminal offences of sexual assault, sexual interference, invitation to sexual touching, sexual exploitation by touching, sexual exploitation by invitation to touch and attempting to obtain the sexual services of a minor for a consideration.

> I understand that a preliminary hearing regarding some of these offences has been scheduled to begin on April 8, 1999 and your first court appearance on the new charges is also scheduled for April 8, 1999.
>
> A file has been opened in the Department of Audit & Investigation and I have been authorized to monitor this matter through the court proceedings.
>
> Would you please advise me if you have retained counsel in order that I may correspond with him or her? In the alternative, please advise me if you would prefer that I communicate directly with you?
>
> In the event that you are convicted of these charges or should there be a finding of guilt, this matter will be brought before a Proceedings Authorization Committee in order to determine whether or not an Application will be issued alleging that you have breached Section 33 of the Law Society Act by engaging in professional misconduct or conduct unbecoming a barrister and solicitor. Should the Law Society determine to pursue disciplinary action against you, I will report this matter to the Discipline Department by way of a counsel brief and document book.

The appellant testified that he understood from this letter that he was put on notice of the possible consequences of a conviction in relation to the criminal charges, as an eventual conviction could affect his standing as a member of the LSUC and his ability to practise law in the province of Ontario.

After receiving the letter from the LSUC, the appellant retained a criminal lawyer to defend himself against the criminal charges. The appellant said that at the time he had two things in mind. First, he wanted to prove that he was not guilty of the conduct alleged, and second, he knew that if he was to be found guilty on these criminal charges, it could terminate his professional life and his ability to earn income as the LSUC could then decide to revoke his licence to practise law.

To date there have been no proceedings started under section 33 of the Law Society Act, R.S.O. 1990, chapter L.8, as amended ("LSA"). As a matter of fact, the appellant's legal practice as a whole has continued to thrive and in 2003 it registered the highest gross income in its history. It should be pointed out, however, that at the time of the present hearing the trial on the merits with respect to the criminal charges had not yet taken place.

After several years of litigation regarding the criminal charges, the appellant has incurred significant legal expenses (the $140,000 at issue in the present appeal) in defending himself in procedural matters before the courts.

The appellant testified that he became the target of allegations related to the Project Truth investigation (of which mention is made in the decision of the Court of Appeal for Ontario referred to in the Admitted Statement of Facts) as a result of being involved as counsel in sexual misconduct cases. He believes that the charges against him arose out of some form of conspiracy.

...

The appellant submits that the legal expenses are deductible against his income earned from a business. That position is based on the argument that if he did not defend himself against the charges and was convicted, he would lose his licence to practise law. Although he admits that he was also motivated by an urge to prove his innocence and stay out of jail, he submits that his ancillary intention to preserve his ability to earn income is sufficient for the deduction to be allowed.

...

The Minister argues that pursuant to section 18 of the ITA the expenses are not deductible because they were not incurred "for the purpose of gaining or producing income from [a] business" and are personal in nature.

...

The calculation of income from a business is outlined in section 9 of the ITA. Income for a taxation year from a business is the profit from that business for the year. Under section 9, a taxpayer can deduct expenses that are incurred to earn that profit, subject to the limitations set out in the ITA. Paragraph 18(1)(a) contains the general limitation on deductible expenses. An expense is only deductible "to the extent that it was ... incurred by the taxpayer for the purpose of gaining or producing income from the business". This is further restricted by paragraph 18(1)(h), which disallows the deduction of "personal or living expenses of the taxpayer"...

... Thus, in order to be deductible as business expenses, the expenses in question must have been incurred "for the purpose of gaining or producing income from the business" within the meaning of paragraph 18(1)(a) of the ITA. The purpose of a particular expenditure is ultimately a question of fact to be decided with due regard for all the circumstances (*Symes, supra*, paragraph 68). Iacobucci J. referred to some factors to consider in answering such a question. Thus, it may be relevant to consider whether a deduction is ordinarily allowed as a business expense by accountants. That could indicate whether a particular kind of expenditure is widely accepted as a business expense (*Symes, supra*, paragraph 69). Similarly, it may be relevant to consider whether the expense is one normally incurred by others involved in the taxpayer's business (*Symes*, *supra*, paragraph 69). It may also be relevant to consider whether a particular expense would have been incurred if the taxpayer was not engaged in the pursuit of business income. If indeed such is the case, there is a strong inference that the expense has a personal purpose (*Symes*, *supra*, paragraph 70).

It may also be helpful to resort to a "business need" test. Would the need exist apart from the business? If a need exists even in the absence of business activity, then an expense incurred to meet the need would traditionally be viewed as a personal expense (*Symes*, *supra*, paragraph 73).

In this context, it is clear, in my view, that the legal expenses incurred by the appellant to defend himself in the criminal proceedings relating to the sexual assault charges laid against him are personal expenditures. They do not constitute expenses normally incurred by others involved in the appellant's profession. It can also be inferred from the evidence that if the appellant had not been engaged in his professional activities, he would nonetheless have paid the legal fees to defend himself before the courts against the criminal charges. These factors, analyzed in the context of the circumstances of this case, suggest that the legal expenses at issue cannot be classified as business expenses pursuant to section 9 and paragraphs 18(1)(a) and 18(1)(h) of the ITA.

The appellant argues, however, that his ability to carry on the law profession was imperilled by the criminal charges. Indeed, under the LSA, the LSUC has the authority to hold inquiries into such matters and the sanctions that can be imposed include the suspension or revocation of the licence to practise law*.

In the appellant's view, the legal expenses have a personal element but they were also essential and necessary to allow him to carry on his practice of law in the future. The appellant argues that for an expense to be deductible the intention to generate revenue through the incurring of the expense need not be the only motivation for incurring it. The appellant relied on the Supreme Court of Canada's decision in *Ludmer c. Ministre du Revenu national*, 1 C.T.C. 95, (sub nom. *Ludco Enterprises Ltd. v. The Queen*) 2001 D.T.C. 5505, (sub nom. *Ludco Enterprises Ltd. v. Canada*) [2001] 2 S.C.R. 1082 (S.C.C.), in submitting that if one of the appellant's purposes in incurring the legal expenses was to preserve his income–generating capability, this is sufficient for those expenses to be deductible under section 9 of the ITA. In his view, the fact that there is an element of personal motivation in an expense does not result automatically in that expense not being deductible. In *Ludco*, supra, it was decided that an ancillary purpose to earn income was sufficient to meet the purpose test for interest deductibility.

I cannot accept the appellant's argument. First, we saw earlier that the legal expenses at issue are, in the particular circumstances of this case, personal expenses. Indeed, in the absence of evidence to the contrary, it would appear that, had he not practised law, the appellant would nonetheless still have incurred the legal expenses to defend himself before the courts against the criminal charges. Therefore, those expenses are not deductible pursuant to paragraph 18(1)(h) of the ITA. The purpose test analysed in *Ludco*, *supra*, is of no application under paragraph 18(1)(h).

Second, I am not even convinced that one purpose of incurring these legal expenses was to earn income. In *Ludco, supra*, the Supreme Court of Canada established that the requisite test to determine purpose for interest deductibility under subparagraph 20(1)(c)(i) is whether the taxpayer had a reasonable expectation of income at the time the investment was made. If, as suggested by counsel for the appellant, this test should be applicable in the determination of the purpose of an expenditure, I do not find that the legal expenses at issue meet the test. Indeed, the appellant testified that during the period when the legal expenses were incurred his earning capacity from the law profession was not affected at all. On the contrary, his legal practice has continued to thrive. There was no need to incur the legal expenses in order to have an expectation of income, as income was already flowing from the appellant's legal practice.

Furthermore, the appellant's earning capacity was not, in my view, in jeopardy at the time the legal expenses were incurred. The appellant himself acknowledged that the LSUC had not commenced any investigation. He recognized that there was no certainty as to the implications of an LSUC investigation in the event that he is found guilty in the criminal proceedings. Indeed, according to Exhibit A-1, if he is found guilty, the matter will be brought before a Proceedings Authorization Committee in order to determine whether or not an application will be issued alleging that he has breached section 33 of the LSA. Then, should the LSUC determine to pursue disciplinary action against the appellant, the matter will be reported to the Discipline Department. The sanctions available in the event of disciplinary action are listed in subsection 35(1) of the LSA and do not necessarily entail the revocation of a member's membership in the LSUC or the member's being disbarred and having his name struck off the roll of solicitors. Instead, for example, there could be an order that the member obtain treatment or counselling. There are as well other forms of sanctions which may not affect a member's capacity to earn income from his legal practice. The fact that an eventual conviction could possibly affect the appellant's practice in the future is, in my view, purely hypothetical and speculative at this stage and, in any event, too remote to justify the deduction of the legal expenses in the taxation year at issue pursuant to paragraph 18(1)(a) of the ITA.

This case is distinguishable from this Court's decisions in *Vango v. The Queen*, (sub nom. *Vango v. Canada*) [1995] 2 C.T.C. 2757 (T.C.C.) and *Mercille v. The Queen*, [2000] 2 C.T.C. 2434, 2000 D.T.C. 1915 (T.C.C. [General Procedure]), referred to by counsel for the appellant. In those cases, the charges faced by the taxpayers were directly related to their work, as an investment advisor in one case and as a stockbroker in the other. The charges with respect to which they incurred the legal fees were directly related to their functions. In *Vango* , the taxpayer was directly faced with the loss of his licence. It was decided in both cases that the legal fees were deductible as employment expenses pursuant to section 8 of the ITA. In the present case, the criminal offences with which the appellant is charged have nothing to do with his legal practice. The legal expenses paid to defend himself against several sexual offence charges did not arise out of his law practice. The acts regarding which a defence is being mounted do not relate to his business.

As Judge Rip stated in *Thiele Drywall Inc. v. The Queen*, [1996] 3 C.T.C. 2208 (T.C.C.), referred to by counsel for the respondent, at paragraphs 19, 20, 23 and 24:

> 19 The question for me to decide, then, is whether the appellant's evasion to comply with the Act was a normal or ordinary incident of carrying on its business. If so, the legal costs of defending the action, whether the appellant was guilty or not, is deductible; if not, then the costs are not deductible. In my view they are not.
>
> 20 Where the courts have allowed appeals to permit the taxpayers to deduct legal expenses, the expenses were incurred in accordance with sound accounting and commercial practices and were incurred to defend the taxpayers' trade practices in the conduct of their businesses and to preserve the systems that helped produce their incomes: *Caulk*, supra, and *Rolland Paper*, supra. The legal expenses in *Heininger*, supra, also related to a taxpayer's way of doing business ...
>
> ...
>
> For expenses to be deductible, the *Caulk* and *Rolland Paper* cases, supra, require the activities in which expenses were incurred be carried on in the normal course of the taxpayer's income earning operations.
>
> 24 As I wrote in *Matthews*, supra, at p. 1268:
>
> Where a business carries out activities in the normal course of its operations, and the cost of those activities is deductible in computing the income of the business, any expense incurred to defend those activities is a direct result of the activities themselves and is permitted by paragraph 18(1)(a) to be deducted: vide The *Queen v. Phyllis B. Bronfman Trust*, (supra). The legal expenses in the case at bar were incurred to defend a prosecution against the appellant which arose directly from the practice of preparing financial statements in the normal course of business.

One may conclude from the above-cited case law that if the activities that led to the charges were carried on in the normal course of the income-earning operations, then an expense incurred to defend those activities is a direct result of the activities themselves, and hence may be deductible under paragraph 18(1)(a) of the ITA. Consequently, it is the activity that resulted in the charges and its connection to the business that determine the deductibility of the legal expenses associated with the defence.

Furthermore, counsel for the appellant relied on another decision of the Supreme Court of Canada, *65302 British Columbia Ltd. v. The Queen*, [1999] 3 S.C.R. 804, 99 D.T.C. 5799, [2000] 1 C.T.C. 57 (S.C.C.), in arguing that public policy considerations should not dictate that a particular expense ought not to be deductible. Indeed, in *65302 British Columbia Ltd.* it was held that, absent a specific provision to the contrary, the fines or penalties ought to be deductible if they were incurred for the purpose of generating income.

The present case is not like the situation *in 65302 British Columbia Ltd., supra*, referred to by the appellant, where the taxpayer wanted to deduct the payment of levies that were incurred as part of its day-to-day operations and where the decision to produce over quota was a business decision made in order to earn income.

In the present case, the charges did not arise in the course of the appellant's business. In his testimony, the appellant suggested that they arose because of his role as the lawyer for several Catholic priests and the local Catholic diocese. In his capacity as a lawyer he helped reach a settlement regarding a priest's "sexual misconduct". Indeed, his name became highly publicized as the lawyer for the Church. The appellant suggested that his role led to a "conspiracy" to elicit testimony against him.

The appellant's allegations at this stage are pure speculation. There is no evidence as such of any conspiracy. The test as outlined in the case law allows the deduction of legal expenses when the activity that led to charges is shown to be a normal part of the production of income. This is clearly not the case here.

I therefore conclude that the legal expenses at issue were not paid in order to produce income from a business. Those expenses were personal in nature and not deductible in the computation of income.

The appeal is dismissed with costs.

Appeal dismissed.

Notes and Questions

1. If Mr. Benton had done his own housekeeping and had hired a farm labourer to do the farm work, would the labourer's wages have been a deductible business expense? If so, is the characterization of the housekeeping expense somewhat formalistic? What characterization test does the court in *Benton* appear to suggest?
2. Was the taxpayer's characterization of the legal expenses in *Leduc* premised on a "but for" test? Did Lamarre, (T.C.J.) reject the application of a "but for" test as

the basis for characterization of the legal expenses as income earning, or did she simply reject the "but for" proposition implicit in the taxpayer's position?

2. Child Care Expenses

Taxpayers often incur child care expenses while away from home earning income. They — in this case predominantly female taxpayers — have frequently attempted to deduct these expenses as incurred for the purpose of earning income without success. The following is the leading Canadian case on this issue.

SYMES v. THE QUEEN
(1993), [1994] 1 C.T.C. 40, 94 D.T.C. 6001 (S.C.C.)

[The taxpayer was a partner in a large Toronto law firm. She hired a full-time nanny to care for her children and deducted the amount as a business expense. The nanny paid tax on her wages and the taxpayer made C.P.P. and U.I. contributions on the nanny's behalf. The Minister disallowed the deduction on the ground that the nanny's wages were not outlays or expenses incurred for the purpose of gaining or producing income from business, but were personal or living expenses. The taxpayer appealed. The taxpayer argued that the nanny's salary was a legitimate business expense deductible in determining her income from business under subsection 9(1) and the existence of a specific deduction under section 63 did not affect her right to deduct the entire amount as an expense incurred for the purpose of earning income from business. The taxpayer further argued that the denial of a deduction for child care expenses in determining business profits constituted a violation of section 15 of the Charter. The extracts below are limited primarily to the issue of whether child care expenses are deductible business expenses.

By a 7-2 majority, split by gender, the Supreme Court of Canada dismissed the taxpayer's appeal. Not surprisingly, this gender split has generated considerable comment.

Iacobucci, J. wrote the decision of the majority. He began with an analysis of the relevant provisions of the Income Tax Act. *He indicated that the determination of profit was a question of law, to be determined in accordance with "well accepted principles of business (or accounting) practice" or "well accepted principles of commercial trading". He indicated that although child care expenses were traditionally viewed as personal expenses that were not deductible under paragraph 18(1)(h), that was not a sufficient reason to prohibit their deduction today. Iacobucci, J. then considered the impact of paragraph 18(1)(a).]*

Iacobucci J.

... First, it is clear on the facts that the appellant would not have incurred child care expenses except for her business. ...

Second, however, it is equally clear that the need which is met by child care expenses on the facts of this case, namely, the care of the appellant's children, exists regardless of the appellant's business activity. The expenses were incurred to make her available to practice her profession rather than for any other purpose associated with the business itself.

Third, I note that there is no evidence to suggest that child care expenses are considered business expenses by accountants. There is, however, considerable reason to believe that many parents, and particularly many women, confront child care expenses in order to work. ... This demographic picture may increase the likelihood that child care expenses are a form of business expense.

Finally, as a fourth point of analysis, I am uncomfortable with the suggestion that the appellant's decision to have children should be viewed solely as a consumption choice. I frankly admit that there is an element of public policy which feeds my discomfort. In *Brooks v. Canada Safeway Ltd.*, [1989] 1 S.C.R. 1219, Dickson C.J. stated (at p. 1243):

> That those who bear children and benefit society as a whole thereby should not be economically or socially disadvantaged seems to bespeak the obvious. It is only women who bear children; no man can become pregnant. ... it is unfair to impose all of the costs of pregnancy upon one half of the population.
>
> ...

The factors so far analyzed suggest that, considering only ss. 9, 18(1)(a) and 18(1)(h), arguments can be made for and against the classification of the appellant's child care expenses as business expenses. ...

I am aware that if I were compelled to reach a conclusion with respect to the proper classification of child care expenses with reference to only ss. 9, 18(1)(a) and 18(1)(h) of the *Income Tax Act,* such a conclusion would involve competing policy considerations. ... to the extent that traditional income tax law would classify child care expenses as "personal" simply because such expenses are incurred in order to make the taxpayer "available" to the business — and in the absence of s. 63 — it might be correct to assert that the changing composition of the business class and changing social structure demand a reconceptualization.

However, I find it unnecessary to determine whether reconceptualization is appropriate having regard to the presence of s. 63 in the *Income Tax Act.* Section 63 cannot be lightly disregarded...

L'Heureux-Dubé J. (dissenting) ...

I do not agree with my colleague Iacobucci J.'s reasons with regard to s. 63 of the Act, nor to s. 15 of the Charter and the eventual result he reaches.

I do, however, substantially agree with the approach he has taken with regard to the definition of "business expense" through ss. 9(1), 18(1)(a) and (h) of the Act ... In my view, the logical conclusion to my colleague's analysis, although he does not state it as such, is that ss. 9, 18(1)(a) and 18(1)(h) do not prevent the deduction of child care expenses as a business expense. My analysis, therefore, will focus primarily on the clear differences between our two positions, specifically with respect to s. 63 of the Act.

... What, in my view, has traditionally been recognized as a "commercial need", has everything to do with those persons who have traditionally held positions in the commercial sphere — primarily men. Further, a review of the developments in income tax legislation and its interpretation clearly demonstrates that, as the needs of those pursuing business have changed, the definition of what constitutes a business expense has similarly expanded. ...

When we look at the case law concerning the interpretation of "business expense", it is clear that this area of law is premised on the traditional view of business as a male enterprise and that the concept of a business expense has itself been constructed on the basis of the needs of business men. ... one must ask whether the many business deductions available, for cars, for club dues and fees, for lavish entertainment and the wining and dining of clients and customers, and for substantial charitable donations, are so obviously business expenses rather than personal ones. Although potentially personal, each one of these expenses has been accepted as a legitimate business expense and, as each reflects a real cost incurred by certain kinds of business people to produce income from business, a deduction has been allowed. The real costs incurred by business women with children are no less real, no less worthy of consideration and no less incurred in order to gain or produce income from business. ...

In conclusion to the question of whether child care expenses are precluded from being deducted as a business expense under s. 9(1) by the interplay of either s.18(1)(a) or s.18(1)(h) of the Act, I answer that child care may be held to be a business expense deductible pursuant to ss. 9(1), 18(1)(a) and (h) of the Act, all other criteria being respected.

[Lamer C.J.C., La Forest, Sopinka, Gonthier, Cory and Major JJ. concurred with Iacobucci J.; McLachlin J. concurred with L'Heureux-Dubé J.]

Notes and Questions

1. The *Symes* decision does not preclude child care expenses from being characterized as business expenses. Because of section 63, Iacobucci, J. found it unnecessary to decide the characterization issue. See the extended excerpts from *Symes*, and discussion of policy issues with respect to child care expense deductions in Chapter 8.
2. Perhaps more so than any other area of tax law, a gender element permeates the analysis of the deductibility of child care expenses. See generally, Rebecca Johnson, *Taxing Choices: The Intersection of Class, Gender, Parenthood and the Law* (Vancouver: UBC Press, 2002).
3. If child care expenses were deductible business expenses, what about the characterization of other personal expenses that enable taxpayers to engage in income-earning activities?

3. Food and Beverages

Traditionally, the personal consumption of food and beverages has always fallen within the confines of paragraph 18(1)(h) as personal and living expenses for the obvious reason that we all need food and water to survive, regardless of our business. In the following case, however, food and beverage expenses were held to be deductible business expenses.

SCOTT v. M.N.R.
[1998] 4 C.T.C. 103, 98 D.T.C. 6530 (F.C.A.)

McDonald J.A.: (Strayer and Robertson JJ.A. concurring)

The issue to be addressed in this application for judicial review is whether the provisions of the *Income Tax Act* (the Act) governing business expense deductions should be interpreted in a manner that responds to Canada's changing business environment. Specifically, this Court must determine whether a 'foot and transit courier' travelling 150 kms a day throughout the Toronto area and carrying a backpack weighing between 20-50 pounds can deduct as a business expense a modest amount for extra food and water. The Tax Court Judge was of the view that the Act precluded the applicant's food and beverage expenses from being deducted as they are of a personal nature. Paragraph 18(1)(h) of the Act specifically excludes personal and living expenses from being deducted.

The facts of this case are straightforward. During the years under review the applicant was a self-employed foot and public transit courier. He states that his typical working day would begin at 6:45 a.m. when he was advised via a dispatcher of the packages that were waiting to be delivered that day. From

7:45 a.m. to approximately 9:30 a.m. he picked up and dropped off packages on foot in the downtown Toronto core. At 9:30 a.m. he would travel by subway to make deliveries. He travelled north on the subway line picking up and dropping off packages en route. Between subway stations he would travel between buildings on foot. He would continue to make deliveries in this manner until 6:00 p.m.

According to the applicant, he would cover approximately 150 km on foot and by public transportation every day. He regularly worked ten hours per day, five days per week, fifty-two weeks per year. His courier company considered him an independent contractor. He did not receive vacation pay and was not paid for any break or meal times. The applicant claims to have been paid on a commission basis, receiving a percentage of the amount the client paid for its courier services. According to the applicant, the typical cost of delivering a package is based upon its weight, the speed with which it must be delivered and the distance it is being transported. The further the package must go, the more the client pays and the more money the applicant receives for its delivery. In order to make his job financially viable, he must deliver as many packages as possible, as quickly as possible.

The applicant claims that this type of employment requires him to consume what essentially amounts to an extra meal per day. At the tax court he sought to deduct $8.00 of what he terms extra food and $3.00 for extra bottled water and juice. It is important to stress that the above figures represent amounts over and above what the average individual would need to consume on a daily basis. The applicant is not asking this Court to approve a deduction for all food and beverages consumed but only a reasonable amount for the extra food and water his body requires as fuel for his job.

Pursuant to subsection 9(1) of the Act, a taxpayer is required to declare as income profit from a business or property. In calculating one's profit the Act allows for certain business deductions. Other deductions are specifically disallowed. Paragraph 18(1)(a) prohibits a deduction for an outlay or expense "except to the extent that it was made or incurred by the taxpayer for the purpose of gaining or producing income from the business or property." Paragraph 18(1)(h) prohibits the deduction of personal or living expenses. In order to determine whether an expense qualifies as a reasonable business expense or whether it is a personal and living expense the following questions are helpful: (1) what is the need that the expense meets? (2) would the need exist apart from the business? and (3) is the need intrinsic to the business? (See Krishna, The Fundamentals of Canadian Income Tax (5th ed) (Carswell: Scarborough, 1995) at 368). According to Iacobucci J. in *Symes v R.* (1993), [1994] 1 C.T.C. 40 (S.C.C.) at 60:

> If a need exists even in the absence of business activity, and irrespective of whether the need was or might have been satisfied by an expenditure to a third party or by the opportunity cost of personal labour, then an expense to meet the need would traditionally be viewed as a personal expense. Expenses which can be identified in this way are expenses which are incurred by a taxpayer in order to relieve the taxpayer from personal duties and to make the taxpayer available to the business are not considered business expenses since the taxpayer is expected to be available to the business as a quid pro quo for business income recovered.

Traditionally, food and beverages have always fallen within the confines of paragraph 18(1)(h) for the valid reason that we all need food and water to survive, regardless of our business. Applying Professor Krishna's analysis, the rationale for not allowing food and beverages to be deducted as business expenses is as follows: the human need for food and water exists apart from the business. It is not a need that is intrinsic to the business. While appropriate meals may make one available for business or better able to perform at one's business, the need to satisfy thirst and hunger exists independently from the business. Parenthetically I note that the Act allows business persons to deduct up to 50% of their food and beverage expenditures for meals of a business nature [section 67.1]. While presumably these individuals require food regardless of their business needs, the Act specifically allows for this deduction. Similarly, if the applicant worked in a business office which provided water coolers for its employees would not the employer be able to deduct the cost of those coolers as a business expense? Having said this, it is not necessary to consider these allowable business deductions further because my analysis of this case does not turn on them. I simply note them in passing.

Thus, because an expense has been considered personal in the past does not mean that it necessarily follows that it should be classified as personal today. Justice is not served by remaining wedded to concepts which are outdated and in need of change in order to respond to the ever changing framework of our society. As Iacobucci J. stated in *Symes supra* when faced with the argument that the child care expense deduction should be disallowed because it has traditionally been classified as an expense that is personal in nature (at 54):

> This appeal presents a particular expense which has been traditionally characterized as personal in nature. If, in coming to a decision, this Court stated that since such expenses have always been personal they must now be personal, the conclusion could be easily and deservedly attacked. For this reason, proper analysis of this question demands that the relationship between child care expenses and business income be examined more critically, in order to determine whether that relationship can be sufficient to justify the former's

> deductibility. This proposition, in my opinion, leads naturally to paragraph 18(1)(a), which sets out the relationship required by the Income Tax Act.

Iacobucci J. went on to state that:

> In turning to paragraph 18(1)(a), however, I must take pains not to eviscerate needlessly paragraph 18(1)(h) and its related jurisprudence, when faced with a particular expense, and it may be both proper and expedient to refer to past decisions which have characterized the expense as 'personal' within 18(1)(h), such that an extensive analytical approach invoking the words of paragraph 18(1)(a) may not be required. On the facts of this case, paragraph 18(1)(a) may be of greater assistance than the simple prohibition against deducting 'personal expenses' in paragraph 18(1)(h), as I re-examine whether child care expenses truly constitute personal expenses. However, not every expense which has been traditionally characterized as a personal expense will deserve a similar re-examination.

The Minister urges this Court to rely on the latter part of this quotation as well as past jurisprudence that establishes quite correctly that food and beverages are personal expenses. However, the facts of this case are such that a re-examination of the prohibition on this deduction is necessary. Indeed, the reasoning of Iacobucci J. in *Symes* at page 55 is applicable to the case at hand:

> The decision to characterize child care expenses [in this case, food and beverage] as personal expenses was made by judges. As part of our case law, it is susceptible to re-examination in an appropriate case. In *Saluturo v The Queen* [cite omitted] this Court had occasion to state the following:
>
>> Judges can and should adopt the common law to reflect the changing social, moral and economic fabric of the country. Judges should not be quick to perpetuate rules whose social foundation has long since disappeared. Nonetheless, there are significant constraints on the power of the judiciary to change the law. ... The judiciary should confine itself to those incremental changes which are necessary to keep the common law in step with the dynamic and evolving fabric of our society.

I would also note that unlike in *Symes supra* where the Supreme Court analyzed the deductibility of child care expenses generally, this Court is not reconsidering the prohibition on the deduction of the broad category food and beverage expenditures. Instead, it is considering the more limited issue of whether the extra food and beverages consumed by a courier can be deducted when a corresponding deduction in the form of fuel is allowed for couriers using automobiles.

This case would be different from that of an individual who chooses to eat more or more expensive food products which is clearly a personal preference or choice. In this case, the extra food would not have been consumed because the applicant wishes to eat more on a given day. The extra food would be required to enable the applicant to get from point A to point B. He would not be choosing to eat and drink more — he would have to. Just as a courier's automobile requires fuel in the form of gas to move, the applicant alleges that he requires fuel in the form of food and water. The foot and transit courier and the automobile courier are engaged in identical activities the only difference being one uses a car as a means of transport and the other his body or a bicycle. Because the courier who drives the automobile is allowed to deduct his or her fuel, the foot and transit courier should be able to deduct the fuel his body needs. However, because we all require food and water to live, he can only deduct the extra food and water he must consume above and beyond the average person's intake in order to perform his job. This is similar to the automobile courier who is only entitled to deduct that portion of the fuel used for a business purpose. The extra fuel consumed for personal needs cannot be deducted. This result takes into account the different methods by which the same job is done and puts all couriers on an equal footing. Arguably, it also recognizes and encourages [rather than discourages as a prohibition on this expense would] new environmentally responsible ways of producing income.

The concern with this decision is that by moving away from a bright line rule prohibiting the deduction of food and beverage expenses I have opened the floodgates to a myriad of claims for deductions for personal expenses. I would note that the floodgates argument is always referred to when seeking to preserve the status quo. However, in this context, I do not find these concerns valid as the analogy between fuel for an automobile and fuel for the human body provides an appropriate line for the courts to draw. Only where there is a corresponding business deduction allowed for fuel in the form of gasoline for the same type of business will a deduction for the extra food and water a human needs to consume as its fuel be allowed. For instance, a rickshaw driver would be entitled to deduct the extra food and drink he needs to consume to do his job because his corresponding compatriot — the taxi driver — is entitled to a deduction for his gasoline. A construction worker, however, who engages in physically demanding work would not be entitled to deduct his food and beverage expenses despite the fact that his job may require him to eat and drink more because there is no corresponding position where fuel in the form of gasoline would be entitled to a deduction under the Act. Thus, this decision provides a narrow exception for the deduction of food and beverages as business expenses under the Act and should in no way be interpreted as providing a basis to challenge all traditional prohibitions on the deduction of food and beverages as a business expense under the Act.

In light of the above conclusion, the matter must be referred back to the Tax Court Judge for determination of two factual issues not addressed by him because of the position taken on the preliminary legal question: that is as to the deductibility of the expense. Specifically, it was unnecessary to determine whether in fact the taxpayer required extra amounts of food and beverages because of the nature of his business as a "foot and transit courier". Thus, it is open to ask whether there is persuasive evidence to support the allegation that the needs of the taxpayer are, for example, greater than those of a construction worker. As well, if the taxpayer is able to establish what he is alleging then the Tax Court Judge must fix an amount which represents a reasonable deduction. I have doubts as to whether Perrier is necessary in lieu of tap water or commercially bottled water.

For the above reasons I would allow the application for judicial review, set aside the judgment of the Tax Court dated August 6, 1997, and remit the matter to the Tax Court Judge for a determination with respect to the factual issues which remain outstanding.

Notes and Questions

1. Do you agree with the statement in *Scott* that "this decision provides a narrow exception for the deduction of food and beverages as business expenses under the Act and should in no way be interpreted as providing a basis to challenge all traditional prohibitions on the deduction of food and beverages as a business expense under the Act"?
2. To what extent does the reasoning in *Scott* extend *Symes* on the characterization of expenses as business expenses? Was L'Heureux-Dubé in *Symes* correct in suggesting that club dues and fees, lavish entertainment and the wining and dining of clients were fully deductible business expenses?
3. Given that responsibility for child care is traditionally, and continues to be, borne primarily by women, are there any policy reasons for distinguishing between child care and food and beverage expenses?

4. Commuting Expenses

Expenses incurred by taxpayers to travel between home and the work location are generally considered to be personal or living expenses. In effect, the choice where to live is considered a personal consumption decision. On the other hand, travel expenses are a routine cost of doing business and will commonly be unquestioned as deductions for tax purposes, even though there is sometimes a personal element. When a doctor maintains a home office and finds it necessary to travel between that office and a hospital, which is the primary work location, it is not surprising that the revenue authorities will be skeptical about the real purpose of the travel when it involves 12 or 15 trips a day. Is the doctor traveling in the course of a professional practice or simply, as a matter of personal convenience, going home whenever he or she is not busy at the hospital?

CUMMING v. M.N.R.
[1967] C.T.C. 462, 67 D.T.C. 5312 (Exch. Ct.)

Thurlow J.:

The issue in these appeals, which are from re-assessments of income tax for the years 1962 and 1963 respectively, is the extent of the deductions to which the appellant is entitled, in computing his income, for the expenses of operating an automobile and for allowances in respect of its capital cost.

The appellant is a physician and is engaged in practising exclusively in his specialty as an anaesthetist. He holds what is referred to as an appointment to the staff of the Ottawa Civic Hospital and it is there that he renders all of his services to his patients. But there are no emoluments paid to him by the hospital. His income receipts from his practice consist of the amounts which the patients pay him for his services. The billing of these patients and most of what may be classed as the administrative work involved in securing payment for his services is done at his home, which is located about half a mile from the hospital. In both years the appellant used an automobile for the purpose of travelling between his home and the hospital and the principal dispute in the appeals turns on the question whether expenses incurred in maintaining and operating the automobile for this purpose are properly deductible in computing his income from his practice. The Minister's position is that the expenses of ordinary travelling between these points at the beginning and end of the day's scheduled work at the hospital and of travelling between them in response to a call at a time when the appellant happens to be at his home (as opposed to travelling to the hospital on receipt of a call when actually engaged in working on his records at home) are not "incurred for the purpose of gaining or producing income" from the appellant's business within the meaning of the exception to Section 12(1)(a) of the *Income Tax Act* [now 18(1)(a)] but are "personal or living expenses" the deduction of which is prohibited by Section 12(1)(h) [now 18(1)(h)] of the Act. There is also an issue of fact to be determined as to the extent to which the expenses incurred and the use made of the automobile in the years in question were referable to travelling concerned with the appellant's practice as opposed to travelling for purposes in no way referable to it. ...

The appellant's routine was to go to the hospital at about 6:30 each evening to obtain the schedule of operations for the following day and to visit in their rooms the patients to whom he was scheduled to administer anaesthetic the following day and patients to whom he had administered anaesthetic the previous day. This usually took him until about 8:00 o'clock when he would return to his home. The following morning he would return to the hospital in time for the first scheduled operation at which he was to serve and he would remain there until his schedule for the day was completed unless there was a gap in his schedule or cancellations should occur leaving him time to go home to work on his records or to study. If a gap was not long enough to make it worthwhile to go home he might use the time in visiting patients to whom he had administered anaesthetic on the previous day. The schedule for the day was normally completed by 4:00 o'clock in the afternoon when he would again return to his home. Some days there would be no opportunities to go home before the schedule was completed while on others there might be several.

Emergency work was, of course, unscheduled and was in addition to the routine of scheduled or "elective" work. In emergency cases the call for his services might come at any time of the day or night and whether on weekends or other days. It might occur when he was at home or when he was elsewhere whether for social or business reasons. In such cases he was expected to go to the hospital with all necessary dispatch. When he was on emergency call duty, if not already at the hospital in connection with other cases, he was usually at his home and it is there that he was called.

When going to the hospital the appellant carried a booklet in which he would make notes of the names and locations in the hospital of patients that he was to attend and he also carried a supply of cards on each of which, whenever an opportunity to do so occurred, he would enter the name of a patient, his address, next of kin, age, telephone number, location in the hospital, date of operation, surgeon's name, the operation performed, and the time of day, the anaesthetic administered, information as to any insurance coverage which the patient might have and possibly other details concerning the particular patient. From the information on these cards, the appellant would later prepare and send out a bill to the patient for his services. The amount of the fees charged would also be entered on the card and subsequent payments would be recorded on it as well. The work of completing the entries of charges on the cards, making up the bills, preparing insurance claim forms, corresponding with insurance companies, receiving and making entries with respect to payments, preparing and sending out receipts and follow-up bills both for unpaid accounts and for balances not paid by the insurer, the making up of bank deposits, the paying of bills or expenses and the keeping of records of receipts and expenditures, was all done at his home, by the appellant himself and his wife.

The appellant's home was built to serve his needs and to his specifications. In an area of the building designated on its plan as a den, there was a built-in secretary where the appellant kept his business records and stationery, text books and periodicals and other office equipment and it was there that the work of maintaining the records, sending out accounts, and other office work was done. This was also the part of his home where the appellant's professional study and writing were done. His wife estimated that he works about 12 hours a week on his accounts and that she also works about 12 hours a week attending to opening the mail, posting payments, preparing and sending out receipts and follow-up bills, telephone calls to patients who have not paid their accounts and other details.

When patients call at the house, whether to pay bills or to have insurance forms completed, which is not encouraged and is infrequent, they are received in this room but they are not treated there. The room is also said to be out of bounds to the appellant's children.

This was the appellant's system during 1962, the first of the taxation years in question. In 1963 there was a difference in the original billing and collection phases of the operation. During that year the appellant submitted the necessary information to DARMCO Limited, a company organized to render and collect physicians' accounts, which thereupon billed the patients on the appellant's behalf, collected the payments and accounted to the appellant for them. When DARMCO Limited was unable to collect an account it was returned to the appellant who thereafter took steps to collect it by re-billing the patient, telephoning him and if necessary putting the account into the hands of a collection agency. In other respects the operation was carried out in the same way in both years in question.

In both years the appellant maintained two automobiles, one of which, a Vauxhall, was used generally by his wife and by him only when the other was undergoing repairs or when for some reason it was convenient for him to use it. The expenses of operating this car do not enter into the problem. The other car, a 1961 Chevrolet station wagon, was used by the appellant in travelling to and from the hospital, to the bank or to the DARMCO office or elsewhere in connection with his practice and to some extent as well, for purposes not connected with his practice. The appellant considered it to be mandatory for him to have a car available for his use when required to go to the hospital in response to emergency calls and he also said that apart from this without a car the carrying on of his practice would be more complicated and his office work would pile up. There is evidence that the other anaesthetists practising in Ottawa also used automobiles to travel to and from the hospital and that the expenses of operating an automobile for that purpose were regarded as being properly deductible for the purpose of computing profit from the practice on commercial accounting principles. ...

It appears to have become established in England, as well as in Rhodesia and in some other parts of the Commonwealth, that where a professional man lives at a distance from the office or chambers where he carries on his practice the expenses of travelling between his home and his office or chambers are not to be regarded as having been incurred "wholly and exclusively" for the purposes of his practice but on the contrary are personal or living expenses, even though he may do at his home a considerable portion of the work by which his income is earned. ...

... [T]he Minister's contention was that the base of the appellant's operation was the hospital, where the appellant rendered the services for which he was paid. It was, however, admitted in the course of argument that the appellant conducted part of his practice at his home, that the nature of the business was such that the bookkeeping and financial activities had to be carried on at a location different from that where the patients were treated and that there were no office facilities available to him at the hospital where he might have carried out this part of his business.

While I think it might be said in a particular sense that the appellant exercised his profession at the hospital, as I see it, he had no base of his practice there. His services were not performed in any one place in the hospital but in the numerous areas in which anaesthetics were administered, in the recovery rooms, in the areas where resuscitation procedures were carried out and in the various patients' rooms. The appellant had no space there but a locker that he could call his own. There was a cot in the office of the department of anaesthesia where he might go for a nap if he wished and time permitted between cases. There was also a library where he might study and a lounge where he could sit when not engaged with a patient. But these were not his nor were they for his use alone. They were for the use of all the anaesthetists. Nor had he an office or even a desk there to which he could repair to do the administrative work of his practice when he was not immediately engaged with a patient. The operations booking office was also a place to which he might go for some purposes such as to get a copy of the schedule of operations for the next day but I do not regard any of these places or the aggregation of them as having been any more in the nature of a base for his operation of practising his profession than any other room which he may have visited for a purpose associated with the carrying out of his professional activity. And if the whole hospital were to be considered his base I fail to see why the area consisting of the whole hospital plus his house and the distance between them could not just as readily be said to be the base of his practice. As I view the matter the appellant had no more of a base for his professional business at the hospital than a barrister can be said to have at a court house where he attends frequently as required and in the course of a day may have occasion to be engaged in one or more court rooms on one or more cases and incidentally to spend some time in the barristers' robing room and possibly in the court registry office as well. In my view therefore there is no basis for holding that the base of the appellant's practice within the reasoning of *Newsom v. Robertson* was at the Ottawa Civic Hospital.

In my opinion the base of the appellant's practice, if there was any one place that could be called its base, was his home. This was the place from which he was called when required and whence he set forth to serve patients, whether by scheduled appointment or in emergencies. It was the place where the records of his practice were kept, where he worked on them and where his studying for particular cases and for the purpose of keeping up with developments in his specialty was done. It was the place to which he returned during the day whenever the time available was long enough to enable him to make the trip and do some work of the kind which he did there. Indeed, though in fact he went nearly every day, he had no occasion to go to the hospital at all in connection with his practice except when there was some service to be rendered to a patient there. And when he had no work to do there he had no place of his own or base of his practice to repair to but his home where the administrative side of his practice was carried out.

It seems to me that if the appellant had not found it convenient to carry out at his home that part of the work of his practice in fact done there and had maintained an office for the purpose, whether near to or at some distance from the hospital, there could have been little doubt that such office was the base of his practice and that both the reasonable expense of maintaining it and the expense of travelling between it and the hospital would have been expense of his business. The result is, I think, the same where the office, such as it was, was at his home and the work was done there. In the present case it seems to me to be the only single place which could be regarded as the base from which his professional operation was carried on. The case is thus not like that of the barrister travelling from his home to his professional chambers-which, in *Newsom v. Robertson* was the base of his operation-but resembles more closely that of the same barrister's travelling between his chambers and the courts, the expense of which, had it involved expense, would, I apprehend, not have been regarded as personal or living expense and would, I also think, have been allowable as a deduction even under the stringent prohibition of the English statute. As I view the matter therefore *Newsom v. Robertson* affords no guide for the determination of the present case and it seems to me to be necessary to reach a conclusion by applying the words of Section 12(1)(a) and (h) of the Act without assistance from the jurisprudence of other countries.

In my view, since the appellant could not possibly live in or over the hospital so as to incur no expense whatever in getting to and from it when required and since he could not even carry out at the hospital all the activities of his practice necessary to gain or produce his income therefrom, it was necessary for the successful carrying on of the practice itself that he have a location of some sort somewhere off the hospital premises. This necessity of itself carried the implication that travel by him between the two points would be required. Where, as here, the location off the hospital premises was as close thereto as it might reasonably be expected to be from the point of view of his being available promptly when called as well as from the point of view of economizing on the expense of travelling between the two points it is, I think, unrealistic and a straining of the ordinary meaning of the words used in the statute to refer to any portion of the expense of travelling between these points in connection with his practice as "personal or living expenses" and this I think is so whether the taxpayer lives at or next door to his location off the hospital premises or not. There may no doubt be cases where a further element of personal preference for a more distant location has an appreciable effect on the amount of the expense involved in travelling between the two points but I do not think such an element is present here. In the appellant's situation there is, in my view, no distinction to be made either between journeys from his home to the hospital and returning therefrom in the course of his scheduled daily and evening routines and similar journeys made in response to emergency calls or between journeys of either of these types and those made either in response to a call when he was working on his records at home or from the hospital to his home for the purpose of working on his records and then returning to the hospital to attend another patient. In my view whenever he went to the hospital to serve his patients he was doing so for the purpose of gaining income from his practice and the expenses both of going and of returning when the service had been completed were incurred for the same purpose. All such expenses, in my view, fall within the exception to Section 12(1)(a) and are properly deductible and none of them in my opinion can properly be classed as personal or living expenses within the prohibition of Section 12(1)(h).

There remains, however, the question of how much of the amounts claimed by the appellant as deductions was properly referable to the appellant's use of the automobile in question in his practice and how much was referable to his use of the automobile for other purposes.

[The taxpayer had claimed 90 per cent of the operating expenses and capital cost for the Chevrolet. For 1962, this produced a claim of 90 per cent of $993.06 for operating expenses based on a total of 8,071 miles driven in the year in the Chevrolet. On the basis of the taxpayer's own estimate of five round trips daily between his house and the hospital, Thurlow, J. allowed 2,000 miles as the mileage referable to the business and gave the taxpayer 25 per cent of his operating expenses. This resulted in a deduction for the taxpayer of $130 (after elimination of $465 which represented repairs to his wife's Vauxhall, an amount that was included in the taxpayer's claim without explanation of its pertinence to the business).

Thurlow J. dealt with the capital cost allowance claim on a different basis. Applying paragraph 13(7)(c), which provides for situations in which property is used partly to gain or produce income from a business and partly for other purposes, Thurlow J. said:]

On the basis of mileage alone, the use made by the taxpayer of the Chevrolet for the purposes of his practice appears to me to have been no more than 25 per cent of the total use and if this were the only thing to be considered as being "use" of an automobile the basis for calculation of the appellant's capital cost allowance would, it seems, necessarily be limited by Section 20(6)(e) to 25 per cent of the total capital cost of the automobile. The appellant on the other hand, and his accountant, considered that 90 per cent of the use of the car was use for the purposes of the practice and this I think was derived by considering its use from the point of view of the time involved in keeping it available for operation in the practice. Thus on a day when the appellant drove the car to the hospital, left it standing there while he was at the hospital, drove it again to return home and perhaps made several more trips with it to the hospital and back in the course of the day and at no time had any occasion to drive it for any purpose not associated with the practice, the car might well be considered as having been used throughout that day solely for the purposes of the practice. It was urged as well, and it is I think notorious, that an automobile depreciates both from operating it and by becoming obsolete and that the loss in capital value over a year through the latter might well be greater than through the former. I have no difficulty in accepting the evidence that the car was used (in the time sense) a great deal more for the purposes of the practice than it was used for other purposes but I think that an estimate of the proportion of the use to be attributed to the practice must have some regard both to the extent of wear and tear through driving it for the purposes of the practice as compared with the driving done for other purposes and to the extent of the time in which it was in use for the purposes of the practice as compared with the time it was in use for other purposes. On this basis I would fix the proportion of the use made of the car for the purposes of the practice at 50 per cent and the capital cost for the purposes of Section 11(1)(a) and the Regulations at 50 per cent of its capital cost. The appellant is entitled to deductions in each year for capital cost allowance calculated on that basis.

The appeals therefore succeed and they will be allowed to the extent indicated.

Problems, Notes and Questions

1. X is a litigation lawyer, and a sole practitioner. He maintains a home office in Toronto and an office on King Street in Toronto. In computing his income from the law practice, how should X treat expenses in respect of:
   a) travel between his King Street office and the court house,
   b) travel between his home office and the court house,
   c) travel between home and the King Street office,
   d) travel between home and the court house, and

e) travel between his home office and the King Street office?

2. Even after reducing Dr. Cumming's claim for vehicle operating expenses, did Thurlow, J. allow a somewhat inflated claim? If Dr. Cumming returned to his home five times a day to work on his accounts, and, if this work totaled about 12 hours a week, he must have averaged less than 25 minutes of work on the accounts per trip.
3. Of what significance is Thurlow, J.'s observation that Dr. Cumming could have maintained a separate office, in which case he would have been entitled to deduct the cost of maintaining the office as well as his travel expenses between office and hospital? Is it conceivable that a doctor would make five trips to his office to accomplish two hours of work on his accounts? Are we entitled to suspect that some of the trips to his home really represented a "personal or living" decision-i.e., a preference to spend free time at home?
4. In the Supreme Court of Canada, the correctness of *Cumming* was doubted in the judgment of Hall J. in *Henry v. M.N.R.* (1971), [1974] S.C.R. 155, [1972] C.T.C. 33, 72 D.T.C. 6005. The following reasons were cited in the same case, *M.N.R. v. Doctor E. Ross Henry*, [1969] C.T.C. 600, 69 D.T.C. 5395 (Exch. Ct.) to distinguish it from *Cumming*:

   (a) The agreement of June 6, 1961 (Ex. R2) provides that all the anaesthetic services would be performed in the hospital and not elsewhere except with the written consent of the hospital. Writing may have been waived in favour of an oral permission but that is here irrelevant. In any event, no patients were treated at the house in question and all services for which charges were made were performed within the limits of the hospital.

   (b) The information contained in the card (Ex. R3) shows that none of that information was obtained at his house. The first items were obtained from the hospital chart, further items from the knowledge of the respondent in attending the operation and the charges were those fixed by the Medical Association. Therefore no information on the card was necessarily filled out at the house and it was from this card that the secretary made the account charged to the patient.

   (c) This respondent had an office which alone distinguishes the *Cumming* case. All records were kept at the office and the account was made out there and which office the respondent visited only once or twice a week but on those occasions he would deliver to the secretary the card from which she would make out the account to mail to the patient.

   (d) The respondent stated that at the conclusion of the day's operations, around three, five or six o'clock p.m., he returned home to dinner; therefore he returned to his house not as a base of his operations nor for the purpose of completing cards.

5. In *Hogg v. The Queen*, [2002] 3 C.T.C. 177, 2002 D.T.C. 7037 (F.C.A.), a case dealing with deductions in computing income from office or employment, the taxpayer argued that security concerns converted the otherwise personal character of expenses incurred traveling to and from work into deductible expenses. An agent in the administration of justice, he feared assaults while commuting to work. While sympathetic to the taxpayer's concerns, the Court denied the deduction; the matter of personal security, though a function of his work, was not sufficient to render the expense deductible.

5. Expenses of a Home Workspace

Similar to commuting expenses, maintenance of a home office or other workspace used to earn income from business or employment, gives rise to expenses that are difficult to characterize. One taxpayer may find a home office a convenient alternative to staying downtown several evenings each week. Another taxpayer may find maintenance of a home office a business necessity.

The appropriate treatment of a home office for tax purposes has been a difficult issue. Although theoretically space used for business purposes in a home should be tested in the same manner as other business expenses, because the space is part of a home, an inference that the office expenses are of a personal nature is difficult to rebut.

Effective in 1988 and subsequent years, subsection 18(12) was introduced to deal with home office expenses. This provision prohibits the deduction by an individual of home office expenses, unless the home office is either:

(1) is the individual's "principal place of business", *or*

(2) used exclusively for the purpose of earning income from business and used on a regular and continuous basis for meeting clients, customers or patients of the individual in respect of the business.

Where a taxpayer qualifies for a deduction under subsection 18(12), expenses can only be deducted to the extent of the taxpayer's income from the business for the year. A loss cannot be created or increased. However, losses created by the deduction can be carried forward indefinitely by virtue of paragraph 18(12)(c).

The reference to "an otherwise deductible amount" in paragraph 18(2)(a) suggests that the business purpose test of subsection 9(1) and paragraph 18(1)(a) must be met, and provisions such as paragraph 18(1)(h) and section 67 must be complied with. When a home office deduction is available, the question of the appropriate amount of the deduction arises. In general, a deductible amount should be based on a reasonable allocation of costs attributable to the home office. The most common method of allocation is to determine the amount of space occupied by the office compared to the total usable area of the home. A proportionate amount of the expenses of the home are then taken as a business deduction. If the taxpayer is renting a home, a percentage of rent paid, utilities, insurance, etc., would be calculated. If the taxpayer owns the home, it would be a percentage of related expenses such as mortgage interest, insurance, property taxes, maintenance fees, utilities and, if desired, capital cost allowance.

Problem

Taxpayer X is a self-employed lawyer. She owns a house and uses the basement of the house as her law office. During Year 1, X billed $15,000 for legal services rendered and incurred the following expenses in connection with the law practice:

a) $20,000, which is a reasonable portion of the total mortgage interest, property tax, property insurance, and utility cost for the whole house,
b) $1,000 in stationery,
c) $5,000 in salary paid to her part-time assistant
d) $2,000 paid for telephone, fax, and Internet access (X has a separate line for her office).

For Year 1, how much deduction can X claim in computing her income from her law practice? If the amount of expenses remains the same for Year 2, while the revenue is increased to $100,000, what would her income be for Year 2?

6. Entertainment Expenses and Business Meals

Separating the personal and business purposes of entertainment expenses is remarkably difficult. It seems fair to state that many taxpayers would have great difficulty in resolving confidently in their own minds just how much of their entertainment expense reflected a personal consumption decision.

Consider the following excerpt from Neil Brooks, "The Principles Underlying the Deduction of Business Expenses" in *Canadian Taxation*, Hanson and Rendall, eds. at 202-203:

> The courts have not articulated any clear rules to deal with the deductibility of entertainment expenses. The prevailing rule, however, would appear to be that if the principal purpose of the entertainment is business, the expenses are deductible. Entertainment expenses have not generally been allocated on the basis that part of the cost served a business purpose (and is therefore deductible) and part of it served a personal purpose (and is therefore to this extent not deductible). In those cases where part of the expense is disallowed it is usually because the taxpayer cannot substantiate the full amount claimed.
>
> It seems clear that a rule must be formulated in this area allowing all entertainment expenses incurred for a business purpose or disallowing all such expenses. A rule that

> required taxpayers to report for each individual expenditure the amount that represented personal enjoyment would give rise to evidentiary chaos. However, although the prevailing rule is that all entertainment expenses are deductible if the principal purpose for incurring them is business, strong arguments can be made for just the opposite rule, namely that all entertainment expenses should be disallowed. Indeed the present rule would appear to offend virtually every criteria of a good tax law. First, regardless of the existence of a business purpose, there is often a high level of personal enjoyment associated with entertainment. Indeed, in most cases, such expenses must produce personal enjoyment to have their intended effect. Therefore, it is not unrealistic to assume that in most cases entertainment expenses will result in personal satisfaction equal or almost equal to cost. Consequently, a rule permitting the deductibility of entertainment expenses creates horizontal inequities. Those people who are able to incur their entertainment expenses in a business context will pay less tax than those who cannot, even though both will have consumed goods or services of the same value. Second, vertical inequities are created by the present rule since virtually all of the untaxed personal enjoyment that results because entertainment expenses are deductible accrues to the benefit of high-income taxpayers. Furthermore, most of the people who incur entertainment expenses probably also have high untaxed psychic returns from their jobs. Third, a deduction for entertainment expenses undoubtedly gives rise to a considerable amount of abuse. Taxpayers probably deduct a good deal of entertainment expenses incurred solely or mainly for personal purposes, particularly because they realize their business associates will reciprocate their generosity. Fourthly, such a deduction is almost impossible to police. Often, one's business associates are also one's friends and if the taxpayer asserts that a particular expense was incurred for a business purpose, the Department seldom has facts to rely on to prove otherwise. Fifth, allowing deductions for what most people consider the luxuries of life, reduces the moral acceptability of the tax system. Sixth, the deduction probably results in an inefficient allocation of resources; namely, an over-consumption of entertainment type goods and services. For example, the cost of going to a hockey game will be the same whether a person goes alone or with a business associate, if in the latter case the cost is deductible. Therefore, he or she will often choose to take a business associate, even though the value of doing so is less than the after-tax cost of the business associate's ticket. Finally, disallowing all entertainment expenses will not place any taxpayer at a competitive disadvantage (except perhaps those who compete with overseas companies). For these reasons, the courts should have formulated a rule disallowing most entertainment expenses. Such a rule would probably be more just than the present rule. For some entertainment expenses, like business meals at which business matters are discussed, it might be less likely that the personal satisfaction derived equals its cost, and, therefore, a rule arbitrarily allocating the expense to business and personal purpose (for example by allowing only 50 per cent of the expense) might lead to the most just results.

Subsection 67.1(1) limits the deduction of food and entertainment expenses to 50 per cent of the lesser of the actual cost or a reasonable amount. Section 67.1 was first introduced in 1988 and originally allowed the deduction of 80 per cent of food and entertainment expenses. The reduction to 50 per cent was introduced in 1994.

This limitation is linked to paragraph 18(1)(h), which has been amended to take into account subsection 67.1(1). Formerly, that paragraph referred to "traveling expenses (*including the entire amount expended for meals and lodging*) incurred by the taxpayer while away from home in the course of carrying on his business". The amount that is denied as a deduction (i.e., 50 per cent of the expenditure) can be considered a statutory "nothing" in that it is an expenditure incurred for business purposes but not deductible at all. For the CRA's current position on the deductibility of food and entertainment expenses, see Interpretation Bulletin IT-518R: Food, Beverages and Entertainment Expenses (April 16, 1996). An excellent discussion of the parameters of subsection 67.1(1) is found in *Stapley v. Canada*, [2006] 3 C.T.C. 188, 2006 D.T.C. 6075, [2006] F.C.J. No. 130 (F.C.A.).

7. Education Expenses

Education expenses have been characterized as non-deductible personal expenses (see, for example, *Gridley v. M.N.R.* (1951), 4 Tax A.B.C. 122, 51 D.T.C. 178). However, the courts have distinguished between the cost of a post-graduate course and the normal refresher courses taken by professionals. Amounts paid for a post-graduate course were classed as personal expenditure (see *Levin v. M.N.R.*, [1971] C.T.C. 66, 71 D.T.C. 5047 (Exch. Ct.)). Amounts paid for refresher courses may be treated as deductible expenses. Note, however, section 118.5, which provides a tax credit for tuition fees paid for obtaining post-secondary education. See also section 118.62, which provides a tax credit in respect of interest expense on certain student loans. The possible rationales for these tax credits are discussed in Chapter 8.

E. Public Policy Considerations

The prohibitions on deductions discussed thus far are contained in the Act. Sometimes the courts will prohibit the deduction of certain expenses if it would result in a frustration of public policy. "Public policy" here refers to policies that exist outside of the express language of the Act. Absent specific statutory authority, should the judiciary take into account public policy in its determination of the deductibility of an expense? Resolution of this issue requires consideration of the proper roles of the judiciary and the legislature, respectively. It also depends on the definition of "public policy", which could range from vague notions of immorality to deterrence of an activity rendered illegal by a specific statute, such as the *Criminal Code*. A related question concerns the deductibility of expenses incurred in the operation of an illegal business.

The following material invites us to take a fresh look at the extent of the basic statement of deductibility in subsection 9(1). Leaving aside the questions of public policy, how should an accountant treat the expenses of carrying on an illegal business, fines and penalties, illegal payments, theft, burglary or embezzlement losses? When reading these materials, refer to the previous discussion in this chapter of the scope of subsection 9(1) and to the decisions in *Imperial Oil* and *Royal Trust*, *supra*.

1. Expenses of Carrying On an Illegal Business

As seen in Chapter 2 (in particular, the *Buckman* case), the concept of income reflected in section 3 does not distinguish between income derived from legitimate activities and income from illegal business activities. When income from illegal businesses is taxable under the Act, the question becomes whether expenses of carrying on an illegal business are deductible. The following case considers this question.

M.N.R. v. ELDRIDGE
[1964] C.T.C. 545, 64 D.T.C. 5338 (Exch. Ct.)

Cattanach J.:

... The respondent had been carrying on a call girl operation in the City of Vancouver, British Columbia during the taxation years under review and had been so engaged since 1953. She filed her first income tax return for the year 1957 and also filed returns for the three preceding years, 1954, 1955, 1956, following a discussion in 1957 between the respondent and her tax consultant and officers of the Taxation Division of the Department of National Revenue. The respondent had not filed income tax returns and the purpose of the discussion in 1957 was to review the respondent's affairs generally. Because of the nature of the respondent's business, she alleged that she kept no books of account or similar records. At that time the officers of the Taxation Division pointed out the advantages and necessity of maintaining complete records for income tax purposes. However, since such records were apparently lacking, the officers of the Taxation Division obtained net worth statements for the taxation years 1953 to 1957 inclusive.

The respondent filed a net worth return for the years 1958 and 1959 and an incomplete return for the 1960 taxation year, also on a net worth basis.

[In 1960 the appellant was charged under the Criminal Code. As a result certain records were seized and in due course found their way into the hands of the Department of National Revenue. The records were quite detailed, showing incoming moneys and expenditures.]

The respondent freely admits that she was engaged in an illegal and illicit business, nor does she dispute the computation of the gross income received by her. The substance of her objection to the assessments is that further expenses were incurred by her in the operation of her business which should be taken into account and her taxable income reduced to the extent of those expenses.

At this point I would mention it is abundantly clear from the decided cases that earnings from illegal operations or illicit businesses are subject to tax. The respondent, during her testimony, remarked that she expressed the view to the officers of the Taxation Division that it was incongruous that the government should seek to live on the avails of prostitution. However, the complete answer to such suggestion is to be found in the judgment of Rowlatt, J. in *Mann v. Nash*, 16 T.C. 523, where he said at p. 530:

> It is said again: "Is the State coming forward to take a share of unlawful gains?" It is mere rhetoric. The State is doing nothing of the kind; they are taxing the individual with reference to certain facts. They are not partners; they are not principals in the illegality, or sharers in the illegality; they are merely taxing a man in respect of those resources. I think it is only rhetoric to say that they are sharing in his profits, and a piece of rhetoric which is perfectly useless for the solution of the question which I have to decide.

The respondent puts forward as further expenses items in the total amount of $20,255.40, which she claims should have been deducted in the year 1959 to arrive at her taxable income which if allowed, would reduce her taxable income for the year 1959 to $4,391.35.

With respect to the taxation year 1960, the respondent claims additional expenses to the total amount of $22,140 which, if allowed would result in a loss of $336.33 for the 1960 taxation year.

The items put forward by the respondent as operating expenses of her business for the 1959 taxation year, not taken into account in making the assessment on that year, are as follows:

		Cheques	Cash	Total
(1)	Rent paid to Kamlo Hotel	$ 475.00	$ 500.00	$ 975.40
(2)	Rent for apartment at 1095 Bute St.	180.00	1,155.00	1,335.00
(3)	Rent paid to Shirley Miline apt. occupied by her		2,100.00	2,100.00
(4)	Rent paid for additional suites		1,170.00	1,170.00
(5)	Legal fees	425.00	500.00	925.00
(6)	Telephone inspection		1,000.00	1,000.00

(7)	Payment for assistance to girls	100.00	900.00	1,000.00
(8)	Payments to casual employees	150.00		150.00
(9)	Protection fees		9,000.00	9,000.00
(10)	Liquor payment fees		2,600.00	2,600.00
	Totals for 1959 taxation year	$1,330.40	$18,925.00	$20,255.40

[In 1960, besides similar claims, there were also expenses for fees paid for bail bonds, $6,400, and purchase of entire issue of Flash newspaper, $500.]

All such items, with the possible exception of the items for legal fees, the purchase of Flash newspaper and fees paid for bail bonds, are of such a nature that, if proven to have been disbursed, would be proper deductions. With respect to such items as are deductible, if proven, counsel for the Minister contends that the onus, which is on the respondent, that she did so expend such sums, has not been discharged by the production of acceptable evidence. With respect to the payments of legal fees, for Flash newspaper and fees for bail bonds, he contends that even if payment of those fees is proved, they were not outlays or expenses made or incurred by the respondent for the purpose of gaining income from her business and accordingly the deduction thereof in computing income is precluded by Section 12(1)(a) of the *Income Tax Act*.

...

The claim with respect [to] the premises at 1095 Bute Street, occupied by Shirley Milne is in the total amount of $4,025 being $2,100 for twelve months in the year 1959 and $1,925 for eleven months in the year 1960 which is at the rate of $175 per month. These premises were occupied by Shirley Milne as her personal living accommodation. Mrs. Milne was apparently an intimate and trusted friend of the respondent having previously lived with the respondent in her home. Shirley Milne occasionally acted as a call girl and sometimes acted as a telephone operator. However, in addition to being personally occupied by Shirley Milne as her living accommodation, the premises were used as a central location to which the call girls could resort (and did so resort) between calls so as to be readily available and to avoid the necessity of travelling greater distances to places of assignation with a corresponding increase in taxicab fares. Further, the premises were used as a place of assignation when other such places were not available. Therefore, there is no doubt that these premises were used in the conduct of the respondent's business.

... While I am satisfied that a monthly rental of $105 was paid for these premises and that the premises were used in the respondent's business, the evidence with respect to the additional expenses is extremely vague. With respect to the further monthly amount of $75, this was put forth as an estimate for expenses which were not particularized other than by mention in the evidence of the respondent and Mrs. Milne of maid service and groceries and a yearly amount of $185 for utilities, such as electricity and telephone, which was added as an afterthought. The relationship between Mrs. Milne and the respondent was not explained with any degree of exactitude, that is, whether she was the resident manager of the respondent for the operation of these premises and if so the nature of the arrangement for her compensation. I am certain that a portion of the expense incurred were personal living expenses of Mrs. Milne. Further the additional expense put forward is admittedly an estimate unsupported by vouchers, receipts and no proper records or accounts were kept to support the statements. While I am satisfied that the monthly rental of $105 was paid, I have not been satisfied by adequate evidence which is the responsibility of the respondent to produce, as to the additional expenses claimed. Therefore, I would allow as a deduction as a business expense incurred by the respondent for these premises the sum of $1,260 for the year 1959 and the sum of $1,155 for the year 1960.

...

The third item common to the 1959 and 1960 taxation years is an amount of $1,000 in each year for telephone inspections. The respondent, by reason of the nature of her business, suspected that a listening device might be surreptitiously attached to the telephones in her telephone room by the law enforcement authorities to secure information which might lead to the respondent's criminal prosecution and conviction and so hamper or terminate her business. To guard against such possibility she testified that she engaged an employee of the telephone company to ascertain if her telephones had been so tapped. Admittedly, the telephone company employee was prohibited by his employer from conducting such an inspection. The respondent claims that a fee was charged for each such inspection but that no receipt was given to the respondent. The respondent admits that she did not keep records of the number of such inspections or of the total cost thereof. The amount of $1,000 for each year is admittedly only a very rough estimate. Again, such vague generalities as were introduced in evidence are not adequate to discharge the onus on the respondent. That onus can only be discharged by precise and definite evidence. The respondent has not satisfied me by adequate evidence that any such amount was expended and, if so, of the amount so expended.

The fourth item common to the 1959 and 1960 taxation years is the amount claimed for protection fees, being $9,000 in 1959 and $7,500 in 1960. The respondent maintained that she could not conduct her business without the payment of protection to the law enforcement authorities. She alleges that she paid $750 per month for this purpose based on $100 for each call girl in her employ and $50 for the messenger who collected the money which she testified was paid in cash, placed in a white envelope and invariably collected the first of each month by a person who identified himself as Mr. Jones of Seattle. In exchange for such payment the respondent was advised of certain hotels to be avoided by her girls when these hotels were under police surveillance and like information. She also attributed the fact that her business was operated without molestation until November 10, 1960 to these protection payments being made. While the respondent hinted that she knew the recipients of these payments, she refused to identify such persons because, as she stated, she feared for the safety of the lives of her children and her own life if she made such disclosures. I must assume that the law enforcement officers are conscientious in the exercise of their duties and are incorruptible and such assumption can only be rebutted by convincing evidence to the contrary. The evidence which I received was not of this nature and accordingly I have not been satisfied that payments for protection were made.

The concluding item common to the years 1959 and 1960 is for liquor payment fees, being one case of liquor per week purported to have been given to officials of the civic administration amounting to $2,600 for the year 1959 and $2,000 for the year 1960. These amounts are admittedly only an estimate. The respondent, at one stage of her testimony, said she caused to be delivered a case of high quality whisky once a week, but during her examination for discovery she stated deliveries were made once a month. I have not been convinced that these gifts were, in fact, made and even if they were made, no evidence has been adduced from which I could ascertain the number of such gifts and so compute their value. ...

The next item is a claim for $925 paid by the respondent to Mr. N. Mussellem in August 1959 for his services in defending one of the call girls engaged by the respondent on a charge under the Criminal Code. I might mention that Mr. Mussellem is counsel for the respondent in the present appeal and that the accused call girl was acquitted. In my opinion the amount of $925 paid by the respondent for legal expenses is properly deductible for the twofold reason (1) that it was laid out for the purpose of gaining income, the girl upon her acquittal of the charge returned to work which she could not have done if sentenced to imprisonment, and (2) it was part of the girl's arrangement with the respondent that in the event of criminal prosecution as a result of the activities, the respondent would assume the cost of the girl's defence. Compare *M.N.R. v. Goldsmith Bros. Smelting and Refining Company Limited*, [1954] S.C.R. 55; [1959] C.T.C. 28.

The concluding item for the year 1959 is a claim for $1,000 as having been paid for assistance to the girls. It frequently happened that a girl sent on an assignment would encounter difficulty with the customer. In these events the respondent had an arrangement with certain men possessed of physical strength and some guile, which they exercised when sent to extricate a girl from difficulty, for which services these men were paid. By cheque dated July 2, 1959 the respondent paid P. Graham $100 for these services performed by him, which, in my opinion, is properly deductible as a business expense. However, the respondent estimates that she paid a further $900 in cash during 1959 for like services for which there is no confirmation by means of any record. Therefore, the further amount of $900 has not been substantiated to my satisfaction and is not allowed.

There now remains for consideration the items put forward by the respondent for business expenses incurred by her in the 1960 taxation year with which she was not credited by the Minister in making the assessment for that year, but excluding these items which I have already considered as applicable in both taxation years under review.

The first item is a claim for legal fees in the amount of $1,000 paid by the respondent to R. Myers for his services in defending one of the call girls when the respondent and her girls were arrested on November 10, 1960 and charged with conspiring to live from the avails of prostitution. This particular girl wished to be defended by counsel of her own choice. This payment of $1,000 cannot be justified as a legal expense laid out for the purpose of gaining income from the business since the respondent's business has been brought to an end by the wholesale arrests. However, it was a term of the call girl's engagement with the respondent that the respondent would assume responsibility for legal expenses as a part of the girl's remuneration. As such, I am of the opinion that this amount is properly deductible and should be allowed. ...

The next item claimed as a business expense by the respondent is an amount of $500 paid for the entire issue of a newspaper called Flash, which was to be distributed on the British Columbia mainland. This newspaper, which specializes in the publication of scandalous stories, contained a story concerning the respondent which she considered scurrilous and detrimental to her business. The entire issue was, therefore, purchased by her to suppress this article. A copy of the newspaper was not produced but upon asking I was informed that the article had described the respondent as a Czarina of the particular underworld trade in which she was engaged who wished to obtain control of all prostitutes in the area and that the independents had risen against her, kidnapped her and subjected her to loathsome physical indignities which latter statements the respondent testified were completely false. From the brief description of the substance of the article which I received, I am unable to conclude that the respondent could have been of the opinion that the circulation of this newspaper would have been detrimental to her business. I must, therefore, conclude that this expenditure was not laid out for the purpose of earning income and that it must be disallowed.

Notes and Questions

1. The paper contained a lurid story about Ms. Eldridge and her business. Ms. Eldridge testified that the story was entirely false and that she sought to suppress it because she thought it would be detrimental to her business. Cattanach, J. said "I am unable to conclude that the [taxpayer] could have been of the opinion that the circulation of this newspaper would have been detrimental to her business. I must therefore, conclude that this expenditure was not laid out for the purpose of earning income and that it must be disallowed." Consider Cattarach, J.'s rationale for denying the amount spent to buy the entire issue of Flash. What other motive could Ms. Eldridge have had for buying up the newspaper? To what extent, and in what circumstances, may the Minister or a court second-guess a taxpayer's business judgment? Compare *No. 511 v. M.N.R.* (1958), 19 Tax A.B.C. 248, 58 D.T.C. 307.
2. Of the $6,400 paid by Ms. Eldridge as commissions to bail bondsmen, $5,400 was referable to bail bonds arranged for her employees. This amount was allowed because Ms. Eldridge had assumed this responsibility, along with the responsibility for legal fees, as a term of the employment. The $1,000 commission for bail for Ms. Eldridge herself was disallowed. All of the bail bonds were arranged after the arrests of November 10, 1960, which terminated the business. Suppose that Ms. Eldridge had been arrested at an earlier date and none of her employees were arrested, and that the business could continue to operate only if Ms. Eldridge was promptly released from jail. In this situation would a bail bond commission be deductible? Refer to the materials dealing with the statutory limitations on deductions and frame as many arguments as you can for denying a deduction.
3. Cattanach, J. quotes from *Mann v. Nash* in response to the taxpayer's remark that the government was living off the avails of prostitution by subjecting her income to taxation. What arguments could he have relied on to support the taxation of Ms. Eldridge?
4. The "telephone inspection expenses", the "protection fees", and the "liquor payment fees" were disallowed because of a lack of sufficient proof. Do you agree with Cattanach, J. that all of the above items "are of such a nature that, if proven to be disbursed, would be proper deductions"? Should there be a distinction between lawful expenses (e.g., rent) incurred in the operation of a business and unlawful expenses (e.g., protection fees)? For example, if the Lockheed corporation pays millions of dollars in bribes to officials of a foreign government for the purpose of obtaining contracts for Lockheed aircraft, should these amounts be deductible in computing Lockheed's income? See section 67.5.
5. Should the question of deductibility be affected by considerations of illegality or immorality? If illegal expenses (i.e., those which violate a statute) are deductible, does this undermine the criminal law system? Would their non-deductibility result in double punishment? Are there reasons for treating illegal expenses differently

from those expenses considered immoral but not rendered illegal by a specific statute? How do you define immorality? Are notions of immorality within the exclusive purview of the legislature? See *Canadian Imperial Bank of Commerce v. Canada*, 2013 FCA 122, [2013] 4 C.T.C. 218, 2013 D.T.C. 5098 (F.C.A.).

6. The Act is based on a modified concept of net accretion to wealth. Gains from an illegal activity are taxed because they enhance the taxpayer's wealth. It can be argued that it is inconsistent to deny the deduction of illegal expenses since these expenses reduce the wealth of the taxpayer. Neil Brooks, *supra*, argues (at 243), however, that such a position is not illogical: "If people are to be taxed on the basis of their ability to pay, then the lawfulness of their income is an irrelevant factor in determining their tax liability. The income tax must, however, sometimes weigh other interests against the pursuit of equity. ... [I]n deciding whether all expenses should be deductible, a further interest must be considered — the danger that express legislative policy will be frustrated if certain business expenses are held deductible. An analogy to the taxation of illegal gains is not of much assistance when weighing this interest against the need for tax equity. Certainly it does not compel a logician to favour allowing the deduction."
7. In the context of large-scale illegal drug trafficking businesses, how should the courts characterize the seizure and forfeiture of drugs by the state? Do the forfeited substances constitute deductible expenses in the nature of lost or destroyed inventory? What about legal fees incurred by a taxpayer in defending criminal charges related to an underlying illegal business? See *Neeb v. The Queen* (1997), 97 D.T.C. 895 (T.C.C.).

2. Fines and Penalties

If public policy considerations do not prevent the deduction of expenses of carrying on an illegal business, what would be the reasons for disallowing fines and penalties as deductions? Consider the following decision of the Supreme Court of Canada.

65302 BRITISH COLUMBIA LTD. v. THE QUEEN
[2000] 1 C.T.C. 57, 99 D.T.C. 5799 (S.C.C.)

[The taxpayer corporation operated an egg-producing poultry farm. It deliberately produced over-quota in order to maintain its major customer until it could purchase additional quota at what it thought was an affordable price. The taxpayer was assessed an over-quota levy by the British Columbia Egg Marketing Board. The main issue in this case is whether the over-quota levy was deductible in computing the taxpayer's income. The Tax Court of Canada found in favour of the taxpayer. In allowing the Crown's appeal, the Federal Court of Appeal concluded, inter alia, that the taxpayer could have carried on its business so as to avoid the excess

production leading to the levy, but deliberately chose not to do so, and that there was a strong public policy argument precluding the taxpayer from claiming the over-quota levy as a business expense. The taxpayer appealed to the Supreme Court of Canada.

The majority decision written by Iacobucci, J. is included immediately below, which is followed by the minority decision written by Bastarache, J.]

Iacobucci J. (Gonthier, McLachlin, Major and Binnie JJ. concurring):

[Iacobucci, J. held that the appellant incurred the over-quota levy for the purpose of gaining or producing income from its business. To be deductible under paragraph 18(1)(a), expenses need not be incidental in the sense that they were unavoidable, or need to be necessary and inevitable. He then discusses the issue of public policy.]

The most compelling argument put to this Court in the present appeal is that Parliament could not have intended s. 18(1)(a) to permit the deduction of fines and penalties as such a result violates public policy. Therefore, even if fines and penalties are allowable expenses within the ordinary meaning of s. 18(1)(a), this meaning must be modified in order to conform to a broader appreciation of Parliament's intent, and thereby avoid a repugnant disharmony or absurdity. In *Amway of Canada Ltd. v. MNR,* (1996), 193 N.R. 381, the Federal Court of Appeal also took this approach, holding, at para. 31, that even if the fine or penalty in question is unavoidable, its deduction should be disallowed where "that fine or penalty is imposed by law for the purpose of punishing or deterring those who through intention or a lack of reasonable care violate the laws." Similarly, Professor Neil Brooks argues that this consideration is legitimate for courts to invoke even in the absence of statutory language to that effect, because of "the broad interpretative principle that in discharging their function they [courts] should not construe one statute in such a way that the objectives of another statute are frustrated": "The Principles Underlying the Deduction of Business Expenses" in B. Hansen, V. Krishna and J. Rendall, eds., Canadian Taxation 1981), 189, at p. 242.

The United States Supreme Court took this position in *Tank Truck Rentals, Inc. v. Commissioner of Internal Revenue,* 356 U.S. 30 (1958). At issue was whether fines imposed for the operation of trucks in violation of state maximum weight laws were "ordinary and necessary" business expenses under ss. 23(a)(1)(A) of the Internal Revenue Code of 1939. The court held at pp. 33-35 that:

> A finding of "necessity" cannot be made ... if the allowance of the deduction would frustrate sharply defined national or state policies proscribing particular types of conduct, evidenced by some governmental declaration thereof.
>
> ...

> ... It is clear that assessment of the fines was punitive action and not a mere toll for use of the highways: the fines occurred only in the exceptional instance when the overweight run was detected by the police. Petitioner's failure to comply with the state laws obviously was based on a balancing of the cost of compliance against the chance of detection. Such a course cannot be sanctioned, for judicial deference to state action requires, whenever possible, that a State not be thwarted in its policy. We will not presume that the Congress, in allowing deductions for income tax purposes, intended to encourage a business enterprise to violate the declared policy of a State. To allow the deduction sought here would but encourage continued violations of state law by increasing the odds in favor of non-compliance. This could only tend to destroy the effectiveness of the State's maximum weight laws.

However, the court recognized that this presumption against congressional intent to encourage the violation of declared public policy had to be balanced against the congressional intent to tax only net income. The test for non-deductibility therefore turns on "the severity and immediacy of the frustration resulting from allowance of the deduction" (at p. 35). I note that in 1969 Congress amended ss. 162 of the Internal Revenue Code to disallow, *inter alia*, the deduction of "any fine or similar penalty paid to a government for the violation of any law."

Invoking public policy concerns raises the question, as put by Richard Krever, of whose public policy should be furthered by courts in disallowing the deduction of fines and penalties ("The Deductibility of Fines: Considerations From Law and Policy Perspectives" (1984), 13 Austl. Tax Rev. 168, at p. 185). As he notes, "[a] taxpayer may incur a fine in one jurisdiction as a result of activities producing assessable income that are undertaken on a nation-wide basis and allowed in all other States" (p. 185). ...

In this connection, I note that in calculating income, it is well established that the deduction of expenses incurred to earn income generated from illegal acts is allowed. For example, not only is the income of a person living from the avails of prostitution liable to tax, but the expenses incurred to earn this income are also deductible: *M.N.R. v. Eldridge*, [1964] C.T.C. 545 (Exch. Ct.). See also *Espie Printing Co. v. M.N.R.*, [1960] Ex. C.R. 422. Allowing a taxpayer to deduct expenses for a crime would appear to frustrate the Criminal Code; however, tax authorities are not concerned with the legal nature of an activity. Thus, in my opinion, the same principles should apply to the deduction of fines incurred for the purpose of gaining income because prohibiting the deductibility of fines and penalties is inconsistent with the practice of allowing the deduction of expenses incurred to earn illegal income.

This brings us to the crux of the issue. While fully alive to the need in general to harmonize the interpretation of different statutes, the question here arises in the specific context of a tax collection system based on self-assessment. Parliament designed the system and it is open to Parliament, as part of that design, to choose for itself to resolve any apparent conflicts between policies underlying tax provisions and other enactments. Parliament has indicated its intention to perform this role, not only in the design of the self-assessment system, which requires individuals without legal training to work through a complex series of provisions to calculate net income, for which maximum explicit guidance is necessary, but more specifically in its identification in the Act itself of certain outlays which the taxpayer is not permitted to deduct, as discussed below. Having recognized the problem of potentially conflicting legislative policies, Parliament has provided the solution, which is that in the absence of Parliamentary direction in the *Income Tax Act* itself, outlays and expenses are deductible if made for the purpose of gaining or producing income.

The argument is also put to this Court that Parliament did not intend to dilute the deterrent effect of a fine or penalty. If this Court is to accept this argument, then it would have to determine whether any particular fine or penalty was in fact meant to be deterrent in nature. If a fine was instead meant to be compensatory then there is no public policy frustrated by allowing its deduction. ... Furthermore, this argument requires a court to establish that the deduction of the fine or penalty would decrease its intended effect. ...

These difficulties outlined above demonstrate that the public policy arguments ask courts to make difficult determinations with questionable authority. Moreover, they place a high burden on the taxpayer who is to engage in this analysis in filling out his or her income tax return and would appear to undermine the objective of self-assessment underlying our tax system. ...

While various policy objectives are pursued through our tax system, and do violate the principles of neutrality and equity, it is my view that such public policy determinations are better left to Parliament. ...

This approach and conclusion are supported by the fact that Parliament has expressly disallowed the deduction of certain expenses on what appear to be public policy grounds. For example, s. 67.5, added by R.S. 1994, c. 7, Sch. II (1991, c. 40), s. 46, prohibits the deduction of any outlay or expense made for the purpose of doing anything that is an offence under any of sections 119 to 121, 123 to 125, 393 and 426 of the Criminal Code or an offence under section 465 of that Act as it relates to an offence described in any of those sections. In the absence of s. 67.5, bribes to public officials would be deductible (and taxable in the hands of the "bribee"). This is a situation where Parliament, specifically chose to prohibit a deduction which would otherwise have been allowed. In addition, taxpayers are prohibited from deducting payments of interest and penalties levied under the Act itself (s. 18(1)(t) added by R.S. 1990, c. 39, s. 8), statutory royalties (s. 18(1)(m)), and payments required under the *Petroleum and Gas Revenue Act* (s. 18(1)(l.1)). ...

Moreover, given that Parliament has expressly turned its mind to the deduction of expenses associated with certain activities that are offences under the Criminal Code, outlined in s. 67.5 of the Act, I do not find a legitimate role for judicial amendment on the general question of deductibility of fines and penalties. Since the Act is not silent on the issue of restricting the deduction of some expenses incurred for the purpose of gaining income, this is a strong indication that Parliament did direct its attention to the question and that where it wished to limit the deduction of expenses or payments of fines and penalties, it did so expressly. I am also sceptical that the deduction of fines and penalties provides the taxpayer with a "benefit" or "profit" — indeed, their purpose is to calculate the taxpayer's profit, which is then taxed. ...

I therefore cannot agree with the argument that the deduction of fines and penalties should be disallowed as being contrary to public policy. First and foremost, on its face, fines and penalties are capable of falling within the broad and clear language of s. 18(1)(a). For courts to intervene in the name of public policy would only introduce uncertainty, as it would be unclear what public policy was to be followed, whether a particular fine or penalty was to be characterized as deterrent in nature, and whether the body imposing the fine intended it to be deductible. Moreover, allowing the deduction of fines and penalties is consistent with the tax policy goals of neutrality and equity. Although it may be said that the deduction of such fines and penalties "dilutes" the impact of the sanction, I do not view this effect as introducing a sufficient degree of disharmony so as to lead this Court to disregard the ordinary meaning of s. 18(1)(a) when that ordinary meaning is harmonious with the scheme and object of the Act. When Parliament has chosen to prohibit the deduction of otherwise allowable expenses on the grounds of public policy, then it has done so explicitly. ...

Bastarache, J. (L'Heureux-Dubé, J. concurring):

This appeal raises the narrow question of whether a levy imposed pursuant to a provincial egg marketing scheme can be deducted as a business expense for the purposes of the Act. The broader question posed by my colleague Justice Iacobucci is whether fines or other types of payments may be deductible from a taxpayer's income. While I agree with his answer to the narrow question, as well as with his characterization of the payment as a current expense rather than a capital outlay, and adopt his statement of the facts and judgments of the lower courts, I respectfully cannot agree that all types of fines and penalties are deductible as a matter of course. ...

When considering the operation of ss. 9 and 18 in their entire context, I am persuaded that it was not the intention of Parliament to allow all fines to be deductible. I principally reach this conclusion for the simple reason that to so allow would operate to frustrate the legislative purpose of other statutes.

The statute book as a whole forms part of the legal context in which an act of Parliament is passed. As Driedger notes in the second edition, at p. 159, "one statute may influence the meaning of the other, so as to produce harmony within the body of the law as a whole". ... To allow all fines to be deductible as a matter of course would therefore be inconsistent with the modern contextual approach to statutory interpretation, which requires that weight be given to the total context of the Act, including its relationship to other statutes. As N. Brooks argues in "The Principles Underlying the Deduction of Business Expenses", in B. Hansen, V. Krishna and J. Rendall, eds., Essays on Canadian Taxation (1978), 249, at p. 297:

> If the legislative bodies and the courts are perceived as engaged in a cooperative venture of law-making, then the courts must assume the task of ensuring, as much as possible, that the matrix of statutory instruments do not operate at cross purposes.

... [I]t would clearly frustrate the purposes of the penalizing statute if an offender was allowed to deduct fines imposed for violations of the Criminal Code, R.S.C., 1985, c. C-46, or related statutes as business expenses. The deduction of a fine imposed for a Criminal Code violation would suggest that the decision to commit a criminal offence may be a legitimate business decision. Moreover, such a deduction would have the unsavoury effect of reducing the penal and deterrent effect of the penalizing statute.

The Act has since been amended to prohibit the deduction of illegal bribery expenses (s. 67.5, added by 1994, c. 7, Sch. II (1991, c. 49), s. 46) and fines imposed pursuant to the Act itself (s. 18(1)(t), added by 1990, c. 30, s. 8). It is argued that this indicates that Parliament did not intend to prohibit the deduction of other fines and penalties. In my view, this observation does not address the general consistency issue or require that the principles sustaining the coherence of our statutory framework be set aside when deciding whether an expense is incurred for the purpose of producing income under s.18(1)(a). ...

In this case, it is possible to interpret the Act in a manner that is consistent with the object of other legislative enactments. To adopt the position that fines are always or generally deductible, without reference to the Act under which the fine was imposed, ignores the obligation to consider the intention of Parliament and to determine whether the deduction would defeat or impair the effectiveness of other legislative enactments. Absent express provision to the contrary, the presumption that Parliament would not intend to encourage the violation of other laws must be considered.

In my view, it is important not to overlook the importance of the characterization of the expenditure. When considering other types of payments, such as fees levied under regulatory regimes with compensatory aims, it might be wholly consistent with the scheme to allow the charges to be deductible. Such charges, like user fees generally, are costs of engaging in a particular type of business and are levied to compensate for different types of regulated activities or to claw back profits earned in violation of the regulations. Allowing such charges to be deducted does not undermine their function, as the money still goes to the compensatory scheme. Thus, it would not undermine the charging statute for these levies to be deducted from a taxpayer's income. ...

The distinction between deductible and non-deductible payment must therefore be determined on a case-by-case basis. The main factor in such a determination is whether the primary purpose of the statutory provision under which the payment is demanded would be frustrated or undermined. Statutory provisions imposing payments either as punishment for past wrongdoing or as general or specific deterrence against future law-breaking would be undermined if the fine could then be deducted as a business expense.

In contrast, if the legislative purpose behind a provision is primarily compensatory, its operation would not generally be undermined by the deduction of the expense. Where the purpose is mixed and the charging provisions have both a penal and a compensatory aim, a court should look for the primary purpose of the payment. In approaching this task, the court should consider, in particular, the nature of the mischief that the provision was designed to address.

I agree with my colleague, Iacobucci, J., that public policy determinations are best left to Parliament. However, I am not suggesting that the deduction of penal fines be disallowed for public policy reasons, but instead because their deduction, not specifically authorized by the Act, would frustrate the expressed intentions of Parliament in other statutes if they were held to come under s. 18(1)(a) of the Act. In my view, penal fines are not expenditures incurred for the purpose of gaining or producing income in the legal sense. This concern is not so much one of public policy, morality or legitimacy, but one consistent with a realistic understanding of the accretion of wealth concept and the court's duty to uphold the integrity of the legal system in interpreting the *Income Tax Act*. ...

The impugned levy in the case at bar was imposed under s. 6 of the British Columbia Egg Marketing Board Standing Order (Rev. Jan. 1989), which derives its authority from s. 13(1)(k) of the *Natural Products Marketing (BC) Act*, R.S.B.C. 1979, c. 296, (the "Marketing Act") permitting the Lieutenant Governor in Council to vest in a marketing board or commission the power to:

> ... fix and collect levies or charges from designated persons engaged in the production or marketing of the whole or part of a regulated product and for that purpose to classify those persons into groups and fix the levies or charges payable by the members of the different groups in different amounts, and to

use those levies or charges and other money and licence fees received by the commission

(i) to carry out the purposes of the scheme;

(ii) to pay the expenses of the marketing board or commission;

(iii) to pay costs and losses incurred in marketing a regulated product;

(iv) to equalize or adjust returns received by producers of regulated products during the periods the marketing board or commission may determine; and

(v) to set aside reserves for the purposes referred to in this paragraph; ...

In contrast, penalties are authorized by s. 20 of the Marketing Act which contemplates both fines and imprisonment as punishment for failing to comply with the Act or subordinate legislation:

(1) Every person who fails to comply with this Act or the regulations or an order, rule, regulation, determination or decision made by the Provincial board or a marketing board or commission or made by virtue of a power exercisable under the federal Act, is liable on conviction, to a fine of not less than $100 and not more than $500 or to imprisonment not exceeding 6 months or to both a fine and imprisonment.

The comparison of these two provisions confirms that the over-quota levy assessed by the board pursuant to s. 13 of the Marketing Act was primarily compensatory and not penal. I would thus accept the trial judge's determination that this type of levy was akin to a 'fee for service' incurred for the purpose of producing income:

... I do not view the levy imposed by the Board under the authority of paragraph 6(e) of the Standing Order, as a penalty. Indeed, there is a specific section in the B.C. Act dealing with penalties (section 20), and I do not see that these levies are assessed as a punishment imposed by statute as a consequence of the commission of an offence, but rather as an additional cost to the producer in the carrying out of his business.

The deduction of such a levy does not operate to frustrate or undermine the purposes of the Marketing Act or of the British Columbia Egg Marketing Board Standing Order because such levies are not primarily geared towards punishment or deterrence, but instead to the efficient operation of the regulatory scheme.

Thus, as the over-quota levy was a compensatory fee charged primarily to defray the costs of over-production and incurred for the purpose of gaining or producing income, I would allow its deduction for the purposes of the computation of profit.

Notes and Questions

1. Amendments passed in 2005 effectively overrule the decision in *65302 British Columbia Ltd.* Section 67.6, applicable to fines and penalties imposed after March 22, 2004, denies the deduction of fines or penalties (other than prescribed fines or penalties) imposed under federal, provincial (including municipal), territorial or foreign law. To date, no fines or penalties have been prescribed. Given the discussion in *65320 British Columbia Ltd.*, what kinds of fines or penalties might be prescribed and thereby be deductible as business expenses? See generally, Interpretation Bulletin IT-104R3: Deductibility of Fines or Penalties (August 9, 2002).
2. Damages and contractual penalties are generally deductible if they meet the general test of deductibility under section 9, paragraphs 18(1)(a) and (h). See *Imperial Oil*, *supra*, and Interpretation Bulletin IT-467R2: Damages, Settlements and Similar Payments (November 15, 2002).

3. Illegal Payments

As mentioned in the *65302 British Columbia Ltd.*, section 67.5 of the Act imposes restrictions on the deductibility of illegal payments if the payments entail the corruption of officials or employees in the public sector or the bribery of private sector agents or employees where the payment would be an offense under specific provisions of the *Criminal Code*. However, not all illegal payments are non-deductible. For example, illegal payments made during the course of a business activity, whether legal or illegal, which do not fall within subsection 67.5(1) would appear to remain deductible. Do you think this is reasonable in the circumstances?

4. Theft, Burglary or Embezzlement Losses

In dealing with the deductibility of losses suffered by a business through dishonest acts of employees, Canadian and Commonwealth case law appeared to establish a distinction based on the employee's role and function within the business. In *General Stampings of Canada Ltd. v. M.N.R.* (1957), 17 Tax A.B.C. 1, 57 D.T.C. 163, for example, the taxpayer's claim to deduct the sum of $30,000 was disallowed. The taxpayer's general manager had taken more than $36,000 from the taxpayer company's funds for his own use. He owned one share of the company and was a director. When the defalcations were discovered he was discharged, and an agreement was reached by which he was to repay $30,000. The taxpayer's appeal was dismissed by Mr. Fordham who relied on cases such as *Curtis v. J. & G. Oldfield,*

Ltd. (1925), 9 T.C. 319, 41 T.L.R. 373, *Weidman Bros. Ltd. v. M.N.R.* (1950), 2 Tax A.B.C. 223 and *Ash v. Fed. Commissioner of Taxation*, [1938] A.T.D. 76. The governing principle was thought to be revealed in this brief extract from *Ash*:

> Thus, purloinings by office boys and thefts by shop employees should, prima facie, be allowed as deductions. They may be shown to be incidental to, and perhaps inevitable in, the operations which produce income.
>
> But the case is different when income is actually received and then misapplied by the proprietor of a business or a person in the position of such a proprietor, as, for example, the manager of a company.

The CRA's administrative policy in this area, which generally follows the case law, is set out in CRA Income Tax Folio S3-F9-C1: Lottery Winnings, Miscellaneous Receipts, and Income (and Losses) from Crime.

Notes and Questions

1. Is there a difference for tax purposes as between loss by "theft", "burglary", "robbery", "purloinings", "embezzlement", "defalcation", or "misappropriation"? Does it make any difference to the taxpayer whether the employee who caused the loss was a lowly office employee or a general manager? Could there be an unarticulated public policy reason for the different treatment of the thefts according to the type of dishonest employee? Paragraph 4 of Interpretation Bulletin IT-185R states that no deduction will be allowed for losses through theft committed by an employee who is a major shareholder. Is this "piercing of the corporate veil" justifiable? Does this position frustrate a policy of corporate law?
2. How do you treat the expenses incurred to acquire insurance against the above occurrences? What do you do with the amount the insurance company pays if a loss occurs?
3. Could one argument for the Minister be that the deduction of defalcation losses would allow the taxpayer to share the loss with the public according to the taxpayer's marginal rate? For example, a taxpayer in a 40 per cent bracket would only effectively suffer 60 per cent of the loss. If this is a convincing argument, then how does one distinguish deductions for theft from deductions for bad debts (i.e., accounts which are written off because there is no hope of collection)? Even if the prevention of loss-distribution is a meritorious public policy, should it be implemented by the judiciary?

F. Interest Expense

The deduction of interest on borrowed money would normally be prohibited by paragraph 18(1)(b) as a "payment on account of capital". Paragraphs 20(1)(c) and (d) provide statutory exceptions to this general prohibition and allow the deduction of interest expense under certain conditions. The following materials focus on the general rules contained in subparagraphs 20(1)(c)(i) and (ii).

Subparagraph 20(1)(c)(i) allows a taxpayer to deduct amounts paid in the year or payable in respect of the year pursuant to a legal obligation to pay interest on borrowed money used for the purpose of earning income from a business or property (other than exempt income or to acquire a life insurance policy). Subparagraph (ii) permits the deduction of interest payable on the unpaid balance of the purchase price of an asset used by the taxpayer to earn business or property income.

Since the deduction for interest expense is available only under paragraph 20(1)(c), strict compliance with the provisions of that paragraph have been demanded by the courts. This has led to considerable litigation in two areas.

The first area relates to the deductibility of interest where the property or business that the loan was used to finance no longer exists. Paragraph 20(1)(c) permits the deduction only where the interest expense was incurred to gain or produce income. When the income-earning "source" ceases to exist, the courts generally held that the related interest expense is no longer deductible. Although the denial of the deduction is technically correct, given the wording of paragraph 20(1)(c), it may result in undue hardship where a *bona fide* business decision must be made to dispose of a business or income-producing property. Consider, for example, the case of a taxpayer who borrows $50,000 to acquire shares. Within a few months the shares fall in value to $25,000. If the taxpayer sells the shares to avoid a further loss on the investment, he or she will have disposed of the income-producing property necessary to continue deducting the interest on the outstanding principal on the loan. Do you think this result is fair? What if the taxpayer reinvested the $25,000 proceeds in another income-producing property?

In *Tennant v. The Queen*, [1996] 1 S.C.R. 305, [1996] 1 C.T.C. 290, 96 D.T.C. 6121 (S.C.C.), the taxpayer borrowed $1 million in order to acquire shares of a company. Four years later, when the shares were worth only $1,000, the taxpayer transferred the shares to a holding company under section 85 in exchange for common shares of the holding company. The taxpayer continued to deduct interest on his original $1 million loan. The Minister assessed the taxpayer on the basis that the interest deductible under subparagraph 20(1)(c)(i) following the share transfer was limited to the cost to him of the shares of the holding company, that is, $1,000. The taxpayer's appeal to the Federal Court–Trial Division ([1993] 1 C.T.C. 148, 93 D.T.C. 5067) and the Federal Court of Appeal ([1994] 2 C.T.C. 113, 94 D.T.C. 6505) were both dismissed. The Supreme Court of Canada allowed the taxpayer's appeal. Relying on the decision in *The Queen v. Bronfman Trust*, *infra*, the Court concluded that the ability to deduct interest on a loan is not lost simply because the taxpayer sells the income-producing property acquired with the loaned funds, so long as the taxpayer reinvests the proceeds in an eligible use property. As long as the replacement property can be traced to the entire amount of the loan, the interest on the loan remains fully deductible.

Section 20.1 was enacted in 1994 to deal specifically with the continuing deductibility of interest after a source of income ceases to exist. What is the effect of section 20.1 on the decision in *Tennant* and previous case law?

The second area of litigation relates to the condition in subparagraph 20(1)(c)(i) that the borrowed money be used for the purpose of earning income from business or property. This condition does not require that income actually be generated, but an intention and a demonstrable use of the funds for this purpose must be established.

THE QUEEN v. BRONFMAN TRUST
[1987] 1 C.T.C. 117, 87 D.T.C. 5059 (S.C.C.)

The Chief Justice:

... In the present appeal, the trustees of a trust elected to make discretionary capital allocations to Phyllis Barbara Bronfman in 1969 and 1970. Instead of liquidating capital assets to make the allocations, the trustees considered it advantageous to retain the trust investments temporarily and finance the allocations by borrowing funds from a bank.

The issue is whether the interest paid to the bank by the trust on the borrowings is deductible for tax purposes; more particularly, is an interest deduction only available where the loan is used directly to produce income or is a deduction also available when, although its direct use may not produce income, the loan can be seen as preserving income-producing assets which might otherwise have been liquidated. A subordinate issue is whether the answer to this question depends upon the status of the taxpayer as a corporation, a trust, or a natural person. ...

The trust argues that even if the loans were used to pay the allocations, they were also used for the purpose of earning income from property since they permitted the trust to retain income-producing investments until the time was ripe to dispose of them. The end result of the transactions, the trust submits, was the same as if the trustees had sold assets to pay the allocations and then borrowed money to replace them, in which case, it is argued, the interest would have been deductible. The Crown, on the other hand, takes the position that the borrowed funds were used to pay the allocations to the beneficiary, that the amounts of interest claimed as deductions are not interest on borrowed money used for the purpose of earning income from a business or property and as such are not deductible. ...

It is perhaps otiose to note at the outset that in the absence of a provision such as paragraph 20(1)(c) specifically authorizing the deduction from income of interest payments in certain circumstances, no such deductions could generally be taken by the taxpayer. Interest expenses on loans to augment fixed assets or working capital would fall within the prohibition against the deduction of a "payment on account of capital" under paragraph 18(1)(b): *Canada Safeway Ltd. v. M.N.R.*, [1957] S.C.R. 717, [1957] C.T.C. 335, at 722-23 (C.T.C. 339-40) per Kerwin, C.J. and at 727 (C.T.C. 344) per Rand, J.

... Parliament created subparagraph 20(1)(c)(i), and made it operate notwithstanding paragraph 18(1)(b), in order to encourage the accumulation of capital which would produce taxable income. Not all borrowing expenses are deductible. Interest on borrowed money used to produce tax exempt income is not deductible. Interest on borrowed money used to buy life insurance policies is not deductible. Interest on borrowings used for non-income earning purposes, such as personal consumption or the making of capital gains is similarly not deductible. The statutory deduction thus requires a characterization of the use of borrowed money as between the eligible use of earning non-exempt income from a business or property and a variety of possible ineligible uses. The onus is on the taxpayer to trace the borrowed funds to an identifiable use which triggers the deduction. Therefore, if the taxpayer commingles funds used for a variety of purposes only some of which are eligible he or she may be unable to claim the deduction: see, for example, *Mills v. M.N.R.*, [1985] 2 C.T.C. 2334, 85 D.T.C. 632 (T.C.C.), *No. 616 v. M.N.R.*, 22 Tax A.B.C. 31, 59 D.T.C. 247 (T.A.B.).

The interest deduction provision requires not only a characterization of the use of borrowed funds, but also a characterization of "purpose". Eligibility for the deduction is contingent on the use of borrowed money for the purpose of earning income. It is well established in the jurisprudence, however, that it is not the purpose of the borrowing itself which is relevant. What is relevant, rather, is the taxpayer's purpose in using the borrowed money in a particular manner: *Auld v. M.N.R.*, 28 Tax A.B.C. 236, 62 D.T.C. 27 (T.A.B.). Consequently, the focus of the inquiry must be centred on the use to which the taxpayer put the borrowed funds.

In my opinion, the distinction between eligible and ineligible uses of borrowed funds applies just as much to taxpayers who are corporations or trusts as it does to taxpayers who are natural persons. While it is true that corporations or trusts are less likely to be motivated by personal consumption purposes, there remains nevertheless a variety of ineligible uses for borrowed money which apply to artificial persons. A trust may, for example, purchase assets for the purpose of capital gain. Or, as in the present instance, it may distribute capital to a trust beneficiary. It follows, with respect, that I cannot accept the suggestion of the majority of the Federal Court of Appeal that virtually any use of borrowed funds by a trust, rather than by an individual, will satisfy the requirements of the statutory interest deduction. Fairness requires that the same legal principles must apply to all taxpayers, irrespective of their status as natural or artificial persons, unless the Act specifically provides otherwise.

...

The cases are consistent with the proposition that it is the current use rather than the original use of borrowed funds by the taxpayer which is relevant in assessing deductibility of interest payments: see, for example, *Lakeview Gardens Corporation v. M.N.R.*, [1973] C.T.C. 586, 73 D.T.C. 5437 (F.C.T.D.), per Walsh, J., for a correct application of this principle. A taxpayer cannot continue to deduct interest payments merely because the original use of borrowed money was to purchase income-bearing assets, after he or she has sold those assets and put the proceeds of sale to an ineligible use. To permit the taxpayer to do so would result in the borrowing of funds to finance the purchase of income-earning property which could be re-sold immediately without affecting the deductibility of interest payments for an indefinite period thereafter.

Conversely, a taxpayer who uses or intends to use borrowed money for an ineligible purpose, but later uses the funds to earn non-exempt income from a business or property, ought not to be deprived of the deduction for the current, eligible use: [1981] C.T.C. 2599, 81 D.T.C. 465 (T.R.B.); *Attaie v. M.N.R.*, [1985] 2 C.T.C. 2331, 83 D.T.C. 613 (T.C.C.) (presently under appeal). For example, if a taxpayer borrows to buy personal property which he or she subsequently sells, the interest payments will become prospectively deductible if the proceeds of sale are used to purchase eligible income-earning property.

There is, however, an important natural limitation on this principle. The borrowed funds must still be in the hands of the taxpayer, as traced through the proceeds of disposition of the preceding ineligible use, if the taxpayer is to claim the deduction on the basis of a current eligible use. Where the taxpayer has expended the borrowings on an ineligible use, and has received no enduring benefit or saleable property in return, the borrowed money can obviously not be available to the taxpayer for a subsequent use, whether eligible or ineligible. A continuing obligation to make interest payments to the creditor therefore does not conclusively demonstrate that the borrowed money has a continuing use for the taxpayer.

In the present case the borrowed money was originally used to make capital allocations to the beneficiary for which the trust received no property or consideration of any kind. That use of the borrowings was indisputably not of an income-earning nature. Accordingly, unless the direct use of the money ought to be overlooked in favour of an alleged indirect income-earning use, the trust cannot be permitted to deduct the interest payments in issue in this appeal.

...

As I have indicated, the respondent trust submits that the borrowed funds permitted the trust to retain income-earning properties which it otherwise would have sold in order to make the capital allocations to the beneficiary. Such a use of borrowings, it argues, is sufficient in law to entitle it to the interest deduction. In short, the Court is asked to characterize the transaction on the basis of a purported indirect use of borrowed money to earn income rather than on the basis of a direct use of funds that was counter-productive to the trust's income-earning capacity.

In my view, neither the *Income Tax Act* nor the weight of judicial authority permits the courts to ignore the direct use to which a taxpayer puts borrowed money. One need only contemplate the consequences of the interpretation sought by the trust in order to reach the conclusion that it cannot have been intended by Parliament. In order for the trust to succeed, subparagraph 20(1)(c)(i) would have to be interpreted so that a deduction would be permitted for borrowings by any taxpayer who owned income-producing assets. Such a taxpayer could, on this view, apply the proceeds of a loan to purchase a life insurance policy, to take a vacation, to buy speculative properties, or to engage in any other non-income-earning or ineligible activity. Nevertheless, the interest would be deductible. A less wealthy taxpayer, with no income-earning assets, would not be able to deduct interest payments on loans used in the identical fashion. Such an interpretation would be unfair as between taxpayers and would make a mockery of the statutory requirement that, for interest payments to be deductible, borrowed money must be used for circumscribed income-earning purposes.

One finds in the Act not only the distinction within subparagraph 20(1)(c)(i) between eligible and ineligible uses of funds, but other provisions which also require the tracing of funds to particular uses in a manner inconsistent with the argument of the trust. Subsection 20(3) (formerly subsection 11(3b)) stipulates, for example, that interest on money borrowed to repay an existing loan shall be deemed to have been used for the purpose for which the previous borrowings were used. This provision would, of course, be unnecessary if interest on borrowed money were deductible when the taxpayer had income-earning properties to preserve. On the contrary, however, for taxation years prior to the enactment of subsection 11(3b) in S.C. 1953-54, c. 57, s. 2(6), it had been held that such interest was not deductible since the borrowings were used to repay a loan and not to earn income: *Interior Breweries Ltd. v. M.N.R.*, [1955] C.T.C. 143 at 148, 55 D.T.C. 1090 at 1093 (Exch. Ct.).

It is not surprising, therefore, that the cases interpreting subparagraph 20(1)(c)(i) and its predecessor provisions have not favoured the view that a direct ineligible use of borrowed money ought to be overlooked whenever an indirect eligible use of funds can be found. See *Sternthal and also Garneau Marine Co. v. M.N.R.*, [1982] C.T.C. 21, 82 D.T.C. 1171 (T.R.B.).

In a similar vein, it has been held repeatedly that an individual cannot deduct interest paid on the mortgage of a personal residence even though he or she claims that the borrowing avoided the need to sell income-producing investments. Some of the more recent cases include: *Toolsie v. The Queen*,

[1986] 1 C.T.C. 216, 86 D.T.C. 6117 (F.C.T.D.), *Jordanov v. M.N.R.*, [1986] 1 C.T.C. 2183, 86 D.T.C. 1136 (T.C.C.), *Day v. M.N.R.*, [1984] C.T.C. 2200, 84 D.T.C. 1184 (T.C.C.), *Eelkema v. M.N.R.*, [1983] C.T.C. 2311, 83 D.T.C. 253 (T.R.B.), *Zanyk v. M.N.R.*, [1981] C.T.C. 2042, 81 D.T.C. 48 (T.R.B.), *Holmann v. M.N.R.*, [1979] C.T.C. 2653, 79 D.T.C. 594 (T.R.B.), *Huber v. M.N.R.*, [1979] C.T.C. 3161, 79 D.T.C. 936 (T.R.B.), *Dorman v. M.N.R.*, [1977] C.T.C. 2355, 77 D.T.C. 251 (T.R.B.), and *Verhoeven v. M.N.R.*, [1975] C.T.C. 2292, 75 D.T.C. 230 (T.R.B.). It has also been held in a number of cases that an estate cannot deduct interest paid on borrowings used to pay succession duties or taxes even though the estate claims to have borrowed in lieu of selling income-producing investments: *Shields v. M.N.R.*, [1968] Tax A.B.C. 909, 68 D.T.C. 668, *Auld v. M.N.R.*, *Cutten v. M.N.R.*, 16 Tax A.B.C. 1, 56 D.T.C. 454, *No. 228 v. M.N.R.*, 12 Tax A.B.C. 83, 55 D.T.C. 39, *No. 185 v. M.N.R.*, 11 Tax A.B.C. 173, 54 D.T.C. 395.

The leading case from this Court on the availability of the interest deduction, *Canada Safeway Ltd. v. M.N.R.*, also demonstrates a reluctance to overlook a clearly ineligible direct use of borrowed money in order to favour the taxpayer by characterizing the transaction on the basis of a less direct eligible use of borrowings. The taxpayer corporation in that case sought to deduct the interest on a series of debentures which the corporation used to finance the purchase of shares in another, related corporation. In the period in question, 1947-1949, dividends from shares of Canadian corporations were exempted from taxable income. To the extent to which the debentures were used to produce dividend income from shares, the taxpayer was accordingly ineligible for the interest deduction. The taxpayer corporation argued however that the share purchase not only provided dividend income, but also increased the taxpayer's income from its existing business operations by giving it control over a wholesale supplier. This conferred a considerable advantage on the taxpayer relative to its competitors and allowed it to increase significantly its net income. Nevertheless, the Court held that the interest payments were not deductible, Locke, J. dissenting. Justice Rand stated, at 726 (C.T.C. 343):

> No doubt there is in fact a causal connection between the purchase of the stock and the benefits ultimately received; but the statutory language cannot be extended to such a remote consequence; it could be carried to any length in a chain of subsidiaries; and to say that such a thing was envisaged by the ordinary expression used in the statute is to speculate and not interpret.

Referring to the interest expense deduction for borrowed money used for the purpose of earning income from business, Rand, J. concluded at 727 (C.T.C. 345):

> What is aimed at by the section is an employment of the borrowed funds immediately within the company's business and not one that effects its purpose in such an indirect and remote manner.

Turning to borrowings used to generate income from property, he said:

> There is nothing in this language to extend the application to an acquisition of "power" annexed to stock, and to the indirect and remote effects upon the company of action taken in the course of business of the subsidiary.

Although the *Canada Safeway* case did not relate specifically to an alleged indirect use of funds to preserve income-producing assets, the emphasis on directness of use of borrowed funds in the reasons of Justice Rand is antithetical to the submission of the taxpayer in the present appeal.

The respondent trust prefers the decision of Jackett, P. in *Trans-Prairie*. In that case, as I have already indicated, Jackett, P. relied on the proposition, perfectly correct in so far as it goes, that it is the current use and not the original use of borrowed money that determines eligibility for a deduction. As stated previously, however, the fact that the taxpayer continues to pay interest does not inevitably lead to the conclusion that the borrowed money is still being used by the taxpayer, let alone being used for an income-earning purpose. For example, an asset purchased with borrowed money may have been disposed of, while the debt incurred in its purchase remains unpaid.

With the exception of *Trans-Prairie*, then, the reasoning of which is, in my opinion, inadequate to support the conclusion sought to be reached by the respondent trust, the jurisprudence has generally been hostile to claims based on indirect, eligible uses when faced with direct but ineligible uses of borrowed money.

I acknowledge, however, that just as there has been a recent trend away from strict construction of taxation statutes (see *Stubart Investments Ltd. v. The Queen*, [1984] 1 S.C.R. 536 at 573-79, [1984] C.T.C. 294 at 313-316 and *The Queen v. Golden*, [1986] 1 S.C.R. 209 at 214-15, [1986] 1 C.T.C. 274 at 277), so too has the recent trend in tax cases been towards attempting to ascertain the true commercial and practical nature of the taxpayer's transactions. There has been, in this country and elsewhere, a movement away from tests based on the form of transactions and towards tests based on what Lord Pearce has referred to as a "common sense appreciation of all the guiding features" of the events in question: *B.P. Australia Ltd. v. Commissioner of Taxation of Australia*, [1966] A.C. 224 at 264, [1965] 3 All E.R. 209 at 218 (P.C.). See also *F.H. Jones Tobacco Sales Company Ltd.*, [1973] F.C. 825 at 834, [1973] C.T.C. 784 at 790 (T.D.) per Noël, A.C.J.; *Hallstroms Pty. Ltd. v. Federal Commissioner of Taxation* (1946), 8 A.T.D. 190 (High Ct.) at 196 per Dixon, J.; and *Cochrane*

Estate v. M.N.R., [1976] C.T.C. 2215, 76 D.T.C. 1154 (T.R.B.), per Mr. A. W. Prociuk, Q.C.

This is, I believe, a laudable trend provided it is consistent with the text and purposes of the taxation statute. Assessment of taxpayers' transactions with an eye to commercial and economic realities, rather than juristic classification of form, may help to avoid the inequity of tax liability being dependent upon the taxpayer's sophistication at manipulating a sequence of events to achieve a patina of compliance with the apparent prerequisites for a tax deduction.

This does not mean, however, that a deduction such as the interest deduction in subparagraph 20(1)(c)(i), which by its very text is made available to the taxpayer in limited circumstances, is suddenly to lose all its strictures. It is not lightly to be assumed that an actual and direct use of borrowed money is any less real than the abstract and remote indirect uses which have, on occasion, been advanced by taxpayers in an effort to achieve a favourable characterization. In particular, I believe that despite the fact that it can be characterized as indirectly preserving income, borrowing money for an ineligible direct purpose ought not [to] entitle a taxpayer to deduct interest payments.

The taxpayer in such a situation has doubly reduced his or her long run income-earning capacity: first, by expending capital in a manner that does not produce taxable income; and second, by incurring debt financing charges. The taxpayer, of course, has a right to spend money in ways which cannot reasonably be expected to generate taxable income but if the taxpayer chooses to do so, he or she cannot expect any advantageous treatment by the tax assessor. In my view, the text of the Act requires tracing the use of borrowed funds to a specific eligible use, its obviously restricted purpose being the encouragement of taxpayers to augment their income-producing potential. This, in my view, precludes the allowance of a deduction for interest paid on borrowed funds which indirectly preserve income-earning property but which are not directly "used for the purpose of earning income from ... property".

Even if there are exceptional circumstances in which, on a real appreciation of a taxpayer's transactions, it might be appropriate to allow the taxpayer to deduct interest on funds borrowed for an ineligible use because of an indirect effect on the taxpayer's income-earning capacity, I am satisfied that those circumstances are not presented in the case before us. It seems to me that, at the very least, the taxpayer must satisfy the Court that his or her bona fide purpose in using the funds was to earn income. In contrast to what appears to be the case in Trans-Prairie, the facts in the present case fall far short of such a showing. Indeed, it is of more than passing interest that the assets which were preserved for a brief period of time yielded a return which grossly fell short of the interest costs on the borrowed money. In 1970, the interest costs on the $2.2 million of loans amounted to over $110,000 while the return from an average $2.2 million of trust assets (the amount of capital "preserved") was less than $10,000. The taxpayer cannot point to any reasonable expectation that the income yield from the trust's investment portfolio as a whole, or indeed from any single asset, would exceed the interest payable on a like amount of debt. The fact that the loan may have prevented capital losses cannot assist the taxpayer in obtaining a deduction from income which is limited to use of borrowed money for the purpose of earning income.

Before concluding, I wish to address one final argument raised by counsel for the trust. It was submitted — and the Crown generously conceded — that the trust would have obtained an interest deduction if it had sold assets to make the capital allocation and borrowed to replace them. Accordingly, it is argued, the trust ought not to be precluded from an interest deduction merely because it achieved the same effect without the formalities of a sale and repurchase of assets. It would be a sufficient answer to this submission to point to the principle that the courts must deal with what the taxpayer actually did, and not what he might have done: *Matheson v. The Queen*, [1974] C.T.C. 186 at 189, 74 D.T.C. 6176 at 6179 (F.C.T.D.) per Mahoney, J. In any event, I admit to some doubt about the premise conceded by the Crown. If, for example, the trust had sold a particular income-producing asset, made the capital allocation to the beneficiary and repurchased the same asset, all within a brief interval of time, the courts might well consider the sale and repurchase to constitute a formality or a sham designed to conceal the essence of the transaction, namely that money was borrowed and used to fund a capital allocation to the beneficiary. In this regard, see *Zwaig v. M.N.R.*, [1974] C.T.C. 2172, 74 D.T.C. 1121 (T.R.B.), in which the taxpayer sold securities and used the proceeds to buy a life insurance policy. He then borrowed on the policy to repurchase the securities. Under subparagraph 20(1)(c)(i) the use of borrowed money to purchase a life insurance policy is not a use entitling the taxpayer to an interest deduction. The Tax Review Board rightly disallowed the deduction sought for interest payments, notwithstanding that the form of the taxpayer's transactions created an aura of compliance with the requirements of the interest deduction provision. The characterization of taxpayers' transactions according to their true commercial and practical nature does not always favour the taxpayer. The taxpayer trust in this appeal asks the Court for the benefit of a characterization based on the alleged commercial and practical nature of its transactions. At the same time, however, it seeks to have the commercial and practical nature of its transactions determined by reference to a hypothetical characterization which reflects the epitome of formalism. I cannot accept that it should be allowed to succeed.

[*Appeal allowed.*]

The courts since *Bronfman* are reluctant to recognize an indirect use of borrowed funds in characterizing interest expense as income-earning. In *The Queen v. Attaie*, [1990] 2 C.T.C. 157, 90 D.T.C. 6413 (F.C.A.), the taxpayer moved from Iran to

Canada and borrowed funds to purchase a house. Initially, the house was rented out and the rental income declared on his tax return. He deducted expenses related to the property including the interest paid pursuant to the mortgage. The taxpayer subsequently moved into the property, occupying it as his residence. Shortly thereafter, he received $200,000 from Iran. Rather than use this money to pay off the mortgage, the taxpayer chose to invest the $200,000 in term deposits because the rate of interest on the investments was significantly higher than the interest payable under the mortgage. On his income tax returns for the years in which he occupied the house, the taxpayer sought to offset the interest payable under the mortgage against the interest generated by the term deposits. In denying the deduction of mortgage interest, the court looked to the direct use of the borrowed funds. The money was borrowed to finance a personal residence, an ineligible use; therefore, the taxpayer could not deduct the mortgage interest. Contrast *The Queen v. Attaie* with the following case.

SINGLETON v. THE QUEEN
[2002] 1 C.T.C. 121, 2001 D.T.C. 5533 (S.C.C.)

The judgment of the court was delivered by:

Major J.

...

The respondent is a partner in the law firm Singleton Urquhart. On October 27, 1988 the amount in the respondent's capital account at the law firm was at least $300,000. The respondent's original capital contributions had not been financed with borrowed funds. On October 27, 1988 the respondent wanted to do a number of things. He wanted to use $300,000 of his equity in the law firm to assist in the purchase of a house. He then wanted to borrow that same amount and use it to refinance his partnership capital account.

There is less than full agreement on how the respondent achieved these results and the record is unclear as to the sequence of the transactions that occurred on October 27, 1988. While not central to this appeal, the transactions occurred in one of two possible ways.

One way was that found by the Tax Court Judge, that is that $298,750 of money borrowed from the Bank of British Columbia, along with $1,250 of the respondent's own money, went into the firm trust account. A cheque for $300,000 was then paid into the partnership general account and credited to the respondent's capital account. The partnership then paid $300,000 by cheque to the respondent, who deposited this money into his personal bank account. The respondent then issued a cheque drawn on his personal bank account, payable to the firm, for $300,000. This amount was deposited into a client trust account. The respondent's spouse deposited $147,901 into the same account.

The firm issued a cheque for $440,451 drawn on the client trust account and payable to the solicitors for the vendors of the house.

The other way as found by the Court of Appeal, was that on October 27, 1988, the firm paid the respondent Singleton $300,000 from his capital account. He used the $300,000 to assist in the purchase of a house registered in his wife's name. Later that same day, the respondent borrowed $400,000 from the Bank of British Columbia, only $298,750 of which is relevant to this appeal, and together with $1,250 of his own money, paid $300,000 back into his capital account at the law firm.

Counsel for the respondent conceded that the record is unclear as to whether the $300,000 came out of the firm before the money was borrowed. However, it is undisputed that the respondent had at least $300,000 in his capital account on October 27, 1988. Furthermore, all of the relevant cheques were deposited and honoured.

The respondent paid interest of $3,688.52 in 1988 and $27,415.46 in 1989 and deducted the interest on his tax return for those years, pursuant to s. 20(1)(c)(i) of the Act. The Minister reassessed and denied the interest deduction on the grounds that the borrowed money was used to finance the purchase of the house. The Tax Court of Canada dismissed the respondent's appeal. The majority of the Federal Court of Appeal allowed the respondent's appeal.

...

Was the borrowed money "used for the purpose of earning income from a business" such that the interest is deductible pursuant to s. 20(1)(c)(i) of the Act?

...

Bowman J.T.C.C. concluded that it was an "inescapable factual determination that the true economic purpose for which the borrowed money was used was the purchase of a house" (p. 2878). Linden J.A., in dissent, held that this was a factual determination which should not be interfered with. I respectfully disagree. I adopt the conclusion of Rothstein J.A. That is, this appeal raises the issue of what is the proper legal test under s. 20(1)(c)(i). That is a question of law. For the reasons outlined, the Tax Court Judge, in searching for the "true economic purpose", applied the wrong legal test.

...

The law with regard to s. 20(1)(c)(i) was recently clarified in *Shell Canada Ltd. v. Canada*, [1999] 3 S.C.R. 622, [1999] 4 C.T.C. 313, 99 D.T.C. 5669 (S.C.C.). The decision in Shell is determinative of the issue in this case. The key principles from that case bear repeating.

In *Shell*, *supra*, McLachlin J. (later Chief Justice), writing for the Court, confirmed that s. 20(1)(c)(i) contains four elements (at para. 28):

> (1) the amount must be paid in the year or be payable in the year in which it is sought to be deducted; (2) the amount must be paid pursuant to a legal obligation to pay interest on borrowed money; (3) the borrowed money must be used for the purpose of earning non-exempt income from a business or property; and (4) the amount must be reasonable, as assessed by reference to the first three requirements.

Only the third element is at issue in this appeal: the borrowed money must be used for the purpose of earning non-exempt income from a business. The *Shell* case confirmed that the focus of the inquiry is not on the purpose of the borrowing per se, but is on the taxpayer's purpose in using the money. McLachlin J. agreed with Dickson C.J. in *Bronfman Trust* that the inquiry must be centred on the use to which the taxpayer put the borrowed funds. McLachlin J. made it clear that the deduction is not available where the link between the borrowed money and the eligible use is indirect. However, she made it equally clear that "[i]f a direct link can be drawn between the borrowed money and an eligible use" this third element is satisfied (para. 33).

In examining the Minister's argument about the need to consider the economic realities of a transaction rather than being bound to its strict legal effects, McLachlin J. recognized that the courts must be sensitive to the economic realities of a transaction. However, she stated that (at paras. 39-40):

> ... this Court has never held that the economic realities of a situation can be used to recharacterize a taxpayer's bona fide relationships. To the contrary, we have held that, absent a specific provision of the Act to the contrary or a finding that they are a sham, the taxpayer's legal relationships must be respected in tax cases. ...
>
> Second, it is well established in this Court's tax jurisprudence that a searching inquiry for either the "economic realities" of a particular transaction or the general object and spirit of the provision at issue can never supplant a court's duty to apply an unambiguous provision of the Act to a taxpayer's transaction. Where the provision at issue is clear and unambiguous, its terms must simply be applied. [References omitted.]

The Court in *Shell* emphasized that taxpayers are entitled to structure their transactions in a manner that reduces taxes (see for example paras. 45 and 46). The fact that the structures may be complex arrangements does not remove the right to do so.

It is now plain from the reasoning in *Shell* that the issue to be determined is the direct use to which the borrowed funds were put. "It is irrelevant why the borrowing arrangement was structured the way it was or, indeed, why the funds were borrowed at all" (*Shell, supra*, para. 47).

...

The appellant, the Minister in Right of the Crown, relied on the reasons of the Tax Court Judge and Linden J.A., in dissent, and urged the Court to examine the "economic realities" of the taxpayer's transactions in determining whether the requirements of s. 20(1)(c)(i) had been met.

Applying *Shell*, I decline to do so. This Court must simply apply s. 20(1)(c)(i) rather than search for the economic realities of the transaction.

In applying s. 20(1)(c)(i) here, the relevant question is: to what use were the borrowed funds put? The Tax Court Judge found that the purpose in using the money was to purchase a house and that this purpose could not be altered by the "shuffle of cheques" that occurred on October 27, 1988. I respectfully disagree. It is this "shuffle of cheques" that defines the legal relationship which must be given effect. The respondent had at least $300,000 of his own money in the law firm. Surely it follows that the $300,000 invested in the law firm was not frozen for all time in the form of its original investment. The respondent was free to change his mind and decide whether to use his own money or borrowed money to finance the business of his law firm. In reviewing what the respondent did, it is clear that the relevant cheques were deposited and honoured. There is no suggestion that the transaction was a sham. Giving effect to the legal relationships in this case, it is clear that the respondent used the borrowed funds to refinance his capital account.

This characterization of the use of the funds is not altered by the fact that the respondent used the money he withdrew from the firm to purchase a house. Nor is it altered by the fact that the transactions occurred on the same day.

In my respectful opinion, it is an error to treat this as one simultaneous transaction. In order to give effect to the legal relationships, the transactions must be viewed independently. When viewed that way, on either version of the facts (i.e. regardless of the sequence), what the respondent did in this case was use the borrowed funds for the purpose of refinancing his partnership capital account with debt. This is the legal transaction to which the Court must give effect. In this regard, I adopt the following reasons of Rothstein J.A. (at para. 54):

> In the case at bar, the direct use of the borrowed funds was to refinance the appellant's capital account at the firm. Treating the borrowed funds as used for financing the purchase of the home ignores what the appellant actually did, i.e. used the borrowed funds to replace the funds required for his capital account at the firm. As stated by Dickson C.J. in Bronfman Trust, the Court cannot ignore the direct use to which the appellant put the borrowed money.

The fact that the money was borrowed in order to allow the respondent to use his own money to purchase the house is of no moment. The Shell decision decided that why the money was borrowed is irrelevant. The fact that money was transferred from the firm to the respondent for the purchase of a residential property has no impact on the application of s. 20(1)(c)(i) to the interest incurred on borrowed money which was used directly for the purpose of refinancing the capital, and as such used for the purpose of earning income from the law firm.

...

If a direct link can be drawn between the borrowed money and an eligible use, then the money was used for the purpose of earning income from a business or property. That is clearly the case in this appeal. The respondent was entitled to deduct the relevant interest payments from his income.

The appellant submitted that even if there is a direct link between the borrowed funds and an eligible use, the respondent must still demonstrate that his bona fide purpose in using the funds was to earn income. However, as explained in *Ludmer c. Ministre du Revenue national*, [2002] 1 C.T.C. 95, (sub nom. *Ludco Enterprises Ltd. v. The Queen*) 2001 D.T.C. 5505, (sub nom. *Ludco Enterprises Ltd. v. Canada*) [2001] 2 S.C.R. 1082 (S.C.C.), the appellant's overriding concern for determining the respondent's bona fide purpose in using the funds is not consistent with the express wording of s. 20(1)(c)(i). Absent a sham or window-dressing or other vitiating circumstances, none of which was alleged in this case, the respondent does not have to demonstrate a bona fide purpose.

The appellant also relied upon the following obiter dicta statement in *Bronfman Trust* to support the position that even if there is a direct eligible use, the interest is not deductible (at pp. 54-55):

> Before concluding, I wish to address one final argument raised by counsel for the Trust. It was submitted – and the Crown generously conceded – that the Trust would have obtained an interest deduction if it had sold assets to make the capital allocation and borrowed to replace them. Accordingly, it is argued, the Trust ought not to be precluded from an interest deduction merely because it achieved the same effect without the formalities of a sale and repurchase of assets. It would be sufficient answer to this submission to point to the principle that the courts must deal with what the taxpayer actually did, and not what he might have done. ... In any event, I admit to some doubt about the premise conceded by the Crown. If, for example, the Trust had sold a particular income-producing asset, made the capital allocation to the beneficiary and repurchased the same asset, all within a brief interval of time, the courts might well consider the sale and repurchase to constitute a formality or a sham designed to conceal the essence of the transaction, namely that money was borrowed and used to fund a capital allocation to the beneficiary. In this regard, see *Zwaig v. M.N.R.*, [1974] C.T.C. 2172, 74 D.T.C. 1121 (T.R.B.), in which the taxpayer sold securities and used the proceeds to buy a life insurance policy. He then borrowed on the policy to repurchase the securities. Under s. 20(1)(c)(i) the use of borrowed money to purchase a life insurance policy is not a use entitling the taxpayer to an interest deduction. The Tax Review Board rightly disallowed

> the deduction sought for interest payments, notwithstanding that the form of the taxpayer's transactions created an aura of compliance with the requirements of the interest deduction provision. The characterization of taxpayers' transactions according to their true commercial and practical nature does not always favour the taxpayer. The taxpayer Trust in this appeal asks the Court for the benefit of a characterization based on the alleged commercial and practical nature of its transactions. At the same time, however, it seeks to have the commercial and practical nature of its transactions determined by reference to a hypothetical characterization which reflects the epitome of formalism. I cannot accept that it should be allowed to succeed.

The appellant has over-stated the importance of this statement. It is clear that Dickson C.J. was simply responding to a hypothetical question in a somewhat tentative way. This was more musing than jurisprudence. As well, it is noteworthy that in the Shell decision the Court, although invited to, declined to follow other obiter dicta statements from Bronfman Trust that similarly suggested that sophisticated transactions designed to minimize tax liability should not be given effect.

In summary, it is irrelevant that by his own admission the respondent structured the transaction for tax purposes. Courts cannot search for the "economic reality" or the "bona fide" purpose of the transaction in this case. In giving effect to the legal relationships underlying the transactions here, it is obvious that the borrowed money was used directly to refinance the respondent's capital account. This is a direct, eligible use within the meaning of s. 20(1)(c)(i) of the Act. The respondent was entitled to deduct the interest expenses.

...

Problems, Notes and Questions

1. In what respects do the circumstances of *Singleton* differ from those in *Attaie*? Is there any significant difference between a taxpayer who uses personal savings stored up in a bank account to purchase a house and at the same time borrow funds to invest in a business and Singleton's withdrawal of equity in his law firm to purchase a home and the subsequent borrowing to replenish the capital account?
2. Can a taxpayer deduct interest as a business expense when the interest expense grossly exceeds the income that the borrowed funds generate? See *Ludco Enterprises et al., supra*, and subsection 9(3).
3. X borrows $10,000 and uses it to buy common shares. Is the interest deductible? What if
   - the shares do not pay any dividends for several years?
   - X sells the shares for $10,000 and uses the proceeds to take a vacation?
   - X sells the shares for $5,000 (i.e., at a loss) and repays $5,000 of the loan? Is the interest on the balance of the loan deductible?

- X owns shares worth $10,000 and borrows $10,000 to take a vacation?
- X sells the shares, uses the proceeds to take a vacation and then borrows and reacquires the shares?
- X borrows to repay an existing loan? See subsection 20(3)?
- X borrows to pay the outstanding interest on an existing loan?

4. Why is a specific authorization necessary for the deduction of interest? Would interest be deductible as an ordinary business expense in the absence of paragraph 20(1)(c)? What is the policy underlying the deductibility of interest? Is paragraph 20(1)(c) broad enough?
5. Under paragraph 20(1)(c), the amount of the interest paid or payable or a reasonable amount in respect thereof, whichever is the lesser, may be deducted. What is a reasonable amount of interest in any particular case?
6. Paragraph 20(1)(c) permits the deduction of interest in the year in which it is paid or in the year in respect of which it is payable. What is the difference? The deduction of interest expense on either a paid or payable basis must accord with "the method regularly followed by the taxpayer in computing his income". How does this condition restrict a taxpayer's option with respect to the year in which interest expense may be deducted? See *Crown Forest Industries Ltd. v. The Queen*, [2006] 2 C.T.C. 2332, 2006 D.T.C. 2321 (T.C.C.). What is the relationship between the timing rules in paragraph 20(1)(c) and subsections 18(9) and (9.2)?
7. Interest on money borrowed or property acquired to produce exempt income is not deductible. Under the pre-1972 Act, this restriction prevented a corporation from deducting interest on borrowed money used to acquire shares in another corporation, as intercorporate dividends were within the definition of "exempt income" in the predecessor to subsection 248(1). That definition was amended in 1972 to expressly exclude intercorporate dividends. Consequently, interest on borrowed money used to acquire shares in another corporation is now deductible under paragraph 20(1)(c). The former restriction was sharply criticized as one of the causes of the numerous takeovers of Canadian corporations by foreign corporations. In effect, there was an apparent competitive disadvantage for Canadian corporations, since other countries generally permitted the deduction of interest expense incurred in a takeover.
8. In *Ludco Enterprises Ltd. v. Canada*, [2001] 2 S.C.R. 1082, [2002] 1 C.T.C. 95, 2001 D.T.C. 5505, the Court held that the text of subparagraph 20(1)(c)(i) did not indicate that the income-earning purpose had to be the exclusive, primary or dominant purpose of the borrowed funds so as to qualify the interest for deductibility. As long as one of the purposes was to earn income, this is sufficient to engage subparagraph 20(1)(c)(i).

G. The Requirement of Reasonableness

Section 67 provides that no deduction shall be made in respect of an outlay or expense otherwise deductible under the Act, except to the extent that the outlay or expense was reasonable in the circumstances. The section does not prohibit an unreasonable deduction but rather operates to reduce it to a reasonable amount.

In most cases in which section 67 has been applied, it has served to curb a contrived reduction of income through the deduction of expenses that are largely personal in nature, or where amounts have been diverted to persons who are not at arm's length.

MULDER BROS. v. M.N.R.
[1967] Tax A.B.C. 761, 67 D.T.C. 475

J.O. Weldon, Q.C.:

... Incidentally, it is plainly the responsibility of the Minister under Section 12(2) [currently section 67] of the Act, in the first instance, to decide when an outlay or expense otherwise deductible is reasonable in the circumstances, and it should be assumed that he is aware of the current rates of salaries in various industries and occupations.

It was after receiving the above-quoted letter of Dirk Mulder, dated February 11, 1965, outlining his wife's duties and status in the company, that the Minister issued his Notice of Reassessment dated May 5, 1965 in which he disallowed the sum of $7,000 of the $13,000 salary paid to Mrs. Mulder by the appellant in its 1963 taxation year. In other words, with the information contained in Dirk Mulder's letter before him, the Minister's assessor, presumably, concluded that the sum of $6,000 was what he considered to be a proper amount to be deducted from the taxpayer's income as a salary expense in the circumstances having in mind that it had to pass the test of reasonableness, as prescribed by section 12(2) of the Act. Prima facie, that conclusion does not appear to be entirely without merit. However, the Board has now been furnished with a much more complete picture of Mrs. Velma Mulder's duties and position in Mulder Bros. in the taxation year in question than could possibly have been available to the assessor. Before her marriage in 1947, Mrs. Mulder had obtained a good practical commercial background and had actually held for several years a position of some responsibility in the branch office of a forwarding company. So, she was accustomed to dealing with the practices and problems related to the trucking business. In the beginning, Mrs. Mulder probably knew a great deal more than her husband about running an office and, since she set out to be just as helpful to him as she could possibly be, she must have been invaluable indeed.

In the result, I have come to the conclusion that, under the economic conditions of the past few years and, bearing in mind that the Minister has not questioned a salary of $20,000 to Everett Mulder in the 1963 taxation year even though he seems to have devoted himself primarily to his and Dirk Mulder's market gardening business, the facts of this matter amply justify the appellant charging a salary of $8,500 to Mrs. Velma Mulder as an item of expense in the said taxation year. Accordingly, the $7,000 amount disallowed by the Minister in connection with her salary, which is the subject matter of this appeal, should be reduced to the sum of $4,500.

Before completing these reasons there are several comments which I would like to make. First, it is my considered opinion that it was not open to Dirk Mulder to cause his salary in the 1963 taxation year to be set at the sum of $13,000 or $7,000 less than the $20,000 salary set for his brother Everett Mulder so that the salary of his wife, Mrs. Velma Mulder, could be set with the approval of his said brother (the other principal shareholder of the appellant) at the same amount as his own, namely, $13,000. To permit him to do that would, in effect, give him the right to juggle his income to attract a minimum of tax which would most certainly be contrary to the spirit of the Act as presently constituted. Secondly, even though I was duly impressed with Mrs. Mulder's services to Mulder Bros. both in the years preceding its incorporation in January 1958 and in the years subsequent thereto, I do not think that it is sound for a corporation to add something directly into the salary of one of its officers for past services, although it should, in my view, place due importance on the value of the training and experience of such company officer which was gained in the years of his or her employment in the corporation. Mrs. Velma Mulder, as a key member of the company's management, had, of course, a firsthand picture of its finances and, consequently, had the assurance at all times that she was helping her husband and his brother build a strong, reliable and expanding business for the security of the two families in the future. Thirdly, if a corporate taxpayer, such as the appellant, still has profits available for distribution to its working shareholders, after paying reasonable salaries to them in the circumstances, such profits can, of course, be paid out to the shareholders as cash dividends which could be considered as a return on the capital invested in the company.

NO. 511 v. M.N.R.
(1958), 19 Tax A.B.C. 248, 58 D.T.C. 307

Maurice Boisvert, Q.C.:

... On July 4, 1956, the taxpayer served on the Minister a Notice of Objection stating that the disallowance of a sum of $22,500 by the Department of National Revenue was improper because that sum represented the cost of the sponsoring of a baseball team for the purpose of advertising the company's product in the western Provinces. It is also stated that the expenditure was incurred for the purpose of producing or maintaining income and that the company had gained considerable publicity from this form of advertising. ...

In view of all this, I am obliged to declare that the appellant company is entitled to a deduction with respect to the expenditure incurred in sponsoring the X Baseball team. Of course, the deduction must be within the provisions of subsection (2) of Section 12 of said Act, [currently section 67] that is to say "reasonable in the circumstances".

Advertising today is a necessity of trade but it does not mean that one engaged in a business must spend on advertising all the profits produced from his business activity. It is legitimate to promote goodwill, the quality of goods, the efficiency of a service, even the name of a commercial firm, but, for the purpose of the *Income Tax Act*, the legitimacy of the thing does not always legitimate the expenditures. In determining the reasonableness of an advertising expense, it is well to take cognizance of the size of the business, the patronage to be expected in the future, the form of advertising, the locality where it is done, the size of population reached by the advertising.

The circumstances revealed by the evidence do not give an opening to accept the full amount spent by the taxpayer as the result of its sponsorship as deductible from its income for the taxation year 1954. The size of the appellant company's business does not justify the Board to allow the full amount. If the Board did so, it would mean that the appellant company would deduct, for 1954, the sum of $22,500 out of a net income of $42,874, which is more than one-half of the said income. This would be unreasonable and in complete derogation of the letter and the spirit of Section 12 of said Act.

I see nothing in the evidence to permit me to arrive at such a conclusion. On the contrary, the evidence discloses that the advertising started in the month of July instead of in the month of May when it should have. Moreover, it must be accepted also, from the evidence, that the appellant company was a producer of lumber, and that the advertising was in relation to the name of the firm rather than to the marketable product which was sold through agencies. To be deductible, advertising expenditures must have some relation to the business in which one is engaged.

After having taken into consideration all the facts and the circumstances in this case, I arrive at a figure of $5,000 which would be about the expenditure of an advertising campaign during the summer in question in the daily newspaper and over the radio station of the City of which the appellant is a resident.

On the whole, may I say that it is difficult to define the type or form of advertising which is to be employed by a company to keep before the public its name, its products, the services offered. Each case must be considered in regard to the evidence adduced. It appears to me, after a careful examination of the facts disclosed by the evidence, that I have no other alternative except to reach the conclusion that the assessment should be varied and that a sum of $5,000, representing a portion of the sum of $22,500 which the appellant claimed as advertising expenditures, should be made deductible from its income for the taxation year 1954.

Appeal allowed in part.

Notes and Questions

1. In a recent case covering many issues, A.C.J. Rossiter (as he then was) set out a succinct summary of section 67 in only four paragraphs. See *Garber v. Canada*, 2014 TCC 1, [2014] 4 C.T.C. 2077, 2014 D.T.C. 1045 (T.C.C.) at paragraphs 415-418. See also the leading case on section 67, *Gabco Limited v. M.N.R.*, [1968] 2 Ex. C.R. 511, [1968] C.T.C. 313, 68 D.T.C. 5210.
2. Do you think the purpose of section 67 is to encourage economic efficiency in business decision-making and likewise discourage imprudence? For example, if a corporate president determined that he wanted an office as big as a football field in order to hold shareholders' meetings, could a deduction for the costs incurred for the office be reduced under this section? Similarly, could a mother be told that there are less expensive day care centres, or a student advised that the same course could be studied for a lesser amount elsewhere and thus be denied a full deduction or credit for their costs?
3. In determining what is "reasonable", the CRA will closely scrutinize the facts surrounding payments to related individuals. The Tax Review Board decided in *Cohen v. M.N.R.* (1963), 31 Tax A.B.C. 216, 63 D.T.C. 237 (T.A.B.) that a payment of $12,000 by the taxpayer to his wife as rent for a dental office in their home was unreasonable. The Board rejected the taxpayer's argument that accommodation in the local Medical Arts Building would have equalled the claimed deduction and reduced the allowable portion to $5,000. Would this have been decided the same way if the payments had been made to a stranger?
4. In *Beauchemin v. M.N.R.*, [1977] C.T.C. 2029, 77 D.T.C. 26 (T.R.B.), the taxpayer, a plastic surgeon, gave the following testimony:

> I therefore thought about purchasing a car to meet very specific requirements. The first requirement was safety, so that I could make the same trips with less fatigue and greater peace of mind. You tend to think about safety when you spend many hours driving, particularly when you treat a large number of victims of automobile accidents, and I thought I could provide just as available service if I used an automobile built by a firm whose reputation for the comfort, safety and reliability of the models it builds is legendary. I also considered that an automobile with some prestige could only have the effect of increasing the size of my practice and, consequently my income.

> I chose a 1972 Porsche 911, which is the safest of all the models produced by this manufacturer — with a hard top, brakes, responsiveness and with the same suspension as the more powerful 911S.

Despite the taxpayer's obvious knowledge about automobiles, he apparently did not sufficiently comprehend the severity of Canadian winters. As a result he found it desirable to purchase another, 4-wheel drive vehicle.

When faced with the deduction of the expenses of maintaining the two vehicles the Minister disallowed capital cost allowance on the Porsche and allowed only 25 per cent of the business expenses claimed.

The Tax Review Board overturned the Minister's assessment and allowed the business expenses claimed by the taxpayer — namely 75 per cent of the expenses of operating the vehicles. The Board also stated that "the use of a special vehicle appropriate for winter driving, namely, the Blazer jeep, was justified". In respect of the Porsche, the Board stated:

> The appellant's argument to the effect the purchase of an automobile with a certain prestige could only promote an increase in the size of his practice does not convince the Board, just as such arguments did not satisfy the courts. The Board accordingly allows, in respect of a second automobile, half the cost of the Porsche, namely $5,627.

Is it open to a taxpayer to deduct expenses if it can be established to the satisfaction of the Board that earnings were increased by a luxury element?

5. Could the Minister use section 67 to challenge the production costs of a taxpayer involved in manufacturing? If so, how would the Minister determine what is a reasonable cost for doo-dads in the manufacture of thingamabobs? What about reasonable labour costs? Consider the following comments of Linden, J.A. in *Tonn v. The Queen*, [1996] 1 C.T.C. 205, 96 D.T.C. 6001 (Fed. C.A.), (at 219; 6009, footnotes omitted):

> But do the Act's purposes suggest that deductions of losses from *bona fide* businesses be disallowed solely because the taxpayer made a bad judgment call? I do not think so. The tax system has every interest in investigating the *bona fides* of a taxpayer's dealings in certain situations, but it should not discourage, or penalize, honest but erroneous business decisions. The tax system does not tax on the basis of a taxpayer's business acumen, with deductions extended to the wise and withheld from the foolish. Rather, the Act taxes on the basis of the economic situation of the taxpayer — as it is in fact, and not as it should be, subject to what is said below.
>
> It seems to me that for most cases where the department desires to challenge the reasonableness of a taxpayer's transactions, they need simply refer to section 67. This section provides that an expense may be deducted only to the extent that it is reasonable in the circumstances. They need not resort to the more heavy-handed *Moldowan* test.

In fact, in many cases, resorting to section 67 may well be more appropriate. This point has been made more than a few times by Bowman T.C.C.J. In *Cipollone v. R.* [(*sub. nom. Cipollone v. Canada*) [1995] 1 C.T.C. 2598], for example, the taxpayer attempted to deduct a variety of large expenditures as part of her "humour therapy" business. Despite the unusual nature of the business, Bowman, T.C.C.J. found the business to be *bona fide* and thus not a candidate for the application of *Moldowan*. He added:

> The reason her losses were as great as they were was not because the business had no reasonable expectation of profit or because she was not expending money for the purpose of gaining or producing income from a business. I find as a fact that she was spending money in order to earn a profit and that her expectation of earning a profit was reasonable, if she had chosen to claim reasonable expenses. The problem lies not in the absence of a reasonable expectation of profit-businesses of this sort can be quite lucrative — but rather in the attempt to deduct unreasonable expenses.

6. The Act also imposes a number of limitations on automobile expense deductions. Section 67.2 limits the amount of interest expense deductible in respect of the acquisition of a "passenger vehicle", as defined in subsection 248(1), which may otherwise be deductible in computing income from a business or, in certain circumstances an office or employment (paragraph 8(1)(j)). The interest deductible is limited to an amount prescribed by regulation, currently prescribed at $300 per month. Section 67.3 limits the deductible costs of leasing a passenger vehicle, currently prescribed at $800 per month (plus applicable federal and provincial sales tax). For capital cost allowance purposes, paragraph 13(7)(g) restricts the capital cost of a passenger vehicle to an amount prescribed by regulation, currently prescribed by regulation 7307(1) at $30,000 (plus applicable federal and provincial sales tax).

   The restrictions in sections 67 to 67.3 can be said to displace the business judgment of the taxpayer. Nevertheless, the tax regime must balance the principle that a taxpayer's business judgment should be respected against protection from abuses which pass off as business judgments those decisions which really reflect personal consumption choices. Provisions such as sections 67.2 and 67.3 are a rough and ready attempt to fix a level beyond which "business expenditures" will be presumed to involve personal benefit to the individuals use of the vehicle. The amounts in the provisions are arbitrary amounts; they presume that sound business judgment would not lead to a decision to, for instance, buy or lease a vehicle worth more than $30,000. Is it a poor business decision, or unreasonable, for a movie producer to use a car worth more than $30,000 in his or her business?

6

Computation of Profit and Timing Principles for the Recognition of Revenue and Expense

I. SIGNIFICANCE OF TIMING PRINCIPLES

What constitutes income from a business or property is discussed in Chapter 5. This chapter examines how profit is computed for income tax purposes. Because the Act requires profit to be computed annually, when an item of revenue or expense must be included in computing profit is fundamentally important. Taxpayers strongly prefer to pay their taxes later rather than sooner because they retain the use of the money longer. Consider a taxpayer who can choose between paying $1,000 of taxes today and paying $1,000 of taxes a year from now. Assuming an interest rate of 8 per cent, the present value — the value today — of $1,000 due in one year is $926. In other words, the sum of $926 invested at 8 per cent today will grow to $1,000 at the end of one year. The taxpayer will need to put aside only $926 now in order to meet the tax obligation of $1,000 next year. If the taxpayer can postpone the tax payment — in other words, postpone the recognition of income giving rise to $1,000 of tax — for one year, he or she will have saved $74. The government, of course, sees the matter in opposite terms: a year's delay "costs" the government $74. As described in Part IV.B. of Chapter 1, the concepts of tax deferral and the time value of money are critical in the design of income tax systems. Not surprisingly, achieving tax deferral is one of the main objectives of tax planning. Deferral can be achieved in two ways: accelerating the deduction of expenses or delaying the recognition of revenue.

Timing principles for the recognition of revenue and expense are at the heart of many of the provisions in Division B of Part I of the Act. For example, there is no question that the cost of inventory ought to be deductible in the calculation of "profit" from a retail business. Should the cost be deducted when the inventory is bought or later when it is sold by the taxpayer? Similarly, there is no question the cost of a machine that has a limited life span should be deductible from the revenues produced by the machine in the calculation of "profit" from a manufacturing business. Should the cost be deducted when the machine is bought or later, say, in equal annual amounts over the estimated life span of the machine? The deduction of the costs of inventories and depreciating assets are two of the important issues studied in this chapter.

II. RELEVANCE OF FINANCIAL ACCOUNTING PRACTICE

Section 9 of the Act provides that income from a business of a taxpayer is the taxpayer's profit therefrom but, the Act does not define the term "profit". As mentioned in Chapter 5, "profit" for purposes of the Act is considered a net concept. Costs and expenses incurred in earning income are deductible in computing profit. In the absence of statutory provisions governing the treatment of specific items of revenue or expense, the question arises as to what extent financial accounting principles govern the computation of profit for income tax purposes.

CANDEREL LTD v. THE QUEEN

[1998] 2 C.T.C. 35, 98 D.T.C. 6100 [1998] 1 S.C.R. 147

Iacobucci J.: In a narrow sense, this appeal raises one issue: how is a taxpayer to treat a payment made to a prospective tenant for the purpose of inducing that tenant to lease space in the taxpayer's premises? More specifically, is the expenditure, commonly referred to as a tenant inducement payment ("TIP"), to be deducted from income entirely in the year in which it was made, or is it to be amortized over the term of the lease to which it relates?

More broadly, however, this Court is required to revisit the fundamental concept of profit computation for income tax purposes. The appeal raises serious questions about the ability of the taxpayer to calculate his or her income in accordance with well-accepted principles of business practice and with the provisions of the *Income Tax Act,* as interpreted by the courts. In the absence of statutory provisions or overriding legal principles to the contrary, is the Minister of National Revenue entitled to insist on a particular method of profit computation? Put another way, what is the analytical framework within which taxpayers can compute, and the Minister can dispute, profit?

...

It is appropriate to begin the consideration of profit with s. 9(1) of the Act, which defines a taxpayer's income for a taxation year from a business or property source as "his profit therefrom for the year". Significantly, "profit" is not defined in s. 9(1) or anywhere else in the Act. It seems to me that this approach was a deliberate legislative choice, particularly given that the Act contains exhaustive definitions of numerous other concepts and terms with which it deals. This choice reflects the reality that no single definition can adequately apply to the millions of different taxpayers bound by the Act. Under our self-assessment system, each taxpayer must be able to compute his or her income in such a way as to constitute an accurate picture of his or her income situation, subject, of course, to express provisions in the Act which require specific treatment of certain types of expenses or receipts.

What, then, is the true nature of "profit" for tax purposes? While the concept has been variously expressed, perhaps the clearest and most concise articulation of the term is to be found in the oft-quoted decision of this Court in *Irwin v. Minister of National Revenue*, [1964] S.C.R. 662 (S.C.C.), at p. 664, where profit in a year was taken to consist of "the difference between the receipts from the trade or business *during such year* ... and the expenditure laid out to earn those receipts". (emphasis in original) ...

... The starting proposition, of course, must be that the determination of profit under s. 9(1) is a question of law, not of fact. Its legal determinants are two in number: first, any express provision of the *Income Tax Act* which dictates some specific treatment to be given to particular types of expenditures or receipts, including the general limitation expressed in s. 18(1)(a), and second, established rules of law resulting from judicial interpretation over the years of these various provisions.

Beyond these parameters, any further tools of analysis which may provide assistance in reaching a determination of profit are just that: interpretive aids, and no more. Into this category fall the "well-accepted principles of business (or accounting) practice" which were mentioned in *Symes* [[1994] 1 C.T.C. 40, 94 D.T.C. 6001 (S.C.C.)], also referred to as "ordinary commercial principles" or "well-accepted principles of commercial trading," among other terms. A formal codification of these principles is to be found in the "generally accepted accounting principles" ("G.A.A.P.") developed by the accounting profession for use in the preparation of financial statements. These principles are accepted by the accounting profession as yielding accurate financial information about the subject of the statements, and become "generally accepted" either by actually being followed in a number of cases, by finding support in pronouncements of professional bodies, by finding support in the writings of academics and others ... What must be remembered, however, is that these are non-legal tools and as such are external to the legal determination of profit, whereas the provisions of the Act and other established rules of law form its very foundation.

The reason for this is simple: generally speaking, well-accepted business principles will have their roots in the methodology of financial accounting, which ... is motivated by factors fundamentally different from taxation. Moreover, financial accounting is usually concerned with providing *a comparative* picture of profit from year to year, and therefore strives for methodological consistency for the benefit of the audience for whom the financial statements are prepared: shareholders, investors, lenders, regulators, etc. Tax computation, on the other hand, is solely concerned with achieving an accurate picture of income for each individual taxation year for the benefit of the taxpayer and the tax collector. Depending on the taxpayer's commercial activity during a particular year, the methodology used to calculate profit for tax purposes may be substantially different from that employed in the previous year, which in turn may be different from that which was employed the year before. Therefore, while financial accounting may, as a matter of fact, constitute an accurate determinant of profit for some purposes, its application to the legal question of profit is inherently limited. Caution must be exercised when applying accounting principles to legal questions.

I do not wish to be taken, however, as minimizing the role of G.A.A.P. in the determination of profit for income tax purposes. ... G.A.A.P. will generally form the very foundation of the "well-accepted business principles" applicable in computing profit. It is important, however, for the courts to avoid delegating the criteria for the *legal* test of profit to the accounting profession, and therefore a distinction must be maintained. That is, while G.A.A.P. may more often than not parallel the well-accepted business principles recognized by the law, there may be occasions on which they will differ, and on such occasions the latter must prevail. ...

Moreover, there will, of course, be situations in which G.A.A.P. will offer various acceptable options in the preparation of financial statements, and the taxpayer will be free, for financial accounting purposes, to adopt whichever option best suits his financial objectives at the given time. In such cases, G.A.A.P. will surely not be determinative as to the method by which an accurate picture of profit may be obtained for taxation purposes, though it may still be useful as a guide to the various acceptable methods of computation, one of which may yield the appropriate result for taxation.

A good example of the relationship among the provisions of the Act, the principles developed in the case law, and G.A.A.P. or well-accepted business principles can be found in s. 18(9) of the Act, which requires the amortization of certain prepaid expenses over the periods of time to which they relate. It is possible, although I express no specific opinion on this matter, that some of these expenses could be treated otherwise for the purposes of G.A.A.P. or business practice; perhaps they might be deducted entirely in the year incurred, or even capitalized. However, this possibility is negated for tax purposes by their specific legislative treatment.

...

Having established an appropriate framework for analysis, I should now like to discuss what exactly is the question that must be answered when attempting to assess a taxpayer's profit for tax purposes. A good place to begin is with the decision of the Federal Court of Appeal in *West Kootenay* [see *infra*], where MacGuigan J.A. stated at p. 6028:

> The approved principle is that whichever method presents the "truer picture" of a taxpayer's revenue, which more fairly and accurately portrays income, and

> which "matches" revenue and expenditure, if one method does, is the one which must be followed.

In the court below, Stone J.A. took this passage as grounding his conclusion that the matching principle of accounting has been elevated to a rule of law. Obviously, in light of my previous comments, I do not, with respect, subscribe to that point of view. To my mind, the significance of this statement is to confirm a much sounder proposition: that the goal of the legal test of "profit" should be to determine which method of accounting best depicts the reality of the financial situation of the particular taxpayer. If this is accomplished by applying the matching principle, then so be it. On the other hand, if some other method is appropriate, is permissible under well-accepted business principles, and is not prohibited either by the Act or by some specific rule of law, then there is no principled basis by which the Minister should be entitled to insist that the matching principle — or any other method, for that matter — be employed. MacGuigan J.A. in *West Kootenay* seemed to advert to this notion at pp. 745-46, in the passage immediately following the above-quoted portion:

> The result often will not be different from what it would be using a consistency principle, but the "truer picture" or "matching approach" *is not absolute in its effect, and requires a close look at the facts of a taxpayer's situation.* [Emphasis added.]

...

To the extent that they may be applicable to particular circumstances, well-accepted business principles are to be assessed and applied only on a case-by-case basis, and only for the purpose of achieving an accurate picture of profit for the year in question for income tax purposes. In this light, I have no hesitation in finding that to the extent that the majority decision of the Federal Court of Appeal was premised on the view of the matching principle as a rule of law, it was clearly in error.

...

It follows from all of this that in calculating his or her income for a taxation year, the taxpayer must adopt a method of computation which is not inconsistent with the Act or established rules of law, which is consistent with well-accepted business principles, and which will yield an accurate picture of his or her income for that year. In the simplest cases, it will not even be necessary to resort formally to the various well-accepted business principles, as the simple formula by which revenues are set against the expenditures incurred in earning them is always the basic determinant.

However, where the income picture is more complicated, as is frequently the case, the taxpayer is free to employ whichever well-accepted business principles will be most useful in depicting profit, provided again that the method adopted is not inconsistent with the law. As a general rule, and as I have already stated, the Minister is in no position to insist on the application of one principle or another, in the absence of some legal rule so requiring, unless, as I shall discuss next, the application of an alternative rule would yield a more accurate picture of income than that which was obtained by the taxpayer.

Revenue Canada is free to indicate its disapproval of the taxpayer's chosen method of computation by means of assessment. In *Johnston v. M.N.R.*, [1948] S.C.R. 486, this Court held that the onus is on the taxpayer, in the face of an assessment, to establish that the factual findings on which the assessment is based are wrong. However, to satisfy this onus where the dispute is over the appropriate method of computation, the taxpayer need only show that his or her income was calculated in a manner consistent with the foregoing paragraph, that is, that the figure attained was in conformity with the then-existing legal framework and represents an accurate picture of his or her financial position for the year in question. The onus then shifts to the Minister to prove either that the figure does *not* constitute an accurate picture of income or that some other method of computation would yield a *more* accurate picture. In so doing, however, I emphasize that the Minister is not entitled to rely on particular well-accepted business principles as being *inherently* preferable over others. If the method chosen by the taxpayer is otherwise acceptable by law and in accordance with such well-accepted principles, then it is no answer for the Minister to say that other principles should have been employed unless to do so would have yielded a more accurate picture of income.

The outlined framework for analysis is, of course, only as useful as its application to actual cases. Turning to the facts of this case will illustrate how this principled approach to the computation of income is intended to operate. Before I do this, however, it may be both convenient and useful to summarize the principles which I have set out above:

(1) The determination of profit is a question of law.

(2) The profit of a business for a taxation year is to be determined by setting against the revenues from the business for that year the expenses incurred in earning said income: *M.N.R. v. Irwin*, *supra*, Associated Investors, *supra*.

(3) In seeking to ascertain profit, the goal is to obtain an accurate picture of the taxpayer's profit for the given year.

(4) In ascertaining profit, the taxpayer is free to adopt any method which is not inconsistent with

(a) the provisions of the *Income Tax Act*;

(b) established case law principles or "rules of law"; and

(c) well-accepted business principles.

(5) Well-accepted business principles, which include but are not limited to the formal codification found in G.A.A.P., are not rules of law but interpretive aids. To the extent that they may influence the calculation of income, they will do so only on a case-by-case basis, depending on the facts of the taxpayer's financial situation.

(6) On reassessment, once the taxpayer has shown that he has provided an accurate picture of income for the year, which is consistent with the Act, the case law, and well-accepted business principles, the onus shifts to the Minister to show either that the figure provided does not represent an accurate picture, or that another method of computation would provide a more accurate picture.

...

It is evident that the method of income calculation adopted by Canderel in the instant case was not inconsistent with any provision of the *Income Tax Act* or other rule of law. The general income provision, s. 9(1), provides no definition of "profit," and no other section of the Act touches, either directly or indirectly, upon the income treatment to be given TIPs [Tenant inducement payments]. Section 18(9) of the Act does require the amortization of certain "prepaid expenses," but TIPs are not included in this provision.

To my mind, this exclusion not only exempts TIPs from any statutory amortization requirement, but also provides a valuable hint as to Parliament's lack of intention to require such treatment of TIPs. I do not mean to suggest that the *expressio unius* maxim of statutory interpretation applies here, as s. 18(9) certainly does not purport to be an exhaustive compendium of amortizable expenses, and it is arguable that TIPs do not really fall into the same category as the prepaid expenses touched upon by the section, but the fact that Parliament has directed its mind to requiring the amortization of some expenses without requiring this of TIPs is nonetheless telling to some extent. Parliament would be free to institute this requirement, but has not done so. ...

At this stage, then, Canderel was free to deduct the payments entirely in the year incurred. But that does not end the matter. It remains to be seen whether the method chosen by Canderel was in accordance with the case law principles as outlined above and with well-accepted business principles, and whether it provided an accurate picture of its income for the year in question. Even if that were so, the Minister would still be entitled to insist on an alternative treatment of the expenditures if it could be shown that such would provide a *more* accurate picture. To answer these questions will require an examination of the evidence and the findings of the trial judge.

The accounting evidence adduced by the parties was somewhat inconclusive at best. It disclosed that at the time of the payments, G.A.A.P. allowed for three alternative and acceptable methods of accounting for TIPs. The payer was entitled to treat the payments either as operating expenses, fully chargeable to the results of operations in the year incurred, as capital expenditures to be added to the cost of the building and depreciated, or as deferred expenses to be amortized over the life of the relevant leases. The experts called by Canderel were of the opinion that the first option was to be preferred because the expenditures were incurred in the ordinary course of generating revenue from Canderel's business and that this method would thus give the most accurate picture of income. Those called by the Minister, as might be expected, testified that the preferred method was the third, as the payments were causally linked to rental revenue while any other benefits to which they gave rise were not revenue and could not be the subject of "matching". To my mind, this evidence is useful only to demonstrate that G.A.A.P. at the time endorsed the options contended for by both parties. However, I cannot draw from this alone any specific conclusion as to which method was preferable in terms of yielding the more accurate picture of Canderel's income.

But the findings of fact made by the trial judge are more instructive. Brulé J. found that the payments yielded four primary benefits for Canderel: the prevention of a "hole in income" which otherwise would have been caused by maintaining a vacant building, the ability to satisfy the underlying requirements of its interim financing and to obtain permanent financing, the ability to meet its competition and to maintain its market position and reputation, and the generating of revenues through rentals and through management and development fees (which were to some extent contingent upon the rate of lease-up). From this, he concluded that the payments constituted "running expenses," as they could not be causally linked to any single or specific stream of revenue, and that the matching principle therefore did not apply in the circumstances, as contended for by the Minister. ...

In light of all of this, I find it difficult, particularly given the findings of the trial judge as to the various benefits generated by the TIPs, to conclude that the amortization of the payments over the terms of the leases, as contended for by the Minister, would provide a more accurate picture of Canderel's income than would their immediate deduction in the year expended. In such a case, where no one method emerges as clearly superior or more properly applicable than another, the taxpayer should retain the option of ordering its affairs in accordance with any method which is in accordance with well-accepted business principles and which is acceptable in light of the reality of its business. ...

Indeed, in my view, the fact that in the instant case, Brulé J. found that the TIPs were properly attributable to a number of different expenses makes inevitable the conclusion that they constituted running expenses. As I have already noted, I do not see how, under these circumstances, it is possible with any accuracy to amortize the payments over the term of the lease, in the absence of an established formula acceptable for tax purposes, which was not advanced by the Minister. It follows, then, that the TIPs were not referable to any particular items of income, i.e., they cannot be correlated directly, or at least not principally, with the rents generated by the leases which they induced. They therefore qualify as running expenses to which the matching principle does not apply: see *Oxford Shopping Centres, supra.* The findings of fact made by Brulé J. in this regard are entitled to considerable deference. There is no indication that these findings were unsupported by the evidence, and I can see no reason to reject them.

In light of the foregoing, I am compelled to the view that the Federal Court of Appeal erred in requiring that the TIPs be amortized over the terms of the leases which they induced, rather than being deducted entirely in the year incurred. ...

Note

For a discussion of *Canderel* and its companion cases, *Toronto College Park Ltd. v. The Queen*, [1998] 2 C.T.C. 78, 98 D.T.C. 6088 (S.C.C.) and *Ikea Limited v. The Queen*, [1998] 2 C.T.C. 61, 98 D.T.C. 6092 (S.C.C.), see B. Carr, "Current Receipts and Expenses after *Canderel, Toronto College Park* and *Ikea*" (1998), 46 Can. Tax J. 954.

III. TAX ACCOUNTING

A. Annual Accounting Requirement

The first question that must be addressed in designing tax accounting rules is the definition of the taxation period. As a practical matter, income taxes must be collected on a periodic basis. The period normally selected is the taxation year.

Section 249 defines "taxation year" for corporations and individuals. For corporations, the taxation year is its "fiscal period". For individuals, it is the calendar year. Where a source of income is a business or a property, the income from that source must be calculated for its fiscal period. As a general rule, income from business is included in the taxation year in which the fiscal period ends (see section 11 and paragraph 96(1)(f)).

The "fiscal period" of a business or property of a person or partnership is defined in subsection 249.1(1). A corporation may choose any period not exceeding 53 weeks as its fiscal period. For individuals who operate businesses as sole proprietors and any partnership in which an individual is a partner, the fiscal period must end in the calendar year in which it began, unless an election is made to use an "off-calendar" fiscal period.

This definition of fiscal period was introduced in 1996, applicable to fiscal periods commencing after 1994. Previously, individual taxpayers (including partners of partnerships) benefited from a significant deferral opportunity. Consider an individual's business with a fiscal period of February 1 – January 31. Under the former rules, the income of the fiscal period February 1, 1994 – January 31, 1995 would be included in the individual's income for the 1995 calendar year, for which the tax return was not due until April 30, 1996. Thus, the taxpayer had the benefit of the 11 months of business income earned in 1994 for an additional year before the tax related to it was due. Now, under the general rule, if a business's fiscal period begins on February 1, it cannot end after December 31 of the same year.

Subsection 249.1(4) permits individuals who operate businesses and partnerships to retain an off-calendar fiscal period. However, section 34.1 eliminates the deferral opportunity. For example, if an individual elects to keep the fiscal period February 1 – January 31, section 34.1 requires the individual to include in income of a calendar year an estimate of the business income for the period February 1 – December 31.

Consider the implications of annual recognition of income for tax purposes, particularly where a taxpayer's income is "bunched" — that is, a significant amount of income falls in one year rather than being spread out over a number of years — or where the taxpayer realizes an overall loss in a particular year. Taxpayer A and Taxpayer B engage in transactions that have the same economic income of $50,000 over a two-year period. Taxpayer A has income of $25,000 in each year. Taxpayer B has income of $50,000 in the first year and nothing in the second year. Alternatively, Taxpayer B has income of $100,000 in the first year and a loss of $50,000 in the second year. Should the taxpayers be treated the same in terms of tax policy?

B. Methods of Accounting

The methods of accounting are crucial for income tax purposes because revenues and expense must be accounted for each year. There are two basic methods of accounting: the cash method and the accrual method.

1. Cash Method

Under the cash method, all that is accounted for in the accounting period are revenues actually received by the taxpayer and expenses actually paid by the taxpayer. Income from office or employment is generally computed on a cash basis. Section 28 expressly permits the use of the cash method for computing income from a farming or fishing business.

There is usually not much doubt about the time for inclusion or deduction under this method. Payments received by a third person (such as an escrow agent) on the taxpayer's behalf are generally considered to be received by the taxpayer. Payment can be made in cash, in kind or by setting off an existing obligation. Disputes may arise, however, when a taxpayer receives a cheque at the end of a year but does not cash the cheque until early in the following year. Cheques, which are viewed as mechanisms for making payments, are generally treated like cash; thus, under the cash basis, revenue is recognized when the cheque is received.

2. Accrual Method

Under the accrual method, income is recognized in the year in which it is earned, regardless of when payment is actually received, and deductions are claimed in the year in which they are incurred, regardless of when they are paid. The accrual method is used by corporations and in computing income of most businesses. The timing of recognition of revenue and expense under the accrual method is considered further, *infra.*

Problems

1. Mary is a lawyer. In 2010, Mary received $50,000 in fees for professional services rendered. At the end of the year, Mary has accounts billed but unpaid of $10,000 and work that is completed but not yet billed of $5,000. Mary also has the following expenses: secretary's salary, $16,000; office supplies, payable in 2011, $1,000; insurance for 3 years commencing in 2010, $3,000; and photocopier, $10,000. What is Mary's income for each of 2010 and 2011 under the cash method or accrual method? Consider section 34.
2. Robert has a computer store. During 2010, Robert buys a computer at a cost of $1,000. On December 1, 2010, Robert sells the computer for $3,000 on a deferred payment basis. The $3,000 is received on January 15, 2011. Assume these are the only transactions for 2010 and 2011. What is Robert's income for each of 2010 and 2011 under the cash method or accrual method?
3. X Corporation owes an employee $10,000 in unpaid salary for 2010. Is the employee required to include the $10,000 in computing his or her income for 2010? Can the corporation deduct the $10,000? If the amount is still unpaid as of July 2011, what is the result? See subsection 78(4).

IV. TIMING OF THE RECOGNITION OF REVENUE AND EXPENSE

The Act does not contain any general timing provisions with respect to the computation of income from business or property. Subsection 9(1) simply provides that the income for a taxation year from a business or property is the profit therefrom for the year. Although, the Act contains timing rules governing specific situations, the Act is generally silent on this fundamental issue. For taxpayers using the accrual method of accounting, the recognition of income generally depends on when the income is "earned" or becomes receivable, and the recognition of expenses generally depends on when the expenses are "incurred" or become payable. These general timing rules are considered first, and then a number of modifications provided in the Act are reviewed.

A. Timing of the Recognition of Revenue

Income from the sale of property and the provision of services are two of the most important types of income from a business. The timing of recognition of these two types of income is governed by paragraph 12(1)(b) of the Act. Pursuant to this provision, revenues from the sale of goods or services in the course of a business are included in computing profit when they become receivable. The Act does not define "receivable", and its meaning has therefore been left to the courts.

M.N.R. v. J. COLFORD CONTRACTING CO.
[1960] C.T.C. 178, 60 D.T.C. 1131 (Ex. Ct)

Kearney J.: ...

The taxpayer is engaged in the furnishing and installation of plumbing, heating, air conditioning and ventilation equipment. In the computation of its taxable income for its fiscal year ended March 31, 1953, which is the only year in issue, the taxpayer excluded therefrom all receipts and expenditures (but we are here concerned only with gross receipts) directly related to three then in-completed contracts. The issue is not whether the excluded amounts are taxable but when they are taxable. The amounts in question fall into two categories: progress payments actually received and unreceived holdbacks. According to the taxpayer, the provisions of the contract were such that profits and losses in connection therewith could only be determined if and when each entire project had been completed to the satisfaction of the owner, as witnessed by a certif-icate to that effect signed by an architect or engineer selected by the owner and mentioned in the contract. ...

As "amount receivable" or "receivable" is not defined in the Act, I think one should endeavour to find its ordinary meaning in the field in which it is employed. If recourse is had to a dictionary meaning, we find in the *Shorter Oxford,* Third Edition, the word "receivable" defined as something "capable of being received". This definition is so wide that it contributes little towards a solution. It envisages a receivable as anything that can be transmitted to anyone capable of receiving it. It might be said to apply to a legacy bestowed in the will of a living testator, but nobody would regard such a legacy as an amount receivable in the hands of a potential legatee. In the absence of a statutory definition to the contrary, I think it is not enough that the so-called recipient have a precarious right to receive the amount in question, but he must have a clearly legal, though not necessarily immediate, right to receive it. A second meaning, as mentioned by Cameron, J., is "to be received", and Eric L. Kohler, in *A Dictionary for Accountants*, 1957 edition, page 408, defines it as "collectible, whether or not due". These two definitions, I think, connote entitlement.

This leads to a consideration of whether, legally speaking, each of the holdbacks in the instant case possessed the quality required to bring it within the meaning of a receivable. Speaking of the quality required to constitute income, the learned president of this Court stated in *Robertson Ltd. v. M.N.R.*, [1944] C.T.C. 75 at page 91:

> " ... Did such amounts have, at the time of their receipt, or acquire, during the year of their receipt, the quality of income, to use the phrase of Mr. Justice Brandeis in *Brown v. Helvering* [(1934) 291 U.S. 193]. In my judgment, the language used by him, to which I have already referred, lays down an important test as to whether an amount received by a taxpayer has the quality of income. Is his right to it absolute and under no restriction, contractual or otherwise, as to its disposition, use or enjoyment? To put it in another way, can an amount in a taxpayer's hands be regarded as an item of profit or gain from his business, as long as he holds it subject to specific and unfulfilled conditions and his right to retain it and apply it to his own use has not yet accrued, and may never accrue?"

...

In this case each contract must be scrutinized in order to ascertain whether in law the clause dealing with the procurement of an architect's or engineer's certificate either expressly or by implication constitutes a binding condition precedent on the taxpayer which prevents him from claiming a holdback until the certificate is issued. In Ontario it has been held that the contractor has no legal right to the amount of the holdback until the issuance of the certificate, and no suit can be properly commenced by him before certification unless it is clear that the certificate has been improperly withheld by the architect. See *McDonald v. Oliver,* 3 O.R. 310; *Quaintance v. Howard,* 18 O.R. 95 (C.A.); *Coatsworth v. Toronto*, 7 O.R. 490 (C.A.), see 8 U.C.C.P. 364; *Ferguson v. Galt*, 23 U.C.C.P. 66 (C.A.).

The above-mentioned jurisprudence deals with the relationship between a contractor and the owner, but I think it applies with even greater force between a sub-contractor and a prime contractor. Mr. W. E. Williams who has been engaged in the construction business for several years and is a past president of the Montreal Building Exchange gave evidence as an independent expert regarding the usual provisions found in construction contracts and how they operate. He stated that a sub-contractor is never paid by the prime contractor until the latter has secured the certificate of the engineer or architect appointed by the owner and until the whole construction, which may include the work of many sub-contractors, has been completed to the satisfaction of the owner, and a certificate of the architect or engineer chosen by him has been issued. It will be seen therefore that, notwithstanding that a sub-contractor may have carried out his sub-contract perfectly, insofar as payment is concerned, he must wait until every other sub-contractor has done so to the satisfaction of the prime contractor and the latter has received a certificate to that effect from the architect or engineer. ...

It is provided in article 3 of the Dominion Bureau of Statistics contract that the amount of the holdback is to be 15 per cent of the progress payments, and the article concludes in these words:

> "Final payment to be made within 30 days after satisfactory completion of the entire building and acceptance by the architect."

Although it does not add that such completion and acceptance by the architect are conditions precedent which must be fulfilled before the taxpayer is entitled to final payment of the holdback, in my opinion, under the jurisprudence such meaning is to be implied. As a corollary, I consider that the holdback does not, as far as the taxpayer is concerned, take on the quality of a receivable until the work has been accepted by the architect. This does not, however, dispose of the issue in regard to the contract under consideration.

Ross, Patterson, Townsend and Fish, as appears by the contract, had been named by the owner as the "architect;" and on March 9, 1953, the above-mentioned firm, per J. K. Ross, certified that all the work in connection with the Dominion Bureau of Statistics, which totalled some $6,000,000, had been completed by the prime contractor according to plans and specifications; and that no holdback was to be retained. The above-mentioned certificate, of course, covered the work done by several sub-contractors, including the taxpayer. It will thus be seen that the condition precedent ceased to exist before the termination of the taxpayer's fiscal year 1953 and the holdbacks payable under it acquired the quality of a receivable as of the date of the certificate. It is to be recalled that final payment was to fall due thirty days after the issuance of the certificate which would bring it into the taxpayer's subsequent fiscal year, and it was in fact paid on April 11, 1953. I do not think that the latter can rely on the delay allowed for payment as justification for bringing the amount of the holdback into the fiscal year in which it fell due. In my opinion, a term or instalment account must be included in the taxation year in which it could be said that it had the quality of a receivable since Section 85B(1)(b) [now paragraph 12(1)(b)] provides that it shall be thus included "notwithstanding that the amount is not receivable until a subsequent year."

It was alleged by counsel for the taxpayer that, because of article 4 of the contract, the holdback in question did not become a receivable in the true sense of the word until April 11, 1953, the date on which the taxpayer received it from the general contractor, since the taxpayer was not aware of the issuance of the architect's certificate to the prime contractor until he had received payment of the holdback. ...

... Article 4 of the contract reads in part as follows:

> "No payment made under this contract shall be conclusive evidence of the performance of this contract, either wholly or in part, and no payment shall be construed to be an acceptance of defective work or improper materials or to relieve Sub-Contractor of responsibility for any guarantee or maintenance for which he may be liable under this contract or the specification applicable thereto."

In my opinion, article 4 notwithstanding, the architect's certificate given in the present case on March 9 is sufficiently conclusive to give to the holdback in question the character of a receivable as of that date.

On April 11, the taxpayer could have ascertained, as he did later, that the architect's certificate had been issued on March 9. It is not the date on which he obtains knowledge of the existence of the certificate but the date of its execution which governs. I am accordingly of the opinion that the holdback of approximately $56,000 which was paid on April 11, about thirty days after the issuance of the architect's certificate, as contemplated in the contract, must be considered as an amount receivable in the taxpayer's fiscal year 1953. ...

M.N.R. v. BENABY REALTIES LTD.
[1967] C.T.C. 418, 67 D.T.C. 5275 (S.C.C.)

Judson J. (all concur): The sole question in this appeal is whether a profit of $263,864.03 was properly assessed in the taxation year 1955. The judgment of the Exchequer Court holds that this profit must be excluded in assessing the profits for the taxation year 1955 on the ground that it should have been assessed in the taxation year 1954.

The facts are simple. On January 7, 1954, the Crown in right of Canada expropriated two parcels of land belonging to the respondent company, Benaby Realties Limited, on the Island of Montreal. The company's 1954 fiscal year ended on April 30, 1954. On November 9, 1954, as a result of an agreement fixing the amount of compensation, the Crown paid the sum of $371,260. This happened during the company's 1955 fiscal year, which ended on April 30, 1955. The profit of $263,864.03 is the difference between the cost of the land and the amount of compensation.

It was argued in the Exchequer Court that the profit was not taxable but the judgment of the Exchequer Court was against this and the appeal in this

Court was argued on the assumption that this was a taxable profit. The only issue was the appropriate year of assessment.

The taxpayer's argument in this Court is that from the moment of expropriation, the taxpayer no longer had its land but had instead the right to receive compensation. This is set out in Section 23 of the *Expropriation Act*, which reads:

> The compensation money agreed upon or adjudged for any land or property acquired or taken for or injuriously affected by the construction of any public work shall stand in the stead of such land or property; and any claim to or encumbrance upon such land or property shall, as respects Her Majesty, be converted into a claim to such compensation money or to a proportionate amount thereof, and shall be void as respects any land or property so acquired or taken, which shall, by the fact of the taking possession thereof, or the filing of the plan and description, as the case may be, become and be absolutely vested in Her Majesty.

The taxpayer conducted its business on the accrual basis under Section 85B(1)(b) [now paragraph 12(1)(b)]. ...

The Crown's argument is that the general rule under the *Income Tax Act* is that taxes are payable on income actually received by the taxpayer during the taxation period; that there is an exception in the case of trade receipts under Section 85B(1)(b), which include not only actual receipts but amounts which have become receivable in the year; that the taxpayer's profit from this expropriation did not form part of its income for the year 1954 because it was not received in that year and because it did not become an amount receivable in that year.

In my opinion, the Minister's submission is sound. It is true that at the moment of expropriation the taxpayer acquired a right to receive compensation in place of the land but in the absence of a binding agreement between the parties or of a judgment fixing the compensation, the owner had no more than a right to claim compensation and there is nothing which can be taken into account as an amount receivable due to the expropriation. ...

My opinion is that the Canadian *Income Tax Act* requires that profits be taken into account or assessed in the year in which the amount is ascertained.

Try v. Johnson, [1946] 1 All E.R. 532, is much closer to the point in issue here. The claim was for compensation under legislation which imposed restrictions on "Ribbon Development." When the case reached the Court of Appeal, the amount of compensation was admitted to be a trade receipt. The argument in that Court was directed to the appropriate year of assessment. The judgment was that the right of the frontager to compensation under the Ribbon Development Act contained so many elements of uncertainty both as to the right itself and the quantum that it could not be regarded as a trade receipt for the purpose of ascertaining the appropriate year of assessment until the amount was fixed either by an arbitration award or by agreement.

Under the Canadian *Expropriation Act*, there is no doubt or uncertainty as to the right to compensation, but I do adopt the principle that there could be no amount receivable under Section 85B(1)(b) until the amount was fixed either by arbitration or agreement. ...

I would therefore allow the appeal, set aside the judgment of the Exchequer Court and restore the assessment of the Minister, with costs in this Court and in the Exchequer Court.

WEST KOOTENAY POWER AND LIGHT COMPANY LIMITED v. THE QUEEN

[1992] 1 C.T.C. 15, 92 D.T.C. 6023 (F.C.A.)

MacGuigan J.A.: The issue in this case is one of tax timing: whether estimates of unbilled revenue at December 31, the end of the taxpayer appellant's taxation year, must be included in its income from business in that year.

The appellant is ... engaged in the business of generating and distributing hydro-electric power in southeastern British Columbia and subject to regulation, including as to its rates, by the British Columbia Utilities Commission ("the BCUC"). Its residential customers were on a two-month billing cycle, and meter readings were made on a bi-monthly basis.

At the relevant fiscal year-ends, 1983 and 1984, the appellant had delivered some electricity for which, as of those year-ends, the customers had not yet been billed. In fact, the BCUC-approved tariff did not permit the appellant to issue bills for electricity supplied to December 31 until the completion of the billing cycle ending after that date.

Until 1979, the accounting practice followed by the appellant did not take account of unbilled revenue, but in that year, on the advice of accountants, the appellant changed its practice and recorded income based on estimates of the revenue anticipated to be received, both for financial statements of its operation and for tax purposes. This accrual basis was continued through 1982.

In 1983, while maintaining the accrual basis for calculating income for its annual statements, the appellant changed from an accrual to a "billed" basis for its income tax return, eliminating from its income the estimate of revenue unbilled at year-end, and reported revenues only as billed.

The estimated sale price of the delivered but as yet unbilled electricity at year-end was $3,919,176 as of the end of 1983, and $3,874,834 as of the end of 1984 ("the unbilled revenue"). This unbilled revenue was added to the appellant's income by the Minister of National Revenue for the 1983 and 1984 taxation years by reassessments dated May 21, 1987.

...

The principal question remaining is as to whether the unbilled revenues in question come under the provisions of paragraph 12(1)(b) of the Act as an amount receivable, and, if so, whether they are exempted from that provision by the unless clause.

The word "receivable" is nowhere defined in the Act. The respondent's witness Culver acknowledged that, under GAAP, unbilled revenue at the end of a year is not considered an amount receivable for that year (Transcript at pages 129-30). That is, of course, relevant, but not decisive, as to the legal concept. ...

The *locus classicus* for the concept of "receivable" is *M.N.R. v. John Colford Contracting Co.* ... where Kearney J. said:

> As "amount receivable" or "receivable" is not defined in the Act, I think one should endeavour to find its ordinary meaning in the field in which it is employed. If recourse is had to a dictionary meaning, we find in the Shorter Oxford, Third Edition, the word "receivable" defined as something "capable of being received." This definition is so wide that it contributes little towards a solution. It envisages a receivable as anything that can be transmitted to anyone capable of receiving it. It might be said to apply to a legacy bestowed in the will of a living testator, but nobody would regard such a legacy as an amount receivable in the hands of a potential legatee. In the absence of a statutory definition to the contrary, I think it is not enough that the so-called recipient have a precarious right to receive the amount in question, but he must have a clearly legal, though not necessarily immediate, right to receive it. A second meaning as mentioned by Cameron, J., is "to be received", and Eric L. Kohler, in *A Dictionary for Accountants,* 1957 edition, page 408, defines it as "collectible, whether or not due." These two definitions, I think, connote entitlement.

...

Applying the *Colford* rule to the facts at hand, at first blush the unbilled revenue would seem to qualify as receivable because based on appellants "clearly legal, though not necessarily immediate, right to receive it." Electricity produced, sold and consumed is a commodity or good: *Quebec Hydro-Electric Commission v. M.N.R.*, [1970] S.C.R. 30. It also falls under the definition of property in subsection 248(1) of the Act. Where property is sold, delivered and consumed, the rendering of an account is not a precondition to the right to payment: sections 31 and 32, *Sale of Goods Act*, R.S.B.C. 1979, c. 370.

The language of paragraph 12(1)(b) itself makes a distinction between "receivable" and "due" so that an amount may be receivable even though not due until a subsequent year. As this Court said in *The Queen v. Derbecker*, [1984] C.T.C. 606, 84 D.T.C. 6549 per Hugessen, J.A. "the words due to him look only to the taxpayer's entitlement to enforce payment and not to whether or not he has actually done so" (at page 607 (D.T.C. 6549)).

The only contrary argument is that the unbilled revenue was not receivable because, for practical purposes, it could not be known exactly. Viscount Simon in *Commissioners of Inland Revenue v. Gardner Mountain & D'Anbrumenil, Ltd.* (1947), 29 T.C. 69, at page 93 was willing to accept 'an estimate of what the future remuneration will amount to" and even "a discounting of the amount to be paid in the future." In my opinion the amount here is sufficiently ascertainable to be included as an amount receivable.

I can have no doubt that the appellant was absolutely entitled to payment for any electricity delivered, and in an amount reasonably estimated. Suppose, for example, that a customer's residence was destroyed by fire at midnight on December 31. The appellant would surely have a legal right as of the due date to reimbursement for the electricity supplied since the previous billing, viz, through December 31, and a court would be prepared to fix the amount of entitlement, probably using something like the appellant's prorated method.

I must therefore conclude that the appellant had a clear legal right to payment: the amounts in question were sufficiently ascertainable to be receivables even though not yet billed or due, and therefore had to be included in income for the year then ending, provided only they are not exempted by the "unless" clause in paragraph 12(1)(b).

In my opinion, this clause does not provide an exemption because of the words "accepted for the purpose of this Part." As previously set forth, I believe the principle to be applied for purposes of this Part of the Act is the "truer picture" or "matching" principle, which, as applied here, has the effect of denying the appellant the right to use the billed account method.

In the light of this holding, it would be inappropriate to consider the applicability of subsection 9(1) taken apart from paragraph 12(1)(b) or of subsection 12(2).

In the result the appeal should be dismissed with costs.

MARITIME TELEGRAPH AND TELEPHONE COMPANY, LIMITED v. THE QUEEN

[1992] 1 C.T.C. 264, 92 DTC 6191 (F.C.A.)

[The taxpayer provided telephone and other telecommunication services, for which it billed its clients on a monthly basis for local and long distance charges. The billing periods did not generally correspond to the calendar month. The taxpayer's taxation year was the calendar year. For financial accounting purposes and for regulatory agency reporting purposes, the taxpayer used the "earned method", under which it estimated the amount of revenue earned by year-end even though some of its cus-

tomers had not been billed for these amounts. Beginning in 1984, the taxpayer adopted the "billed method" for tax purposes, so that it reported only the income that it had billed in the calendar year. The Minister reassessed the taxpayer and included in its income for tax purposes all income computed in accordance with the "earned method". The taxpayer appealed.]

MacGuigan J.A. (Heald and Linden JJ.A. concurring): This case deals with an issue of tax timing similar to that recently decided by this Court in *West Kootenay Power and Light Company Limited v. The Queen* (1991), 92 DTC 6023, but raises for resolution questions which as a matter of judicial economy were not found necessary for decision in *West Kootenay.* ...

On the factual question the learned Trial Judge said (Appeal Book at 155):

> It is clear from the evidence that both methods of accounting are in accordance with Generally Accepted Accounting Principles. At the same time, while there is some evidence that the billed method is used by some utility companies, there was no evidence that any large Canadian telephone company uses the billed method for its general financial statements. Also, it is fair to conclude that the earned method accords a "truer" picture of the company's income for the year in question than does the billed method. The plaintiff is engaged in providing a continuing service which by its very nature results in revenue accruing daily.

On the *Kathy K* standard, this finding of fact could be upset only in the presence of palpable and overriding error: *Stein v. The Ship "Kathy K"*, [1976] 2 S.C.R. 802. The appellant did succeed in showing that there is evidence going both ways, but was unable to establish an error of the requisite magnitude.

The appeal can, therefore, succeed only if the appellant can establish, as it contended, that the 1983 amendment to par. 12(1)(b) [which added the deeming rule applicable to the provision of services] must change the result.

Whatever the 1983 amendment may mean, its language makes clear that it applies only to the provision of services. It is common ground that it is services, i.e., telecommunications services, that the appellant supplies to its customers, and so the amendment prima facie applies. *West Kootenay* did not have to consider this issue because the taxpayer there supplied electricity, which, it was held, is properly classified as a good rather than a service. ...

Stated in more detail, the appellant's position was as follows. The general rule of par. 12(1)(b) is that a taxpayer is required to include any amount receivable in respect of property sold or services rendered in the year, notwithstanding that the amount may not be due until the next year. *West Kootenay* held that a reasonable estimate of the amount earned at a year-end is sufficiently ascertainable to be an amount receivable, but that case dealt with the passing of goods, whereas the 1983 amendment makes a specific exception with respect to the providing of services. This new deeming provision, it was argued, must therefore be conclusive in determining whether an amount for telecommunications services rendered is an amount receivable for purposes of the general rule; in other words, amounts relating to the provision of all services should be conclusively deemed not to be amounts receivable for the purposes of par. 12(1)(b). S. 12(2) cannot be interpreted to frustrate the obvious meaning of par. 12(1)(b), especially since it long predates the 1983 amendment.

In my opinion, and as the respondent argued, such an interpretation could not be accepted without first locating par. 12(1)(b), including the amendment to it, in the scheme of the Act.

The determinative provision for the definition of income is s. 9, which equates income for a year with profit for a year. It was common ground that the purpose of s. 12 of the Act was only to specify what should be included in income, but there was no agreement between the parties as to whether exclusions from income were created in the course of the delineating of inclusions in s. 12(1).

In my view, the statutory language and structure support the respondent's position. That is particularly true of s. 12(2), which explains that the purpose of s. 12(1) is only to provide greater certainty, obviously by specifying with more exactitude what is to be included in income, and which clearly forbids any construction that would have the effect of excluding income that would otherwise be included. This interpretation is also confirmed by s. 12(1) itself, which begins with the words "*there shall be included in computing the income of a taxpayer for a taxation year*..." [Emphasis added].

In my opinion, s. 12(1) operates so as to expand s. 9(1)'s ambit of inclusion. Obviously, at the boundary line of inclusion there may logically be some exclusions, but the joint thrust of s. 9 and s. 12(1) is to include, not exclude, and s. 12(2) has the effect of ensuring, at the very least, that nothing clearly included in s. 9 is henceforth excluded.

This interpretation is, I believe, supported by the only extrinsic evidence available. ... The technical note accompanying the 1983 amendment reads as follows:

> 1982 TN — Paragraph 12(1)(b) of the Act requires any amount receivable in respect of property sold or services rendered in the course of a business in a year to be included in that year's income. This paragraph is amended to add a provision that treats an amount as having become receivable for services performed on the day the account would have been rendered had there been no undue delay in rendering the account for the services. This rule, which previously applied only to services rendered in the course of a professional business under section 34 of the Act, has been expanded to apply to all services.

Not only is there no suggestion in the note of such a major change in the law as would completely exempt all services from the application of the earned method of computation, but the emphasis of the note is entirely upon subpar. 12(1)(b)(ii), relating to an imputed billing date where there is undue delay. This suggests to me that the principal intention of the amendment was to prevent undue extension of billing times in rendering accounts for services rather than to establish any exclusion from income. ...

... The purpose of par. 12(1)(b) is to ensure that income from a business is computed on the accrual basis, not a cash basis, with certain specified exceptions. It applies in cases where profit is not otherwise required to be computed on the accrual basis. In the present case, it has no application, because of the Trial Judge's factual finding that the earned method was the appropriate accounting method for this taxpayer. The appellant's earned revenues to the end of each taxation year were receivables in law, and therefore income for the ending year. As I pointed out in *West Kootenay* ... the case at bar is a weaker case for the taxpayer than that of the taxpayer in *West Kootenay*, because the appellant's records indicate the exact times at which its services were rendered, making the amounts more readily quantifiable at year-end. The receivables already being recognized as profit under s. 9(1), s. 12(2) requires that that status be maintained. ...

The appeal must therefore be dismissed with costs.

B. Timing of the Recognition of Expense

The Act uses words such as "paid", "payable", "payments made" and "incurred" to indicate the timing of the recognition of expenses. However, the Act does not define any of these terms. In general, the timing of "paid" and "payable" is related to the timing of "received" and are necessary to "receivable". The time when an expense is incurred and is therefore deductible is when all the events have occurred that are necessary to establish the taxpayer's liability to make the payment and the amount of the expense can be determined with reasonable accuracy. This principle is derived primarily from the following case.

J. L. GUAY LTÉE v. M.N.R.
[1971] C.T.C. 686, 71 D.T.C. 5423 (F.C.T.D.)

[The taxpayer was a building contractor. Under the terms of its contracts with subcontractors, the taxpayer was entitled to withhold 10 per cent of the amount due under the contracts until the work was completed. This amount became payable at the end of 35 days after a certificate of acceptance was issued by the architects and engineers to the effect that the work was completed in accordance with the contract.

In its 1965 taxation year, the taxpayer deducted over $277,000 as holdbacks. The Minister denied the deductions and the taxpayer appealed.]

Noël A.C.J. (official translation): ...

Referring to the decision of this Court by Kearney J. in *John Colford Contracting Co. Ltd. v. M.N.R.*, ... the learned member of the Tax Appeal Board stated that, although the facts in that case were the opposite of those established in the present case, he nevertheless felt obliged to apply the principles contained therein. In *Colford,* in fact, Kearney J. refused to include in a construction company's income amounts withheld during the current year and payable on the architect's approval. In Kearney J.'s opinion, these amounts were not "receivables"; for them to be receivables they must, in the learned judge's view, be amounts which *"the intended recipient has a clearly legal, though not necessarily immediate, right to receive."*

According to Mr. Boisvert, applying that decision to the case which now concerns us, if the amount withheld could not constitute a debt due and payable to be included in a taxation year, because it represented a contingent debt, similarly an amount withheld which is due and payable in the future can only constitute an allowable deduction in the year in which it becomes certain and mandatory. Only then does it meet the condition set forth in s. 12(1)(a) [now paragraph 18(1)(a)], i.e. It becomes an outlay incurred by the taxpayer for the purpose of gaining income from a business, or, to go back to the argument of the learned counsel for the respondent, Mr. Boivin, if, in Kearney J.'s opinion, these amounts could not be regarded as income, it is because they were not due as long as the architect's certificate had not been issued; and for the same reasons they could not be regarded as due and payable in the hands of the person owing them. If they were not payable, then they could not be deducted from appellant's income for 1965. ...

As stated by appellant, the contract does provide that, if the work is not found satisfactory by the architect, the sub-contractor will nevertheless have the right to be paid in full at the current market price for the work already done; this does not mean, however, that the contractor will always have to pay the amount so withheld in full. In fact, it must not be forgotten that the purpose of the provision which permits withholding of a certain percentage of the contract price is to ensure the payment of any damages the owner or the general contractor may incur from the subcontractor's failure to perform the work or its faulty performance of it. If such damages correspond to, or exceed, the amounts so withheld, the owner or the general contractor may keep the entire amount; if, on the other hand, the damages are less, the sub-contractor will be entitled to receive the difference.

It seems to me, therefore, that it is far from certain that the amounts so withheld will be paid in full to the sub-contractor. in fact, the payment of these amounts to the sub-contractor is perhaps to be regarded, if damages are incurred, as contingent. It is true that, once fixed, such damages may be offset by the amounts withheld, and that the general contractor will not benefit therefrom, but the damages have not yet been liquidated for 1965, and compensation cannot be paid until they are. Until then, and even after, until the architect has issued his certificate and 35 days have elapsed, the general contractor is under no obligation to pay this amount, and it is not claimable by the sub-contractor. ...

In most tax cases only amounts which can be exactly determined are accepted. This means that, ordinarily, provisional amounts or estimates are rejected, and it is not recommended that data which is conditional, contingent or uncertain be used in calculating taxable profits. If, indeed, provisional amounts or estimates are to be accepted, they must be certain. But then it is always difficult to find a procedure by which to arrive at a figure which is certain. Accountants are always inclined to set aside reserves for unliquidated liabilities, for, if they do not do so, the financial statement will not reflect the true position of the client's affairs. The difficulty arises from the fact that making it possible to determine the taxpayer's tax liability is not the main purpose of accounting. The accountant's report is, in fact, intended to give the taxpayer a general picture of his affairs so as to enable him to carry on his business with full knowledge of the facts. To achieve this end, it is not necessary for the profit shown to be exact, but it must be reasonably close, while the *Income Tax Act* requires it to be exact, and it is thus necessarily arbitrary. ... What is the situation when the amounts involved are certain, but are not due until a subsequent accounting period? Such amounts were involved in *The Naval Colliery Ltd. v. I.R.C.,* 12 T.C. 1017, and the Court decided nevertheless that they could not be deducted so long as the outlay had not been made. ...

As a general rule, if an expenditure is made which is deductible from income, it must be deducted by computing the profits for the period in which it was made, and not some other period.

The procedure adopted by appellant, of deducting from its income amounts withheld by it, which it may one day be required to pay its sub-contractor, but which the latter may not claim until 35 days after the work is approved by the architect, is, as we have just seen, contrary to the rule that an expenditure may only be deducted from income for the period in which it was made, and this would suffice to dispose of the present appeal. However, as we have seen above, there is an additional reason for dismissing the appeal: this is that we are dealing with amounts withheld which are not only uncertain as to quantum if partial damages result from badly done work, but which will no longer even be due or payable if damages exceed the amounts withheld. How can it be claimed in such circumstances that a certain and current expense is involved, and that the amounts withheld, which appellant has full enjoyment of until it pays the amounts owing to the subcontractor, "or until compensation becomes due, may be deducted by appellant as it receives them from the owner.

The appeal is therefore dismissed ...

[Noël A.C.J.'s decision was affirmed without reasons by both the Federal Court of Appeal, [1973] C.T.C. 506, 73 D.T.C. 5373, and the Supreme Court of Canada, [1975] C.T.C. 97, 75 D.T.C. 5094.]

Notes and Questions

1. It was suggested above that, as a general rule, an expense is deductible in the year in which it is incurred and, according to *J.L. Guay Ltée*, an expense is incurred in the year in which the taxpayer has a legal and unconditional, though not necessarily immediate, obligation to pay the amount. It does not follow that all expenses that relate to the income earning process are deductible in the year in which they are incurred. Recall the discussion in *Canderel*, *supra*, of the matching principle. To what extent, apart from the specific rules in subsection 18(9), is the matching principle recognized for tax purposes? Consider *M.N.R. v. Tower Investment Inc.*, [1972] C.T.C. 182, 72 D.T.C. 6161 (F.C.T.D.); and *Oxford Shopping Centres Ltd. v. The Queen*, [1980] C.T.C. 7, 79 DTC 5458 (F.C.T.D.), aff'd [1981] C.T.C. 128, 81 D.T.C. 5065 (F.C.A.).
2. See the tax treatment of inventory in Part V and the treatment of capital expenditures in Part VI.

C. Modification of General Timing Rules

The general timing rules discussed above are subject to statutory exceptions, a number of which are discussed below.

1. Advance Payments for Unearned Income or Prepaid Income

When should an accrual basis taxpayer include in income amounts that have actually been received but have not yet been earned? Under generally accepted accounting principles (GAAP), the income is properly accrued (i.e., recognized) when earned by delivery of goods or performance of services, notwithstanding that an amount has already been received. Under paragraph 12(1)(a), however, such amounts must be included in the taxpayer's income in the year in which they are received, even though they have not been earned in that year because the taxpayer has not obtained the absolute and unconditional right to retain the amount. Therefore, paragraph 12(1)(a) is an exception to the general timing rule. Paragraph 20(1)(m) allows the taxpayer to deduct a reasonable reserve in respect of such unearned income; the administrative practice of the Canada Revenue Agency (the "CRA") permits a reasonable reserve equal to the "gross proceeds" (i.e., the full amount included in income): see Interpretation Bulletin IT-154R: Special Reserves (February 19, 1988), paragraph 4. When paragraph 12(1)(a) and paragraph 20(1)(m), as interpreted by the CRA, are considered together, the net result is effectively the same as that derived under financial accounting principles: the unearned income is not included in computing income until earned.

2. Prepaid Expenses

The payment of amounts for goods or services to be received in future years is generally regarded as prepaid expenses. For accounting purposes, such prepaid expenses are carried as assets on the financial statements and deducted as expenses in computing profit in the year or over the years in which the services are rendered. For income tax purposes, subsection 18(9) prohibits deductions in computing income for a particular year in respect of prepayments made in that year for certain items: (a) services to be rendered after the end of the year, (b) interest, taxes, rent, or royalties with respect to a period after the end of the year, and (c) insurance with respect to a period after the end of the year. Such prepayments are deductible only in the subsequent year or years to which the amount reasonably relates. Therefore, expenses in respect of a future year could be matched with the revenue earned in that year. The rules in subsection 18(9) are a clear adaptation of the "matching principle" and are consistent with financial accounting principles.

3. Reserves

Under financial accounting principles, if revenue is earned in a particular year but has not actually been received — for example, because the contract specifically provides for payment over a number of years — an amount may be currently deductible as a "reserve". The reserve essentially represents the possibility that the earned income may never be received. Similarly, if there is a reasonable probability that an amount will have to be expended in the future that relates to the revenue earned in the year — for example, under warranties of goods sold in the year — an amount may be currently deductible as a reserve on account of this contingency. These reserves stem primarily from the conservative nature of financial accounting: the concern not to overstate the profit of the business.

For tax purposes, the general rule is that no deductions are permitted on account of reserves or contingent liabilities: paragraph 18(1)(e). Amounts set aside in anticipation of future events cannot generally be deducted in computing income because such amounts are too contingent or uncertain for income tax purposes. The Act provides several exceptions to this general rule. It authorizes the deduction of a reasonable amount as a reserve in several situations, which include the following:

- Paragraph 20(1)(m) reserve, discussed above.

- Paragraph 20(1)(n) reserve in respect of deferred payments for property sold. A similar reserve is available under paragraph 40(1)(a) for the sale of capital property. These reserves are designed to apportion the profit or capital gain over the period during which the proceeds of sale are receivable, although there are limitations.
- Paragraph 20(1)(l) reserve for doubtful debts, which represents an attempt to reduce the value of an account receivable to the amount likely to be realized. Paragraph 20(1)(p) permits a deduction for bad debts. The distinction between 'doubtful' and 'bad' debts is discussed below in the notes.

Reserves taken in one year must normally be included in income in the next year. For example, if a reserve for doubtful debts is claimed under paragraph 20(1)(l) in one year, this amount must be included in income in the following year (see paragraph 12(1)(d)). If the debt remains uncollected and doubtful in the following year, another reserve can be claimed for that year.

Notes and Questions

1. The CRA's administrative practice with respect to the reserves in paragraph 20(1)(m) and (n) is set out in IT-154R, *supra.* As noted above, a reasonable reserve under paragraph 20(1)(m) is generally considered to be the "gross proceeds" received by the taxpayer and included in income under paragraph 12(1)(a).
2. What is the effect of subsections 20(6) and (7)?
3. X receives $10,000 in 2010 for goods to be manufactured in 2011. In 2010, it is expected that the total cost of the manufactured goods will be $9,000. The goods are manufactured and delivered in 2011 for $9,000. What is X's income for 2010 and 2011? What if the actual cost incurred in 2011 for manufacturing the goods was $8,000? What if it was $10,000? Consider paragraphs 12(1)(a) and (e) and 20(1)(m).
4. The reserve under paragraph 20(1)(n) departs from GAAP in a number of respects. First, no reserve is permitted in respect of goods sold unless the terms of the sale provide that at least part of the amount due is not due for at least two years from the day on which the property was sold. This limitation does not apply to a sale of land. What is the effect of the limitation in subsection 20(8)?
5. In contrast to paragraph 20(1)(m), the reserve under paragraph 20(1)(n) relates only to the profit element in the amount due. The CRA's administrative position is set out in IT-154R, paragraphs 11 and 12:

> 11. The only requirement in regard to the allowable amount of a reserve in respect of the profit element in such an amount due is that the reserve must be a reasonable amount. Normally, it is considered reasonable to assume that the profit element in any amount due is that proportion of such amount that the gross profit on the sale bears to the gross selling price; thus a reserve might

be allowed equal to the full amount of the profit if no part of the selling price had been received. Stated as a formula, the foregoing would be:

$$\frac{\textit{gross profit}}{\text{gross selling price}} \times \text{amount due} = \text{reserve}$$

12. Where the profit element in an amount due is determined on some other basis and the amount is greater than it would be if it had been calculated on the above basis, the taxpayer must submit reasons for considering that the reserve is a reasonable amount. A claim for a reserve equal to the lesser of the gross profit on the sale and the amount due will not be allowed as it is not considered reasonable to assume that the vendor receives no profit until after the full investment in the property sold has been recovered.

6. On June 1, 2010, X, a real estate developer, sells land for $100,000, $30,000 payable immediately and $35,000 on June 1, 2011 and $35,000 on June 1, 2012. The land was acquired by X in 2000 at a cost of $60,000. What is X's income for 2010, 2011 and 2012? Consider paragraphs 12(1)(b) and (e) and 20(1)(n).
7. What if, in question 6, $20,000 was payable immediately and a further $20,000 was payable in each of 2011, 2012, 2013 and 2014? What would X's income be in each of 2010 through 2014?
8. What if, in question 6, X was a manufacturer of specialty machinery and the asset sold in 2010 (on the same terms as in question 6 with the same cost to manufacture) was a custom-made hydraulic lift?
9. The CRA's administrative practice with respect to the reserve for doubtful debts in paragraph 20(1)(l) and the deduction for bad debts in paragraph 20(1)(p) is set out in Interpretation Bulletin IT-442R: Bad Debts and Reserves for Doubtful Debts (September 6, 1991). What is the difference between a "bad" debt and a "doubtful" debt? According to IT-442R, paragraph 23:

> 23. ... For a debt to be classed as a bad debt, there must be evidence that it has in fact become uncollectible. It is sufficient, however, that there is reasonable doubt about the collectibility of a debt for it to be included in a reserve for doubtful debts. ...

10. IT-442R, paragraph 24 provides:

> 24. For a taxpayer to establish that a reserve for doubtful debts is reasonable in amount it is necessary to identify the debts that are doubtful of collection having regard for such indications as the period of arrears or default, the financial status and prospects of the debtor, the debtor's past credit record both with the taxpayer and, if available, with other creditors, the value of any security taken and any other factor that is relevant in judging the debtor's

ability or willingness to pay. Once having identified which debts are doubtful, the maximum amount of the reserve should be calculated based on an estimate as to what percentage of the doubtful debts will probably not be collected. This calculation should preferably be based on the taxpayer's past history of bad debts, the experience in the industry if that information is available, general and local economic conditions, costs of collection, etc. This procedure may result in a reserve being calculated as a percentage of the total amount of the doubtful debts or a series of percentages relating to an age-analysis of those debts. However, a reserve that is merely based on a percentage of all debts, whether doubtful or not, a percentage of gross sales or some similar calculation is not considered to be a reserve determined on a reasonable basis as required by subparagraph 20(1)(l)(i). However, a reserve for doubtful debts that is less than the amount that could have been claimed in accordance with a determination such as that described above will be viewed as a "reasonable" amount.

11. X renders services in 2010 and sends a bill for $1,000. X incurred expenses of $600 in rendering the services. The bill is not paid by the end of 2010. What are the income tax consequences? What if the bill is not paid in 2011? What if the bill will never be paid? Consider paragraphs 20(1)(l), 20(1)(p), 12(1)(d) and 12(1)(i).
12. Where stock in trade (i.e., inventory), including land, is sold on a deferred payment basis, a reserve for the profit element in the amount receivable may be claimed under paragraph 20(1)(n); a reserve in respect of the debt itself may also be claimed under paragraph 20(1)(l). How should these two reserves interact?

4. Allowances

The Act permits the deduction of allowances in respect of the capital cost of depreciable property (paragraph 20(1)(a)) and eligible capital expenditures (paragraph 20(1)(b)). The effect is that capital expenditures are deducted over several taxation years. The rationale is that these expenditures provide a lasting benefit to the taxpayer's business and only a portion of the expenditure can be deducted each year during the useful life of the capital property. This view is consistent with the matching principle. These allowances are considered in more detail, *infra*.

5. Inventory

The cost of inventory is not necessarily deducted in the year in which the cost is incurred. Rather, an attempt is made to match the costs to the year in which the inventory is sold. The tax treatment of inventory is considered in detail, *infra*.

6. Modified Accrual for Professionals: Section 34 Election

Paragraph 12(1)(b) provides that income from services must be recognized when it is receivable, notwithstanding that it is not received until a subsequent year. Paragraph 12(1)(b) was amended in 1983 to add the proviso that

> an amount shall be deemed to have become receivable in respect of services rendered in the course of a business on the day that is the earlier of
>
> (i) the day on which the account in respect of the services was rendered, and
>
> (ii) the day on which the account in respect of those services would have been rendered had there been no undue delay in rendering the account in respect of the services.

The extent to which this proviso modified or superceded the general principle that income from services must be recognized when it is earned was considered in *Maritime Telegraph and Telephone Company, Limited v. The Queen, supra.*

Based on this case, a professional generally must recognize income from services as it is earned, notwithstanding that an account has not been sent. In order to determine when the amount is "earned", all of the circumstances, including the contract governing the provision of services, must be considered. Generally speaking (although the contract may provide otherwise), income from services is earned as the services are performed, and not necessarily when the contract is completed. Accordingly, a professional must generally recognize service income from "work-in-progress" at the end of the fiscal period. Furthermore, under subsection 10(5), work-in-progress of a professional is considered part of inventory and as such, the expenses associated with work-in-progress cannot be deducted until the work-in-progress is completed (i.e., it is no longer part of the inventory of the taxpayer). Subsection 10(4) provides that, for the purpose of determining the value of closing inventory (see the discussion of inventory, *infra*), work-in-progress must be valued at its realizable value in order to avoid an argument that the fair market value of work-in-progress has a negligible value.

Section 34 permits certain listed professionals to elect not to include any amount on account of work-in-progress in determining income for tax purposes. Professionals permitted to make the election are limited to doctors, lawyers, accountants, dentists, veterinarians and chiropractors. This election has ramifications both for the revenue side and the expense side of income computation. On the revenue side, the value of work-in-progress need not be included in income until a bill is rendered. On the other hand, expenses to generate work-in-progress can be deducted when the expenses are incurred rather than being included in the computation of closing inventory. Thus, professionals who can make the election have a distinct advantage over professionals (such as engineers and architects) who cannot.

The meaning of work-in-progress was considered in the following case.

BROCK V. M.N.R.
[1991] 2 C.T.C. 2121, 91 D.T.C. 1079 (T.C.C.)

[The taxpayer was a lawyer in Kitchener, Ontario who had made a section 34 election. The taxpayer periodically sent to his clients statements of account, which indicated that payment was due within 10 days of receipt. The taxpayer took the position that these statements of account were interim statements, representing work in progress, and that the amounts billed did not have to be included in income until a final statement of account was rendered. The Minister reassessed the taxpayer, including the amount of the accounts in income, but allowed a doubtful debt reserve under paragraph 20(1)(l). The taxpayer appealed.]

Proulx T.C.J. ...

There was no evidence adduced about the terms of the contracts between the clients and the law practice relating to the billing practice and the understanding that the clients should have had about the distinction between interim and final accounts. ...

After my reading of the *Law Society Act* [R.S.O. 1980 c. 23] and the *Solicitors Act* [R.S.O. 1980 c. 478] and the regulations thereunder, it appears to me that in the Ontario law, the general contract law governs the solicitor and client agreement except to the extent modified by these acts and the regulations. In these acts, there does not seem to be any distinction between interim and final accounts respecting their enforceability. I am not aware of anything that prevents a lawyer from sending bills on a recurrent basis and nothing that prevents a lawyer from enforcing them in accordance with the provisions of the *Solicitors Act* as to proper notice [Section 2 of the *Solicitors Act*.] I cannot therefore agree with the argument that only accounts sent at the completion of the lawyer's mandate can be enforced by virtue of the aforementioned acts.

If I refer to the two judgments cited by counsel for the Appellant, it appears to me that in the Ontario law an interim bill is enforceable except that it is not considered final for the purposes of taxation and for the purposes of calculating the limitation period under section 10 of the *Solicitors Act*. ...

The statements of account of the Appellant's law practice are so worded that they cannot, in any event, be considered as true interim bills or non-enforceable bills. They are worded as accounts in respect of services rendered of which payment is requested and owed. They are not worded as pieces of information for the fees and disbursements incurred on work-in-progress. If the nature of these accounts were to be true interim accounts, this should have been made clear on the face of the document. The note at the bottom of the page should have read in clear terms that the statement is sent for information purposes only, that the bill is an interim bill, and that no payments are expected. It is impossible to believe that clients receiving statements of account, as those previously described, could have understood that they did not have to pay and that the account was an interim account, not a final account. Moreover, it has to be remembered that there was no evidence adduced in respect of the agreements with the clients. ...

Counsel for the Appellant also made the submissions that they were statements for work-in-progress. This cannot stand either.

What is work in progress? It is not defined in the Act. It should then be given a meaning that is consistent with the natural meaning of these words in the context of subsection 34(1) of the Act. It has to consist of services rendered about which an account has not been rendered or should not have been rendered if there had not been an undue delay. Because the services have been rendered, a proportionate amount of the fees should be included in the receivables but because they have not been invoiced, or should not have been invoiced, they may be excluded from the computation of income if an election is made to this effect by the taxpayer. This is the extent of the reserve allowed under subsection 34(1) of the Act since that reserve is allowed "except as otherwise provided by this section". This section stipulates that an amount is deemed to be receivable in respect of that part of the services rendered that is invoiced or that should have been invoiced if it had not been for an undue delay, and therefore the part that remains for the exclusion of the work in progress is that part of the services rendered but not invoiced.

I am therefore of the view that the words "work in progress" mean that part of the services rendered which have not yet been invoiced or should not have been invoiced. In the case at bar, the services rendered have been invoiced. The Appellant submits that it constitutes in fact work in progress because the invoices are not invoices. As previously explained, this is a statement that is not correct in fact and in law, in the circumstances of the case at bar.

The appeal is therefore dismissed.

Notes and Questions

1. Consider an architect who runs a business in which she employs a number of other architects and draftspersons. What costs are included in her work in progress? Would a portion of the salaries paid to her employees be included? If the individual were a lawyer who employed a number of associates, what would be the effect of making a section 34 election?
2. What is the policy rationale for section 34? Why is the election available only to certain professionals?

V. TAX TREATMENT OF INVENTORY

A. Definition of "Inventory"

Inventory accounting is an important aspect of the accrual method of accounting. For taxpayers engaged in a merchandising or manufacturing business, the cost of inventory — or more precisely, the cost of goods sold — is likely the most significant item of deduction in computing profit. The term "inventory" is defined in subsection 248(1) to mean "a description of property the cost or value of which is relevant in computing a taxpayer's income from a business for a taxation year". This definition is so broad that it provides little assistance in developing criteria for determining whether a particular cost is to be treated as inventory for tax purposes.

In general, however, inventory may be described as property acquired or produced by a taxpayer for the purpose of resale at a profit. Inventory also includes partially finished goods ("work in progress") and property to be used in the production of goods for sale (raw materials and component parts). What assets constitute inventory generally depend on the nature of the business. For example, for a used car dealer, cars will be inventory. For a computer manufacturer, the manufactured computer, spare parts, partially completed computers and component parts will be inventory. For a professional, work-in-progress is generally treated as inventory, although certain professionals can elect to exclude work in progress, as discussed above.

B. Inventory Accounting

Under generally accepted accounting principles, a business that derives profits from the sale of goods must, in determining its income at the end of the taxation year, divide its inventory costs between those costs which are properly allocable to the current year's operations and those costs which should be deferred to subsequent periods. The fundamental focus of inventory accounting is the timing of the deduction of the cost of assets included in inventory. The main objective of inventory accounting is to match appropriate costs against revenues in order that there may be a proper determination of the realized income. Section 10 of the Act contains a number of rules on inventory accounting for tax purposes. It is not a comprehensive regime and appears to assume that inventory accounting for income tax purposes is largely the same as that for commercial accounting purposes, except as modified by that section.

Under inventory accounting, gross profit from the sale of inventory is computed by deducting from proceeds of sale an amount commonly referred to as the "cost of goods sold". Expressed as a formula:

$$\text{Gross Profit} = \text{Revenues from sales} - \text{Cost of Goods Sold}$$

From gross profit, allowable expenses are then deducted to determine the business's profit. Cost of goods sold ("CGS") is determined by taking the opening inventory ("OI") of the business at the beginning of the year, adding to it the cost of goods acquired ("CGA") during the year and subtracting the closing inventory ("CI") at the end of the year. Expressed as a formula:

$$CGS = OI + CGA - CI$$

A number of questions must be answered in order to apply this formula.

- What is the opening inventory at the beginning of the year?
- What is the cost of inventory acquired during the year?
- Which goods remain on hand at the end of the year and what is their value?

When a taxpayer has thousands of nuts and bolts, how can the cost of each item be established? What are the general principles guiding inventory valuation? These questions are addressed in the following excerpt.

TIMING AND INCOME TAXATION: THE PRINCIPLES OF INCOME MEASUREMENT FOR TAX PURPOSES, 2d ed.

Brian J. Arnold, Colin Campbell, Michael Hiltz, Richard Marcovitz, Shawn D. Porter, and James R. Wilson

(Toronto: Canadian Tax Foundation, 2015) (footnotes omitted)
Reproduced with permission of the Canadian Tax Foundation

Subsection 10(1) governs the use of inventory accounting for tax purposes. ... The inventory provisions of the Act are surprisingly brief and do not provide specific guidance as to their application in various situations. Most of the case law on section 10 and other inventory provisions relates to the interpretation of subsection 10(1). The Canada Revenue Agency (CRA) interprets section 10 by reference to accounting principles and practices [see CRA, Interpretation Bulletin IT-473R, now archived on the Internet].

In recent years, the CRA's interpretation and application of the provisions of section 10 have not generated much controversy. For the most part, taxpayers appear to adhere to accounting principles and practices with respect to the treatment of inventory, and the CRA generally accepts the application of such accounting principles and practices, even where they conflict with its published administrative positions.

Basic Rules of Inventory Valuation

The basic statutory rules for the valuation of inventory are contained in section 10. ... The method of valuation to be applied in respect of a business (other than an adventure in the nature of trade) is set out in subsection 10(1), which reads as follows:

> For the purpose of computing a taxpayer's income for a taxation year from a business that is not an adventure or concern in the nature of trade, property described in an inventory shall be valued at the end of the year at the cost at which the taxpayer acquired the property or its fair market value at the end of the year, whichever is lower, or in a prescribed manner.

The "prescribed manner" under regulation 1801 is that taxpayers may choose to value property at fair market value. Prior to January 15, 1987, taxpayers were also able to value inventory at cost, but this option is no longer available. Regulation 1802 sets out a special rule for the valuation of animals owned by breeders. ...

In considering how the statutory options for inventory valuation operate, it is important to understand the effect of each method on profit for tax purposes. If all property in inventory is valued at its fair market value, profit or loss will result if the fair market value of the property at the end of the taxation year is different from the value at the commencement of the taxation year or, where property is acquired during the year, from the value, usually the cost, at the time of acquisition. If the property has appreciated in value during the taxation year, the amount of the appreciation reduces the cost of goods sold (or results in a negative inventory cost) and thereby increases income for tax purposes. Conversely, if the property has declined in value during the year, the amount of the reduction is reflected in an increased cost of goods sold and a reduction in income. Under the lower-of-cost-and-fair-market-value rule, if the value of property declines below its cost, the amount of the decrease in value increases the cost of goods sold and reduces the amount of income for the year. Appreciation in the value of property above its original cost does not, however, have the converse effect.

Subsection 10(1) differs from most tax provisions in that it allows taxpayers to recognize unrealized gains and losses in respect of property. The use of the lower-of-cost-and-fair-market-value method allows taxpayers to claim unrealized losses if the value of inventory declines to an amount that is less than the cost of the property. The use of the fair market value method requires taxpayers to recognize both gains and losses. Taxpayers who have previously written down inventory to a fair market value below its cost are required to recognize income to the extent that the fair market value of the inventory subsequently increases up to the amount of its original cost. ...

The computation of the cost of goods sold under subsection 10(1) depends in particular on the meaning of the words "cost" and "fair market value". The determination of the cost of items included in inventory has important consequences. If an expense is included in the cost of inventory, the cost is deductible when the goods are sold or when the fair market value declines. If an expense is not a capital expense and is not included in the cost of inventory, it is generally deductible in the year in which it is incurred. Moreover, when a taxpayer regularly acquires and disposes of many similar or identical properties and cannot determine cost on an item-by-item basis, some method or formula must be used to determine the cost of inventory properties owned at the end of the year. The determination of fair market value involves subjective judgments even in the simplest situations. However, with respect to inventory, a taxpayer must determine fair market value on the basis of the particular circumstances in order for the rule in subsection 10(1) to operate as intended. For example, a retailer of apples will determine a fair market value for its unsold apples sitting on a shelf that is different from the value used by the farmer who grew and picked them; otherwise, subsection 10(1) would produce results that are not in accordance with well-established business principles.

The Determination of Cost
Which Expenses are Included in Costs of Inventory?

Although valuing inventory at the lower of cost and fair market value is widely accepted, the mechanics of determining both the cost and the fair market value of property included in inventory involve several difficult and contentious issues. There is no statutory definition of "cost" for income tax purposes. Consequently, the cost of property included in inventory for tax purposes is determined largely by reference to accounting principles that deal with the issue in the context of financial reporting, and a limited body of case law that has shown considerable deference to accounting practice.

The accounting rules for the determination of the cost of an item of property included in inventory have generally been accepted by the CRA as an acceptable basis to compute cost under subsection 10(1). In Interpretation Bulletin IT-473R, the CRA describes the cost of inventory as follows:

> "Cost" as used in the phrase "cost at which the taxpayer acquired the property" in section 10 means the original cost of the particular item of inventory plus all costs which may reasonably be considered as having been incurred to bring that particular item of inventory to its condition and location at the end of the taxation year.

This meaning of "cost" is similar to the definition that applies for accounting purposes. ...

The computation of cost in actual situations reflects a large number of small decisions made by employees who administer the financial accounting system of a business. Each such decision is likely to be made in reliance on accounting principles and practices without regard to the tax consequences. If, for example, transportation costs are small in relation to the cost of the materials purchased and it is expensive and time-consuming to allocate those costs to the particular materials, such transportation costs may be deducted in the taxation year in which they are incurred, particularly if such amounts are not material for financial accounting purposes. In short, the CRA should, and apparently does, accept a taxpayer's determination of the cost of inventory property, unless that determination violates generally accepted accounting practices or is not applied consistently from one taxation year to the next. ...

Under GAAP, the cost of inventory comprises three types of costs:

1. costs of purchase,
2. costs of conversion, and
3. other costs incurred in bringing the inventories to their present location and condition.

The costs of purchase include the purchase price, import duties and other non-recoverable taxes, transport, handling, and other costs directly attributable to the *acquisition* (as opposed to storage) of finished goods, materials, and services. The CRA uses the term "laid-down costs" instead of "costs of purchase", but the terms have the same meaning, except that, according to the CRA, significant storage costs are included in laid-down costs. Discounts and rebates should be deducted from the costs of purchase for accounting purposes and also for tax purposes. Costs of purchase or laid-down costs do not usually include indirect costs of acquisition such as purchasing and accounting department costs.

The costs of conversion are costs that enhance the value of the particular items of inventory and certain other costs. These costs are generally included by taxpayers in the cost of inventory for tax purposes. For accounting purposes, costs of conversion that are fixed production costs are allocated to particular items of inventory on the basis of normal rates of production. The amount allocated to a particular item of inventory is not increased during periods of abnormally low production but may be decreased during periods of high production.

"Other costs" included in inventory for accounting purposes include only expenses that are "incurred in bringing the inventories to their present location and condition" — for example, expenses incurred in designing inventory for a specific customer. The following expenses are not included in the cost of inventory as other costs:

a) abnormal amounts of wasted materials, labour, or other production costs;
b) storage costs, unless those costs are necessary in the production process before a further production stage;

c) administrative overheads that do not contribute to bringing inventories to their present location and condition; and
d) selling costs.

Borrowing costs related to inventory may have to be included in the cost of inventory that is produced by the taxpayer, unless the inventory is produced in a short period of time. ...

The foregoing accounting rules and administrative positions suggest a complex meaning for the term "cost" in connection with inventory that is relevant only for the purposes of subsection 10(1). Generally, when the word "cost" is used in the Act, it essentially means laid-down cost — what a taxpayer pays to acquire the item — plus perhaps some expenses directly incurred in making the purchase. However, in the context of inventory, the concept of cost includes most of the expenses required to produce a saleable item. ...

Overhead Costs

The determination of which indirect costs must be added to the costs of purchase or laid-down costs involves a range of small, seemingly insignificant problems, which cumulatively may be significant. Provided that costs are treated consistently and in accordance with established accounting and tax principles, in most situations the CRA should accept the taxpayer's determination of the cost of inventory.

The most contentious issue in the determination of the cost of inventory property for accounting and income tax purposes is the extent to which overhead expenses (or, more generally, expenses incurred indirectly in connection with the production of goods for sale) should be included in the cost of inventory. Specifically, the question is how variable expenses (such as heat, light, power, and maintenance) and fixed expenses (such as depreciation, taxes, and insurance) should be reflected in the cost of inventory. The accounting rules require a business to undertake a "systematic allocation of fixed and variable production overheads that are incurred in converting materials into finished goods". Fixed production overheads are those that are incurred in any case, such as factory depreciation and the costs of management based on normal capacity. Variable costs, including variable overhead costs, relate directly to, and vary with, production, such as the cost of labour or the cost of electricity used to produce a particular item.

In general, there are three possible methods for determining the share of overhead costs to be allocated to inventory:

1. *Prime costs method.* Under this method, only the costs of direct labour and materials are charged to inventory. All overhead expenses are deducted from income in the period in which they are incurred. The prime costs method is not in accordance with GAAP and is not accepted

by the CRA. This method results in the lowest closing cost of inventory and therefore the lowest profit.

2. *Full or absorption costs method.* At the other extreme from the prime costs method is full or absorption costing, under which all overhead expenses are charged to work in progress and finished goods, usually on the basis of a predetermined formula. Overhead costs are estimated and included in the cost of inventory; they are not increased during periods of low production but may be decreased during periods of high production. Full or absorption costing is the method required under GAAP because the costs of conversion incurred to bring goods to their location and condition include costs directly related to the units of production.
3. *Direct or variable costs method.* Under the direct or variable costs method, the cost of inventory includes only expenses directly related to the production of that property. Consequently, variable expenses such as heat, light, and power are included in the cost of inventory, but depreciation is not included, since it is an expense incurred whether or not any goods are produced. Direct costing is not permitted under GAAP, although in the past it was permitted in certain circumstances.

[T]he CRA's published position is that both absorption costing and direct costing are acceptable.

Cost Formulas

After a taxpayer determines the expenses included in the cost of inventory, it must also determine the cost of inventory owned at the end of the period in order to compute the cost of goods sold. Where the inventory consists of items that can be specifically identified, such as works of art or automobiles, the actual cost of the particular items of inventory sold during the year and of those items still held at the end of the year can be tracked to compute the cost of goods sold for tax purposes. This method is known as the specific identification method and is always the preferred method for tax purposes because it accords with the actual facts.

The specific identification method is not always practical for taxpayers that own a large number of indistinguishable items acquired at different costs and times. It is difficult and potentially expensive, if it is possible at all, to trace the physical flow of particular goods to determine the actual cost of the goods sold during the year. In these situations, accounting rules may not require, or even permit, the use of the specific identification method, and may require instead the use of what are referred to ... as "cost formulas". These cost formulas are sometimes referred to as "cost flow assumptions".

Although there are many methods or formulas for determining the cost of closing inventory, not all of them are acceptable ... for the purposes of subsection 10(1). For accounting purposes, businesses must employ the same cost formulas for inventory with the same nature and use, but can employ different formulas for inventory with a different nature and different use.

The major methods or formulas are

- the average-cost method;
- the first in, first out (FIFO) method;
- the last in, first out (LIFO) method; and
- the retail (or gross margin) method.

Under the average-cost method, an average cost is computed for all items of inventory available for sale during a particular period. Closing inventory is calculated as the average cost multiplied by the number of inventory units on hand at the end of the period. In an inflationary period, the average-cost method results in the sale of inventory that has a cost that is lower than current prices, because the average cost of goods reflects the cost of items of inventory that were acquired earlier at lower prices. Advances in technology have made it practical to constantly update the average cost of inventory. When record systems were less advanced, businesses might have computed the average cost of inventory less frequently, possibly only at the end of the year.

Under the FIFO method, an assumption is made that goods in inventory are sold in the same order in which they were acquired. Consequently, the cost of closing inventory is the cost of the most recently acquired inventory property. In contrast to the average-cost method, it does not matter how frequently the cost is computed because it is assumed that the oldest inventory is always sold first and the items of inventory on hand at the end of the year are always the last items acquired.

Under the LIFO method, an assumption is made that the most recently acquired goods are sold first; consequently, the cost of closing inventory is the cost of the oldest units of inventory. If the number of units of closing inventory does not change from one year to the next, the cost of closing inventory will remain unchanged even if the replacement cost and the fair market value of the goods increase during the same period owing to inflation.

The retail method, which is a variation of a category of methods that compute the cost of inventory on the basis of gross margins, is used for accounting purposes in the retail sector. The retail method is not identified as a cost formula under GAAP and does not depend on assumptions regarding the flow of goods. It is often used for practical reasons by taxpayers who sell many types of goods and face difficulties in determining the precise number of items owned at year-end.

Given the limited case law, the CRA's position on the use of cost formulas in [paragraph 15 of] IT-473R is of great practical importance:

> 15. Where it is practical to identify costs by reference to specific items, the cost is determined by ascertaining the laid-down cost of the specific items. If it is not practical to determine cost by reference to specific items, it is necessary to use an arbitrary cost selection method which has the effect of making a presumption as to the order in which inventory is sold. Among the methods most commonly used in determining cost are:
>
> - specific item
> - average cost
> - first in, first out (FIFO)

The last in, first out method (LIFO) and the base stock method [that is, a method valuing a portion of inventory at purchase price and the rest using LIFO] are not accepted for income tax purposes as methods of determining cost.

Notes and Questions

1. Subsection 10(2.1) addresses problems surrounding inventory valuation uncertainty to a certain extent by requiring taxpayers to use the same valuation method every year unless permission is granted by the Minister. Forcing taxpayers to use the same valuation method each year encourages consistent tax obligations and likely inhibits possible abuses associated with valuing inventories in such a way as to temporarily lower tax liabilities.
2. Taxpayer A has a retail business and the fiscal period for the business is the calendar year. She has the following amounts in respect of her inventory:

December 31, 2009	closing inventory (CI) = $20,000
January 1, 2010	opening inventory (OI) = $20,000
During 2010	cost of goods acquired or CGA = $5,000
December 31, 2010	cost of CI = $20,000
	FMV of CI = $18,000

   What is the value of the closing inventory under subsection 10(1)? What is the cost of goods sold for the purpose of computing profit?

3. Mary carries on business manufacturing and selling children's clothing. At the end of 2010, she has the following inventory on hand: finished goods with a cost (and replacement cost) of $10,000 and a fair market value of $20,000; work-in-progress with a cost (and replacement cost) of $8,000 and a fair market value of $3,000; and raw materials with a cost of $4,000 and a fair market value of $3,500. What is Mary's closing inventory at the end of 2009 assuming that she uses the method required under subsection 10(1)?

FRIESEN v. THE QUEEN
[1995] 2 C.T.C. 369, 95 D.T.C. 5551 (S.C.C.)

[In 1982, the appellant and several other taxpayers acquired a parcel of vacant land as an adventure in the nature of trade. In the years following its acquisition, the property decreased substantially in value and in 1986 the mortgagee foreclosed on the property. In 1983 and 1984, the taxpayer deducted the decline in the fair market value of the property as a business loss. The Minister disallowed the deductions and the taxpayer's appeals to the Federal Court–Trial Division and Federal Court of Appeal were dismissed. The issue was whether the taxpayer was entitled to write down the value of property held as an adventure or concern in the nature of trade under subsection 10(1) and claim a business loss under section 9 or whether the loss could be claimed only in the year the property was disposed of.]

Major J.: ... The central question on this appeal of whether the appellant is entitled to take advantage of the inventory valuation method in s. 10 of the Act involves a careful examination of the wording of the provisions of the Act and a consideration of the proper interpretation of these sections in the light of the basic structure of the Canadian taxation scheme which is established in the *Income Tax Act.*

In interpreting sections of the *Income Tax Act,* the correct approach, as set out by Estey, J. in *Stubart Investments Ltd. v. The Queen*, [1984] 1 S.C.R. 536, is to apply the plain meaning rule [discussed *infra* in Chapter 10]. ...

The primary section whose interpretation is in dispute is s. 10:

> 10. (1) For the purpose of computing income from a business, the property described in an inventory shall be valued as its cost to the taxpayer or its fair market value, whichever is lower, or in such other manner as may be permitted by regulation.

The plain reading of this section is that it is a mandatory provision requiring a taxpayer who computes income from a business to value the inventory at the lower of cost or market value or as permitted by regulation. Thus, *prima facie*, the taxpayer must meet two requirements in order to use this section: the venture at issue must be a "business" and the property in question must be "inventory."

[Major J. considered the meaning of "business" in subsection 248(1) and the concept of an adventure or concern in the nature of trade and concluded that the appellant's activities constituted an adventure. He then considered whether the property was inventory in 1983 and 1984.]

Reduced to its simplest terms, the income or profit from the sale of a single item of inventory by a sales business is the ordinary tracing formula calculated by subtracting the purchase cost of the item from the proceeds of sale. This is the basic formula which applies to the calculation of profit before the value of inventory is taken into account, as is made clear by Abbott, J. in *Minister of National Revenue v. Irwin*, [1964] S.C.R. 662, at pp. 664-65:

> The law is clear therefore that for income tax purposes gross profit, in the case of a business which consists of acquiring property and reselling it, is the excess of sale price over cost, subject only to any modification effected by the "cost or market, whichever is lower" rule.

Thus, for any particular item:

Income = Profit = Sale Price – Purchase Cost.

It is clear from the formula above that the cost of an item of property sold by a business is relevant in computing the income from the business in the taxation year in which it is sold. As discussed above, an adventure in the nature of trade constitutes a business under the Act. Therefore, an item of property sold as part of an adventure in the nature of trade is relevant to the computation of the taxpayer's income from a business in the taxation year of disposition and so is inventory according to the plain language of the definition in s. 248(1).

The respondent argued that even if the Styles Property were inventory in the year of disposition it would not qualify as inventory in preceding years. Specifically the respondent urged that the phrase "relevant in computing a taxpayer's income from a business for a taxation year" requires that the characterization of each item of property as inventory (or not) be made on an annual basis on the basis of the relevance of the item to the computation of income for that taxation year. ...

In my opinion, the interpretation urged by the respondent runs contrary to the natural meaning of the words used in the definition of inventory in s. 248(1) and to common sense. The plain meaning of the definition in s. 248(1) is that an item of property need only be relevant to business income in a single year to qualify as inventory: "relevant in computing the taxpayer's income from a business for a taxation year." In this respect the definition of inventory in the *Income Tax Act* is consistent with the ordinary meaning of the word. In the normal sense, inventory is property which a business holds for sale and this term applies to that property both in the year of sale and in years where the property remains as yet unsold by a business. ...

The respondent is asking this Court to interpret the definition of inventory as though it read:

> "inventory" [for a taxation year] means a description of property the cost or value of which is relevant in computing a taxpayer's income from a business for [the] taxation year;

The principal problem with the respondent's interpretation is that the bracketed words do not appear in the definition in the *Income Tax Act*. The addition of these words to the definition effects a significant change to the sense of the definition. It is a basic principle of statutory interpretation that the court should not accept an interpretation which requires the insertion of extra wording where there is another acceptable interpretation which does not require any additional wording. Reading extra words into a statutory definition is even less acceptable when the phrases which must be read in appear in several other definitions in the same statute. If Parliament had intended to require that property must be relevant to the computation of income in a particular year in order to be inventory in that year, it would have added the necessary phraseology to make that clear. ...

[Major J. also considered the Crown's argument inconsistent with the division in the Act between business income and capital gain. In this discussion, Major, J. incorrectly stated that subsections 13(7) and 45(1) apply to conversions of real property from inventory to capital property and vice versa. This proposition was not the crux of his reasoning and it is therefore unlikely that the error would have affected the remainder of his decision. Major, J. continued:]

... the interpretation proposed by the respondent is inconsistent with the commonly understood definition of the term. In the ordinary sense of the term, an item of property which a business keeps for the purpose of offering it for sale constitutes inventory at any time prior to the sale of that item. The ordinary sense of the word also reflects the definition of inventory which is accepted according to ordinary principles of commercial accounting and of business. The Canadian Institute of Chartered Accountants has defined "inventory" as including, inter alia "[i]tems of tangible property which are held for sale in the ordinary course of business": Terminology for Accountants (3rd ed. 1983), at p. 81. In the specific context of real estate the Canadian Institute of Public Real Estate Companies states that land held for sale and land held for future development and sale is inventory: *Canadian Institute of Public Real Estate Companies Recommended Accounting Practices for Real Estate Companies* (November 1985), at p. 204-1.

It was held in *Bailey*, and is accepted by Iacobucci, J., that single pieces of real estate held for sale as an adventure of the nature of trade meet the definitions of inventory accepted by the commercial and accounting worlds. These definitions are consistent with the plain meaning interpretation of the definition in the Act which would require only that the item of property be relevant to the computation of income in a single year. However, the interpretation sought by the respondent is considerably more restricted because it would require a connection to income in years prior to sale. I agree with my colleague that the express wording of the *Income Tax Act* is capable of overruling accounting and commercial principles where it is sufficiently explicit. Nevertheless, the Court should be cautious to adopt an interpretation which is clearly inconsistent with the commonly accepted usage of a technical term particularly where an interpretation consistent with common usage is more natural on a plain reading of the definition. ...

... I conclude that the correct interpretation of the term of inventory in s. 248(1) is the one which appears most obvious on a literal reading of the wording that an item of property is inventory if it is relevant to the computation of business income in a year. As a general principle, items of property sold by a business venture will always be relevant to the computation of income in the year of sale. ...

The Styles Property was relevant to the computation of business income in the taxation year of disposition and therefore it is correctly categorized as "inventory" for the purposes of the *Income Tax Act* both in that year and in preceding years.

...

The final argument of the respondent which should be addressed is that the inventory valuation method in s. 10(1) is simply a codification of the common law and so is restricted to stock-in-traders. The respondent is correct to note that the common law recognized an exception to the realization principle by allowing inventory to be valued at the lower of cost or market value in the case of stock-in-trade ...

[Major J. reviewed the jurisprudence and history of subsection 10(1) and continued:]

The appropriate focus in determining whether s. 10(1) is a mere codification of the common law is upon the wording of the section itself. ... The common law rule was restricted to stock-in-traders. Section 10(1) on the other hand explicitly states that it applies to the inventory of a business. As discussed above, the word business is defined in the Act and specifically includes adventures in the nature of trade. If Parliament had wanted to simply codify the common law it could and would have used the term "ordinary trading business" or "stock-in-trader" both of which had judicially established definitions. Since Parliament chose to use the broader term "business," there is simply no basis on which to assume that s. 10(1) was no more than a codification of a common law rule. To place such a judicial limit on the clear and unambiguous wording of the statute is an usurpation of the legislative function of Parliament.

... The restriction placed upon this section by [Iacobucci, J.] is based on his view that the object and purpose of the section is to provide a limited exception to the realization principle for stock-in-traders as was provided for at common law. However, as discussed at the beginning of these reasons, the clear language of the *Income Tax Act* takes precedence over a court's view of the object and purpose of a provision. ...

Therefore, the object and purpose of a provision need only be resorted to when the statutory language admits of some doubt or ambiguity. In this case, there is no doubt or ambiguity in the statutory language of s. 10(1) which clearly applies to the inventory of a business including an adventure in the nature of trade. ...

I would allow the appeal with costs in this Court and in the courts below ...

[Iacobucci J., in dissent, agreed that the appellant's activities constituted an adventure or concern in the nature of trade, and therefore a business. However, he disagreed with the majority's interpretation of subsection 10(1) and the meaning of "inventory" in subsection 248(1).]

Iacobucci J. ... The respondent correctly notes, however, that the principle of realization in the computation of profit and loss is subject to an exception in the case of stock-in-trade ... In Canada, this exception is presently codified in s. 10(1) of the *Income Tax Act: Minister of National Revenue v. Irwin*, [1964] S.C.R. 662 (referring to the former version of s. 10(1), s. 14(2)). Such stock-in-trade can be valued at the lower of cost and fair market value and, consequently, can permit a dealer therein to deduct unrealized losses through the cost of goods sold formula. The result of this principle is effectively to enable a business to increase its cost of goods sold and thus reduce its profits (or increase its losses) in a given year by the amount by which the market value of its inventory at the end of the year falls below the cost of that inventory. The effect of this is to permit a business to recognize as a loss the decline in the value of its inventory in the year in which this decline occurs as opposed to the year in which the inventory is actually sold. However, the commercial principles and jurisprudential authority underpinning the *Income Tax Act* do not recognize that this exception to the realization principle should operate for unsold single pieces of land that are held by adventurers in trade and alleged to be inventory. ...

... the respondent makes the following submission, which I fully endorse:

> The introduction of section 10 in the Act was intended only to recognize statutorily the rule that only "ordinary trading businesses" could properly use the lower of cost or market rule. The section was not intended to extend the use of that rule to cases such as the present one where there is only a single transaction.

[Iacobucci J. further stated that subsection 10(1) was limited to taxpayers who carry on a business and therefore excluded persons involved in an adventure or concern in the nature of trade. After further discussion of the rationale for limiting subsection 10(1) to stock-in-traders, Iacobucci, J. concluded:]

In closing, I emphasize my discomfort with a ruling that would permit speculative investments constituting "adventures in the nature of trade" to be written down to the lower of cost and market value in years in which their value declines yet they are not sold. This discomfort appears to be shared by the drafters of the Act as well as the authors of much of the jurisprudence and academic commentaries dealing with the computation of profit under s. 9 of the Act. Both the application of s. 10(1) as well as the definition of "inventory" must be very sensitive to these considerations.

[Iacobucci, J. then reviewed the definition of "inventory" in subsection 248(1) and concluded that property held in an adventure or concern in the nature of trade was not inventory in years prior to its disposition since it was not relevant in computing the taxpayer's business income for those particular years.]

I would therefore dismiss the appeal with costs. It should, however, be noted that, by rejecting this taxpayer's appeal, this Court is not denying him the right to claim any losses (that are otherwise available) on the Styles Property as business losses. Rather, this Court is simply ensuring that these losses can only be recorded on his 1986 tax return, the only year in which they actually relate to his income. ...

[Sopinka and L'Heureux-Dubé JJ. concurred with Major J.; Gonthier J. concurred with Iacobucci J.]

Note

The result in *Friesen* has been overruled by amendment to subsection 10(1) and the introduction of subsection 10(1.01). Subsection 10(1.01) requires that property described in the inventory of a business that is an adventure or concern in the nature of trade be valued at the end of year at cost and not, for example, at the lower of cost and fair market value as permitted by subsection 10(1). Is there a defensible tax-policy rationale for maintaining the lower of cost and fair market value rule in subsection 10(1) for inventory of a business other than an adventure in the nature of trade?

VI. CAPITAL EXPENDITURE

In determining the proper tax treatment of an expenditure, the analysis first should determine whether an expense is a current expense or a capital expense. If it is a current expense, it is fully deductible in the year incurred. In most cases the characterization is an easy one, but in some situations the distinction is difficult. If it is concluded that an expense is a capital expense, then its deduction is, subject to the application of section 20, prohibited by paragraph 18(1)(b). Section 20 contains various exceptions to the general prohibition in paragraph 18(1)(b), the two most common of which are the deduction permitted under paragraph 20(1)(a) in respect of a taxpayer's depreciable property ("capital cost allowance", more commonly referred to as "depreciation") and the deduction permitted under paragraph 20(1)(b) in respect of a taxpayer's "eligible capital expenditures". Where applicable, these provisions generally permit a deduction in respect of the capital expenditure over a period of years. If an expenditure is not a current expense and does not come within one of the exceptions in section 20, then it is a "nothing" and no deduction is permitted.

Since a full deduction in the current year is usually preferable to a deduction over time, taxpayers generally seek to have expenses treated as current expenses rather than capital expenses, but this is not always the case. Sometimes a taxpayer will claim an expense is a capital outlay (normally because it is advantageous to do so) while the CRA contends it is a current expense (see, e.g., *Denison Mines, infra*).

This part will first deal with the distinction between current expenses and capital expenses. It will then review the tax treatment of a capital expense under the capital cost allowance and eligible expenditure rules.

A. Current Versus Capital Expenditure

1. The Basic Test: Enduring Benefit

The following cases discuss the basic distinction between a current and a capital expenditure.

BRITISH INSULATED AND HELSBY CABLES, LIMITED v. I.R.C.
[1926] A.C. 205 (H.L.)

[The appellant agreed with its employees when setting up a pension fund that it would contribute to the fund. To form a nucleus for the fund and to ensure that older employees ranked proportionately, the company made a large lump sum payment to the fund. The company then sought to deduct this sum as a current expenditure.]

Viscount Cave, L.C. ...

But there remains the question, which I have found more difficult, whether, apart from the express prohibitions, the sum in question is (in the words used by Lord Sumner in *Usher's* case [1915] A.C. 468) a proper debit item to be charged against incomings of the trade when computing the profits of it; or, in other words, whether it is in substance a revenue or a capital expenditure. This appears to me to be a question of fact which is proper to be decided by the Commissioners upon the evidence brought before them in each case; but where, as in the present case, there is no express finding by the Commissioners upon the point, it must be determined by the Courts upon the materials which are available and with due regard to the principles which have been laid down in the authorities. Now, in *Vallambrosa Rubber Co. v. Farmer*, 1910 S.C. 519, 525; 5 Tax Cas. 529, 536 Lord Dunedin, as Lord President of the Court of Session, expressed the opinion that "in a rough way" it was "not a bad criterion of what is capital expenditure - as against what is income expenditure - to say that capital expenditure is a thing that is going to be spent once and for all, and income expenditure is a thing that is going to recur every year"; and no doubt this is often a material consideration. But the criterion suggested is not, and was obviously not intended by Lord Dunedin to be, a decisive one in every case; for it is easy to imagine many cases in which a payment, though made "once and for all," would be properly chargeable against the receipts for the year. Instances of such payments may be found in the gratuity of £1500 paid to a reporter on his retirement, which was the subject of the decision in *Smith v. Incorporated Council of Law Reporting for England and Wales*, [1913] 3 K.B. 674, and in the expenditure of £4994 in the purchase of an annuity for the benefit of an actuary who had retired, which, in *Hancock v. General Reversionary and Investment Co.*, [1919] 1 K.B. 25, was allowed, and I think rightly allowed, to be deducted from profits. But when an expenditure is made, not only once and for all, but with a view to bringing into existence an asset or an advantage for the enduring benefit of a trade, I think that there is very good reason (in the absence of special circumstances leading to an opposite conclusion) for treating such an expenditure as properly attributable not to revenue but to capital. For this view there is already considerable authority. Thus, moneys expended by a brewing firm with a view to the acquisition of new licensed premises: *Southwell v. Savill Brothers*, [1901] 2 K.B. 319; "flitting expenses" incurred in transferring a manufacturing business to new premises: *Granite Supply Association v. Kitton*, S.F. 55; 5 Tax Cas. 168; costs incurred in promoting a Bill which was dropped on the desired facilities being obtained by agreement: *A.G. Moore & Co. v. Hare*, 1913 S.C. 91; 6 Tax Cas. 572; and expenditure incurred by a shipbuilding firm in deepening a channel and creating a deep water berth (not on their own property) to enable vessels constructed by them to put out to sea: *Ounsworth v. Vickers, Ltd.*, [1915] 3 K.B. 267, have been held to be in the nature of capital expenditure and not to be deductible under the *Income Tax Acts*; and *Rowntree & Co. v. Curtis*, [1925] 1 K.B. 328 is to the same effect. I think that the principle to be deduced from this series of authorities rests on sound foundations and may properly be adopted by this House.

My Lords, in my opinion the present case falls within the same principle. The payment of £31,784, which is the subject of dispute, was made, not merely as a gift or bonus to the older servants of the appellant company, but (as the deed shows) to "form a nucleus" of the pension fund which it was desired to create; and it is a fair inference from the terms of the deed and from the Commissioners' findings that without this contribution the fund might not have come into existence at all. The object and effect of the payment of this large sum was to enable the company to establish the pension fund and to offer to all its existing and future employees a sure provision for their old age, and so to obtain for the company the substantial and lasting advantage of being in a position throughout its business life to secure and retain the services of a contented and efficient staff. I am satisfied on full consideration that the payment was in the nature of capital expenditure, and accordingly that the deduction of the amount from profits, although not expressly prohibited by the Act, was rightly held by the Court of Appeal not to be admissible.

For these reasons I move your Lordships that this appeal be dismissed with costs.

Lord Blanesburgh, dissenting: ... As to the suggestion that the £31,784 representing the notional payments made over a number of years must be treated as capital because that sum was paid in one year and in one amount, I find myself in entire agreement with Lush, J., when in *Hancock v. General Reversionary Interest and Investment Co.*, [1919] 1 K.B. 25, 37 he said: "It seems to me as impossible to hold that the fact that a lump sum was paid instead of a recurring series of annual payments alters the character of the expenditure as it would be to hold that, if an employer made a voluntary arrangement with his servant to pay the servant a year's salary in advance instead of paying each year's salary as it fell due, he would be making a capital outlay. ..."

Notes and Questions

1. Viscount Cave is correct in stating that singularity ("once and for all") or recurrence of an expenditure is not a sufficient criterion in all cases for determining whether an expenditure is capital in nature. If the expenditure is of a non-recurring nature and if it also purchases an asset "for the enduring benefit of the trade", that additional factor obviously tends to confirm that it is a capital outlay. However, Viscount Cave's test has led to a great deal of confusion in later cases.
2. Did Viscount Cave need to add the "asset or advantage" gloss to the *Vallambrosa* test in order to distinguish the *Smith* and *Hancock* cases?

DENISON MINES LIMITED v. M.N.R.
(1972), [1972] C.T.C. 521, 72 D.T.C. 6444 (F.C.A.)

[The taxpayer owned and operated a uranium mine. The mine included numerous "throughways", which led to "rooms" where the ore was mined. The throughways provided the means of removing ore from the mine, provided necessary ventilation to the areas where mining was being carried on, and provided a means of access by personnel. All of the throughways were driven through the orebody and not in the waste rock beneath. The value of the ore extracted from the throughways exceeded the cost of opening them. The cost of removing the ore that resulted in leaving the throughways in the four years 1958 to 1961 was approximately $21 million. In its 1961 return, the company sought to deduct about $9 million of this amount as capital

cost allowance, but the Minister disallowed the deduction. The company contended that throughways were depreciable property included in Class 12(f) of Schedule B to the Regulations, and that accordingly, it was entitled to deduct up to 100 per cent of the cost of the throughways under section 11(1)(a) [now paragraph 20(1)(a)] in computing its 1961 income.]

Jackett C.J. (orally from the Bench) (Thurlow J. concurring): ...

The appellant's claim for capital cost allowance is based upon the fact that, as a result of the way in which the ore was extracted during the first part of the first phase, these throughways have been created for a use during subsequent operations that is intended to continue long into the future. The jumping-off point for the appellant's claim for capital cost allowance is its contention that these throughways are capital assets of the mining operation that are commonly known as haulageways. Not only is the validity of its claim based on the validity of that contention but it is also essential to its argument that it succeed in its further contention that the expense of removing the ore from the space where the haulageways are is the "capital cost" of such "assets."

As far as the ore removed from the "rooms" is concerned, there is no difference between the parties as to the position under the *Income Tax Act*. It is common ground that the proceeds of disposition of such ore less the costs of its extraction is profit from the operation of the mine.

With reference to the ore removed from the "haulageways," however, while the respondent says that the position is the same (i.e., that the proceeds of disposition of such ore less the costs of its extraction is profit from the operation of the mine), the appellant says

(a) that the proceeds of disposition of such ore without any deduction in respect of its extraction is profit from the operation of the mine, and

(b) that the cost of extraction of such ore is the "capital cost" of the haulageways that resulted from its removal.

Prima facie, this would seem to be an unlikely position for a taxpayer to take as, if it is sustained, it would force the appellant to give up a deduction of expenses in the year incurred in favour of capital cost allowance, which, in principle, is deductible over a period of years. In the peculiar circumstances of this case, however, that disadvantageous position would not arise if the appellant is correct in its further claim, which is that it is entitled to take a capital cost allowance in one year of 100 per cent. This would mean that the full cost of extraction could be taken in the year incurred where it is desirable. Moreover, if correct, the appellant's contention has the advantage, from its point of view, that, during a period of three years when income from operating the mine was "exempt," it will have been building up capital cost to be taken as a deduction in subsequent years.

In our view, the correctness of the appellant's position must be determined by sound business or commercial principles and not by what would be of greatest advantage to the taxpayer having regard to the idiosyncrasies of *the Income Tax Act.*

In considering that question, it must be emphasized that, as far as appears from the pleadings or the evidence, no more money was spent on extracting the ore the extraction of which resulted in the haulageways than would have been spent if no long term continuing use had been planned for them.

One business or commercial principle that has been established for so long that it is almost a rule of law is that "The profits ... of any transaction in the nature of a sale must, in the ordinary sense, consist of the excess of the price which the vendor obtains on sale over what it cost him to procure and sell, or produce and sell, the article vended ..." (See *The Scottish North American Trust, Ltd. v. Farmer* (1910), 5 T.C. 693, per Lord Atkinson at page 705.)

Our difficulty, at the outset, with the appellant's claim for capital cost allowance is, therefore, that we cannot accept the submission of the appellant that, while the profit from the mining operation, as far as the ore taken from its rooms is concerned, is the net of proceeds of disposition over costs of extraction, the profit from the mining operation, as far as the ore taken from the "haulageways" is concerned, is the proceeds of disposition without deducting the costs of extraction of such ore. That submission is contrary to a long line of authority.

In the second place, if we are correct in our view that the deduction of such costs is required in preparing the profit and loss account for the year in which they are incurred, it would not seem that any sound system of accounting could show them also as a "capital cost" of something other than the ore. No single disbursement can be reflected twice in the accounts, if the result is to be an accurate reflection of the state of the businessman's affairs.

That conclusion is sufficient to dispose of the appeal because if there is no "capital cost" of property, paragraph 11(1)(a) does not authorize capital cost allowance.

There is, however, a further question that should be discussed. If the appellant is correct in its contention that removal of the ore from the spaces in question brought into existence capital assets known as haulageways, how can one avoid the conclusion that there was a substantial capital cost of such assets?

In the first place, it should be said that we are not convinced that there is involved any acquisition or creation of property. The situation is, we assume, that the appellant already owned the property in question with the ore *in situ* and it did nothing except that it removed the ore so that there was remaining the waste rock bed that it previously owned. We doubt that it can be said that

that brought into existence any property that did not previously exist and, as it would seem to us, if no new property was created or acquired, there cannot be any "cost" of "property" within the meaning of paragraph 11(1)(a) of the *Income Tax Act*.

On the other hand, if we assume for the sake of argument that the removal of the ore in question brought into existence something that did not previously exist, namely a haulageway, in our view the cost of removing the ore is not a cost to the appellant of that property.

We recognize that there are cases where a single operation has two objectives and two results and that the cost of such an operation would normally be divided in a sound system of accounts.

If, for example here, there were merged into one operation the activities necessary to remove the ore and the activities necessary to bring in and install some plant and equipment of a permanent character, the cost of that operation would have to be appropriately divided.

Where, however, a businessman does nothing but carry on his ordinary current operations but so plans those operations, without increasing the costs of those operations, that he has an asset of an enduring nature at the end of a period of operation, we are of the view that the situation is of a different kind. Where, for example, a businessman deliberately plans his operations so as to acquire a very valuable goodwill (both by his advertising and by his manner of doing business), we should have no hesitation in saying that ordinary business principles would nevertheless require the deduction of all the costs of his operations that are ordinarily regarded as current costs in determining his annual profits and would attribute none of such costs to the acquisition of his goodwill.

Similarly, we are of the view that, even though the appellant planned his extraction operations so as to leave it in the result with "haulageways" that are of enduring benefit to its business, the cost of such extraction operations is, in accordance with ordinary business principles, the costs of earning the profits made by selling the ore extracted from them. If that is right, there was no cost, and therefore no "capital cost," of acquiring the haulageways.

For the aforesaid reasons, we are of opinion that the appeal should be dismissed with costs.

[The taxpayer's appeal to the Supreme Court of Canada was dismissed, [1974] C.T.C. 737, 74 D.T.C. 6525. Martland J., who wrote the unanimous opinion of the Court, quoted extensively from the trial and appeal judgments and simply agreed with the quoted reasons from the lower courts.]

JOHNS-MANVILLE CANADA INC. V. THE QUEEN
[1985] 2 C.T.C. 111, 85 D.T.C. 5373 (S.C.C.)

Estey J: The question on appeal is whether the taxpayer-appellant has the right under the *Income Tax Act* of Canada to charge to expense rather than to capital, the cost of purchase of land at the periphery of an open pit mine, in the course of its mining operations. The issue concerns the taxation years ending in 1969 (two fiscal periods) and 1970. The pre-1972 *Income Tax Act* applies. ...

... The evidence was that for almost 40 years mining operations have required a progressive acquisition of land so as to maintain the walls of the conically-shaped mining pit at a safe angle. As the pit deepens in the course of mine operations its mouth at the surface must widen in order to maintain a safe angle of slope. Consequently, additional land was regularly acquired and any buildings thereon were removed. The soil was then stripped away so that the wall of the pit was pushed back or outwards from its prior location. In the conventional sense of "land," all that remains of the acquired area is a part of a sloped wall, well below the original surface, between the top of the mine and the exposed ore body at the bottom of the pit. As additional land was acquired, the sloping wall was pushed further outward and consequently the actual location of the surface of each acquisition moves down the wall although the sloped angle of its surface remains generally constant. Any roadways located on the "steps" cut into the face of the wall likewise disappear on each enlargement of the pit and are re-established on the new sloping wall after the surface of the additional lands has been stripped off. All these changes proceed as the removal of the ore body progresses.

The mining operations are extensive. During the relevant time period, production was 33,000 tons of ore and 60,000-65,000 tons of overburden and waste material daily. Thus about 100,000 tons of material were removed from the base of the pit in these mining operations every day. ...

The learned trial judge concluded that these land expenditures were not in the nature of capital outlays but rather were expenses incurred in the mining operations and should be taken into account in the computation of net income in connection therewith. In the course of so determining, the learned justice stated: "The evidence also discloses that the acquisition of property at the periphery of its mining pit has been a constant part of the mining operations of Johns-Manville and purchases of land have occurred annually for almost 40 years. The acquisition cost of the purchases of such lands represent only ..." about three per cent of the average of the cost of sales of the appellant during the eight-year period from 1966 to 1973 inclusive. He continued:

> The subject expenditures did not add to or preserve the ore body. Instead, the lands purchased by these expenditures were in essence consumed for all

practical purposes in the course of and as part of the mining operations of Johns-Manville and as a consequence were expenditures "incidental to the production and sale of the output of the mine" (cf *Denison Mines Limited v. M.N.R.* [[1976] 1 S.C.R. 245]) and were part of the cost in the determination of profits.

His Lordship concluded:

> Therefore, after considering the whole of the evidence, and as stated, looking at the character or quality of the expenditures based upon business or commercial practice rather than the character of the asset acquired by the expenditures, the conclusion is that the subject expenditures in the taxation years 1969 and 1970 were not on capital account within the meaning of section 12(1)(b) of the *Income Tax Act.*

The Court of Appeal, Ryan J writing on behalf of the Court, reversed the trial court and concluded that these expenditures were of a capital nature and could not be charged as an expense in the computation of profit from the appellant's mining operations. ...

The Court of Appeal, in the course of its judgment, distinguished the judgment of this Court in *Denison Mines Limited v. M.N.R., supra*. In that case this Court found that the creation of corridors and haulage ways in a mine in the course of removing the ore body entailed expenditures which were not capital in nature but were expenses to be deducted from the sale of ore once removed. The Court found that on ordinary commercial principles the cost of removing the ore was deductible in the computing of the annual profit or loss of the mining operation. The passageways, haulage ways and corridors were really created or resulted as a by-product of the mining operation. The court below distinguished this case because there the taxpayer was required to expense the expenditures which were made in the very extraction of the ore.

The fact that the expenditures here involved were made for the purchase of land is perhaps an important if not vital part of the reasoning which led the court below to its conclusion that they were capital expenditures.

[In his judgment, Ryan, J. had emphasized that " ... new assets were acquired by the [taxpayer's] purchase of the lots ... The lots, even when stripped of their overburden, continue as part of the business structure ... and have value as such."

Estey, J. reviewed Canadian and foreign jurisprudence concerning the distinction between current expenses and capital expenditures and continued:]

After this review of the authorities it can be seen that the principles enunciated by the courts and the elucidation on the application of those principles is of very little guidance when it becomes necessary, as it is here, to apply those principles to a precise set of somewhat unusual facts.

The question remains for answer, therefore, what is the proper application of the relevant provisions of the *Income Tax Act* to the facts of this case?

[Estey J. then reviewed paragraphs 12(1)(a) and (b), now paragraphs 18(1)(a) and (b), and turned to paragraph 11(1)(a), now paragraph 20(1)(a) of the Act.]

The allowance for depreciation or depletion stems from paragraph 11(1)(a) of the Act which authorizes the deduction of "such part of the capital cost to the taxpayer of property, or such amount in respect of the capital cost to the taxpayer of property, if any, as is allowed by regulation. ..." Regulation 1100(1) creates a series of capital cost allowances and Schedule B sets forth the classes of property to which these rates of allowances may be applied. The property here in question is not to be found in Schedule B and hence no capital cost allowance can be taken under section 11 with reference to the cost of these land acquisitions. Furthermore, subject to any concession made by the Minister, no depletion allowance is available on these lands as they are not used for mining purposes. Consequently, the taxpayer is in the position of either being permitted by paragraph 12(1)(a) to deduct these expenditures as expenses "for the purpose of gaining or producing income," or being left with no tax relief of any kind with respect to these ongoing expenditures. ... [I]f the interpretation of a taxation statute is unclear, and one reasonable interpretation leads to a deduction to the credit of a taxpayer and the other leaves the taxpayer with no relief from clearly *bona fide* expenditures in the course of his business activities, the general rules of interpretation of taxing statutes would direct the tribunal to the former interpretation. That is the situation here, in my view of these statutory provisions. These expenditures were clearly made for *bona fide* purposes. They clearly are not disqualified by paragraph 12(1)(a) nor by any other section of the *Income Tax Act* dealing with expenditures in the course of operating a business. The only possible basis in the statute for a denial of these *bona fide* expenditures closely associated with the conduct of the taxpayer's mining operations is the prohibition in paragraph 12(1)(b) relating to capital expenditures ...

In this situation, and in analyzing those facts, it may be helpful to observe:

1. The purpose of these expenditures, when viewed from the practical and business outlook, was the removal of a current obstacle in the operation of the taxpayer's mine and was not the acquisition of a capital asset;

2. These expenditures were incurred year in and year out as an integral part of the day-to-day operations of the undertaking of the taxpayer;

3. These expenditures form an easily discernible, more or less constant, element and part of the daily and annual cost of production;

4. These lands were not acquired for any intrinsic value but merely by reason of location, and after the mining operation for the year in question had

been completed, the land had acquired no intrinsic value, and indeed, as was found below, was "consumed" in the mining process;

5. These expenditures produced a transitional benefit and one which had no enduring value because similar expenditures were required in the future if the mining operation was to be continued at all;

6. The lands acquired in any given year do not produce a permanent wall or perimeter to the mining operation but are simply a transitional location of the wall representing the cone surrounding the mining undertaking; and to the extent that the wall of the cone is used for haulage of materials from the bottom of the pit on temporary roads, there may be some transitional asset created, but this asset disappears as the wall of the cone recedes in ensuing taxation years;

7. The nature of these expenditures is made clear when it is appreciated that they have been incurred annually for almost 40 years and there is no evidence whatever to indicate that mining operations can continue in the future without this annual expenditure;

8. The capitalization of these expenditures will not produce for the mining operator an asset which may be made subject to either capital cost or depletion allowances, the former because no asset recognized in the *Income Tax Act* is produced, and the latter because these lands contain no minerals which are being removed by the mining operations of the taxpayer;

9. These expenditures did not add to the ore body, nor did they increase the productive capacity of the mine, nor do they bear any relation to any asset engaged in the mining operation, but are simply expenditures for the removal of overburden which, if not removed, would bring the mining operation to a halt;

10. The expenditures relative to the cost of operating the mine are small and are directly related to the cost of operation averaging over a long period about three per cent per annum.

The circumstances of this case evoke in the mind many parallels or analogies. These lands, peripheral to the mouth of the open pit operation, perform a function not unlike that of a catalyst such as platinum used in the refinement of petroleum for the production of gasoline. The purchase of the platinum no doubt produces, in the hands of the refiner, an identifiable asset of value. At the end of the day, the asset has either physically disappeared or lost its desired physical characteristics. The refiner no longer possesses the original platinum asset but he has produced marketable gasoline by its use in the processing of petroleum. If not for the explicit addition of Class 26, "Property that is a catalyst," to Schedule B of the *Income Tax Regulations* in March 1970, the platinum in this example was qualified for deduction as an expense. The property at issue in the case at bar, however, has not been included in Schedule B. The legislators, therefore, have not precluded it from being treated as an expense if such treatment is appropriate in all the circumstances. By further analogy, a mining operator faced with the presence of a body of water above an ore body is in a somewhat similar position to that of the appellant here. The removal of the water to lay bare the minerals on the floor of the lake could hardly be seen as the creation of an asset. The cost of pumping would be an expenditure which would not create an asset in the hands of the operator. Indeed, as mining progresses and water, by the forces of nature, returns to the pit on the bottom of the lake, the water must be removed by successive pumping. The cost of this pumping would likely be, without further complicating factors, an expense properly incurred by the taxpayer to gain income and could not be seen as creating another asset. In the case at bar the land all but disappeared, as did the catalyst in the refining operation and the water in the mining operation on the floor of the lake. In none of these situations, at the end of the day, is an asset produced, nor does an asset remain. Here the taxpayer, at the end of the mining operations, is the owner of a large hole in the surface of the earth. The acquired lands represent segments down the wall of the hole, the older purchases being further down than the last purchases. There is no asset in the sense of a surface which can, by itself, be sold. The hole once filled in, at a likely considerable expense, would produce a surface which might have value in the market. Although the hole itself, and that part of the wall with which we are here concerned, might conceivably have some value, it can hardly be described as an asset which by itself has a real value. The evidence indicates that the life of this mine will end in the 1990s. Both courts below have concluded that at that time these lands will have disappeared for all practical purposes. ...

The characterization in taxation law of an expenditure is, in the final analysis (unless the statute is explicit which this one is not), one of policy. In the mining industry, where the undertaking is underground mining with its associated assets such as vertical shafts and horizontal transportation elements not created directly by the removal of commercial ore, the tax treatment of capitalization is invoked. On the other hand, open pit or strip mining requiring none of these fixed facilities leads to the attribution of the associated expenditures to the revenue account. Strip mining or open pit mining with conical access (as we have here) and its associated expenditures falls in between these two rough categories of mining undertakings. The assessment of the evidence and the conclusions to be derived therefrom, and the application of the common sense approach to the business of the taxpayer in relation to the tax provisions, leads, in my respectful view, to the conclusion that the mining operations here approximate the circumstances encountered in the traditional open pit mining more than underground mining and so I conclude, with all respect to those who have otherwise concluded, that the appropriate taxation treatment is to allocate these expenditures to the revenue account and not to capital. Such a determination is, furthermore, consistent with another basic concept in tax law that where the taxing statute is not explicit, reasonable uncertainty or factual ambiguity resulting from lack of explicitness in the statute should be resolved in favour of the taxpayer. This residual principle must be the more readily applicable in this appeal where otherwise, annually recurring expenditures completely connected to the daily business operation of the taxpayer, afford the taxpayer no credit against tax either by way of capital cost or depletion allowance with reference to a capital expenditure, or an expense deduction against revenue.

In summary, therefore, it can be said without fear of contradiction from this record that these expenditures by the taxpayer were incurred *bona fide* in the course of its regular day-to-day business operations. Common sense dictated that these expenditures be made, otherwise the taxpayer's operations would, of necessity, be closed down. These expenditures were not part of a plan for the assembly of assets. Nor did they have any semblance of a once and for all acquisition. These expenditures were in no way connected with the assembly of an ore body or a mining property which could itself be developed independently of any ore body, hence the inability to find entitlement for depletion or capital cost allowance for this expenditure under the statute. These expenditures are not disqualified by paragraph 12(1)(a) and indeed that provision of the Act favours the inclusion of these expenditures in authorized expenses because there is no other provision made in the Act for these items which are, beyond contention, incurred of necessity by the taxpayer in conducting its mining operations according to good business and engineering practice. ...

Appeal allowed.

Notes and Questions

1. Although Estey, J. said that the characterization of an expenditure as a deductible current expense or a non-deductible capital outlay is a question of policy, he adopted a conventional analysis in his finding that the expenses made by the taxpayer did not produce an asset. In the Federal Court of Appeal, Ryan, J. had said that new assets were acquired by the purchase of the lots which remained as "part of the business structure". Is a hole in the ground an asset that can be shown on the balance sheet of an open-pit mining business? Is a bigger hole more valuable? Whether or not a hole in the ground would normally be a balance sheet asset, Estey, J. suggests, quite correctly, that it could be a depreciable property for tax purposes if it were included in one of the scheduled classes of property for capital cost allowance purposes.
2. Businesses often spend money on research or feasibility studies. The Act includes incentives for "scientific research and experimental development" by allowing certain expenses that would otherwise be capital expenses to be deducted in the year incurred as current expenses. What is the policy rationale for such incentives?

3. How are research expenses other than scientific research treated for tax purposes? Should it depend on whether the research concerns:
   - the existing business of the taxpayer;
   - whether the business should be expanded; or
   - whether a new business should be started?

   See Interpretation Bulletin IT-475: Expenditures on Research and for Business Expansion (March 31, 1981).
4. In *Algoma Central Railway v. M.N.R.*, [1967] C.T.C. 130, 67 D.T.C. 5091 (Exch. Ct.), Jackett, P. considered that a taxpayer's cost of "a mammoth advertising campaign designed to attract substantial amounts of new customers by some spectacular appeal to the public" would be deductible as a current expense. Is he right? Do accountants regard all advertising expenses as current expenses? Would it affect the tax result if the Minister could show that accountants regard some advertising expenses as having a carry-over or long range effect but tend, nevertheless, to deduct the expenses on a current basis because of uncertainty as to the real value and duration of such effect? If a taxpayer had spent little on advertising for many years and then engaged in one year in a "mammoth campaign" to restore his or her business image, would the cost be deductible?
5. In *Gifford v. Canada*, [2004] 1 S.C.R. 411, [2004] 2 C.T.C. 1, 2004 D.T.C. 6120, a financial advisor who was an employee of Midland Walwyn paid an amount to a departing employee (who was also a financial advisor) in order to obtain a list of the departing employee's clients, a favourable endorsement to those clients from the departing employee and the covenant of the departing employee not to provide retail investment advice to those clients for a period of 30 months. The Supreme Court of Canada applied the principles established in *Johns-Manville* to conclude that the amount paid to acquire the customer list was a non-deductible capital expenditure.
6. In some cases the courts have recognized that certain expenses are not current expenses, yet they have not been treated as capital expenses. Rather, a middle approach has been adopted which involves part of the expense being deferred to future years. In *M.N.R. v. Tower Investment Inc.*, [1972] C.T.C. 182, 72 D.T.C. 6161 (F.C.T.D.) the Court allowed the taxpayer to deduct the cost of an advertising campaign over three years. The Minister did not argue that the expense was on account of capital; the Minister's argument was that the entire expenditure had to be deducted in the year it was incurred because the accounting principle of deferral of prepaid expenses was not authorized by paragraph 18(1)(a). Nevertheless, the Court allowed the deferral of the deductions. See also, *Neonex International v. The Queen* (1978), [1978] C.T.C. 485, 78 D.T.C. 6339 (F.C.A.).
7. An amount paid for the assignment of a supply agreement that entitled the taxpayer over the term of the agreement to purchase raw materials for use in its business at an advantageous rate was found to be a current expense which the

taxpayer could properly amortize over the term of the supply agreement. See *Basell Canada Inc. v. Canada*, [2008] 1 C.T.C. 2369, 2008 D.T.C. 2108 (T.C.C.).

2. Protection of Intangible Assets

M.N.R. v. THE DOMINION NATURAL GAS CO. LTD.
[1940-41] C.T.C. 155, 1 D.T.C. 499-133 (S.C.C.)

[In 1904, Barton Township granted the taxpayer a perpetual exclusive licence to supply natural gas to its inhabitants. The United Gas and Fuel Co. had an exclusive franchise to supply gas in the City of Hamilton. Portions of Barton Township were subsequently annexed to Hamilton. Dominion continued to supply gas to those inhabitants in the annexed areas. United brought an action for a declaration of its rights and an injunction to restrain Dominion from supplying gas in the annexed areas. If the claim had succeeded Dominion would have lost part of its franchise. Dominion successfully defended the action all the way to the Privy Council. After crediting all costs recovered from United, the litigation costs paid by Dominion in 1934 amounted to $48,560.94 which Dominion claimed as a deduction in 1934. The Minister denied the deduction and the taxpayer appealed.]

Duff C.J.C.: ...

There are two broad grounds upon which I think the Minister is entitled to succeed. First, in order to fall within the category "disbursements or expenses wholly, exclusively and necessarily laid out or expended for the purpose of earning the income," expenses must, I think, be working expenses; that is to say, expenses incurred in the process of earning "the income." ...

Again, in my view, the expenditure is a capital expenditure. It satisfies, I think, the criterion laid down by Lord Cave in *British Insulated v. Atherton,* [1926] A.C. 205 at 213. The expenditure was incurred "once and for all" and it was incurred for the purpose and with the effect of procuring for the company "the advantage of an enduring benefit." The settlement of the issue raised by the proceedings attacking the rights of the respondents with the object of excluding them from carrying on their undertaking within the limits of the City of Hamilton was, I think, an enduring benefit within the sense of Lord Cave's language. As Lord Macmillan points out in *Van den Berghs Ltd. v. Clark*, [1935] A.C. 431, at 440:

> Lord Atkinson indicated that the word "asset" ought not to be confined to "something material" and, in further elucidation of the principle, Romer L.J. has added that the advantage paid for need not be "of a positive character" and may consist in the getting rid of an item of fixed capital that is of an onerous character: *Anglo-Persian Oil Co. v. Dale*, [1932] 1 K.B. 446.

The character of the expenditure is for our present purposes, I think, analogous to that of the expenditure in question in *Moore v. Hare*, 1914-1915 S.C. 91, where promotion expenses incurred by coalmasters in connection with two parliamentary bills giving authority to construct a line to serve the coalfield were held to be capital expenditures. Lord Skerrington at p. 99 says:

> One can figure a case where a firm of coalmasters in the position of the appellants might incur Parliamentary or other preliminary expenses with a view to constructing a railway which was to be the private property of the firm, and which when constructed would be useful and would in fact be used wholly and exclusively for the purposes of their trade as coalmasters. Such expenditure would be of the same legal character as the actual cost of building the railway. It would be capital employed in the firm's trade as coalmasters, and therefore would not be a legitimate deduction from profits.

I do not perceive any distinction between expenditures incurred in procuring the company's by-laws authorizing the undertaking and the expenses incurred in their litigation with the City of Hamilton.

In the ordinary course, it is true, legal expenses are simply current expenditure and deductible as such; but that is not necessarily so. The legal expenses incurred, for example, in procuring authority for reduction of capital were held by the Court of Sessions not to be deductible in *Thomas v. Batty*, 1919 S.C. 289.

The appeal should be allowed and the assessment restored with costs throughout.

[Crocket J. concurred in allowing the appeal, but on the first issue (i.e., that the expenses were prohibited by paragraph 6(a), the forerunner to present paragraph 18(1)(a)).

Kerwin and Hudson JJ. also agreed to allow the appeal, basing themselves on the second issue (i.e., paragraph 6(b), the forerunner to paragraph 18(1)(b)).]

KELLOGG COMPANY OF CANADA LIMITED v. M.N.R.
[1942] C.T.C. 51, 2 D.T.C. 548 (Exch. Ct.)

[Kellogg, in carrying on its business, marketed a product under the name Shredded Wheat. A competitor alleged trademark rights in the name and commenced an action against Kellogg. In due course Kellogg incurred a substantial expenditure for legal fees in its successful defence and this case arose out of its attempt to deduct the amount of these fees. During the action, no income was derived from products using the name Shredded Wheat.]

Maclean J.:

... [The Minister argued that] the expenditures in question were made by Kellogg, (1) to preserve its right to carry on a portion of its business, (2) to assert and defend its common law right to manufacture and sell certain cereal products under the descriptive name of such products, (3) to maintain the right to earn future profits as distinguished from current profits, to secure an "asset" or "an advantage or enduring benefit" for its business, by making an expenditure "once and for all," and (4) that the expenses incurred for such purposes were not deductible in computing the annual profits or gains to be assessed for the income tax, and were of a capital nature and properly attributable to capital. It will at once be observed that the grounds advanced by [counsel for the Minister] are of a familiar character, and that he had in mind a line of well known cases which I shall have occasion to mention later on. On the other hand, Kellogg is claiming that the items of disbursements in question were expenses properly attributable to income. ...

The present case is somewhat analogous to that of *M.N.R. v. Dominion Natural Gas Co. Ltd.* ... If I understand the view of the Supreme Court to be as I have stated it, then the "advantage of an enduring benefit," and the preservation of "an asset or advantage," must have been intended to relate to the franchise rights or privileges under which the company commenced and continued its undertaking, which comprised the foundation and totality of all its assets, and which rights or privileges were the means of making profits though they themselves did not yield profits, and that therefore the expenses in question were directly related to capital assets. I think there is a distinction between that case and the present case, and as my reasons for thinking so will presently appear in my discussion of the present case, and will, I think, differentiate the two cases, I need not anticipate them just at this stage.

Now turning to the specific question here to be determined. The broad principle laid down by Lord Cave in *British Insulated and Helsby Cables Ltd. v. Atherton*, [1926] A.C. 205 at 213 is not, in my opinion, of any assistance in the present case. Applying that test to the present case, the payment here made was not, I think, an expenditure incurred or made "once and for all," with a view of bringing a new asset into existence, nor can it, in my opinion, properly be said that it brought into existence an advantage for the enduring benefit of Kellogg's trade within the meaning of the well known language used by Lord Cave in a certain passage of his speech in that case. What the House of Lords was considering in that case was a sum irrevocably set aside as a nucleus of a pension fund established by a trust deed for the benefit of the company's clerical staff, and, as was said by Lawrence L.J. in the *Anglo Persian Oil* case, *supra*, I have no doubt that Lord Cave had that fact in mind when he spoke of an advantage for the enduring benefit of the company's trade. Such an expenditure differs fundamentally from the expenditure with which we are concerned in the present case. Here, the expenditure brought no such permanent advantage into existence for the taxpayer's trade. I do not think it can be said that the expenditure in question here brought into existence any asset that could possibly appear as such in any balance sheet, or that it procured an enduring advantage for the taxpayer's trade which must presuppose that something was acquired which had no prior existence. No "material" or "positive" advantage or benefit resulted to the trade of Kellogg from the litigation except perhaps a judicial affirmation of an advantage already in existence and enjoyed by Kellogg. I do not think that the Crown can be heard to say that because the litigation affirmed a right which Kellogg, in common with others, was already entitled to and enjoyed, that therefore Kellogg acquired something which should be treated as an asset or an enduring advantage to its trade. Such reasoning would lead to many strange and undesirable results. In any event, Kellogg never disbursed any money to acquire something, and it would appear hardly tenable to say that the payment of the legal expenses in question was something paid to acquire an asset or a trade advantage. That was an involuntary expense, not a disbursement incurred once and for all, or for the benefit of a trade, within the meaning of such cases as I have earlier discussed. Again, this is not a case of a payment, as no such payment was ever made by Kellogg, and equally true is it, I think, that the expenses here were not incurred for the purpose of earning future profits. In all the decided cases I have mentioned the taxpayer voluntarily made specific disbursements, for one reason or other connected with his trade; whether they were held to be attributable to capital or revenue is presently irrelevant, the important and relevant thing being that they were made in pursuance of settled business policy. Kellogg made no such comparable disbursement; the disbursement here was one virtually imposed upon the taxpayer. It is to be remembered that the plaintiff in the action against Kellogg claimed the choice of either an account and payment to it of the profits or income which Kellogg had gained in its trade, or an enquiry as to damages alleged to be occasioned by the wrongful conduct of Kellogg. The profits of Kellogg were made by the sale of certain cereal products in cartons, on which was printed the common name of the product, as, I think, is required by regulations made under the *Food and Drugs Act*. That is part of the selling mechanism and not of the production mechanism of Kellogg, almost the final step in the selling of the product itself and in the earning of profits, or gains. It was to maintain this trading and profit-making position that Kellogg was obliged to make the expenditure in question. It was against actual sales, the earning of income, that the Canadian Shredded Wheat Company sought an injunction against Kellogg, and also against its customer Bassin to whom it had actually sold its goods for resale.

... Here, Kellogg had encountered a business difficulty, one associated directly with the sales branch of its business, which it had to get rid of, if possible, in order to continue the sales of its products as it had in the past. I have no doubt that there are many cases in which legal expenses incurred are properly attributable to capital and not revenue, in computing the profits or gains assessable for the income tax. ...

The conclusion which I have reached is that the appeal herein should be allowed, and with costs to the appellant.

Judgment accordingly.

[The Crown's appeal to the Supreme Court of Canada was dismissed with brief reasons: [1943] C.T.C. 1, 2 D.T.C. 601. According to Duff C.J.:

> *... The right upon which the respondents relied was not a right of property, or an exclusive right of any description, but the right (in common with all other members of the public) to describe their goods in the manner in which they were describing them.*
>
> *It was pointed out in The Minister of National Revenue v. The Dominion Natural Gas Company, supra, at p. 25, that in the ordinary course legal expenses are simply current expenditures and deductible as such. The expenditures in question here would appear to fall within this general rule.]*

CANADA STARCH CO. LTD. v. M.N.R.
[1968] C.T.C. 466, 68 D.T.C. 5320 (Exch. Ct.)

[During 1963 and 1964, the taxpayer spent more than $80,000 in an effort to develop the most desirable name under which to market a new brand of cooking oil. The name selected was "Viva", and the $80,000 represented the cost of advertising, container and label design, and a great deal of market research to test the consumer reaction to "Viva" as compared with other possible names. In August 1963, the taxpayer was informed that the Registrar of Trade Marks considered "Viva" to be confusing with a trade mark registered by Power Super Markets Ltd. Early in 1964, the taxpayer paid $15,000 to Power for its agreement to withdraw its opposition to registration by the taxpayer of the trade mark "Viva". The Minister disallowed a claim to deduct the $15,000 on the ground that it was prohibited by paragraph 18(1)(b).]

Jackett P.: ...

In effect, in the course of putting a new product on the market, the appellant, in addition to spending money on market research, industrial designs and advertising, spent money on obtaining the registration of a trade mark that it was adopting for the new product; and that expenditure included this amount of $15,000 that it paid to induce another company to drop its opposition to such registration being granted to it. ...

For the purpose of the particular problem raised by this appeal, I find it helpful to refer to the comment on the "distinction between expenditure and outgoings on revenue account and on capital account" made by Dixon, J. in

Sun Newspapers Ltd. et al. v. The Federal Commissioner of Taxation, (1938) 61 C.L.R. 337 at page 359, where he said:

> The distinction between expenditure and outgoings on revenue account and on capital account corresponds with the distinction between the business entity, structure, or organization set up or established for the earning of profit and the process by which such an organization operates to obtain regular returns by means of regular outlay, the difference between the outlay and returns representing profit or loss.

In other words, as I understand it, generally speaking,

(a) on the one hand, an expenditure for the acquisition or creation of a business entity, structure or organization, for the earning of profit, or for an addition to such an entity, structure or organization, is an expenditure on account of capital, and
(b) on the other hand, an expenditure in the process of operation of a profit-making entity, structure or organization is an expenditure on revenue account.

Applying this test to the acquisition or creation of ordinary property constituting the business structure as originally created, or an addition thereto, there is no difficulty. Plant and machinery are capital assets and moneys paid for them are moneys paid on account of capital whether they are

(a) moneys paid in the course of putting together a new business structure,
(b) moneys paid for an addition to a business structure already in existence, or
(c) moneys paid to acquire an existing business structure.

In my opinion, however, from this point of view, there is a difference in principle between property such as plant and machinery on the one hand and goodwill on the other hand. Once goodwill is in existence, it can be bought, in a manner of speaking, and money paid for it would ordinarily be money paid "on account of capital." Apart from that method of acquiring goodwill, however, as I conceive it, goodwill can only be acquired as a by-product out of the process of operating a business. Money is not laid out to create goodwill. Goodwill is the result of the ordinary operations of a business that is so operated as to result in goodwill. The money that is laid out is laid out for the operation of the business and is therefore money laid out on revenue account.

Basically, as I understand it, a trade mark or trade name is merely one facet of the goodwill of a business. A trade mark or trade name is a mark or name which distinguishes the businessman's wares or services from those of others. It so distinguishes his goods or services because, by virtue of his business operations, including the use of the name or mark, his goods or services have become distinct from those of others in the public mind. ...

... Huge sums must be spent on market surveys before a decision can be made as to what product to market or as to what trade mark or trade name to adopt. Industrial designers are employed at great expense to choose a colour and design for a label. Lawyers, accountants and economists find employment in the highly complicated process that has replaced the decisions that an individual would have made "by the seat of his pants." Nevertheless, from the point of view of what are current business operations and what are capital transactions, as it seems to me, the distinction follows the same line.

In my view, the advertising expenses for launching the new product in this case were expenses on revenue account. ...

The respondent says that the payment of $15,000 was made "with a view of bringing into existence an advantage for the enduring benefit of the appellant's business" because it made the payment in order to acquire a registered trade mark with all the statutory rights to which the owner of a registered trade mark is entitled. Looking only at the *Trade Marks Act*, there is much force in this contention. However, in distinguishing between a capital payment and a payment on current account, in my view, regard must be had to the business and commercial realities of the matter. When the intricate conditions of the *Trade Marks Act* are properly understood, they operate so that the statute only provides protection for a trade mark that is distinctive of the owner's wares or services. If it does not distinguish them, the registration is invalid (Section 18), and the protection afforded by Section 19 does not apply. The situation is, therefore, that if, as a result of the ordinary current operations of a business, a trade mark is distinctive, the action of passing off (and Section 7 of the *Trade Marks Act*) operates to give automatic protection; and additional protection can be obtained by registration. The trade mark, as an advantage for the enduring benefit of the business, is the product of the current operations of the business and is not the result of registration. Registration merely facilitates the businessman in enforcing the rights that accrued to him from his business operations. Either "VIVA" will be found, if it is ever tested, to have become distinctive of the appellant's wares by virtue of its trading operations, or its registration will be found to be invalid. Mere registration is an empty right if it is not based on a trade mark that has business or commercial reality as an incidental consequence of the current operations of the business. In my view, therefore, the trade mark in question as an "advantage for the enduring benefit of the ... business," if it is such an advantage, was not acquired by the payment of $15,000.

Putting my view another way, it is that, while a trade mark, once it becomes a business or commercial reality, is a capital asset of the business giving rise to it, just like goodwill, of which it is merely a concrete manifestation, a trade mark is not a capital asset that has been acquired by a payment made for its acquisition, but is a capital asset that arises out of, and can only arise out of, current operations of the business; and registration of a trade mark does not create a trade mark that is such a business or commercial reality, but is merely a statutory device for improving the legal protection for it.

The appeal will be allowed. ...

Notes and Questions

1. An analogy may be drawn between expenditures to "defend" or "protect" an intangible asset, such as the franchise to deliver natural gas in Barton Township, and amounts spent to "repair" or "maintain" physical assets such as a ship or a building. Compare *Dominion Natural Gas* with *Canada Steamship Lines Ltd. v. M.N.R.*, *infra*, and *The Queen v. Shabro Investments Ltd.*, *infra*.
2. In *Inskip v. M.N.R.*, [1987] 1 C.T.C. 2009, 86 D.T.C. 1837 (T.C.C.), the taxpayer was a cattle rancher whose business depended on a water licence to use lake water for irrigation purposes. He was required to contribute $38,000 to the reconstruction by the government of the dam which formed the lake. It was held that the amount was deductible as a current expense. According to Kempo, T.C.J.:

> The advantage being sought, in the circumstances of this case, was in respect of the current operations of the appellant. The expenditure in question prevented that operation from being severely crippled. There is no evidence that the value of the farming operation was any different from its value before the dam reconstruction. Rather than enhancing the business, and thus acquiring an advantage of enduring nature likened to an assembly of assets in the capital structure of the business, the expenditure was shown to have merely maintained what was had before.

3. Amounts paid to a retail leasing consultant for advice and assistance in connection with the taxpayer's acquisition of new retail store leases and the extension of existing leases were found to be current expenses on the basis that the payments were of a recurring nature and were required to insure the ongoing operation of the taxpayer's business. See *Pantorama Industries Inc. v. The Queen*, [2005] 2 C.T.C. 336, 2005 D.T.C. 5230 (F.C.A.).
4. Legal fees paid in connection with an action brought by the taxpayer to secure the return of mining rights were found to be current expenses on the basis that the mining rights were held by the taxpayer as a trading asset and not a capital asset. See *Bolen v. The Queen*, 2007 D.T.C. 5559 (F.C.A.).
5. Would *Dominion Natural Gas* be decided the same way today? See *Farmers Mutual Petroleum Ltd. v. M.N.R.*, [1967] C.T.C. 396, 67 D.T.C. 5277 in which the Supreme Court of Canada drew a distinction between expenses incurred to protect a right to income and expenses incurred to protect a capital asset which produces income.

3. Repair of Tangible Assets

CANADA STEAMSHIP LINES LTD. v. M.N.R.
[1966] C.T.C. 255, 66 D.T.C. 5205 (Exch. Ct.)

Jackett P.:

... The only question to be decided in the appeals is whether certain expenditures made during the years in question on ships operated by the appellant in the course of its business of operating ships for the transportation of goods are outlays of capital the deduction of which, as such, is prohibited by Section 12(1)(b) of the *Income Tax Act* [now paragraph 18(1)(b)] or are expenditures for the repair of capital assets used in the business which are deductible in the computation of profit from the business in accordance with ordinary business or commercial principles and the deduction of which is not prohibited by Section 12(1)(b).

The expenditures fall into two classes:

(a) the expense of replacing what are, in effect, floors and walls of cargo-carrying holds in certain ships and of incidental work in respect of the apparatus or members whereby such floors and walls were joined to the outside surface or "skin" of the ship - such work having been made necessary by the wear and tear arising out of the loading, carrying and unloading of cargoes; and
(b) the expense incurred in the replacement of boilers in one of the ships.

So far as the first class of expenditures is concerned, I do not, myself, have much difficulty in reaching the conclusion that these expenditures are deductible. ... So long as the ship survives as a ship and damaged plates are being replaced by sound plates, I have no doubt that the ship is being repaired and it is a deductible current expense. (I exclude, of course, a possible replacement by something so different in kind from the thing replaced that it constitutes a change in the character — an upgrading — of the thing upon which the money is expended instead of being a mere repair.) ...

The Minister's argument against the conclusion that I have just expressed may, as I understand it, be summarized as follows: the expenditures are in respect of the replacement of a substantial part of the ship's holds, which are of "signal" importance in the operation of a cargo-carrying ship, and the cost of the replacement is substantial when compared with the value of the ship and the cost of repairs done to the ship in other years; such expenditures would, therefore, be regarded as being for capital repairs or renewals and not as being for current repairs. I have tried unsuccessfully to appreciate the full significance of the Minister's submission. I have not, however, been able to escape the conclusion that a replacement of a worn or damaged board or plate that is an integral part of an asset used in a business is a repair and that the costs of repairs are current expenses and not outlays of capital. I cannot accept the view that the cost of repairs ceases to be current expenses and becomes outlays of capital merely because the repairs required are very extensive or because their cost is substantial. ...

With reference to the expenditures in replacing the boilers in one of the appellant's ships, I have more difficulty. ...

Things used in a business to earn the income — land, buildings, plant, machinery, motor vehicles, ships — are capital assets. Money laid out to acquire such assets constitutes an outlay of capital. By the same token, money laid out to upgrade such an asset — to make it something different in kind from what it was — is an outlay of capital. On the other hand, an expenditure for the purpose of repairing the physical effects of use of such an asset in the business — whether resulting from wear and tear or accident — is not an outlay of capital. It is a current expense.

The problem arises here because, depending on one's conception of the facts, an expenditure made in replacing the boilers of a ship when they have worn out may be regarded as

(a) being nothing more than an expenditure for the repair of the ship by replacing a worn out part, or

(b) the acquisition of a new piece of plant or machinery to replace an old piece of plant or machinery which has an existence separate and distinct from the ship even though it is used in the ship and as part of the equipment by which the ship is propelled.

In the case of ordinary plant or machinery in a factory or a machine shop, I should have thought that there is no doubt that each engine and each machine is a capital asset quite separate and distinct from the building in which it is installed and in which it is used. The cost of acquisition of such an asset is, I should have thought, an outlay of capital. On the other hand, in the case of a ship, the function of which involves movement, I should have thought that it was a tenable or arguable view that the equipment or machinery required to effect such movement is, from a businessman's point of view, an integral part of the ship as a capital asset. If this were the right view, I should have thought that it would follow that the cost of the replacement of the whole of the propulsion machinery or of some unit thereof would be a current expense even though the thing replaced were an asset that, by itself, was an engine or machine that could be installed in a factory as a distinct and separate capital asset. I do not, however, feel free to consider whether I should adopt that approach in disposing of the present problem having regard to two previous decisions of this Court. I refer to *Thompson Construction (Chemong) Limited v. M.N.R.*, [1957] Ex. C.R.

96, [1957] C.T.C. 155, 57 D.T.C. 1114 and *M.N.R. v. Vancouver Tugboat Company, Limited*, [1957] Ex C.R. 160; [1957] C.T.C. 178, 57 D.T.C. 1126. In each of these cases the result would have been different if the power plant, whereby the structure in which it was installed was moved from place to place, had been regarded as being merely an integral part of that structure. I think I am bound to approach the matter in the same way as the similar problem was approached in each of these cases until such time, if any, as a different course is indicated by a higher Court. When I say bound, I do not mean that I am bound by any strict rule of *stare decisis* but by my own view as to the desirability of having the decisions of this Court follow a consistent course as far as possible.

...

THE QUEEN v. SHABRO INVESTMENTS LTD.
[1979] C.T.C. 125, 79 D.T.C. 5104 (F.C.A.)

Jackett C.J.: ...

The principal question that has to be decided is whether an amount spent by the appellant in replacing a substantial part of the floor of the lower storey of a two-storey building that was owned by the appellant as a rental property was a revenue expenditure on "repairs" or an expenditure on account of capital.

As I understand them, the relevant facts may be summarized briefly as follows:

(1) when the building, which was built on a site created by fill consisting of garbage and earth, was originally constructed, while the peripheral walls of the building were supported by piles sunk through the garbage fill to solid earth, the bottom floor was concrete slabs reinforced by "wire mesh" laid on the fill and *dependent on the fill for support*;

(2) after some years, the fill compacted causing the floor to subside and break, with the result that the lower storey of part of the building in question became unusable as rental space and "the waterlines, storm drains, plumbing, weeping tile and electric wiring" settled and broke under the weight of the floor;

(3) it was recognized that

  (a) having regard to the character of the site on which it was located, the damaged floor could not be repaired as, or replaced by, a floor consisting of concrete slabs dependent upon the fill for support, and

  (b) for a floor on that part of the site it was necessary to have

    (i) support of the same character as had been provided for the peripheral walls — i.e., steel piles sunk through the fill to solid earth, and

    (ii) a floor consisting of a concrete slab reinforced by steel so that it could be supported by such piles;

(4) the space in question, as I understand it, was, accordingly, made usable, in the taxation year 1973, by
   (a) breaking up and removing the sunken and fractured floor,
   (b) installing steel piles to be used as support for a substitute floor,
   (c) creating a new floor by constructing a concrete slab reinforced with steel resting on the steel piles, and
   (d) repairing or replacing the waterlines, storm drains, weeping tile and electric wiring that had been damaged or destroyed by the subsidence and fracturing of the old floor, and
(5) the total cost of such operation was $95,198.10, which was treated by the appellant as an operating expense for the 1973 taxation year and was disallowed as such by the Minister of National Revenue who treated it as an outlay on account of capital.

...

I know of no single test to distinguish between

(a) "repairs," the cost of which is a revenue expenditure in the year during which they are carried out, and
(b) additions or improvements, the cost of which is an outlay on account of capital.

Generally speaking, replacements of worn or damaged parts, even though substantial, are repairs and are to be contrasted with changes designed to create an enduring addition or improvement to the structure. In ordinary cases, the difference is evident. Unfortunately, this is not such an ordinary case. ...

When that part of the building in question was erected, there was a hidden defect in the structure thereof which adversely affected its intrinsic value but, being unrecognized, would not have affected its market value. When that defect became apparent, it seriously diminished, if it did not destroy, the market value of the part of the building involved. The installation of supporting piles for the basic floor was necessary to eliminate the defect, which had always existed but had just become apparent. Elimination of the defect was necessary to give the building the character of a long term usable asset that it had previously seemed to have but did not actually have. In my view, installation of the piles was a permanent addition to the structure of the building of a foundation that had not previously existed and was not a repair to the building as it had existed prior to their installation. ...

In so far as the outlay of $95,198.10 is reasonably attributable to the removal of the damaged floor and its replacement by a floor supported by the steel piles, I have more difficulty.

... Damage caused by accident or vandalism, just as much as that caused by deterioration from wear and tear or aging, can call for "repairs" in the profit and loss sense; and, similarly, "repairs" do not become disqualified as "repairs" in that sense merely because they are carried out in the light of technology unknown when the original structure was built or because they take into account conditions (such as dampness) not taken into account when the original structure was built.

I am of the view that, if the replacement of the floor could otherwise be regarded as being the remedying of damage to the fabric of the building, it would have been properly deducted as a current expense on repairs notwithstanding

(a) that the damage arose from a hidden defect in the original structure and not from wear and tear, aging of materials or some accidental or malicious happening in the course of use, or

(b) that the damage was remedied in accordance with technology or knowledge as of the time thereof that incidentally effected an improvement in the structure over what it was when originally built.

The real problem, in my view, with regard to that part of the $95,198.10 that can reasonably be attributed to the replacement of the floor, is whether the replacement of the floor was merely the remedying of damage to the fabric of the building as it had theretofore existed or whether it was an integral component of a work designed to improve the building by replacing a substantial part thereof by something essentially different in kind.

My conclusion is that, prior to the change, the part of the building in question had a *floor* (consisting of concrete slabs resting on garbage fill) which made the lower floor of that part of the building unusable and that to remedy that situation and to improve the building by making the space in question usable it was necessary to replace that floor by a floor consisting of a concrete slab reinforced by steel resting on steel piles. With some hesitation, my view is that the improvement operation was the whole replacement work and not merely the sinking of the steel piles. ...

There is no doubt that, in this case, from the point of view of the persons making physical use of the building, once the floor was replaced, it was essentially the same as the old floor as it was before it subsided. So regarded, the replacement of the floor could be regarded as a repair of damage to the building. However, from the point of view of the owner or tenant of the building as such, a building the floor of which was "floating" on garbage fill has been changed into a substantially improved building namely, a building the floor of which is supported by steel piles. Moreover, the removal of the old floor and construction of a floor consisting of a single concrete slab reinforced by steel so as to be suitable for being supported by piles was an essential part of that change. As already indicated, with some hesitation I have come to the conclusion that the problem must be so regarded and that the removal of the old floor, the sinking of the piles and the placing thereon of a concrete slab reinforced by steel was a single operation whereby an improvement was made to the building that was essentially different in kind from a repair to the building as it originally was.

In so far as the balance of the amount in question is concerned (viz., that part of the $95,198.10 that can reasonably be regarded as the cost of replacing or repairing of the waterlines, etc.), the learned Trial Judge was of the view that the cost attributable to them must be disallowed because what was done was not due to wear, aging or deterioration resulting from use or passage of time. I am of the view that that was not a reason for disallowing them. Whether or not this part of the amount in dispute or some part of it qualifies for deduction on current account, in my view, depends on whether, apart from what made the expenditures necessary, they are to be regarded as the cost of repairs or as an outlay on account of capital. In my view it has been shown that this portion of the amount was disallowed on a wrong basis and that the matter should be referred back for reconsideration thereof on a proper basis.

I would allow the appeal, set aside the judgment of the Trial Division and the assessment in question and refer that assessment back for reassessment on the basis that any part of the $95,198.10 that is not reasonably attributable to the replacement of the old floor by a floor supported by steel piles and that would otherwise be deductible as a current expense should be allowed notwithstanding that its expenditure became necessary as a result of the subsidence or fracturing of the original floor.

[Urie J. and Kelly D.J. concurred with Jackett C.J.].

GOLD BAR DEVELOPMENTS LTD. v. THE QUEEN
[1987] 1 C.T.C. 262, 87 D.T.C. 5152 (F.C.T.D.)

[The taxpayer owned an apartment building the exterior of which was constructed of brick veneer. Bricks began to fall from the building. Inspection revealed that an entire wall was unsound, and that the primary cause was inferior work of the original subcontractor. On the advice of professional engineers, the taxpayer made the necessary repairs, using metal cladding instead of brick veneer, at a cost of $242,000. The taxpayer deducted that sum as a business expense. The Minister treated it as a capital outlay.]

Jerome J.: ...

I do not think the solution to this problem can be found in the effect of the expenditure. It is expected that repairs to a capital asset should improve it. Where the source of income is a residential apartment building, that is always the case, especially where the repairs are substantial. Nor do I find the "once-in-a-lifetime" approach of much assistance. The more substantial the repair, the less likely it is to recur (certainly the fervent hope of the building owner) but it remains a repair expenditure nonetheless.

I think it is more helpful to emphasize the purpose of the outlay by the taxpayer. What was in the mind of the taxpayer in formulating the decision to spend this money at this time? Was it to improve the capital asset, to make it different, to make it better? That kind of decision involves a very important elective component — a choice or option which is not present in the genuine repair crisis.

It is not in dispute that the plaintiff discovered in 1979 that the bricks were coming loose and falling on the ground around the building used by tenants and passersby. Obviously, it was a risk that would be unacceptable to the public, but also one likely to meet a reaction from city officials, in the extreme even closure of the premises. In the circumstances, I cannot conclude that the plaintiff had any real choice. To ignore that condition would certainly have brought about a reduction in occupation, or in rental income.

It is also common ground that the cause of the premature break-down of the brick veneer was faulty work by the original subcontractor when the plaintiff had arranged to have the building constructed some ten years earlier. That is not directly relevant to the taxation issue, but certainly verifies the fact that the plaintiff had this decision forced upon him and did not initiate it. This was not a voluntary expenditure with a view to bringing into existence a new capital asset for the purpose of producing income, or for the purpose of creating an improved building so as to produce greater income. The plaintiff was faced with an unexpected deterioration in the walls of the building which put the viability of the property at risk. The decision to spend the money was a decision to repair to meet that crisis and despite the fact that I am sure the plaintiff's expectation was, and still is, that it will not recur in the lifetime of the building, it remains fundamentally a repair expenditure.

There remain two other considerations that arise from the jurisprudence. An expenditure which is in the nature of repair will not be allowed as a deduction from income if it becomes so substantial as to constitute a replacement of the asset. See *Canada Steamship Lines Limited v. M.N.R.*, [1966] C.T.C. 255; 66 D.T.C. 5205; *M.N.R. v. Haddon Hall Realty Inc.*, [1961] C.T.C. 509; 62 D.T.C. 1001; and *M.N.R. v. Vancouver Tugboat Company, Limited*, [1957] C.T.C. 178; 57 D.T.C. 1126. Here, however, while the sum of money is certainly substantial, the undisputed evidence is that this building's value at the material time was in the range of $8 million so that the sum in issue represents less than three per cent of the value of the asset. There is no justification therefore to reclassify the expenditure on that basis.

Finally, there have been a number of decisions in which repairs, either alone or in combination with other work, have rendered the capital asset not simply restored to its original condition, but greatly improved because of its new-found resistance to those factors which caused the deterioration. See *Shabro Investments Ltd. v. The Queen*, [1979] C.T.C. 125; 79 D.T.C. 5104 and *Sydney Harold Healey v. M.N.R.*, [1984] C.T.C. 2004; 84 D.T.C. 1017.

Counsel for the defendant invites me to reach that conclusion here because the walls to the plaintiff's building were not replaced with brick as before, but with a metal cladding that went beyond answering the defects, and made the building not only fully resistant to the problem of falling bricks, but also substantially improved in appearance. I cannot accept the suggestion, however, that once the decision to repair is forced upon the taxpayer, he must ignore advancements in building techniques and technology in carrying out the work. In remedying the situation, the plaintiff was given two or three options, including the replacement of the original brick. In pursuing the option of curtain-wall cladding, the plaintiff adopted an extremely popular modern construction technique. I am not satisfied that the appearance of the building was any better than it would have been had the original brick been replaced.

Nothing in this repair project attempted to change the structure of the building. What was done was neither more nor less than was required to replace the deteriorating and dangerous brick condition. The Minister was therefore in error in requiring the taxpayer to treat this as an expenditure on account of capital. The appeal is allowed ...

Notes and Questions

1. In characterizing an expenditure as a repair or a capital outlay, is it relevant that the expenditure was involuntary? Assuming the appropriate business purpose, why does it matter whether the taxpayer chose to make the outlay?
2. As the *Shabro* case illustrates, part of an expenditure might constitute a capital expense and part might constitute a current expense. A close analysis of the repair or renovation work may reveal that some of the expenditure resulted in an upgrade. However, as indicated in *Shabro* and *Gold Bar*, new technology may be used to effect a repair.
3. In *Canada Steamship Lines Ltd., supra*, Jackett P. indicated that the amount of the expenditure is not determinative of the question of whether it is a repair or a replacement. In *M.N.R. v. Vancouver Tugboat Company Ltd.*, [1957] C.T.C. 178, 57 D.T.C. 1126, the taxpayer expended $42,000 on a new engine for one of its boats and attempted to deduct the amount as a current expense. The Exchequer Court considered the cost of the replacement in relation to the cost of ordinary repairs to determine that the expenditure was of a capital nature. The CRA generally accepts small expenditures without questioning whether they represent a payment that should be treated as a capital outlay.

4. In *MacMillan Bloedel (Alberni) Ltd. v. M.N.R.*, [1973] C.T.C. 295, 73 D.T.C. 5264 (F.C.T.D.), the taxpayer carried on a logging business which required it to operate its trucks over very rough roads. The useful life of the truck tires averaged 12 1/ 2 months. New trucks cost $50,000 to $60,000 each; the tires represented 10 per cent to 15 per cent of this cost. In 1966, the total cost of tires on new trucks purchased by the taxpayer was about $140,000; in 1967, it was about $53,000. The taxpayer deducted those amounts as current expenses in the two taxation years. The Minister disallowed the current deductions and added the amounts to the value of the trucks, which were Class 10 assets for the purpose of capital cost allowance. The taxpayer's appeal was dismissed. Collier, J. said:

> The appellant contends that because of the short life of the tires on these particular units their initial cost and replacement cost is a recurring annual expense which is deductible. Mr. Rushton, the Manager of the Tax Section of the appellant and its associated companies, and also a chartered accountant, expressed the view that treating the initial cost of the tires as an expense incurred in the year of purchase of the unit was in accordance with ordinary commercial principles or well accepted principles of business and accounting practice. The appellant says its method is in accordance with the "matching" principle, that is the proper matching of revenue and expense in the years in question.
>
> In my view, the method adopted by the appellant here is not a true application of the matching principle. It is not disputed that the logging units are capital assets. They cannot function without tires. It is also admitted there is other equipment or materials that require replacement or repair within the first year. Some examples are fan belts and lubricating oil of various kinds. No attempt has been made by the appellant to claim those items as an initial expense, presumably because the cost is small in respect to the overall cost of the unit. In my view it is purely an arbitrary procedure to segregate these tires from the rest of the unit. This equipment was purchased as a package, not as a number of individual parts later assembled to form an operational machine.

5. The cost of replacing damaged electrical transforms used by the taxpayer in its electrical distribution system was determined to be a current expense since the purpose of the expenditure was to maintain the operation of the distribution system and the overall cost of the expenditure was relatively small, representing only 1 per cent of the taxpayer's revenue. This conclusion was reached notwithstanding that the average usable life of a transformer was 33 years. See *Atco Electric Ltd. v. Canada*, [2007] 4 C.T.C. 2297, 2007 D.T.C. 974 (T.C.C.), affirmed on other grounds [2008] 4 C.T.C. 255, 2008 D.T.C. 6438 (F.C.A.).

6. The cost of repairing a severely damaged building in order to return it to a habitable state and expenses incurred in the substantial reconstruction of a portion of a building to make the building space rentable were both considered to be

capital expenditures. See *Fotherby v. Canada*, 2008 D.T.C. 4186 (T.C.C.); *Nguyen v. Canada*, [2008] C.T.C. 2321 (T.C.C.).

7. Are the following expenditures capital or current?
   - the cost of cash registers for a large department store
   - the cost of a car for a travelling salesperson
   - the cost of cars for a new or used car dealership
   - the cost of building an outdoor patio for a restaurant
   - the cost of repairing an outdoor patio for a restaurant
   - the cost of reshingling the roof of a rental property
   - the cost of painting rooms for a hotel (the rooms are repainted every 5 years)
   - the cost of advertising a new beer

B. Capital Cost Allowance

1. Fundamentals of the Statutory Regime

"Depreciation" is the accounting term for the loss in value of certain assets attributable to their use in the income-earning process. A taxi, for example, may wear out in two or three years of use, and the amount of its value that is "used up" each year should be deducted from the gross income for that year in order to obtain an accurate statement of net income (that is, to match the cost of the taxi to the revenue that it produces). The depreciation of an asset thus serves two purposes: the first is to attribute the wear and tear on assets to the proper accounting period; the second is to provide an estimate of the value for the asset at any given time. In theory, by deducting the total amount of depreciation recognized over the years from the original value of the asset, the current value can be obtained. However, as a matter of practice the "written-down value" or "book value" of an asset generally does not equal the actual market value, due to inflation, depression, supply and demand, or particularly good or poor maintenance of the asset. Through long experience, the accounting profession has developed various rates for depreciating various types of assets. The Act, however, sets out specific rates that may differ from the rates used for financial accounting purposes. These statutory rates must be followed in computing income for tax purposes.

Paragraph 20(1)(a) of the Act allows a taxpayer to deduct an amount to reflect "depreciation" under the title of capital cost allowance ("CCA"). The paragraph specifically states that, notwithstanding paragraph 18(1)(a), (b) or (h), an amount which is allowed by the regulations is deductible. However, no deduction is permitted for expenditures that are not for the purpose of earning income or that are of a personal nature (regulation 1102(1)(c)).

The amounts allowed by the regulations are deductible regardless of whether they reflect the actual depreciation of the assets involved. In an attempt to provide logical capital cost allowances, all assets are divided into numerous different classes set out in Schedule II to the regulations, with a specific rate applicable to each class. There appears to be a general attempt to classify assets according to their normal expected life. However, government, social, economic or political policy may affect these rates: see, for example, the assets described in paragraphs (o) and (p) of Class 12, Schedule II.

Two methods of depreciation that are generally permitted for financial accounting purposes are:

(a) "straight-line" method, under which the cost of the asset is allocated evenly over the asset's useful life; and

(b) "declining balance" method, under which the annual amount of depreciation is based on a fixed percentage of the asset's written down cost (after taking into account depreciation from previous years).

The distinction between the two methods is that, under the latter, the amount of depreciation is generally greater in earlier years. CCA varies from accounting depreciation in two major respects, apart from possible distinctions in rates. First, only the declining balance method is used for tax purposes, except for certain property such as a leasehold interest, patent, concession, franchise or licence, for which the straight-line method is used (see regulation 1100(1)(b) and (c) and Schedule III). Second, CCA is a permitted deduction, in that a taxpayer may claim as a deduction any amount up to the maximum amount (see regulation 1100(1)(a)). The taxpayer may choose not to claim capital cost allowance in a given year but rather defer its deduction to a subsequent year (although the amount claimed in a year is limited to the percentage of the asset's written-down cost or "undepreciated capital cost" at the end of that year; the taxpayer cannot "double up" the amount of CCA claimed by deferring to a later year).

The Act requires all assets in respect of a particular business that are within a particular class to be pooled, and then CCA is claimed on the entire class or pool. There are, however, exceptions to this pooling requirement. For instance, automobiles that are "passenger vehicles" with a cost above a certain prescribed amount (currently $30,000 - see regulation 7307) must be treated separately (see regulation 1101(1af)); in addition each rental property acquired at a cost of $50,000 or more is treated as a separate class (see regulation 1101(1ac) and the discussion of the rental and leasing property restrictions, below).

Certain items of property are not mentioned in Schedule II and, therefore, no CCA is allowed. All tangible assets not in any other class are included in class 8. Regulation 1102 specifically excludes a number of items from the classes of property in Schedule II. As noted above, the major limitation is found in regulation 1102(1)(c), which requires that an asset be acquired by the taxpayer for the purpose of gaining or producing income. Other significant exclusions are assets the cost of which are currently deductible (regulation 1102(1)(a)), inventory (regulation 1102(1)(b)) and land (regulation 1102(2)).

2. Calculation of Capital Cost Allowance

The amount of the CCA deduction available under paragraph 20(1)(a) is determined by regulation 1100(1)(a). Under regulation 1100(1)(a), the amount is equal to the appropriate percentage of the undepreciated capital cost ("UCC") of each class of depreciable assets. Because the UCC of a class at the end of a taxation year is determinative, the timing of the deduction for CCA is fixed at the end of the taxation year.

"Undepreciated capital cost" is defined in subsection 13(21). In simplified terms, the definition provides that the UCC of a class is the aggregate of "A" (the cost of all acquisitions of property in the class) and "B" (recapture (see below)) minus "E" (the aggregate of all CCA previously claimed in respect of the class, which includes any "terminal loss" (see below) previously deducted in respect of the class) and "F" (the lower of the cost and proceeds of disposition of assets of the class that have been disposed of). The UCC account is thus cumulative and reflects all acquisitions and dispositions of property in a particular class since the first asset in the class was acquired. In practice, in computing UCC for a particular year, a taxpayer simply needs to take the UCC of the class at the end of the previous year, deduct CCA claimed for the previous year, add the cost of new purchases in that year and subtract the proceeds of disposition (up to the cost) of property disposed of in that year.

The computation of CCA is complicated somewhat by the "50 per cent rule" or "half-year rule" in regulation 1100(2), which applies to acquisitions in 1982 and subsequent years. The rule overcomes a perceived inequity which resulted when taxpayers purchased assets late in the taxation year yet claimed CCA for the full year. Rather than adopting a complicated pro-rata formula, a simplistic "averaging" approach was taken. Regulation 1100(2) only has application when depreciable property has been acquired in the taxation year and its effect is limited to that year only. It operates to limit the maximum CCA claim in respect of the net increase in the UCC of the class in a year to one-half of the amount that would normally be deductible. Accordingly, only the amount by which purchases in the year exceed proceeds of sale (up to cost) in the year of property in the class is subject to the one-half treatment. Regulation 1100(2) creates a notional UCC for the first year any asset is added to the class. The CCA is calculated for that year on the basis of the notional UCC. The notional UCC is determined by the following formula:

Notional UCC = Year-end UCC otherwise determined – 1/2 (acquisitions minus dispositions in the year)

Thus, if dispositions in the year exceed acquisitions, regulation 1100(2) has no application. Certain property is exempt from the application of regulation 1100(2).

The following example illustrates a basic capital cost allowance calculation.

Example

In year one, a taxpayer buys three buses for a total price of $75,000 for use in a transportation business. The price paid for each bus was $20,000, $25,000 and $30,000 respectively. The taxpayer also bought a concrete building in which to garage the buses for $100,000. Assuming these are the taxpayer's only depreciable capital assets, two capital "pools" must be established, one for the buses and the other for the building. Schedule II sets out the relevant classes and regulation 1100(1)(a) provides the maximum capital cost allowance that can be taken each year for the assets in each class. The UCC at a given time is determined by the application of the formula in the definition of UCC in subsection 13(21). The term "year-end UCC" is used to refer to the UCC at the end of a particular taxation year before CCA is deducted at that time. CCA is calculated as a percentage of the UCC at the end of the taxation year and it is assumed in the example that the maximum amount possible will be claimed as a deduction.

Class 10 (30%)	*Class 1 (4%)*
Buses	Building
$75,000	$100,000

For year one, the taxpayer may claim CCA as follows:

(1) Class 10 – buses

Year-end UCC $ 75,000

UCC = (A+B) − (E + F)
A (cost of the property): 75,000
B (previous recapture): nil
E (CCA previously claimed): nil
F (proceeds of disposition up to cost): nil

Does the half year rule apply?

Yes: acquisitions (additions to A) exceed dispositions (additions to F).
Notional UCC = $75,000 – 1/2 ($75,000 – 0) $ 37,500

CCA at 30% $ 11,250

CCA = Notional UCC (37,500) × 30%

(2) Class 1 – building

Year-end UCC $100,000

UCC = (A+B) – (E + F)
A: $100,000
B: n/a
E: n/a
F: n/a

Does the half-year rule apply? Yes

Notional UCC = \$100,000 − 1/2 (\$100,000 – 0) — \$ 50,000

CCA at 4% — \$2,000

CCA = Notional UCC (\$50,000) × 4%

Therefore, the amount of CCA deductible under paragraph 20(1)(a) in calculating income, is \$11,250 + \$2,000 or \$13,250.

In year 2, assume the taxpayer sells the bus that originally cost \$20,000 for \$18,000.

(1) Class 10 – buses

Year-end UCC — \$45,750

UCC = (A+B) − (E + F)
A: \$75,000
B: n/a
E: \$11,250
F: \$18,000

Does the half-year rule apply? No

CCA at 30% — \$13,725

CCA = UCC (\$45,750) × 30%

(2) Class 1 – building

Year-end UCC — \$98,000

UCC = (A+B) − (E+F)
A: \$100,000
B: n/a
E: \$2,000
F: n/a

Does half-year rule apply? No

CCA at 4% — \$3,920

CCA = UCC (\$98,000) × 4%

Therefore, the amount of CCA that can be claimed as a deduction in year 2 is \$13,725 + \$3,920, or \$17,645.

Suppose in year 3 the taxpayer purchases another bus for \$50,000 and sells the bus that originally cost \$25,000 for \$15,000:

(1) Class 10

Year-end UCC — \$67,025

UCC = (A+B) − (E+F)
A: \$125,000 (\$75,000 + \$50,000)
B: n/a
E: \$24,975 (\$11,250 + \$13,725)
F: \$33,000 (\$18,000 + \$15,000)

Does the half-year rule apply? Yes

Notional UCC = \$67,025 – 1/2 (\$50,000 – \$15,000)	\$49,525
CCA at 30%	\$14,857
CCA = Notional UCC (\$49,525) × 30%	

(2) Class 1

Year-end UCC	\$94,080
UCC = (A+B) – (E+F)	
A: \$100,000	
B: n/a	
E: 5,920 (\$2,000 + \$3,920)	
F: n/a	
CCA at 4%	\$3,763

Therefore, the amount of CCA that may be claimed as a deduction in year 3 is \$14,857 + \$3,763 or \$18,620.

3. Disposition of Depreciable Assets

The capital cost allowance system is based on the average useful life of each particular class of assets. In other words, assets have been assigned to classes generally based on an estimate of their useful lives. Thus, a bus which depreciates quickly is a Class 10 (30 per cent) asset, while a building which has a longer useful life is normally a Class 1 (4 per cent) asset. The problem to be discussed here arises when the actual life of the asset differs from the estimated useful life as provided for in the Act. If we assume that the assets did depreciate somewhat before being disposed of, there may have been an over-allowance or an under-allowance by the mechanical formula in the Act.

These differences are dealt with in two sections of the Act:

- subsection 20(16), which permits a deduction for a "terminal loss"; and
- subsection 13(1), which requires the taxpayer to include recapture in income.

Because the UCC of a class is a running account, any previous terminal loss or recapture with respect to that class must be incorporated into the computation of UCC. How are these two items dealt with? See the definition of "total depreciation" in subsection 13(21) and term "B" of the definition of UCC.

Example

If we continue with the example above, we find that, at the beginning of year 4, the UCC of Class 10 is \$52,168 (\$67,025 – \$14,857) and the UCC of Class 1 is \$90,317 (\$94,080 – \$3,763).

Suppose, in year 4, the two remaining buses (which cost \$30,000 and \$50,000, respectively) are sold for \$24,000 each and no new buses are purchased. The UCC of Class 10 at the end of year 4 would be as follows:

Class 10

Year-end UCC $ 4,168

UCC = (A+B) − (E+F)
A: $125,000
B: n/a
E: $39,832 ($11,250 + $13,725 + $14,857)
F: $81,000 ($18,000 + $15,000 + $24,000 + $24,000)

The UCC of Class 10 is $4,168, even though there are no assets in the class at year-end. The buses declined in value by a total of $44,000 ($125,000 aggregate cost less $81,000 aggregate proceeds of disposition) but the taxpayer was able to claim an aggregate of only $39,832 as CCA while the buses were owned. The positive balance that arises in these circumstances is fully deductible as a "terminal loss" under subsection 20(16). Study the provision carefully; note its reference back to the definition of "undepreciated capital cost" in subsection 13(21). Also note that the deduction is mandatory.

Subsection 20(16) deals with the situation where an asset actually depreciates at a rate faster than the relevant CCA rate (or, more specifically, the amount of CCA claimed by the taxpayer is less than the amount that the asset actually depreciated in value). Subsection 13(1) concerns the situation where an asset does not, in reality, depreciate as quickly as it is written off for tax purposes. If an asset is disposed of for more than the UCC of the class, the excess must be included in income.

Example

In the above example, the building used to house the buses had a UCC of $90,317 at the beginning of year 4. Suppose the building is sold in year 4, for $95,000:

Class 1

Year-end UCC ($ 4,683)

UCC = (A+B) − (E+F)
A: $100,000
B: n/a
E: $9,683 ($2,000 + $3,920 + $3,763)
F: $95,000

On examining the definition "undepreciated capital cost" in subsection 13(21), you will note that the UCC can never be a negative figure. See, in this respect, section 257. Nevertheless, the net effect of subsection 13(1) is to bring this negative balance into the taxpayer's income if the negative balance exists at year-end. This amount is commonly called "recapture".

Subsection 13(1) applies generally where, at the end of a taxation year, the aggregate of the total depreciation allowed to the taxpayer and the lesser of proceeds of disposition and capital cost of the property sold exceeds the capital cost of property. Expressed using the simplified mathematical formula for UCC, subsection

13(1) applies to include in income the amount by which (E+F) exceeds (A+B). In the above example, this is the case at the end of year 4 to the extent of $4,683, and that is the amount that must be included in the taxpayer's income under subsection 13(1) as recapture of excessive CCA deductions. To look at it another way, the taxpayer was able to claim an aggregate of $9,683 as deductions over the 3 years when the property had in reality declined in value by only $5,000. The difference should be added back to the taxpayer's income when the asset is sold.

Recapture occurs whenever the UCC has a notional negative balance at year end, regardless of whether there are assets remaining in the class. In contrast, a terminal loss will only occur if there are no assets in the class at the end of the year.

Note that in the definition of "undepreciated capital cost" in subsection 13(21), the amount deducted under term "F" is the lesser of

(a) the proceeds of disposition of the particular property less any expenses of disposition, and

(b) the original capital cost of the particular property.

By limiting the amount to no more than the capital cost of the asset, the Act prevents the "recapture" or inclusion in income of the amount by which the proceeds of disposition exceed the original cost of the property. This excess is taxed as a capital gain. The taxation of any capital gain is dealt with by other provisions of the Act, discussed in Chapter 7.

Keep in mind that the purpose of both subsections 13(1) and 20(16) is to correct errors created by the mechanical application of the CCA regulations. The Act requires the recognition of recapture based on UCC at the end of a taxation year. Consequently, recapture can be deferred if the class is suitably "replenished" prior to the end of the taxation year in question. This can be done by purchasing in the year another asset of the same class at a price that exceeds the amount that would otherwise be included in income as recapture. Suppose, in the above example, that the taxpayer acquired another Class 1 asset in year 4 for $70,000.

Class 1

Year-end UCC	$65,317
UCC = (A+B) – (E+F)	
A: $170,000	
B: n/a	
E: $9,683	
F: $95,000	

In this example, recapture was deferred by purchasing another asset of the same class, which had the effect of maintaining a positive UCC. In effect, the amount of the recapture ($4,683) otherwise determined reduces the UCC of the class and therefore the amount of CCA that can be claimed as a consequence of the acquisition of the $70,000 asset. Would the half-year rule apply when determining CCA in year 4?

One further point. Assume that there was recapture of $4,683 in year 4 (that is, that no other building was acquired in the year as in the example immediately above). The UCC at the beginning of year 5 would be nil (because of term "B" in the definition of UCC). Assume that during year 5 an asset of the same class is purchased for $10,000. What is the closing UCC for the year?

Class 1

Year end UCC	$10,000
UCC = (A + B) − (E + F)	
A: $110,000	
B: $4,683	
E: $9,683	
F: $95,000	

Would the half-year rule apply in year 5?

Problems

1. X purchased a Class 1 (4%) building in year 1 at a cost of $100,000. It is her only Class 1 asset. X took maximum CCA in respect of the building in year 1 and year 2. In year 3, she sold the building for $80,000.
   (a) What are the tax consequences to X for year 3?
   (b) What if X acquired another Class 1 building later in year 3 at a cost of $50,000?
   (c) Ignoring (b), rather than being sold, what if the building was destroyed by flood in year 3 and X had no flood insurance? See subsection 20(16) and the definitions of "disposition" and "proceeds of disposition" in subsections 248(1) and 13(21), respectively.
   (d) Ignoring (b) and (c), what if X gave the property to her brother in year 3 and it can be established that the building had a fair market value of $100,000? Would the result be different if she sold the building to her brother for $50,000 rather than giving it to him?
2. Y purchased a Class 8 (20%) asset in year 1 at a cost of $5,000. It is his only Class 8 asset. Y took maximum CCA in respect of the asset in year 1 and year 2. In year 3, Y sold the asset for $4,500.
   (a) What are the tax consequences to Y for year 3?
   (b) What if Y acquired another Class 8 asset later in year 3 at a cost of $10,000?
   (c) Ignoring (b), what if Y had disposed of the asset in year 3 for $5,500?
   (d) Ignoring (b) and (c), what if Y gave the asset to his sister in year 3, and it can be established that it had a fair market value at the time of $5,500? What if Y sold the asset to his sister for $3,000?

4. Replacement Property Rules

Sometimes a taxpayer intends to replace a depreciable property but is unable to do so prior to a year end. In these circumstances, subsection 13(1) may require the inclusion of recapture in income. After income tax has been paid on the recapture, the taxpayer may be unable to acquire a replacement for the disposed asset. To alleviate this difficulty — or, more precisely, to eliminate the tax costs from the decision to replace — subsection 13(4) permits the deferral of recapture where the disposition was involuntary (that is, fire, expropriation, etc.) or the property disposed of was a "former business property". Subsection 13(4) applies only where a "replacement property", defined in subsection 13(4.1), is acquired within a specified time period. See Interpretation Bulletin IT-259R4: Exchange of Property (September 23, 2003) for the CRA's views on the scope of this and other similar replacement property provisions.

Problem

Dumpsons is a department store in Saskatoon. Its operations are carried on in an eight-storey building which is owned by the company. The original cost of the building to Dumpsons in year 1 was $400,000. The company has been taking maximum CCA on the structure on the basis that it is a Class 1 asset. In year 2, a fire virtually destroyed the building. The only asset which was recovered was an IBM computer and it was substantially damaged. The computer had been purchased by Dumpsons in year 1 at a cost of $75,000 and $3,750 of CCA was claimed in year 1.

In year 2, under an insurance policy with the Nostale Insurance Company, Dumpsons received $400,000 for the destruction of the building and $25,000 for the damage to its computer. Dumpsons had the computer repaired in year 2 at a cost of $23,000. In year 3, construction began on a new building. A total of $170,000 was expended in year 3 and another $430,000 was required in year 4 to complete the building.

What are the tax consequences to Dumpsons?

What if Dumpsons received $460,000 of insurance proceeds for the destroyed building and the same amounts as above were expended to rebuild the building? See section 44 (discussed in Part III of Chaper 7), which provides similar replacement property rules for capital gain arising from an involuntary disposition or a disposition of a former business property.

5. Rental and Leasing Property Restrictions

Certain provisions in the Act and the Regulations limit the amount of CCA otherwise available. The restrictions are usually an attempt to negate undue tax advantages derived from CCA claims for certain kinds of property. These limitations are often legislated in response to perceived abusive tax planning. The most notable limitations are those in respect of "rental" and "leasing" properties.

Under regulation 1100(11), the amount of otherwise deductible CCA in respect of "rental properties" is limited to the taxpayer's net income from all such properties, ignoring CCA. A taxpayer is thus prevented from creating a rental property loss, or increasing a loss, through CCA. The rationale is to eliminate the ability to use CCA to reduce income from other sources and effectively lower the after-tax cost of investing in rental properties. A "rental property" is defined in regulation 1100(14) as a building used principally for the purpose of producing gross revenue that is rent. A restriction similar to that for rental properties applies to income derived from the leasing of personal property. See regulations 1100(15) to (17). Certain corporations are excluded from the rental property and leasing property restrictions (see regulations 1100(12) and (16), respectively).

6. The Meaning of "Cost"

Under term "A" of the definition "undepreciated capital cost" in subsection 13(21), the cost of a depreciable asset is added to the UCC of a class for CCA purposes. Although undefined in the Act, the "cost" of an asset is ordinarily the amount expended to acquire it. As the following case illustrates, this simple principle can raise some difficult interpretative issues in certain circumstances.

BEN'S LTD. v. M.N.R.
[1955] C.T.C. 249, 55 D.T.C. 1152 (Exch. Ct.)

Cameron J.: ... The main facts are not in dispute. The appellant owns and operates a bakery on Pepperell Street in Halifax. In January, 1952, it purchased three adjoining residential properties, each consisting of land and a dwelling house; the total cost of acquiring the three properties was $42,832.65. Early in June of the same year it sold the three buildings for $1,200 and shortly thereafter they were removed from the land. The business of the appellant company had increased and it became necessary to provide additional accommodation for its bakery and equipment. The three properties in question were acquired with the intention that the houses thereon would be removed and the land used as a site for the extension of the main building. At the time of the purchase, however, this scheme could not be carried out as all the properties were located in R2 Zone (Second Density Residential) under the existing by-laws of the city of Halifax and could not be changed from residential use to commercial or business purposes unless and until the property was re-zoned. Accordingly, on May 21, 1952, the appellant lodged a petition (Exhibit 10) with the council of the city of Halifax and the Town Planning Board to re-zone the properties to

C2 Zone (General Business Zone). In the result the proposed amendment to the zoning by-law was passed by the City Council on September 11, 1952, and approved by the Minister of Municipal Affairs on September 20, 1952. Shortly thereafter a contract was awarded for the construction of a concrete extension to the main factory and office building and the new extension was completed early in 1953.

In its T2 income tax return for the year 1952, the appellant stated its costs of acquisition of the three properties (after allowing $1,200 for the amount received on the sale of the buildings) to be $41,632.85, which it apportioned as follows: land — $3,000; buildings — $38,632.85. In respect of these buildings it deducted 10 per cent of that amount ($3,863.28) for capital cost allowance, but the full amount thereof (*inter alia*) was disallowed and added to the declared income in the re-assessment dated January 11, 1954. The appellant was advised that the disallowance was made on the ground that the entire amount had been expended for the purpose of acquiring the site on which the plant addition had been erected and that no portion of the payment was expended for the purpose of acquiring depreciable assets.

Subsequently, in its Notice of Objection, the appellant admitted that the value of the land was $6,000 and the appeal to the Income Tax Appeal Board was on the basis of a capital cost allowance of $35,632.85. The appeal to this Court is based on the same amount. ...

I shall first consider the main submission of the appellant, namely, that it is entitled to the maximum capital cost allowance of 10 per cent provided for "frame buildings" in Class 6 of Schedule B. The inclusion of that type of building in a class, however, is not conclusive of the right to capital cost allowance in view of [regulation 1102(1)(c)] ...

In my view, therefore, the question is not whether the appellant's outlay as a whole was for the purpose of gaining or producing income, but rather this: Was the property referred to in Class 6 as "a building of frame" acquired by the appellant for the purpose of gaining or producing income? ...

On the evidence as a whole, I am satisfied that the sole purpose in making the purchase was to acquire a site for the extension of the factory. There never was any intention to acquire the frame houses for gaining or producing income; the sole intention in regard to the houses was to have them torn down and removed at the earliest possible moment, and that purpose was carried out. The mere fact that certain amounts of rental were obtained from one is attributable to the existing leases and does not affect in any way the real purpose of acquisition. Section 1102(1)(c) of the Regulations therefore bars the frame houses, under the circumstances, from being property which was subject to capital cost allowance. The appeal on this point is therefore disallowed. ...

Notes and Problems

1. In the absence of a statutory definition, "cost" is generally the amount expended by a taxpayer to acquire property. There are, however, several situations where this general principle does not apply.
   (a) Where property is acquired by gift or bequest, the taxpayer is deemed to have acquired it at a cost equal to its fair market value at the time of the gift or bequest (paragraph 69(1)(c)).
   (b) Where property originally acquired for a purpose, other than to produce income, is subsequently used for the purpose of producing income, the taxpayer is deemed to have acquired it at a cost equal to its fair market value if the fair market value is less than its cost. If the fair market value is greater than its cost, capital cost is limited to:
      (i) the actual cost of the property to the taxpayer; plus
      (ii) one-half of any capital gain realized on the change in use to the extent that a capital gains exemption was not claimed (paragraph 13(7)(b)).
   (c) Where property is used partly for the purpose of gaining or producing income and partly for some other purpose, the taxpayer's capital cost is apportioned according to the percentage of income-earning use (paragraph 13(7)(c)).
   (d) Where depreciable property is transferred in a non-arm's length transaction, and the transferee's cost at the time of acquisition otherwise determined is greater than the transferor's cost or capital cost, the transferee is deemed to have acquired the property at an amount equal to the total of:
      (i) the transferor's cost or capital cost; plus
      (ii) one-half of any capital gain realized by the transferor to the extent that a capital gains exemption was not claimed (subparagraphs 13(7)(e)(i) and (ii)).
   (e) Where depreciable property is acquired in a non-arm's length transaction and the transferee's capital cost at the time of acquisition otherwise determined is less than the transferor's cost or capital cost, the transferee is deemed to have acquired the property at the transferor's cost, and the difference between the transferee's acquisition cost otherwise determined and the transferor's capital cost of the property is treated as having been previously claimed by the transferee as capital cost allowance (subparagraph 13(7)(e)(iii)). The difference will, therefore, be subject to recapture to the transferee if the property is ultimately disposed of for an amount in excess of the transferee's actual capital cost.
   (f) Where the property is a "passenger vehicle", as defined in subsection 248(1), a $30,000 limit (plus GST and PST) is imposed on the cost (paragraph 13(7)(g) and regulation 7307(1)) for CCA purposes. No recapture occurs and

no terminal loss may be taken on a disposition of passenger vehicles to the extent that the cost exceeds the limit (subsections 13(2) and 20(16.1)).

2. Examine the above statutory provisions carefully. What is the reason behind each of them? Compare the above provisions with those in section 45. Does section 45 apply to depreciable property? Does the rule in paragraph 69(1)(c) make sense? Should a taxpayer who acquires depreciable property by gift or bequest, that is, at no cost, be entitled to any CCA?
3. Is cost restricted to the actual purchase price of property? What about legal or other professional fees? What about interest on money that the taxpayer has borrowed to acquire the property? Can the cost of demolishing an old building be added to the cost of the new building for CCA purposes? See Interpretation Bulletin IT-285R2: Capital Cost Allowance — General Comments (March 31, 1994). What about amounts expended by a taxpayer on repairs or replacement parts at the time of the acquisition of a depreciable asset? What if those expenses are incurred to put the asset in suitable condition for use?
4. When a taxpayer purchases a number of assets, both depreciable and non-depreciable, the allocation of the purchase price between the two types of assets assumes great importance. The purchaser, of course, wants to allocate as much of the purchase price as possible to the depreciable assets in order to increase the CCA claim. Does the seller care how the purchase price is allocated between depreciable and non-depreciable property? Review section 68 and subsection 13(21.1).
5. In *The Queen v. Golden*, [1986] 1 C.T.C. 274, 86 D.T.C. 6138 (S.C.C.), the Supreme Court held that, as section 68 refers to the disposition of "any property", it would apply to both depreciable and non-depreciable property. See also *H. Baur Investments Limited v. M.N.R.*, [1988] 1 C.T.C. 2067, 88 D.T.C. 1024 (T.C.C.), affirmed [1990] 2 C.T.C. 122, 90 D.T.C. 6371 (F.C.T.D.); and *R.L. Petersen v. M.N.R.*, [1988] 1 C.T.C. 2071, 88 D.T.C. 1040 (T.C.C.) where the Minister used section 68 to challenge the allocation asserted by the taxpayer. In *Baur*, the allocation set out in the agreement between the vendor and the purchaser was upheld; in the *Petersen* case it was struck down. Although the Minister is not bound by an allocation arrived at by the parties through arm's-length bargaining, it is an important consideration. In the *Golden* case, the Federal Court of Appeal stated [1983] C.T.C. 112, 83 D.T.C. 5138 at 5142:

> Where, as in this case, as found by the trial judge, the transaction is at arm's length and is not a mere sham or subterfuge, the apportionment made by the parties in the applicable agreement is certainly an important circumstance and one which is entitled to considerable weight.

6. Do you agree with the result in *Ben's*? It has been followed rather consistently since 1955. Does the court's interpretation of regulation 1102(1)(c) make sense?

Can you suggest an alternative interpretation? Could the taxpayer have added the cost of the removed buildings to the cost of the addition to its factory?

7. When is Depreciable Property Acquired?

If an asset is acquired during the taxation year, its cost is generally added to the UCC of the class and CCA may be claimed. Not surprisingly, a number of decisions have addressed the question of whether an asset was acquired and a "cost" incurred before the end of the taxation year under review or in the following taxation year.

The generally accepted test for the determination of when an asset is acquired was described by Cattanach, J. in *M.N.R. v. Wardean Drilling Ltd.*, [1969] C.T.C. 265, 69 D.T.C. 5194 (Exch. Ct.):

> As I have indicated above, it is my opinion that a purchaser has acquired assets of a class in Schedule B when title has passed, assuming that the assets exist at that time, or when the purchaser has all the incidents of title, such as possession, use and risk, although legal title may remain in the vendor as security for the purchase price as is the commercial practice under conditional sales agreements. In my view the foregoing is the proper test to determine the acquisition of property described in Schedule B to the Income Tax Regulations.

In *Wardean*, the agreement between the parties read "title to pass and notes issued as at the date of shipment". The clause was interpreted to mean that the intention of the parties was that the taxpayer would acquire the property on the date of shipment, which was after the end of the taxation year rather than in December when the agreement was signed. On that basis, the taxpayer was not entitled to claim CCA for the year of purchase.

The test in *Wardean* was also applied in *The Queen v. Henuset Bros. Ltd. (No. 2)*, [1977] C.T.C. 228, 77 D.T.C. 5171 (F.C.T.D.). There the conditional sales agreement between the parties provided that the buyer was obligated to insure against risk as of December 29 when the agreement was executed. The buyer was also entitled to take delivery of the property as of December 29, although such delivery did not occur until the following year. Bastin, D.J. determined on these facts that the taxpayer had gained constructive possession of the tractors before the end of the year and was entitled to claim CCA.

In both cases, the intention of the parties as to when property was to pass was determined from their agreement. What tests will be used when the intention of the parties is unclear? What effect will the *Wardean* test have on a claim for CCA if depreciable assets are still under construction at the end of the taxation year? In this respect, see *Schultz v. M.N.R.*, [1979] C.T.C. 2328, 79 D.T.C. 279 (T.R.B.) where the taxpayer purchased an apartment building under construction in 1975, but was not entitled to possession until its completion in 1976. The Tax Review Board held that to claim CCA the taxpayer must have legal acquisition and legal possession of the property. Thus, despite the fact that legal title to the building had been transferred in 1975, CCA was disallowed on the basis that it was not possible to have in fact and in law the possession of a building before its completion.

Subsections 13(26) to (32) of the Act contain some statutory rules dealing with the timing of acquisition of depreciable property for CCA purposes. Subsection 13(26) provides that, for the purposes of paragraph 20(1)(a) and the related regulations, no addition may be made to the UCC of a class in respect of the acquisition of property until the property has become "available for use" by a taxpayer.

Subsection 13(27) states that property, other than a building, acquired by a taxpayer is considered available for use at the earliest of the following general times:

(a) the time at which the property is first used for the purpose of earning income;
(b) the time which is the beginning of the first taxation year commencing more than 357 days after the taxation year in which the property was acquired (the two-year "rolling start" rule);
(c) the time immediately before the property is disposed of by the taxpayer; and
(d) the time the property is delivered or made available for the use or benefit of the taxpayer and is capable of producing a saleable product or performing a saleable service.

Subsection 13(28) provides a similar rule for buildings and includes the following general times:

(a) the time at which all or substantially all of the building is used by the taxpayer for its intended purpose;
(b) the time at which the construction of the building is complete;
(c) the time which is the beginning of the first taxation year commencing more than 357 days after the taxation year in which the property was acquired; and
(d) the time immediately before the property is disposed of by the taxpayer.

Special rules are set out for public corporations and their subsidiaries, property acquired as part of a long-term project, partially available rental buildings, pollution abatement equipment, property acquired for use in a farming or fishing business, certain transportation equipment, and offshore oil production facilities.

The "available-for-use" rules apply to property acquired after 1989. It is important to remember that subsection 13(26) applies only in determining the UCC of a class for the purposes of calculating the maximum CCA available for deduction under paragraph 20(1)(a) and the Regulations. For all other purposes, such as the determination of recapture and terminal loss, UCC additions are to be made as property of a class is acquired. Similarly, the application of subsection 13(4) continues to depend on the time at which a replacement property is acquired.

With the introduction of the "available-for-use" rules, the half-year rule in regulation 1100(2)(a) was amended to take into account additions of specific property as acquired or as it becomes available for use. The amendment ensures that different properties added to the same class on different bases because of their acquisition dates are similarly added to the class for the purpose of the half-year rule. However, property added to the UCC of a class on the basis of the two-year rolling start rule is excepted from the application of the half-year rule (regulation 1100(2)(a)(vii)). What is the reason for this exception?

Notes

1. In *Thomas P. McQuillan v. M.N.R.*, [1981] C.T.C. 2657, 81 D.T.C. 618 (T.R.B.), the taxpayer was involved in the production of a film, "Lies My Father Told Me," in the years 1972 to 1976. Based on paragraph 20(1)(a) and class 18, the taxpayer argued that he was entitled to CCA during the production years. The Tax Review Board held that, in order for a film maker to qualify for the 60 per cent CCA provided for in regulation 1100(1), the film must be a motion picture film which is ready to be shown to the public. Consequently, the film did not qualify as a depreciable asset until it was completed.
2. The test established in *Wardean* is based on the common law view of property rights and in particular the ability to separate those rights between the legal and beneficial owner of a property. Since a similar concept of separable property rights is not generally recognized under civil law, it has been observed that some situations may lead to different conclusions under the civil law of Québec and the common law of the other provinces. The potential for inconsistent results was arguably resolved by the decision of the Federal Court of Appeal in *Construction Bérou Inc.* v. *Canada*, [2000] 2 C.T.C. 174, 99 D.T.C. 5868 (F.C.A.) which confirmed that the test established in *Wardean* also governed the acquisition of property in Quebec. Although this appears to have resolved the issue, it has been recently argued that the decision of the FCA may have been explicitly overruled by the introduction of section 8.1 of the *Interpretations Act*, R.S., 1985, c. I-21., which came into force on June 1, 2001. Section 8.1 reads as follows:

> Both the common law and the civil law are equally authoritative and recognized sources of the law of property and civil rights in Canada and, unless otherwise provided by law, if in interpreting an enactment it is necessary to refer to a province's rules, principles or concepts forming part of the law of property and civil rights, reference must be made to the rules, principles and concepts in force in the province at the time the enactment is being applied

See David Duff, "Canadian Bijuralism and the Concept of an Acquisition of Property in the Federal Income Tax Act" (2009) 54 McGill L.J. 423-462.

C. Eligible Capital Expenditures

1. Fundamentals of the Statutory Regime

Under the pre-1972 Act, expenditures related to certain intangible assets, such as goodwill, were not deductible even if they were incurred in connection with a business. These expenditures were normally considered capital outlays, but the property acquired was not included in the CCA Regulations and the costs were not specifically deductible under any other provision of the Act.

The Act now attempts to deal with the cost associated with such assets by providing a separate amortization system for the deduction of the cost as well as a system of income inclusion for the taxpayer who realizes a gain on the sale of the assets.

The amounts subject to this special system are referred to as "eligible capital expenditures", which are defined in subsection 14(5) to include the portion of any outlay or expense made or incurred, as a result of a transaction occurring after 1971, on account of capital, for the purpose of gaining or producing income from a business. A number of types of property which are specifically excluded from this special system are listed in paragraphs (a) to (f) and should be reviewed. You will note in particular, that the cost of tangible property of the taxpayer and intangible depreciable property, as well as any other property for which a deduction is otherwise provided in the Act, are listed in the exceptions.

Eligible capital expenditures qualify for deduction by virtue of subsection 14(5). The provision operates in conjunction with paragraph 20(1)(b) to create a system that has attributes similar to those of the CCA and capital gains systems. The concept on which this system is based is "cumulative eligible capital", as defined in subsection 14(5). Three-quarters of an eligible capital expenditure is added to this account and three-quarters of the proceeds of disposition (referred to as an "eligible capital amount") is deducted from the account. Under paragraph 20(1)(b), the taxpayer may deduct up to 7 per cent of the balance in the account at the end of the year. The amounts deducted under paragraph 20(1)(b) reduce the balance of the cumulative eligible capital account so that the deduction under paragraph 20(1)(b) is calculated on a declining-balance basis.

Where the aggregate of the deductions in computing cumulative eligible capital (that is, eligible capital amounts and deductions under paragraph 20(1)(b)) exceeds the additions (three-quarters of eligible capital expenditures), subsection 14(1) requires the taxpayer to include in computing its income at the end of the year an amount equal to the total of:

(a) all amounts previously deducted by the taxpayer under paragraph 20(1)(b); and

(b) two-thirds of the amount, if any, by which the excess exceeds the amount determined in paragraph (a) above.

Subsection 14(1) therefore creates a result similar to the disposition of a depreciable property in that it first requires the taxpayer to include in computing income any amount previously deducted under paragraph 20(1)(b) (this is similar to "recapture") and thereafter requires the inclusion of one-half of the amount, if any, by which the aggregate eligible capital expenditures (analogous to "proceeds of disposition") exceed the aggregate eligible capital amounts (analogous to "cost").

The effect of these rules is illustrated by the following simple example.

Example

Assume that a taxpayer buys goodwill in year 1 at a cost of $10,000 and deducts the maximum amount possible under paragraph 20(1)(b) for years 1, 2 and 3. Assume further that the taxpayer can sell the goodwill in year 4 for proceeds of $18,000 or $6,000.

(a) Assuming the sale for $18,000

Cumulative eligible capital		
Addition in year 1 (3/4 × $10,000)		$7,500
year 1 – paragraph 20(1)(b) deduction (7% of cumulative eligible capital)		525
	balance	6,975
year 2 – paragraph 20(1)(b) deduction		488
	balance	6,487
year 3 – paragraph 20(1)(b) deduction		454
	balance	6,033
year 4 – eligible capital amount (3/4 × $18,000)		13,500
Excess amount under subsection 14(1)		(7,467)
Inclusion under paragraph 14(1)(a):		
Previous deductions under 20(1)(b): (i.e., $525 + $488 + $454)		1,467
Inclusion under paragraph 14(1)(b):		
2/3 of excess amount net of previous deductions (i.e., 7,467 − 1,467)		4,000
Total inclusion under subsection 14(1)		5,467

In this example, the net effect is the inclusion in income of an amount equal to the total of amounts previously deducted under paragraph 20(1)(b) and one-half of the gain (the amount by which the aggregate eligible capital expenditures exceeds the aggregate eligible capital amounts) realized on the goodwill. The following calculation shows this effect.

Proceeds of sale of goodwill	$18,000
Cost of goodwill	10,000
Gain	$ 8,000

One-half thereof		4,000
Amount included in income under 14(1)		$ 5,467
Less: Aggregate of deduction allowed under 20(1)(b): ($525 + $488 + $454)		1,467
Net inclusion in income		$ 4,000

(b) Assuming the sale for $6,000

Cumulative eligible capital		
Addition in year 1 (3/4 × $10,000)		$ 7,500
year 1 – paragraph 20(1)(b) deduction		525
	balance	6,975
year 2 – paragraph 20(1)(b) deduction		488
	balance	6,487
year 3 – paragraph 20(1)(b) deduction		454
	balance	6,033
year 4 – eligible capital amount (3/4 × $6,000)		4,500
		1,533

In this example, no amount is required to be included in income under subsection 14(1). The treatment of the $1,533 balance of cumulative eligible capital depends on whether the taxpayer continues to carry on the business to which the eligible capital property relates. If so, the taxpayer will be entitled to continue to amortize the balance under paragraph 20(1)(b). If the business is discontinued, the taxpayer may be entitled to an immediate deduction equal to that balance in the year in which the business ceases (subsection 24(1)). The effect in this case is to allow the taxpayer a deduction equal to three-quarters of the actual net loss from the property.

Cost of eligible capital property	$10,000
Proceeds of sale	6,000
Net loss	$ 4,000
Three-quarters thereof	$ 3,000
Deductions allowed under 20(1)(b) in previous years ($525 + $488 + $454)	$ 1,467
Future deductions available	1,533
	$ 3,000

There are a number of points worth noting about these rules.

(1) The portion of the proceeds of disposition of eligible capital property deducted from the cumulative eligible capital account is not limited by reference to the original cost of the property to the taxpayer. Why?

(2) Even if there was no addition to the cumulative eligible capital with respect to the particular property (e.g., because the property had no cost), three-quarters of the proceeds is deducted from the cumulative eligible capital account balance.

(3) In certain circumstances, a taxpayer may elect under subsection 14(1.01) to report the disposition of an eligible capital property as a capital gain rather than an income inclusion under subsection 14(1).

(4) Where income would be created under subsection 14(1) as a result of the sale of eligible capital property and new eligible capital property is acquired for the same or similar use in connection with the same or a similar business, subsection 14(6) may be used to defer the recognition of that income provided that the replacement property is acquired in the year following the disposition of the former property. This "replacement property rule" for eligible capital property is discussed in Interpretation Bulletin IT-259R4: Exchange of Property (September 23, 2003).

(5) Where a taxpayer discontinues a business, but the business is subsequently carried on by a spouse or by a corporation controlled by the taxpayer, the balance in the cumulative eligible capital account may not be deductible under section 24. Instead, it may effectively be transferred to the spouse or controlled corporation, and the transferee becomes entitled to further deductions under paragraph 20(1)(b). See subsection 24(2).

Problem

1. A taxpayer purchases the goodwill of Business A in year 1 for $20,000 and commences to operate the business. In year 2, the taxpayer acquires a trademark to use in the business for $40,000. In year 3, the taxpayer sells the trademark for $60,000. What are the effects of these transactions on the taxpayer's income from business in years 1, 2 and 3?

2. What Is An "Eligible Capital Expenditure"?

Subsection 14(5) defines "eligible capital expenditure" to include nearly all expenses that are incurred after 1971 for the purpose of gaining or producing income from a business, are capital in nature and are not otherwise deductible under the Act. Generally, the most frequent expenditures which arise are those for goodwill, customer lists, some franchises and expenses of incorporation and reorganization. Interpretation Bulletin IT-143R3: Meaning of Eligible Capital Expenditure (August 29, 2002) sets out the CRA's views in this area. The cases below consider this issue.

ROYAL TRUST CORPORATION OF CANADA v. THE QUEEN
[1982] C.T.C. 79, 82 D.T.C. 6076 (F.C.T.D.)

[A corporate predecessor of the taxpayer sold shares of its capital stock to a broker for resale to the public. It granted the broker a commission on the selling price and claimed deductions for eligible capital expenditures in relation to the commission. The Minister disallowed the deductions and the taxpayer appealed.]

Jerome A.C.J.: ...

The agreement between United Trust and Pitfield was executed on September 7, 1972 and it is common ground that this agreement constituted sale by United Trust and purchase by Pitfield of 325,000 shares with a par value of $5. The agreement recites a price of $8 per share and a commission of 541/2 per share and pursuant to the agreement, two purchases were made by Pitfield: the first upon the date of the agreement for 300,000 shares for which Pitfield issued a cheque payable to United Trust for $2,400,000; the second, in October, 1972, for the remaining 25,000 shares for which Pitfield issued a cheque payable to United Trust for $200,000. On the date of the first transaction, United Trust issued a cheque to Pitfield in payment of the 541/2 commission in the amount of $162,000, and for the same purpose, issued a cheque in the amount of $13,500 on the date of the second transaction.

On the basis that these payments represented the cost of issuing the shares to the public, United Trust in filing its 1972-73-74 and 1975 returns, treated the amounts as eligible capital expenditures within the meaning [in subsection 14(5)] of the *Income Tax Act* and claimed 10% of one-half of $175,000 as a deduction in those years. ...

In disallowing the deduction, the Minister contended that United Trust had never actually made an outlay or expense and that the 541/2 per share was simply a discount or reduction in the purchase price. ...

The evidence discloses that in 1972, United Trust had carried on negotiations with more than one broker but, ultimately, negotiated an agreement with Pitfield to underwrite an issue of 325,000 shares at a price of $8 each, with a commission of 541/2 per share. Both the share price and the commission were arrived at after extensive negotiations between the parties. The purpose of the transaction was, beyond any question, to achieve a distribution of the shares to the public and there is some evidence that the plaintiff had requested, even insisted on, as broad as possible a distribution, particularly to financial institutions with the intent of increasing its potential clientele. ...

Returning then to [the definition of "eligible capital expenditure" in subsection 14(5)]. I find that United Trust, in 1972, issued 325,000 shares all of which were purchased by the public at $8 per share, a capital transaction entered into for the purpose of gaining or producing income from the business. In connection with the share issue, United Trust entered into an agreement with Pitfield, pursuant to which Pitfield served as a distribution vehicle by taking title from United Trust in two certificates and issuing new certificates to the individual purchasers but which involved a number of other services to United Trust including advice in establishing the $8 price, public identification as underwriter at that price and a successful sales promotion, as a result of which the issue was fully taken up by the public. The 541/2 per share commission negotiated between the parties constituted compensation to Pitfield for all such services rendered and was therefore a cost of the share issue, and as such, an expense to United Trust in 1972, in the amount of $175,500, clearly an eligible capital expenditure within the meaning of [subsection 14(5)(b)].

Accordingly, the appeal is allowed and the matter is referred back to the Minister for the appropriate reassessment for the taxpayer's 1972-73-74 and 1975 taxation years. The plaintiff is entitled to costs.

The decision was affirmed by the Federal Court of Appeal, [1983] C.T.C. 159, 83 D.T.C. 5172. The specific expenses in issue are now treated as a deductible expense under paragraph 20(1)(e).

THE QUEEN v. SASKATOON DRUG & STATIONERY COMPANY LIMITED
[1978] C.T.C. 578, 78 D.T.C. 6396 (F.C.T.D.)

[In 1969, the taxpayer purchased seven drugstores in Regina as going concerns. In addition to the tangible assets, inventory and fixtures, for which it paid $353,980, the taxpayer acquired a number of rights and intangible assets, to which no portion of the $290,000 balance of the purchase price was specifically attributed. These included: the leases assigned or granted by the vendor; the vendor's agreement not to compete for five years; the right of first refusal to buy a chain of convenience stores operated by the vendor; non-assignable rights of first refusal to buy, during the terms of the leases, the properties leased as the Rexall, Broad Street and Lorne (R, B and L) stores; and the right to use the vendor's trade name. The agreement also contained a "fire clause" which provided that in the event of total destruction of the R, B and L stores, the vendor would pay to the purchaser, by way of liquidated damages, the proportionate share of $30,000 in respect of the lease covering the R store, the proportionate share of $120,000 in respect of the lease covering the B store, and the proportionate share of $35,000 in respect of the lease covering the L store, provided that the purchaser was still carrying on business on the premises when they were destroyed by fire. The "proportionate share" was defined as the number of whole months remaining in the term of the lease at the date of the total destruction divided by 60. Immediately upon closing the transaction, the taxpayer disposed of four of the seven stores. The value of the goodwill applicable to the three remaining stores was $207,500, an amount which was shown in the taxpayer's books as "premiums on lease purchased". In computing its income in the 1969 and 1970 taxation years, the taxpayer claimed capital cost allowance on the $207,500 on the basis that it was a leasehold interest within the meaning of Class 13 of Schedule B to the Regulations, and also sought to deduct legal and other expenses incurred in the purchase of the drugstores. The Minister disallowed the claim for capital cost allowance on the basis that the $207,500 was paid for goodwill not attributable to the leases, nor for a leasehold interest, and further disallowed the taxpayer's claim for a deduction for expenses incurred in acquiring the drugstores. The taxpayer

appealed, arguing that the lease assigned in respect of the South Albert Street store and the lease given to the purchaser by the vendor in respect of the Broad Street store were especially favourable, and that any goodwill associated with these locations was part of the leasehold interest, and that therefore the $207,500 was paid as a premium for the leases because of these factors and was a leasehold interest upon which it could claim capital cost allowance. The Board held that an amount of 50 per cent of the sum of $207,500 was paid for the leasehold interest and could be written off accordingly. The Minister appealed and the taxpayer cross-appealed.]

Mahoney J.:

... [W]hile ... the South Albert lease was a relatively favourable lease from a tenant's point of view, the evidence does not establish that it was so favourable, in relation to the market, that a prospective tenant would pay anything for it over and above the assumption of the tenant's obligations under it. [Similarly] the evidence does not establish that the Board Street lease was so favourable to the tenant, relative to the market, that a prospective sub-lessee would pay anything for it beyond assumption of the tenant's obligations under it. ...

The only evidence I have as to the local [i.e. locational] goodwill attaching to the South Albert store is the opinion of the plaintiff's expert, Catty, that it was $67,500. ... I accept $67,500 as the correct figure. ...

As to the Broad Street store, the evidence establishes clearly that there was, in fact, a particular advantage to its location. That advantage had a value. ... If the store had been totally destroyed a moment after closing and, in consequence, the lease had terminated, the defendant would have been entitled to recover $120,000 of the $290,000 paid for goodwill. That $120,000 was intended to compensate the defendant for something intangible it had bought from McNeill and would lose as a result of the lease's termination. ... It would have lost only two intangible assets: its right of first refusal on the sale of the Broad Street property and its right to operate its drugstore at that location for the next 25 years.

The $120,000 figure had been arrived at in a process of hard bargaining between parties dealing at arm's length, both professionally advised and both knowledgeable of the location and of the business conducted and to be conducted thereon. The agreement is conclusive that $120,000 was the value of those two intangible assets. [Since] the value of the right of first refusal was, at best, nominal, ... I accept, as did Catty, that the $120,000 ... was paid entirely for ... goodwill of location. ...

I am unable to divorce the goodwill of a location from the other advantages accruing to the person entitled to possession of that location. When it accrues under a lease, it is part of the leasehold interest and the price paid for it is part of the capital cost of that leasehold interest.

There is no basis for disturbing the assessment disallowing the claimed deduction of the expenses incurred in negotiating the McNeill transaction. ...

The defendant's 1969 and 1970 income tax returns will be referred back to the Minister for reassessment on the basis that $187,500 was the capital cost of the leasehold interests ... in respect of which the defendant is entitled to claim capital cost allowance. The remaining $20,000 in issue was not proved to have been paid for any leasehold interest.

Appeal dismissed.

Cross-appeal allowed in part.

Questions

1. Why would a taxpayer prefer to treat a capital outlay as subject to the CCA system, rather than as an eligible capital expenditure?
2. The *Saskatoon Drug* case discusses the problem of goodwill of location. What other kinds of goodwill are there?
3. What problems in valuing goodwill might occur when a business is sold?

7

Capital Gains

I. PREFERENTIAL TAX RATE FOR CAPITAL GAINS

Capital gains currently receive more favourable tax treatment than most forms of employment, business or property income. A capital gain may occur on the sale of a capital property such as shares or land held as an investment. Similarly, a capital gain may arise in a business context such as upon the sale of a fixed capital asset used in a business. In the personal context, a capital gain may arise on the sale of a valuable painting held for investment or enjoyment. In each case the gain is treated as capital for tax purposes, but to the individual taxpayer, there is not necessarily any qualitative difference between the financial benefit of receiving a capital gain as distinct from receiving other types of income — the taxpayer receives something of equivalent economic value. Yet history and current policy dictate that a capital gain is different from other income gains for tax purposes, and is subject to its own particular set of rules.

Until the 1971 tax reform, capital gains were completely outside the definition of income and were therefore exempt from tax. Capital losses were correspondingly not deductible. The path by which capital gains and losses were brought into the calculation of taxable income began with the *Report of the Royal Commission on Taxation* in 1966. The Commission took the view that a capital gain was just as much an accretion to a taxpayer's wealth as ordinary income was — or, to quote the popular catch-phrase that was used to sum up the Commission's thinking, "a buck is a buck is a buck".

The Commission buttressed this premise by identifying three principal policy reasons for taxing capital gains. First, it results in greater equity. Horizontal equity is improved because the taxpayer who realizes a $1,000 capital gain on the stock market is put more nearly in the same tax position as the taxpayer who earns $1,000 from employment. Vertical equity is enhanced because rich taxpayers deriving a large part of their income from capital transactions are made to assume a more appropriate burden of taxation as compared with poorer taxpayers earning their livelihood from employment. Secondly, it makes the tax system more neutral by reducing the incentive for taxpayers to structure their transactions to look like capital transactions rather than income-producing transactions. For example, before 1972, the fact that capital gains were tax-free encouraged shareholders in companies with substantial accumulated surpluses to sell their shares rather than receive the surplus in the form of dividends. The gain on the shares was a tax-free capital gain whereas the dividends were taxable income (albeit subject to a dividend tax credit). This problem was revived in 1985 with the introduction of the lifetime capital gains exemption. More stringent anti-avoidance rules were enacted as a result. The third policy factor that the Commission emphasized was certainty. The notoriously elusive distinction between capital gains and business income would cease to be significant if capital gains were taxable in full. According to the *Report of the Royal Commission* (Vol. 3, at 336), the change "would render obsolete the many guidelines that have been established over the years for determining what was in the taxpayer's mind, an exercise which was at its best unsatisfactory, and at its worst an arbitrary, inequitable and capricious way to determine tax liability".

In the 1969 White Paper, *Proposals for Tax Reform*, the government opened its case on capital gains circumspectly:

> [A]lthough the government does not accept the "buck is a buck" theory in all its splendid simplicity, neither does it believe that the distinction between a so-called "capital gain" and an income receipt is either great enough or clear enough to warrant the tremendous difference between being completely exempt and being completely taxable.

The government's proposal was for full inclusion of capital gains, except for gains on principal residences and personal-use property, which would be partly exempt, and gains on shares of widely-held Canadian corporations, which would be included in income only to the extent of one-half. The last type of gain would also be subject to a special deemed realization every time the taxpayer owning the shares reached an age divisible by five (an "unhappy birthday"). Deemed realization every five years would reduce taxpayers' control over the timing of gain or loss, and would reduce the "lock- in" effect of reluctance to sell successful investments with overly large accrued gains that were liable to be triggered by a sale. Taxpayers could refer to the financial pages for valuations of publicly-traded shares, but might be forced to sell investments simply to raise cash to pay tax owing on unrealized "paper" gains. Capital losses would be fully deductible on all property except principal residences and most other property held for personal use, and would be one-half deductible in the case of shares of widely-held Canadian corporations.

The public generally, and provincial governments and the Commons Committee in particular, were opposed to the full taxation of capital gains, primarily on the ground that such a tax burden would discourage investment both by individuals and by corporations. The government was persuaded to abandon the proposals for full inclusion and to settle for inclusion of half the gain. Only one-half of a capital loss would be deductible, however. The one-half inclusion would apply to the disposition of all forms of capital property, making the effective tax rate on capital gains 50 per cent of that on other income. The government also gave up the proposal for quinquennial revaluation of shares of widely-held Canadian corporations. The adoption of a preferential rate of inclusion for all capital gains meant that the distinction between income and capital gains remained important, and that the simplification that the Commission saw as one of the great benefits of eliminating the distinction was lost.

A further step away from the neutral treatment of capital gains was taken in 1985, with the introduction of a lifetime exemption for capital gains realized by individuals. The avowed purpose was to "encourage risk-taking and investment in small and large businesses and to assist farmers". Until 1994 the deduction was not restricted to gains on investment properties and farm property, but extended to gains on the disposition of any capital property, including personal-use property and property situated abroad (although certain real property was excluded from the exemption in 1992). In 1987, the capital gains deduction was capped at $100,000 (with the exception of shares in small business corporations and family farms) and, in 1994, completely abolished (again with the exception of those two types of property). In more recent years, the lifetime capital gains exemption entered an expansive phase. Fishing property was added to farm property and shares in a small business corporation in 2006. In 2007, the upper limit was increased to $750,000 from $500,000 (equivalent to $375,000 of otherwise taxable capital gains). For 2014, the upper limit was raised to $800,000 of capital gains on the three types of property (or $400,000 of taxable capital gains). For 2015 onwards, the upper limit is indexed for inflation.

While the inclusion rates applicable to capital gains and losses appeared to be moving towards neutrality, that trend was reversed in 2000. From 1972 to 1987, the rate of inclusion of capital gains and losses was one-half of the gain or loss. As a result of the 1987 federal budget, the rate of inclusion rose to two-thirds in 1988 and 1989, and to three-quarters from 1990. However, the 2000 budget reduced the inclusion rate for capital gains and losses to two-thirds for dispositions after February 28, 2000 and the October 18, 2000 economic statement reduced the inclusion rate back to one-half. The 2000 budget papers stated that the reduction was necessary to respond to lower rates of capital gains taxation elsewhere (particularly the United States), and to further encourage risk-taking in Canada.

The one-half inclusion rate means that capital gains are taxed at half the effective rates of tax applicable to such forms of investment (property) income as interest, rents, and royalties. Changes to the tax regime on dividends from Canadian public companies, introduced in 2006, have lowered the effective rate of tax on these dividends below that on capital gains at all marginal rates, except for the highest marginal rates where the tax on capital gains and dividends is roughly equivalent.

Capital losses receive less tax relief than other types of losses because, with one exception, capital losses are deductible only from capital gains, and not from any other type of income. Allowable business investment losses, which may be deducted against ordinary income, recognize the need for more generous tax relief for losses on venture capital investments in small businesses (paragraphs 3(d) and 38(c)). Allowable business investment losses (capital losses on shares or debt issued by small businesses) are deductible from all sources of income. However, with the reduction of the capital gains inclusion rate to one-half, the preference attached to allowable business investment losses was similarly reduced.

There is no question that the taxation of capital gains since 1972 has improved the equity of the Canadian tax system, because capital gains are a source of income enjoyed primarily by the wealthy. The regime of capital gains taxation at any particular time reflects a constantly shifting balance of conflicting policy considerations. Fundamentally, the goal of taxing capital gains is the improvement of tax equity. Other goals conflict with this objective, and have largely overtaken it, however. Encouragement of such activities as home ownership, small business, farms and fishing, savings for retirement, and investing in securities have undercut the equity of capital gains taxation, and reduced its significance. The tax preference for capital gains, consisting of the one-half rate of inclusion is a significant tax expenditure that benefits primarily higher-income taxpayers. Few issues in tax policy have been the topic of as much debate and rhetoric, both political and academic.

II. DISTINCTION BETWEEN ORDINARY INCOME AND CAPITAL AMOUNTS

A. Significance of the Distinction and its Conceptual Basis

Undoubtedly, the greatest amount of jurisprudence in tax law concerns the question of whether a gain or loss is of an income or capital nature. The uncertainty arises, in part, because the *Income Tax Act* (the "Act") does not define "income". Rather, it simply describes "income" and provides some rules with respect to what is included in that term (section 3). Similarly, a capital gain is defined only insofar as the legislation states that a capital gain is not income from a source within the meaning of section 3 or section 56 (paragraph 39(1)(a)).

REPORT OF THE ROYAL COMMISSION ON TAXATION, 1966

Volume III, at 62-67

The Distinction Between Capital and Income

One of the fundamental rules of the present Canadian system is that a distinction must be drawn between gains of an income and those of a capital nature. Only the former are brought into tax. Capital gains have never been taxed under Canadian income tax law, although some gains that had at certain times been regarded as being of a capital nature have lost that character by legislative amendments or by court decisions. The exclusion of capital gains from tax is not provided for in the legislation, and the terms "capital" or "capital gains" are not defined therein; but the principle of the exclusion is clearly established in decisions of the courts.

The most important application of this general rule is that gains arising from the disposition of property, other than in the course of business, are not ordinarily taxable.

However there are many types of gains that do not necessarily arise from the disposition of property but which may be treated as being of a capital nature and are therefore not regarded as income. Thus, compensation for loss of an office or employment, which is now treated as income, was not originally taxable. However, by statutory provision, retiring allowances which include compensation for loss of office or employment must be brought into income. The proceeds of life insurance policies are ordinarily treated as capital receipts. Also, the position under the decided cases appears to be that under most circumstances if indebtedness of a business nature is forgiven, the amount forgiven is not income of the debtor.

Many other amounts may be treated as income or capital, depending on the circumstances; examples are premiums for the granting of leases, discounts or premiums on loans, amounts received as a result of the breach or cancellation of a contract, the proceeds of insurance (apart from life insurance), foreign exchange profits, payments of damages, government subsidy payments, and the proceeds of expropriation of property. This list is by no means exhaustive. In many cases difficulties have arisen in determining whether particular gains, in the circumstances of particular cases, are properly regarded as being of an income or of a capital nature, and disputes of this sort continue to arise.

...

Influence of the United Kingdom

In considering the Canadian tax system, it is desirable to keep in mind that it has been greatly influenced by the tax system of the United Kingdom. Income tax was introduced in the United Kingdom in 1799 and has been imposed there without interruption since 1842. The word income is not defined in the legislation, but the tax applies to income from particular sources and to other designated types of receipts. There are basic similarities, although there are also significant differences, between the tax bases in the two countries. The United Kingdom legislation as amended over the years has been extensively interpreted in judicial decisions. These decisions have had persuasive effect in the Canadian courts, with the result that many of the principles and rules established in United Kingdom jurisprudence have been followed in Canada. The same is true to a lesser extent of decisions of tribunals in other parts of the Commonwealth.

...

The distinction between amounts of an income nature and those of a capital nature for tax purposes was established in the United Kingdom long before income tax was first imposed in Canada. Even there, however, the basis for the distinction is not entirely clear. It may be that introduction of an income tax in that country when its economy was primarily agricultural gave rise to the view that income was the yield from a productive source. The British came to regard the basic sources of income, that is, property, businesses, and offices and employment, as things which were inherently productive of income, and as being capital substances from which income emerged. The source itself and the proceeds of a disposition of such a source were capital and not subject to income tax; it was the yield from the source which was income and subject to tax. The analogy often used was that of the fruit and the tree. The fruit (or its value) was income, but the tree (or the proceeds of its disposition) was capital and not income.

...

In the United Kingdom, gifts, inheritances and windfalls have not been subject to income tax. Here again, the reason for their original exclusion is not clear, although a contributing factor may have been that gifts and windfalls did not emanate from a specified source held by the recipient. In any event the Canadian practice has again followed that of the United Kingdom.

...

Appraisal of Present System

The present Canadian tax system, when examined from the point of view of what is brought into tax, is seriously defective in many respects.

The Act does not contain, nor have the courts in interpreting the legislation evolved, any clear, consistent concept of income. What is brought into income is determined under a collection of rules which have been developed over a period of time, to a considerable extent on an *ad hoc* basis; some of them are statutory, others are based on the practice of the tax authorities in administering the legislation, and still others are based on judicial interpretation of the statutes.

It is clear that many items which increase the economic power of the recipient, that is, his ability to pay, and which in our view should in equity be taxed, are not included in the present income tax base. These include, as we have noted, certain gains from the disposition of property, other capital receipts, the proceeds of life insurance, the benefit arising from the forgiveness of business indebtedness, gifts, inheritances and windfall receipts. Other illustrations of exclusions from the tax base and of the preferential treatment of particular types of income will appear in the chapters which follow. The omission of these items from the present tax base is, we are convinced, most inequitable.

It is not surprising in the circumstances that great uncertainty has existed over the years as to what receipts, gains and benefits are properly regarded as being of an income nature for tax purposes. This has led to continual litigation and to frequent changes in the statute law. It has also meant that in many instances the form rather than the substance of a transaction has been important for tax purposes. By careful attention to matters of form, liability to tax has been avoided or minimized. To cite a simple example, the sale of the assets of a company may lead to substantial tax, while the sale of the shares of the company will ordinarily result in a tax-free gain. We believe that these difficulties, and the resultant inequities of the present system, cannot be overcome without radical changes in the present system. What is required is a new comprehensive tax base.

...

B. Drawing the Distinction: Characterization of a Transaction as an Adventure or Concern in the Nature of Trade

Most of the cases dealing with the distinction between business income and capital gain turn on whether a transaction can be characterized as an "adventure or concern in the nature of trade" within the definition of "business" in subsection 248(1). The following Interpretation Bulletin issued by the Canada Revenue Agency (the "CRA") is a convenient summary of the jurisprudence on the characterization of a gain or loss as an ordinary income amount arising from an adventure in the nature of trade. Following the Interpretation Bulletin, a few of the leading cases on the distinction between capital gains and ordinary income are excerpted.

INTERPRETATION BULLETIN IT-459 (ARCHIVED)
September 8, 1980

Adventure or Concern in the Nature of Trade

1. It is a general principle that when a person habitually does a thing that is capable of producing a profit, then he is carrying on a trade or business notwithstanding that these activities may be quite separate and apart from his ordinary occupation. An example is that of a dentist who habitually buys and sells real estate.

2. Where such a thing is done only infrequently, or possibly only once, rather than habitually, it still is possible to hold that the person has engaged in a business transaction if, in accordance with the definition of "business" in subsection 248(1), it can be shown that he has engaged in "an adventure or concern in the nature of trade". That phrase has been interpreted in numerous decisions of the Courts and some of those decisions, where the transactions involved real estate, are reflected in IT-218, entitled ["Profit, Capital Gains and Losses from the Sale of Real Estate."]

3. Although an adventure or concern in the nature of trade is included in the definition of the term "business" in section 248, it does not necessarily mean that a taxpayer who is engaged in an adventure or concern in the nature of

trade is "carrying on" a business or has "carried on" a business. Where these phrases are used in the Act, a determination is made based on the degree of activity and each situation must be considered in the light of its own particular facts.

4. In determining whether a particular transaction is an adventure or concern in the nature of trade the Courts have emphasized that all the circumstances of the transaction must be considered and that no single criterion can be formulated. Generally, however, the principal tests that have been applied are as follows:

(a) whether the taxpayer dealt with the property acquired by him in the same way as a dealer in such property ordinarily would deal with it;

(b) whether the nature and quantity of the property excludes the possibility that its sale was the realization of an investment or was otherwise of a capital nature, or that it could have been disposed of other than in a transaction of a trading nature; and

(c) whether the taxpayer's intention, as established or deduced, is consistent with other evidence pointing to a trading motivation.

Comments on the significance of the above tests appear below under the headings "Taxpayer's Conduct," "Nature of the Property" and "Taxpayer's Intention."

Taxpayer's Conduct

5. The primary consideration is whether the taxpayer's actions in regard to the property in question were essentially what would be expected of a dealer in such a property. What is required, therefore, is to compare what dealers in the same kind of property ordinarily do with what the taxpayer did when he purchased the property, when he sold it and during the time when it was in his possession. Where the property is real estate, some relevant factors are set out in IT-218.

6. Evidence that efforts were soon made to find or attract purchasers or that a sale took place within a short period of time after the acquisition of the property by the taxpayer points to a trading intention.

7. During the time the taxpayer owned the property it is significant whether steps were taken with the intended result of improving its marketability. Where the property consisted of an operating business, such steps might involve various changes in the way the business was operated so as to improve the profit potential. The listing of the business for sale when the improved marketability was achieved would suggest that the business had not been acquired as an investment but had been acquired, improved and offered for sale in a manner similar to procedures followed by a dealer in businesses.

8. The fact that the taxpayer has a commercial background in similar areas or has had previous experience of a similar commercial nature has been held to be a pertinent consideration in some circumstances.

Nature of the Property

9. Where property acquired by a taxpayer is of such a nature or of such a magnitude that it could not produce income or personal enjoyment to its owner by virtue of its ownership and the only purpose of the acquisition was a subsequent sale of the property, the presumption is that the purchase and sale was an adventure or concern in the nature of trade. This was a finding of the courts for instance, where the property acquired was a large quantity of one kind of goods.

10. The property acquired may be capable of producing income but only if the taxpayer is in a position to operate or lease it, as for example, a cargo ship. If the taxpayer is not in a position to operate it and could make use of it only by selling it, the presumption again would be that the purchase and subsequent sale was an adventure or concern in the nature of trade.

11. Some kinds of property (e.g., a business, a security) are prima facie of an investment nature in that they are normally used to produce income through their operation or mere possession. Where property is of this kind and the taxpayer was in a position, if he so wished, to have operated or held it but he chose to sell it, then the manner in which he dealt with it and the intention when he acquired it must be the governing factors in deciding whether the transaction was an adventure or concern in the nature of trade.

Taxpayer's Intention

12. A taxpayer's intention to sell at a profit is not sufficient, by itself, to establish that he was involved in an adventure or concern in the nature of trade. That intention is almost invariably present even when a true investment has been acquired, if circumstances should arise that would make it financially more beneficial to sell the investment than to continue to hold it. Where, however, one or other of the above tests clearly suggests an adventure or concern in the nature of trade, and, in addition, it can be established or inferred that the taxpayer's intention was to sell the property at the first suitable opportunity, intention will be viewed as corroborative evidence. On the other hand, inability to establish an intention to sell does not preclude a transaction from being regarded as an adventure or concern in the nature of trade if it can otherwise be so regarded pursuant to one of the above tests.

13. It must be recognized that a taxpayer may have more than one intention when a property is acquired. If the primary intention is said to be the holding of the property as an investment, regard must be had to whether, at the time of the acquisition, there was a secondary intention to sell the property if the primary intention could not be fulfilled. Secondary intention is particularly

significant when the circumstances suggest that there was little likelihood of the property being retained by the taxpayer because of a lack of financial resources or for some other reason. Further, a taxpayer's intentions are not limited to the purposes for acquiring the property but extend to the time at which the disposition was made. A taxpayer's intention, if any, at the time of acquisition of the property may change at any time during ownership and up to disposition because the taxpayer may form an intention or otherwise change or abandon the primary, dominant or secondary intention with respect to the property.

Isolated Transactions

14. The following factors, in and of themselves, are not sufficient to prevent a finding that a transaction was an adventure or concern in the nature of trade:

(a) the transaction was a single or isolated one;

(b) the taxpayer did not create any organization to carry out the transaction;

(c) the transaction is totally different from any of the other activities of the taxpayer and he never entered into such a transaction either before or since.

Losses

15. A taxpayer who embarks on what is established as an adventure or concern in the nature of trade may suffer a loss rather than the anticipated gain. Such a loss constitutes a loss from business and enters into the calculation of the taxpayer's non-capital loss for the year.

...

CALIFORNIAN COPPER SYNDICATE v. HARRIS

(1904), 6 F. (Ct. of Sess.) 894, 41 S.L.R. 691, 5 T.C. 159 (Scot. Ct. of Ex.)

The Lord Justice Clerk: ... It is quite a well settled principle in dealing with questions of assessment of Income Tax, that where the owner of an ordinary investment chooses to realise it, and obtains a greater price for it than he originally acquired it at, the enhanced price is not profit in the sense of Schedule D of the Income Tax Act of 1842 assessable to Income Tax. But it is equally well established that enhanced values obtained from realisation or conversion of securities may be so assessable, where what is done is not merely a realisation or change of investment, but an act done in what is truly the carrying on, or carrying out, of a business. The simplest case is that of a person or association of persons buying and selling lands or securities speculatively, in order to make gain, dealing in such investments as a business, and thereby seeking to make profits. There are many companies which in their very inception are formed for such a purpose, and in these cases it is not doubtful that, where they make a gain by a realisation, the gain they make is liable to be assessed for Income Tax.

What is the line which separates the two classes of cases may be difficult to define, and each case must be considered according to its facts; the question to be determined being — Is the sum of gain that has been made a mere enhancement of value by realising a security, or is it a gain made in an operation of business in carrying out a scheme for profit-making?

This Syndicate was formed with a capital of £30,000, *inter alia*, to acquire copper and other mines, and certain mines named in particular, and to prospect and explore for the purpose of obtaining information, and to enter into treaties, contracts, and engagements with respect to mines, mining rights, and a number of other matters in the United States and elsewhere. It was also to carry on mercantile, commercial, financing and trading businesses, and to work minerals, to establish and form companies for such objects, to subscribe for purchase, or otherwise acquire, shares or stock of any company, and accept payment in shares for property sold or business undertaken or services rendered, and to hold, sell, or dispose of the same, to promote companies for the purpose of acquiring the undertaking, property, and liabilities of the Company, or carrying on business deemed conducive to the prosperity of the Company.

These are shortly some of the main purposes of the Company, and they certainly point distinctly to a highly speculative business, and the mode of their actual procedure was in the same direction. Of the £28,332 realised by shares which were subscribed for, £24,000 was invested in a copper-bearing field in the United States, and the balance was spent in development of the field, and in preliminary and head office expenses.

The Company then was successful in selling the property to the Fresno Company — 300,000 in fully paid up shares being given by the Fresno Company for the property. Although that was a sale, the price to be paid in shares, I feel compelled to hold that this Company was in its inception a Company endeavouring to make profit by a trade or business, and that the profitable sale of its property was not truly a substitution of one form of investment for another. It is manifest that it never did intend to work this mineral field with the capital at its disposal. Such a thing was quite impossible. Its purpose was to exploit the field, and obtain gain by inducing others to take it up on such terms as would bring substantial gain to themselves. This was that the turning of investment to account was not to be merely incidental, but was ... the essential feature of the business, speculation being among the appointed means of the Company's gains.

In these circumstances I am of the opinion that the finding of the Commissioners was right.

Notes and Questions

1. What relevance is the fact that the taxpayer is a corporation? In *Canadian Marconi Company v. The Queen*, [1986] 2 C.T.C. 465, 86 D.T.C. 6526, the Supreme Court held that, where income is received or generated by an activity done in pursuit of an object set out in the corporation's articles of incorporation, there is a rebuttable presumption that such income is from a business.
2. In *Friesen v. The Queen*, [1995] 2 C.T.C. 369, 95 D.T.C. 5551 (S.C.C.), Major J. said that the first requirement of an adventure in the nature of trade is a transaction of purchase and sale involving a "scheme for profit-making".

REGAL HEIGHTS LIMITED v. M.N.R.
[1960] C.T.C. 384, 60 D.T.C. 1270 (S.C.C.)

[A businessperson learned that a property site in Calgary, bordering the proposed route of the Trans-Canada Highway, was for sale. Thinking the site ideal for a shopping centre, the individual formed a partnership with several other associates, purchasing the land on September 8, 1952. The association later incorporated itself as Regal Heights Limited, the appellant. Inquiries were made among commercial firms for possible tenants of the shopping centre, further property was purchased to facilitate traffic conditions around the proposed enterprise and other steps were taken to forward the venture until September 1954. At that time a national company announced plans to build a shopping centre only two miles from the appellant's property. Consultants previously retained to advise on the matter informed the appellant that under these circumstances it was impractical to build the shopping centre on the company's land. The appellant's land was therefore sold in three lots at a profit of some $140,000, which was treated by the company as a capital gain. The Minister, however, regarded it as income. The Tax Appeal Board dismissed the appeal. The Exchequer Court dismissed a further appeal and the company appealed to the Supreme Court of Canada.]

Judson J.: ...

The question is whether the appellant's profit from the sale of this real estate in the 1955 taxation year was profit derived from a venture or concern in the nature of trade and was therefore income from a business within the meaning of Sections 3, 4 and 139(1)(e) of the *Income Tax Act,* R.S.C. 1952, c. 148.

There is no doubt that the primary aim of the partners in the acquisition of these properties, and the learned trial judge so found, was the establishment of a shopping centre but he also found that their intention was to sell at a profit if they were unable to carry out their primary aim. It is the second finding which the appellant attacks as a basis for the taxation of the profit as income. The Minister, on the other hand, submits that this finding is just as strong and valid as the first finding and that the promoters had this secondary intention from the beginning.

The appellant adduced much evidence concerning the efforts of the promoters to establish what was described as a "regional shopping centre." This means the largest of this type of enterprise and requires an area of from 30 to 60 acres. These promoters undoubtedly had the necessary land but a scheme of this kind involves an expenditure of anything from $2,000,000 to $5,000,000 and its financing and establishment depend upon the negotiation of leases with satisfactory tenants, and above all, upon the negotiation of a lease with a major department store as the centre of attraction.

It is necessary to set out the efforts made by the promoters to develop this property in this way. The acquisition of the two additional properties, the one for the purpose of easy access and the other for the purpose of advertising the centre, fits into the scheme. In February 1953 they secured a favourable opinion from the Calgary Planning Board that the property would be rezoned from residential to commercial purposes although the Board withheld formal approval until there should be some indication that construction would begin. In addition, they had sketches made to show what the centre would look like. These sketches were no more than promotional literature. They made studies of other shopping centres; with professional help they compiled lists of prospective tenants; they entered into discussions with four department stores, although the evidence shows that there was only one which might possibly be interested; they had discussions with one of the banks concerning the financing of the project; they had a special survey made at a fee of $3,000 for the purpose of influencing one particular department store; and they incorporated this company.

These efforts were all of a promotional character. The establishment of a regional shopping centre was always dependent upon the negotiation of a lease with a major department store. There is no evidence that any such store did anything more than listen to the promoters' ideas. There is, understandably, no evidence of any intention on the part of these promoters to build regardless of the outcome of these negotiations. There is no evidence that these promoters had any assurance when they entered upon this venture that they could interest any such department store. Their venture was entirely speculative. If it failed, the property was a valuable property, as is proved from the proceeds of the sales that they made. There is ample evidence to support the finding of the learned trial judge that this was an undertaking or venture in the nature of trade, a speculation in vacant land. These promoters were hopeful of putting the land to one use but that hope was not realized. They then sold at a substantial profit and that profit, in my opinion, is income and subject to taxation.

Throughout the existence of the appellant company, its interest and intentions were identical with those of the promoters of this scheme. One of the objects stated in the memorandum of association of the company was

> To construct and operate apartment houses, blocks, shopping centres and to otherwise carry on any business which may be conveniently carried on in a shopping centre.

Nothing turns upon such a statement in such a document. The question to be determined is not what business or trade the company might have carried on but rather what business, if any, it did in fact engage in. *[authority cited]*... What the promoters and the company did and intended to do is clear to me on the evidence, as it was to the learned trial judge. They failed to promote a shopping centre and they then disposed of their speculative property at a profit. This was a venture in the nature of trade and the profit from it is taxable within the meaning of Sections 3, 4 and 139(1)(e) of the *Income Tax Act.* These cases must all depend on their particular facts and there is no analogy between the sale of long-held bona fide capital assets ... and the realization of a profit from this speculative venture in the nature of trade.

[The appeal was dismissed with costs. Fauteux, Martland and Ritchie JJ. concurred; Cartwright J. dissented.]

Notes and Questions

1. In *Riznek Construction Ltd. v. The Queen*, [1979] C.T.C. 197, 79 D.T.C. 5131 (F.C.T.D.), the taxpayer assembled land with the intention of building a shopping plaza. The project was approved by the municipality, subject to compliance with certain planning department requirements. The taxpayer was unable to meet one of the requirements when the owner of a small parcel of land changed his mind at the last moment. The development was frustrated, and the taxpayer sold part of the land for profit in response to an unsolicited offer. The Court held that the profit was not income. There was no evidence of any secondary intention at the time of purchase to resell if development was frustrated, and the transaction was held not to be an adventure in the nature of trade.
2. What is the distinction between the situations in *Riznek Construction* and *Regal Heights*? Could one argue that the sale in *Regal Heights* came about only after the taxpayer's failure to negotiate a lease with a major department store led to the frustration of his shopping centre development? Compare *Regina Shoppers Mall v. M.N.R.*, [1984] C.T.C. 2091, 84 D.T.C. 1081 (T.C.C.) (appeal dismissed [1986] 1 C.T.C. 261, 86 D.T.C. 6091 (F.C.T.D.)), where, in circumstances similar to those in *Regal Heights*, the gains from the sale of property were held to be income. Unlike *Regal Heights*, however, where the Court found a secondary intention to sell at the time of acquisition, the Tax Court in *Regina Shoppers Mall*

seemed to hold that the secondary intention to sell did not arise until the time that the primary intention was frustrated. The development of a secondary intention to sell for profit after the time of acquisition was sufficient to characterize the whole gain as income. The difficulties with the doctrine of secondary intention are perhaps indicated by the fact that on appeal, the Federal Court found a secondary intention at the time of acquisition.

3. Is the Tax Court's decision in *Regina Shoppers Mall* a more accurate characterization of cases where resale occurs only after the primary investment intention is frustrated? In *Hughes v. The Queen*, [1984] C.T.C. 101, 84 D.T.C. 6110 (F.C.T.D.), the taxpayer purchased an apartment building, financing the purchase by a mortgage, as an income-earning investment. In the Court's view, it was clear from the beginning that the mortgage payments would exceed revenue. When it became apparent to the taxpayer that the venture was unlikely to produce income, she successfully applied to have the apartment converted to strata title in order to sell the units individually for profit. The Court accepted that the taxpayer's only intention at the time of acquisition was to hold the apartment as an investment. When that became frustrated, there was a change of intention to one of selling for profit. Unlike *Regina Shoppers Mall*, where a subsequent development of an intention to sell was sufficient to treat the entire gain as income, the Court in *Hughes* ordered an apportionment between income and capital so that only the gain accrued after the change in intention was treated as ordinary income. The other part was treated as a capital gain. See also Interpretation Bulletin IT-218 (archived): Profit, Capital Gains and Losses from the Sale of Real Estate, including Farmland and Inherited Land, and Conversion of Real Estate from Capital Property and Vice Versa (September 16, 1986), paragraphs 10–15.

4. The taxpayer is in the business of operating a chain of retail grocery stores, and does not develop real estate projects. A mall developer offered the taxpayer the potential of a prime location for one of its stores, if it would finance development of the mall in which the store would be located. The taxpayer entered into a joint venture with the developer, to provide the financing, in return for a half-interest in the mall, and a long-term leasehold for its store. From the outset, the taxpayer intended to keep the store but dispose of the joint venture interest, after the mall was developed and its premises leased to tenants. Shortly after the mall was successfully completed, the taxpayer disposed of its joint venture interest to an investor. What principles apply to determine the tax treatment of the gain to the taxpayer on its sale of the half-interest in the mall? See *Canada Safeway Ltd. v. The Queen*, [2008] 2 C.T.C. 149, 2008 D.T.C. 6074 (F.C.A.).

IRRIGATION INDUSTRIES LIMITED v. M.N.R.
[1962] C.T.C. 215, 62 D.T.C. 1131 (S.C.C.)

[The appellant was incorporated in 1947 to purchase farm property and to construct and operate an alfalfa mill in Alberta. This project was never carried out and the company remained dormant for some years. About February 6, 1953, the company purchased 4,000 shares of the common stock of Brunswick Mining and Smelting Corporation Ltd., a company having a number of mining claims in New Brunswick. The appellant arranged to pay for these shares through its bank, which allowed an overdraft of nearly $40,000. The appellant had no other asset at this time. The appellant's president gave evidence that the bank called upon the appellant to pay up its overdraft within two or three weeks of the purchase of the shares, and that between March 10 and March 13, 1953 2,400 of the shares were sold for $38,513.50, which sum was deposited with the bank, paying off the overdraft in full. The remaining 1,600 shares were sold in June 1953 for $28,345, which was credited to a bank loan that the appellant had obtained to purchase certain property.]

... Martland J. (for the majority): The issue in this appeal is as to whether an isolated purchase of shares from the treasury of a corporation and subsequent sale thereof at a profit, not being part of the business carried on by the purchaser of the shares, or in any way related to it, constitutes an adventure in the nature of trade so as to render such profit liable to income tax.

... Cameron J. [in the Exchequer Court] held that there was an adventure in the nature of trade and the basis of his decision is stated as follows:

> On the facts in evidence and drawing what I consider to be the proper inferences therefrom, I have reached the conclusion that the purchase in question was not an investment, but a purely speculative purchase, and was entered into with the intention of disposing of the stock at a profit as soon as there was a reasonable opportunity of so doing. It was therefore an adventure or concern in the nature of trade.

The reasons leading to his conclusion that the purchase was not an investment are:

1. the fact that the appellant borrowed the funds necessary to effect the purchase of the shares;
2. the inference that the nature of Brunswick indicated that its shares were speculative in value and that dividends could not be expected for some years.

With respect, I would not think that the question of whether securities are purchased with the purchaser's own funds, or with money borrowed by him, is a significant factor in determining whether their purchase and subsequent sale is or is not an investment.

Similarly, the fact that there was no immediate likelihood of dividends being paid on the shares should not have much significance, for there are many corporate ventures, financed by the sale of shares to the public, in which immediate payment of dividends may not be anticipated, and yet the purchase of the treasury shares of a company embarking on a new enterprise is a well recognized method of making an investment.

However, assuming that the conclusion was correct that this purchase was speculative in that it was made, not with the intention of holding the securities indefinitely, with a view to dividends, but made with the intention of disposing of the shares at a profit as soon as reasonably possible, does this, in itself, lead to the conclusion that it was an adventure in the nature of trade?

It is difficult to conceive of any case, in which securities are purchased, in which the purchaser does not have at least some intention of disposing of them if their value appreciates to the point where their sale appears to be financially desirable. If this is so, then any purchase and sale of securities must constitute an adventure in the nature of trade, unless it is attempted to ascertain whether the primary intention at the time of purchase is to retain the security or to sell it. This, however, leads to the difficulty mentioned by my brother Cartwright that the question of taxability is to be determined by seeking to ascertain the primary subjective intention of the purchaser at the time of purchase.

I cannot agree that the question as to whether or not an isolated transaction in securities is to constitute an adventure in the nature of trade can be determined solely upon that basis. In my opinion, a person who puts money into a business enterprise by the purchase of the shares of a company on an isolated occasion, and not as a part of his regular business, cannot be said to have engaged in an adventure in the nature of trade merely because the purchase was speculative in that, at that time, he did not intend to hold the shares indefinitely, but intended, if possible, to sell them at a profit as soon as he reasonably could. I think that there must be clearer indications of "trade" than this before it can be said that there has been an adventure in the nature of trade. ...

The positive tests to which [Thorson, P. in *M.N.R. v. Taylor*, *infra*] refers as being derived from the decided cases as indicative of an adventure in the nature of trade are: (1) Whether the person dealt with the property purchased by him in the same way as a dealer would ordinarily do and (2) whether the nature and quantity of the subject-matter of the transaction may exclude the possibility that its sale was the realization of an investment, or otherwise of a capital nature, or that it could have been disposed of otherwise than as a trade transaction.

I will deal first with the second of these tests, which, if applied to the circumstances of the present case, would not, in my opinion indicate that there had been an adventure in the nature of trade.

The nature of the property in question here is shares issued from the treasury of a corporation and we have not been referred to any reported case in which profit from one isolated purchase and sale of shares, by a person not engaged in the business of trading in securities, has been claimed to be taxable. ...

Corporate shares are in a different position because they constitute something the purchase of which is, in itself, an investment. They are not, in themselves, articles of commerce, but represent an interest in a corporation which is itself created for the purpose of doing business. Their acquisition is a well recognized method of investing capital in a business enterprise.

Were the operations involved in the present case ... carried on in the same way as those which are characteristic of ordinary trading in the line of business in which the venture was made?

The only operations of the appellant in the present case were the purchase of 4,000 treasury shares directly from Brunswick and their subsequent sale, presumably through brokers. This is not the sort of trading which would be carried on ordinarily by those engaged in the business of trading in securities. The appellant's purchase was not an underwriting, nor was it a participation in an underwriting syndicate with respect to an issue of securities for the purpose of effecting their sale to the public, and did not have the characteristics of that kind of a venture. What the appellant did was to acquire a capital interest in a new corporate business venture, in a manner which has the characteristics of the making of an investment, and subsequently to dispose, by sale, of that interest.

But it may be contended that persons may make a business merely of the buying and selling of securities, without being traders in securities in the ordinary sense, and that the transactions involved in that kind of business are similar, except in number, to that which occurred here. It has, however, been pointed out in the well known case of *Californian Copper Syndicate v. Harris* (1904), 5 T.C. 159 at 165, that, where the realization of securities is involved, the taxability of enhanced values depends on whether such realization was an action done in the carrying on of a business. In that case the Commissioners had held that the transaction there in question was an adventure or concern in the nature of trade. The judgments on appeal make no reference to that point, but are based on the ground that the turning of the investment to account in that case was not merely incidental, but was the essential feature of the appellant's business. ...

In my opinion, the transaction in question here does not fall within either of the positive tests which the authorities have suggested should be applied.

The only test which was applied in the present case was whether the appellant entered into the transaction with the intention of disposing of the shares at a profit so soon as there was a reasonable opportunity of so doing. Is that a sufficient test for determining whether or not this transaction constitutes an adventure in the nature of trade? I do not think that, standing alone, it is sufficient. I agree with the views expressed on this very point by Rowlatt, J., in *Leeming v. Jones*, [[1930] 1 K.B. 279] at page 284. That case involved the question of the taxability of profits derived from purchase and sale of two rubber estates in the Malay Peninsula. The Commissioners initially found that there was a concern in the nature of trade because the property in question was acquired with the sole object of disposing of it at a profit. Rowlatt, J., sent the case back to the Commissioners and states his reason as follows:

> I think it is quite clear that what the Commissioners have to find is whether there is here a concern in the nature of trade. Now, what they have found they say in these words (I am reading it in short): That the property was acquired with the sole object of turning it over again at a profit, and without any intention of holding the property as an investment. That describes what a man does if he buys a picture that he sees going cheap at Christie's, because he knows that in a month he will sell it again at Christie's. That is not carrying on a trade. Those words will not do as a finding of carrying on a trade or anything else. What the Commissioners must do is to say, one way or the other, was this — I will not say carrying on a trade ... but was it a speculation or a venture in the nature of trade? I do not indicate which way it ought to be, but I commend the Commissioners to consider what took place in the nature of organizing the speculation, maturing the property, and disposing of the property, and when they have considered all that to say whether they think it was an adventure in the nature of trade or not.

The case was returned to the Commissioners who then found as a fact that there had not been a concern in the nature of trade. Ultimately it reached the House of Lords [1930] A.C. 415, where the main issue was as to whether the profits were taxable under Case VI of Schedule D of the *Income Tax Act,* 1918. There is, however, a general statement of principle by Lord Buckmaster, at 420, which aptly applies to the present case, when he says:

> ... an accretion to capital does not become income merely because the original capital was invested in the hope and expectation that it would rise in value; if it does so rise, its realization does not make it income.

In my opinion, therefore, the appeal should be allowed, with costs here and in the Court below, and the matter should be referred to the respondent with the direction that he deduct from the income of the appellant, for the taxation year 1953, the sum of $26,897.50.

[Taschereau and Locke JJ. concurred.].

Cartwright J. dissenting

... On the facts as found by Cameron, J. in the case at bar, the profit realized was not the enhancement in price of an ordinary investment but rather "a gain made in an operation of business in carrying out a scheme for profit-making." To hold otherwise would appear to me to be contrary to the reasoning of the majority in the *Regal Heights case, supra* ...

[Judson J. concurred with Cartwright, J.]

Notes and Questions

1. Was the decision of the majority in *Irrigation Industries* consistent with *Regal Heights*? Was it significant that *Irrigation Industries* concerned a gain from the sale of shares while *Regal Heights* concerned a sale of raw land? See generally, J.W. Dunford, "Profits on the Sale of Shares: Capital Gains or Business Income? A Fresh Look at *Irrigation Industries*" (1987), 35 Can. Tax J. 837.
2. Tax-exemption through a tax-free savings account ("TFSA") applies to corporate shares and other securities, but not to real estate: subsection 207.01(1) ["qualified investment"]. If the holder of the TFSA has a significant interest (10 per cent) in the corporation, its shares are a prohibited investment, with adverse tax consequences to the holder: subsection 207.01(1) ["prohibited investment"].
3. Under subsection 39(4) of the Act, a taxpayer may elect to characterize gains and losses from the disposition of Canadian securities as capital gains and capital losses. Once the election has been made, any gain or loss on a "Canadian security" in that year and every subsequent year is deemed to be a capital gain or capital loss. A "Canadian security" is defined in subsection 39(6) to include shares of corporations resident in Canada and debt issued by persons resident in Canada. Securities that do not qualify for the election are described in Income Tax Regulation section 6200.
4. Subsection 39(5) prohibits a "trader or dealer in securities" and certain other taxpayers (e.g., financial institutions) from making the election. In *The Queen v. Vancouver Art Metal Works Ltd.*, [1993] 1 C.T.C. 346, 93 D.T.C. 5116 (F.C.A.), (leave to appeal refused (1993), 160 N.R. 314n (S.C.C.)), the Federal Court of Appeal held (at paragraph 17) that a taxpayer loses the right to make the election when "... he becomes a trader or dealer, that is to say when his dealings amount to carrying on a business and can no longer be characterized as investor's transactions or mere adventures or concerns in the nature of trade". In making this determination, the court stated (at paragraph 13):

> I have no doubt that a taxpayer who makes it a profession or a business of buying and selling securities is a trader or a dealer in securities within the meaning of paragraph 39(5)(a) of the Act. As Cattanach, J. stated in *Palmer v. Minister of National Revenue*, [[1973] C.T.C. 323, 73 D.T.C. 5248 (F.C.T.D.) at page 325 (D.T.C. 5249)], "it is a badge of trade that a person who habitually does acts capable of producing profits is engaged in a trade or business". It is, however, a question of fact to determine whether one's activities amount to carrying on a trade or business. Each case will stand on its own set of facts. Obviously, factors such as the frequency of the transactions, the duration of the holdings (whether, for instance, it is for a quick profit or a long term investment), the intention to acquire for resale at a profit, the nature and quantity of the securities held or made the subject matter of the transaction, the time spent on the activity, are all relevant and helpful factors in determining whether one has embarked upon a trading or dealing business.

In *Kane v. The Queen* (1994), [1995] 1 C.T.C. 1, 94 D.T.C. 6671 (F.C.T.D.), the taxpayer's special knowledge of the market in which the shares were traded made him a trader or dealer in securities and therefore he could not benefit from the election in 39(4). In *Sandnes v. The Queen*, [2004] 2 C.T.C. 3139, 2004 D.T.C. 2466, the Tax Court said that to characterize a taxpayer as a trader requires a finding of a course of conduct amounting to carrying on a business of buying and selling securities with particular or special knowledge. Relevant factors include intention, frequency of transactions, duration of holdings, nature and quality of securities, time spent and particular knowledge. What effect do the results in these cases have on the scope of an election under subsection 39(4)?

5. Rowlatt J.'s dictum to the effect that the purchase and resale of a painting by auction could result in business income has contemporary application to the CRA's efforts to identify and impose tax on Canadians selling their goods and services over online auction websites: see *eBay Canada Ltd. v. The Queen* (2008), [2009] 2 C.T.C. 141, 2008 D.T.C. 6728 (F.C.A.).

M.N.R. v. JAMES A. TAYLOR
[1956] C.T.C. 189, 56 D.T.C. 1125 (Exch. Ct.)

[The taxpayer was the president and general manager of a company engaged throughout Canada in fabricating various products from non-ferrous metals, including lead. The company was permitted by its parent in the United States to have on hand only a 30-day supply of raw metals and as a result experienced considerable difficulties from time to time due to shortages in supply. In 1949 when lead prices broke sharply and the metal became available abroad, Taylor requested permission from the parent company for the Canadian subsidiary to import foreign lead and to buy it for three months' future delivery. The parent company refused because it was against policy for the Canadian subsidiary to deal in futures. Taylor then asked the

parent company whether he could purchase the lead himself and was granted this permission. He believed that he could obtain the foreign lead and thereby supplement the inadequate Canadian supply. Accordingly, Taylor decided to buy 1,500 tons of lead (22 carloads) himself, sell it to the company and assume personally whatever risk might be involved in the transaction. Lead was duly purchased by Taylor and sold to the company through brokers. Taylor did not himself put up any money for the purchase of the lead. Taylor made a profit on the transaction of $83,712.24 which was assessed to him in 1949 and 1950. The Income Tax Appeal Board allowed the respondent's appeal. The Minister appealed to the Exchequer Court. The issue was whether Taylor's transaction in the lead was an "adventure or concern in the nature of trade" and thereby taxable as income from a business within the meaning of section 3 and paragraph 127(1)(e) of the Income Tax Act, 1948.]

Thorson P.: ...

The case is of considerable importance by reason of the fact that it is the first one in which the meaning of the term "adventure or concern in the nature of trade" falls to be considered by this Court.

... It is, I think, plain from the wording of the Canadian Act, quite apart from any judicial decisions, that the terms "trade" and "adventure or concern in the nature of trade" are not synonymous expressions and it follows that the profit from a transaction may be income from a business within the meaning of Section 3 of the Act, by reason of the definition of business in Section 127(1)(e), even although the transaction did not constitute a trade, provided that it was an adventure or concern in the nature of trade.

... The first definition of "trade" in the United Kingdom cases is that of Lord Davey in *Grainger and Son v. Gough* (1896), 3 R.T.C. 462 at 474. There he said, in his speech in the House of Lords:

> Trade in its largest sense is the business of selling, with a view to profit, goods which the trader has either manufactured or himself purchased.

This definition is only partially helpful. It indicates that "trade" is included in "business" which latter term is of wider import than that of trade in that it embraces any gainful activity, but it does not define the term "trader."

An advance was made by the Lord Justice Clerk (Macdonald) of the Court of Exchequer (Scotland) in the famous case of *Californian Copper Syndicate Limited v. Harris* (1904), 5 T.C. 159. ...

The [*Californian Copper Syndicate*] decision is subject to certain comments. In the first place, I think it is clear that when the Lord Justice Clerk used the expression "scheme of profit-making" he did not imply that the word "scheme" meant a multiplicity of transactions. There could be a scheme of profit-making even if there were only one transaction. The difficulty involved in the term "scheme of profit-making" came before the Court inferentially, if not directly, in *T. Beynon and Co., Limited v. Ogg* (1918), 7 T.C. 215. There a company carrying on business as coal merchants, ship and insurance brokers and as sole selling agents for various collier companies, in which latter capacity it purchased wagons for its clients, made a purchase of wagons on its own account as a speculation and subsequently sold them at a profit. It contended that since the transaction was an isolated one the profit was in the nature of a capital profit on the sale of an investment and should be excluded in computing its liability to income tax. It was held, however, that it was made in the operation of the company's business and properly included in the computation of its profits therefrom. Sankey, J., put the matter thus, at page 132:

> The only question one has to determine is which side the line this transaction falls on. Is it ... in the nature of capital profit on the sale of an investment? Or is it ... a profit made in the operation of the Appellant Company's business?

As I see it, the test thus put is to the same effect and essentially the same as that laid down by the Lord Justice Clerk in the *Californian Copper Syndicate* case (*supra*). ...

The case is also of importance for the stress which the Lord Justice Clerk put on the element of speculation as the determining factor in the decision that the transaction was not the realization of an investment and its transfer into another form but the gaining of profit by the sale of the property and thus a transaction that was characteristic of what a trader would do. This stress on the speculative element is of particular importance when it is coupled with the finding that the sale of a property, which by itself is productive of income and might be regarded as an investment, can be a trade in the property rather than a realization of an investment.

Finally, I must confess that I find it strange that although the Commissioners had denied the Company's appeal against its assessment on the ground that the profits made by it were from a transaction of purchase and sale that was an adventure or concern in the nature of trade and the court was unanimous in the opinion that they were right in their finding, there is not a word in the judgments bearing on what is an adventure or concern in the nature of trade as distinct from what is a trade. But it is obvious, it seems to me, that if the Court considered the transaction in question a trading transaction, as it clearly did, it must, a *fortiori,* be considered as an adventure or concern in the nature of trade, as the Commissioners had found it to be.

I now come to the decision in *C.I.R. v. Livingston et al.* (1926), 11 T.C. 538, in which an attempt was made to define the expression "adventure in the nature of trade." ... While all the judges agreed that the finding of the Commissioners should be reversed the case loses much of the value that it might otherwise have by reason of the divergence in the four reasons for judgment. In my opinion, the Lord President (Clyde) made the most useful contribution to the jurisprudence. At page 542, he said:

> I think the profits of an isolated venture, such as that in which the Respondents engaged, may be taxable under Schedule D provided the venture is "in the nature of trade." I say, "may be," because in my view regard must be had to the character and circumstances of the particular venture. If the venture was one consisting simply in an isolated purchase of some article against an expected rise in price and a subsequent sale of it, it might be impossible to say that the venture was "in the nature of trade"; because the only trade in the nature of which it could participate would be the trade of a dealer in such articles, and a single transaction falls as far short of constituting a dealer's trade as the appearance of a single swallow does of making a summer. The trade of a dealer necessarily consists of a course of dealing, either actually engaged in or at any rate contemplated and intended to continue. But this principle is difficult to apply to ventures of a more complex character such as that with which the present case is concerned.

And then Lord Clyde put the test of whether a venture was in the nature of trade as follows:

> I think the test, which must be used to determine whether a venture such as we are now considering is, or is not, "in the nature of trade," is whether the operations involved in it are of the same kind, and carried on in the same way, as those which are characteristic of ordinary trading in the line of business in which the venture was made. If they are, I do not see why the venture should not be regarded as "in the nature of trade," merely because it was a single venture which took only three months to complete.

And he went on to say that the operations were the same as those which characterized the trade of converting and refitting second-hand articles for sale and that the transaction was "in the nature of trade." Lord Sands took a different view. In his view it was the operation done on the ship that made the transaction a trading one. At page 543 he said:

> But I am disposed to think that it would introduce the element of carrying on a trade if the purchaser were, by himself or his own employees or by a contractor, to carry through a manufacturing process which changed the character of the article.

...

A great step towards clarification of the meaning of the expression under review was taken by the Court of Session in *Rutledge v. C.I.R.* (1929), 14 T.C. 490. There the appellant, who was a moneylender and also interested in a cinema company and other businesses, being in Berlin on business connected with the cinema company, purchased very cheaply a large quantity of toilet paper from a bankrupt German firm and within a short time after his return to London sold the whole consignment to one person at a considerable profit. On being assessed on this profit he appealed to the Commissioners who found that the profit made was liable to assessment as being profit in the nature of trade and the Court unanimously dismissed the appeal from their finding. The judgment of the Lord President (Clyde) is illuminating. ...

> ... But the question here is not whether the appellant's isolated speculation in toilet paper was a trade, but whether it was an "adventure ... in the nature of trade"; and in the opinion referred to I said that, in my opinion, "the profits of an isolated venture ... may be taxable under Schedule D provided the venture is 'in the nature of trade'." I see no reason to alter that opinion. It is no doubt true that the question whether a particular adventure is "in the nature of trade" or not must depend on its character and circumstances, but if ... as in the present case ... the purchase is made for no other purpose except that of resale at a profit, there seems little difficulty in arriving at the conclusion that the deal was "in the nature of trade," though it may be wholly insufficient to constitute by itself a trade.

Then the Lord President put his conclusion clearly, at page 497:

> It seems to me to be quite plain (1) that the Appellant, in buying the large stock of toilet paper, entered upon a commercial adventure or speculation; (2) that this adventure or speculation was carried through in exactly the same way as any regular trader or dealer would carry through any of the adventures or speculations in which it is his regular business to engage; and therefore (3) that the purchase and resale of the toilet paper was an "adventure ... in the nature of trade" within the meaning of the *Income Tax Act,* 1918.

... [T]he singleness or isolation of a transaction cannot be a test of whether it was an adventure in the nature of trade. ... This does not mean that the isolation or singleness of a transaction has no bearing on whether it was a business or trading transaction. On the contrary, it might be a very important factor.

But "trade" is not the same thing as "an adventure in the nature of trade" and a transaction might well be the latter without being the former or constituting its maker a "trader." And whatever merit the singleness or isolation of a transaction may have in determining whether it was a trading or business transaction, it has no place at all in determining whether it was an adventure in the nature of trade. The very word "adventure" implies a single or isolated transaction and it is erroneous to set up its singleness or isolation as an indication that it was not an adventure in the nature of trade. ...

Nor is it essential to a transaction being an adventure in the nature of trade that an organization be set up to carry it into effect. ...

[A] transaction may be an adventure in the nature of trade even though nothing was done to the subject matter of the transaction to make it saleable, as in *C.I.R. v. Livingston et al.* (*supra*).

Likewise, the fact that a transaction is totally different in nature from any of the other activities of the taxpayer and that he has never entered upon a transaction of that kind before or since does not, of itself, take it out of the category of being an adventure in the nature of trade. What has to be determined is the true nature of the transaction and if it is in the nature of trade, the profits from it are subject to tax even if it is wholly unconnected with any of the ordinary activities of the person who entered upon it and he has never entered upon such a transaction before or since.

And a transaction may be an adventure in the nature of trade although the person entering upon it did so without any intention to sell its subject matter at a profit. The intention to sell the purchased property at a profit is not of itself a test of whether the profit is subject to tax, for the intention to make a profit may be just as much the purpose of an investment transaction as of a trading one. Such intention may well be an important factor in determining that a transaction was an adventure in the nature of trade but its presence is not an essential prerequisite to such a determination and its absence does not negative the idea of an adventure in the nature of trade. The considerations prompting the transaction may be of such a business nature as to invest it with the character of an adventure in the nature of trade even without any intention of making a profit on the sale of the purchased commodity. And the taxpayer's declaration that he entered upon the transaction without any intention of making a profit on the sale of the purchased property should be scrutinized with care. It is what he did that must be considered and his declaration that he did not intend to make a profit may be overborne by other considerations of a business or trading nature motivating the transaction.

Consequently, the respondent in the present case cannot escape liability merely by showing that his transaction was a single or isolated one, that it was not necessary to set up any organization or perform any operation on its subject matter to carry it into effect, that it was different from and unconnected with his ordinary activities and he had never entered into such a transaction before or since and that he purchased the lead without any intention of making a profit on its sale to the Company. ...

In addition to the negative propositions established by the cases they also lay down positive guides. There is, in the first place, the general rule that the question whether a particular transaction is an adventure in the nature of trade depends on its character and surrounding circumstances and no single criterion can be formulated.

But there are some specific guides. One of these is that if the transaction is of the same kind and carried on in the same way as a transaction of an ordinary trader or dealer in property of the same kind as the subject matter of the transaction it may fairly be called an adventure in the nature of trade. The decisions of the Lord President in the *Livingston* case (*supra*) and the *Rutledge* case (*supra*) support this view. Put more simply, it may be said that if a person deals with the commodity purchased by him in the same way as a dealer in it would ordinarily do, such a dealing is a trading adventure: *vide* Lord Radcliffe's reasons for judgment in *Edwards v. Bairstow* (*supra*).

And there is the further established rule that the nature and quantity of the subject matter of the transaction may be such as to exclude the possibility that its sale was the realization of an investment or otherwise of a capital nature or that it could have been disposed of otherwise than as a trade transaction: *vide* the reasons for judgment of Lord Sands in the *Rutledge* case (*supra*). And there is the statement of Lord Carmont in the *Reinhold* case *(supra)* that there are cases "where the commodity itself stamps the transaction as a trading venture."

In my opinion, the principles laid down in the *Rutledge* case (*supra*), the *Fraser* case (*supra*) and the *Edwards v. Bairstow* case (*supra*) are applicable to the present case and I have no hesitation in holding that the respondent's purchase and sale of 1,500 tons of lead was an adventure in the nature of trade. I do not see how it could possibly have been anything else. His transaction was certainly an adventure, a bold and imaginative one and highly successful, both for the Company and for himself, and the only question is whether it was in the nature of trade. If the alternatives are whether it was of a capital nature or in the nature of trade I am unable to see how there can be any doubt of which it was. The nature and quantity of its subject matter, namely, 1,500 tons of lead requiring 22 carloads to carry it, excluded any possibility that it was of an investment nature involving the realization of a security or resulted in a fortuitous accretion of capital or was otherwise of a capital nature. It is plain that the respondent had no considerations of a capital nature in mind. The nature and quantity of the subject matter of the transaction were such as to exclude the possibility that it was other than a transaction of a trading nature. The respondent could not do anything with the lead except sell it and he bought it solely for the purpose of selling it to the Company. In my judgment, the words of Lord Carmont in the *Reinhold* case *(supra)* that "the commodity itself stamps the transaction as a trading transaction" apply with singular force to the respondent's transaction.

Moreover, he dealt with the lead in exactly the same manner as any dealer in imported lead would have done. He bought it from abroad and sold it to a user of lead in Canada, namely, the Company. If it had bought the lead it would have been subject to tax on the profit made by it on the sale of its products fabricated from the lead so bought. The respondent merely did what the Company would have done if his judgment in the matter had prevailed. But since the Company was not permitted by the parent company to deal in the lead the respondent dealt in it himself and did so exactly in the same manner as a trader or dealer in imported lead would have done. ... It was a dealing in lead and, as such, it was ... essentially a trading adventure.

It is of no avail to the respondent that when he purchased the lead he did so without any intention of selling it to the Company at a profit. He did not pretend that his purchase was for an investment purpose. All his reasons were business reasons of a trading nature. His adventure was a speculative one. When lead prices broke, others in the industry were unwilling to gamble, but he did not hesitate. He saw advantages of a business nature in the transaction and these outweighed with him the risk of loss which he undertook. He calculated that the advantages outweighed the risk and he deliberately assumed it. He was justified in his speculative venture. The Company got the benefit of a substantial drawback of approximately $30,000. The respondent was rehabilitated with the Company and in his own self esteem. He made up for his remissness in making a bad deal causing a substantial loss to the Company through relying on a verbal agreement with the Canadian supplier. And he succeeded in getting better supply terms from the Canadian supplier. As for himself his venture brought him the personal satisfaction of victory as well as an increase in salary and pension rights. These possible advantages were all contemplated by him. The evidence indicates that he entered into the transaction for a variety of purposes but they were all of a business nature and many of them were similar to those that would have motivated a trader. His transaction was a dealing in lead and nothing else.

I am, therefore, of the opinion that the respondent's transaction was an adventure in the nature of trade within the meaning of Section 127(1)(e) of The 1948 *Income Tax Act,* and that his profit from it was profit from a business within the meaning of Section 3 of the Act and that the Minister was right in including it in the assessment. ...

[The appeal was allowed with costs, except that the amount of profit to be assessed was set at $70,098.80 instead of $83,712.24.]

Notes and Questions

1. The CRA's administrative position concerning the taxation of transactions in commodity futures and certain commodities is set out in Interpretation Bulletin IT-346 (archived): Commodity Futures and Certain Commodities (November 20, 1978). According to this bulletin, where taxpayers trade in commodities or commodity futures as part of their business operations or where the taxpayers have some special information about the commodity, the transactions are treated on income account. However, for other taxpayers — referred to in the bulletin as "speculators" — the CRA considers it acceptable to treat the gains and losses on

capital account provided that the taxpayer does so on a consistent basis. Is the CRA's administrative position consistent with the jurisprudence?

2. Futures contracts and other types of derivatives do not qualify for tax exemption through a tax-free savings account.

III. THE CAPITAL GAINS FRAMEWORK

Paragraph 40(1)(a) provides that a gain equals the amount by which a taxpayer's proceeds realized on a disposition of property exceed the adjusted cost base of the property and any associated expenses of disposition. Conversely, paragraph 40(1)(b) defines a loss as the excess of the adjusted cost base of a property and any expenses of disposition over the proceeds of disposition. This concept of a net gain and a net loss requires the development of four concepts that are the legislative core of the capital gains regime: (1) "adjusted cost base"; (2) "disposition"; (3) "proceeds of disposition"; and (4) "expenses of disposition". Other important features of the capital gains regime concern: (1) capital gains reserve where the taxpayer does not immediately receive all of the proceeds of disposition (similar to the reserve available to business persons under paragraph 20(1)(n)); (2) limitations on the recognition of losses; (3) exempt treatment of certain gains; and (4) maintenance of the tax base applied to non-resident taxpayers.

A. Adjusted Cost Base

The adjusted cost base ("ACB") of depreciable property at any given time is its "capital cost" to the taxpayer as of that time (section 54, "adjusted cost base", paragraph (a)), whereas the ACB of capital property other than depreciable property is its "cost", adjusted as of the relevant time in accordance with section 53 (section 54, "adjusted cost base", paragraph (b)). Capital gains can apply to the disposition of depreciable property for proceeds greater than its cost and expenses of the disposition, but there cannot be a capital loss on the disposition. If the proceeds are less than capital cost, a terminal loss under under subsection 20(16) may result.

1. Capital Cost and Actual Cost

Neither of the terms "capital cost" or "cost" is defined in the Act. The CRA considers "capital cost" to mean the full cost to the taxpayer of acquiring depreciable property, including costs like legal, accounting, engineering and other fees: Interpretation Bulletin IT-285R2 (archived): Capital Cost Allowance — General Comments (March 31, 1994), paragraph 8. The cost of property includes all amounts paid, and debts incurred, by the vendor at the time of acquisition. For a debt incurred by the taxpayer to form part of the cost, it must be a "real" debt, not a contingent liability that depends on the happening of a future uncertain event. The taxpayer cannot include in the cost any amounts paid to the vendor by third parties.

The capital cost of depreciable property must be reduced by the amount of any investment tax credit or any government assistance that is received in respect of the property's acquisition (subsection 13(7.1)). The taxpayer may also elect to reduce the capital cost of depreciable property (subsection 13(7.4)) or the cost of other capital property that is used to earn income (subsection 53(2.1)) by an amount received in respect of the cost of that property, as a grant, reimbursement or other form of assistance within paragraph 12(1)(x). If the taxpayer does not elect to treat the amount in question as a reduction of the cost of capital property, the amount will be included in income under that paragraph.

Capital expenditures to improve property after acquisition are also included in its cost. Capital expenditures must be in money or money's worth; the taxpayer's own labour in improving the asset will not increase its cost base. Except where the Act specifically provides otherwise, expenses of ownership such as interest, property taxes, storage charges and maintenance may not be added to the cost of the property. However, if the taxpayer chooses, interest and borrowing costs incurred to acquire depreciable property may be added to the capital cost (section 21). Interest and taxes paid in relation to raw land, whose deduction is disallowed under subsection 18(2) because they exceed revenue from the land, must be so capitalized (subsections 18(2) and (3) and paragraph 53(1)(h)). Similar treatment is mandatory for certain land ownership and construction costs ("soft costs") incurred during the construction of a building (subsections 18(3.1) – (3.7)). Because it only goes to reduce a capital gain that is in part taxable, an expenditure added to the cost of non-depreciable capital property is less valuable than a currently deductible expense.

If property is acquired in an arm's-length exchange for another property owned by the taxpayer or for services rendered by the taxpayer (i.e., a barter transaction), determining the cost of the new property may be problematic. If property that is difficult to value (such as a disputed legal claim) is acquired in exchange for property that can be valued easily, there is a presumption that the properties have the same value, and accordingly the cost to the taxpayer of the former property will equal the value of the latter property. This is because the cost of property is the value of what the taxpayer gives up to acquire it, and the taxpayer can be presumed to have given up something equal in value to what was received. If the property given up or the services rendered can be easily valued, that value will be the cost of the acquired property.

Questions

1. Taxpayer owned a controlling block of shares in T Ltd. In 1973, in order to attract C to an executive position with T Ltd., Taxpayer granted C an option to acquire 340,000 T Ltd. shares. C left T Ltd. in 1975. In 1976 Taxpayer purported to

cancel C's stock option. C brought an action for specific performance of the option agreement, which was eventually settled by Taxpayer paying C $1.3 million. Subsequently, C discovered that Taxpayer knew at the time of the settlement agreement that T Ltd. would be the target of a takeover bid, which later materialized. C brought a second action in respect of Taxpayer's nondisclosure, both at common law and under the insider trading provisions of the provincial securities legislation. Taxpayer was held liable to C in this second action for $2.5 million. Can Taxpayer add either of the amounts paid to C to the cost of his shares in T Ltd.? See *Bodrug Estate v. Canada*, [1991] 2 C.T.C. 347, 91 D.T.C. 5621 (F.C.A.).

2. A mortgagor defaults on payment of interest and is eventually in arrears by $50,000. The mortgagee attempts to foreclose, which is resisted by the mortgagor. Eventually the mortgagee purchases the mortgagor's property for $150,000, paying only $100,000, the statement of adjustments reflecting the $50,000 arrears of interest. Has the mortgagee received $50,000 interest, and if so, what is the cost to it of the property? (See *The Queen v. Greenington Group Ltd.*, [1979] C.T.C. 31, 79 D.T.C. 5026 (F.C.T.D.)).
3. A taxpayer buys certain bonds for $1,200, of which $200 represents accrued interest. A month after his acquisition of the bonds, he receives interest of $210. Must the seller of the bonds include $200 in his income? Are his proceeds of disposition $1,000 or $1,200? Does taxpayer include $210 or $10 in his income? Is the cost of the bonds to the taxpayer $1,000 or $1,200? See subsection 20(14) and paragraph 53(2)(l).

2. Cost of Property Acquired before 1972

The basic purpose of the transitional provisions introduced with the 1971 tax reform is to ensure that when capital property that was acquired before the new system came into effect is disposed of, the "pre-system" gains and losses — those accrued before 1972 — are excluded from the "post-system" gains and losses so that only the post-system ones are included. The proposition is simple enough, but the rules necessary to put it into effect are somewhat complicated. They are contained for the most part in section 26 of the Income Tax Application Rules (ITAR).

3. Deemed Cost of Property Acquired After 1971

In most situations, taxpayers use the purchase price (actual cost) as the primary component of the ACB, but sometimes the Act imposes a deemed cost instead. Depending on the transaction, the Act may substitute fair market value, nil cost, or ACB, for the actual cost:

- Examples of the fair market value rule include: dividends in kind (subsection 52(2)) non-arm's length transactions, gifts, bequests, inheritances (subsection 69(1)), other acquisitions of capital property on death (paragraph 70(5)(b)), lottery prizes (subsection 52(4)), and various deemed dispositions and reacquisitions of property. Starting with a cost of fair market value ensures that the taxpayer acquiring property only pays tax on gains accruing after the time of acquisition. If a taxpayer acquires a capital property in circumstances where the cost is deemed to be fair market value, may the taxpayer add to fair market value any initial capital outlays in respect of the property? For example, if the taxpayer is given a capital property with fair market value of $1,000 and incurs $500 in freight charges, the cost ought to be $1,500. However, if the outlay was made before the deemed acquisition of the property, the taxpayer's expenses may be excluded from the cost base because the Act prescribes fair market value as the cost of acquisition: *Allison v. Murray*, [1975] 1 W.L.R. 1578, [1975] 3 All E.R. 561 (Ch. D.).
- Examples of the nil cost rule include: bad debts of a capital nature, or shares in a bankrupt or insolvent corporation (subsection 50(1)). Deeming the cost to be nil renders any subsequent proceeds chargeable as capital gains and disallows future capital losses. This nil cost is the consequence of a tax write-off (i.e., deemed disposition for proceeds of nil) in respect of the worthless property.
- Examples of the ACB rule include: transfers to a spouse or spouse trust (subsections 70(6) and 73(1)), transfers of fishing or farm property (subsections 70(9) and 73(3)), and the conversion of certain convertible investments (section 51). In order to postpone taxation of an accrued gain (or the deduction of an accrued loss), the Act provides a "rollover" in these circumstances. On a transfer, the transferee's cost is deemed to be equal to the transferor's ACB. The transferor realizes no capital gain or loss, and whatever gain or loss has accrued to the time of transfer will form part of the capital gain or loss when the transferee disposes of the property. Rollovers are discussed further in the section, "Disposition and Proceeds of Disposition", below.

4. Adjustments to Cost

The various adjustments that the Act requires to be made to actual or deemed cost in order to arrive at the ACB are designed to ensure that the taxation of capital gains and losses is integrated with other parts of the Act. Additions to cost are necessary in cases where the taxpayer has made further capital expenditures on the asset that do not come within the description of "cost" (for example, contributions of capital to a corporation of which the taxpayer is a shareholder or contributions of capital to the taxpayer's partnership). They are also necessary if the taxpayer has made what would ordinarily be deductible expenditures in connection with the property but were disallowed because of a special rule. They are necessary as well if the taxpayer has already paid tax on a part of the capital value of the property, for example, by having part of the value of the property included in income (subsection 52(1)). Deductions from cost are required in a variety of circumstances: for example, if part of the cost of the property was a deductible expense.

A negative ACB is precluded, except in the case of certain partnership interests, by subsection 40(3). If at any time in a taxation year, deductions from cost exceed the property's ACB immediately prior to such deductions, the excess is deemed to be proceeds of disposition and a capital gain at that time. The capital gain is then added to ACB, restoring it to zero for future gain or loss computations (paragraph 53(1)(a)). The rule takes effect at any time that the ACB notionally becomes a negative figure (that is, notwithstanding subsequent additions to cost in the same taxation year that would otherwise increase the ACB above zero).

(a) Additions to Cost

Leaving aside the more technical adjustments, which relate to shares, property owned by a corporation the control of which has changed, interests in trusts, interests in partnerships, and certain obligations, the following are the adjustments of more general interest.

Amounts that relate to the value of the property and that were included in income may be added to the cost of the property under subsection 52(1). When the asset is sold, the amount previously included in income will reduce the amount of the gain and may create a capital loss. As with dividends in kind and deemed dispositions at fair market value, the taxpayer has already been subject to tax in respect of the amount included in income, so it becomes a part of the "cost" of the property, to prevent double taxation of that same amount.

Disallowed amounts, such as superficial losses (paragraph 53(1)(f)), interest and property taxes and restricted farm losses (paragraphs 53(1)(h) and (i)), are added to cost. Reasonable costs of surveying or valuing the property for the purpose of its acquisition or its disposition are also added to the ACB, unless they are deducted in computing income or are attributable to other property (paragraph 53(1)(n)).

(b) Deductions from Cost

Most deductions from cost are technical adjustments relating to shares, interests in partnerships, interests in trusts, and certain obligations. Other reductions include the following. Government grants, subsidies or other public assistance to finance property are subtracted from its cost (paragraphs 53(2)(k) and (s)). If some of the cost of property is deductible in computing income, it must be subtracted from cost, for capital gains purposes, to prevent taxpayers from deriving double relief for the same outlay (paragraph 53(2)(m)). Thus, subsections 20(14) and (14.1) require both the transferor and transferee of a bond or other interest-earning obligation that is transferred with accrued interest to apportion their proceeds of disposition and cost, respectively, between the capital and income elements of the transferred property. The accrued interest must be included in the transferor's income (paragraph 20(14)(a)) and deducted from proceeds (paragraph 39(1)(a)). The transferee may deduct the amount of the accrued interest from income in a year the obligation was acquired (paragraph 20(14)(b)), and this amount must then be deducted from the cost base of the obligation to the transferee (paragraph 53(2)(l)).

B. Disposition and Proceeds of Disposition

1. Statutory Definitions

The Supreme Court of Canada has said that the "definitions of 'disposition of property' and 'proceeds of disposition' are not exhaustive; these expressions must bear both their normal meaning and their statutory meaning; it would be wrong to restrict the former because of the latter": *The Queen v. Compagnie Immobilière BCN Ltée.*, [1979] C.T.C. 71 at 76, 79 D.T.C. 5068 at 5072 (S.C.C.). Under subsection 248(1), the definition of a "disposition" includes "any transaction or event entitling a taxpayer to proceeds of disposition of property"; the definition of "proceeds of disposition" in section 54 describes various types of dispositions.

Subsection 248(1) also contains a sweeping definition of "property". The overall effect of these provisions is that "[i]n principle, any right that is convertible into cash is likely to result in a disposition when it is converted": *RCI Environment Inc. v. The Queen* (2008), 2008 FCA 419, 2009 D.T.C. 5105 (F.C.A.), leave to appeal dismissed 2009 CarswellNat 1832 (S.C.C.).

Perhaps the most obvious kind of disposition is a sale at arm's length. On such a sale, the proceeds of disposition equal the amount of the sale price of the property sold. Where, in respect of the property acquired, the purchaser assumes as part of the purchase price liability for the vendor's "separate existing debt" or the vendor's mortgage, it would form part of the vendor's proceeds of disposition and of the purchaser's cost: *Daishowa-Marubeni International Ltd. v. R.* 2013 SCC 29, [2013] 4 C.T.C. 97, 2013 D.T.C. 5085 (sale of a timber resources company). The CRA takes the position that if the vendor promptly assigns consideration such as a promissory note, mortgage or agreement for sale, only the value received rather than the face amount would be included in the proceeds.

Notes and Questions

1. A vendor agrees to sell land to a purchaser for $10,000, of which $5,000 is payable in cash and the balance is secured by a mortgage in favour of the vendor.

The vendor assigns the mortgage for $4,000. What are the tax consequences to the vendor of assigning the note?

2. In 1979, Taxpayer bought an interest in a multiple-unit residential building (MURB) from Developer. Developer continued to manage the project for Taxpayer and her fellow investors. Taxpayer's purchase price was $250,000, which consisted of $30,000 cash paid on closing, a $40,000 promissory note given to Developer, and the assumption of a $180,000 mortgage debt owing to Bank. The MURB project ran into financial difficulties, and in 1981 Developer insisted that Taxpayer was liable under the contract to indemnify Developer for $65,000 of operating losses, which Taxpayer denied. After much wrangling, it was agreed in 1982 that Developer would repurchase Taxpayer's interest for (a) $1 cash; and (b) assumption by Developer of Taxpayer's mortgage debt, which now stood at $160,000. At the same time Developer agreed to cancel Taxpayer's $40,000 promissory note, and to abandon the claim against Taxpayer for an indemnity of $65,000. Which amounts must Taxpayer include in her proceeds of disposition? See *Robert v. M.N.R.*, [1990] 1 C.T.C. 2407, 90 D.T.C. 1281 (T.C.C.).
3. What if the vendor, rather than the purchaser, assumes an obligation or otherwise suffers a detriment as part of the sale? Suppose Charlie, who owns all the shares in X Co., sells those shares to Fred for a sale price of $7.8 million, but it is one of the terms of the sale that Charlie pay to X Co. a $1.4 million debt owing to X Co. from another firm. X Co. assigns this debt to Charlie. Its fair market value is only $600,000. Are Charlie's proceeds of disposition (a) $7.8 million, (b) $7 million, or (c) $6.4 million? See *The Queen v. Fradet*, [1986] 2 C.T.C. 321, 86 D.T.C. 6411 (F.C.A.).

The sale price of property would include the value of any non-cash consideration such as property or services. A sale, whether voluntary or compelled by court order, involves a transfer of property to another for consideration: *Corbett v. The Queen*, [1997] 1 C.T.C. 2 at 7 (F.C.A.). But a "disposition" is broader and includes involuntary transfers such as expropriation, where the compensation paid is the proceeds. Even though property or title to the capital asset has not passed to another person, the taxpayer may have disposed of it, or a part of it, for tax purposes. Where property has been unlawfully taken, destroyed or damaged, the taxpayer is treated as having disposed of it for the amount received by way of compensation or insurance. For example, an award of damages to a taxpayer for breach of a long-term dealer agreement was subject to tax as a capital gain when received by the dealer. If the taxpayer had succeeded in characterizing the award as tortious damages, it might have been tax-free, but the taxpayer's claim and the judge's award established contractual breach as the basis of compensation: *Valley Equipment Ltd. v. The Queen*, [2008] 3 C.T.C. 36, 2008 D.T.C. 6200 (F.C.A.). However, where property is damaged, the taxpayer may exclude from proceeds any amount spent within a reasonable time to repair the damage (section 54, "proceeds of disposition" paragraph (f)).

Question

X recovers $7,000 from his insurance company in respect of fire damage to her painting and spends $5,000 of that sum to restore the painting. Her proceeds would be $2,000 ($7,000 – $5,000). If, however, A pays the $5,000 out of her own pocket before recovering the $7,000, would her proceeds be $2,000 or $7,000?

Example

X owns two adjacent plots of land, Blackacre and Whiteacre. On Blackacre, X operates a manufacturing plant and on Whiteacre, he stores his raw materials and provides his employees with parking. If a government were to expropriate Whiteacre, the value of Blackacre would diminish. X would probably be entitled to compensation under two distinct heads: (1) for the expropriation of Whiteacre, and (2) for the injurious affection of Blackacre. Thus the Act provides for separate dispositions of the two pieces of land for proceeds equal to the compensation in respect of each property.

The Act provides for dispositions where there is a change in ownership without proceeds (for example, gifts) and where there is no change in ownership but there are proceeds (e.g., a destruction of the property followed by insurance proceeds). Theft is a disposition, on the grounds that ownership has changed *de facto*, if not *de jure,* and that there are usually proceeds in the form of insurance. See Income Tax Folio S3-F9-C1: Lottery Winnings, Miscellaneous Receipts, and Income (and Losses) from Crime. But what about an uninsured building that burns down, or a building that is simply knocked down by the owner? In *The Queen v. Compagnie Immobilière BCN Ltée*, *supra*, the Supreme Court of Canada stated that the term "dispose of" should be given its broadest possible meaning, and was wide enough to include parting with, or destroying, or extinguishing property, although no proceeds were received in return. The CRA accepts this proposition, and is prepared to treat as a disposition any "event or transaction where possession, control and all other aspects of property ownership are relinquished": Interpretation Bulletin IT-460 (archived): Disposition — Absence of Consideration (October 6, 1980).

Aside from cases where property is lost or destroyed without proceeds, there are other situations that require an interpretation of "disposition" in its general sense. Is a conversion of property from capital to inventory a disposition? Suppose, for instance, that a farmer decides to subdivide his farm and sell it in small lots. The CRA takes the view that no disposition takes place at the time the decision is taken, presumably because to hold the contrary would involve taxing accrued capital gains. However, when the property is sold, the taxpayer will have to calculate both the trading profit, and the capital gain. The trading profit will be computed on a notional cost of acquisition equal to the fair market value of the property at the time it was converted to inventory. The capital gain will be based on the original ACB and proceeds equal to the fair market value at the time of conversion. See Interpretation Bulletin IT-218R (archived): Profit, Capital Gains and Losses from the Sale of Real

Estate, Including Farmland and Inherited Land and Conversion of Real Estate from Capital Property to Inventory and Vice Versa (September 16, 1986), paragraphs 15–22.

If the issuer of a security changes its terms significantly, the change may trigger a disposition for the holder. According to the CRA, a debenture or share is disposed of if the rights attached to it are altered so fundamentally as to change the nature or identity of the property. Examples given are a change in repayment or maturity date of a debt, or a change in voting rights attached to shares that results in a change of control: Interpretation Bulletin IT-448 (archived): Dispositions — Changes in Terms of Securities (June 6, 1980, and Special Release dated June 21, 1982). Paragraph 50(1)(b) provides that shareholders may elect to have a deemed disposition of shares for nil proceeds if a corporation becomes bankrupt, winds-up, or ceases business because of insolvency.

2. Transactions that are not Dispositions

Some changes of legal ownership do not result in a disposition for capital gains tax purposes. For example, the following transactions are non-dispositions.

- Transfers securing a loan or debt or returning the security to the borrower are not dispositions (subsection 248(1), "disposition", paragraph (h)). Thus, a transfer of property by a debtor to a creditor for the purpose of securing a debt or loan, and the creditor's return of such property on repayment of the indebtedness, are not dispositions. Neither the granting of a mortgage nor its discharge on payment of the debt has capital gains consequences so far as the mortgaged property is concerned (but it does so far as the debt is concerned). If, however, property given as security is acquired outright by the creditor as a consequence of the debtor's default, there is a disposition by the debtor of the property and a disposition by the creditor of the debt. See *Halbauer v. Canada*, [1998] 3 C.T.C. 115, 98 D.T.C. 6275 (F.C.A.). The Act contains detailed rules for determining the tax consequences to each party.
- Transfers of bare legal title to property generally are not dispositions (subsection 248(1), "disposition", paragraphs (e) and (f)). Transfers of property to agents or nominees without any change in beneficial ownership do not constitute dispositions. Transfer of a legal title to a trust will trigger a disposition unless the trust is a bare or passive trust that acts as agent for the beneficiaries. Transfers from one trust to another trust trigger dispositions unless both the transferor and transferee are passive trusts for the same beneficiaries. On the disposition of the property by the agent or bare trustee on behalf of the transferor taxpayer, the capital gain or loss would be included in the income of the transferor, not that of the trust. If the trust were for the benefit of the transferor and some other person, however, then the change in the beneficial

interest would result in a disposition. A transfer of property to a person who had established herself by court action as a beneficiary of a constructive trust in the property, was held not to be a disposition because the constructive trust amounted to beneficial ownership: *Anderson Estate v. The Queen*, [1995] 1 C.T.C. 2454 (T.C.C.). Some transfers that do not involve a change in beneficial ownership nevertheless constitute dispositions. One type is a transfer of property by a Canadian resident trust to an offshore trust. Other transactions are transfers between a beneficiary and a registered retirement savings plan (RRSP), a deferred profit-sharing plan, an employee profit-sharing plan, or a registered retirement income fund, if the taxpayer was a beneficiary under the plan or fund. The taxpayer is deemed to realize a gain on such a transfer as well as a deductible contribution to the plan, assuming that it otherwise qualifies for deduction. One cannot generate a capital loss by transferring declining investments to an RRSP, a TFSA, or other similar plan in trust for oneself.

- Transactions such as the bailment of a chattel or a lease of realty or personality, do not involve a change in either the legal or beneficial ownership, and therefore are not dispositions by the owner of the property, though a lease is an acquisition of property for the lessee. The granting of a lease with an option to purchase is not a disposition of the leased property, unless the transaction is, in substance, a sale. Does a bailee acquire property? If the chattel is destroyed while in the bailee's possession, has the bailee or the bailor disposed of it? Consider whether any of the following would constitute a disposition: a bare licence; a licence coupled with a grant; an easement; a profit à prendre; or the exercise of a power of appointment.
- Partitions of co-owned property are not dispositions (subsections 248(20), (21)) Where co-owned property is partitioned so that each owner receives a new separate interest that represents exactly the same share of the fair market value of the whole property as the old undivided interest, there is no disposition and the new interest is deemed to be a continuation of the old (subsection 248(21)). In any other partition, there is a part disposition of the old undivided interest if the fair market value of the new interest is less than the fair market value of the old one. Thus, for example, if A and B are equal joint owners of a $100,000 property (each has a half-interest worth $50,000) and they partition it so that A's part is worth $60,000 and B's $40,000, A is deemed not to have disposed of any of her old interest but B is deemed to have disposed of 20 per cent of his old interest to A, and A is deemed to have acquired it (subsection 248(20)). Actual or deemed proceeds to B and cost to A are determined in the usual way, depending on whether A paid B for the addition to her interest, received it as a gift, etc.
- The granting of an option is not a disposition of the property to which it relates, but it is a disposition of the option, which has a deemed ACB of nil (subsection

49(1)). If the option is exercised, the granting of it is retroactively treated as not having been a disposition (subsections 49(3), (4)).

- A corporation does not dispose of anything when it issues its own stock or other securities (subsection 248(1), "disposition" paragraphs (i), (j)). Nor does it dispose of anything when it issues shares in return for the surrender of convertible shares or other instrument or when it buys its own shares and resells or cancels them (section 51). This rule reflects accounting rather than legal theory. There are tax consequences to the shareholder when a corporation purchases or redeems its own shares; these consequences may take the form of a deemed dividend or a capital gain. See Chapter 9. Under subsection 39(3), an issuer of any bond, debenture or similar obligation, on purchasing the obligation in the open market in the manner in which such obligation would normally be purchased in the open market, must account for the capital gain or loss on the purchase.

Example

A corporation borrowed $100 and issued a debt instrument at a face amount of $100 with interest at current rates to secure repayment of the loan. Because of an increase in interest rates, the company was able to repurchase the bond for $90. The difference of $10 would be a capital gain.

3. Deemed Dispositions

To prevent tax avoidance and reduce the "lock-in" effect of permitting capital gains to accrue over long periods of time, the Act provides for certain fictional realizations, or deemed dispositions at fair market value, most of which are associated with an event or transaction that changes the tax status of the property or the taxpayer. These are: (1) change in the use of capital assets from income-earning to non-income-earning and vice versa (section 45); (2) death of the taxpayer (subsection 70(5)); (3) giving up Canadian residence (paragraph 128.1(4)(b)); and (4) deemed dispositions by a trust of trust property every 21 years (paragraphs 104(4)(b), (c)).

4. Timing of Dispositions

For many reasons, it is important to know precisely when a disposition takes place. For example, timing of a disposition may determine whether the seller or the buyer is entitled to claim depreciation in respect of the asset for the year. Similarly, timing may determine the year in which a gain or loss must be brought into income or the date as of which the fair market value of consideration other than cash must be appraised. The moment of disposition may fix the date from which a time period starts to run, for example, the 10-day period that a non-resident vendor has to report a disposition under subsection 116(3), or the 61-day period for defining superficial losses (section 54, definition of "superficial loss"). Since a disposition is an event that triggers the realization for tax purposes of capital gains and losses, to the extent that taxpayers can control these events, they can plan their strategy for gains and losses.

The general rule is that taxpayers must report capital gains and losses from dispositions that occur in a taxation year. The date of a sale of property may in some cases be a matter of dispute. The timing of dispositions is discussed in *Hewlett Packard (Canada) Ltd. v. R.* 2004 FCA 240, [2004] 4 C.T.C. 230, 2004 D.T.C. 6490, a case on capital cost allowance. A disposition occurs when the beneficial ownership of the capital property passes from the taxpayer. The passing of a bare legal title or absolute entitlement to the proceeds of disposition are not determinative. A disposition and acquisition of capital property occurs simultaneously. The incidents of ownership include possession, use and risk. A disposition occurs when these incidents pass to the other party to the transaction, even though legal title remains with the taxpayer.

Notes and Questions

1. In 2010, V agreed to sell certain land to P for $850,000. The price was payable $70,000 on the closing date, October 31, 2010, and the balance upon the fulfillment of certain conditions precedent, within two years. P had possession from the closing date for purposes of construction. The last of the conditions precedent was fulfilled in 2012. In which year did V dispose of the property? Does it make any difference that the conditions precedent could be waived by P? See *The Queen v. Imperial General Properties Ltd.*, [1985] 1 C.T.C. 40, 85 D.T.C. 5045 (F.C.A.). See also *Mintenko v. The Queen* (1988), [1989] 1 C.T.C. 40, 88 D.T.C. 6537 (F.C.T.D.); *Johnstone v. The Queen*, [1988] 1 C.T.C. 48, 88 D.T.C. 6032 (F.C.T.D.); *Kozan v. M.N.R.*, [1987] 1 C.T.C. 2258, 87 D.T.C. 148 (T.C.C.); and *Ryan v. M.N.R.*, [1992] 2 C.T.C. 2288, 92 D.T.C. 2027 (T.C.C.).
2. V leased certain property to P in 2005, and P took possession. Under the terms of the agreement P was obliged to purchase the property for $225,000 by the end of the five year term, which P did in 2010. Did V dispose of the property in 2000 or 2005? See *Robert Bédard Auto Ltée v. M.N.R.*, [1985] 2 C.T.C. 2354, 85 D.T.C. 642 (T.C.C.).
3. In the case of shares traded on a stock exchange, the CRA takes the view that the date of disposition is not the "trade date", the date on which the sale goes through the exchange, but the "settlement date", the date on which the seller is required to deliver the share certificates and the purchaser is required to pay for the shares.
4. The timing of certain involuntary dispositions, including theft, accidental destruction and expropriation, is defined by subsection 44(2), discussed below.

5. Part Dispositions

On the sale of an entire capital property, the vendor calculates the capital gain or loss by deducting the full amount of the ACB from the proceeds. When a taxpayer disposes of part of a capital property, the taxpayer must deduct only a proportionate part of the total ACB from the proceeds. The taxpayer must allocate a reasonable portion of the cost base to the part sold (subsection 43(1)). Only that reasonable portion is deductible from the proceeds. After deducting the reasonable portion of the cost base allocated to the part disposed of, the taxpayer allocates the rest of the cost base to the unsold part of the property (paragraph 53(2)(d)).

Example

Verna purchased a two-hectare parcel of waterfront land for $100,000 on which to build her dream home. Because the north hectare was right on the water it was worth 80 per cent of the value. The south hectare, on the other hand, was not immediately adjacent to the water and was only worth 20 per cent of the total. Two years later, Verna built her home on the waterfront hectare, and sold the south hectare for $25,000. Verna's ACB for the south part would be $20,000 (20 per cent of $100,000) and her capital gain on the sale would be $5,000 ($25,000 proceeds – $20,000 ACB). Following the part disposition, Verna's ACB for the north part that she retained would be $80,000 ($100,000 – $20,000).

6. Combined Proceeds for More Than One Property

An amount may be paid in a single transaction as consideration for more than one item including: depreciable property, non-depreciable property, services and something else that is not property, like know-how. Where the vendor and purchaser agree on the allocation of the price among the various items of property or other things being paid for, and that allocation is *bona fide* and reasonable, it will define the proceeds attributable to each property that is being purchased. Problems arise where the parties fail to make an allocation, or make one that is self-serving or unreasonable.

If the parties agree on an allocation of the price, but the allocation is in some way unreasonable, the CRA has recourse to section 68, which applies to apportion any amount received or receivable in part as proceeds of disposition of a particular property and in part as consideration for services or proceeds of disposition of another property. The proceeds of disposition of the particular property, or the consideration for particular services, is deemed to be "the part of the amount that can reasonably be regarded" as consideration for the disposition of that property or for those services.

In *The Queen v. Golden*, [1986] 1 C.T.C. 274, 86 D.T.C. 6138 (S.C.C.), the taxpayer sold land and an apartment building for $5,850,000, of which $5.1 million was allocated to the land and $750,000 to the building. The trial judge accepted expert evidence that a reasonable allocation of the total value to the land alone would have been $2,320,000, and applied section 68 to reassess the vendor for recaptured depreciation on the basis that the building had been sold for $3,530,000. This was reversed by the Federal Court of Appeal, [1983] C.T.C. 112, 83 D.T.C. 5138, which held that the trial judge had erred in approaching the question of allocation from the point of view of the vendor alone. Heald J. said:

> It is my opinion that the correct approach to a section 68 determination would be to consider the matter from the viewpoint of both the vendor and the purchaser and to consider all of the relevant circumstances surrounding the transaction. Where, as in this case, as found by the trial judge, the transaction is at arm's length and is not a mere sham or subterfuge, the apportionment made by the parties in the applicable agreement is certainly an important circumstance and one which is entitled to considerable weight. Furthermore, in this case, the trial judge made a specific finding of fact ... that the figure of $5,100,000, which the parties apportioned to land in the agreement, was not an unreasonable price for the purchaser to pay for the land alone in March 1973. Accordingly, based on that specific finding and on the other circumstances appearing from the evidence and addressing the question from the point of view of both the appellant and its purchaser, I am of the opinion that the amount that can reasonably be regarded as having been paid and received for the land apart from the buildings, etc., was $5,100,000 and for the building, equipment, roads, sidewalk, etc., was $750,000.

On appeal, a majority of the Supreme Court of Canada held that this was the correct application of section 68. It is therefore clear that a reasonable allocation of the combined consideration under section 68 need not be proportional to the respective fair market values of the items of property taken by themselves. If the parties bargain at arms' length over the allocation of the price among the items being sold and the valuations are reasonable, their agreed allocation is entitled to considerable weight, and the CRA will have difficulty attacking the allocation under section 68. In the case of a sale of land and depreciable building, paragraph 13(21.1)(a) sets a base amount that must be allocated to the proceeds for the building. Why is this particular allocation rule necessary?

Where a building is demolished shortly after or before a sale of the underlying land, the proceeds can be allocated entirely to the land, because only bare land is being paid for: *The Queen v. Malloney's Studio Ltd.*, [1979] C.T.C. 206, 79 D.T.C. 5124 (S.C.C.).

A taxpayer sold a single asset for the entire consideration. After the sale, the taxpayer purported to reallocate some of the proceeds to another asset, using section 68, to achieve a more favourable tax result. The Federal Court of Appeal held that, if the parties to the transaction allocate all the proceeds to one asset, section 68 cannot apply: *Robert Glegg Investment Inc. v. The Queen*, 2009 D.T.C. 5009.

7. Rollover Treatment on the Reinvestment of Proceeds in a Replacement Property

Section 44 provides non-recognition or rollover treatment for owners who receive proceeds on certain dispositions if they reinvest the proceeds in a replacement asset and elect to defer tax until the disposition of the replacement. Basically, the taxpayer can deduct the capital gain from the cost of the replacement asset, deferring tax until the replacement asset is disposed of, without a further replacement. The provision extends to the following dispositions:

(a) unlawful taking;

(b) destruction;

(c) taking under statutory authority, or sale to a person by whom notice of an intention to take it under statutory authority was given; and

(d) replacement of a "former business property", that is, real property or an interest therein (other than a leasehold interest) used primarily for the purpose of gaining or producing business income (not including rent), that was disposed of in any manner (subsection 248(1) definition of "former business property").

The rationale for including (a) to (c) is that the involuntary nature of the disposition makes it unfair to assess a capital gain if the proceeds are reinvested in similar property. The rationale for (d) is presumably to permit businesses to change location without the disincentive of a tax liability for capital gains realized on the old premises. The provision applies to depreciable as well as non-depreciable property, with subsection 13(4) addressing the CCA consequences. See Chapter 6.

Section 44 requires the taxpayer to reinvest the proceeds in a replacement property promptly within certain time limits.

Subsection 44(5) defines replacement property. It must be "reasonable to conclude that the property was acquired by the taxpayer to replace the former property". The replacement property must be bought for the same or a similar use as the former property, and must be used for the purpose of gaining or producing income from the same business as the former property was used (if the former property was used in a business).

Section 44 operates by reducing any capital gain on the former property to the amount, if any, by which the proceeds of disposition of the former property exceed the cost of the replacement property (plus any expenses of the disposition of the former property). In effect, the taxpayer is deemed to have no capital gain if all the proceeds are used in acquiring the replacement property. If some proceeds are left over, that amount will be the amount of the capital gain, up to the maximum of the capital gain calculated without reference to section 44. Whatever amount of gain is exempted by operation of these rules must be subtracted from the cost of the replacement property, so it will eventually form part of the capital gain when the replacement property is disposed of in a taxable transaction. The rules apply only if the taxpayer so elects in the return for the year in which the replacement property is acquired.

Taxpayers can also defer gains on the sale of small business shares by reinvesting the proceeds (see section 44.1). The provision extends non-recognition treatment to dispositions of shares that qualify as eligible small business investments if the proceeds are reinvested in other shares that also qualify as an eligible small business investment. The rationale for this rollover is to assist small companies in accessing financing from venture capitalists.

Question

An earthquake destroyed Taxpayer's factory, which was worth $500,000. Immediately before the disaster, capital cost and ACB of the factory was $300,000 and its undepreciated capital cost (UCC) was $150,000. Taxpayer received insurance proceeds of $500,000. What are the tax consequences if Taxpayer uses the entire proceeds to build a new factory? What if Taxpayer uses only $475,000?

8. Other Rollover or Non-Recognition Transactions

In some circumstances, for various policy reasons, the Act allows property with accrued capital gains or losses to be transferred to another taxpayer without tax consequences. The transferor is deemed to have received proceeds of disposition that remove or reduce the capital gain or loss that would occur without the deeming provision, and the figure that is used for proceeds is also deemed to be the transferee's cost. Because the transferor's deemed proceeds are deemed to be the transferee's cost, the gain or loss that is eliminated for the transferor is built into the transferee's cost base. It becomes a deferred gain or loss that increases or reduces what would otherwise be the capital gain or loss when the transferee disposes of the property.

Rollovers can be mandatory or elective. An example of a mandatory rollover is the *inter vivos* transfer of farm property from parent to child (subsection 73(3)). Elective rollovers take various forms. The rollover for transfers of property between spouses and common-law partners, both *inter vivos* (subsection 73(1)) and on death (subsections 70(6) and (6.2)), is automatic unless the transferor elects not to have the rollover apply. If a taxpayer donates capital property to a charity, subsection 118.1(6) provides an elective rollover. A transferor of property to a corporation in return for consideration that includes shares can take advantage of a rollover if the transferor and the corporation jointly elect (subsection 85(1)).

9. Reserve for Future Proceeds

A seller of appreciated capital property faces the prospect of a capital gain in the year of sale. However, if the terms of sale provide for the seller to receive the selling price in a series of instalments, the taxpayer may claim a reserve for future proceeds (subparagraphs 40(1)(a)(ii), (iii)). By claiming a reserve, the seller can reduce the amount of gain in the year of disposition and can defer the balance of the gain to future taxation years as the proceeds become due. In effect, the capital gain is taxable by instalment. The reserve is available to a taxpayer who sells an asset on credit, whether the buyer's promise to pay is unsecured or secured.

Assume that a taxpayer disposes of capital property in the current year for a capital gain. The agreement provides that the purchaser does not have to make one or more payments until after the end of the year. The taxpayer may compute and deduct a capital gains reserve in determining the capital gain on the transaction in the tax return for the year of sale (year 1). The taxpayer must report the reserve claimed in year 1 in year 2's tax return and may deduct a reserve for any proceeds that will be payable in subsequent years, and so on (subject to limitations discussed below) until the entire capital gain has been allocated to a taxation year.

The CRA accepts the following formula for calculating a reasonable reserve:

$$\frac{\text{Capital gain} \times \text{Amount not due until after the end of the year}}{\text{Proceeds of disposition}}$$

The taxpayer deducts this reserve in calculating the capital gain to be reported in each taxation year. The formula allocates the capital gain to a taxation year in proportion to the fraction of the total proceeds that are payable in that year.

A taxpayer may choose to claim any amount up to the maximum reserve, but the amount claimed in one year limits the amount that may be claimed in the following year. There is no obligation to claim a reserve and a taxpayer claims a capital loss fully in the year of disposition, even though the buyer will pay the proceeds in later years. Claiming a reserve defers reporting the vendor's capital gain but has no effect on the purchaser's ACB of the asset.

A nine-year limit applies to sales to the taxpayer's child of family farm or fishing property (including corporate stock or partnership interests) or small business corporation shares. For instalment sales of other capital property, the taxpayer may claim a reserve up to a maximum of four years. The maximum reserve for each year is the lesser of:

Either

$$\text{Capital gain} \times \frac{\text{Amount not due until after the end of the year}}{\text{Proceeds of disposition}}$$

Or

Capital gain ×
4/5 (year of disposition)
3/5 (second year)
2/5 (third year)
1/5 (fourth year)

0 (fifth year)

Question

X sold a capital property for $100,000. The property had an ACB of $70,000. Y paid X $25,000 on closing of the sale, with the balance of the sale price to be paid in annual instalments of $15,000 each over the next five years. What amounts may X claim as a capital gains reserve in each year following the year of sale?

C. Expenses of Disposition

In computing a capital gain or loss, the taxpayer may add to the ACB any outlays or expenses to the extent that they were made or incurred for the purpose of making the disposition (subparagraphs 40(1)(a)(i), (b)(i)). An expenditure made for another purpose, such as the taxpayer's use and enjoyment of the asset, is not allowable as an expense of the disposition on the sale of the asset shortly thereafter.

Most outlays for the purpose of putting property into saleable condition and expenses incurred in connection with the disposition itself are deductible in computing the gain or loss. They include certain "fixing-up" expenses, finder's fees, commissions, surveyor's fees, transfer taxes and other reasonable expenses directly attributable to facilitating the disposition. Fixing-up expenses would include minor and incidental expenses to enhance the marketability of a capital property, such as painting or repairing a building for sale (even though such expenses might otherwise be current expenses and fully deductible in the event that no sale was contemplated). Outlays to make more extensive improvements or renovations would be added to the cost.

Since a deemed disposition is a concept for income tax purposes only, expense is seldom incurred on such a disposition (although appraisal costs to establish fair market value for tax purposes may qualify as an expense of a deemed disposition). The costs of transferring title subsequent to a deemed disposition on death are not deductible as expenses of the deemed disposition: see *White Estate v. The Queen*, [1999] 4 C.T.C. 99, 99 D.T.C. 5005 (F.C.T.D.); *Akenhead Estate v. M.N.R.*, [1983] C.T.C. 2111, 83 D.T.C. 105 (T.R.B.).

D. Capital Losses

1. Netting and Carryover of Allowable Capital Losses

A taxpayer realizes a capital loss on a disposition of capital property for proceeds less than the ACB and any expenses of disposition. Just as only one-half of a capital gain is taxable, only one-half of a capital loss ("allowable capital loss") is deductible. Capital losses are initially deductible in the year of disposition, to the extent of realized taxable capital gains. If they cannot be used up in that year, excess capital losses are deductible in other years. Relief in the current year is described as "netting", that is, offsetting allowable capital losses against taxable capital gains and, in certain circumstances, against ordinary income, arising in that year. The exceptional deduction of allowable capital losses against ordinary income applies to allowable business investment losses and to unused losses on a taxpayer's death. Relief in other years is called "carry over", that is, offsetting excess allowable capital losses in the particular year (referred to as a "net capital loss") against taxable capital gains arising in prior or subsequent years. Allowable business investment losses and unused losses on death are also deductible from sources of income other than capital gains by way of loss carryover.

The maximum period for carrying back an allowable capital loss is three years. There are two restrictions on a taxpayer's right to carry such losses back to previous years. First, an earlier year's loss must be deducted before a later year's loss (paragraph 111(3)(b)). For example, all of a taxpayer's net capital loss incurred in year 1 must be deducted before carrying back year 2's net capital loss. Second, each item of loss can be deducted only once. Allowable capital losses can be carried forward indefinitely to subsequent taxation years.

2. Non-Recognition of Capital Losses

(a) Depreciable Property

The ACB of a depreciable property is its capital cost. If a taxpayer disposes of a depreciable asset for proceeds greater than capital cost, a taxable capital gain will result. A disposition for proceeds less than capital cost does not result in an allowable capital loss (paragraph 39(1)(b)), because the CCA provisions of the Act deal with proceeds below the property's capital cost.

(b) Personal-Use Property and Listed Personal Property

Personal-use property is subject to two restrictions. First, a capital loss on personal-use property is generally deemed to be nil, which prevents the deduction of capital losses attributable to personal consumption (subparagraph 40(2)(g)(iii)). As an exception to this rule, section 41 permits losses on listed personal property to be deducted from gains on such property. Second, a $1,000 exemption applies to dispositions of personal-use property (including listed personal property) (subsection 46(1)). If both the proceeds of disposition and the ACB of a property are less than $1,000, the capital gain (or loss on listed personal property) is exempt. If the ACB is less than $1,000 but the proceeds are greater than $1,000, the gain is computed as though the ACB were $1,000. If the proceeds of disposition are less than $1,000 and the ACB is greater than $1,000, a loss (on listed personal property only) is computed as though the proceeds were $1,000. If both proceeds and ACB are greater than $1,000, the exemption is inapplicable and gain or loss is computed in the ordinary way.

Example:

	A	B	C	D
ACB of property	$ 800	$1,800	$ 100	$ 900
Proceeds of disposition	$1,200	$ 400	$ 900	$ 200
Calculation of Capital Gain (Loss)				
Deemed proceeds of disposition (greater of proceeds or $1,000)	$1,200	$1,000	$1,000	$1,000
Deemed ACB (greater of cost or $1,000)	$1,000	$1,800	$1,000	$1,000
Capital gain (loss)	$ 200	($ 800)	$ Nil	$ Nil
Actual gain (loss)	$ 400	($1,400)	$ 800	($ 700)

Note: The loss in "B" would be deductible only if the asset sold was "listed personal property".

As defined in section 54, "personal-use property" means capital property owned by a taxpayer and used primarily for the personal use or enjoyment of the owner or any individual related to the owner. Most personal-use property consists of chattels, such as clothing, personal effects, hobby assets, cars, boats, furniture and listed personal property. Also, interests in certain real property are personal-use property, such as the family home, summer cottage or other recreational property. Two kinds of choses in action that relate to personal-use property are themselves personal-use property: an option to acquire personal-use property or the unpaid balance of the sale price on the disposition of such property. Property owned by a trust, partnership or corporation is personal-use property if the property is primarily for the personal use or enjoyment of certain individuals. If a taxpayer disposes of an interest in a trust or a partnership, or of shares in a corporation, and the proceeds are adversely affected by a decline in value of personal-use property owned by the trust, partnership or corporation, the adverse effect is disregarded as personal expense in computing the gain or loss. Part of an asset may be personal-use property, such as a family home that contains an office or a rental suite. An asset may be converted from personal use to commercial or investment purposes and *vice versa*. A change in use triggers a deemed disposition (section 45).

A debt owing to a taxpayer for the disposition of a capital property is itself a capital property. In the year in which the debt becomes uncollectible, and the taxpayer so elects, the outstanding balance can be realized as a capital loss (subsection 50(1)). On the sale of personal-use property, the vendor may extend credit to the purchaser. Such a debt arising out of the disposition of personal-use property is also personal-use property, and any capital loss on the bad debt is disallowed. But to recognize the fact that the taxpayer may have paid tax on a gain that will not be realized, a bad debt on personal-use property is deductible to the extent of the gain reported on the disposition, if the taxpayer and debtor dealt at arm's length (subsection 50(2)).

Although listed personal property is also personal-use property, it is different from other personal-use property because, as a "collectible", its value does not inevitably decline through use (section 54 "listed personal property"). If its value falls, it may be for essentially the same reasons that cause any capital loss, such as changing market conditions. Nevertheless, losses on listed personal property may be deducted only from gains on listed personal property (section 41).

If a taxpayer disposes of part of a personal-use property, the ACB of the part disposed of is deemed to be the greater of the ACB as determined under subsection 43(1) or the proportion of $1,000 that the ACB of the part disposed of bears to the ACB of the whole property (paragraph 46(2)(a)). Similarly, the proceeds of disposition are deemed to be the greater of the proceeds or the same proportion of $1,000 (paragraph 46(2)(b)).

In certain circumstances, subsection 46(3) deems a number of personal-use properties, which a taxpayer has separately disposed of, to be one personal-use property and each disposal to be a part disposition. First, the properties must be of the type that would normally be disposed of as a set. Whether a number of articles constitute a set is a question of fact, comprising various factors: the items should match or belong together, they should have been produced or issued at roughly the same time and, ordinarily, they are worth more collectively than individually. Even though a taxpayer may have purchased the items individually, as long as two or more were owned at any time, they would constitute a set. Second, the taxpayer must have disposed of all the items by more than one disposition, either to one person or to the members of a group who are not at arm's length with each other. Third, the aggregate fair market value of the assets must be more than $1,000.

Questions

1. X purchased antique dining room furniture, consisting of four matching chairs and a matching table. X paid $100 for each chair and $400 for the table. Years later the chairs are worth $200 each and the table is worth $800 as separate items, but as a unit they are worth $2,400. X wishes to give the furniture to Y. Should X do so by one gift or several? What is the effect of subsection 46(3)?

2. X sold his collection of approximately 1,000 stamps for $15,000. The stamps had been acquired by X at various times since 1972 at a total cost of $23,000. At the same time X sold his car, which originally cost $3,000, for $1,000 and 6 dining room chairs for $400 apiece. The chairs cost $300 each. What are the tax consequences to X? What if X had sold the car for $4,000 rather than $1,000? What if X had sold a painting, which cost $10,000 for $15,000? What if the stamps were hockey cards?

(c) Superficial Loss

A superficial loss is a loss realized on a transaction in which a taxpayer sells property at a loss and repurchases the same or identical property. The purpose of the transaction is to trigger a loss by temporarily parting with property that has declined in value. The superficial loss rule disallows the loss that would otherwise result, and requires its addition to the ACB of the "substituted property". Recognition of the loss is postponed, therefore, to a subsequent disposition of the substituted property.

A superficial loss is defined in section 54 as a capital loss arising from the taxpayer's disposition of property if the same or identical property (the "substituted property") or a right to acquire such property is acquired by the taxpayer, or by a person affiliated with the taxpayer, within 30 days before or after the disposition of the original property. The substituted property, or the right to acquire it, must still be owned by the taxpayer or the affiliated person 30 days after the disposition that resulted in the loss. The definition of superficial loss excludes losses arising on certain deemed dispositions. Affiliated persons include spouses, controlled corporations and partnerships (section 251.1).

E. Capital Gains Deduction

The capital gains deduction, also known as the lifetime capital gains exemption, exempts up to a base amount of $800,000 for 2014, indexed for inflation thereafter. For 2015, the limit is $813,600 ($800,000 × index factor of 1.017) of capital gains on the disposition of shares of a qualifying small business corporation or qualified farm or fishing property. Under the one-half inclusion rate for taxable capital gains, the exemption covers up to $400,000 (in 2014) of taxable capital gains as a cumulative lifetime total. The exemption is a Division C deduction that may be taken in calculating taxable income for the year. It is available only to an individual (other than a trust) who was resident in Canada throughout the year. A taxpayer who was resident for only part of the taxation year in question is deemed to have been resident throughout that year if he or she was resident throughout either the immediately preceding or the immediately following year (subsection 110.6(5)).

Until 1994, section 110.6 distinguished between three types of property on which capital gains were eligible for the deduction. First, there was "qualified farm property" (subsection 110.6(1)). Up to $500,000 of capital gains on such property could be offset by the deduction in subsection 110.6(2). Second, there were "qualified small business corporation shares" (subsection 110.6(1)) which are, basically, shares of a Canadian-controlled private corporation (CCPC) substantially all of whose assets are used in an active business carried on in Canada. Gains on these shares were entitled to the $500,000 deduction (subsection 110.6(2.1)) to encourage investment in small businesses. Third, subsection 110.6(3) allowed the capital gains deduction to be claimed in respect of gains on any other capital property. In 1992, gains on investments in most real estate ceased to qualify under the third category. Moreover, the lifetime maximum amount of capital gains exempted under the third category was to be $500,000 when it was introduced in 1985 (although phased in over five years), but was capped at $100,000 in 1988. Henceforth the third category was commonly called the "$100,000 exemption". It was eliminated in 1994.

Qualified fishing property became eligible for the exemption in 2006. In 2007, the lifetime maximum rose to $750,000 ($375,000 of taxable capital gains), from the previous $500,000 maximum. In 2014, the maximum rose to $800,000 ($400,000 of taxable capital gains). For 2015 onwards, the maximum of $800,000 is indexed for inflation.

There are certain limitations on a taxpayer's ability to claim the capital gains deduction if the taxpayer has claimed certain expenses or realized losses from property (see the definitions of "cumulative net investment loss" and "investment expense" in subsection 110.6(1)). The deduction must be taken after all other Division C deductions, including non-capital and net capital losses from other years (section 111.1), which, however, are discretionary. Occasionally, a taxpayer may have to decide whether it is better to "save" net capital losses for use in another taxation year and use the capital gains deduction in the year in question or vice versa.

F. International Aspects

1. Non-Residents and Capital Gains

A disposition of taxable Canadian property by a non-resident is taxed under Part I rather than under the withholding tax provisions in Part XIII of the Act. See Chapter 3. The non-resident disposing of such property must file a Canadian tax return, and is liable to pay tax that is due. Relief for non-residents may involve exemption by treaty, entitlement to claim the principal residence exemption for years of residence in Canada, or applicability of a tax rollover provision. Non-residents cannot claim the capital gains deduction under section 110.6, however. To address the obvious problems of collecting tax from non-residents after the fact, section 116 establishes an elaborate withholding scheme. The ultimate responsibility is imposed on the purchaser to ensure that a non-resident vendor of taxable Canadian property prepays a required amount near the time of the disposition towards the ultimate tax liability. Section 116 applies to most forms of taxable Canadian property (most often to transactions in Canadian real estate) and applies regardless of whether the purchaser of taxable Canadian property is resident or non-resident.

2. Deemed Disposition or Acquisition on Change of Residence

Canadian residents are taxable in respect of gains on capital property generally, regardless of whether it is located within or beyond Canadian borders. In principle, an immigrant to Canada should face Canadian tax consequences on dispositions of taxable Canadian property even though the gains and losses accrued before the taxpayer became resident in Canada. Like other residents, the immigrant should also face Canadian tax consequences on world-wide capital gains and losses that accrue during the owner's residence in Canada. On the other hand, an emigrant leaving Canada should, on becoming non-resident, remain subject to the Canadian tax system for gains or losses on taxable Canadian property, but not on other capital property.

Before 1996, the Act tried to realize these principled results by providing for deemed dispositions and acquisitions of capital property other than taxable Canadian property at fair market value upon becoming resident in Canada and upon ceasing to be a resident of Canada. For those entering Canada, the deemed disposition did not trigger liability for Canadian tax on the gains because they related to a period of non-residence. It did, however, fix the initial cost base for the property to exclude gains and losses that accrued during the period of non-residency. For any property other than taxable Canadian property that the taxpayer owned before becoming a Canadian resident, the cost was deemed to be equal to the property's fair market value when the taxpayer became a resident. Even before taking up residence in Canada, the immigrant was liable to tax in Canada on the disposition of taxable Canadian property, so those accrued gains and losses should be brought into any computation of future Canadian tax when the property is ultimately sold. On emigrating from Canada, a taxpayer was liable for tax as a consequence of a deemed disposition of capital property other than taxable Canadian property (the "departure tax"). Those gains or losses that accrued during Canadian residence would otherwise escape from the Canadian tax system unless they were deemed to be realized immediately before the change in residence, that is, while the taxpayer was still a Canadian resident. The deemed disposition and acquisition rules applied to any taxpayer that changed residence, including a corporation or a trust.

The current rules, which took two years to develop, apply on changes in residence status after October 1, 1996. The rules do not change the tax consequences of immigration, because after becoming a Canadian resident, world-wide gains and losses are taxable in Canada, including those previously accruing on taxable Canadian property. As before, a person immigrating to Canada is still deemed to acquire capital property other than taxable Canadian property at its fair market value when the person becomes resident in Canada (see subsection 128.1(1)).

Under the current rules, however, an individual emigrant faces a more comprehensive departure tax than previously, covering virtually all capital property, including many types of taxable Canadian property (see subsection 128.1(4)). This change was necessary to prevent emigrants from escaping Canadian tax on taxable Canadian properties by moving to a country with which Canada had concluded a tax treaty, and claiming exemption from Canadian tax under treaty provisions. For example, as a resident of a treaty country, the taxpayer could often claim exemption from Canadian tax on the disposition of movable capital property such as corporate shares. There are a few exceptions from the departure tax for certain taxable Canadian properties, however. These properties, notably real property in Canada and capital property used to carry on business in Canada through a permanent establishment, remain subject to Canadian tax on disposition by non-residents located in treaty countries.

The rigors of the "departure tax" are mitigated in various ways. Immigrants who are resident in Canada for 60 months or less out of the 120 months preceding their departure from Canada are not subject to the departure tax in respect of capital property owned when they entered Canada. Second, an individual (other than a trust) who emigrated from Canada and returns to Canada within 60 months of emigrating may elect to undo the earlier deemed disposition upon becoming non-resident. A taxpayer can also elect to have a deemed disposition and reacquisition at fair market value of any item of taxable Canadian property that would not normally be deemed to be disposed of upon losing Canadian residence. A taxpayer might make the election to claim accrued losses on the taxable Canadian property (to offset gains on other property). Also, the election might be useful if taxable Canadian property has accrued gains that are eligible for the capital gains exemption, which can only be claimed while the taxpayer is a Canadian resident. The elections cannot be used selectively to generate an overall reduction of income (paragraph 128.1(4)(f)). Finally, if an emigrant disposes of capital property that declined in value following the departure tax, the loss can be carried back and deducted from the previous capital gain triggered by the emigration, without any limitation period.

IV. INTRA-FAMILY TRANSFERS

A. Realization Versus Rollover Treatment

If a donor gives a capital property such as shares or land to a donee, should the transfer be taxed as if it were a sale at fair market value? Who should be taxed: the donor or the donee? Generally, the Act imposes tax on the transfer and the donor bears the tax liability. A donor of capital property is deemed to have sold it for fair market value proceeds and the donee is deemed to acquire the property at an equivalent cost (paragraphs 69(1)(b) and (c)). The donor must compute and pay tax on a capital gain if the fair market value exceeds its ACB. If the property declined in value, the donor will be able to claim a capital loss, subject to the superficial loss rule described above.

In contrast to the fair market value rule, a "rollover" exempts the transfer from tax, and preserves the accrued gain or loss until the donee subsequently disposes of the property. Transfers of capital property to a transferor's spouse or spouse trust and of farm property to a child benefit from rollover treatment. The increase or decline in value remains excluded from the computation of a capital gain or loss until the donee disposes of the property in a taxable transaction. To preserve any accrued and potential gain or loss, the donee is deemed to acquire the property at a cost equal to the donor's ACB at the time of the transfer. When the donee disposes of the property in a taxable disposition, the capital gain or loss will be the difference between the proceeds of disposition and the donee's deemed cost. Such gains or losses will reflect both the appreciation or decline in value accrued during the donor's ownership and any appreciation or decline in value accrued during the donee's ownership.

Rollover treatment for inter-spousal transfers is premised on an assumption that spouses are an economic unit. The same treatment for farm property attempts to preserve the family farm as a way of life. Although a family may be viewed as a single economic and social unit, it is generally regarded for income tax purposes as composed of distinct individual taxpayers. Taxpayers who view the family as a unit may wish to transfer properties for both fiscal and personal reasons. A high-income taxpayer may give an income-producing property to a lower-income family member in order to split income while keeping the property in the family. An older taxpayer may give property on which a gain likely will accrue to a younger member of the family to avoid the taxation of accrued gain on death. A taxpayer whose capital property has declined in value may transfer it to a family member so as to claim a deduction for the capital loss while keeping the asset within the family. Taxpayers may seek to use trusts and corporations as intermediaries for the benefit of present family members or future generations. The deemed disposition at fair market value achieves the following goals: (1) equivalent treatment of gifts and sales; (2) prevention of avoidance or deferral of tax on accrued but unrealized gains; and (3) prevention of the shifting of income to family members taxable at lower rates.

The transfer of property between family members may result in the attribution of income, gain or loss back to the transferor. See Chapter 2 for a discussion of the income attribution rules as an additional response to income shifting.

B. Gifts and Non-Arm's Length Transactions

For tax purposes, a gift is a gratuitous transfer of property. A sale at an undervaluation is not a gift: *The Queen v. Littler*, [1978] C.T.C. 235, 78 D.T.C. 6179 (F.C.A.). Subsection 69(1) deals specifically with both gifts and sales. On a gift of anything, the donor is deemed to receive proceeds of disposition equal to fair market value and the donee is deemed to have acquired it at a cost equal to that value.

If property is sold in a non-arm's length transaction and the actual selling price is greater than fair market value, the proceeds to the vendor remain the selling price but the deemed cost to the purchaser is the fair market value. If the actual price is less than fair market value, the deemed proceeds to the vendor are fair market value, but the cost to the purchaser remains the actual cost. In effect, where a vendor and purchaser do not deal at arm's length, the Act replaces a price that does not correspond to fair market value with the fair market value for only one of the parties. If they understate the price, the vendor's proceeds are increased. If they overstate the price, the purchaser's cost is lowered. There is no explicit provision for an offsetting correction for the other party. Although there is a general presumption in the case law against taxing the same amount of income twice, here, two taxpayers, the non-arms' length buyer and seller, are being taxed on the same amount and the presumption may not extend to them.

In anticipation of a dispute with the CRA over the price chosen for a non-arm's length sale, the parties may use a "price adjustment clause", whereby they agree to accept the ultimate determination of fair market value (for example, by the CRA upon reassessment, or as determined by subsequent objection or appeal) if it should be different from their own. The CRA's guidelines for price adjustment clauses are set out in Income Tax Folio S4-F3-C1: Price Adjustment Clauses (January 14, 2014); see also *Seaman (R.) v. M.N.R.*, [1990] 2 C.T.C. 2469, 90 D.T.C. 1909 (T.C.C.). If agreement cannot be reached with a taxpayer as to the fair market value of property and the dispute goes to court, the trial becomes a "battle of experts", in which the appraisers' opinions on both sides are scrutinized by the judge who must ultimately determine fair market value as a question of mixed fact and law, to be determined by applying the legal definition of "fair market value" to the findings of fact from the evidence adduced: *Nash v. Canada* (2005), [2006] 1 C.T.C. 158, 2005 D.T.C. 5696 (F.C.A.).

Because section 69 applies to transfers for consideration between taxpayers who are not dealing at arm's length (as well as to gifts), the meaning of "non-arm's length" must be considered. There are two rules for determining if parties do not deal at arm's length.

First, "related persons" are not at arm's length: paragraph 251(1)(a). Individuals connected by blood relationship, marriage or adoption and corporations connected by common control are related persons. An individual is connected by blood with his or her grandparents, parents, siblings, children, successive descendants and in-laws (brother, sister, son or daughter, grandparents and parents) (paragraph 251(6)(a) and subsections 252(1) and (2)). By marriage, a taxpayer is connected to his or her spouse, spouses of the siblings of his or her spouse and siblings of spouses of his or her siblings (paragraph 251(6)(b) and subsection 252(2)). Since 1993, common-law spouses, and since 2001, same-sex partners, have been treated the same as married couples. A common-law partner is defined by section 248 ("common-law partner") as a person who is living with the taxpayer in a conjugal relationship and either had been living in such a relationship with the taxpayer for at least 12 months or, if the period of cohabitation is less than 12 months, is the parent (broadly defined) of a child of whom the taxpayer is a parent. Relatives who are not related to the taxpayer include an aunt or uncle, nephew or niece, and cousin of any degree. A person is not considered related to someone who is deceased.

Second, unrelated persons may not deal at arm's length as a question of fact (paragraph 251(1)(c)). In determining whether persons do not deal at arm's length, the CRA considers the following criteria:

(a) the existence of a common mind that directs the bargaining for both parties to the transaction;

(b) parties acting in concert without separate interests (or in a highly interdependent manner);

(c) *de facto* control, in the sense of excessive or constant advantage, authority or influence by one party over the other; and

(d) price different from fair market value.

See Income Tax Folio S1-F5-C1: Related persons and dealing at arm's length (May 2, 2014); see also *Penner v. The Queen*, [1994] 2 C.T.C. 253, 94 D.T.C. 6566 (F.C.T.D.).

C. Spousal Transfers

Under subsection 73(1), the transfer by an individual of capital property to the taxpayer's spouse or to a spouse trust will automatically benefit from rollover treatment, unless the transferor elects otherwise. On a rollover of capital property, the proceeds of disposition are deemed to be the ACB of the transferred property. If the property is depreciable, the proceeds are deemed to equal the UCC, although for the CCA provisions, the property is deemed to have a capital cost equal to its cost to the transferor (in order to preserve the potential for recapture). The transferee is deemed to acquire the property at the same amount so that the actual gain or loss is deferred rather than permanently excluded. The transferor may elect in the income tax return for the taxation year in which the transfer occurs not to apply the rollover. If so, the proceeds to the transferor and the cost to the transferee will be determined under the general rules in subsection 69(1) (subject, in the case of depreciable property, to special rules in paragraph 13(7)(e)). The transferor will report the capital gain or loss resulting from the disposition and the transferee spouse or spouse trust is not taxable on the transfer.

To qualify for rollover treatment, there must be a transfer of capital property, and the transferor and transferee must be resident in Canada. The recipient of the property must be one of the following:

(a) the transferor's spouse or common-law partner;

(b) the transferor's former spouse or common-law partner, if the transfer is in settlement of rights arising out of their marriage or common law partnership; or

(c) a "spouse trust".

On a marriage breakdown, a property settlement qualifies for the rollover if it occurs before the divorce decree, because the parties are still spouses. After the decree, the parties are no longer spouses, but the rollover applies if the transfer is in settlement of rights arising out of the marriage. It is arguable that a court-ordered division of matrimonial property or an interest in matrimonial property created by provincial legislation is not a "transfer" because it is involuntary. To ensure that the rollover applies, the word "transfer" is defined to include a court-ordered division and the vesting of an interest in property by law on a marital break-up (subsection 73(1.1)).

D. Transfer of Farm or Fishing Property

Subsections 73(3) and (4) provide rollover treatment on transfers of farm or fishing property to a child of the transferor. When the child disposes of the property, he or she will include the postponed gain or loss on the transfer in calculating his or her gain or loss on the disposition. If at the time of disposition by the child, the child is under 18 years of age, the gain or loss is attributed back to the transferor (section 75.1). See Chapter 2. To qualify for rollover treatment, the child must be a Canadian resident immediately before the transfer, and the property must be used in a farming or fishing business that actively engaged the transferor or the spouse or child of the transferor on a regular and continuous basis. "Child" is defined broadly in subsection 252(1). The rollover applies to assets, shares of the capital stock of a corporation, or an interest in a partnership.

On a transfer of capital property such as farmland, the transferor is deemed to have received, at the very least, proceeds of disposition equal to the ACB; for depreciable property, proceeds equal to the UCC; and, for eligible capital property, proceeds equal to four-thirds of the cumulative eligible capital. Therefore, the transferor cannot create a capital loss or a terminal loss. The child's cost equals the deemed proceeds.

V. THE PRINCIPAL RESIDENCE

For individuals, the most significant exemption from capital gains is the principal residence. Any gains realized on a disposition of a property that qualifies as a "principal residence" may be exempt from tax. If the dwelling qualifies as the taxpayer's principal residence throughout the period of ownership, the entire gain is exempt. If it is a principal residence for some of that period, a corresponding portion of the gain is exempt. The Act provides a formula that apportions the realized gain over the entire period of the taxpayer's ownership (paragraph 40(2)(b)). The exemption applies to the portion of the gain that corresponds to the period that the dwelling qualified as a principal residence and the person was resident in Canada. A capital loss on the disposition of an owner-occupied dwelling is disallowed as a loss on personal-use property.

A taxpayer may not claim CCA on the family home because it is not held to produce income. The typical homeowner cannot deduct interest on a mortgage to finance the acquisition of the home or any property taxes because such expenses are not incurred to produce income. However, some astute taxpayers, by borrowing for investment or business purposes on the security of a mortgage on the family home have rendered their mortgage interest deductible. Physicians, lawyers and other self-employed professional or business taxpayers who have home offices may be able to deduct overhead expenses attributable to the office. See Chapter 5.

A. The Elements of the Principal Residence Exemption

"Principal residence" is defined in section 54 as a housing unit, leasehold interest or share of the capital stock of a co-operative housing corporation owned (jointly or otherwise) by the taxpayer, and ordinarily inhabited by the taxpayer, his or her spouse, former spouse, common-law partner, former common-law partner, or child. A "housing unit" may include a house, condo apartment or townhouse, mobile home, camper, trailer, cottage or houseboat. The phrase "ordinarily inhabited" requires that the housing unit must be "in most cases, usually or commonly occupied as an abode", and includes seasonal or recreational occupation. Therefore, if only half of a duplex is occupied by the owner, only half of the land and building comprise the principal residence. On the other hand, where a taxpayer owns a house containing three apartment units, one of which he or she occupies, the whole building may qualify as a principal residence if the division of units is internal and the occupiers share common facilities. A vacant lot cannot qualify as a principal residence until it contains a housing unit.

The principal residence includes up to one-half hectare (1.24 acres) of surrounding land that may reasonably be regarded as contributing to the taxpayer's use and enjoyment of the housing unit as a residence. This test, as now applied by the courts and the CRA, accepts without proof that land up to one-half hectare does contribute to the taxpayer's use and enjoyment, unless the taxpayer uses the land to earn income. Claiming the principal residence exemption over larger areas of land is more difficult, however. To exempt the gain on land in excess of half a hectare, the taxpayer faces "a formidable task", for the excess is deemed not to have contributed to the use and enjoyment of the housing unit as a residence unless the taxpayer establishes that it was necessary to such use and enjoyment. The test of necessity for excess land is primarily objective, to which evidence of the taxpayer's lifestyle is almost irrelevant. As Christie A.C.J.T.C. stated in *Rode v. M.N.R.*, [1985] 1 C.T.C. 2324, 85 D.T.C. 272 (T.C.C.):

> ... the proper approach ... is to objectively consider all of the relevant circumstances adduced in evidence which were in existence immediately prior to the disposition of the property and in the light of that answer this question: have the [taxpayers] established on a balance of probabilities that without the area of land for which they contend constituting the subjacent and immediately contiguous land component of their housing unit they could not practically have used and enjoyed the unit as a residence?

The taxpayer has to show that the excess land not merely contributed, but was indispensable to the use and enjoyment of the housing unit as a residence. Evidence of an expert appraiser that the highest and best use of the excess land was for the use and enjoyment of the housing unit is relevant, but not conclusive.

Applying this approach, the courts have held that, if a zoning by-law imposed minimum lot sizes or forbade subdivision into smaller parcels and these limits prevent the taxpayer from selling part of the land, the excess is considered necessary. In *The Queen v. Yates*, [1983] C.T.C. 105, 83 D.T.C. 5158 (F.C.T.D.); appeal dismissed, [1986] 2 C.T.C. 46, 86 D.T.C. 6296 (F.C.A.), the taxpayers purchased 10 acres of land and built their home on the property, actually using less than one acre for the home and renting the other nine acres to a neighbouring farmer. They bought the 10 acres because the zoning by-law specified that minimum lot size. Fourteen years later, they sold the vacant land to the city under threat of expropriation. Mahoney J., upheld the taxpayer's claim of the principal residence exemption in respect of the land and expressed the initial approach when he wrote "[i]n my opinion, the critical time is the moment before disposition."

In *Cassidy v. Canada* (2011), 2011 FCA 271, [2012] 1 C.T.C. 105, 2011 D.T.C. 5160 (F.C.A.), the Court rejected that approach, holding that the taxpayer must make the designation of the property as a principal residence year-by-year throughout the period of ownership. In most circumstances, the designation does not need to be filed with the CRA.

The CRA adopts the year-by-year approach to determine the principal residence. In Income Tax Folio S1-F3-C2: Principal Residence (February 3, 2015) at paragraph 2.13 it is stated as follows:

> 2.13 For a property to be a taxpayer's principal residence for a particular year, he or she must designate it as such for the year and no other property may have been so designated by the taxpayer for the year.

If the property does not satisfy the requirements to be a principal residence in a year, the gain on disposition may not be completely exempted.

Despite the foregoing expressions of judicial scepticism towards allowing the principal residence to exempt gains on large plots of land, a contrary decision of the Federal Court of Appeal suggested that the taxpayer's task may be less "formidable" than had previously been thought. In *Carlile v. The Queen*, [1995] 2 C.T.C. 273, 95 D.T.C. 5483 [cited to C.T.C.], the Federal Court of Appeal indicated that, contrary to previous authority, a taxpayer could establish that a large piece of land was necessary to the use and enjoyment of the residence exclusively on a subjective basis, that is, on matters of lifestyle. The Court also accepted rather equivocal evidence regarding local land use practice and politics to establish necessity on an objective test. The following dictum by the majority suggested another approach to considering the taxpayer's lifestyle:

> One way of establishing that land in excess of one acre [now one-half hectare] is necessary to the use and enjoyment of the housing unit as a residence is by reference to what is known as an objective test. Where the land does not qualify on the objective test it may, however, qualify as part of the principal residence by recourse to a subjective test. [At 275.]

In *Stuart Estate v. The Queen*, [2004] 2 C.T.C. 332, 2004 D.T.C. 6173, the Federal Court of Appeal was dismissive of the majority's reasoning in *Carlile*, preferring objective evidence. According to *Stuart*, objective evidence is relevant to support a claim that land in excess of one-half hectare was necessary to the use and enjoyment of the housing unit as a residence, and subjective evidence is only marginally relevant. Thus, the taxpayer disposing of a larger estate could make a more cogent argument for complete exemption based on zoning restrictions, barriers to subdivision, accessibility to roads and utilities as justifying the need for a super-sized lot, whereas the taxpayer's personal preference for more space or privacy would be less persuasive. The CRA requires the taxpayer to establish that excess land must "clearly be necessary" to the proper functioning of the residence, not merely desirable: Income Tax Folio S1-F3-C2: Principal Residence (February 3, 2015) at paragraph 2.33.

The exemption applies to only one dwelling, or co-interest therein, for each taxation year. A taxpayer may buy, renovate, occupy and sell a series of principal residences over the years; but if the transactions become too numerous, the houses would become the subject of an adventure in the nature of trade: see for example, *Isaaks v. The Queen*, [2001] 3 C.T.C. 2190, 2001 D.T.C. 645 (T.C.C.), appeal dismissed [2003] 4 C.T.C. 183, 2003 D.T.C. 5494 (F.C.A.); *Nowoczin v. Canada*,

[2007] 5 C.T.C. 2086, 2007 D.T.C. 949 (T.C.C.); *Scopacasa v. The Queen*, [2004] 5 C.T.C. 2530, 2004 D.T.C. 3455 (T.C.C.); and *Vogan v. The Queen* (2004), [2005] 1 C.T.C. 2372, 2004 D.T.C. 3459 (T.C.C.). A taxpayer who owns more than one principal residence (e.g., a house and cottage) must, when the first property is disposed of, designate one of the properties as the principal residence for each year in which both were owned. The taxpayer should determine which of the properties has enjoyed the greatest increase in value over the years of ownership since 1972 and should designate that property as the principal residence to make the best use of the exemption. The taxpayer claiming the principal residence exemption must be resident in Canada during the year of designation, but the property may be located outside Canada.

Until December 31, 1981, each spouse could claim a principal residence. Therefore, until then, if each spouse owned a property separately and not as a joint tenant with the other spouse (for example, one spouse owned the primary residence and the other spouse owned a summer cottage or other seasonal property), they could claim two principal residences between them. After 1981, only one principal residence may be claimed by a family, comprising the two spouses and unmarried children under 18 years. Spouses living together are therefore limited to one principal residence, but those who are legally separated and living apart may each claim a principal residence. Common-law spouses living together could claim two principal residences up to 1993, but for 1993 and subsequent years, they are subject to the one residence limitation as a result of the extended definition of spouse in subsection 252(4). Since 2001, same-sex couples have also been limited to one principal residence.

On marriage breakdown, if one spouse or former spouse receives exclusive possession of the matrimonial home, the other spouse, who owns the property, may continue to claim the exemption for the period during which he or she is not in possession. Similarly, if a child of the taxpayer occupies the dwelling, it qualifies for exemption.

A homeowner who vacates the principal residence and rents it out may continue to claim the dwelling as a principal residence for a maximum period of absence of four years as long as the owner elects under subsection 45(2) (see below) to treat the dwelling as personal-use property while renting it out. A period of absence greater than four years is permissible on work relocation. In particular, a homeowner who vacates the dwelling in order to move at least 40 kilometres closer to a new place of employment may continue to claim the principal residence exemption for the property for the duration of the relocated job plus one year or until death during the term of employment. The owner must elect to treat the dwelling as personal-use property (section 54.1).

As noted above, the principal residence exemption is determined after the taxpayer has computed the capital gain in the ordinary way. Paragraph 40(2)(b) provides a deduction from the gain based on the number of years of ownership that the taxpayer occupied the property as his or her principal residence. The formula uses whole years, so that if a taxpayer owns or occupies a property for part of a year, it constitutes a whole year for the purpose of the formula. The formula favours the taxpayer because it includes one extra year as a principal residence. What is the rationale for the extra year? Consider the common situation in which a taxpayer sells a residence and buys a new residence in the same year. See generally Income Tax Folio S1-F3-C2: Principal Residence (February 3, 2015).

Questions

1. In 1982, H and W purchased a large house in Toronto at a cost of $40,000. In 1993 they had a swimming pool installed in the backyard at a cost of $10,000. In 1995 H died and the house, which H and W had held as joint tenants, became the sole property of W. W continued to live in the house until 2015 when she sold the house for $1,500,000. Advise W as to the income tax consequences of the sale of the house.
2. X purchased a house for $300,000 and occupied it as a principal residence within the meaning of the Act for several months. Then X was moved to another city as part of a job relocation and sold the house for $325,000. What are the income tax consequences? What if X bought a house at the new location and then sold it at a gain later in the same calendar year when X was once again moved for job reasons?

B. Deemed Disposition on Change in Use

Under subsection 45(1), a disposition at fair market value is deemed to occur when a taxpayer changes the use of property from personal-use to income-earning purposes or vice versa. The deemed disposition on change in use applies to any type of capital property owned by a taxpayer, although in practice, it applies most often to dwellings. For example, a taxpayer may decide to stop using the family home as such and to turn it into a real estate development. The taxpayer's home would cease to be a personal capital asset and would become the subject-matter of the taxpayer's real estate development business. There is some uncertainty about when a change in use occurs. A clear and unequivocal positive act evidencing a change of intention is necessary to change the use of land. A mere expression of intention by the taxpayer to develop the land is insufficient. The test would be satisfied by the commencement of construction work or other physical change in the use of the land. Preliminary meetings, hiring consultants or the expenditure of the taxpayer's time and money examining the feasibility of development may be sufficient acts of a positive nature to demonstrate the change of use, even though the project never advances beyond the preliminary stage: see, for example, *Duthie Estate v. The Queen*, [1995] 2 C.T.C. 157, 95 D.T.C. 5376 (F.C.T.D.).

Sometimes, a taxpayer purchases a dwelling, rents it for years to tenants and then, after giving the current occupant notice to quit, occupies it as his or her personal residence. Even though there are no proceeds, the taxpayer may be required to recognize a capital gain because, on moving into the house, there is a deemed disposition for proceeds equal to fair market value. In *Leib v. M.N.R.*, [1984] C.T.C. 2324, 84 D.T.C. 1302 (T.C.C.), Taylor, T.C.C.J. suggested that the deemed disposition achieved equity as between the taxpayer who moves into a house that was formerly rented out and the taxpayer who sells the rental house and uses the proceeds (net of tax) to purchase another house for personal occupation:

> ... Using simple numbers for illustration purposes, if the taxpayer had paid $50,000 for the property in 1972, and sold it in 1976 to a third party for $100,000 and paid $10,000 income tax on the $50,000 gain, he would then have ended up with $90,000 net.
>
> Now, let us assume that there were only two houses available: the subject one at 275 Greenwood, and an identical one at 277 Greenwood, all other things were equal and he had a choice between the two houses, he could have reclaimed 275 Greenwood as his principal residence, and faced the problem before the Court, or he could have sold 275 Greenwood, and acquired 277 Greenwood instead. Since 277 Greenwood would cost him $100,000 he would only have $90,000 available and would be required to put up $10,000 of his own funds (or provide some other satisfaction) in order to acquire 277 Greenwood and make it "his" house. In simple terms, he would have found it necessary to replace the $10,000 income tax he had paid in order to have an equivalent property. As I see it, section 45 of the Act as it applies to these appeals merely ensures equal treatment (no less and no more) to taxpayers changing the use of a property with those taxpayers who acquire a principal residence in the manner outlined. ...

Subsection 45(3) permits a taxpayer to elect out of the deemed disposition at fair market value that would otherwise apply where a property is converted from an income-earning use to a personal use. The election is available only where the property, having previously been used for an income-earning purpose, becomes the taxpayer's principal residence. The election cannot be made if the taxpayer, the taxpayer's spouse, or a trust of which either of them was a beneficiary, has claimed CCA in respect of the property for a taxation year ending after 1984 and on or before the change in use (subsection 45(4)). The election must be filed with the Minister in writing within 90 days after a demand or by the deadline for filing the tax return for the year in which the property is actually disposed of (in other words, the election applies retroactively). In addition to the deferral of any accrued gain that would otherwise have been realized on a deemed disposition, the election under subsection 45(3) permits the property to qualify as the taxpayer's principal residence for a maximum of four previous years during which it was used for an income-earning purpose and was not occupied by the taxpayer, the taxpayer's spouse, former spouse, or child (section 54 "principal residence", subparagraph (b)(ii) and paragraph (d)).

Subsection 45(2) permits a taxpayer to elect out of the deemed disposition at fair market value that otherwise applies where property is converted from personal use to income-earning use. After the change in use, the taxpayer must report income earned from the property, after deducting applicable expenses; however CCA may not be claimed. In deciding whether to make this election, the taxpayer must weigh the advantage of postponing tax on any accrued gain against the disadvantage of being prevented from claiming CCA in respect of the asset. If, after making an election, the taxpayer revokes it, a disposition is deemed to occur on the first day of that year for proceeds equal to the fair market value at that time.

In the absence of an election under subsection 45(2), when the taxpayer, after having vacated the principal residence and leased it to a tenant, moves back into the house and reoccupies it, there would be another deemed disposition at fair market value when the use changes from income-producing to personal occupation. The principal residence exemption would not cover the accrued gain during the period that the taxpayer did not personally occupy the dwelling. However, if the taxpayer moves back into the family home while an election is in effect, and within four years (or longer if a change in workplace was involved), the gain during the period that the home was a rental property would be covered by the principal residence exemption. Even if the taxpayer does not move back into the property, the election under subsection 45(2) permits the property to qualify as the taxpayer's principal residence for a maximum of four more years (section 54 "principal residence" subparagraph (b)(i) and paragraph (d)).

A taxpayer who acquires a capital asset for both income-producing and non-productive purposes must allocate the cost according to the relative use for each purpose, and on disposing of the asset must allocate the proceeds on the same basis. This allocation rule applies when there is a change in the relative use between productive and non-productive purposes. The taxpayer is deemed to receive proceeds equal to the fair market value of the asset at that time multiplied by the amount of the change in use (expressed as a fraction of the whole). This rule may apply to a homeowner who acquires a home partly for the purpose of earning income or, after acquisition of the residence begins to use part for the purpose of earning income. Examples include doctors, lawyers, accountants and others who maintain offices in their homes, homeowners who let rooms in their houses, and store proprietors who live on the premises.

The CRA permits a taxpayer to install a home office or to take in boarders or otherwise begin to use a portion of the home for the purpose of earning income without triggering a deemed disposition or losing any portion of the principal residence exemption so long as: (1) the income use remains ancillary to the personal use; (2) the taxpayer does not make structural changes to the house; and (3) the taxpayer does not claim any CCA in respect of the house. Presumably, the taxpayer can claim CCA on furniture and equipment used in the home office. See Income Tax Folio S1-F1-C2, *supra*, paragraphs 2.58–2.59.

Example

X acquires an asset at a cost of $4,000 intending to divide its use equally between income production and personal consumption. When its fair market value rises to $8,000 he decides to increase the proportion of income production to 75 per cent of its total use. Under subparagraph 45(1)(c)(ii), he must recognize a gain of:

Deemed Proceeds:	25% of $8,000 or	$2,000
Deemed Cost:	25% of $4,000 or	$1,000
Deemed Gain (½ taxable):		$1,000

Question

X purchased a house at a cost of $50,000. This year, X decides to rent the upstairs portion of the house. What are the tax consequences if X makes the election contemplated by subsection 45(2)? What happens if next year X sells the house for $200,000? What if this year X rents out the entire house?

8

Refining What Is Taxed — In Search of an Ideal Income Tax System

I. INTRODUCTION

Provisions that Refine the Tax System's Structure and Advance Social Policy Goals

How does an ideal income tax system distribute the tax burden and achieve government social and economic policy goals? The government answers this question largely through the subdivision e deductions (ITA sections 60-66.8) and Division E tax credits (ITA sections 117-127.4). The provisions discussed in this chapter establish a minimum tax-free threshold for the progressive tax rate system; refine the tax unit by recognizing dependency; adjust income for expenses that straddle the line between personal and income earning purposes; promote saving for retirement; subsidize higher education and extraordinary medical expenses; and deliver government programs.

The provisions fall into two broad categories: structural provisions define who, what, when and how much we tax, and tax expenditure provisions carry out the government's social and economic policy goals. Structural provisions make up the normative or benchmark tax system. Tax expenditure provisions deliberately depart from the benchmark and spend government revenues by foregoing taxes if the taxpayer meets the expenditure's policy-based criteria.

We recommend that you revisit portions of Chapter 1 as you read this chapter. Chapter 1 sets the stage for understanding this chapter's provisions in two ways. First, it canvases the income tax system's multiple roles: raising revenue, redistributing income, stabilizing the economy, and delivering economic and social policy. Chapter 1 links to questions raised in this chapter, such as: How should government measure an individual's ability to pay? When and how should government recognize individual and family circumstances? Are tax measures that support private choices, like saving for retirement or attending university, primarily subsidies? Or do they achieve other social and economic goals by correcting market failures, or stabilizing the economy? When should the government choose tax reduction over direct spending to achieve its goals?

Second, Chapter 1 explains the evaluative criteria that policy makers apply to the structural and tax expenditure provisions. Budgetary spending criteria – clear objectives, proper targeting and fair distribution, measurable costs, and reasonable administrative costs – apply primarily to expenditure provisions. And remember Chapter 1's proviso that all tax policy decisions require tradeoffs between competing objectives and criteria.

When you evaluate the provisions covered in this chapter, consider whether they are properly cast as a deduction or credit. Subdivision e deductions reduce the amount of income that is taxed, whereas tax credits reduce the amount of tax that is paid. In a progressive tax rate system, a deduction is more valuable to a person in a high tax bracket than to a person in a low tax bracket. On the other hand, a tax credit has equal value to all taxpayers, assuming they owe enough tax to use the full credit amount. Ask yourself questions like: What is the rationale for structuring moving expenses, child care expenses, and pension and retirement contributions as deductions? Are some credits missing their target because too many otherwise eligible individuals owe little or no taxes? Should more credits be refundable?

In 1967, Stanley S. Surrey popularized dividing tax provisions into benchmark and tax expenditure provisions as a tool to better evaluate and account for government spending. Today, the Department of Finance publishes tax cost estimates, research papers, and reference documents that add transparency to fiscal policy. *Tax Expenditures and Evaluations*, an annual accounting of both benchmark and tax expenditures, answers the question, "How much does the provision cost?" Each year research papers on specific tax measures such as small business taxation (2012) and the public transit credit (2011) accompany the tax expenditure document. *Tax Expenditures: Notes to the Estimates/Projections*, published periodically, is a reference document summarizing each expenditure's objective and how Finance calculates the expenditure estimates and projections. These Department of Finance publications start us off with information we can build on to evaluate whether the provisions are fair, too narrow or to broad, achieve their objectives, easy to understand, or too complicated for people to apply.

We start with two early articles on the tax expenditure concept written by well-known tax scholars Stanley S. Surrey and William D. Andrews. We then turn to more current writing. Robin Boadway refines our understanding of the benchmark-expenditure dichotomy. Economist Frances Woolley confronts the partisan political agenda that sometimes motivates tax expenditures.

Stanley S. Surrey's *Pathways To Tax Reform* explains: (1) the two functions of the structural or "benchmark" provisions, (2) the government policy decisions required to create the tax structure, and (3) how tax expenditures differ from benchmark provisions. Surrey uses a medical expense deduction to illustrate a deduction's "upside-down" subsidy effect in a progressive tax rate system. In Canada the medical expense deduction was replaced by a credit in 1988, but the ideas Surrey discusses are still relevant. Surrey's analysis paves the way for your own thinking about which items should be deductions or credits.

In *Personal Deductions In An Ideal Income Tax*, William D. Andrews shakes up the tax expenditure analysis by adding a new initial inquiry: Is the provision simply a personal subsidy or is it "intrinsic" to a government tax policy? Andrew suggests that if the provision's objective links to a larger government policy goal by subsidizing individuals, then the upside-down subsidy effect may be justified. In the full article, Andrews discusses both medical expenses and charitable contributions. The excerpt focuses mostly on charitable contributions, which in Canada have, for individuals, been a credit since 1988. However, Andrews' review will be relevant to your study of the underlying rationales for the charitable credit. More importantly, Andrews' idea that we can justify deductions, despite their upside-down subsidy effect, if the government has a larger economic or social agenda, will give you food for thought when you ponder why moving and child care expenses remain deductions.

Robin Boadway's article *Policy Forum: The Annual Tax Expenditure Accounts – A Critique* highlights another conceptual problem with the benchmark-expenditure dichotomy: the line between benchmark and expenditure is a blurry one. Boadway makes us think more precisely about how we characterize and calculate the net tax costs of incentive provisions.

Finally, Frances Woolley's newspaper commentary *Why Politicans Love Boutique Tax Credits* berates the government for proliferating politically motivated personal tax credits that have little real economic value or capacity to change behaviour. Keep Woolley's commentary in mind when you read about the proposed Income-Splitting Credit and the Child Fitness Credit.

*PATHWAYS TO TAX REFORM**

Stanley S. Surrey

(Cambridge: Harvard University Press, 1973)pages 6-28 (footnotes omitted)

The [U.S.] federal income tax system consists really of two parts: one part comprises the structural provisions necessary to implement the income tax on individual and corporate net income; the second part comprises a system of tax expenditures under which Governmental financial assistance programs are carried out through special tax provisions rather than through direct Government expenditures. This second system is grafted on to the structure of the income tax proper; it has no basic relation to that structure and is not necessary to its operation. Instead, the system of tax expenditures provides a vast subsidy apparatus that uses the mechanics of the income tax as the method of paying the subsidies. The special provisions under which this subsidy apparatus functions take a variety of forms, covering exclusions from income, exemptions, deductions, credits against tax, preferential rates of tax, and deferrals of tax.

...

The tax expenditure concept in essence considers these special provisions as composed of two elements: the imputed tax payment that would have been made in the absence of the special provision (all else remaining the same) and the simultaneous expenditure of that payment as a direct grant to the person benefited by the special provision. The exemption, deduction, or other type of tax benefit is thus seen as a combined process of assumed payment of the proper tax by the taxpayer involved and an appropriation by the Government of an expenditure made to that taxpayer in the amount of the reduction in his actual tax payment from the assumed payment-that is, the tax reduction provided by the special provision.

...

The building of an income tax requires two types of provisions that collectively perform the following two functions: *First,* they provide the answers to questions that would essentially be treated in much the same way by any group of tax experts building the structure of an income tax and being governed in that task by all the requirements implicit in such a tax because it is an *income tax.* These answers then become the structural provisions which shape a normative income tax. As an illustration, in this first category all matters relating to the measurement of net income and the time periods for inclusion of that income. *Second,* they provide the answers to ... questions that likewise are necessary to building an income tax but could, in the view of such a group of tax experts, conceivably be treated differently from country to country depending on the views and policies shaped by other goals in the particular society, rather than by factors special to an income tax. These answers, in view of these possible differences, are not part of a normative income tax. However, these answers, once they are determined, do become structural parts of an income tax — and essential to the operation of that tax — and therefore are not tax expenditures. For example, as the Treasury analysis indicates, the treatment of the family — e.g., the tax burden on married couples in relation to single persons — is not part of a normative income tax. There is no preordained method of treatment that follows from the decision to adopt an income tax. Countries properly differ in the treatment depending on their attitudes toward marriage or women in the labor force and other such social and economic questions. The levels of personal exemptions and tax rates, and the degree of rate progressivity, are other examples mentioned in the Treasury analysis that would fall in this second category. The treatment of the corporation — as a separate entity or its income integrated with that of the shareholders in some fashion — is still another example. The provisions incorporating the decisions in these areas are not tax expenditures. But the decisions have to be made before the structure of the income tax is complete and the tax is ready to be applied. As a consequence, this set of provisions, while necessary to the construction of an income tax, is shaped by processes different in character from the processes determining the provisions in the first category, also relating to the inherent structure of an income tax. The tax expenditure provisions are, then, the provisions that may be found in an income tax law but that do not serve the two functions set forth above.

...

When medical expenses and charitable contributions are tested against the generally accepted definition of income, most economists would classify these items as tax expenditures. Hence their place in the Tax Expenditure Budget.

Another approach that should be mentioned is the view that a medical expense deduction is, shall we say, appropriate under an income tax since the deduction is needed to equalize the "ability to pay" an income tax between a family with an illness and a family without an illness. Proponents of this view would acquiesce in the listing of the medical expense deduction as a tax expenditure, since they both accept the Simons definition of income and recognize that, under that definition, the fact that funds are spent for medical care does not reduce the amount of "income". In this sense the medical expense deduction is not a theoretically necessary deduction in an income tax. But supporters of this view find this particular tax expenditure to be proper on policy grounds since they believe that, in the case of medical care, income is an imperfect measure of ability to pay, or an imperfect measure of horizontal equality between the above two families. This appears, for example, to be Joseph Pechman's tax policy justification for accepting a medical expense deduction.

... [W]hile I find understandable Pechman's concern about the medical bills of ill family A compared with the lack of such bills in healthy family B, I dislike the end consequences of his using a tax deduction and hence the tax system to equalize the two families. Essentially, he is saying that the Government as a creditor should yield a tax claim against family A — since Pechman accepts the Simons definition — in order that funds otherwise required to pay that tax claim may be used to pay a doctor's bill. But the amount of funds thus made available to pay that doctor's bill depends on the marginal tax bracket of family A. For a 70 per cent bracket family, the tax deduction — the yielding of the tax claim — means the Government is in effect paying 70 per cent of the doctor's bill. For a 14 per cent bracket family, it is through the deduction paying only 14 per cent of that bill. This is the inevitable upside-down quality that any tax expenditure phrased as a deduction has under a progressive income tax, and why such a tax expenditure is not as fair or efficient a way of meeting a national goal — here financial assistance in the payment of medical expenses — as is a direct expenditure program. Certainly, no direct program for medical care would have this upside-down effect.

*PERSONAL DEDUCTIONS IN AN IDEAL INCOME TAX**

William D. Andrews
(1972), 86 Harv L Rev 309

pages 309-346 (footnotes omitted)

A variety of provisions in the income tax law are now described as tax expenditures and evaluated as if they involved direct government expenditures equivalent in amount and distribution to the revenue reduction they produce. The medical expense deduction, for example, is described as the equivalent of a direct expenditure program by which the federal government provides partial reimbursement for extraordinary medical expenses. So viewed, of course, the provision seems to reflect an upside-down idea of policy because the rate of reimbursement is the taxpayer's marginal tax rate; this results in relatively generous rates of reimbursement for the well-to-do, while it provides nothing at all for the very poor who presumably have the greatest need.

Similarly, the charitable contribution deduction has been described as a kind of government matching gift program for the support of taxpayers' charities. Again the distribution of matching grants is effectively skewed to favor the charities of the wealthy because of their higher marginal tax rates: in the 70 per cent bracket, for example, the Government contributes $70 to match the taxpayer's $30 contribution, while in the 20 per cent bracket the Government's matching grant is only $20 for each $80 contributed by the taxpayer. Furthermore, there are other difficulties. Presumably, we would not permit direct government expenditures to provide matching gifts for churches. And if we were to have programs of direct support for other charities, it seems likely that we would insist upon a much more rigorous evaluation of priorities than the tax expenditure mechanism provides.

These are devastating criticisms. If they are correct, it seems to me the provisions in question are indefensible. But my feeling is that the criticisms are somehow overstated and that more sense can be made out of these two provisions than tax expenditure analysis immediately indicates. ...

The principal lesson to be derived from the tax expenditure analysis, I think, is that deductions (or exclusions) in the individual income tax are inferior devices for implementing objectives extraneous to those of the tax itself. This is mostly because of graduated rates. It will not generally make sense to distribute government funds according to the graduated rates in the personal income tax unless the purpose of the distribution is intrinsically related to the distribution of tax burdens that those rates are designed to effect.

But this lesson makes it imperative to focus very carefully upon the question whether the purposes underlying a particular provision are indeed extraneous to the purposes of the tax. Put the other way, it makes it imperative to consider carefully whether a provision can be defended by reference to intrinsic matters of tax policy before evaluating it as if it were something else. The tax expenditure analysis itself does not lead us to focus on that question because characterization as a tax expenditure and analogy to a direct expenditure generally imply that the provision serves purposes outside those of the tax system. The crucial judgment about underlying purpose tends, therefore, to get made by implication when a provision is classified as a tax expenditure, before the analysis itself begins.

Approaching the problem from the standpoint of any particular provision, therefore, the question that the tax expenditure analysis makes it urgent to consider is whether the provision can intelligently be seen as reflecting a refinement in our notion of an ideal personal income tax, rather than a departure from it. Only if that question is answered in the negative can the provision be adequately evaluated as if it were a direct expenditure unrelated to the collection of taxes.

These considerations have led me to re-examine the content of our notion of an ideal personal income tax in relation to the question of personal deductions to try to see whether, and under what conditions, deductions can be regarded as refinements instead of departures from the ideal.

...

Henry Simons advanced what is now the most widely accepted definition of personal income for tax purposes, defining it not in terms of sources but of uses. In its oft-quoted long form the definition states:

> Personal income may be defined as the algebraic sum of (1) the market value of rights exercised in consumption and (2) the change in the value of the store of property rights between the beginning and end of the period in question.

In its short form, as Simons repeated it throughout his book, income is consumption plus accumulation.

...

Identification of an ideal personal tax base as aggregate personal consumption plus accumulation makes good sense in terms of the purpose and effect of a personal tax. The primary intended effect of a direct, personal tax must be to divert economic resources away from personal consumption and accumulation. Some part of the national output which would otherwise be consumed or accumulated by private individuals is to be devoted to public purposes. Government expenditures are the device by which particular goods and services are devoted to public use, and taxation is the mechanism for imposing and distributing the corresponding reduction in private consumption and accumulation which must accompany the commitment of part of the aggregate national product to public purposes.

If the primary intended effect of the tax is to cause a reduction of private consumption and accumulation of real goods and services, then it makes sense to distribute the reduction in some kind of uniform (though graduated) relationship to the amount of consumption and accumulation people would otherwise enjoy. The effect of imposing direct personal taxes on the basis of aggregate consumption plus accumulation is to treat all people at any particular level of consumption and accumulation alike without regard to differences in the means by which their consumption and accumulation are financed. The result is that people at any given level of consumption plus accumulation before the tax will remain at the same level as one another after the tax, having borne an equal reduction by reason of the tax.

...

There is a more familiar way of stating the purpose of the income tax that may seem to point in a somewhat different direction: taxes are to be levied according to ability to pay, and such ability is shown by the receipt of income whether or not it is devoted to personal consumption and accumulation. But ability to pay expresses only a most vague and general idea of tax policy. It expresses a rejection of a benefit approach in which one tries to assess taxes in relation to the distribution among taxpayers of the benefits of government services. But it hardly goes any further because it fails to specify how ability is to be measured. There is no warrant for an a priori assumption that money income without adjustments is an ideal index of ability.

One way to measure ability to pay taxes is in terms of aggregate personal consumption and accumulation because this is what it is assumed will ultimately be sacrificed to pay the tax.

...

The *charitable contribution* deduction is generally described as a subsidy to charitable giving and thus to the activities of qualified charitable organizations. The effect of the deduction has been likened to a matching gift program under which an employer makes matching gifts to charities supported by its employees. There is something peculiar, of course, about the Government spending funds with so little control over their allocation or use. Furthermore, this is an unusual matching gift program because the rate at which gifts are matched varies directly with the taxpayer's marginal tax rate bracket: wealthy taxpayers find their gifts much more generously matched than do lower bracket taxpayers. A 70 per cent bracket taxpayer can make a $100 contribution at an after-tax cost of only $30; by way of tax reduction, therefore, the Government can be seen as contributing $70 to match the taxpayer's $30, for a matching rate of 233 per cent. By similar computation, a 40 per cent bracket taxpayer will find that the Government provides a matching grant of only $40 for his charitable contributions of $60, or a 662/ 3 per cent matching rate; a 20 per cent bracket taxpayer will find the Government's rate for matching his contributions to be only $1 for every $4 he contributes, or 25 per cent; and one too poor to pay any income tax in any event will find the Government unwilling to make any matching grant at all. ...

But I do not believe, nor do I think most serious practical students of the subject believe, that the charitable contribution deduction is as irrational as this explanation makes it sound. ...

... [T]here are substantial grounds for excluding from our definition of taxable personal consumption whatever satisfactions a taxpayer may get from making a charitable contribution. The charitable contribution deduction is quite different from the medical expense deduction since there is no reason to view the charitable contribution as offsetting some particular personal hardship like disease or injury. But there are other good reasons why a charitable contribution may rationally be excluded from the concept of taxable personal consumption. In the case of alms for the poor, for instance, the charitable contribution results in the distribution of real goods and services to persons presumably poorer and in lower marginal tax brackets than the donor. These goods and services, therefore, should not be taxed at the higher rates intended to apply to personal consumption by the donor. In the case of philanthropy more broadly defined — the support of religion, education, and the arts — benefits often do not flow exclusively or even principally to very low bracket taxpayers. But the goods and services produced do have something of the character of common goods whose enjoyment is not confined to contributors nor apportioned among contributors according to the amounts of their contributions. There are a number of reasons for defining taxable personal consumption not to include the benefit of such common goods and services. The personal consumption at which progressive personal taxation with high graduated rates should aim may well be thought to encompass only the private consumption of divisible goods and services whose consumption by one household precludes their direct enjoyment by others.

POLICY FORUM: THE ANNUAL TAX EXPENDITURE ACCOUNTS — A CRITIQUE

Robin Boadway
(2007) 55 Can. Tax. J. 106

Pages 107-108, 110, 114, 118-120 (footnotes omitted)

This article provides a critical review of the Department of Finance's annual publication *Tax Expenditures and Evaluations* (herein referred to as "the document"). The intent of the document is to inform Parliament and the public about the revenue costs of pursuing government policy objectives using special measures in the tax system. Economists have long recognized the equivalence of direct subsidies (which appear as expenditures in the public budget) and implicit subsidies offered as tax breaks of various sorts (which are not itemized in the budget). Both are intended to further public policy, and both entail costs to the government — direct subsidies in the form of costs to general revenue, and implicit subsidies in the form of forgone general revenues. Direct spending comes under parliamentary and public scrutiny through the normal process of budgetary approval. The idea of publishing an annual tax expenditure report is to enable comparable levels of scrutiny to apply for policies delivered indirectly through the tax system.

The main problem in achieving that objective is a conceptual one: how to identify the sources of forgone revenue that constitute tax expenditures. Once identified, the calculation of costs for particular tax expenditures is more or less routine, albeit subject to the many well-known problems — statistical and otherwise — of measuring forgone revenues.

...

Conceptual Issues

Defining what is meant by a "tax expenditure" raises issues of a conceptual nature for which there are no clearcut solutions, and this is recognized in the document. The implication is that considerable judgment is involved in deciding how tax expenditures should be classified in order to provide the best information to Parliament and the public. In this section, I will explore these conceptual issues, discuss alternative ways of addressing the problems they raise, and describe the conceptual basis for tax expenditure reporting adopted in the document.

The main problem arises because tax expenditures are essentially revenues that the government has chosen to forgo by legislating some measure of tax relief in order to achieve a particular policy objective. As the document points out, this necessarily requires that one define the benchmark tax system as the system that would be in place in the absence of tax expenditures. There are several reasons why this is problematic. The most basic one is that any benchmark tax system is itself a matter of government policy. The issue then is how to distinguish between policy objectives that are embodied in the tax system and those that should be treated as deviations from the benchmark. Somehow, the principles that are applied in designing a tax system that is both efficient and equitable must be distinguished from tax measures that are based on considerations other than optimal tax design, but nonetheless are delivered through the tax system.

This is much easier said than done. There is no consensus on what an optimal tax system looks like, so basing the definition of a benchmark system on the ideal system is not possible. Moreover, even if there were a consensus on what an optimal tax system should be in theory, judging which observed deviations from the optimal system are a matter of policy is not easy. Some deviations are the result of administrative feasibility. Thus, excluding the imputed rent on owner-occupied housing and other durables from the personal tax base may reflect problems of measurement as opposed to a specific policy choice. The same might be said for the special treatment afforded to capital gains to account for the fact that they are not indexed, or the limited extent to which the dividend tax credit reflects taxes paid at the corporate level. Other deviations represent tax measures that are introduced to pursue social objectives or to favour particular groups. For example, the basic personal exemption can be interpreted as being part of the rate structure, and as such it might be considered part of the benchmark system, encompassing standard equity objectives. What about other tax credits that effectively introduce progressivity into the tax structure, such as the spouse credit, the disability credit, the age credit, or the dependant credit? Are these elements of the benchmark tax structure intended to achieve equity in the personal tax system, or are they a matter of social policy? After all, optimal tax theory can be used to argue in favour of including special measures to deal with family circumstances in the tax system. Similar ambiguities arise with many other tax credits or deductions, including those for education, medical expenditures, and charitable donations.

...

At the same time, some policies delivered through the tax system are more clearly motivated by objectives other than the efficiency and equity of the tax system per se. Selectively sheltering some retirement savings from taxation is an example. This is evidently intended to encourage individuals to save for their retirement, rather than to achieve optimal taxation. It might be argued that credits for political contributions are similarly intended to serve as an incentive.

It seems clear that it is virtually impossible to define a benchmark tax system that lacks ambiguity for use as a basis for presenting tax expenditures. It also seems clear that many of the items that are listed as tax expenditures could just as well be treated as part of the benchmark system on efficiency and equity grounds. One must look a little further than optimal tax theory to define a benchmark system. Given the lack of agreement on what constitutes an optimal tax system to begin with, one might reasonably take the view that a benchmark should be defined as expansively as possible, and based on transparent and understandable principles. Then there would be no need to be precise about the various reasons for deviating from the benchmark, such as administrative feasibility, providing incentives for certain types of behaviour, or favouring certain types of persons. The information provided to policy makers would simply be the amount of deviation from a broadly defined benchmark for each type of tax, and they could judge whether the deviations were justified or not.

...

The second issue with respect to the benchmark tax rates concerns the definition of the rate structure in the case of the income tax. To an economist, the rate structure includes both the full set of tax brackets and rates and those tax credits and/or exemptions that are intended to make the tax structure more equitable. In this context, "equitable" can include both vertical equity as reflected in the progressivity of the tax structure and horizontal equity in the sense that equals are treated equally. The problem is that the actual set of tax credits and exemptions includes some that serve purposes other than — or in addition to — enhancing taxpayer equity. Thus, child tax credits can be viewed as enhancing horizontal equity across families, but they can also be viewed as supporting other social objectives, such as equal opportunity or family formation. Moreover, even credits that are intended to serve taxpayer equity may do so in a non-optimal way. Credits may be in place for horizontal equity reasons where exemptions would be more suitable. And credits may be restricted in ways that detract from equity objectives; thus, some credits (education, health) have restrictions on their size and some (charitable) have differential rates. As well, some credits are refundable while others are not, a distinction that might be viewed as a fundamental violation of equity. Resolving this by classifying some credits as part of the benchmark and others as tax expenditures is fraught with difficulty, since judgments must be made that are not clearcut. In these circumstances, the principle of providing information in the most transparent way suggests that all credits should be treated as tax expenditures regardless of their apparent role in defining the rate structure.

...

A more controversial issue concerns the refundability of personal tax credits. The income tax system distinguishes between tax credits that are refundable (the GST credit and the Canada child tax benefit) and those that are not (the basic personal credit, the age credit, the spouse or common-law partner credit, the eligible dependant credit, etc.). From an economic point of view, there is no compelling reason why some credits should be refundable and others not, despite the distinction in income tax treatment; all are, to some extent, intended to achieve progressivity in the tax system. On the other hand, a possible defence of the limited refundability of tax credits is that it represents a decision based on government policy. Regardless, from the point of view of consistency among the various types of credits, one could argue that non-refundable credits should be recognized as negative tax expenditures, even if evaluating them is challenging.

...

Another questionable item is the treatment of sheltered retirement savings that take the form of RRSPs and registered pension plans (RRP). (Deferred profit-sharing plans are also recognized as a source of tax expenditure, but no figures are presented.) The treatment consists of a mix of accrual accounting and cash accounting. The accrual component is the forgone return on registered assets, which constitutes the main source of sheltering and as such is a legitimate tax expenditure. The cash component consists of deductions of contributions less the taxation of withdrawals. This gives rise to a tax cost to the government to the extent that a higher tax rate applies when contributions are made than when funds are withdrawn. Should this be treated as a tax expenditure? No clear justification is presented. The argument against treating it as a tax expenditure is that the use of registered savings can be thought of as a system of lifetime averaging that the tax system makes available to households. Of course, as a system of averaging it is very crude, especially since negative RRSPs are not available to average incomes between high-tax periods later in life and low tax periods at the beginning. Despite that, the case for including the net tax cost arising from differential tax rates in retirement and during contribution years as a tax expenditure seems tenuous. (By the same argument, calculating the full present value of tax assistance for retirement savings plans as an alternative to cash accounting seems questionable.)

WHY POLITICIANS LOVE BOUTIQUE TAX CREDITS

Frances Woolley
(Professor of Economics, Carleton University)

SPECIAL TO THE GLOBE AND MAIL

Published Thursday, Mar. 24 2011, 12:25 PM EDT
Last updated Monday, Sep. 10 2012, 1:39 PM EDT

There are economic statements that amount to full-fledged budgets. And then there are budgets, like this one, that barely amount to an economic statement.

Budget 2011 continues the trend towards an ever more personalized tax system with a new Volunteer Firefighters Tax Credit, a Family Caregiver Tax Credit, and a Children's Art Tax credit. Coming soon: the Marginal Riding Tax Credit, available to all voters in must-win constituencies.

The irritation such credits generate among economists is completely disproportionate to their fiscal impact. The Children's Art Tax Credit, for example, is projected to cost $100-million in 2011-12, or a miniscule 0.035 per cent of the $278.7-billion the federal government is planning to spend that year. The importance of the credits is symbolic: they show that smart politics, bad economics outplays bad politics, smart economics every time.

These boutique credits are bad economics for any number of reasons. If the aim of the Children's Art Tax Credit is to make activities affordable, it's not enough money to make much difference: the maximum credit, 15 per cent of $500, is just $75. Charities like the Max Keeping Foundation are better at targeting support to families in need.

If the Credit aims to support families with children, it would be simpler to increase the child amount tax credit by $500. This would benefit almost all families, from those who are stretched to find $100 for art classes, to those who don't think twice about paying $500 for violin lessons, and would not require the creation of millions of tax receipts. Plus, as Tim Cestnick points out in his Tax Matters column, all of these boutique credits only add to the complexity of the tax system.

But boutique credits are smart politics. First, they appeal to people's sense that they deserve a break, validate their choices, and reaffirm their sense of self-worth. The Children's Art Tax Credit goes to good parents, ones who enroll their children in Suzuki violin lessons, not bad parents who spend their money on beer and popcorn. Second, they give people a sense of control. Tax liabilities stop being something outside of an individual's control. Instead, the plethora of credits available mean that taxes can be reduced through planning and wise choices.

Policies are smart politics for a reason: they appeal to voters. If economists want to have a positive influence on the policy debate, they have to understand voter psychology: why do voters like special tax credits so much? "Smart politics" isn't a criticism. Sometimes it's a way of saying "I don't understand why people like this policy". At other times, it's a way of saying, "I understand why this policy appeals to people, but if they were well-informed, they would think otherwise".

There's no point in telling politicians that a particular policy is "smart politics, bad economics". They'll take it as a compliment, and keep on making the same kind of policy choices.

Notes and Questions

1. How well do you understand the difference between deductions and credits? As Surrey points out, in a progressive marginal rate system, deductions benefit persons taxed at the highest marginal rate more than persons taxed at the lowest marginal rate.

   Consider two tax taxpayers, Ms. High, who pays at the highest federal marginal tax rate (29 per cent), and Ms. Low, who pays at the lowest federal marginal tax rate (15 per cent). Both contribute $1,000 to their Registered Retirement Savings Plan (RRSP), which they each deduct from their income for the year under ITA paragraph 60(i). Ms. High saves $290 in federal taxes while Ms. Low saves only $150. Surrey refers to the unequal savings as the "upside-down effect".

   In contrast, a tax credit directly reduces the taxes owed by Ms. High and Ms. Low by the same amount. If Ms. High and Ms. Low each contribute $1,000 to the Canada Pension Plan, they each receive a tax credit of $150 [$1000 × 15 per cent ("the appropriate percentage")] under ITA section 118.7. The tax credit has the same value to Ms. High and Ms. Low with one proviso. As Boadway points out, if Ms. Low's income is so low that she owes no taxes, she gets no benefit from the tax credit, unless it is a refundable tax credit.

2. In 1988, many of the items discussed in this chapter were converted from deductions to tax credits using the lowest marginal tax rate for the "appropriate percentage". After the conversion, a taxpayer in the lowest marginal tax bracket has the same tax savings as he or she did when the item was a credit. In contrast, all other taxpayers now spend at the highest marginal rate but receive tax support at the lowest marginal rate. For example, if Ms. H spends $1,000 on medical expenses, she will pay $290 in federal tax on the earnings she uses to pay for her medical expenses, but her tax credit will be $150, because the credit is calculated using the lowest marginal rate. (In fact, Ms. H will not be eligible for the credit unless her medical expenses exceed 3% of her net income.)

3. Policy makers must carefully consider whether a provision should be a deduction or credit. As Andrews points out, if the provision's primary goal is to deliver a subsidy, it does not make good policy sense to give high-income earners a greater subsidy than low-income earners. But what if, as Andrews suggests, the provision's primary goal is to adjust the tax system itself? What if the provision removes tax barriers to labour mobility (moving expense deduction), adjusts income to recognize expenses that prevent mothers from staying in the workforce (child care expenses deduction), or corrects a disincentive for saving (RRSP contribution deduction)? Are deductions for moving expenses, child care expenses, and RRSP contributions properly characterized as individual subsidies or adjustments to the benchmark itself? You will have a chance to answer this question for yourself later in the chapter.

How difficult do you think it is to decide whether a deduction is "an expenditure analogous to direct spending"? Do you agree with Andrews that the key to answering the question lies in the deduction's purpose? What happens when the deduction serves multiple purposes?

4. The provisions in this chapter are dizzyingly detailed and often complex because the government must carefully target and limit who qualifies and under what circumstances. Also, credit amounts and thresholds change every year based on inflation. The chapter references are to the 2015 values. We recommend that rather than learn every detail, you concentrate on understanding each provision's rationale, overall structure, and effect.

II. SUBDIVISION E DEDUCTIONS

Subdivision e deductions (sections 60–66.8) serve a mixed bag of policy objectives. Some, like moving expenses (section 62), child care expenses (section 63), and attendant care expenses (section 64), recognize costs that could be either income earning or personal living expenses. The deduction for alimony, maintenance, and support payments (paragraphs 60(b) and (c.2) and section 60.1) recognize the impact of divorce and separation on a taxpayer's ability to pay. Deductions for contributions to registered pension plans and registered retirement savings plans (paragraph 60(i)) stabilize retirement income and government revenues over a generation, and mitigate what some critics claim is an inherent bias against saving in an income tax system.

A. Moving Expenses

Are moving expenses personal living or income earning expenses? Where you live in relation to where you work is a personal, lifestyle choice. For a long time the tax treatment of moving expenses paralleled that of commuting expenses; both were non-deductible personal expenses. But is it good economic policy for the tax system to ignore moving expenses? If the tax system does not recognize moving expenses, then people have difficulty going where the jobs are. They cannot move between regions of high and low unemployment, and the economy loses labour productivity.

Today, the moving expense deduction in section 62 promotes labour mobility and allows entrepreneurs to move anywhere in Canada to carry on business. The deduction is limited to the income earned after the move. Full-time students who move for post-secondary education can also deduct their moving expenses, but only to the extent that they have taxable income from scholarships, bursaries or research grants.

Section 62 defines eligible moving expenses and sets overall deduction limits. Subsection 248(1) defines the purpose, change of residence, and distance required for an "eligible relocation".

Moving expenses must satisfy three key criteria to take them out of the "personal living expense" category:

Purpose: You must move because of work rather than for personal reasons.

Change of Residence: You must actually relocate, and not just commute between a primary and temporary residence.

Distance: The move must bring your residence at least 40 km closer to your new work location.

As you read the moving expense case summaries, pay attention to the statutory amendments and their effect on whether the courts apply the provision narrowly or broadly.

Purpose: Causal Connection and Timing

Subsection 248(1) requires a causal connection between a taxpayer's reason for moving and his or her work:

> [the] relocation occurs to *enable* the taxpayer to carry on a business or be employed *at a location in Canada ... referred to as 'the new work location' ... (italics added)*

What does moving to "enable" employment mean? Must the move connect to a new job? Or is "enable" broad enough to allow taxpayers to deduct moving expenses when they decide to move closer to their current employment because they have new work responsibilities?

And when must the move take place? Do taxpayers meet the causal connection between moving and work if they wait several years after starting a new job before they move? Does the move qualify if you move before you find a job?

The italicized word "enable" replaced the phrase "commenced to be employed", starting in 1999. An earlier 1984 amendment eliminated a prerequisite that the taxpayer "ceased to be employed" at the old location. As you read the case examples, consider whether these changes in language justify courts interpreting moving expense eligibility liberally.

Cases pre-dating the amended language set out four conditions to qualify for the moving expense deduction. Chief Judge Christie's often quoted standard in *Bracken v. Minister of National Revenue*, [1984] C.T.C. 2922 at para 15, 84 D.T.C. 1813 states:

> My reading of subsection 62(1) is that it contemplates the existence of four separate elements: old work location, new work location, old residence and new residence, and the comparison of two distances, i.e. the distance from the old residence to the new work location with the distance from the new residence to the new work location the former of which must exceed the latter by 40 or more kilometers in order for the moving expenses to be deductible.

After the amendments, the Tax Court in *Gelinas v. The Queen*, 2009 TCC 111, [2009] 4 C.T.C. 2232, 2009 D.T.C. 1091 reviewed the four-part Bracken test in a case that presented, in the Court's words, "a unique situation". The taxpayer, a nurse working part-time, moved closer to the hospital she already worked at after she obtained a new, full-time position. The Court emphasized that: the nurse went from two shifts a week to a 40-hour workweek; she competed for the job; the position was in a different unit; and her new duties required additional training. With these facts in mind, the Tax Court judge gave the moving expense provision a "flexible" interpretation, stating in paragraphs 12-16:

> I have concerns with any rigid interpretation requiring both an old and a new work location. Firstly, "new work location" is simply a term defining the words preceding it. Why should it be elevated to introduce a whole new concept that is not contained in the operative words. The words preceding it are "to enable the taxpayer to be employed at a location in Canada". Those are the critical words, not "new work location". There is no reference in the operative words to a new location or new employment, though the context is a move of residence by the taxpayer due to fulfilling employment requirements. This certainly suggests something had to have changed in the taxpayer's work to result in the taxpayer's move. And, indeed, with respect to Ms. Gelinas, there was something new — a new job.
>
> The term "new work location" used to describe the concept of enabling a taxpayer to be employed at a location in Canada should not, I respectfully suggest, restrict that very concept. As Chief Justice Rip indicated in *Dalisay v. Canada*:
>
>> 17. The phrase "the new work location" is not to be interpreted with any rigidity. The words "to carry on a business or to be employed at a location in Canada" have a very broad meaning. The words allow for flexibility in interpretation depending on the facts. ...
>
> "New work location" is simply a term defining the actual requirement, and nothing more.
>
> By interpreting the term "new work location" as not introducing a requirement for an old work location, I am not injecting into the definition of eligible relocation words that are simply not there. I note that former Chief Justice Christie in *Bracken*, while identifying an old work location as a requirement, actually goes on in applying the eligible relocation definition to rely on only three elements, the location called the new work location, an old residence and a new residence. This suggests to me that this case does not set any rigid rules to be slavishly followed. I believe the appropriate approach generally in determining deductions, such as moving expenses, is the more flexible approach suggested by Chief Justice Rip. It is unnecessary to get hung up on "new work location" as demanding an old work location. What is necessary is to ask if the taxpayer moved to enable the taxpayer to be employed at a location in Canada. Ms. Gelinas meets that requirement.

> This conclusion is not intended to open doors for taxpayers who have no change in their work to claim moving expenses if they move 40 kilometres closer to work. In such situations, there is clearly no change in work that such a taxpayer could rely on to successfully claim the move was to enable such a taxpayer to be employed at the location. Ms. Gelinas' circumstances are entirely different. Her new job required unacceptable travel: she had to move. What she could handle part-time, she could not handle full-time.

In *Wunderlich v. The Queen* (2011), 2011 TCC 539, 2012 D.T.C. 1040, Justice Webb went further than the Court in *Gelinas* and allowed moving expenses for a taxpayer who moved closer to work because he was promoted to a management position. The promotion occurred four years after the taxpayer started working for the company. Canada Revenue Agency denied Mr. Wunderlich's moving expenses because he did not have a "new work location".

The Tax Court judge allowed the taxpayer's moving expenses on several alternative grounds. First, the judge interpreted the phrase "new work location" as a "label" and not part of the definition. Then the judge found *Wunderlich's* facts to be analogous to *Gelinas*, relying on the taxpayer's statement that his commute was barely manageable even before the promotion and that he "felt that he needed to be closer to his work" to fulfill his new managerially responsibilities.

As a final alternative ground, the judge decided that the taxpayer could apply his 2008 moving expenses to his initial, 2004 employment start date. At paragraph 19, the judge noted that the moving expense provision did not specify a timeframe for the move:

> The current wording is that there must be a relocation which enables the person to be employed at a 'new work location'. Just as the previous version of section 62 of the Act did not provide any time period within which a move must occur following the commencement of employment at a 'new work location', the current version of section 62 of the Act and the definition of 'eligible relocation' in subsection 248(1) of the Act do not provide any time period within which a move must occur following the commencement of employment at a 'new work location'.

The *Wunderlich* decision cited *Beyette v. M.N.R.* (1989), [1990] 1 C.T.C. 2001, 89 D.T.C. 701 (T.C.C.) as an example where moving expenses were allowed for a move several years after the taxpayer started work. In *Beyette*, the taxpayer commuted 110 kilometres round trip for 5 years before moving closer to work. The Minister considered five years too long for the move to be causally connected to starting new employment. The Tax Court judge disagreed on both the facts and the statute's language. First, the judge held that the taxpayer presented "good reasons" for the delay based on illness, lack of housing at the new location, and an inactive real estate selling market at the old location. Second, the judge noted that the statute only required that the taxpayer "commenced to be employed", and did not give a time limit for the move. The *Beyette* decision pre-dated the change from "commenced to be employed" to "enable". The *Wunderlich* decision follows *Beyette* to give the moving expense criteria the widest possible interpretation.

Two recent Tax Court cases disagree with how widely the judge in *Wunderlich* interprets the moving expense criteria and pinpoint the potential abuse arising from interpreting the section too broadly. In *Langelier v. The Queen* (2013), 2013 TCC 322, [2014] 3 C.T.C. 2231, 2013 D.T.C. 1256, the taxpayer argued that his moving expenses should be deductible because he had new work responsibilities – transferring financial and accounting data from old software to new software, and training and supervising a newly hired payroll clerk. The Tax Court judge noted Justice Webb's interpretation in *Wunderlich* but concluded in paragraph 12:

> Based on the modern approach of interpretation of taxing statutes, as enunciated by the Supreme Court of Canada in *Canada Trustco Mortgage Co. v. Canada*, [2005 D.T.C. 5523] 2005 SCC 54, I do not believe that Parliament's intent was to permit a taxpayer to deduct moving expenses in circumstances where a taxpayer performed new duties with the same employer at the same business location.

Similarly, in *Dueck v. The Queen*, 2014 TCC 187, 2014 D.T.C. 1183, the Tax Court judge did not accept the taxpayer's argument that his deteriorating health and inability to maintain his old residence justified his deducting his expenses to move closer to work. In paragraph 15, the Tax Court gave the following example of how applying the moving expense deduction too broadly could lead to abuse:

> In my opinion, it is not sufficient for a taxpayer to declare that he moved to get closer to work and to continue working when there are no changes in his employment conditions. He must provide evidence as to the circumstances surrounding the move so as to enable the Court to decide whether the declaration of his subjective intent is accurate. If this were not required it would be easy for taxpayers to deduct moving expenses incurred for personal reasons by moving shortly before retirement rather than doing so after retirement.

Change of Residence

The move must be from one residence at which the taxpayer "ordinarily resided" to another residence at which, after the move, he or she "ordinarily resided". In other words, the deduction is for actual relocation costs and not for expenses connected to temporary stays away from home or job-related commuting expenses. The courts look closely at the taxpayer's connections to the old and new residences.

If the taxpayer leaves family behind and only moves for a period of weeks or months, the court is likely to treat the moving expenses as non-deductible incidental travel expenses to a new worksite. The Tax Court denied a moving expense deduction in *MacDonald v. The Queen*, 2007 TCC 250, [2007] 4 C.T.C. 2166, where the taxpayer returned to his family in Cape Breton after working for six weeks in Alberta, and also in *Sampson v. The Queen*, 2009 D.T.C. 1142, where the taxpayer moved back and forth between Nova Scotia and three different provinces.

On the other hand, in *Persaud v. The Queen*, 2007 TCC 474, 2007 DTC 1432, the Tax Court decided that a taxpayer who stayed for four months in Alberta before moving back to New Brunswick had established a residence in Alberta because he opened bank accounts and visited with his children living in the area. And in *Calvano v. The Queen*, 2004 TCC 227, [2004] 2 C.T.C. 3004, 2004 D.T.C. 2471, the taxpayer was "ordinarily resident" during his 19-month stay in rental accommodation because he and his family established a social life at the new location that demonstrated the move was more than a "transitory lay-by".

Sometimes taxpayers make a series of moves before taking up their final residence. Some judges have allowed the expenses in multiple moves if the taxpayer demonstrates that he or she had not become ordinarily resident in the "temporary" location. See *Jaschinski v. The Queen* (2002), [2003] 1 C.T.C. 2571, 2002 D.T.C. 2183 (T.C.C.), on accepting the taxpayer's first move as an interim stay.

Distance

How should the 40 km distance between the old and new residence be measured? Do we use the taxpayer's normal route, or the shortest route, or do we simply draw a straight line on the map to measure "as the crow flies"? Early cases, like *Cameron v. M.N.R.*, [1993] 1 C.T.C. 2745, 93 D.T.C. 437 (T.C.C.), measured the distance, "as the crow flies", without regard to the actual driving distance.

The Federal Court of Appeal in *Giannakopoulos v. M.N.R.*, [1995] 3 F.C. 294, [1995] 2 C.T.C. 316, 95 D.T.C. 5477 (T.C.C.), replaced the "as the crow flies" standard with "the shortest normal route open to the travelling public". In the Court's words, the new test "would prevent a taxpayer from being expected to use an extraordinary route such as a neglected or unpaved road. It would also leave room to consider travel not only on roads, but on ferries and rail lines" (paragraph 9).

In *Nagy v. The Queen*, 2007 TCC 394, [2007] 5 C.T.C. 2642, 2007 D.T.C. 1208, at paragraph 11, the Tax Court rejected the Minister's argument that a "mechanical measurement of all possible routes should be made and the shortest chosen, regardless of whether any reasonable person would follow such a route". The Minister suggested a route with 18 left turns, 19 right turns, travelling on 40 roads, and driving through the heavily congested City of Brampton. The Tax Court rejected the "38 turn slalom suggested by the Crown" as "neither realistic, nor normal, nor reasonable, nor commonsensical", and noted that *Gianakopoulos* was the Federal Court of Appeal's attempt to "substitute a measure of common sense and rationality" for the previous "unthinking mechanical approach".

Notes and Questions

1. How liberal should the moving expense deduction be? Did the 1999 amendment changing "commence" to "enable" employment give the courts more room to allow moving expenses even when the taxpayer continues to work for the same employer? Or should the courts be more vigilant to weed out moves motivated by personal circumstances and lifestyle choices?
2. *Dueck v. The Queen*, *supra*, cautions that if courts interpret "eligible relocation" too broadly, it could open up claims for personal, retirement-related moving expense. Can you think of other situations where a broad interpretation could lead to moving expenses claims for purely personal moves?
3. *Beyette, v. M.N.R.*, *supra*, allowed a deduction for a move five years after the taxpayer started work. Other cases have allowed moves after even longer delays. See also *Beaudoin v. The Queen*, 2005 TCC 94, [2005] 1 C.T.C. 2821, 2005 D.T.C. 282 (deduction allowed eight years after the employee started work at the employer's new location); and *Dierckens v. The Queen*, 2011 TCC 169, [2011] 3 C.T.C. 2328, 2011 D.T.C. 1136 (moving expenses and real estate commissions allowed 10 years after employment started).

   Can the taxpayer move first and then find employment? In *Abrahamsen v. The Queen*, 2007 TCC 95, [2007] 3 C.T.C. 2001, 2007 D.T.C. 412, the Tax Court interpreted the amended language to give "more latitude" to the taxpayer and to allow moving expenses where the taxpayer moved sixteen months before beginning work. See also *Evangélist v. The Queen,* 2013 TCC 62, 2013 D.T.C. 1095, on allowing moving expenses when the taxpayer found a job two years after the taxpayer moved.

   Do you agree with these results?
4. **What expenses qualify?** Subsection 62(3) defines moving expenses to include expenses incurred "as or on account of":
   - travel, transportation, and storage of household effects,
   - lease cancellation,
   - up to 15 days of meals and lodging,
   - legal fees and taxes (excluding GST) related to the purchase of a new residence, and
   - selling costs of the old residence including up to $5,000 of mortgage interest, property taxes, insurance premiums and heat and power paid to maintain the vacant former residence while reasonable efforts are being made to sell it.

   Subsection 62(3) is an inclusive list leaving it to the courts to decide what falls within the scope of each item. Early cases took a narrow view of moving expense. *Storrow v. Canada* (1978), [1979] 1 F.C. 595, [1978] C.T.C. 792, 78 D.T.C. 6551 (Fed. T.D.) disallowed land registry fees paid on the purchase of the new home, and limited moving expenses to "ordinary out-of-pocket expenses incurred by the taxpayer in the course of physically changing his residence" (paragraph 14). *Séguin v Canada* (1997), 221 N.R. 321, [1998] 2 C.T.C. 13, 97 D.T.C. 5457 (F.C.A.) disallowed mortgage interest on the old residence while it was vacant pending sale, on the grounds that moving expenses did not include an "amount intended to compensate for accessory damages that are unrelated to the actual move to and resettlement in the new residence" (paragraph 8).

After *Storrow* and *Séquin,* subsection 62(2) was changed from "*incurred in the course of moving from his old residence to his new residence*" to "*expenses incurred in respect of an eligible relocation*". And the specific amounts disallowed in *Storrow* and *Séquin* are now allowed under subparagraphs 62(3)(f) and (g).

5. If the section is intended to encourage workforce mobility, as a matter of policy, should moving expenses be given a liberal interpretation? Should the benefit of the doubt go to the taxpayer? Think about these questions in the context of the facts and case examples below. How would you decide each one?

   What should be included in the transportation of household effects? Should the cost of moving a mobile home qualify? (Interpretation Bulletin IT-178-R3.) What about transporting the family dog or horses? Are dogs and horses members of the household? See *Critchley v. M.N.R.,* [1983] C.T.C. 2365, 83 D.T.C. 278 (T.R.B.) and *Yaeger v. MNR*, [1986] 1 C.T.C. 2282, 86 D.T.C. 1217 (T.C.C.).

   How about the cost to repair or replace personal goods damaged or lost in shipping? See *Fardeau v. The Queen,* [2002] 3 C.T.C. 2169 (T.C.C.) and *Rath v. The Queen*, [1978] C.T.C. 2425, 78 D.T.C. 1327 (T.R B.), affirmed [1979] C.T.C. 183, 79 D.T.C. 5140 (Fed. T.D.), affirmed [1982] C.T.C. 207, 82 D.T.C. 6175 (Fed. C.A.)

   And what about costs incurred to fix up the old residence for sale? Compare *Faibish v. The Queen*, 2008 TCC 241, 2008 D.T,C, .3554, disallowing the cost of mold removal prior to listing the old residence for sale, with *Trigg v. The Queen*, 2009 TCC 194, [2010] 1 C.T.C. 2091, allowing the cost to replace asbestos with suitable insulation where the replacement was a condition of the sale.

6. Should there be a time limit on storage? What if the taxpayer stores household goods for 18 months while a new home is being built? See *Christian v. The Queen* (2010), 2010 TCC 458, [2011] 1 C.T.C. 2111, 2010 D.T.C. 1316 (Eng.). In *Hasan v. The Queen*, 2004 TCC 502, [2004] 4 C.T.C. 2420, 2004 D.T.C. 3001, appeal dismissed 2005 FCA 114, [2005] 2 C.T.C. 181, 2005 D.T.C. 5220, a McGill University student was not permitted to claim her rent payments as fees for storing household effects, when she moved from Montreal to Toronto for summer employment.

7. What about expenses incurred to job- and house-hunt at the new location when the taxpayer eventually relocates there for the job? The Tax Court judge in *Ball v. The Queen*, [1996] 3 C.T.C. 2178 (T.C.C.) held that these expenses were not

"moving expenses in the ordinary meaning of that term" even though the taxpayer moved to the new location for employment in the same year.

Ball was decided before the 1999 amendment. Do you think that the amended language could change the result in *Ball* so that job-hunting expenses might now be deductible if the taxpayer eventually moves for a job? What abuse might this lead to? Can you draft a provision that clearly extends the moving expense deduction to employment-related job-hunting, but does not become a subsidy for vacation expenses?

8. **Other Limits:** The statute limits moving expenses to the amount of income earned at the new location, although unused expenses can be carried over to the subsequent year. Amounts reimbursed by an employer cannot be claimed.

   Compare moving expenses under subsection 62(1) with the more generous treatment of employer reimbursed moving expenses which do not have any limits based on income. Then consider the relatively recent provisions allowing employers to reimburse $15,000 of housing losses and half of the losses above that on a tax-free basis. Subsection 62(3) is unlikely to recognize the loss on the sale of a house as a moving expense. Should this anomaly be addressed?

9. Moving expenses are also limited to moves within Canada. However section 64.1 provides a special rule for moving, child care and attendant care expenses of taxpayers who, although physically absent from Canada, are considered to be resident for income tax purposes. These taxpayers are permitted to deduct expenses incurred to move to or from a location outside Canada as well as amounts paid for child or attendant care provided outside Canada.

10. **Students:** You may be interested in carefully reviewing the moving expense deduction available to persons who move to take up full-time attendance as students at universities. You may be eligible to deduct the costs of moving each year to the extent that you have taxable income from scholarships, bursaries or research grants. The relatively recent exemption for scholarship income in subsection 56(3) will, by and large, limit the moving expense deduction for students.

    But what if you have a part-time job while in school? Can you claim moving expenses against your part-time job earnings? And what about the expense of moving to take on a summer job or paid internship? Do you think your expenses moving back and forth between school and summer employment qualify? Also, do not forget to keep track of your expenses when you move to take up your first job after graduation.

11. **Receipts:** Taxpayers now have the option of using a simplified method, which does not require receipts, to determine meal and vehicle expenses incurred during the course of moving. See Interpretation Bulletin IT-178R3 (consolidated, archived).

B. Child Care Expenses

The child care expense deduction in Section 63 sparks critical questions on every possible plane.

- Should we characterize the child care expense deduction as a benchmark or tax expenditure item? Benchmark because it defines net profit from business or employment and corrects a market failure, or expenditure because it subsidizes personal expenses of a subset of taxpayers?
- Is the policy goal of removing child care as a barrier to workforce participation best accomplished by delivering tax benefits to individuals or through direct spending to create low-cost child care spaces?
- Does a deduction deliver benefits to the right people and in the right form, or should child care expenses become a credit or a refundable credit?

Keep these questions in mind as you read about section 63.

Early case law characterized child care expense as personal and non-deductible. It was only in 1972, following the Carter Commission's recommendations and the Government White Paper, "Proposal for Tax Reform" (1969), that women could deduct child care expenses up to $2,000. The two most often cited policy rationales for the provision are to recognize the impact on the family's ability to pay, and to lower a significant barrier to women participating in the paid work force. Initially men could only deduct child care expenses if the "female member of the household" was ill, disabled, in school, imprisoned, or the parents were separated.

In 1982, as part of the government's *Charter* review, the provision became ostensibly gender-neutral. Rather than explicitly targeting women, the provision now targets the household's "secondary" income earner. In the first instance, the "supporting person" with the lower income can take the deduction, except when they are unavailable under the same circumstances as before. Given the persistent gender wage gap, women are still more likely to qualify for the deduction.

Section 63 has several other limitations. The deduction only reduces "earned" income, including employment, business, and the taxable part of scholarships, bursaries, fellowships, and research grants. There is an overall limit of two-thirds of the supporting individual's earned income. Payments made to the child's own parent, the taxpayer's dependent, or a relative under the age of 18 do not qualify. And there is a per child cap, currently $7,000 per child under the age of 7, $4,000 per child between the ages of 7 and 16, and $10,000 per child eligible for the Disability Tax Credit. Pending amendments will increase these per child caps to $8,000, $5,000, and $11,000 respectively, effective 2015, for the first time since 1998.

Eligible child care expenses include fees paid for babysitting, day nursery services, daycare centres, the portion of fees paid to an educational institution for non-educational child care services, day camps and day sports schools, and boarding school or camp to a maximum of $100 per week per child ($175 a week for children under age seven).

Tax Subsidy or a Cost of Earning Income?

Section 63 recognizes child care as an income earning expense for working parents. We can easily state several policy goals for the deduction: increasing financial security for working families; removing barriers to workforce participation, particularly for women; and ensuring an adequate labour supply and workforce productivity. What is more debatable is whether the deduction is a tax expenditure implementing a federal child care policy or a structural adjustment to the benchmark needed to properly define net income.

The debate on how child care expenses should be characterized ignited in *Symes v. Canada* (1993), [1993] 4 S.C.R. 695, [1994] 1 C.T.C. 40, 94 D.T.C. 6001, 161 N.R. 243. Toronto lawyer Beth Symes claimed the salary she paid to her child care provider as a business expense. The Minister disallowed the deduction on the grounds that the expenses were personal living expenses. Symes argued that the current social and economic realities of women in the work force made child care expenses a legitimate business expense, crossing the hurdles of both ITA paragraphs 18(1)(a) and (h). She further argued that denying child care expenses as a business expense violated section15 of the *Charter*.

At the Federal Court–Trial Division ([1989] 3 F.C. 59, [1989] 1 C.T.C. 476, 89 D.T.C. 5243), Cullen J. allowed Symes' appeal, agreeing with the taxpayer that her child care costs were a legitimate expense to determine business profit under ITA subsection 9(1) and, alternatively, that section 15 of the *Charter* prevented section 9 from being applied to women entrepreneurs in a discriminatory fashion. The Federal Court of Appeal ([1991] 3 F.C. 507, [1991] 2 C.T.C. 1, 91 D.T.C. 5397, 127 N.R. 348), reversed and disallowed the expense. The Supreme Court of Canada dismissed the taxpayer's appeal by a 7-2 majority. Notably both women judges, McLachlin J. and L'Heureux-Dubé, J. dissented.

The *Symes* case is studied in Chapter 5, to illustrate how courts interpret subsection 9(1), and paragraphs 18(1)(a) and (h). We use the case in this chapter as a backdrop to the subsidy-expenditure debate on child care and the purpose of section 63.

Both Justice Iacobucci's majority and Justice L'Heuerux-Dubé's dissenting opinions deal at length with whether child care is a personal or business expense, and with Parliament's reasons for enacting section 63. Justice Iacobucci's opinion sidesteps the characterization issue by holding that Parliament intended section 63 as a "code in itself complete and independent" addressing child care costs for both employed and self-employed persons. L'Heureux-Dubé's dissent places child care expenses in a modern context reflecting women's participation in the paid workforce.

She explicitly finds that self-employed taxpayers can deduct child care as a business expense.

If we see child care as subsidizing a personal expense of working parents, then we lean towards an expenditure analysis. If on the other hand, we take L'Heureux-Dubé's perspective that in a modern context, child care is a cost of earning income, then we lean towards a benchmark analysis. As you read the case, think about why the characterization as expenditure or benchmark matters. We will return to this question in the notes.

SYMES v. THE QUEEN

(1993), [1993] 4 S.C.R. 695, 161 N.R. 243, [1994] 1 C.T.C. 40, 94 D.T.C. 6001

Iacobucci J. ...

This appeal presents a particular expense which has been traditionally characterized as personal in nature. ... Why, in this case, is it appropriate to re-examine extensively whether child care expenses are appropriately characterized as personal expenses? Relying upon the evidence of the expert witness, Armstrong, the trial judge had this to say (at p. 72):

> ... there has been a significant social change in the late 1970's and into the 1980's, in terms of the influx of women of child-bearing age into business and into the workplace. This change post-dates the earlier cases dismissing nanny expenses as a legitimate business deduction and therefore it does not necessarily follow that the conditions which prevailed in society at the time of those earlier decisions will prevail now. ...

The increased participation of women in the Canadian workforce is undoubtedly a change in the "social foundation". .... Accordingly, I do not feel that I must slavishly follow those cases which have characterized child care expenses as personal in nature. It now falls to be considered whether the alternative is appropriate. In other words, are child care expenses not prohibited by s. 18(1)(a) of the Act? ...

It may be relevant in a particular case to consider whether a deduction is ordinarily allowed as a business expense by accountants. ... Similarly, it may be relevant to consider whether the expense is one normally incurred by others involved in the taxpayer's business. If it is, there may be an increased likelihood that the expense is a business expense. ... It may also be relevant to consider whether a particular expense would have been incurred if the taxpayer was not engaged in the pursuit of business income.

I note that in a tax system which is at least partly geared toward the preservation of vertical and horizontal equities ("[h]orizontal equity merely requires that 'equals' be treated equally, with the term 'equals' referring to equality of ability to pay" and "vertical equity merely requires that the incidence of the tax burden should be more heavily borne by the rich than the poor ...), one seeks to prevent deductions which represent personal consumption. To the extent that a taxpayer can make a lifestyle choice while maintaining the same capacity to gain or produce income, such choices tend to be seen as personal consumption decisions, and the resultant expenses as personal expenses. ...

It remains to consider the appellant's child care expenses in light of this discussion. First, it is clear on the facts that the appellant would not have incurred child care expenses except for her business. It is relevant to note in this regard that her choice of child care was tailored to her business needs. As a lawyer, she could not personally care for her children during the day since to do so would interfere with client meetings and court appearances, nor could she make use of institutionalized daycare, in light of her working hours. ...

Second, however, it is equally clear that the need which is met by child care expenses on the facts of this case, namely, the care of the appellant's children, exists regardless of the appellant's business activity. The expenses were incurred to make her available to practise her profession rather than for any other purpose associated with the business itself.

Third, I note that there is no evidence to suggest that child care expenses are considered business expenses by accountants. There is, however, considerable reason to believe that many parents, and particularly many women, confront child care expenses in order to work. There is, first of all, the evidence of the expert witness, already discussed above. In addition, the record before this Court includes a report by Status of Women Canada, entitled the Report of the Task Force on Child Care (1986), which demonstrates that a very large number of working parents require non-parental care for their children (see, e.g., Table 4.2). As well, the intervener the Canadian Bar Association presented this Court with survey information which specifically addresses the experience of lawyers in Ontario. That information suggests that for lawyers with children, a significant proportion of child care responsibility is borne by paid child care workers, and the mean proportion is over 250 percent greater for women (25.56 hours per week) than for men (9.53 hours per week): Law Society of Upper Canada, Transitions in the Ontario Legal Profession (1991). This demographic picture may increase the likelihood that child care expenses are a form of business expense.

Finally, as a fourth point of analysis, I am uncomfortable with the suggestion that the appellant's decision to have children should be viewed solely as a consumption choice. I frankly admit that there is an element of public policy which feeds my discomfort. In Brooks v. Canada Safeway Ltd., [1989] 1 S.C.R. 1219, Dickson C.J. stated (at p. 1243):

> That those who bear children and benefit society as a whole thereby should not be economically or socially disadvantaged seems to bespeak the obvious. It is only women who bear children; no man can become pregnant ... it is unfair to impose all of the costs of pregnancy upon one half of the population. ...

The factors so far analyzed suggest that, considering only ss. 9, 18(1)(a) and 18(1)(h), arguments can be made for and against the classification of the appellant's child care expenses as business expenses. ... [I]n general terms, I am of the view that child care expenses are unique: expenditures for child care can represent a significant percentage of taxpayer income, such expenditures are generally linked to the taxpayer's ability to gain or produce income, yet such expenditures are also made in order to make a taxpayer available to the business, and the expenditures are incurred as part of the development of another human life. It can be difficult to weigh the personal and business elements at play. ...

I am aware that if I were compelled to reach a conclusion with respect to the proper classification of child care expenses with reference to only ss. 9, 18(1)(a) and 18(1)(h) of the Act, such a conclusion would involve competing policy considerations. On the one hand, there is value in the traditional tax law test which seeks to identify those expenses which simply make a taxpayer available to the business, and which proceeds to classify such expenses as "personal" for the reason that a "personal need" is being fulfilled. On the other hand, however, it is inappropriate to disregard lightly the policy considerations which suggest that choice and consumption have no role to play in the classification of child care expenses. ...

However, I find it unnecessary to determine whether reconceptualization is appropriate having regard to the presence of s. 63 in the Act. ...

Considering first the language of s. 63, it is readily apparent that the Act's definition of "child care expenses" specifically comprehends the purpose for which the appellant incurred her nanny expenses. ...

The fact that this language accurately describes the situation at hand — i.e., a law partner paying child care in order to work — is itself persuasive reason to suppose that ss. 9, 18(1)(a) and 18(1)(h) cannot be interpreted to permit a child care business expense deduction. Décary J.A., in the Federal Court of Appeal below, considered this language to be "clear and not open to question", and suggested that s. 63 is "really a code in itself, complete and independent" (p. 525). In addition to the plain language of the quoted provisions, however, there are other reasons to believe that this is the correct interpretation.

One such reason is the structure of s. 63 itself. Section 63 places a number of limitations upon the child care deduction. ...To the extent that s. 63 intends to limit child care expense deductions to lower earning supporters, the appellant's position could substantially undermine that intent.

In this case, the appellant and her husband admittedly made a "family decision" to the effect that the appellant alone bears the financial burden of child care: see Federal Court of Appeal judgment, at p. 513. By proffering evidence on this point, the appellant would seek to avoid the definition of "supporting person" in s. 63(3)(d) of the Act, which would statutorily define her husband as such a person, notwithstanding the "family decision". In the result, she would take a complete deduction of the child care expenses, free from the consideration of whether or not she is the lower earning supporter.

The appellant's approach is unworkable. For example, consider the case of two spouses living with an eligible child, one of whom is an employee earning a low income, and the other of whom is a businessperson earning a higher income. The approach of the appellant clearly invites this couple to make a "family decision" in order to establish that the cost of child care is the sole responsibility of the taxpayer with business income. Without casting aspersions upon the appellant, I fear that in many cases there would be more bookkeeping than reality about such a decision. The courts being poorly suited to assess the validity of "family decisions" of this sort, I am inclined to believe that the intent of s. 63 is to prevent the need for such assessments. Further, by statutorily defining both parents to be responsible for child care expenses for tax purposes, s. 63(3)(d) is entirely congruent with a contemporary understanding of parental obligations in that regard. ...

Although it is unnecessary to my conclusion, I wish to note, finally, that evidence of Parliamentary intent appears to support my view. ... I wish ... to make particular note of the proposals which directly led to the 1972 introduction of s. 63. In Proposals for Tax Reform (1969) (E. J. Benson, Minister of Finance), the following approach to child care expenses is advocated (at p. 15):

> 2.7 We propose to permit deduction of the child care expenses that face many working parents today. The problem of adequately caring for children when both parents are working, or when there is only one parent in the family and she or he is working, is both a personal and a social one. We consider it desirable on social as well as economic grounds to permit a tax deduction for child care expenses, under carefully controlled terms, in addition to the general deduction for children. ...
>
> 2.9 This new deduction for child care costs would be a major reform. While it is not possible to make an accurate forecast of the number who would benefit from this new deduction, it seems likely to be several hundred thousand families. It would assist many mothers who work or want to work to provide or supplement the family income, but are discouraged by the cost of having their children cared for.

These proposals suggest to me that s. 63 was intended by Parliament to address comprehensively child care expenses. I cannot imagine that a system which allowed some parents to deduct expenses under general provisions respecting business income, but which confined others to a s. 63 regime, would permit deductibility "under carefully controlled terms" within the meaning of the above quotation. Further, I am not impressed by the suggestion that Parliament intended s. 63 to limit deductibility only for employees. The proposals do not specify the kind of "work" which is to be encouraged, and the language of s. 63 clearly addresses income from business.

For these reasons, a straightforward approach to statutory interpretation has led me to conclude that the Act intends to address child care expenses, and does so in fact, entirely within s. 63. It is not necessary for me to decide whether, in the absence of s. 63, ss. 9, 18(1)(a) and 18(1)(h) are capable of comprehending a business expense deduction for child care. Given s. 63, however, it is clear that child care cannot be considered deductible under principles of income tax law applicable to business deductions

L'heureux-Dubé ... J. (dissenting): —

...The arguments of the parties and interveners make it clear that, though ostensibly about the proper statutory interpretation of the Act, this case reflects a far more complex struggle over fundamental issues, the meaning of equality and the extent to which these values require that women's experience be considered when the interpretation of legal concepts is at issue. The answer, with regard to the statutory interpretation of the Act, requires that the Court consider the reality of the relationship of both women and men to child care and to work, as well as the impact of concepts of equality on the interpretation of legislation. As Professor Claire F. L. Young has written in "Impact of Feminist Analysis on Tax Law and Policy" in Feminist Analysis: Challenging Law and Legal Processes (1992 Institute of Continuing Legal Education, Canadian Bar Association — Ontario, January 31, 1992), at p. 1

> The tax system is ... a powerful tool used to direct social and economic activity in Canada.

The role that this "powerful tool" may play in the prevention of the attainment of substantive equality for women cannot be overlooked. ....

V. Statutory Interpretation

At this time, I would like to make a brief comment on the gendered analysis entangled in the statutory interpretation in this case ... s. 9 of the Act is gender neutral. [A] claim may also have been made by a businessman in the same situation as Ms. Symes. If such a businessman were, for example, the primary caretaker of his children, the rationale as well as the end result would have been the same. The ability to deduct a legitimate business expense that one incurs in order to gain or produce income from business should not be based on one's sex. Any businessperson would be entitled to a deduction if he or she can prove that such expenses have been incurred for business purposes.

The reality, however, is that generally women, rather than men, fulfill the role of sole or primary caregiver to children and, as such, it is they alone who incur and pay for such expenses. ... Regardless of this future possibility, [that more men would take on child care responsibilities] at this time the reality is that it is primarily women who incur the cost, both social and financial, for child care and this decision cannot, as such, ignore the contextual truth when examining whether child care may be considered a business expense.

Courts in the past, and the Court of Appeal in this case, have also always assumed that commercial needs were an objectively neutral set of needs. As a consequence, they did not examine the close relationship between child care and women's business income. It is crucial, in my view, to examine the link between child care and the generation of income from business. ...

Dr. Armstrong testified that dramatic and fundamental changes have been taking place in both the labour market and the family structure over the past 40 years. In 1951, only 24 percent of Canadian women participated in the labour force. By 1987, this number had risen to 56 percent. With respect to how the increase took place Dr. Armstrong testified that:

> It's been quite rapid from the mid-'70s - early '70s on. It was fairly slow to increase in the '50s, but then the '60s, the acceleration was faster and it increased in the '70s.

Further, the increase was most dramatic for women in their childbearing years, with nearly three-quarters of women between the ages of 16 and 44 being counted as members of the labour force, particularly in the 1980s. Today, a majority of women, even those with very young children, are now in the labour force. Fully 70 percent of employed mothers with children younger than six years old work full time, as do 75 percent of employed mothers with school-age children (6 to 15 years). Current forecasts suggest that by the year 2000, fully 88 percent of women aged 25 to 34 years will be in the work force. This increasing trend is particularly noteworthy, since women aged 25 to 34 years are the group most likely to have young children at home, thus requiring child care. It is evident that for most Canadian families, the issue of child care is of crucial importance. ...

In the past, the scope of deductible business disbursements has been expanded constantly. It has been held to include a wide array of expenditures, such as club dues, meals and entertainment expenses, car expenses, home office expenses, legal and accounting fees, to name only a few. ... When we look at the case law concerning the interpretation of "business expense", it is clear that this area of law is premised on the traditional view of business as a male enterprise and that the concept of a business expense has itself been constructed on the basis of the needs of businessmen. ... The definition of "business expense" was shaped to reflect the experience of businessmen, and the ways in which they engaged in business. ... As a consequence, the male standard now frames the backdrop of assumptions against which expenses are determined to be, or not to be, legitimate business expenses. Against this backdrop, it is hardly surprising that child care was seen as irrelevant to the end of gaining or producing income from business but rather as a personal non-deductible expense.

.... [O]ne must ask whether the many business deductions available, for cars, for club dues and fees, for lavish entertainment and the wining and dining of clients and customers, and for substantial charitable donations, are so obviously business expenses rather than personal ones. Although potentially personal, each one of these expenses has been accepted as a legitimate business expense and, as each reflects a real cost incurred by certain kinds of business people to produce income from business, a deduction has been allowed. The real costs incurred by businesswomen with children are no less real, no less worthy of consideration and no less incurred in order to gain or produce income from business.

In conclusion to the question of whether child care expenses are precluded from being deducted as a business expense under s. 9(1) by the interplay of either s. 18(1)(a) or s. 18(1)(h) of the Act, I answer that child care may be held to be a business expense deductible pursuant to ss. 9(1), 18(1)(a) and 18(1)(h) of the Act, all other criteria being respected. This result leads me to the most crucial consideration in this appeal, that is whether s. 63 of the Act precludes the deduction of child care expenses as a business expense. Here, I part company with my colleague since, in my view, s. 63 of the Act, properly interpreted, is no such bar.

D. Section 63 of the Income Tax Act

Recognition that laws are not neutral is not new. As the interpretation of "business expense" has been shown to be wrought with male perspective and subjectivity, so is an interpretation of business expense that is limited by s. 63 of the Act. Section 63 was implemented in order to adapt to the needs of a society at that time. In 1972, when that section was enacted, societal ideals with regard to equality of the sexes and the equal participation of women in all aspects of society had not evolved to the point where they have today. Now, in 1993, as we approach the interpretation of laws, one hopes, as is observed by Joan Brockman in "Social Authority, Legal Discourse, and Women's Voices" (1992), 21 Man. L.J. 213, at p. 233, that "[t]he myth of law's neutrality has been largely eroded". An interpretation which holds that s. 63 prevents the deduction of child care costs which would otherwise constitute a valid business expense is guided, in my opinion, by the myth of neutrality, a matter I will now examine.

(ii) Section 63 Interplay with Section 9(1)

According to my colleague ... since the wording of s. 63 of the Act clearly includes the appellant's nanny expenses, s. 63 acts as a complete bar, rendering the appellant Symes ineligible to deduct her child care expenses as a business expense. I do not interpret s. 63 of the Act in such a fashion. Sections 63 and 9(1), in my view, may co-exist. The fact that Parliament enacted a section to benefit all parents in the paid work force without distinction does not prevent a taxpayer who is in business from deducting an expense which can be legitimately claimed as a business expense. Section 63 provides general relief to parents, but nothing in its wording implies that deductions available under s. 9(1) are abolished or restricted in this respect. Had Parliament intended to submit the deduction of child care expenses to the application of s. 63 it would have expressed it in clear language. In providing that none of the deductions permitted by ss. 60 to 63 are applicable to a particular source of income, s. 4(2) of the Act clearly provides for some deductions which may legitimately fall under two sections of the Act. In addition, it is not insignificant that the text of s. 63 is permissive as opposed to the negative wording of ss. 18(1)(b) and 18(1)(e), which are clearly intended to limit the allowable deductions to only those permitted under these paragraphs. Finally, it is important to note that the taxpayer in this case is not seeking to claim a s. 63 deduction from a source, but is seeking a source deduction, independent of the s. 63 deduction for child care, for a business expense. ....

(iii) Historical and Purposive Perspective

The 1966 report of the Carter Commission recommended that tax credits for working mothers be instituted (Report of the Royal Commission on Taxation, vol. 3, Taxation of Income: Part A - Taxation of Individuals and Families (1966), at p. 19). Six years later, in 1972, s. 63 formed part of a tax reform package, in which Parliament extended to employees a number of new deductions. After noting that six out of seven Canadian taxpayers earn wages or salaries, a limited deduction for child care expenses, together with a number of other employee deductions for tools and travelling expenses, was announced by E. J. Benson the then Minister of Finance in Proposals for Tax Reform (1969), at p. 10, para. 1.33, as follows:

> Costs of looking after young children when both parents are working, or when there is only one parent and that parent is working, would be allowed as a deduction subject to certain conditions. This new plan is intended primarily to benefit mothers who need to work to support their families. ...

Benson, as quoted by Iacobucci J., further noted supra, at p. 15, paras. 2.7 and 2.9:

> We propose to permit deduction of the child care expenses that face many working parents today. The problem of adequately caring for children when both parents are working, or when there is only one parent in the family and she or he is working, is both a personal and a social one. We consider it desirable on social as well as economic grounds to permit a tax deduction for child care expenses, under carefully controlled terms, in addition to the general deduction for children. ...
>
> This new deduction for child care costs would be a major reform. While it is not possible to make an accurate forecast of the number who would benefit from this new deduction, it seems likely to be several hundred thousand families. It would assist many mothers who work or want to work to provide or supplement the family income, but are discouraged by the cost of having their children cared for.

The deduction available under s. 63 has consistently been described in relation to employed mothers as a "special tax allowance to working mothers" (House of Commons Standing Committee on Finance, Trade and Economic Affairs, Minutes of Proceedings and Evidence, June 23, 1970, at p. 70:145).

It is not insignificant that, as discussed earlier, the number of women in the work force in 1972 was ostensibly less than it is today and the number of women who were in business was minimal. It is highly probable that the legislators did not even put their mind to the fact that women may some day enter into business and the professions in large numbers and that these women may approach the world of business differently than did their male predecessors. Most importantly, it was certainly not within the legislators' frame of mind that child care would be viewed as anything other than a personal expense.

Secondly, I wish to address the concern raised by many commentators, including my colleague Iacobucci J., that to allow child care expenses to be deducted as a business expense would defeat and undermine the purpose of the provision of s. 63, to allow a general deduction of child care expenses to all parents, whether employed or self-employed. Clearly, this analysis is very much tied to the purpose one attaches to the legislation. In a very thoughtful response to these concerns, Audrey Macklin, supra, notes that, even under the s. 63 deduction, the more income a person has and consequently, the higher tax bracket one falls into, the higher the deduction available. This fact also undermines the goal of equity. Further, the concern that employed persons and business people will not be treated in the same manner is a fact which stems from the rationale of the Act itself; business deductions generally are restricted to those in business and are not available to an employed person. An employee cannot deduct an office at home, car expenses, meal and entertainment expenses, nor club dues or fees. In addition, employers who hire staff can deduct their salaries and employers who provide day care for their employees may deduct the expense (D. Goodison, "Nanny Means Business", CGA Magazine, September 1989, 15). Employees enjoy no such comparable deductions.

As my colleague has indicated, our tax system is based on principles of horizontal and vertical equity. The former requires that we tax individuals in similar circumstances the same, while the latter focuses on the similar taxation of individuals in different circumstances. These are important objectives and were recognized as of the highest priority in the Report of the Royal Commission on Taxation, supra. The Carter Commission stated in vol. 2, at p. 17:

> We assign a higher priority to the objective of equity than to all the others. ... our task requires us to make recommendations that would lead to an equitable distribution of the burden of taxation. We are convinced that unless this objective is achieved to a high degree all other achievements are of little account. Thus the need for an equitable tax system has been our major concern and has guided us in all our deliberations.

At the same time as we value equity under the income tax system, however, it is apparent that the system creates and perpetuates many inequalities. As Professor Claire Young notes, supra, at pp. 108-9:

> Income tax legislation is, by its very nature, both overtly and systemically discriminatory. For example, in Canada, the Act discriminates in favour of Canadian residents and against non-residents by imposing higher rates of tax on some forms of income realised by the latter. It discriminates in favour of the self-employed and against employees by allowing the self-employed a greater range of deductions from income. It discriminates in favour of investors in equity and against investors in debt by taxing capital gains at a lower rate than interest income and giving every resident a lifetime exemption from tax on $100,000 of capital gains.

The basic premise upon which discussion with respect to the differential treatment between employees and businesspersons must be laid is the recognition that the Act can be viewed to operate in a discriminatory fashion. While the Act may never have attempted to maintain equilibrium between persons in business and those who are employed, one must recognize that the realities of doing business cannot be ignored. Employees do not incur overhead expenses while businesses do. Employees are not able to deduct any expenses that they incur in order to work because their income is based on their gross salary, whereas business income is based on the calculation of the net profit or gain of the business. As a result, deductions are a regular occurrence. What constitutes a business expense for tax purposes is not cast immutably in stone. The concept of business expense should be interpreted in a way that takes into account the realities of businesswomen's expenses in relation to child care. However, in recognizing the distinction between the treatment of employees and businesspersons under the Act, in no way am I indicating that this may not constitute a real difficulty within our taxation system.

This said, this case is most fundamentally not about the many vertical inequities that may exist, but rather a question of horizontal equity and the need to treat all businesspersons alike. Further, the fact that the government has provided that a deduction for child care expenses be available to all parents, including employed persons, who ordinarily enjoy very few deductions, indicates governmental recognition that child care is a legitimate expense of working parents, in particular mothers. Finally, we must not assume that most self-employed entrepreneurs, whom the Act favours, are multi-millionaires — they are not, as the evidence of Dr. Armstrong demonstrates. Dr. Armstrong indicated that self-employed women generally work in small businesses of three to four persons. Their businesses are mostly in the service sector, where, if they are not physically present at the work site, the business could not operate, for example: beauty salons, shops, doctors, lawyers, caterers, etc. As a result of long hours and the requirement to work at the place of business, rather than at home, child care needs are extremely critical for these women. Business-women and, for that matter, men who legitimately incur child care expenses for the purpose of gaining or producing income from business must not be deprived of the benefit of a business deduction for their expenses.

E. Conclusion on Statutory Interpretation of the Income Tax Act

In conclusion, ss. 63 and 9(1) of the Act may, in my view, co-exist. There is nothing in the wording of s. 63 that excludes the application of s. 9. In addition, any such interpretation is contrary to the purpose and historical basis for the enactment of s. 63 and to traditional approaches to diverse deductions under the Act. In any analysis involving the examination of the interplay between ss. 9(1) and 63, one cannot overlook the effect of an interpretation which concludes that s. 63 overrides the possibility of a business deduction for child care. Although apparently neutral, such an interpretation may be shaped by a selective perspective. Though legislators, no doubt, strive toward objectivity, laws are inevitably drafted on the basis of the law makers' own vision of society and their own experience, experience which leads them to perceive certain interpretations and results as being obvious or neutral. ....

Notes and Questions

1. Although they disagree on the case outcome, both Justice Iacobucci and Justice L'Heureux-Dubé agree that the deduction for work-related child care expenses responds to massive changes in women's workforce participation. Both justices also note that section 63 targets the lower-income parent in a two-earner house-

hold. Do these two points make you more or less inclined to see the child care expense deduction as a subsidy or a benchmark adjustment?

2. The *Symes* case stirred up considerable controversy. On the one hand, the gender split on the Supreme Court brings home Justice L'Heureux-Dubé's point; The majority decision fails to recognize the realities of business women because predominately male lawmakers (and judges) draft laws and interpret statutes based on their own experiences and "partisan" perspectives.

   On the other hand, as Justice Iacobucci points out, if *Symes* had prevailed, employees – who make up the majority of working women - would still be limited by section 63's dollar cap and other restrictions. Also, if *Symes* had prevailed, self-employed men in two-earner households could arguably claim child care as a business expense, arguably undermining the provision's goal of removing barriers for women in the workforce. What do you think of Justice L'Heureux-Dubé's response to these objections?

   See also Audrey Macklin, "*Symes v. M.N.R.*: Where Sex Meets Class" (1992) 5 C.J.W.L. 498; and Claire Young, "Child Care and the *Charter*: Privileging the Privileged" (1994) 2 Rev. Const. Stud. 20.

3. Why does it matter if we view section 63 as an expenditure or benchmark adjustment?

   Consider the deduction-credit debate. Would a child care expense credit be more appropriate than the current deduction? All deductions have the upside-down effect described in the readings at the beginning of the chapter. Your perspective on this question depends in part on whether you think child care expenses should be deducted to determine profit from business or employment, or whether you think the deduction is more properly characterized as a subsidy for an otherwise personal expense of working parents.

   If you think a credit is better than a deduction, should it be a refundable credit and if so, how would the credit be paid? Monthly? Annually? Based on actual costs, average costs, or just a set amount regardless of actual costs?

   Some credit proponents go further and support replacing the deduction with a targeted, diminishing credit that would decrease until it disappears as family income increases. A diminishing credit would primarily support low- and moderate-income earning families.

   What might be the unintended consequences of a diminishing credit? What about women in low and modest paid jobs who depend on child care but who live with high income earning spouses? Removing child care costs as a financial barrier to women's workforce participation gives women financial security and economic independence, promotes women's professional networking and skills retention, and capitalizes on society's investment in women workers. Would a diminishing credit undermine these important objectives?

C. What Expenses Qualify?

The next case considers whether child care expenses include fees for activities with a recreation or education component. As you read the case, think about other types of child care situations that might raise the same issue. For example, what if the Levine children attended an after-school care program at a community centre where the children participated in organized art, music, or ballet activities and went on outings for swimming, skating, or other sports? Or what about sports or arts programs for older children who would otherwise be latch key kids? Should age-appropriate activities be considered child care expenses for older children?

LEVINE v. THE QUEEN
(1995), [1996] 2 C.T.C. 2147, 1995 CarswellNat 1394 (T.C.C.)

Archambault J.T.C.C.:

Mrs. Sharon Levine is appealing an assessment by the Minister of National Revenue (Minister) for the 1992 taxation year in which the Minister disallowed a sum of $2,397 out of the $13,206 claimed by her as child care expenses.

Facts

In 1992, Mrs. Levine was a flight attendant working for Air Canada. Although she had been in Air Canada's employ for 15 years, she was still on call and had to accept flight assignments with very short notice. She went anywhere in the world and could be away as long as five days at a time. She usually worked 18 days per month and she was off 13 days. However, she could be asked to replace sick co-workers on her days off.

Her husband, who testified on her behalf, estimated that she worked during weekends about half the time. Mr. Levine was a chartered accountant, an expert in forensic accounting, who worked long hours. His services could also be required on very short notice. He usually worked on Saturdays and sometimes on Sundays. In January 1992, the Levines had two children, aged seven and four. They had a live-in nanny to look after the children. The nanny worked no more than 50 hours a week and generally not on weekends. Mrs. Levine was able to make special arrangements with her to take into account her days off and trade weekend days for weekdays. The Levines also hired extra help from neighbours or got help from relatives for evenings and weekends.

As Mrs. Levine was expecting twins in the month of June, 1992, she stopped flying at the end of March and assumed ground duties until May 25 when the twins were born. Unfortunately for the Levines, the nanny decided to leave her employ soon after and they had a lot of difficulty finding a replacement. Many were hired but did not stay very long. They had to hire an agency to find a replacement. After two failures, the agency found a new nanny who is still working for them. They paid a finder's fee of $500 for this service. After the birth of the twins, Mrs. Levine took a 6-month maternity leave which was extended to March 1993.

In computing Mrs. Levine's income for 1992, the Minister refused the deduction of the following expenses:

Cost	**Course**
$169.00	Ballet Lessons
$ 77.00	Hampstead-Swimming
$155.79	Nautilus Plus Swimming
$135.00	Visual Arts Centre
$318.00	Mount Royal Ballet Lesson
$135.00	Ville Montréal Skating
$ 36.00	Hampstead-Swimming
$ 45.00	McGill University Tennis
$ 47.00	Pointe-Claire Swimming
$455.00	Hampstead Ski School
$170.00	Questo-Gymnastics
$ 50.00	Club Flexart-Gymnastics
$ 70.00	Côte St-Luc Skating
$ 35.00	Brownies
$500.00	Women's Domestic Service

The recreational activities described above represent lessons of a duration of one hour to one hour and a half once a week over a 12- to 13-week period, and in some instances over an 8-month period. The only exception is the ski school activity which was a whole day affair. They were either the activities of the seven year old or the four year old, but not both, except for the Nautilus swimming. They usually took place right after kindergarten or during the weekend. The Levines had an arrangement with friends and neighbours to share the duties for the transportation of their children as is often done in communities across Canada. Mr. Levine estimated that he and his wife did about 40% of the transportation.

Analysis

Are the recreational expenses and the finder's fee deductible as childcare expenses under section 63 of the Income Tax Act (Act)? The answer to this question depends on the application of the definition of child care expenses found in paragraph 63(3)(a) of the Act ...

This paragraph [d] lists certain exceptions:

> for greater certainty, any expenses described in subsection 118.2(2) and any other expenses that are paid for medical or hospital care, clothing, transportation or education or for board and lodging (except as otherwise expressly provided in this paragraph) are not child care expenses;

It is useful to refer to the French version of the key words in paragraph 63(3)(a):

> "frais de garde d'enfants" s'entend *des frais engagés* au cours d'une année d'imposition *dans le but de faire assurer au Canada la garde de tout enfant admissible* du contribuable, *en le confiant à des services de garde d'enfants*, y compris des services de gardienne d'enfants ou de garderie ou encore des services assurés dans un pensionnat ou dans une colonie de vacances, si les services étaient assurés. ...

What is the meaning and scope of "care" in English and "garde" in the French version? In the *Concise Oxford Dictionary,* "care" means, inter alia, "4 a. protection, charge. b. Brit. = child care". In *Le Petit Robert,* "garde" means:

> Action de veiller sur un être vivant, soit pour le protéger (V. Défense, protection), soit pour l'empécher de nuire, (V. Surveillance). Confier un enfant à la garde de quelqu'un.

To better understand the scope of these words, it is useful to read them within the object and spirit of section 63 of the Act. This is in conformity with the teleological approach recently reiterated by the Supreme Court of Canada in *Québec (Communauté urbaine) v. Corporation Notre-Dame de Bon-Secours* [see Chapter 10, *infra]*.

> A legislative provision should be given a strict or liberal interpretation depending on the purpose underlying it, and that purpose must be identified in light of the context of the statute, its objective and the legislative intent: this is the teleological approach;

We can find a review of the legislative intent of Parliament respecting section 63 in *Symes v. R.,* another decision of the Supreme Court of Canada. Iacobucci J. there refers to the Proposals for Tax Reform, 1969 where the following approach to child care expenses is described at page 15, para. 2.7:

> We propose to permit deduction of the child care expenses that face many working parents today. The problem of adequately caring for children when both parents are working, or when there is only one parent in the family and she or he is working, is both a personal and a social one. We consider it desirable on social as well as economic grounds to permit a tax deduction for

child care expenses, under carefully controlled terms, in addition to the general deduction for children.

In *McCluskie v. R.,* Judge Rip of this Court made the following comments on the approach to be followed in interpreting section 63:

> Child care expenses were permitted by Parliament "under carefully controlled terms" and it is not for the courts to vary explicit terms. Where Parliament has drafted a provision of law in general terms, the Courts must use common sense in interpreting the provision. ...

However, not all expenses incurred for the care of children are deductible. In particular, subparagraph [63(3)(d)] stipulates for greater certainty that education, medical and transportation costs are not child care expenses. I do not think that the recreational expenses disallowed by the Minister are child care expenses or "frais de garde d'enfants" within the meaning of paragraph 63(3)(a) of the Act. These expenses were not incurred for the purpose of watching over the children to protect them, and therefore to enable the parents to earn income from employment. They were incurred to develop the physical, social and artistic abilities of the children. These expenses would have been incurred whether or not the parents had been working. The evidence has shown that these activities were carried out even if both parents were not working, that is, both during the period when Mrs. Levine was working and during her maternity leave. The fact that these activities were for a limited period of time, one hour to one hour and a half per week, sometimes just for a few weeks, also supports this conclusion. Attending a one-hour lesson can hardly be considered an effective way of watching over the children to protect them. It is, however, a very effective means of teaching children new physical and artistic abilities.

It was argued on behalf of the Appellant that these recreational activities had the benefit of providing care for the children, thereby freeing the nanny to devote more time to the twins. It is true that the children, once they have been transported to the location of their lesson, are under the supervision of a responsible person. However, this person's primary role is not to watch over the children to protect them, but to teach ballet, swimming, skating, arts, etc. In my view, the children's being watched over is only an incidental benefit of the lessons. I do not believe that this type of expense was intended by the Canadian Parliament to be deductible. They are outside the scope of the "carefully controlled terms" of the Act. In conclusion, the recreational activities are not child care expenses within the meaning of paragraph 63(3)(a) of the Act.

For these reasons, this appeal is allowed and the assessment is referred back to the Minister for reassessment on the basis that the sum of $500 is a child care expense and that $1,897 of recreational expenses are not deductible in computing income for the 1992 taxation year.

Appeal allowed.

Notes and Questions

1. Some of the expenses claimed by Ms. Levine would now qualify for the Children's Fitness Tax Credit (effective 2007) and Children's Art Tax Credit (effective 2012) discussed later in this chapter. However, these two new credits have overall dollar limits ($1,000 and $500 respectively) and detailed definitions on what activities qualify.
2. If section 63's underlying policy goal is to enable parents to work, should it matter that the child care program is educational or recreational? Compare *Levine* with *Lessard v. The Queen*, 2003 TCC 266, [2003] 4 C.T.C. 2097, where the Tax Court allowed board and supervision fees paid to the Royal Winnipeg Ballet School. The Tax Court disagreed with the Minister disqualifying the fees because the mother chose the RWBS primarily to further her daughter's dance education. The Tax Court stated in paragraph 12:

> The Court considers that, in applying the *Act*, it must determine whether the child is eligible, and whether the parent performed the duties of an office or employment or was in other circumstances set out in the definition of child care expenses. In the Court's opinion, the *Act* does not require that the parent's choice of childcare services be justified by the parent's work needs. The taxpayer is responsible for choosing the boarding school at which he or she wishes the child to study, or the child care services he or she wishes to use; the taxpayer makes this choice on the basis of the child's needs, and this choice is an exercise of parental discretion. In the Court's opinion, the *Act* does not require that questions be asked about whether a particular form of child care is chosen on the basis of the parent's work needs or the child's needs.

3. Can you reconcile *Levine* and *Lessard*? Cases similar to *Levine* that disallowed child care deductions for recreational or educational activities include: *Keefer v. The Queen*, [2000] 2 C.T.C. 2622 (T.C.C.) (piano, pottery, equestrian lessons); *Sykes v. The Queen*, [2005] 3 C.T.C. 2054 (TCC [Informal Procedure]) (gymnastic and dance programs); and *Malecek v. The Queen*, 2007 TCC 271, [2007] 4 C.T.C. 2391, 2007 D.T.C. 833 (sports activities and music lessons).

   Cases allowing a deduction include: *Bailey v. The Queen*, 2005 TCC 305, [2005] 3 C.T.C. 2170, 2005 DTC 673 (primary school program for a pre-school age child were "reasonably priced child care services" and any education received was only an incidental benefit); and *Jones v. R.* (2006), 2006 TCC 501, [2007] 1 C.T.C. 2137, 2006 D.T.C. 3531 (after-school gymnastic programs for a pre-teen child who refused to stay home alone until her mother returned from work).

4. The child care expense must "enable" the parents to be employed, carry on a business, research, or attend school. When a parent is on maternity leave, should child care expenses for older children be allowed? In *D'Amour v. M.N.R.*, [1990] 2 C.T.C. 2355, 90 DTC 1827 (T.C.C.) at paragraph 17, the Tax Court allowed the expense of a babysitter who had worked continuously for the taxpayer before and during her maternity leave for her fourth child:

> The object of this legislation is, without any doubt, to enable parents who work to deduct child care expenses. It may happen that parents are unable to dismiss a babysitter or interrupt day care services not merely for personal reasons but because of economic reality. If a babysitter is dismissed, there may be little chance that she can be rehired at the end of the maternity leave. If a child is removed from day care, it may lose its priority on the waiting list and it may not be possible to have it re-admitted to the day care at the desired time. This does not create the desirable permanence and quality of care for children that working parents need to enable them to perform their own jobs. In the circumstances, these expenses were not incurred for personal purposes but for purposes of employment.

See also *McLelan v. The Queen*, [1995] 1 C.T.C. 2673, 95 D.T.C. 856 (T.C.C.) at paragraph 7, allowing the expenses of a nanny hired in the middle of a maternity leave where the Court acknowledged: "although the appellant may not have required the nanny for the entire period, owing to market conditions relative to secure a good nanny, especially in her residential area, she felt that it was the most prudent thing to do to hire the nanny in question as soon as the nanny was available".

Contra Spar McCluskie v. The Queen, [1994] 1 C.T.C. 2401, 94 D.T.C. 1735 (T.C.C.), disallowed the expenses to secure a nanny who arrived in Canada two months before the taxpayer's maternity leave ended, on the basis that the expenses were paid for the taxpayer's "personal convenience" as a "standby fee" and not to enable her to perform her job.

5. How liberally do you think section 63 should be interpreted? In *Labrecque v. The Queen* (2007), 2007 TCC 195, [2008] 1 C.T.C. 2318, 2008 D.T.C. 3275, both parents were working professionals with an autistic child who needed care on Saturdays. Because neither parent was physically at work on the weekend, the Minister disallowed the child care expense. The Tax Court reversed the Minister's decision and stated that:

> In a context where one of the members of a family of four is an autistic child, it must be understood that none of the usual domestic tasks, such as housekeeping, shopping and groceries, can be done with Simon present. In these circumstances, Simon has to be taken into care on Saturdays to allow the appellant to hold full-time employment from Monday to Friday. Without child care services for Simon on Saturdays, the appellant would have to give up her employment or hold part-

time employment, which is not at all easy to do in the case of a professional (para. 25).

What do you think of the Tax Court judge's reasoning? How would the judge's reasoning apply to child care expenses paid when a parent is temporarily unemployed and looking for work?

6. **Other Policy Issues and Initiatives:**

More Direct Support and Creating More Daycare Spaces

Are there better ways to support parents in the workforce and to address a widely acknowledged shortage in daycare spaces? Instead of an income tax deduction, would it be more equitable and efficient to directly fund universal, affordable, quality daycare?

Quebec takes the direct subsidy approach. Since 1997, Quebec's early childhood education and care program provides universal low-fee child care for children under five. The Quebec program has three major goals: to increase mothers' participation in the labour market, to balance the needs of workplace and home, and to enhance child development and equal opportunity for children. A qualitative evaluation by Pierre Lefebvre, Philip Merrigan, & Francis Roy-Desrosiers, "Québec's Childcare Universal Low Fees Policy 10 Years After: Effects, Costs and Benefits" (2011) *Centre Interuniversitaire sure le Risque, les Politiques Economiques et l'Emploi (CIRPEE)* recommends some changes, but gives the program an overall positive review.

The federal government uses an investment tax credit to encourage businesses to create licensed child care spaces for both children of employees and the greater community. Starting in 2007, subsection 127(9) provides a non-refundable tax credit of 25 per cent for defined expenditures up to a maximum of $10,000 for each additional child care space created.

As a future policy maker or commentator, how would you evaluate the investment tax credit's impact? How would you compare the tax credit approach to a direct subsidy approach?

Women Caring For Their Own Children At Home

Families in which only one parent, usually the father, is in the full-time work force criticize the child care expense deduction as unfairly favouring women in the paid workforce over women who choose to look after their children themselves. The Tax Court has dismissed several section 15 *Charter* challenges brought by single income earning families. See *Copeland v. The Queen*, [1993] 2 C.T.C. 3046 (T.C.C.) (two-parent families where one parent chooses to stay at home to bring up the children are not a discrete and insular minority) and *Ross v. The Queen*, [1993] 2 C.T.C. 2197, (T.C.C.) (the *Charter* does not support a deduction for payments to a mother looking after her children in the family's home).

In 2006, the federal government introduced the Universal Child Care Benefit (UCCB) to "foster choice" in child care arrangements. Currently, the UCCB pays a $100 per month ($1,200 annually) taxable amount for each child under age six, regardless of whether the parents choose institutional daycare or looking after their own children in their home. Subsection 56(6) includes the benefit payment in the taxable income of the spouse or common-law partner with the lower net income, regardless of which parent received the payment. The government promotes the UCCB as creating fairness by supporting diversity in a family's choice of child care.

Under proposed legislation, the government will increase and expand the UCCB starting in 2015. The UCCB payment will increase to $1,920 per year for each child under the age of six. The program will pay another $720 per year for children 6-17 years old. The UCCB will be included in the taxable income of the lower-income spouse. Single parents can choose to include the UCCB in either their own or their dependent's income.

D. Alimony and Maintenance Payments

In 1942, Parliament enacted a tax credit for child and spousal support payments because it was concerned that many divorced and separated men would be unable to pay both high wartime taxes and alimony. Shortly after, in 1944, the credit was replaced by a deduction-inclusion regime that stayed in place until the federal government enacted the 1997 child support guidelines.

The Child Support Payment Reform

Under the deduction-inclusion provisions in paragraphs 60(b) and 56(1)(b), support payers deduct support payments and support recipients include the payments in taxable income. When Parliament enacted the deduction-inclusion provisions, it assumed that men in high marginal tax brackets would pay support to women with either low or no income. The difference in marginal tax brackets would create an overall tax savings beneficial to the separated or divorced family. Over time, the overall tax savings assumption became controversial, particularly for child support payments.

Today, the deduction-inclusion provisions no longer apply to child support payments made under a written agreement or court order entered into or varied after April 30, 1997. The deduction-inclusion regime continues to apply to clearly designated spousal support payments.

The history behind removing child support payments from the deduction-inclusion scheme illustrates the political side of tax expenditures and how court cases can affect the policy agenda — even when the taxpayer loses. In the 1980s and 1990s, organizations concerned with the high rate, depth, and duration of poverty of single custodial mothers put the income tax treatment of child support on the policy reform agenda. Much had changed since 1942: divorce and separation were more frequent; women custodial parents were either already in the workforce or re-entered the workforce shortly after a separation or divorce; and women's disproportionate child-rearing responsibilities was severely affecting women's long-term economic well-being. Women's organizations and scholars viewed child support taxation as undermining custodial mothers' ability to support their children, making mother-led families more vulnerable to poverty.

The child support reform agenda was pushed along after the Supreme Court upheld the constitutionality of paragraph 56(1)(b). In *Thibaudeau v. The Queen*, [1995] 2 S.C.R. 627, [1995] 1 C.T.C. 382, 95 D.T.C. 5273, the taxpayer, Suzanne Thibaudeau, a divorced mother with two children, challenged the requirement that separated custodial parents must include child support payments in their taxable income. Thibaudeau only challenged the inclusion side of the deduction-inclusion system so that a decision in her favour would have left the payer's deduction untouched.

The Supreme Court majority viewed the inclusion provision in the context of both the tax deduction and the family law system. The Supreme Court accepted the government's position that the deduction-inclusion scheme created a tax subsidy that would benefit most separated and divorced families. The Court assumed that the family law system would then make appropriate adjustments to ensure that the total support payment covered the mother's increased liability in respect of the support payment.

A tax-subsidy only exists if the custodial mother is in a lower tax bracket than the father paying support. In fact, over the years, the tax differential had become far less likely. First, more custodial mothers were in the paid workforce. Second, the government had reduced the number of tax brackets, making it more likely that both parents would be in the same tax bracket. See Glenn Feltham & Alan Macnaughton, "Who Benefitted from the Deduction-Inclusion Regime for Taxing Child Support?" (1999) 47 Can. Tax J. 1479, a theoretical and empirical analysis confirming earlier research that child support recipients were disadvantaged in most cases.

Suzanne Thibaudeau's own case showed the difficulty custodial mothers had getting properly tax-adjusted child support awards. The Family Court judge underestimated Thibaudeau's federal tax burden on her child support by $2,500 — leaving her with far less money to meet her children's needs. The Supreme Court assumed that the Family Court would get it right, or that it was easy to go back to Family Court to get it fixed.

The *Thibeaudeau* decision came in the midst of a concerted effort to overhaul the child support system by enacting guidelines. Federal Child Support Guidelines calculate the payer's contribution towards child support using three components: (1) a "basic amount" based on the parent's income and the number of children; (2) a proportionate share of special expenses such as child care expenses, health care expenses and expenses for extraordinary extracurricular activities; (3) a further possible adjustment based on undue hardship of either parent which might include unusually high debts or significant costs associated with access.

While the guidelines were being developed, women's organizations were pressuring the government to eliminate child support taxation as part of the guideline reform. The government responded; when it introduced the Federal Child Support Guidelines, it also prospectively repealed the deduction-inclusion system for child support.

The Basic Rules

The deduction-inclusion provisions still apply to spousal support and to pre-May 1, 1997 child support orders. The provisions are highly detailed and there is a large body of case law interpreting each requirement. Support payments only qualify if the payer and recipient are living apart and the payments are (1) an allowance (2) paid on a periodic basis (3) made pursuant to a court order or written agreement. Taxpayers who want to take advantage of the deduction-inclusion provisions must pay close attention to each element in the definition.

A support payment qualifies as an allowance if it is a predetermined amount and the recipient has full discretion on how to use it. Payments made directly to third parties for typical items like mortgage payments, tuition fees, car lease payments, rent, or dental fees will not ordinarily qualify as an allowance because the recipient does not control the money. Subsections 56.1(2) and 60.1(2) create an exception if the order or agreement specifically states that the deduction-inclusion subsections apply. In other words, the parties must have actively turned their minds to the tax treatment of the third party payments and made sure that the order or agreement reflects their understanding that the third party payments are periodic support. The subsections deem the recipient to have discretion over the third party payments.

How specific does the agreement or order have to be for the third party payments to qualify as an allowance? Early cases required a specific reference to the two subsections by number. However, more recently, courts have been less strict, as long as the agreement shows the parties intended that the payments come within the provision. See *Veilleux v. Canada* (2002), 2002 FCA 201, [2003] 1 C.T.C. 138, lawyers must take great care to ensure their clients obtain the tax treatment they expected.

Courts distinguish between a "periodic" payment and a lump sum capital payment that happens to be paid in installments. For example, In *Maheu v. Canada*, 2013 TCC 279, 2013 D.T.C. 1261, the Court held that $208,000 paid in weekly installments over four years compensated the wife for releasing her interest in the husband's company. The installments were not deductible periodic support payments. In *Ostrowski v. The Queen*, 2002 FCA 299, [2002] 4 C.T.C. 196, 2002 D.T.C. 7209 (T.C.C.), the taxpayer was ordered to pay his former wife a lump sum of $88,800 from his share of the matrimonial home sales proceeds as "security" for the maintenance and support payments that would be due over the next two years. The issue was whether the advanced "security" payment still met the definition of a deductible "periodic" payment. The Court held that the advanced payment retained its original character as maintenance payable on a periodic basis, because the original court order for monthly payments was not varied. Again, careful attention to drafting is important to avoid a costly tax appeal.

What happens when a payer, who has been in arrears on support payments, makes a lump sum catch-up payment in a subsequent year? In a progressive tax rate system, the recipient of a lump sum payment could pay more tax than if she had received the original payment on time over more than one tax year. Subsection 110.2(2) now allows limited retroactive income averaging when the lump sum received is at least $3,000.

The deduction and inclusion provisions are detailed and exacting. The courts continue to review cases involving child support where orders pre-date May 1997 to see whether the payments still meet the deduction criteria. Later in the chapter, when we look at credits for dependent children, you will learn that a parent who pays child support is ineligible for certain dependent credits, regardless of whether the payer-parent can deduct the child support payment from income under paragraph 60(b). Family lawyers must be up to date on all the tax consequences of support payments.

E. Retirement Savings: Tax-Assisted Private Pension Plans

Canada pursues a three-pronged, public-private strategy to prevent late-life poverty and income insecurity among seniors, and to smooth out seniors' income drop post-retirement.

- **Publically Financed Income Support Transfer Programs:** Old Age Security (OAS), Guaranteed Income Supplement (GIS), and Spousal Allowance provide a minimum level of income for persons over 65. Payments are income-tested so that they are reduced, or "clawed-back", when income exceeds a threshold amount. OAS is paid back at 15 per cent when an individual's income is over $71,592 (2014). GIS is clawed back by 50 cents for every dollar of income until it is no longer paid once a single person's net income reaches $17,088. Different "net family income" thresholds apply for couples, depending on whether one or both receive the GIS.
- **Mandatory Public Pension Plans:** The Canada Pension Plan (CPP) and the Quebec Pension Plan (QPP) provide pensions for employees and self-em-

ployed persons based on how much and how long a person contributes to the plan. Both employees and employers contribute. Section 118.7 gives taxpayers a tax credit based on their annual contributions. Taxpayers include CPP and QPP payments in taxable income. The payments are neither income-tested nor clawed back.

- **Tax-Assisted Private Retirement Pensions and Savings:** Registered Pension Plans (RPPs), Deferred Profit Sharing Plans (DPSPs), Registered Retirement Savings Plans (RRSPs), and Tax-Free Savings Accounts (TFSAs) encourage private savings for retirement. Taxes are deferred on the taxpayer's contributions to RPPs, DPSPs, and RRSPs and on the income earned in the plans, until the taxpayer withdraws money, usually after retirement. A taxpayer does not pay tax on income earned in a TFSA.

The government's strategy relies heavily on the tax-assisted private pension and savings plans. The government income support programs and public pensions only replace about 38 per cent of an average wage-earner's pre-retirement income, far less than the estimated 60-70 per cent seniors need to maintain their standard of living after retirement. The private plans are expected to fill in the gap.

There are three types of tax-subsidized private plans: employer-sponsored pension plans, individually funded retirement plans, and the relatively recent TFSA. Two rationales are often given for the tax subsidy. First, the deduction is a government expenditure to encourage retirement savings. Second, a less accepted rationale views the tax concession to correct an income tax system's inherent bias against savers.

Employer-sponsored pension plans (RPPs and DPSPs) have several tax advantages: employers' contributions are not taxed as an employee benefit (paragraph 6(1)(a)) and employees and employers can deduct their contributions from income under paragraphs 8(1)(m) and 20(1)(q). The RPP or DPSP is not subject to tax on its earnings; benefits paid to members of the plan are taxed as income.

RRSPs defer taxes on retirement savings until the taxpayer withdraws funds from the plan. RRSPs are funded through the taxpayer's contributions deducted under paragraph 60(i) from the current year's income. There is no tax on the investment earnings as they accrue in the RRSP. Thus, taxpayers get both an immediate tax saving from the contribution deduction and the retirement fund can grow faster because no taxes are paid on the fund's investment income until it is withdrawn. Taxpayers who contribute to an RRSP when their earnings are taxed at a high marginal rate and who later withdraw funds when their income is taxed at a lower marginal rate, have an overall tax savings, not just a deferral.

The RRSP annual contribution limit is 18 per cent of the previous year's earned income up to an overall annual maximum of $24,930 in 2015. The overall maximum increases are based on increases in average wages. The RRSP is designed to provide consistency and equity between plans funded by employers and those funded by individuals. The contribution amount is also limited when a person is a member of an RPP or DPSP. There is also a catch-up provision that allows a person who cannot make his or her maximum contribution for the year to make the contribution any time in the future.

Tax-Free Savings Accounts are a more generalized savings vehicle designed to encourage both savings for retirement and other major purchases. Taxpayers can put a modest annual amount ($5,500 in 2014) into a TFSA and are not taxed on the investment income. The annual TFSA contribution is not tax deductible. When taxpayers withdraw the contributed amounts and any investment income, they are not subject to tax. The annual contribution amount accumulates so that a taxpayer who does not contribute the full amount in a given year can contribute it in a subsequent year.

Notes and Questions

Do Tax-Assisted Private Plans Meet the Government's Policy Goals?

Canada's public-private strategy gets mixed reviews in terms of both reducing elder poverty rates and creating a buffer against retirement income deficits.

1. **Elder Poverty Rates and the Gender Gap:** Elder poverty rates were reduced significantly from close to 21 per cent in the 1980s to less than 5 per cent in 2009. Recent research cautions that there was an increase in 2010 to between 5.2 and 7.2 per cent, depending on what is measured. However, even with the recent increase, Canada's overall elder poverty rate is still among the lowest in OECD countries and is considerably below the international average of 12 per cent.

   Researchers consistently point out that poverty is still acute among elderly women, especially those who are divorced or separated. Higher poverty rates for women stem from historically lower wages, more part-time work, more gaps in women's work histories, and longer life expectancy. Many women are not able to save enough for a modestly comfortable retirement.

   Addressing the poverty gap for women requires strengthening the OAS and GIS safety net and changing CPP eligibility and payments to take into account women's employment patterns. Overall the government would need to increase the publically-funded portion of retirement support. See Claire Young, "Pensions, Privatization, and Poverty: The Gendered Impact" (2011) 23:2 C.J.W.L. 661; Monica Townson, "Poverty Issues for Canadian women: Background Paper" (2005) Status of Women Canada; Philip Bazel & Jack Mintz, "Income Adequacy Among Canadian Seniors: Helping Singles Most" (2014) 7 SPP Research Papers 4.

2. **High Marginal Effective Tax Rates for Low Income Seniors:** In 2003, social policy researcher Richard Shillington documented a now widely acknowledged problem; low income seniors who followed government advice and put savings into RRSPs are taxed at high effective marginal rates — over 50% and as high

as 100% — when they withdraw their RRSP savings in retirement. In *New Poverty Traps: Means-Testing and Modest-Income Seniors* (Toronto: CD Howe Institute, 2003) at 4, Shillington writes:

> ... [Taxpayers have] fallen for the bad advice coming from governments and the financial community: that everyone should save in an RRSP. These households have sacrificed current consumption to accumulate, on average, $23,000 in an RRSP ($38,000 if we include other pensions). The primary beneficiary of this saving will be the federal and provincial governments because most of the income from it will be confiscated by income-tested programs and income taxes. To the extent that these households were misled, they have been defrauded.

Shillington points out that low and modest income earners receive negligible tax savings from their RRSPs. Earners whose incomes fall in the lowest marginal tax bracket when they make the contribution will likely be in the same tax bracket when they withdraw the funds, and so they have no overall saving and only a small deferral of tax on the investment income.

More importantly, Shillington demonstrates the plight of the "futile savers" — people who sacrifice current consumption in order to contribute to an RRSP, but then find themselves worse off when they withdraw the funds. Because RRSP withdrawals are treated as income, low and modest income seniors have their GIS, OAS, GST credit, and other income-tested benefits clawed back. They may also become ineligible for services and benefits such as subsidized nursing homes, "meals on wheels", and prescription drug plans.

The TFSA, introduced in 2009, now gives low and modest income households a way to save for retirement that will not penalize them on withdrawal. But it does not address the high-marginal rate problem for people who already took the government's advice and saved through an RRSP.

For more on the relationship between retirement savings and low income seniors, see Michael Veall, "Estimates of the Number of Guaranteed Income Supplement Recipients Who Receive Income from Registered Retirement Savings Plans" (2014) 62:2 Can. Tax J. 383; Alexandre Laurin & Finn Poschmann, "Who Loses Most? The Impact of Taxes and Transfers on Retirement Incomes" (2014) CD Howe e-brief 189.

3. **Modest Income Earners — Still Insecure:** Research suggests that, currently, modest income earners do not have adequate retirement income. Researchers estimate that 80% of current retired persons are adequately protected, taking into account government transfers, registered pension plans, RRSP investments, and ownership equity in their homes. However, modest income earners ($25,000 - $50,000) have inadequate retirement income. There is concern that future retirees will have difficulty recovering from the economic downturn that began in 2009.

For an overview of corrective measures under consideration see, Jack Mintz & Thomas Wilson, "Reform Proposals For Replenishing Retirement Savings" (2013) 6:9 SPP Research Papers.

III. TAX CREDITS

Tax credits function as both part of the progressive tax system's design and as tax expenditures. Personal credits determine the starting point for the progressive tax rate system, redistribute income within society, and refine the individual tax unit by recognizing some dependency relationships. Medical expense, disability, and elder care credits recognize unequal personal financial burdens that affect a person's ability to pay taxes. Education and tuition credits, child fitness credits and children's art credits encourage people to spend money to develop their "human capital" and to keep their children mentally and physically healthy and active. Charitable donation credits subsidize support for registered charities such as hospitals, schools, religious organizations, food-banks, museums, recycling initiatives, community centres, and a myriad of other institutions and activities benefiting society at large.

Tax credits directly reduce the taxes you owe dollar for dollar. You calculate the credit and then subtract the credit amount from what you would otherwise pay in tax. Because all taxpayers get the same dollar benefit, credits avoid the subdivision e deduction "upside-down subsidy" effect. The 1988 tax reform converted many items described in this chapter from subdivision e deductions into tax credits to make them more equitable.

Most credits are calculated by applying an "appropriate percentage" to a base amount. The base amount can be a set dollar amount (basic personal credit), can fluctuate with the dependent's income (spousal and equivalent-to-spousal credits), or can be based on how much you spend within defined limits (medical expenses, tuition fees, children's fitness and art programs, and charitable donations). For most credits, the "appropriate percentage" corresponds with the lowest tax bracket — 15% (in 2015). Most credits are adjusted annually for inflation. The government also occasionally increases the credit amount to adjust the rate structure or to increase benefit amounts.

Refundable credits are used to deliver social benefits. Most refundable credits are tied to family income so that the benefit amount gradually reduces and then disappears when family income exceeds an eligibility threshold. Keep in mind that most credits are non-refundable, which means that if a taxpayer's income is so low that he or she owes little or no tax, he or she gets little or no value from the credit. Boadway, *supra*, raises the question whether most personal credits should be refundable to achieve their economic purpose more equitably.

For this chapter we chose a cross section of tax credits with both benchmark and expenditure rationales. As you study the credits, consider which ones might be better as refundable credits and which ones are best left as non-refundable.

A. Personal Credits for Individuals and Dependants

Basic Personal Credit — Spouse, or Common-Law Partner Credit — Wholly Dependent Person Credit — Other Dependants Credit

Personal credits for individuals and dependants reflect the ability-to-pay principle. The $1,699 basic personal credit refines the progressive tax rate structure by setting an $11,327 tax-free threshold (in 2015). The spousal and equivalent-to-spousal credits, and the dependant tax credit modify the individual as the basic tax unit by creating a higher tax-free threshold based on family circumstances.

The personal credits reflect policy choices on the tax unit and how the tax system should respond to different family, household, and personal circumstances. And what might seem straightforward becomes complicated when family circumstances change because of separation or divorce. In recent years, the personal credits have been in a state of flux. Amendments and new provisions address some gaps. And a proposed "family tax cut credit" in the Conservative 2011 election platform would move the income tax structure away from an individual taxation unit and closer towards marital unit taxation.

The personal tax credit amount and structure present several related questions: Should a person have a minimum standard of living before he or she pays tax? How should a minimum standard of living be set? Should the personal credits become refundable — as a negative income tax — to guarantee a minimum standard of living?

The basic personal credit is straightforward; it applies to every taxpayer. The spousal, equivalent-to-spousal, and dependant relative credits in paragraphs 118(1)(a), (b), (c.1), (d), (d.1) and subsections 118(4)-(7) have exacting details on who qualifies as a spouse and dependant and who can claim the credit.

Dependant Spouses

The old saying, "two can live as cheaply as one" is a romantic notion not borne out by most people's personal experiences. Taxpayers supporting a spouse or common-law partner with little or no income can claim a $1,699 credit that shields an additional $11,327 from tax. Because the spousal credit is targeted for households where one spouse fully supports a non-working spouse, the credit gradually reduces and completely disappears when the supported spouse has income over $11,327.

There is also a parallel "equivalent to spouse" credit under paragraph 118(1)(b) for a single or separated taxpayer supporting a minor child, parent, grandparent, or certain other defined close relatives. The taxpayer must provide a home and support for the dependant. The spouse and equivalent-to-spouse credits recognize that an additional, non-income earning household member affects a person's ability to pay.

Dependant Minors

Tax credits and income-support transfer payments to parents supporting dependent minor children have seen the greatest number of recent changes. A patchwork of credits and transfers, each with its own terms and delivery mode, and sometimes with similar names, make it difficult to track the overall effect of each change. You may need a scorecard to keep track of what's in and what's out.

On October 2014, the federal government announced it was replacing the non-refundable Child Tax Credit (a $315 credit for each child under age 18, paragraph 118(1)(b.1)) with an enhanced, taxable Universal Child Care Benefit (UCCB). Assuming the changes receive royal assent, effective January 1, 2015, parents will receive $160 per month ($1,920 annually) of taxable income for each child under age 6 and $60 per month ($720 annually) for children ages 6 through 18.

The enhanced UCCB will not affect the child care expense deduction for working parents. And eligible parents will still receive the Canada Child Tax Benefit (CCTB) — a non-taxable amount paid monthly to low- and moderate-income families with children under age 18. Eligibility for the CCTB is income-tested based on family income. Some parents may also qualify for extra support for children with mental or physical disabilities. The CCTB also incorporates the National Child Benefit Supplement (NCBS), a monthly amount per child targeted towards low-income families.

Other Dependants

Taxpayers supporting relatives over age 18 who are dependent because of age, or mental or physical infirmity, can claim additional credits defined in paragraphs 118(1)(c.1) and (118(1)(d). Watch out for some confusing terms. First, there are non-refundable caregiver credits if the taxpayer maintains a home for a parent or grandparent over age 64 or an infirm adult relative. The caregiver credits are income-tested based on the dependant's income. Then, a Family Care Giver amount can be added to the spousal, spousal equivalent, and caregiver credit if the dependent is physically or mentally impaired. Need some help? The CRA's website has a step-by-step series of questions taxpayers can use to see whether they are eligible.

Notes and Questions

1. **The Income-Splitting Credit — The Individual vs Marital Tax Unit Question:**

   Canada chose the individual as the basic tax unit rather than the family or married and common-law couple. Chapter 1 canvases some of the arguments for and against the individual tax unit in light of the progressive tax rate system. Those who support family or marital unit taxation often argue that in a fair tax system, two families with the same combined income should pay the same amount of tax regardless of whether the income is earned by one or both spouses. On the other hand, those who support the individual as the basic tax unit stress that dual income earning families have extra income earning costs and have to purchase many goods and services provided for free by the spouse who stays at home. Individual unit taxation also supports women's autonomy and work force participation. With marital unit taxation, women face being taxed at their spouses' higher marginal tax rate, which is a disincentive to women entering or staying in the workforce. Most countries use the individual as the basic tax unit.

The income-splitting credit, dubbed the "Family Tax Cut", proposes to fix a perceived inequity between families with children where one person earns all the income and families where there are two income earners. If the provision receives royal assent, the credit will in effect allow the higher-income earning spouse to transfer up to $50,000 of taxable income to a spouse in a lower income tax bracket and claim a maximum credit of $2,000.

Critics of the credit point out that the largest benefits will go to income earners in the highest income brackets who support spouses who do not work. Couples with both spouses in the same tax bracket and single parents gain nothing from the proposed credit. Jonathan Rhys Kesselman, an economist and tax policy scholar, points out that 87 per cent of Canadian households gain nothing. Another 6 per cent have overall tax savings of $500 or less. The largest benefit amounts go to 7 per cent of couples with children who have very high incomes. Families with one spouse at home and an average income over $155,999 gain over $3,000, and families with household incomes over $311,000 gain over $5,000 (Jonathan Rhys Kesselman, "Family Tax Cuts: How Inclusive a Family?" (2014) Caledon Institute of Social Policy).

One of the rationales for the income-splitting credit is to assist families who choose to have a parent stay home to care for children. If the majority of families where one parent stays home get minimal or no benefits, would it be better to further enhance the tax credits for children? Can you think of other ways to equitably support families raising children?

2. **Common-law partners:** The spousal credit in paragraph 118(1)(a) includes "common-law partner" defined in subsection 248(1) as a person with whom the taxpayer "cohabits in a conjugal relationship" for more than 12 months or, if the couple has cohabited for less than 12 months, is a parent of the taxpayer's child. The common-law partner definition applies to many other provisions, including disability and income-tested transfer credits. The definition sometimes leads to counterintuitive results. For example, under section 63, the lower income person in the household must take the child care expense deduction; as a result, a common-law step-parent who does not contribute to his or her stepchild's daycare cost may get the tax benefit.

When judges apply the common-law partner definition, they sometimes get drawn into examining the intimate details of the taxpayer's life. In *Savory v. Canada*, 2008 TCC 69, [2008] 5 C.T.C. 2033, the Minister disallowed the taxpayer's claim for child care expenses and the equivalent to spousal credit, and recouped child tax benefit and GST credit overpayments, based on the taxpayer's intermittent common-law relationship with her children's father. The taxpayer and the children's father initially lived together for four months in 1998, when they separated. Then starting in August 2001, they lived in the same apartment building but in different apartments. For a six-month period (September 2004 to February 2005), they lived in the same apartment. The Tax Court judge examined, in minute detail, the financial, emotional, and physical aspects of the taxpayer's relationship with the children's father. To determine which, if any, periods the taxpayer was in a "conjugal relationship", the judge considered whether the father performed household services, what social supports he provided, and what interactions he had with the children.

Are you comfortable with the judge's approach in *Savory*? Can you think of an alternative standard or a simple administrative process?

Personal Credits and Separation and Divorce: The equivalent to spousal credit in paragraph 118(4)(b) prohibits two taxpayers from taking a credit for the same dependant ("supported person). Subsection 118(5) disqualifies a parent who pays child support from claiming the equivalent-to-spousal credit, without regard to whether the parent can deduct child support under paragraph 60(b). The provisions prevent taxpayers from double-counting the same child for credits and deductions.

What happens when parents have joint or shared custody? When parents share custody of two or more children, if they both meet the criteria, each parent can claim the equivalent-to-spouse credit for one of the children. In some situations, subsection 118(5) prevents either parent from claiming the credit. Take, for example, *de Moissac v. The Queen* (2006), [2007] 1 C.T.C. 2001, 2006 D.T.C. 3502 (T.C.C.), where each parent had custody for six months of the year and each paid the other child support for part of the year. Neither parent qualified for the paragraph 118(1)(b) credit because of subsection 118(5). Subsection 118(5.1) now remedies the *de Moissac* situation by allowing one of the parents to claim the credit. However, the parents must agree on which one takes the credit. Neither can take the credit if they cannot agree.

In many instances, separation and divorce increases the overall costs of raising children who live part-time with each parent or visit frequently with a non-custodial parent. Should these economic facts of life be taken into account in the paragraph 118(1)(b) regime? Now that child support payments are no longer deductible, should there be an entirely different credit regime to cover non-custodial parents who make support payments?

B. Charitable Donations

There are over 161,000 registered charities and non-profit organizations in Canada engaged in diverse, public-oriented activities. The sector's activities include: social services for children, youth, seniors, and people with disabilities, operating museums, hospitals, schools, food banks, low-income housing, and daycare centres; maintaining places of worship and centres for community activities; researching cures for diseases; and running literacy, conservation, and disaster relief programs. The charity and non-profit sector generates over $112 billion annual revenue and employs over 2 million people. Each year almost half of all Canadians work for charities and non-profits as volunteers.

Registered charities have two tax advantages: they are tax-exempt and they can issue charitable donation tax receipts that donors need to claim a charitable tax credit under section 118.1. The Department of Finance Canada, *Tax Expenditures and Evaluations* (2013) estimates the tax expenditure on individual charitable giving was over $2 billion in 2013.

When charitable contributions were converted from a deduction to a credit in 1988, the new credit preserved its original value for high-income taxpayers. The charitable credit is calculated using two rates: the lowest marginal rate (15%) applies to the first $200 of eligible donations and the highest marginal rate (29%) applies to the balance. There is an annual cap on the donation amount of 75% of a donor's income. The credit is non-refundable. However, donors can carry unused donations forward for five years.

The 2013 federal budget introduced a temporary First-Time Donor's Super Credit that gives first-time donors an additional 25% federal tax credit on up to $1,000 of donations. The credit may only be claimed once in the 2013 to 2017 taxation years.

Special valuation and capital gains rules apply to donations of property. Enhanced incentives apply to donations of corporate securities, certified Canadian cultural property, and ecologically sensitive lands.

Why does the income tax system recognize charitable contributions? Tax scholars most often cite three policy rationales: (1) gifts to charity should be excluded from the taxpayer's income tax base because the funds are used for the public good rather than for the taxpayer's personal needs; (2) donation credits are government subsidies or matching grants for underfunded charitable activities that are worthy of support; and (3) donation credits promote the public good by rewarding altruism and selflessness.

The first rational — that amounts given to charity are not part of a person's economic wealth — is in line with William D. Andrews' argument that removing charitable gifts from taxable income could be a benchmark or normative adjustment. (“*Personal Deductions in an Ideal Income Tax*”, *supra)*. The matching fund and reward for altruism rationales are more in line with a tax expenditure-subsidy view. See David Duff, "Tax Treatment of Charitable Contributions in Canada: Theory, Practice, and Reform" (2004) 42:1 Osgoode Hall L.J. 47.

And finally, the chapter discusses another possible rationale, using the charitable credit to indirectly purchase non-market public goods. We look at the eco-gift program as an inexpensive way for the government to preserve ecologically sensitive land for the public good.

When is a Donation not a Donation?

Donations are gifts — the giver voluntarily transfers money or property to a recipient without expecting anything in return. To what extent should a donor's charitable motivations affect his or her eligibility for the credit? What about a mixed motive? What if I give land to a University for new buildings, knowing that eventually property I own nearby will increase in value because people will want to live close to the University? Have I made a charitable gift?

What if the donor receives something back from the charity, either something incidental, like a T-shirt or mug with the charity's logo, or something more substantial like the donor's name on a plaque or on the face of a building? Should someone who pays $2,000 to attend a charity dinner, where the value of the meal is $50, receive a full or partial tax credit? Keep these questions in mind as you read the *McBurney* case.

THE QUEEN v McBURNEY
[1985] 2 C.T.C. 214, 85 D.T.C. 5433 (F.C.A.)

[McBurney claimed charitable donations for payments he made to three Christian religious schools attended by his children. The school requested the payments and parents were expected to pay, but no child had been turned away if the parents were unable to pay. The CRA disallowed the charitable donation claim on the basis that the payments were tuition fees.]

Stone J.: ....

[T]he main question here is whether these payments were "gifts" within the meaning of subparagraph 110(1)(a)(i) of the statute. To conclude, as did the learned trial judge, that they were not "tuition", of course, leaves this question unanswered for even if they were not tuition it remains to be determined whether they were "gifts" within the statute. The learned trial judge appears not to have addressed this question directly, having concluded that they were deductible from income because they did not represent tuition or material consideration paid or given in respect of the respondent's children.

The word "gifts" is not defined in the statute. I can find nothing in the context to suggest that it is used in a technical rather than in its ordinary sense. This latter sense was attributed to that word by courts of Australia as it appeared in a like context of an Australian taxing statute allowing "gifts" to be deducted from income in certain circumstances. (*Commissioner of Taxation of the Commonwealth v. McPhail* (1967-68), 41 A.L.J.R. 346 at 347; *Leary v. Federal Commissioner of Taxation* (1980), 32 A.L.R. 221 at 221, 237 and 241). The same approach was taken by the Trial Division of this Court in *The Queen v. Zandstra (supra)*. It adopted the views expressed by Owen, J. in the *McPhail* case which decided that payments made by a parent to the building fund of a school attended by his son were not deductible as "gifts". At 348 of the report, Owen, J. stated:

> But it is, I think, clear that to constitute a "gift", it must appear that the property transferred was transferred voluntarily and not as the result of a contractual obligation to transfer it and that no advantage of a material character was received by the transferor by way of return.

The judges of the Federal Court of Australia who heard the *Leary* case, while generally agreeing with Owen, J., placed some qualification on the test he enunciated. Thus, after referring to the above passage, Deane, J. in his concurring reasons for judgment stated (at 243):

> I would question the unqualified nature of his Honour's comments. Ordinarily, a gift will not be made in pursuance of a contractual obligation: the mere fact that a person has made a contractually binding promise to make a gift may not, however, necessarily deprive it of its character as such when it is made: see, e.g., the illustration of the father of the prospective bride given by Ridley J. in *Attorney-General v. Holden*, [1903] 1 K.B. 832 at 837. Ordinarily, a gift will be without valuable material return; again, the mere fact that a donor receives, either from a stranger or the donee, a valuable return which he may or may not welcome may not prove conclusively that there was no gift: see, e.g. *Collector of Imposts (Vic) v. Peers, supra*, at 121-2.
>
> If a transfer of property is in return for valuable consideration received by the transferor from the transferee, it will not be a gift by the transferor. If the relevant property is not, for that reason, precluded from being properly regarded as a gift, the above-mentioned considerations indicate usual attributes of a gift, namely, that a gift will ordinarily be by way of benefaction, that a gift will usually be not made in pursuance of a contractual obligation and that a gift will ordinarily be without any advantage of a material character being received in return. I would add to those usual attributes of a gift, the attribute that a gift ordinarily "proceeds from a 'detached and disinterested generosity', *Commissioner v. LoBue* (1956) 351 U.S. 243, 246; 'out of affection, respect, admiration, charity or like impulses'. *Robertson v. United States* 343 U.S. 711, 714"; See also *Overseers Etc. of the Savoy v. Art Union of London*, [1896] A.C. 296 at 308 and 312; *Collector of Imposts (Vic) v. Cuming Campbell Investments Pty. Ltd., supra*, at 641. In the clear case, one will be able to determine from overall

> impression of the circumstances whether the relevant transfer can properly be described as a gift. In a borderline case involving dispute as to whether a particular transaction constitutes a gift ... the presence or otherwise of these usual attributes of a gift will provide the reference point for answering. The essential question remains, however, ... namely, whether the transfer in question can as a matter of ordinary language, properly be described as a gift.

Apart from this qualification (which I would not consider material), the approach taken by Owen, J. in the *McPhail* case has stood through the years and has found favour in the Trial Division of this Court in the *Zandstra* case. That case also involved annual payments made by a taxpayer to a charitable organization of which he was a member. That organization, as here, operated a Christian school which two of the taxpayer's children attended in the years the payments were made. The amount of payments was arrived at in much the same manner as in the present case, being based upon projected school operating costs and the number of children attending. Parents were assessed on the basis of family income. It was their view that payments were made out of a sense of moral obligation rather than a legal or contractual one. In holding that these payments were not "gifts" within the meaning of subparagraph 27(1)(a)(i) of the *Income Tax Act* (being in all relevant respects similar to subparagraph 110(1)(a)(i)), Mr. Justice Heald stated (at 252; C.T.C. 509):

> It seems clear from the evidence of most of the witnesses that they considered they had a primary duty to their own children to provide them with a Christian education in a separate Christian school and that obligation has been discharged by the payments to the Jarvis School. Such a factual situation clearly, in my view, removes these payments from the "gift" category.

There can be little doubt that here, too, the respondent saw it as his Christian duty to ensure his children receive the kind of education these schools provided. The payments were made in pursuance of that duty and according to a clear understanding with the charities that while his children were attending these schools he would contribute within his means toward the cost of operating them. I cannot accept the argument that because the respondent may have been under no legal obligation to contribute, the payments are to be regarded as "gifts". The securing of the kind of education he desired for his children and the making of the payments went hand-in-hand. Both grew out of the same sense of personal obligation on the part of the respondent as a Christian parent to ensure for his children a Christian education and, in return, to pay money to the operating organizations according to their expectations and his means. In my judgment the Minister was correct in refusing to treat these payments as "gifts" under subparagraph 110(1)(a)(i) of the *Income Tax Act*.

It is significant, in my view, that in the years after his children were no longer attending the OCSA school, the respondent's payments to that charity declined dramatically. With respect, I am unable to draw from this evidence the inferences that the learned trial judge was able to draw, namely (at 477; D.T.C. 6504) that "there is nothing to be made" of this fact and, specifically, that "no inference of his paying a tuition fee can be drawn in these circumstances". On the contrary, this evidence supports the appellant's contention that the payments made by the respondent in 1976 and 1977 were directly related to the presence of his children at this school where they received the Christian education he felt in conscience bound to secure for them.

Notes and Questions

1. *McBurney* was followed by *Woolner v. The Queen* (1999), [2000] 1 C.T.C. 35, 99 D.T.C. 5722 (F.C.A.), affirming (1997), [1999] 4 C.T.C. 2512, 2000 D.T.C. 1956 (T.C.C.), (disallowed donations to a Mennonite Church that funded school bursaries for the donor's children; and *Coleman v. Canada*, 2010 TCC 109, [2010] 3 C.T.C. 2311, 2010 D.T.C. 1096, affirmed [2011] 3 C.T.C. 149, 2011 D.T.C. 5040 (F.C.A.), leave to appeal refused 2011 Carswell Nat 4679 (S.C.C.) (donations to a fund funneled back to the donor's children and grandchildren) Similarly, in *Burns v M.N.R.*, [1988] 1 C.T.C. 201, 88 D.T.C. 6101 (F.C.T.D.), appeal dismissed [1990] 1 C.T.C. 350, 90 D.T.C. 6335 (F.C.A.), a parent's donations to the Canadian Ski Association during the years that his daughter was a member of the training squad were disallowed on the basis that the payments were made for the purpose of securing a material advantage and were not gifts.
2. In *McBurney*, Justice Stone uses the phrase "no advantage of a material character" as part of the gift criteria. If the CRA strictly applied this requirement, many common charity fundraising events would fail. Charities routinely invite donors to pay large amounts to attend an event where there is food, entertainment, or even a chance to meet a celebrity. For many years, the CRA made an administrative concession when the donor received a nominal benefit. The CRA also allowed charities to issue charitable donation receipts for the price of a fundraising event ticket, less the value of the meal, show, or other benefit. See Interpretation Bulletin IT-110R3: Gifts and Official Donation Receipts (20 June 1997) at paragraphs 5-10.
3. After over 10 years in limbo, the "split receipting" provision was enacted in 2013. The amendments were originally proposed in 2002 and were given retroactive effect.

   The split receipting provision is carefully worded to retain the classic common-law gift criteria, while at the same time allowing a charity to give a donation receipt when the donor receives some benefit. Subsections 248(30) to (38) provide that the receipt of an "advantage" will not *"in and of itself"* disqualify a donation. The charity can give a receipt in the amount of the gift, less the amount of the "advantage". The language leaves it open for the CRA to challenge a gift if it lacks donative intent.

The provision has two basic rules based on the size of the advantages relative to the gift:

- Relatively small advantages (*de minimis)* do not need to be deducted from the amount of the tax receipt. The charity can ignore an advantage that is worth no more than $75 and 10% of the gift's value.
- On the other side of the equation, if there is a large advantage, the charity cannot issue any tax receipt. If the advantage is worth more than 80% of the gift's value, then the benefit outweighs the donor's gift intention.

Donors who make gifts that fall between the *de minimis* and 80% values can receive a "split receipt" for the difference between the value of the gift and the advantage.

4. The CRA does not recognize gifts of services. See IT-110R3, *supra*, and *Slobodrian v. The Queen* (2003), 2003 FCA 350, [2004] 1 C.T.C. 124, 2003 D.T.C. 5632. Conceptually the person who performs services for a charity is foregoing taxable income.

   Perhaps there should be a credit for volunteering?

   See "Debate over Volunteer Tax Credits: Good for Some, Bad for Others?" *Evolution* (2011), online: Volunteer Canada <http://volunteer.ca/content/volunteer-tax-credits-goodsome- bad-others>; Clifford Spyker & John Peloza, *The Potential Impact of Canadian Federal and/or Provincial Tax Credit Incentives for Volunteer Participation* (Edmonton: Volunteer Alberta, 2009).

Gifts of Property – Valuation and Abuse Problems

Taxpayers often donate property to charities. Property like corporate shares can earn income or be sold to support the charity's work. Sometimes the property directly relates to the charity's activities: artwork or artifacts to museums; a residential property to a social service agency; medical supplies to an aid organization; or ecologically sensitive land to a conservation authority.

Charities issue donation receipts based on the property's fair market value defined as:

> [T]he highest price obtainable in an open and unrestricted market between informed and prudent parties, acting at arm's length, under no compulsion to act, expressed in terms of money, or money's worth.

Establishing fair market value is important for both the charitable donation amount and the taxpayer's capital gain or loss from the gift. Gifts to charities are deemed disposition under subsection 69(1). The donor is deemed to have sold the item to the charity at fair market value. Special rules effectively eliminate the capital gain for certain "eligible property": publically traded securities, certified cultural property, and ecologically sensitive land. Taxpayers must carefully consider the capital gains effect when they donate capital property. The taxpayer can avoid or minimize a capital gain by electing a deemed proceeds amount between the property's adjusted cost base and its fair market value. The elected amount then becomes the taxpayer's donation credit amount.

The CRA recommends using an independent appraiser or valuator to determine the fair market value of property worth more than $1,000. Because cultural and ecological properties get special tax treatment, there are specific appraisal requirements. Cultural gifts must be certified and valued by The Canadian Cultural Property Export Review Board. Ecological gifts must be valued by an experienced independent appraiser and then recommended to the Minister of Environment by an Appraisal Review Panel.

Buy-Low, Donate-High Flips

From time to time tax "promoters" devise schemes to take advantage of the charitable donation rules. *Klotz v. The Queen* illustrates the buy-low, donate-high charitable receipts scheme. The judge relies on "common sense" to deny the taxpayer a charitable credit based on an inflated appraisal value. As you read the case, think about whether common sense is enough, or would you recommend tighter rules?

The excerpt includes the Court's discussion on whether the art prints are personal use property. To understand how the taxpayer (or the tax promoter) structured the scheme so as to avoid any capital gains, you will need to remember the special "*de minimis*" rule in subsection 46(1) that effectively eliminates capital gains from dispositions of low-value (under $1,000) personal use property.

KLOTZ v. THE QUEEN

2004 TCC 147, [2004] 2 C.T.C. 2892, 2004 D.T.C. 2236, appeal dismissed 2005 FCA 158, [2005] 3 C.T.C. 78, 2005 D.T.C. 5279, leave to appeal refused (2006), 355 N.R. 392, [2005] S.C.C.A. No. 286.

Bowman A.C.J.T.C.: Mr. Klotz is one of about 660 individual Canadian taxpayers who participated in a program called Art for Education or AFE ...

Under the AFE program the Canadian taxpayers acquired limited edition prints which they donated to colleges and universities that were prescribed for the purposes of paragraph 118.1(1)(f) of the Act. They bought the prints from the promoters of the program for about $300 per print and immediately donated them to the universities or colleges and received a receipt for $258,400 or approximately $1,000 per print, which they used to support a claim for a charitable gift tax credit under subsection 118.1(3).

... Curated, through a person Hazel Hett, who retained Ms. Krawczyk, acquired prints from artists or dealers. Ms. Krawczyk's instructions were pay no more than US$50 and this was the price typically paid. Novak Graphics Ltd., a Canadian source, was paid CDN$50, $55, $70 or $75 per print. Ms. Krawczyk testified that she was sometimes able to acquire prints for less than US$50 - in some cases as little as US$5, in others $20. Prints were acquired in large quantities. In 1997, 1998 and 1999 when the program was in effect, over 63,000 prints were acquired.

In light of the prices for which Ms. Krawczyk, on behalf of Curated, was able to obtain the prints the other instruction to Ms. Hett may seem a little strange. It was that the prints she acquired should have a value of CDN$1,000 or more. I say strange because the man on the Clapham omnibus might find it anomalous that a person could be instructed to acquire prints having a value of at least CDN$1,000 for a price not exceeding US$50. But then, the man on the Clapham omnibus would probably not be familiar with the art scene in New York in the 1990s or the methods devised to make mass charitable gifts of art a profitable endeavour. ...

Mr. Klotz's donation to FSU comprised 250 prints created by 30 artists. They were bought for $75,000 on December 28, 1999 and donated on December 30, 1999 for which he received a charitable donation receipt of $258,400. He never saw the prints, never had possession of them and had no role in choosing them. They were shipped directly to FSU ...

One thing is clear, albeit probably irrelevant to what has to be decided here, and it is that Mr. Klotz's motivation in participating in this program was purely the anticipated tax benefit. The broadening of the cultural or intellectual horizons of the students at FSU was not a factor. He never asked what FSU was going to do with the prints. In 1999, FSU received 1,450 prints from various donors and presumably issued receipts for at least $1,450,000.

He received substantial promotional materials from the AFE program. They contain a page or two of idealistic and somewhat hifalutin verbiage about the social benefit of giving art to educational institutions but the bulk of the material has to do with the tax advantages. Two opinions from well-known law firms were received. The opinions are carefully drafted but like most legal opinions that I have seen in respect of transactions in which the reduction of tax is a significant factor, they are more in the nature of a dissertation on the various provisions of the Act in the government's arsenal that might be used to attack the intended tax result. Such opinions are stated to be subject to so many qualifications, provisos and assumptions that it is difficult to see how a client could derive much comfort from them. ...

The principal question here is: what was the fmv of these prints at the date they were donated? It is not suggested that they increased over 300 per cent in value between December 28, 1999 and December 30, 1999. The argument is that in December 1999 they were worth $1,000 and it is irrelevant that Ms. Krawczyk or other purchasing agents managed to persuade hundreds of artists or art dealers to part with thousands of limited edition prints for US$50 (or less, sometimes as little as US$5) or that Curated was able to sell over 63,000 prints to about 660 Canadians for about $300 per print.

The basis upon which the $1,000 per print value is advanced is the valuation made by Ms. Laverty. ...

Of the 250 prints valued in the Klotz donation, 201 are valued at exactly $1,000 each, 13 at $1,100, 16 at $1,200, 11 at $1,400, five at $1,500, three at $1,800 and one at $2,000. One is struck by how many come in at exactly $1,000 each. Ms. Laverty's reports that are given to the donors appear to be identical in every case except for numbers.

...

In *Aikman*, supra, I stated:

> The intent or expectation of obtaining a tax advantage does not vitiate the charitable gift. Nonetheless an appellant in such circumstances runs a risk that the Board or the court may conclude that the best evidence of fair market value is the price at which the object was bought.

I continue to be of that view. It is one thing serendipitously to pick up for $10 a long lost masterpiece at a garage sale and give it to an art gallery and receive a receipt for its true value. It is another for Curated to buy thousands of prints for $50, create a market at $300 and then hold out the prospect of a tax writeoff on the basis of a $1,000 valuation. Mr. Mathew presented the appellant's case with consummate skill and persuasiveness but ultimately his case foundered on the shoals of common sense.

I turn now to the question whether the prints were personal-use property. The significance of this is that if I had agreed with the appellant's valuation of $1,000 per print but held that the prints were not personal use property the appellant would have lost the benefit of paragraph 46(1)(a) and would have realized a capital gain of the difference between his actual cost of $75,000 and his deemed proceeds of $258,400. The reason this question was not relevant on assessing was that since the Minister's assumed value of the prints ($75,000) was equal to the appellant's cost, no capital gain or loss would have arisen on the Minister's theory. I raise parenthetically the rather interesting question what the court could do if it had agreed with the appellant's value (thereby supporting the tax credit claimed under subsection 118.1(3)), but held that the prints were not personal use property, so that a capital gain of $183,400 arose. I have not calculated the comparative benefit of the tax credit and the detriment of the loss of the protection afforded by subsection 46(1). It is of course trite law that the court cannot increase the tax assessed. In light of the conclusion I have reached, it is not necessary for me to deal with the question. ...

I have concluded that the prints are personal-use property. Even if I had accepted the narrower interpretation advanced by the Crown I would still have held that the prints were personal use property. One way of using an object is to give it away, whether the motive be altruistic, charitable or fiscal.

Finally, I come to the question of penalties. The penalties were based upon the premise that the appellant's claim was made in circumstances amounting to gross negligence. I have already held that the value of the gift to FSU was overstated by a significant amount. Does this amount to a misrepresentation that is attributable to gross negligence? Counsel argued that the appellant did not make the sort of enquiries that he should have and that he knew or ought to have known that the prints were over valued. It is important to emphasize that failure to exercise due diligence is not the same as gross negligence. Gross negligence connotes a much greater degree of negligence amounting to reprehensible recklessness. ...

I have concluded that this is not an appropriate case for a penalty under subsection 163(2). The AFE program was admittedly aggressive. Counsel submitted that Mr. Klotz was cavalier about checking the values. Cavalier may be an accurate enough expression. Counsel noted that he sought no independent advice and did not pay sufficient attention to the advice in the legal opinions that he examined to the effect that he should independently verify the appraisals.

Counsel's criticism of Mr. Klotz has some validity. He was careless about verifying the value. Nonetheless a penalty under subsection 163(2) for gross negligence is a punishment for reprehensible behaviour. Here he relied upon his financial advisor Mr. Brill. He had what on the face of it was an appraisal by a qualified appraiser. He had two legal opinions which, however qualified they might be, would be taken by the average layman as implicitly putting the imprimatur of two major law firms on the program.

In light of these considerations, I am allowing the appeal and referring the assessment back to the Minister for reassessment solely for the purpose of deleting the penalties under subsection 163(2).

Notes and Questions

1. The art-flip industry was very active for a time. An early case, *Friedberg v. The Queen*, [1992] 1 C.T.C. 1, 92 D.T.C. 6031 (F.C.A.), affirmed [1993] 2 C.T.C. 306, 93 D.T.C. 5507 (S.C.C.), paved the way for art-flip promoters. In *Friedberg*, the taxpayer was asked by the Royal Ontario Museum's staff to purchase two lots of rare Islamic and Coptic textiles for $67,500 and $12,000 and then immediately donate them to the museum at fair market values of $496,175 and $229,437 respectively. Both lots were certified under the *Cultural Property Export and*

Import Act. The Court looked closely at the transaction documents and allowed the donation credit at the appraised fair market value for the one lot where title clearly passed from the seller to the taxpayer and then to the museum.

Other cases affirming the taxpayer's donation credit at the flipped-appraised fair market value include, *Whent v. The Queen*, [2000] 1 C.T.C. 329, 2000 D.T.C. 6001 (F.C.A.), leave to appeal refused 2000 CarswellNat 2397 (S.C.C.) (donations of art work created by the famous native artist, Norval Morrisseau, to public art galleries in Ontario); and *Nguyen v. The Queen* (2008), 2008 TCC 401, [2009] 1 C.T.C. 2438, 2008 D.T.C. 4390; The taxpayers were unsuccessful in *Nash v. The Queen* (2005), 2005 FCA 386, [2006] 1 C.T.C. 158, 2005 D.T.C. 5696, leave to appeal refused 2006 CarswellNat 932 (S.C.C.).

2. The government substantially dampened the buy-low/donate-high art-flip arrangements by adding subsections 248(35) and (36). If the taxpayer owned the donated property for less than three years, the new subsections deem the fair market value to be the lesser of its cost or its fair market value. If one of the main reasons the taxpayer acquired the property was to make a charitable gift, then the deemed fair market rule applies for ten years.

3. **Leveraged Gifts, the Tax Shelter Registration, and Planner and Preparer Penalties:** The "leveraged gift" arrangement is another scheme that takes advantage of the charitable donation rules. Tax promoters set up complex arrangements where "donors" are promised "returns" on their charitable gifts. Typically, the arrangement includes a pre-arranged loan that funds a portion of the taxpayer's donation. The promoters structure the loan so that the taxpayer never has to repay it.

The CRA has successfully argued that leveraged gifts do not meet the basic gift criteria. In *Maréchaux v. The Queen* (2010), 2010 FCA 287, [2011] 2 C.T.C. 77, 2010 D.T.C. 5174, leave to appeal refused 2011 CarswellNat 1911 (S.C.C.), the Federal Court of Appeal upheld the Tax Court judge's ruling that Mr. Maréchaux had not made a "gift" within the meaning of section 118.1:

> [B]ecause he made the payment to the foundation expecting to receive, and in fact did receive, a significant benefit, namely an interest-free loan of $80,000 from a lender (not the foundation), repayable in twenty years (paragraph 3).

See also *Kossow v. the Queen*, 2012 TCC 325, [2012[6 C.T.C. 2140, 2012 D.T.C. 1266, affirmed [2014] 2 C.T.C. 1, 2014 D.T.C. 5017 (F.C.A.), leave to appeal refused 2014CarswellNat 1529 (S.C.C.); *Berg v. Canada*, 2014 FCA 25, [2014] 3 C.T.C. 1, 2014 D.T.C. 5028.

For a review of the art-flip and leveraged loan problems, see D. Sandler & T. Edgar, "The Tax Expenditure Program for Charitable Giving: Kicking a Gift Horse in the Teeth" (2003) 51 Can. Tax J. 2193.

4. New tax shelter registration requirements for "gifting arrangements" and tax preparer and tax planner penalties are the government's latest vehicles to shut down leveraged gift schemes. The tax shelter definition under subsection 237.1(1) now includes "gifting arrangements" where taxpayers contribute property to a charity and the property was purchased with no-risk loans.

   Tax shelters must be registered with the CRA and the promoters must report the names of taxpayers who participate. The CRA tracks and audits tax shelters. In 2013, the CRA announced it would not assess taxes owed or provide a refund to taxpayers who claim a tax credit under a gifting tax shelter scheme until the CRA audits the tax shelter.

5. The tax preparer and tax planner penalties target persons who knowingly make, or participate in making, false statements that another person could use for the purpose of the *Income Tax Act*, under circumstances amounting to "culpable conduct". Subsection 163.2(1) defines culpable conduct as "an act or a failure to act, that is (a) is tantamount to intentional conduct; (b) is indifferent to whether the *Income Tax Act* is complied with; or (c) shows a willful, reckless or wanton disregard of the law". The penalty for a false statement is the greater of

   (a) $1,000, and

   (b) the lesser of

      (i) the penalty to which the other person would be liable under subsection 163(2) if the other person made the statement in a return filed for the purposes of this Act and knew that the statement was false, and

      (ii) the total of $100,000 and the person's gross compensation, at the time at which the notice of assessment of the penalty is sent to the person, in respect of the false statement that could be used by or on behalf of the other person.

6. *Guindon v. Canada*, 2013 FCA 153, 446 N.R. 154, [2013] 5 C.T.C. 1, 2013 D.T.C. 5113, leave to appeal allowed 2014CarswellNat 654 (S.C.C.) applied the tax planner penalty to a lawyer involved in a leveraged gift scheme. Guindon, a family lawyer, provided a favourable tax opinion for the promoter of a leveraged donation scheme. Guindon was also a director of the charity and signed the charity's donation receipts. The CRA imposed a $546,757 penalty based on the taxes that each of the 134 donors would have owed. The Federal Court of Appeal upheld the penalty provision.

   Guindon challenged the tax planner penalties for being so severe that they amount to criminal penalties. She argued that she is entitled to *Charter* protections including the standard of proof beyond a reasonable doubt. *Guindon v. Canada* was heard by the Supreme Court of Canada in December 2014.

7. Many taxpayers have had to repay the full tax credit plus interest after a CRA audit of leveraged tax arrangements. Taxpayers have started class actions seeking

damages for negligence or negligent misrepresentation from the lawyers and accountants who gave favorable opinions to the tax shelter promoters. The Ontario courts certified class actions in *Cannon v. Funds for Canada Foundation*, 2012 ONSC 399, [2012] 3 C.T.C. 132 (S.C.J.), additional reasons 2012 ONSC 3009 (S.C.J.), leave to appeal refused 2012 ONSC 6101 (Div. Ct.) and *Lipson v. Cassels Brock & Blackwell LLP*, 2013 ONCA 165, 114 O.R. (3d) 481, [2013] 4 C.T.C. 116, additional reasons 2013 ONCA 391. In 2013, the *Cannon* case settled against some defendants for about $28.2 million; the class action continues against the non-settling defendants.

8. The charity and non-profit sector performs important public functions and is a large and vital component of the Canadian economy. The sector is underfunded and organizations are constantly under financial pressure to fundraise. Financial pressures make participating in aggressive tax planning schemes tempting. However, charities participating in tax planning schemes risk losing their charitable status.

   Lawyers are often asked to sit on charities' boards. As a lawyer-board member, would you apply a business risk/benefit analysis to the decision to take donations generated through a tax shelter arrangement? Or would you apply a higher standard?

9. **Using the Charitable Contribution Provisions to Fund Government Purchases and Correct Market Failures:** The Ecological Gifts Program conserves important natural habitats across Canada by providing enhanced charitable income tax incentives for donations of full or partial interests in ecologically sensitive land ("eco-gifts") made to eligible conservation charities, municipalities, and federal and provincial agencies. Taxpayers donating eco-gifts receive extra incentives: eco-gifts are not subject to an annual net charitable donation limit; the carry forward for unused credits is 10 years compared to the usual 5 years; and eco-gifts are fully exempt from capital gains. Eco-gifts are routinely discussed as a charitable-giving incentive. The Federal Finance Department's expenditure budget accounts for eco-gifts in the charitable donation category.

   But are the tax incentives for eco-gifts really a charitable giving expenditure, or is the government in effect purchasing ecological goods and services at a discount rate using charitable credits? Is the Ecological Gifts Program an example of using income tax incentives to correct a potential market failure stemming from the lack of a commercial market for important "public goods"?.

   The Ecological Gifts Program is a specific national conservation program with Environment Canada as the lead partner. Working in concert with provincial officials, the Minister of Environment must certify that the donated property is "ecologically sensitive land", important to "the preservation of Canada". The program preserves "sites that have significant current ecological value", "lands that are zoned or designated for biodiversity objectives", "natural buffers around environmentally sensitive areas such as water bodies, streams or wetlands", lands that are "significant habitats", "sites with enduring geological features that contribute to biodiversity" and "areas of wildlife concentration".

The Minister of Environment working with its provincial and territorial counterparts oversees every aspect of the Ecological Gifts Program. Environment Canada defines the criteria for qualified ecologically sensitive property, approves recipient organizations, and determines the eligibility and donation value of each ecological gift. Only organizations approved by the Minister are eligible to receive an eco-gift. Approved organizations must have among their primary objects both the conservation and protection of Canada's environmental heritage and the acquisition and management of real estate for conservation purposes. The Environment Canada website lists approved recipients.

What does the government "buy" through the eco-gift tax charitable tax credits? Forest areas and wetlands, which account for the majority of eco-gifts, provide an impressive range of ecological services including ensuring water quality and supply, providing flood control, preventing runoff, supporting soil formation and retention, ensuring nutrient recycling and insect pollination, and providing recreation and cultural areas.

Eco-gifts also contribute to an effective greenhouse gas emissions and climate change strategy. There is a relationship between protecting existing ecosystems, biodiversity, and climate change mitigation and adaption. Healthy and intact ecosystems are more resilient and can withstand damage and adapt better to climate change than degraded and fragmented land. Forests, grasslands, and wetlands function as carbon sinks, removing carbon dioxide from the atmosphere and maintaining natural vegetative cover in and around agricultural land. They prevent the release of natural carbon stored, and thus, reduce green-house gas emissions.

While it is difficult to compare the value of the goods and services gained from eco-gifts, we know that the ecological services provided are potentially indefinite, and by using the charitable tax credit, the government pays only a percentage of the eco-gift's fair market value.

The government "purchase" rationale is similar to the standard rationale that donation credits are government subsidies or matching grants for underfunded charitable activities that are worthy of support. What makes ecological gifts different than how charitable credits usually subsidize worthy activities is Environment Canada's extensive oversight.

C. Medical Expense Tax Credit (METC)

The Medical Expense Tax Credit recognizes medical expenses beyond what the average person might incur for the things Canada's publicly funded health care system does not cover. Prescription drugs, prescription eyeglasses, braille readers, and home renovations that ensure accessibility are examples of costs that must be privately purchased and that can qualify for the METC.

Tax scholars debate whether and to what extent medical expenses should be eligible for a tax credit. Has the taxpayer made a voluntary personal consumption choice that the tax system should not recognize? Or has the taxpayer spent money on a non-discretionary basic health need that reduces his or her ability to pay tax?

The METC's structure reflects its purpose — support for taxpayers facing greater than ordinary non-discretionary medical costs. Taxpayers can only claim medical expenses for themselves, family members, and other dependants for costs exceeding a threshold amount: either 3 per cent of net income or a fixed amount ($2,208), whichever is less. And subsection 118.2(2) confines eligible medical expenses to an exclusive list that draws a tight line between items that will be publicly supported and items that remain private expenses.

Eligible medical expenses include: payments to hospitals and health professionals; devices such as prosthetic limbs, hearing aids, prescription eye glasses, and oxygen tanks; full-time care either in a nursing home or in the patient's home; home renovations for disabled persons; prescription drugs; and private health insurance premiums. In recent years, the list expanded to include gluten-free food for persons with celiac disease, organ transplant costs, and animals trained to assist persons with restricted use of their arms and legs.

The government continuously revises eligible expenses to add new treatments and technology, but carefully restricts items to those that are medically required. Subsection 118.2(2) and regulation 5700 use complicated qualifiers and dollar caps to confine expenses to non-discretionary items. For example, a person with a "severe chronic ailment, disease, or disorder" can claim the lesser of $1000 or 50% of an air conditioner's cost, but only if a medical practitioner prescribes the air conditioner. Similarly, travel costs for medical treatment can qualify if the taxpayer must travel at least 80 km and substantially equivalent medical services are not available near the taxpayer's home.

Judges interpreting the medical expense provision must apply narrowly worded language to compelling taxpayer stories. Decisions balance Parliament's intent to assist taxpayers' serious and prolonged mental and physical impairments with Parliament's intent to prevent abuse. Home renovation costs are an example where a series of cases interpreting the METC liberally to allow credits for hot tubs and hardwood floors prompted the 2005 amendments to curtail these types of expenses.

As you read, *Sotski v. Canada* — a post-2005 renovation amendment case — think about the challenge faced by the Court. Do you think judges should have more leeway to interpret the METC rules liberally based on particular taxpayers' circumstances, or is a more "rigorous" definition of medical expenses needed to prevent abuse?

SOTSKI V CANADA
2013 TCC 286; 2013 D.T.C. 1229

PIZZITELLI T.C.J. (orally): — The only issue to be decided in this case is whether the Appellant can deduct the sum of $3,675 expended in 2010 to install engineered hardwood flooring in her home pursuant to paragraph 118.2(2)(l.2) of the Income Tax Act (the "Act").

The facts are not generally in dispute. The Appellant's husband suffers from the progressively debilitating Parkinson's disease that, without dispute by either party, constitutes a severe and prolonged physical disability, which makes walking on surfaces that offer friction like carpets both difficult and unsafe due to risks from falling. Due to both the difficulty in raising his feet above a friction offering surface like carpeting and the forward leaning posture of her husband due to the disease, as well as the added problem of his psoriatic arthritis which causes his toes to turn in, the husband was at serious risk of having the carpet arrest his feet and forcing him into a fall; essentially risking injuring himself, the Appellant as his in-home caregiver and any outside caregivers who try to assist him. As a result, the Appellant, a person with experience in caregiving, attended at a flooring centre, and after obtaining the advice of the dealer having regard to her husband's needs, replaced the fairly new carpet in their five-year old home with very modestly-priced engineered smooth laminate flooring to eliminate the resistance and hence reduced the physical effort and resulting fatigue as well as the risk of fall to all as mentioned.

The Respondent agrees that the Appellant has a medical reason and justification for installing the flooring and agrees with the Appellant that the new laminate flooring would enable the Appellant's husband to be more mobile and function within the dwelling as contemplated by the above paragraph 118.2(2)(l.2) of the Act. The only dispute between the parties is the Respondent's position that the other two conditions of the above paragraph are not met, namely, those found in the portion of the above paragraph that reads:

> (l.2) ... provided that such expenses
>
> (i) are not of a type that would typically be expected to increase the value of the dwelling, and
>
> (i) are of a type that would not normally be incurred by persons who have normal physical development or who do not have a severe and prolonged mobility impairment;

In order for the Appellant to succeed in this appeal, both the above conditions must be met.

The Respondent takes the position that the installation of laminate flooring is a type of renovation that would typically be expected to increase the value of the dwelling unit and that the installation of laminate floors is a type of expense normally incurred by persons who have normal physical development or who do not have a severe and prolonged mobility impairment, although led no evidence in this regard. The onus to rebut the Minister of National Revenue's (the "Minister") assumption of course rests on the Appellant and the Appellant argued that while the installation of solid hardwood floors could typically be expected to increase the value of a dwelling unit the installation of modestly-price engineered floors would not, as the existing carpet was relatively new. The Appellant also testified that she replaced only the 800 square foot area utilized by her husband and not the remainder of the carpets in the house. The Appellant also testified that her personal preference is a quality carpet as she had before over the laminate but that the laminate was the only affordable option she had to address her husband's medical condition. The Appellant's testimony was sincere and consistent and I found her to be highly credible.

Frankly, the Appellant has demonstrated to my satisfaction that the installation of modestly-priced laminate flooring instead of solid hardwood flooring cannot be said to typically increase the value of the dwelling. The issue of flooring is, as she suggested and which I accept as being most reasonable, a personal consumption decision at best, and although I would find it reasonable to conclude that the replacement of an old and stained carpet would likely increase the value of a dwelling unit, I cannot agree that the replacement of a fairly new quality carpet with low-end laminate flooring would achieve the same result. I must say, from my personal experiences, that the cost of quality carpeting can be substantially higher than some types of laminate flooring and that engineered flooring with a wood veneer is substantially less expensive than full-quality hardwood flooring. In my view, the Appellant has demonstrated she has met the first condition of paragraph 118.2(2)(l.2) of the Act and the Respondent led no evidence to the contrary.

The second condition the Appellant must meet in the above paragraph is more problematic in my view. The Appellant must demonstrate that this type of expenditure is of "a type that would not normally be incurred by persons who have normal physical development or who do not have a severe and prolonged mobility impairment" to paraphrase the clause. The Respondent had argued that Parliament's intention was clear that the installation of hardwood flooring was one of those types of expenses that would normally be incurred by those without the requisite impairment. The Respondent led into evidence the Annex to the Budget Plan of 2005 where the Minister of Finance acknowledged on page 19 that recent decisions of this Court interpreted the former section more broadly so as to include in some cases the cost of hardwood floors or installing a hot tub, which went beyond the policy intent of the Medical Expense Tax Credit because:

> ... it subsidizes renovation expenses that increase the value of the home, and extends tax recognition to expenses with a substantial element of personal consumption and personal choice. ...

To stop this recognition, Parliament added the two conditions in question above, which the Respondent pointed out was to have overruled previous Tax Court of Canada decisions which allowed hardwood flooring expenses and hot tub expenses. While Budget Papers and Technical Notes are not law, they should be given good weight when Parliament was aware at the time the legislation was passed that the Department of Finance was aware of the issue and intended to deal with it.

The Respondent, relying on the above, states that the type of expense intended to be disallowed then was that of the installation of hardwood floors and hence the Appellant should be denied here. In addition, the Respondent points out that recent cases decided after the change in legislation, which was effective as of February 23, 2005, the Budget date, support its position. In *Hendricks v. Canada*, 2008 TCC 497, 2008 D.T.C. 4852, Paris J. denied as a medical expense deduction of the cost of hardwood flooring citing the clear intent of Parliament found in the Budget Papers and in *Barnes v. Canada* 2009 TCC 429, 2009 D.T.C. 1282, Boyle J., also citing the clear intent of Parliament evidenced by the Department of Finance's Explanatory Notes and Budget Papers accompanying the 2005 amendments to the legislation, denied the deduction of a swimming pool installation expenses.

The Appellant, however, has argued that in keeping with the intention of Parliament, her expense is not an expense reflecting an element of personal consumption or personal choice as the caution in the Budget Papers above alluded to. She testified she simply had no choice if she wished to address her husband's medical impairments due to Parkinson's.

Frankly, I am in agreement with the position of Appellant in this matter. The Budget Papers and explanatory notes make it clear the two conditions were inserted to ensure the taxpayer was not subsidizing personal consumption and personal choices. I agree with the Appellant that if her only choice was to install low-cost laminate floors to deal with her husband's condition, then there is no element of personal consumption or choice here that the taxpayer is being asked to fund. I note as well that in the Hendricks case above, in paragraphs 8 and 9, Paris J. found that the Appellant had not disproven the Minister's assumption that the installation of hardwood flooring was an alteration that would typically be expected to increase the value of the dwelling and that, as stated in paragraph 9:

> 9 ... I would also add that, as a matter of common sense, it would seem that the installation of new hardwood floors in the place of 23 year old carpets in this case, could typically be expected to increase the value of a dwelling.

Paris J. decided that case on the basis the first condition had not been met.

In the case at hand, we have a situation where the Appellant replaced fairly new carpets, only five years old, in only part of the home which her impaired husband utilizes, with low-end engineered laminate flooring, not solid flooring and I have found the first condition had been met.

Moreover, in dealing with the second condition, Boyle J. in the Barnes case above, stated at paragraph 13 thereof:

> 13 This is not to say that, in an appropriate case, a swimming pool especially designed or altered for a person for therapeutic physiotherapy purposes will be unable to qualify.

Accordingly, Boyle J. recognized that the legislation is not solely geared to prohibiting "types" of expenditures as the Respondent contends, but types of expenditures that fail to meet the condition of Parliament having regard to its stated policy. In my view, if as Boyle J. stated, a specially-designed pool for the disabled Appellant in that case may have qualified, I fail to see why flooring that needs no special design, but which meets the requirements, purchased and installed without bells and whistles so to speak, should not. It would indeed seem an absurd result that if the Appellant here hired an engineer to design a super smooth concrete floor or "medical floor" to use the Respondent's term, with no resistance to specifically suit the needs of the Appellant at great expense, that that would qualify while using the most modest means to achieve the same result would not.

In interpreting the provisions of the paragraph, one cannot lose sight of the policies of Parliament, both in enacting the Medical Expense Tax Credit and in the amendments. The Medical Expense Tax Credits were designed to grant relief to taxpayers who suffer from serious and prolonged mental and physical impairments, to assist them with dealing with the extra costs incurred by them as a result of their condition. The amendments to the provisions in 2005 were to avoid abuses of those provisions. The Respondent in this case does not disagree with the existence of the Appellant husband's impairments and even agrees that the installation of the engineered laminate flooring assists in alleviating his symptoms and addressing his condition. The Respondent does not take issue with the Appellant's purpose and intent in having the flooring installed to assist her husband with mobility and reduce fatigue and risk of injury by providing a surface of lesser resistance in her dwelling, those requirements spelled out in subsection 118.2(2). The Respondent only relies on his technical interpretation of the two conditions in such paragraph (l.2) pointing to the Budget Papers and Technical Notes to suggest the intention of Parliament was to categorize the types of expenditures in general, including all hardwood flooring. I simply do not agree.

Parliament, having regard to its policy of avoiding abuse in medical expenditures, set out two conditions designed to avoid abuse. It did not specifically categorize expenditures such as hardwood floorings, or hot tubs or swimming pools are being prohibited in its language and while the language of the Budget Papers and Explanatory Notes made mention of these types of abuses, these were the types being set out as examples because they were the types that were the subject matter of the cases the Department of Finance took issue with as being abusive in those circumstances. In the circumstances at hand, I do not find that replacing a quality carpet flooring of only five years old with modestly-priced engineered laminate flooring instead of higher-priced solid hardwood to be abusive. The Appellant did not attempt to buy a luxury floor or upgrade the quality of her dwelling by installing the floor she did. She instead only put in what was necessary, without the intent or expectation of having the taxpayer fund her personal consumption choices. Had she installed, say high-end solid mahogany instead of lower-end engineered flooring, one could question her motives and arrive at a reasonable conclusion that this would not only increase the value of his dwelling but also be of the type of higher-end material most taxpayers would no doubt be happy to have his fellow taxpayers fund. This was not the case here. There is no abuse and the conditions of paragraph 118.2(2)(l.2), interpreted with the policies of Parliament in mind, have been met so the appeal is allowed in full.

Notes and Questions

1. Do you think the judge in *Sotski* got it right? Other cases decided subsequent to the amendment of paragraph 118.2(2)(l.2) disqualified renovation expenses because a non-disabled person would have made the same type of improvement and the home's value increased. For example, *Chobotar v. The Queen*, 2009 TCC 260, 2009 D.T.C. 1174 denied the cost of adding a wheelchair-accessible bathroom for a taxpayer with multiple sclerosis who was confined to wheelchair. *Barnes, supra*, denied the cost of a modest-sized swimming pool recommend by a physiotherapist for a teenager with cerebral palsy and severe epileptic seizures that affected her ability to walk, talk, dress herself and use the bathroom on her own. And *Anthony v. Queen,* 2012 TCC 334, 2012 D.T.C. 1275 denied the cost of a hot tub even though it was configured specifically for the taxpayer's ailment and alleviated her severe chronic back pain, giving her a greater ability to walk.

   Do you think that the restrictions on renovation expenses are realistic or do they create an unfair hurdle for individuals with disabilities?

2. Taxpayers can claim the METC for any 12-month period ending in the taxation year. This expanded period ensures that taxpayers with large expenses incurred over two taxation years can still meet the threshold requirement.
3. How liberal should the METC be? Would it be better to have fewer restrictions and substitute an overall dollar cap for any 12-month period?
4. **Cosmetic Procedures:** As of March 4, 2010, new subsection 118.2(2.1) eliminates the credit for "purely cosmetic medical and dental expenses". The amendment is another example of Parliament's attempt to draw the line between personal choice items and non-discretionary medical costs. As you read the provision, consider what interpretation issues leap out:

   > 118.2(2.1) The medical expenses referred to in subsection (2) do not include amounts paid for medical or dental services, nor any related expenses, provided purely for cosmetic purposes, unless necessary for medical or reconstructive purposes.

   When will a procedure be "purely for cosmetic purposes"? The budget and Tax Folio S1-F1-C1: Medical Expense Tax Credit (modified: 2014-09-02) list liposuction, wrinkle removal, tooth whitening, and chin, cheek, and lip augmentation as examples of procedures that "generally" will not qualify for the METC. What about cosmetic surgery recommend by a physician to relieve psychological distress?

   For a comprehensive legal and policy review of the new provision, including comparisons with other jurisdictions, see Ling Chu, Alan MacNaughton & Nicole Verlinden, "Curtailing Income Tax Relief for Cosmetic Medical Expenses" (2010) 58:3 Can. Tax J. 529. The article also summarizes the debate on whether it is good tax policy to recognize medical expenses.
5. **Complementary and Alternative Medicines:** According to Health Canada, 71% of Canadians have used natural health products like vitamins and minerals, herbal products, and homeopathic medicines. Statistics Canada estimated that in 2003, one-fifth of Canadians over age 11 (5.4 million people) had used some form of alternative therapy during the previous year. Chiropractic therapy was the most popular (11%), followed by massage therapy (8%). Acupuncture, homeopathy, and naturopathy were each used by 2%.

   Do alternative medicines fall within the METC? Paragraph 118.2(2)(n) was amended in 2008 to tighten the restrictions on over-the-counter remedies. The new paragraph 118.2(2)(n) and changes to regulation 5701 specify that over-the-counter remedies are not eligible for the medical expense credit unless the substance can only be lawfully obtained by prescription.

   Similarly, subsection 118.4(2) only provides METC credits for fees paid to non-physicians (chiropractors, dental hygienists, dieticians, midwives, optometrists and naturopaths) that are licensed in a province or territory. As of 2015, naturopaths are licensed in only six provinces, (Alberta, British Columbia, Saskatchewan, Manitoba, Ontario and Nova Scotia); massage therapists in only four (British Columbia, New Brunswick, Newfoundland and Labrador and Ontario); and Traditional Chinese Medicine Practitioners in only two (British Columbia and Ontario).

Do the METC restrictions keep up with the times?

6. **Surrogacy Costs:** What about costs related to surrogacy arrangements for women dealing with infertility problems? Most cases deny the taxpayer who uses a surrogate any METCs for medical procedures for the surrogate and for surrogacy fees, because the surrogate is not the taxpayer's dependant under subsection118(6), nor is she a patient receiving a transplant under paragraph 118.2(2)(a).

   See *Ismael v. The Queen*, 2014 TCC 157, [2014] 6 C.T.C. 2098, 2014 DTC 1140; *Warnock v. The Queen*, 2014 TCC 240, 2014 D.T.C. 1176; and *Zanatta v. Canada*, 2014 TCC 293, 2014 D.T.C. 1206.

   Are these case results appropriate? Or, keeping in mind L'Heureux-Dubé's discussion in *Symes*, are the cases examples of gender-biased rules and decisions?

7. **Medical Travel:** When a taxpayer travels for medical services that are unavailable where he or she lives, paragraph 118.2(2)(h) allows transportation and living expenses for the taxpayer and an accompanying person provided (1) the distance travelled is at least 80 kilometers away from the taxpayer's home and (2) substantially equivalent medical services are unavailable locally.

   What does it mean for services to be unavailable locally? Should the taxpayer's expense for travel to the United States be allowed if there is a two-year wait for the same services locally or if the taxpayer wants to use an alternative treatment not available in Canada?

   How would you apply the METC to situations where the taxpayer is choosing to travel to a place where he or she has family to provide support during treatment?

D. Disability Credit

Disabled persons incur a multitude of extra, unavoidable expenses that are difficult to itemize and that are not faced by others. The Disability Tax Credit (DTC) in section 118.3 recognizes these extra costs of daily living through a non-refundable credit. Once taxpayers meet the DTC criteria, they also likely meet the threshold criteria for other tax benefits and programs including the disability tax supplement for children, Registered Disability Savings Plan (RDSP), Disability Bonds and Disability Grants.

The DTC is restricted to persons with "severe and prolonged mental or physical impairment" who are "markedly restricted" in their ability to perform one or more "basic activities of daily living". A medical doctor or other specified medical practitioner must certify that the taxpayer's impairment meets the standard. Sections 118.3 and 118.4 set detailed criteria — sometimes down to the hours of the day and week — on what qualifies as an impairment. The statute goes to great length to draw the line between persons with diminished capacity who are ineligible and persons who are severely impaired who qualify. For example:

- Basic activities of daily living are narrowly defined to include: mental functions necessary for everyday life; feeding or dressing oneself; speaking or hearing in a quiet setting with a familiar individual; bowel or bladder functions; and walking.
- Paragraph 118.4(1)(d) specifically excludes working, housekeeping, and social or recreational activity from the list of basic activities of daily living. In other words, it does not matter whether your disability prevents you from working or socializing; if you can function at home, you are not eligible.
- The "prolonged" impairment must last at least 12 continuous months.
- "Markedly restricted" is defined as not being able to perform an activity of daily living "substantially all the time", even with the help of therapy, medication, and adaptive devices. The CRA interprets "substantially all" as 90 per cent of the time.
- A person has the "equivalent of marked restriction" if they can only function when they spend an "inordinate amount of time" on "life sustaining" therapy. The therapy must be:
  - (i) essential to sustain a vital function
  - (ii) administered at least three times each week for a total duration averaging not less than 14 hours a week, and
  - (iii) unlikely to be of significant benefit to persons without the disability.

Bowman T.C.J explained the DTC's purpose and the Court's interpretative task in *Radage v. R.*, [1996] 3 C.T.C. 2510, 96 D.T.C. 1615 (T.C.C.), an often-cited case. The quote below is sometimes referred to as the "compassionate" approach to interpreting the DTC:

> In a recent case, I concluded that a combination of extreme depression, anorexia and severe, prolonged and frequent migraines that rendered an otherwise intelligent person incapable of any type of rational thought during the frequent attacks qualified the taxpayer for the credit. In another, I allowed the appeal of a person suffering from severe bi-polar disorder. Each case depends on its own facts and to a degree upon the court's perception of the severity of the problem. If asked "Where do you draw the line?" I can only answer that I draw the line in any given case where my own common sense, based on the evidence and on a compassionate view of what I think Parliament was trying to achieve in section 118.3, tells me to draw it.

I do not mean by the foregoing to imply by any means that the determination be based on an arbitrary and subjective knee-jerk reaction. It must be based not only on the facts of the particular case but upon appropriate legal principles. I shall try to state briefly those principles upon which this decision is based:

(a) The legislative intent appears to be to provide a modest amount of tax relief to persons who fall within a relatively restricted category of markedly physically or mentally impaired persons. The intent is neither to give the credit to everyone who suffers from a disability nor to erect a hurdle that is impossible for virtually every disabled person to surmount. It obviously recognizes that disabled persons need such tax relief and it is intended to be of benefit to such persons.

(b) The court must, while recognizing the narrowness of the tests enumerated in sections 118.3 and 118.4, construe the provisions liberally, humanely and compassionately and not narrowly and technically. ...

If the object of Parliament, which is to give to disabled persons a measure of relief that will to some degree alleviate the increased difficulties under which their impairment forces them to live, is to be achieved the provision must be given a humane and compassionate construction. Section 12 of the Interpretation Act reads as follows:

> Every enactment is deemed remedial, and shall be given such fair, large and liberal construction and interpretation as best ensures the attainment of its objects.

(c) If there is doubt on which side of the line a claimant falls, that doubt should be resolved in favour of the claimant.

Gibson v. The Queen illustrates how deeply courts delve into the taxpayer's condition and the supporting medical evidence. As you read *Gibson*, think about the burden a disability case appeal puts on the taxpayer and his or her physician.

GIBSON v. THE QUEEN
2014 TCC 236, 2014 D.T.C. 1177

Woods J.:

I Background

Joan Gibson is a retired psychologist who was diagnosed many years ago with severe chronic fatigue syndrome. In 2012, Ms. Gibson made an application for the disability tax credit under the *Income Tax Act*, which was denied by notice of determination dated June 14, 2013. The appeal relates to this determination.

Ms. Gibson represented herself at the hearing and was the only witness. It was clear at the hearing that Ms. Gibson's disability quite severely hampered her ability to conduct this appeal.

Counsel for the Crown dealt with this situation commendably. Instead of conducting a lengthy cross-examination of Ms. Gibson, counsel relied on the doctors' certificates provided to the Canada Revenue Agency (CRA). There were four such documents. ...

III Discussion

The only issue raised in the Reply is whether Ms. Gibson actually has the impairments that Dr. Flor-Henry certified.

I will start with Ms. Gibson's testimony. Ms. Gibson testified as to having a great many symptoms, including that her brain is often foggy. She also testified that her fatigue is so profound that she is in bed or in a state of inertia most of the time. However, she also testified that the level of severity of her symptoms does fluctuate from time to time.

Overall, I found that Ms. Gibson's testimony was not detailed enough to give a good picture of the disability. In particular, I cannot determine how often Ms. Gibson has good periods and how well she functions in these periods. Unfortunately, the impression that I had was that Ms. Gibson did not have the stamina to properly present sufficient detail of her circumstances.

Counsel for the Crown suggested that the best evidence of Ms. Gibson's disability is the information provided by the doctors. I agree with this.

I turn now to Dr. Flor-Henry's certificate. ... Dr. Flor-Henry appears to be highly qualified as a medical practitioner knowledgeable about chronic fatigue syndrome. He is a Clinical Professor at the University of Alberta and was a member of a panel that determined a clinical case definition of chronic fatigue syndrome ...

The certificate is a prescribed form requiring that the doctor state:

(1) whether the patient is markedly restricted in one basic activity of daily living (as defined) and whether this impairment is present all or substantially all of the time, or

(2) whether the patient is significantly restricted in at least two basic activities of daily living (as defined), and whether these impairments are present all or substantially all of the time and taken together are tantamount to a marked restriction in one basic activity of daily living.

The certificate by Dr. Flor-Henry gave positive responses to both these categories.

A Marked impairment

With respect to ... a marked impairment in one basic activity, Dr. Flor-Henry identified the impairment as 'mental functions necessary for everyday life.'

Dr. Flor-Henry also identified 'walking' as a marked impairment but he neglected to check the box as to whether this restriction was present all or substantially all of the time, as required by the legislation. This may have been inadvertent and if it were necessary I would give Ms. Gibson time to have this question answered by Dr. Flor-Henry. This type of fo low up was specifically sanctioned in the *Buchanan* case.

B Significant impairment

With respect to... significant impairments in at least two basic activities of daily living, Dr. Flor-Henry certified that Ms. Gibson has significant impairments in feeding, walking, elimination, walking and mental functions necessary for everyday life.

Although Dr. Flor-Henry's certificate was a positive certificate for purposes of the legislation, it failed to provide details as to the effects of the impairment. This is required information in the prescribed form and would assist the CRA in verifying that the legislative requirements were satisfied.

Since these details were not provided, the CRA requested that Dr. Flor-Henry fill out another check-the-box form. The evidence from Ms. Gibson was that Dr. Flor-Henry was not happy that the CRA wanted more information. In any event, the answers given by Dr. Flor-Henry in the second form are not helpful to Ms. Gibson (Exhibit R-3). In general, they paint a picture of someone who is functioning well except during 'periods of exacerbation or in stressful situations.' This seems to suggest that Ms. Gibson is not severely impaired all or substantially all of the time, as required.

This is not the end of the matter, however, because Dr. Flor-Henry subsequently filed an amended form (Exhibit R-4). In it, Dr. Flor-Henry changed his answers to two questions and indicated that Ms. Gibson had severe impairment all or substantially all of the time with respect to judgment and ability to plan daily activities.

The Crown suggests that impairments only with respect to judgment and planning daily activities are not sufficient impairments to qualify for the disability tax credit. As I understand it, the Crown relies on the definition in s. 118.4(1)(*c*.1) of the Act which reads:

118.4

For the purposes of subsection 6(16), sections 118.2 and 118.3 and this subsection, [...]

(c.1) mental functions necessary for everyday life include

(i) memory,

(ii) problem solving, goal-setting and judgement (taken together), and

(iii) adaptive functioning;

The Crown suggests that Ms. Gibson's disability does not qualify because she has only two of the three disabilities listed in clause (*c*.1)(ii) above. It is submitted that all three impairments described in (*c*.1)(ii) must be satisfied. Ms. Gibson is capable of problem-solving, and this is fatal to her claim, according to the Crown.

I disagree with this view. The phrase 'taken together' in clause (*c*.1)(ii) implies that one look at all three mental functions together and decide whether the combination results in a severe impairment. This is the interpretation that makes the most sense.

This is sufficient to dispose of this appeal but I would also note that the CRA forms have their shortcomings and it is appropriate to take this into account. For example, the prescribed form is in a check-the-box format. This may be a practical way for the CRA to obtain information, but it does not give a very accurate picture in some cases. Taxpayers should not be denied tax relief simply because the questions in the prescribed form do not neatly fit the circumstances.

In addition, I have a concern that physicians generally would not have first hand knowledge of a patient's daily activities. The form, however, requires the doctor to give an opinion on this if the impairment is with respect to mental functions. Since this is the legislative scheme that Parliament has put in place, a physician may have to rely to a certain extent on information provided by the patient. I would imagine that some physicians would be reluctant to give an opinion on this basis, and this is something that should be taken into account.

In this case, a highly-qualified medical specialist stated an opinion that Ms. Gibson has a disability that severely impacts her ability to perform mental functions necessary for every day life. The disability is present all or substantially all of the time. In my view, the opinions expressed in the forms sent by Dr. Flor-Henry adequately establish that Ms. Gibson satisfies the legislative requirements for the disability tax credit.

I would also observe that:

a. Ms. Gibson has been diagnosed with a severe form of chronic fatigue, which suggests that her symptoms are particularly debilitating
b. Ms. Gibson did not call Dr. Flor-Henry to testify, but this should generally not be necessary unless the medical practitioner has not given a positive certificate;
c. the severity of Ms. Gibson's disability was evident at the hearing; and
d. the disability tax credit provisions should be interpreted in a compassionate manner.

For these reasons, the appeal will be allowed.

Notes and Questions

1. The DTC adopts a "medical model", which defines disability in terms of how far an individual's condition deviates from a standard based on the healthy non-

impaired person. The medical model requires that a person must be so impaired that he or she is incapable of normal activities.

An alternative and more modern "social theory perspective" sees persons with disabilities as "being restricted in performing daily activities because of a complex set of interrelating factors, some pertaining to the person and some pertaining to the person's immediate environment and social/political arrangements". See Human Resources and Skills Development Canada, *Advancing the Inclusion of Persons with Disabilities* (Gatineau (QB): Publication Services, 2002) at 10-11. The social theory model would recognize the extra burden society places on persons who currently bear the cost of navigating a world designed without taking persons like them into account.

2. Raquel Chisholm, "The Disability Tax Credit and Amputees: It's Time for a Reality Check" (2003) 2 U.T.J.L. & Eq'y 156 at 156, 178-179, explains the effects of the "over medicalization" of disability in the context of amputees:

> ... the current DTC regime fails to recognize the reality of the lives of disabled Canadians. First, many disabled Canadians live in poverty. Despite this poverty and despite their disabilities, many of these Canadians live independent lives. Additionally, whether poor or rich, disabled Canadians incur costs that others in society do not. Given these realities, the goals of the DTC should be twofold: firstly, in the name of tax fairness and horizontal equity, the DTC should recognize the reality of the non-discretionary costs incurred by these taxpayers; and, secondly, it should contribute to social equality as a tax expenditure. Moreover, it should achieve these goals in a way that maintains and even heightens the dignity of disabled Canadians by improving their socio-economic status. The current DTC regime does not do so. Instead, it perpetuates myths about disability through its reliance on the medical model of disability. Today, disabled Canadians are encouraged to be independent and to participate in all aspects of society. Organizations such as The War Amputations of Canada have films demonstrating how even a seriously disabled multiple-amputee can take up activities like skiing. These initiatives reinforce positive images of the disabled. Yet, in order for the same multiple-amputee to convince the CCRA that she is entitled to the DTC, she must tug the heartstrings of the tax adjudicators by portraying herself as fitting neatly into the stereotype of the dependent invalid. The tax system should not treat disabled Canadians in this manner. ...
>
> Over and above the affronts to their dignity, amputees encounter other difficulties with the DTC. First, section 118.4(1)(b) makes it clear that as long as taxpayers can perform the activities of daily living "with ... the use of appropriate devices", they will not qualify for the DTC. Most leg amputees and many arm amputees wear artificial limbs, and these certainly are considered "appropriate devices". The technological advances in these limbs have led to wonderful independence for even the most severely disabled, such as multiple amputees. However, the limbs are expensive, ranging in the tens of thousands of dollars. Amputees incur these costs and yet, in doing so, they could be disqualified from the DTC.

> While artificial limbs are recognized under the Medical Expenses Tax Credit (METC), the credit only amounts to "roughly 25 cents for each dollar of eligible medical expenses exceeding the applicable threshold, "which is the lesser of $1,637 or 3 per cent of net income. This could still leave amputees paying thousands for their limbs with little tax relief for these non-discretionary costs. Indeed, the average amputee may not even be aware that their limbs are listed under this credit, entitling him or her to take advantage of this tax relief.
>
> There are many other devices used by amputees that do not qualify under the METC. Amputees without arms, for example, use devices to help them eat, such as scoop plates and special jar openers. To dress themselves, they require dressing sticks and zipper pull rings. In the bathroom, they use toothpaste squeezers or hand-held shower nozzles. To help them walk in icy and slippery conditions, leg amputees purchase ice cleats for their shoes and boots. To drive, they may require parking brake extensions, left foot accelerators, or hand controls. The costs of all of these devices add up (for example, one scoop plate can cost up to $60), and yet they are the "appropriate devices" that allow amputees to perform the activities of daily living. The very costs incurred by the amputee, which should be recognized by the DTC and its emphasis on both horizontal equity and ability to pay, end up potentially disqualifying the amputee from the credit. The irony is disconcerting.

3. Not everyone who is eligible for the DTC applies, either because they do not realize they are eligible or they find the process too complex. The CRA estimates that only 620,000 of the 1.1 million people eligible for the DTC receive it.

   The CRA's "Taxpayer Relief Provisions" now respond to the uptake problem by allowing a person eligible for the DTC to request a retroactive filing going back as long as 10 years. The potential for large retroactive refunds created a new business, "DTC promoters" who assist disabled persons to apply. Reports that some DTC promoters charge as much as 30% of the disabled person's expected refund led the government to pass the *Disability Tax Credit Promoters Restrictions Act*, aimed at regulating promoter's maximum fees. The Act will come into effect following public consultations on maximum fees and how to simplify the application process.

4. A person does not qualify if he or she can perform the basic activities of daily life with the aid of therapy, medication, or adaptive devices. But what if the therapy that lets you function takes up a significant amount of time?

   Subparagraphs 118.3(1)(a.1)(i) to (iii) carve out an exception if the therapy:

   (1) is life sustaining;

   (2) is administered three times a week for not less than 14 hours a week;

   (3) requires the individual to take time away from their normal activities; and

   (4) does not include time spent on activities related to dietary or exercise restrictions or regimes.

Is the exception realistic and fair? Consider *Corbett v. The Queen* (2008), 2008 TCC 499, [2009] 3 C.T.C. 2222, 2008 D.T.C. 4858, denying the DTC to a taxpayer whose AIDS therapy regime included monthly blood tests, 29 different medications administered twice daily which take an hour to self-administer, and a two 4-hour daily exercise regime. How should the DTC respond to individuals with HIV/AIDS and other immuno-suppressed diseases who spend many hours a day on exercise and diet to remain healthy?

5. Can you design a series of provisions that is more in keeping with the modern social theory of disability? What new issues would need to be addressed?
6. Should the DTC be expanded to give a tax credit to persons with impairments or chronic ailments, who currently absorb the costs of participating fully in work and social activities?

E. Tuition and Education Credits

Governments invest in higher education for the benefit of both individuals and society as a whole. Secondary education contributes to increased individual earning power, economic growth in an increasingly knowledge- and technologically-driven economy, civic engagement, and poverty reduction. Direct government investment often takes the form of student loan programs, study grants, scholarships, and bursaries for individuals, and infrastructure and program support for colleges and universities.

Traditionally the income tax system views educational expenses as non-deductible personal expenses or non-deductible capital outlays. Government spending on higher education through the income tax system has equity, economic efficiency, and market-failures rationales. Tax relief for education costs supports students with limited resources, encourages greater overall enrollment, and corrects the tax system's bias favouring capital investment in business assets over human capital.

Students attending post-secondary institutions can claim four separate education-related non-refundable tax credits; tuition (section 118.5), an education amount (subsection 118.6(2)), textbooks (subsection 118.6(2.1)), and interest on student loans (section 118.62). Qualifying tuition fees must be paid for post-secondary education at a university or college, or an institution recognized by Human Resources and Skills Development Canada. The full amount paid for tuition is eligible, with no upper limit. The education and textbook credits are calculated based on the number of months in school multiplied by a set amount that varies for full- and part-time studies. The student loan-interest credit applies to interest paid on federally or provincially sponsored loans.

Two design features — carry forwards and credit transfers — address the problem that students often do not earn sufficient income to be liable for tax while they are in school. Students can carry unused credits to future tax years when their earnings are higher. As well, up to $5,000 of the amount on which the credit is based can be transferred to a spouse, common-law partner, parents, or grandparents.

Does the carry forward and credit transfer make higher education more affordable? Would a refundable credit be a better way to support students while in school?

Notes and Questions

1. **The Case for a Refundable Credit:** How effective are the education-related credits? Do the credits reduce barriers to secondary education and increase enrollment? A 2013 CD Howe research commentary by Christine Neill estimates that in 2012-2013, the combined federal and provincial credits hypothetically had the potential to offset 31-43 per cent of university tuition and 60 per cent of college tuition costs.

   The potential to offset tuition costs exists, but the more important question is how are the credits used? The same research commentary notes that students increasingly could not use the tax credit in the same year as they attended school. By 2012, two-thirds of students either deferred using the credits until they were out of school and earning income, or transferred them to an eligible family member.

   Looking more closely at who takes the credit, 42 per cent of total credits that were transferred went to the 10 per cent of taxpayers who earn over $80,000 a year. Only 7 per cent of credits were transferred to family members whose income was under $30,000, although this taxpayer-group represents about one-half of all tax filers. If most students cannot use the credits to offset tuition costs while they are in school, and if higher-income taxpayers used most of the transferred credits, how likely is it that the credits reduce barriers for low-income students and increase enrollment?

   Christine Neill recommends fixing the credit's design flaws by making the credits refundable. "Refundability would help ensure that the benefits go more quickly to students who need them most, even though they would come at the end of the academic year after the expenses had been incurred". (Christine Neill, " What You Don't Know Can't Help You: Lessons of Behavioural Economics for Tax-Based Student Aid" CD Howe Institute commentary No 363 (November 2013)).

   Are there any disadvantages to Neill's recommendation? Could you design a mechanism to deliver the credits in time for students to make tuition payments?

2. **The Case for More Direct Public Funding:** Some critics note that compared to other countries, Canada relies more heavily on tax credits for individual students to fund post-secondary education as compared to direct public funding. Some countries with higher levels of public financing offer low or no tuition fees and therefore have less need to offer tax relief to subsidize education on the individual level. Ross Finnie and Alex Usher offer three pragmatic reasons for Canada's approach:

> The first is that, unlike investments in student loans and grants, tax credits can be implemented unilaterally by the federal government, without the need to negotiate changes in shared policy rules with the provinces. The second is that the assistance flows directly from the Government of Canada to the individual citizen. This is a bonus not only in terms of post-referendum 'visibility', but also means that federal programme changes cannot be 'swallowed' up by the provinces, as happened when the Canada Millennium Scholarship Foundation was created. ... The third reason is that tax credits possess a certain useful political versatility in that they can be described either as 'spending' or 'tax cuts', depending on how the government wishes to present the changes". "The Canadian Experiment in Cost-Sharing and Its Effects on Access to Higher Education, 1990-2002" in BD Johnstone, et al., eds, *Cost-Sharing and Accessibility in Higher Education: A Fairer Deal? Higher Education Dynamics* (The Hague: Springer, 2006) 159 at 162.

Which do you think meets the government's multiple objectives for supporting post-secondary education the best: overall direct support to post-secondary institutions, individual tax credits that can be deferred to later tax years, or refundable tax credits?

3. **Other Tax-Related Support for Post-Secondary Education:**

Tax-Free Scholarships

Students can exclude from income the full amount of scholarships, fellowships, or bursaries connected to their attendance in an educational program that qualifies for the education tax credit: ITA paragraph 56(3)(a).

Registered Education Savings Plans, Grants, and Bonds

The government encourages individuals to invest in post-secondary education through tax-deferred savings plans, government grants, and income-tested grants and bonds.

The Registered Education Savings Plan (RESP) encourages families to save for post-secondary education through a tax-deferred investment and government grants. Taxpayers can open an RESP for any child and contribute up to $50,000 until the plan beneficiary turns 31 years old. Unlike an RRSP, contributions are not tax-deductible. Income earned in an RESP is not taxed.

The federal government boosts the RESP through the Canada Education Savings Grant (CESG) paid directly into a RESP. A basic CESG grant increases the RESP by the equivalent of 20% of the annual RESP contributions up to $500 a year ($7,200 a lifetime) per child. The basic CESG is paid regardless of family income. Low- and moderate-income parents (family income under $43,954 and 87,908 respectively) can apply for an additional CESG of 10% or 20% on the first $500 of RESP annual contribution.

Many low-income families cannot contribute even a minimal amount to an

RESP. The Canada Learning Bond program provides low-income families who opened an RESP an initial payment of $500 per child if the family is entitled to the National Child Benefit (NCB) supplement. An additional $100 will be added each year up to a total of $2,000 per child.

Encouraging private savings and targeting low- and modest-income earners for extra support all sounds positive, unless it turns out that the program is too complex for the intended users to access. How likely do you think it is that low-income families can take advantage of either the additional CESG or the Learning Bond? Were you aware of these programs?

F. Child Fitness Tax Credit and Children's Art Tax Credit

The Child Fitness Tax Credit, introduced in 2006, aims to promote physical fitness of children up to age 16. Originally, a tax credit of 15 per cent on up to $500 per child in fees paid for eligible physical activity programs was provided by former ITA section 118.03. For 2015, the maximum eligible fees per child is doubled to $1,000 and the credit is refundable (ITA section 127).

Qualifying programs must be supervised, run for a minimum of 8 consecutive weeks or 5 consecutive days, and contribute to "cardio-respiratory endurance, plus one or more of: muscular strength, muscular endurance, flexibility, or balance".

The Children's Arts Tax Credit (ITA 118.031, introduced in 2011) gives a 15 per cent credit on up to $500 of eligible expenses for supervised children's programs with artistic, cultural, recreational and developmental activities. The maximum credit is $75. The government has not proposed either increasing the CATC amount or making it refundable.

Who would quarrel with tax benefits encouraging parents to put their children in physical activity and artistic programs? And yet, in the introductory reading, economist Alice Woolley calls these credits, "smart politics, bad economics". Why?

The Child Fitness Tax Credit has been around long enough for researchers to evaluate whether the credit achieves its policy objective, and whether it is equitably distributed. The Children's Arts Tax Credit is still too new to evaluate. Here is what the research on the CFTC shows:

High Income Earners Benefit Disproportionately:

Families in the bottom income quartile are the least likely to enroll a child in organized sports or eligible physical activity programs and the least likely to claim the credit. Survey research in 2007 reported that:

- 63 per cent of Canadian parents in the lowest income quartile spend less than $100 or more on their children's sport and physical activities. (John Spence et al., (2012) 103:3 Can. J. Pub. Health)

- 28 per cent of parents in the lowest income quartile claimed the CFTC compared to approximately 55 per cent of parents in the highest income quartile. (John Spence et al,. "Uptake and effectiveness of the Children's Fitness Tax Credit in Canada: the rich get richer" (2010) BMC Public Health.)

Research using both survey and tax filer data spanning from 2007 to 2009 also confirms that higher income households disproportionately benefit from government spending through the credit:

- The average household income of families that claimed the credit was approximately $115,000 compared to the population average income of $80,000.
- 46 per cent of families claiming the credit earned more than $100,000.
- Parents under the age of 30, who because of their age are more likely to be modest income earners, were less likely to claim the credit. Fewer than 20 per cent of parents in the under-30 age group and families with a single child claimed the credit.

  See Koren Fisher et al., "Awareness and Use of Canada's Children's Fitness Tax Credit" (2013) 61:3 Can. Tax J. 599.

Weak Correlation Between the Credit and its Policy Objectives:

The CFTC expects to address the growing incidence of childhood obesity by increasing physical fitness activities. However, the 2007 survey reports that only 16 per cent of parents who claimed the CFTC stated that the credit influenced them to increase their children's organized physical activities. The majority who claimed the credit would have enrolled the children without the credit. John Spence et al., 2010, *supra.*

Will a credit, even a refundable credit, actually reach the majority of families? Will a refundable credit really remove the financial barrier for low-income parents? Not likely. Consider that to claim the $150 credit, a parent must spend $1,000 upfront and have enough money in the family budget to spend $850 after tax, per child, on eligible fitness programs.

Notes and Questions

1. The Department of Finance's *Tax Expenditures and Evaluations* (2013), estimates that the CFTC cost $110 million in 2011 and projects this will increase to $115 million for 2012 and 2013. Critics say the money would be better spent on spaces and facilities such as parks, trails, arenas, rinks, and pools. Other critics say the money should be used directly to reduce sports and physical activity fees. Do you see any problems with these proposals?

How else can the government's objectives be achieved in a more effective and equitable way? For instance, could the federal government work with provincial governments to fund daily gym programs in public schools?

2. The Children's Art Tax Credit is estimated to cost $100 million in each of 2011-2012 and 2012-2013. Given what we already know about which families benefit from the Child Fitness Tax Credit, is there any reason to think that the CATC will be used by families with limited means?
3. What do you think about the government's proposal to increase the Child Fitness Tax Credit but not the Children's Art's Tax Credit? Does this difference in treatment reflect Canadian values, political polling, or the government's failure to appreciate the contribution of arts education to children's physical and intellectual growth?
4. For more readings on the CFTC see: Barbara von Tigerstrom, Tamara Larre & JoAnne Sauder, "Using the Tax System to Promote Physical Activity: Critical Analysis of Initiatives in Canada" (2011) 101 Am. J. Pub. Health e10 (online only) online: AJPH <ajph.aphapublications.org/content/vol101/issue8/index.dtl>; Tamara Larre, "The Children's Fitness Tax Credit: Right Message, Wrong Policy?" in Lisa Phillips, Neil Brooks & Jinyan Li, eds., *Tax Expenditures: State of the Art* (Canada: Canadian Tax Foundation, 2011); John Spence et al., "Uptake and effectiveness of the Children's Fitness Tax Credit in Canada: The rich get richer (2010) 10:356 BMC Public Health online: BMC Public Health <www.biomedcentral.com/content/pdf/1471-2458-10-356.pdf> [Spence, "Uptake"]; John Spence et al., "Non-refundable Tax Credits are an Inequitable Policy Instrument for Promoting Physical Activity among Canadian Children" (2012) 103:3 Can. J. Pub. Health 175.

G. Other Credits

The credits discussed so far are a mixed-bag: they redistribute income by establishing the progressive tax rate system's starting point; smooth out inequalities by recognizing dependency, medical expenses, and disability; create equal opportunity by encouraging investing in education; establish retirement income policies; promote altruism, and fund charitable activities. We suggested different ways to evaluate a credit's policy goals, fairness, and effectiveness.

To round out this section on credits, here is a précis of some other credits you might study and evaluate on your own. Our list is not comprehensive, but it does illustrate how the income tax system uses credits to respond to new and diverse demands for government spending.

Social Transfers

The Working Income Tax Benefit (WITB): A refundable income-tested tax credit targeted for low-income individuals and families who are in the paid workforce. The WITB addresses income insecurity of the "working poor" through an income supplement to employment and business earnings. The credit encourages people to stay in the workforce by smoothing out welfare benefits lost in the transition from welfare to work. To kick start your readings on the WITB see: Ken Battle & Sherri Torjman, "Enhancing the working income tax benefit" (Ottawa: Caledon Institute for Social Policy, 2012).

GST/HST Credit: A refundable income-tested amount targeted towards low- and moderate-income individuals and families to address the regressive effect of the GST/HST on goods and services. The credit amount is calculated based on the previous year's income and is paid in quarterly installments.

Environmental Externalities

Public Transit Pass Credit (PTPC): A non-refundable credit based on what a taxpayer actually spends on monthly or annual public transit passes. Taxpayers must keep their receipts and transit passes to prove the expense. As an example, if a taxpayer spends $800 annually on monthly transit passes, he or she will benefit from a $120 tax credit, provided he or she owes tax. The public transit pass credit is intended to improve the environment by reducing greenhouse gas emissions and making public transportation more affordable. For a critical review on the PTPC's ability to achieve its environmental goal see Office of the Auditor General of Canada, *2008 Report of the Commissioner of Environmental and Sustainable Development* (2008) online: <http://www.oag-bvg.gc.ca/internet/English/parl_cesd_200812_01_e_31818.html#hd5g>. For a review of the distributional affects, see Department of Finance Canada's *Tax Expenditures and Evaluations 2011: Tax Evaluations and Research Reports Evaluation of the Public Transit Pass Credit* (2011).

Recognizing Volunteers

Volunteer firefighters and search and rescue volunteers receive a $450 non-refundable credit if they complete at least 200 hours of eligible volunteer firefighting services or eligible search and rescue volunteer services in the year. Volunteer service includes being on call, attending meetings and training.

Political Contributions

The political contribution tax credit encourages broad financial support from the electorate for the federal political parties. The subsection 127(3) credit is calculated on a sliding scale: 75 per cent of the first $400, 50 per cent on the next $350 and 33 1/3 per cent of any contribution over $750, up to $1,275.

The Adoption Expense Tax Credit

This credit recognizes adoption-related expenses such as adoption agency and legal fees, and reasonable travel and living expenses, up to a maximum of $15,000 ($2,250 credit).

IV. ALTERNATIVE MINIMUM TAX

The public needs confidence that the income tax system is fair. If the average income earner thinks that high-income earners somehow escape paying taxes, even if there are excellent policy objectives behind every deduction and credit they claim, the overall income tax system will lack credibility. The Alternative Minimum Tax ("AMT") was introduced in 1986 to remedy the situation where high-earning individuals pay little or no tax because they can take advantage of certain provisions commonly referred to as "tax preferences".

The AMT ensures that all Canadians pay some tax. There are many tax preferences, not covered in this chapter, designed for specific economic and social objectives. Examples include special treatment for losses from investments in certified Canadian films, Canadian exploration expenses, the non-taxable portion of capital gains, losses from limited or tax shelter partnerships, and certain employee stock option deductions. The AMT applies when the savings from tax preferences, like the ones mentioned, reduces a person's tax liability below an alternative calculation that includes the preference items.

The original discussion paper, released in the pre-introduction consultation period, documented the relatively low percentage of high-income persons who paid little or no tax. The paper also analyzed the items that most frequently resulted in taxpayers paying average federal tax rates of 10 per cent or less. See Department of Finance Canada, *A Minimum Tax for Canada*, budget papers (Ottawa: Public Works and Government Services, 1985), at Table I and Table 7.

Determining the best design to achieve the tax fairness goal requires a balance between ensuring income earners with substantial incomes are taxed, while not stifling the appropriate use of important tax incentives. To this end, the government set a basic exemption level to ensure that taxpayers who used a few preference items would not be subject to the AMT. As well, it was important that no one tax preference item, on its own, should trigger the AMT, to prevent undoing the very effect intended by the item in the first place. See "Alternative Minimum Tax" in *Expenditures and Evaluations 2000* (Ottawa: Department of Finance, 2000).

In essence, the AMT tax recalculates the tax liability on "adjusted taxable income", which adds back into income certain tax preferences originally used to reduce taxable income. The taxpayer pays the higher of the original tax or the alternative tax. Sections 127.5-127.55 set out the details. There is a basic $40,000 deduction and a tax rate of 15 per cent corresponding to the current lowest tax rate.

The AMT tax is often a prepayment of future taxes owed because the taxpayer gets a credit against regular federal income tax owed for the next seven years based on the amount the AMT exceeds the taxpayer's original tax calculation.

Notes and Questions

1. *Netupsky v. The Queen* (1994), [1995] 1 C.T.C. 2321, 95 D.T.C. 210 (T.C.C.), appeal dismissed [1996] 2 C.T.C. 29, 96 D.T.C. 6129 (F.C.A.) considered a challenge of the AMT as discriminatory based on age in violation of section 15 of the *Charter*. The taxpayer contended that because many seniors' incomes drop post-retirement, they will be unable to use the AMT credit within the seven years provided for in section 120.2. The Tax Court rejected this reasoning based on the AMT's application to any taxpayer based solely on income and not on any personal characteristics of the taxpayer.

   According to "Alternative Minimum Tax", *supra,* 28.6 per cent of AMT is paid by persons age 60 and above. Does this give any weight to the taxpayer's argument in *Netupsky*?

   The data also shows that in some years a small number of filers with gross income below $25,000 paid AMT. What if these AMT payers are also retirees, living on a reduced income? Should retirees be treated differently under the AMT?

2. Critics of the AMT argue a wealth tax is needed because even with the AMT in place, some high-income earners still pay no tax. Wealth taxes in their various forms are often controversial. GN Larin & MN Jacques, "Is the Alternative Minimum Tax a Paper Tiger?" (1994) 42 Can. Tax J. 804 at 822 note that Canada, along with the United States, is unique worldwide for imposing an AMT in this format. Some countries impose a minimum tax on an individual's net wealth, while others tax the net worth of businesses each year.

   Do you think that wealth taxes are preferable to AMT as a means of redistributing the tax burden and funding the delivery of social benefits?

9

Taxation of Intermediaries and the Relevance of Income Tax to Other Areas of Law

The previous chapters have focused on issues of income tax policy, theory and the general principles that underlie the Canadian income tax system. Most of this book deals with the taxation of individuals, as is appropriate for an introductory casebook. It is a fact, however, that most businesses are operated through partnerships and corporations. In addition, trusts are often used to own property. This chapter provides an overview of the taxation of these entities. Moreover, because income taxes are imposed on all forms of transactions, taxation issues are relevant to the practice of law generally. This chapter is also intended to provide a starting point in alerting you to income tax issues that impact selected areas of the law.

I. TAXATION OF INTERMEDIARIES

A. Taxation of Trusts and Beneficiaries

1. Definitions

The term "trust" is not defined in the *Income Tax Act* (the "Act"). Subsection 104(1) provides that a reference to a trust or estate (both of which are to be treated as trusts for income tax purposes) includes a reference to the trustee or executor (administrator, liquidator of a succession, heir or other legal representative) who has ownership or control of the trust property. Therefore, the Act appears to adopt the equitable concept of a trust as being the relationship that exists whereby one party (the trustee) holds legal title to property for the benefit of the equitable owner (the beneficiary).

The Act categorizes trusts as "testamentary" or "*inter vivos*" and "personal" or "commercial". A "testamentary trust" is one that arises upon the death of the individual who created the trust. All other trusts are *inter vivos* trusts. A testamentary trust can become an *inter vivos* trust if property is contributed to it otherwise than on the death of an individual. A "personal trust" is defined as a testamentary trust or *inter vivos* trust of which (subject to limited exceptions for related parties) no beneficial interest was acquired for consideration payable to the trust or to a person who contributed property to the trust. The Act does not define a "commercial trust", but the term is used generally to refer to any *inter vivos* trust that is not a personal trust. There also are a myriad of other specially defined types of trusts, for example, mutual fund trusts, each with a particular set of rules.

A "beneficiary" of a trust is any person "beneficially interested" in the trust. Subsection 248(25) defines the phrase "beneficially interested" in an extremely broad manner.

2. Overview of the Taxation of Trusts and Beneficiaries

Subsection 104(2) provides that a trust is taxed as an individual. Therefore, the first issue is to determine whether the trust is subject to tax as an individual resident in Canada. As noted in Chapter 3, the Act does not provide express rules for determining the residency of a trust (or an individual for that matter). The case law, which generally has been accepted by the Canada Revenue Agency (the "CRA"), indicates that the central management and control test that applies to corporations is also appropriate in determinging the residence of a trust (*Garron Family Trust v. The Queen*, 2012 SCC 14, [2012] 3 C.T.C. 265, 2012 D.T.C. 5063). Prior to the Garron decision it was generally accepted that the residence of the trustees is important, if not determinative in establishing residence, assuming the trustees are exercising management and control over the trust property. For a discussion of the residence of a trust, see also *Thibodeau Family Trust v. The Queen*, [1978] C.T.C. 539, 78 D.T.C. 6376 (F.C.T.D.); and Interpretation Bulletin IT-447: Residence of a Trust or Estate (May 30, 1980). Certain trusts are deemed to be resident in Canada for purposes of Part I of the Act if (subject to numerous detailed rules) one or more persons resident in Canada are beneficially interested in the trust or property has been transferred to the trust by one or more persons resident in Canada (paragraph 94(3)(a)). The discussion below is limited to the taxation of trusts that are resident in Canada.

The progressive rate schedule for individuals applies to determine the tax liability of a testamentary trust prior to 2016. However, subsection 122(1) now provides that, in place of the progressive rates, all testamentary trusts other than graduated rate estates (GREs) and qualified diability trusts (QDTs) are subject to federal tax at a flat rate equal to the highest marginal rate for individuals. This rate for testamentary trusts will match the highest marginal rate of tax that applies to all *inter vivos* trusts. Neither testamentary nor *inter vivos* trusts are eligible for the tax credits provided in section 118. If substantially all of the property of two or more trusts has been received from one person and the conditions of the trust provide that the income of the various trusts will accrue to the same beneficiary or group of beneficiaries, subsection 104(2) provides that all of the trusts may be taxed as one individual (thus preventing multiple use of the marginal income tax brackets by identical testamentary trusts).

Part XII.2 imposes a special tax of 36 per cent on the designated income of *inter vivos* trusts, other than mutual fund trusts and certain tax-exempt trusts. Designated income includes income from real property in Canada, timber resource properties, certain Canadian resource properties, businesses carried on in Canada, and taxable capital gains from the disposition of taxable Canadian property. Because Part XII.2 is intended to tax income distributed to non-resident beneficiaries, an offsetting credit is provided to resident beneficiaries.

A trust may be considered a flow-though vehicle in the sense that it is subject to tax on its income only to the extent that the income is not paid or is not payable to a beneficiary, or is not the subject of a preferred beneficiary election. If income of a trust is subject to taxation in the trust, after-tax amounts can be distributed to Canadian resident beneficiaries without further tax. If income of a trust is paid or is made payable to a beneficiary or is the subject of a preferred beneficiary election, it is taxable in the hands of the beneficiary and is not taxed to the trust.

All of the normal rules apply in calculating the income and taxable income of a trust. In general, property of a trust (other than certain types of commercial trusts and a trust for a spouse) is subject to a deemed disposition every 21 years and on the happening of certain other events, such as the death of a spouse in the case of a spouse trust or the death of the settlor in the case of an alter ego trust. A number of specific rules attempt to prevent the use of arrangements that would otherwise result in an avoidance of the deemed disposition provisions.

An amount will be considered payable to a beneficiary in a year if it is paid to the beneficiary, or if the beneficiary is entitled to enforce payment. Even if payable to a beneficiary, income or capital gains may be taxed to the trust where the trust so designates (subsections 104(13.1) and (13.2)). In that case, the income is deemed not to be payable to the beneficiary. The inclusion of such an amount in the income of the trust instead of a beneficiary is particularly advantageous where the trust has loss carryovers that may be deducted in calculating its taxable income. It also facilitated interprovincial planning if the beneficiary was resident in a province with higher tax rates than those where the trust was a tax resident. For 2016 and subsequent years the ability to designate an amount under these provisions is effectively limited to circumstances where a trust or estate uses its tax losses to reduce the taxable income of the trust to zero.

A "preferred beneficiary" election accommodates mentally or physically-impaired beneficiaries. Provided an appropriate election is made, income may accumulate in a trust in favour of such beneficiaries and can still be deducted by the trust and included in the beneficiaries' income.

The beneficiary of a trust is required to include in income all amounts of trust income that are paid or made payable to the beneficiary in the year or with respect to which a preferred beneficiary election has been filed (subsections 104(13) and (14)). To the extent that trust income is taxed to the beneficiaries, the trust acts as a conduit. In this respect, paragraph 108(5)(a) provides that the income of a beneficiary from a trust constitutes income from a property that is an interest in the trust. This provision is subject, however, to a number of exceptions that, under certain conditions, attribute the underlying source of trust income to the beneficiaries. The most important of those exceptions are: taxable dividends (subsection 104(19)), tax-free capital dividends (subsection 104(20)), taxable capital gains (subsections 104(21) and (21.2)), foreign-source income (which allows access to the appropriate foreign tax credits) (subsection 104(22)), and pension and death benefits (subsections 104(27) and (28)). Each of these designations may be made only to the extent that amounts from the particular source may reasonably be considered to have been distributed to the beneficiary.

Subsection 105(1) requires that the value of all benefits provided to a taxpayer by a trust be included in income. Amounts excepted from inclusion under subsection 105(1) include any amount deducted from the adjusted cost base of a beneficiary's trust interest and amounts the value of which have already been included in income. The provision operates as a penalty in that amounts included in the taxpayer's income are not deductible by the trust. In *Cooper v. The Queen,* [1989] C.T.C. 66, 88 D.T.C. 6525, the Federal Court — Trial Division held that an interest-free loan from a trust was not a benefit within the meaning of subsection 105(1). Subsection 105(2) also provides that, where the terms of a trust require that trust property be maintained for the use of a beneficiary or life tenant, any income of the trust used to pay the costs of such maintenance must be included in the income of the beneficiary or tenant. In the case of subsection 105(2), such amounts are deductible to the trust in computing its income.

3. Transfers of Property to a Trust

A taxpayer is deemed by subsection 251(1) not to deal at arm's length with the particular trust if the taxpayer (or any person not dealing at arm's length with the taxpayer) is beneficially interested in the trust. Accordingly, transfers of property to a trust are generally recognition events that occur at the fair market value of the property transferred (subsection 69(1)). Property can be transferred, however, to a trust on a non-recognition or rollover basis in the following circumstances:

- *Inter vivos* or testamentary transfers to a trust for a spouse or common-law partner ("conjugal trust") — section 73 and subsection 70(6): Generally, a "conjugal trust" is a trust created by the transferor where, under the terms of the trust, the spouse or common-law partner of the transferor is entitled to receive all of the income of the trust that arises before the spouse's or common-law partner's death and no person except the spouse or common-law partner may, before the death of the spouse or common-law partner, receive or otherwise obtain the use of any of the income or capital of the trust. See the discussion in Part II. B, below. Income for this purpose is income determined under trust law (subsection 108(3)). This rollover is restricted to capital property and occurs automatically if the above conditions are satisfied. The transferor is deemed to have received proceeds of disposition equal to the adjusted cost base of the property to the transferor, and the trust is deemed to have received the property at an equivalent cost. The attribution rules in subsections 74.1(1) and 74.2(1) may apply to deem any amount paid or payable to the spouse or common-law partner or otherwise included in the spouse's or common-law partner's income to be income of the transferor (subsection 74.3(1)). It is possible to elect to not have the rollover provisions apply. If such election is filed and if the transferor has received fair market value consideration, the attribution provisions generally will not apply (subsection 74.5(1)).

- *Inter vivos* transfers to "alter ego" trusts — section 73: Rollover treatment is provided on an *inter vivos* transfer of capital property to an "alter ego trust". Generally, such a trust exists where the trust is created by the transferor who is 65 years old or older and, under the terms of the trust, the transferor is entitled to receive all of the income of the trust that arises before the transferor's death and no person except the transferor may, before the transferor's death, receive or otherwise obtain the use of any of the income or capital of the trust. Income for this purpose generally is income determined under trust law (subsection 108(3)). The attribution rule in subsection 75(2) may apply to deem any income, loss, taxable capital gain or allowable capital loss earned or realized by the trust in respect of any transferred property or property substituted for such property to be that of the transferor. A similar rollover is available if the settlor is younger than 65 (subparagraph 73(1.02)(b)(ii)), however as a condition of this rollover there must be no change in the beneficial ownership of the property and no other person can be beneficially interested in the trust while the settlor is alive.
- *Inter vivos* transfers to joint conjugal trusts — section 73: Rollover treatment is also available on an *inter vivos* transfer of capital property to a trust that combines the elements of an alter ego trust and a conjugal trust. Generally, such a trust exists where the trust is created by the transferor and, under the terms of the trust, any combination of the transferor or transferor's spouse or common-law partner is entitled to receive all of the income of the trust that arises before the death of the latter and no person except the transferor or spouse or common-law partner may, before the death of the latter, receive or otherwise obtain the use of any of the income or capital of the trust.
- Qualifying dispositions — section 107.4: Property can also be rolled to a trust as the result of a "qualifying disposition" by a beneficiary to a trust. Generally, such a disposition will occur where property has been transferred to a trust in circumstances where there is a change in the legal ownership of the property but no change in the beneficial ownership. The provision accommodates

certain trust-to-trust transfers including a transfer from a Registered Retirement Savings Plan (RRSP) to a Registered Retirement Income Fund (RRIF).

4. Transfers of Beneficial Interests and Distributions of Trust Property

A taxpayer may dispose of a beneficial interest under a trust in either of two general ways: a transfer to another person, or in exchange for trust property. The tax consequences of either transaction vary depending on whether the interest is an income or a capital interest.

For a personal trust, a beneficiary may have an "income" or "capital interest". The Act defines an "income interest" as any right to receive all or part of the income of the trust (subsection 108(1)). A "capital interest" is defined as all other rights as a beneficiary (subsection 108(1)). For the purpose of the definition of an income interest, the concept of income as a matter of trust law is determinative (subsection 108(3)). For a commercial trust, all beneficial interests are capital interests.

If a beneficiary transfers an income interest to another person, the proceeds of disposition must be recognized as ordinary income to the transferor (paragraphs 106(2)(a) and (b)). In calculating income from the interest, the purchaser may deduct the cost (subsection 106(1)). If the income interest is acquired otherwise than from a person who was a beneficiary of the trust, the cost of the interest is deemed to be nil. If property is distributed by the trust in satisfaction of an income interest, the beneficiary is not required to include any amount in income (paragraph 106(2)(a)). In these circumstances, the trust is deemed to have disposed of the property distributed for proceeds equal to its fair market value (subsection 106(3)).

For the purpose of calculating any taxable capital gain on the disposition of a capital interest in a personal trust, the adjusted cost base of the interest is the greater of its adjusted cost base otherwise determined and its "cost amount" (paragraph 107(1)(a)). Subsection 108(1) defines the "cost amount" of a capital interest (other than for purposes of a deemed disposition every 21 years) as either:

- in the case of a distribution of trust property, the aggregate of any money received and the cost amount to the trust of the distributed property; or
- in any other case, the capital beneficiary's proportionate share of the cost amount of all trust properties less any debt or other obligations of the trust.

Unless a beneficiary acquired the capital interest from a previous beneficiary or for fair market value consideration payable to the trust, the cost of the interest is deemed to be nil (subsection 107(1.1)). Consequently, a taxpayer may realize a capital gain on the transfer to another person of a capital interest in a personal trust, depending on the amount of proceeds, the actual cost of the interest and the cost amount of the underlying trust property. However, a capital loss may be realized only if the taxpayer has an actual cost (paragraph 107(1)(b) and subsection 107(1.1)).

If property of a personal trust is distributed to a capital beneficiary in partial or complete satisfaction of the interest, subsection 107(2) generally provides a rollover, with the recognition of income, gain or loss deferred until the beneficiary disposes of the property (although an election can be made to have the distribution taxed in the same manner as distributions by a commercial trust). In the case of a commercial trust, the distribution of property to a beneficiary is a disposition by the trust for proceeds equal to the fair market of the property. The beneficiary also experiences a disposition of a capital interest on such distribution generally for proceeds equal to the proceeds of disposition to the trust, less the amount of the gain realized by the trust on the disposition (subsection 107(2.1)). This reduction of the proceeds of disposition for the beneficiary prevents the cascading of income tax.

B. Taxation of Partnerships and Partners

1. Definitions

The term "partnership" is not defined in the Act. Case law has held that the applicable provincial law is the appropriate reference for determining whether a partnership exists (see, for example, *Backman v. The Queen*, [2001] 2 C.T.C. 11, 2001 D.T.C. 5149 (S.C.C.)). The definitions of partnership in the various provincial statutes are remarkably similar, all having been derived from the late nineteenth century U.K. legislation, which itself was largely a codification of the common law. Generally, the following separate elements are necessary in order to establish the existence of a partnership:

- there must be a relationship between two or more persons (generally individuals, the trustees of a trust, or corporations);
- those persons must carry on a business in common; and
- the business must be carried on with a view to profit.

The provincial statutes provide a number of factors that will not, by themselves, result in the existence of a partnership but must be considered when determining whether a partnership exists. As a practical matter, it can be difficult to distinguish a partnership from co-ownership or a joint venture. Generally, the CRA accepts the relevant provincial law as persuasive (see Interpretation Bulletin IT-90: What is a Partnership? (February 3, 1973) and Income Tax Technical News No. 25 (October 30, 2002)).

The CRA and the courts have generally accepted that a foreign commercial relationship or entity that is formed under and governed by foreign law is a partnership for the purposes of the Act where that relationship or entity displays the essential elements of a partnership as determined under Canadian provincial law (see, generally, *Backman* and IT-90, *supra*, and Income Tax Technical News No. 38 (September 22, 2008)). However, difficult characterization issues may arise where a foreign commercial relationship or entity displays elements of both Canadian corporations and Canadian partnerships.

2. Overview of the Taxation of Partnerships and Partners

While it may have to file a yearly informational return pursuant to regulation 229 (but see the current version of T4068(E) Guide to the Partnership Information Return (T5013 Forms) for CRA Administrative Exceptions to this requirement), a partnership is not subject to tax (except under certain specialized Parts of the Act, such as the special tax on certain resource income levied under Part XII.1 of the Act and the special tax on certain income earned by types of investment partnerships levied under Part IX.1 of the Act). Tax is imposed instead on the partners, who are required to include their share of each type of income or loss of the partnership, regardless of the actual distributions from the partnership. The general rule in subsection 96(1) requires that partnership income or loss that is allocated to the partners be calculated as if:

(a) the partnership were a separate person resident in Canada;

(b) the taxation year of the partnership were its fiscal period; and

(c) each partnership activity (including the ownership of property) were carried on by the partnership as a separate person and a computation were made of the amount of:

(i) each taxable capital gain and allowable capital loss of the partnership from the disposition of property, and

(ii) each income or loss from each other source or from sources in a particular place, for each taxation year of the partnership.

Since income of a partnership is determined at the partnership level (with some specific exceptions), most deductions in computing income must be claimed at the partnership level, including optional deductions such as capital cost allowance.

As the partnership is not itself subject to tax, the partnership is, in effect, treated as a conduit. While the computation of income is required by the Act to be made at the partnership level, this does not prevent a partner from deducting any expenses incurred personally to earn a share of partnership income. Partners may thus use their own property (as distinct from partnership property) in the partnership business and deduct the relevant expenses, including capital cost allowance, in computing their income from the partnership. Where amounts are expended by a partnership that would, if paid by a partner, be deductible in computing taxable income or tax payable, those amounts are allocated separately to the partners based on their proportionate shares (see, for example, subsections 110.1(4) (taxable income deduction for charitable donations of corporations), 118.1(8) (tax credit for charitable donations of individuals), subsection 127(4.2) (tax credit for political contributions) and subsection 127(8) (investment tax credit)). Unlike the general treatment of trust income distributed to its beneficiaries, partnership income retains its characterization to its partners.

While provincial partnership legislation acknowledges that the partners are entitled to agree to allocate profits and losses other than equally (which is the default rule), section 103 contains rules designed to address tax-avoidance arrangements involving unreasonable allocations of partnership profits or losses. Where the principal reason for an agreement by partners to share profits, losses or other amounts in a certain manner may reasonably be considered to be the reduction or postponement of tax, that agreement may be ignored for tax purposes. In this situation "the amount that is reasonable having regard to all the circumstances, including the proportions in which the members have agreed to share the profits and losses of the partnership from other sources or from sources in other places", can be substituted for the amount agreed to by the partners (subsection 103(1)). Where the partners do not deal with one another at arm's length, any agreed sharing of profits, losses, etc., should take into account the capital invested and work performed by each partner to avoid being overturned pursuant to subsection 103(1.1).

A partnership may select any date for its fiscal period, but, once selected, it may not change that date without the consent of the Minister of National Revenue. For fiscal periods beginning after 1994, this ability to select a fiscal period is severely limited for most partnerships that have individuals or professional corporations as partners (subsection 249.1(1) definition of a "fiscal period"). Further, where a partnership has a different-year-end than its partners there may be an income inclusion for the "stub period" pursuant to section 37.1 (for individual partners) and section 34.2 (for corporate partners). To avoid this result, a partnership with a corporate partner can elect pursuant to subsections 249.1(8)-(11) to align its fiscal period with (one of) its corporate partner(s).

A retired partner often is entitled to receive a share of partnership profits. In the absence of a special rule, such amounts likely would not be deductible in computing the partnership's income as an expense and would be taxed in the hands of the continuing partners. Subsection 96(1.1) provides special rules that address allocations and distributions to retired partners to prevent double taxation on distributions to retired partners. Subsection 96(1.01) also provides for the ability of a partnership to allocate income and losses for a particular fiscal period of the partnership to partners who cease to be partners during that fiscal period.

For the most part, the rules in the Act apply equally to general and limited partnerships. With limited partnerships, special "at-risk" rules restrict the flow-through of tax benefits in excess of the actual amount of a limited partner's investment. Under subsection 96(2.1), limited partners can deduct their share of investment tax credits, business losses (other than farm losses) and property losses of the partnership only to the extent of their "at-risk amount". Business and property losses that are not deductible in the year may be carried forward indefinitely and applied against a limited partner's share of partnership income in future years. The "at-risk amount" of a limited partner is defined in subsection 96(2.2) generally as the adjusted cost base of the partner's interest plus the share of partnership income for the current year less debts owing to the partnership and any amounts intended to protect the partner from loss. These rules apply only to limited partners as defined in subsection 96(2.4).

3. The Partnership Interest

The partnership interest is treated for income tax purposes as a property separate from the underlying assets of the partnership. The case law suggests that a partnership interest is usually capital property (see, for example, *Continental Bank of Canada v. The Queen*, [1998] 4 C.T.C. 119, 98 D.T.C. 6505 (S.C.C.). As with other capital properties, the gain or loss on a disposition of a partnership interest is determined by comparing the adjusted cost base of the partnership interest and the relevant proceeds of disposition.

The Act provides a number of special rules relevant to the calculation of the adjusted cost base of a partnership interest. The adjusted cost base adjustments with respect to a partnership interest are set out in paragraphs 53(1)(e) and 53(2)(c) of the Act. The starting point for these adjustments is the cost of the interest to the partner. Some of the more important adjustments are the following:

(a) A partner's share of partnership income is added in computing the adjusted cost base of the partnership interest (since it will have previously been included in the partner's income). Conversely, a partner's share of losses reduces the adjusted cost base of the partnership interest. The adjusted cost base of a limited partner's partnership interest is reduced by losses only to the extent that the deduction of the losses is not restricted by the at-risk rules.

(b) Contributions of capital to the partnership by the partner are added to the adjusted cost base of the interest.

(c) Amounts received by the partner as a distribution of partnership profits or capital are subtracted from the adjusted cost base of the partnership interest.

For the purposes of the adjusted cost base adjustments, partnership profits and losses are calculated in accordance with special rules that accommodate various matters such as the inclusion rates for capital gains and eligible capital amounts. This prevents the non-taxable portions of such amounts being taxed indirectly on the disposition of the partnership interest.

It is important to recognize that certain of the adjusted cost base inclusions and deductions only occur *after* a particular fiscal period of a partnership while others occur *during* the particular fiscal period. For example, income allocated by a partnership only increases the adjusted cost base of the applicable partnership interest after the end of the relevant fiscal period of the partnership while distributions of that income reduce adjusted cost base at the time the distributions are made. This mismatch may result in unintended and adverse tax consequences. Subsection 96(1.01) provides for certain deemed fiscal period ends in an attempt to remedy some of the unintended consequences from this timing mismatch.

Partnership interests are excepted from the rule in subsection 40(3), which requires the negative amount of any adjusted cost base to be realized as a capital gain. A negative adjusted cost base that would otherwise trigger a deemed gain on a partnership interest is accounted for only on the disposition of the interest. This general exception for partnership interests is subject to subsection 40(3.1), which deems limited partners and certain passive partners ("specified members" as defined in subsection 248(1)) to realize a capital gain at any time that there is a negative balance in the adjusted cost base of the partnership interest.

4. Transfers of Property to a Partnership

Transfers of property to a partnership generally constitute a disposition for proceeds equal to the fair market value of the property (subsection 97(1)). As an exception to this general rule, subsection 97(2) provides that a person may elect to transfer property to a partnership at an amount that is less than the fair market value of the subject property if:

- immediately after the transfer, the partnership was a Canadian partnership (defined in section 102 to require all members to be resident in Canada) of which the transferor was a member;
- the property transferred is capital property, resource property, eligible capital property or inventory (other than specified participating interests as defined in subsection 248(1)); and
- a joint election is made by the transferor and all other members of the partnership to have subsection 97(2) apply (see subsections 96(3) to (6) for the administrative requirements applicable to the election).

Where these conditions are satisfied, the proceeds of disposition to the transferor and the cost of the property to the partnership may be designated, within certain limits, in the election. These limitations generally preclude the elected amount from being lower than the tax cost of the transferred property or greater than its fair market value. As well, the elected amount cannot be greater than the amount of non-partnership consideration received by the transferor. Specific anti-avoidance rules discourage the conferral of a benefit by the transferor on other related partners by transferring property for consideration that is lower than the fair market value of the transferred property. These limitations are identical to those applying on a transfer of property to a taxable Canadian corporation. See Part I. C, below.

5. Transfers of Partnership Interests or Partnership Property

A partner may dispose of a partnership interest to another person, in which case the gain or loss on the disposition of the interest is calculated under the rules in section 40 and subsection 100(2). Alternatively, the partner's interest may be reduced in value upon a distribution of partnership property. In that case, subsection 98(2) deems the partnership to have realized proceeds of disposition equal to the fair market value of the distributed property, and the partner to have acquired the property at a cost equal to that amount.

Where a partnership has ceased to exist, but the distribution of partnership property has not been completed, subsection 98(1) provides a number of special rules. Until the distribution is completed, the partnership is deemed to continue to exist, the former partners are deemed to continue as partners, and their rights to share in the partnership property are deemed to be partnership interests. As property is distributed, the adjusted cost base of a partner's interest is reduced pursuant to subsection 53(2). Where, however, the deductions under subsection 53(2) exceed the aggregate of the cost and the additions under subsection 53(1), the "negative adjusted cost base" must be recognized as a gain.

A similar rule is provided in section 98.1, where the partnership continues to exist but a taxpayer ceases to be a partner. In those circumstances, until such time as all of any rights to receive distributions of partnership property, other than a right to receive an income allocation under subsection 96(1.1), are satisfied, the partnership interest is deemed not to have been disposed of and to continue to exist as a residual interest in the partnership. If all of the rights are satisfied before the end of the fiscal period in which the taxpayer ceased to be a partner, the interest is deemed to have been disposed of at the end of that fiscal period.

As is the case when subsection 98(1) applies, section 98.1 does not permit the deferral of the recognition of a capital gain on the residual interest. That is, when the deductions in computing the adjusted cost base of the interest under subsection 53(2) exceed the aggregate of the cost and the additions under subsection 53(1), a gain equal to the amount of the excess is deemed to have been realized at the end of the fiscal period of the partnership. Where section 98.1 applies, the taxpayer with the residual interest is deemed not to be a partner except for certain limited purposes.

Property of a partnership can be distributed by the partnership on a rollover basis, subject to numerous specific rules, in any of the following circumstances:

- *Transfer of partnership property to a corporation:* Subsection 85(2) permits a partnership to transfer property to a corporation on a rollover basis in the same manner as an individual or corporation. The ability to defer the recognition of the gain would be negated, however, if the property received by the partnership as consideration for the transfer was deemed on a subsequent distribution to the partners to be disposed of by the partnership for proceeds equal to its fair market value. Subsection 85(3) avoids this effect, by providing a rollover of property to the partners where the affairs of the partnership are wound up within 60 days after the initial transfer of partnership property to a corporation, and, immediately before the winding up, the partnership had no property except money or property received from the corporation as consideration for the transfer.

- *Distribution to all partners:* Subsection 98(3) provides a rollover in circumstances where proportional undivided interests in each partnership property are distributed to the partners on the cessation of the partnership and the requisite election is made.
- *Continuation of partnership business by a sole proprietor:* Where the former business of the partnership is carried on by one (but not more than one) of the former partners, subsection 98(5) provides a rollover for partnership property transferred to that particular partner.
- *Continuation of partnership by new partnership:* Where, after 1971, a Canadian partnership has ceased to exist and all of its property is transferred to a new partnership consisting of the same partners of the predecessor, the new partnership is deemed to be a continuation of the predecessor and the partners' interests in the new partnership are deemed to be a continuation of their interests in the predecessor (subsection 98(6) and section 98.1). As a result, there will be no disposition of property by the partnership, and no disposition of the partnership interests by the partners.

C. Taxation of Corporations

1. Definitions

The Act does not provide an exhaustive definition of a corporation. Subsection 248(1) merely defines a corporation to include an "incorporated company". The CRA generally considers the presence of separate legal personality as the hallmark of a corporation (see Interpretation Bulletin IT-343R: Meaning of the Term "Corporation" (September 26, 1977)).

The Act contains special rules that effectively classify corporations for income tax purposes. The major types of corporations are "private corporations", "public corporations" and "Canadian-controlled private corporations" ("CCPCs"). Subsection 89(1) defines a "private corporation" generally as a corporation resident in Canada, other than a public corporation or a corporation controlled by one or more public corporations. A "public corporation" is also defined in subsection 89(1) as a corporation resident in Canada whose shares are traded on a designated stock exchange in Canada (subsection 262(5)). A corporation may elect to be, or cease to be, a public corporation within certain conditions (regulation 4800). Under subsection 125(7), a CCPC is defined as a private corporation that is a Canadian corporation whose shares do not trade on a prescribed foreign stock exchange and is not controlled, directly or indirectly, in any manner whatever, by one or more non-residents or by one or more public corporations or by a combination of non-residents and public corporations. Subsection 89(1) defines a "Canadian corporation" as either a corporation resident and incorporated in Canada or a corporation resident in Canada throughout the period beginning June 18, 1971. A "taxable Canadian corporation" is defined in subsection 89(1) generally as a Canadian corporation that is not exempt from tax.

The definitions of a "private corporation" and a "Canadian-controlled private corporation" depend on the concept of control. While "control" is defined specifically for a number of provisions under the Act (for example, subsections 112(6) and 186(2)), it is not defined generally for the purposes of the Act. In accordance with well-established jurisprudence, control means *de jure* control — that is, ownership of a sufficient number of shares to elect a majority of the board of directors. Control for this purpose may be affected by corporate constating documents including a unanimous shareholder agreement (USA) to the extent that the USA impacts the control of the corporation (*Duha Printers (Western) Ltd. v. R.*, [1998] 3 C.T.C. 303, 98 D.T.C. 6334, [1998] S.C.J. No. 41 (S.C.C.)). For the purposes of the definition of a CCPC in subsection 125(7), the concept of control begins with *de jure* control but is modified significantly by subsections 251(5) and subsection 256(5.1). The former provision requires that certain rights with respect to shares, other than full ownership rights, be considered in determining *de jure* control. The latter provision imposes a concept of *de facto* control in addition to the *de jure* test.

Not all corporations are either public or private corporations. For example, subsidiaries of public corporations are neither public corporations nor private corporations. Such corporations are subject generally to the regime applicable to public corporations.

2. Overview of the Taxation of Corporations — Rules Applicable to all Corporations

(a) Computation of Income and Taxable Income

A corporation is a taxpayer and a person and its income for a taxation year is computed in much the same way as the income of an individual. Obviously, some provisions, such as those governing the treatment of moving expense, alimony payments and child care expenses are not applicable to corporations. Further, there are some differences between the computation of income of a corporation and that of an individual. For example, because a corporation cannot be an employee, its sources of income are generally limited to businesses, property and taxable capital gains. Moreover, unlike an individual, the taxation year of a corporation is its fiscal period, which may be different from the calendar year, but cannot exceed 53 weeks (see the definition of a "taxation year" in subsection 249(1) and the definition of a fiscal period in subsection 249.1(1)). The fiscal period (and hence the taxation year) of a professional corporation must be the calendar year (subsection 249.1(1)).

Taxable dividends received by a corporation, like taxable dividends received by other taxpayers, must be included in income. However, such dividends received by a corporation are not subject to the gross-up and credit mechanism in paragraph 82(1)(b) and section 121. Instead, in order to prevent cascading of tax, dividends received by a corporation are generally deductible in the computation of the recipient's taxable income (subsection 112(1)). Special refundable taxes under Part IV of the Act are imposed on dividends received by private corporations and certain public corporations (subsection 186(4)).

(b) Tax Rates

The basic federal rate of tax on corporate income is 38 per cent (section 123) less the provincial abatement (discussed below) of 10 per cent. The federal corporate tax rate has been reduced annually since 2000 in respect of income that is not subject to other special income tax credits (section 123.4). The result is a general federal tax rate reduction of 13 per cent in 2015, which results in a 15 per cent federal tax rate for corporations other than CCPCs. Most importantly for CCPCs, the general rate reduction does not apply to income subject to the lower small business deduction tax rate or to investment income, which is, in addition to the basic federal rate, subject to a refundable tax of 6 2/3 per cent (section 123.3), resulting in a total federal rate of 34.7 per cent for 2015 on such income of CCPCs.

(c) Income Tax Credits

A corporation resident in Canada is entitled to claim various tax credits, including the following:

- *Provincial abatement.* Subsection 124(1) entitles a corporation to deduct from its income tax otherwise payable an amount equal to 10 per cent of its taxable income earned in the year in a province, including the Yukon Territory, the Northwest Territories and Nunavut. This deduction from tax is designed to allow for provincial tax on the earnings of a corporation.
- *Small Business Tax Credit.* Section 125 (discussed further below) provides for an additional tax credit of 17 per cent on the active business income of CCPCs (up to $500,000) that is earned in Canada. Such income is taxed at a federal rate of 11 per cent in 2010.
- *Other Credits.* The income tax credits for foreign taxes (section 126), logging taxes (subsection 127(1)), political donations (subsection 127(3)) and certain

investments (subsection 127(5)) are available for corporations as well as for individuals.

3. Special Rules for Private Corporations and CCPCs

(a) General Concepts

The Canadian tax system has historically provided special treatment for CCPCs and, to a lesser extent, private corporations. In the case of private corporations, the special rules apply to dividends received from portfolio investments. In the case of CCPCs, the rules apply to all investment income, that is, income from property and from businesses, the principal purpose of which is to earn income from property. The objective of these rules is to provide integration — that is, a system where one is indifferent, from a tax perspective, between earning passive income directly or through a corporation. To implement integration, the Act provides for a number of taxes that are refundable to CCPCs and private corporations when the relevant income is distributed as taxable dividends.

Eligible CCPCs enjoy a further advantage (commonly referred to as "the small business deduction" or "SBD"): that is, a credit against corporate tax otherwise payable equal to 17 per cent of active business income, up to a maximum of $500,000 per year (which limit must be shared among associated CCPCs). This reduces the federal tax rate on active business income to approximately 11 per cent. The actual combined federal-provincial rate will depend on the applicable provincial rates, which vary considerably and range from a low of 0 per cent in Manitoba to a high of 8 per cent in Quebec.

(b) Investment Income other than Inter-Corporate Dividends Earned by CCPCs

Investment income, other than inter-corporate dividends earned by CCPCs, is taxed at the basic federal corporate rate of 38 per cent (less the 10 per cent provincial abatement). In addition, a special tax equal to 6 2/3 per cent of the income is levied under section 123.3. This special tax was added to the Act in 1995 to remove any benefit of deferral from having investment income taxed at corporate, rather than presumed higher individual tax rates. An amount equal to 26 2/3 per cent of aggregate investment income is added to the "RDTOH" account of a CCPC. RDTOH is refundable on the basis of $1 for each $3 of taxable dividends paid (subsection 129(1)). The logic underlying this part of the refund is integration of the corporate and shareholder-level taxes. In theory, the total tax paid on the income initially earned by the corporation, taxed at the corporate level, and distributed as taxable dividends to a taxpayer in the highest tax bracket should approximate that which an individual would pay had the income been earned directly. The mechanics of the refund process are set out in section 129.

"Aggregate investment income" is defined in subsection 129(4) for purposes of calculating the amount of RDTOH and generally includes: (i) taxable capital gains in excess of allowable capital losses; (ii) income from property (other than intercorporate dividends) less losses from property; and (iii) income or loss from a "specified investment business" ("SIB") carried on in Canada. A SIB is defined in subsection 125(7) as a business, the principal purpose of which is to derive income from property, unless the corporation employs throughout the year more than five full-time employees or could reasonably be expected to require more than five full-time employees but for the fact that managerial, administrative, financial, maintenance or other similar services are provided by an associated corporation.

The characterization of income as either investment income or active business income is important since:

- active business income is not subject to the RDTOH mechanism; and
- most investment income is not subject to the small business deduction.

Income from property that is used in an active business or income that is incident or pertains to an active business is excluded from investment income (subsection 129(4)), definition of "income or loss from a source that is property") and is considered income from an active business for purposes of the small business deduction discussed below.

Dividends are excluded from the investment income of CCPCs under paragraph 129(3)(a) and instead may be subject to a special tax under Part IV of the Act that is added to RDTOH separately under paragraph 129(3)(b).

Notwithstanding the complex definition in subsection 129(3), RDTOH of a private corporation can be summarized as: (i) the amount of Part IV tax paid by the corporation plus, (ii) in the case of a CCPC, 26 2/3 per cent of the corporation's investment income (other than intercorporate dividends). RDTOH is a cumulative account that carries over to a subsequent year to the extent that it is not refunded in a previous year. The balance carries over to a subsequent year only if the particular corporation maintains its status as a private corporation at the end of the immediately preceding year. Once a corporation ceases to be a private corporation, its RDTOH disappears and is not revived even if the corporation subsequently becomes a private corporation.

The non-taxable portion of the capital gains realized by a private corporation in excess of its capital losses is added to the corporation's capital dividend account (subsection 89(1)), which can be distributed to the shareholders in the form of a tax-free dividend under subsection 83(2), upon making an appropriate election. The combined effect of the RDTOH and capital dividend account is that the aggregate of the tax payable by a corporation and the tax payable by the shareholder on a distribution of a capital gain realized by the corporation is approximately the same as the tax that would have been payable by the shareholder had the capital gain been realized directly (i.e., integration is achieved).

(c) Inter-Corporate Dividends — Part IV Tax

Part IV of the Act imposes a special tax on private corporations and certain other corporations, referred to as "subject corporations" (essentially a public corporation controlled by an individual or family). This tax is intended to prevent any deferral benefit from the earning of dividend income on portfolio ("non-controlling") investments through a closely-held corporation. This goal is realized by imposing Part IV tax at a rate approximating the highest marginal personal rate (combined federal-provincial) on tax-free inter-corporate dividends received by the relevant corporations, and then refunding the tax when the dividends are distributed to shareholders who are individuals. The current rate of Part IV tax is 33 1/3 per cent.

The Part IV tax base may be reduced by one-third of the amount of business losses (current-year losses as well as loss carryovers). Once a business loss has been used to reduce Part IV tax payable, it cannot be deducted in computing the corporation's taxable income (subparagraph 111(3)(a)(ii)).

(d) Small Business Deduction

As noted above, a CCPC is entitled to deduct from its tax payable for a year an amount equal to 17 per cent in respect of up to $500,000 of income from an active business carried on in Canada.

(i) Active Business Income

Only income from an active business carried on in Canada qualifies for the SBD. The term "active business" is defined in subsection 125(7) to mean "any business carried on by the corporation, other than a specified investment business or a personal services business" (also defined in subsection 125(7)). An adventure in the nature of trade is specifically included in the definition. Income of the corporation for the year from an active business is also defined in subsection 125(7) to include income pertaining to or incident to the active business.

In determining whether income earned by a CCPC is active business income or investment income, the case law has held that there is a rebuttable presumption that income earned by a corporation from an activity permitted by its objects as set out in the constating documents is income from a business. A series of cases has held that interest earned on surplus cash of a business is investment income if the business does not rely on the cash. The key juridical test is whether the property on which the investment income is earned is employed or risked in the business in the sense that its removal would have a decidedly destabilizing effect on the business.

(ii) Associated Corporations

The small business deduction is limited to the first $500,000 of active business income earned in a taxation year by a CCPC. One obvious way of avoiding this limit would be to create multiple corporations, each earning $500,000 of active business income in any particular year. To prevent this type of abuse, subsections 125(2) and (3) provide that associated CCPCs are entitled to one small business deduction, which they may allocate among themselves. If they fail to do so, the Minister of National Revenue shall make the allocation (subsection 125(4)).

Section 256 provides a set of detailed rules for determining whether corporations are associated for purposes of the Act.

(iii) Corporate Partnerships

To prevent CCPCs from extending their entitlement to the small business deduction by carrying on business in partnership, paragraph 125(1)(a) and the definition of "specified partnership income" in subsection 125(7) limit a corporation's share of the income of a partnership eligible for the small business deduction. A $500,000 limit is applied to each partnership with one or more corporate partners, and this limit is allocated to each partner in proportion to its share of the total active business income of the partnership.

D. Corporate Distributions

The basic scheme for the taxation of corporate earnings is to impose tax at two points in the income stream. The first of these is imposed on the corporation at the time that the income is earned; the second is imposed on the shareholder when the after-tax income of the corporation is distributed as a dividend. The potential for the "double-taxation" of corporate income has been significantly reduced by the system of integration as discussed below.

1. Ordinary Taxable Dividends

Under subsection 82(1), taxpayers are required to include in income all amounts received as "taxable dividends" from corporations resident in Canada. A "taxable dividend" is defined in subsection 89(1) as any dividend other than certain non-taxable dividends and capital dividends.

The term "dividend" is not defined in the Act apart from the fact that it includes stock dividends (subsection 248(1)). Therefore, the term must be given its ordinary meaning for corporate law purposes, which generally includes all *pro rata* distributions to shareholders other than those made in certain specified circumstances described in subsections 84(2) to (4.1).

Subsection 82(1) requires a shareholder who is an individual to include in income all taxable dividends received in the year from resident corporations plus either one-quarter or 44 per cent of of the amount received based on whether the dividend is eligible or ineligible. The additional amount is commonly referred to as the "gross-up". Under section 121, individuals may deduct from the tax otherwise payable for the year, two-thirds of the amount of the gross-up or 16.67 per cent of the amount of a dividend received if the dividend was ineligible (gross-up of one-quarter) or 10/17 of the amount in the case of eligible dividends where the gross-up is 44 per cent.

The dividend gross-up and tax credit provisions are designed to provide a measure of integration between corporate and personal taxes. The eligible dividend rules and enhanced gross-up were introduced in 2005 to recognize that the then existing gross-up and credit system did not provide for a full credit in respect of corporate tax paid at the general corporate tax rate. The rules were also intended to provide comparable tax treatment in respect of different business structures (in particular, between corporations and income trusts). The result is that income that was subject to the small business tax rate remains subject to the ineligible dividend tax regime, while income subject to the general corporate tax rate benefits from the enhanced regime.

Taxable dividends received by a corporation resident in Canada from another resident corporation are included in the recipient's income under paragraph 82(1)(a) without any gross-up and dividend tax credit. Instead, the corporate recipient is generally entitled to deduct such dividends in calculating taxable income (subsection 112(1)). In the absence of such a deduction or some other relieving mechanism, corporate income paid through a chain of corporations would be subject to multiple levels of corporate tax.

As described above, taxable dividends received by a private corporation are subject to a special 33 1/3 per cent refundable tax under Part IV of the Act. The tax is intended to prevent individuals from deferring tax on dividend income by having the income paid to a corporation. In the absence of Part IV tax, the dividends would not be subject to any tax for the recipient corporation because of the inter-corporate dividend deduction.

2. Dividends in Kind and Stock Dividends

If a corporation distributes assets other than cash by way of a dividend ("dividend in kind"), the shareholders are considered to have received a dividend in an amount equal to the fair market value of such assets (definition of "amount" in subsection 248(1)). Under subsection 52(2), the distributing corporation is considered to have disposed of the property for proceeds equal to its fair market value, and the recipient shareholder is considered to have acquired the property at an equivalent cost. These rules ensure that the tax consequences on the payment of a dividend in kind are equivalent to those on a sale of a corporate asset followed by a distribution of the proceeds as a dividend.

A "stock dividend" is defined in subsection 248(1) to include any dividend paid by a corporation by the issue of its shares. The amount of a stock dividend is generally the amount by which the paid-up capital of the corporation increases as a result of the dividend payment (definition of "amount" in subsection 248(1)). That amount also becomes the cost to the shareholder of the shares received. These rules ensure that the tax consequences on the payment of a stock dividend are equivalent to the payment of a cash dividend followed by an issue of shares for the amount of that cash. However, consideration must be given to the potential application of subsection 15(1.1) whenever a stock dividend is declared. This anti-avoidance provision generally prevents the use of stock dividends to shift value between significant shareholders (i.e., by the declaration of stock dividends of shares with high value but low paid-up capital). When applicable, subsection 15(1.1) generally includes the fair market value of the shares issued as stock dividends in the income of the recipient. Section 86.1 provides for a tax-deferred rollover in certain circumstances where shares of a U.S. corporation are distributed as a dividend-in-kind on shares of another U.S. corporation. Where section 86.1 applies, the general rules for dividends in kind in subsection 52(2) are displaced.

3. Capital Dividends

The definition of a "taxable dividend" in subsection 89(1) excepts two major categories of dividends: (1) certain dividends paid out of a corporation's surplus accounts; and (2) capital dividends. The first category is a transitional feature of the 1972 tax reform and is now mainly of historical interest. The second category is the more significant one. The capital dividend account is designed to permit private corporations to flow through the untaxed portion of certain amounts to shareholders with no tax consequences.

Under subsection 83(2), a private corporation may elect to pay a tax-free capital dividend to its shareholders out of its capital dividend account. Capital dividends are primarily advantageous to Canadian-resident shareholders, since non-residents are liable to a 25 per cent withholding tax on such dividends (subsection 212(2)). The capital dividend account is defined in subsection 89(1) and includes the following amounts determined on a cumulative basis:

(a) The non-taxable portion of capital gains in excess of the non-deductible portion of capital losses during the period. The idea is to permit private corporations to distribute tax-free the untaxed portion of net capital gains realized after 1971. However, gains or losses accrued during a period when the corporation was not a private corporation are generally excluded from the capital dividend account.

(b) The amount of any capital dividends received by the corporation.

(c) The mortality proceeds of life insurance policies acquired by the corporation to the extent that such proceeds exceed the adjusted cost base of the policy.

(d) The untaxed portion of the proceeds of disposition of eligible capital property in excess of the non-deductible portion of the cost of all such property.

To prevent a private corporation from distributing amounts in excess of its capital dividend account, a penalty tax is levied under Part III of the Act equal to 75 per cent of the excess of the dividend over the account balance. Proposed amendments reduce this penalty tax to 60 per cent of the excess. Problems may arise in this regard where a corporation's capital dividend account is adjusted retroactively as a result of subsequent events such as a capital loss carryback or a replacement property election under section 44. If Part III tax applies to any portion of a dividend, an election may be made to treat such excess as a regular taxable dividend and thereby avoid the application of the tax.

4. Deemed Dividends

In general terms, the Act permits shareholders to receive a tax-free return of capital at any time. However, any amount received in excess of that capital is taxed as a dividend under the "deemed dividend rules" in section 84. These rules are designed to prevent shareholders from converting what would otherwise be a dividend distribution into a preferentially taxed capital gain. A deemed dividend is generally treated as a dividend for all purposes of the Act.

A transaction giving rise to a deemed dividend often results in the disposition of a share, with capital gain or loss consequences. To ensure that an amount received by a shareholder is not taxed as both a dividend and a capital gain, the Act reduces the proceeds of disposition by the amount of any deemed dividend (paragraph (j) of the definition of "proceeds of disposition" in section 54). Where a transaction giving rise to a deemed dividend does not result in the disposition of a share, the Act requires a reduction of the adjusted cost base to reflect any recovery of cost by the shareholder (paragraph 53(2)(a)).

(a) Paid-Up Capital

A dividend is deemed to arise to the extent that the amount distributed in certain circumstances exceeds the paid-up capital ("PUC") of a share. The definition of "paid-up capital" is critical, therefore, in the application of the deemed dividend rules. In essence, the concept represents the amount that may be returned as a capital receipt to a shareholder at any time. Subsection 89(1) defines "paid-up capital" in terms of a share, a class of shares, and all of the shares of the corporation. The definition of PUC of a share or all the shares of the corporation is defined by reference to PUC of a class.

The tax law concept of PUC is based on the corporate law concept of capital or stated capital, subject to a number of specified adjustments for tax purposes. Where the PUC of a class of shares is reduced pursuant to any of the rules in the Act, the amount of the reduction is added back to PUC to the extent that any deemed dividends subsequently arise on the particular class of shares as a result of a redemption, acquisition or cancellation of shares or a reduction of capital. The purpose of this add-back is to offset the original reduction in PUC once that reduction has been subject to tax.

(b) Capitalization of Surplus

Under subsection 84(1), a corporation is deemed to have paid a dividend if it increases the PUC of a class of shares otherwise than by:

(a) the payment of a stock dividend;

(b) a net contribution of assets to the corporation;

(c) a reduction of PUC of another class; or

(d) the conversion of contributed surplus.

There are also some additional special provisions that apply to insurance corporations and banks.

The amount of the deemed dividend under subsection 84(1) is the amount by which the increase in the PUC of the class of shares exceeds the amount determined under paragraphs (b), (c) and (d) above. The deemed dividend is considered to have been paid to, and received by, all shareholders of the class. The amount of the deemed dividend is added to the adjusted cost base of the affected shares to ensure that it is not taxed again when distributed to the shareholder on a return of capital (paragraph 53(1)(b)).

Subsection 84(1) prevents a corporation from increasing its PUC, and then distributing the increase as a return of capital to the shareholders. In the absence of subsection 84(1), corporate income could be distributed to shareholders as capital by capitalizing such income prior to a redemption of shares or a reduction of capital.

(c) Distributions On Winding-Up, Discontinuance or Reorganization

Where an amount is distributed by a corporation resident in Canada to its shareholders of a class on the winding-up, discontinuance or reorganization of a business, subsection 84(2) deems a dividend to have been paid equal to the amount by which the value of the distributed assets or funds exceeds any reduction in the PUC of the relevant shares. The shareholders are deemed to have received a proportionate share of the dividend based on the number of shares of the class owned immediately before the distribution. The terms "winding-up", "discontinuance" and "reorganization" have been interpreted to have their ordinary commercial meanings and not technical legal meanings.

When property is distributed to shareholders on the winding-up of a corporation, the corporation is deemed to have disposed of the property for proceeds equal to its fair market value and the shareholder is deemed to have acquired it at a cost equal to the same amount (subsection 69(5)). For purposes of determining the amount of the deemed dividend under subsection 84(2), it is the fair market value of the property distributed that is taken into account and not its cost to the corporation or its book value. However, where the corporation distributes its own shares, the value of the shares for purposes of determining the amount of the deemed dividend under subsection 84(2) is deemed to be the PUC in respect of the shares (subsection 84(5)). Subsection 84(2) does not apply to a transaction to the extent that subsection 84(1) applies or to a purchase by a corporation of its own shares in the open market (subsection 84(6)). Where subsection 84(2) applies, subsection 15(1), dealing with benefits conferred on a shareholder, does not apply.

Where a corporation is liquidated, the shareholders will usually be considered to have disposed of their shares (subparagraph (b)(i) of the definition of "disposition" in subsection 248(1). By virtue of paragraph (j) of the definition of "proceeds of disposition" in section 54, any deemed dividend arising under subsection 84(2) is not treated as proceeds of disposition.

(d) Redemption, Acquisition or Cancellation of Shares

Where a corporation resident in Canada redeems, acquires or cancels its shares of any class, subsection 84(3) deems a dividend to have been paid equal to the amount distributed in excess of the PUC of the shares. The shareholders are deemed to have received a proportionate share of the dividend based on the number of the affected shares owned immediately before the redemption, which results in the disposition of the shares for capital gains purposes (subparagraph (b)(i) of the definition of "disposition" in subsection 248(1). However, the amount of the proceeds of disposition is reduced by the amount of any deemed dividend arising under subsection 84(3) (paragraph (j) of the definition of "proceeds of disposition" in section 54). Where a corporation issues new shares in consideration of the redemption of other shares of the corporation, the amount paid is equal to the increase in the PUC of the corporation resulting from the issue of the shares (paragraphs 84(5)(b) and (d)). Subsection 84(3) does not apply to any transaction to the extent that subsection 84(1) applies (paragraph 84(6)(a)) or to which subsection 84(2) applies.

Similarly, subsection 84(3) does not apply where a shareholder sells the shares to the corporation in the open market (paragraph 84(6)(b)).

With the introduction of the lifetime capital gains exemption, a public corporation could distribute its earnings as a tax-preferred capital gain rather than a dividend through a very simple arrangement. The corporation would first issue stock dividends with a nominal PUC but a substantial fair market value. The PUC of such shares would be included in the shareholder's income as a dividend. On a subsequent repurchase of the shares by the corporation in the open market at their fair market value, the difference between the fair market value and the PUC would be a capital gain, not a deemed dividend, because of the exception in paragraph 84(6)(b). To address these surplus stripping transactions, a special tax under Part II.1 was enacted. It applies where a corporation whose shares are publicly traded pays an amount to its shareholders as proceeds of disposition that can reasonably be regarded as a substitute for taxable dividends that would otherwise have been paid in the normal course.

(e) Reduction of Capital

Where a corporation resident in Canada, other than a public corporation, distributes an amount on a reduction in the PUC of its shares of any class, subsection 84(4) deems a dividend to have been paid equal to the amount distributed in excess of the reduction in PUC. Historically, where a public corporation paid an amount to its shareholders after April 10, 1978 on a reduction of its PUC, the total amount paid, and not just the amount in excess of the reduction in capital, was deemed to be a dividend (subsection 84(4.1)). This provision effectively prohibited the shareholders of a public corporation from receiving a tax-free return of capital on a reduction in PUC. It was intended to prevent public corporations from extending the ability to pay certain tax-deferred dividends after 1978. However, subsection 84(4.1) now permits public corporations to make tax-free returns of PUC in certain extraordinary circumstances.

Subsections 84(4) and (4.1) do not apply to any payment on a reduction in PUC to which subsection 84(2) or (3) applies.

5. Stripping Transactions

Because the Act treats dividends differently from capital gains, opportunities are available for taxpayers to arrange their affairs to achieve tax savings by deriving income in one form or the other. Not surprisingly, the Act contains specific anti-avoidance rules to address some of these avoidance opportunities. Two of the significant ones are the dividend stripping rules and capital gains stripping rules.

(a) Dividend Stripping

Dividend stripping transactions attempt to avoid or reduce the shareholder-level tax on dividend distributions by converting such distributions into a capital gain realized on the disposition of the shares. To counter these schemes, the Act includes the deemed dividend rules discussed immediately above and sections 84.1 and 212.1, which apply on certain non-arm's length sales of shares.

The necessity for rules to prevent dividend stripping depends on the relative tax rates for dividends and capital gains. If dividends are taxed more than capital gains, taxpayers will attempt to strip the surplus of a corporation by converting dividends into capital gains. Since 1972, the tax rates on dividends and capital gains have varied widely.

(b) Capital Gains Stripping

Capital gains stripping transactions attempt to convert what would otherwise be a capital gain realized on a disposition of a share into a tax-free inter-corporate dividend. The most obvious situation to which this type of planning could be applied is where a parent corporation is considering the sale of shares of a subsidiary. If the contemplated sale would result in a capital gain, the gain may be avoided or reduced if the parent corporation causes the subsidiary, prior to the sale, to declare a dividend on the shares held by the parent. This dividend, which would be received tax-free by the parent, would have the effect of reducing the sale price, and thereby the amount of the gain that would have been subject to tax.

Subsections 55(1) to (5) provide a complex set of rules designed to prevent the conversion of a taxable capital gain into a tax-free inter-corporate dividend. They operate to deem certain dividends to be proceeds of disposition for the shares on which the dividends were received. Where the shares have not been disposed of, the dividend is deemed to be a gain on the disposition of capital property. Because of the complexity of these rules, an advance ruling from the CRA is often necessary.

6. Shareholder Benefits and Loans

(a) Shareholder Benefits

Where a corporation confers a benefit on a shareholder or a person in contemplation of becoming a shareholder, the amount of the benefit must be included in computing the recipient's income under subsection 15(1). The provision does not apply to benefits conferred on a shareholder by way of the payment of a dividend, including a deemed dividend, a reduction of capital, certain rights offerings, or the capitalization of contributed surplus. Some of the most frequently encountered shareholder benefits include: (i) the sale of corporate property to a shareholder for an amount less than the fair market value of the property; (ii) the sale of property by a shareholder to the corporation for an amount in excess of the fair market value of the property; (iii) the rent-free use of corporate property by a shareholder; and (iv) the payment by a corporation of a shareholder's personal expenses.

Benefits included in income under subsection 15(1) are not treated as a dividend. Consequently, the recipient is not entitled to the benefit of the dividend tax credit. The amount included in a shareholder's income under section 15 is also not deductible to the corporation. Subsection 15(1) thus serves as a deterrent to shareholders seeking to avoid the tax on dividends by receiving distributions of corporate property in a form other than a dividend.

(b) Shareholder Loans

A shareholder (or certain other persons specified by subsection 15(2)) who receives a loan from, or incurs indebtedness to, a corporation may be required to include the amount of the loan or indebtedness in income. Exceptions apply where certain conditions are met, including: (i) the loan was made for certain specified purposes (for example, the purchase of a dwelling by an officer of the corporation) and *bona fide* arrangements have been made for the repayment of the loan within a reasonable time; (ii) the loan was repaid within one year from the end of the taxation year in which it was made and the repayment is not part of a series of loans and repayments; or (iii) it is reasonable to conclude that the debtor received the loan as a result of a person's capacity as an employee and not as a shareholder.

As with subsection 15(1), the amount of a loan included in income under subsection 15(2) is not treated as a dividend. Various exceptions apply for certain shareholder-employee housing loans, stock purchase loans, automobile loans, and in other limited instances.

E. Corporate Reorganizations

Some forms of corporate reorganizations are contemplated explicitly by provisions of the Act: transfers of property to a corporation (section 85), share takeovers (section 85.1), the exercise of conversion rights (section 51), reorganizations of capital (section 86), amalgamations (section 87), and liquidations (section 88). Tax-deferred rollovers are provided by most of these provisions, but not all; for example, the dissolution of a corporation, other than a 90 per cent owned subsidiary that is dissolved into a taxable Canadian corporation, exposes all accrued gains and deferred income to taxation. Other forms of reorganization are not explicitly contemplated by the Act. For example, to achieve rollover treatment for many types of acquisitive reorganizations, the transaction has to be carried out in steps, one or more of which may qualify for rollover treatment.

1. Section 85 - Transfers of Property to a Corporation

When a taxpayer disposes of property, any accrued gain or loss generally must be recognized. Subsection 85(1), however, allows taxpayers, in certain circumstances, to transfer assets to a corporation without the recognition of accrued gain provided the transferee receives consideration that includes shares of the transferee. (As noted above in Part I. B, subsection 85(2) provides an equivalent rollover for transfers by a partnership to a corporation.) Subsection 85(1) applies when all of the following conditions are satisfied:

- a taxpayer has disposed of eligible property (as defined in subsection 85(1.1) to a taxable Canadian corporation;
- the consideration for the transfer includes shares of the transferee corporation; and
- the taxpayer and the corporation have jointly elected in prescribed form and within the time contemplated in subsection 85(6).

The rollover in section 85 allows the corporation and the transferor to jointly elect the transfer price, within certain limits. The elected amount plays an important role in the transfer because that amount is deemed to be:

- the proceeds of disposition to the transferor of the transferred property (paragraph 85(1)(a));
- the adjusted cost base to the corporation of the property (paragraph 85(1)(a)); and
- the cost to the transferor of the consideration received for the property (paragraphs 85(1)(f), (g) and (h)).

By electing the appropriate amount, any gain that would otherwise be realized by the transferor on the disposition of the property can be deferred until either the transferor disposes of the consideration (i.e., shares) received for the property, or the corporation disposes of the property.

The rollover in subsection 85(1) does not automatically apply to all property transferred to a corporation, nor does it apply to all transfers in exactly the same manner. The following types of property, listed in subsection 85(1.1), generally may be transferred under subsection 85(1): depreciable property, non-depreciable capital property (except real property owned by a non-resident), eligible capital property, inventory (except for real property), and certain resource property. Subsection 85(1.11) denies eligible property status for certain resource properties and specified participating interests (as defined in subsection 248(1)) in certain instances.

Section 85 does not dictate the elected amount for the parties, but it allows them to select from a range of values. The upper limit is the fair market value of the property transferred to the corporation (paragraph 85(1)(c)). One lower limit is the fair market value of any non-share consideration received from the corporation (paragraph 85(1)(b)).

If the elected amount exceeds the fair market value of the transferred property, paragraph 85(1)(c) deems the parties to have chosen the fair market value of the property as the elected amount. If the elected amount is less than the fair market value of any non-share consideration, paragraph 85(1)(b) deems the parties to have chosen the fair market value of that consideration as the elected amount. If the fair market value of the non-share consideration is greater than the fair market value of the transferred property, paragraph 85(1)(b) is expressly subject to paragraph 85(1)(c), and the elected amount may be no greater than the fair market value of the transferred property. Subsection 15(1) can apply in such a situation to deem the transferor to have received a benefit to the extent that the fair market value of the non-share consideration exceeds the fair market value of the transferred property.

In addition to the limits in paragraphs 85(1)(b) and (c), there are special minimum election rules in paragraphs 85(1)(c.1), (d) and (e), which apply to the broad categories of inventory and non-depreciable capital property, eligible capital property and depreciable property. In general, these special provisions ensure that the elected amount cannot be less than the lesser of the fair market value and tax cost of the transferred property. As a result, on a transfer under section 85, a taxpayer must realize an accrued loss but cannot create an "artificial" loss by electing an amount less than the tax cost of the transferred property if its fair market value is greater.

Paragraph 85(1)(e.3) provides that when the fair market value of any non-share consideration received for an asset is different from the deemed proceeds under paragraphs 85(1)(c.1), (d) or (e), the parties are deemed to have elected an amount equal to the greater of: (i) the amount deemed by paragraph 85(1)(c.1), (d) or (e); and (ii) the amount deemed by paragraph 85(1)(b). In short, when the transferor receives non-share consideration, the lower limit on the elected amount is at least equal to the fair market value of the non-share consideration.

Under paragraphs 85(1)(f), (g) and (h), the transferor is deemed to acquire the share or non-share consideration received for the transferred property at a cost equal to the deemed proceeds of disposition. These provisions allocate the elected amount to the different types of consideration in the following order:

(a) to the non-share consideration, up to the lesser of its fair market value and the fair market value of the property exchanged for it;

(b) to any preferred shares, up to the fair market value of the shares immediately after the transfer of the property to the corporation; and

(c) to any common shares received on the transfer.

This allocation method ensures that any deferred gain will normally be reflected in the share consideration.

The cost that can be allocated to preferred shares is limited by their fair market value. No such limit applies with common shares. If only preferred share consideration is received on a section 85 transfer, and for some reason the fair market value of the shares is found to be less than the cost assigned to them, that cost will be lost.

It may be possible to use section 85 to obtain capital gains treatment on the indirect disposition of property (through a sale of the shares of a corporation to which the property has been "rolled" under subsection 85(1)) whose direct disposition would otherwise be treated as ordinary income if realized by the transferor. However, some jurisprudence suggests that the character of the shares received as consideration is coloured by the character of the property for which the shares were issued (see, for example, *Fraser v. M.N.R.*, [1964] C.T.C. 372, 64 D.T.C. 5224 (S.C.C.)). On that basis, a rollover of inventory to a corporation followed by a sale of the shares of the corporation may still give rise to business income to the transferor. More recent jurisprudence provides more generous treatment, however (see, for example, *Continental Bank of Canada v. The Queen*, [1998] 4 C.T.C. 119, 98 D.T.C. 6505 (S.C.C.)).

Where the greater of the fair market value of the consideration received and the elected amount is less than the fair market value of the transferred property, paragraph 85(1)(e.2) may apply to increase the proceeds of disposition by the amount of the excess. This provision applies only if any part of the excess may reasonably be considered a benefit that the transferor desired to confer on a related person, other than a wholly-owned corporation of the transferor. Because this indirect benefit rule applies only to increase the amount of the proceeds realized by the transferor, there is an element of double taxation that arises when the related persons dispose of their shares and also recognize the value of the benefit.

Subsection 85(2.1) applies on a transfer of property under section 85 (other than a non-arm's length sale of shares subject to section 84.1 or 212.1). This provision reduces the PUC of the share consideration to the extent that the aggregate of the increase in the paid-up capital and the fair market value of any non-share consideration exceeds the elected amount. The significance of PUC for tax purposes is discussed in Part I. D above.

A transfer of property with an accrued loss to a corporation (whether or not under section 85) results generally in the recognition of the loss. If the transferor and the transferee are "affiliated", recognition of the accrued loss may be deferred until the property is transferred by the transferee corporation to an unaffiliated person: see subsections 13(21.2), 14(12), 18(15), 40(3.3) and (3.4), the superficial loss rule in subparagraph 40(2)(g)(i), and the definition of "affiliated persons" in section 251.1.

The rollover that may otherwise be obtained under section 85 is denied if the anti-avoidance rule in subsection 69(11) applies. Subsection 69(11) is a broadly worded anti-avoidance provision that deems a disposition of property to occur for proceeds of disposition equal to fair market value in certain instances involving transfers of property to unaffiliated persons. Since subsection 69(11) only deems the proceeds of disposition on a transfer to occur for fair market value proceeds, and does not adjust the cost of the property to the transferee, great care must be taken to ensure that the provision does not apply, otherwise an element of double taxation will result.

2. Section 85.1: Share-for-Share Exchanges

Section 85.1 provides rollover treatment on certain share-for-share exchanges. Like all rollover provisions, the provision only applies under specified conditions, including the following:

(a) the vendor shareholder has exchanged shares of the acquired corporation for shares of the purchaser corporation;

(b) the exchanged shares are held as capital property by the vendor shareholder;

(c) the purchaser corporation is a Canadian corporation;

(d) the acquired corporation is a taxable Canadian corporation; and

(e) the vendor shareholder and purchaser corporation have not filed a joint election under section 85 with respect to the exchange.

In addition to these conditions, the vendor shareholder and the purchaser corporation must deal with each other at arm's length immediately before the exchange. Paragraph 85.1(2)(b) further provides that the rollover is unavailable if the shareholders of the acquired corporation, separately or together with non-arm's length persons, controlled, directly or indirectly in any manner whatever, the purchaser corporation, or owned more than 50 per cent of the issued shares of the purchaser corporation immediately before the exchange. Unless the prospective shareholders of the purchaser corporation are related to each other, or control is sufficiently concentrated, this requirement should not be an obstacle. If some of the shareholders are not dealing at arm's length, they will be denied the rollover, while those who do deal at arm's length will be able to take advantage of it.

Paragraph 85.1(2)(d) also provides that the rollover is unavailable to any shareholders who receive consideration from the purchaser corporation other than shares of one class. This is true even if the consideration for the old shares was shares of several classes, or a combination of debt and shares.

Where section 85.1 applies, the vendor shareholder is deemed to have disposed of the shares for proceeds equal to their adjusted cost base and to have acquired the new shares for a cost equal to that cost base, unless the shareholder elects to report any gain or loss in a return for the year of the exchange. The purchaser corporation is deemed to have acquired each of the exchanged shares at a cost equal to the lesser of its fair market value and its paid-up capital.

This cost rule for the purchaser corporation applies whether or not a particular vendor shareholder has elected to recognize any gain or loss on the exchange. It is for this reason that numerous public takeover transactions are structured as acquisitions of shares of the target in exchange for shares of the bidder plus nominal cash. The use of cash effectively forces the target shareholders to file an election under section 85 with the bidder if rollover tax treatment is desired. Where a significant portion of the target's shareholders do not need a rollover (for example, if the shares have declined in value below cost or if tax-exempts hold a meaningful percentage of shares), the bidder obtains an adjusted cost base equal to the fair market value of the target shares.

Subsection 85.1(2.1) limits the increase in the PUC of the shares of the purchaser corporation to the total PUC of the exchanged shares of the acquired corporation.

3. Section 51: Conversion Rights

Section 51 provides a rollover on the disposition of a debt obligation where the disposition is made pursuant to the exercise of a conversion right attached to the security. The same rollover is provided where shares of a corporation are exchanged for new shares of the same corporation, without the need for a conversion right. In both cases, the rollover is available provided that the exchanged property is capital property for the holder, and no consideration other than shares of the issuer is received on the exchange. Section 51 applies automatically where these conditions are satisfied. If applicable, subsection 51(1) deems the exchange not to be a disposition of the exchanged property (except for certain enumerated purposes). The cost of the shares received on the exchange is equal to the adjusted cost base of the exchanged property. Where more than one class of shares is received, the adjusted cost base is allocated among the different classes based on their relative fair market value.

Subsection 51(2) contains an anti-avoidance rule similar to that in paragraph 85(1)(e.2) applicable where the fair market value of the shares received on an exchange is less than that of the exchanged property. If the shortfall can reasonably be considered a benefit that the holder intended to confer on a related person, it must be recognized as proceeds of disposition of the exchanged property, along with the adjusted cost base of the property.

Subsection 51(3) ensures that the PUC of the issued shares does not exceed the PUC of any exchanged shares.

Consistent with proposed revisions to other reorganization provisions, proposed amendments provide that subsection 51(1) will not apply to exchanges of specified participating interests (as defined in subsection 248(1)).

4. Section 86: Capital Reorganizations

Section 86 provides rollover treatment on an exchange of shares that occurs in the course of a reorganization of the share capital of a corporation. To qualify for the rollover, the shareholder must dispose of all shares of a class held as capital property (the "old shares") and receive "new shares". Capital gains are recognized on the exchange only to the extent that the value of any non-share consideration received by the shareholders exceeds the adjusted cost base of the old shares.

Where the relevant conditions are met, section 86 applies automatically without the need for an election. The application of the provision is subject to subsections 85(1) to (3) where those provisions apply (subsection 86(3)). On the other hand, the application of section 86 takes precedence over section 51 (subsection 51(4)). Consistent with proposed revisions to other reorganization provisions, proposed amendments provide that subsection 86(1) will not apply to exchanges of specified participating interests (as defined in subsection 248(1)).

Under section 86, the cost to the shareholder of any non-share consideration received on the exchange is deemed to be its fair market value at the time it was received. The cost of the new shares is deemed to be the cost of the old shares less the fair market value of any non-share consideration. The proceeds of disposition of the old shares is deemed to be the aggregate of the cost of the new shares and non-share consideration. If no consideration other than shares is received, section 86 provides a straightforward rollover in that the cost of the old shares becomes the cost of the new shares, and this amount also serves as the proceeds of the old shares. Thus, any gain or loss on the old shares is deemed to be nil, and recognition of potential gain or loss is deferred until the disposition of the new shares.

Subsection 86(2) contains an anti-avoidance rule similar to that in paragraph 85(1)(e.2) and subsection 51(2). If the total value of the consideration received for the old shares is less than their fair market value and that shortfall can reasonably be regarded as a benefit that the shareholder intended to confer on a related person, the amount of the shortfall must be recognized as proceeds for the old shares.

Subsection 86(3) ensures that the PUC of the new shares does not exceed the PUC of the old shares less the fair market value of any non-share consideration received on the exchange.

Section 86.1 provides special rules that may result in a rollover for certain U.S. corporate reorganizations involving Canadian shareholders.

5. Section 87: Amalgamations

All Canadian corporate statutes provide for both statutory and court-ordered amalgamations. Generally, the first step in amalgamating two or more corporations is to prepare an amalgamation agreement which must be approved by the shareholders of the amalgamating corporations. The terms of the agreement cover all of the items that are found in the articles of incorporation, plus the provisions that are being made for shareholders of the various corporations. When the certificate of amalgamation is issued, all of the amalgamating corporations become combined in one amalgamated corporation. For corporate law purposes, the amalgamating corporations are generally deemed to continue to exist as the amalgamated corporation and the amalgamated corporation is deemed to have existed previously as the predecessor corporations (see, for example, *The Queen v. Black and Decker Manufacturing Co. Ltd.*, [1975] 1 S.C.R. 411 (S.C.C.)). The property owned by the amalgamating corporations continues to be the property of the amalgamated corporation. Liabilities, actions, claims, obligations, proceedings, etc., that were enforceable against the amalgamating corporations are enforceable against the amalgamated corporation, as are convictions, rulings, judgments or orders against the amalgamating corporations.

Section 87 of the Act provides rollover treatment on certain amalgamations. The provision applies where two or more taxable Canadian corporations ("predecessor corporations") merge or amalgamate to form one successor corporation (the "new corporation") and the following conditions are met:

(a) all of the property owned by the predecessor corporations becomes the property of the new corporation;

(b) all of the liabilities of the predecessor corporations, other than debts or obligations owed to another predecessor corporation, become the liabilities of the new corporation;

(c) all shareholders of the predecessor corporations, other than a predecessor corporation, receive shares of the new corporation; and

(d) the amalgamation is not realized by way of an asset purchase or a distribution of property on the liquidation of a corporation.

Where section 87 applies, the recognition of tax liability at both the corporate and shareholder level is deferred. At the corporate level, the tax attributes of the predecessor corporations are transferred to the new corporation. Cost bases for depreciable property, capital property, cumulative eligible property, reserves, debts, prepayments, benefit plans, etc. are all deemed to have passed to the new corporation at their current tax costs under subsection 87(2). Accounts that have special tax significance, such as the capital dividend account and RDTOH, are also aggregated at prior tax values in the new corporation. Perhaps most important, the loss carryovers of the predecessor corporations are transferred to the new corporation under subsection 87(2.1), subject to the conditions, described below, that apply on the winding-up of a subsidiary into its parent corporation. This transfer permits the amalgamated corporation to carry forward losses of a predecessor for offset against income that the corporation realizes in later taxation years. In this respect, subsection 87(2.11) is a special provision that applies on the amalgamation of a parent corporation and one or more of its wholly-owned subsidiaries ("a vertical amalgamation"). In that case, the amalgamated corporation is deemed to be the same corporation as the predecessor subsidiary for a number of purposes, including loss carryovers. This deeming rule permits losses of a predecessor subsidiary to be carried back for offset against income and gains of the parent, which can also be done on the winding up of a subsidiary into its parent under subsection 88(1). Although a vertical amalgamation and a winding up are similar in effect, the carry back of losses would not otherwise be available on an amalgamation, because the amalgamated corporation is considered a new corporation under paragraph 87(2)(a) with no prior income.

At the shareholder level, subsection 87(4) permits the tax-free exchange of shares of the predecessor corporations for shares of the new corporation. However, the shares must be capital property of the shareholder and the shareholder may receive no consideration other than shares in the new corporation. Subsections 87(3) and (3.1) ensure that the PUC of the shares of the new corporation do not exceed the PUC of the shares of the predecessor corporations, other than shares held by a predecessor corporation.

A rollover similar to that for shareholders of the predecessor corporations is also provided for holders of debt or options to acquire shares of the predecessor corporations (subsections 87(5) and (6)).

6. Section 88: Winding-Up

The winding-up of a corporation ordinarily results in the realization of accrued gains or losses and deferred income by the corporation. It also results in the realization of gain or loss and deemed dividends for shareholders whose shares are cancelled.

On the winding-up of a corporation, paragraph 69(5)(a) deems the corporation to have disposed of its assets that it distributes to its shareholders at their fair market value immediately before the winding-up. The deemed disposition is for the purpose of calculating the corporation's income in its final taxation year. The shareholders are deemed to acquire the assets at a cost equal to the deemed proceeds (paragraph 69(5)(b)).

On a winding-up of a resident corporation, subsection 84(2) deems a dividend to have been paid on a class of shares equal to the excess of the fair market value of funds or property distributed to the shareholders over the PUC of the class. Where such a "winding-up dividend" has been paid by a Canadian corporation, paragraph 88(2)(b) provides ordering rules that determine the composition of the dividend. The amount of any separate dividend deemed to be paid on the winding-up is attributed to the shareholders *pro rata* based on the number of shares of the class which they hold. The cancellation of the shares on the winding-up constitutes a disposition under the Act (subparagraph (b)(i) of the definition of a "disposition" in subsection 248(1)). The amount of the deemed dividend under subsection 84(2) is not treated as proceeds of disposition of the cancelled shares (paragraph (j) of the definition of "proceeds of disposition" in section 54). In effect, only the PUC and pre-1972 capital surplus on hand (basically, the pre-1972 accrued gain on capital property of the corporation: see subsection 88(2.1)) are treated as proceeds.

A rollover is available under subsection 88(1) on the winding-up of a subsidiary corporation into its parent. Subsection 88(1) applies when the subsidiary is a taxable Canadian corporation and the parent owns at least 90 per cent of the issued shares of each class of stock, provided that any shares of the subsidiary not owned by the parent are owned by persons dealing at arm's length with the parent. The overall effect is to transfer the subsidiary's property to the parent at the subsidiary's tax cost. When the parent disposes of the property, all deferred and accrued gains or income amounts will be recognized by the parent.

On the winding-up of a subsidiary, a corporation's assets will not necessarily be liquidated; the usual pattern is for the property to be distributed to the parent. Potentially all of the subsidiary's property, therefore, will be deemed to have been sold at fair market value by paragraph 69(5)(a). When the corporation that is winding up is a qualifying subsidiary, paragraph 88(1)(a) generally nullifies the effect of paragraph 69(5)(a). To the extent that the subsidiary disposes of property to a shareholder, other than its parent, paragraph 69(5)(a) continues to operate. Thus, it is possible, when the subsidiary corporation is not wholly owned, for the realization of some gains and losses and income amounts on distributions to minority shareholders.

Paragraph 88(1)(d.1) provides that subsection 84(2) does not apply to the winding-up of a subsidiary corporation. Paragraph 88(1)(c) further provides that the cost base of the property for the subsidiary generally becomes the parent's tax cost. Thus, a distribution in kind results in a rollover of the subsidiary's property to its parent. However, to the extent that the adjusted cost base of the parent's shares in the subsidiary exceed the tax cost of the subsidiary's assets, cash on hand and any previously paid tax-free inter-corporate dividends, the excess may be added, within limits, to the cost of certain non-depreciable capital property distributed to the parent (see paragraphs 88(1)(c) and (d)). This cost bump transfers to the cost of the particular underlying assets of a subsidiary the amount of any unrecovered share premium that the parent may have paid on a previous acquisition of the subsidiary. A similar "bump" is available for certain "vertical" amalgamations (subsection 87(11)). Special rules apply to transfers of a resource property or partnership interest on a winding-up (see subparagraph 88(1)(a)(i) and paragraph 88(1)(a.2)).

Even though the primary purpose of subsection 88(1) is to provide a rollover of the subsidiary's property to its parent, paragraph 88(1)(d.1) appears to apply to distributions of the subsidiary's property to its minority shareholders as well. This can present serious problems in some cases as there is no deemed dividend on the winding-up, with the result that none of the distribution can be designated as a capital dividend or a distribution of pre-1972 capital surplus on hand. If a minority shareholder receives a distribution in kind, then the cost base of the property to the shareholder is its fair market value at the time of the transfer.

Tax accounts are not considered to be assets and, in any event, they normally cannot be transferred from one taxpayer to another. However, on the winding-up of a subsidiary corporation, subsection 88(1) permits not only special surplus accounts, but a whole host of other tax attributes of the subsidiary corporation, to be transferred to its parent. These tax attributes include prepaid expenses, employee benefit plans, various reserves, undepreciated capital cost and other attributes. All of the special surplus accounts are transferred at current levels to the parent; the subsidiary's capital dividend account, RDTOH and pre-1972 capital surplus on hand are all added to the parent's tax accounts in the year of the rollover. In addition, the parent corporation may carry over (either forward or back) the subsidiary's net capital losses, non-capital losses and limited partnership losses as if they were incurred by the parent. Loss carryovers are eligible for this treatment only if there is some continuity in the control of both the parent and subsidiary corporations. When there has been a change in control of either corporation, net capital losses become completely non-deductible. Non-capital losses are not treated quite so harshly; under subsection 88(1.1), a parent can deduct its subsidiary's non-capital losses and limited partnership losses after an acquisition of control if the business that generated the losses continues to be carried on for profit. However, even if a non-capital loss or limited partnership loss meets this requirement, it can be applied only against income from the same business that generated it or from any other substantially similar business. It can also be applied against net taxable capital gains on capital property that the parent acquired from the subsidiary corporation. See Part IV of Chapter 2 for a brief description of the loss carryover rules that apply on the acquisition of control of a corporation.

Paragraph 88(1)(b) completes the rollover by deeming the parent to have disposed of its shares of the subsidiary for proceeds that normally avoid recognition of gain or loss. The proceeds are deemed to be equal to the greater of two amounts. The first amount is the lesser of the paid-up capital of the subsidiary's shares or the tax value of its net assets. The second amount is the parent corporation's adjusted cost base of the shares of the subsidiary. Thus, it is impossible for the parent corporation to have a loss on the disposition of the subsidiary's shares. If the tax value of the subsidiary's net assets is greater than the parent's cost base of its shares, the parent will recognize a capital gain on the difference.

Subsection 88(3) provides special rules that may result in a rollover for certain cross-border windings-up of foreign corporations into Canadian parent corporations.

II. RELEVANCE OF INCOME TAX TO OTHER AREAS OF LAW

The importance of appreciating the potential impact of income tax cannot be over-emphasized. Virtually no area of law is immune from income tax issues. In many areas its relevance is obvious — for example, in a corporate practice. In other areas of the law, such as immigration, family, criminal or environmental law, lawyers are often not fully aware of the impact that income tax issues, both positive and negative, may have on their clients. This part is intended to alert you to some of these issues.

A. Corporate and Commercial Law

1. Choosing A Business Format

Although the particular structure that is selected to carry on a business should not be governed by income tax considerations, income tax may play an important role in determining the appropriate business vehicle.

Sole proprietorship or incorporation? There can be some significant tax advantages to choosing a corporate format. These include:

- tax deferral on business income that is eligible for the small business deduction, Canadian manufacturing and processing profits deduction or the general rate reduction, assuming the individual is in the highest personal tax bracket;
- income splitting potential with family members as employees or shareholders;
- estate planning advantages on the transfer of future growth in value to children;
- stabilization of income of the individual through salary payments or greater flexibility in the timing of the receipt of income subject to personal tax; and
- potential access to the $800,000 capital gains exemption (for the 2014 taxation year, indexed thereafter) on a disposition of the shares of a qualifying small business corporation.

Incorporating a business also can result in various tax disadvantages, including:

- a prepayment of tax if the corporate income is ineligible for the small business deduction, Canadian manufacturing and processing credit or the general rate reduction, and the individual is not in the highest personal tax bracket;
- the additional costs of maintaining a corporation including the cost of administrative filings and tax filings; and
- a loss of the availability of business and capital losses to offset personal income.

Often, the income tax benefits will outweigh the disadvantages of incorporating. Careful planning around the optimum mix of salary/dividends also can provide significant benefits to owner-managed businesses.

The main reason for the tax advantages or disadvantages is that a corporation is taxed as a separate entity, whereas a sole proprietorship is not. Business income earned through a sole proprietorship is taxed directly to the proprietor.

Incorporation or partnership? The use of a partnership can provide some benefits compared to the use of a corporate form of business organization, including:

- the potential ability to flow through losses, investment tax credits, and, where applicable, scientific research and experimental development costs and claim them against personal income;
- no double taxation of income on the distribution of profits; and
- distribution of an amount in excess of contributed capital without immediate adverse tax consequences.

Potential disadvantages of a partnership compared to the corporate form of organization include:

- no access to the small business deduction, Canadian manufacturing and processing profits credit or the general rate reduction;
- no access to the $800,000 enhanced capital gains exemption (for the 2014 taxation year, indexed thereafter) on the disposition of the business (although, it may be possible to transfer the business to a corporation on a rollover basis and sell the shares of the corporation at capital gains tax rates (see section 54.2)); and
- limited income-splitting opportunities.

2. Corporate Finance

The capitalization of a corporation generally consists of a combination of debt and equity financing. However, in recent years, hybrid instruments that have characteristics of both debt and equity have become increasingly prevalent.

(a) Debt Financing

The use of debt instruments traditionally has been a favoured form of corporate finance for both tax and non-tax reasons. From a non-tax perspective, the use of debt provides leverage that can produce increased returns on investment for the equity holders of a corporation; however, leverage also increases the risk of business failure. From a tax perspective, the use of debt to capitalize a corporation has a clear advantage to the corporation as interest on the debt is deductible by the corporation if the requirements of paragraph 20(1)(c) are satisfied. Interest is generally taxable to holders of the debt instrument.

When considering the issuance of debt by a corporation to a non-resident, two tax issues need to be considered: application of non-resident withholding tax and the thin capitalization rules. With respect to the first issue, payments of interest to non-residents with whom the payer deals at arm's length are not subject to Canadian withholding tax pursuant to subsection 212(1). Payments of interest to non-arm's length (as defined in section 251) non-residents will be, so long as the interest is not a participating debt interest (as defined in subsection 212(3)). With respect to the second issue, subsection 18(4) denies the deduction of interest expense in circumstances where the total debt owing to "specified non-residents" of a corporation (defined in subsection 18(5)) exceeds 1.5 times the corporation's "equity amount" (also defined in subsection 18(5)). In addition to subsection 18(4) permanently denying the interest expense deduction, paragraph 214(16)(a) deems the non-deductible interest to be a dividend to both the paying corporation and recipient specified non-resident. As such, the deemed dividend will be subject to Canadian withholding tax pursuant to subsection 212(2) as modified by an applicable tax treaty. Subsection 18(8) provides an exception to subsection 18(4) and allows an interest deduction where the corporation must report foreign accrual property income pursuant to subsection 91(1) in respect of the interest.

(b) Equity Financing

Unlike interest payments, dividend payments are not deductible by the payer. Therefore, there is potential for some "double tax" as recipients of dividends must include them in income under paragraph 12(1)(j). However, the impact of this income inclusion and potential for double tax is addressed by the "gross-up" and "dividend tax credit" mechanisms in subsection 82(1) and section 121 and the tax-free treatment of inter-corporate dividends.

Where an interest deduction is not valuable to the borrower, equity financing may be preferred in order to permit the creditor to receive tax-free dividends rather than taxable interest income. The tax savings realized by substituting non-taxable dividends for taxable interest income can be split between the borrower and the creditor. An example is the use of "taxable preferred shares" to capitalize a corporation where such corporation does not need any interest deductions (say, if it has losses) and so is willing to pay non-deductible dividends in return for a lower cost of capital (i.e., the dividend rate on the shares would be lower than that on an equivalent amount of debt). As a result of the distribution taxes in Parts IV.1 and VI.1, taxable preferred shares are tax effective only in very limited situations. A key exception to these taxes is where the equity holder has a "substantial interest" in the corporation (a condition defined in subsection 191(2) that is essentially based upon ownership of shares that comprise at least 25 per cent of the votes and value of the corporation). This exception generally protects equity investments by related persons, and effectively limits the distribution taxes to those situations in which preferred shares are used as substitutes for an arm's length borrowing by taxpayers who are effectively tax exempt.

(c) Hybrid Financing

The financial markets have evolved to a point where the use of hybrid debt/equity instruments (i.e., instruments that have features associated with both debt and equity, such as participating debt, convertible debt, equity-linked debt, etc.) is significant. The provisions of the Act generally have not kept pace with changes in financial markets. Accordingly, a measure of uncertainty exists as to the proper characterization of debt-equity hybrids. Moreover, there is only limited jurisprudence in the area. However, the weight of the existing jurisprudence is that a hybrid instrument should be characterized as debt or equity based upon its predominant characteristics rather than being bifurcated into separate debt and equity components.

(d) Financing Owner-Managed Businesses

A closely-held corporation gives rise to different financing considerations. These corporations and their shareholders typically have significant transactions with each other centered on a tax-effective mix of interest, salary and dividend payments. For ease of flexibility, most such transactions are not paid in cash but rather through adjustments to the appropriate shareholder loan accounts. It is important that the terms of such advances and repayments are properly documented. Further, shareholder loans should provide at least a nominal interest rate. This will strengthen the position that any loss that may be suffered on a disposition of a shareholder loan (say, if the business fails) will not be deemed to be nil under subparagraph 40(2)(g)(ii). Because of the need for flexibility in advances and repayments of investment capital, small business corporations tend not to be financed using significant amounts of equity. Careful attention must be paid to any equity financing and shareholder agreements to ensure that *de jure* control of the corporation resides in the appropriate persons and that the desired status of the corporation (e.g., a CCPC) is unaffected.

3. Corporate Distributions and Reorganizations

See Parts I. D and E of this chapter.

4. Petroleum and Natural Gas

Although most of the provisions of the Act that apply to the computation of business income apply to the petroleum and natural gas sector, the Act contains many provisions that are tailored to the resource industry.

(a) Intangible Expenditures

One unique aspect of resource taxation is the treatment of expenditures on intangible assets. Exploration and development of petroleum and natural gas properties requires significant expenditures that are on account of capital but do not directly relate to the acquisition of tangible property. For income tax purposes, all such costs are classified and aggregated into pools as either "Canadian exploration expenses" ("CEE"), Canadian development expenses ("CDE"), foreign resource expenses ("FRE"), or Canadian oil and gas property expenses ("COGPE") (see the definitions of the above in subsections 66.1(6), 66.2(5), 66.21(1), 66(15) and 66.4(5), respectively). Generally, these resource expenditure pool balances may be deducted based on the following declining balance rates: CEE – 100 per cent; CDE – 30 per cent; FRE – 10 per cent (or 30 per cent of foreign resource income, whichever is greater); COGPE – 10 per cent. These deductions are permissive and any amount up to the maximum may be claimed. The definitions of each type of intangible expenditure are extensive. In general terms, CEE includes expenditures that relate to exploration; CDE includes expenditures that relate to development; FRE includes expenditures that relate to foreign exploration or development; and COGPE includes expenditures that relate to the acquisition of petroleum and natural gas property interests.

(b) Flow-Through Shares

The flow-through share provisions create an exception to the fundamental principle that a corporation is a taxpayer that is separate and apart from its shareholders. Where certain conditions are satisfied, resource expenditures that are incurred by a corporation may be renounced by the corporation in favour of its shareholders, and such expenditures are deemed to have been made by the shareholders. This effectively transfers resource expenditure pools from the corporation that incurs them to the shareholders who finance such expenditures. This tax sheltering feature makes them an attractive financing tool (see subsections 66(12.6) – (12.75)). There is scope for a corporation to renounce prospectively expenditures that it will make in the first 60 days of the following year. This provides an acceleration of deductions. There are also provisions whereby up to $1,000,000 of CDE may be renounced by a corporation but treated as CEE to the shareholders. The adjusted cost base of flow-through shares is deemed to be nil. This results in the entire proceeds of disposition being treated as a capital gain.

(c) Successor Rules

The successor rules in section 66.7 are both beneficial and limiting, depending upon the circumstances. The successor rules allow a taxpayer who has acquired all or substantially all of the Canadian resource properties of another taxpayer to deduct the resource expenditure pools of the first taxpayer (i.e., an important exception to the general principle that a taxpayer can only deduct expenses that the taxpayer incurs). However, where control of a taxpayer has changed (say, from a sale of shares of a corporation), the resource expenditure pools of the corporation become "streamed" and can only be used to shelter income from production from the particular properties. Care must be taken when transferring resource properties or shares of petroleum and natural gas corporations to ensure that all potential benefits from the successor rules are obtained and any unfortunate streaming effects are minimized.

(d) Disposition of Resource Properties

Dispositions of petroleum and natural gas Canadian resource properties are treated in a manner that is somewhat similar to depreciable assets. Generally, that portion of the proceeds that are attributable to intangible assets are credited first to COGPE to the extent of that pool, then subsequently to CDE to the extent of that pool. Any remaining amount is included in the income of the taxpayer.

5. Commercial Real Estate

The Act contains numerous provisions that impact the tax treatment of commercial real estate transactions. The structure and circumstances of a real estate transaction must be carefully considered in order to maximize potential benefits and to avoid pitfalls.

(a) Characterization of Gains and Losses

An enduring issue is whether a gain or loss from the disposition of real property is on account of income or capital. Given that capital gains are taxed at an effective tax rate that is half of that applicable to business income, one can expect that this issue will continue to be litigated well into the future. When real property is disposed of, it will be critical to undertake a detailed review of the circumstances surrounding its acquisition and ownership to ascertain if the desired tax characterization of the gain or loss is possible. See Chapter 7 generally.

(b) Reallocation of Proceeds

Assuming that a gain from the disposition of real property is capital in nature, the proper allocation of proceeds of disposition between land and a building is essential. In this regard, subsection 13(21.1) can be a trap for the unwary. This provision applies where a terminal loss would otherwise result from the disposition of a building but a capital gain would result from the disposition of the underlying land (i.e., the value of the land has appreciated but the value of the building has declined). Subsection 13(21.1) effectively reallocates proceeds of disposition from the land to the building to reduce the terminal loss to the extent of any capital gain.

(c) Inventory Valuation

Subsection 10(1.01) requires land that is held as an adventure or concern in the nature of trade to be valued at cost. Where an ongoing business exists (rather than an adventure or concern in the nature of trade), the taxpayer may continue to apply the lower of cost and fair market value rule in subsection 10(1) and thereby deduct accrued losses on land inventory. See Chapter 6.

(d) Limitations on Deductions

The deduction of costs, expenses and losses is limited in certain circumstances:

- *Carrying costs.* Subsections 18(2) and (2.1) provide important limits on the ability of a taxpayer to deduct property taxes and interest on debt related to the acquisition of land. Generally, these provisions restrict the deduction of interest and property taxes to the net income (i.e., gross revenue less other related expenses) earned from the property. That is, losses cannot be created by deducting interest or property taxes. An exception exists where the land is used in carrying on a business other than a resale or development business. If the principal business of the taxpayer is the rental, lease or development of property, the taxpayer may deduct interest and property taxes in excess of net income to the extent of the developer's "base level deduction". A base level deduction is defined in subsection 18(2.2) as the amount of interest that would be calculated on debt of $1,000,000 at prescribed rates. Provisions require that the base level deduction must be shared among associated corporations (similar to the sharing of the small business deduction limit). Where interest and property taxes are disallowed, the Act provides for an increase to the adjusted cost base of the underlying property (paragraph 53(1)(h)). As a result, any gain on a subsequent disposition is reduced. Where the land is held by a corporation or partnership, the adjusted cost base of the shares of the corporation or partnership interest may also be increased, in certain circumstances.

- *Construction period interest.* Subsection 18(3.1) requires that interest incurred during the period of construction, renovation or alteration of a building be added to the cost of the building. An exception is available where the principal business of the taxpayer is the leasing, rental, sale or development of real property. Specific provisions deal with the determination of the period of construction.
- *Capital cost allowance.* Regulation 1100(11) precludes a taxpayer from deducting capital cost allowance on rental properties in excess of the net income from all rental properties that are held by the taxpayer. Exceptions exist for life insurance corporations or corporations whose principal business is the leasing, rental, sale or development of real property.

(e) Separate Depreciable Property Classes for Rental Properties

Regulation 1101(1ac) requires that rental properties with a capital cost of $50,000 or more be held in separate classes for purposes of capital cost allowance. The effect of this is that, when a building is sold and a terminal loss arises, the taxpayer may deduct the terminal loss even if the taxpayer continues to hold other buildings. In the ordinary case, a terminal loss from the disposition of one asset would be absorbed in the remaining pool balance in the class before being deducted from income. On the other hand, if recapture of depreciation results from a disposition, the amount must be included in income and cannot be offset against other class balances attributable to other buildings.

(f) Tenant Inducement Payments

The Supreme Court of Canada in *Canderel Ltd. v. The Queen,* [1998] 2 C.T.C. 35, 98 D.T.C. 6100 held that a lessor who made a payment to induce tenants to enter into leases of real property could deduct the entire amount of the payment in the year incurred rather than amortize such payments and deduct them over the course of the lease. The recipient of such payments generally must include the same in income as receivable (see *Ikea Ltd. v. The Queen,* [1998] 2 C.T.C. 61, 98 D.T.C. 6092 (S.C.C.)). See Chapter 6.

(g) Replacement Property

The Act allows for a deferral of the recognition of a capital gain and recaptured depreciation where property that is "former business property" (for example, building or equipment) is disposed of and replaced within a certain time frame. Generally, for voluntary dispositions of property, the replacement property must be acquired before the later of the end of the next taxation year and 12 months following the end of the initial year. This is extended by a further 12 months where the disposition was involuntary in nature (e.g., an expropriation). The term "former business property" is defined in subsection 248(1) to mean real property (other than rental property) that is used by the taxpayer or a related person primarily for the purpose of gaining or producing income from a business. Where the rules apply, the acquisition cost of the replacement property absorbs the gain or income from the disposition of the former business property. The replacement property thus has a reduced adjusted cost base and a reduced undepreciated capital cost (subsections 44(1) and 13(4)). See Chapters 6 and 7.

(h) Non-Residents

Unless the property constitutes "treaty-protected property" (as defined in subsection 248(1)) or "excluded property" (as defined in subsection 116(6), a non-resident who disposes of taxable Canadian property, which includes real property located in Canada, is liable to pay as a tax 25 per cent of the gain realized on the disposition pursuant to paragraph 2(3)(c) and section 115. In addition, section 116 generally requires the non-resident vendor to notify the Minister at any time prior to (subsection 116(1)) or within 10 days following (subsection 116(3)) the disposition of the purchaser and the property, including the estimated (if in advance) or actual proceeds of disposition and its adjusted cost base. While not required by the Act, this is typically accomplished by completing and filing Form T2062 with the Tax Services Office responsible for the area where the property is located (see the current version of Information Circular 72-17 for further details).

Where the anticipated (where notice is given in advance) or actual proceeds of disposition exceed the property's adjusted cost base, then the non-resident is additionally required to pay to the Receiver General, or provide security for, 25 per cent of the difference. This entitles the non-resident to a certificate, which can protect the purchaser from being liable to pay 25 per cent (50 per cent in certain cases pursuant to subsection 116(5.3)) of the proceeds of the disposition (without any deductions) asa tax pursuant to subsection 116(5) on behalf of the non-resident (assuming the "certificate limit" as referred to in subsection 116(2) is equal to or greater than the actual proceeds of disposition).

To protect itself, the purchaser should insist that the contract for sale include: (a) the vendor's representation s to its residency status for Canadian income tax purposes, and (b) the purchaser's right to withhold 25 per cent of the purchase price (to remit to the Receiver General pursuant to subsection 116(5)) if the vendor represents that it is a non-resident and does not provide the purchaser with a certificate as described above. The purchaser should also make (and document) "reasonable inquiries" of the residency status of the vendor as of the time of sale as subsection 116(5) absolves the purchaser from personal liability in respect of a non-resident vendor's Canadian income tax liability where after making such inquiries the purchaser had no reason to believe that the vendor was not a Canadian resident.

The provisions in Canada's bilateral tax treaties that allow gains from the alienation of property to be subject to tax only in the state where the alienator is resident typically do not extend to dispositions of real property or shares of corporations whose value is dependent on real property (see, for example, Article XIII of the *Canada-U.S. Income Tax Convention, 1980*). The withholding rules and liability provisions in section 116 generally do not apply if the property disposed of is treaty-protected property (as defined in subsection 248(1)) and the transferor is resident in the appropriate jurisdiction (see subsection 116(5.01)).

Rental payments earned by a non-resident are subject to a 25 per cent withholding tax under Part XIII of the Act (paragraph 212(1)(d)). This rate is typically reduced in Canada's bilateral tax treaties other than for rents on real property situated in Canada. Under section 216, a non-resident can elect to file a Canadian income tax return and be taxed under Part I of the Act with respect to the rental income. This allows for taxation at Part I rates on net income rather than 25 per cent on gross income.

(i) Farm and Fishing Property

The Act is replete with provisions concerning the taxation of farmers and farm income. Of particular relevance are the provisions that: (i) allow a taxpayer to transfer farm property on a rollover basis to a child by way of either a testamentary or *inter vivos* trust (subsection 73(3)); and (ii) exempt $800,000 (for the 2014 taxation year, indexed thereafter) of capital gain realized on the disposition of certain farm property (section 110.6). Simliar rules apply to a fishing property transferred to a child of the taxpayer under subsection 73(4).

(j) Life Estates

Section 43.1 provides rules that apply when a taxpayer disposes of real property while reserving a life estate in the property (with exceptions for certain charitable donations, Crown gifts and transactions to which subsection 73(3) would otherwise apply. The taxpayer is deemed to have disposed of the life estate for fair market value proceeds and to immediately reacquire the same. Therefore, there is a full fair market realization (of both the life and remainder interest) on the transaction. On the subsequent death of the taxpayer, the taxpayer is deemed to have disposed of the life estate for proceeds of disposition equal to its adjusted cost base (thus no gain should result) and the remainder interest holder, if she did not deal at arm's length with the taxpayer, may receive an increment to the adjusted cost base of the land.

B. Taxation on Death

The Canadian income tax regime affects all estates regardless of their size. Under the current regime unrealized capital gains, as well as other amounts of unrealized income, are subject to a deemed disposition immediately prior to death and are, therefore, taxable in the year of death (subsection 70(5)). This tends to produce a "bunching" effect that, in turn, affects the rate at which income tax is levied. The rules affecting taxation on death can be influenced to a large extent by the terms of a will.

The amount of income tax due also may vary depending upon the decisions made by the personal representative. Planning for income tax liability in the terminal year can be an important factor in will drafting, estate administration and estate planning. Some of the more significant considerations are discussed below. They are divided into four general categories.

First, the rules for computing income for the terminal year vary in a number of important respects from those that apply during a taxpayer's lifetime. The most significant of these provide the personal representative with a number of options or elections. Others deem certain types of property to have been disposed of by the deceased immediately prior to his or her death for fair market value proceeds.

Second, a number of provisions provide special tax treatment for specific types of income and capital property. These include provisions regulating rights to income that is accruing at the date of the death, other "rights or things" that would have produced income if disposed of before death, capital property, eligible capital property, resource properties and land inventory.

Third, rules throughout the Act provide special treatment with respect to reserves, the use of capital losses and other deductions and credits in the year of death. Finally, there are a number of provisions that allow for the filing of separate returns.

1. Income

In computing the income of a taxpayer for the year of death, amounts that would have been income for that year if the taxpayer had lived must be included. As well, there may be certain amounts that, although not accrued during his or her lifetime, will be deemed to be income for the terminal year. Under subsection 70(1), income that is payable periodically but that is still accruing at the date of death is, in effect, subject to a notional severance and deemed to have accrued in equal amounts from day-to-day. The amount deemed to have accrued before death is included in income for the terminal year. The remainder will be income of the estate for its first taxation year or income of any beneficiary to whom it is payable. Examples include wages or salaries, interest from bonds, rents, royalties or annuity payments.

If at the time of death the taxpayer had rights to income that do not fall within subsection 70(1), such amounts will, as a general rule, produce income for the deceased's terminal year. Such rights are commonly referred to as "rights or things". Examples of rights or things cited by the CRA in Interpretation Bulletin IT-212R3: Income of Deceased Persons — Rights or Things (March 21, 1990) include dividends declared but unpaid, deferred cash purchase tickets, uncashed matured bond coupons and amounts in respect of which an amount has been deducted in computing income, such as a "cash basis" inventory. Common to each is that the amount "when realized or disposed of would have been included in computing [the deceased's] income". Capital property, eligible capital property, land inventory, resource properties, interests in life insurance policies, and certain participating interests in foreign investment entities are not rights or things for the purposes of the relevant provisions in subsections 70(2) and (3).

From the taxpayer's viewpoint, subsection 70(2) is usually more attractive than inclusion under subsection 70(1). In particular, the deceased's personal representative may:

(a) file a separate return for rights or things (and so access an additional set of marginal tax rates and credits);

(b) transfer rights or things to a beneficiary in whose hands they will be taxed when received and thereby remove their value from the income of the deceased; or

(c) include the net value of the rights or things in the deceased's income for the year of death.

If the personal representative does not choose either the first or the second alternative within one year of the deceased's death or 90 days from the mailing of a notice of assessment, whichever is the later day, the third alternative will become mandatory.

2. Property

(a) Capital Property

The policy of sweeping all unrealized income of the deceased into income applies to unrealized taxable capital gains. Subsection 70(5) deems all capital property owned by the taxpayer immediately prior to his or her death to have been disposed of at that time for proceeds equal to the fair market value of the property. It follows that there may be a capital gain or capital loss and, in the case of depreciable property, either recapture of capital cost allowance or a terminal loss. Correspondingly, the recipient of such property will acquire it at a cost equal to its fair market value immediately before the deceased taxpayer's death.

If the property is depreciable property of a prescribed class, a further adjustment will be required if the fair market value of the property immediately prior to death is less than the capital cost of the property to the deceased. In that case, the recipient will be deemed by paragraph 70(5)(c) to have acquired the property at a capital cost equal to that of the deceased and the excess of the deceased's capital cost over the deemed proceeds of disposition will be treated as if it had been claimed by the recipient as capital cost allowance in previous years.

Capital gains on shares of a qualifying small business corporation or on qualifying farm and fishing property that arise by virtue of a deemed disposition under subsection 70(5) can qualify for the $800,000 (as of 2014, indexed thereafter) capital gains exemption. In addition, if the same capital property is transferred to a spouse trust, the spouse trust is entitled to claim a capital gains exemption for the taxation year in which the deceased's spouse died, to the extent the spouse would have been able to claim an exemption if the eligible capital gains of the trust had been realized by the deceased's spouse directly (subsection 110.6(12)(c)).

There are three issues that generally arise around the operation of subsection 70(5).

(a) What is the fair market value of property at death and, in particular, what factors affect the value?

(b) What assets are considered "owned" by a taxpayer immediately prior to death for purposes of subsection 70(5)?

(c) When and under what circumstances will property be viewed for purposes of the relieving provisions in subsection 70(5) as being transferred as a consequence of death?

(b) Property Transferred to, or in Trust for, a Spouse or Common-Law Partner

(i) To a Spouse or Common-Law Partner

Capital property transferred to a deceased's spouse or common-law partner as a consequence of death is not subject to the deeming provisions in subsection 70(5) if the following conditions are met:

(a) the deceased and his or her spouse or common-law partner were resident in Canada immediately before the death of the deceased; and

(b) the property vests indefeasibly in the spouse within 36 months of the deceased's death and the fact of this vesting is established within 36 months of the death or such longer period as the Minister determines is reasonable in the circumstances upon written application for any extension made within the period.

If these conditions are met, the property is deemed by subsection 70(6) to be transferred to the spouse or common-law partner at its tax cost unless the personal representative elects under subsection 70(6.2) to have subsection 70(5) apply. Such an election might be made to absorb capital losses or terminal losses in the deceased's terminal year.

Subsection 70(6) requires that the property "vest indefeasibly" in the transferee. (Subsection 70(9) imposes a similar requirement for transfers of qualifying farm and fishing property to a child.) *Boger Estate v. M.N.R.*, [1993] C.T.C. 81, 93 D.T.C. 5276 (F.C.A.) suggests that "to be vested indefeasibly an interest must not be subject to a condition subsequent or a determinable limitation set out in the grant". In this respect, there is some authority for the proposition that shares subject to a mandatory buy-sell agreement do not vest indefeasibly in the spouse or common-law partner for purposes of the rollover. In contrast, a right of first refusal in an agreement which imposes an obligation to buy on the survivor, but no obligation to sell on the beneficiary spouse, has resulted in vesting and a rollover of the property. The CRA's views on the meaning of "vested indefeasibly" are set forth in Technical Interpretations 2007-0235171E5 (Jan. 15, 2008) and 9526815 (May 24, 1996) and now archived in Interpretation Bulletin IT-449R: Meaning of "Vested Indefeasibly" (September 25, 1987).

Capital property that is transferred to a testamentary trust for a spouse or common-law partner ("conjugal trust") is also eligible for rollover treatment if the property vests indefeasibly in the trust within the stipulated period and the following requirements are met:

1. the property is property of a taxpayer who was resident in Canada immediately before his or her death;
2. on or after the taxpayer's death, and as a consequence thereof, the property is transferred or distributed to the trust;
3. the conjugal trust is created by the taxpayer's will;
4. the conjugal trust is resident in Canada immediately after the time the property vested indefeasibly in the trust;
5. the spouse or common-law partner is entitled to receive all of the income of the trust that arises before his or her death;
6. no person except the spouse or common-law partner may, before his or her death, receive or otherwise obtain the use of any income or capital of the trust; and
7. it can be established, within the period ending 36 months after the death of the taxpayer, that the property vests indefeasibly in the conjugal trust.

An encroachment on capital for the benefit of the spouse or common-law partner is entirely acceptable; however, the mere possibility of anyone else receiving a "benefit" from the trust assets during the lifetime of the spouse or common-law partner would appear to prevent rollover treatment.

(ii) Tainted Conjugal Trusts

A testamentary instrument that directs the personal representative to pay the debts and discharge the liabilities of the testator, other than those specifically referred to in subsection 108(4), would, according to the CRA, taint a testamentary conjugal trust and prevent rollover treatment. Relieving provisions are available, however, in subsections 70(8) and (9), which permit the personal representative to cure a tainted conjugal trust. The general scheme of the relieving provisions is to permit the trust to qualify as a conjugal trust if the personal representative so elects by listing properties of the deceased at least equal to the value of the debts. These listed properties are then deemed to have been disposed of immediately prior to death for proceeds equal to their fair market value. The mechanics of these rules to qualify a spouse trust can be found in Interpretation Bulletin IT-305R4: Testamentary Spouse Trusts (October 30, 1996) at paras 18–29.

(c) Other Property

The recipient of the mortality gain under a life insurance policy is not subject to tax. However, any savings element equal to the difference between the value of the interest and the adjusted cost basis of the policy must be included in computing the income of the holder in the terminal year (paragraph 148(2)(b)).

A taxpayer owning a registered retirement savings plan ("RRSP"), registered pension plan ("RPP"), registered retirement income fund ("RRIF") or deferred profit sharing plan ("DPSP") may have a tax liability on death. As a general rule, all amounts received by a taxpayer from an RRSP are fully taxable as ordinary income in the year of receipt, whether received as retirement income in the form of annuity payments, as a return of premiums on the collapse of the plan (subsection 146(8)), or upon the annuitant's death (subsection 146(8.8)). Notwithstanding this general rule, special provision has been made for the receipt of RRSP proceeds on the death of the annuitant. If the plan has not matured during the deceased's lifetime, the amount in the plan is included in the deceased's income for the terminal year unless all or a portion of the plan qualifies as a "refund of premiums" (subsection 146(8.9)). To qualify as a refund of premiums, the amount must be paid to, or deemed to have been received by, the surviving spouse or common-law partner of the annuitant or, to children or grandchildren of the deceased who were financially dependent on the deceased.

In contrast, a taxpayer owning a tax-free savings account ("TFSA") will not have a tax liability on death. The value of the TFSA at the time of death will remain tax-free to the deceased with only the income earned after the taxpayer's death being taxable to the estate or the beneficiary of the TFSA. If the taxpayer designates a surviving spouse or common-law partner as the successor of the TFSA either within the TFSA itself or pursuant to his will the surviving spouse or common-law partner will be able to continue enjoying the tax-free benefits of the deceased's TFSA and will not have to report post-mortem income from the TFSA on her return.

3. Deductions, Credits and Exemptions

(a) Deductions

Subject to a few special rules, the deductions that would have been available to the deceased if he or she had lived may be taken for the purpose of computing income for the terminal year. In addition, a number of options or elections are available to relieve some of the tax burden that results from the deemed disposition rules. These options provide more flexibility than the general taxing provisions would otherwise allow.

(i) Reserves

During a taxation year prior to the year of death, the taxpayer may have been entitled to one or more of a variety of deductions with respect to amounts that would otherwise have been included in his or her income for the year but which would not have become payable until sometime in the future. For example, under subparagraph 40(1)(a)(iii), a taxpayer who disposes of a capital property is, in effect, permitted to claim a reserve with respect to that part of the proceeds that is not due until a future year. Similar reserves are permitted for unpaid installments of the purchase price of property sold by the deceased in a business and for unearned commissions of insurance agents or brokers. Consistent with the policy of taxing the value of the deceased's unrealized rights to income in the year of his or her death, such reserves are generally not deductible in the year of death. An exception is made if the right to the amount in respect of which the reserve was allowed is transferred or distributed to the spouse or common-law partner of the deceased or to a conjugal trust as a consequence of the death. If that is the case a deduction in respect of a reserve may be claimed for the terminal year if the personal representative and the transferee so elect. Thereafter the reserve will be treated as if it had been acquired originally by the spouse or common-law partner or the conjugal trust as the case may be (subsection 72(2)).

(ii) Capital Loss Utilization

Allowable capital losses incurred by the deceased in his or her lifetime cannot be transferred to the deceased's estate or to the deceased's successors. Allowable capital losses in the year of death and net capital losses carried over from prior years may be deducted from income from any source in the year of death and the previous taxation year (subsection 111(2)). Allowable capital losses used against other income must first be reduced by the total capital gains exemptions previously claimed by the deceased. Thus, any allowable capital losses that cannot be offset against taxable capital gains realized are only deductible against other income to the extent they exceed the total of all capital gains exemptions previously claimed.

The deceased's personal representative may also elect under subsection 164(6) to treat all or part of certain allowable capital losses and terminal losses realized by the deceased's estate in its first taxation year as those of the deceased in his or her terminal year. Allowable capital losses transferred in this manner may affect the capital gains exemption of the deceased under section 110.6 and result in a reduction in the deceased's income tax. The allowable capital losses that are eligible for this transfer are generally those which exceed the estate's capital gains in its first taxation year. The legal representative must, at or before the time of the election to transfer the losses, file an amended return for the deceased for the terminal year.

Unlike losses incurred in the year of death, which may be carried back to the prior year, losses transferred under subsection 164(6) may only be deducted in computing the taxable income of the deceased in the year of death.

(b) Computation of Tax

(i) Charitable Donations

The rules with respect to charitable donations on death will change for deaths occurring after 2015. Currently, under subsection 118.1(4), charitable gifts made in the year of death (which, by virtue of subsection 118.1(5), include gifts made by will), are deemed to have been made in the immediately preceding taxation year to the extent that a credit is not actually taken in the year of death. This means that the unutilized portion of a donation may be used in calculating the tax credit available for the preceding year. To ensure that gifts made by will qualify for the credit in the terminal year or prior year, the extent of the gift and the charity to whom the gift is to be made should be clearly identifiable. The CRA has also taken the view that if a will grants the executor discretion to donate within a specified range, only the minimum in the range will qualify for a credit in the return for the terminal year or the prior year. A donation over the minimum is considered to be at the trustee's discretion and may be claimed in the estate return only.

For deaths that occur after 2015, donations made by will and designated donations (under an RRSP, RRIF, Tax Free Savings Account or life insurance policy) will no longer be deemed to be made by an individual immediately before the individual's death. Instead, the donation will be deemed to have been made by the estate at the time at which the property is transferred to a qualified donee. In addition, the personal representative of the individual's estate (assuming it is designated as a graduated rate estate) will have the flexibility to allocate the available donation among any of the following: the taxation year of the estate in which the donation is made; an earlier taxation year of the estate, or in the last two taxation years of the individual. The donation must be made in the first 36 months following the death of the individual.

A number of options are available with respect to gifts of capital property. Under the normal rules in paragraph 70(5)(a), capital property is deemed to have been disposed of for proceeds equal to fair market value. However, if the deceased makes a charitable or ecological gift of that capital property, by will or otherwise, and the property has appreciated in value, the legal representative may elect to designate the amount of the gift at an amount not greater than the fair market value of the property and not less than the greater of the property's adjusted cost base and any advantage received by the taxpayer as a result of making the gift. A similar rule applies to works of art described in an inventory and donated by artistes. The designated amount is deemed to be the value of the gift for purposes of determining the credit for charitable or ecological gifts and the proceeds of disposition of the property. The amount chosen should take into consideration the taxpayer's other capital gains or losses, charitable donations and income for the year, and the capital gains deduction under section 110.6.

If the deceased makes a gift of Canadian cultural property as certified by the Canadian Cultural Property Export Review Board, by will or otherwise, its value is used in determining the credit for cultural gifts. A capital gain on the disposition of property that is a cultural gift is specifically exempt from tax provided that the property is disposed of within 36 months after death (see Interpretation Bulletins IT-288R2: Gifts of Capital Properties to a Charity and Others (January 16, 1995); and IT-407R4 (Consolidated): Dispositions of Cultural Property to Designated Canadian Institutions (October 12, 2001)).

(ii) Medical Expenses

The 12-month period within which medical expenses may be claimed is extended in the case of a deceased individual. The legal representative may claim, in the year of a taxpayer's death, medical expenses paid by the representative or the taxpayer within any 24-month period that includes the day of death. This concession recognizes the heavy medical expenses often incurred before the death of an individual, some of which may not be paid until after his or her death. The CRA also has indicated that, if the legal representative of a deceased individual has filed a return for the year of death and subsequently pays additional medical expenses, an adjustment of qualifying medical expenses and the medical expense tax credit can be made, if requested, to reflect such payments.

4. Other Separate Returns

In addition to the separate returns that may be filed for rights and things, separate returns may be filed if the deceased had income from a testamentary trust, a partnership of which he or she was a member, or a business of which he or she was the proprietor, if the death occurred after the close of the taxation year of the trust, partnership or business and before the end of the calendar year in which the taxation year ended. Such occurrences are, except in the case of a beneficiary of a testamentary trust, somewhat limited.

Subsection 150(4) provides that income tax on the income reported in a separate return shall be paid as if the income were the income of another person. However, a number of special rules apply. For example, the deductions that may be claimed on those returns include the stock option deductions, the prospector's and grubstaker's deduction, certain payments such as workmen's compensation and social assistance, unemployment insurance benefit repayments, the home relocation loan deduction, and gifts to a religious order. These deductions may be divided among the terminal returns, but the total amount deducted among all returns must not exceed what could have been deducted if all income of the deceased was reported on the ordinary return. The personal credits (that is, basic personal, married, dependent children, and other dependants) and the age credit may be claimed on each separate return as well as on the ordinary return. The ability to claim multiple credits is one of the main reasons for filing separate returns. Certain other credits may be claimed on the separate returns and may be divided among the terminal returns; but again the total amount claimed is limited to what could have been claimed if all the deceased's income was reported on the ordinary return (see Interpretation Bulletin IT-326R3: Returns of Deceased Persons as Another Person (November 13, 1996)).

C. Family Law

Marriage is a form of economic partnership that, upon dissolution, presents a unique set of family law, economic and income tax problems. Family law practitioners are required to address multiple tax issues including, but not limited to, the deductibility of support payments and legal fees, division of matrimonial property (including the timing of property transfers), the benefit of rollover provisions, and the avoidance of the application of the income attribution rules. Clients are concerned about many issues such as which person can claim the equivalent-to-spouse tax credit, the effect of support payments on the deductibility of child care costs and so forth. Other issues, including the treatment of support payments from or to non-residents, also commonly arise. Counsel should be aware of the basic issues affecting their clients and, with complex family law files, would be well-advised to consult tax experts.

Family law matters have also become more complex with the introduction of federal and provincial legislation in respect of same-sex couples and adult interdependent relationships. Many of the rights and obligations normally associated with marriage have now also been extended to unmarried cohabitants, and it has been judicially recognized that many of the rights accorded to heterosexual cohabitants must also be extended to same-sex cohabitants. For the purposes of the income tax treatment of spousal support, for example, there is no distinction between married and unmarried same or opposite sex couples.

Other financially dependent relationships are also being recognized at the provincial level. In 1999, the British Columbia Law Institute recommended expanding marriage-like rights and obligations to non-conjugal dependent relationships through the vehicle of Domestic Partnership Agreements, either registered or non-registered. Similarly, in 2001, the Law Commission of Canada published, *Recognizing and Supporting Close Personal Adult Relationships*, recommending the expansion of marriage-like rights and obligations to non-conjugal dependent relationships through the vehicle of Registered Domestic Partnerships. In 2003, the province of Alberta formally recognized same-sex and other close non-conjugal dependent relationships in enacting the *Adult Interdependent Relationships Act*, with the primary reason for the use of different nomenclature being the debate over same-sex marriage in that province.

Notwithstanding these provincial measures, for income tax purposes, a spouse is considered to be a legally married person or a person who is a party to a void or voidable marriage. A common-law partner includes a person of the same or opposite sex with whom the taxpayer has been cohabitating in a conjugal relationship for the last twelve months (or for twelve months ending in a prior year without legally separating for at least ninety days thereafter) or for less than twelve months if the taxpayer has a child with the other person. As noted above, for income tax purposes, there is no distinction made in the treatment of these conjugal units. For ease of discussion, therefore, we refer to both spouses and common-law partners as "conjugal partners" and to support payments for either as "conjugal payments".

1. Support Payments

The income tax consequences associated with support payments can vary significantly depending upon the specific terms of the agreement or order and its operative date. Counsel will be required to pay close attention to these items when assessing a client's income tax position. To assist taxpayers and their advisors, the CRA has published Income Tax Folio S1-F3-C3: Support Payments (March 5, 2015).

The income tax treatment of alimony and maintenance was completely overhauled in 1997. Under the current regime, child support payments under agreements or orders made after April 1997 are not included in the recipient's income and no deduction can be claimed by the payer. However, conjugal support continues to be included in the income of the recipient (pursuant to paragraph 56(1)(b)) and is deductible from the income of the payer (pursuant to paragraph 60(6)). The distinction between these amounts is obviously significant. See generally the discussion in Chapter 8. For income tax purposes, "child support" is defined in subsection 56.1(4) (as a "child support amount") as a support amount that is not identified in the agreement or order under which it is receivable as being solely for the support of a spouse or common-law partner or former spouse or common-law partner or person who is a parent of a child of whom the payer is a legal parent. If support payments do not distinguish between conjugal and child support, all support paid will be treated as child support (subsection 56.1(4)).

Conjugal support is under the jurisdiction of the federal *Divorce Act*. Conjugal support payments are taxable to the recipient and deductible to the payor if the payments are made pursuant to an order or written agreement (paragraphs 56(1)(b) and 60(b) as supplemented by sections 56.1 and 60.1). In litigation, the income tax implications of support payments should be considered by the court when it determines the amount of these payments. The recipient will need enough support to cover the additional income tax he or she must pay as a result of receiving that additional income. At the same time, the payer's ability to pay support will be increased by the fact that his or her income tax payments will be reduced because of the deductibility of the support payments. The court order or agreement mandating support payments should be registered with the CRA (Form T1158: Registration of Family Support Payments) to support both the obligation to pay support and the quantum of support for which the conjugal partner is claiming a deduction.

With conjugal support payments, caution must be exercised to ensure that the conditions for deduction are met. Generally speaking, to meet these conditions, the payments must be:

- identified in a written agreement or court order as being solely for the support of a recipient who is a conjugal partner, former conjugal partner, or the parent of a child of whom the payer is a legal parent,
- payable on a periodic basis to such recipient (as opposed to a third party) for his or her maintenance (as opposed to expenditures on a self-contained domestic establishment in which the payer resides or expenditures for the purchase of tangible property or for civil law corporeal property (with some limited exceptions set out in subsection 60.1(2)), and
- usable at the recipient's discretion.

Where all of the conditions are not satisfied, which is often the case when conjugal partners begin the process to dissolve their legally recognized relationship, then absent legislative relief, conjugal support payments made during this time will not be deductible. To minimize the likelihood of a successful negligence action, family law practitioners should advise their clients of all of these conditions (and possible strategies to satisfy them) prior to any payments being made.

Lump sum payments and payments for amounts in arrears may or may not be deductible depending on the circumstances. A lump sum payment, paid either at once or in installments over a specified time, is generally not deductible by the payer, with exceptions for the lump sum payment of arrears of periodic payments.

Caution also must be exercised when making payments to third parties on behalf of a conjugal partner, if the deductibility of those payments is not to be compromised. In general terms, an amount paid to a third party for the benefit of the recipient partner is deemed to have been paid to and received by the recipient only if the recipient has discretion as to the use of the amount paid. A deeming provision also may assist the payer to obtain a deduction under paragraph 60(b) for such third-party payments provided they otherwise qualify (subsection 60.1(2)). In order for these provisions to apply, however, the court order or written agreement must specifically so state.

Child support payments fall under the jurisdiction of the federal Child Support Guidelines, which were enacted May 1, 1997. The objectives of the Guidelines are to establish a fair standard of support, to reduce conflict by standardizing the calculation of support payments, and to improve the efficiency of the legal process through the promotion of settlement while providing both objectivity and consistency. The Child Support Tables (which were most recently updated on December 31, 2011), which are schedules to the Guidelines, set out the amount of basic monthly child support payments as calculated on the basis of the annual income of the payer and the number of children for whom support is being paid. There is a separate table for each province and territory, and the amounts vary for each jurisdiction due to differences in provincial income tax rates. The Tables are based on the income of the payer alone. In calculating child support, the courts use the table for the province in which the payer ordinarily resides at the time the application is made. If the payer is a non-resident, the courts use the table for the province in which the applicant ordinarily resides at the time of the application.

With the coming into effect of the federal Child Support Guidelines, the income tax treatment of child support is dependent upon the commencement date specified by the separation agreement or court order. Counsel with clients who had an agreement or order in place prior to the enactment of the new Guidelines may need to determine whether a variation would be beneficial for income tax purposes, as the weightiest factor may be the change to the tax treatment of the child support payments. A careful analysis of each party's financial position will be warranted if one or the other is asking questions regarding the variation of a pre-May 1997 agreement or order. Any variation will bring the support matter into the jurisdiction of the new Guidelines such that the receiving parent will no longer pay tax on child support received and the paying parent will no longer receive a tax deduction for the amount paid. Any adjustment of child support payments will be made in light of the financial position of the parties, with the overriding consideration being, as always, the best interests of the child.

Generally speaking, unless modified by an applicable tax treaty, support amounts are treated the same under Canadian income tax law despite the payer or recipient being non-resident. Further, there is no requirement for a resident payer to withhold income tax from any support amounts (whether conjugal or child support) paid to a non-resident.

2. Division of Matrimonial Property

The legislative trend in Canada has been to view marriage, in many respects, as an economic partnership of broad scope. The various provincial and territorial statutes all seek an orderly, equitable and fair settlement of property and financial matters on marital breakdown. The income tax consequences for transfers of matrimonial property must be carefully considered and measured by family law practitioners for equalizing purposes. This will be an especially important tool for counsel during negotiations.

(a) The Principal Residence Exemption

While the disposition of a matrimonial home can result in a taxable capital gain (where the fair market value of the home at the time of the disposition exceeds its original cost), this gain can be reduced or even eliminated where the home is properly designated as the couple's principal residence (as defined in section 54) and the principal residence exemption is claimed (pursuant to paragraph 40(2)(b)). For property to be eligible to be designated as a principal residence for a particular year, the property must constitute a housing unit, a leasehold interest in a housing unit or a share of the capital stock of a co-operative housing corporation and must have been ordinarily inhabited by the couple or any of their children during the year (see Chapter 7). Further, for taxation years after 1981, conjugal partners are allowed only to designate only one property as their principal residence each year until the year after separation. If the conjugal partners in the face of a marriage breakdown own more than one property that might qualify as a principal residence, they should agree which property should be designated as the principal residence for each of the relevant years.

(b) RRSPs

If an RRSP or RRIF is transferred as a result of a marital breakdown pursuant to a separation agreement or court order, no income will be triggered and no taxes will be payable by virtue of the conjugal rollover provisions (paragraph 146(16)(b) and Form T2220). Given this preferable result, parties will frequently use this rollover provision to equalize RRSPs on a breakdown of a marriage or common-law partnership. Counsel will need to carefully scrutinize any RRSPs being rolled over to make sure that they can be dealt with by the recipient in a tax-effective manner. Locked-in plans will require special attention because they differ substantially from RRSPs that are not locked-in. When drafting a separation or settlement agreement, it will be prudent for counsel to include the exact nature of all RRSPs in a schedule to the clause dealing with the RRSP rollover.

The recipient (the holder of the RRSPs upon equalization) will require a discount for the amount of tax that will inevitably be paid on them when they are collapsed and taken into income. As the payment of tax on RRSPs is inevitable, where RRSPs are not to be equalized in a matrimonial property division, it has become customary to arbitrarily apply a 25 per cent tax discount to the value. In other words, where a conjugal partner is retaining his or her RRSPs on marriage breakdown, the value is to be discounted by approximately 25 per cent in determining net family property (NFP).

(c) Pensions

In a matrimonial property division, the key issue with respect to pensions is their current valuation on an after-tax basis. The proper amount of tax to be deducted (the discount) will be debated and negotiated and obviously, the higher the rate of tax to be deducted at valuation, the lower the present value of the pension. To assist in this regard, the Canadian Institute of Actuaries has enumerated standards with respect to long- and short-term interest, mortality tables and methodology for valuing pensions for family law purposes. Counsel would be well-advised to seek specialized assistance in valuing pension benefits.

(d) The Canada Pension Plan ("CPP")

CPP contributions are mandatory for most income earners, as governed by the terms of the federal Canada Pension Plan. The CPP is structured to reflect increases in the Consumer Price Index, and contributions are made by both employer and employee, as well as by individuals who are self-employed. As contributions vest immediately and may not be withdrawn, members do not benefit until they are eligible to receive monthly pension benefits. Upon the breakdown of the conjugal relationship, CPP provides for equal splitting of unadjusted pensionable earnings ("credits") earned during cohabitation. All credits earned are essentially pooled and divided equally between conjugal partners. When each party receives CPP benefits, he or she receives the adjusted amount. Parties can only opt out of credit splitting by express written agreement that has not been invalidated by a subsequent court order.

3. Conjugal Rollovers

There is an automatic rollover for transfers of capital property between conjugal partners who are both residents at the time of transfer during their relationship or as part of a family law settlement pursuant to section 73. In this case, while there is still a disposition for tax purposes, the disposition is deemed to occur at the transferor's adjusted cost base, thereby postponing the recognition of the gain and associated tax consequences until the recipient disposes of the property.

If the conjugal partners do not want this result, they may choose to opt out of the automatic rollover provisions by having the transferor simply report the disposition at fair market value. In this case, the transferor will be liable for the tax on any capital gains from the time of the original acquisition to the date of transfer (and the recipient will acquire the property with a cost base equal to the fair market value at the time of transfer). Given that the transferor must report the transfer at fair market value to avoid the automatic rollover, counsel for the recipient should strongly consider including this treatment by the transferor in the settlement agreement or court order.

4. Income Attribution

The income attribution rules do not apply after a divorce or termination of a common-law partnership. During the period that the conjugal partners are living separate and apart by reason of a breakdown in their relationship, the income attribution rule in section 74.1 also will not apply (paragraph 74.5(3)(a)). However, the capital gains attribution rule in section 74.2 will continue to apply during the legal separation unless the couple jointly elects that it not apply, and the transferor partner reports the transfer at fair market value in his or her tax return (paragraph 74.5(3)(b)).

5. Legal Fees

Legal fees incurred by a payer on account of child or conjugal support are not deductible in the computation of income under any circumstances. Legal fees incurred by a recipient may be deductible, however, depending upon the relief sought. Historically, legal fees incurred in establishing a right to conjugal support or in obtaining a divorce were not deductible as such costs were considered on account of capital or were personal or living expenses. Legal fees incurred to obtain an increase in support were also non-deductible. However, the courts' and the CRA's current position is that legal fees and other costs (i.e., accounting fees) incurred to obtain support, to increase support amounts, to enforce a pre-existing right to support, and to update a pre-May 1997 child support award so it will be non-taxable are now deductible (see the comments in paragraphs 3.81–3.84 in Folio S1-F3-C3: Support Payments (March 5, 2015)). Legal fees in relation to custody and access remain non-deductible.

6. Domestic Contracts

Any contract arising out of a relationship breakdown, be it a separation agreement or a matrimonial settlement, must contain clauses that address the income tax implications of what has been agreed to, including support payments and property transfers. Before a settlement is finalized, the particular circumstances of the individual client must be carefully reviewed to determine the impact on both conjugal partners. It is clear that a court cannot disregard an agreement. In fact, section 15.2(4) of the *Divorce Act* provides that, in making a conjugal support order, the court shall take into consideration any previous order, agreement or arrangement relating to the support of either conjugal partner. The courts cannot vary a previous agreement or order made under the *Divorce Act*, unless the applicant for the variation has established a material change in circumstances since the agreement was made. Once a material change has been established, a court will consider what amount of support, if any, is justified under the Act.

In dividing matrimonial property, the parties must consider whether or not they wish the automatic conjugal rollover provisions discussed above to apply to the transfer of various properties. If they do not want the provisions to apply, then they must specifically opt out of the provisions (subsection 73(1)), and the transferring spouse or common-law partner must agree to file the appropriate election (for which there is no official election form) with his or her income tax return for that year, all of which should be captured within a clause of a filed or registered domestic contract so as to avoid confusion, expense and future litigation. If the transferring spouse or common-law partner files his or her tax return electronically, then the written election that would normally be attached to the paper return must be sent to the CRA. If the automatic rollover provisions will apply, then the parties should take steps to protect each other from potential capital gains attribution by agreeing to sign and file the appropriate joint election with their income tax returns (subsection 74.5(3)). If the parties own more than one property that could qualify for the principal residence exemption, they should agree in writing which property will be designated as their principal residence for each of the relevant taxation years.

D. Civil Litigation

1. Damages, Interest and Other Payments

(a) Damage Awards

Generally, amounts received by a taxpayer as special or general damages for personal injury or death are not included as income for taxation purposes. General damages may, however, be taxable if they are to compensate for income from a source that would have been taxable had it been received. See Chapter 2.

(b) Interest

As a general rule, both pre- and post-judgment interest will be taxable to the recipient pursuant to paragraph 12(1)(c) if it is in "the nature of interest", which has been described by the courts as "the return or consideration or compensation for the use or retention by one person of a sum of money belonging to ... or owed to another". (See, for example, Income Tax Technical News No. 30 (May 21, 2004); and *Tourigny v. The Queen*, 2008 D.T.C. 2213 (T.C.C.). However, pre-judgment interest was held to be tax-free in *Ahmad v. The Queen*, [2002] 4 C.T.C. 2497, 2002 D.T.C. 2065 (T.C.C.) on the basis that there was "no principal" on which interest could accrue before judgment. Administratively, the CRA's current position appears to be that pre-judgment interest will be taxable if the underlying award is taxable pursuant to the "surrogatain principle" described by the Supreme Court of Canada in *Tsiaprailis v. Canada*, [2005] 1 S.C.R. 113, 2005 SCC 8, 2005 CarswellNat 431, 2005 CarswellNat 432 (see, for example, Income Tax Technical News No. 30, *supra*, and Technical Interpretation 2013-0475631I7 "Treatment of Settlement Amounts" (February 12, 2013)). As such, pre-judgment interest for wrongful dismissal will be considered taxable, while such interest on an award for personal injury or death, or retroactive workers' compensation claims, will not. Further, interest earned on a damage award for personal injury will be tax-free through to the end of the year in which the plaintiff turns 21 (paragraph 81(1)(g.1)). The same will apply to interest earned on that interest (paragraph 81(1)(g.2)), and to capital gains on investments or other property purchased with the award (subsection 81(5)); these rules apply to other income from the property as well, including dividends or rent.

(c) Legal Fees

In the context of civil litigation, the question of whether legal fees are deductible depends on the purpose for which they were incurred. Counsel will look both to the specific provisions of the Act and to general commercial principles when advising clients as to the deductibility of legal fees. In the employment law context, legal fees incurred to collect or establish a right to collect, an amount that, if received, would be included in computing the taxpayer's income under subdivision a, are deductible (paragraph 8(1)(b)). Expenses paid to protect a right to employment through a wrongful dismissal suit are generally not deductible (but see below); nor, generally, are legal fees incurred in defending against charges of professional misconduct (*Blagdon v. The Queen*, [2003] 4 C.T.C. 107, 2003 D.T.C. 5491 (F.C.A.)). Legal fees incurred to collect a "retiring allowance" (which is defined in subsection 248(1) to include a wrongful dismissal award, severance pay and a termination payment, whether awarded by a court or settled out of court will be partially deductible to the extent that the taxpayer has income from the retiring allowance in that year, subject to carry-forward (paragraph 60(o.1)).

2. Employment Litigation

Litigation surrounding breach of contract in the employment context raises several income tax issues. Much employment litigation is based upon either loss of employment or wrongful dismissal, where compensation is based upon a requisite notice period and may come in the form of a lump sum. Before 1978, damages from loss of employment were received free of tax, because an award of damages in breach of contract or tort was not considered to be remuneration for the performance of the duties of the employment and therefore was not considered income for tax purposes. The Act has now been amended to subject all types of severance payments to tax.

(a) Retiring Allowances

Subsection 248(1) defines a "retiring allowance" as an amount received "on or after retirement of a taxpayer from an office or employment in recognition of the taxpayer's long service" or "in respect of a loss of an office or employment whether or not received as, on account or in lieu of payment of, damages or pursuant to an order or judgment of a competent tribunal". A retiring allowance is taxed not as income from employment but rather as "other income". and includes any amount paid to an employee, former employee or third party on behalf of the employee or former employee, so long as the amount is paid in respect of loss of office or employment (see generally Interpretation Bulletin IT-337R4 (consolidated): Retiring Allowances (February 1, 2000)). A portion of a payment received as a retiring allowance in respect of years of employment before 1996 may be transferred to an RRSP or RPP free of tax (paragraph 60(j.1)).

(b) Non-Taxable Amounts

Not all amounts paid on loss of employment will be taxable. For example, damages for defamation will be tax-free (*Bedard v. M.N.R.*, [1991] 1 C.T.C. 2323, 91 D.T.C. 573 (T.C.C.)). Further, the Supreme Court of Canada has held that a settlement in compensation for loss of intended employment is not taxable where a prospective employer terminates an employment contract before a taxpayer's employment has actually commenced (*Schwartz v. The Queen* [1996] 1 C.T.C. 303, 96 D.T.C. 6103, excerpted in Chapter 2). In other words, damage awards for breach of an employment contract before the employment has actually commenced will escape tax. Damages for physical or mental injuries suffered at the hands of an employer may be tax-free where the complaint is a "claim existing apart from the loss of employment" (*Dunphy v. The Queen*, [2010] 2 C.T.C. 2335, 2010 D.T.C. 1028 (T.C.C.)). Similarly, amounts paid to persons as compensation for having been the victim of a crime will, in most cases, be exempt from taxation (paragraph 81(1)(q)).

Amounts paid on account or in lieu of general damages for loss of self-respect, humiliation, mental anguish etc. may not be taxable if the amounts are unrelated to the loss of employment (see Interpretation Bulletin IT-337R4 (Consolidated): Retiring Allowances (February 1, 2006)). This exception may also apply to exclude a reasonable amount in respect of general damages when a loss of employment involves a human rights violation. The CRA's position is that the issue of whether a human rights violation has occurred (and whether a portion of the settlement or award reasonably relates to the violation) is a question of fact. A portion of the settlement or award may be non-taxable where the CRA is satisfied that the damages relate to events or actions separate from the loss of employment. In making such a determination, the CRA provides that the amount of severance that the employee would reasonably be entitled to will be taken into account. In order to secure the most favourable tax position for a client, counsel will have to draft minutes of settlement that carefully enumerate the grounds upon which the settlement is based.

3. Personal Injury Awards

(a) Pecuniary Loss

Damages for pecuniary loss will be awarded by the courts to cover loss of future earning capacity, loss of income, pre-trial expenses, cost of future care, and familial claims such as loss of consortium and housekeeping. The largest component of this head of damages is frequently loss of future earning capacity, particularly in litigation involving young plaintiffs. No deduction for income taxes will be taken from this head of damages, on the policy basis that a defendant must still make full restitution, not something less (see *Jennings v. Cronsberry*, [1966] S.C.R. 532; *Cunningham v. Wheeler*, [1994] 1 S.C.R. 359). One exception may be fatal accident cases, where income tax is taken into account by the court prior to setting an award. As confirmed in paragraph 2 of Interpretation Bulletin IT-365R2 (archived): Damages, Settlements and Similar Receipts (May 8, 1987), such damage awards are generally not taxable to the recipient.

(b) Non-Pecuniary Loss and Non-Compensatory Damages

Unlike damage awards for pecuniary losses, which are meant to replace or provide income, awards for non-pecuniary loss are intended to compensate an injured plaintiff for non-financial damage such as pain and suffering. Tax will not normally be taken into account or "built-in" by the courts in making non-pecuniary awards. As with damage awards for pecuniary losses, these damage awards will also not be taxable to the recipient.

(c) Structured Settlements

A structured settlement is a CRA-approved mechanism (see Interpretation Bulletin IT-365R2, *supra*, at paragraph 5) for disbursing damage awards, particularly used in the context of serious personal injuries, whereby funds for a plaintiff's care are invested to produce an annuity, which is entirely tax-free to the plaintiff throughout his or her lifetime, even though a portion of the annuity would normally have been taxable as interest. Structured settlements typically offer significant tax savings to a plaintiff, particularly when the plaintiff is in a high income tax bracket. A structured settlement will likely be composed of two elements, namely, lump sum payments and periodic payments, each paid at specified intervals, depending upon the particular circumstances of the plaintiff. Often, payments will increase each year by a fixed percentage, to partially protect against inflation. Once the value of an award for personal injury has been determined, counsel will need to advise the client of the various methods for disbursing the award. Options include: a) using the award to make capital purchases; b) investing in a portfolio of financial assets; and/ or c) receiving a stream of income in the form of a structured settlement.

Will a client who has sustained personal injuries in an automobile accident be subject to tax on an out-of-court settlement made with an insurer in circumstances where benefits are structured as ongoing periodic payments? The answer appears to be no. Generally, amounts received by a taxpayer as special or general damages for personal injury are excluded from income. See Chapter 2. The award should remain non-taxable notwithstanding that damages have been determined with reference to the loss of earnings of the taxpayer or that they are ongoing and periodic. This is particularly the case where a settlement is structured so that the defendant purchases an annuity in the name of a plaintiff, with no tax payable on the interest generated by the investment, depending upon payment periods and the value of payments.

One exception to this general rule is in the context of disability insurance plans. The same result will not occur where an out-of-court settlement is made with an insurance company under a disability insurance plan to which the individual's employer contributed with regard to a long-term disability claim. A lump-sum payment received by a taxpayer in lieu of overdue periodic payments in these circumstances is taxable (paragraph 6(1)(f)), as the lump sum does not alter the character of the payment. Further, if the settlement includes a lump sum for wrongfully withheld back-payments, the taxpayer may be in a much worse position than if the disability payments were made annually. Had such payments been made annually, the income tax for each year would have been paid at progressive rates as the payments were received. Lump-sum payments may attract higher rates, leaving individuals with less after-tax income. In some cases, section 110.2 (in connection with section 120.31) can alleviate this hardship by allowing the taxpayer to have the portion of the lump sum relating to previous taxation years effectively taxed at the rates that would have been applicable had the payments actually been received and taxed in those years (plus an interest charge).

E. Criminal Law

1. Taxation of Illegal Income

All income, whether legally or illegally earned, is taxable if it constitutes income from the carrying on of a business. Thus, income generated from the sale of illegal drugs, bookmaking, fraud or extortion, to take obvious examples, is subject to tax. See Chapters 2 and 5. Most clients, however, will not have reported such illegal income for income tax purposes. The CRA often attempts to collect outstanding income taxes with respect to such income-earning activities once criminal charges are laid. The collection process often begins by the issuance of a net worth assessment. This assessment can extend back several years and may lead to substantial income tax liability in addition to the criminal charges faced by the client.

2. Net Worth Assessments

The statutory basis for a net worth assessment is found in subsections 152(4) and (7). The latter provision provides that, in making an assessment, the Minister of National Revenue is not bound by a return or information supplied by or on behalf of the taxpayer and may, notwithstanding the return or information so supplied, or if no return has been filed, assess the tax payable. The Minister is entitled to make this assessment estimating the taxpayer's income based on the best available evidence. Once assessed, the initial legal burden is on the taxpayer to disprove the assessment on a balance of probabilities (see, for example, *Johnston v. M.N.R.*, [1948] C.T.C. 195, 3 D.T.C. 1182 (S.C.C.)).

Case law suggests that the traditional method of calculating taxable income using the net worth method is to determine (or attempt to determine) the taxpayer's net worth at the beginning and end of each year in question and add to the difference the taxpayer's expenditures. Obviously, this method of determining a taxpayer's income may be somewhat imprecise.

3. Garnishment

Funds seized during criminal prosecutions also may become subject to a garnishment order issued by the CRA. Subsection 224.3(1) enables the Minister of National Revenue to issue a garnishment order in instances where moneys have been seized from a taxpayer by the police in the course of administering or enforcing the criminal law of Canada under circumstances where the moneys may be restored to the taxpayer. A receipt issued by the Minister operates to discharge the police from the requirement to return the seized money to the debtor.

4. Defence of Charges under the Act

Criminal lawyers may also be called on to represent clients charged with an offence under the Act. The Act is replete with both criminal and quasi-criminal offences relating to both taxpayers and, more recently, their advisors. An important issue is the extent to which information gleaned by the CRA during an audit of a taxpayer may be used to support the criminal prosecution of that taxpayer under the Act. The Supreme Court of Canada has determined that a warning must be given to the taxpayer by the CRA that the taxpayer has constitutional rights against self-incrimination when the predominant purpose of the audit shifts and becomes a criminal investigation (see *The Queen. v. Jarvis* (2002), [2003] 1 C.T.C. 135, 2002 D.T.C. 7547 (S.C.C.)).

5. Legal Fees

The income tax treatment of legal costs incurred to defend against criminal charges may also be of importance to clients. Two of the more common issues include: (1) whether a payment made on behalf of an employee to defend him or her on criminal charges constitutes a taxable benefit to the employee; and (2) whether legal fees paid to defend the payer against criminal charges are deductible. With respect to the first issue, the courts have held that, to avoid the inclusion of the amount as a taxable benefit, there must be a nexus between the outlay and the requirements of the taxpayer's position as employee or director. With respect to the second issue, the courts have held that where the primary purpose of the conduct which led to the criminal charges was an income (as opposed to a personal) purpose, the legal fees incurred to defend against the charges will be deductible for tax purposes. See Chapter 5.

F. Aboriginal Law

See Chapter 3 at Part VI.

G. Environmental Law

In recent years, individuals and governments around the world have become very concerned with the current state of our environment and the steps that should be taken to preserve and enhance it for future generations. In response to these concerns, Canada, like many other nations, has implemented a variety of programs to reduce environmental damage and promote positive environmental behaviour. The following are some of the more common measures in the Act.

1. Accelerated CCA Claims for Environmentally Friendly Assets (Paragraph 20(1)(a))

Environmentally friendly (i.e., renewable or energy efficient) assets that fall within Classes 34, 43.1, and 43.2, are eligible for accelerated capital cost allowance claims than would otherwise be allowed under Classes 1, 2, or 8. In each of its last four budgets (beginning in 2010), the federal government has expanded these classes to further encourage businesses to invest in clean energy generation and energy efficient equipment.

2. Canadian Renewable and Conservation Expenses (Sections 66 and 66.1 and Regulation 1219)

Generally speaking, "Canadian renewable and conservation expenses" are expenses that are incurred in projects for developing clean energy (i.e., renewable or energy efficient) where at least 50 per cent of the depreciable assets used in such projects would properly belong in Classes 43.1 and 43.2 referred to above. Such expenses are generally deductible in the year incurred as opposed to being treated as non-deductible capital expenditures. They may be deducted by the taxpayer who incurs the expenses or, where such expenses are incurred by certain corporations that have issued flow-through shares to their shareholders, by the shareholders.

3. Contributions to or Acquisition of a Qualifying Environmental Trust (Paragraphs 20(1)(ss) and (tt))

A "qualifying environmental trust" is a trust that is maintained for the sole purpose of funding the reclamation of a site that had been used primarily for, or in combination with, the operation of a mine, the extraction of clay, peat, sand, shale, or aggregates (including dimension stone and gravel) or the deposit of waste in the province in which the trust is resident. A contribution to a qualifying environmental trust is deductible in the year that the contribution is made rather than in the year that the reclamation expense is incurred. Similarly, the costs to acquire a beneficial interest in a qualifying environmental trust are deductible in the year the interest is acquired. These provisions alleviate potential timing problems arising from taxpayers being required by governments to fund their reclamation expenses in advance of actually performing the reclamation.

4. Gifts of Ecologically Sensitive Land (Paragraphs 38(a.2) and 110.1(1)(d) and Section 118.1)

When a taxpayer makes a gift or other transfer of property, the taxpayer is required to calculate and include in income any gain in the value of the gifted (or transferred) property from the time the property was acquired to the time the gift or transfer was made. However, where the property is land (including a servitude, a covenant, or a conservation easement) that is certified by the Minister of the Environment to be "ecologically sensitive land, the conservation and protection of which is, in the opinion of the Minister, important to the preservation of Canada's environmental heritage", any gain in the value of such land or other listed real property interests will be deemed for tax purposes to be nil (see Chapter 8). This tax treatment makes such gifts appealing to taxpayers as they will still be eligible to deduct the fair market value of the gift (if the gift is made by a corporation) or claim a tax credit (if the gift is made by an individual either in the taxation year in which the gift is made or up to 10 years in the future). According to the Environment Canada website, since 1995 (when the Canadian Ecological Gift Program was created), there have been over 1,110 ecogifts valued at over $716 million protecting over 166,000 hectares of wildlife habitat.

5. Public Transit Pass Credit (Section 118.02)

The public transit pass credit gives a taxpayer who acquires an "eligible transit pass" (typically a monthly pass) for use of "public commuter transit services" for either the taxpayer, the taxpayer's spouse or common-law partner or child under the age of 19 years, a non-refundable tax credit equal to the price of the pass (less any reimbursements, allowance, or any other forms of assistance) multiplied by the "appropriate percentage" (that is, the lowest federal marginal rate of 15 per cent in 2015). The purpose of this credit, as announced in the 2006 Budget, is "to encourage individuals to use public transit, ease traffic congestion in urban areas and improve the environment".

10

Dispute Resolution, Statutory Interpretation and Tax Avoidance

This chapter covers several topics, all loosely connected with tax planning. Tax planning involves the review of a client's proposed plan of action to ensure that it is carried out so as to minimize the overall tax consequences and avoid any unintended tax consequences. If the tax system were neutral, a client's business decisions would be made without regard to tax consequences. However, the tax system is not neutral; in many cases, the same business objective can be achieved in different ways with different tax consequences depending on the method chosen. A tax professional's job is to ensure that the client is aware of the consequences, and of any alternative arrangements that can achieve the same results but in a more tax efficient manner.

Tax planning often involves "tax avoidance": open attempts to take advantage of the tax laws by arranging a taxpayer's affairs to reduce the amount of tax payable. Certain types of tax planning are viewed by the Canada Revenue Agency ("the CRA") and the courts as constituting acceptable tax planning, and therefore legitimate tax avoidance, while others are not. The line between the two types is not always clear, and the grey area is often the subject of dispute between taxpayers and the tax authorities.

Such disputes generally come to light in the context of an audit of the taxpayer. The resolution of such disputes involves both the interpretation of the relevant provisions of the *Income Tax Act* ("the Act") and their application to a particular situation. The court's approach to statutory interpretation thus plays a crucial role in the outcome of much tax litigation.

It is sometimes difficult to distinguish between the judicial approach to the rules of statutory interpretation and their approach to tax avoidance. This confusion arises partly because tax avoidance schemes often depend on an interpretation of the wording of the income tax legislation or the absence of provisions specifically prohibiting the taxpayer's treatment of the transactions under consideration. In other words, all tax avoidance cases necessarily involve statutory interpretation; however, not all cases involving statutory interpretation are tax avoidance cases.

This chapter begins with an overview of the dispute resolution process. It then considers the approach of Canadian courts to the interpretation of tax legislation and reviews other statutes that affect the interpretation of the Act. Tax avoidance, as distinguished from tax evasion, is then considered. Finally, the lawyer's ethical and professional responsibilities in advising clients in tax planning are briefly considered.

I. DISPUTE RESOLUTION

A. Returns and Assessment

The tax process begins with the filing of a return by the taxpayer with the CRA. The CRA is a quasi-independent agency of the Government of Canada which exercises the powers given to the Minister of National Revenue in the Act. The CRA is headed by the Commissioner of Revenue whose position corresponds to that of the Deputy Minister in a government department. The requirement to file a return is contained in section 150 of the Act. In general, an individual who has tax payable or who has disposed of a capital property or realized a taxable capital gain must file. A corporation must file whether or not tax is payable. The CRA may also demand that a taxpayer file a return, in which case the taxpayer is obligated under subsection 150(2) to do so. The return is filed by sending it to the Taxation Centre for the region in which the taxpayer lives. Most taxpayers' returns can also be filed electronically, as permitted in section 150.1 and the returns for larger corporations must be filed electronically. Most commercial tax preparers are also required to file returns electronically. Electronic filing can be made by

- EFILE, by which the return is filed by an approved electronic filer; or
- NETFILE , by which qualified taxpayers can file their returns using the Internet. The returns must be prepared using software approved by the CRA.

Returns of individuals are processed by the Taxation Centre. They are checked first to ensure that all appropriate documents have been enclosed (in the case of a paper return) and the information has been correctly entered. If information is missing or otherwise incomplete, the taxpayer is contacted. Once the return is complete, it is entered into the electronic database, where arithmetical and similar types of errors are corrected. A notice of assessment is then issued and sent to the taxpayer (either by mail or, if the taxpayer chooses, electronically), together with a refund of any overpayment where applicable. The initial assessments generated at the Taxation Centre are based on the mechanical accuracy of the return and the correspondence of the return and the other information included with it. The date of sending of the initial notice of assessment is the starting point for the statute-barring period during which further assessments or reassessments can be made. Subsection 244(14) contains a rebuttable presumption that the date of sending of the notice is the date printed on the notice. A small number of the returns filed are subsequently subject to audit by the CRA District Offices, and if the auditors believe a change in tax liability is warranted, notices of reassessment are issued. The taxpayers who are audited are generally selected from categories of "high-risk" taxpayers considered to be most likely to under-report their income.

The CRA has very broad statutory powers in carrying out an audit, including the right to enter business premises, to require taxpayers to produce records and documents and to answer any questions relevant to the administration of the Act (even if they relate to other taxpayers). *Charter*-based attempts to challenge those powers have been generally unsuccessful, except in two cases – where the powers are being used to gather evidence for use in a criminal prosecution or where they impinge on solicitor-client privilege.

What constitutes an assessment? This definition is important not only because the original assessment starts the clock for the statutory limitation period, but also because assessments are an essential foundation for the appeal process. The difficulty was particularly significant in the case of an assessment showing no tax owing (i.e., a "nil assessment") and revolved around the question of whether this document was in fact an assessment from which the taxpayer could appeal. In *Okalta Oils Ltd. v. M.N.R.*, [1955] C.T.C. 271, 55 D.T.C. 1176, a decision under the *Income War Tax Act*, the Supreme Court of Canada held that an assessment stating that no tax was payable was not an assessment for purposes of the appeal process. In a later decision under the Act, *Anjulin Farms Limited v. M.N.R.*, [1961] C.T.C. 261, 61 D.T.C. 1182, the Exchequer Court held that, for certain purposes, a nil assessment was an assessment. The Federal Court of Appeal, however, confirmed in *The Queen v. Garry Bowl Limited*, [1974] C.T.C. 457, 74 D.T.C. 6401, that no appeal lies from a nil assessment. In order for a taxpayer to start the statutory limitation period with respect to losses (e.g., unused non-capital, net capital, or limited partnership losses), the taxpayer may request a determination under subsection 152(1.1), in which case the general rules applicable to reassessments (including subsection 152(4)) apply to the determination. Otherwise, the limitation period will not begin until an assessment is received for the year in which the losses are used.

The Minister's right to reassess a taxpayer is subject to certain limits. Under subsection 152(4), the Minister may reassess an individual or a Canadian-controlled private corporation within three years from the day of sending of the original assessment or the date of the notification that no tax is owing. For corporations other than Canadian-controlled private corporations, the limitation period is four years. This three- or four-year period is defined as the "normal reassessment period" in subsection 152(3.1). After the expiry of the normal reassessment period, the Minister can reassess only if:

(a) in filing the return, the taxpayer has made a misrepresentation attributable to neglect, carelessness or wilful default or has committed fraud; or

(b) the taxpayer has filed a waiver within the normal reassessment period.

In addition, paragraph 152(4)(b) sets out a number of circumstances in which the normal reassessment period is extended by a further three years, including reassessments made as a consequence of a non-arm's length transaction between the taxpayer and a non-resident or where a taxpayer subsequently is allowed to amend a return under subsection 152(6) to, for example, carry back losses from a subsequent taxation year.

B. Refunds, Interest and Penalties

A refund may be claimed by a taxpayer to the extent that any tax payments made exceed the tax owing. If tax has been overpaid, interest is paid to the taxpayer on the overpayment, running from the latest of certain dates (subsection 164(3)). Interest is payable by the taxpayer on a late payment of the balance of tax owing and on deficient instalments.

The Act includes both civil and criminal penalties. Civil penalties are found in sections 162 to 163.2. For example, a taxpayer who files a return late is subject to a late filing penalty of 5 per cent of the tax unpaid plus a further 1 per cent per month (not exceeding 12 months) until the return is filed (subsection 162(1)). Other civil penalties are imposed for the failure to file a return, to provide required information and to pay instalments of tax. In certain circumstances, increased penalties are provided for repeat offences. The most commonly used civil penalty provision is subsection 163(2), which applies in circumstances where the taxpayer knowingly or through "gross negligence" has filed a return that results in the calculation of a tax liability less than the actual liability. This provision is widely used because it is not necessary to demonstrate *mens rea* on the part of the taxpayer. Under sections 238 and 239, which impose criminal penalties and carry higher fines, *mens rea* is required. The criminal penalties are discussed further below.

Section 163.2 imposes civil penalties (so-called "adviser penalties") on persons other than the particular taxpayer whose tax liability is concerned. The CRA's administrative guidelines on the application of section 163.2 are found in Information Circular 01-1: Third-party civil penalties (Information Circulars set out, for the benefit of the public, the CRA's administrative policy on various topics). Prior to the enactment of section 163.2, persons other than the taxpayer were liable only to criminal charges of tax evasion if they assisted or participated in another taxpayer's tax evasion activity (see sections 238 and 239 of the Act and section 380 of the *Criminal Code*). The third-party civil penalties apply to persons who make, participate in, or acquiesce in a false statement made with respect to another person's tax situation, either knowingly, or in circumstances amounting to "culpable conduct". Culpable conduct is defined as conduct that is tantamount to intentional conduct, which shows an indifference as to whether the Act is complied with, or shows a wilful, reckless or wanton disregard of the law. A false statement includes a statement that is misleading because of an omission. The penalty is imposed by assessment, and is the greater of $1,000 and 50 per cent of the other person's understatement of tax owing, subject to a cap of $100,000 plus the gross compensation received in respect of the statement. If the false statement is made in the context of a "planning activity" or "valuation activity", the penalty is the greater of $1,000 and the person's gross entitlements in respect of the planning or valuation activity. The onus is on the Minister to establish the facts justifying the assessment of a penalty. The third-party civil penalties are ostensibly aimed at promoters of tax shelters and overly aggressive tax advisers and tax return preparers, but they may be applied to a much wider group, including employees of corporate taxpayers and law and accounting firms and other professionals. There are exemptions for clerical staff other than bookkeepers and an exception where an adviser acts in good faith on information provided to the adviser.

C. Waiver of Interest and Penalties

The Minister has discretion to provide relief to taxpayers who have failed to comply with provisions of the Act, including making refunds to individual taxpayers beyond the normal limitation period (subsection 152(4.2)), waiving interest and penalties of a taxpayer (subsection 220(3.1)) and allowing taxpayers to make, amend or revoke certain elections (listed in regulation 600) beyond their normal filing deadline (subsection 220(3.2)).

The CRA's administrative practice regarding the exercise of discretion under these provisions is set out in Information Circular 07-1: Taxpayer Relief Provisions (May 31, 2007). A taxpayer who has applied for relief under these provisions and who is not satisfied with the CRA's response can seek judicial review of the CRA exercise of discretion in the Federal Court. In general, courts will require the CRA to exercise the discretion in accordance with the published guidelines CRA has set down.

D. Voluntary Disclosure Program (VDP)

The CRA operates a form of amnesty program where a taxpayer has voluntarily disclosed a previous failure to comply with the provisions of the Act, for example, by failing to disclose certain items of income on a return. Where the disclosure is made voluntarily (that is, before any CRA audit or investigation) and fully discloses all of the relevant facts, and the taxpayer undertakes to pay any additional tax owing, the CRA will refrain from imposing either criminal or civil penalties and will generally give at least limited relief in respect of accumulated interest. The CRA's administrative practice in respect of the VDP Program is set out in Information Circular 00-1R3 (March 21, 2013).

E. Objections and Appeals

A taxpayer who wishes to dispute the tax, interest or penalties assessed by the CRA (or who wishes to dispute a determination of losses) may, within 90 days of an assessment or reassessment (or determination or redetermination of loss), file a notice of objection. There is no prescribed form for the notice of objection, although subsection 165(1) indicates that it must set out the reasons for the objection and all relevant facts. A "large corporation" (as defined in subsection 225.1(8)) must provide a more detailed notice of objection, including a statement of the precise amount in issue (which will then provide the upper limit on any recovery). The CRA has broad powers to collect tax, interest or penalties assessed and can begin collection action 90 days after the date of the reassessment. These include the power to seize property and to garnish amounts owing to the taxpayer by third parties. Where a taxpayer has failed to remit amounts withheld at source from employees like tax deductions or Canada Pension Plan contributions, the CRA's right of collection will outrank even secured creditors of the taxpayer.

Filing a notice of objection will generally suspend collection action by the CRA (except in the case of a large corporation, which must pay at least one-half of the amount in dispute). While other taxpayers are not required to pay the amount in dispute, interest continues to accrue and will be payable to the extent that the taxpayer's objection or appeal is unsuccessful. The notice of objection is normally considered by the appeals section within the District Office and by the regional appeals office. Following the review of the notice of objection, the assessment may be confirmed, modified by a further reassessment or vacated.

A taxpayer who has filed a notice of objection may appeal the assessment or reassessment (or determination or redetermination) to the Tax Court of Canada within the following time limits:

(a) 90 days after the filing of the notice of objection if the Minister has not notified the taxpayer of the confirmation or vacation of the assessment, or has not reassessed the taxpayer; or

(b) within 90 days of the day that the Minister confirmed the assessment or reassessed

In most cases a taxpayer will take the opportunity to make submissions to the CRA appeals officer. If the taxpayer chooses not to do so, or is dissatisfied with the CRA's response to the objection, and in either case appeals to the Tax Court, the CRA's collection powers will again be suspended until the appeal has been heard and disposed of.

Since January 1, 1991, the Tax Court has had exclusive original jurisdiction to hear appeals of income tax assessments. There are two methods of procedure before the Tax Court: the Informal Procedure and the General Procedure. The Informal Procedure is very similar to a small claims court procedure in the provincial court systems. The taxpayer can elect the Informal Procedure if the amount of federal tax and penalties in dispute in respect of a taxation year (notwithstanding that appeals of several taxation years may be joined in a single appeal in the court) does not exceed $25,000, if the amount of a loss in dispute does not exceed $50,000, or if only interest is in issue. As in most small claims court procedures, a taxpayer can also access the Informal Procedure by abandoning the appeal in respect of amounts in excess of the monetary limits. In an Informal Procedure appeal, the taxpayer may appear in person or be represented by an agent who is not a lawyer. The proceedings are informal in that there is no special form of pleadings and the Court is not bound by the normal rules of evidence. Generally, a taxpayer will not be liable to pay costs to the Crown if unsuccessful in the appeal but may recover costs on a tariff basis if successful.

In a General Procedure appeal, the taxpayer must appear in person or be represented by a lawyer. Procedure in a General Procedure appeal is similar to that in the Federal Court or in the provincial superior courts. Both parties will be required to make pre-trial discovery (disclosure) of relevant documents and, in most cases, there will be examinations for discovery.

At trial, the taxpayer must lead evidence first, since the onus rests on the taxpayer to prove that the assessment or reassessment was in error. Furthermore, where the Minister has relied on certain assumptions in making the assessment or reassessment, these assumptions will be presumed to be correct unless specifically disproved by the taxpayer. The foundation for this principle is found in the following extract from the majority judgment in *Johnston v. M.N.R.*, [1948] S.C.R. 486, [1948] C.T.C. 195, 3 D.T.C. 1182:

> Notwithstanding that it is spoken of in section 63(2) as an action ready for trial or hearing, the proceeding is an appeal from the taxation; and since the taxation is on the basis of certain facts and certain provisions of law either those facts or the application of the law is challenged. Every such fact found or assumed by the assessor or the Minister must then be accepted as it was dealt with by these persons unless questioned by the appellant. If the taxpayer here intended to contest the fact that he supported his wife within the meaning of the Rules mentioned he should have raised that issue in his pleading, and the burden would have rested on him as on any appellant to show that the conclusion below was not warranted. For that purpose he might bring evidence before the Court notwithstanding that it had not been placed before the assessor or the Minister, but the onus was his to demolish the basic fact on which the taxation rested. Any such assumptions therefore, must be carefully analyzed and evidence prepared to meet them. It will be noted that those assumptions presumed to be correct are assumptions relating to facts and not to law. If the Minister has made assumptions as to law the onus rests on the Crown to prove these assumptions correct, rather than on the taxpayer.

At trial, a special burden of proof is imposed on the Minister in certain circumstances. First, if the Minister imposes a penalty on the taxpayer under section 163 (repeated failure to report income, or knowingly or negligently making a false statement or omission) or on a third person under proposed section 163.2, subsection 163(3) requires the Minister to establish the facts that justify the assessment of the penalty. Second, if the Minister assesses a taxpayer outside the normal reassessment period on the basis that the taxpayer made a misrepresentation attributable to neglect, carelessness or wilful default or has committed fraud, the onus of proving the misrepresentation or fraud lies with the Minister: *M.N.R. v. Taylor*, [1961] C.T.C. 211, 61 D.T.C. 1139 (Ex. Ct.). Third, if the Minister alleges new facts other than those that formed the basis of the assessment or reassessment, the onus is on the Minister to prove the new facts: *Pillsbury Canada Ltd. v. M.N.R.*, [1964] C.T.C. 294, 64 D.T.C. 5184 (Ex. Ct.).

The Tax Court can dismiss the appeal or allow it in whole or in part (in which case it will be sent back to the Minister for appropriate reassessment). Where an appeal raises more than one issue, the Tax Court, with the consent of both parties, can similarly dispose of one or more issues, while leaving others to be dealt with later. This ability to make partial judgements can facilitate settlement of the remaining issues. A decision of the Tax Court made under the General Procedure may be appealed as of right to the Federal Court of Appeal. However, where the decision of the Tax Court has been made under the Informal Procedure, it is subject only to judicial review by the Federal Court of Appeal. A decision of the Federal Court of Appeal may be appealed to the Supreme Court of Canada with leave. Where the taxpayer is unsuccessful in an appeal to the Tax Court, the CRA will be entitled to use its collection powers in respect of amounts assessed, whether or not the taxpayer appeals further to the Federal Court of Appeal.

F. Settlements

Informal negotiation between the taxpayer (or an advisor) and the CRA can begin at the audit stage and many disputes are settled without recourse to the formal objection and appeal procedures.

However, there are certain limitations on the taxpayer's ability to obtain a binding settlement from the Minister. According to the Federal Court of Appeal in *Galway v. M.N.R.*, [1974] C.T.C. 454, 74 D.T.C. 6355:

> ... the Minister has a statutory duty to assess the amount of tax payable on the facts as he finds them in accordance with the law as he understands it. It follows that he cannot assess for some amount designed to implement a compromise settlement and that, when the Trial Division, or this Court on appeal, refers an assessment back to the Minister for re-assessment, it must be for re-assessment on the facts in accordance with the law and not to implement a compromise settlement.

The case concerned a single issue: whether an amount which was not in dispute, must be included in the taxpayer's income. The settlement reached by the taxpayer and Revenue Canada (now the CRA) appeared to include only a portion of the amount in income (i.e., a "compromise settlement"). Consider the application of *Galway* in the following case.

COHEN v. THE QUEEN
[1980] C.T.C. 318, 80 D.T.C. 6250 (F.C.A.)

Pratt J. (Ryan J. and Lalande D.J. concurring): ...

It was first argued on behalf of the appellant that the judge below had erred in deciding that the profit realized on the sale of the Bourret Street property was not a capital gain. There is, in my view, no substance in that argument. A mere reading of the record shows that there is ample evidence supporting the finding of the Trial Division on this point.

The appellant's second argument was that the Minister could not legally reassess the appellant on the basis that the profit in question was income because he had previously agreed to treat that profit as a capital gain. Counsel submitted that this agreement had been made during the course of negotiations between representatives of the appellant and officers of the Department of National Revenue concerning the appellant's assessments for the years 1961 to 1964. The appellant had agreed, said counsel, not to appeal his assessments for the 1961 to 1964 taxation years on the understanding that his income tax for 1965 would be computed on the basis that the profit here in question was a capital gain. Counsel argued that the Minister could not repudiate that understanding, particularly after the expiry of the time within which the appellant might have appealed the 1961 to 1964 assessments.

In my view, the Trial judge correctly dismissed that argument. "... the Minister has a statutory duty to assess the amount of tax payable on the facts as he finds them in accordance with the law as he understands it. It follows that he cannot assess for some amount designed to implement a compromise settlement ...", (*Galway v. M.N.R.*, [1974] 1 F.C. 600 at page 602, [74 D.T.C. 6355 at page 6357]). The agreement whereby the Minister would agree to assess income tax otherwise than in accordance with the law would, in my view, be an illegal agreement. Therefore, even if the record supported the appellant's contention that the Minister agreed to treat the profit here in question as a capital gain, that agreement would not bind the Minister and would not prevent him from assessing the tax payable by the appellant in accordance with the requirements of the statute.

Notes and Questions

1. Was the nature of the settlement reached by the taxpayer and the Minister in *Cohen* similar to that in *Galway*?
2. In *Consoltex Inc. v. The Queen*, [1997] 2 C.T.C. 2846, 97 D.T.C. 724 (T.C.C.), Bowman, J. permitted the taxpayer to appeal a reassessment even though the reassessment arose from a settlement reached by the taxpayer with the Minister. The settlement agreement reflected a compromise that, under *Galway* and *Cohen*, was not binding on the Minister. After reviewing *Cohen*, Bowman, J. suggested (at paragraph 36): "It is unconscionable enough that the Minister should be able to renege on settlements that he or she has made. It would be doubly indefensible that a taxpayer should be unilaterally bound to honour agreements that the Minister is free to repudiate."
3. Tax legislation in both the United States and the United Kingdom as well as in some provinces expressly permits the tax authorities to settle cases on the basis of litigation risk or cost rather than strict statutory principles. Should similar legislation be introduced in the Act?
4. Pending amendments to the Tax Court General Procedure Rules provide for costs penalties to a party which rejects a settlement offer where the eventual disposition of the appeal is no more favourable to that party than if it had accepted the offer. The amendments also allow the Court, at its initiative or at that of a party, to convene a settlement conference to explore the possibility of settlement before trial. The current practice of the Court is to conform to the proposed amendments. See Practice Note No. 17 (January 18, 2010).

II. INTERPRETATION OF TAX STATUTES

A. Strict Interpretation

Early U.K. and Canadian cases established that the words of a taxing statute must be strictly construed, and the taxpayer must fall clearly within a charging provision to be liable for tax. This approach was premised largely on the view that a tax was to some degree equivalent to a penalty and therefore tax legislation was analogous to other forms of penal legislation, and should be construed literally on the basis of the words of the statute alone. The use of strict construction was further supported by the perception that the sole purpose of tax legislation was the raising of government revenue. As such, taxing statutes had no other object or purpose that would support them being given a more liberal or equitable construction. For example, in *Partington v. Attorney-General* (1869-70), L.R. 4 H.L. 100 at 122, it was said:

> If the person sought to be taxed comes within the letter of the law he must be taxed, however great the hardship may appear to the judicial mind to be. On the other hand, if the Crown, seeking to recover the tax, cannot bring the subject within the letter of the law, the subject is free, however apparently within the spirit of the law the case might otherwise appear to be. In other words, if there be admissible, in any statute, what is called an equitable construction, certainly such a construction is not admissible in a taxing statute, where you can simply adhere to the words of the statute.

The nature of the words necessary to render a citizen liable to tax was further examined in *The Cape Brandy Syndicate v. C.I.R.* (1920), 12 T.C. 358, where the following statement was made (at 366):

> But it is often endeavoured to give that maxim a wide and fanciful construction. It does not mean that words are to be unduly restricted against the Crown or that there is to be any discrimination against the Crown in such Acts. It means this, I think: it means that in taxation you have to look simply at what is clearly said. There is no room for any intendment; there is no equity about a tax; there is no presumption as to tax; you read nothing in; you imply nothing, but you look fairly at what is said and at what is said clearly and that is the tax.

Accordingly, in the event there was any ambiguity in the application of a provision in a taxing statute, such ambiguity was resolved on the basis of a presumption that favoured the taxpayer where the issue related to the application of a charging provision and favoured the state in the case or a provision providing for an exemption or deduction. The latter is illustrated by *Witthuhn v. M.N.R.* (1957), 17 Tax A.B.C. 33, 57 D.T.C. 174, in which the taxpayer sought to deduct the expenses of a full-time attendant for his spouse. Such expenses were deductible under subparagraph 27(1)(c)(iv)of the 1952 *Income Tax Act* if the spouse was "necessarily confined by reason of illness, injury or affliction to a bed or wheelchair". The taxpayers' spouse could sit for a few hours each day in a special rocking chair designed for her but was otherwise confined to bed. In denying the deduction, W.S. Fisher stated (at 35; 176):

> I do not know what particular virtue there is in sitting in a wheelchair as opposed to an ordinary chair or a rocking chair, but nevertheless that is a specific requirement which Parliament has put into the legislation ... It is not for this Board or for the Courts to attempt to give a very broad interpretation to the legislation as enacted by Parliament when the language used is quite clear and explicit, as to do so would be to enter upon the field of legislation which, of course, is the exclusive right and prerogative of Parliament and certainly is not the function of a board or court. However much one may consider that, in equity, a taxpayer should be entitled to a deduction in circumstances such as those present in this appeal, nevertheless if those circumstances do not coincide with the strict wording of the legislation, this Board has no jurisdiction to extend the provisions of the statute by granting the deductions claimed.

Contrast *Johns-Manville Canada Inc. v. The Queen*, [1985] 2 C.T.C. 111, 85 D.T.C. 5373, in which the Supreme Court of Canada indicated that all statutory ambiguities, even those in exempting clauses, should be resolved in favour of the taxpayer. Estey, J., speaking for the Court, said (at paragraph 27):

> ... if the interpretation of a taxation statute is unclear, and one reasonable interpretation leads to a deduction to the credit of a taxpayer and the other leaves the taxpayer with no relief from clearly *bona fide* expenditures in the course of his business activities, the general rules of interpretation of taxing statutes would direct the tribunal to the former interpretation.

He went on to add (at paragraph 43):

> The characterization in taxation law of an expenditure is, in the final analysis (unless the statute is explicit which this one is not), one of policy. ... Such a determination [deductibility of the expense] is, furthermore, consistent with another basic concept in tax law that where the taxing statute is not explicit, reasonable uncertainty or factual ambiguity resulting from lack of explicitness in the statute should be resolved in favour of the taxpayer.

B. The Modern Approach

Consideration of the judiciary's modern approach to interpreting tax legislation usually begins with the Supreme Court of Canada decision in *Stubart*, which involved a complex series of transactions designed solely to reduce the taxpayer's tax liability. The Supreme Court's approach to statutory interpretation is discussed in the excerpt below. The Court's approach to tax avoidance is reproduced in Part III below.

STUBART INVESTMENTS LTD. v. THE QUEEN
[1984] C.T.C. 294, 84 D.T.C. 6305 (S.C.C.)

[For the facts of the case and further extracts from the judgment, see Part III.B.1 below]

Estey J.: ...

In all this, one must keep in mind the rules of statutory interpretation, for many years called a strict interpretation, whereby any ambiguities in the charging provisions of a tax statute were to be resolved in favour of the taxpayer; the taxing statute was classified as a penal statute. See Grover & Iacobucci, *Materials on Canadian Income Tax*, 5th ed, (1981), pp 62-65.

At one time, the House of Lords, as interpreted by Professor John Willis, had ruled that it was "not only legal but moral to dodge the Inland Revenue"

(51 *Canadian Bar Review* 1 at 26), referring to *Inland Revenue Commissioners v. Levene*, [1928] A.C. 217, at 227. This was the high water mark reached in the application of Lord Cairns' pronouncement in *Partington v. Attorney-General* ...

The converse was, of course, also true. Where the taxpayer sought to rely on a specific exemption or deduction provided in the statute, the strict rule required that the taxpayer's claim fall clearly within the exempting provision, and any doubt would there be resolved in favour of the Crown. See *Lumbers v. M.N.R.*, [1944] C.T.C. 67; [1943] C.T.C. 281; 2 D.T.C. 631 (Exch. Ct.), affirmed [1944] S.C.R. 167; and *W. A. Sheaffer Pen Co. Ltd. v. M.N.R.*, [1953] Ex. C.R. 251; [1953] C.T.C. 345; 53 D.T.C. 1223. Indeed, the introduction of exemptions and allowances was the beginning of the end of the reign of the strict rule.

Professor Willis, in his article, supra, accurately forecast the demise of the strict interpretation rule for the construction of taxing statutes. Gradually, the role of the tax statute in the community changed, as we have seen, and the application of strict construction to it receded. Courts today apply to this statute the plain meaning rule, but in a substantive sense so that if a taxpayer is within the spirit of the charge, he may be held liable. ...

While not directing his observations exclusively to taxing statutes, the learned author of *Construction of Statutes*, 2nd ed., (1983), at 87, E.A. Driedger, put the modern rule succinctly:

> Today there is only one principle or approach, namely, the words of an Act are to be read in their entire context and in their grammatical and ordinary sense harmoniously with the scheme of the Act, the object of the Act, and the intention of Parliament.

The question comes back to a determination of the proper role of the court in construing the *Income Tax Act* in circumstances such as these where the Crown relies on the general pattern of the Act and not upon any specific taxing provision. The Act is to be construed, of course, as a whole, including section 137 [a former provision denying deductions that unduly or artificially reduced income] but, for reasons already noted, without applying that section specifically to these assessments. The appellant stands to save taxes if its program is successful. The Crown loses revenue it might otherwise receive. At least in theory, the burden falls on other taxpayers to make up the lost revenue. Lord Simon of Glaisdale had this to say in not dissimilar circumstances:

> It may seem hard that a cunningly advised taxpayer should be able to avoid what appears to be his equitable share of the general fiscal burden and cast it on the shoulders of his fellow citizens. But for the Courts to try to stretch the law to meet hard cases (whether the hardship appears to bear on the individual taxpayer or on the general body of taxpayers as represented by the

> Inland Revenue) is not merely to make bad law but to run the risk of subverting the rule of law itself. Disagreeable as it may seem that some taxpayers should escape what might appear to be their fair share of the general burden of national expenditure, it would be far more disagreeable to substitute the rule of caprice for that of law.
>
> *Ransom v. Higgs*, 50 T.C. 1 at 94 (1974).

All this may reflect the tradition of annual amendments to the *Income Tax Act* when the government budget for the ensuing year is presented to Parliament for approval. Perhaps the facility of amendment to the *Income Tax Act* is one of the sources of the problem since the practice does not invite the courts to intervene when the legislature can readily do so.

Nonetheless, some guidelines can be discerned for the guidance of a court faced with this interpretative issue.

1. Where the facts reveal no *bona fide* business purpose for the transaction, section 137 may be found to be applicable depending upon all the circumstances of the case. It has no application here.
2. In those circumstances where section 137 does not apply, the older rule of strict construction of a taxation statute, as modified by the courts in recent years, (*supra*), prevails but will not assist the taxpayer where:
   (a) the transaction is legally ineffective or incomplete; or;
   (b) the transaction is a sham within the classical definition.
3. Moreover, the formal validity of the transaction may also be insufficient where:
   (a) the setting in the Act of the allowance, deduction or benefit sought to be gained clearly indicates a legislative intent to restrict such benefits to rights accrued prior to the establishment of the arrangement adopted by a taxpayer purely for tax purposes;
   (b) the provisions of the Act necessarily relate to an identified business function. This idea has been expressed in articles on the subject in the United States:

   > The business purpose doctrine is an appropriate tool for testing the tax effectiveness of a transaction, where the language, nature and purposes of the provision of the tax law under construction indicate a function, pattern and design characteristic solely of business transactions.
   >
   > Jerom R. Hellerstein, "Judicial Approaches to Tax Avoidance", 1964 Conference Report, p. 66.

   (c) "the object and spirit" of the allowance or benefit provision is defeated by the procedures blatantly adopted by the taxpayer to synthesize a loss, delay or other tax saving device, although

> these actions may not attain the heights of "artificiality" in section 137. This may be illustrated where the taxpayer, in order to qualify for an "allowance" or a "benefit" takes steps which the terms of the allowance provisions of the Act may, when taken in isolation and read narrowly, be stretched to support. However, when the allowance provision is read in the context of the whole statute, and with the "object and spirit" and purpose of the allowance provision in mind, the accounting result produced by the taxpayer's actions would not, by itself, avail him of the benefit of the allowance.

These interpretative guidelines, modest though they may be, and which fall well short of the *bona fide* business purpose test advanced by the respondent, are in my view appropriate to reduce the action and reaction endlessly produced by complex, specific tax measures aimed at sophisticated business practices, and the inevitable, professionally-guided and equally specialized taxpayer reaction. Otherwise, where the substance of the Act, when the clause in question is contextually construed, is clear and unambiguous and there is no prohibition in the Act which embraces the taxpayer, the taxpayer shall be free to avail himself of the beneficial provision in question.

...

[Wilson J. wrote a concurring judgment.]

In the years following *Stubart*, the Supreme Court has struggled with the application of the modern approach to tax statutes. In particular, the modern approach leaves unclear what relative weight should be given to the ordinary meaning, context and purpose. For example, in *Antosko v. The Queen*, [1994] 2 C.T.C. 25, 94 D.T.C. 6314 (S.C.C.), Iacobucci J., speaking for a unanimous Supreme Court, stated (at paragraph 29):

> While it is true that the courts must view discrete sections of the Income Tax Act in light of the other provisions of the Act and of the purpose of the legislation, and that they must analyze a given transaction in the context of economic and commercial reality, such techniques cannot alter the result where the words of the statute are clear and plain and where the legal and practical effect of the transaction is undisputed ...

In the following year, the Supreme Court of Canada in *Corporation Notre-Dame de Bon-Secours v. Quebec (Communauté Urbaine)*, [1995] 1 C.T.C. 241, 95 D.T.C. 5017 (S.C.C.) applied a "teleological" approach to the interpretation of tax legislation. Under the "teleological" approach, the court begins with the underlying purpose of the legislative provision and then interprets the words of the provision in a manner that best accomplishes this purpose.

A year after *Bon-Secours*, the "plain meaning" approach of *Antosko* was adopted by the majority of the Supreme Court of Canada in *Friesen v. The Queen*,

[1995] 2 C.T.C. 369, 95 D.T.C. 5551 (S.C.C.): see Chapter 6. Subsequent cases have tried to reconcile the teleological approach and the plain meaning approach. For example, in *The Queen v. Province of Alberta Treasury Branches*, [1996] 1 C.T.C. 395, 96 D.T.C. 6245, Cory J., writing for the majority of the Court, stated (at paragraph 15):

> Thus, when there is neither any doubt as to the meaning of the legislation nor any ambiguity in its application to the facts then the statutory provision must be applied regardless of its object or purpose ... Even if the ambiguity were not apparent, it is significant that in order to determine the clear and plain meaning of the statute it is always appropriate to consider the "scheme of the Act, the object of the Act, and the intention of Parliament".

Major J., in dissent, referred back to his majority decision in *Friesen*, and suggested (at paragraph 100) that "the words of a taxing statute are to be read strictly for their plain and ordinary meaning and that only if there is a true ambiguity is the intention of Parliament to be considered."

In its first case considering the general anti-avoidance rule in section 245, the Supreme Court of Canada revisited the modern approach, restating it as a "textual, contextual and purposive analysis". The Supreme Court's approach to statutory interpretation is considered in the excerpt below. The Court's approach to the general anti-avoidance rule is reproduced in Part III below.

CANADA TRUSTCO MORTGAGE CO. v. THE QUEEN
[2005] 5 C.T.C. 215, 2005 D.T.C. 5547 (S.C.C.)

[For the facts of the case and further extracts from the judgment, see Part III.B.2 below.]

5. Analysis

5.1 *General Principles of Interpretation*

It has been long established as a matter of statutory interpretation that "the words of an Act are to be read in their entire context and in their grammatical and ordinary sense harmoniously with the scheme of the Act, the object of the Act, and the intention of Parliament": see *65302 British Columbia Ltd. v. Canada*, [1999] 3 S.C.R. 804, at para. 50. The interpretation of a statutory provision must be made according to a textual, contextual and purposive analysis to find a meaning that is harmonious with the Act as a whole. When the words of a provision are precise and unequivocal, the ordinary meaning of the words play a dominant role in the interpretive process. On the other hand, where the words can support more than one reasonable meaning, the ordinary meaning of the words plays a lesser role. The relative effects of ordinary meaning, context and purpose on the interpretive process may vary, but in all cases the court must seek to read the provisions of an Act as a harmonious whole.

As a result of the Duke of Westminster principle (*Commissioners of Inland Revenue v. Duke of Westminster*, [1936] A.C. 1 (H.L.)) that taxpayers are entitled to arrange their affairs to minimize the amount of tax payable, Canadian tax legislation received a strict interpretation in an era of more literal statutory interpretation than the present. There is no doubt today that all statutes, including the *Income Tax Act*, must be interpreted in a textual, contextual and purposive way. However, the particularity and detail of many tax provisions have often led to an emphasis on textual interpretation. Where Parliament has specified precisely what conditions must be satisfied to achieve a particular result, it is reasonable to assume that Parliament intended that taxpayers would rely on such provisions to achieve the result they prescribe.

The provisions of the *Income Tax Act* must be interpreted in order to achieve consistency, predictability and fairness so that taxpayers may manage their affairs intelligently. As stated at para. 45 of *Shell Canada Ltd. v. Canada*, [1999] 3 S.C.R. 622:

> [A]bsent a specific provision to the contrary, it is not the courts' role to prevent taxpayers from relying on the sophisticated structure of their transactions, arranged in such a way that the particular provisions of the Act are met, on the basis that it would be inequitable to those taxpayers who have not chosen to structure their transactions that way. [Emphasis added.]

See also *65302 British Columbia*, at para. 51, *per* Iacobucci J. citing P. W. Hogg and J. E. Magee, *Principles of Canadian Income Tax Law* (2nd ed. 1997), at pp. 475-76:

> It would introduce intolerable uncertainty into the Income Tax Act if clear language in a detailed provision of the Act were to be qualified by unexpressed exceptions derived from a court's view of the object and purpose of the provision.

[In its subsequent discussion of the general anti-avoidance rule, particularly subsection 245(4), the Supreme Court further commented on the interaction between text, context, and purpose:]

Even where the meaning of particular provisions may not appear to be ambiguous at first glance, statutory context and purpose may reveal or resolve latent ambiguities. "After all, language can never be interpreted independently of its context, and legislative purpose is part of the context. It would seem to follow that consideration of legislative purpose may not only resolve patent ambiguity, but may, on occasion, reveal ambiguity in apparently plain language." See P. W. Hogg and J.E. Magee, *Principles of Canadian Income Tax Law* (4th ed. 2002), at p. 563. In order to reveal and resolve any latent ambiguities in the meaning of provisions of the *Income Tax Act*, the courts must undertake a unified textual, contextual and purposive approach to statutory interpretation.

...

Following *Canada Trustco*, all subsequent cases involving statutory interpretation issues, whether tax avoidance has been alleged or not, have referenced the "textual, contextual and purposive" approach. See, for example, *Ontario (Minister of Finance) v. Placer Dome Canada Ltd.*, 2006 D.T.C. 6532 (S.C.C.); *The Queen v. Imperial Oil Ltd.*, [2007] 1 C.T.C. 41, 2006 D.T.C. 6639 (S.C.C.), in which the Supreme Court of Canada applied the "textual, contextual and purposive" approach in cases that did not involve allegations of tax avoidance. The relative emphasis that a court places on text, context, and purpose remains problematic in both tax avoidance and non-tax avoidance cases.

Notes and Questions

1. Brian Arnold, in a critical review of Supreme Court of Canada decisions since *Stubart*, "Statutory Interpretation: Some Thoughts on Plain Meaning" 1998 *Conference Report* (Toronto: Canadian Tax Foundation, 1999), 6:1 at 6:20 stated:

> The only conclusion that can be drawn from an analysis of the recent judgments of the Supreme Court about statutory interpretation is that no conclusions are possible. The views of the judges range from strict interpretation to the modern approach to something in between. All of these approaches may be called the plain meaning approach by judges. Confusing matters is the fact that despite what the judges call their approach to statutory interpretation, they may apply a different approach. The only consistent thing about the court's comments about statutory interpretation is the lack of analysis to support the conclusion that a particular approach is appropriate. Most of the cases simply repeat the relevant excerpts concerning statutory interpretation from the *Stubart* and *Friesen* cases as authority for whatever interpretative approach the court uses.
>
> [footnotes omitted]

   Has Arnold's concern been addressed by the Supreme Court decision in *Canada Trustco*?

2. Consider the Supreme Court of Canada decision in *Will-Kare Paving & Construction Ltd. v. The Queen*, [2000] 3 C.T.C. 463, 2000 D.T.C. 6467 (S.C.C.). The taxpayer operated a paving business. In 1988 it constructed its own asphalt plant so that it would not have to rely on third-party suppliers. In the 1988-1990 taxation years, the taxpayer included the plant and additions made to it as Class 39 assets, which were entitled to an accelerated rate of capital cost allowance. The taxpayer also claimed investment tax credits on the basis that the plant was "qualified property" under subsection 127(9). In both cases, the preferential tax

treatment was dependent on the plant being used primarily for the purpose of manufacturing or processing goods for sale or lease. In the taxation years in issue, approximately 75 per cent of the asphalt from the plant was used in Will-Kare's own paving business and approximately 25 per cent was sold to third parties. Both the Tax Court and Federal Court of Appeal dismissed the taxpayer's appeal on the basis that most of the asphalt from the plant was used by the taxpayer in its own business (as goods supplied through contracts for work and materials) and was not therefore "goods for sale". In dismissing the appeal, the majority of the Supreme Court of Canada (per Major, J.) adopted a narrow meaning of "sale", relying on common law and statutory sale of goods concepts. Binnie, J., writing for the dissent, concluded that the term "sale" should be given its "plain meaning" as understood by the ordinary taxpayer. Both the majority and dissent relied on the modern approach to statutory interpretation and both considered the intent of Parliament for the conclusion reached. Which judgment do you find more persuasive and why?

C. Other Legislation Affecting the Interpretation of Tax Statutes

Three statutes — the federal and provincial *Interpretation Acts*, the *Official Languages Act* and the *Canadian Charter of Rights and Freedoms* — affect the interpretation and application of statutes in Canada.

Interpretation Acts

The *Interpretation Act*, R.S.C. 1985, c. I-21 applies to all federal statutes unless specifically excepted. The Act has no special status. Each of the provinces has also enacted its own *Interpretation Act* that governs the application and interpretation of provincial legislation and is generally similar to the federal statute. The provisions of the federal *Interpretation Act* range from general rules of statutory construction to specific mechanical details. Section 12 provides: "[E]very enactment is deemed remedial, and shall be given such fair, large and liberal construction and interpretation as best ensures the attainment of its objects." This provision has been largely ignored in the interpretation of income tax legislation. Other provisions, such as sections 29 and 33, are much more specific: section 29 defines "standard time" for federal statutes, and section 33 deems that words importing male persons to include female persons and corporations, and deems words in the singular to include the plural and *vice versa*.

Official Languages Act

The *Official Languages Act*, R.S.C. 1985, c. 31 (4th Supp.) requires all federal statutes to be "enacted, printed and published in both official languages" (section 6). Section 13 provides that:

> Any journal, record, Act of Parliament, instrument, document, rule, order, regulation, treaty, convention, agreement, notice, advertisement or other matter referred to in this Part that is made, enacted, printed, published or tabled in both official languages shall be made, enacted, printed, published or tabled simultaneously in both languages, and both language versions are equally authoritative.

Subsection 18(1) of Schedule B of the *Constitution Act*, 1982 similarly states: "[T]he statutes ... of Parliament shall be printed and published in English and French and both official versions are equally authoritative."

The existence of two equally authentic versions of a federal statute presents a number of interesting problems and issues in statutory interpretation. For example, what if the two versions differ in their respective meanings, or alternatively, the meaning in one version is clear but ambiguous in the other? Robert Couzin, in "What Does It Say in French?" (1985), 33 Can. Tax J. 300-306, offers these comments:

> In several decided cases ... courts have used one version of a statute to enlighten the reading of the other version. For example, a court may find an ambiguity in the English version of the text. It may decide which reading seems better to accord with the spirit and intent of the Act, and find itself fortified in this view by the French text.
>
> ... One can conclude that where it is not clear from the context of the *Income Tax Act* which of two or more possible interpretations of the English text is likely to correctly render the intention of the legislator, a reading of the French text may well be of assistance. This is not to relegate the French text to a subservient role. There are also cases in which even a tolerably clear English version must be rethought because the French version simply cannot accommodate the apparent meaning of the other... Two linguistic versions are not always better than one, because they may create ambiguities that would not otherwise be there. On many occasions, however, they provide two chances to divine the meaning.

Canadian Charter of Rights and Freedoms

The *Canadian Charter of Rights and Freedoms*, Part I of the *Constitution Act, 1982*, being Schedule B to the *Canada Act 1982* (U.K.), 1982, c. 11 ("the *Charter*") applies to both federal and provincial legislation and expressly overrides any such legislation to the extent that there are any inconsistencies between it and the *Charter* (*Charter*, subsection 52(1)). The validity of all legislation must be tested against the

Charter, subject to an express declaration in the legislation that it (or a provision thereof) operates "notwithstanding a provision included in section 2 or sections 7 to 15 of this *Charter*" (*Charter*, subsection 33(1)).

The *Charter* is intended to guarantee an enumerated set of civil liberties. That protection is provided through the courts, which are charged with the duty of assessing the validity of legislation against the *Charter* where a particular statutory provision has been challenged (*Charter*, subsection 24(1)). The judicial assessment is basically a two-step process in which the court must first determine if the application of the impugned legislation violates one of the enumerated civil liberties. In such a case, the legislation is invalid and must be struck down unless the violation may, in effect, be characterized as a reasonable limit justifiable in a free and democratic society (*Charter*, section 1).

The *Charter* may also be used by the courts as an interpretative aid. If, and only if, a statutory provision is found to be ambiguous, the court will give preference to the interpretation that is consistent with *Charter* values over an interpretation that would run contrary to them.

The interpretation and application of all provisions of the Act are potentially subject to challenge by a taxpayer under the *Charter*. The *Charter's* effect has been particularly significant for the search and seizure provisions in the Act, which have been amended to ensure that they are consistent with the protection against unreasonable search or seizure provided by section 8 of the *Charter*.

Even with the amendments to the search and seizure provisions, the manner in which the CRA actually gathers information may violate section 8 of the *Charter* in certain circumstances. For example, in *The Queen v. Norway Insulation Inc. and Norman Jurchison*, [1995] 2 C.T.C. 451, 95 D.T.C. 5328 (Ont. Gen. Div.), a tax evasion case under section 239 of the Act, information obtained by an auditor under the warrantless inspection and audit procedures in subsection 231.1(1) of the Act was held to have been obtained in violation of the taxpayers' right to freedom from unreasonable search or seizure. The information was obtained by the auditor at the request of the Special Investigations division of the CRA, the division responsible for investigating tax evasion. Norman Jurchison had not been advised that he and his company were the subjects of a criminal investigation. He believed that he was legally obliged to produce the documents and answer questions under the regulatory inspection procedures in subsection 231.1(1). The Court excluded the tainted evidence under section 24 of the *Charter* and both accused were acquitted. The taxpayers were also successful in obtaining an order excluding the tainted evidence in the appeal against their reassessments: *Jurchison v. M.N.R.*, [2000] 1 C.T.C. 2762, 2000 D.T.C. 1660 (T.C.C.). In addition, the Tax Court of Canada shifted the burden of establishing the correctness of the reassessments to the Minister.

In *Gernhart v. The Queen*, [2000] 1 C.T.C. 192, 99 D.T.C. 5749 (F.C.A.), the Federal Court of Appeal struck down subsection 176(1) of the Act on the grounds that it violated section 8 of the *Charter*. Subsection 176(1) requires the Minister to forward to the Tax Court copies of the returns, notices of assessment, notices of objection and notifications that are relevant to an appeal. The appellant's tax returns were thus effectively made public documents, and any person could view them and make copies under the Tax Court Rules. In addition, the Tax Court Judge would have the opportunity to review the returns and other documents even where neither party introduced them in evidence. The Court held that the taxpayer had a reasonable expectation of privacy of the information in her return arising from section 241 of the Act, which prohibits the disclosure of taxpayer information except for purposes of administration or enforcement of the Act (and certain other related statutes). Subsection 176(1) therefore represented a significant intrusion on the privacy interests of an appellant. The Federal Court of Appeal noted with approval the Tax Court Judge's recognition that appeals from assessments could be inhibited by the public disclosure of returns mandated by subsection 176(1).

The application of the advisor penalties in section 163.2 is another provision of the Act that has recently been the subject of a challenge under section 11 of the *Charter*, which provides certain rights to a person charged with an offence including, in paragraph (d), the right "to be presumed innocent until proven guilty according to law in a fair and public hearing by an independent and impartial tribunal".

In *Julie Guindon v. The Queen*, [2013] 1 C.T.C. 2007, 2012 DTC 1283 (T.C.C.), the Minister assessed penalties under section 163.2 of the Act in the amount of $546,747 in connection with the issuance of 135 charitable tax receipts that the taxpayer, Ms. Guindon, knew, or would reasonably be expected to have known, constituted false statements that could be used to claim an unwarranted tax credit under the Act. In her appeal to the Tax Court of Canada, Ms. Guindon argued that the imposition of a penalty under section 163.2 involved by its very nature a criminal proceeding in respect of which the protection under section 11 of the *Charter* would apply to guarantee fundamental substantive and procedural legal rights to any individual so charged. In particular, the individual charged would have the right to be presumed innocent, the effect of which would be to raise the burden of proof from that of proof on a balance of probabilities to proof beyond a reasonable doubt (paragraph 5). The taxpayer's appeal was allowed by Justice Bédard of the Tax Court of Canada, who vacated the Minister's assessment. In reaching his conclusion, Justice Bédard determined that section 163.2 went beyond the mere imposition of an administrative penalty, intended to ensure compliance with the Act, and should be considered as creating a criminal offence, intended to "promote public order and protect the public at large" (paragraph 70). Furthermore, the characterization of section 163.2 as an offence required that it be prosecuted in provincial court under the criminal procedure provided for in the *Criminal Code*. Notwithstanding that Justice Bédard vacated the Minister's assessment, on the basis that section 163.2 created a criminal offence, he went on to find that the evidence submitted by the Minister conclusively demonstrated Ms. Guindon's culpable conduct, and that the penalty under section 163.2 would have been applicable if that penalty were a civil one (paragraph 102). The Minister appealed the decision to the Federal Court of Appeal ([2013] 5 C.T.C. 1, 2013 D.T.C. 5113) which held that Justice Bédard's finding would require a ruling that, as a constitutional matter, some or all of section 163.2 was invalid, inoperable or inapplicable, and that the jurisdiction to make such a ruling is present only when a notice of constitutional question has been served on the Attorneys General (paragraph 29). Given that Ms. Guindon had failed to serve a notice of constitutional question, Justice Bédard lacked the jurisdiction to find that section 163.2 created an offence, triggering the rights under section 11 of the *Charter* (paragraphs 28 and 32). In result, the FCA allowed the Minister's appeal and dismissed Ms. Guindon's appeal from the Minister's assessment of penalties (on the basis that Justice Bédard concluded that the penalty would have been applicable if that penalty were a civil one) (paragraph 62). Leave to appeal by the Supreme Court of Canada has been allowed (2014 CarswellNat 654 (S.C.C.)).

Arguably, the *Charter* provision with the most significance for the interpretation and application of statutes is subsection 15(1), which provides that:

> Every individual is equal before and under the law and has the right to the equal protection and equal benefit of the law without discrimination and, in particular, without discrimination based on race, national or ethnic origin, colour, religion, sex, age or mental or physical disability.

The determination of whether a statutory provision is contrary to subsection 15(1) of the *Charter* involves a four-step process. First, does the impugned provision establish an inequality based upon a personal characteristic? Second, if an inequality is found, does it result in discrimination? Third, if an inequality and discrimination are found, is the personal characteristic at issue either an enumerated or analogous ground for the purposes of subsection 15(1) of the *Charter*? If so, is the provision saved by section 1 of the *Charter*? The government bears the burden of proving under section 1 that a *Charter* infringement is a reasonable limit, demonstrably justified in a free and democratic society.

In a number of cases, taxpayers have challenged various provisions of the Act as discriminatory under subsection 15(1) of the *Charter*. In most of these cases, the taxpayers were unsuccessful: see, for example, *Symes v. The Queen* (1993), [1994] 1 C.T.C. 40, 94 D.T.C. 6001 (S.C.C.) (concerning the deduction of child care expenses in section 63) and *The Queen v. Thibaudeau*, [1995] 1 C.T.C. 382, 95 D.T.C. 5273 (S.C.C.) (concerning the tax treatment of child support payments under paragraphs 56(1)(b) and 60(b)). These two cases are reviewed in detail in Part II of Chapter 8.

However, in *Re Rosenberg et al. and the Attorney General of Canada*, [2000] 2 C.T.C. 83, 98 D.T.C. 6286 (Ont. C.A.), the taxpayer successfully challenged the definition of "spouse" in subsection 252(4) on the basis that it discriminated against same-sex couples in the context of the registered pension plan provisions. The appropriate remedy, according to the court (at paragraph 53), was "to read the words 'or the same sex' into the definition of 'spouse' in subsection 252(4) for the purpose of the registration of pension plans and amendments to registered pension plans".

Following this decision, the Minister of Finance announced that the definition of spouse would be amended to include same-sex couples for all purposes. Amendments to the Act to incorporate this change were included in the *Modernization of Benefits and Obligations Act*, S.C. 2000, c. 12, which amends a number of federal acts that provide for benefits or obligations that depend on an individual's relationship to another family member. Effective 2001, this statute amended subsection 248(1) to add definitions of "common-law partner" and "common-law partnership". The extended definition of "spouse" in subsection 252(4) was also deleted (although the term retains its ordinary meaning). Finally, all references in other provisions of the Act to a spouse or marriage were amended to references to a spouse or common-law partner or marriage or common-law partnership, respectively.

D. The "Hansard Rule"

The "*Hansard* rule" excludes the use by the courts of parliamentary debates and other legislative history as aids to statutory interpretation. The *Hansard* rule originated in 18th century U.K. jurisprudence and remains a part of Canadian jurisprudence, although certain exceptions to the rule are well recognized. For example, it is permissible to look at legislative history for the purpose of determining the mischief or evil which the legislation was intended to correct or for the purpose of determining the constitutional validity of a statute or for interpreting the *Constitution Act*, 1982.

In the United Kingdom, the rule was modified in *Pepper v. Hart* (1992), [1993] 1 All E.R. 42, in which the House of Lords held that parliamentary debates can be used as aids to statutory interpretation where the legislation is ambiguous or absurd, the statements relied on are made by a minister or other sponsor of the legislation, and the statements are clear.

One commentator has suggested that section 12 of the *Interpretation Act* (the predecessor of which was first enacted in 1869) implicitly requires judges to look at parliamentary debates and other legislative history in order to determine the purpose of legislation (G. Bale, "Parliamentary Debates and Statutory Interpretation: Switching on the Light or Rummaging in the Ashcans of the Legislative Process" (1995) 74 *Can. Bar Rev.* 1-28). In practice, many Canadian judges have been considering legislative history in one way or another for many years. In *The Queen v. Fibreco Export Inc.*, [1995] 2 C.T.C. 172, 95 D.T.C. 5412 (F.C.A.), the Court suggested that the use of administrative practice and parliamentry history was a "question of weight rather than admissibility".

Consider the decisions in *Lor-Wes Contracting Ltd. v. The Queen*, [1985] 2 C.T.C. 79, 85 D.T.C. 5310 (F.C.A.); *Edmonton Liquid Gas Ltd. v. The Queen*, [1984] C.T.C. 536, 84 D.T.C. 6526 (F.C.A.); and *Canterra Energy Ltd. v. The Queen*, [1985] 1 C.T.C. 329, 85 D.T.C. 5245 (F.C.T.D.). Is a distinction readily apparent between the use of extrinsic materials to ascertain the evil that a provision is intended to remedy as opposed to the intention of Parliament evidenced in the provision? Can extrinsic materials be used to determine the "object and spirit" of the legislative provision, in accordance with the *Stubart* guidelines? Can extrinsic materials be used in order to determine whether a transaction would result in a misuse of the provisions of the Act or an abuse of the Act under subsection 245(4)?

III. TAX EVASION VERSUS TAX AVOIDANCE

The Canadian income tax system is one of self-assessment. As a result, it relies on the honesty of taxpayers. It is recognized, however, that there will be attempts by some to evade or improperly avoid tax under the Act. The terms "tax evasion" and "tax avoidance" are not easily defined. Obviously, the object of both is the reduction or elimination of income tax. The major distinction is illustrated by the different consequences to a taxpayer of an unsuccessful attempt to evade or avoid tax. In the case of tax evasion, the consequences are criminal in nature and lead to the imposition of a fine or incarceration in addition to civil consequences, which involve the payment of the tax that has been evaded, interest and penalties. An unsuccessful attempt to avoid tax involves no criminal penalty in the nature of a fine or incarceration, but merely payment of the tax, interest and, perhaps, the imposition of civil penalties. In other words, tax evasion has a criminal connotation while tax avoidance does not.

A. Tax Evasion

Somewhat simplistically, one might define tax evasion as the wilful attempt by a taxpayer to suppress or not disclose income where the law clearly stipulates the obligation to report the income and pay the tax. Tax evasion inevitably involves an element of non-disclosure of some kind. In more difficult cases, there will be either partial disclosure with the omission of significant information or complete or partial misrepresentation of significant facts.

Ordinarily, tax evasion involves the following:

(1) not filing a tax return;

(2) filing a tax return but wilfully omitting income;

(3) filing a tax return containing a wilful misrepresentation of the nature or amount of income;

(4) arranging for the receipt of income in a jurisdiction or form whereby that income will not come to the attention of the CRA and, of course, wilfully omitting reference to the income in the tax return (e.g., receiving payment for services in cash, which the taxpayer believes cannot be traced); and/ or

(5) characterizing a transaction both in the books of account and the tax return in a manner so as to disguise the real object or benefit of the transaction (e.g., recording an expense which has not been incurred in the income-earning process).

However, the offence of tax evasion leading to criminal penalty does not extend to the disclosure of income and the non-payment of the resulting tax, unless there is a deliberate attempt to secrete assets to avoid execution (paragraph 239(1)(d)). Collection of income tax is a civil matter for which the criminal process is seen as an inappropriate mechanism. The heart of culpable tax evasion goes to the wilful attempt by a taxpayer to suppress an accurate determination of the nature and amount of the liability for tax.

Information Circular No. 73-10R3: Tax Evasion (February 13, 1987) sets forth the organization and attitude of the CRA in matters of tax evasion and is also a handy reference guide to the relevant statutory provisions.

Review sections 238 and 239 of the Act, then read the following decisions.

REGINA v. BRANCH

[1976] C.T.C. 193, 76 D.T.C. 6112 (District Court of Alberta)

[The accused practised dentistry in Calgary and admittedly had not filed tax returns for the years 1970-1973 inclusive. He had kept books and had filed returns for 1968 and 1969.]

Medhurst D.J.:

... The Accused gave evidence to the effect that he filed his tax returns for 1968 and 1969 and in 1970 he encountered marital problems. His first marriage broke up and a subsequent remarriage also ended after a short period. The Accused stated he was washed up emotionally and the burden became too much. He was ashamed to consult an accountant. This is the explanation given by the Accused for his failure to comply with the numerous demands made on him to file a tax return.

Counsel for the Appellant and for the Crown have referred me to recent reported decisions respecting prosecutions under this section of the *Income Tax Act*.

In *Regina v. Baker*, 45 D.L.R. (3d) 247, Nova Scotia County Court Judge McLellan had this to say:

... It seems obvious, then, that Parliament did not intend the word 'evasion' in s. 239(1)(d) to mean simple avoidance, and, therefore, I think that the other meaning given by the dictionaries in explanation of evade'-to avoid by craft, artifice or strategy-is the meaning of the word 'evade' as used in s. 239(1)(d).

I am supported in this view by the definition of 'evasion' in Black's Law Dictionary-'artifice or cunning is implicit in the term as applied to contest between citizen and government over taxation'.

I come to the same decision if I take the view that, as there is more than one choice of meaning for the word 'evade', I must, in a penal section of a taxation statute, use the meaning most favourable to the accused. In this case, it would be the meaning of 'avoiding by artifice, craft, or strategy'. ...

...

It is noted that paragraph 239(1)(d) of the *Income Tax Act* actually creates two offences. The first is wilfully, in any manner, evading or attempting to evade compliance with the Act. The second offence is wilfully, in any manner, evading or attempting to evade payment of taxes imposed by the Act.

Many decisions have been given on the interpretation to be placed on words used in a statute and it is an accepted principle that such words shall be given the meaning ordinarily attached to them.

The Accused has been charged with wilfully evading payment of taxes imposed by the *Income Tax Act*. This is an offence punishable on summary conviction and *mens rea* is an essential element. Furthermore Counsel for the Crown readily conceded that the offence must be proven beyond a reasonable doubt. It was submitted on behalf of the Crown that the circumstances of the failure to file the tax returns as required and the failure to pay any tax constitute an evasion of obligations as contemplated by the Act.

...

In my opinion the word evade implies something of an underhanded or deceitful nature. In other words a deliberate attempt to escape the requirement of paying tax on income that had been earned. This intention can be inferred from acts of omission or commission. Certainly failure to file tax returns and to pay taxes for four successive years might suggest an attempt to evade in some way the payment of taxes.

However in the case of the Accused we have other factors to consider. There is no suggestion that there was anything secretive about his default. He was convicted in 1972, 1973 and 1974 of failing to file tax returns. He had received numerous demands to file returns and he knew that he was under surveillance. It also appears that the records were intact when finally taken over by the Tax Department for examination. The explanation given by the Accused is that during this period he was having personal problems and was emotionally washed up.

On a consideration of all of the circumstances I am unable to conclude that the Accused has wilfully evaded payment of income tax. I find the Accused not guilty of the charge and allow the appeal against conviction.

REGINA v. HUMMEL
[1971] C.T.C. 803, 76 D.T.C. 6114 (B.C. Prov. Ct.)

[Hummel was charged with wilful evasion of the payment of taxes in Count 1 of an indictment. The other four counts related to making false and deceptive statements in his tax returns.]

Robinson J.: ...

Both counsel presented arguments as to the matter of whether or not *mens rea* was an integral part of the offence; that is, an essential ingredient that the Crown must prove in order to support a conviction.

There was little argument with respect to *mens rea* concerning Count 1. The main issue was whether or not it was necessary for the Crown to prove mens rea-namely, a guilty intent, to support a conviction under Counts 2 to 5 inclusive.

... I hold that *mens rea* is an integral part of the defence, and for the Crown to succeed-that is, to make out a case to support a conviction-they would have to prove a guilty intent on the part of the accused.

Now, it is important to look carefully at the particulars in Counts 2 to 5 with respect to *mens rea*-guilty intent. First, there is the matter of the gain on the sale of shares of the Park Royal Holdings and the Red Lion Motor Inn. I have before me the evidence of Mr. Thorsteinsson who was called by the Crown as an expert on the subject of income tax, and he gave evidence that the gain on the sale of shares, whether capital or income, presented problems of indissoluble difficulty, and that this was a problem to the Tax Department, the Exchequer Court and the Supreme Court of Canada.

In summary, a number of these types of cases are borderline. They are in the grey area, and certainly, if the taxpayer decides it is capital this does not necessarily mean that this is evidence of guilty intent, or evidence from which an inference of guilty intent may be inferred, as opposed to the matter of obvious income that has not been disclosed.

Another item in Counts 2 to 5 is the matter of salary paid to the accused's wife. Again, Mr. Thorsteinsson, the expert, gave evidence as to the salary of a wife in a corporate body, and the question is — "Is this salary reasonable and justified?"

Mr. Stokes again confirmed this, and Mr. Marquardt and Mr. Warren gave evidence for the Crown; they gave evidence of Mrs. Hummel's participation in the business enterprises; of her knowledgeability and various other items. Again, whether this salary is justified depends on the circumstances. The taxpayer says it is reasonable and justified. The Department says — no. Surely this in itself is not evidence of guilty intent or evidence from which guilty intent can be inferred.

Another item dealt with in Counts 2 to 5 is the matter of car expenses and allowances. Allowances from companies depend on circumstances and reasonableness and the amount of it. Again Mr. Thorsteinsson and Mr. Stokes confirmed this, and there was evidence adduced from Mr. Marquardt as to the extent to which the vehicles of the accused were used with respect to the various business enterprises. The question is, "Is it income or proper reimbursement of expenses?" Again, it depends upon the circumstances and is not a simple matter of drawing the inference of guilty intent.

The other item in Counts 2 to 5 is funds appropriated by the accused as a shareholder from the Victoria Private Hospitals Ltd., and the question is whether the Victoria Private Hospitals Ltd. got proper value for its money; namely, approximately $104,000. This again depends on the fair market value; again a questionable item. A fair market value at the time the transaction took place.

Now, all of these items are not obviously income but, as I have stated before, are borderline cases depending on the circumstances. In my opinion, from the evidence adduced with respect to them, there is no evidence of guilty intent, or evidence.

In summary on that point, it simply means this: the taxpayer says they are not income and the Tax Department says they are and the circumstances of each one would determine whether they are or not.

...

There was clear evidence that the family arrangements and agreements were entered into. There was always considerable delay in reducing these arrangements and agreements to writing. There is no evidence of any sham, scheme, gimmick, hiding of facts, mis-stating the true picture or falsification of documents or accounts for the purpose of evading taxes of falsifying returns.

There was evidence that chartered accountants were employed for the various companies, which was the firm of Roberts, Benson & Hill and another chartered accountant was also employed at the Red Lion. There was considerable evidence adduced regarding the financial problems — the financing of the various enterprises and the manoeuvres to accomplish this. But, these manoeuvres were for the purpose of financing and not for the purpose of evading income tax or falsifying returns.

From the whole of the evidence, and having examined it minutely and weighed with care the arguments of counsel on behalf of the Crown and the accused, ... I can find no evidence of *mens rea*, guilty intent, or any evidence from which I can infer guilty intent.

Accordingly, I would grant the motion of Mr. Spencer on behalf of the accused and find the accused not guilty on all five counts and would dismiss all five counts accordingly.

In *Regina v. Lundy* (1972), 72 D.T.C. 6093, a decision of the British Columbia Provincial Court, the court reviewed the activities of the taxpayer, his background and the surrounding circumstances and found that his sale of certain shares was an adventure in the nature of trade which had not been reported as such in his return for the appropriate year. The Court said (at 6116):

> Having found that Lundy's sale of his shares in Sterling and Paragon was an adventure in the nature of trade and profit derived therefrom reportable as income, that, together with my findings as to his credibility as a witness, and his extensive background and experience in dealing with securities and security matters, I am satisfied beyond any reasonable doubt that Lundy, if he did not know then he should have known, that the profits from the sale of his shares in Sterling and Paragon was income to him and should have been reported as such by him in his income tax returns ... for the taxation years 1965 and 1966 and this he failed to do.
>
> I am also satisfied beyond any reasonable doubt that, in omitting this additional income from his income tax returns in the amounts so found for the taxation years 1965 and 1966, it was done deliberately and deceitfully by Lundy and with that specific intent to evade the payment of income tax on it.
>
> I am also satisfied beyond any reasonable doubt that the income reported by Lundy in his income tax returns for each of the years 1965 and 1966 was false and the omission of additional income for each of those years was done deliberately and with an intent to deceive in order to escape liability for the further payment of income tax in those two years.

The taxpayer was convicted of an offence under section 239 (as it now is) of the Act. Consider the implication of the statement that it is sufficient that the taxpayer knew or "should have known" that the profit on the sale of shares was income in order to find the necessary *mens rea* for conviction. Is that a suitable test of *mens rea* for the purposes of a criminal prosecution? Is it the same as the "wilful blindness" test in *R. v. Sault Ste Marie*, [1978] 2 S.C.R. 1299? Can the decision be rationalized in light of the findings in the *Hummel* decision, specifically, that part which deals with the borderline nature of cases involving the definition of income and capital? In the years in question in *Lundy* the Act did not impose liability on a capital gain. Therefore, many taxpayers did not report such gains in those situations where they alleged that the gain was not income for the purposes of the Act. *Lundy* was convicted in such a circumstance. Since the major amendments to the Act in 1972, a portion of a capital gain is treated as income and must be reported as such. If the taxpayer in *Lundy* had declared his gains as capital and had disclosed all surrounding facts, would the court have been able to find the offence under section 239? Can the characterization by a taxpayer of facts and circumstances fully disclosed ever amount to tax evasion?

B. Tax Avoidance

As mentioned previously, tax avoidance consists of open attempts to take advantage of the tax laws by arranging a taxpayer's affairs to reduce the amount of income tax payable. The list of tax avoidance techniques, whether successful or unsuccessful, is very long. The following are some common types of tax avoidance:

(1) splitting income between two or more taxpayers so as to reduce the marginal rate of tax exigible thereon;

(2) shifting income from one taxpayer to another lower-taxed legal entity in which the taxpayer has the beneficial interest, such as a corporation or a trust or partnership;

(3) shifting losses from one taxpayer to another taxpayer;

(4) deferring the payment of tax on income currently earned;

(5) sheltering of income either in a "tax haven" country which imposes a lesser rate of tax or no tax at all or through the use of shelters implicit in the domestic tax scheme (e.g., capital cost allowance or retirement plans);

(6) converting otherwise taxable income into capital which may remain untaxed or taxed at a lesser rate; or into some form of intangible benefit to the recipient, the receipt of which will be untaxed; or into some form of income otherwise exempt from tax by the provisions of the Act;

(7) converting capital expenditures into apparently current expenses;

(8) utilizing valuation techniques designed to offer maximum advantage to the taxpayer;

(9) passing on property with accrued capital gains or losses by one taxpayer to another so that tax consequences arise only when the other taxpayer disposes of the property in a chargeable transaction (e.g., rollovers); and/or

(10) the structuring of a commercial transaction in a manner designed to minimize the tax burden.

Judicial Limits on Tax Avoidance

The judicial response to tax avoidance is directly related to the approach of the judiciary to the interpretation of the Act. Historically, the judicial response to tax avoidance was relatively sympathetic as a consequence of the judiciary's strict interpretation of statutory provisions. The following case is the seminal case cited in support of the application of the strict approach to statutory interpretation in the context of tax avoidance.

C.I.R. v. THE DUKE OF WESTMINSTER
[1936] A.C. 1, 19 T.C. 490, 51 T.L.R. 467 (H.L.)

[The respondent executed several deeds relating to payments to be made by him to named persons; the deeds were substantially similar. By a deed made in August 1930, the respondent covenanted to pay Allman, a gardener in his employment, a yearly sum of £98 16s. by weekly payments of £1 18s. for a period of seven years or during the joint lives of the parties, and it was agreed that the payments were without prejudice to the remuneration to which Allman should be entitled for services, if any, thereafter rendered.

Before the deed was executed, the respondent's solicitors, on his instructions, wrote to Allman a letter the material parts of which were as follows: "On the 6th inst. we read over with you a deed of covenant which the Duke of Westminster has signed in your favour. ... We explained that there is nothing in the deed to prevent your being entitled to and claiming full remuneration for such further work as you may do, though it is expected that in practice you will be content with the provision which is being legally made for you for so long as the deed takes effect with the addition of such sum, if any, as may be necessary to bring the total periodical payment while you are still in the Duke's service up to the amount of the salary or wages which you have lately been receiving. You said that you accepted this arrangement, and you accordingly executed the deed. ... If you are still quite satisfied, we propose to insert the 6th inst. as the date of the deed, and we shall be obliged by your signing the acknowledgment at the foot of this letter and returning it to us." Allman signed the acknowledgment accepting the provision made for him and agreeing to the deed being dated and treated as delivered and binding on the parties thereto. The acknowledgment was stamped with a sixpenny stamp.

The question was whether certain payments made by the Duke of Westminster under the above documents were annual payments within section 27 of the Income Tax Act, 1918 and so admissible as deductions in arriving at the liability of the Duke for surtax for the years 1929-1930, 1930-1931 and 1931-1932.]

Lord Atkin (dissenting):

... It was not, I think, denied — at any rate it is incontrovertible — that the deeds were brought into existence as a device by which the respondent might avoid some of the burden of surtax. I do not use the word device in any sinister sense, for it has to be recognized that the subject, whether poor and humble or wealthy and noble, has the legal right so to dispose of his capital and income as to attract upon himself the least amount of tax. The only function of a Court of law is to determine the legal result of his dispositions so far as they affect tax. In the present case Finlay J., affirming the Commissioners, decided in favour of the Crown, while the Court of Appeal have set aside that decision and given judgment in favour of the respondent. ...

... I do not myself see any difficulty in the view taken by the Commissioners and Finlay J. that the substance of the transaction was that what was being paid was remuneration. Both the Commissioners and Finlay J. took the document of August 13 into consideration as part of the whole transaction, and in my opinion rightly. I agree that you must not go beyond the legal effect of the agreements and conveyances made, construed in accordance with ordinary rules in reference to all the surrounding circumstances. So construed the correct view of the legal effect of the documents appears to me to be the result I have mentioned. I think the difficulty has probably arisen from the wording of the Commissioners' finding that "the payments made under the deed were in substance" payments by way of remuneration. Standing alone I do not think that phrase would be justified. But reference to the immediately preceding sentence indicates that the Commissioners had taken into consideration the letters and form of acknowledgment before expressing their finding as above. Though they have not analysed the transaction as fully as I have endeavoured to do, I have little doubt that they and Finlay J. arrived at the same result as I, and it may be noted that so far as there is any question of fact involved, the finding of the Commissioners, if there is evidence, is final. ...

Lord Tomlin: ... Apart, however, from the question of contract with which I have dealt, it is said that in revenue cases there is a doctrine that the Court may ignore the legal position and regard what is called "the substance of the matter", and that here the substance of the matter is that the annuitant was serving the Duke for something equal to his former salary or wages, and that therefore, while he is so serving, the annuity must be treated as salary or wages. This supposed doctrine (upon which the Commissioners apparently acted) seems to rest for its support upon a misunderstanding of language used in some earlier cases. The sooner this misunderstanding is dispelled, and the supposed doctrine given its quietus, the better it will be for all concerned, for the doctrine seems to involve substituting "the incertain and crooked cord of discretion" for "the golden and streight metwand of the law". Every man is entitled if he can to order his affairs so as that the tax attaching under the appropriate Acts is less than it otherwise would be. If he succeeds in ordering them so as to secure this result, then, however unappreciative the Commissioners of Inland Revenue or his fellow taxpayers may be of his ingenuity, he cannot be compelled to pay an increased tax. This so-called doctrine of "the substance" seems to me to be nothing more than an attempt to make a man pay notwithstanding that he has so ordered his affairs that the amount of tax sought from him is not legally claimable.

The principal passages relied upon are from opinions of Lord Herschell and Lord Halsbury in your Lordships' House. Lord Herschell L.C. in *Helby v. Matthews* observed: "it is said that the substance of the transaction evidenced by the agreement must be looked at, and not its mere words. I quite agree;" but he went on to explain that the substance must be ascertained by a consideration of the rights and obligations of the parties to be derived from a consideration of the whole of the agreement. In short Lord Herschell was saying that the substance of a transaction embodied in a written instrument is to be found by construing the document as a whole.

Support has also been sought by the appellants from the language of Lord Halsbury L.C. in *Secretary of State in Council of India v. Scoble.* There Lord Halsbury said: "Still, looking at the whole nature and substance of the transaction (and it is agreed on all sides that we must look at the nature of the transaction and not be bound by the mere use of the words), this is not the case of a purchase of an annuity." Here again Lord Halsbury is only giving utterance to the indisputable rule that the surrounding circumstances must be regarded in construing a document.

Neither of these passages in my opinion affords the appellants any support or has any application to the present case. The matter was put accurately by my noble and learned friend Lord Warrington of Clyffe when as Warrington L.J. in *In re Hinckes, Dashwood v. Hinckes* he used these words: "It is said we must go behind the form and look at the substance ... but, in order to ascertain the substance, I must look at the legal effect of the bargain which the parties have entered into." So here the substance is that which results from the legal rights and obligations of the parties ascertained upon ordinary legal principles, and, having regard to what I have already said, the conclusion must be that each annuitant is entitled to an annuity which as between himself and the payer is liable to deduction of income tax by the payer and which the payer is entitled to treat as a deduction from his total income for surtax purposes.

There may, of course, be cases where documents are not *bona fide* nor intended to be acted upon, but are only used as a cloak to conceal a different transaction. No such case is made or even suggested here. The deeds of covenant are admittedly bona fide and have been given their proper legal operation. They cannot be ignored or treated as operating in some different way because as a result less duty is payable than would have been the case if some other arrangement (called for the purpose of the appellants' argument, "the substance") had been made.

I find myself, therefore, in regard to the annuities other than that of Blow, unable to take the same view as the noble and learned Lord upon the Woolsack.

In my opinion in regard to all the annuities the appeal fails and ought to be dismissed with costs.

Lord Russell of Killowen: My Lords, I would dismiss this appeal. ...

The result is that payments, the liability for which arises only under the deed, are not and cannot be said to be payments of salary or wages within Sch. E. They cannot with any regard to the true legal position be said to arise from an employment. They are, and can only be said to be, annual payments within Sch. D. Tax was deductible on payment; they are income of the recipient, and are accordingly not part of the Duke's total income for the purpose of calculating his liability for surtax.

The Commissioners and Finlay J. took the opposite view on the ground that (as they said) looking at the substance of the thing the payments were payments of wages. This simply means that the true legal position is disregarded, and a different legal right and liability substituted in the place of the legal right and liability which the parties have created. I confess that I view with disfavour the doctrine that in taxation cases the subject is to be taxed if, in accordance with a Court's view of what it considers the substance of the transaction, the Court thinks that the case falls within the contemplation or spirit of the statute. The subject is not taxable by inference or by analogy, but only by the plain words of a statute applicable to the facts and circumstances of his case. As Lord Cairns said many years ago in *Partington v. Attorney-General*: "As I understand the principle of all fiscal legislation it is this: If the person sought to be taxed comes within the letter of the law he must be taxed, however great the hardship may appear to the judicial mind to be. On the other hand, if the Crown, seeking to recover the tax, cannot bring the subject within the letter of the law, the subject is free, however apparently within the spirit of the law the case might otherwise appear to be." If all that is meant by the doctrine is that having once ascertained the legal rights of the parties you may disregard mere nomenclature and decide the question of taxability or non-taxability in accordance with the legal rights, well and good. That is what this House did in the case of *Secretary of State in Council of India v. Scoble*; that and no more. If, on the other hand, the doctrine means that you may brush aside deeds, disregard the legal rights and liabilities arising under a contract between parties, and decide the question of taxability or non-taxability upon the footing of the rights and liabilities of the parties being different from what in law they are, then I entirely dissent from such a doctrine.

The substance of the transaction between Allman and the Duke is in my opinion to be found and to be found only by ascertaining their respective rights and liabilities under the deed, the legal effect of which is what I have already stated.

The case of Mr. Blow's deed, which is uncomplicated by any letter, is necessarily decided, in my view, in the same way as Allman's case.

For these reasons I am of opinion that the order of the Court of Appeal was right and ought to be affirmed.

[Lord Macmillan and Lord Wright also wrote judgments dismissing the appeal.]

The *Duke of Westminster* has been considered by the House of Lords and the Supreme Court of Canada on a number of occasions, some of which are discussed below. The *Stubart* decision, with its adoption of the modern approach to statutory interpretation, was thought to have dealt a harsh blow to a burgeoning tax avoidance industry. The following extract from *Stubart* includes a discussion of the various judicial approaches to tax avoidance in Canada.

STUBART INVESTMENTS v. THE QUEEN
[1984] C.T.C. 294, 84 D.T.C. 6305 (S.C.C.)

[The appellant, a wholly-owned profitable subsidiary of Finlayson, sold its assets to Grover, a sister subsidiary which had incurred substantial losses, so that the appellant's profits might be offset by the losses with a resulting reduction in tax payable. The Act allows losses from one business to be offset against gains from another business within the same entity. However, it does not permit consolidated tax returns for related corporations. Grover appointed the appellant to carry on business as its agent for and to the account of Grover. The appellant did so and at the end of the fiscal years for 1966, 1967 and 1968 paid to Grover the net income from the business. Grover included that amount in its corporate tax return, but the Minister reassessed the appellant, set aside the transfer of income to Grover and included it in the appellant's income. At issue was whether a corporate taxpayer, with the avowed purpose of reducing its taxes, could establish an arrangement whereby future profits would be routed through a sister subsidiary in order to avail itself of the latter corporation's loss carry-forward. Two subsidiary issues dealt with whether or not the transaction was a sham, and whether or not it was complete. The Crown advanced no argument based on former section 137 (a provision that denied deductions which unduly or artificially reduced income) of the Act.]

Estey, J.: ... No section of the Act was isolated by the Attorney General of Canada as clearly authorizing the assessments which gave rise to these proceedings. Assuming for the moment there is no sham, the respondent asks the Court to find, without express statutory basis, that no transaction is valid in the income tax computation process that has not been entered into by the taxpayer for a valid business purpose. The respondent asserts that by definition, an independent business purpose does not include tax reduction for its own sake.

...

The simple question, therefore, is whether a corporate group can avail itself of a tax loss in one of the family subsidiaries by rerouting the income from another corporate member into that subsidiary. Clearly, the corporation can do so by buying assets from any business, corporate or unincorporate, and putting these profit-generating assets into a company with an accepted loss position. The purchase of the shares of another company which has a loss carry-forward might prevent its utilization by the purchaser. With that we are not here concerned. If the taxpayer can expand an existing business to create earnings to make use of a loss carry-forward, then one must find some prohibition in the Act to say that the purchase of such additional assets may not come through a non-arm's length transaction; apart from section 137 which has not been relied upon by the respondent here. To this consideration I will return.

The main issue is already set forth, but there are two subsidiary issues.

1. A sham transaction: This expression comes to us from decisions in the United Kingdom, and it has been generally taken to mean (but not without ambiguity) a transaction conducted with an element of deceit so as to create an illusion calculated to lead the tax collector away from the taxpayer or the true nature of the transaction; or, simple deception whereby the taxpayer creates a facade of reality quite different from the disguised reality. ...

2. The application of section 137 of the *Income Tax Act*, *supra*, (section 245 in the new Act) [since repealed and replaced by the general anti-avoidance rule in section 245, discussed in Part III.B.2., *infra*]: This is an anti-tax avoidance section which states that no "disbursement" which "artificially" reduces the income of a taxpayer shall be taken into account in determining tax liability. The section provides in part as follows:

> ...
>
> In computing income for the purposes of this Act, no deduction may be made in respect of a disbursement or expense made or incurred in respect of a transaction or operation that, if allowed, would unduly or artificially reduce the income.

While it is at least arguable that this section covers the "disbursement" by the appellant of the profits earned for the account of Grover in the operation of the business, the Attorney General of Canada expressly, in response to a question from the Court during the hearing of the appeal, said that the Crown was not relying upon section 137. Clearly the cheque transferring the profit from the appellant to Grover at the end of the year is a disbursement, and it is a disbursement the deduction of which leaves no taxable income in the appellant from the business. The Crown does not advance this argument in this appeal presumably in the hope that the tax liability of the appellant will be founded on the "genuine business purpose" principle or the "abuse of rights" principle which are said to form part of the taxation principles in the laws of the United Kingdom and the United States and elsewhere, and which the respondent submits are equally applicable in the interpretation of the *Income Tax Act of Canada*, *supra*.

Returning then to the main issues in this appeal, the respondent asserts the right to tax here on two bases:

A. The transfer is, in any event, incomplete, and therefore should be disregarded and the transferor and transferee taxed according to their respective positions as though this transaction had not taken place;

B. Canadian cases have already established the principle recently stated in the United Kingdom in *Ramsay v. Inland Revenue Commissioners*, *infra*, in *Commissioners of Inland Revenue v. Burmah Oil Company*, *infra*, and in *Furniss (Inspector of Taxes) Appellant v. Dawson*, *et al.*, *infra*, namely, that a transaction without a valid business purpose is not to be taken into account in the computation of liability for tax under the ITA.

...

It is acknowledged that the transferor, the appellant, and the transferee, Grover, completed thirty legal steps in the transfer of the business to Grover. These included the contract of purchase and sale, the implementing documentation all of which has been enumerated above. The purchase price for the business was paid by the assumption by Grover of the secured indebtedness of the appellant to the Bank and by the issuance of secured notes. The respondent did not question the appellant's assertion that the Bank of Nova Scotia, on the default of Grover, would have had the clear right in law to recover from the transferred assets the unpaid balance of the debt assumed by Grover on the purchase of the business from the appellant.

Nevertheless, the Crown says that the following matters were not attended to in relation to the transfer of assets between the parties to the contract and that, therefore, the contract of purchase and sale was not completed. ...

[Estey, J. reviewed the evidence and concluded as follows:]

In my view, these facts and circumstances all lead inexorably to the conclusion that the transfer and sale of the business by the appellant to Grover in 1966 was, in law, fully complete. Grover became the owner of the business, and the appellant operated the business on behalf of and for the account of Grover.

...

What then is the law in Canada as regards the right of a taxpayer to order his affairs so as to reduce his tax liability without breaching any express term in the statute? Historically, the judicial response is found in *Bradford Corporation v. Pickles*, [1895] A.C. 587 where it was stated:

> If it was a lawful act, however ill the motive might be, he had a right to do it. If it was an unlawful act, however good his motive might be, he would have no right to do it (*per* Lord Halsbury LC at 594)
>
> No use of property, which would be legal if due to a proper motive, can become illegal because it is prompted by a motive which is improper or even malicious (*per* Lord Watson at 598).

In the field of taxation itself the traditional position was re-echoed in *I.R.C. v. Duke of Westminster*, [1936] A.C. 1 at 19 where it was stated:

> Every man is entitled if he can to order his affairs so as that the tax attaching under the appropriate Acts is less than it otherwise would be. If he succeeds in ordering them so as to secure this result, then, however unappreciative the Commissioners of Inland Revenue or his fellow taxpayers may be of his ingenuity, he cannot be compelled to pay an increased tax.

[American, Australian and the recent English authorities were considered by Estey, J.].

Secondly, and more importantly, the doctrines developing in *Ramsay and Burmah*, *supra*, reflect the role of the court in a regime where the legislature has enunciated taxing edicts in a detailed manner but has not superimposed thereon a general guideline for the elimination of mechanisms designed and established only to deflect the plain purpose of the taxing provision. The role that the judiciary must play in such a regime to control tax avoidance was recognised by Lord Reid, who, in *Greenberg v. I.R.C.* (1971), 47 T.C. 240, at 272, stated:

> We seem to have travelled a long way from the general and salutary rule that the subject is not to be taxed except by plain words. But I must recognize that plain words are seldom adequate to anticipate and forestall the multiplicity of ingenious schemes which are constantly being devised to evade taxation. Parliament is very properly determined to prevent this kind of tax evasion, and if the Courts find it impossible to give very wide meanings to general phrases the only alternative may be for Parliament to do as some other countries have done and introduce legislation of a more sweeping character, which will put the ordinary well-intentioned person at much greater risk than is created by a wide interpretation of such provisions as those which we are now considering.

Here the appellant has bound itself contractually to pay over the net profits of the business to Grover. Grover was already entitled to set off future earnings against a loss position recognized as valid by the administrators of the *Income Tax Act*. The earnings of Grover, under these valid arrangements, were gains realized in the market-place and were recognized as such by the terms of the Act. The application of the accumulated losses of Grover to reduce tax attributable to these gains is not denied by any provision in the Act. The tax administrators do not invoke section 137. Parliament has nowhere else in the Act expressed an interest in the appellant's accounting and corporate practices in question. At issue is the role and function of a court in these circumstances.

The examination of tax avoidance schemes continued in the House of Lords in *Furniss (Inspector of Taxes) Appellant v. Dawson, et al.* [[1984] A.C. 474 (H.L.)], forwarded to the Court by the respondent after the hearing of this appeal. ...

... It may well be that each of the three House of Lords decisions, *supra*, can be simply distinguished on the basis that in each case, a plan was adopted whereby the taxpayer took affirmative action to create the "loss" or "gain" by a procedure not otherwise required in the ordinary course of business; or that the taxpayer designed an accounting holding tank to delay artificially the receipt by the vendor of the proceeds of sale under an agreement for sale reached directly between the true parties to the transaction before the accounting scheme was established. Here the appellant was legally bound to pay a defined amount to another company which held a valid right of allowance under the *Income Tax Act* against tax liability which would otherwise arise upon the receipt of bona fide future earnings. It is not the taxability of the receipt which is in issue; it is the right of the appellant payor to deduct the amount from its income account and thereby free itself from taxation on the amount so paid out to Grover. There is nothing in the *Income Tax Act* of Canada which expressly prevents the appellant from obligating itself to pay over the sum in question. Section 137 might arguably apply on the grounds that the transaction falls within the reach of the expression "artificial transaction" but the taxing authority has not advanced this position in support of the tax claim here made. However, there remains the larger issue as to whether Canadian law recognizes, as a principle of interpretation, that the conduct of the taxpayer, not dictated by a genuine commercial or business purpose, and being designed wholly for the avoidance of tax otherwise impacting under the statute, can be set aside on the basis of *Furniss*, *supra*, or *Helvering*, *supra*, as though the transaction were, in fact and in law, a "sham."

The scene in Canada is less clear and has not, until this appeal, reached this Court.

[Estey J. reviewed the Canadian jurisprudence.]

The effect of the interworking of all these considerations or rules may be that a court must apply a taxing statute so as to bar the claim of entitlement to an allowance, deduction or other advantage or benefit where the taxpayer created entities or rights and obligations in order to revise the character, under the statute, of the income or earnings already achieved by the taxpayer. The claim would not necessarily be barred, however, where the new alignment of the taxpayer's affairs is adopted only to reduce or avoid taxation of earnings or income thereafter arising independently from the establishment of the arrangements in question.

Before returning to the immediate issue in this appeal, the state of the tax law under section 137, *supra*, as it has evolved in Canada should be briefly examined. Although this section is not invoked by the respondent in this appeal, it is relevant to note that to date the section has not been interpreted so as to incorporate "the *bona fide* business purpose test". Cattanach, J., in the Federal Court – Trial Division, after finding that the transaction in question was not a sham, determined that a tax advantage was not a benefit under subsection 137(2):

> What the defendant has done has been to order its affairs as to attract a lesser tax at a subsequent time as it is entitled to do ... The defendant has effected a tax advantage to itself as is its right and accordingly it is incongruous that that advantage should be construed as a "benefit" to the defendant within the meaning of s. 137(2).

The Queen v. Esskay Farms Ltd., [1976] C.T.C. 24; 76 D.T.C. 6010 at 36-37 [6018].

Notwithstanding that the taxpayer there deferred and reduced taxes otherwise payable on the sale of his land by interposing an independent trust company between himself and the purchaser, and by contract with the trust company delayed his receipt of the proceeds of sale over a period of years commencing several years after the sale, the proceeds of sale were not found to be taxable income. There was no purpose in all these arrangements other than the lessening of the impact of taxation on the transaction. No "independent business purpose test" emerged, and section 137 was found to be inapplicable. *Vide* also Pratte, J. in *Produits LDG Products Inc. v. The Queen*, [1976] C.T.C. 591; 76 D.T.C. 6344 at 598 [6349]:

> There is nothing reprehensible in seeking to take advantage of a benefit allowed by the law. If a taxpayer has made an expenditure which, according to the Act, he may deduct when calculating his income, I do not see how the reason which prompted him to act can in itself make this expenditure non-deductible. I therefore believe that in the case at bar, there is no reason to apply s. 137(1).

To the same effect is *The Queen v. Alberta and Southern Gas Co. Ltd.*, [1977] C.T.C. 388; 77 D.T.C. 5244 at 397 [5249] where Jackett, C.J. stated:

> ... a transaction which clearly falls within the object and spirit of [a given section of the Act] cannot be said to unduly or artificially reduce income merely

because the taxpayer was influenced in deciding to enter into it by tax considerations.

The courts, in applying section 137, and in applying general principles of statutory interpretation, seem, thus far at least, to have fallen short of adopting the "*bona fide* business purpose test". The Richardson case, supra, like the *Atinco* and *Rose* cases, *supra*, falls into the category of incomplete or legally ineffective transactions. The allowance or benefits sought by the taxpayer in those cases were simply not available by the procedures adopted by the taxpayer. Leon, supra, at its highest, is a modification of the sham test, but it seems to have been isolated on its factual base by *Massey-Ferguson*, *supra*.

...

With respect to the courts below, it seems to me that there may have been an unwitting confusion between the incomplete transaction test and the sham test. Earlier I have enumerated the many public registrations effected by the parties in the course of this transaction. The documents establishing and executing the arrangement between the parties were all in the records of the parties available for examination by the authorities. There has been no suggestion of backdating or buttressing the documentation after the event. The transaction and the form in which it was cast by the parties and their legal and accounting advisers cannot be said to have been so constructed as to create a false impression in the eyes of a third party, specifically the taxing authority. The appearance created by the documentation is precisely the reality. Obligations created in the documents were legal obligations in the sense that they were fully enforceable at law. The courts have thus far not extended the concept of sham to a transaction otherwise valid but entered into between parties not at arm's length. The reversibility of the transaction by reason of common ownership likewise has never been found, in any case drawn to the Court's attention, to be an element qualifying or disqualifying the transaction as a sham. If the factual possibility of reversibility were a test as to the legal effect of a transaction under the "sham" doctrine, a retail store's sales policy of guaranteed return of goods found to be unsatisfactory ("Goods satisfactory or money refunded") would render a transaction incomplete, unenforceable and a sham, whether or not the goods were ever returned to the vendor. In fact, of course, we know the transaction was not reversed but was indeed relied upon by the third party purchaser of the assets and undertaking of Grover. There is, in short, a total absence of the element of deceit, which is the heart in these circumstances of the doctrine of sham as it has developed in the case law of this country.

Returning then to the issue of interpretation now before this Court, there are certain broad characteristics of tax statute construction which can be discerned in the authorities here and in similar jurisdictions abroad. The most obvious is the fact that in some jurisdictions, such as Canada and Australia, the legislature has responded to the need for overall regulation to forestall blatant practices designed to defeat the Revenue. These anti-tax avoidance provisions may reflect the rising importance and cost of government in the community, the concomitant higher rates of taxation in modern times, and hence the greater stake in the avoidance contests between the taxpayer and the state. The arrival of these provisions in the statute may also have heralded the extension of the *Income Tax Act* from a mere tool for the carving of the cost of government out of the community, to an instrument of economic and fiscal policy for the regulation of commerce and industry of the country through fiscal intervention by government. Whatever the source or explanation, measures such as section 137 are instructions from Parliament to the community on the individual member's liability for taxes, expressed in general terms. This instruction is, like the balance of the Act, introduced as well for the guidance of the courts in applying the scheme of the Act throughout the country. The courts may, of course, develop, in their interpretation of section 137, doctrines such as the bona fide business purpose test; or a step-by-step transaction rule for the classification of taxpayers' activities which fall within the ban of such a general tax avoidance provision.

In jurisdictions such as the United States and the United Kingdom, such doctrines have developed in the courts, usually in the guise of canons of construction of the tax statutes. These have included the business purpose test, step-by-step transactions analysis, substance over form, and expanded sham rules. Whether the development be by legislative measure or judicial action, the result is a process of balancing the taxpayer's freedom to carry on his commercial and social affairs however he may choose, and the state interest in revenue, equity in the raising of the revenue, and economic planning. In Canada the sham concept is at least a judicial measure for the control of tax abuse without specific legislative direction. The judicial classification of an ineffective transaction is another. In the United States, these doctrines have expanded to include the business purpose test. The United States tax code is, as we have seen, replete with benefits in the form of special relief from general tax measures, but the problem is whether the bona fide business purpose test will, in a given circumstance, descend upon the taxpayer ex post facto. See Surrey et al., "Federal Income Taxation", *Cases and Materials* (Foundation Press 1973) at p. 644. In sharp contrast is the approach of Noël, J., as he then was, in *Foreign Power Securities Ltd. v. M.N.R.*, [1966] C.T.C. 23 at 52, 66 D.T.C. 5012 at 5027, where he stated:

> There is indeed no provision in the *Income Tax Act* which provides that, where it appears that the main purpose or one of the purposes for which any transaction or transactions was or were effected was the avoidance or reduction of liability to income tax, the Court may, if it thinks fit, direct that such adjustments shall be made as respects liability to income tax as it considers appro-

> priate so as to counteract the avoidance or reduction of liability to income tax which would otherwise be effected by the transaction or transactions.

Perhaps the high water mark in the opposition to the introduction of a business purpose test is found in the reasoning of the learned authors, Ward and Cullity, *supra*, who stated, at 473-75, in answer to the question: can it be a legitimate business purpose of a transaction to minimize or postpone taxes?:

> If taxes are minimized or postponed, more capital will be available to run the business and more profit will result. Surely, in the penultimate decade of the twentieth century it would be naive to suggest that businessmen can, or should, conduct and manage their business affairs without regard to the incidence of taxation or that they are not, or should not, be attracted to transactions or investments or forms of doing business that provide reduced burdens of taxation.

I would therefore reject the proposition that a transaction may be disregarded for tax purposes solely on the basis that it was entered into by a taxpayer without an independent or *bona fide* business purpose. A strict business purpose test in certain circumstances would run counter to the apparent legislative intent which, in the modern taxing statutes, may have a dual aspect. Income tax legislation, such as the federal Act in our country, is no longer a simple device to raise revenue to meet the cost of governing the community. Income taxation is also employed by government to attain selected economic policy objectives. Thus, the statute is a mix of fiscal and economic policy. The economic policy element of the Act sometimes takes the form of an inducement to the taxpayer to undertake or redirect a specific activity. Without the inducement offered by the statute, the activity may not be undertaken by the taxpayer for whom the induced action would otherwise have no bona fide business purpose. Thus, by imposing a positive requirement that there be such a bona fide business purpose, a taxpayer might be barred from undertaking the very activity Parliament wishes to encourage. At minimum, a business purpose requirement might inhibit the taxpayer from undertaking the specified activity which Parliament has invited in order to attain economic and perhaps social policy goals. Examples of such incentives I have already enumerated.

Indeed, where Parliament is successful and a taxpayer is induced to act in a certain manner by virtue of incentives prescribed in the legislation, it is at least arguable that the taxpayer was attracted to these incentives for the valid business purpose of reducing his cash outlay for taxes to conserve his resources for other business activities. It seems more appropriate to turn to an interpretation test which would provide a means of applying the Act so as to affect only the conduct of a taxpayer which has the designed effect of defeating the expressed intention of Parliament. In short, the tax statute, by this interpretative technique, is extended to reach conduct of the taxpayer which clearly falls within "the object and spirit" of the taxing provisions. Such an approach would promote rather than interfere with the administration of the *Income Tax Act, supra*, in both its aspects without interference with the granting and withdrawal, according to the economic climate, of tax incentives. The desired objective is a simple rule which will provide uniformity of application of the Act across the community, and at the same time, reduce the attraction of elaborate and intricate tax avoidance plans, and reduce the rewards to those best able to afford the services of the tax technicians ...

Wilson J: I agree with my colleague Mr. Justice Estey that the transaction involved in this appeal was an effectual transaction and that it was not a sham. Indeed, I cannot see how a sham can be said to result where parties intend to create certain legal relations (in this case the purchase and sale of a business and a nominee arrangement to operate it) and are successful in creating those legal relations.

As I understand it, a sham transaction as applied in Canadian tax cases is one that does not have the legal consequences that it purports on its face to have. For example, in *Susan Hosiery Ltd. v. M.N.R.*, [1969] 2 Ex. C.R. 408, [1969] C.T.C. 533, 69 D.T.C. 5346 Mr. Justice Gibson found a purported employees' pension plan to be a mere "simulate" that was "masquerading" as a pension plan; the actions of the taxpayers in question "never established a pension plan, nor any relationship of trustee, *cestui que trust*, nor any other legal or equitable rights or obligations in any of the parties and none of the parties intended at any material time that there should be any" (at 420-21 [544]). In *M.N.R. v. Shields*, [1963] Ex. C.R. 91, [1962] C.T.C. 548, 62 D.T.C. 1343 Mr. Justice Cameron held that an alleged partnership agreement between the taxpayer and his son was "not a reality, but a mere simulate agreement" (at 114 [570]); the parties never intended that it should give rise to a partnership and in law it did not do so. And in *M.N.R. v. Cameron*, (*supra*), Mr. Justice Martland declined to find a contract for services between an employer and a company incorporated by his former employees to be a sham because "the legal rights and obligations which it created were exactly those which the parties intended" (at 1069 [384]).

I am also of the view that the business purpose test and the sham test are two distinct tests. A transaction may be effectual and not in any sense a sham (as in this case) but may have no business purpose other than the tax purpose. The question then is whether the Minister is entitled to ignore it on that ground alone. If he is, then a massive inroad is made into Lord Tomlin's dictum that "Every man is entitled if he can to order his affairs so that the tax attaching under the appropriate Acts is less than it would otherwise be": *I.R.C. v. Duke of Westminster*, (*supra*), at 19. Indeed, it seems to me that the business purpose test is a complete rejection of Lord Tomlin's principle.

The appellant would clearly be liable to pay tax on the income from the flavourings business if the business purpose test is part of our law since it is freely admitted that the saving of tax for the Finlayson conglomerate was the sole motivation for the transaction. In my opinion, the Federal Court of Appeal in *Leon v. M.N.R.*, (*supra*), characterized a transaction which had no business purpose other than the tax purpose as a sham and was in error in so doing. I do not view that case as introducing the business purpose test as a test distinct from that of sham into our law and, indeed, if it is to be so viewed, I do not think it should be followed. I think Lord Tomlin's principle is far too deeply entrenched in our tax law for the courts to reject it in the absence of clear statutory authority. No such authority has been put to us in this case.

For these reasons I concur in my colleague's disposition of the appeal.

[Beetz and McIntyre JJ. concurred with Estey J., and Ritchie J. concurred with Wilson J.]

Despite the fact that the Supreme Court of Canada in *Stubart* refused to adopt a "business purpose test," it is clear that Estey, J. considered the "object and spirit" test to be "a simple rule which will provide uniformity of application of the Act across the community, and at the same time, reduce the attraction of elaborate and intricate tax avoidance plans, and reduce the rewards to those best able to afford the services of the tax technicians".

However, Supreme Court of Canada decisions since *Stubart* suggest that the *Duke of Westminster* remains alive and well in Canada (at least for transactions undertaken prior to the introduction of the general anti-avoidance rule in section 245). The "plain meaning" approach to statutory interpretation, emphasized in cases such as *Antosko*, *supra* and *Friesen*, *supra* has undermined the application of the "object and spirit" test to tax avoidance transactions. Consider also *Duha Printers (Western) Ltd. v. The Queen*, [1998] 3 C.T.C. 303, 98 D.T.C. 6334 (S.C.C.). In this case, a profitable company entered into a series of transactions by which its *de jure* control was acquired by the controller of a loss company, following which the two corporations were amalgamated to form the taxpayer. Following the amalgamation, *de jure* control of the taxpayer was reacquired by the individuals who controlled the predecessor profitable company. The taxpayer claimed the losses of the predecessor loss company, since the transactions technically fell outside the loss limitation provisions in subsection 111(5) (which limits the ability to claim losses following a change in control of a loss company). The Supreme Court of Canada allowed the taxpayer to use the losses. In doing so, the court stated (at paras. 86-7):

> ... it is not necessary to consider whether the Federal Court of Appeal erred in considering the object and spirit of *the Income Tax Act* provisions, the intentions of the parties, and the commercial reality of the transactions, given that the relevant provisions of the Act are clear and unambiguous. However, I would like to comment briefly on the suggestion by the appellant that Linden J.A. would have denied the taxpayer the

benefit of the provisions of the Act "simply because the transaction was motivated solely for tax planning purposes".

It is well established in the jurisprudence of this Court that no "business purpose" is required for a transaction to be considered valid under the Income Tax Act, and that a taxpayer is entitled to take advantage of the Act even where a transaction is motivated solely by the minimization of tax: *Stubart Investments Ltd. v. The Queen*, [1984] 1 S.C.R. 536. Moreover, this Court emphasized in *Antosko, supra*, at p. 327 that, although various techniques may be employed in interpreting the Act, "such techniques cannot alter the result where the words of the statute are clear and plain and where the legal and practical effect of the transaction is undisputed".

A similar, rather permissive, approach to tax avoidance is illustrated in other decisions of the Supreme Court of Canada such as *The Queen v. Continental Bank of Canada*, [1998] 4 C.T.C. 77, 98 D.T.C. 6501; *Neuman v. The Queen*, [1998] 3 C.T.C. 177, 98 D.T.C. 6297 (reproduced in Part III. of Chapter 2); *Mara Properties Limited v. The Queen*, [1996] 2 C.T.C. 54, 96 D.T.C. 6309; *Shell Canada v. The Queen*, [1999] 4 C.T.C. 313, 99 D.T.C. 5669; and *Singleton v. The Queen*, [2002] 1 C.T.C. 121, 2001 D.T.C. 5533 (S.C.C.). All of these cases conclude that the court cannot consider either the "economic realities" of a particular transaction or the general object and spirit of the provisions of the Act if the provisions applicable to the taxpayer's transactions are clear and unambiguous; where the provisions are clear and unambiguous, they must simply be applied. These decisions effectively relegate the "object and spirit" approach of *Stubart* to an historic footnote, a far cry from the anti-avoidance tool that Estey, J. had intended.

Judicial anti-avoidance doctrines are thus rather constrained in Canada, essentially limited to the ineffective transaction and sham transaction doctrines. The following is a brief review of the main anti-avoidance doctrines that have been considered by Canadian courts.

Ineffective Transactions

The tax consequences of a transaction are determined in accordance with the legal relationships created by the parties. If the legal relationships claimed by the taxpayer do not, in fact, exist, then the tax consequences will depend on the true legal position. In short, taxpayers are taxed on the basis of what they do and not what they *intend* to do. The doctrine has been applied where an essential legal formality has not been carried out or has not been carried out on a timely basis. For example, in *The Queen v. Daly*, [1981] C.T.C. 270, 81 D.T.C. 5197 (F.C.A.), the Court refused to recognize any contractual relationship between a radio station and the taxpayer's personal service corporation because of the lack of legal documentation establishing a contract between the two and rescinding the employment agreement between the radio station and the taxpayer. In *Atinco Paper Products Ltd. v. The Queen*, [1978] C.T.C. 566, 78 D.T.C. 6387 (F.C.A.), the Court refused to recognize the existence of a trust because the settlor did not attach any conditions to her original gift and did not make any property settlement at the time the trust agreement was formally concluded. How technically defective the transactions must be before the doctrine applies remains unclear.

Sham Transaction

A sham was defined in *Snook v. London and West Riding Investments Ltd.*, [1967] 2 Q.B. 786 at 802 (C.A.) as:

> ... acts done or documents executed by the parties to the "sham" which are intended by them to give to third parties or to the court the appearance of creating between the parties legal rights and obligations different from the actual legal rights and obligations (if any) which the parties intend to create.

This definition was adopted by the Supreme Court of Canada in *M.N.R. v. Cameron*, [1972] C.T.C. 380, 72 D.T.C. 6325 and affirmed in *Stubart*. According to the Supreme Court of Canada in *Stubart*, deceit is at the "heart and core of a sham". A sham will be disregarded for tax purposes.

The sham doctrine, as defined above, has a narrow application. An earlier suggestion in *M.N.R. v. Leon*, [1976] C.T.C. 532, 76 D.T.C. 6299 (F.C.A.) that transactions which lacked a *bona fide* business purpose constituted a sham was rejected by subsequent cases. However, a few cases have called into question the scope of the sham doctrine. For example in *The Queen v. Bronfman Trust*, [1987] 1 C.T.C. 117, 87 D.T.C. 5059 (reproduced in Part IV of Chapter 5), the Supreme Court of Canada denied an interest deduction to a trust which borrowed money to make a capital distribution. The Crown conceded that had the trust used existing assets to make the capital distribution and borrowed to replace those assets, the interest would have been deductible. The Court stated (at paragraph 53):

> ... In any event, I admit to some doubt about the premise conceded by the Crown. If, for example, the trust had sold a particular income-producing asset, made the capital allocation to the beneficiary and repurchased the same asset, all within a brief interval of time, the courts might well consider the sale and repurchase to constitute a formality or a sham designed to conceal the essence of the transaction, namely that money was borrowed and used to fund a capital allocation to the beneficiary. ...

In *Friesen*, *supra*, which did not concern a tax avoidance scheme, Major, J. stated (at paragraph 92):

> ... Schemes entered into with the intention of creating a business loss would not qualify as adventures in the nature of trade and would be tantamount to a sham ...

The use of the term sham in these two cases appears anomalous. Most recent decisions limit the sham doctrine to the classical *Snook* definition: see, for example, *The Queen v. McClurg*, [1991] 1 C.T.C. 169, 91 D.T.C. 5001 (S.C.C.); *R. v. Cancor Software Corp. et al.* (1991), 92 D.T.C. 6090, 6 O.R. (3d) 577 (Gen. Div.), aff'd [1994] 1 C.T.C. 237, 94 D.T.C. 6102 (Ont. C.A.); *Lutheran Life Insurance Society of Canada v. The Queen*, [1991] 2 C.T.C. 284, 91 D.T.C. 5553 (F.C.T.D.); *Antosko v. The Queen*, *supra*; and *Continental Bank Leasing Corp. v. The Queen*, [1997] 1 C.T.C. 13, 96 D.T.C. 6355 (F.C.A.), reversed [1998] 4 C.T.C. 119, 98 D.T.C. 6505 (S.C.C.). Consider the application of the sham doctrine in *Faraggi v. The Queen*, [2009] 3 C.T.C. 77, 2009 D.T.C. 5585 (F.C.A.), leave to appeal refused 2009 CarswellNat 1152 (S.C.C.).

Substance Over Form

The scope of the substance over form doctrine is difficult to determine primarily because it is a difficult doctrine to define. In the *Duke of Westminster*, the U.K. Inland Revenue argued that the substance of the transaction was that the taxpayer continued to pay a salary to his employees and that this substance should take precedence over the legal form, being payments under an annuity. The House of Lords rejected this argument. Lord Russell of Killowen stated ([1936] A.C. 1 at 25):

> ... If all that is meant by the doctrine is that having once ascertained the legal rights of the parties you may disregard mere nomenclature and decide the question of taxability or non-taxability in accordance with the legal rights, well and good. ... If, on the other hand, the doctrine means that you may brush aside deeds, disregard the legal rights and liabilities arising under a contract between parties, and decide the question of taxability or non-taxability upon the footing of rights and liabilities of the parties being different from what in law they are, then I entirely dissent from such a doctrine.

Some commentators have suggested that the doctrine of substance over form is therefore quite narrow in that it permits a court to disregard the terminology employed by the parties. The court must ascertain the true legal consequences of the transactions according to the relevant documents and any relevant facts and circumstances. In this respect, the doctrine of substance over form is sometimes confused with the ineffective transaction principle.

Some courts have given the doctrine of substance over form a broader meaning: that the tax consequences of a transaction should be determined based on the economic substance of a transaction rather than its legal form, at least in certain circumstances. Those who argue that the legal form of a transaction should determine the tax consequences believe that a taxpayer has the right to organize the form of his or her affairs in a manner that will minimize tax, even though the transaction depends on the use of a highly technical approach to the words of the statute. Those who argue that the economic substance should govern believe that the transaction must be examined to determine whether its economic substance fits within the language and purpose of the legislation strictly construed. These approaches have been the subject of much debate, and the courts have not been consistent in the adoption of one or the other.

The doctrine of substance over form was not discussed by the Supreme Court of Canada in *Stubart*. However, in *Bronfman Trust, supra*, the Supreme Court appeared to expand the "object and spirit" test from *Stubart* as follows (at paragraphs 48-49):

> I acknowledge, however, that just as there has been a recent trend away from strict construction of taxation statutes (see *Stubart Investments Ltd. v. The Queen*, [1984] 1 S.C.R. 536 at 573-79, [1984] C.T.C. 294 at 313-316 and *The Queen v. Golden*, [1986] 1 S.C.R. 209 at 214-15, [1986] 1 C.T.C. 274 at 277), so too has the recent trend in tax cases been towards attempting to ascertain the true commercial and practical nature of the taxpayer's transactions. There has been, in this country and elsewhere, a movement away from tests based on the form of transactions and towards tests based on what Lord Pearce has referred to as a "common sense appreciation of all the guiding features" of the events in question: ... *B.P. Australia Ltd. v. Commissioner of Taxation of Australia*, [1966] A.C. 224 at 264, [1965] 3 All E.R. 209 at 218 (P.C.).
>
> This is, I believe, a laudable trend provided it is consistent with the text and purposes of the taxation statute. Assessment of taxpayers' transactions with an eye to commercial and economic realities, rather than juristic classification of form, may help to avoid the inequity of tax liability being dependent upon the taxpayer's sophistication at manipulating a sequence of events to achieve a patina of compliance with the apparent prerequisites for a tax deduction.

However, in the same manner as the Court has confined any consideration of the "object and spirit" of statutory provisions, so too has it limited any consideration of the "economic realities" of a taxpayer's transactions. As the Supreme Court of Canada stated in *Shell Canada Limited v. The Queen, supra*, (at paragraphs 39-40):

> This Court has repeatedly held that courts must be sensitive to the economic realities of a particular transaction, rather than being bound to what first appears to be its legal form: *Bronfman Trust, supra*, at pp. 52-53, *per* Dickson C.J.; *Tennant, supra*, at para. 26, *per* Iacobucci J. But there are at least two *caveats* to this rule. First, this Court has never held that the economic realities of a situation can be used to recharacterize a taxpayer's *bona fide* legal relationships. To the contrary, we have held that, absent a specific provision of the Act to the contrary or a finding that they are a sham, the taxpayer's legal relationships must be respected in tax cases. Recharacterization is only permissible if the label attached by the taxpayer to the particular transaction does not properly reflect its actual legal effect: *Continental Bank Leasing Corp. v. Canada*, at para. 21, per Bastarache J.
>
> Second, it is well established in this Court's tax jurisprudence that a searching inquiry for either the "economic realities" of a particular transaction or the general

object and spirit of the provision at issue can never supplant a court's duty to apply an unambiguous provision of the Act to a taxpayer's transaction. Where the provision at issue is clear and unambiguous, its terms must simply be applied: *Continental Bank, supra*, at para. 51, per Bastarache J.; *Tennant, supra*, at para. 16, *per* Iacobucci J.; *Canada v. Antosko*, [1994] 2 S.C.R. 312, at pp. 326-27 and 330, *per* Iacobucci J.; *Friesen v. Canada*, [1995] 3 S.C.R. 103, at para. 11, *per* Major J.; *Alberta (Treasury Branches) v. M.N.R.*, [1996] 1 S.C.R. 963, at para. 15, *per* Cory J.

Business Purpose Test

Under the business purpose test, transactions lacking a non-tax purpose are disregarded. The doctrine is well-developed in U.S. jurisprudence. In the United Kingdom and Canada, the *Duke of Westminster* decision is generally considered authority that there is no judicial business purpose test.

In *Stubart*, the Supreme Court of Canada reviewed the American, English and certain Canadian authorities and unanimously rejected the business purpose test as a separate judicial anti-avoidance doctrine. However, the Court suggested that a business purpose test could be used in determining whether former section 245 applied to a particular transaction or where "the provisions of the Act necessarily relate to an identified business function". Its rejection as a general principle ultimately led to the introduction of the general anti-avoidance rule (discussed below) in 1987.

Since *Stubart*, the business purpose test has been applied to avoidance schemes only in the context of certain statutory provisions that incorporate a business purpose element, such as paragraph 20(1)(c) (see, for example, *Mark Resources v. The Queen*, [1993] 2 C.T.C. 2259, 93 D.T.C. 1004 (T.C.C.) and *Canwest Broadcasting Ltd. v. The Queen*, [1995] 2 C.T.C. 2780 (T.C.C.)). Contrast these decisions with that in *722540 Ontario Inc. v. The Queen*, [2003] 3 C.T.C. 1, 2003 D.T.C. 5195 (Fed. C.A.), leave to appeal refused (2003), 321 N.R. 193 (note) (S.C.C.).

General Anti-Avoidance Rule

The Act contains numerous anti-avoidance provisions. Some are very specific relating to specific sections or problems; others operate in a broader context. Many of these statutory limits are discussed in other chapters: see, for example, Chapter 2 (income splitting and the attribution rules) and Chapter 7 (arm's length concept).

As part of its White Paper on Tax Reform issued on June 18, 1987, the federal government proposed to introduce a general anti-avoidance rule ("GAAR"), now found in section 245. According to the White Paper, such a rule was necessary to prevent taxpayers from engaging in aggressive tax planning that undermines the integrity of the Canadian self-assessment system and the stability of tax revenues.

GAAR clearly represents the most powerful weapon in the Act to control abusive tax avoidance. However, it is generally considered a provision of last resort. As Bowman, T.C.C.J. suggested in *Jabs Construction Limited v. The Queen,* [1999] 3 C.T.C. 2556, 99 DTC 729 (at paragraph 48):

> Section 245 is an extreme sanction. It should not be used routinely every time the Minister gets upset just because a taxpayer structures a transaction in a tax effective way, or does not structure it in a manner that maximizes the tax.

Since the enactment of section 245 in 1988, the GAAR has been the subject of over 50 court cases. The Supreme Court of Canada has now considered the application of the GAAR in four different cases, the most commonly cited of which is the following case.

CANADA TRUSTCO MORTGAGE CO. v. THE QUEEN
[2005] 5 C.T.C. 215, 2005 D.T.C. 5547 (S.C.C.)

[On December 17, 1996, the taxpayer purchased trailers from Transamerica Leasing Inc. ("TLI") for their fair market value of $120 million. The taxpayer funded the purchase with a $100 million loan from the Royal Bank of Canada ("RBC") and $20 million of its own money. The taxpayer leased the trailers to Maple Assets Investments Limited ("MAIL"), who subleased them to TLI. TLI then prepaid all amounts due to MAIL under the sublease. MAIL placed on deposit an amount equal to the loan for purposes of making the lease payments, and a bond was pledged as security to guarantee a purchase option payment to the taxpayer at the end of the lease. The circular nature of the transactions allowed the taxpayer to substantially minimize its financial risk while claiming capital cost allowance on the trailers as the owner. The CRA denied the taxpayer's capital cost allowance claim on the basis that the taxpayer did not acquire title to the trailers or, alternatively, under GAAR. The former basis was abandoned at trial, and the taxpayer's appeal was allowed by the Tax Court, which concluded that GAAR did not apply to deny the capital cost allowance claim. The Federal Court of Appeal unanimously dismissed the Crown's appeal.]

1. Introduction

This appeal and its companion case, *Mathew v. Canada*, [2005] 2 S.C.R. 643, 2005 SCC 55 (hereinafter "*Kaulius*"), raise the issue of the interplay between the general anti-avoidance rule ("GAAR") and the application of more specific provisions of the *Income Tax Act*, R.S.C. 1985, c. 1 (5th Supp.). The Act continues to permit legitimate tax minimization; traditionally, this has involved determining whether the taxpayer brought itself within the wording of the specific provisions relied on for the tax benefit. Onto this scheme, the GAAR has superimposed a prohibition on abusive tax avoidance, with the effect that the literal application of provisions of the Act may be seen as abusive in light of their context and purpose. The task in this appeal is to unite these two approaches in a framework that reflects the intention of Parliament in enacting the GAAR and achieves consistent, predictable and fair results.

...

The *Income Tax Act* remains an instrument dominated by explicit provisions dictating specific consequences, inviting a largely textual interpretation. Onto this compendium of detailed stipulations, Parliament has engrafted quite a different sort of provision, the GAAR. This is a broadly drafted provision, intended to negate arrangements that would be permissible under a literal interpretation of other provisions of the *Income Tax Act*, on the basis that they amount to abusive tax avoidance. To the extent that the GAAR constitutes a "provision to the contrary" as discussed in *Shell* (at para. 45), the Duke of Westminster principle and the emphasis on textual interpretation may be attenuated. Ultimately, as affirmed in *Shell*, "[t]he courts' role is to interpret and apply the Act as it was adopted by Parliament" (para. 45). The court must to the extent possible contemporaneously give effect to both the GAAR and the other provisions of the *Income Tax Act* relevant to a particular transaction.

5.2 *Interpretation of the GAAR*

The GAAR was enacted in 1988, principally in response to *Stubart Investments Ltd. v. The Queen*, [1984] 1 S.C.R. 536, which rejected a literal approach to interpreting the Act. At the same time, the Court rejected the business purpose test, which would have restricted tax reduction to transactions with a real business purpose. Instead of the business purpose test, the Court proposed guidelines to limit unacceptable tax avoidance arrangements. Parliament deemed the decision in *Stubart* an inadequate response to the problem and enacted the GAAR.

The *Explanatory Notes to Legislation Relating to Income Tax* issued by the Honourable Michael H. Wilson, Minister of Finance (June 1988) ("Explanatory Notes") are an aid to interpretation. The Explanatory Notes state at the outset that they "are intended for information purposes only and should not be construed as an official interpretation of the provisions they describe". They state the purpose of the GAAR at p. 461:

> New section 245 of the Act is a general anti-avoidance rule which is intended to prevent abusive tax avoidance transactions or arrangements but at the same time is not intended to interfere with legitimate commercial and family transactions. Consequently, the new rule seeks to distinguish between legitimate tax planning and abusive tax avoidance and to establish a reasonable balance between the protection of the tax base and the need for certainty for taxpayers in planning their affairs.

The GAAR draws a line between legitimate tax minimization and abusive tax avoidance. The line is far from bright. The GAAR's purpose is to deny the tax benefits of certain arrangements that comply with a literal interpretation of the provisions of the Act, but amount to an abuse of the provisions of the Act. But precisely what constitutes abusive tax avoidance remains the subject of debate. Hence these appeals.

The application of the GAAR involves three steps. The first step is to determine whether there is a "tax benefit" arising from a "transaction" under s. 245(1) and (2). The second step is to determine whether the transaction is an avoidance transaction under s. 245(3), in the sense of not being "arranged primarily for *bona fide* purposes other than to obtain the tax benefit". The third step is to determine whether the avoidance transaction is abusive under s. 245(4). All three requirements must be fulfilled before the GAAR can be applied to deny a tax benefit.

5.3 *Tax Benefit*

The first step in applying the GAAR is to determine whether there is a tax benefit arising from a transaction or series of transactions of which the transaction is part.

"Tax benefit" is defined in s. 245(1) as "a reduction, avoidance or deferral of tax" or "an increase in a refund of tax or other amount" paid under the Act. Whether a tax benefit exists is a factual determination, initially by the Minister and on review by the courts, usually the Tax Court. The magnitude of the tax benefit is not relevant at this stage of the analysis.

If a deduction against taxable income is claimed, the existence of a tax benefit is clear, since a deduction results in a reduction of tax. In some other instances, it may be that the existence of a tax benefit can only be established by comparison with an alternative arrangement. For example, characterization of an amount as an annuity rather than as a wage, or as a capital gain rather than as business income, will result in differential tax treatment. In such cases, the existence of a tax benefit might only be established upon a comparison between alternative arrangements. In all cases, it must be determined whether the taxpayer reduced, avoided or deferred tax payable under the Act.

5.4 *Avoidance Transaction*

The second requirement for application of the GAAR is that the transaction giving rise to the tax benefit be an avoidance transaction within s. 245(3). The function of this requirement is to remove from the ambit of the GAAR transactions or series of transactions that may reasonably be considered to have been undertaken or arranged primarily for a non-tax purpose. The majority of tax benefits claimed by taxpayers on their annual returns will be immune from the GAAR as a result of s. 245(3). The GAAR was enacted as a provision of last resort in order to address abusive tax avoidance, it was not intended to introduce uncertainty in tax planning.

A "transaction" is defined under s. 245(1) to include an arrangement or event. Section 245(3) specifically defines "avoidance transaction" as a transaction that results in a tax benefit, either by itself or as part of a series of transactions, "unless the transaction may reasonably be considered to have been undertaken or arranged primarily for *bona fide* purposes other than to obtain the tax benefit". These two underlined expressions warrant further discussion.

5.4.1 Series of Transactions

...

The meaning of the expression "series of transactions" under s. 245(2) and (3) is not clear on its face. We agree with the majority of the Federal Court of Appeal in *OSFC* and endorse the test for a series of transactions as adopted by the House of Lords that a series of transactions involves a number of transactions that are "pre-ordained in order to produce a given result" with "no practical likelihood that the pre-planned events would not take place in the order ordained": *Craven v. White*, [1989] A.C. 398, at p. 514, *per* Lord Oliver; see also *W. T. Ramsay Ltd. v. Inland Revenue Commissioners*, [1981] 1 All E.R. 865.

Section 248(10) extends the meaning of "series of transactions" to include "related transactions or events completed in contemplation of the series". The Federal Court of Appeal held, at para. 36 of *OSFC*, that this occurs where the parties to the transaction "knew of the ... series, such that it could be said that they took it into account when deciding to complete the transaction". We would elaborate that "in contemplation" is read not in the sense of actual knowledge but in the broader sense of "because of" or "in relation to" the series. The phrase can be applied to events either before or after the basic avoidance transaction found under s. 245(3). As has been noted:

> It is highly unlikely that Parliament could have intended to include in the statutory definition of "series of transactions" related transactions completed in contemplation of a subsequent series of transactions, but not related transactions in the contemplation of which taxpayers completed a prior series of transactions.
>
> (D. G. Duff, "Judicial Application of the General Anti-Avoidance Rule in Canada: *OSFC Holdings Ltd. v. The Queen*" (2003), 57 I.B.F.D. Bulletin 278, at p. 287)

5.4.2 Primarily for *Bona Fide* Purposes

According to s. 245(3), the GAAR does not apply to a transaction that "may reasonably be considered to have been undertaken or arranged primarily for *bona fide* purposes other than to obtain the tax benefit". If there are both tax and non-tax purposes to a transaction, it must be determined whether it was reasonable to conclude that the non-tax purpose was primary. If so, the GAAR cannot be applied to deny the tax benefit.

While the inquiry proceeds on the premise that both tax and non-tax purposes can be identified, these can be intertwined in the particular circumstances of the transaction at issue. It is not helpful to speak of the threshold imposed by s. 245(3) as high or low. The words of the section simply contemplate an objective assessment of the relative importance of the driving forces of the transaction.

Again, this is a factual inquiry. The taxpayer cannot avoid the application of the GAAR by merely stating that the transaction was undertaken or arranged primarily for a non-tax purpose. The Tax Court judge must weigh the evidence to determine whether it is reasonable to conclude that the transaction was not undertaken or arranged primarily for a non-tax purpose. The determination invokes reasonableness, suggesting that the possibility of different interpretations of the events must be objectively considered.

The courts must examine the relationships between the parties and the actual transactions that were executed between them. The facts of the transactions are central to determining whether there was an avoidance transaction. It is useful to consider what will not suffice to establish an avoidance transaction under s. 245(3). The Explanatory Notes state, at p. 464:

> Subsection 245(3) does not permit the "recharacterization" of a transaction for the purposes of determining whether or not it is an avoidance transaction. In other words, it does not permit a transaction to be considered to be an avoidance transaction because some alternative transaction that might have achieved an equivalent result would have resulted in higher taxes.

According to the Explanatory Notes, Parliament recognized the *Duke of Westminster* principle "that tax planning — arranging one's affairs so as to attract the least amount of tax — is a legitimate and accepted part of Canadian tax law" (p. 464). Despite Parliament's intention to address abusive tax avoidance by enacting the GAAR, Parliament nonetheless intended to preserve predictability, certainty and fairness in Canadian tax law. Parliament intends taxpayers to take full advantage of the provisions of the *Income Tax Act* that confer tax benefits. Indeed, achieving the various policies that the *Income Tax Act* seeks to promote is dependent on taxpayers doing so.

Section 245(3) merely removes from the ambit of the GAAR transactions that may reasonably be considered to have been undertaken or arranged primarily for a non-tax purpose. Parliament did not intend s. 245(3) to operate simply as a business purpose test, which would have considered transactions that lacked an independent *bona fide* business purpose to be invalid.

The expression "non-tax purpose" has a broader scope than the expression "business purpose". For example, transactions that may reasonably be considered to have been undertaken or arranged primarily for family or investment purposes would be immune from the GAAR under s. 245(3). Section 245(3) does not purport to protect only transactions that have a real business purpose. Parliament wanted many schemes that do not have any business purpose to endure. Registered Retirement Savings Plans (RRSPs) are one example. Parliament recognized that many provisions of the Act confer legitimate tax benefits notwithstanding the lack of a real business purpose. This is apparent from the general language used throughout s. 245, as opposed to language which would have adopted a broad anti-avoidance test subject to exemptions for specific schemes like RRSP transactions.

If at least one transaction in a series of transactions is an "avoidance transaction", then the tax benefit that results from the series may be denied under the GAAR. This is apparent from the wording of s. 245(3). Conversely, if each transaction in a series was carried out primarily for *bona fide* non-tax purposes, the GAAR cannot be applied to deny a tax benefit.

...

5.5 *Abusive Tax Avoidance*

The third requirement for application of the GAAR is that the avoidance transaction giving rise to a tax benefit be abusive. The mere existence of an avoidance transaction is not enough to permit the GAAR to be applied. The transaction must also be shown to be *abusive* under s. 245(4).

...

5.5.1 "Misuse and Abuse": Two Different Concepts?

We turn first to the debate about "misuse" and "abuse" which has arisen from the different English and French versions of s. 245(4). This arises from the apparently disjunctive version of the subsection in English ("misuse of the provisions of this Act" or "abuse having regard to the provisions of this Act ... read as a whole") and the non-disjunctive French version ("*d'abus dans l'application des dispositions de la présente loi lue dans son ensemble*"). This discrepancy led the majority of the Federal Court of Appeal to conclude in *OSFC* that s. 245(4) mandates two different inquiries. The first was whether there was a misuse of the particular provisions of the Act that were relied upon to achieve the tax benefit. The second was whether there was an abuse of any policy of the Act read as a whole. The term "policy" was used to refer collectively to purpose, object, spirit, scheme or policy (*OSFC*, at para. 66).

With respect, we cannot agree with this interpretation of s. 245(4). Parliament could not have intended this two-step approach, which on its face raises the impossible question of how one can abuse the Act as a whole without misusing any of its provisions. We agree with the Tax Court judge, in the present case, at para. 90, that "[i]n effect, the analysis of the misuse of the provisions and the analysis of the abuse having regard to the provisions of the *Act* read as a whole are inseparable." As discussed more fully below, the interpretation of specific provisions of the Act cannot be separated from contextual considerations arising from other provisions. The various provisions of the *Income Tax Act* must be interpreted in their contextual framework, so that the Act functions as a coherent whole, with respect to the particular statutory scheme engaged by the transactions.

There is but one principle of interpretation: to determine the intent of the legislator having regard to the text, its context, and other indicators of legislative purpose. The policy analysis proposed as a second step by the Federal Court of Appeal in *OSFC* is properly incorporated into a unified, textual, contextual, and purposive approach to interpreting the specific provisions that give rise to the tax benefit.

The courts cannot search for an overriding policy of the Act that is not based on a unified, textual, contextual and purposive interpretation of the specific provisions in issue. First, such a search is incompatible with the roles of reviewing judges. The *Income Tax Act* is a compendium of highly detailed and often complex provisions. To send the courts on the search for some overarching policy and then to use such a policy to override the wording of the provisions of the *Income Tax Act* would inappropriately place the formulation of taxation policy in the hands of the judiciary, requiring judges to perform a task to which they are unaccustomed and for which they are not equipped. Did Parliament intend judges to formulate taxation policies that are not grounded in the provisions of the Act and to apply them to override the specific provisions of the Act? Notwithstanding the interpretative challenges that the GAAR presents, we cannot find a basis for concluding that such a marked departure from judicial and interpretative norms was Parliament's intent.

Second, to search for an overriding policy of the *Income Tax Act* that is not anchored in a textual, contextual and purposive interpretation of the specific provisions that are relied upon for the tax benefit would run counter to the overall policy of Parliament that tax law be certain, predictable and fair, so that taxpayers can intelligently order their affairs. Although Parliament's general purpose in enacting the GAAR was to preserve legitimate tax minimization schemes while prohibiting abusive tax avoidance, Parliament must also be taken to seek consistency, predictability and fairness in tax law. These three latter purposes would be frustrated if the Minister and/or the courts overrode the provisions of the *Income Tax Act* without any basis in a textual, contextual and purposive interpretation of those provisions.

For these reasons we conclude, as did the Tax Court judge, that the determinations of "misuse" and "abuse" under s. 245(4) are not separate inquiries. Section 245(4) requires a single, unified approach to the textual, contextual and purposive interpretation of the specific provisions of the *Income Tax Act* that are relied upon by the taxpayer in order to determine whether there was abusive tax avoidance.

5.5.2 Abusive Tax Avoidance: A Unified Interpretative Approach

The heart of the analysis under s. 245(4) lies in a contextual and purposive interpretation of the provisions of the Act that are relied on by the taxpayer, and the application of the properly interpreted provisions to the facts of a given case. The first task is to interpret the provisions giving rise to the tax benefit to determine their object, spirit and purpose. The next task is to determine whether the transaction falls within or frustrates that purpose. The overall inquiry thus involves a mixed question of fact and law. The textual, contextual and purposive interpretation of specific provisions of the *Income Tax Act* is essentially a question of law but the application of these provisions to the facts of a case is necessarily fact-intensive.

This analysis will lead to a finding of abusive tax avoidance when a taxpayer relies on specific provisions of the *Income Tax Act* in order to achieve an outcome that those provisions seek to prevent. As well, abusive tax avoidance will occur when a transaction defeats the underlying rationale of the provisions that are relied upon. An abuse may also result from an arrangement that circumvents the application of certain provisions, such as specific anti-avoidance rules, in a manner that frustrates or defeats the object, spirit or purpose of those provisions. By contrast, abuse is not established where it is reasonable to conclude that an avoidance transaction under s. 245(3) was within the object, spirit or purpose of the provisions that confer the tax benefit.

Once the provisions of the *Income Tax Act* are properly interpreted, it is a question of fact for the Tax Court judge whether the Minister, in denying the tax benefit, has established abusive tax avoidance under s. 245(4). Provided the Tax Court judge has proceeded on a proper construction of the provisions of the Act and on findings supported by the evidence, appellate tribunals should not interfere, absent a palpable and overriding error.

The first part of the inquiry under s. 245(4) requires the court to look beyond the mere text of the provisions and undertake a contextual and purposive approach to interpretation in order to find meaning that harmonizes the wording, object, spirit and purpose of the provisions of the *Income Tax Act*. There is nothing novel in this. Even where the meaning of particular provisions may not appear to be ambiguous at first glance, statutory context and purpose may reveal or resolve latent ambiguities. "After all, language can never be interpreted independently of its context, and legislative purpose is part of the context. It would seem to follow that consideration of legislative purpose may not only resolve patent ambiguity, but may, on occasion, reveal ambiguity in apparently plain language." See P. W. Hogg and J. E. Magee, *Principles of Canadian Income Tax Law* (4th ed. 2002), at p. 563. In order to reveal and resolve any latent ambiguities in the meaning of provisions of the *Income Tax Act*, the courts must undertake a unified textual, contextual and purposive approach to statutory interpretation.

As previously stated, the predominant issue in this and its companion appeal is what constitutes abusive tax avoidance. The Explanatory Notes state in part, at pp. 464-65:

> Subsection 245(4) recognizes that the provisions of the Act are intended to apply to transactions with real economic substance, not to transactions intended to exploit, misuse or frustrate the Act to avoid tax. It also recognizes, however, that a number of provisions of the Act either contemplate or encourage transactions that may seem to be primarily tax-motivated. ... It is not intended that section 245 will apply to deny the tax benefits that result from these transactions as long as they are carried out within the object and spirit of the provisions of the Act read as a whole. Nor is it intended that tax incentives expressly provided for in the legislation would be neutralized by this section.
>
> Where a taxpayer carries out transactions primarily in order to obtain, through the application of specific provisions of the Act, a tax benefit that is not intended by such provisions and by the Act read as a whole, section 245 should apply. This would be the case even though the strict words of the relevant specific provisions may support the tax result sought by the taxpayer. Thus, where applicable, section 245 will override other provisions of the Act since, otherwise, its object and purpose would be defeated.
>
> ... Thus, in reading the Act as a whole, specific provisions will be read in the context of and in harmony with the other provisions of the Act in order to achieve a result which is consistent with the general scheme of the Act.
>
> Therefore, the application of new subsection 245 must be determined by reference to the facts in a particular case in the context of the scheme of the Act. ... This can be discerned from a review of the scheme of the Act, its relevant provisions and permissible extrinsic aids.

In all cases where the applicability of s. 245(4) is at issue, the central question is, having regard to the text, context and purpose of the provisions on which the taxpayer relies, whether the transaction frustrates or defeats the object, spirit or purpose of those provisions. The following points are noteworthy:

(1) While the Explanatory Notes use the phrase "exploit, misuse or frustrate", we understand these three terms to be synonymous, with their sense most adequately captured by the word "frustrate".

(2) The Explanatory Notes elaborate that the GAAR is intended to apply where under a literal interpretation of the provisions of the *Income Tax Act*, the object and purpose of those provisions would be defeated.

(3) The Explanatory Notes specify that the application of the GAAR must be determined by reference to the facts of a particular case in the context of the scheme of the *Income Tax Act*.

(4) The Explanatory Notes also elaborate that the provisions of the *Income Tax Act* are intended to apply to transactions with real economic substance.

As previously discussed, Parliament sought to address abusive tax avoidance while preserving consistency, predictability and fairness in tax law and the GAAR can only be applied to deny a tax benefit when the abusive nature of the transaction is clear.

The interpretation of the provisions giving rise to the tax benefit must, in the words of s. 245(4) of the Act, have regard to the Act "read as a whole". This means that the specific provisions at issue must be interpreted in their legislative context, together with other related and relevant provisions, in light of the purposes that are promoted by those provisions and their statutory schemes. In this respect, it should not be forgotten that the GAAR itself is part of the Act.

In general, Parliament confers tax benefits under the *Income Tax Act* to promote purposes related to specific activities. For example, tax benefits associated with business losses, CCA and RRSPs, are conferred for reasons intrinsic to the activities involved. Unless the Minister can establish that the avoidance transaction frustrates or defeats the purpose for which the tax benefit was intended to be conferred, it is not abusive.

Care must be taken in assessing the purposes for which the provisions at issue confer a tax benefit. "The [*Income Tax Act*] is a complex statute through which Parliament seeks to balance a myriad of principles" (*Shell*, at para. 43). The conferring of particular tax benefits can serve a variety of independent and interlocking purposes. These range from imposing fair business accounting principles and promoting particular kinds of commercial activity, to providing family and social benefits.

In interpreting the provisions of the *Income Tax Act*, the statutory language must be respected and should be interpreted according to its well-established legal meaning. In some cases, a contextual and purposive interpretation may add nuance to the well-established legal meaning of the statutory language. Section 245(4) does not rewrite the provisions of the *Income Tax Act*; it only requires that a tax benefit be consistent with the object, spirit and purpose of the provisions that are relied upon.

In summary, s. 245(4) imposes a two-part inquiry. The first step is to determine the object, spirit or purpose of the provisions of the *Income Tax Act* that are relied on for the tax benefit, having regard to the scheme of the Act, the relevant provisions and permissible extrinsic aids. The second step is to examine the factual context of a case in order to determine whether the avoidance transaction defeated or frustrated the object, spirit or purpose of the provisions in issue.

The Explanatory Notes elaborate that the provisions of the *Income Tax Act* are intended to apply to transactions with real economic substance. Although the expression "economic substance" may be open to different interpretations, this statement recognizes that the provisions of the Act were intended to apply to transactions that were executed within the object, spirit and purpose of the provisions that are relied upon for the tax benefit. The courts should not turn a blind eye to the underlying facts of a case, and become fixated on compliance with the literal meaning of the wording of the provisions of the *Income Tax Act*. Rather, the courts should in all cases interpret the provisions in their proper context in light of the purposes they intend to promote.

Courts have to be careful not to conclude too hastily that simply because a non-tax purpose is not evident, the avoidance transaction is the result of abusive tax avoidance. Although the Explanatory Notes make reference to the expression "economic substance", s. 245(4) does not consider a transaction to result in abusive tax avoidance merely because an economic or commercial purpose is not evident. As previously stated, the GAAR was not intended to outlaw all tax benefits; Parliament intended for many to endure. The central inquiry is focussed on whether the transaction was consistent with the purpose of the provisions of the *Income Tax Act* that are relied upon by the taxpayer, when those provisions are properly interpreted in light of their context. Abusive tax avoidance will be established if the transactions frustrate or defeat those purposes.

Whether the transactions were motivated by any economic, commercial, family or other non-tax purpose may form part of the factual context that the courts may consider in the analysis of abusive tax avoidance allegations under s. 245(4). However, any finding in this respect would form only one part of the underlying facts of a case, and would be insufficient by itself to establish abusive tax avoidance. The central issue is the proper interpretation of the relevant provisions in light of their context and purpose. When properly interpreted, the statutory provisions at issue in a given case may dictate that a particular tax benefit may apply only to transactions with a certain economic, commercial, family or other non-tax purpose. The absence of such considerations may then become a relevant factor towards the inference that the transactions abused the provisions at issue, but there is no golden rule in this respect.

Similarly, courts have on occasion discussed transactions in terms of their "lack of substance" or requiring "recharacterization". However, such terms have no meaning in isolation from the proper interpretation of specific provisions of the *Income Tax Act*. The analysis under s. 245(4) requires a close examination of the facts in order to determine whether allowing a tax benefit would be within the object, spirit or purpose of the provisions relied upon by the taxpayer, when those provisions are interpreted textually, contextually and purposively. Only after first, properly construing the provisions to determine their scope and second, examining all of the relevant facts, can a proper conclusion regarding abusive tax avoidance under s. 245(4) be reached.

A transaction may be considered to be "artificial" or to "lack substance" *with respect to specific provisions* of the *Income Tax Act*, if allowing a tax benefit would not be consistent with the object, spirit or purpose of those provisions. We should reject any analysis under s. 245(4) that depends entirely on "substance" viewed in isolation from the proper interpretation of specific provisions of the *Income Tax Act* or the relevant factual context of a case. However, abusive tax avoidance may be found where the relationships and transactions as expressed in the relevant documentation lack a proper basis relative to the object, spirit or purpose of the provisions that are purported to confer the tax benefit, or where they are wholly dissimilar to the relationships or transactions that are contemplated by the provisions.

A proper approach to the wording of the provisions of the *Income Tax Act* together with the relevant factual context of a given case achieve balance between the need to address abusive tax avoidance while preserving certainty, predictability and fairness in tax law so that taxpayers may manage their affairs accordingly. Parliament intends taxpayers to take full advantage of the provisions of the Act that confer tax benefits. Parliament did not intend the GAAR to undermine this basic tenet of tax law.

...

5.6 *Burden of Proof*

The determination of the existence of a tax benefit and an avoidance transaction under s. 245(1), (2) and (3) involves factual decisions. As such, the burden of proof is the same as in any tax proceeding where the taxpayer disputes the Minister's assessment and its underlying assumptions of facts. The initial obligation is on the taxpayer to "refute" or challenge the Minister's factual assumptions by contesting the existence of a tax benefit or by showing that a *bona fide* non-tax purpose primarily drove the transaction: see *Hickman Motors Ltd. v. Canada*, [1997] 2 S.C.R. 336, at para. 92. It is not unfair to impose this burden, as the taxpayer would presumably have knowledge of the factual background of the transaction.

By contrast, the inquiry into abusive tax avoidance under s. 245(4) involves a textual, contextual and purposive analysis of the provisions on which the tax benefit is based. We see no reason to maintain the distinction between a theoretical and practical perspective on the burden of proof, adopted by the majority of the Federal Court of Appeal in *OSFC*. The Federal Court of Appeal held that there is no burden on either party at the stage of interpreting the provisions at issue, since this is a question of law, which is ultimately for the court to decide. It went on to state at para. 68 that "from a practical perspective, ... [t]he Minister should set out the policy with reference to the provisions of the Act or extrinsic aids upon which he relies".

For practical purposes, the last statement is the important one. The taxpayer, once he or she has shown compliance with the wording of a provision, should not be required to disprove that he or she has thereby violated the object, spirit or purpose of the provision. It is for the Minister who seeks to rely on the GAAR to identify the object, spirit or purpose of the provisions that are claimed to have been frustrated or defeated, when the provisions of the Act are interpreted in a textual, contextual and purposive manner. The Minister is in a better position than the taxpayer to make submissions on legislative intent with a view to interpreting the provisions harmoniously within the broader statutory scheme that is relevant to the transaction at issue.

5.7 *Summary*

The approach to s. 245 of the *Income Tax Act* may be summarized as follows.

1. Three requirements must be established to permit application of the GAAR:

(1) A *tax benefit resulting from a transaction* or part of a series of transactions (s. 245(1) and (2));

(2) that the transaction is an *avoidance transaction* in the sense that it cannot be said to have been reasonably undertaken or arranged primarily for a *bona fide* purpose other than to obtain a tax benefit; and

(3) that there was *abusive tax avoidance* in the sense that it cannot be reasonably concluded that a tax benefit would be consistent with the object, spirit or purpose of the provisions relied upon by the taxpayer.

2. The burden is on the taxpayer to refute (1) and (2), and on the Minister to establish (3).

3. If the existence of abusive tax avoidance is unclear, the benefit of the doubt goes to the taxpayer.

4. The courts proceed by conducting a unified textual, contextual and purposive analysis of the provisions giving rise to the tax benefit in order to determine why they were put in place and why the benefit was conferred. The goal is to arrive at a purposive interpretation that is harmonious with the provisions of the Act that confer the tax benefit, read in the context of the whole Act.
5. Whether the transactions were motivated by any economic, commercial, family or other non-tax purpose may form part of the factual context that the courts may consider in the analysis of abusive tax avoidance allegations under s. 245(4). However, any finding in this respect would form only one part of the underlying facts of a case, and would be insufficient by itself to establish abusive tax avoidance. The central issue is the proper interpretation of the relevant provisions in light of their context and purpose.
6. Abusive tax avoidance may be found where the relationships and transactions as expressed in the relevant documentation lack a proper basis relative to the object, spirit or purpose of the provisions that are purported to confer the tax benefit, or where they are wholly dissimilar to the relationships or transactions that are contemplated by the provisions.
7. Where the Tax Court judge has proceeded on a proper construction of the provisions of the *Income Tax Act* and on findings supported by the evidence, appellate tribunals should not interfere, absent a palpable and overriding error.

6. Application to the Facts of This Case

...

We are of the view that the appellant's arguments do not reflect a proper interpretation of the GAAR and that the respondent's position should prevail. We are led to this conclusion by a textual, contextual and purposive interpretation of the relevant provisions of the *Income Tax Act*.

Textually, the CCA provisions use "cost" in the well-established sense of the amount paid to acquire the assets. Contextually, other provisions of the Act support this interpretation. Finally, the purpose of the CCA provisions of the Act, as applied to sale-leaseback transactions, was, as found by the Tax Court judge, to permit deduction of CCA based on the cost of the assets acquired. This purpose emerges clearly from the scheme of the CCA provisions within the Act as a whole. The appellant's argument was not that the purpose of these provisions was unclear, but rather that the GAAR ought to override their accepted purpose and effect, for reasons external to the provisions themselves.

The appellant suggests that the usual result of the CCA provisions of the Act should be overridden in the absence of real financial risk or "economic cost" in the transaction. However, this suggestion distorts the purpose of the CCA provisions by reducing them to apply only when sums of money are at economic risk. The applicable CCA provisions of the Act do not refer to economic risk.

They refer only to "cost". Where Parliament wanted to introduce economic risk into the meaning of cost related to CCA provisions, it did so expressly, as, for instance, in s. 13(7.1) and (7.2) of the Act, which makes adjustments to the cost of depreciable property when a taxpayer receives government assistance. "Cost" in the context of CCA is a well-understood legal concept. It has been carefully defined by the Act and the jurisprudence. Like the Tax Court judge, we see nothing in the GAAR or the object of the CCA provisions that permits us to rewrite them to interpret "cost" to mean "amount economically at risk" in the applicable provisions. To do so would be to invite inconsistent results. The result would vary with the degree of risk in each case. This would offend the goal of the Act to provide sufficient certainty and predictability to permit taxpayers to intelligently order their affairs. For all these reasons, we agree with the Tax Court judge's conclusion that the "cost" was $120 million, not zero as argued by the appellant.

The appellant's submissions on this point amount to a narrow consideration of the "economic substance" of the transaction, viewed in isolation from a textual, contextual and purposive interpretation of the CCA provisions. It did not focus on the purpose of the CCA provisions read in the context of the Act as a whole, to determine whether the tax benefit fell outside the object, spirit or purpose of the relevant provisions. Instead, it simply argued that since there was (as it alleged) no "real economic cost", the GAAR must apply. As discussed earlier, the application of the GAAR is a complex matter of statutory interpretation in which the object, spirit and purpose of the provisions giving rise to the tax benefit are assessed in light of the requirements and wording of the GAAR. While the "economic substance" of the transaction may be relevant at various stages of the analysis, this expression has little meaning in isolation from the proper interpretation of specific provisions of the Act. Any "economic substance" must be considered in relation to the proper interpretation of the specific provisions that are relied upon for the tax benefit.

The appellant originally suggested that the GAAR should be used to override the usual effect of the CCA provisions for a second reason — namely that the relationships and transactions that are expressed in the documents are abusive of the provisions of the *Income Tax Act* and should be set aside. It properly abandoned this argument and the submission that the transaction was a sham before the Federal Court of Appeal. Here the documents detailing the transaction left no uncertainty as to the relationships between the parties. CTMC paid $120 million to TLI for the equipment, partly with borrowed funds and partly with its own money. Having become the owner of the equipment, it leased it to MAIL. MAIL then subleased it back to the vendor, TLI. The relationships between the parties as expressed in the relevant documentation were not superfluous elements; they were the very essence of the transaction.

As the Tax Court judge concluded, under the CCA scheme, "[l]eases of such [exempt] properties will continue to be viewed as acceptable means of providing lower cost financing" (para. 67). TLI's use of the money ultimately reduced the risk, but a company in the financing business is expected to do what it can to reduce risk. Therefore, the way the borrowed money was used provided no grounds for concluding that there was abusive tax avoidance. The Tax Court judge, after considering all the circumstances, found that the transaction was not so dissimilar from an ordinary sale-leaseback to take it outside the object, spirit or purpose of the relevant CCA provisions of the Act and Regulations.

In determining the result in this appeal, the Tax Court judge's conclusions on matters of fact should not be displaced provided that they are based on the correct legal analysis and find support in the evidence.

The Tax Court judge's analysis on the issue of abuse under s. 245(4) is largely consistent with the approach to the application of the GAAR we have adopted. He rejected the two-stage overriding-policy approach to abuse and misuse. He went on to inquire into the policy or purpose underlying the CCA treatment in sale-leaseback arrangements. Construing the CCA provisions as a whole, he rejected the submission that "cost" in the relevant provisions of the Act should be reread as "money at risk", and he also rejected the argument that the "economic substance" of the transaction determined that there was abusive tax avoidance. He conducted a detailed analysis of the transactions to determine whether they fell within the object, spirit or purpose of the CCA provisions. In the end, he concluded that a tax benefit was consistent with the object, spirit and purpose of the CCA provisions and held that the GAAR could not apply to disallow the tax benefit. These conclusions were based on a correct view of the law and were grounded in the evidence. They should be confirmed.

7. Conclusion

We would dismiss the appeal with costs.

Notes and Questions

1. Few cases have considered the meaning of "tax benefit" in subsection 245(1). It includes a "reduction, avoidance or deferral of tax or other amount payable under [the Act]". Against what norm or standard is a tax benefit measured? Is it sufficient simply to contrast the tax result from the challenged transactions to the result had the taxpayer not carried out the transactions? Or must the challenged transactions be contrasted with a "benchmark transaction" that the taxpayer might have carried out? In answering these questions, consider the decision of the Federal Court of Appeal in *Spruce Credit Union v. The Queen*, [2014] 6 C.T.C. 1, 2014 D.T.C. 5079 (F.C.A.).

2. The concept of "series of transactions" is important to the operation of GAAR because in most cases a tax benefit will arise from a number of related transactions rather than a single transaction. As noted in *Canada Trustco*, subsection 248(10) deems a series to "include any related transactions or events completed in contemplation of the series". The degree of inter-connectedness between the related transactions and the series remains problematic. In *Canada Trustco*, the Court suggested that "in contemplation of" does not require actual knowledge, but should be interpreted in the broader sense of "because of" or "in relation to" the series. In *Copthorne Holdings Ltd. v. The Queen*, [2009] 5 C.T.C. 1, 2009 D.T.C. 5101 (F.C.A.), Ryer J.A. stated (at paragraph 46):

   > In my view, if a series is a motivating factor with respect to the completion of a subsequent transaction, the transaction can be said to have been completed "in contemplation of the series" and a direct causal relationship between the series and the transaction, as argued by the appellant, need not be established. In my opinion, this standard is reconcilable with the test as stated in *OSFC* and as broadened in *Canada Trustco*.

   Is a "motivating factor" test different from that enunciated in *Canada Trustco*? The result reached by the Federal Court of Appeal was affirmed by the Supreme Court of Canada ([2012] 2 C.T.C. 29, 2012 D.T.C. 5007). In the unanimous decision, Rothstein J. adopts the "because of" or "in relation to" test established in *Canada Trustco* and does not make reference to the "motivating factor" test applied by Ryer J.A. in the Federal Court of Appeal. With respect to the degree of interconnectedness between the related transaction and the series, Rothstein J. further clarifies that the "because of" or "in relation to" test does not require a strong nexus, but does require more than a "mere possibility" or a connection with "an extreme degree of remoteness".

3. The Supreme Court's interpretation of subsection 245(4) in *Canada Trustco* was based on the provision as it read prior to its amendment in 2005: "For greater certainty, subsection (2) does not apply to a transaction where it may reasonably be considered that the transaction would not result directly or indirectly in a misuse of the provisions of this Act or an abuse having regard to the provisions of this Act, other than this section, read as a whole." The current version of the provision no longer contains the double negative language. Does this change affect the burden of proving abusive tax avoidance? In this respect, contrast the decision in *Canada Trustco* with the majority decision in *Lipson v. The Queen*, [2009] 1 C.T.C. 314, 2009 D.T.C. 5015 (S.C.C.).

4. It can be difficult to reconcile judicial application of the misuse or abuse requirement in subsection 245(4). For example, in the companion case to *Canada Trustco*, *Mathew v. The Queen*, [2005] 5 C.T.C. 244, 2005 D.T.C. 5538, the Supreme Court of Canada characterized as abusive a series of transactions using

a partnership structure to transfer losses between arm's length parties. Similarly, a series of transactions intended to provide the taxpayer with a mortgage interest deduction was characterized as abusive in *Lipson* because the desired result depended on the application of the income attribution rule. Yet, the series of transactions in *Canada Trustco*, which resulted in a sale and purchase of capital cost allowance between arm's length parties, was not considered abusive. Is inconsistency of result an inevitable feature of the identification of prohibited tax avoidance transactions as the outcome of an exercise in statutory interpretation?

5. In *Canada Trustco* the Supreme Court of Canada warned against searching for an overriding policy of the Act and restricted its approach to an interpretation of the specific provisions in issue:

> The courts cannot search for an overriding policy of the Act that is not based on a unified, textual, contextual and purposive interpretation of the specific provisions in issue. ... To send the courts on the search for some overarching policy and then to use such a policy to override the wording of the provisions of the *Income Tax Act* would inappropriately place the formulation of taxation policy in the hands of the judiciary, requiring judges to perform a task to which they are unaccustomed and for which they are not equipped.

In the Supreme Court of Canada's most recent GAAR decision, *Copthorne Holdings Ltd. v. The Queen*, [2012] 2 C.T.C. 29, 2012 D.T.C. 5007, Rothstein J. appears to adopt a more flexible approach to determining the object, spirit or purpose of a provision under the GAAR (paragraph 70):

> The object, spirit or purpose can be identified by applying the same interpretive approach employed by this Court in all questions of statutory interpretation — a "unified textual, contextual and purposive approach". ... [w]hile the approach is the same as in all statutory interpretation, the analysis seeks to determine a different aspect of the statute than in other cases. In a traditional statutory interpretation approach the court applies the textual, contextual and purposive analysis to determine what the words of the statute mean. In a GAAR analysis the textual, contextual and purposive analysis is employed to determine the object, spirit or purpose of a provision. Here the meaning of the words of the statute may be clear enough. The search is for the rationale that underlies the words that may not be captured by the bare meaning of the words themselves. However, determining the rationale of the relevant provisions of the Act should not be conflated with a value judgment of what is right or wrong nor with theories about what tax law ought to be or ought to do.

Do you think the reformulation/restatement by the Supreme Court of Canada broadens the potential scope for applying the GAAR? What does Rothstein J. mean when he states that "[t]he search is for the rationale that underlies the words that may not be captured by the bare meaning of the words themselves"? Rothstein

J. refers to the Court's role in determining the object, spirit or purpose of a provision under subsection 245(4) as an "unusual duty". Does this suggest the adoption of a fairly conservative approach in future GAAR cases?

6. Another area of uncertainty in the application of the GAAR is the extent to which it may be relevant to consider the economic substance of a transaction. In *Canada Trustco*, the Supreme Court of Canada stated that "[w]hile the 'economic substance' of the transaction may be relevant at various stages of the analysis, this expression has little meaning in isolation from the proper interpretation of specific provisions of the Act". In two GAAR cases decided after *Canada Trustco*, *Triad Gestco Ltd. v. The Queen* (2012), [2013] 1 C.T.C. 202, 2012 D.T.C. 5156 (F.C.A.) and *1207192 Ontario Ltd. v. The Queen* (2012), [2013] 1 C.T.C. 1, 2012 D.T.C. 5157 (F.C.A.), the Federal Court of Appeal denied a capital loss realized by the taxpayer on the basis that the loss was not an economic loss. The Federal Court of Appeal reached this conclusion notwithstanding that the relevant provisions of the Act did not expressly restrict the taxpayer's loss to its economic loss. In a third case, *The Queen v. Global Equity Fund Ltd*, [2013] 1 C.T.C. 135, 2013 D.T.C. 5007 (F.C.A.), the Federal Court of Appeal concluded that "in order to be used for taxation purposes, business losses must be grounded in some form of economic or business reality". The Supreme Court of Canada denied leave to appeal in *1207192* and *Global Equity*. Does this signal the possibility of an expanded role for economic substance in GAAR cases?

Table of Statutory References

Income Tax Act, R.S.C. 1985, c. 1 (5th Supplement), as amended

Income Tax Act, R.S.C. 1985, c. 1 — *cont'd*

Income Tax Act, R.S.C. 1985, c. 1 — *cont'd*

Income Tax Act, R.S.C. 1985, c. 1 — *cont'd*

Income Tax Act, R.S.C. 1985, c. 1 — *cont'd*

Income Tax Act, R.S.C. 1985, c. 1 — *cont'd*

Income Tax Act, R.S.C. 1985, c. 1 — *cont'd*

Income Tax Act, R.S.C. 1985, c. 1 — *cont'd*

Income Tax Act, R.S.C. 1985, c. 1 — *cont'd*

Income Tax Act, R.S.C. 1985, c. 1 — *cont'd*

Income Tax Act, R.S.C. 1985, c. 1 — *cont'd*

Income Tax Act, R.S.C. 1985, c. 1 — *cont'd*

Income Tax Act, R.S.C. 1985, c. 1 — *cont'd*

Income Tax Act, R.S.C. 1985, c. 1 — *cont'd*

Income Tax Act, R.S.C. 1985, c. 1 — *cont'd*

Income Tax Act, R.S.C. 1985, c. 1 — *cont'd*

Income Tax Act, R.S.C. 1985, c. 1 — *cont'd*

Income Tax Application Rules, R.S.C. 1985, c. 5 (5th Supplement), as amended

Income Tax Regulations

Income Tax Regulations — *cont'd*

Table of Cases

Index

A

E

S